CAPTAIN MARVEL
CAROL DANVERS

THE Ms. MARVEL YEARS

CAPTAIN MARVEL
CAROL DANVERS
THE MS. MARVEL YEARS

WRITER: **BRIAN REED**

GIANT-SIZE MS. MARVEL #1
MS. MARVEL #1-5
PENCILER: **ROBERTO DE LA TORRE**
INKER: **JIMMY PALMIOTTI**

MS. MARVEL #6-8
PENCILER: **ROBERTO DE LA TORRE**
INKER: **JONATHAN SIBAL**

MS. MARVEL #9-10
PENCILER: **MIKE WIERINGO**
INKER: **WADE VON GRAWBADGER**

MS. MARVEL SPECIAL #1
PENCILER: **GIUSEPPE CAMUNCOLI**
INKER: **LORENZO RUGGIERO**

CAPTAIN MARVEL: CAROL DANVERS — THE MS. MARVEL YEARS VOL. 1. Contains material originally published in magazine form as GIANT-SIZE MS. MARVEL #1, MS. MARVEL #1-17 and MS. MARVEL SPECIAL #1. First printing 2018. ISBN 978-1-302-91014-3. Published by MARVEL WORLDWIDE, INC., a subsidiary of MARVEL ENTERTAINMENT, LLC. OFFICE OF PUBLICATION: 135 West 50th Street, New York, NY 10020. Copyright © 2018 MARVEL. No similarity between any of the names, characters, persons, and/or institutions in this magazine with those of any living or dead person or institution is intended, and any such similarity which may exist is purely coincidental. **Printed in the U.S.A.** DAN BUCKLEY, President, Marvel Entertainment; JOHN NEE, Publisher; JOE QUESADA, Chief Creative Officer; TOM BREVOORT, SVP of Publishing; DAVID BOGART, SVP of Business Affairs & Operations, Publishing & Partnership; DAVID GABRIEL, SVP of Sales & Marketing, Publishing; JEFF YOUNGQUIST, VP of Production & Special Projects; DAN CARR, Executive Director of Publishing Technology; ALEX MORALES, Director of Publishing Operations; SUSAN CRESPI, Production Manager; STAN LEE, Chairman Emeritus. For information regarding advertising in Marvel Comics or on Marvel.com, please contact Vit DeBellis, Custom Solutions & Integrated Advertising Manager, at vdebellis@marvel.com. For Marvel subscription inquiries, please call 888-511-5480. **Manufactured between 2/2/2018 and 3/6/2018 by LSC COMMUNICATIONS INC., KENDALLVILLE, IN, USA.**

10 9 8 7 6 5 4 3 2 1

MS. MARVEL #11-12
PENCILERS: ROBERTO DE LA TORRE
WITH PATCH ZIRCHER (#12)
INKER: JON SIBAL

MS. MARVEL #13-17
PENCILER: AARON LOPRESTI
INKER: MATT RYAN

COLORIST: CHRIS SOTOMAYOR
LETTERER: DAVE SHARPE

COVER ART:
ROBERTO DE LA TORRE, CAM SMITH & MORRY HOLLOWELL (GIANT-SIZE);
FRANK CHO & JASON KEITH (#1-5); DAVID MACK (#6-8); MIKE WIERINGO
& CHRIS SOTOMAYOR (#9-10); GIUSEPPE CAMUNCOLI, LORENZO RUGGIERO
& CHRIS SOTOMAYOR (SPECIAL); TRAVEL FOREMAN (#11) ;AND GREG HORN (#12-17)

ASSISTANT EDITORS: MOLLY LAZER, AUBREY SITTERSON,
DANIEL KETCHUM & ALEJANDRO ARBONA
EDITORS: ANDY SCHMIDT & BILL ROSEMANN WITH WARREN SIMONS

COLLECTION EDITOR: MARK D. BEAZLEY ▪ ASSISTANT EDITOR: CAITLIN O'CONNELL ▪ ASSOCIATE MANAGING EDITOR: KATERI WOODY
ASSOCIATE MANAGER, DIGITAL ASSETS: JOE HOCHSTEIN ▪ SENIOR EDITOR, SPECIAL PROJECTS: JENNIFER GRÜNWALD
VP PRODUCTION & SPECIAL PROJECTS: JEFF YOUNGQUIST ▪ RESEARCH: JESS HARROLD ▪ LAYOUT: JEPH YORK ▪ PRODUCTION: SALENA MAHINA
BOOK DESIGNER: JAY BOWEN ▪ SVP PRINT, SALES & MARKETING: DAVID GABRIEL

EDITOR IN CHIEF: C.B. CEBULSKI ▪ CHIEF CREATIVE OFFICER: JOE QUESADA ▪ PRESIDENT: DAN BUCKLEY ▪ EXECUTIVE PRODUCER: ALAN FINE

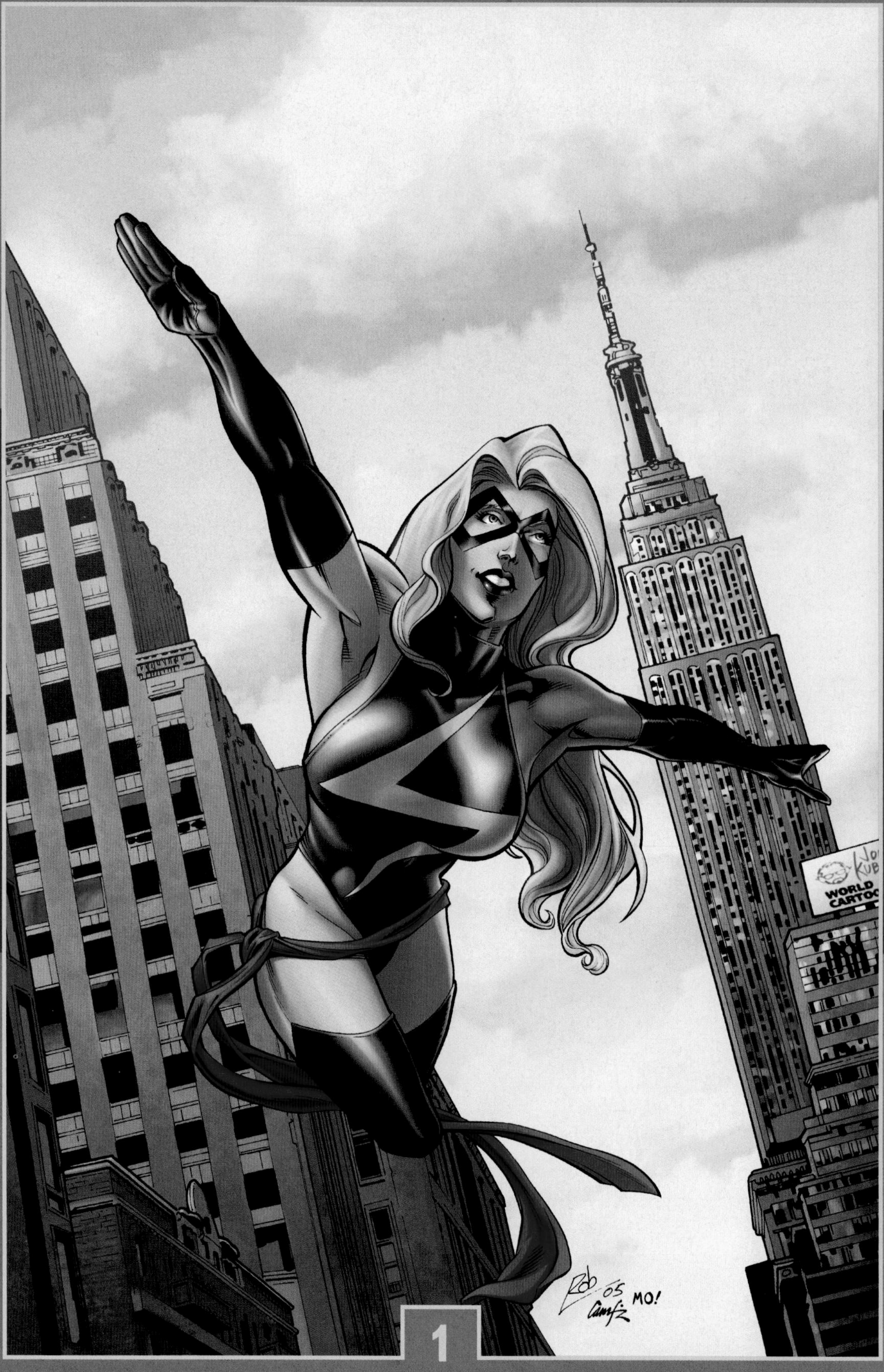

1

GIANT-SIZE MS. MARVEL

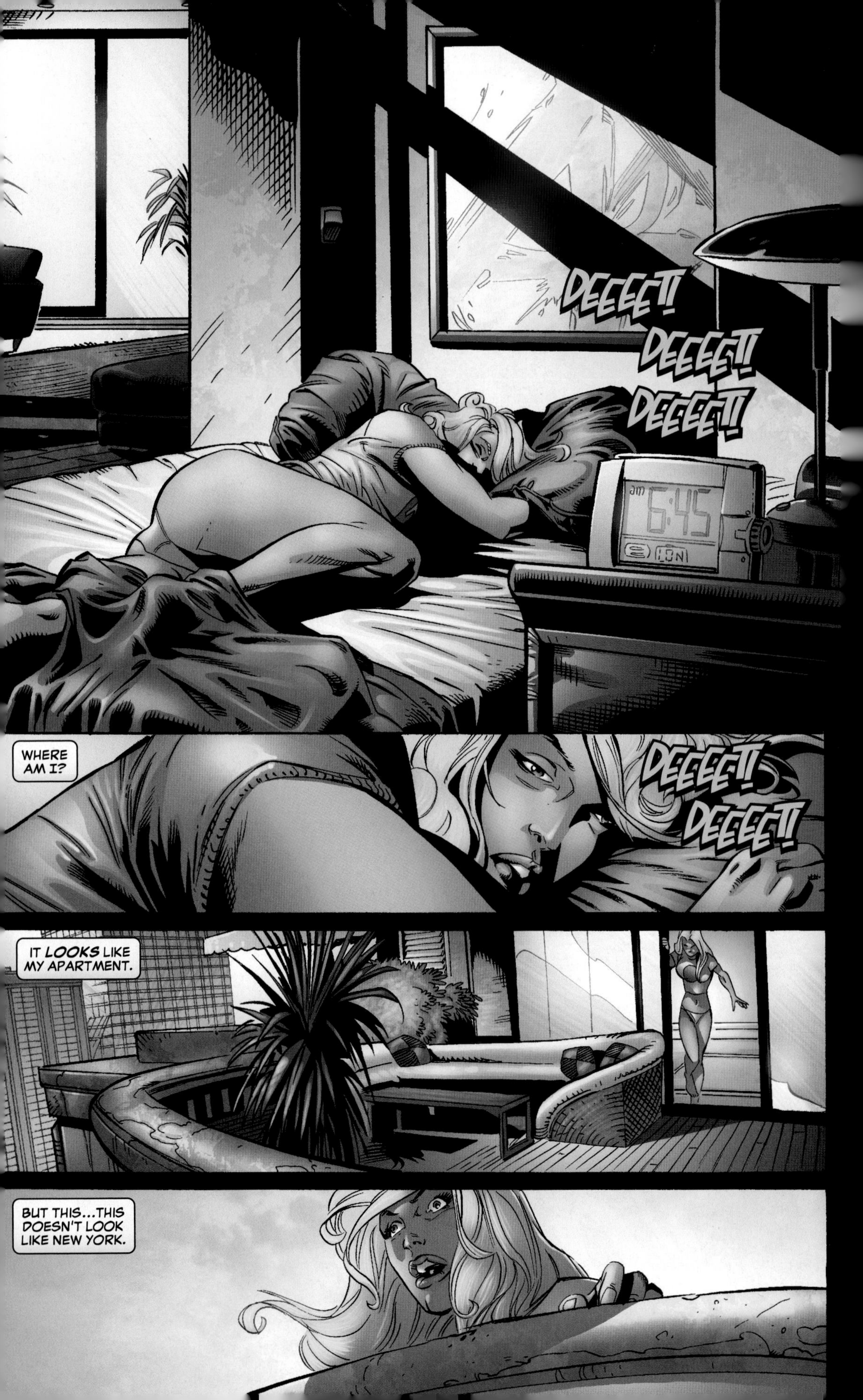
DEEEEET!
DEEEEET!
DEEEEET!
6:45
WHERE AM I?
DEEEEET!
DEEEEET!
IT LOOKS LIKE MY APARTMENT.
BUT THIS...THIS DOESN'T LOOK LIKE NEW YORK.

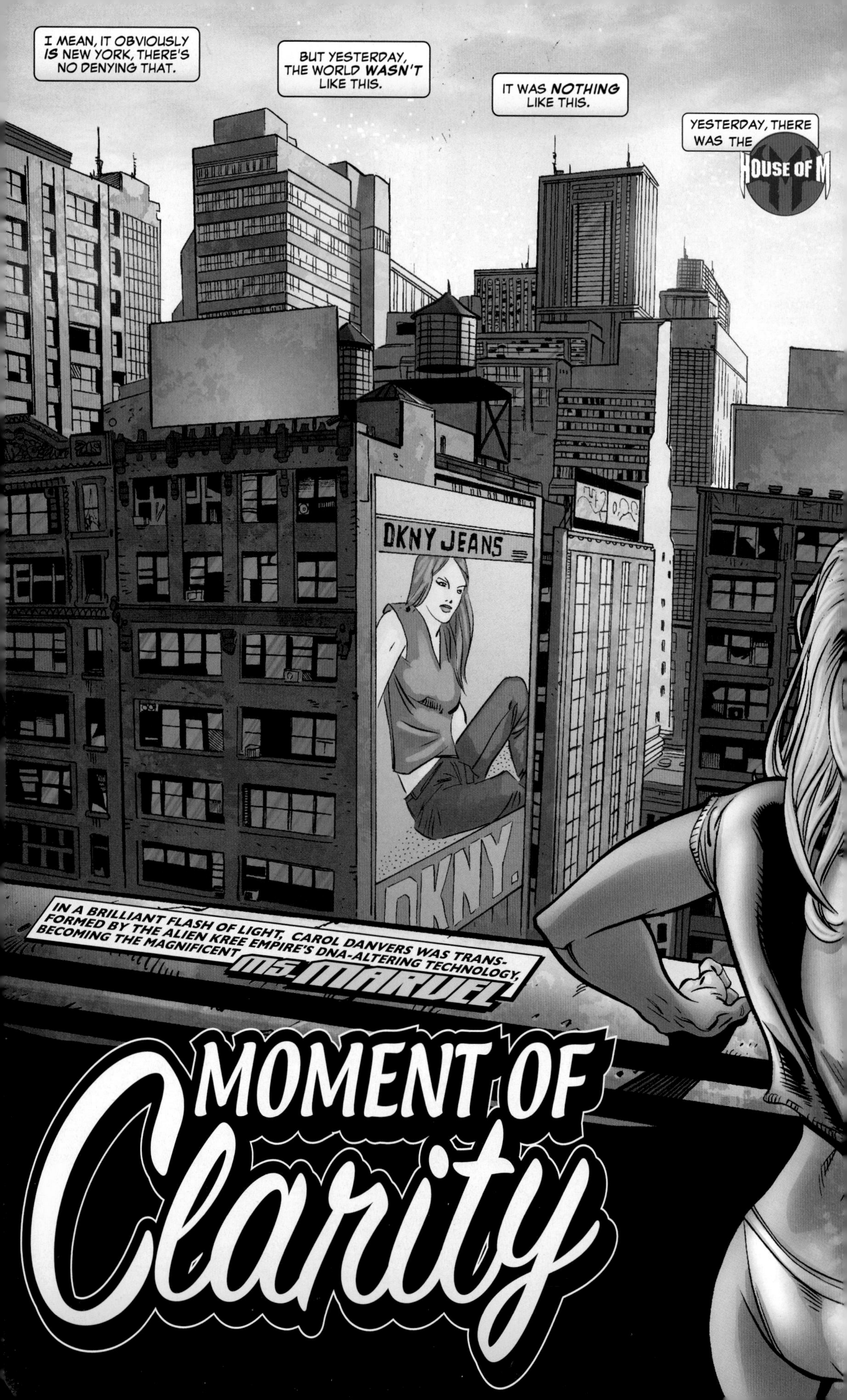
I MEAN, IT OBVIOUSLY IS NEW YORK, THERE'S NO DENYING THAT.
BUT YESTERDAY, THE WORLD WASN'T LIKE THIS.
IT WAS NOTHING LIKE THIS.
YESTERDAY, THERE WAS THE HOUSE OF M
DKNY JEANS
DKNY.
IN A BRILLIANT FLASH OF LIGHT, CAROL DANVERS WAS TRANSFORMED BY THE ALIEN KREE EMPIRE'S DNA-ALTERING TECHNOLOGY, BECOMING THE MAGNIFICENT MS. MARVEL
MOMENT OF Clarity

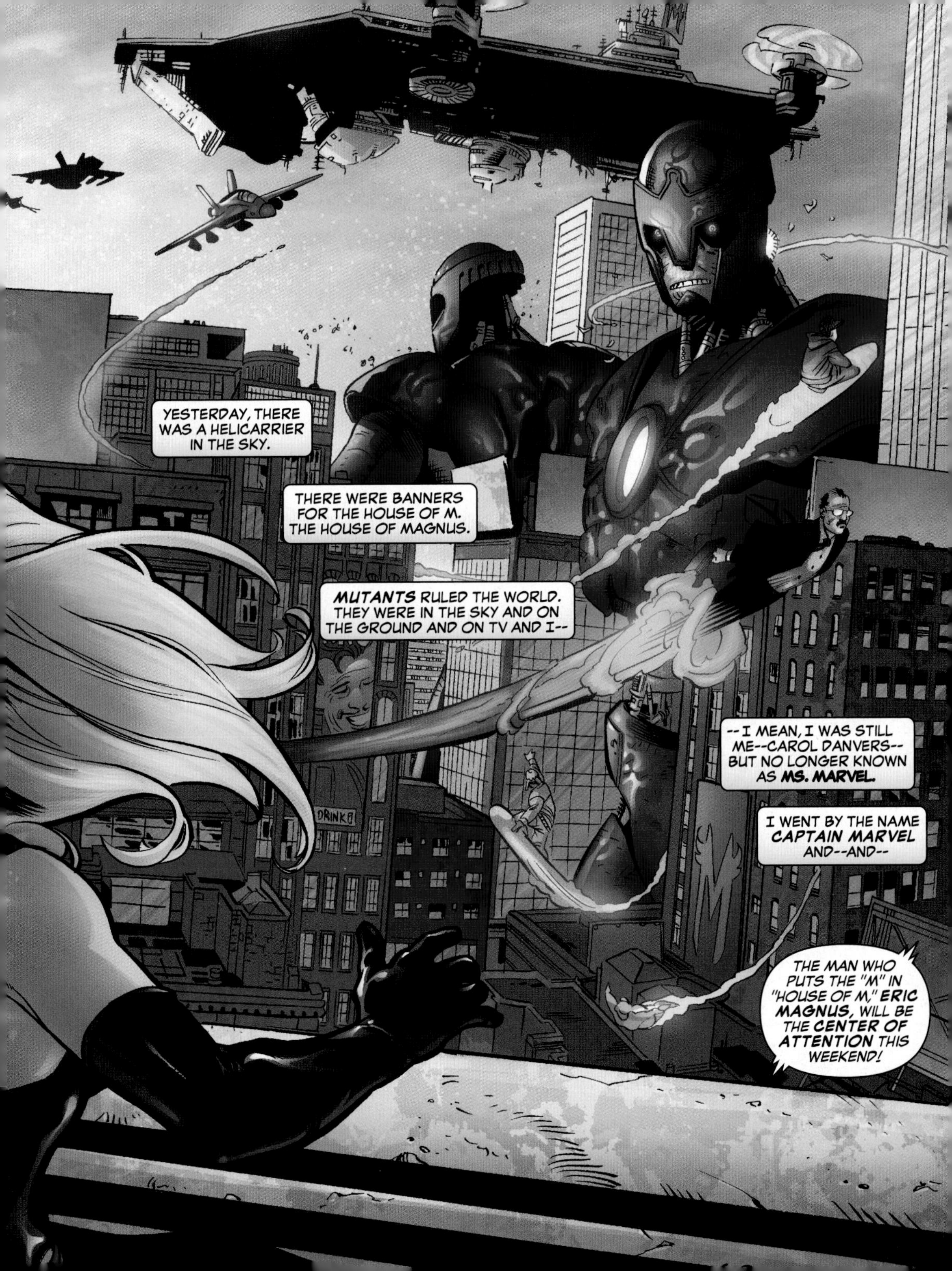

YESTERDAY, THERE WAS A HELICARRIER IN THE SKY.
THERE WERE BANNERS FOR THE HOUSE OF M. THE HOUSE OF MAGNUS.
MUTANTS RULED THE WORLD. THEY WERE IN THE SKY AND ON THE GROUND AND ON TV AND I--
--I MEAN, I WAS STILL ME--CAROL DANVERS--BUT NO LONGER KNOWN AS MS. MARVEL.
I WENT BY THE NAME CAPTAIN MARVEL AND--AND--
THE MAN WHO PUTS THE "M" IN "HOUSE OF M," ERIC MAGNUS, WILL BE THE CENTER OF ATTENTION THIS WEEKEND!
DRINK

PREPARATIONS ARE UNDERWAY FOR A GALA CELEBRATION COMMEMORATING THE ANNIVERSARY OF MAGNUS' REBELLION AGAINST HOMO SAPIENS.

HOUSE OF MAGNUS GALA! SP!

I'M YOUR HOST, LORI GRIFFIN, AND THIS IS SUPER POWERS FOR JULY 20TH!

GOOD EVENING FROM NEW YORK TONIGHT ON SUPE POWERS--

LORI GRIFFIN

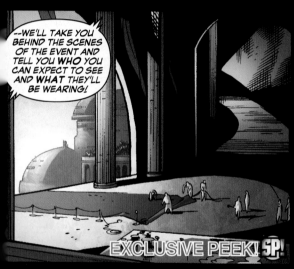

--WE'LL TAKE YOU BEHIND THE SCENES OF THE EVENT AND TELL YOU WHO YOU CAN EXPECT TO SEE AND WHAT THEY'LL BE WEARING!

EXCLUSIVE PEEK! SP!

IS THE WORLD'S MOST ELIGIBLE SAPI BACHELOR A SINGL MAN NO MORE?

IS TONY STARK...

WE LOOK INTO RUMORS OF A SECRET WEDDING TO HOLLYWOOD'S HOTTEST SENSATION, MARY JANE WATSON!

...MARRIED TO A SUPERSTAR! SP!

FROM THE CITY THAT NEVER SLEEPS, THIS IS YOUR SOURCE FOR ALL THE MUTANT NEWS AND VIEWS: SUPER POWERS!

SP!

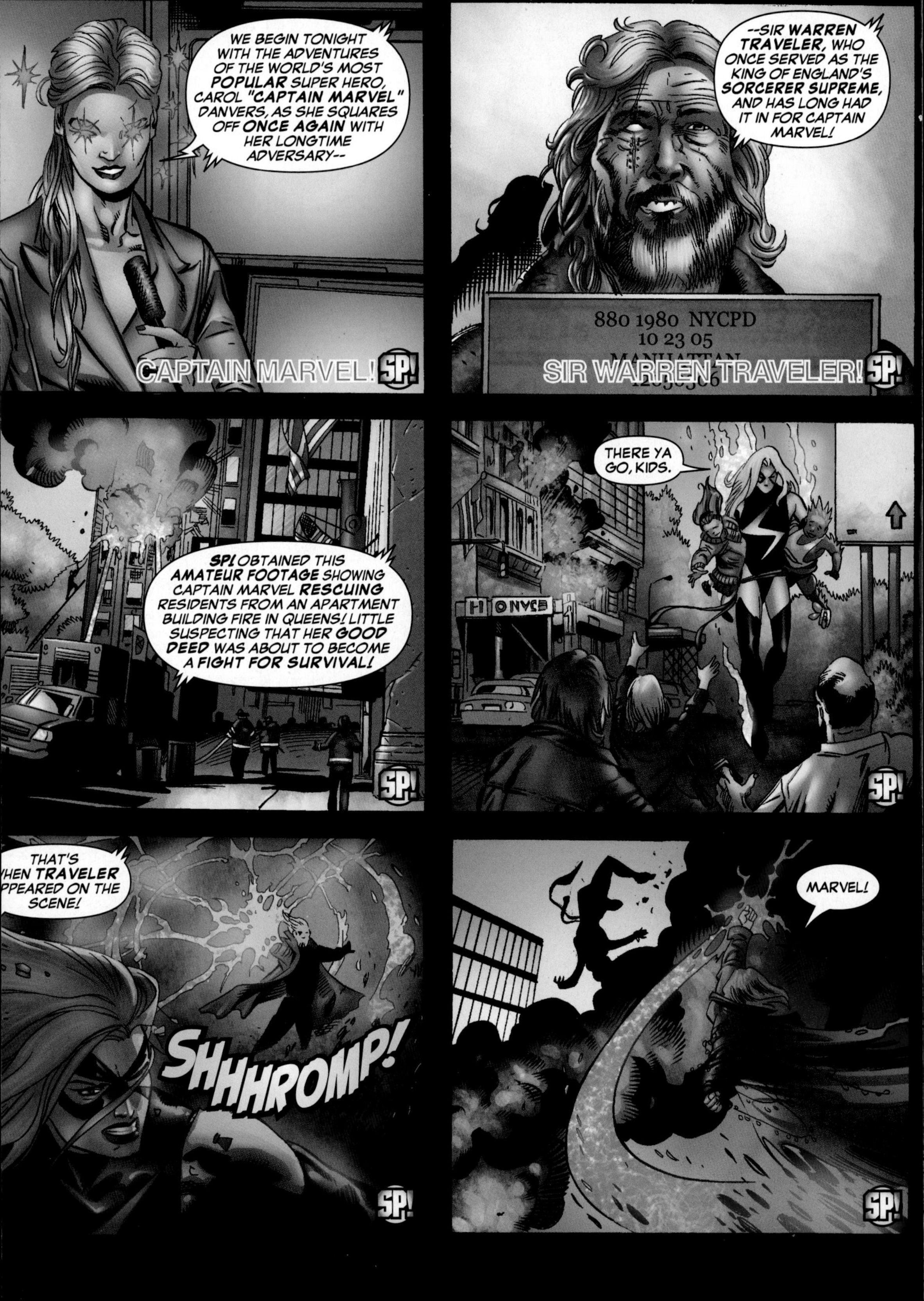
WE BEGIN TONIGHT WITH THE ADVENTURES OF THE WORLD'S MOST POPULAR SUPER HERO, CAROL "CAPTAIN MARVEL" DANVERS, AS SHE SQUARES OFF ONCE AGAIN WITH HER LONGTIME ADVERSARY--
CAPTAIN MARVEL!
SP!
--SIR WARREN TRAVELER, WHO ONCE SERVED AS THE KING OF ENGLAND'S SORCERER SUPREME, AND HAS LONG HAD IT IN FOR CAPTAIN MARVEL!
880 1980 NYCPD
10 23 05
SIR WARREN TRAVELER!
SP!
SP! OBTAINED THIS AMATEUR FOOTAGE SHOWING CAPTAIN MARVEL RESCUING RESIDENTS FROM AN APARTMENT BUILDING FIRE IN QUEENS! LITTLE SUSPECTING THAT HER GOOD DEED WAS ABOUT TO BECOME A FIGHT FOR SURVIVAL!
SP!
THERE YA GO, KIDS.
SP!
THAT'S WHEN TRAVELER APPEARED ON THE SCENE!
SHHHROMP!
SP!
MARVEL!
SP!

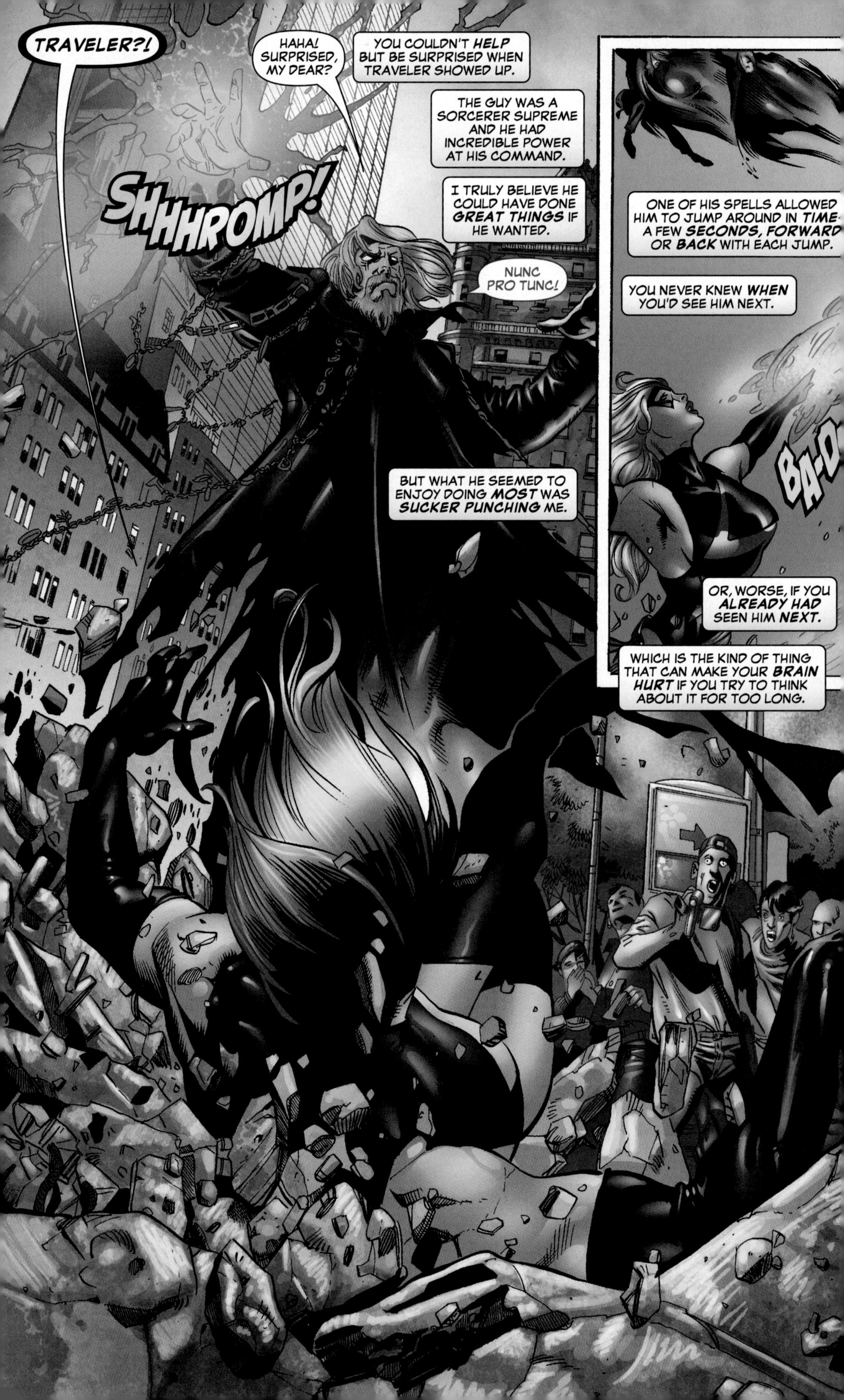
TRAVELER?!
HAHA! SURPRISED, MY DEAR?
YOU COULDN'T HELP BUT BE SURPRISED WHEN TRAVELER SHOWED UP.
THE GUY WAS A SORCERER SUPREME AND HE HAD INCREDIBLE POWER AT HIS COMMAND.
I TRULY BELIEVE HE COULD HAVE DONE GREAT THINGS IF HE WANTED.
SHHHROMP!
NUNC PRO TUNC!
BUT WHAT HE SEEMED TO ENJOY DOING MOST WAS SUCKER PUNCHING ME.
ONE OF HIS SPELLS ALLOWED HIM TO JUMP AROUND IN TIME-- A FEW SECONDS, FORWARD OR BACK WITH EACH JUMP.
YOU NEVER KNEW WHEN YOU'D SEE HIM NEXT.
OR, WORSE, IF YOU ALREADY HAD SEEN HIM NEXT.
WHICH IS THE KIND OF THING THAT CAN MAKE YOUR BRAIN HURT IF YOU TRY TO THINK ABOUT IT FOR TOO LONG.

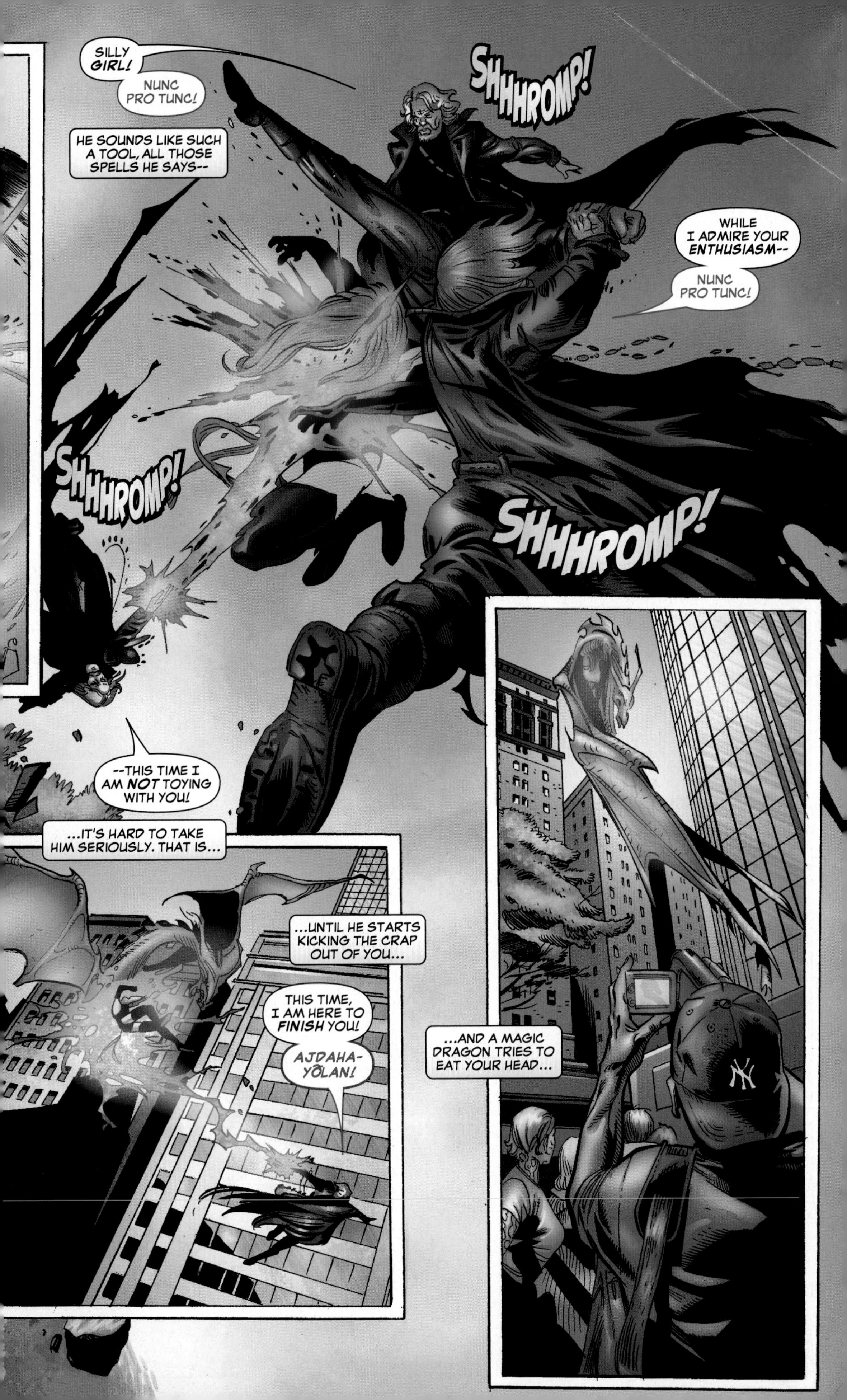

SILLY GIRL!
NUNC PRO TUNC!
SHHHROMP!
HE SOUNDS LIKE SUCH A TOOL, ALL THOSE SPELLS HE SAYS--
WHILE I ADMIRE YOUR ENTHUSIASM--
NUNC PRO TUNC!
SHHHROMP!
SHHHROMP!
--THIS TIME I AM NOT TOYING WITH YOU!
...IT'S HARD TO TAKE HIM SERIOUSLY. THAT IS...
...UNTIL HE STARTS KICKING THE CRAP OUT OF YOU...
THIS TIME, I AM HERE TO FINISH YOU!
AJDAHA-YOLAN!
...AND A MAGIC DRAGON TRIES TO EAT YOUR HEAD...
NY

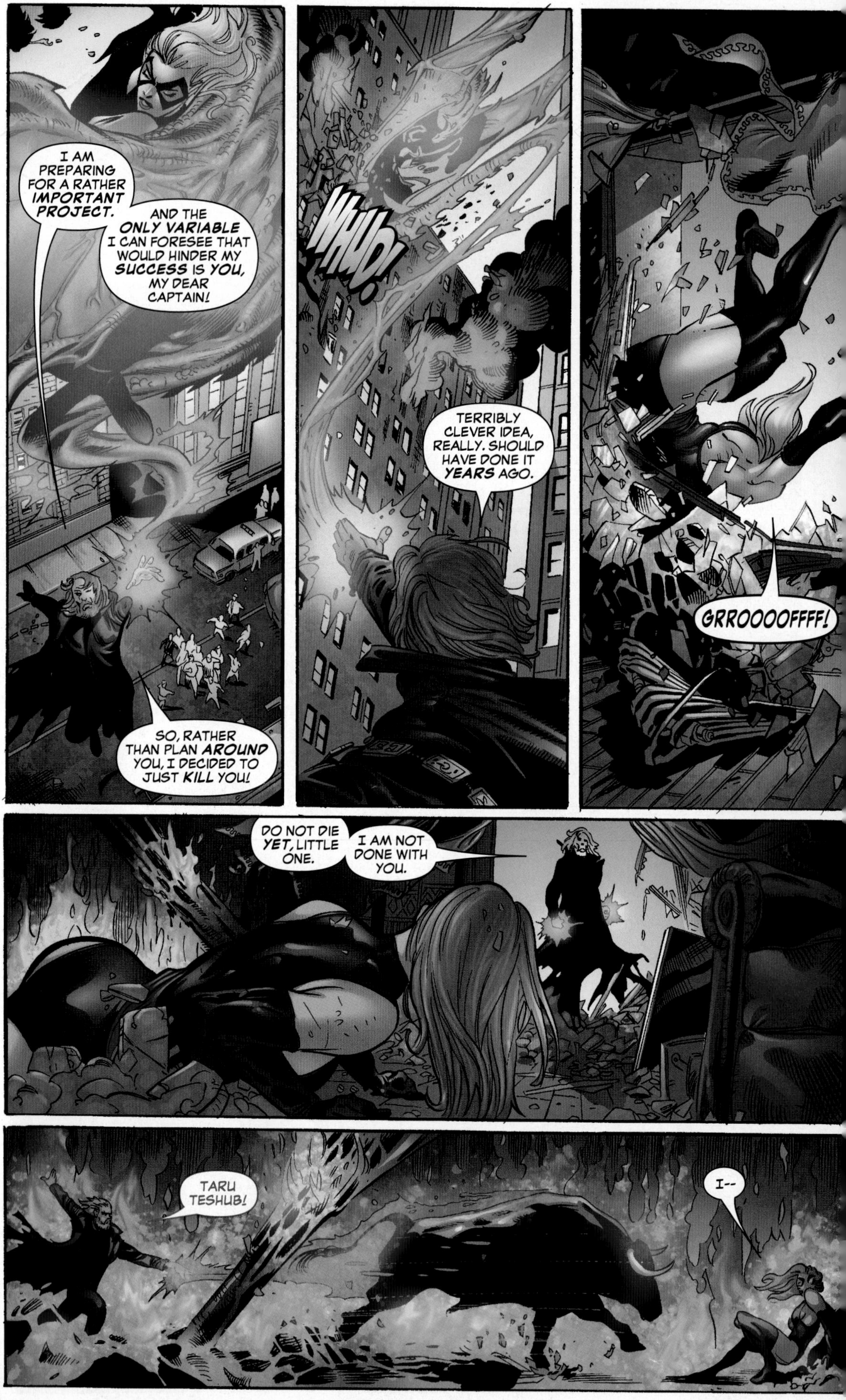
I AM PREPARING FOR A RATHER IMPORTANT PROJECT.
AND THE ONLY VARIABLE I CAN FORESEE THAT WOULD HINDER MY SUCCESS IS YOU, MY DEAR CAPTAIN!
SO, RATHER THAN PLAN AROUND YOU, I DECIDED TO JUST KILL YOU!
WHUD!
TERRIBLY CLEVER IDEA, REALLY. SHOULD HAVE DONE IT YEARS AGO.
GRROOOOFFFF!
DO NOT DIE YET, LITTLE ONE.
I AM NOT DONE WITH YOU.
TARU TESHUB!
I--

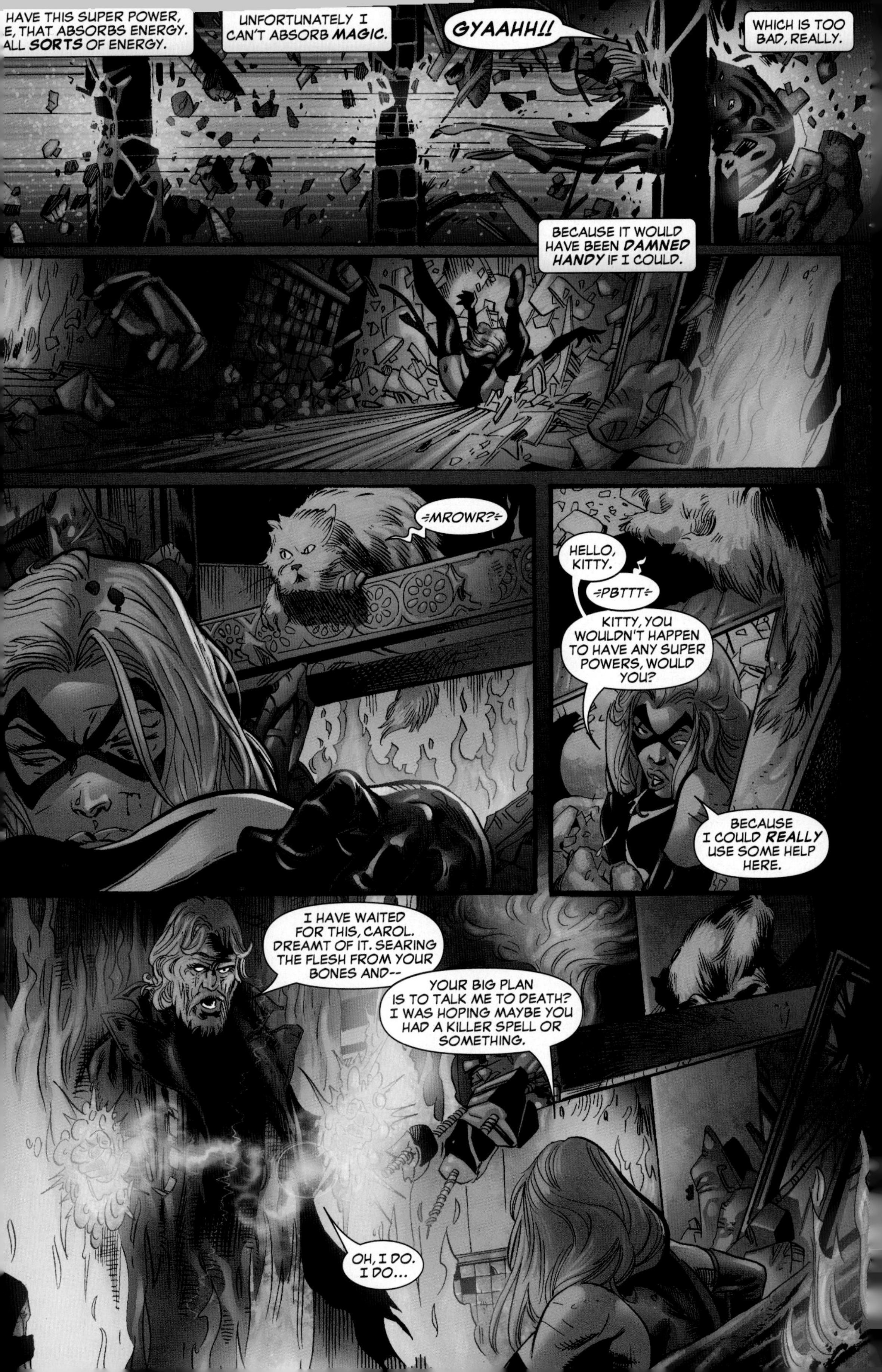
HAVE THIS SUPER POWER, E, THAT ABSORBS ENERGY. ALL SORTS OF ENERGY.
UNFORTUNATELY I CAN'T ABSORB MAGIC.
GYAAHH!!
WHICH IS TOO BAD, REALLY.
BECAUSE IT WOULD HAVE BEEN DAMNED HANDY IF I COULD.
MROWR?
HELLO, KITTY.
PBTTT
KITTY, YOU WOULDN'T HAPPEN TO HAVE ANY SUPER POWERS, WOULD YOU?
BECAUSE I COULD REALLY USE SOME HELP HERE.
I HAVE WAITED FOR THIS, CAROL. DREAMT OF IT. SEARING THE FLESH FROM YOUR BONES AND--
YOUR BIG PLAN IS TO TALK ME TO DEATH? I WAS HOPING MAYBE YOU HAD A KILLER SPELL OR SOMETHING.
OH, I DO. I DO...

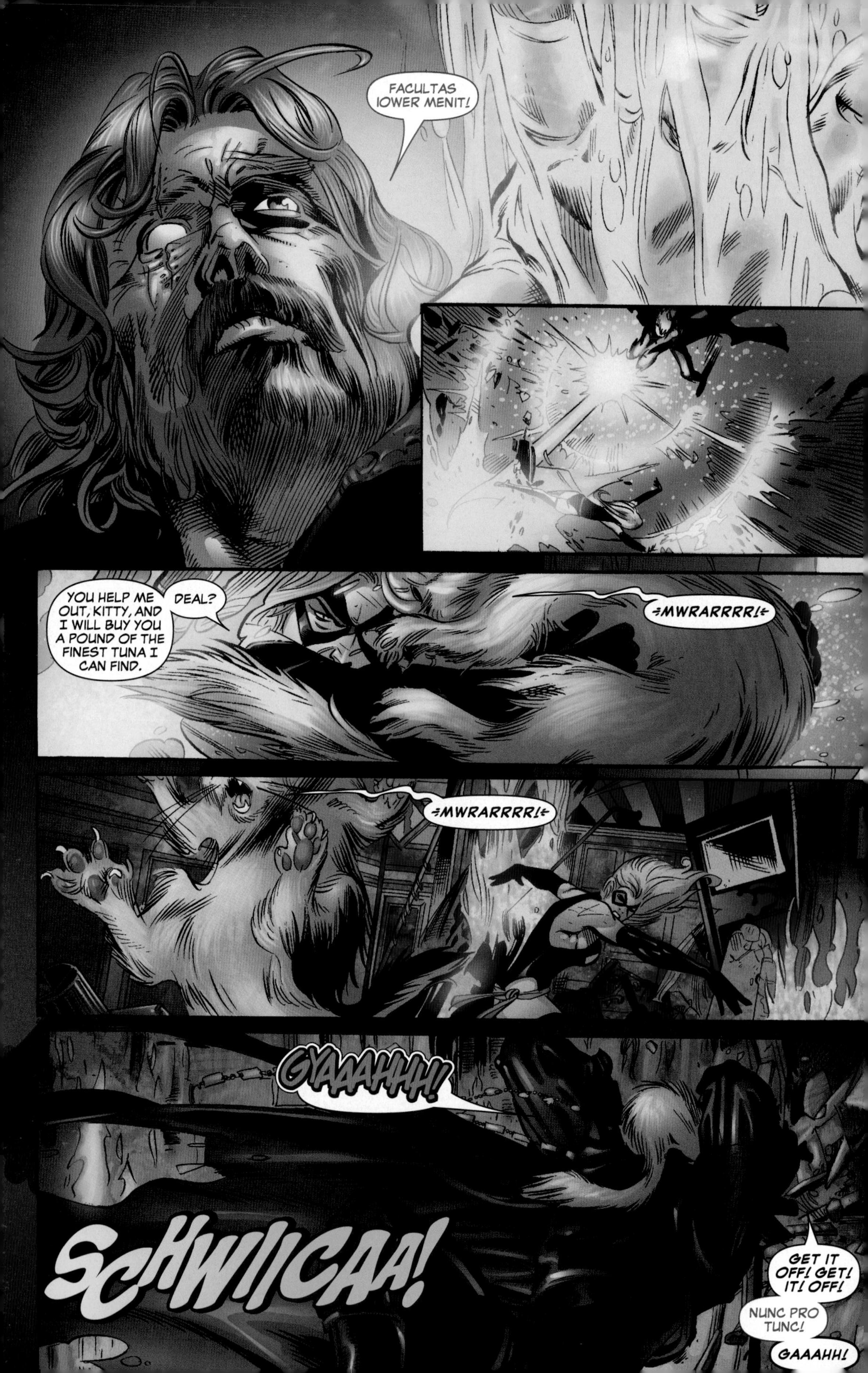

FACULTAS IOWER MENIT!
YOU HELP ME OUT, KITTY, AND I WILL BUY YOU A POUND OF THE FINEST TUNA I CAN FIND.
DEAL?
MWRARRRR!
MWRARRRR!
GYAAAHHH!
SCHWIICAA!
GET IT OFF! GET! IT! OFF!
NUNC PRO TUNC!
GAAAHH!

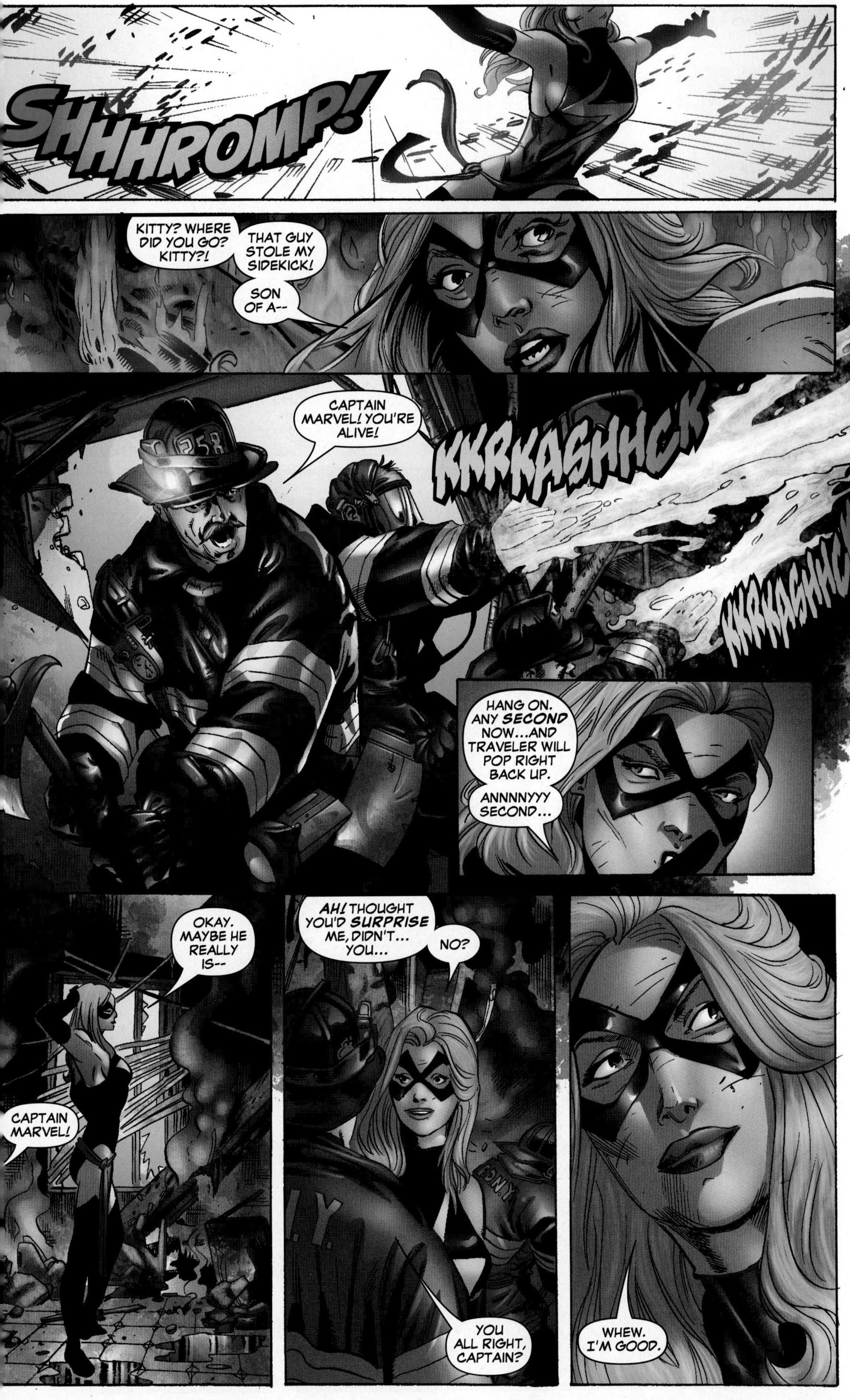
SHHHROMP!
KITTY? WHERE DID YOU GO? KITTY?!
THAT GUY STOLE MY SIDEKICK!
SON OF A--
CAPTAIN MARVEL! YOU'RE ALIVE!
KKRKASHHCK
KKRKASHHCK
HANG ON. ANY SECOND NOW...AND TRAVELER WILL POP RIGHT BACK UP.
ANNNNYYY SECOND...
OKAY. MAYBE HE REALLY IS--
CAPTAIN MARVEL!
AH! THOUGHT YOU'D SURPRISE ME, DIDN'T... YOU...
NO?
YOU ALL RIGHT, CAPTAIN?
WHEW. I'M GOOD.

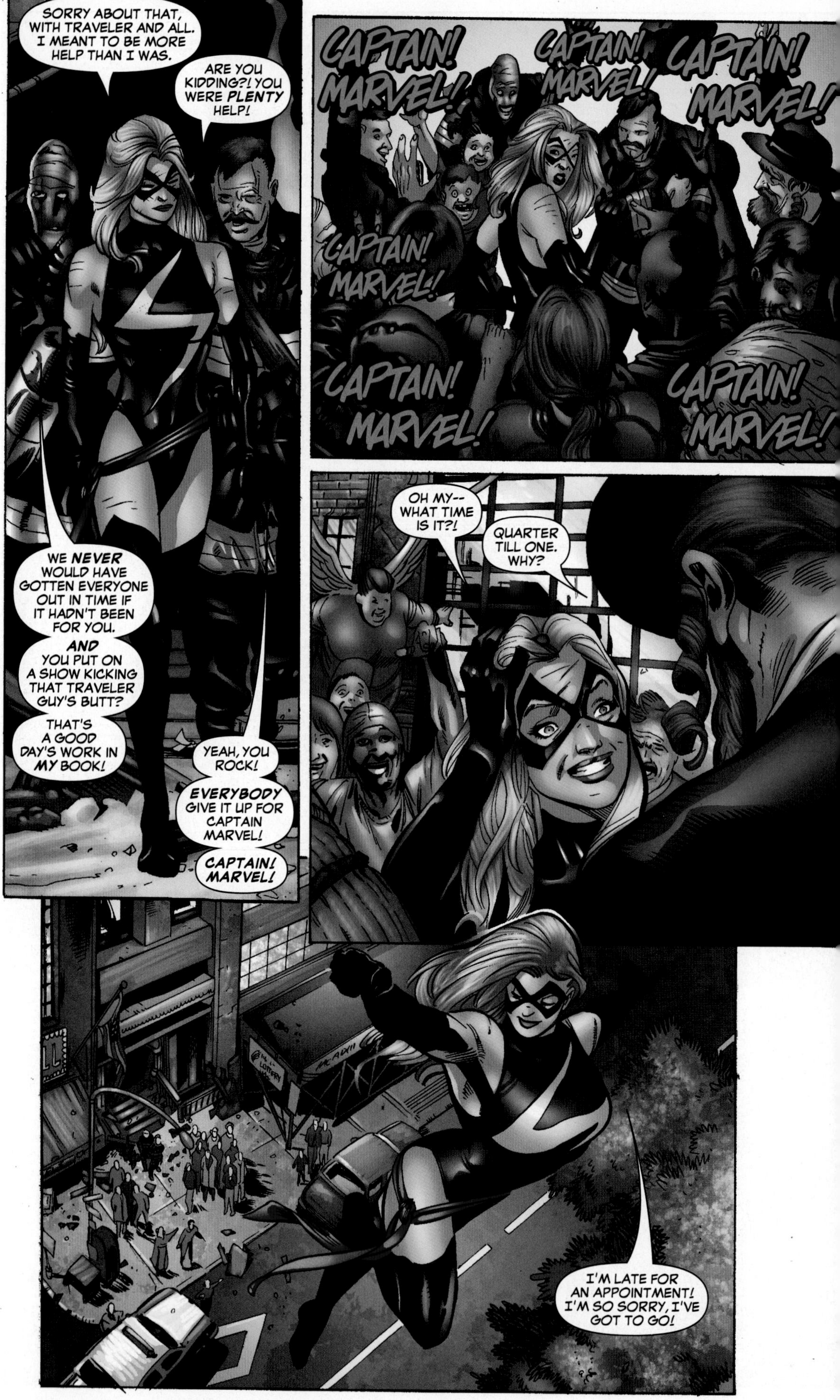
SORRY ABOUT THAT, WITH TRAVELER AND ALL. I MEANT TO BE MORE HELP THAN I WAS.
ARE YOU KIDDING?! YOU WERE PLENTY HELP!
WE NEVER WOULD HAVE GOTTEN EVERYONE OUT IN TIME IF IT HADN'T BEEN FOR YOU.
AND YOU PUT ON A SHOW KICKING THAT TRAVELER GUY'S BUTT?
THAT'S A GOOD DAY'S WORK IN MY BOOK!
YEAH, YOU ROCK!
EVERYBODY GIVE IT UP FOR CAPTAIN MARVEL!
CAPTAIN! MARVEL!
CAPTAIN! MARVEL!
CAPTAIN! MARVEL!
CAPTAIN! MARVEL!
CAPTAIN! MARVEL!
CAPTAIN! MARVEL!
CAPTAIN! MARVEL!
OH MY-- WHAT TIME IS IT?!
QUARTER TILL ONE. WHY?
I'M LATE FOR AN APPOINTMENT! I'M SO SORRY, I'VE GOT TO GO!

SAPIEN CANCER
RESEARCH
FOUNDATION

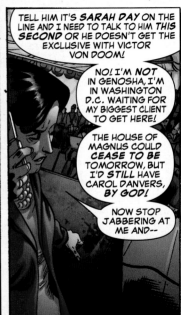

TELL HIM IT'S *SARAH DAY* ON THE LINE AND I NEED TO TALK TO HIM *THIS SECOND* OR HE DOESN'T GET THE EXCLUSIVE WITH VICTOR VON DOOM!

NO! I'M *NOT* IN GENOSHA, I'M IN WASHINGTON D.C. WAITING FOR MY BIGGEST CLIENT TO GET HERE!

THE HOUSE OF MAGNUS COULD *CEASE TO BE* TOMORROW, BUT I'D *STILL* HAVE CAROL DANVERS, BY GOD!

NOW STOP JABBERING AT ME AND--

SORRY I'M LATE!

DEET!

CAROL! YOU CAN *NEVER* BE LATE WHEN AN EVENT *CAN'T START* WITHOUT YOU!

OH MY! WHAT HAPPENED TO YOUR FACE?

WARREN TRAVELER.

AGAIN?!

JUST ANOTHER DAY ON THE JOB, RIGHT?

WELL, LET'S GET SOMEBODY TO PUT THEIR MUTANT WHAMMY ON YOUR FACE AND HEAL YOU UP.

YOU NEED TO LOOK YOUR BEST FOR THE PRESS CONFERENCE.

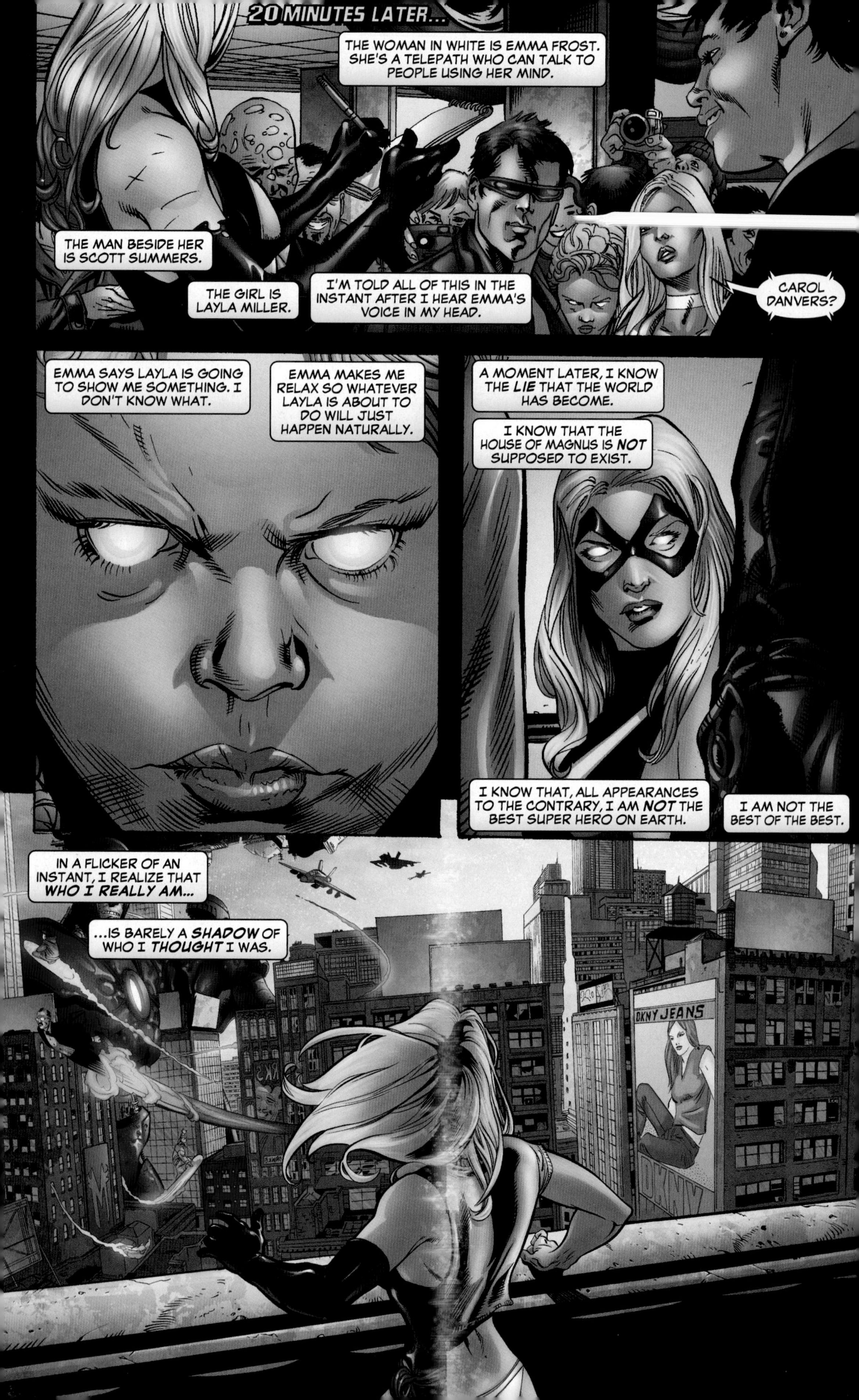
20 MINUTES LATER...
THE WOMAN IN WHITE IS EMMA FROST. SHE'S A TELEPATH WHO CAN TALK TO PEOPLE USING HER MIND.
THE MAN BESIDE HER IS SCOTT SUMMERS.
THE GIRL IS LAYLA MILLER.
I'M TOLD ALL OF THIS IN THE INSTANT AFTER I HEAR EMMA'S VOICE IN MY HEAD.
CAROL DANVERS?
EMMA SAYS LAYLA IS GOING TO SHOW ME SOMETHING. I DON'T KNOW WHAT.
EMMA MAKES ME RELAX SO WHATEVER LAYLA IS ABOUT TO DO WILL JUST HAPPEN NATURALLY.
A MOMENT LATER, I KNOW THE LIE THAT THE WORLD HAS BECOME.
I KNOW THAT THE HOUSE OF MAGNUS IS NOT SUPPOSED TO EXIST.
I KNOW THAT, ALL APPEARANCES TO THE CONTRARY, I AM NOT THE BEST SUPER HERO ON EARTH.
I AM NOT THE BEST OF THE BEST.
IN A FLICKER OF AN INSTANT, I REALIZE THAT WHO I REALLY AM...
...IS BARELY A SHADOW OF WHO I THOUGHT I WAS.
DKNY JEANS

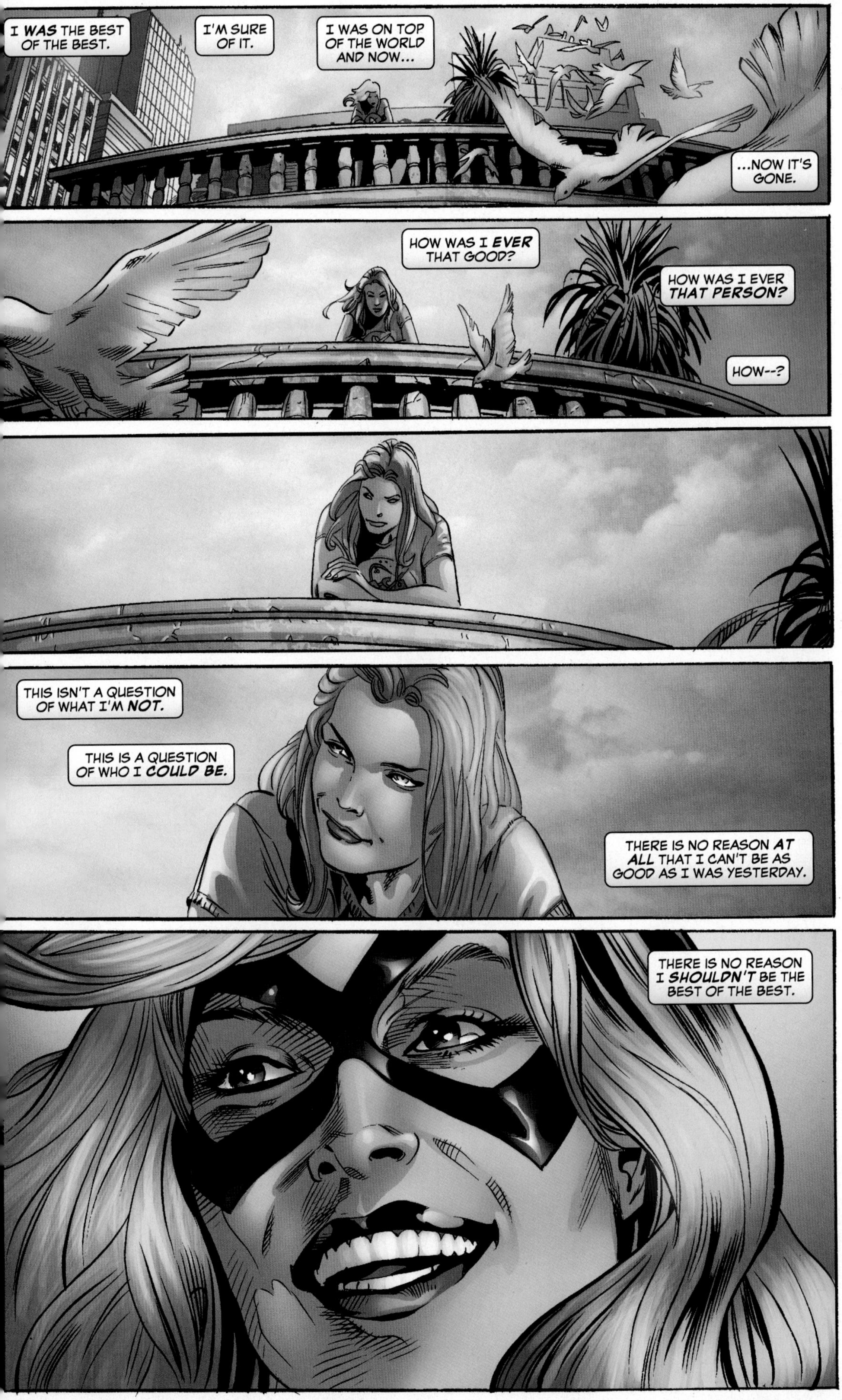

I WAS THE BEST OF THE BEST.
I'M SURE OF IT.
I WAS ON TOP OF THE WORLD AND NOW...
...NOW IT'S GONE.
HOW WAS I EVER THAT GOOD?
HOW WAS I EVER THAT PERSON?
HOW--?
THIS ISN'T A QUESTION OF WHAT I'M NOT.
THIS IS A QUESTION OF WHO I COULD BE.
THERE IS NO REASON AT ALL THAT I CAN'T BE AS GOOD AS I WAS YESTERDAY.
THERE IS NO REASON I SHOULDN'T BE THE BEST OF THE BEST.

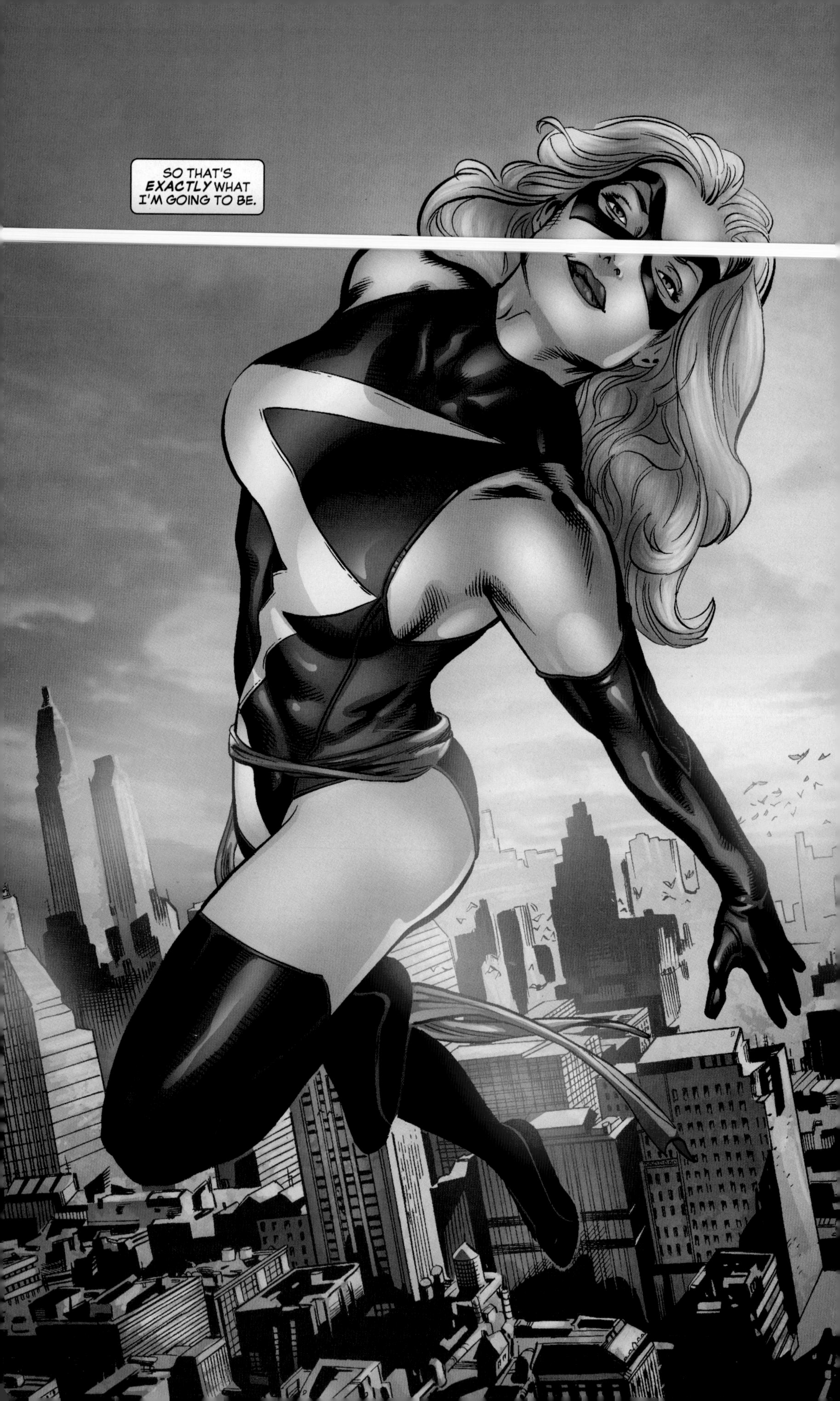
SO THAT'S EXACTLY WHAT I'M GOING TO BE.

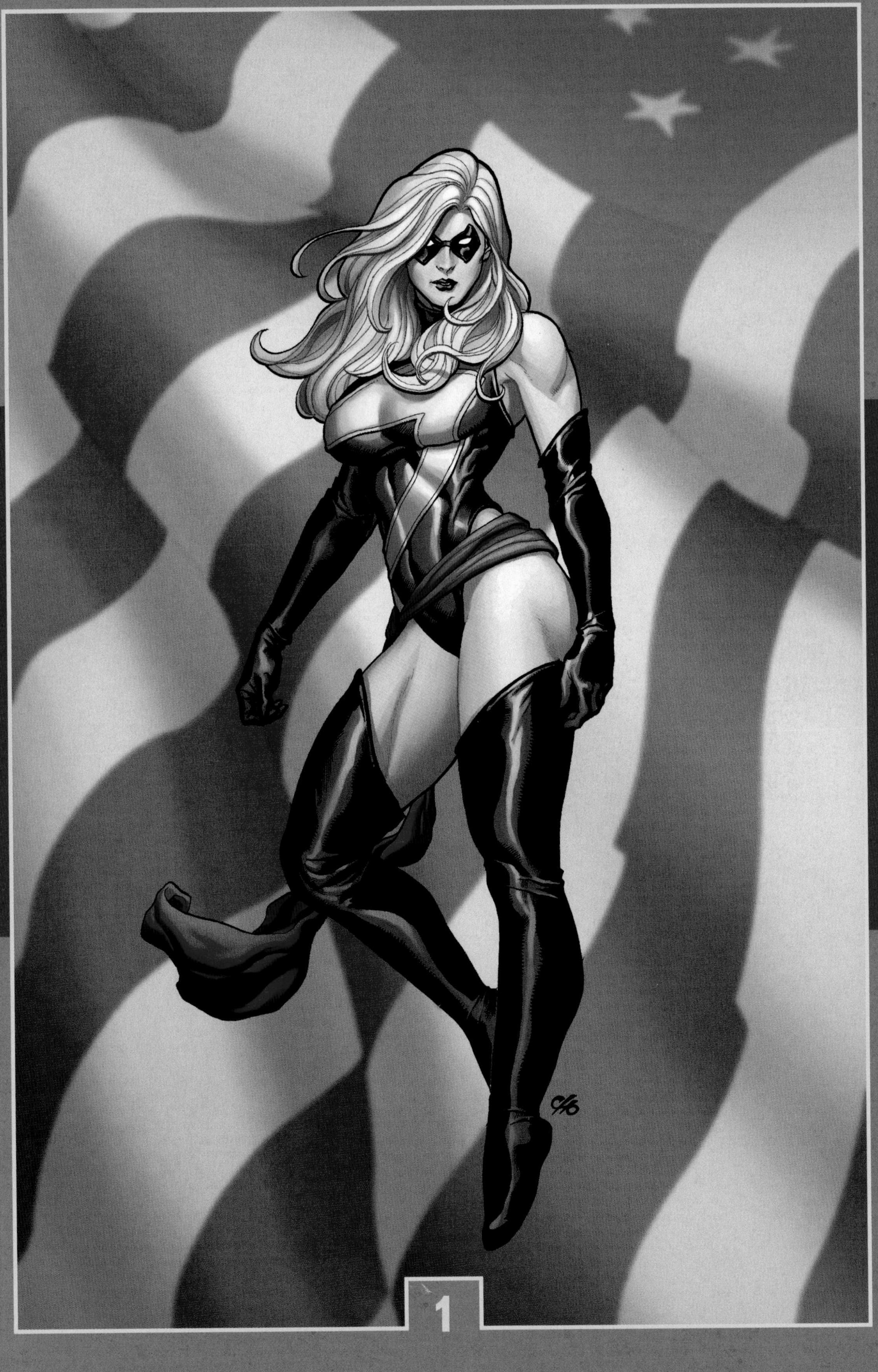

1

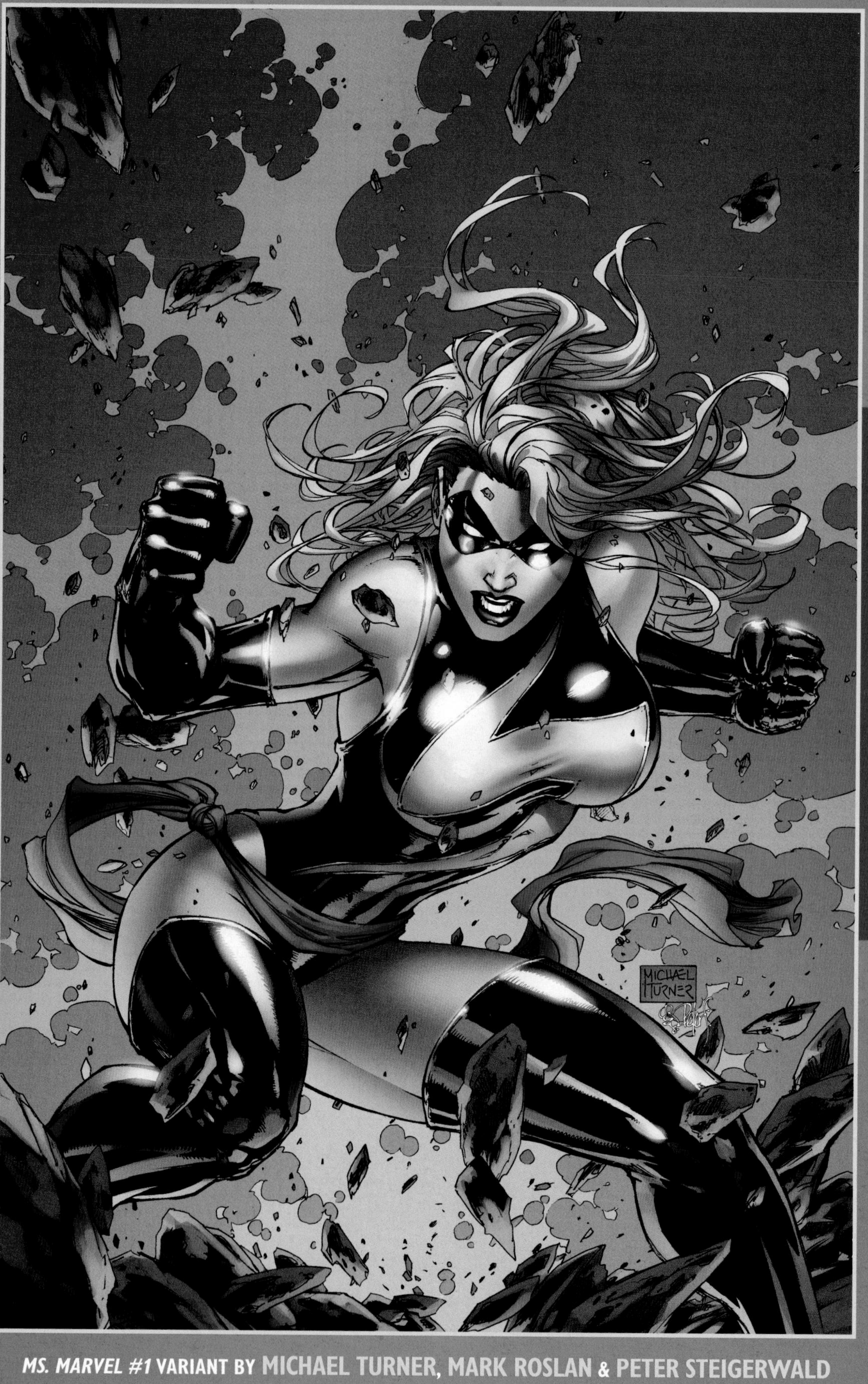
MICHAEL TURNER

MS. MARVEL #1 VARIANT BY MICHAEL TURNER, MARK ROSLAN & PETER STEIGERWALD

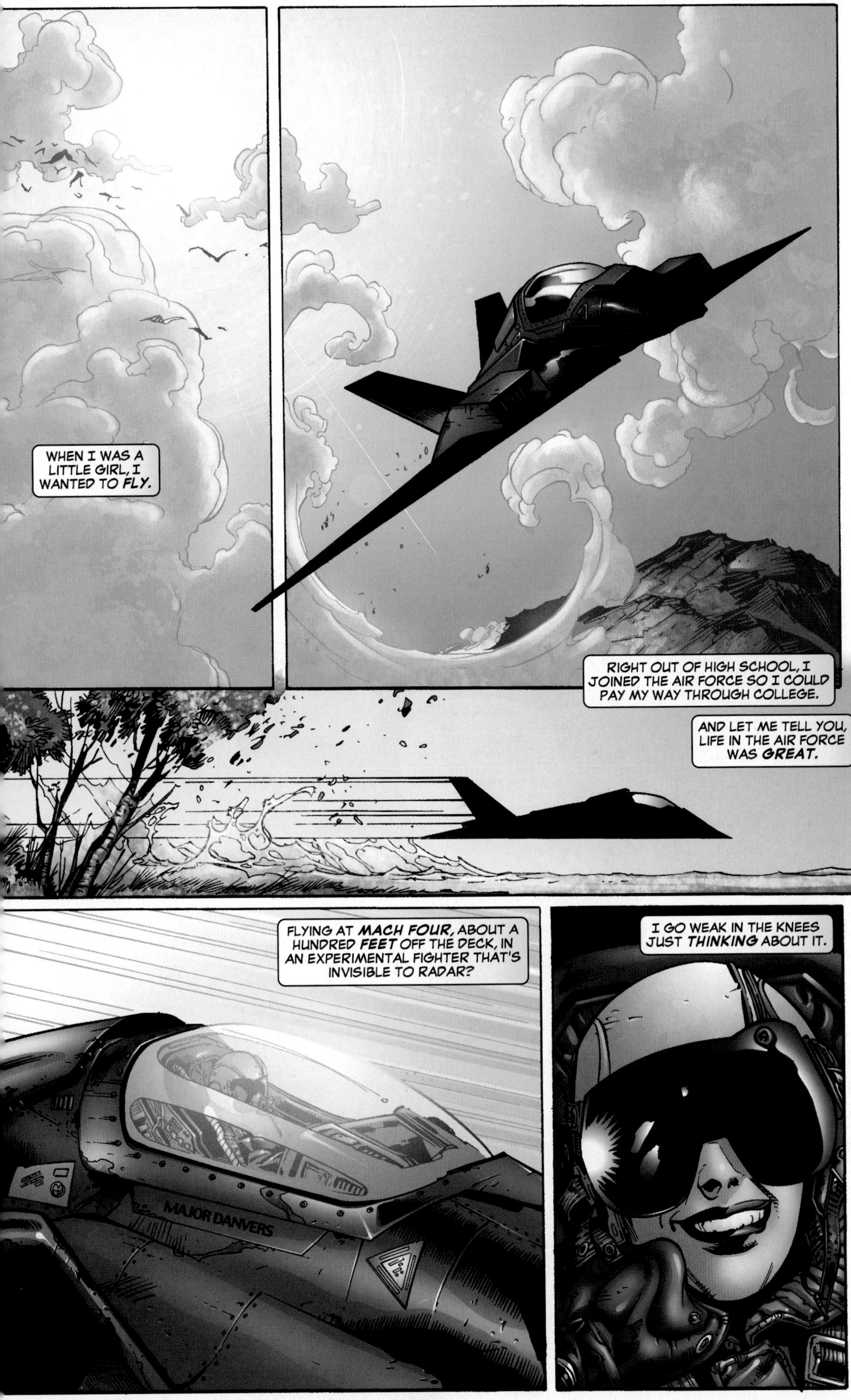
WHEN I WAS A LITTLE GIRL, I WANTED TO *FLY.*
RIGHT OUT OF HIGH SCHOOL, I JOINED THE AIR FORCE SO I COULD PAY MY WAY THROUGH COLLEGE.
AND LET ME TELL YOU, LIFE IN THE AIR FORCE WAS *GREAT.*
FLYING AT *MACH FOUR,* ABOUT A HUNDRED *FEET* OFF THE DECK, IN AN EXPERIMENTAL FIGHTER THAT'S INVISIBLE TO RADAR?
MAJOR DANVERS
I GO WEAK IN THE KNEES JUST *THINKING* ABOUT IT.

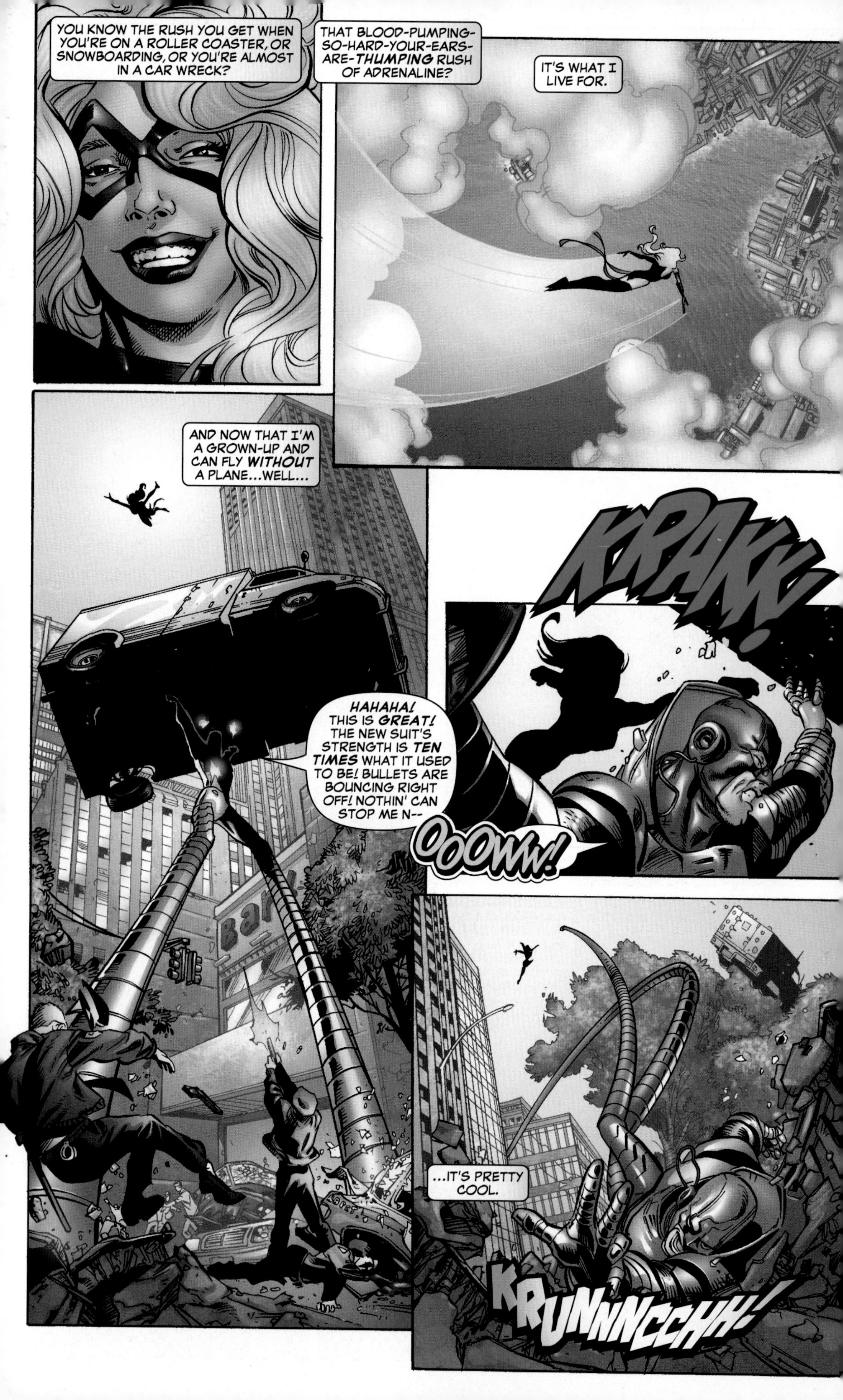
YOU KNOW THE RUSH YOU GET WHEN YOU'RE ON A ROLLER COASTER, OR SNOWBOARDING, OR YOU'RE ALMOST IN A CAR WRECK?
THAT BLOOD-PUMPING-SO-HARD-YOUR-EARS-ARE-*THUMPING* RUSH OF ADRENALINE?
IT'S WHAT I LIVE FOR.
AND NOW THAT I'M A GROWN-UP AND CAN FLY *WITHOUT* A PLANE...WELL...
KRAKK!
HAHAHA! THIS IS *GREAT!* THE NEW SUIT'S STRENGTH IS *TEN TIMES* WHAT IT USED TO BE! BULLETS ARE BOUNCING RIGHT OFF! NOTHIN' CAN STOP ME N--
OOOWW!
...IT'S PRETTY COOL.
KRUNNNCCHH!

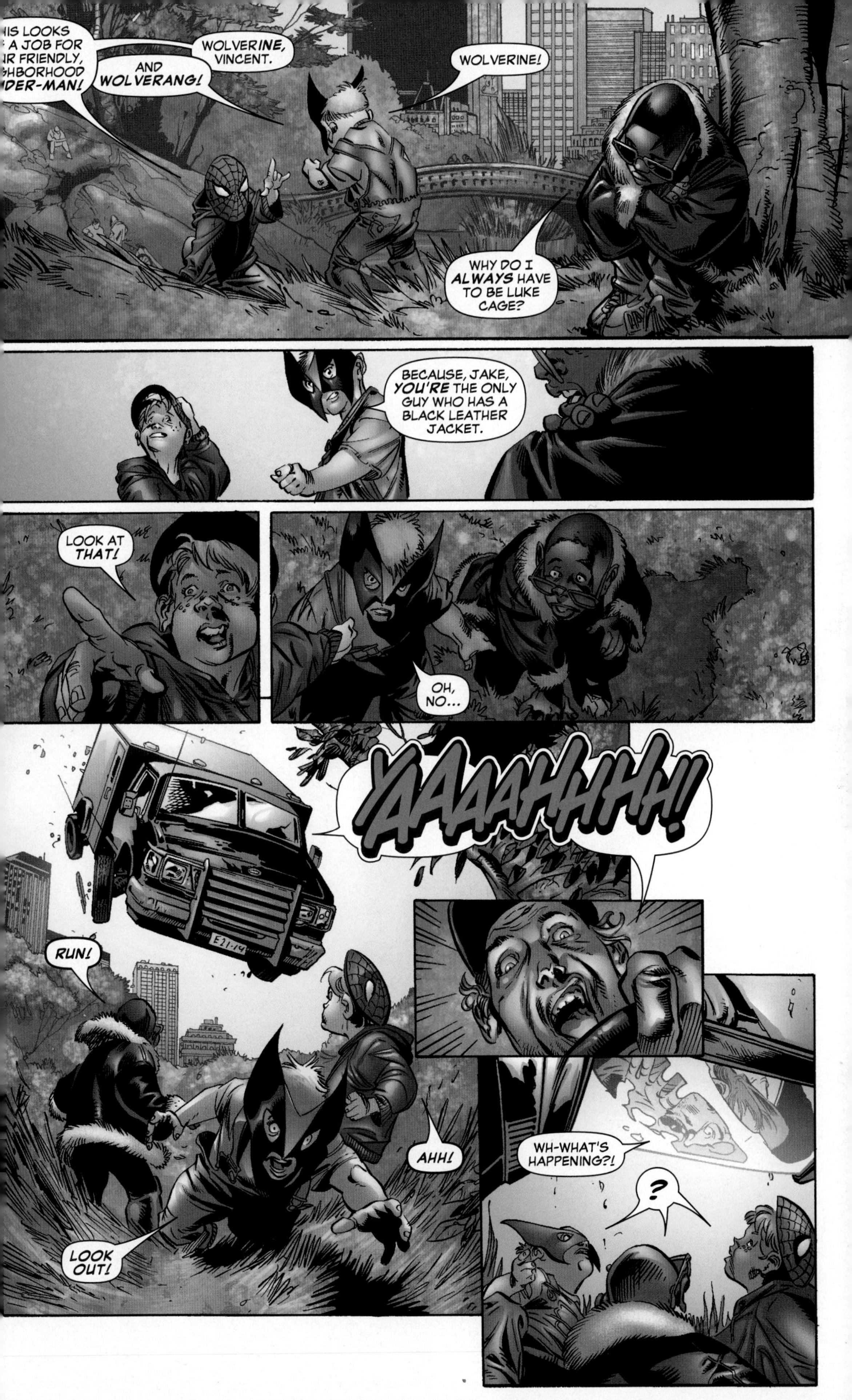
HIS LOOKS
A JOB FOR
R FRIENDLY,
GHBORHOOD
DER-MAN!
AND WOLVERANG!
WOLVERINE, VINCENT.
WOLVERINE!
WHY DO I ALWAYS HAVE TO BE LUKE CAGE?
BECAUSE, JAKE, YOU'RE THE ONLY GUY WHO HAS A BLACK LEATHER JACKET.
LOOK AT THAT!
OH, NO...
YAAAAHHHH!
RUN!
AHH!
LOOK OUT!
WH-WHAT'S HAPPENING?!
?

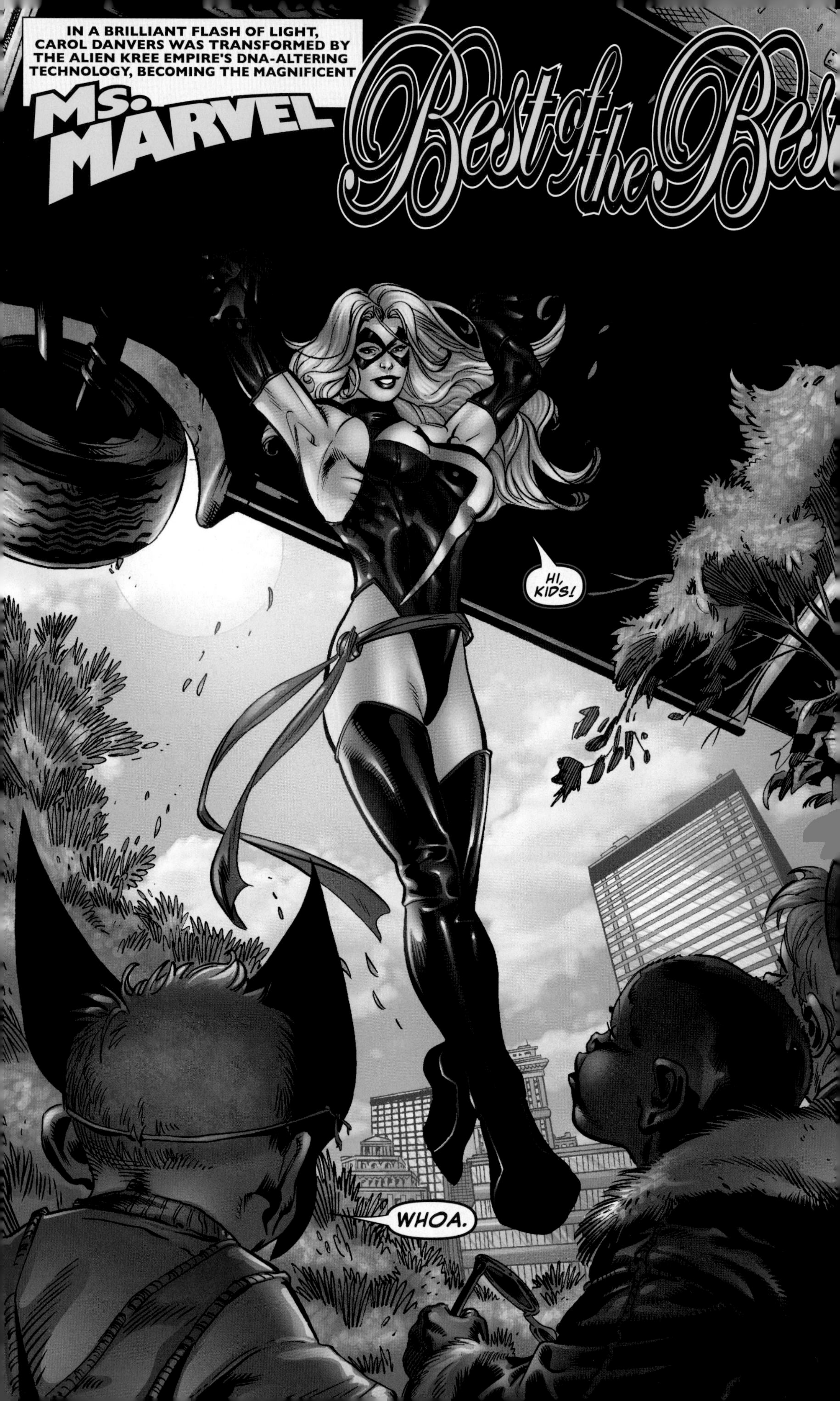
IN A BRILLIANT FLASH OF LIGHT, CAROL DANVERS WAS TRANSFORMED BY THE ALIEN KREE EMPIRE'S DNA-ALTERING TECHNOLOGY, BECOMING THE MAGNIFICENT
MS. MARVEL
Best of the Best
HI, KIDS!
WHOA.

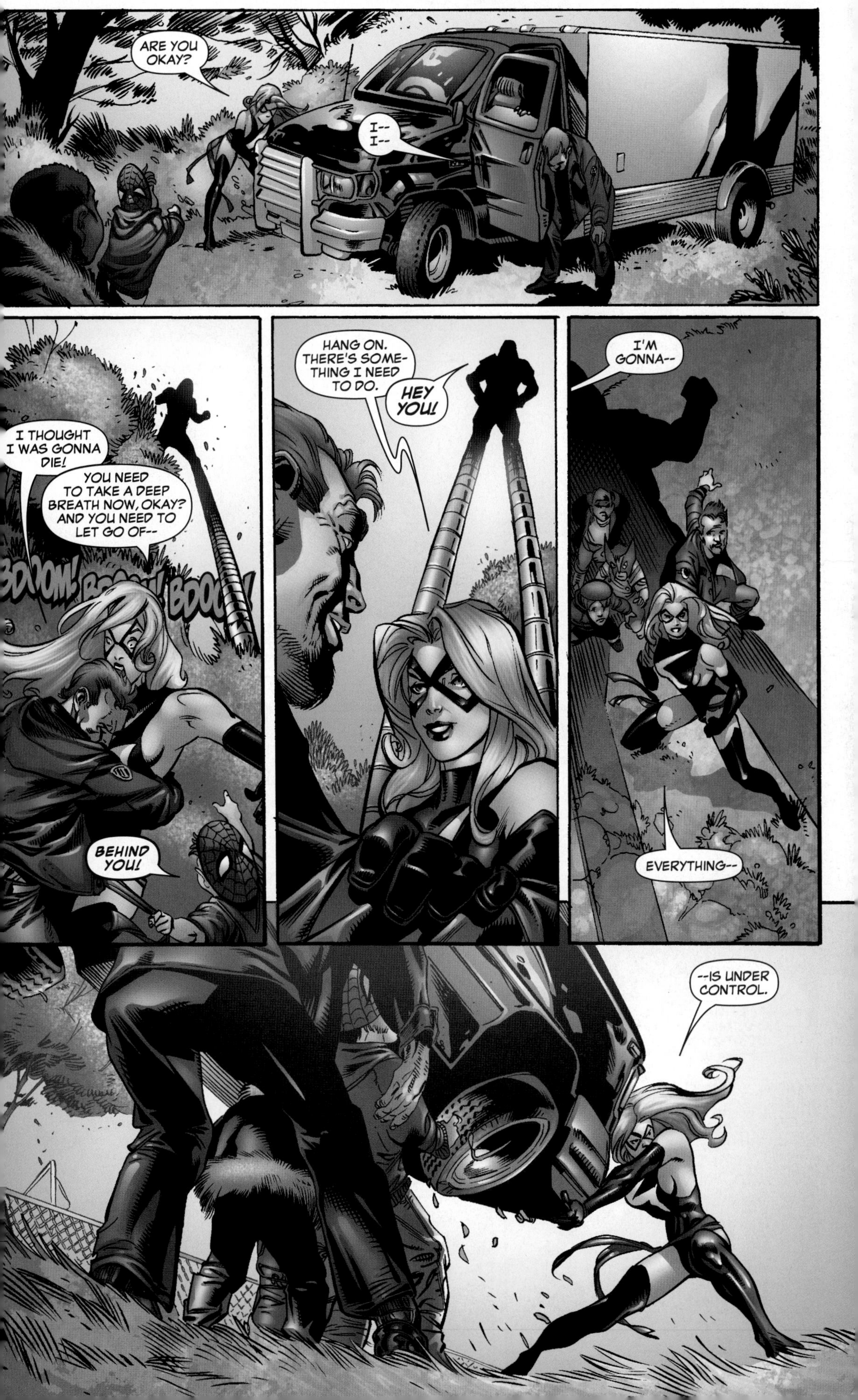
ARE YOU OKAY?
I-- I--
I THOUGHT I WAS GONNA DIE!
YOU NEED TO TAKE A DEEP BREATH NOW, OKAY? AND YOU NEED TO LET GO OF--
BEHIND YOU!
HANG ON. THERE'S SOME-THING I NEED TO DO.
HEY YOU!
I'M GONNA--
EVERYTHING--
--IS UNDER CONTROL.

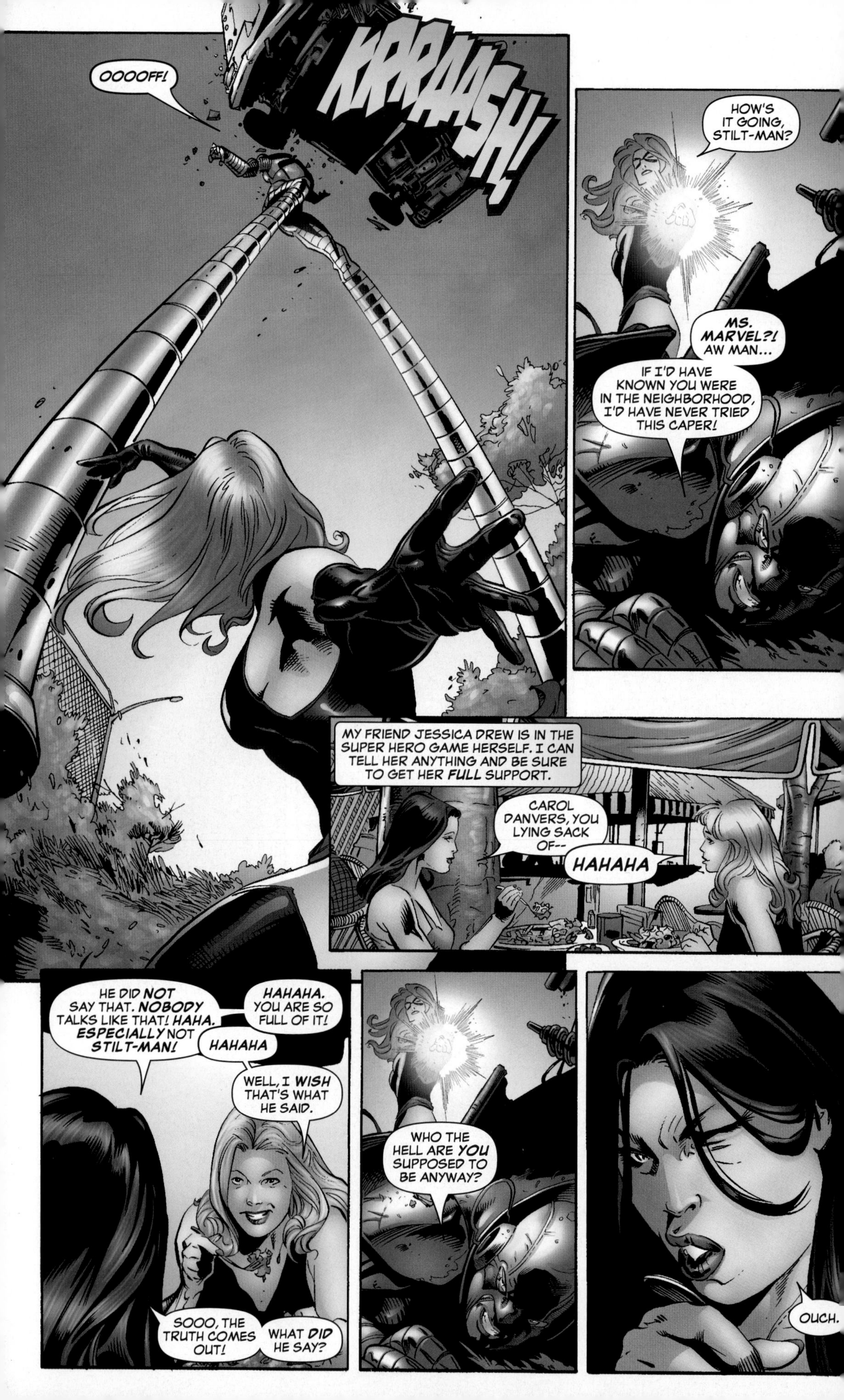
OOOOFF!
KRRAAASH!
HOW'S IT GOING, STILT-MAN?
MS. MARVEL?! AW MAN...
IF I'D HAVE KNOWN YOU WERE IN THE NEIGHBORHOOD, I'D HAVE NEVER TRIED THIS CAPER!
MY FRIEND JESSICA DREW IS IN THE SUPER HERO GAME HERSELF. I CAN TELL HER ANYTHING AND BE SURE TO GET HER FULL SUPPORT.
CAROL DANVERS, YOU LYING SACK OF--
HAHAHA
HE DID NOT SAY THAT. NOBODY TALKS LIKE THAT! HAHA. ESPECIALLY NOT STILT-MAN!
HAHAHA. YOU ARE SO FULL OF IT!
HAHAHA
WELL, I WISH THAT'S WHAT HE SAID.
SOOO, THE TRUTH COMES OUT!
WHAT DID HE SAY?
WHO THE HELL ARE YOU SUPPOSED TO BE ANYWAY?
OUCH.

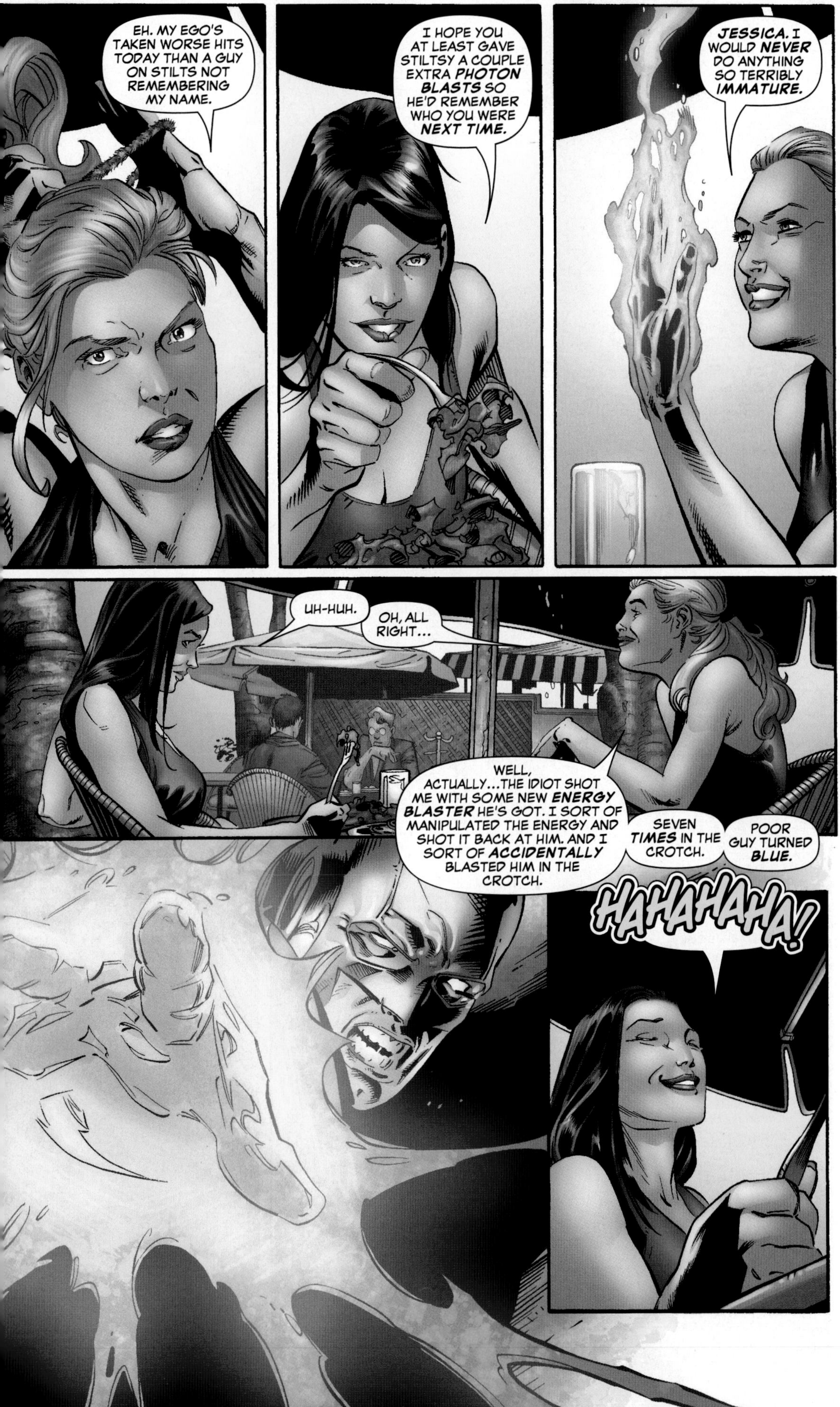
EH. MY EGO'S TAKEN WORSE HITS TODAY THAN A GUY ON STILTS NOT REMEMBERING MY NAME.
I HOPE YOU AT LEAST GAVE STILTSY A COUPLE EXTRA PHOTON BLASTS SO HE'D REMEMBER WHO YOU WERE NEXT TIME.
JESSICA. I WOULD NEVER DO ANYTHING SO TERRIBLY IMMATURE.
UH-HUH.
OH, ALL RIGHT...
WELL, ACTUALLY...THE IDIOT SHOT ME WITH SOME NEW ENERGY BLASTER HE'S GOT. I SORT OF MANIPULATED THE ENERGY AND SHOT IT BACK AT HIM. AND I SORT OF ACCIDENTALLY BLASTED HIM IN THE CROTCH.
SEVEN TIMES IN THE CROTCH.
POOR GUY TURNED BLUE.
HAHAHAHA!

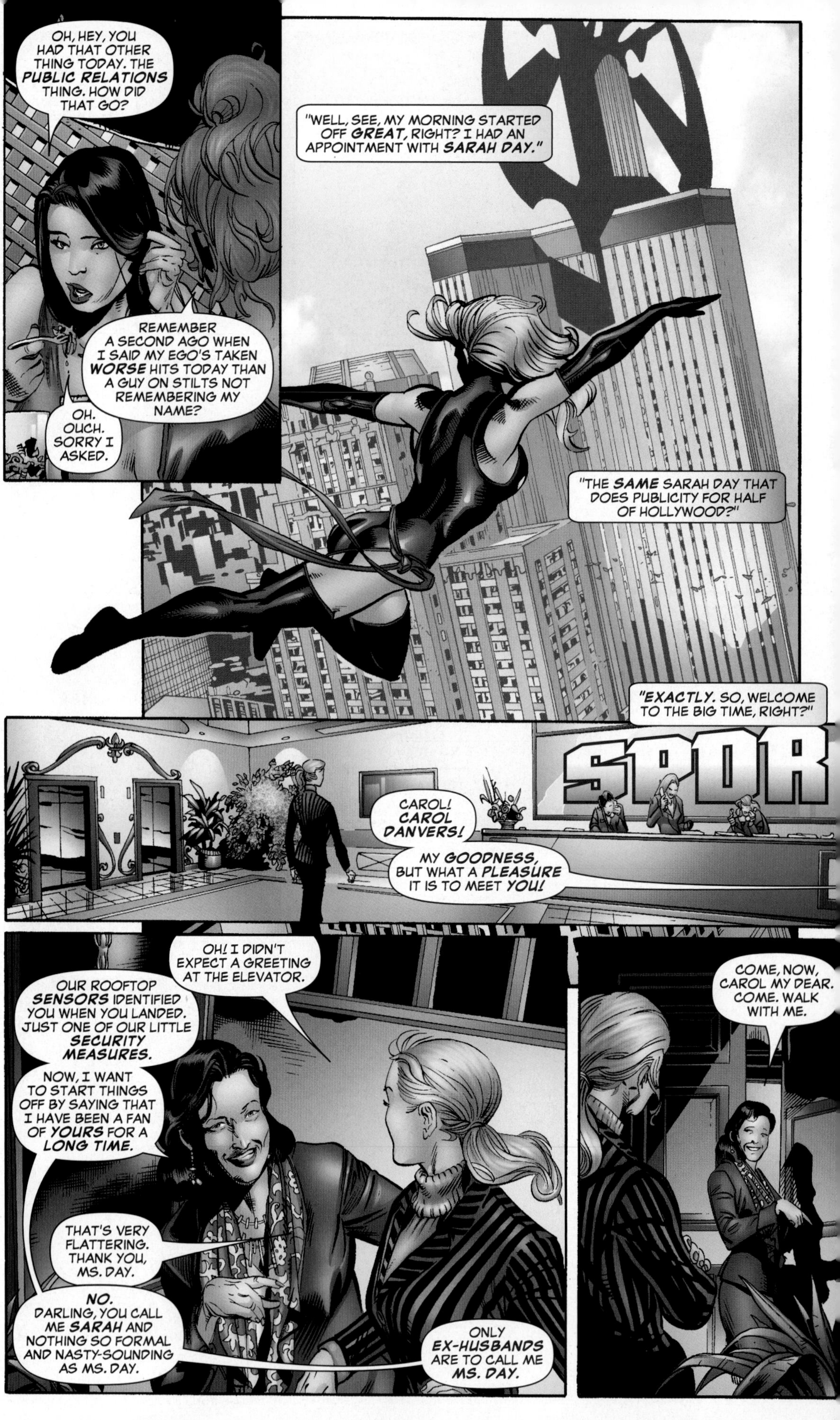

OH, HEY, YOU HAD THAT OTHER THING TODAY. THE PUBLIC RELATIONS THING. HOW DID THAT GO?
REMEMBER A SECOND AGO WHEN I SAID MY EGO'S TAKEN WORSE HITS TODAY THAN A GUY ON STILTS NOT REMEMBERING MY NAME?
OH. OUCH. SORRY I ASKED.
"WELL, SEE, MY MORNING STARTED OFF GREAT, RIGHT? I HAD AN APPOINTMENT WITH SARAH DAY."
"THE SAME SARAH DAY THAT DOES PUBLICITY FOR HALF OF HOLLYWOOD?"
"EXACTLY. SO, WELCOME TO THE BIG TIME, RIGHT?"
SPDR
CAROL! CAROL DANVERS!
MY GOODNESS, BUT WHAT A PLEASURE IT IS TO MEET YOU!
OH! I DIDN'T EXPECT A GREETING AT THE ELEVATOR.
OUR ROOFTOP SENSORS IDENTIFIED YOU WHEN YOU LANDED. JUST ONE OF OUR LITTLE SECURITY MEASURES.
NOW, I WANT TO START THINGS OFF BY SAYING THAT I HAVE BEEN A FAN OF YOURS FOR A LONG TIME.
THAT'S VERY FLATTERING. THANK YOU, MS. DAY.
NO. DARLING, YOU CALL ME SARAH AND NOTHING SO FORMAL AND NASTY-SOUNDING AS MS. DAY.
ONLY EX-HUSBANDS ARE TO CALL ME MS. DAY.
COME, NOW, CAROL MY DEAR. COME. WALK WITH ME.

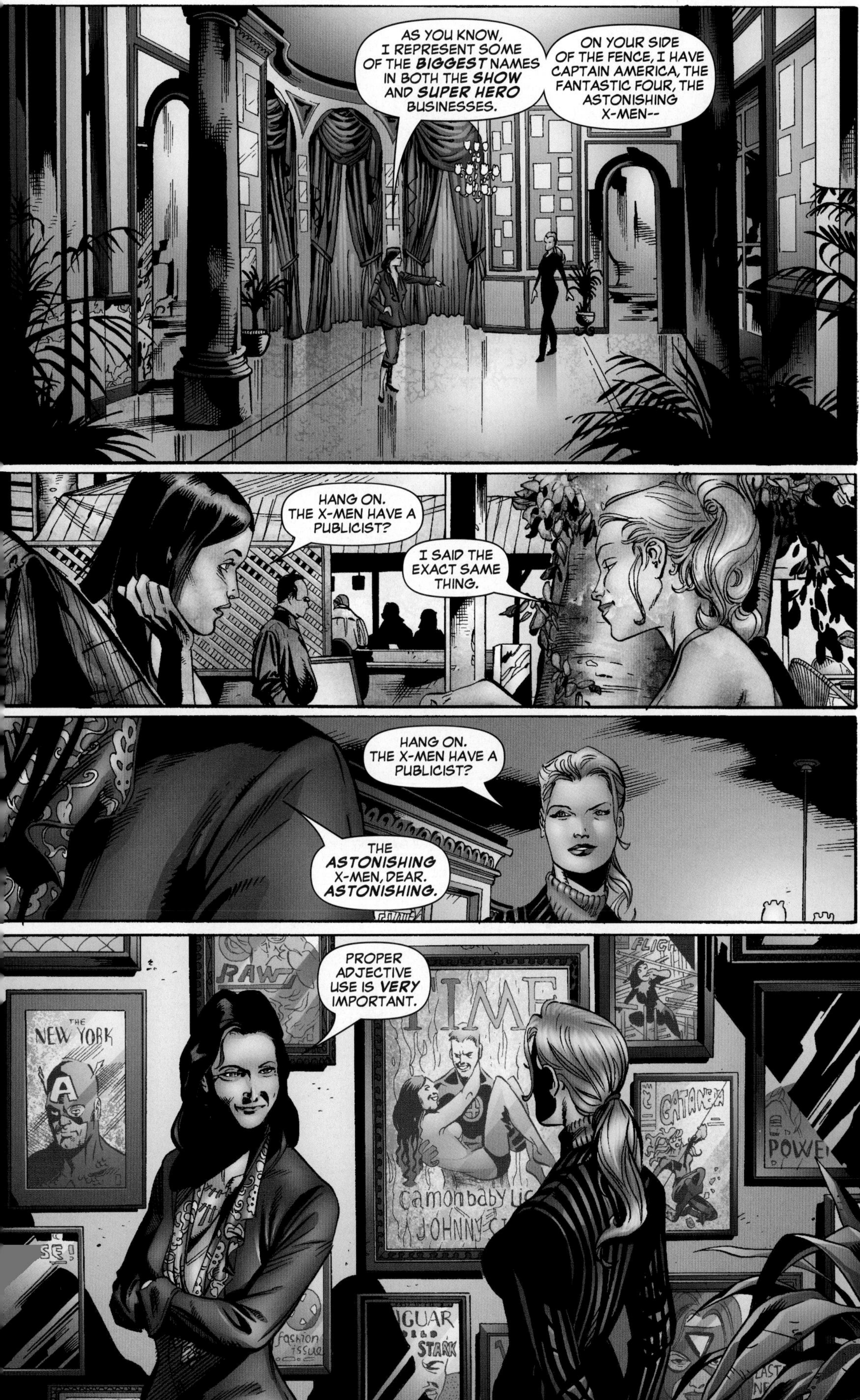

AS YOU KNOW, I REPRESENT SOME OF THE BIGGEST NAMES IN BOTH THE SHOW AND SUPER HERO BUSINESSES.
ON YOUR SIDE OF THE FENCE, I HAVE CAPTAIN AMERICA, THE FANTASTIC FOUR, THE ASTONISHING X-MEN--
HANG ON. THE X-MEN HAVE A PUBLICIST?
I SAID THE EXACT SAME THING.
HANG ON. THE X-MEN HAVE A PUBLICIST?
THE ASTONISHING X-MEN, DEAR. ASTONISHING.
PROPER ADJECTIVE USE IS VERY IMPORTANT.
THE NEW YORK
RAW
TIME
camon baby lic
JOHNNY
STARK
POWE
fashion issue
ELEGANT

SO, HERE'S WHAT I KNOW ABOUT YOU, AND TELL ME IF I'M LEAVING ANYTHING OUT.

EX-AIR FORCE. EX-NASA. EX-AVENGER. AND, AS OF LATE LAST WEEK, EX-HOMELAND SECURITY.

YOU QUIT YOUR HOMELAND SECURITY POST?

I'LL GET TO THAT IN A MINUTE.

YOU BEGAN YOUR SUPER HERO CAREER AS "MS. MARVEL", A NAME I QUITE LIKED, BUT HAVE ALSO GONE BY THE LESS COMPELLING TITLES OF "BINARY" AND, MORE RECENTLY, THE RATHER DREADFUL "WARBIRD".

ALL THE WHILE YOU'VE BEEN WEARING A COSTUME THAT, WELL, COULD BE MORE THAN IT IS, IF I MAY BE FRANK.

ALTHOUGH I *DO* LIKE THE BOOTS. *NOT* EVERYONE HAS THE LEGS FOR THEM. *YOU* DO.

LET'S SEE, WHAT ELSE DO I KNOW? OH, OF COURSE, YOU PUBLISHED A FEW NOVELS THAT GOT SOME ATTENTION.

AND NOW... WHAT?

I, UM--

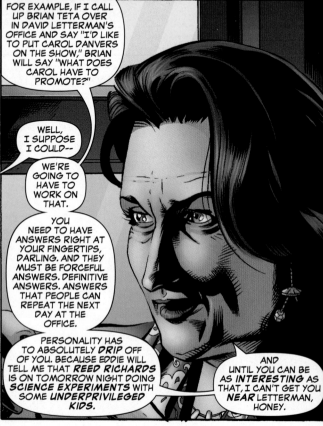

FOR EXAMPLE, IF I CALL UP BRIAN TETA OVER IN DAVID LETTERMAN'S OFFICE AND SAY "I'D LIKE TO PUT CAROL DANVERS ON THE SHOW," BRIAN WILL SAY "WHAT DOES CAROL HAVE TO PROMOTE?"

WELL, I SUPPOSE I COULD--

WE'RE GOING TO HAVE TO WORK ON THAT.

YOU NEED TO HAVE ANSWERS RIGHT AT YOUR FINGERTIPS, DARLING. AND THEY MUST BE FORCEFUL ANSWERS. DEFINITIVE ANSWERS. ANSWERS THAT PEOPLE CAN REPEAT THE NEXT DAY AT THE OFFICE.

PERSONALITY HAS TO ABSOLUTELY *DRIP* OFF OF YOU. BECAUSE EDDIE WILL TELL ME THAT *REED RICHARDS* IS ON TOMORROW NIGHT DOING *SCIENCE EXPERIMENTS* WITH SOME *UNDERPRIVILEGED KIDS.*

AND UNTIL YOU CAN BE AS *INTERESTING* AS THAT, I CAN'T GET YOU *NEAR* LETTERMAN, HONEY.

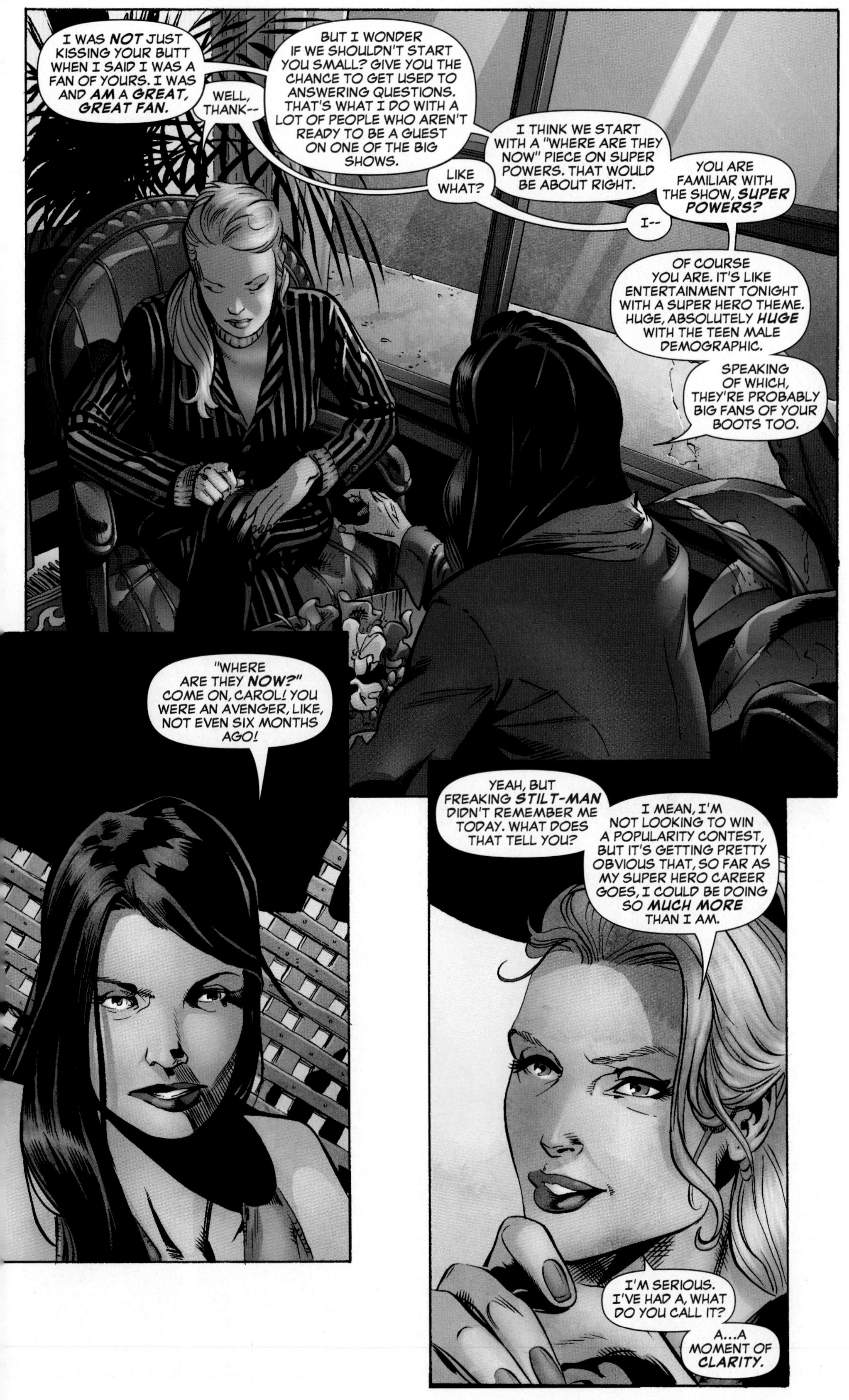
I WAS NOT JUST KISSING YOUR BUTT WHEN I SAID I WAS A FAN OF YOURS. I WAS AND AM A GREAT, GREAT FAN.
WELL, THANK--
BUT I WONDER IF WE SHOULDN'T START YOU SMALL? GIVE YOU THE CHANCE TO GET USED TO ANSWERING QUESTIONS. THAT'S WHAT I DO WITH A LOT OF PEOPLE WHO AREN'T READY TO BE A GUEST ON ONE OF THE BIG SHOWS.
LIKE WHAT?
I THINK WE START WITH A "WHERE ARE THEY NOW" PIECE ON SUPER POWERS. THAT WOULD BE ABOUT RIGHT.
YOU ARE FAMILIAR WITH THE SHOW, SUPER POWERS?
I--
OF COURSE YOU ARE. IT'S LIKE ENTERTAINMENT TONIGHT WITH A SUPER HERO THEME. HUGE, ABSOLUTELY HUGE WITH THE TEEN MALE DEMOGRAPHIC.
SPEAKING OF WHICH, THEY'RE PROBABLY BIG FANS OF YOUR BOOTS TOO.
"WHERE ARE THEY NOW?" COME ON, CAROL! YOU WERE AN AVENGER, LIKE, NOT EVEN SIX MONTHS AGO!
YEAH, BUT FREAKING STILT-MAN DIDN'T REMEMBER ME TODAY. WHAT DOES THAT TELL YOU?
I MEAN, I'M NOT LOOKING TO WIN A POPULARITY CONTEST, BUT IT'S GETTING PRETTY OBVIOUS THAT, SO FAR AS MY SUPER HERO CAREER GOES, I COULD BE DOING SO MUCH MORE THAN I AM.
I'M SERIOUS. I'VE HAD A, WHAT DO YOU CALL IT?
A...A MOMENT OF CLARITY.

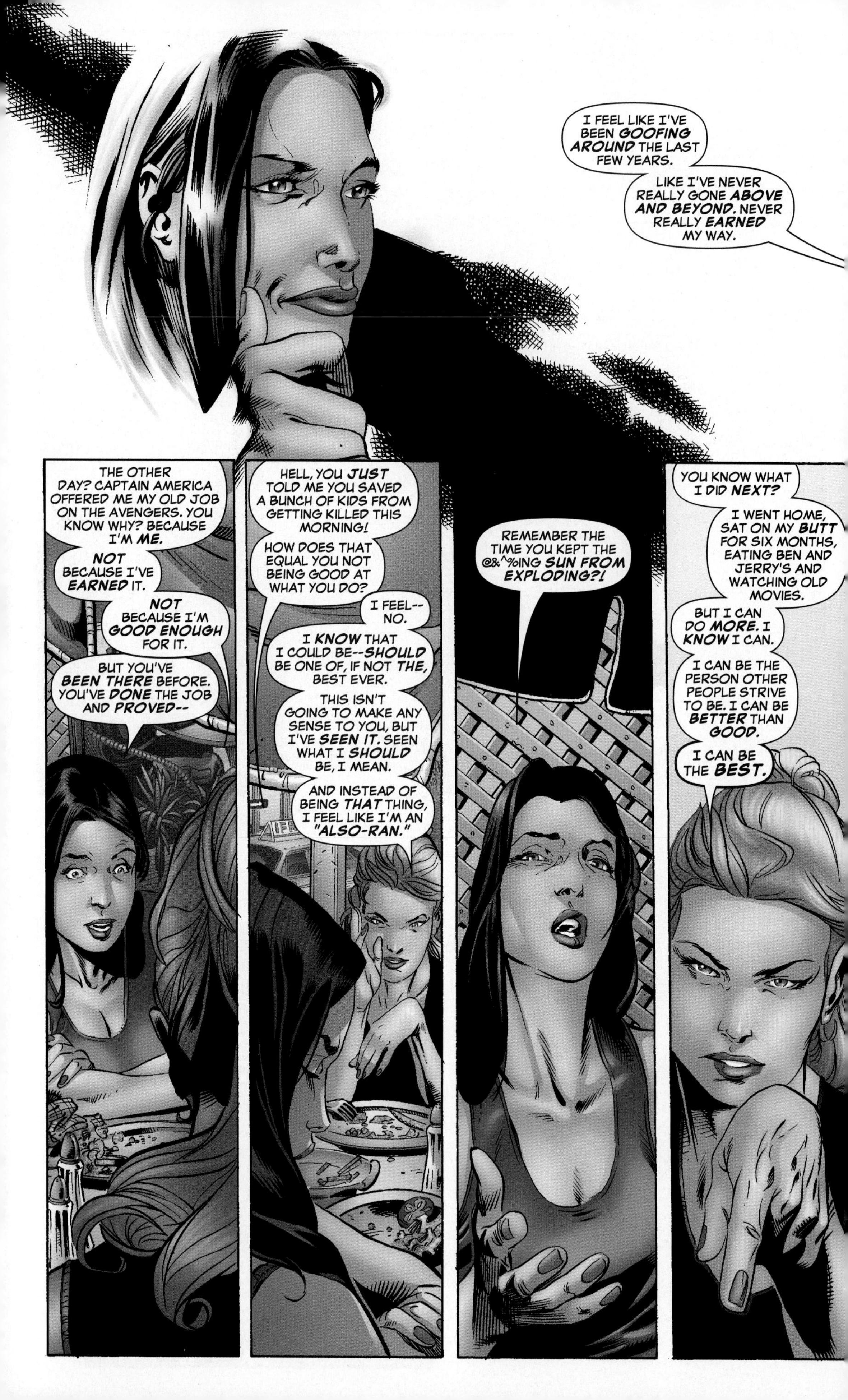
I FEEL LIKE I'VE BEEN GOOFING AROUND THE LAST FEW YEARS.
LIKE I'VE NEVER REALLY GONE ABOVE AND BEYOND. NEVER REALLY EARNED MY WAY.
THE OTHER DAY? CAPTAIN AMERICA OFFERED ME MY OLD JOB ON THE AVENGERS. YOU KNOW WHY? BECAUSE I'M ME.
NOT BECAUSE I'VE EARNED IT.
NOT BECAUSE I'M GOOD ENOUGH FOR IT.
BUT YOU'VE BEEN THERE BEFORE. YOU'VE DONE THE JOB AND PROVED--
HELL, YOU JUST TOLD ME YOU SAVED A BUNCH OF KIDS FROM GETTING KILLED THIS MORNING!
HOW DOES THAT EQUAL YOU NOT BEING GOOD AT WHAT YOU DO?
I FEEL-- NO.
I KNOW THAT I COULD BE--SHOULD BE ONE OF, IF NOT THE, BEST EVER.
THIS ISN'T GOING TO MAKE ANY SENSE TO YOU, BUT I'VE SEEN IT. SEEN WHAT I SHOULD BE, I MEAN.
AND INSTEAD OF BEING THAT THING, I FEEL LIKE I'M AN "ALSO-RAN."
REMEMBER THE TIME YOU KEPT THE @&^%ING SUN FROM EXPLODING?!
YOU KNOW WHAT I DID NEXT?
I WENT HOME, SAT ON MY BUTT FOR SIX MONTHS, EATING BEN AND JERRY'S AND WATCHING OLD MOVIES.
BUT I CAN DO MORE. I KNOW I CAN.
I CAN BE THE PERSON OTHER PEOPLE STRIVE TO BE. I CAN BE BETTER THAN GOOD.
I CAN BE THE BEST.

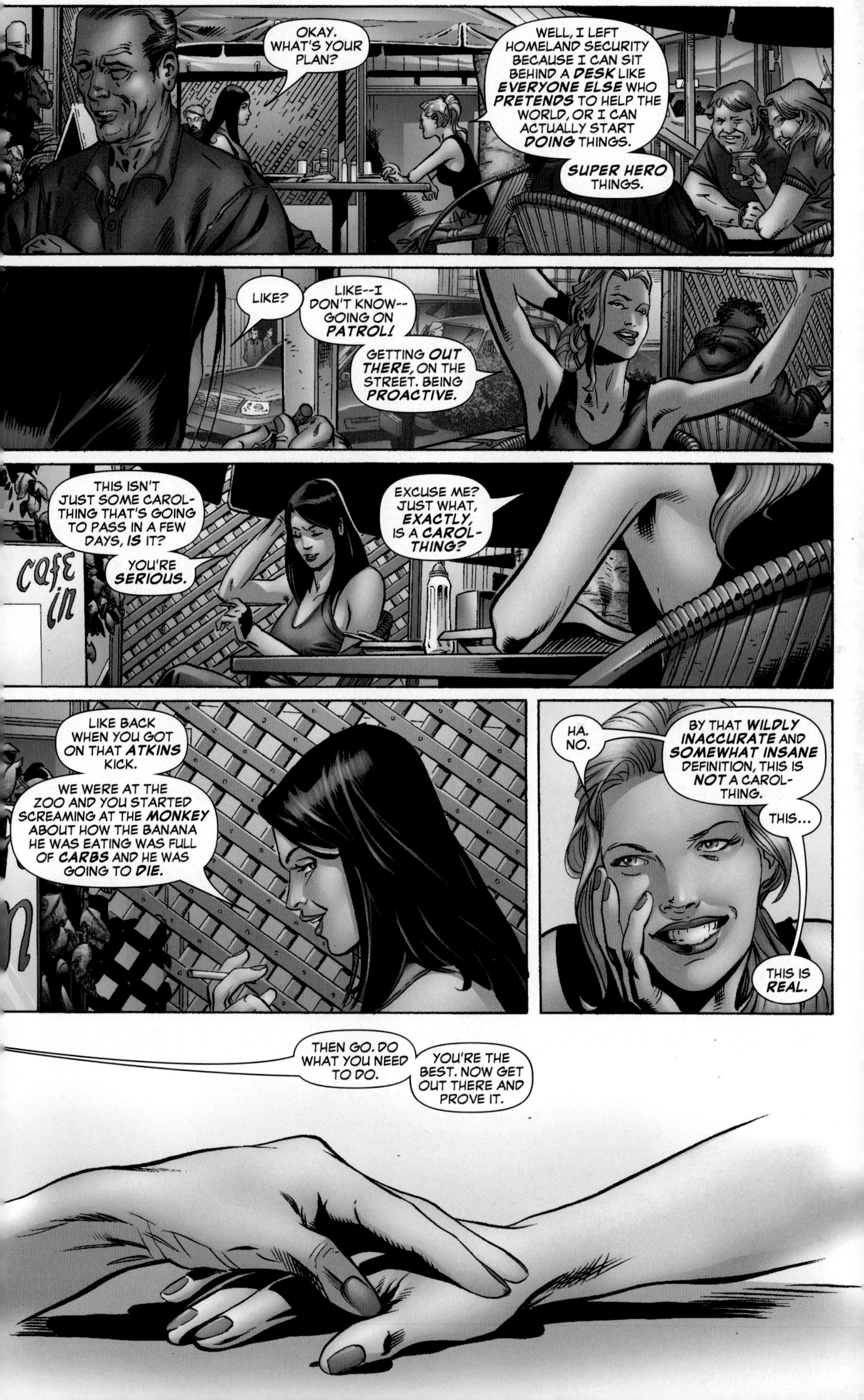
OKAY. WHAT'S YOUR PLAN?
WELL, I LEFT HOMELAND SECURITY BECAUSE I CAN SIT BEHIND A DESK LIKE EVERYONE ELSE WHO PRETENDS TO HELP THE WORLD, OR I CAN ACTUALLY START DOING THINGS.
SUPER HERO THINGS.
LIKE?
LIKE--I DON'T KNOW--GOING ON PATROL!
GETTING OUT THERE, ON THE STREET. BEING PROACTIVE.
THIS ISN'T JUST SOME CAROL-THING THAT'S GOING TO PASS IN A FEW DAYS, IS IT?
YOU'RE SERIOUS.
EXCUSE ME? JUST WHAT, EXACTLY, IS A CAROL-THING?
CAFE
LIKE BACK WHEN YOU GOT ON THAT ATKINS KICK.
WE WERE AT THE ZOO AND YOU STARTED SCREAMING AT THE MONKEY ABOUT HOW THE BANANA HE WAS EATING WAS FULL OF CARBS AND HE WAS GOING TO DIE.
HA. NO.
BY THAT WILDLY INACCURATE AND SOMEWHAT INSANE DEFINITION, THIS IS NOT A CAROL-THING.
THIS...
THIS IS REAL.
THEN GO. DO WHAT YOU NEED TO DO.
YOU'RE THE BEST. NOW GET OUT THERE AND PROVE IT.

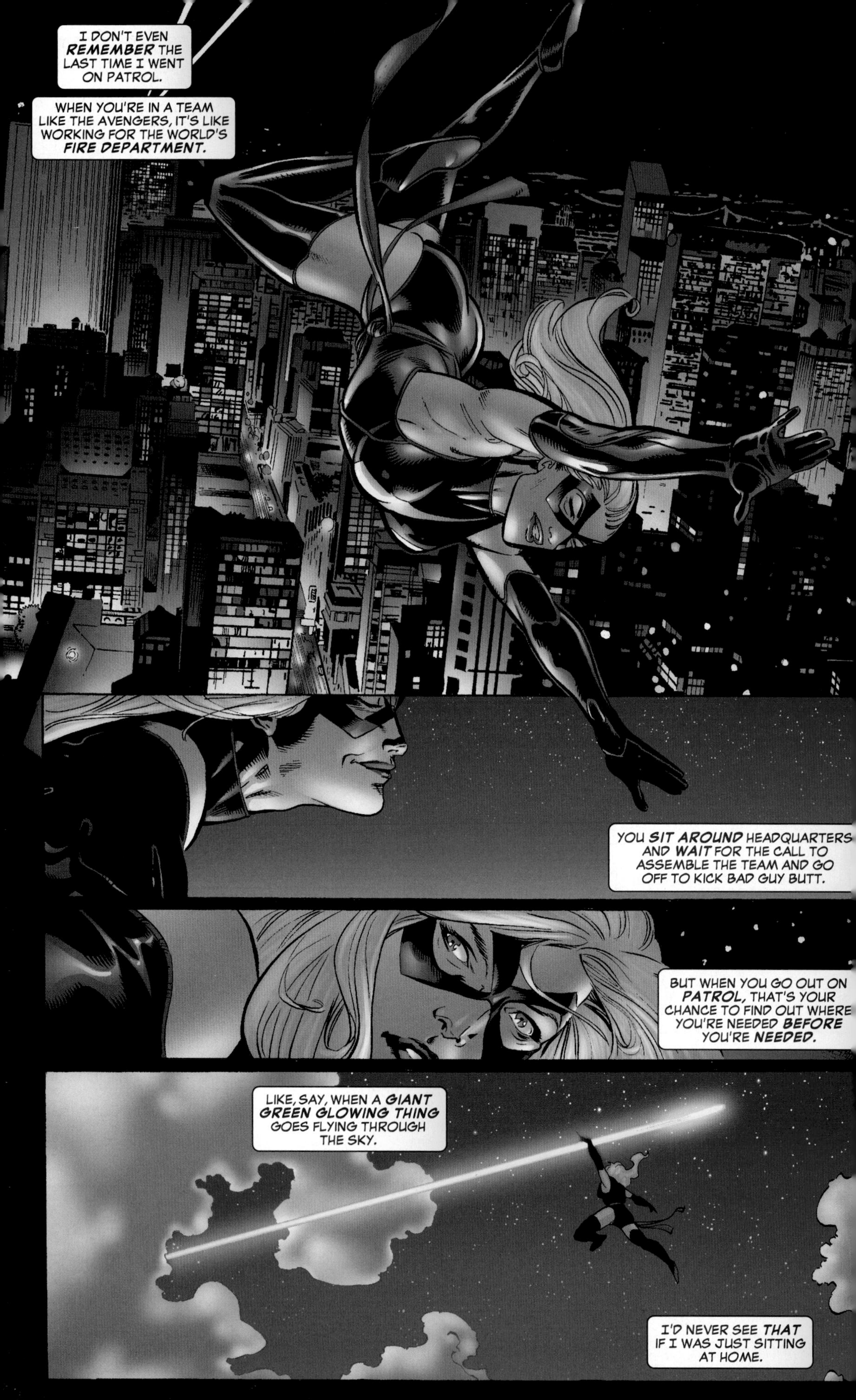
I DON'T EVEN REMEMBER THE LAST TIME I WENT ON PATROL.
WHEN YOU'RE IN A TEAM LIKE THE AVENGERS, IT'S LIKE WORKING FOR THE WORLD'S FIRE DEPARTMENT.
YOU SIT AROUND HEADQUARTERS AND WAIT FOR THE CALL TO ASSEMBLE THE TEAM AND GO OFF TO KICK BAD GUY BUTT.
BUT WHEN YOU GO OUT ON PATROL, THAT'S YOUR CHANCE TO FIND OUT WHERE YOU'RE NEEDED BEFORE YOU'RE NEEDED.
LIKE, SAY, WHEN A GIANT GREEN GLOWING THING GOES FLYING THROUGH THE SKY.
I'D NEVER SEE THAT IF I WAS JUST SITTING AT HOME.

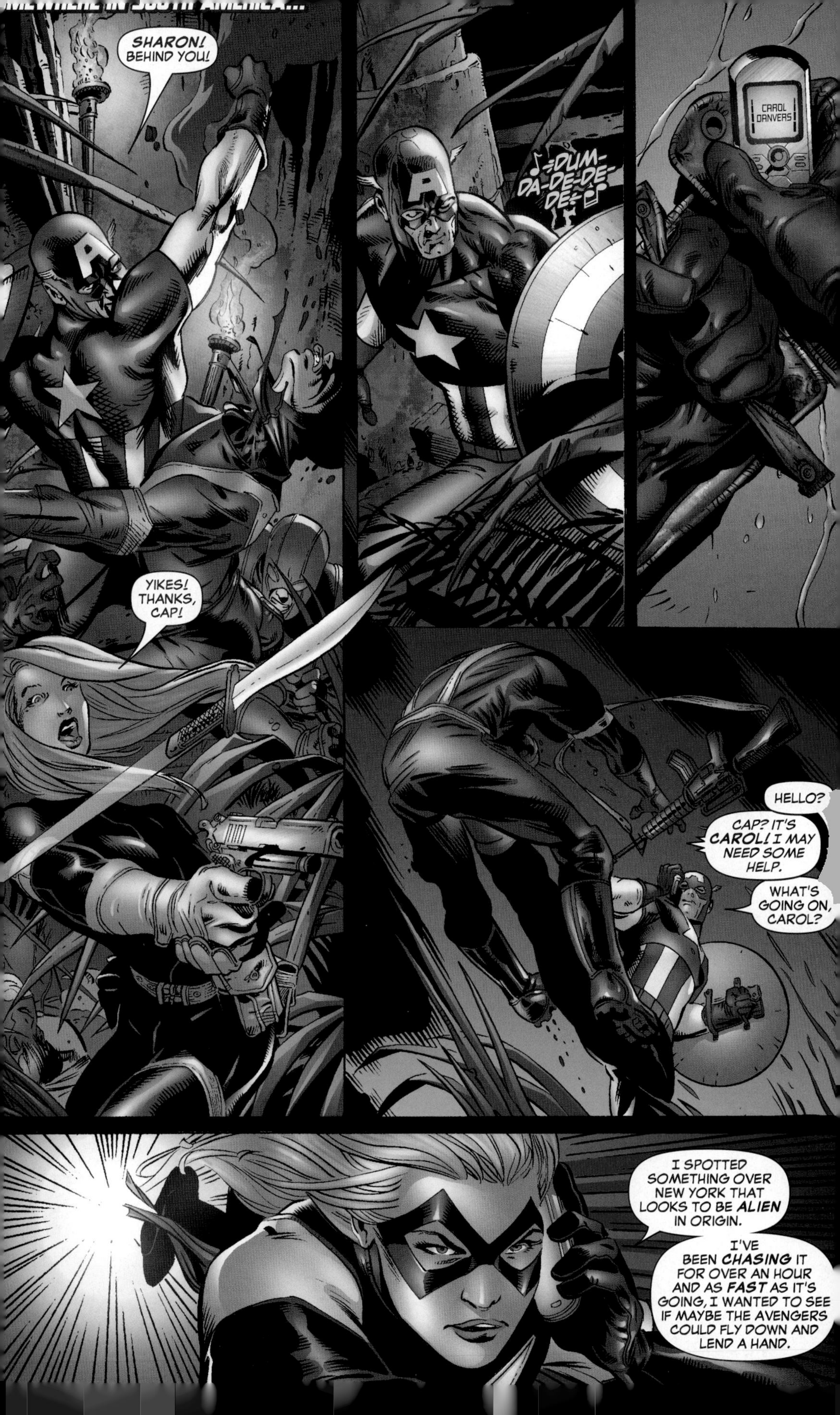

MEWHERE IN SOUTH AMERICA...
SHARON! BEHIND YOU!
YIKES! THANKS, CAP!
DUM-DA-DE-DE-DE
CAROL DANVERS
HELLO?
CAP? IT'S CAROL! I MAY NEED SOME HELP.
WHAT'S GOING ON, CAROL?
I SPOTTED SOMETHING OVER NEW YORK THAT LOOKS TO BE ALIEN IN ORIGIN.
I'VE BEEN CHASING IT FOR OVER AN HOUR AND AS FAST AS IT'S GOING, I WANTED TO SEE IF MAYBE THE AVENGERS COULD FLY DOWN AND LEND A HAND.

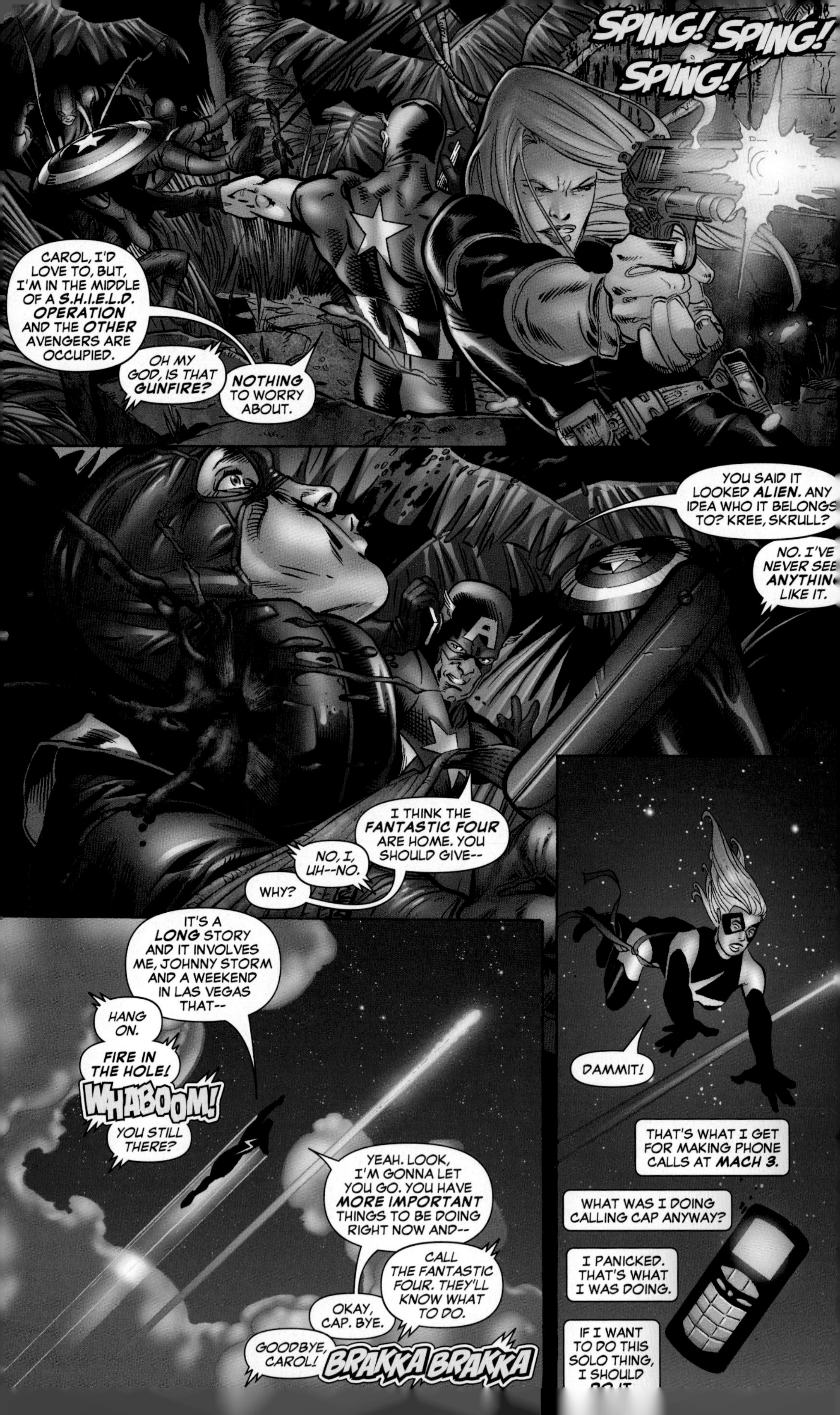
SPING! SPING! SPING!
CAROL, I'D LOVE TO, BUT, I'M IN THE MIDDLE OF A S.H.I.E.L.D. OPERATION AND THE OTHER AVENGERS ARE OCCUPIED.
OH MY GOD, IS THAT GUNFIRE?
NOTHING TO WORRY ABOUT.
YOU SAID IT LOOKED ALIEN. ANY IDEA WHO IT BELONGS TO? KREE, SKRULL?
NO. I'VE NEVER SEE ANYTHIN LIKE IT.
I THINK THE FANTASTIC FOUR ARE HOME. YOU SHOULD GIVE--
NO, I, UH--NO.
WHY?
IT'S A LONG STORY AND IT INVOLVES ME, JOHNNY STORM AND A WEEKEND IN LAS VEGAS THAT--
HANG ON.
FIRE IN THE HOLE!
WHABOOM!
YOU STILL THERE?
YEAH. LOOK, I'M GONNA LET YOU GO. YOU HAVE MORE IMPORTANT THINGS TO BE DOING RIGHT NOW AND--
CALL THE FANTASTIC FOUR. THEY'LL KNOW WHAT TO DO.
OKAY, CAP. BYE.
GOODBYE, CAROL!
BRAKKA BRAKKA
DAMMIT!
THAT'S WHAT I GET FOR MAKING PHONE CALLS AT MACH 3.
WHAT WAS I DOING CALLING CAP ANYWAY?
I PANICKED. THAT'S WHAT I WAS DOING.
IF I WANT TO DO THIS SOLO THING, I SHOULD

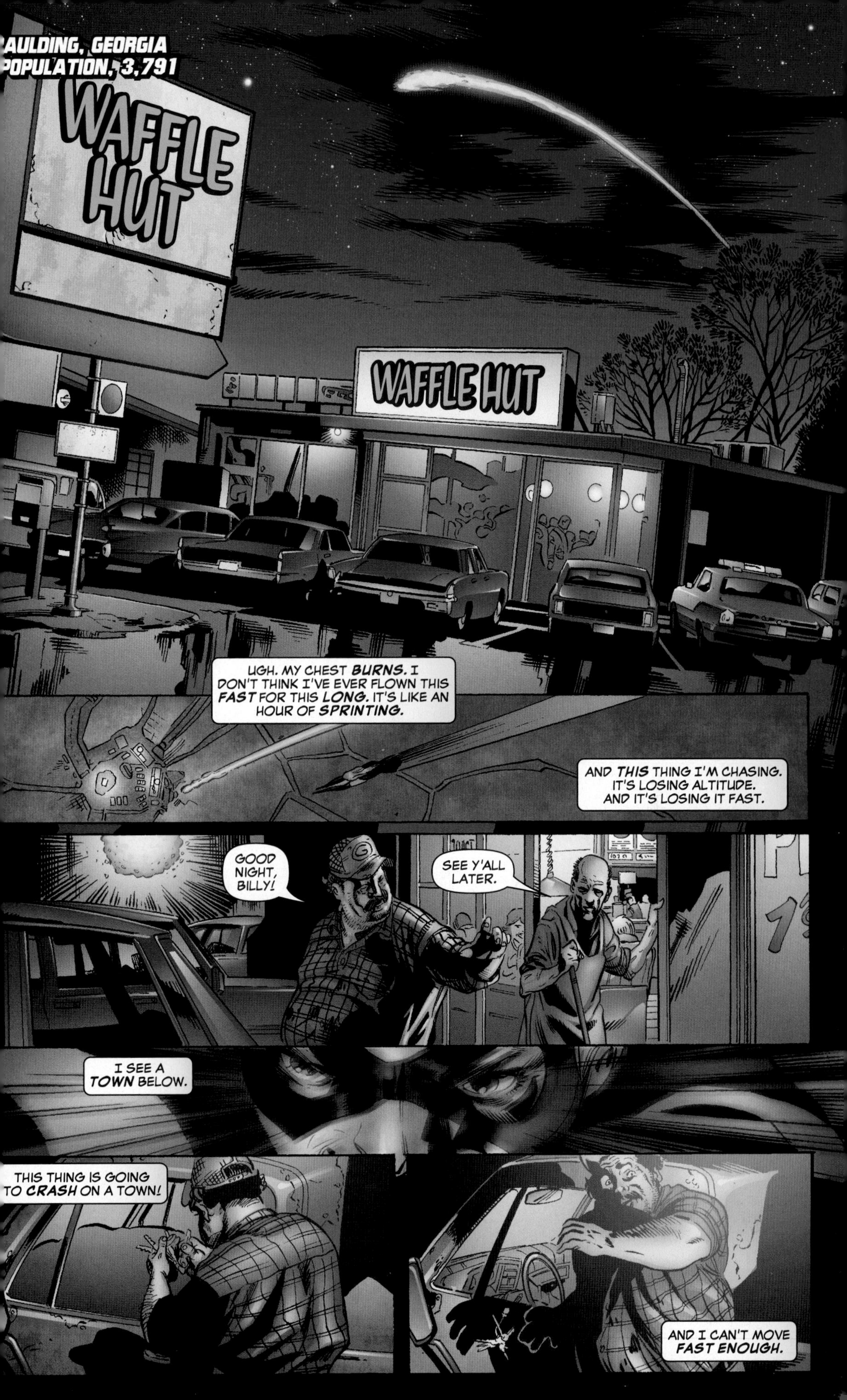

AULDING, GEORGIA
POPULATION, 3,791
WAFFLE HUT
WAFFLE HUT
UGH. MY CHEST BURNS. I DON'T THINK I'VE EVER FLOWN THIS FAST FOR THIS LONG. IT'S LIKE AN HOUR OF SPRINTING.
AND THIS THING I'M CHASING. IT'S LOSING ALTITUDE. AND IT'S LOSING IT FAST.
GOOD NIGHT, BILLY!
SEE Y'ALL LATER.
I SEE A TOWN BELOW.
THIS THING IS GOING TO CRASH ON A TOWN!
AND I CAN'T MOVE FAST ENOUGH.

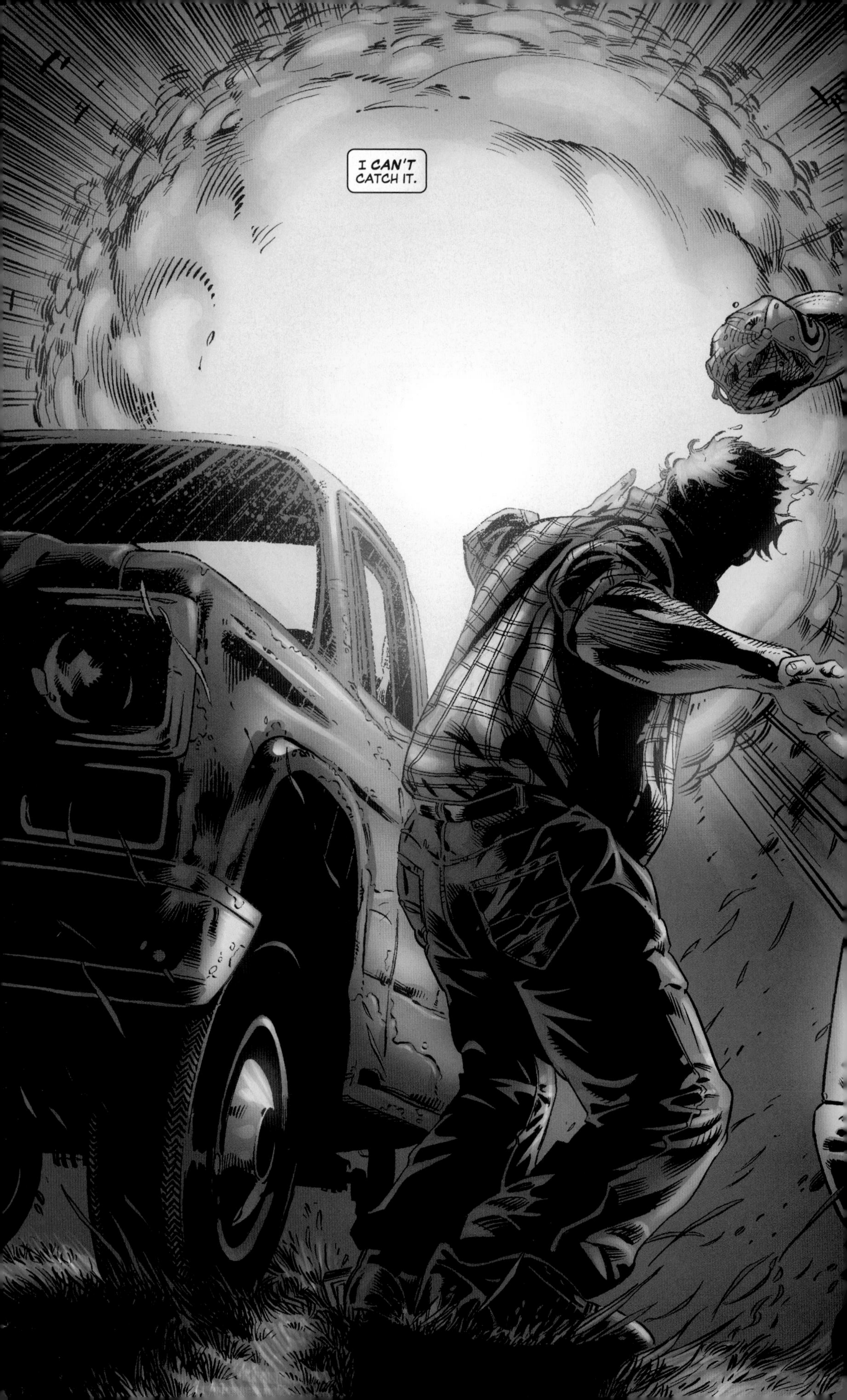
I CAN'T CATCH IT.

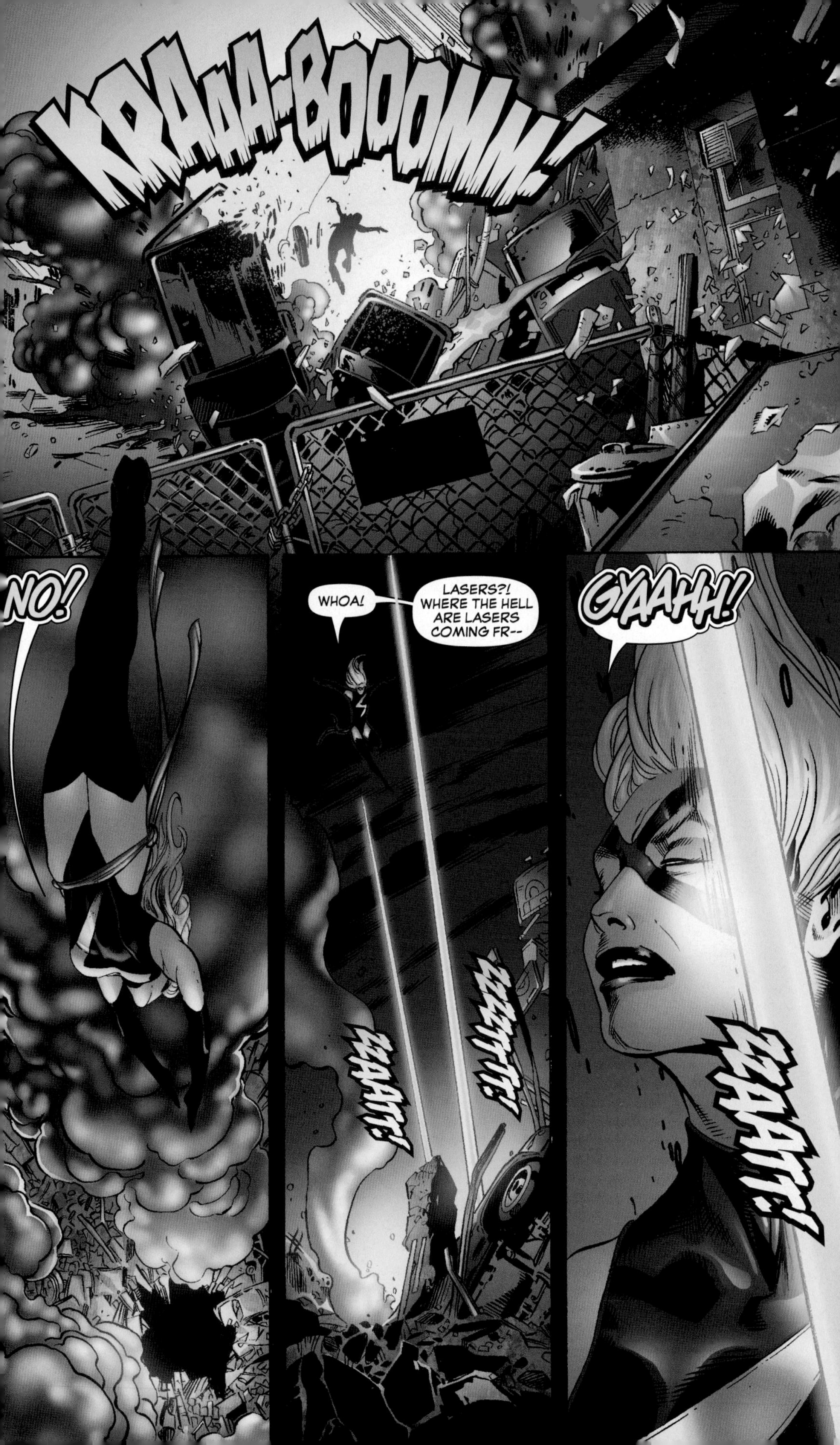
KRAAA-BOOOMM!
NO!
WHOA!
LASERS?! WHERE THE HELL ARE LASERS COMING FR--
ZZAATT!
ZZZZTTTT!
GYAAHH!
ZZAATT!

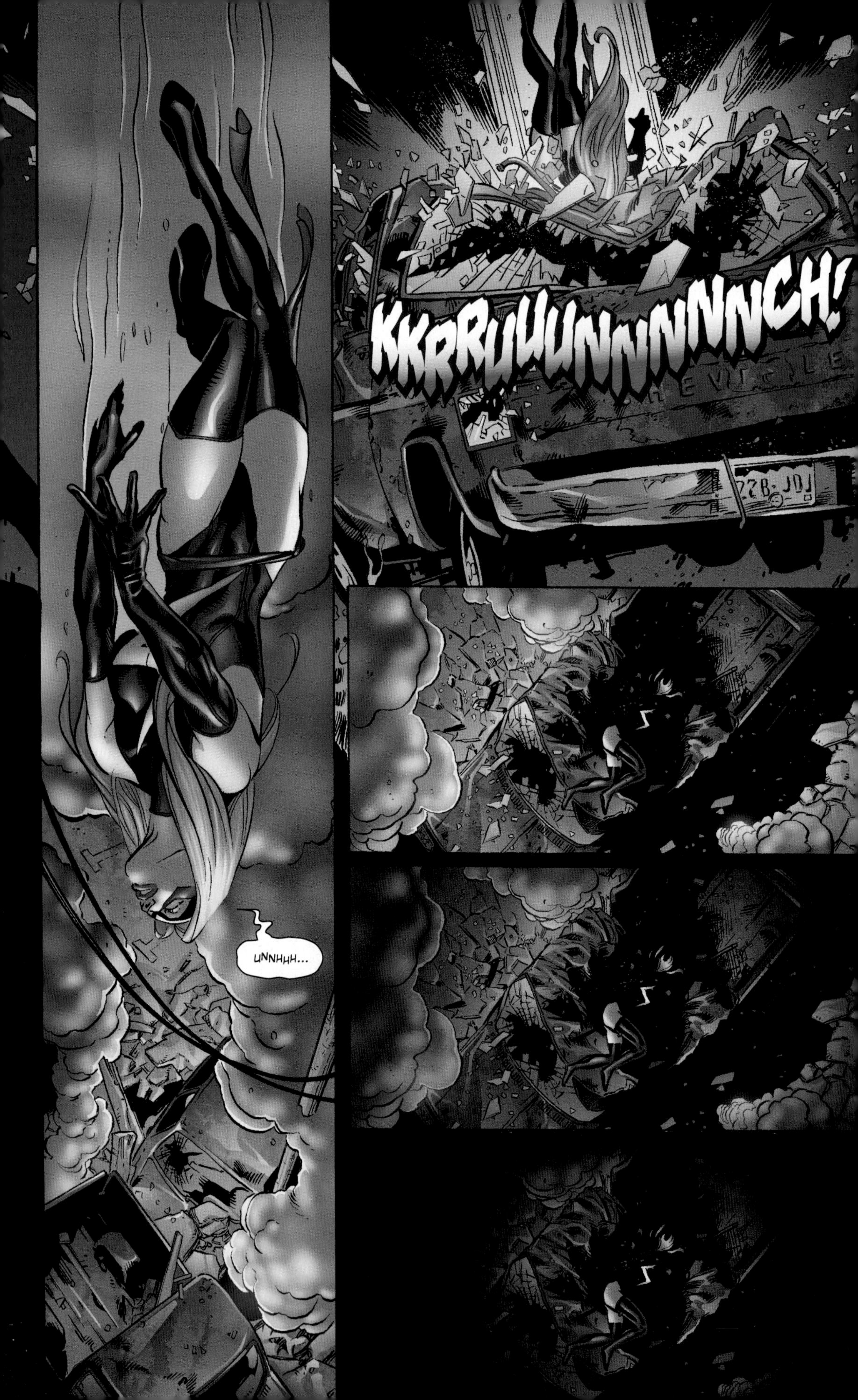
KKRRUUUNNNNNNCH!
UNNHHH...

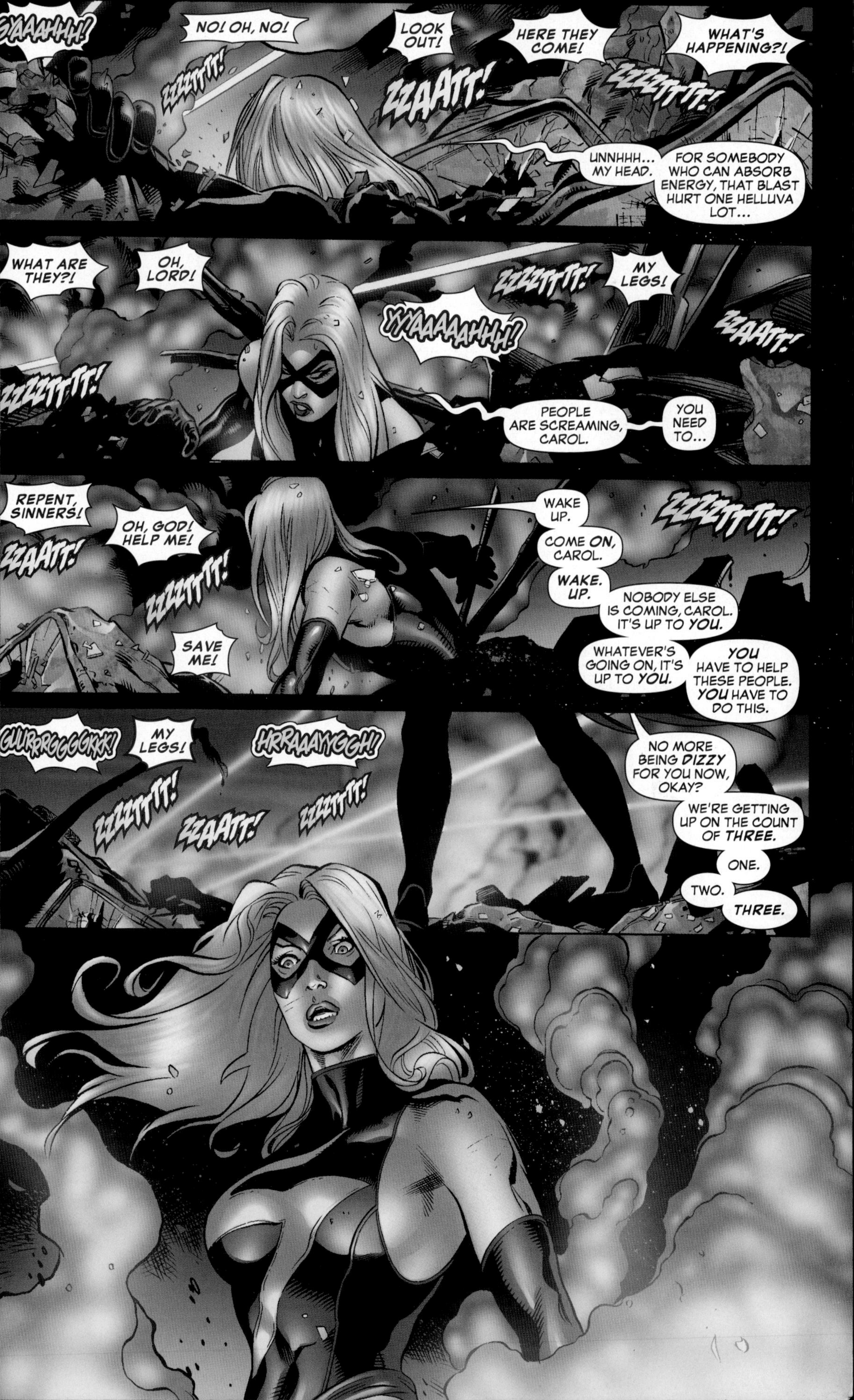
YAAAHHH!
NO! OH, NO!
LOOK OUT!
HERE THEY COME!
WHAT'S HAPPENING?!
ZZZZTTTT!
ZZAATT!
ZZZZTTTT!
UNNHHH... MY HEAD.
FOR SOMEBODY WHO CAN ABSORB ENERGY, THAT BLAST HURT ONE HELLUVA LOT...
WHAT ARE THEY?!
OH, LORD!
ZZZZTTTT!
MY LEGS!
YYAAAAAHHH!
ZZAATT!
ZZZZTTTT!
PEOPLE ARE SCREAMING, CAROL.
YOU NEED TO...
REPENT, SINNERS!
OH, GOD! HELP ME!
ZZAATT!
ZZZZTTTT!
SAVE ME!
WAKE UP.
COME ON, CAROL.
WAKE. UP.
NOBODY ELSE IS COMING, CAROL. IT'S UP TO YOU.
WHATEVER'S GOING ON, IT'S UP TO YOU.
YOU HAVE TO HELP THESE PEOPLE. YOU HAVE TO DO THIS.
ZZZZTTTT!
GUURRRGGGKKK!
MY LEGS!
HRRAAAYYGGH!
ZZZZTTTT!
ZZAATT!
ZZZZTTTT!
NO MORE BEING DIZZY FOR YOU NOW, OKAY?
WE'RE GETTING UP ON THE COUNT OF THREE.
ONE.
TWO.
THREE.

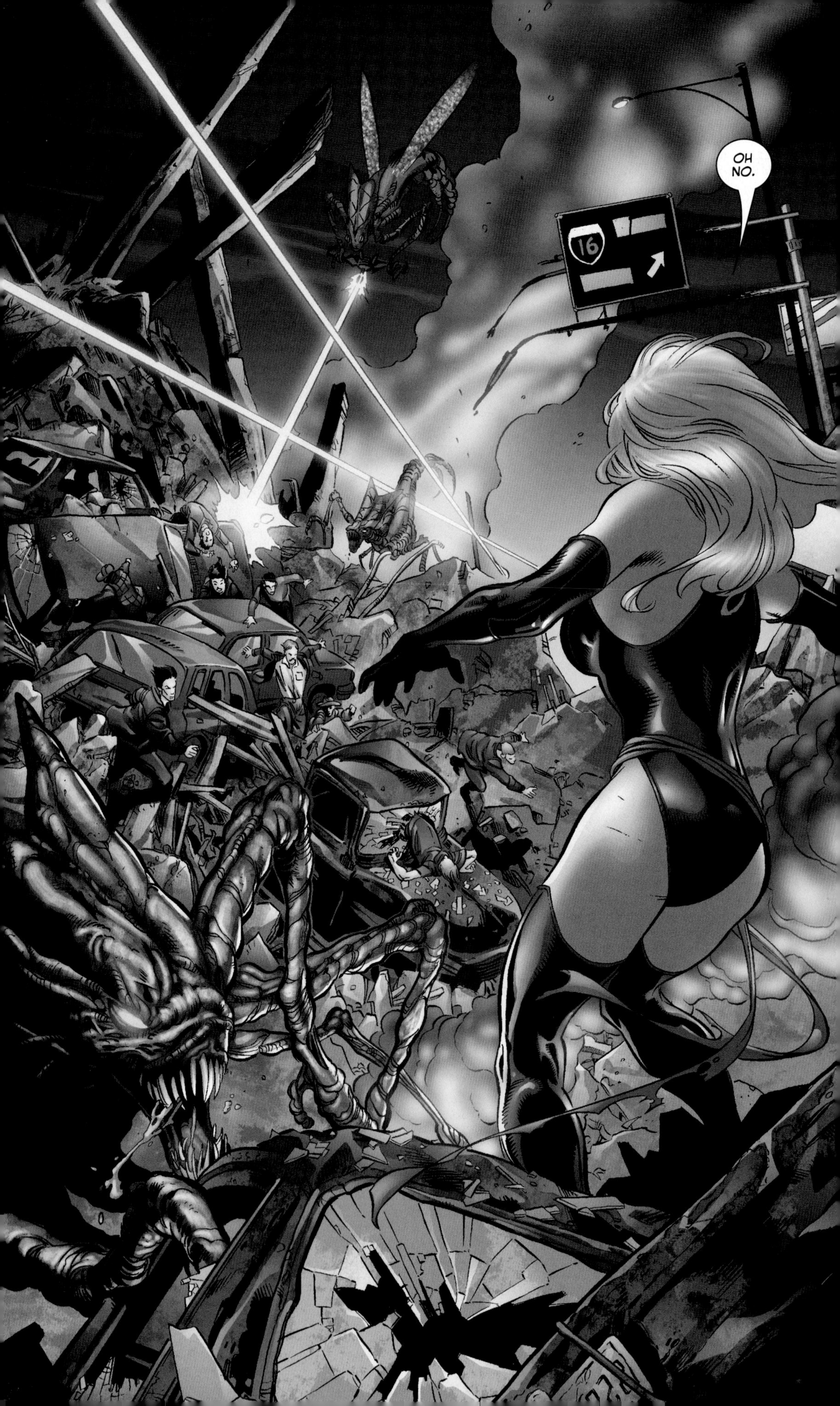
OH NO.
16

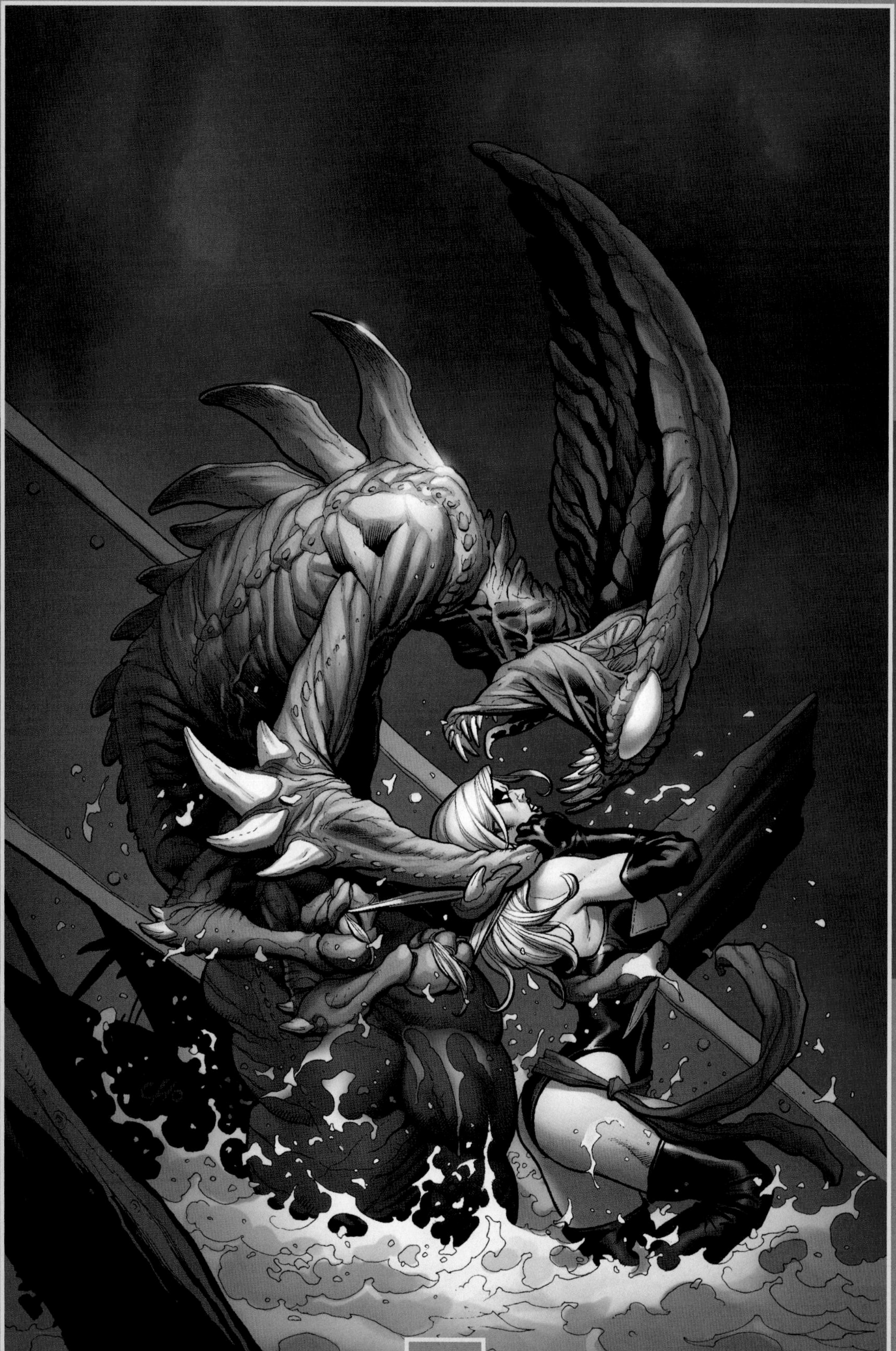

2

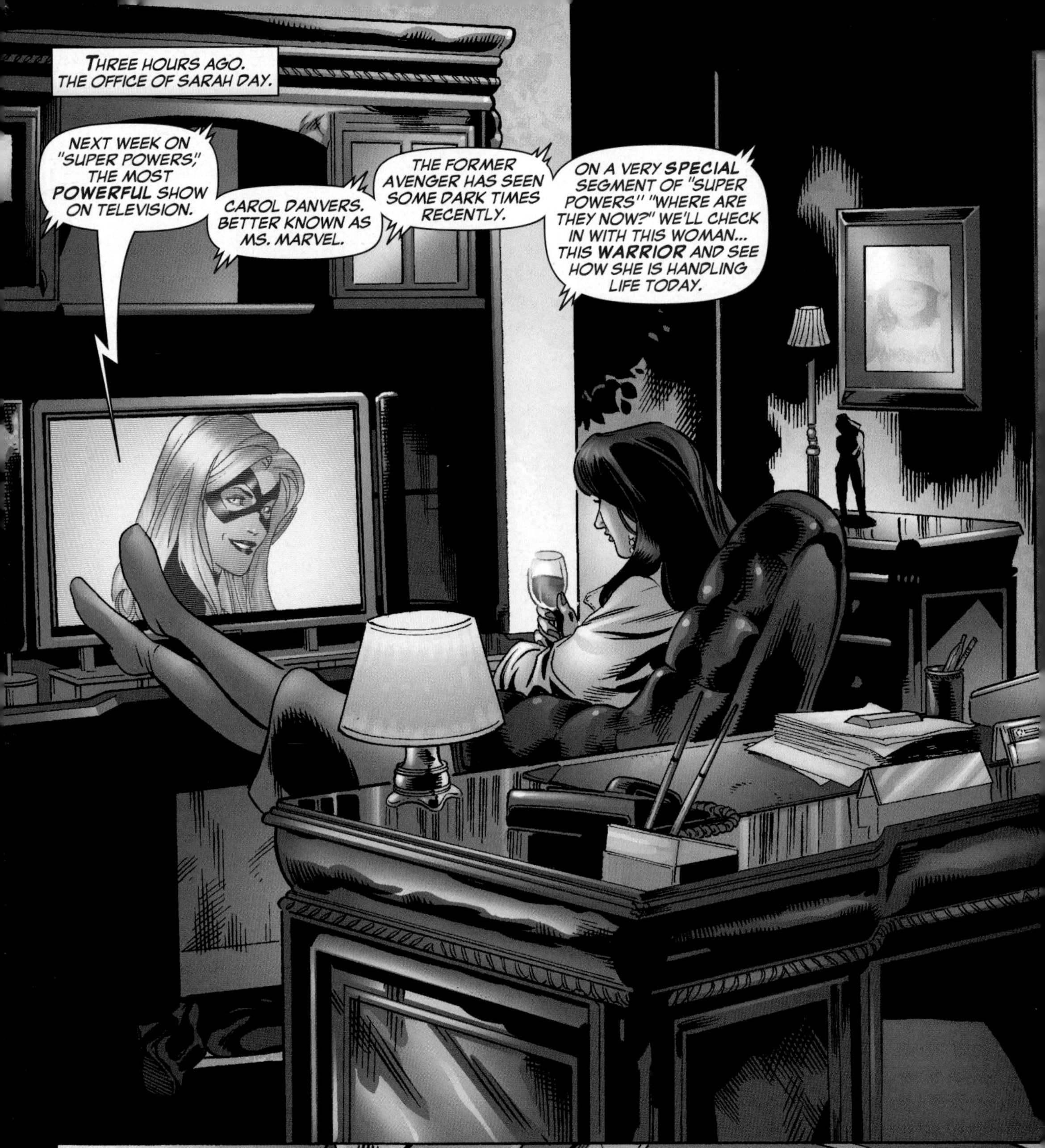

THREE HOURS AGO. THE OFFICE OF SARAH DAY.
NEXT WEEK ON "SUPER POWERS," THE MOST POWERFUL SHOW ON TELEVISION.
CAROL DANVERS. BETTER KNOWN AS MS. MARVEL.
THE FORMER AVENGER HAS SEEN SOME DARK TIMES RECENTLY.
ON A VERY SPECIAL SEGMENT OF "SUPER POWERS'' "WHERE ARE THEY NOW?" WE'LL CHECK IN WITH THIS WOMAN... THIS WARRIOR AND SEE HOW SHE IS HANDLING LIFE TODAY.

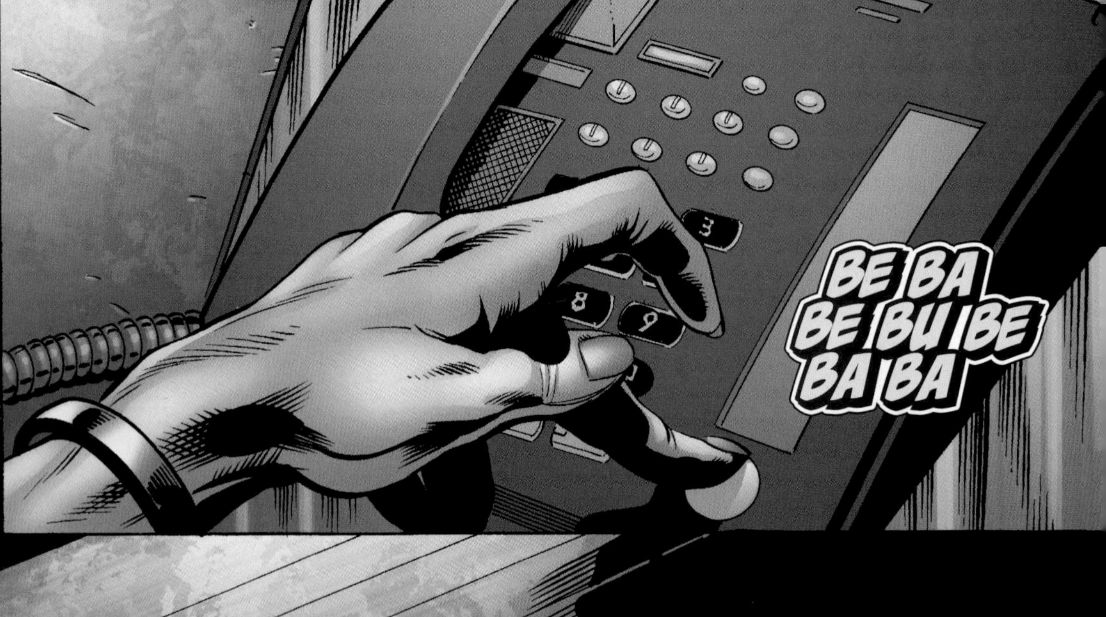

BE BA BE BU BE BA BA

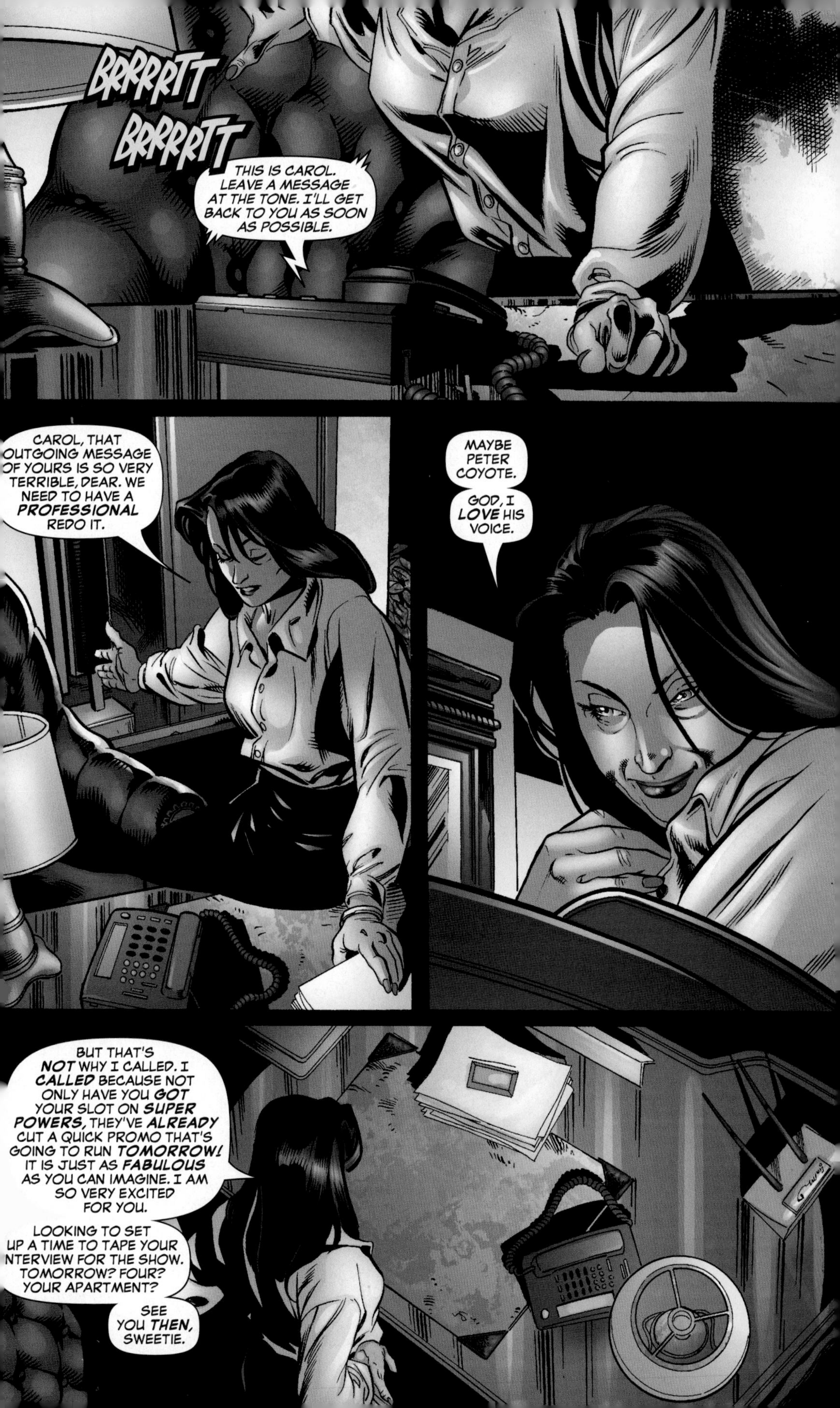
BRRRRTT
BRRRRTT
THIS IS CAROL. LEAVE A MESSAGE AT THE TONE. I'LL GET BACK TO YOU AS SOON AS POSSIBLE.
CAROL, THAT OUTGOING MESSAGE OF YOURS IS SO VERY TERRIBLE, DEAR. WE NEED TO HAVE A PROFESSIONAL REDO IT.
MAYBE PETER COYOTE.
GOD, I LOVE HIS VOICE.
BUT THAT'S NOT WHY I CALLED. I CALLED BECAUSE NOT ONLY HAVE YOU GOT YOUR SLOT ON SUPER POWERS, THEY'VE ALREADY CUT A QUICK PROMO THAT'S GOING TO RUN TOMORROW! IT IS JUST AS FABULOUS AS YOU CAN IMAGINE. I AM SO VERY EXCITED FOR YOU.
LOOKING TO SET UP A TIME TO TAPE YOUR INTERVIEW FOR THE SHOW. TOMORROW? FOUR? YOUR APARTMENT?
SEE YOU THEN, SWEETIE.

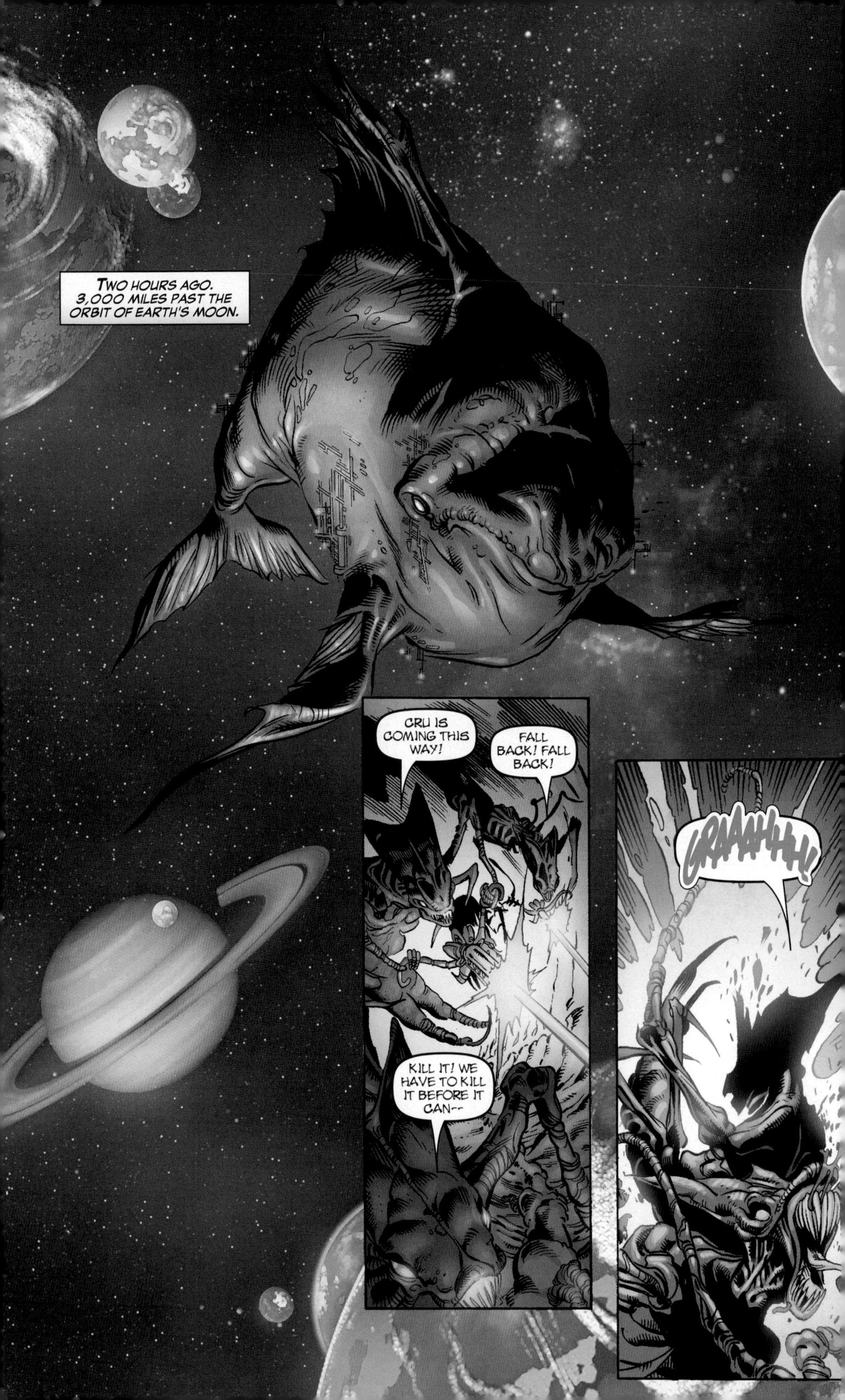
TWO HOURS AGO. 3,000 MILES PAST THE ORBIT OF EARTH'S MOON.
CRU IS COMING THIS WAY!
FALL BACK! FALL BACK!
KILL IT! WE HAVE TO KILL IT BEFORE IT CAN--
GRAAAHHHH!

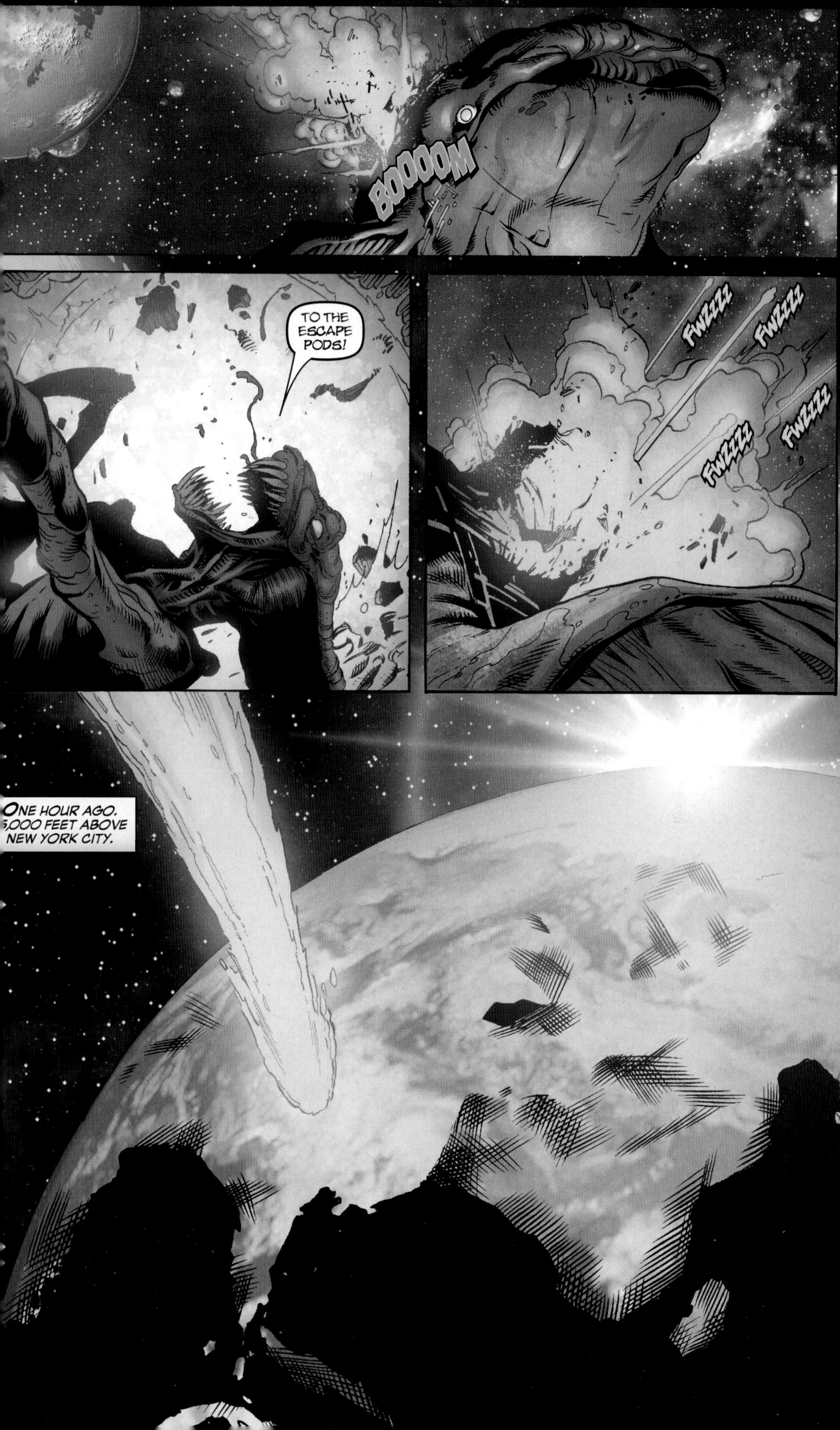
BOOOOM
TO THE ESCAPE PODS!
FWZZZZ
FWZZZZ
FWZZZZ
FWZZZZ
ONE HOUR AGO. 5,000 FEET ABOVE NEW YORK CITY.

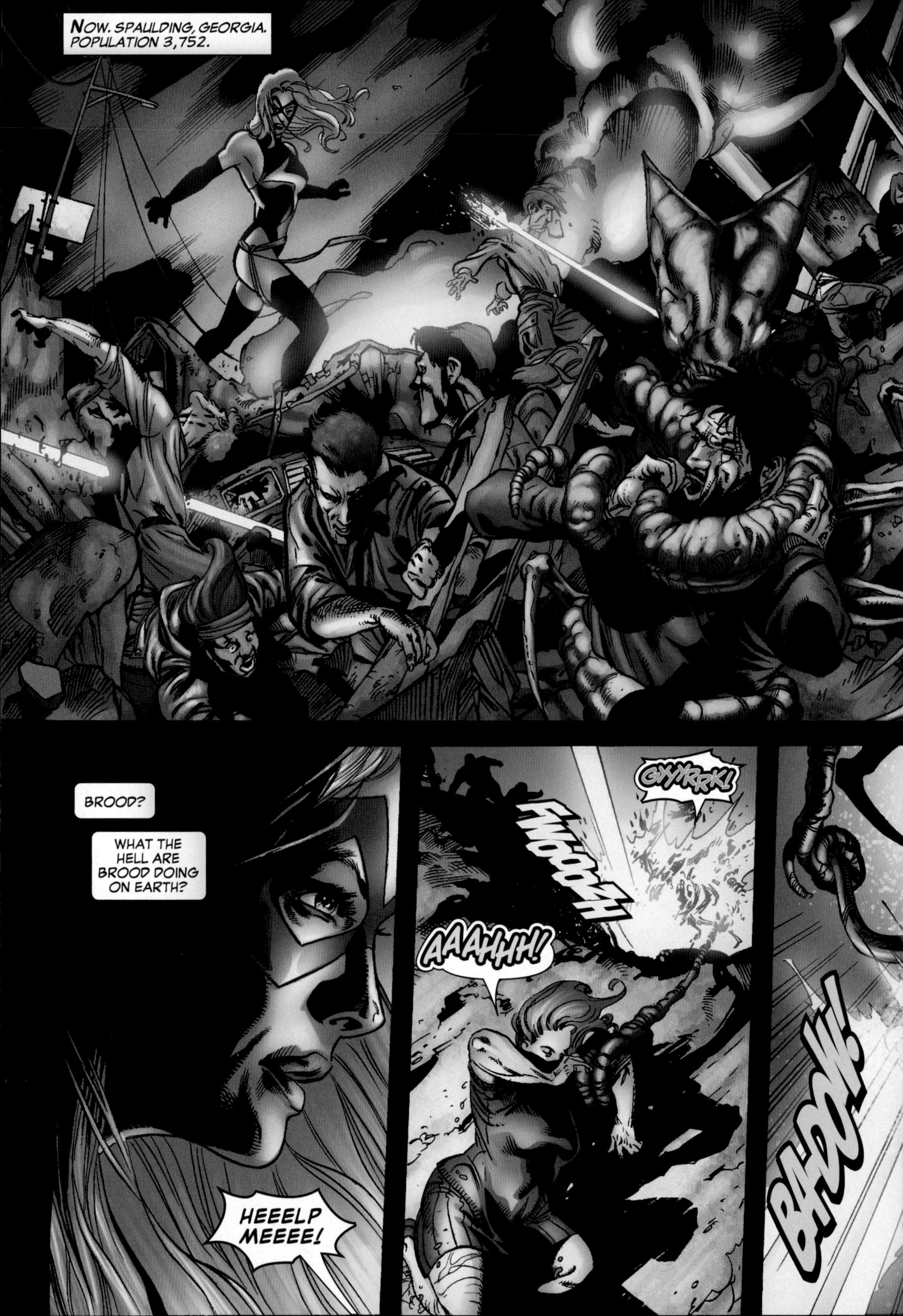

NOW. SPAULDING, GEORGIA. POPULATION 3,752.
BROOD?
WHAT THE HELL ARE BROOD DOING ON EARTH?
HEEELP MEEEE!
GYYRRK!
FWOOOSH
AAAHHH!
BA-DOOM!

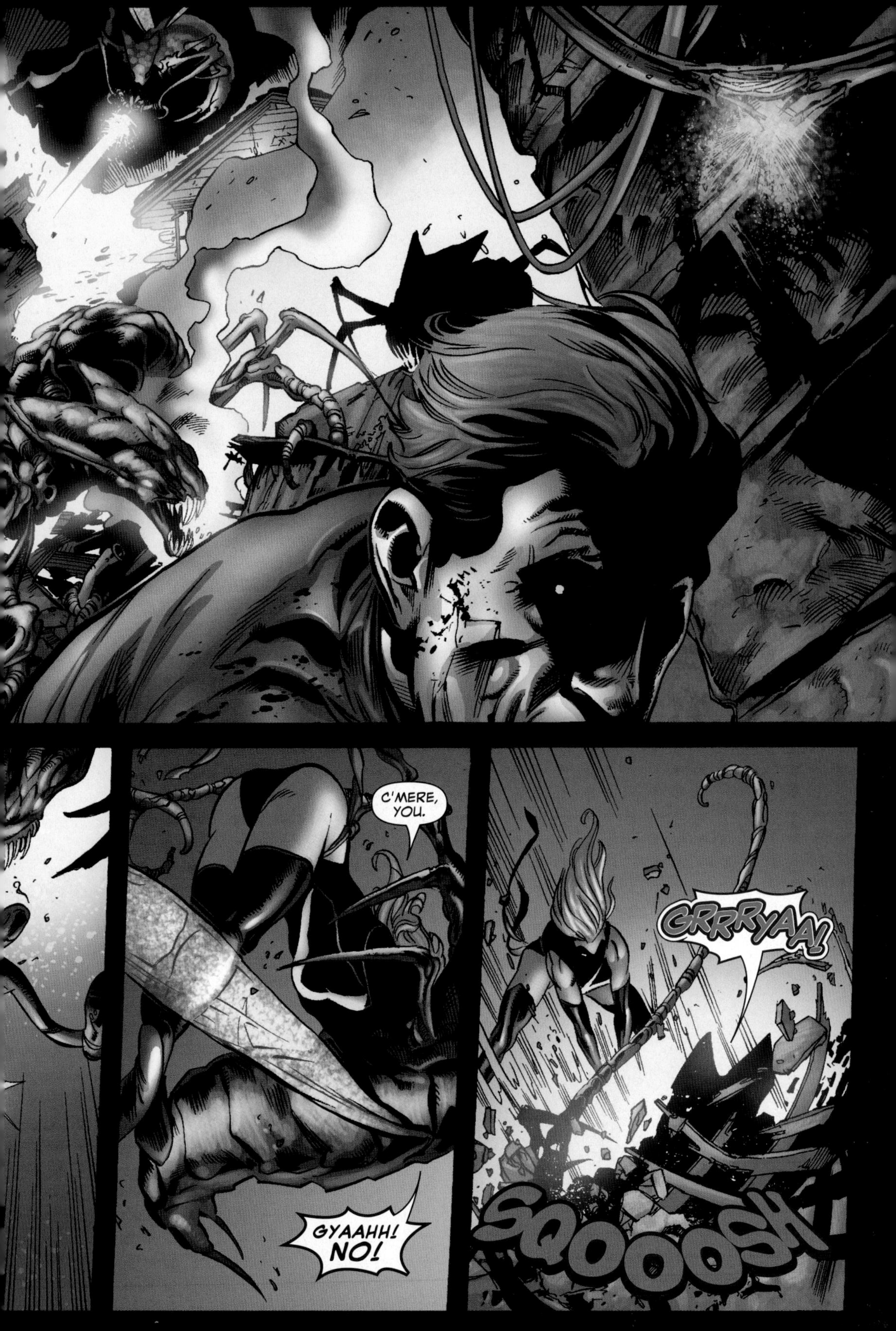
C'MERE, YOU.
GYAAHH! NO!
GRRRYAA!
SQOOOSH

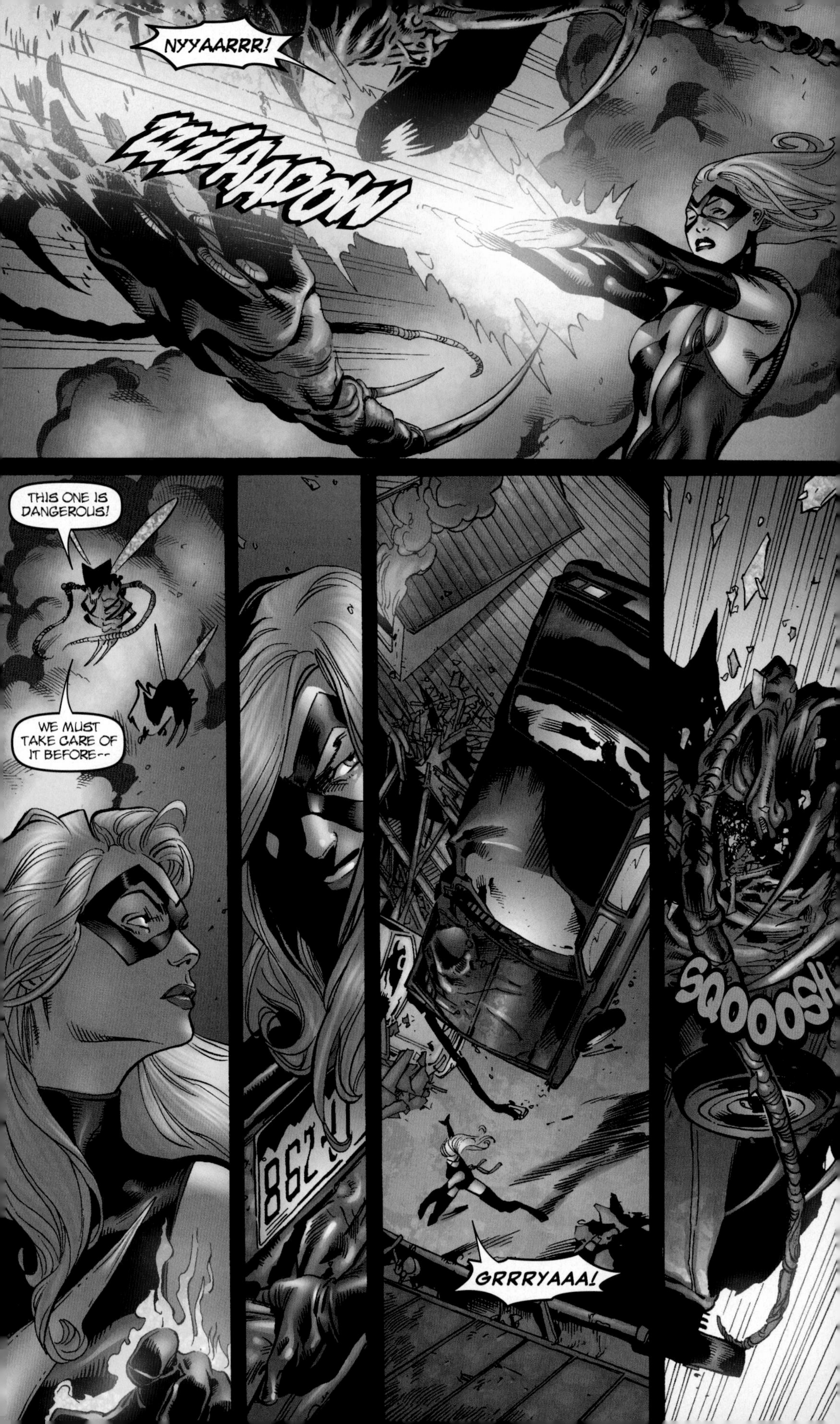
NYYAARRR!
THIS ONE IS DANGEROUS!
WE MUST TAKE CARE OF IT BEFORE--
GRRRYAAA!
SQOOOSH

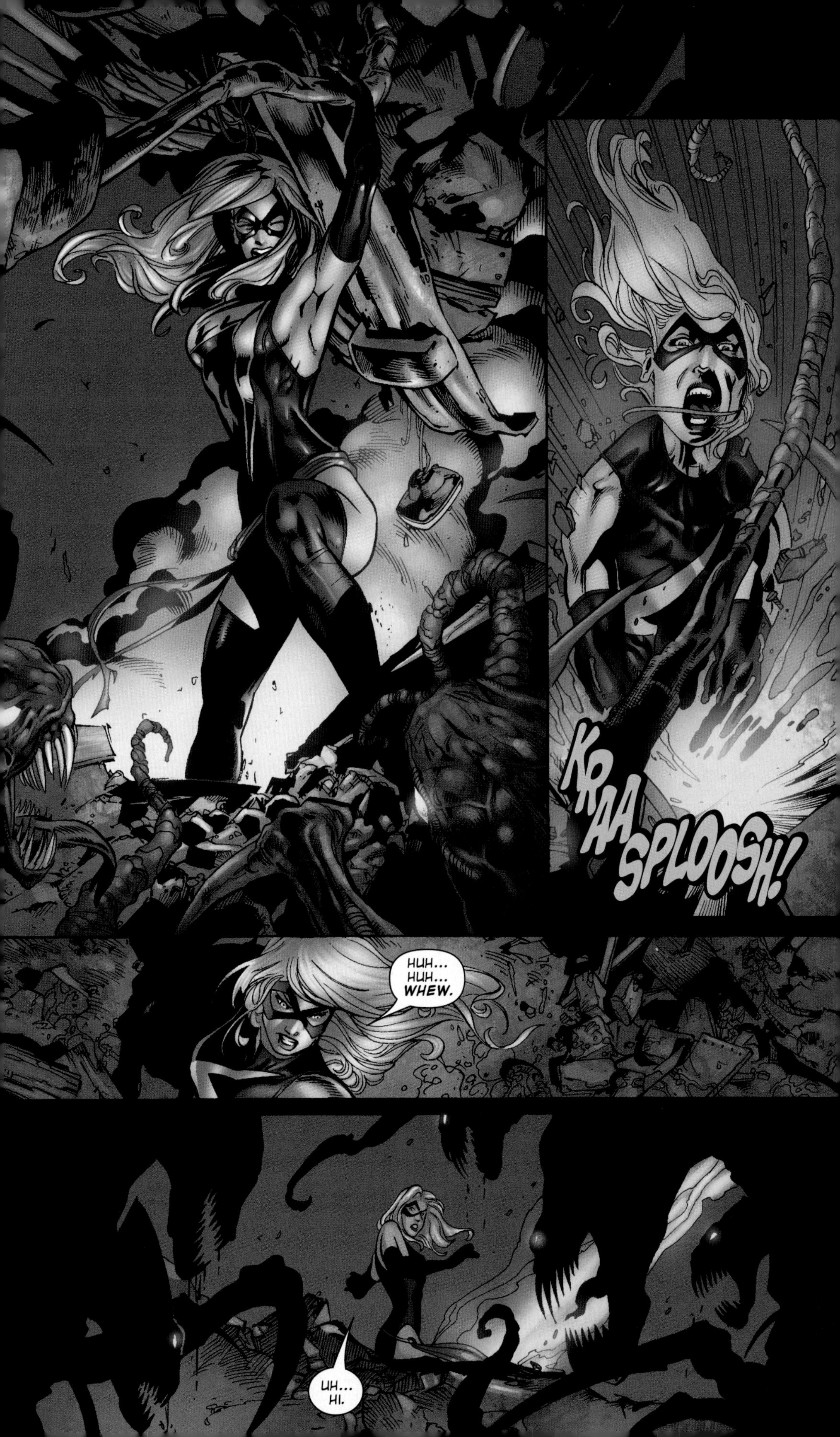
KRAASPLOOSH!
HUH...
HUH...
WHEW.
UH...
HI.

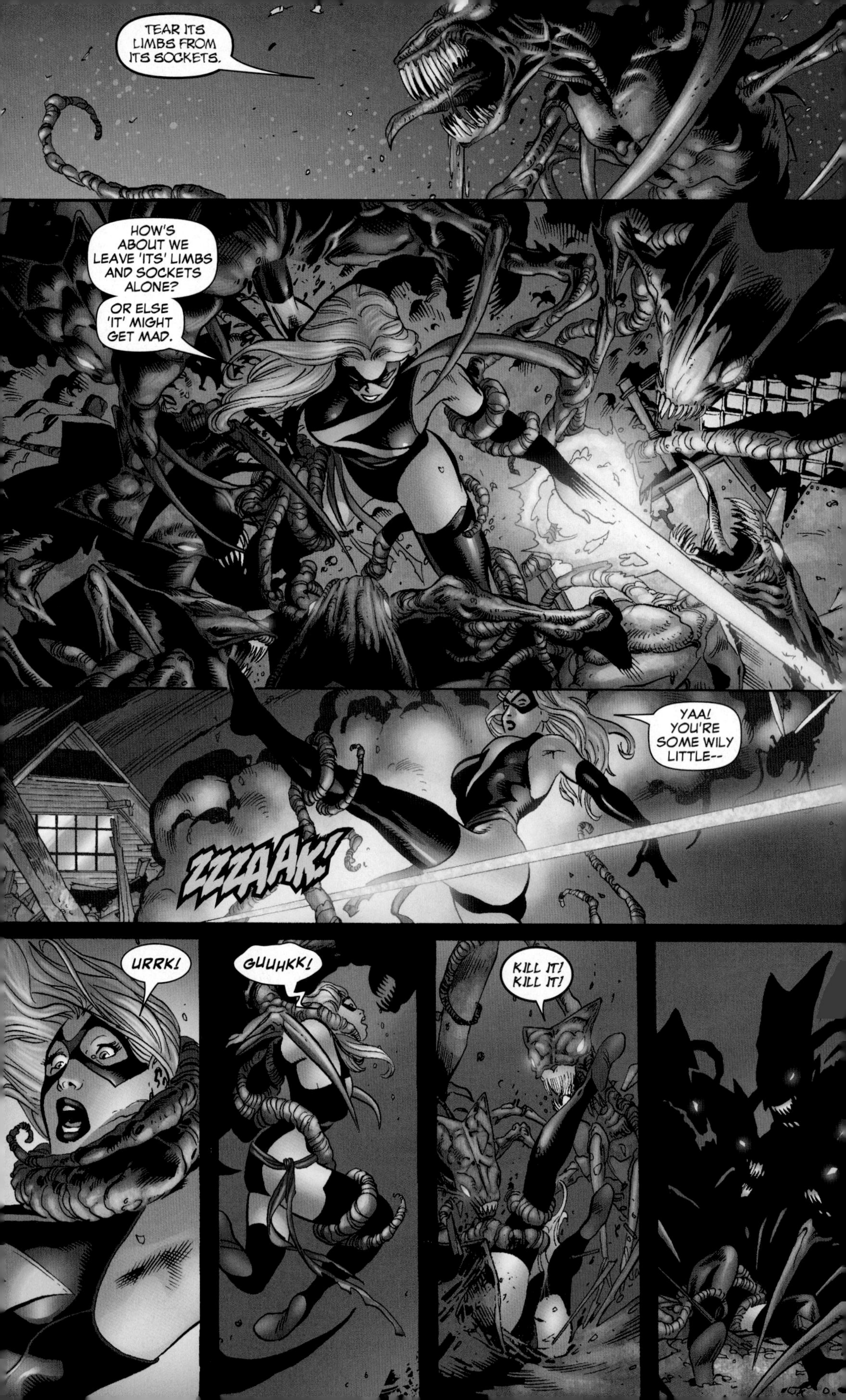
TEAR ITS LIMBS FROM ITS SOCKETS.
HOW'S ABOUT WE LEAVE 'ITS' LIMBS AND SOCKETS ALONE?
OR ELSE 'IT' MIGHT GET MAD.
YAA! YOU'RE SOME WILY LITTLE--
ZZZAAK!
URRK!
GUUHKK!
KILL IT! KILL IT!

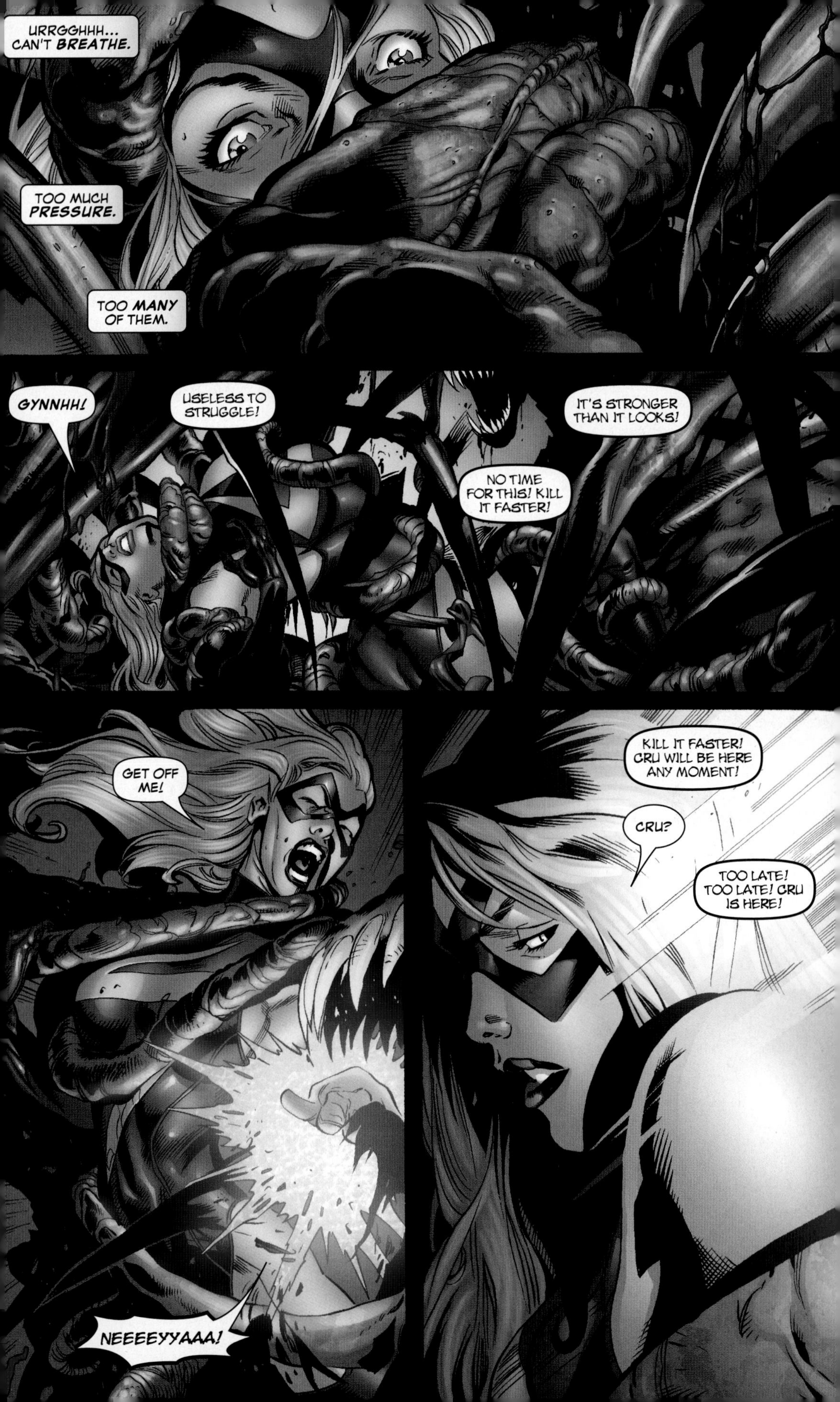
URRGGHHH... CAN'T BREATHE.
TOO MUCH PRESSURE.
TOO MANY OF THEM.
GYNNHH!
USELESS TO STRUGGLE!
IT'S STRONGER THAN IT LOOKS!
NO TIME FOR THIS! KILL IT FASTER!
GET OFF ME!
NEEEEYYAAA!
KILL IT FASTER! CRU WILL BE HERE ANY MOMENT!
CRU?
TOO LATE! TOO LATE! CRU IS HERE!

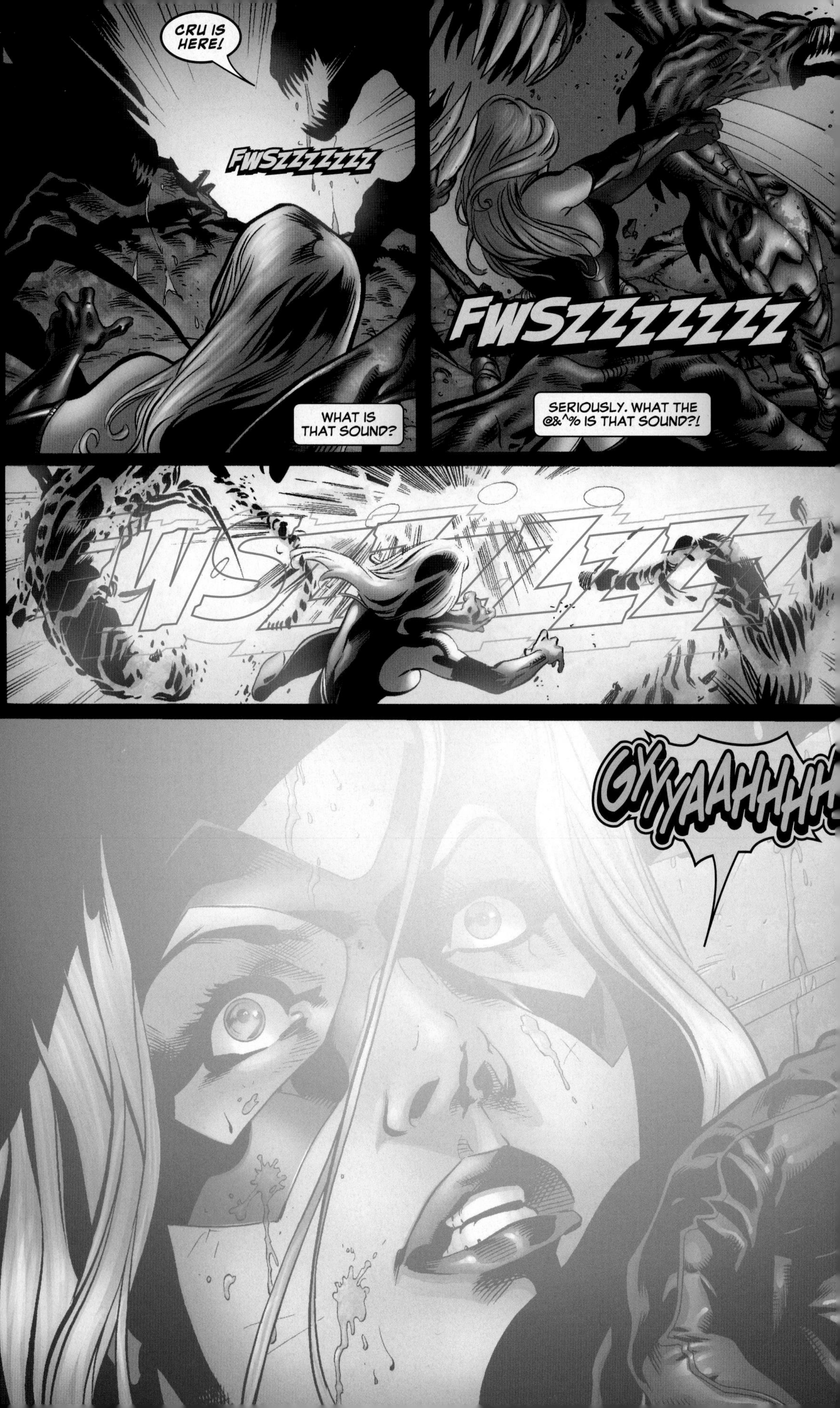
CRU IS HERE!
FWSZZZZZZZ
WHAT IS THAT SOUND?
FWSZZZZZZZZ
SERIOUSLY. WHAT THE @&^% IS THAT SOUND?!
GYYYAAHHHH

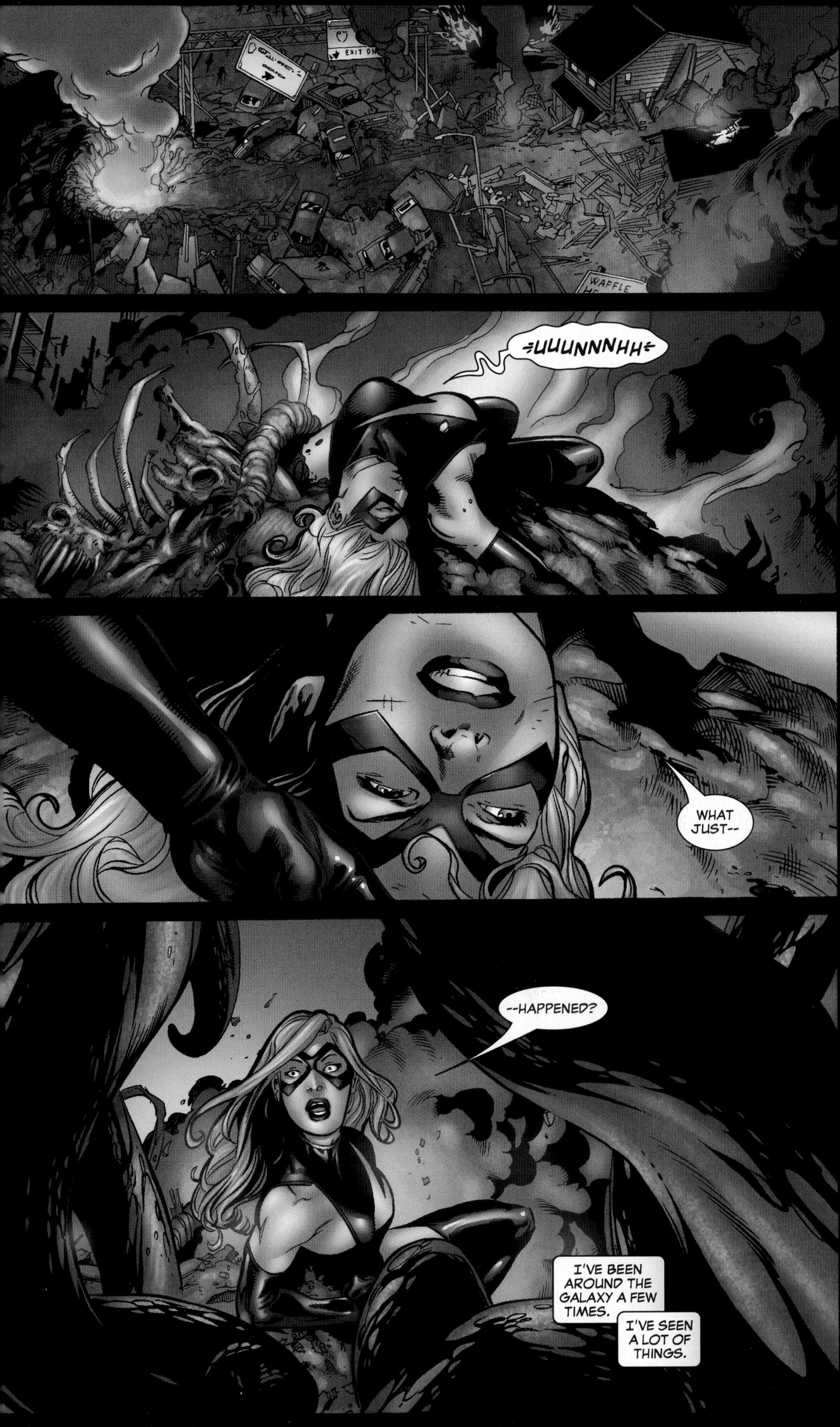
WAFFLE
EXIT ON
UUUNNNHH
WHAT JUST--
--HAPPENED?
I'VE BEEN AROUND THE GALAXY A FEW TIMES.
I'VE SEEN A LOT OF THINGS.

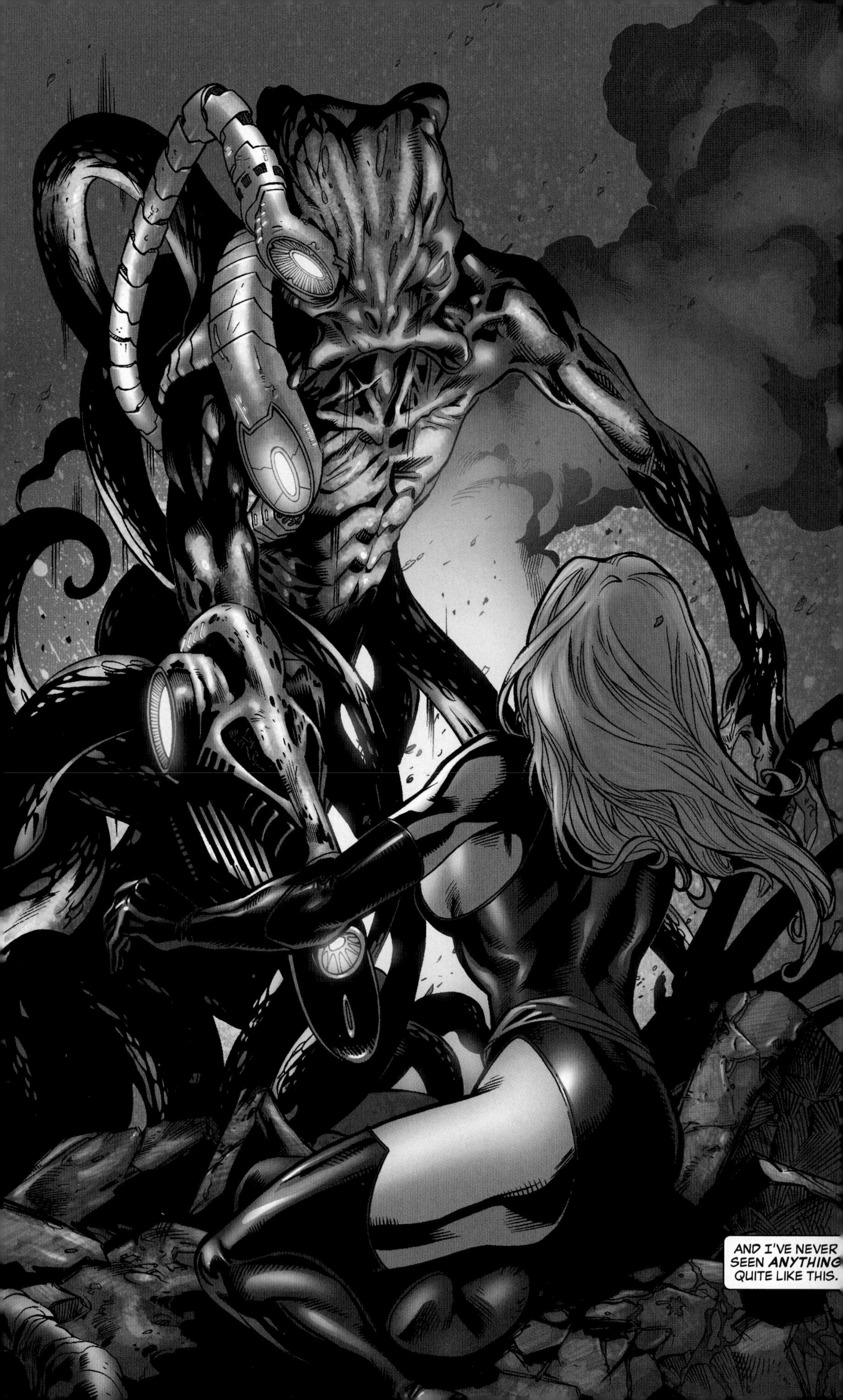
AND I'VE NEVER SEEN ANYTHING QUITE LIKE THIS.

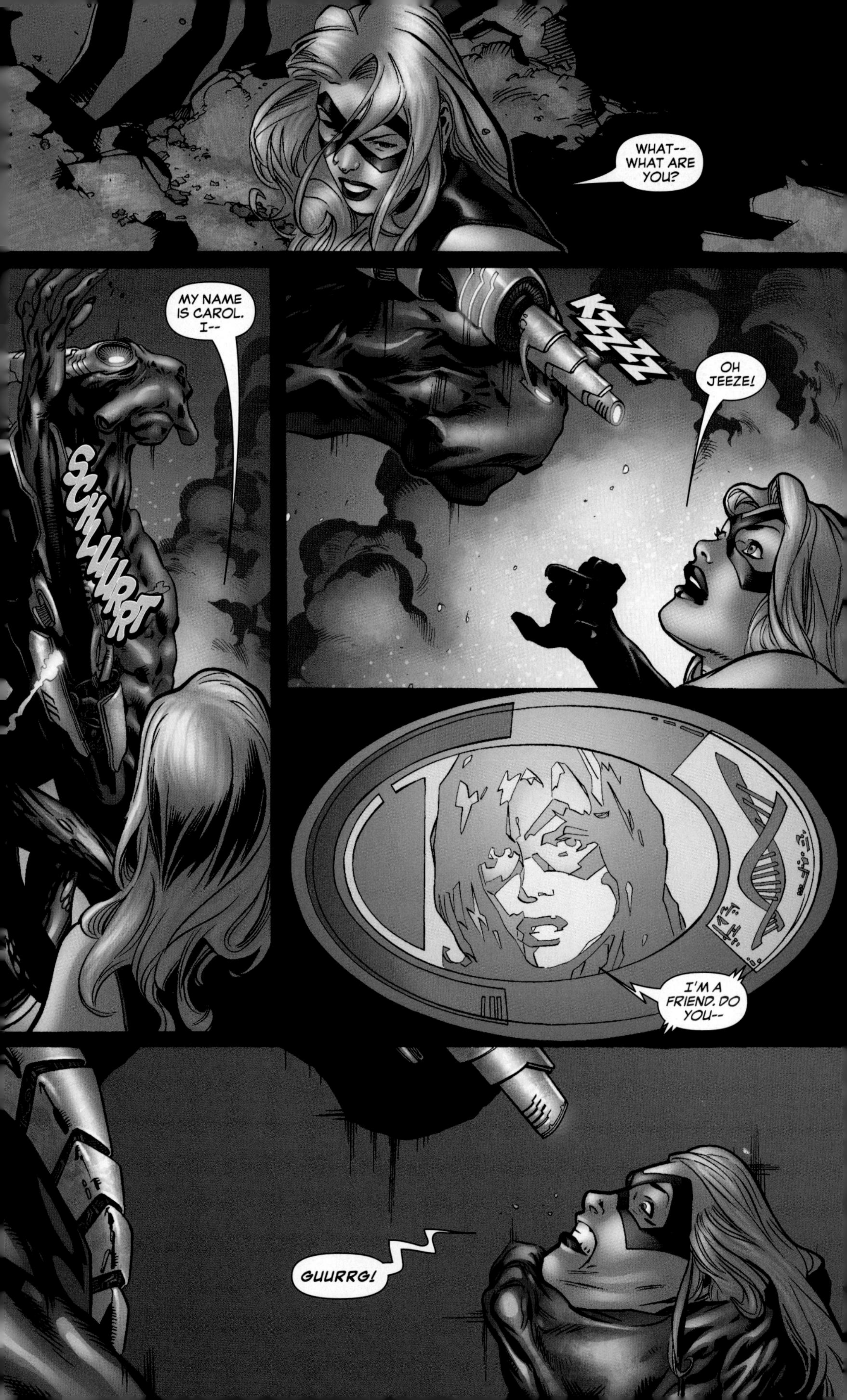
WHAT--
WHAT ARE YOU?
MY NAME IS CAROL. I--
SCHLURRT
KZZZZ
OH JEEZE!
I'M A FRIEND. DO YOU--
GUURRG!

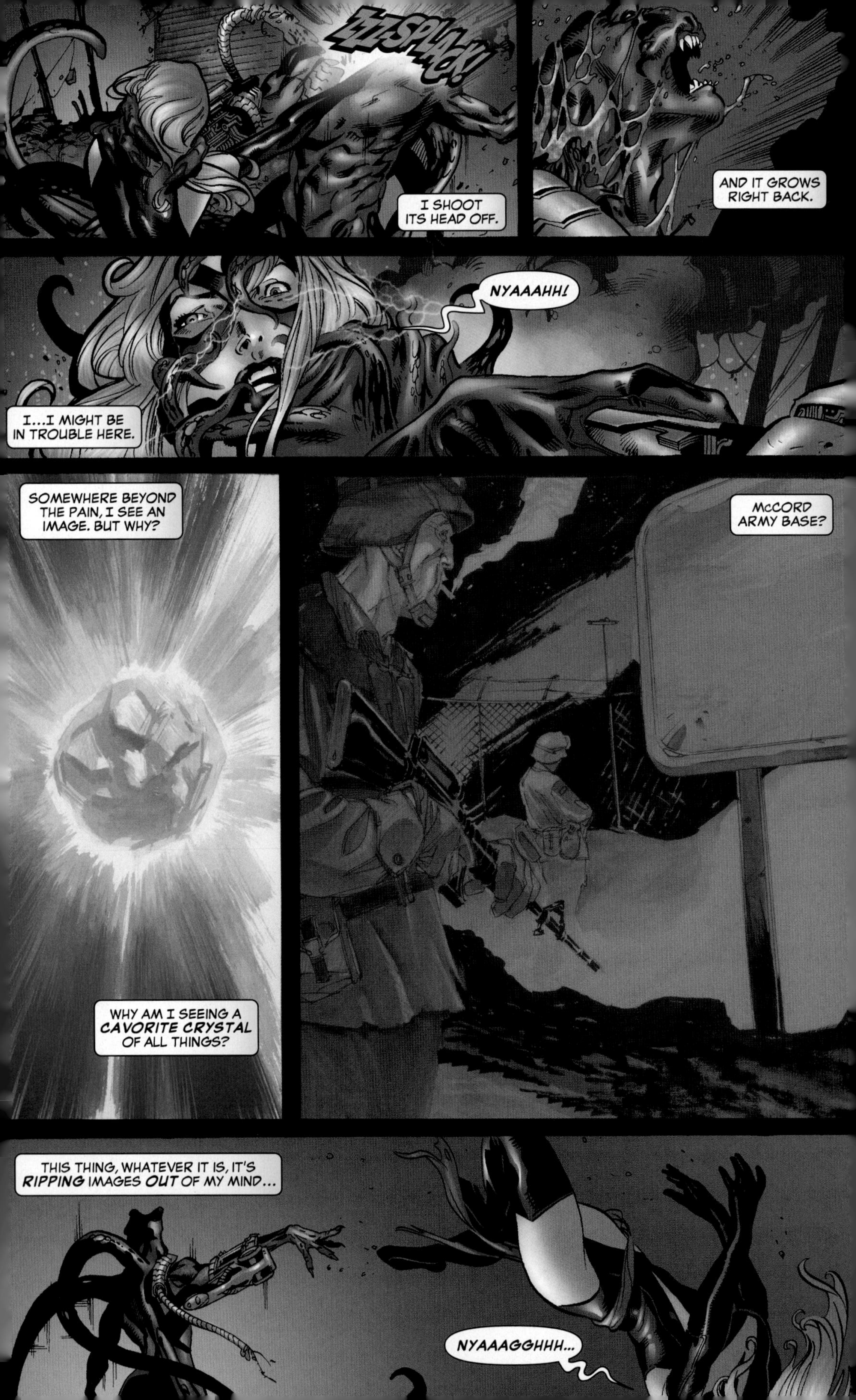
ZZZ-SPLACK!
I SHOOT ITS HEAD OFF.
AND IT GROWS RIGHT BACK.
NYAAAHH!
I...I MIGHT BE IN TROUBLE HERE.
SOMEWHERE BEYOND THE PAIN, I SEE AN IMAGE. BUT WHY?
WHY AM I SEEING A CAVORITE CRYSTAL OF ALL THINGS?
McCORD ARMY BASE?
THIS THING, WHATEVER IT IS, IT'S RIPPING IMAGES OUT OF MY MIND...
NYAAAGGHHH...

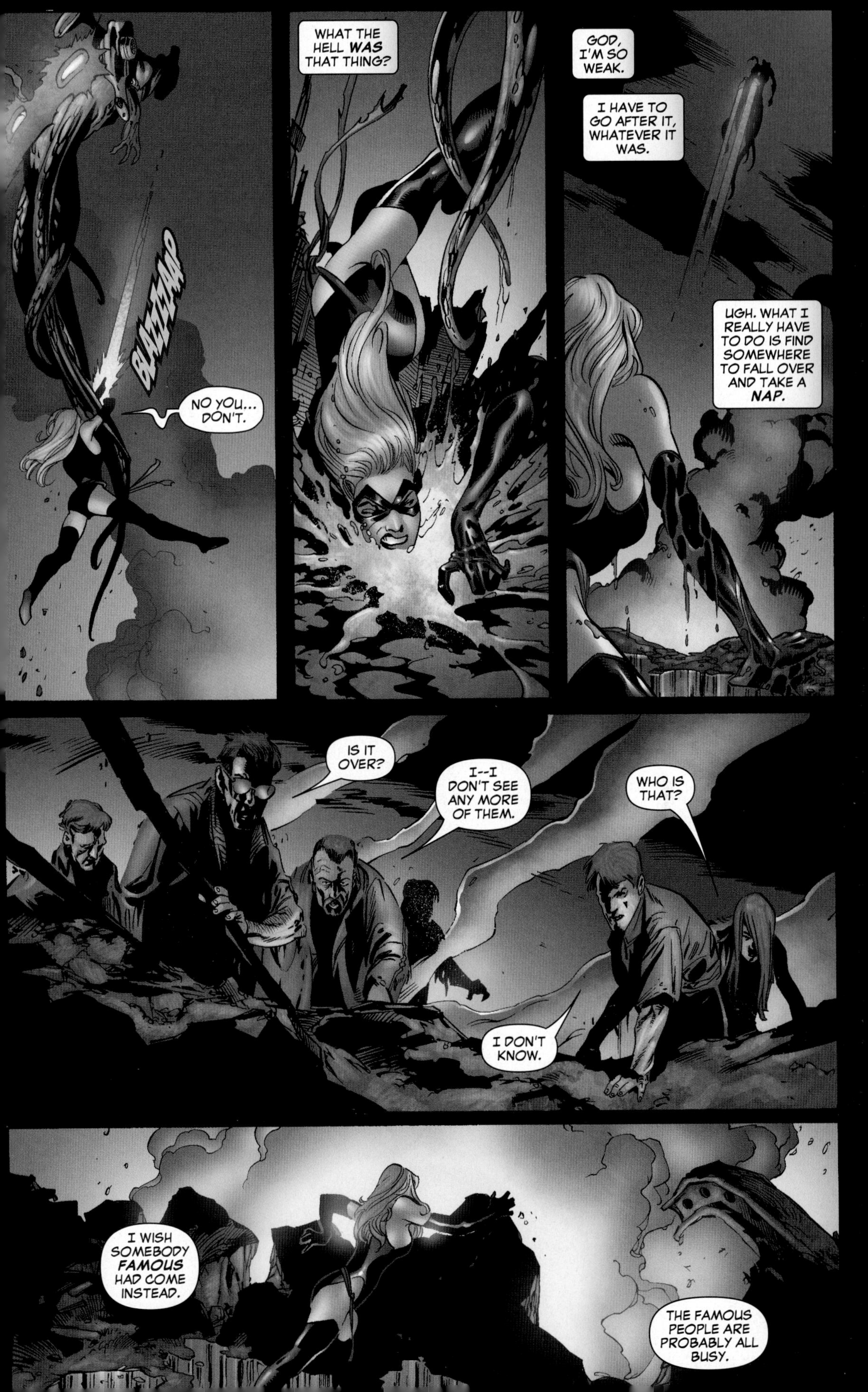
BLAZZZAAP
NO YOU... DON'T.
WHAT THE HELL **WAS** THAT THING?
GOD, I'M SO WEAK.
I HAVE TO GO AFTER IT, WHATEVER IT WAS.
UGH. WHAT I REALLY HAVE TO DO IS FIND SOMEWHERE TO FALL OVER AND TAKE A **NAP**.
IS IT OVER?
I--I DON'T SEE ANY MORE OF THEM.
WHO IS THAT?
I DON'T KNOW.
I WISH SOMEBODY **FAMOUS** HAD COME INSTEAD.
THE FAMOUS PEOPLE ARE PROBABLY ALL BUSY.

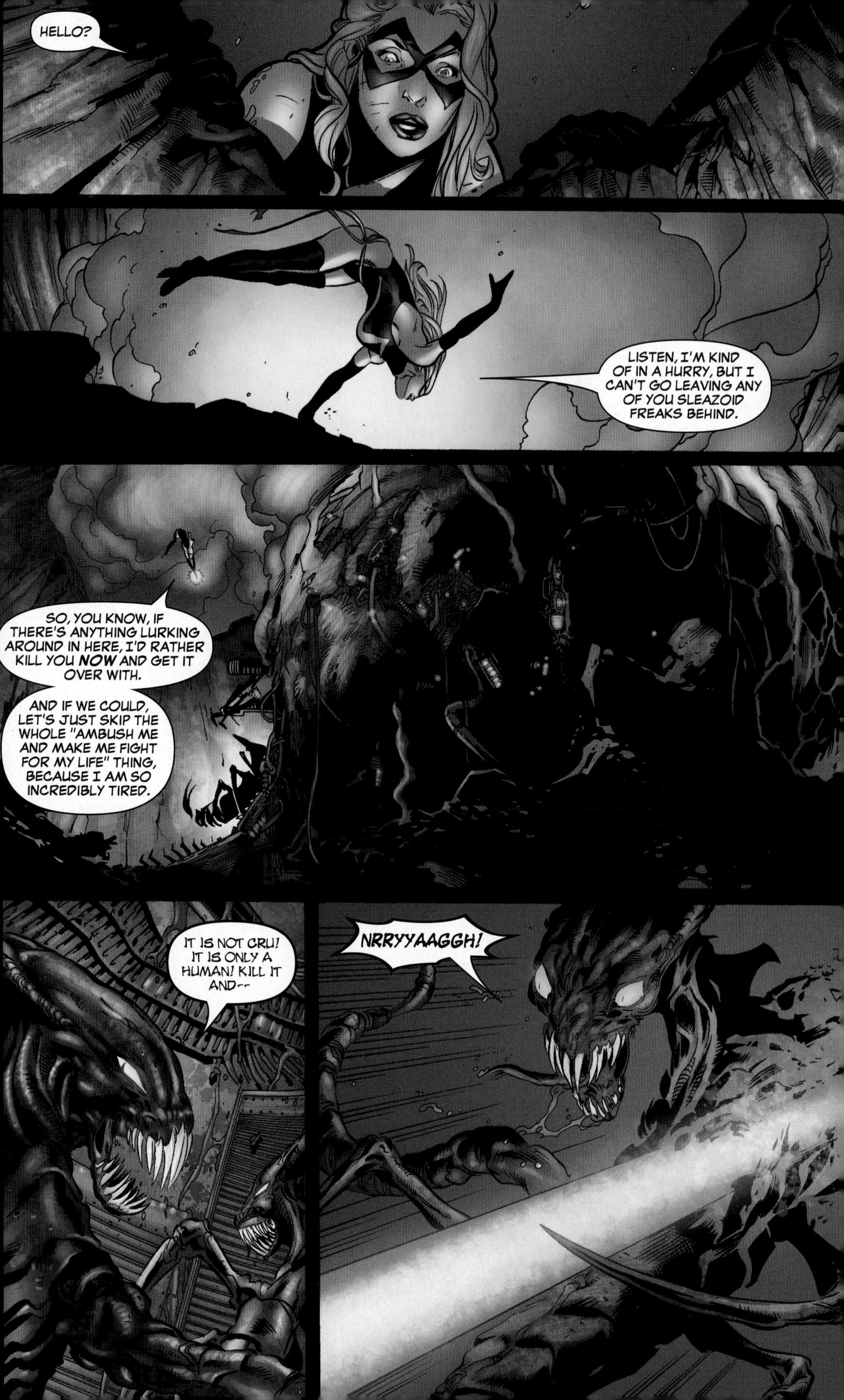
HELLO?
LISTEN, I'M KIND OF IN A HURRY, BUT I CAN'T GO LEAVING ANY OF YOU SLEAZOID FREAKS BEHIND.
SO, YOU KNOW, IF THERE'S ANYTHING LURKING AROUND IN HERE, I'D RATHER KILL YOU NOW AND GET IT OVER WITH.
AND IF WE COULD, LET'S JUST SKIP THE WHOLE "AMBUSH ME AND MAKE ME FIGHT FOR MY LIFE" THING, BECAUSE I AM SO INCREDIBLY TIRED.
IT IS NOT CRU! IT IS ONLY A HUMAN! KILL IT AND--
NRRYYAAGGH!

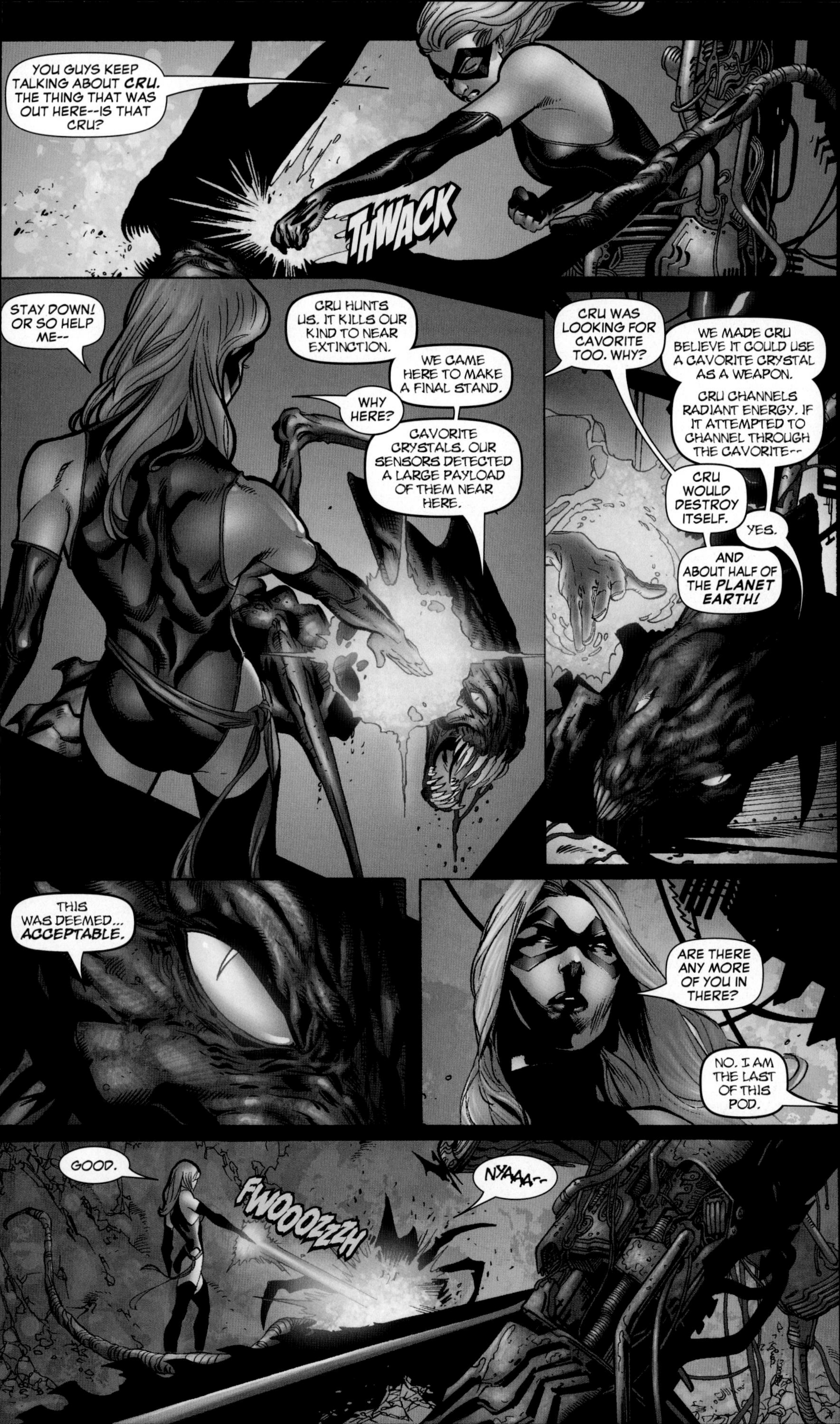
YOU GUYS KEEP TALKING ABOUT CRU. THE THING THAT WAS OUT HERE--IS THAT CRU?
THWACK
STAY DOWN! OR SO HELP ME--
CRU HUNTS US. IT KILLS OUR KIND TO NEAR EXTINCTION.
WE CAME HERE TO MAKE A FINAL STAND.
WHY HERE?
CAVORITE CRYSTALS. OUR SENSORS DETECTED A LARGE PAYLOAD OF THEM NEAR HERE.
CRU WAS LOOKING FOR CAVORITE TOO. WHY?
WE MADE CRU BELIEVE IT COULD USE A CAVORITE CRYSTAL AS A WEAPON.
CRU CHANNELS RADIANT ENERGY. IF IT ATTEMPTED TO CHANNEL THROUGH THE CAVORITE--
CRU WOULD DESTROY ITSELF.
YES.
AND ABOUT HALF OF THE PLANET EARTH!
THIS WAS DEEMED... ACCEPTABLE.
ARE THERE ANY MORE OF YOU IN THERE?
NO. I AM THE LAST OF THIS POD.
GOOD.
FWOOOZZZH
NYAAA--

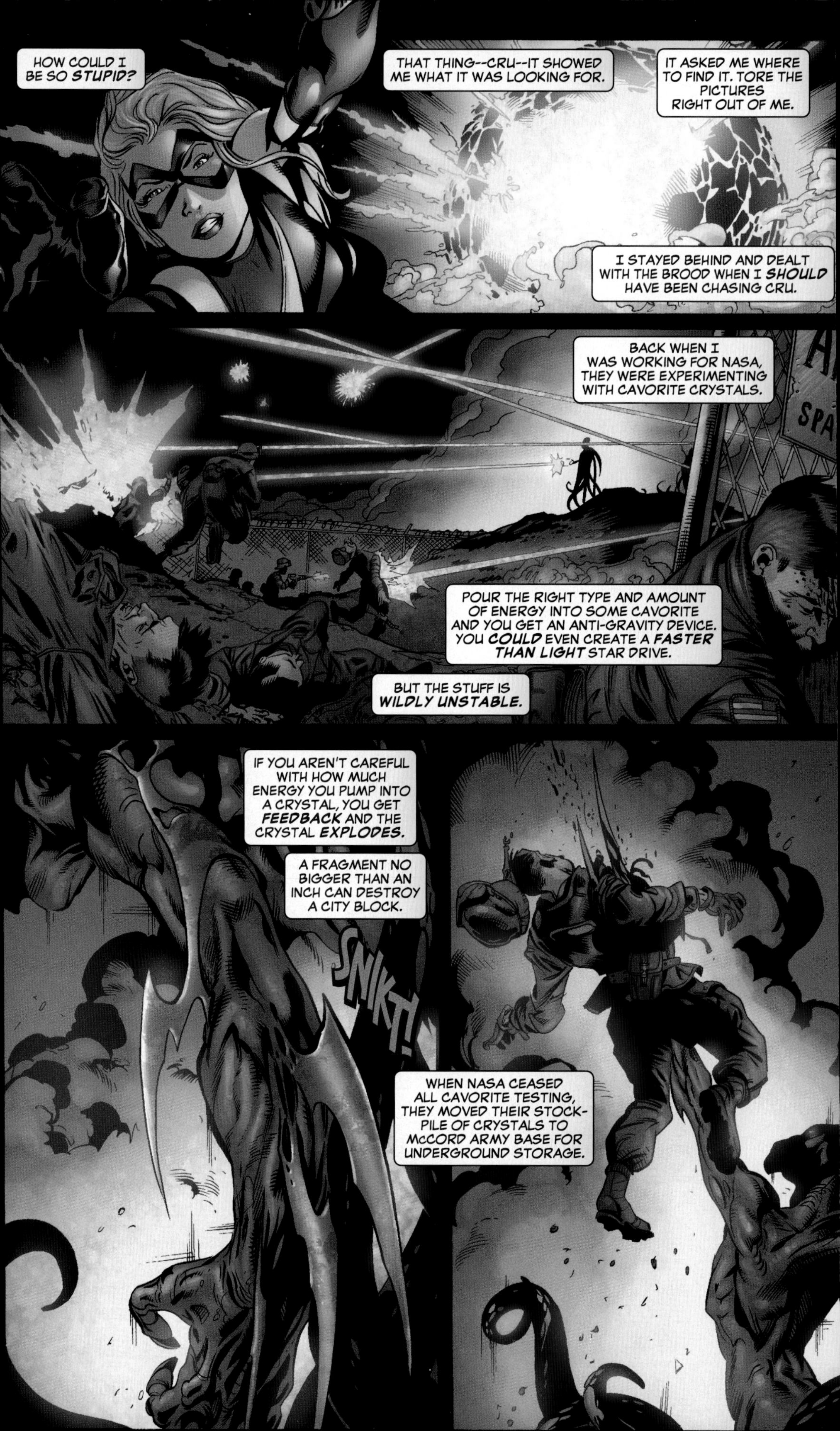
HOW COULD I BE SO STUPID?
THAT THING--CRU--IT SHOWED ME WHAT IT WAS LOOKING FOR.
IT ASKED ME WHERE TO FIND IT. TORE THE PICTURES RIGHT OUT OF ME.
I STAYED BEHIND AND DEALT WITH THE BROOD WHEN I SHOULD HAVE BEEN CHASING CRU.
BACK WHEN I WAS WORKING FOR NASA, THEY WERE EXPERIMENTING WITH CAVORITE CRYSTALS.
POUR THE RIGHT TYPE AND AMOUNT OF ENERGY INTO SOME CAVORITE AND YOU GET AN ANTI-GRAVITY DEVICE. YOU COULD EVEN CREATE A FASTER THAN LIGHT STAR DRIVE.
BUT THE STUFF IS WILDLY UNSTABLE.
IF YOU AREN'T CAREFUL WITH HOW MUCH ENERGY YOU PUMP INTO A CRYSTAL, YOU GET FEEDBACK AND THE CRYSTAL EXPLODES.
A FRAGMENT NO BIGGER THAN AN INCH CAN DESTROY A CITY BLOCK.
SNIKT!
WHEN NASA CEASED ALL CAVORITE TESTING, THEY MOVED THEIR STOCKPILE OF CRYSTALS TO McCORD ARMY BASE FOR UNDERGROUND STORAGE.

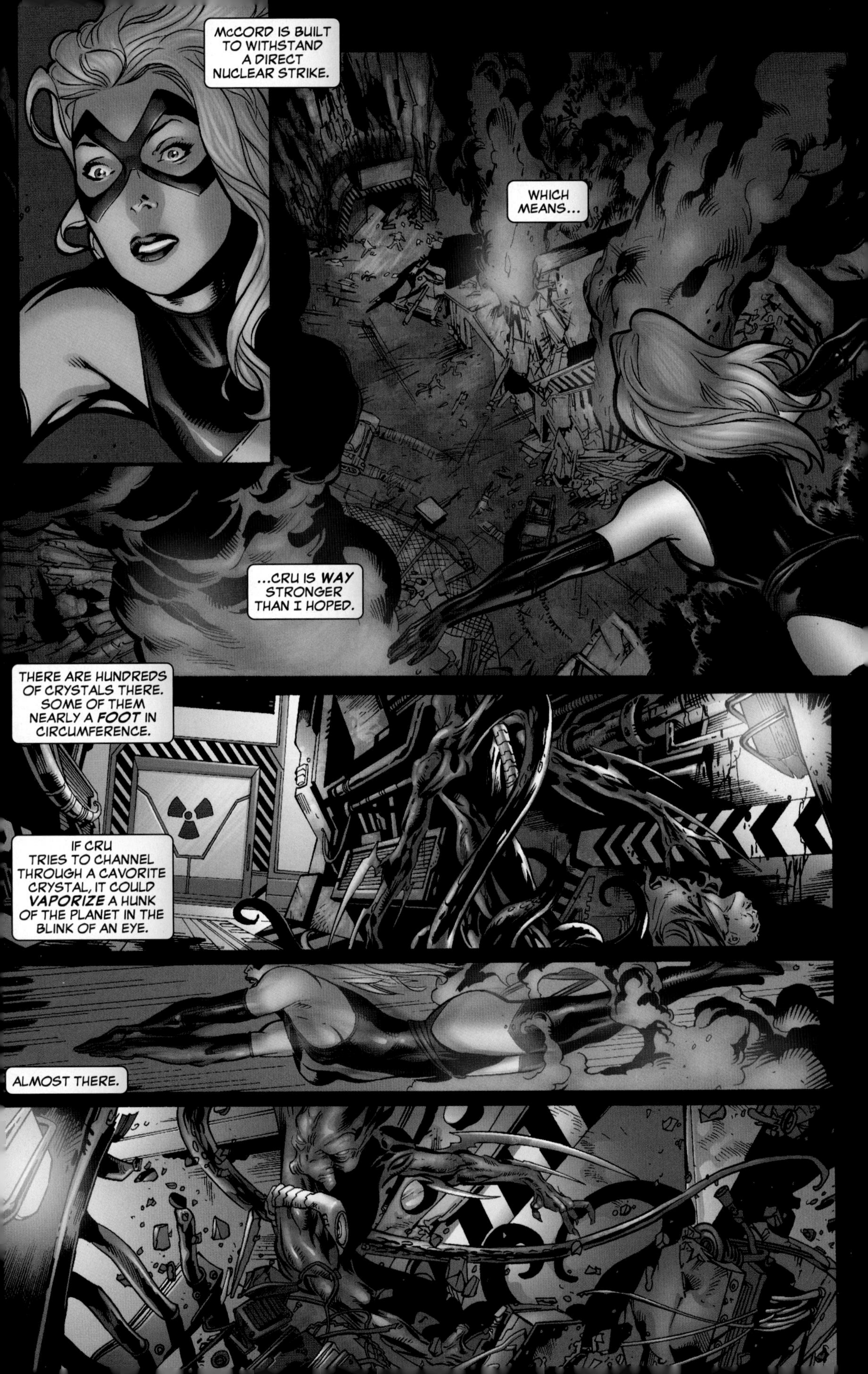
McCORD IS BUILT TO WITHSTAND A DIRECT NUCLEAR STRIKE.
WHICH MEANS...
...CRU IS WAY STRONGER THAN I HOPED.
THERE ARE HUNDREDS OF CRYSTALS THERE. SOME OF THEM NEARLY A FOOT IN CIRCUMFERENCE.
IF CRU TRIES TO CHANNEL THROUGH A CAVORITE CRYSTAL, IT COULD VAPORIZE A HUNK OF THE PLANET IN THE BLINK OF AN EYE.
ALMOST THERE.

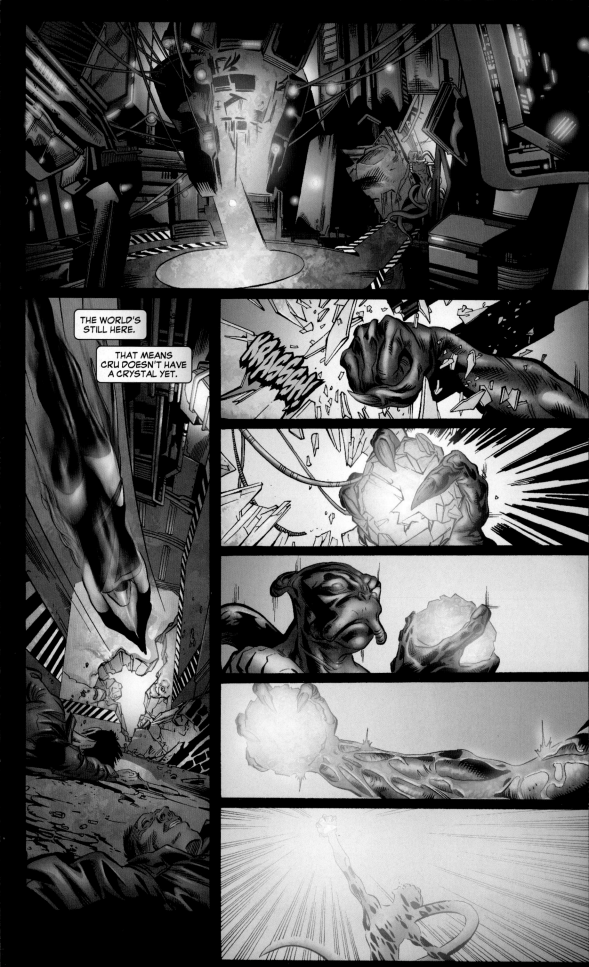

THE WORLD'S STILL HERE.

THAT MEANS CRU DOESN'T HAVE A CRYSTAL YET.

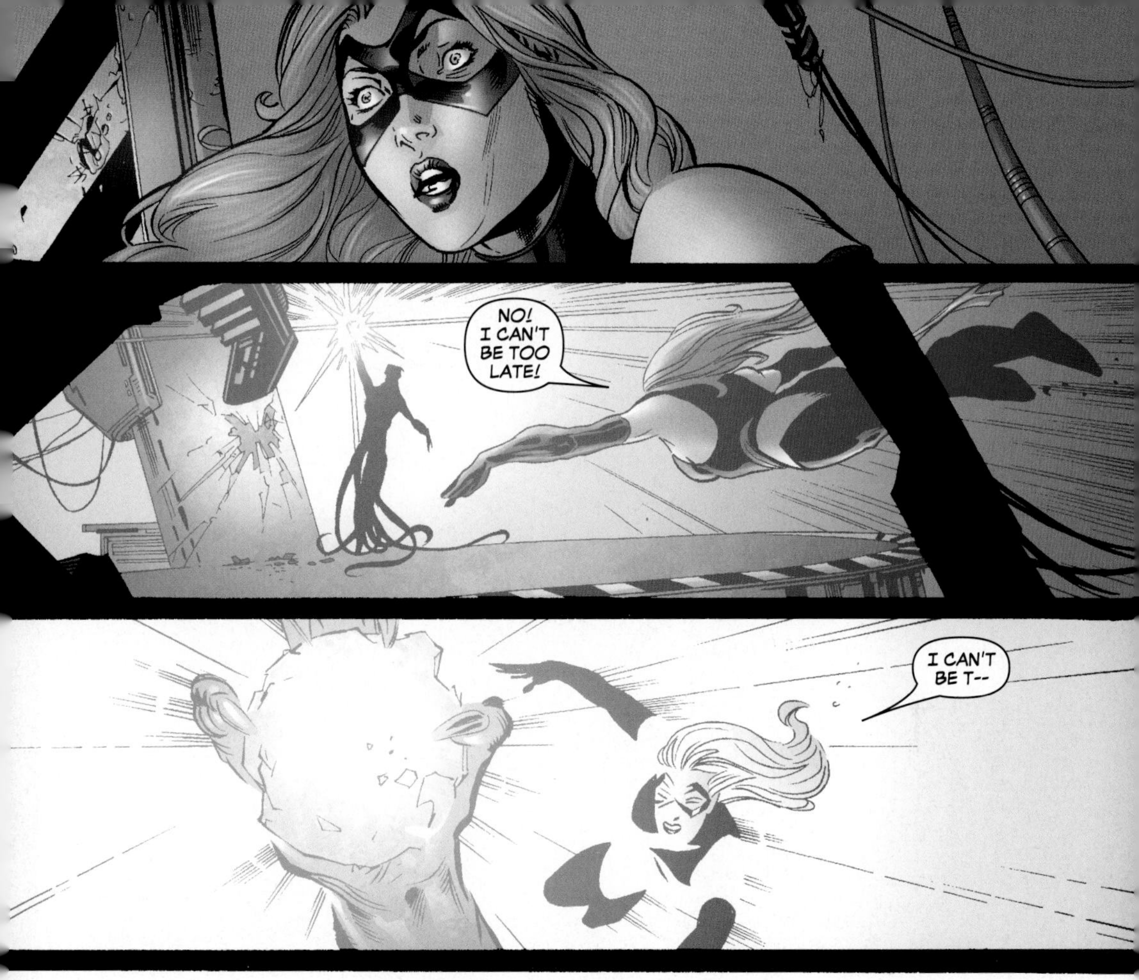
NO! I CAN'T BE TOO LATE!
I CAN'T BE T--

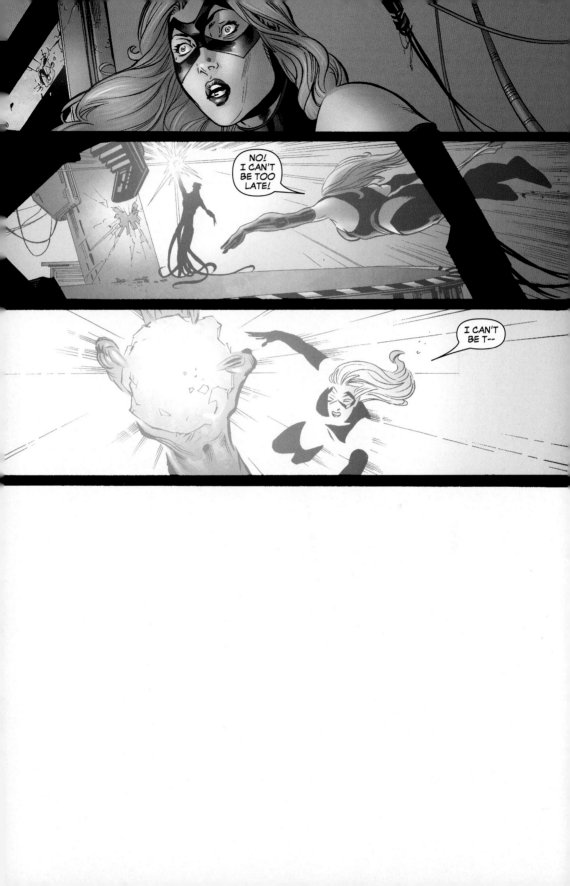

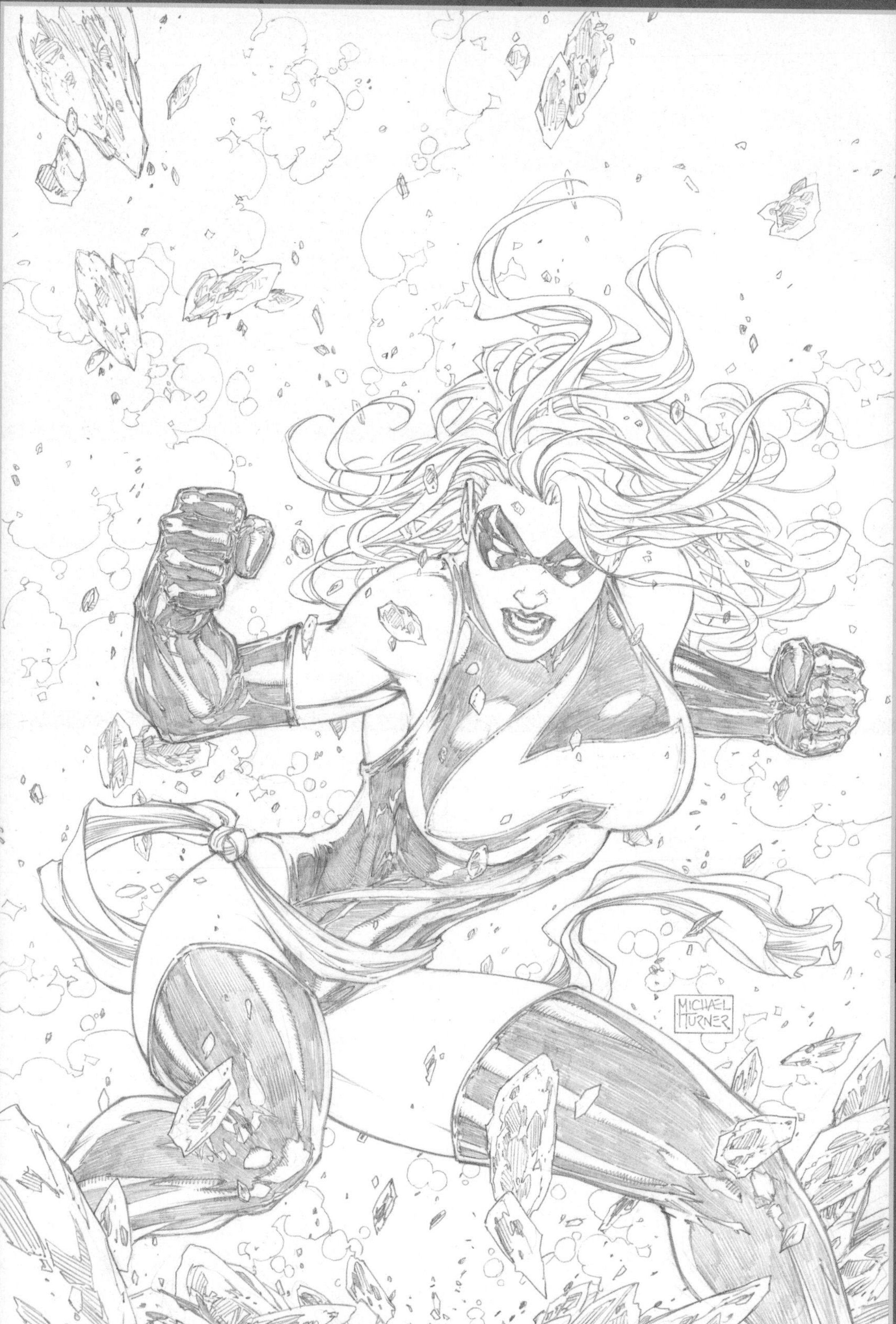
MICHAEL TURNER

MS. MARVEL #1 SKETCH VARIANT BY MICHAEL TURNER

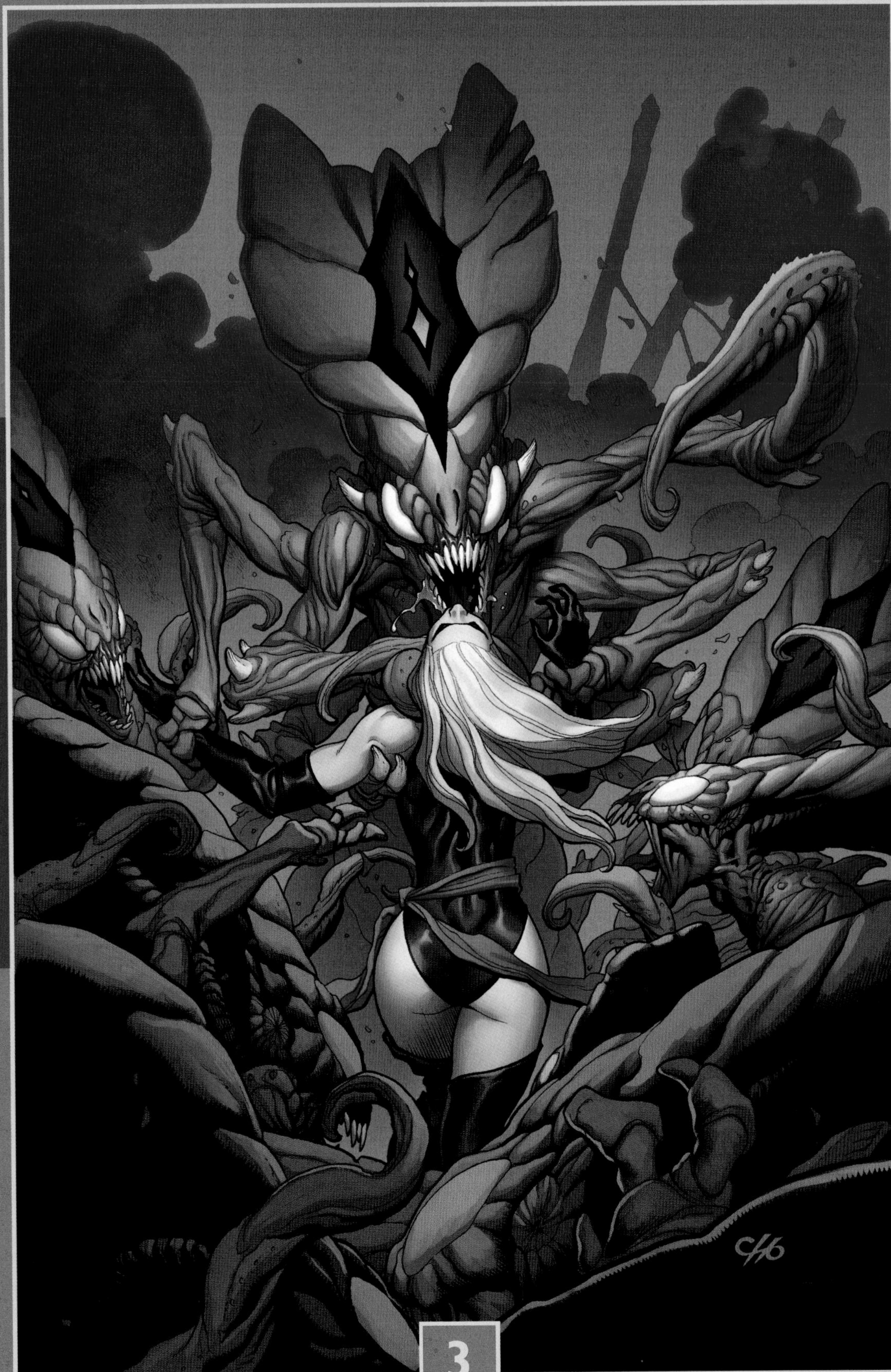

3

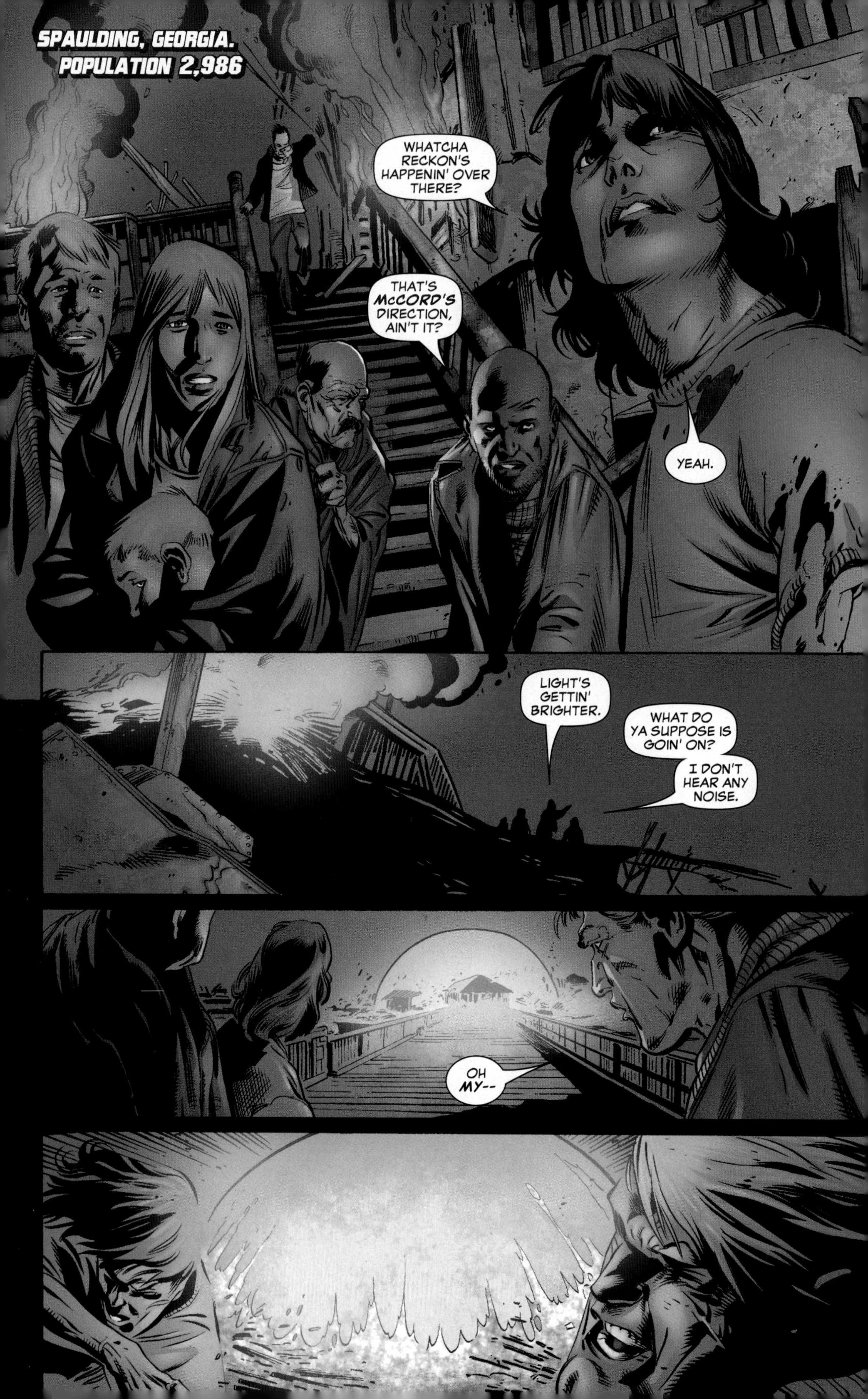
SPAULDING, GEORGIA. POPULATION 2,986
WHATCHA RECKON'S HAPPENIN' OVER THERE?
THAT'S McCORD'S DIRECTION, AIN'T IT?
YEAH.
LIGHT'S GETTIN' BRIGHTER.
WHAT DO YA SUPPOSE IS GOIN' ON?
I DON'T HEAR ANY NOISE.
OH MY--

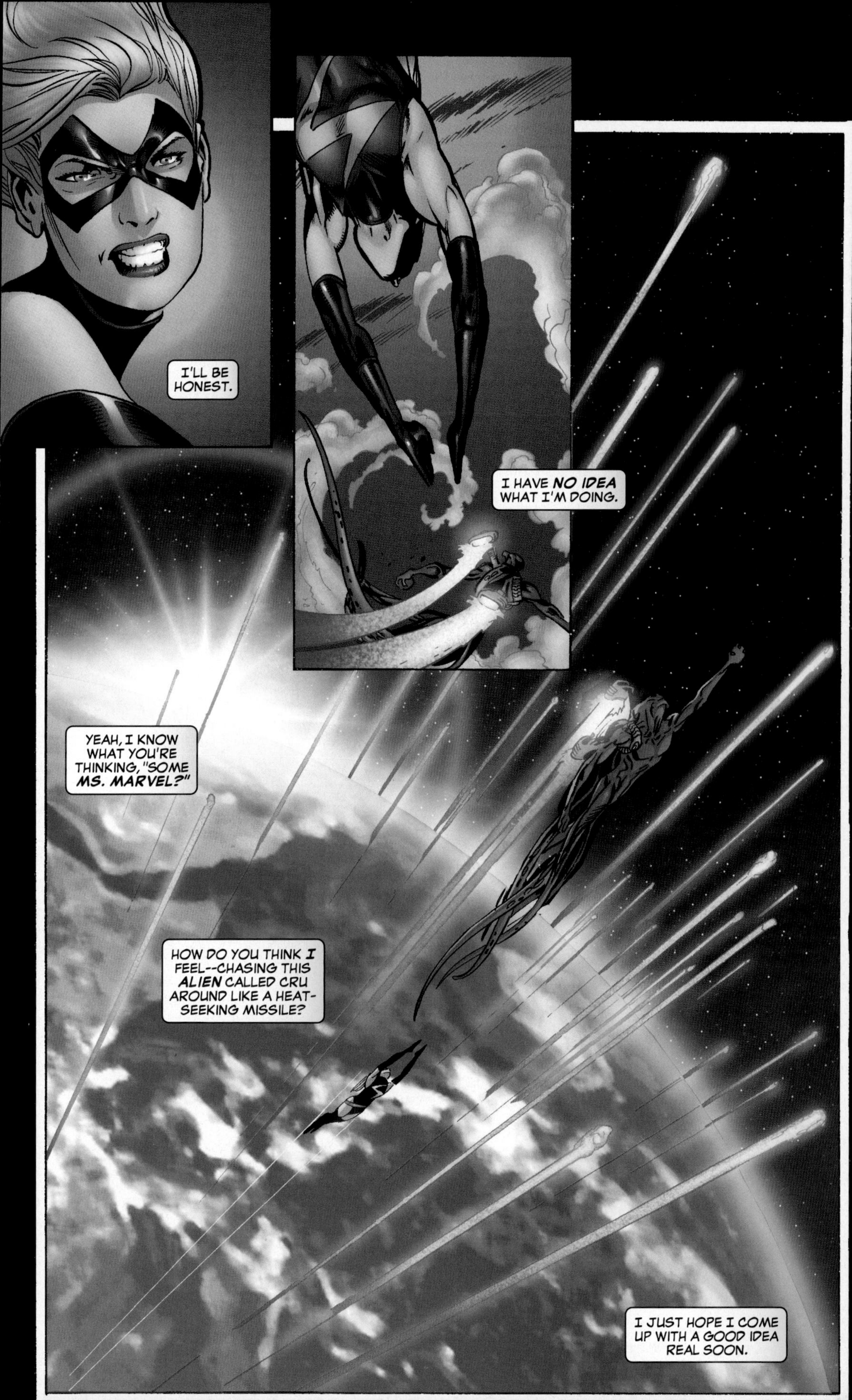
I'LL BE HONEST.
I HAVE NO IDEA WHAT I'M DOING.
YEAH, I KNOW WHAT YOU'RE THINKING, "SOME MS. MARVEL?"
HOW DO YOU THINK I FEEL--CHASING THIS ALIEN CALLED CRU AROUND LIKE A HEAT-SEEKING MISSILE?
I JUST HOPE I COME UP WITH A GOOD IDEA REAL SOON.

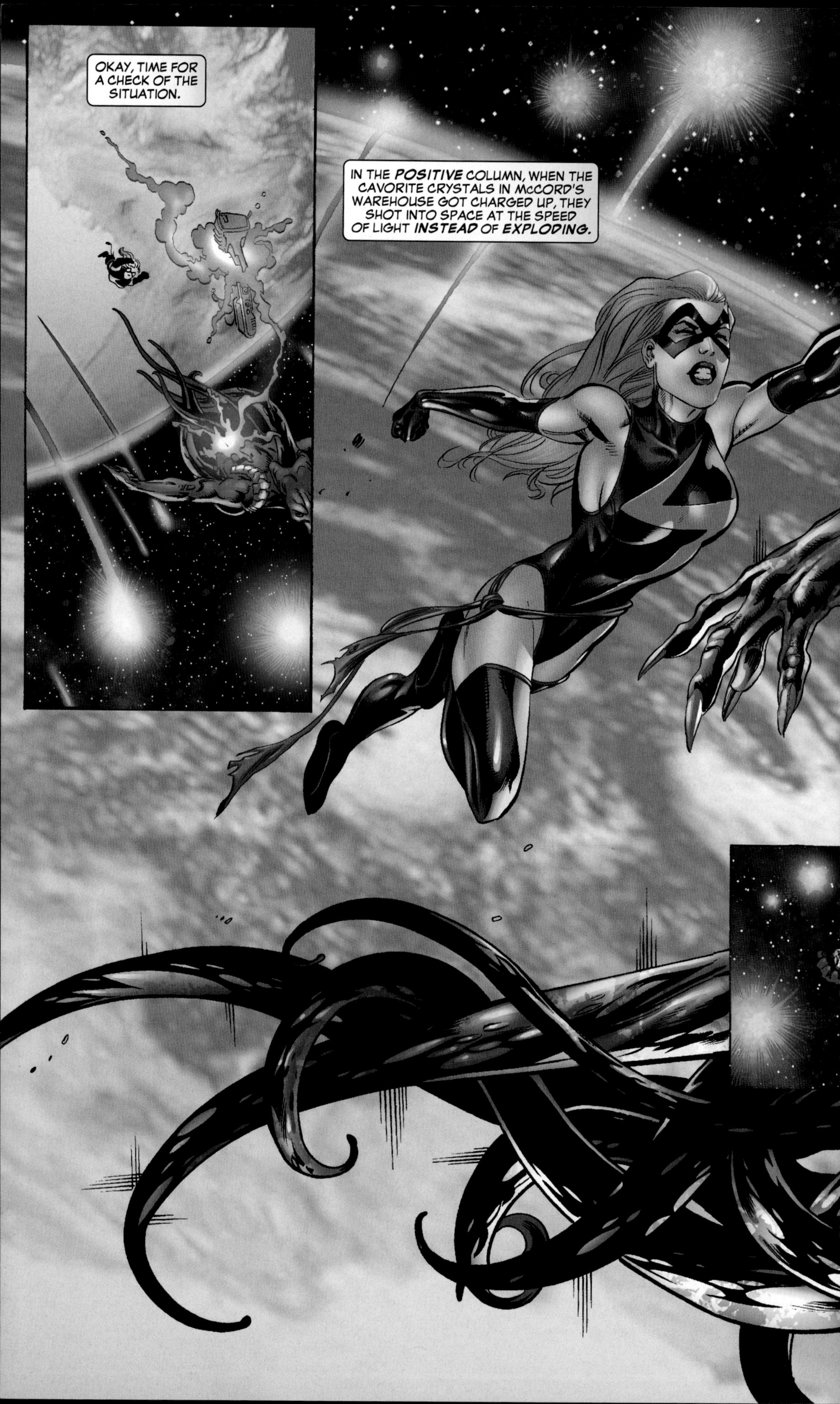
OKAY, TIME FOR A CHECK OF THE SITUATION.
IN THE POSITIVE COLUMN, WHEN THE CAVORITE CRYSTALS IN McCORD'S WAREHOUSE GOT CHARGED UP, THEY SHOT INTO SPACE AT THE SPEED OF LIGHT INSTEAD OF EXPLODING.

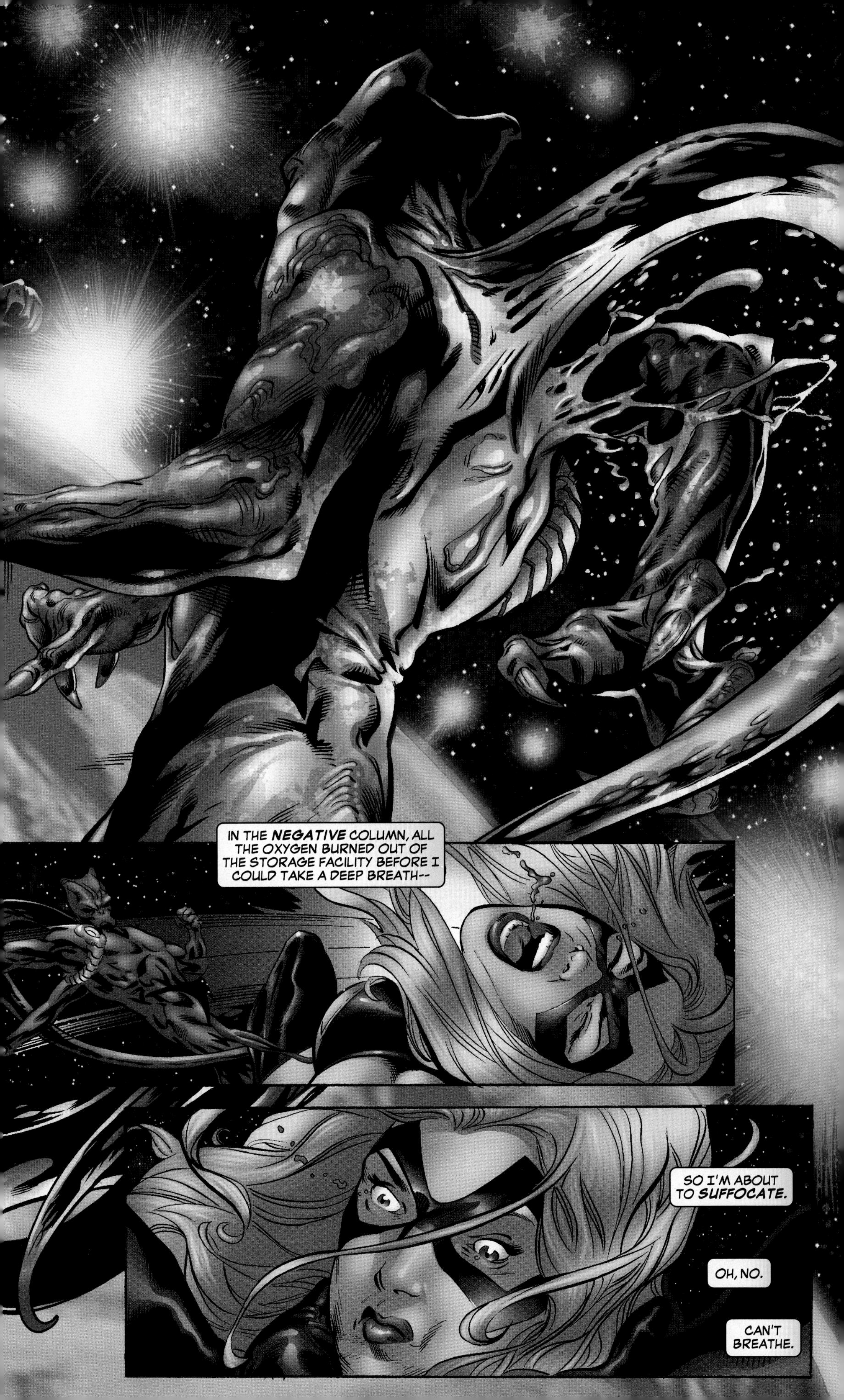
IN THE NEGATIVE COLUMN, ALL THE OXYGEN BURNED OUT OF THE STORAGE FACILITY BEFORE I COULD TAKE A DEEP BREATH--
SO I'M ABOUT TO SUFFOCATE.
OH, NO.
CAN'T BREATHE.

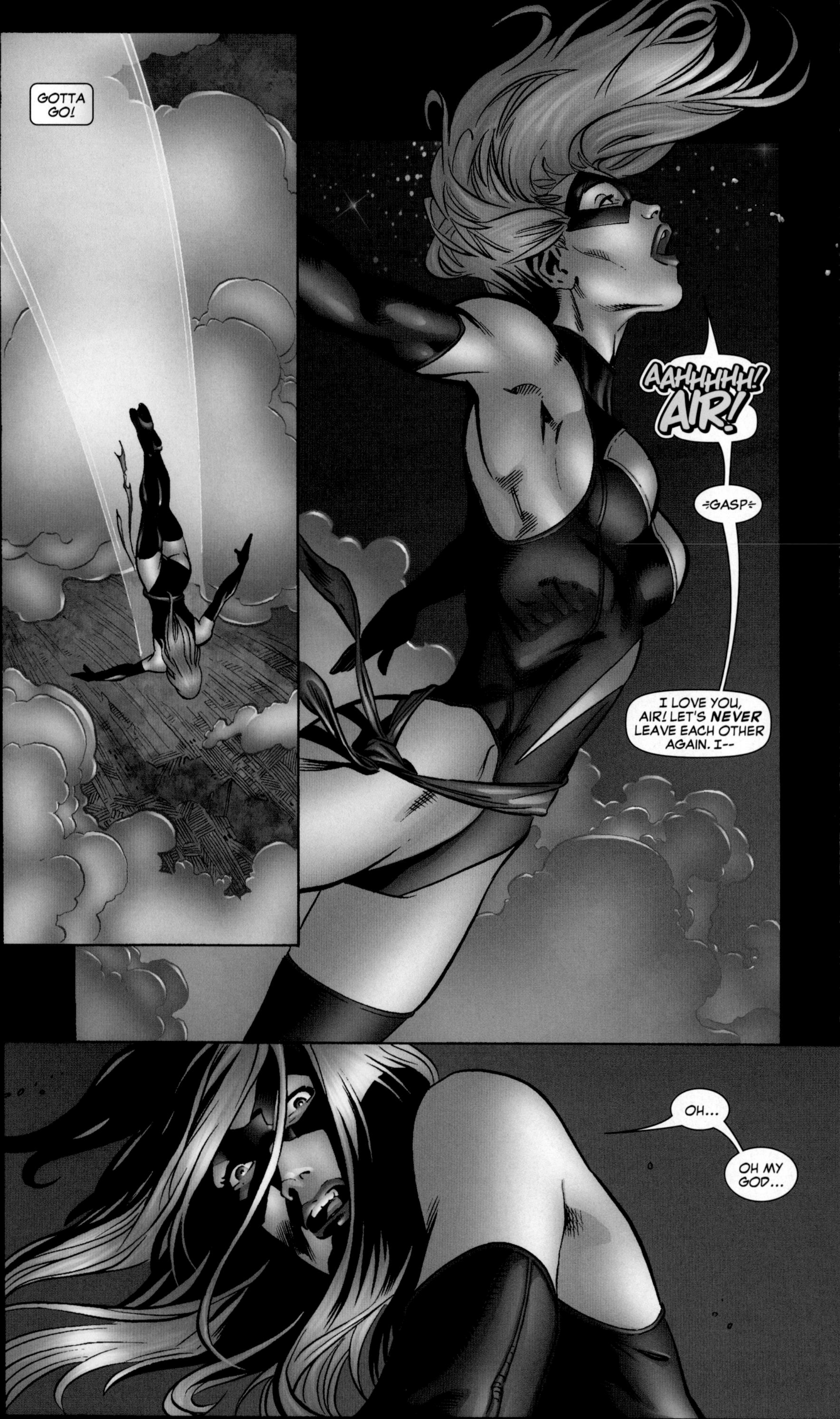
GOTTA GO!
AAHHHHH! AIR!
=GASP=
I LOVE YOU, AIR! LET'S **NEVER** LEAVE EACH OTHER AGAIN. I--
OH...
OH MY GOD...

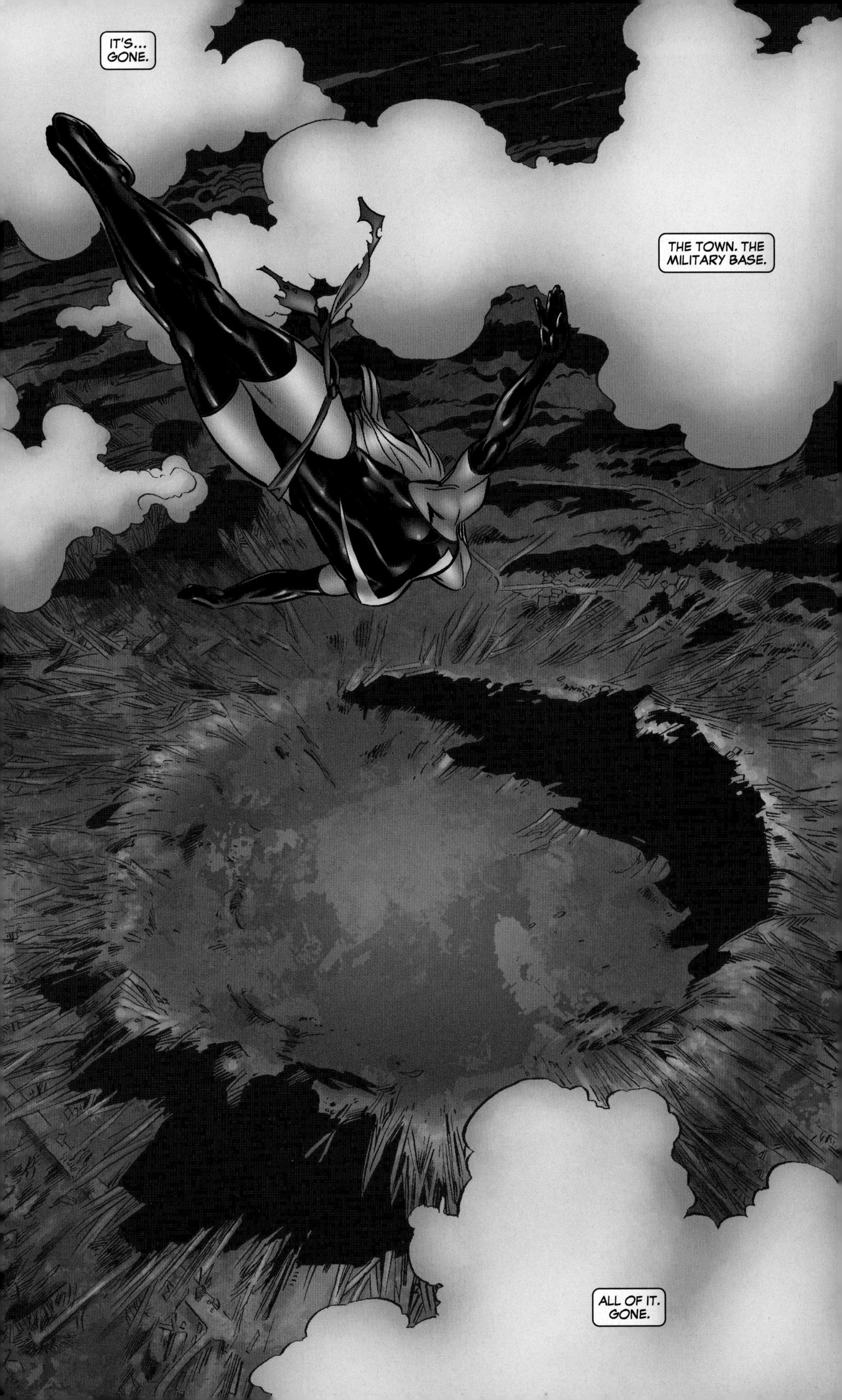
IT'S... GONE.
THE TOWN. THE MILITARY BASE.
ALL OF IT. GONE.

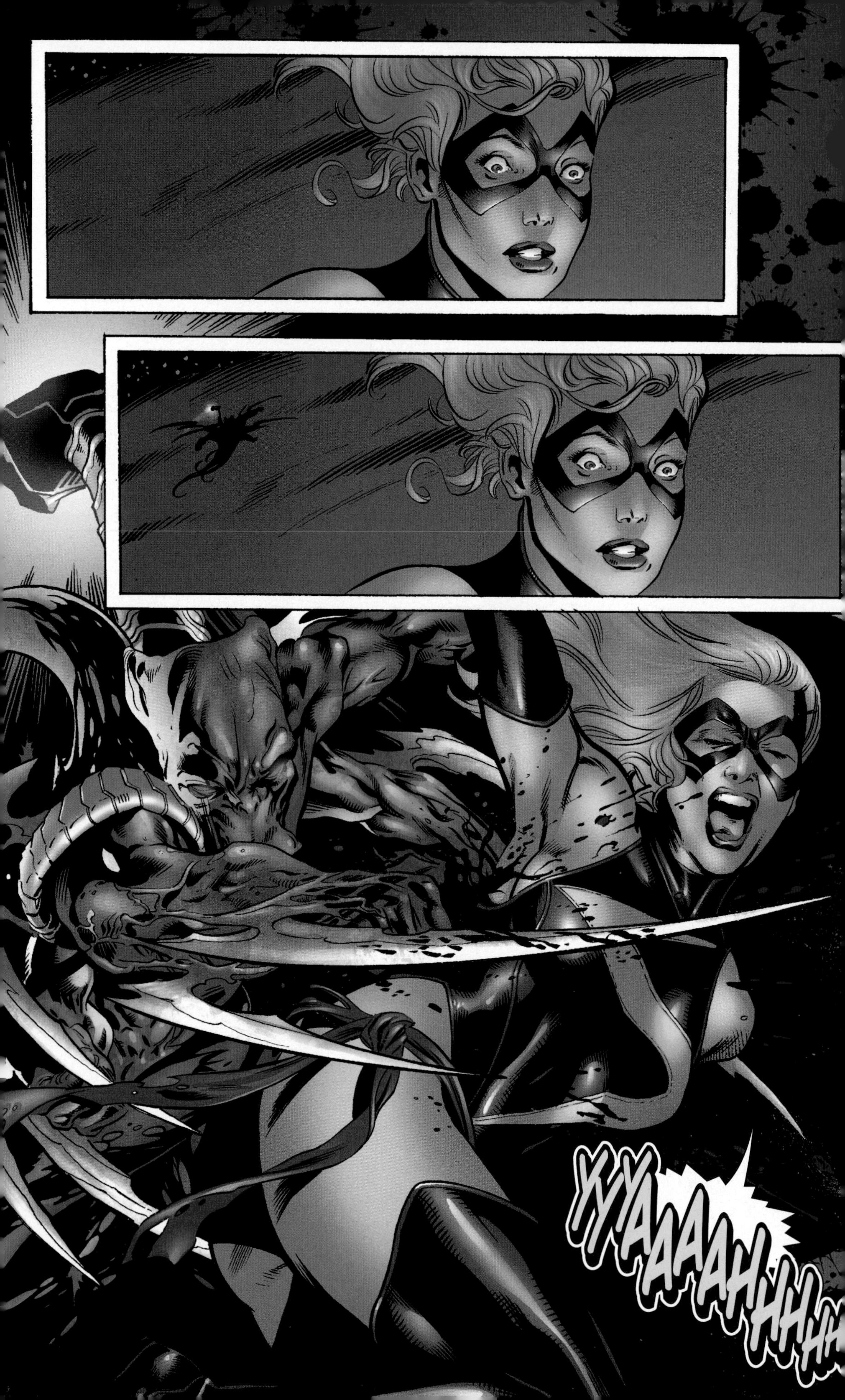
YYAAAAHHHHH

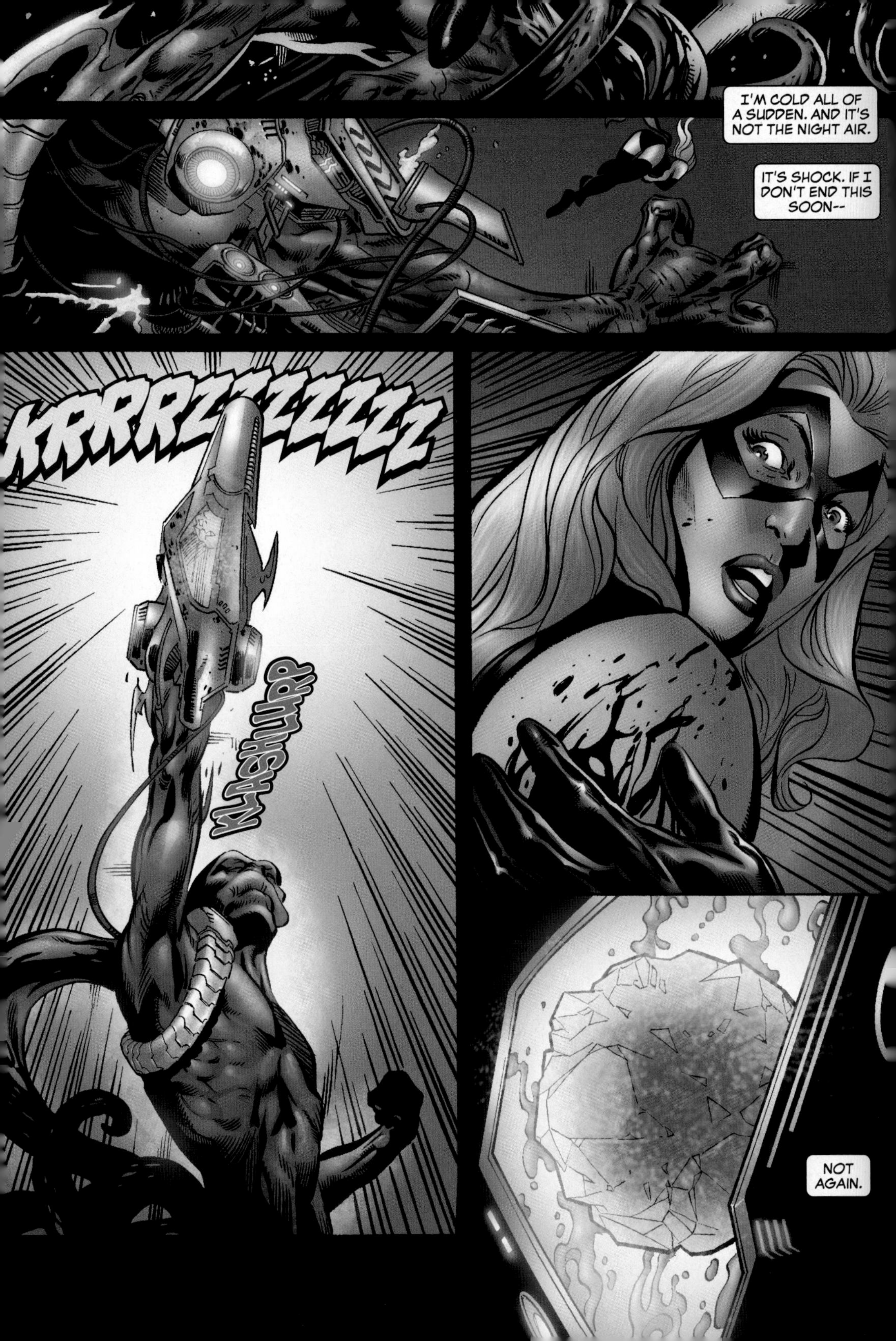
I'M COLD ALL OF A SUDDEN. AND IT'S NOT THE NIGHT AIR.
IT'S SHOCK. IF I DON'T END THIS SOON--
KRRRZZZZZZZ
KLASHLURP
NOT AGAIN.

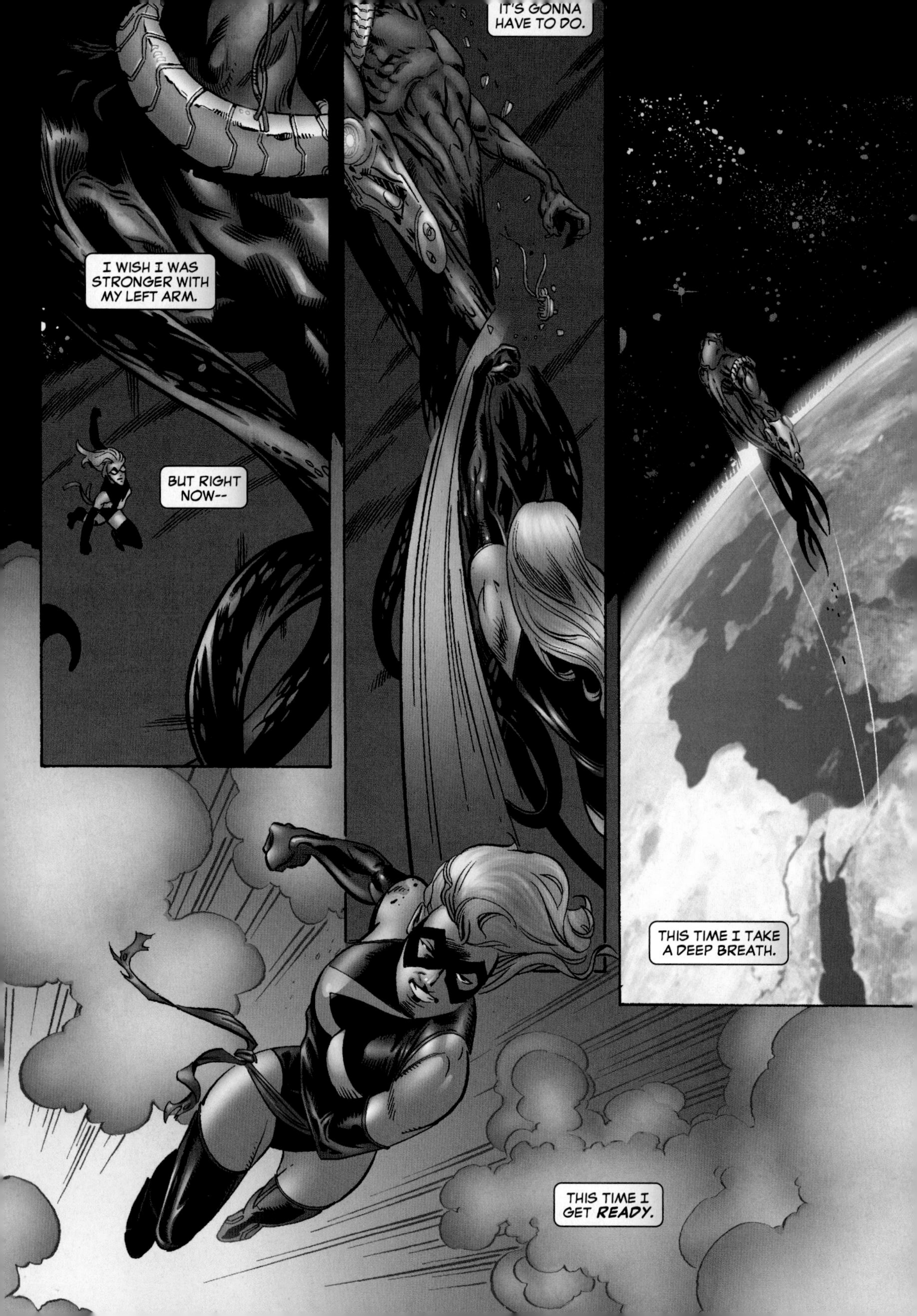
IT'S GONNA HAVE TO DO.
I WISH I WAS STRONGER WITH MY LEFT ARM.
BUT RIGHT NOW--
THIS TIME I TAKE A DEEP BREATH.
THIS TIME I GET READY.

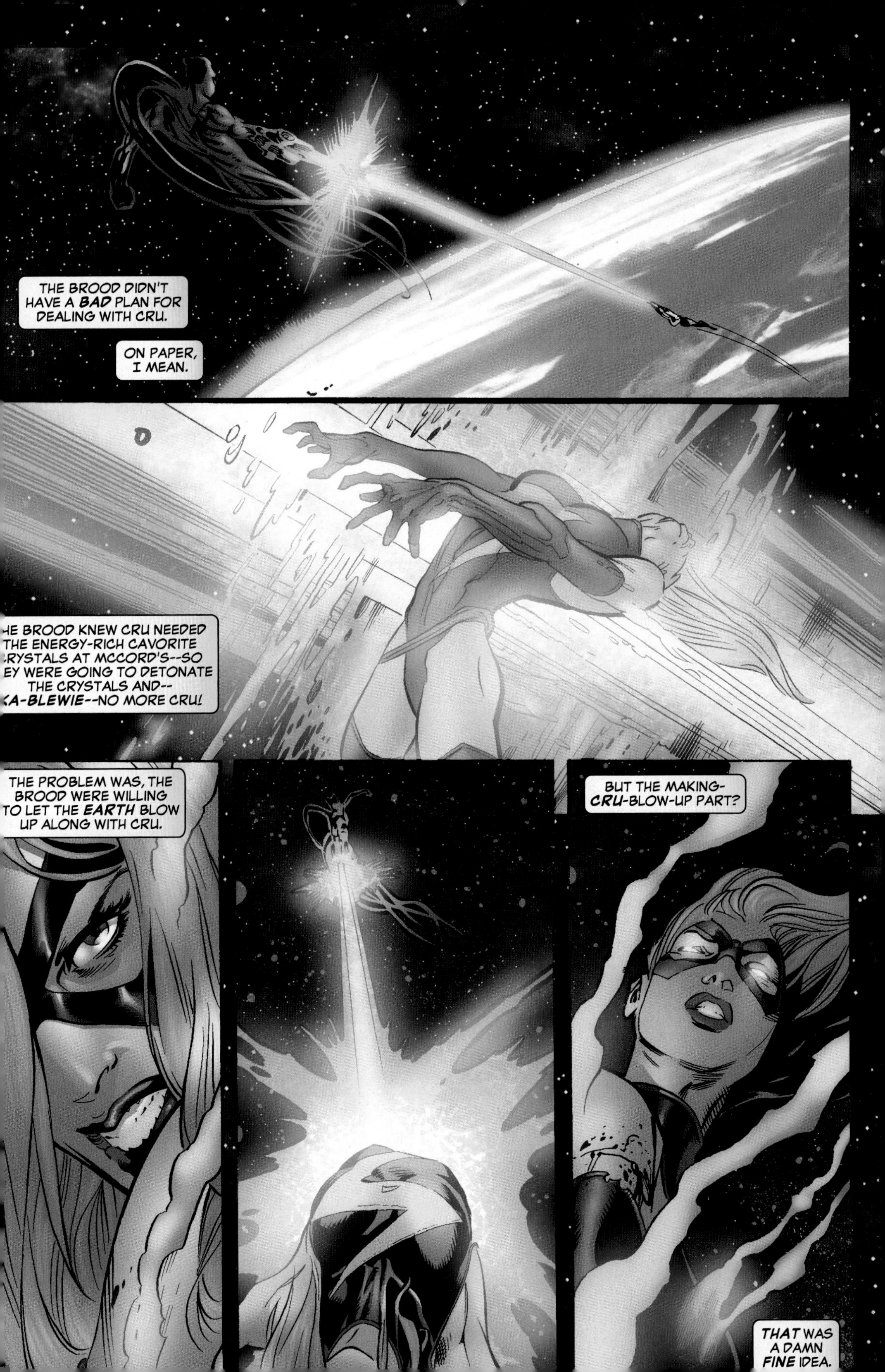
THE BROOD DIDN'T HAVE A BAD PLAN FOR DEALING WITH CRU.
ON PAPER, I MEAN.
HE BROOD KNEW CRU NEEDED THE ENERGY-RICH CAVORITE CRYSTALS AT MCCORD'S--SO EY WERE GOING TO DETONATE THE CRYSTALS AND-- KA-BLEWIE--NO MORE CRU!
THE PROBLEM WAS, THE BROOD WERE WILLING TO LET THE EARTH BLOW UP ALONG WITH CRU.
BUT THE MAKING-CRU-BLOW-UP PART?
THAT WAS A DAMN FINE IDEA.

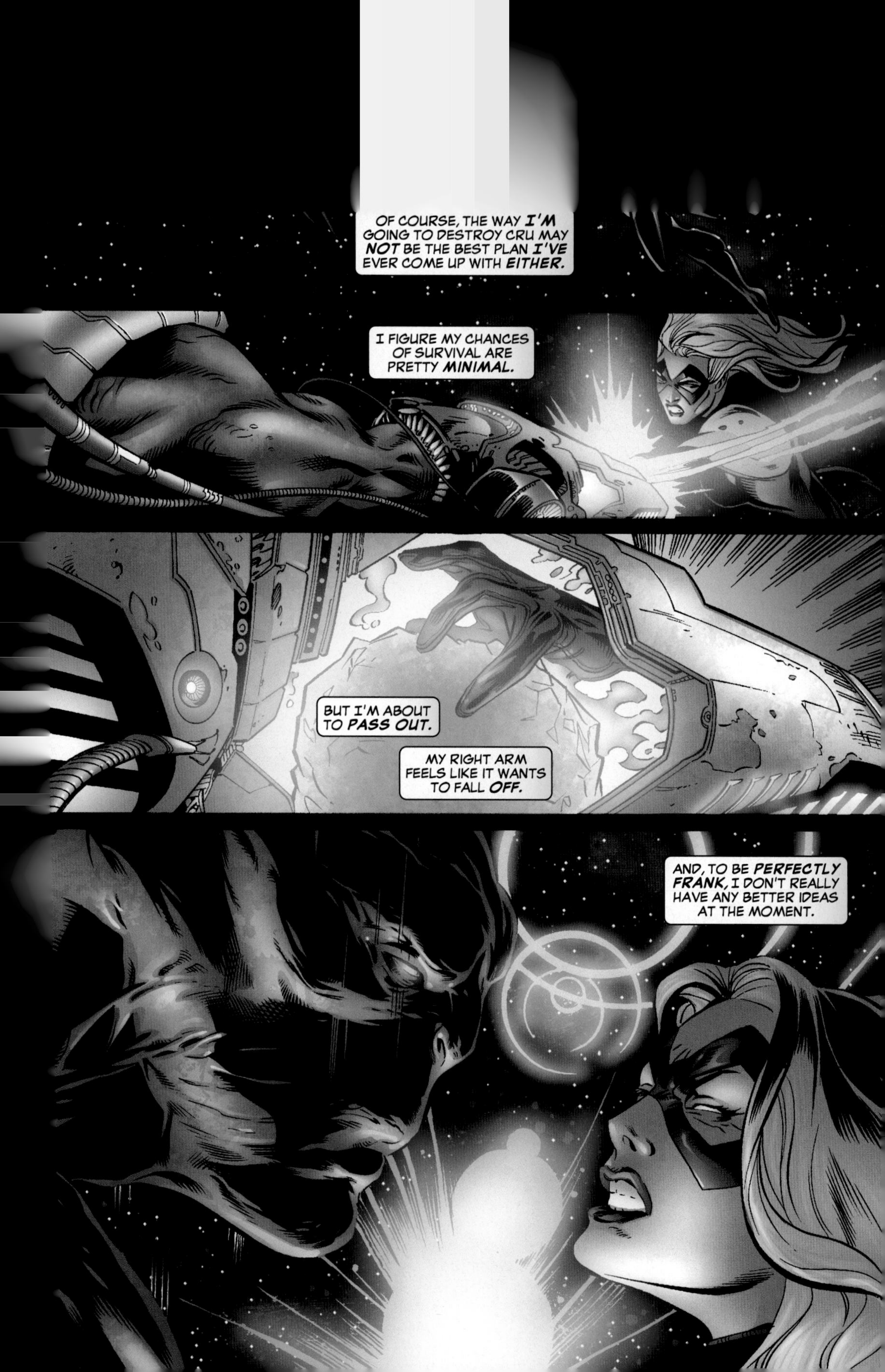

OF COURSE, THE WAY I'M GOING TO DESTROY CRU MAY NOT BE THE BEST PLAN I'VE EVER COME UP WITH EITHER.
I FIGURE MY CHANCES OF SURVIVAL ARE PRETTY MINIMAL.
BUT I'M ABOUT TO PASS OUT.
MY RIGHT ARM FEELS LIKE IT WANTS TO FALL OFF.
AND, TO BE PERFECTLY FRANK, I DON'T REALLY HAVE ANY BETTER IDEAS AT THE MOMENT.

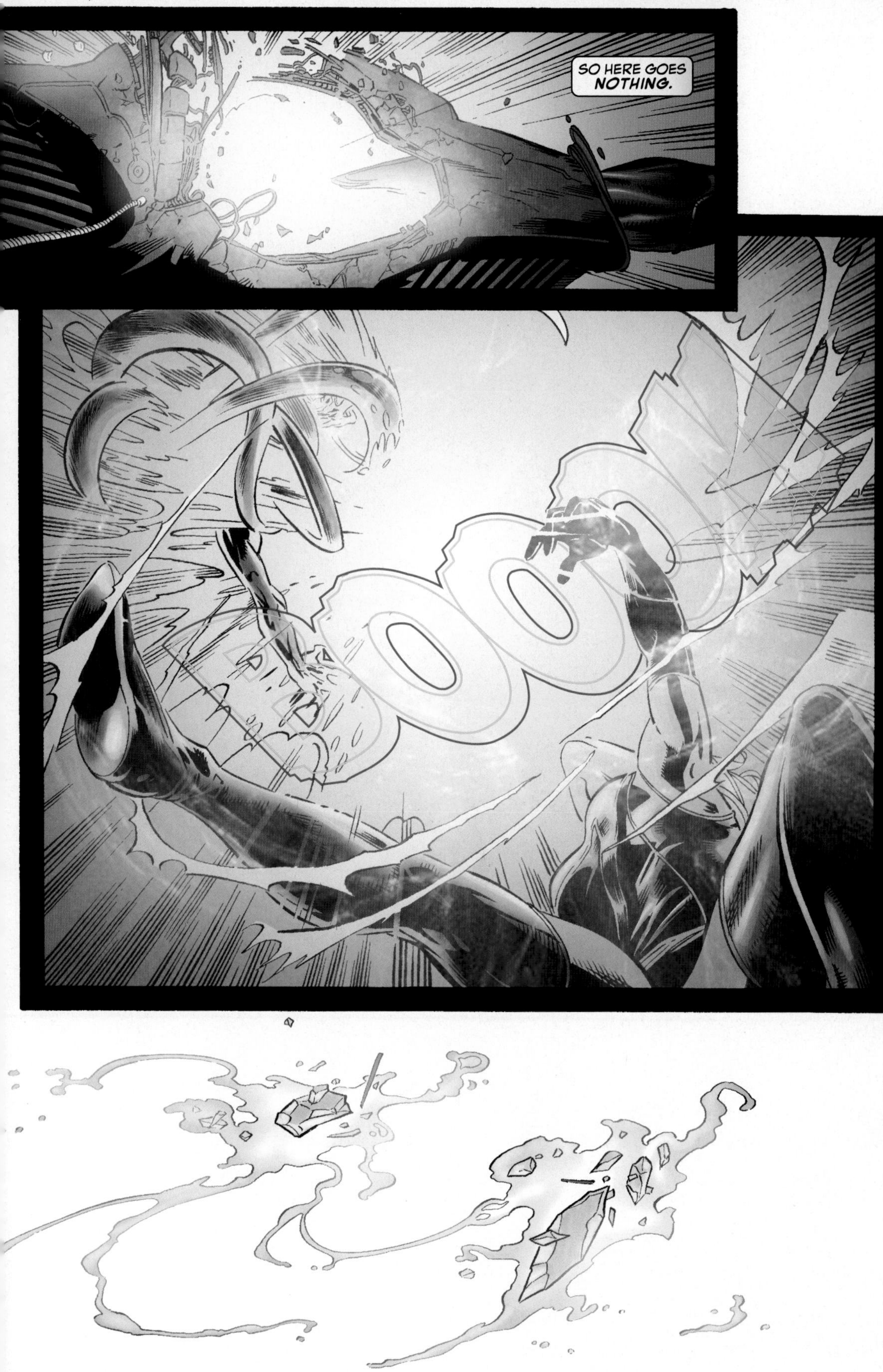
SO HERE GOES NOTHING.

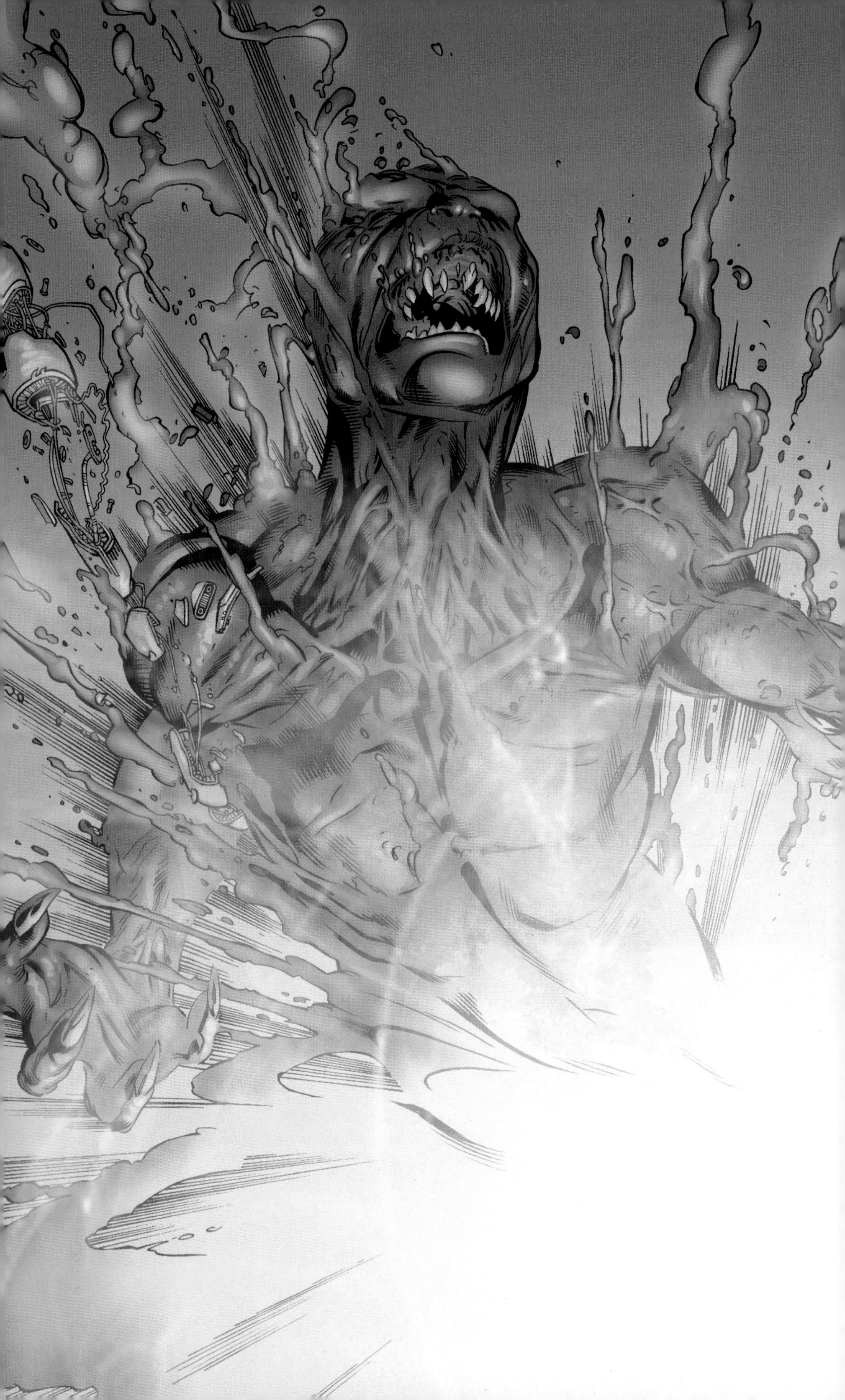

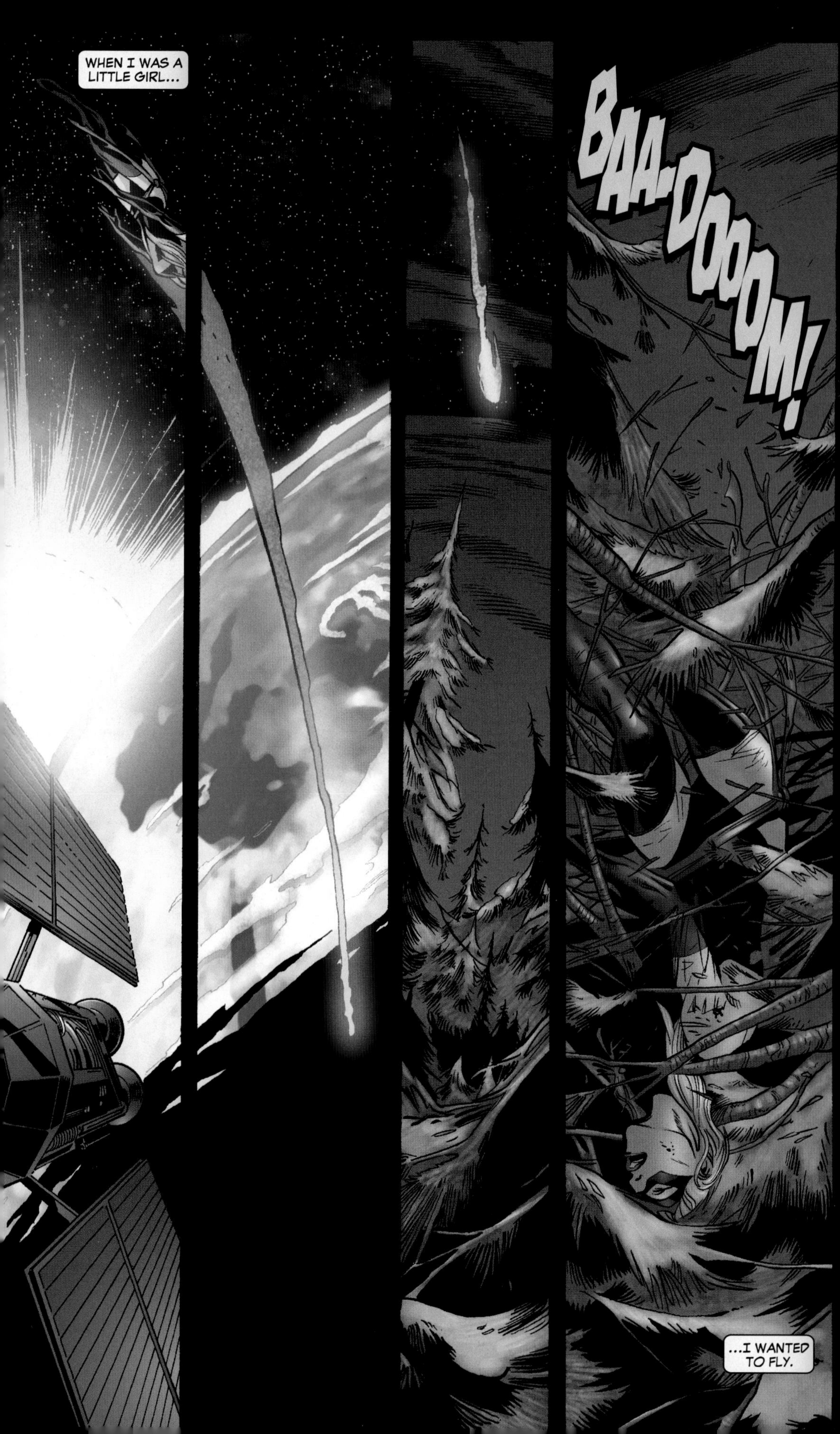
WHEN I WAS A LITTLE GIRL...
BAA-DOOOM!
...I WANTED TO FLY.

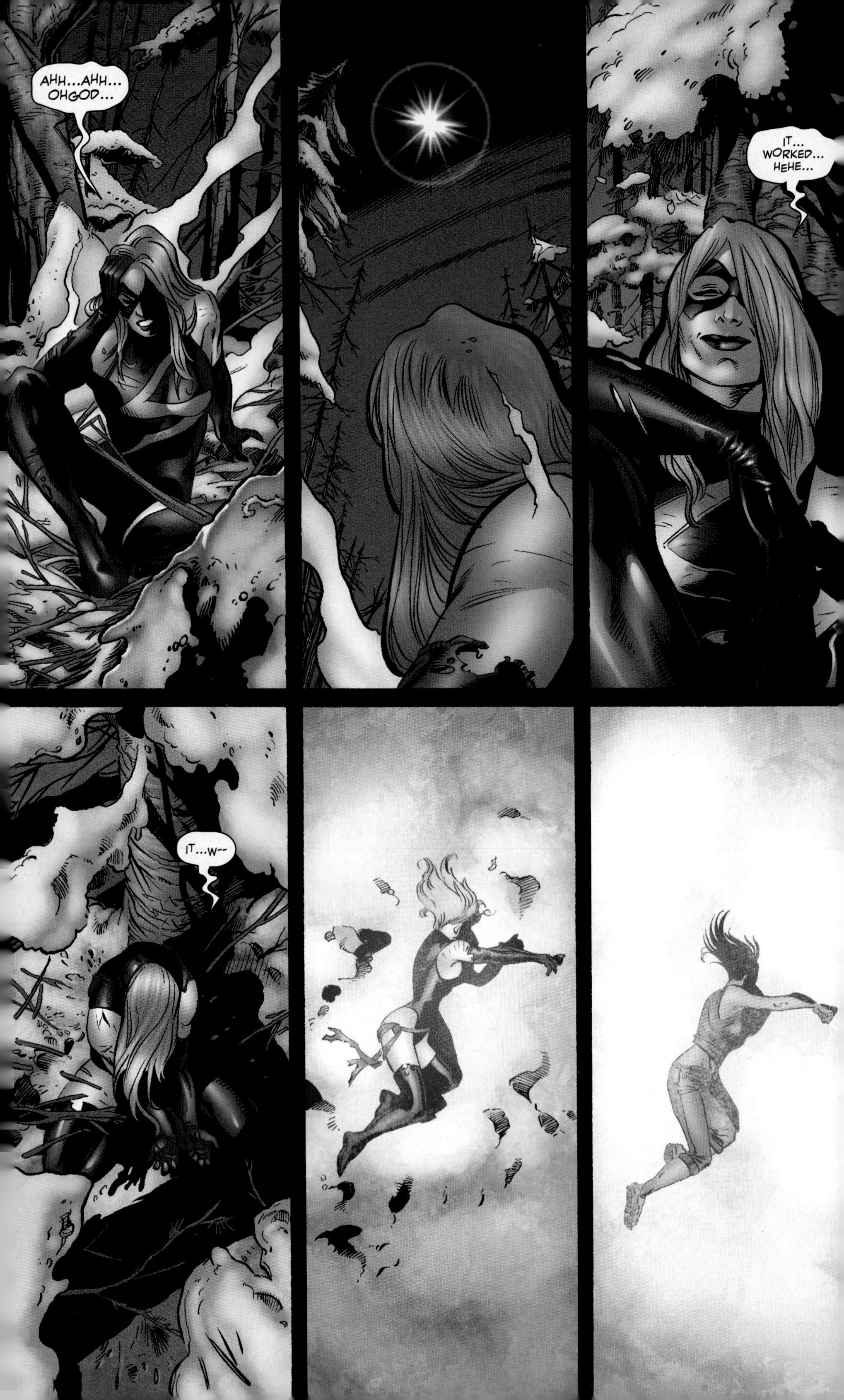
AHH...AHH... OHGOD...
IT... WORKED... HEHE...
IT...W--

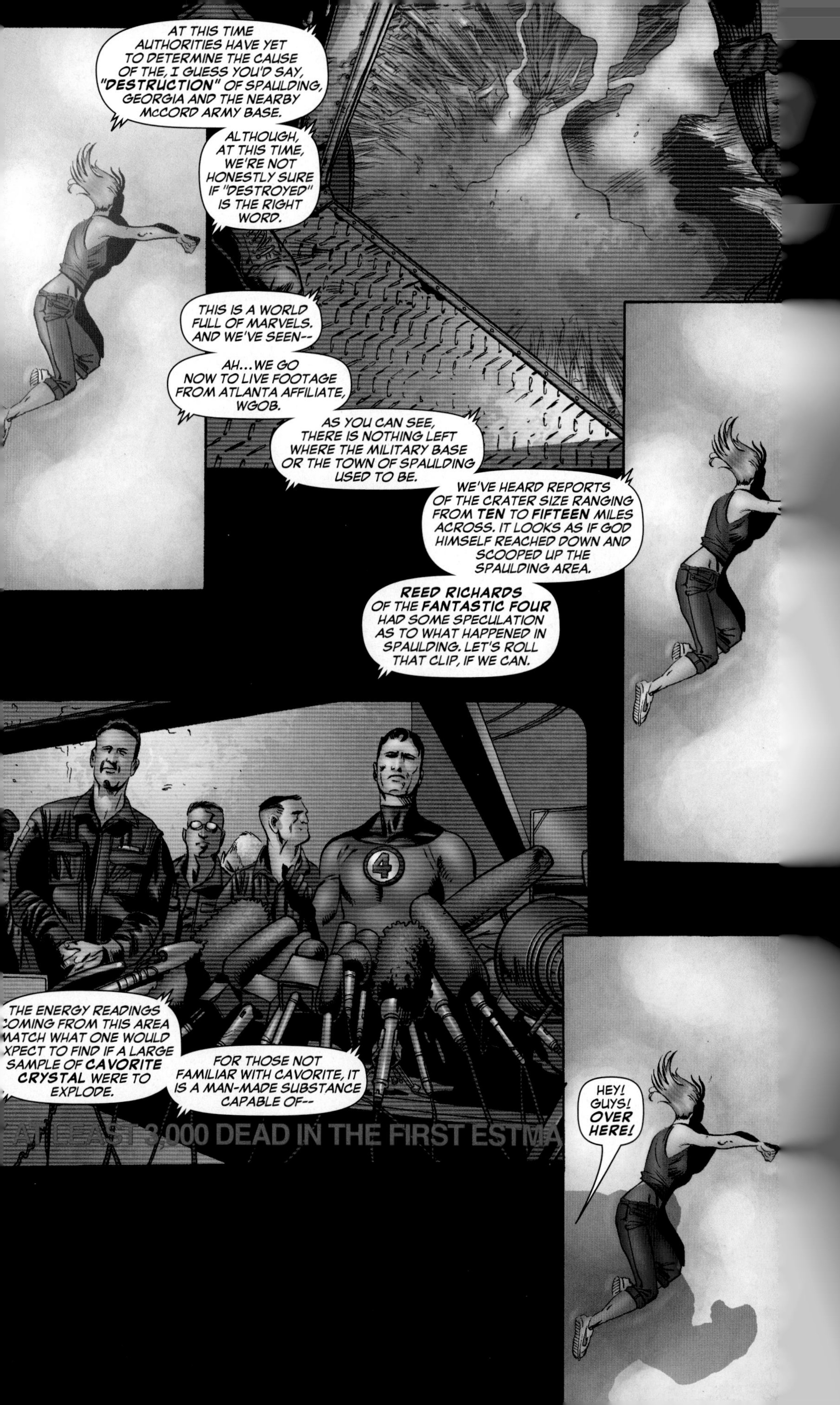
AT THIS TIME AUTHORITIES HAVE YET TO DETERMINE THE CAUSE OF THE, I GUESS YOU'D SAY, "DESTRUCTION" OF SPAULDING, GEORGIA AND THE NEARBY McCORD ARMY BASE.
ALTHOUGH, AT THIS TIME, WE'RE NOT HONESTLY SURE IF "DESTROYED" IS THE RIGHT WORD.
THIS IS A WORLD FULL OF MARVELS. AND WE'VE SEEN--
AH...WE GO NOW TO LIVE FOOTAGE FROM ATLANTA AFFILIATE, WGOB.
AS YOU CAN SEE, THERE IS NOTHING LEFT WHERE THE MILITARY BASE OR THE TOWN OF SPAULDING USED TO BE.
WE'VE HEARD REPORTS OF THE CRATER SIZE RANGING FROM TEN TO FIFTEEN MILES ACROSS. IT LOOKS AS IF GOD HIMSELF REACHED DOWN AND SCOOPED UP THE SPAULDING AREA.
REED RICHARDS OF THE FANTASTIC FOUR HAD SOME SPECULATION AS TO WHAT HAPPENED IN SPAULDING. LET'S ROLL THAT CLIP, IF WE CAN.
THE ENERGY READINGS COMING FROM THIS AREA MATCH WHAT ONE WOULD EXPECT TO FIND IF A LARGE SAMPLE OF CAVORITE CRYSTAL WERE TO EXPLODE.
FOR THOSE NOT FAMILIAR WITH CAVORITE, IT IS A MAN-MADE SUBSTANCE CAPABLE OF--
AT LEAST 3,000 DEAD IN THE FIRST ESTMA
HEY! GUYS! OVER HERE!

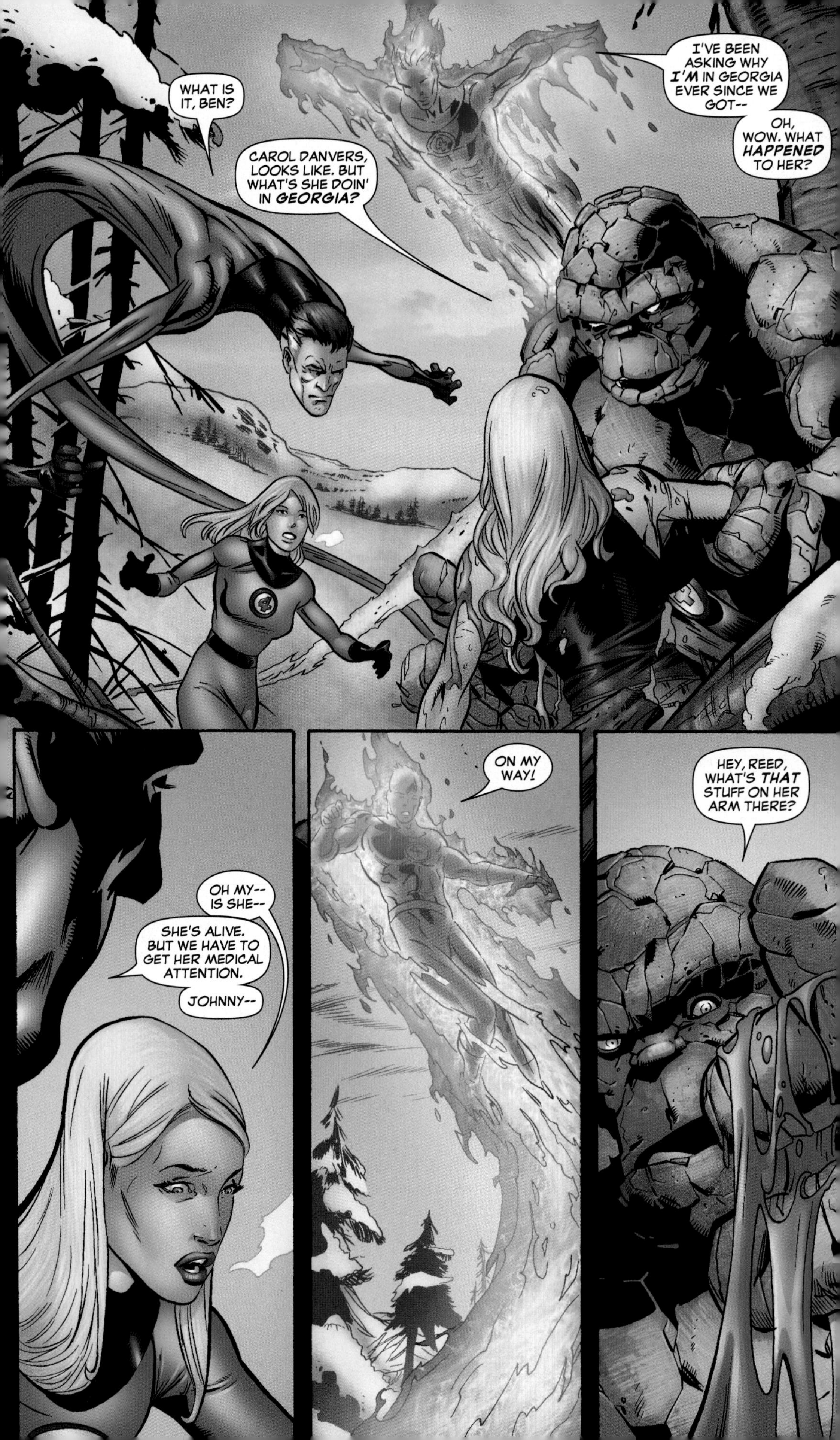
WHAT IS IT, BEN?
CAROL DANVERS, LOOKS LIKE. BUT WHAT'S SHE DOIN' IN GEORGIA?
I'VE BEEN ASKING WHY I'M IN GEORGIA EVER SINCE WE GOT--
OH, WOW. WHAT HAPPENED TO HER?
OH MY-- IS SHE--
SHE'S ALIVE. BUT WE HAVE TO GET HER MEDICAL ATTENTION.
JOHNNY--
ON MY WAY!
HEY, REED, WHAT'S THAT STUFF ON HER ARM THERE?

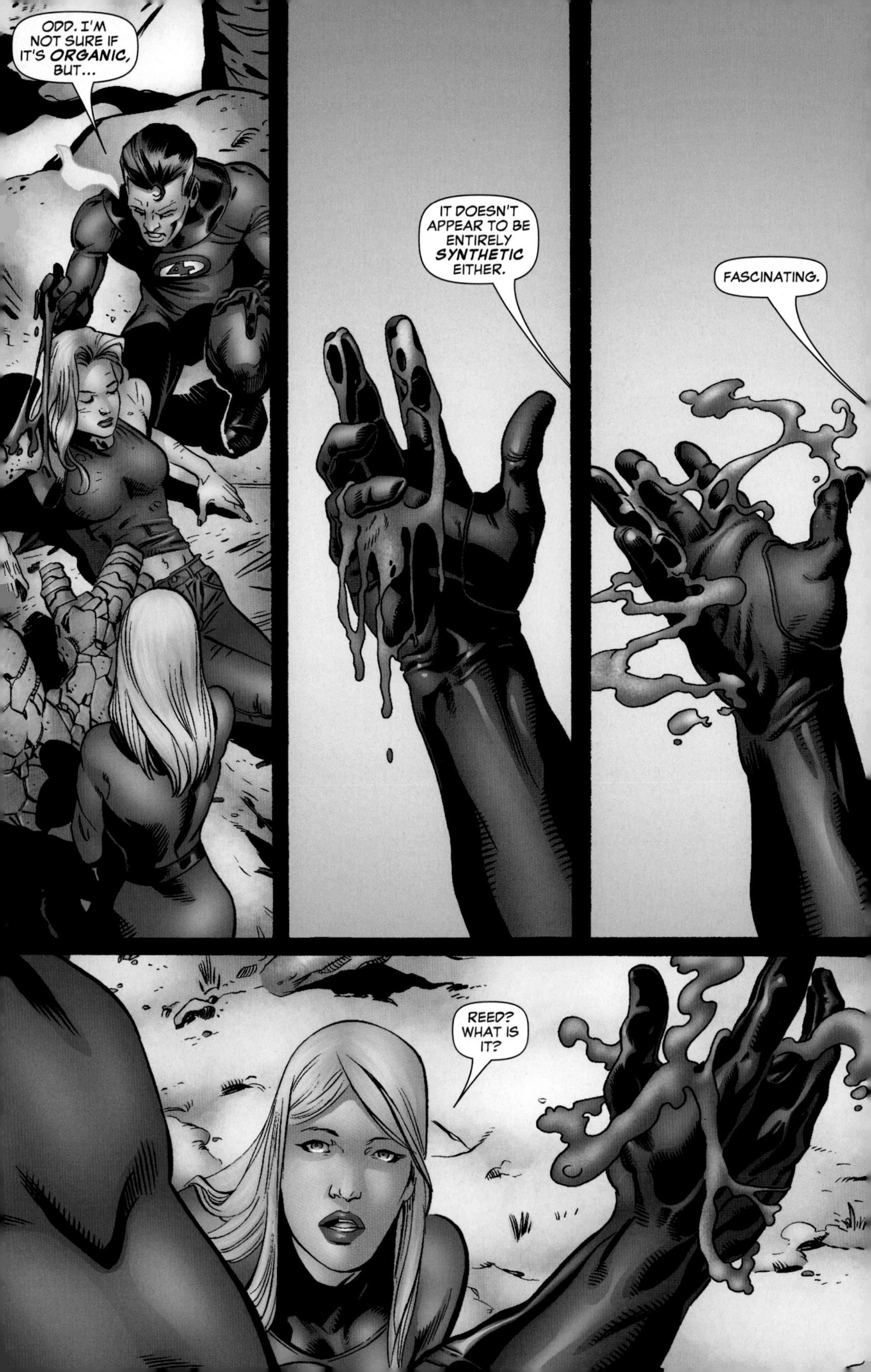
ODD. I'M NOT SURE IF IT'S ORGANIC, BUT...
IT DOESN'T APPEAR TO BE ENTIRELY SYNTHETIC EITHER.
FASCINATING.
REED? WHAT IS IT?

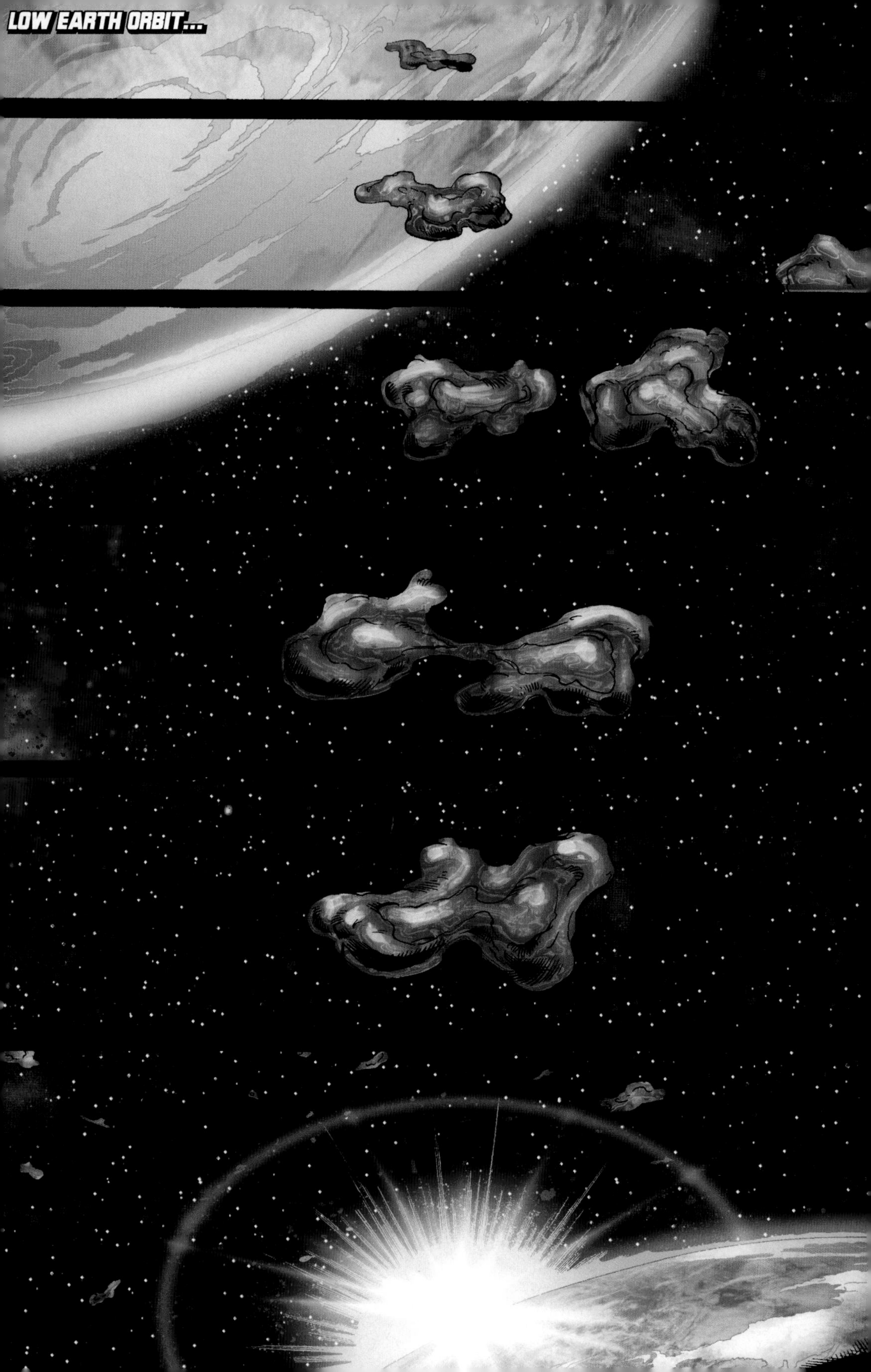
LOW EARTH ORBIT...

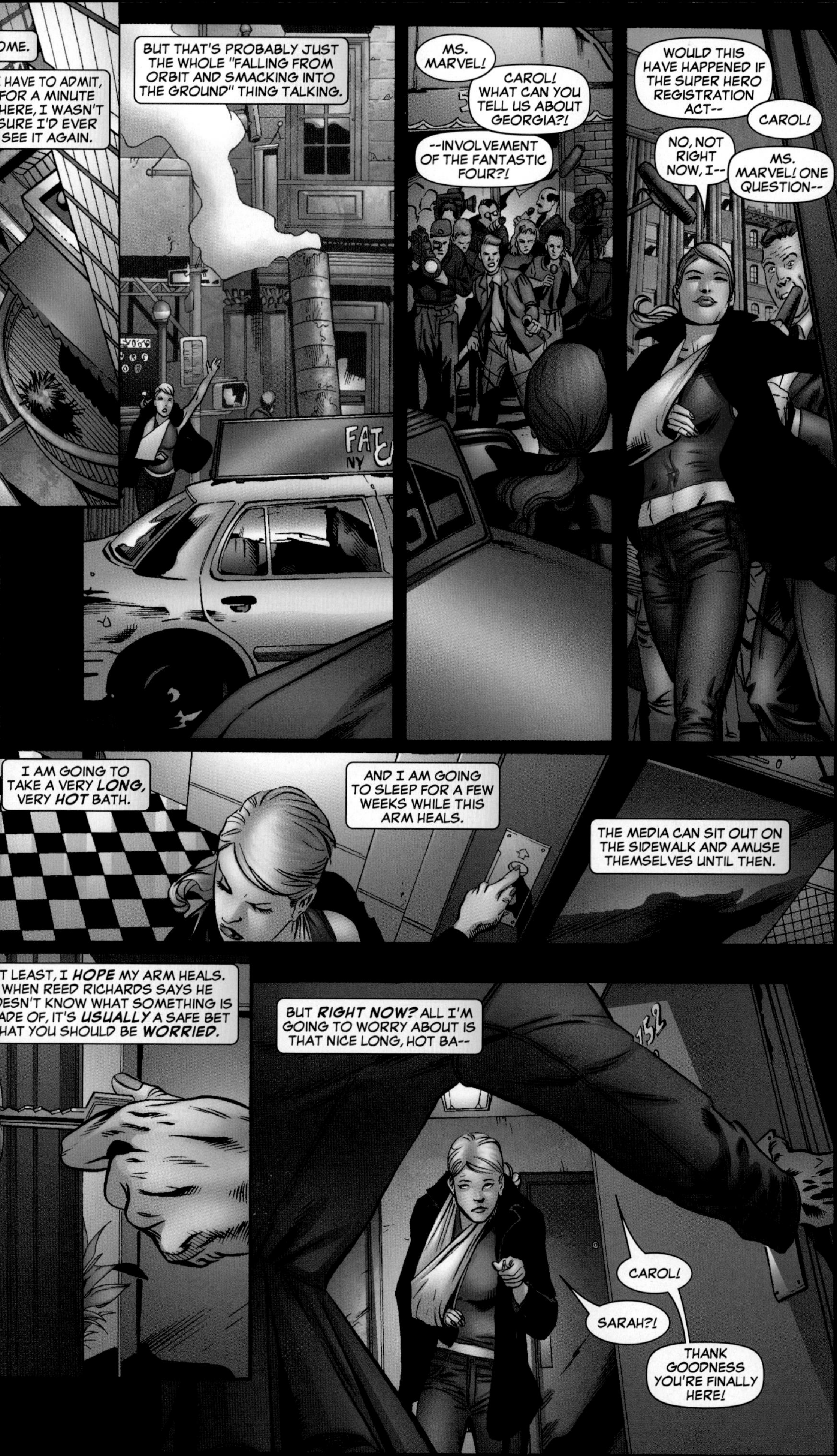
OME.
HAVE TO ADMIT, FOR A MINUTE HERE, I WASN'T SURE I'D EVER SEE IT AGAIN.
BUT THAT'S PROBABLY JUST THE WHOLE "FALLING FROM ORBIT AND SMACKING INTO THE GROUND" THING TALKING.
FAT
NY
MS. MARVEL!
CAROL! WHAT CAN YOU TELL US ABOUT GEORGIA?!
--INVOLVEMENT OF THE FANTASTIC FOUR?!
WOULD THIS HAVE HAPPENED IF THE SUPER HERO REGISTRATION ACT--
CAROL!
NO, NOT RIGHT NOW, I--
MS. MARVEL! ONE QUESTION--
I AM GOING TO TAKE A VERY LONG, VERY HOT BATH.
AND I AM GOING TO SLEEP FOR A FEW WEEKS WHILE THIS ARM HEALS.
THE MEDIA CAN SIT OUT ON THE SIDEWALK AND AMUSE THEMSELVES UNTIL THEN.
T LEAST, I HOPE MY ARM HEALS. WHEN REED RICHARDS SAYS HE DESN'T KNOW WHAT SOMETHING IS ADE OF, IT'S USUALLY A SAFE BET HAT YOU SHOULD BE WORRIED.
BUT RIGHT NOW? ALL I'M GOING TO WORRY ABOUT IS THAT NICE LONG, HOT BA--
152
CAROL!
SARAH?!
THANK GOODNESS YOU'RE FINALLY HERE!

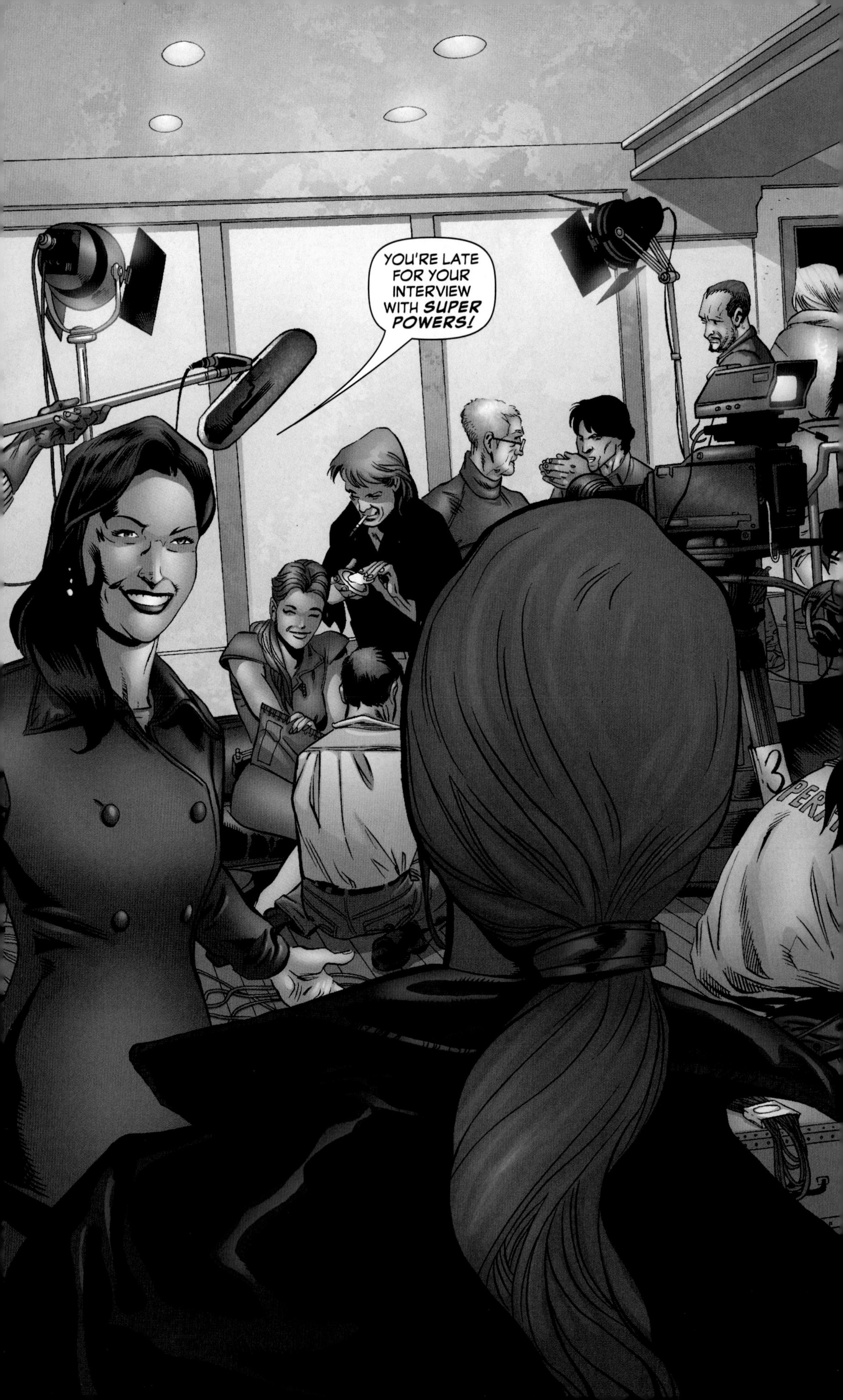
YOU'RE LATE FOR YOUR INTERVIEW WITH SUPER POWERS!

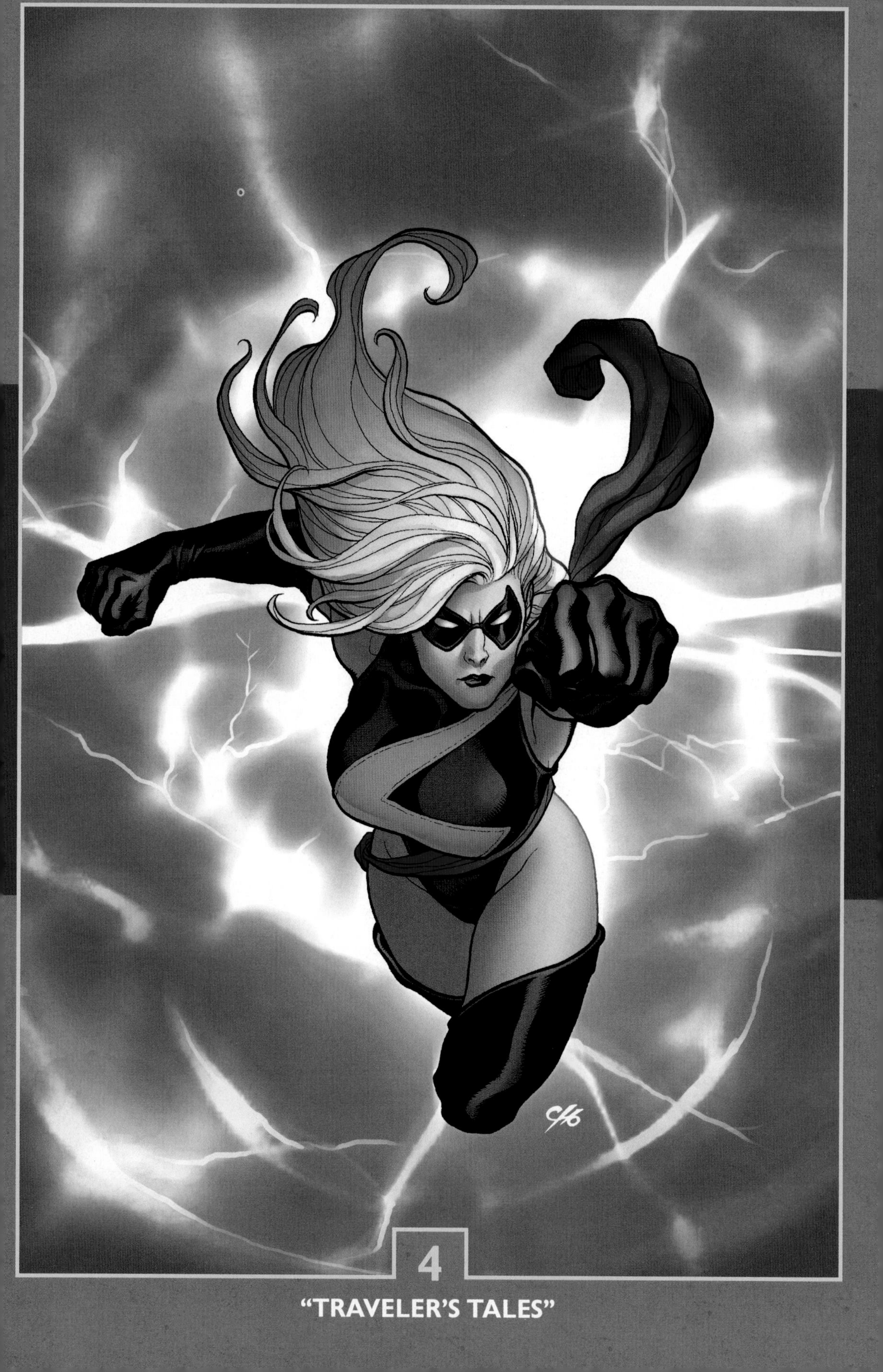

4

"TRAVELER'S TALES"

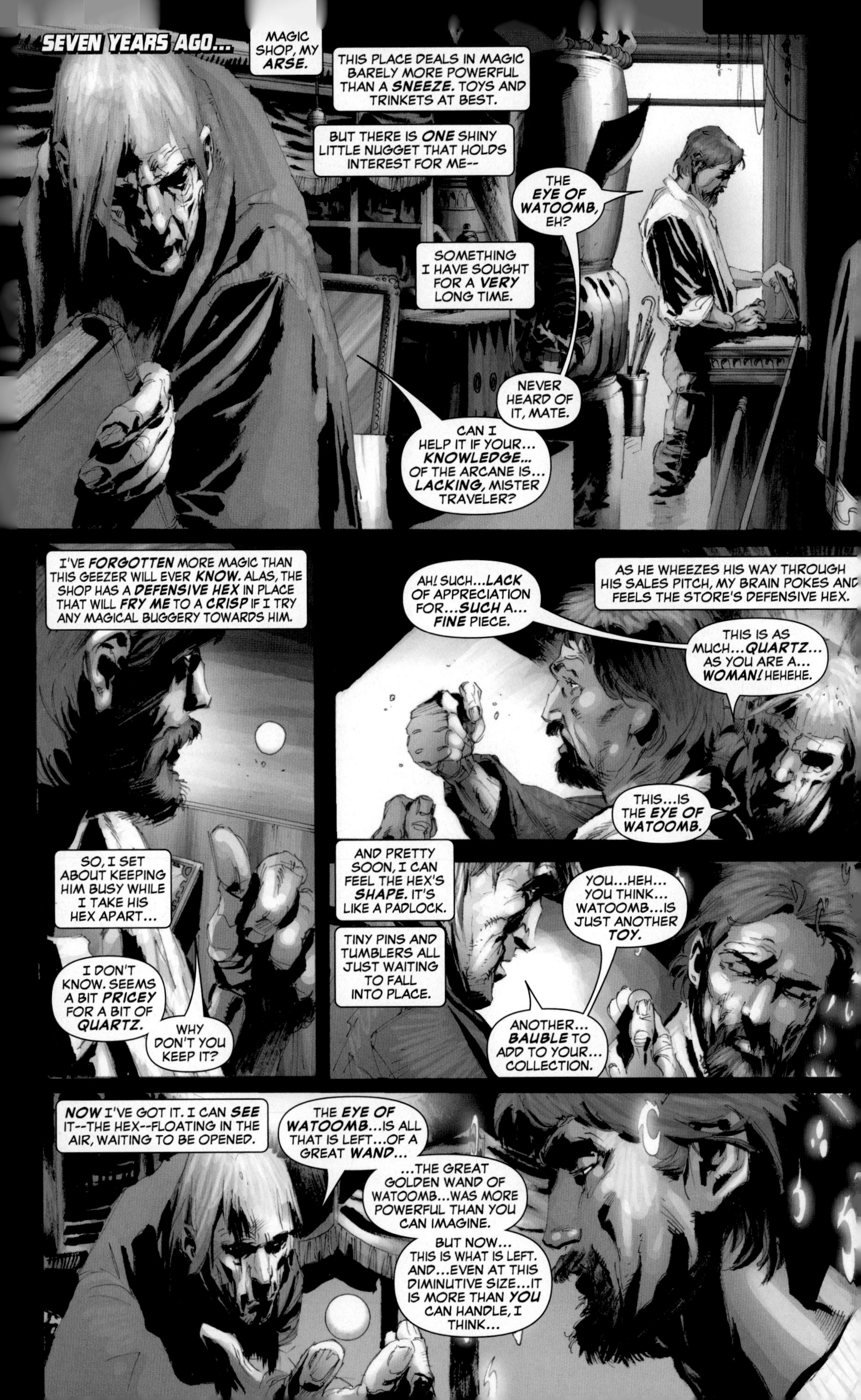

SEVEN YEARS AGO...
MAGIC SHOP, MY ARSE.
THIS PLACE DEALS IN MAGIC BARELY MORE POWERFUL THAN A SNEEZE. TOYS AND TRINKETS AT BEST.
BUT THERE IS ONE SHINY LITTLE NUGGET THAT HOLDS INTEREST FOR ME--
THE EYE OF WATOOMB, EH?
SOMETHING I HAVE SOUGHT FOR A VERY LONG TIME.
NEVER HEARD OF IT, MATE.
CAN I HELP IT IF YOUR... KNOWLEDGE... OF THE ARCANE IS... LACKING, MISTER TRAVELER?
I'VE FORGOTTEN MORE MAGIC THAN THIS GEEZER WILL EVER KNOW. ALAS, THE SHOP HAS A DEFENSIVE HEX IN PLACE THAT WILL FRY ME TO A CRISP IF I TRY ANY MAGICAL BUGGERY TOWARDS HIM.
AS HE WHEEZES HIS WAY THROUGH HIS SALES PITCH, MY BRAIN POKES AND FEELS THE STORE'S DEFENSIVE HEX.
AH! SUCH...LACK OF APPRECIATION FOR...SUCH A... FINE PIECE.
THIS IS AS MUCH...QUARTZ... AS YOU ARE A... WOMAN! HEHEHE.
THIS...IS THE EYE OF WATOOMB.
SO, I SET ABOUT KEEPING HIM BUSY WHILE I TAKE HIS HEX APART...
I DON'T KNOW. SEEMS A BIT PRICEY FOR A BIT OF QUARTZ.
WHY DON'T YOU KEEP IT?
AND PRETTY SOON, I CAN FEEL THE HEX'S SHAPE. IT'S LIKE A PADLOCK.
TINY PINS AND TUMBLERS ALL JUST WAITING TO FALL INTO PLACE.
YOU...HEH... YOU THINK... WATOOMB...IS JUST ANOTHER TOY.
ANOTHER... BAUBLE TO ADD TO YOUR... COLLECTION.
NOW I'VE GOT IT. I CAN SEE IT--THE HEX--FLOATING IN THE AIR, WAITING TO BE OPENED.
THE EYE OF WATOOMB...IS ALL THAT IS LEFT...OF A GREAT WAND...
...THE GREAT GOLDEN WAND OF WATOOMB...WAS MORE POWERFUL THAN YOU CAN IMAGINE.
BUT NOW... THIS IS WHAT IS LEFT. AND...EVEN AT THIS DIMINUTIVE SIZE...IT IS MORE THAN YOU CAN HANDLE, I THINK...

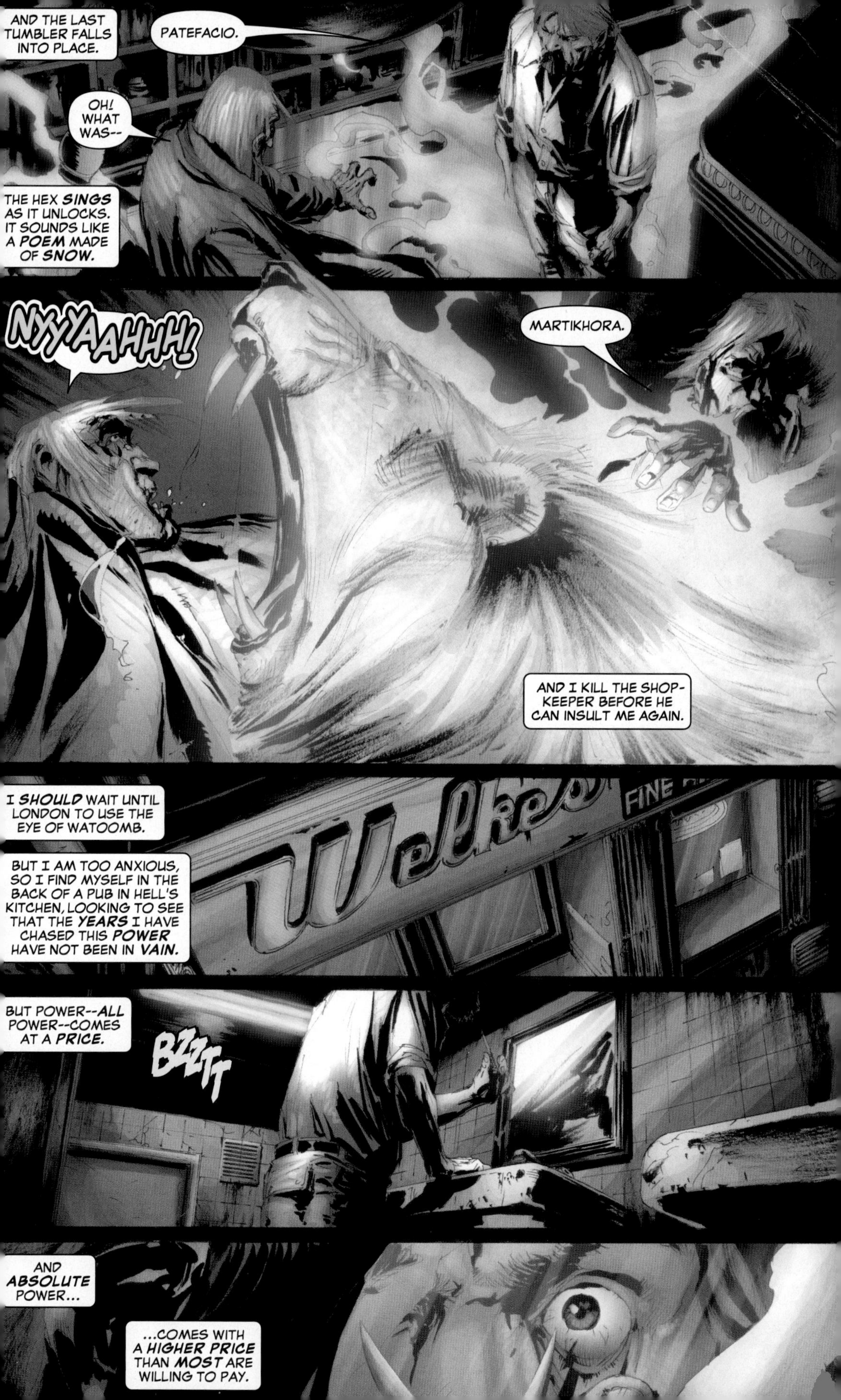
AND THE LAST TUMBLER FALLS INTO PLACE.
PATEFACIO.
OH! WHAT WAS--
THE HEX SINGS AS IT UNLOCKS. IT SOUNDS LIKE A POEM MADE OF SNOW.
NYYAAHHH!
MARTIKHORA.
AND I KILL THE SHOP-KEEPER BEFORE HE CAN INSULT ME AGAIN.
I SHOULD WAIT UNTIL LONDON TO USE THE EYE OF WATOOMB.
BUT I AM TOO ANXIOUS, SO I FIND MYSELF IN THE BACK OF A PUB IN HELL'S KITCHEN, LOOKING TO SEE THAT THE YEARS I HAVE CHASED THIS POWER HAVE NOT BEEN IN VAIN.
Welkes
FINE
BUT POWER--ALL POWER--COMES AT A PRICE.
BZZTT
AND ABSOLUTE POWER...
...COMES WITH A HIGHER PRICE THAN MOST ARE WILLING TO PAY.

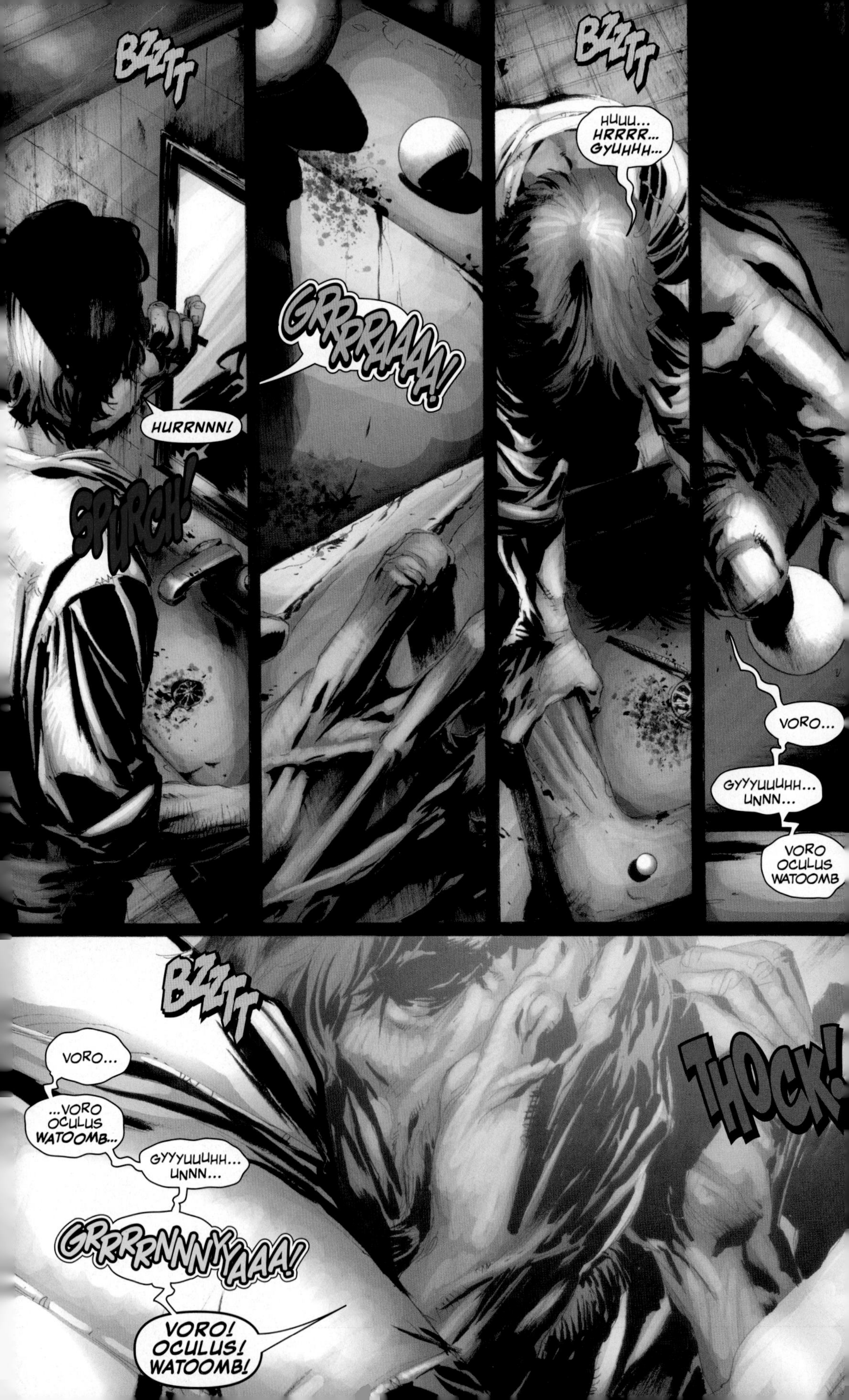
BZZTT
HURRNNN!
SPURCH!
GRRRRAAAAA!
BZZTT
HUUU...
HRRRR...
GYUHHH...
VORO...
GYYYUUUHH...
UNNN...
VORO
OCULUS
WATOOMB
BZZTT
VORO...
...VORO
OCULUS
WATOOMB...
GYYYUUUHH...
UNNN...
GRRRRNNNYAAA!
VORO!
OCULUS!
WATOOMB!
THOCK!

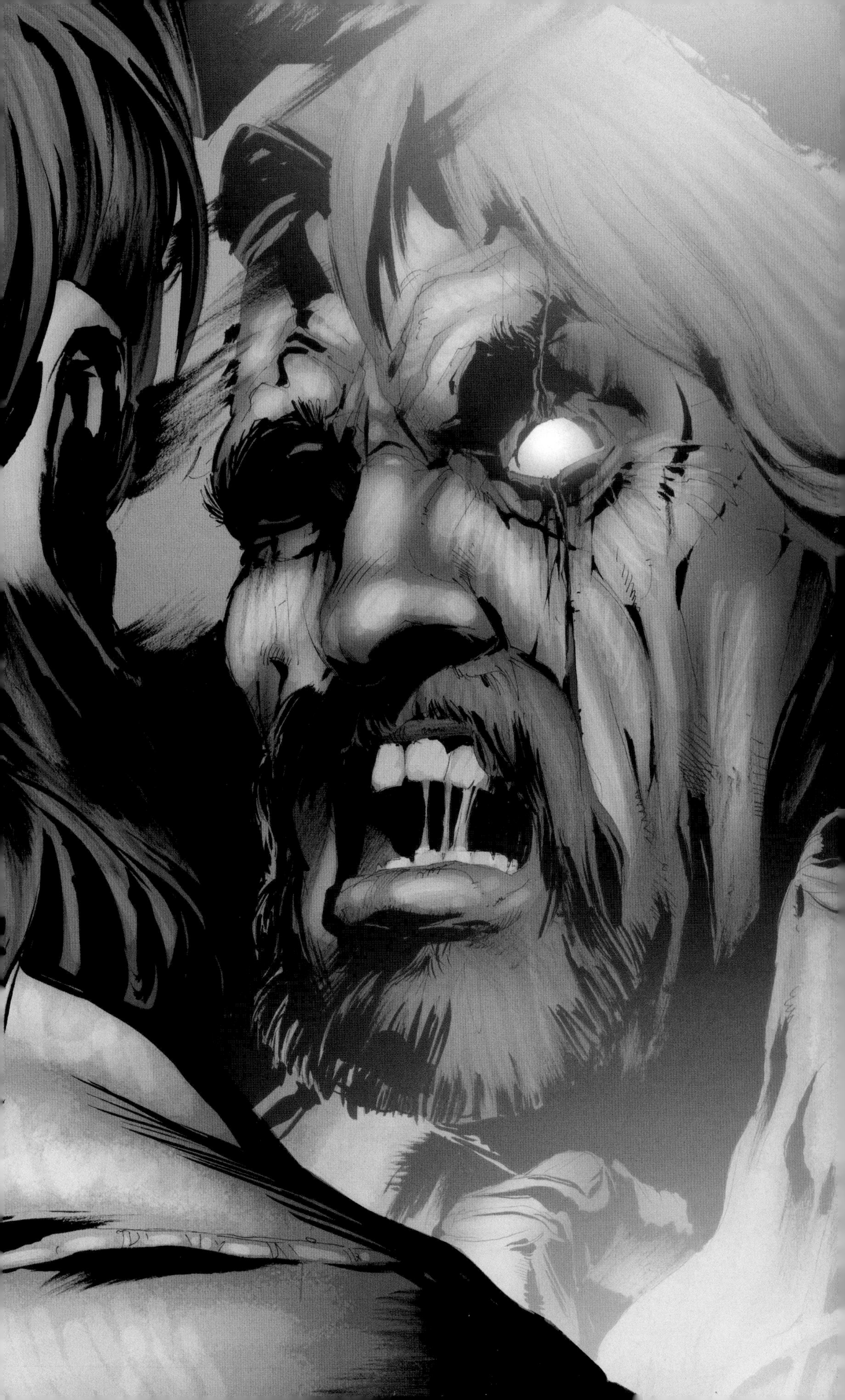

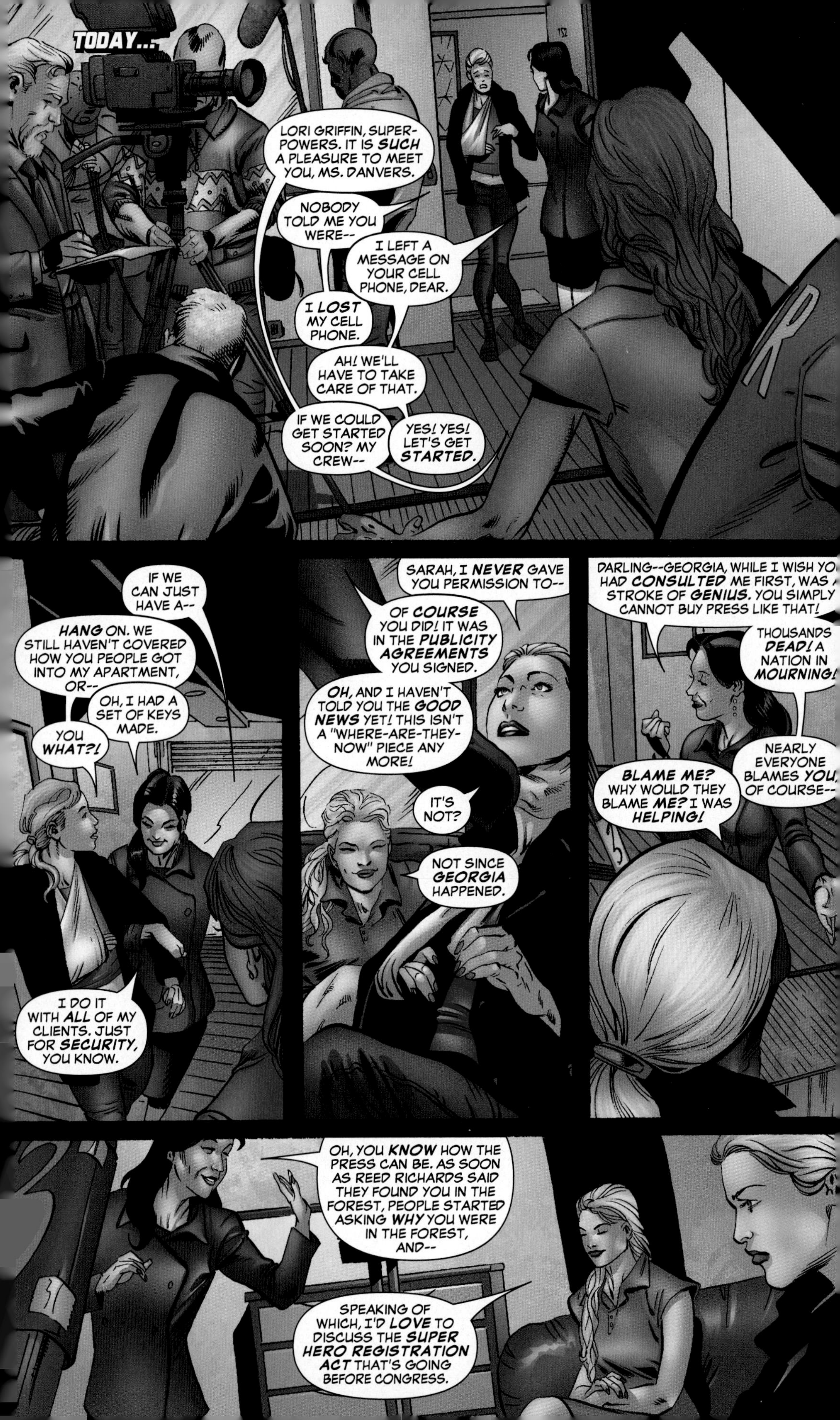
TODAY...
LORI GRIFFIN, SUPER-POWERS. IT IS SUCH A PLEASURE TO MEET YOU, MS. DANVERS.
NOBODY TOLD ME YOU WERE--
I LEFT A MESSAGE ON YOUR CELL PHONE, DEAR.
I LOST MY CELL PHONE.
AH! WE'LL HAVE TO TAKE CARE OF THAT.
IF WE COULD GET STARTED SOON? MY CREW--
YES! YES! LET'S GET STARTED.
IF WE CAN JUST HAVE A--
HANG ON. WE STILL HAVEN'T COVERED HOW YOU PEOPLE GOT INTO MY APARTMENT, OR--
OH, I HAD A SET OF KEYS MADE.
YOU WHAT?!
I DO IT WITH ALL OF MY CLIENTS. JUST FOR SECURITY, YOU KNOW.
SARAH, I NEVER GAVE YOU PERMISSION TO--
OF COURSE YOU DID! IT WAS IN THE PUBLICITY AGREEMENTS YOU SIGNED.
OH, AND I HAVEN'T TOLD YOU THE GOOD NEWS YET! THIS ISN'T A "WHERE-ARE-THEY-NOW" PIECE ANY MORE!
IT'S NOT?
NOT SINCE GEORGIA HAPPENED.
DARLING--GEORGIA, WHILE I WISH YO HAD CONSULTED ME FIRST, WAS STROKE OF GENIUS. YOU SIMPLY CANNOT BUY PRESS LIKE THAT!
THOUSANDS DEAD! A NATION IN MOURNING!
NEARLY EVERYONE BLAMES YOU, OF COURSE--
BLAME ME? WHY WOULD THEY BLAME ME? I WAS HELPING!
OH, YOU KNOW HOW THE PRESS CAN BE. AS SOON AS REED RICHARDS SAID THEY FOUND YOU IN THE FOREST, PEOPLE STARTED ASKING WHY YOU WERE IN THE FOREST, AND--
SPEAKING OF WHICH, I'D LOVE TO DISCUSS THE SUPER HERO REGISTRATION ACT THAT'S GOING BEFORE CONGRESS.

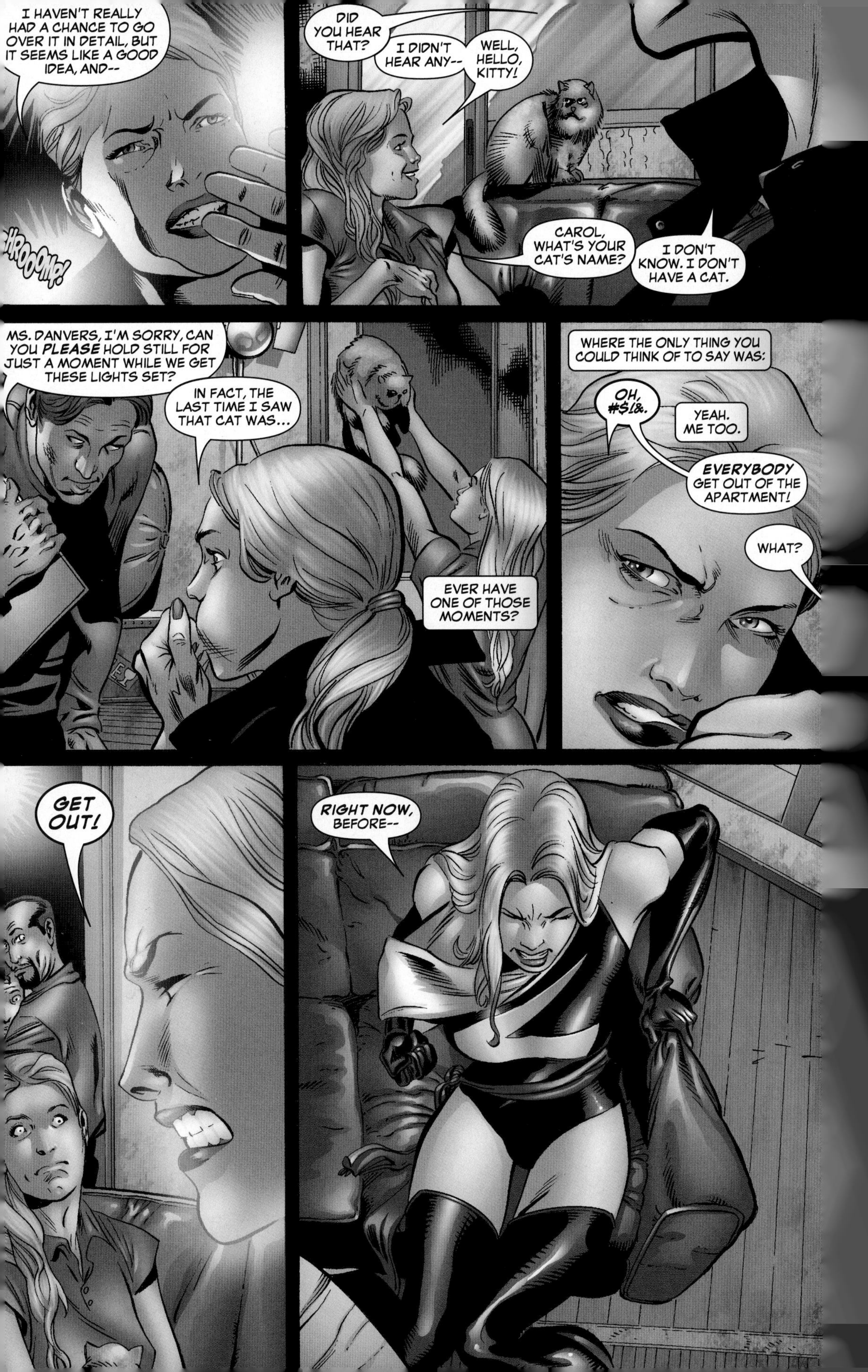

I HAVEN'T REALLY HAD A CHANCE TO GO OVER IT IN DETAIL, BUT IT SEEMS LIKE A GOOD IDEA, AND--
KRROOOMP!
DID YOU HEAR THAT?
I DIDN'T HEAR ANY--
WELL, HELLO, KITTY!
CAROL, WHAT'S YOUR CAT'S NAME?
I DON'T KNOW. I DON'T HAVE A CAT.
MS. DANVERS, I'M SORRY, CAN YOU PLEASE HOLD STILL FOR JUST A MOMENT WHILE WE GET THESE LIGHTS SET?
IN FACT, THE LAST TIME I SAW THAT CAT WAS...
EVER HAVE ONE OF THOSE MOMENTS?
WHERE THE ONLY THING YOU COULD THINK OF TO SAY WAS:
OH, #$!&.
YEAH. ME TOO.
EVERYBODY GET OUT OF THE APARTMENT!
WHAT?
GET OUT!
RIGHT NOW, BEFORE--

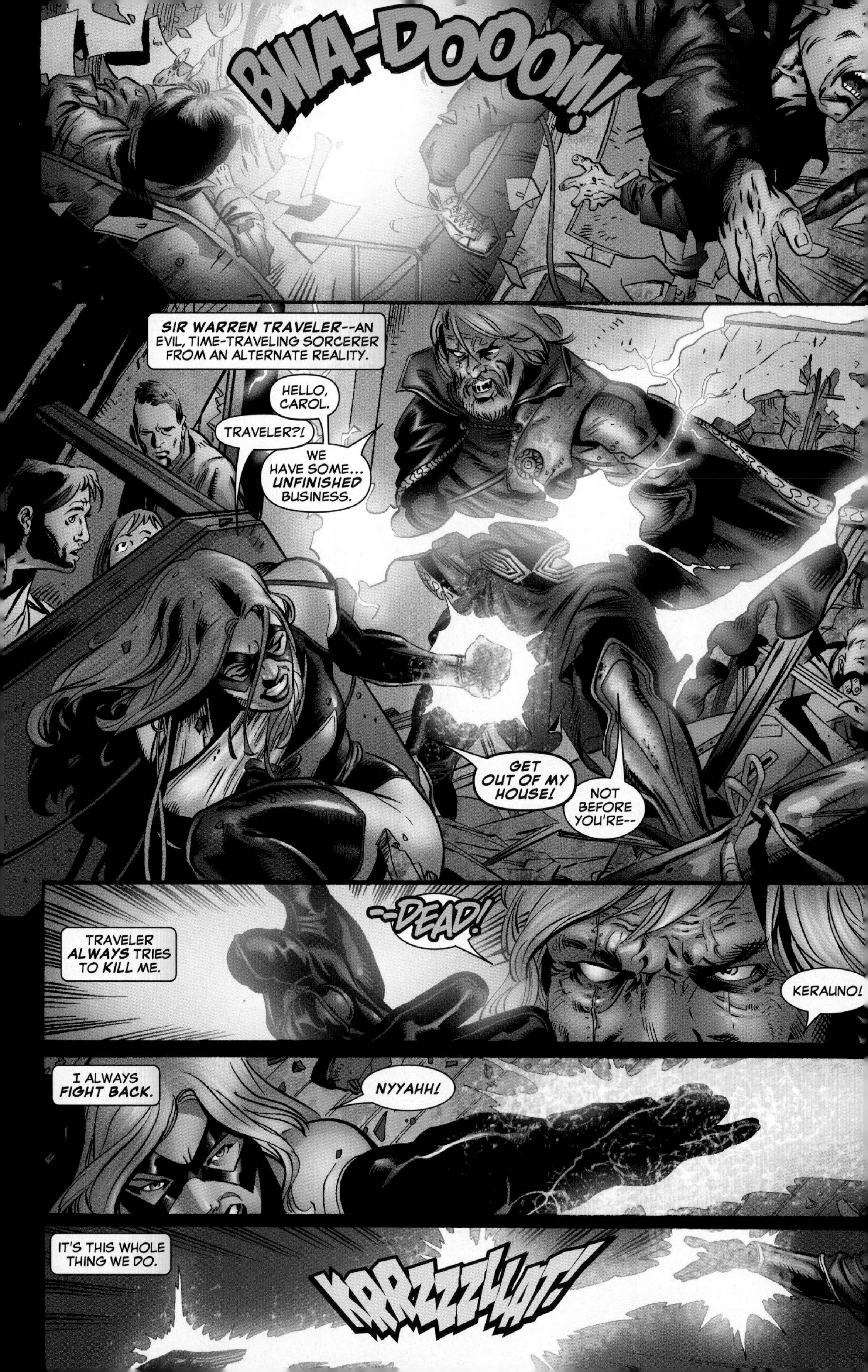
BWA-DOOOM!
SIR WARREN TRAVELER--AN EVIL, TIME-TRAVELING SORCERER FROM AN ALTERNATE REALITY.
HELLO, CAROL.
TRAVELER?!
WE HAVE SOME... UNFINISHED BUSINESS.
GET OUT OF MY HOUSE!
NOT BEFORE YOU'RE--
--DEAD!
TRAVELER ALWAYS TRIES TO KILL ME.
KERAUNO!
I ALWAYS FIGHT BACK.
NYYAHH!
IT'S THIS WHOLE THING WE DO.
KRRZZZLLAT!

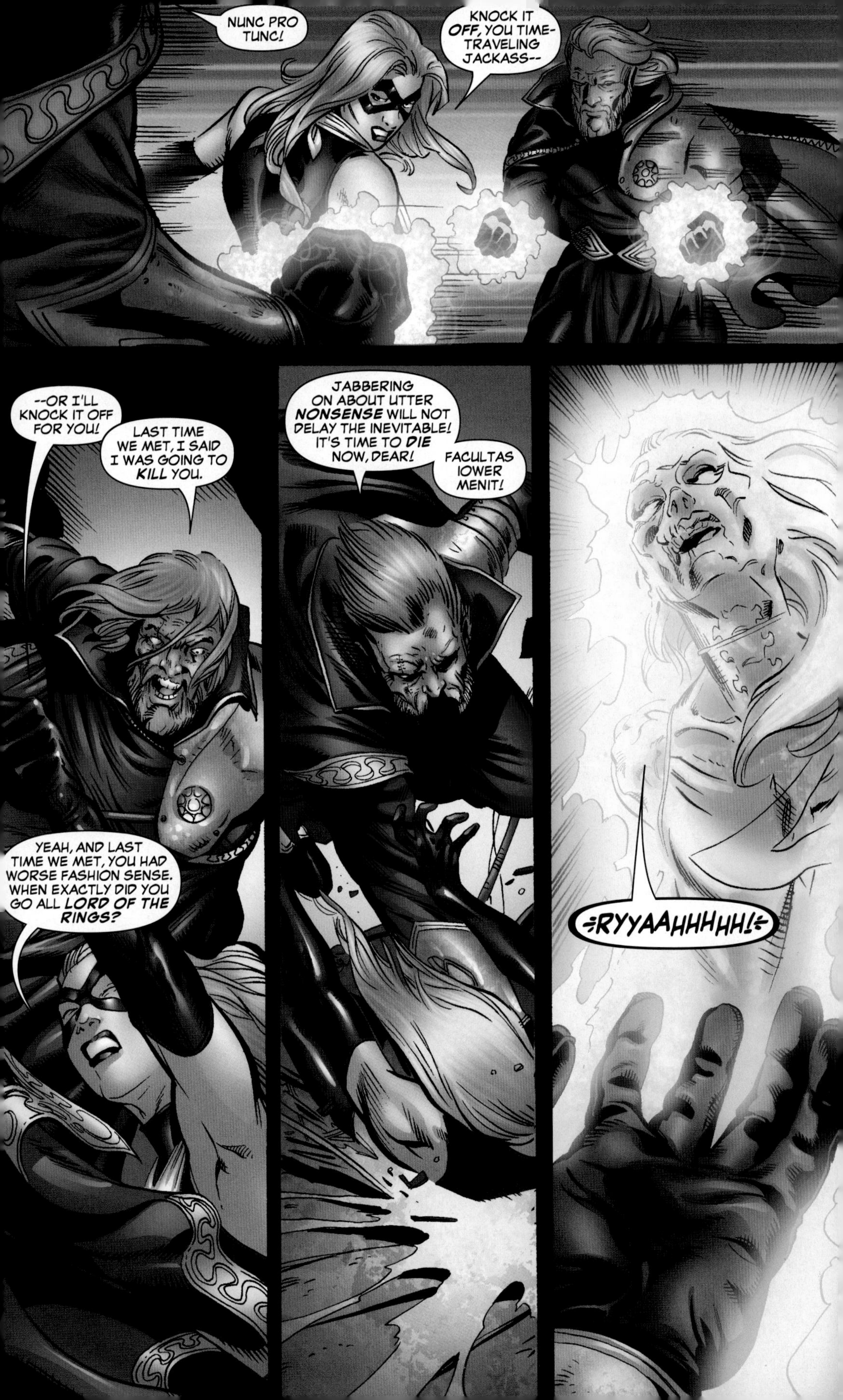
NUNC PRO TUNC!
KNOCK IT OFF, YOU TIME-TRAVELING JACKASS--
--OR I'LL KNOCK IT OFF FOR YOU!
LAST TIME WE MET, I SAID I WAS GOING TO KILL YOU.
YEAH, AND LAST TIME WE MET, YOU HAD WORSE FASHION SENSE. WHEN EXACTLY DID YOU GO ALL LORD OF THE RINGS?
JABBERING ON ABOUT UTTER NONSENSE WILL NOT DELAY THE INEVITABLE! IT'S TIME TO DIE NOW, DEAR!
FACULTAS IOWER MENIT!
RYYAAHHHHH!

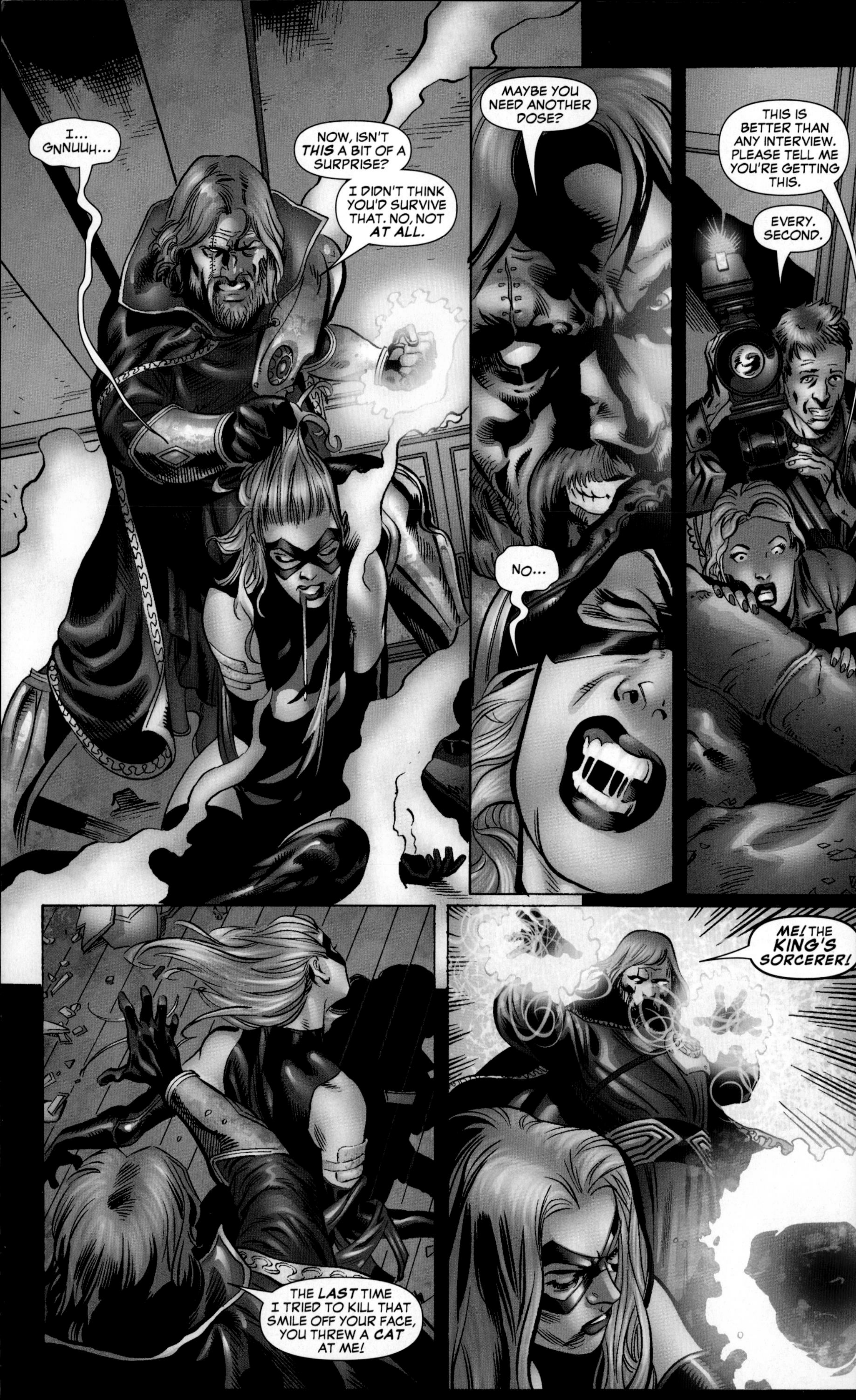
I... GNNUUH...
NOW, ISN'T *THIS* A BIT OF A SURPRISE?
I DIDN'T THINK YOU'D SURVIVE THAT. NO, NOT *AT ALL.*
MAYBE YOU NEED ANOTHER DOSE?
NO...
THIS IS BETTER THAN ANY INTERVIEW. PLEASE TELL ME YOU'RE GETTING THIS.
EVERY. SECOND.
THE *LAST* TIME I TRIED TO KILL THAT SMILE OFF YOUR FACE, YOU THREW A *CAT* AT ME!
ME! THE *KING'S SORCERER!*

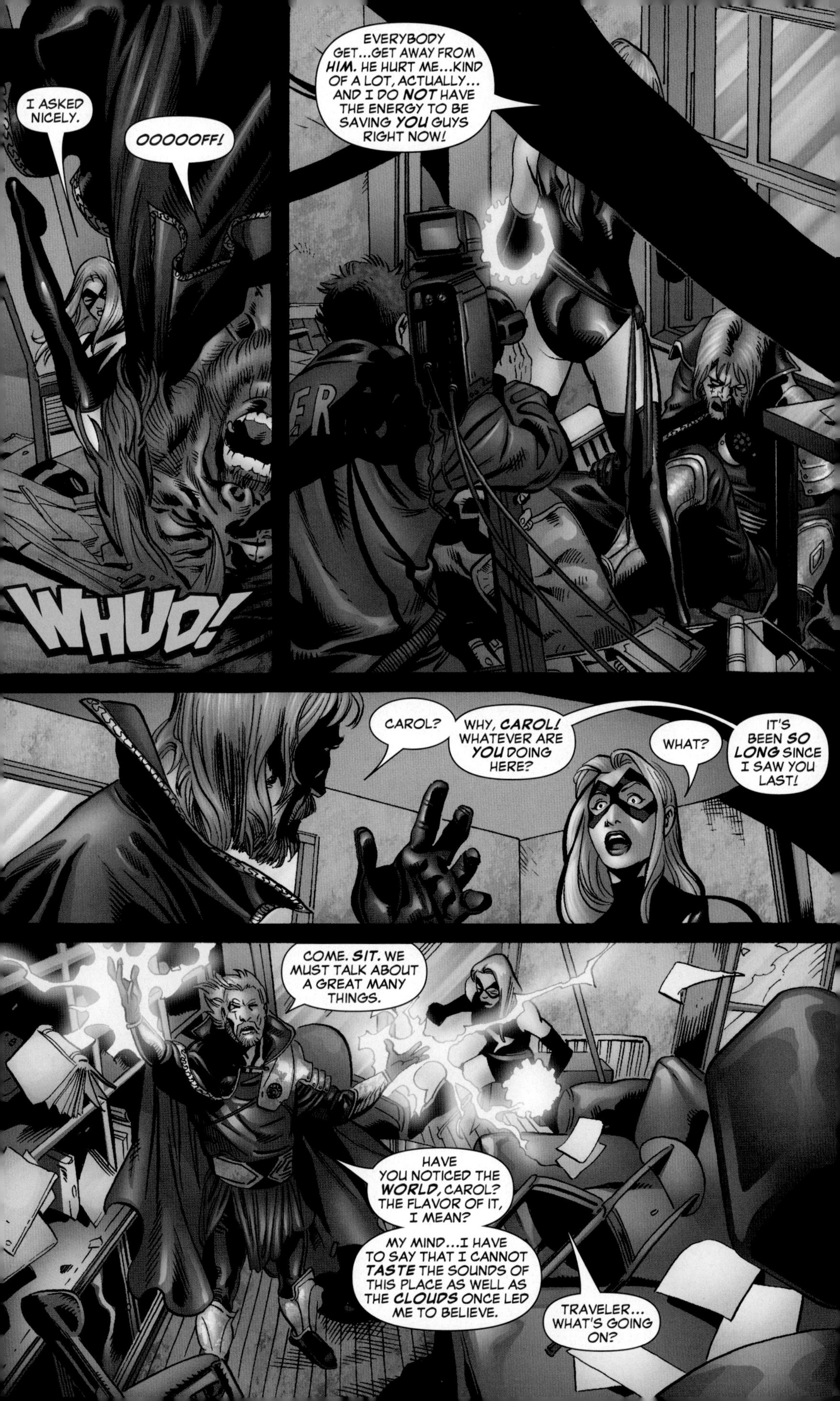
I ASKED NICELY.
OOOOOFF!
WHUD!
EVERYBODY GET...GET AWAY FROM HIM. HE HURT ME...KIND OF A LOT, ACTUALLY... AND I DO NOT HAVE THE ENERGY TO BE SAVING YOU GUYS RIGHT NOW!
CAROL?
WHY, CAROL! WHATEVER ARE YOU DOING HERE?
WHAT?
IT'S BEEN SO LONG SINCE I SAW YOU LAST!
COME. SIT. WE MUST TALK ABOUT A GREAT MANY THINGS.
HAVE YOU NOTICED THE WORLD, CAROL? THE FLAVOR OF IT, I MEAN?
MY MIND...I HAVE TO SAY THAT I CANNOT TASTE THE SOUNDS OF THIS PLACE AS WELL AS THE CLOUDS ONCE LED ME TO BELIEVE.
TRAVELER... WHAT'S GOING ON?

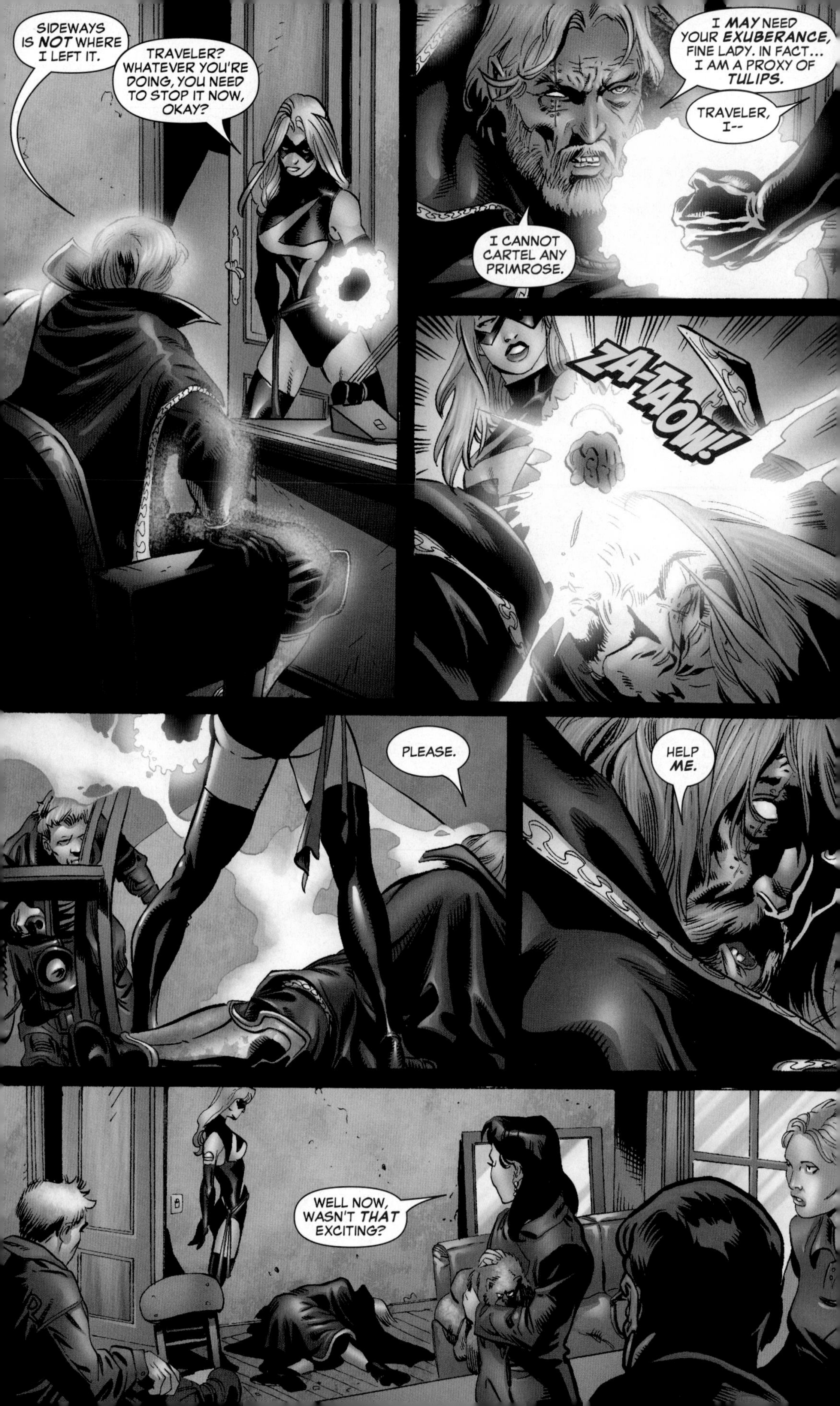

SIDEWAYS IS NOT WHERE I LEFT IT.
TRAVELER? WHATEVER YOU'RE DOING, YOU NEED TO STOP IT NOW, OKAY?
I MAY NEED YOUR EXUBERANCE, FINE LADY. IN FACT... I AM A PROXY OF TULIPS.
TRAVELER, I--
I CANNOT CARTEL ANY PRIMROSE.
ZA-TAOW!
PLEASE.
HELP ME.
WELL NOW, WASN'T THAT EXCITING?

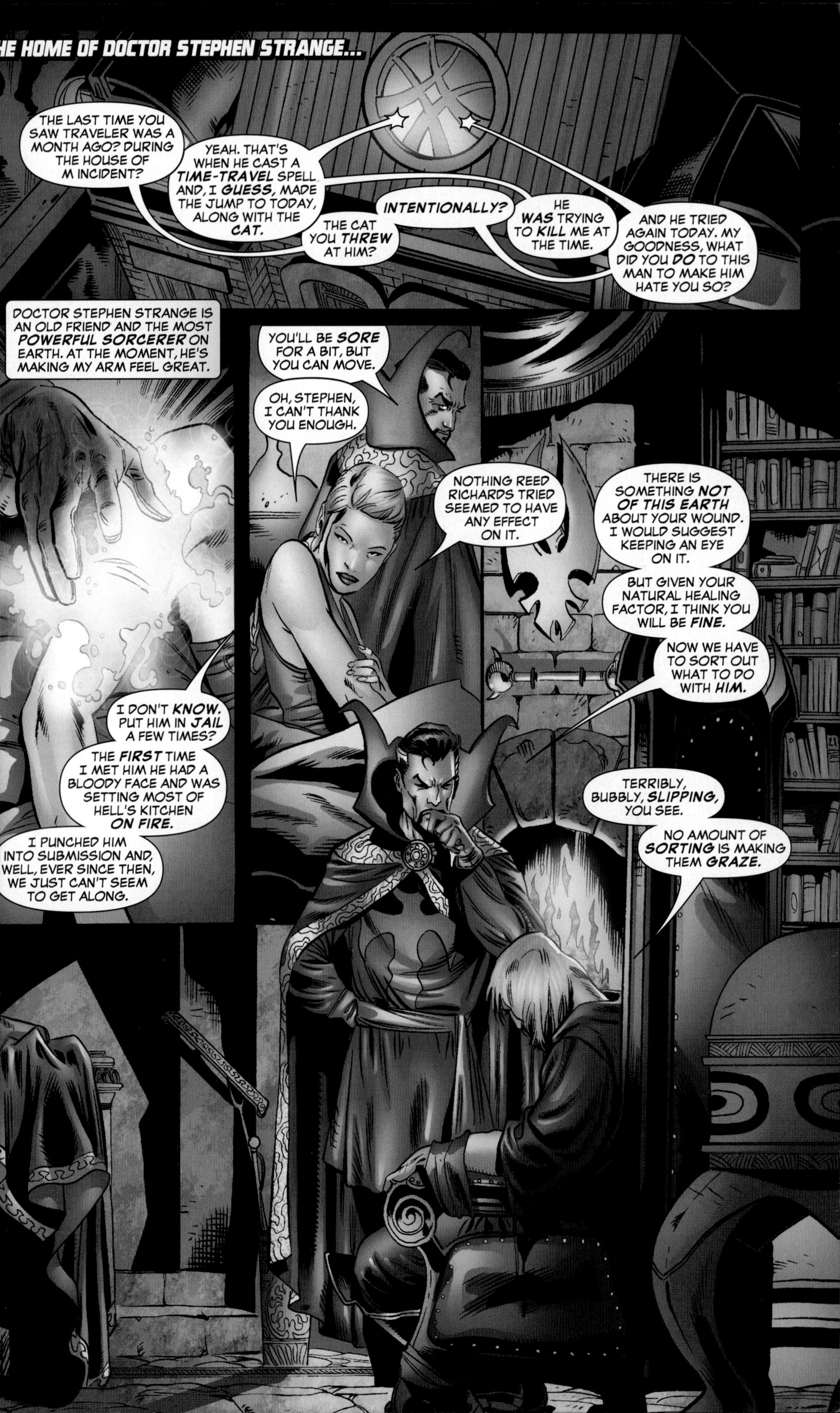
HE HOME OF DOCTOR STEPHEN STRANGE...
THE LAST TIME YOU SAW TRAVELER WAS A MONTH AGO? DURING THE HOUSE OF M INCIDENT?
YEAH. THAT'S WHEN HE CAST A TIME-TRAVEL SPELL AND, I GUESS, MADE THE JUMP TO TODAY, ALONG WITH THE CAT.
THE CAT YOU THREW AT HIM?
INTENTIONALLY?
HE WAS TRYING TO KILL ME AT THE TIME.
AND HE TRIED AGAIN TODAY. MY GOODNESS, WHAT DID YOU DO TO THIS MAN TO MAKE HIM HATE YOU SO?
DOCTOR STEPHEN STRANGE IS AN OLD FRIEND AND THE MOST POWERFUL SORCERER ON EARTH. AT THE MOMENT, HE'S MAKING MY ARM FEEL GREAT.
I DON'T KNOW. PUT HIM IN JAIL A FEW TIMES?
THE FIRST TIME I MET HIM HE HAD A BLOODY FACE AND WAS SETTING MOST OF HELL'S KITCHEN ON FIRE.
I PUNCHED HIM INTO SUBMISSION AND, WELL, EVER SINCE THEN, WE JUST CAN'T SEEM TO GET ALONG.
YOU'LL BE SORE FOR A BIT, BUT YOU CAN MOVE.
OH, STEPHEN, I CAN'T THANK YOU ENOUGH.
NOTHING REED RICHARDS TRIED SEEMED TO HAVE ANY EFFECT ON IT.
THERE IS SOMETHING NOT OF THIS EARTH ABOUT YOUR WOUND. I WOULD SUGGEST KEEPING AN EYE ON IT.
BUT GIVEN YOUR NATURAL HEALING FACTOR, I THINK YOU WILL BE FINE.
NOW WE HAVE TO SORT OUT WHAT TO DO WITH HIM.
TERRIBLY, BUBBLY, SLIPPING, YOU SEE.
NO AMOUNT OF SORTING IS MAKING THEM GRAZE.

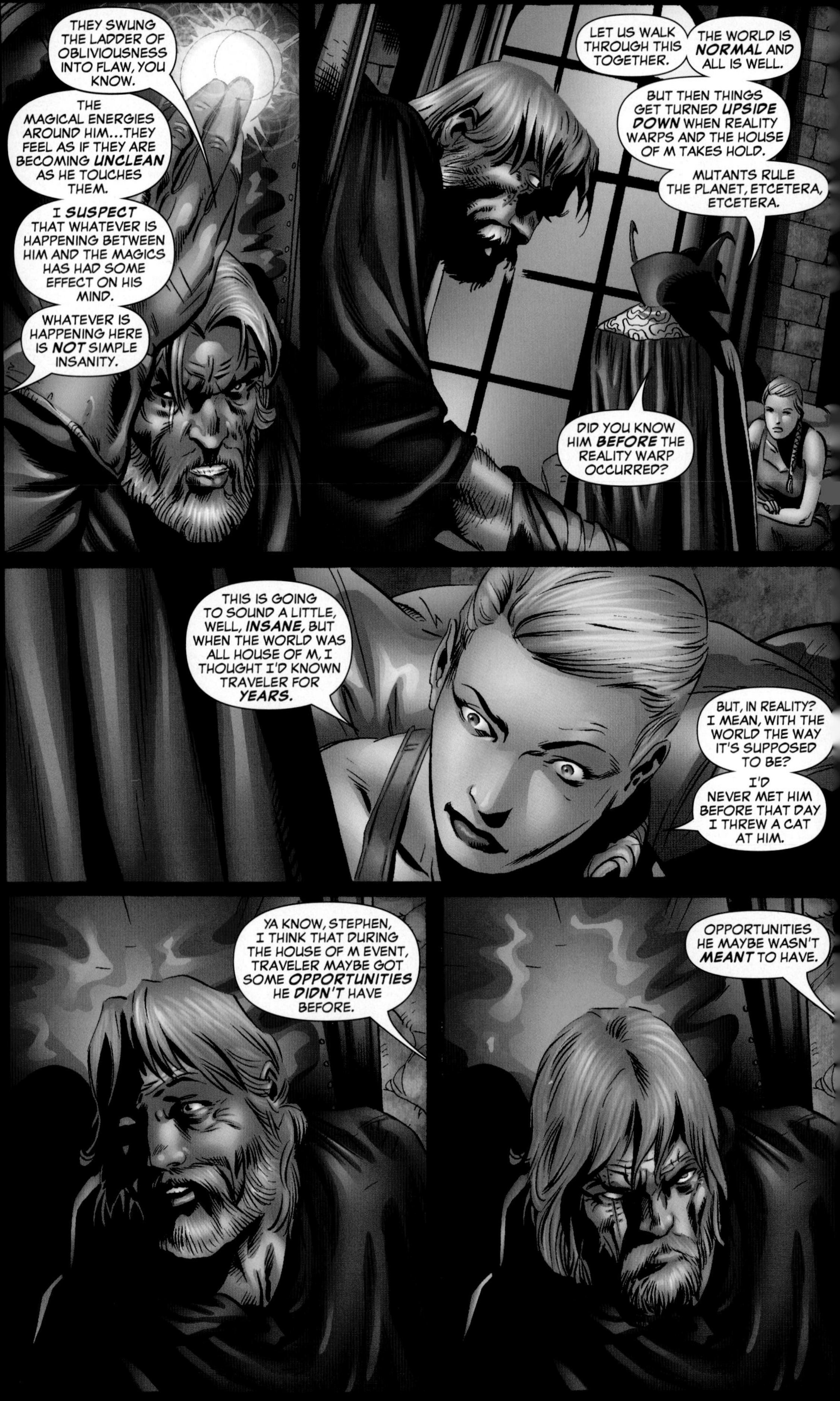
THEY SWUNG THE LADDER OF OBLIVIOUSNESS INTO FLAW, YOU KNOW.
THE MAGICAL ENERGIES AROUND HIM...THEY FEEL AS IF THEY ARE BECOMING **UNCLEAN** AS HE TOUCHES THEM.
I **SUSPECT** THAT WHATEVER IS HAPPENING BETWEEN HIM AND THE MAGICS HAS HAD SOME EFFECT ON HIS MIND.
WHATEVER IS HAPPENING HERE IS **NOT** SIMPLE INSANITY.
LET US WALK THROUGH THIS TOGETHER.
THE WORLD IS **NORMAL** AND ALL IS WELL.
BUT THEN THINGS GET TURNED **UPSIDE DOWN** WHEN REALITY WARPS AND THE HOUSE OF M TAKES HOLD.
MUTANTS RULE THE PLANET, ETCETERA, ETCETERA.
DID YOU KNOW HIM **BEFORE** THE REALITY WARP OCCURRED?
THIS IS GOING TO SOUND A LITTLE, WELL, **INSANE,** BUT WHEN THE WORLD WAS ALL HOUSE OF M, I THOUGHT I'D KNOWN TRAVELER FOR **YEARS.**
BUT, IN REALITY? I MEAN, WITH THE WORLD THE WAY IT'S SUPPOSED TO BE?
I'D NEVER MET HIM BEFORE THAT DAY I THREW A CAT AT HIM.
YA KNOW, STEPHEN, I THINK THAT DURING THE HOUSE OF M EVENT, TRAVELER MAYBE GOT SOME **OPPORTUNITIES** HE **DIDN'T** HAVE BEFORE.
OPPORTUNITIES HE MAYBE WASN'T **MEANT** TO HAVE.

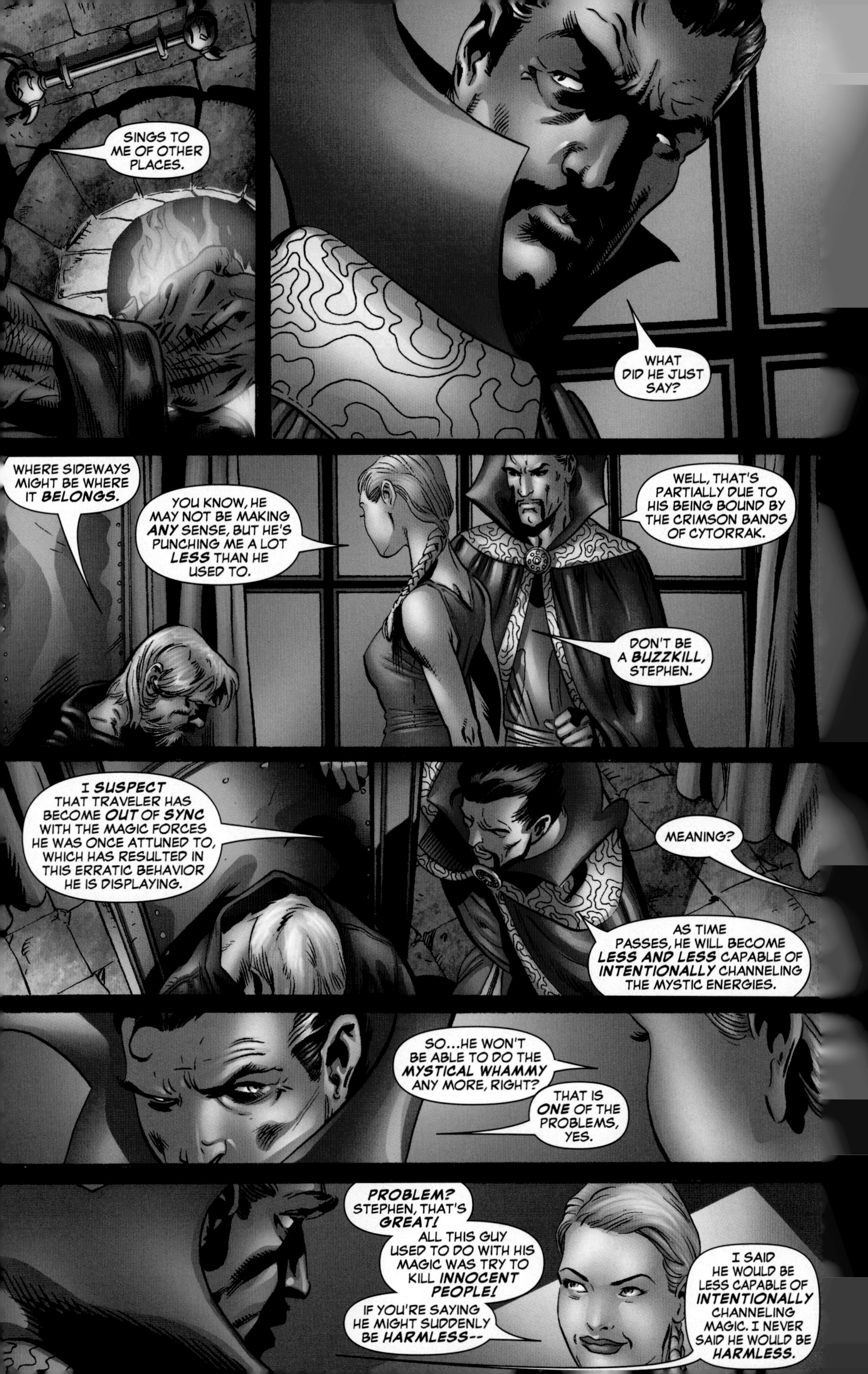
SINGS TO ME OF OTHER PLACES.
WHAT DID HE JUST SAY?
WHERE SIDEWAYS MIGHT BE WHERE IT BELONGS.
YOU KNOW, HE MAY NOT BE MAKING ANY SENSE, BUT HE'S PUNCHING ME A LOT LESS THAN HE USED TO.
WELL, THAT'S PARTIALLY DUE TO HIS BEING BOUND BY THE CRIMSON BANDS OF CYTORRAK.
DON'T BE A BUZZKILL, STEPHEN.
I SUSPECT THAT TRAVELER HAS BECOME OUT OF SYNC WITH THE MAGIC FORCES HE WAS ONCE ATTUNED TO, WHICH HAS RESULTED IN THIS ERRATIC BEHAVIOR HE IS DISPLAYING.
MEANING?
AS TIME PASSES, HE WILL BECOME LESS AND LESS CAPABLE OF INTENTIONALLY CHANNELING THE MYSTIC ENERGIES.
SO...HE WON'T BE ABLE TO DO THE MYSTICAL WHAMMY ANY MORE, RIGHT?
THAT IS ONE OF THE PROBLEMS, YES.
PROBLEM? STEPHEN, THAT'S GREAT!
ALL THIS GUY USED TO DO WITH HIS MAGIC WAS TRY TO KILL INNOCENT PEOPLE!
IF YOU'RE SAYING HE MIGHT SUDDENLY BE HARMLESS--
I SAID HE WOULD BE LESS CAPABLE OF INTENTIONALLY CHANNELING MAGIC. I NEVER SAID HE WOULD BE HARMLESS.

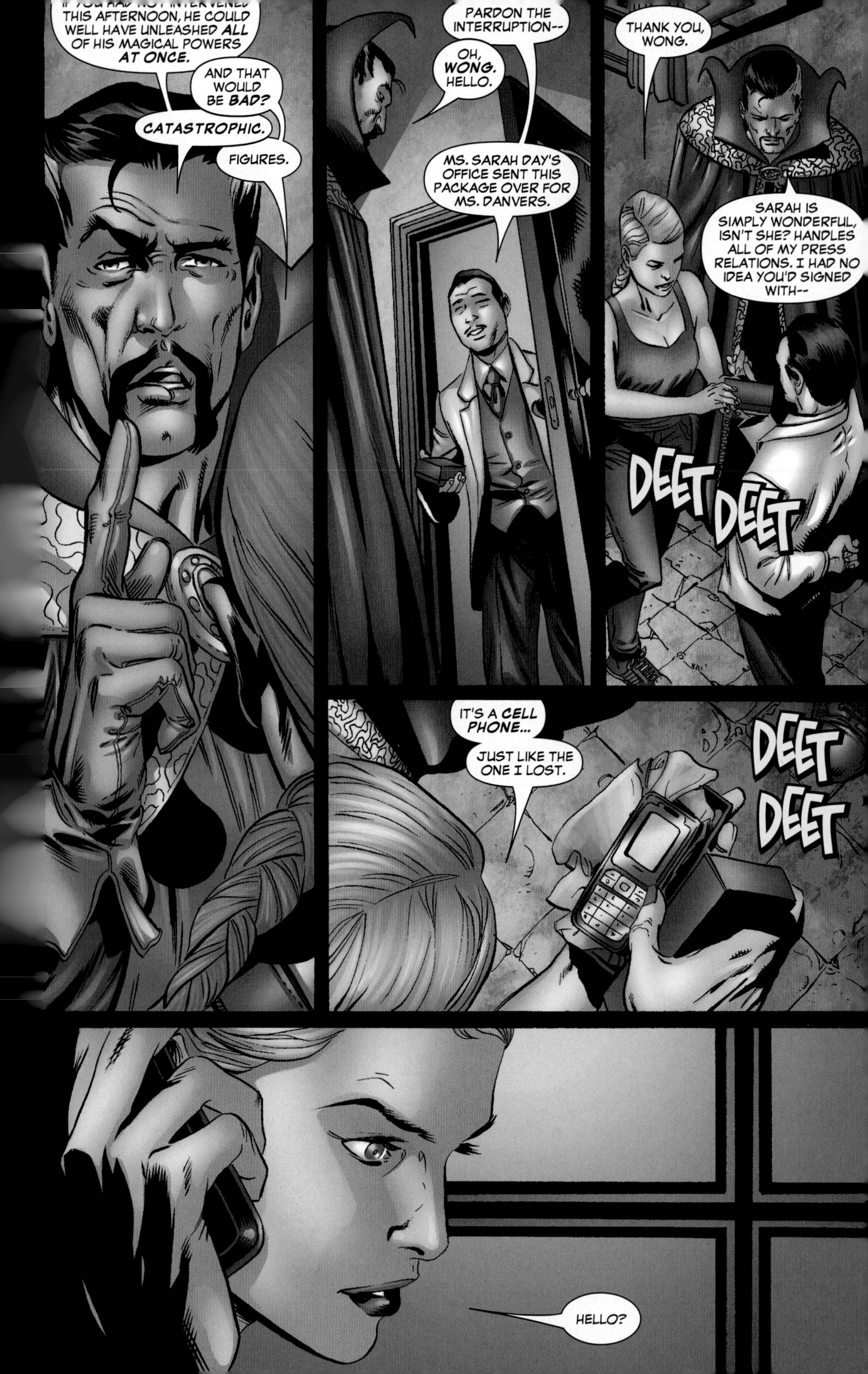
THIS AFTERNOON, HE COULD WELL HAVE UNLEASHED ALL OF HIS MAGICAL POWERS AT ONCE.
AND THAT WOULD BE BAD?
CATASTROPHIC.
FIGURES.
PARDON THE INTERRUPTION--
OH, WONG. HELLO.
MS. SARAH DAY'S OFFICE SENT THIS PACKAGE OVER FOR MS. DANVERS.
THANK YOU, WONG.
SARAH IS SIMPLY WONDERFUL, ISN'T SHE? HANDLES ALL OF MY PRESS RELATIONS. I HAD NO IDEA YOU'D SIGNED WITH--
DEET DEET
IT'S A CELL PHONE...
JUST LIKE THE ONE I LOST.
DEET DEET
HELLO?

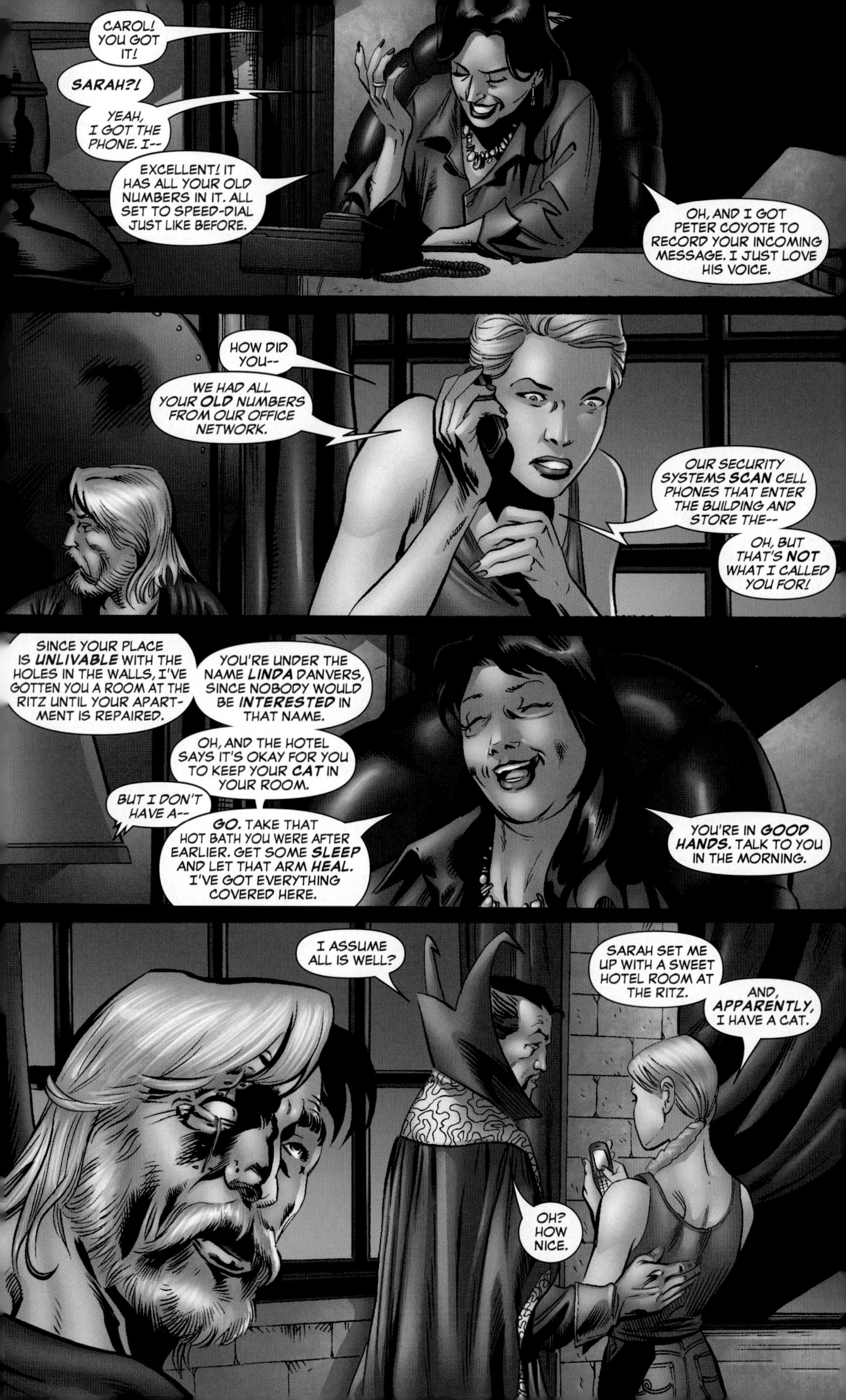

CAROL! YOU GOT IT!
SARAH?!
YEAH, I GOT THE PHONE. I--
EXCELLENT! IT HAS ALL YOUR OLD NUMBERS IN IT. ALL SET TO SPEED-DIAL JUST LIKE BEFORE.
OH, AND I GOT PETER COYOTE TO RECORD YOUR INCOMING MESSAGE. I JUST LOVE HIS VOICE.
HOW DID YOU--
WE HAD ALL YOUR OLD NUMBERS FROM OUR OFFICE NETWORK.
OUR SECURITY SYSTEMS SCAN CELL PHONES THAT ENTER THE BUILDING AND STORE THE--
OH, BUT THAT'S NOT WHAT I CALLED YOU FOR!
SINCE YOUR PLACE IS UNLIVABLE WITH THE HOLES IN THE WALLS, I'VE GOTTEN YOU A ROOM AT THE RITZ UNTIL YOUR APARTMENT IS REPAIRED.
YOU'RE UNDER THE NAME LINDA DANVERS, SINCE NOBODY WOULD BE INTERESTED IN THAT NAME.
OH, AND THE HOTEL SAYS IT'S OKAY FOR YOU TO KEEP YOUR CAT IN YOUR ROOM.
BUT I DON'T HAVE A--
GO. TAKE THAT HOT BATH YOU WERE AFTER EARLIER. GET SOME SLEEP AND LET THAT ARM HEAL. I'VE GOT EVERYTHING COVERED HERE.
YOU'RE IN GOOD HANDS. TALK TO YOU IN THE MORNING.
I ASSUME ALL IS WELL?
SARAH SET ME UP WITH A SWEET HOTEL ROOM AT THE RITZ.
AND, APPARENTLY, I HAVE A CAT.
OH? HOW NICE.

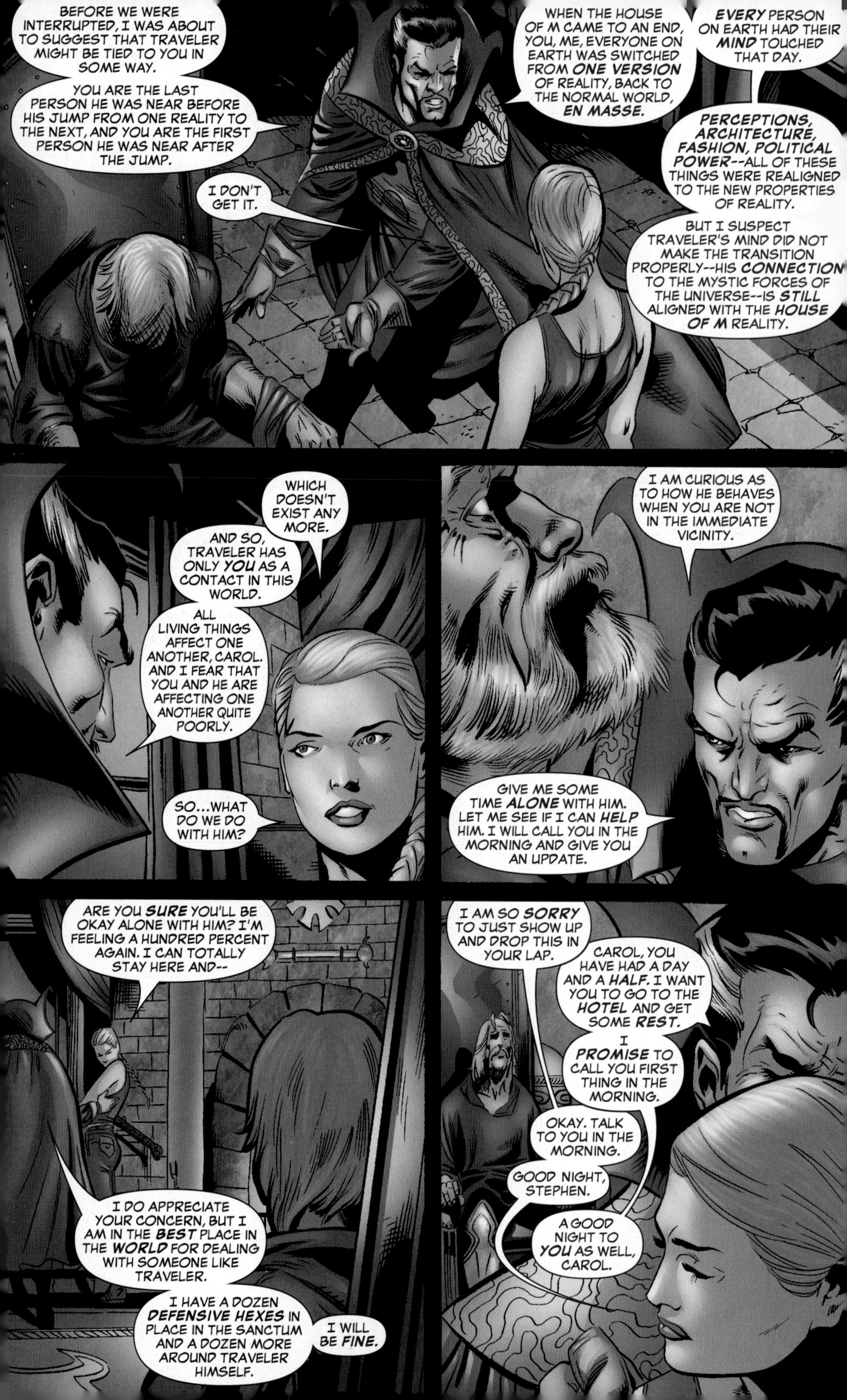
BEFORE WE WERE INTERRUPTED, I WAS ABOUT TO SUGGEST THAT TRAVELER MIGHT BE TIED TO YOU IN SOME WAY.
YOU ARE THE LAST PERSON HE WAS NEAR BEFORE HIS JUMP FROM ONE REALITY TO THE NEXT, AND YOU ARE THE FIRST PERSON HE WAS NEAR AFTER THE JUMP.
I DON'T GET IT.
WHEN THE HOUSE OF M CAME TO AN END, YOU, ME, EVERYONE ON EARTH WAS SWITCHED FROM ONE VERSION OF REALITY, BACK TO THE NORMAL WORLD, EN MASSE.
EVERY PERSON ON EARTH HAD THEIR MIND TOUCHED THAT DAY.
PERCEPTIONS, ARCHITECTURE, FASHION, POLITICAL POWER--ALL OF THESE THINGS WERE REALIGNED TO THE NEW PROPERTIES OF REALITY.
BUT I SUSPECT TRAVELER'S MIND DID NOT MAKE THE TRANSITION PROPERLY--HIS CONNECTION TO THE MYSTIC FORCES OF THE UNIVERSE--IS STILL ALIGNED WITH THE HOUSE OF M REALITY.
WHICH DOESN'T EXIST ANY MORE.
AND SO, TRAVELER HAS ONLY YOU AS A CONTACT IN THIS WORLD.
ALL LIVING THINGS AFFECT ONE ANOTHER, CAROL. AND I FEAR THAT YOU AND HE ARE AFFECTING ONE ANOTHER QUITE POORLY.
SO...WHAT DO WE DO WITH HIM?
I AM CURIOUS AS TO HOW HE BEHAVES WHEN YOU ARE NOT IN THE IMMEDIATE VICINITY.
GIVE ME SOME TIME ALONE WITH HIM. LET ME SEE IF I CAN HELP HIM. I WILL CALL YOU IN THE MORNING AND GIVE YOU AN UPDATE.
ARE YOU SURE YOU'LL BE OKAY ALONE WITH HIM? I'M FEELING A HUNDRED PERCENT AGAIN. I CAN TOTALLY STAY HERE AND--
I DO APPRECIATE YOUR CONCERN, BUT I AM IN THE BEST PLACE IN THE WORLD FOR DEALING WITH SOMEONE LIKE TRAVELER.
I HAVE A DOZEN DEFENSIVE HEXES IN PLACE IN THE SANCTUM AND A DOZEN MORE AROUND TRAVELER HIMSELF.
I WILL BE FINE.
I AM SO SORRY TO JUST SHOW UP AND DROP THIS IN YOUR LAP.
CAROL, YOU HAVE HAD A DAY AND A HALF. I WANT YOU TO GO TO THE HOTEL AND GET SOME REST.
I PROMISE TO CALL YOU FIRST THING IN THE MORNING.
OKAY. TALK TO YOU IN THE MORNING.
GOOD NIGHT, STEPHEN.
A GOOD NIGHT TO YOU AS WELL, CAROL.

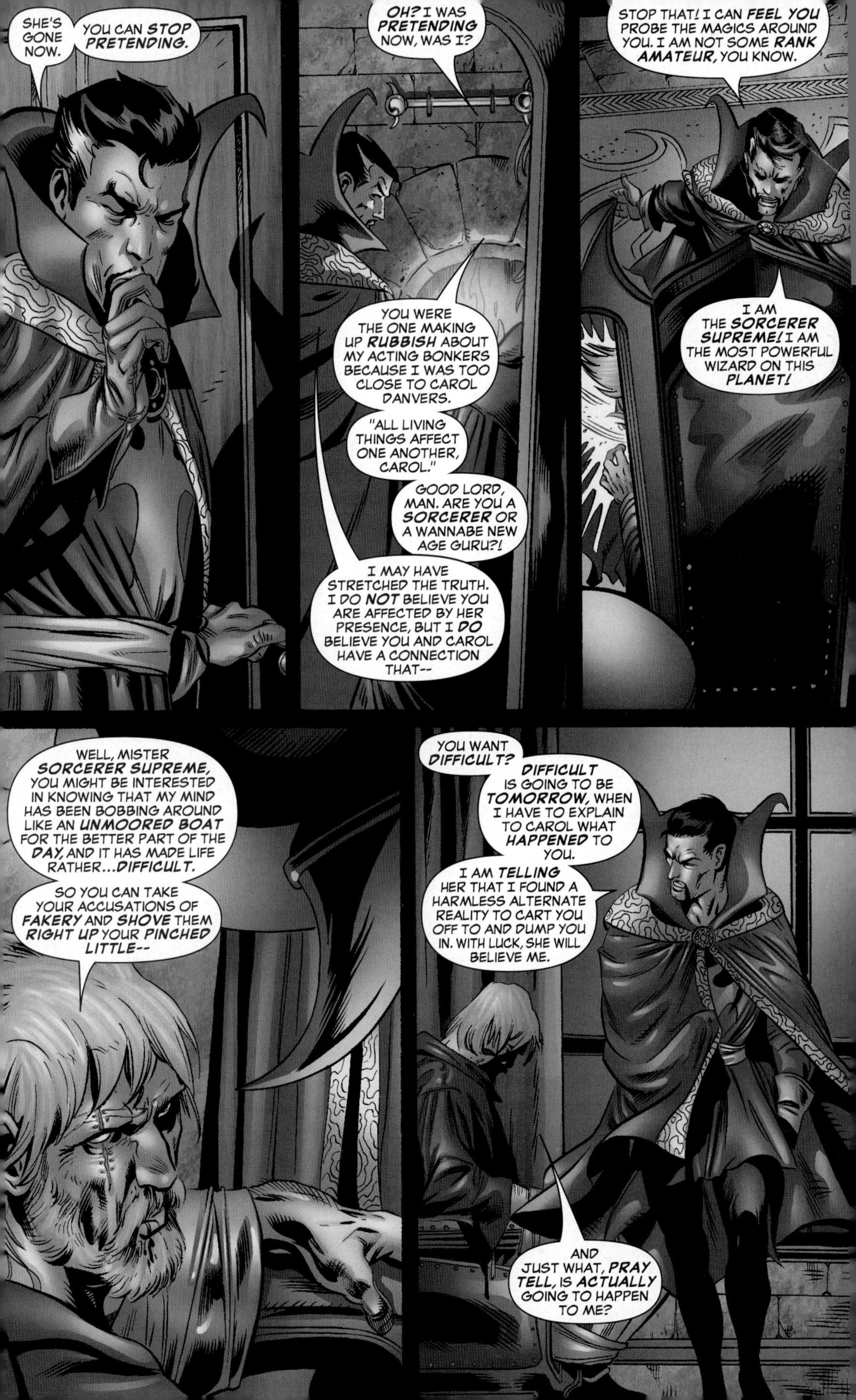
SHE'S GONE NOW.
YOU CAN STOP PRETENDING.
OH? I WAS PRETENDING NOW, WAS I?
YOU WERE THE ONE MAKING UP RUBBISH ABOUT MY ACTING BONKERS BECAUSE I WAS TOO CLOSE TO CAROL DANVERS.
"ALL LIVING THINGS AFFECT ONE ANOTHER, CAROL."
GOOD LORD, MAN. ARE YOU A SORCERER OR A WANNABE NEW AGE GURU?!
I MAY HAVE STRETCHED THE TRUTH. I DO NOT BELIEVE YOU ARE AFFECTED BY HER PRESENCE, BUT I DO BELIEVE YOU AND CAROL HAVE A CONNECTION THAT--
STOP THAT! I CAN FEEL YOU PROBE THE MAGICS AROUND YOU. I AM NOT SOME RANK AMATEUR, YOU KNOW.
I AM THE SORCERER SUPREME! I AM THE MOST POWERFUL WIZARD ON THIS PLANET!
WELL, MISTER SORCERER SUPREME, YOU MIGHT BE INTERESTED IN KNOWING THAT MY MIND HAS BEEN BOBBING AROUND LIKE AN UNMOORED BOAT FOR THE BETTER PART OF THE DAY, AND IT HAS MADE LIFE RATHER...DIFFICULT.
SO YOU CAN TAKE YOUR ACCUSATIONS OF FAKERY AND SHOVE THEM RIGHT UP YOUR PINCHED LITTLE--
YOU WANT DIFFICULT?
DIFFICULT IS GOING TO BE TOMORROW, WHEN I HAVE TO EXPLAIN TO CAROL WHAT HAPPENED TO YOU.
I AM TELLING HER THAT I FOUND A HARMLESS ALTERNATE REALITY TO CART YOU OFF TO AND DUMP YOU IN. WITH LUCK, SHE WILL BELIEVE ME.
AND JUST WHAT, PRAY TELL, IS ACTUALLY GOING TO HAPPEN TO ME?

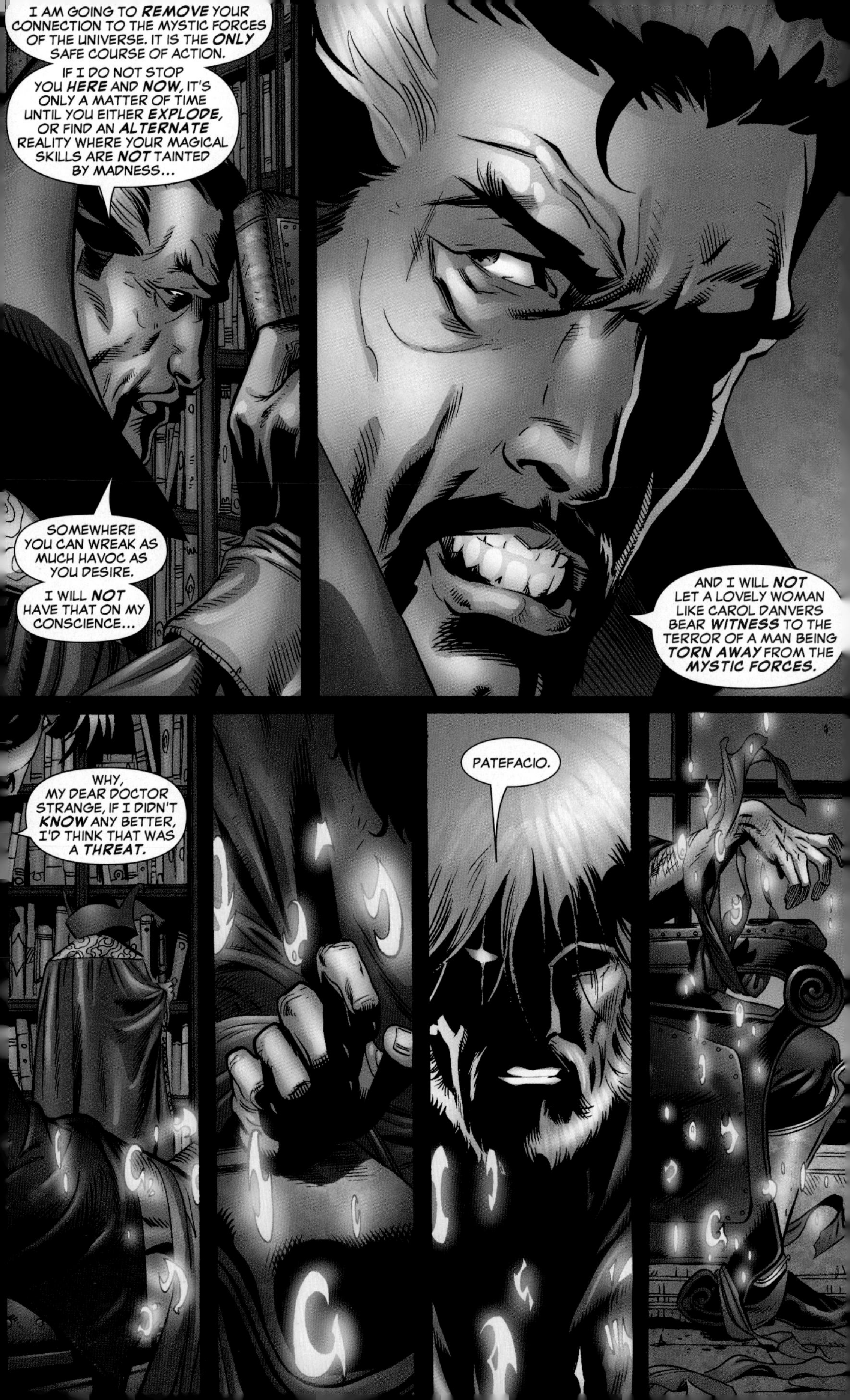
I AM GOING TO REMOVE YOUR CONNECTION TO THE MYSTIC FORCES OF THE UNIVERSE. IT IS THE ONLY SAFE COURSE OF ACTION.
IF I DO NOT STOP YOU HERE AND NOW, IT'S ONLY A MATTER OF TIME UNTIL YOU EITHER EXPLODE, OR FIND AN ALTERNATE REALITY WHERE YOUR MAGICAL SKILLS ARE NOT TAINTED BY MADNESS...
SOMEWHERE YOU CAN WREAK AS MUCH HAVOC AS YOU DESIRE.
I WILL NOT HAVE THAT ON MY CONSCIENCE...
AND I WILL NOT LET A LOVELY WOMAN LIKE CAROL DANVERS BEAR WITNESS TO THE TERROR OF A MAN BEING TORN AWAY FROM THE MYSTIC FORCES.
WHY, MY DEAR DOCTOR STRANGE, IF I DIDN'T KNOW ANY BETTER, I'D THINK THAT WAS A THREAT.
PATEFACIO.

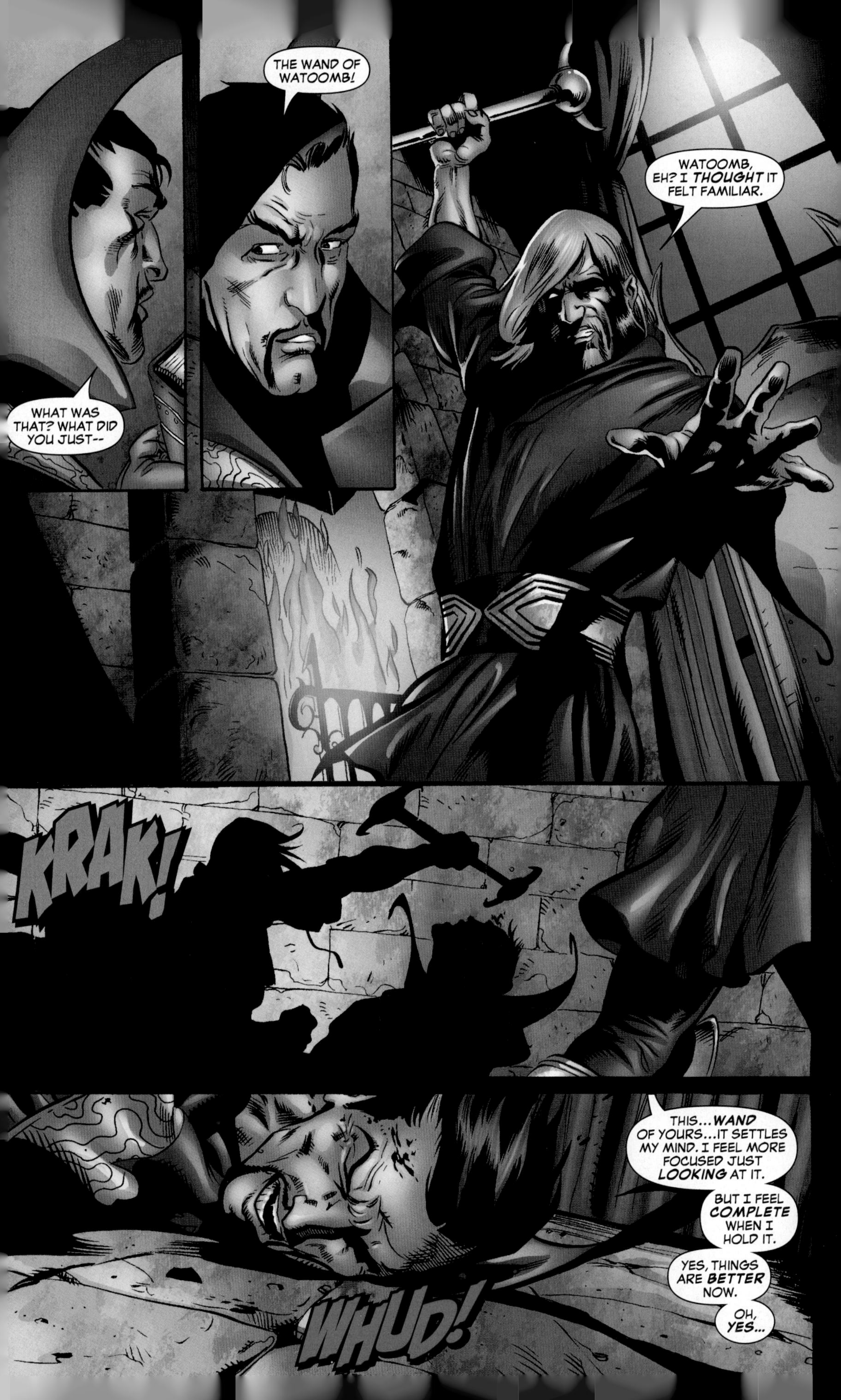
THE WAND OF WATOOMB!
WHAT WAS THAT? WHAT DID YOU JUST--
WATOOMB, EH? I THOUGHT IT FELT FAMILIAR.
KRAK!
THIS...WAND OF YOURS...IT SETTLES MY MIND. I FEEL MORE FOCUSED JUST LOOKING AT IT.
BUT I FEEL COMPLETE WHEN I HOLD IT.
YES, THINGS ARE BETTER NOW.
OH, YES...
WHUD!

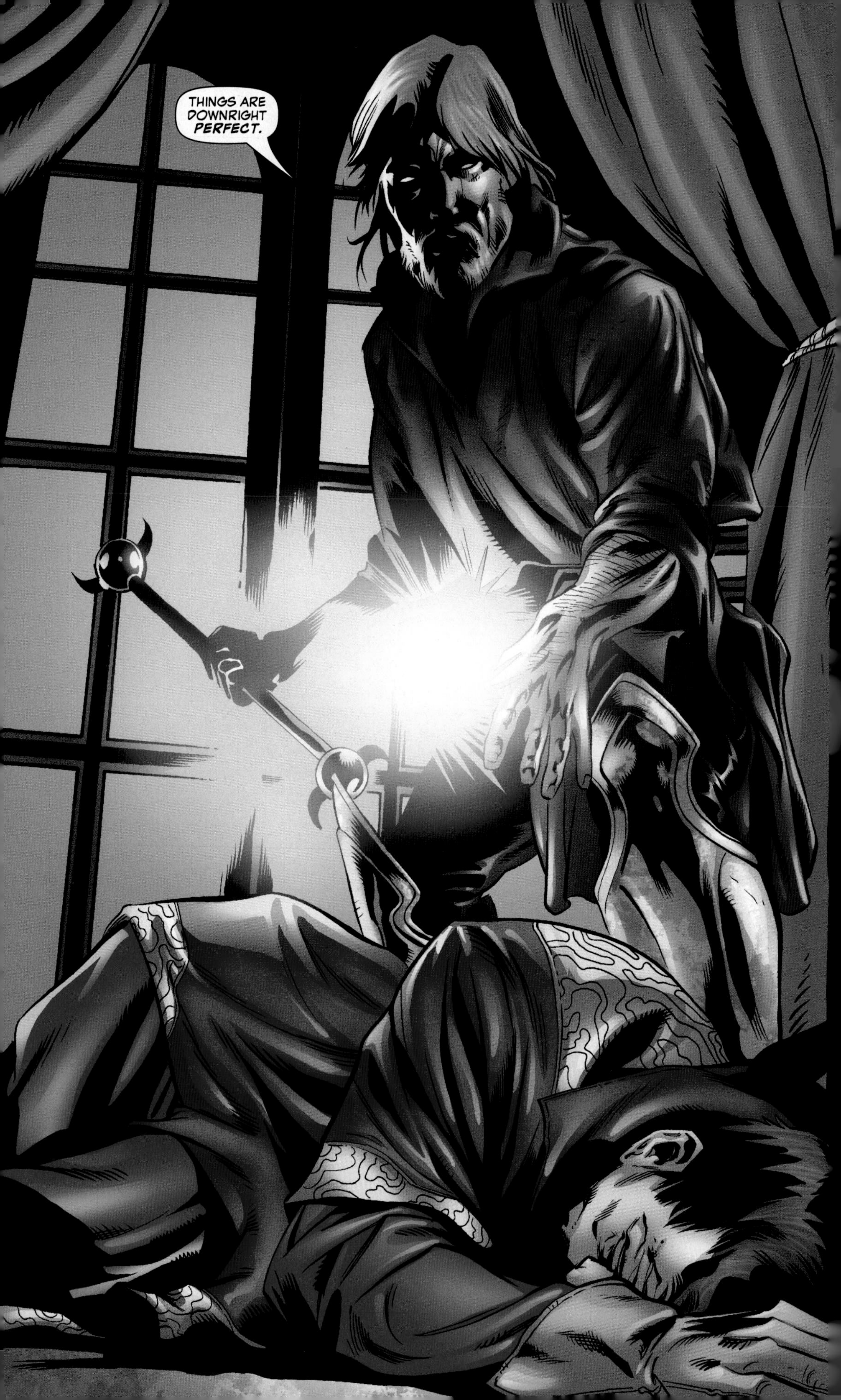
THINGS ARE DOWNRIGHT PERFECT.

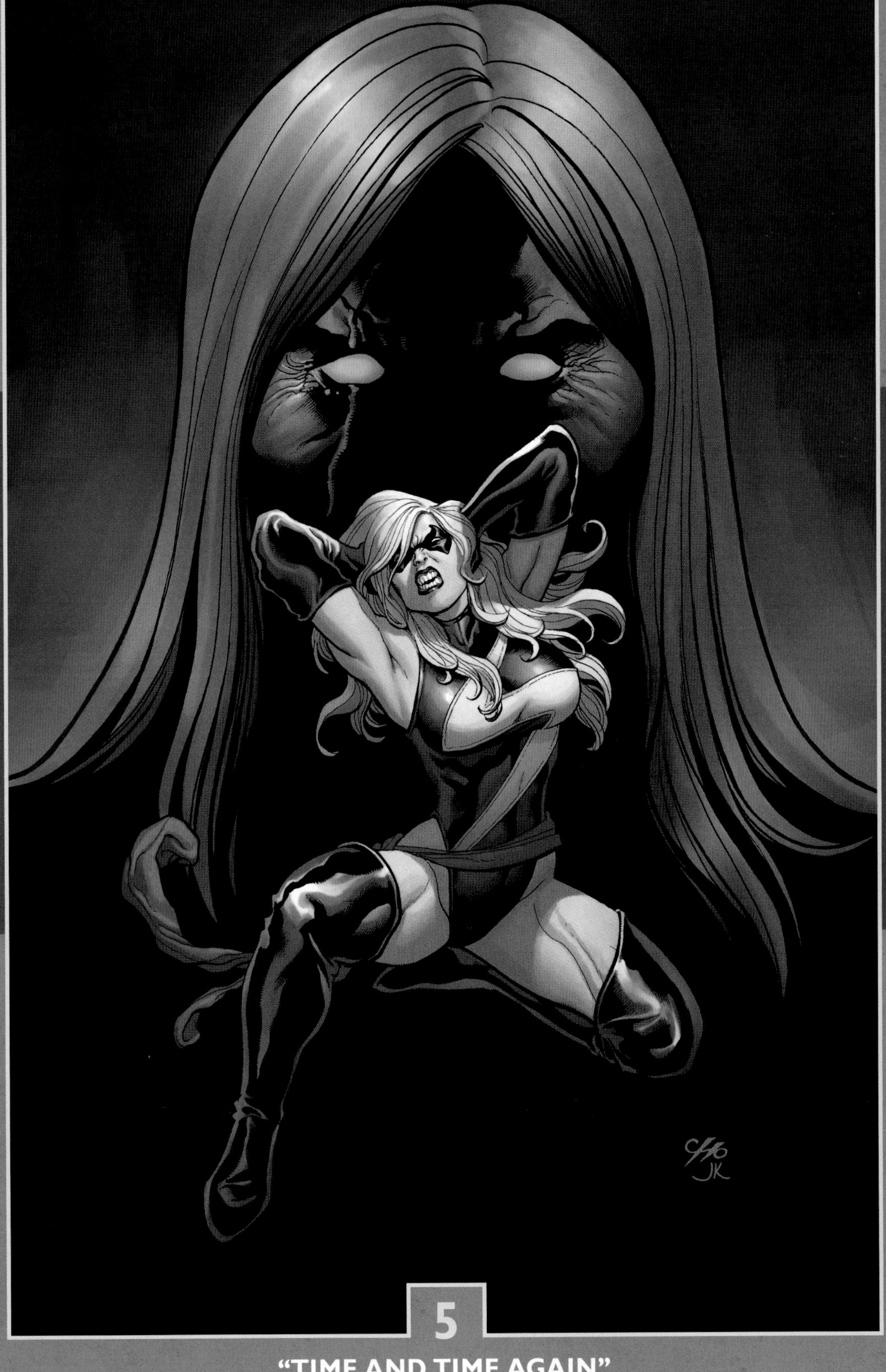

5

“TIME AND TIME AGAIN”

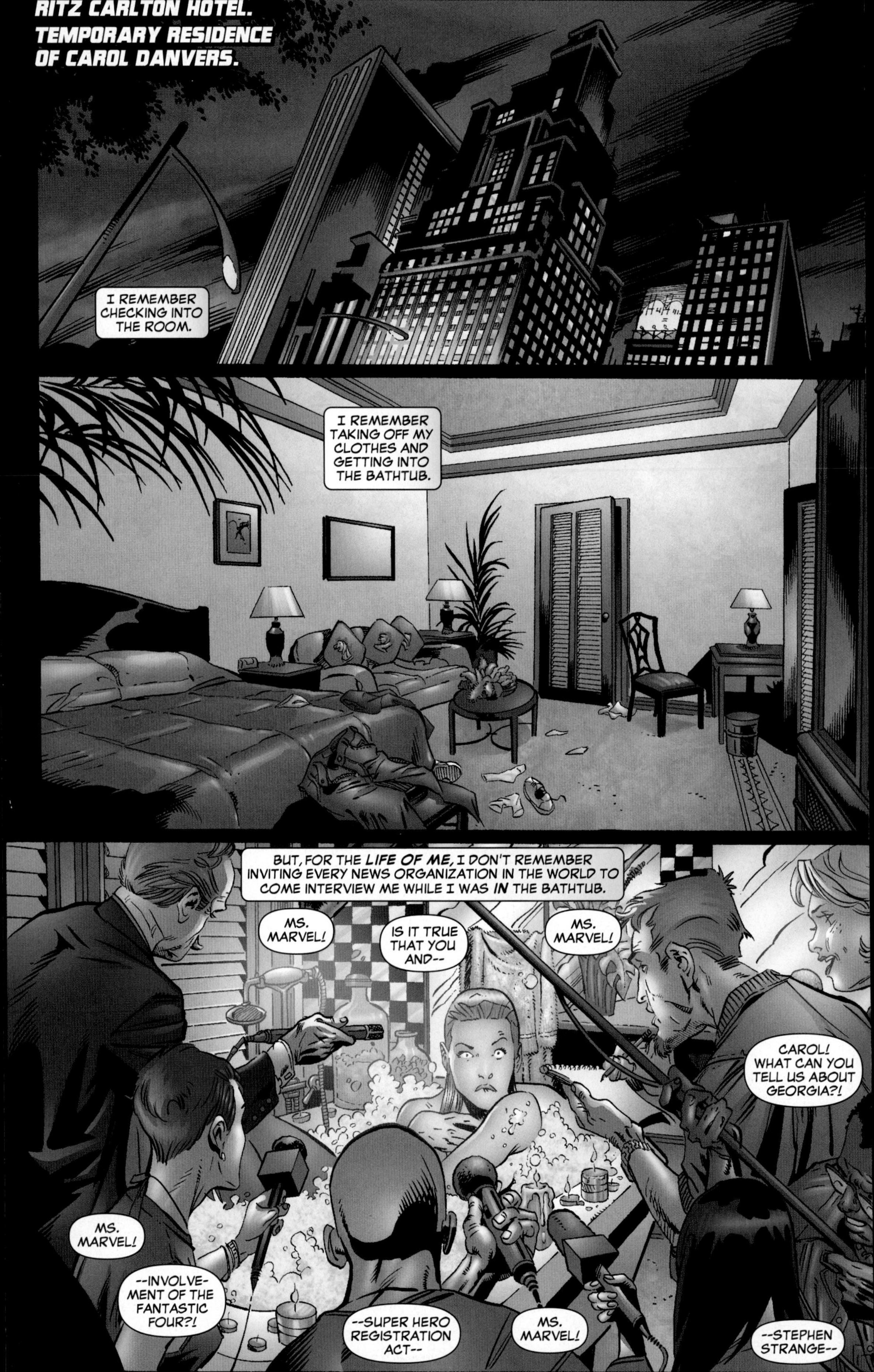
RITZ CARLTON HOTEL. TEMPORARY RESIDENCE OF CAROL DANVERS.
I REMEMBER CHECKING INTO THE ROOM.
I REMEMBER TAKING OFF MY CLOTHES AND GETTING INTO THE BATHTUB.
BUT, FOR THE LIFE OF ME, I DON'T REMEMBER INVITING EVERY NEWS ORGANIZATION IN THE WORLD TO COME INTERVIEW ME WHILE I WAS IN THE BATHTUB.
MS. MARVEL!
IS IT TRUE THAT YOU AND--
MS. MARVEL!
CAROL! WHAT CAN YOU TELL US ABOUT GEORGIA?!
MS. MARVEL!
--INVOLVEMENT OF THE FANTASTIC FOUR?!
--SUPER HERO REGISTRATION ACT--
MS. MARVEL!
--STEPHEN STRANGE--

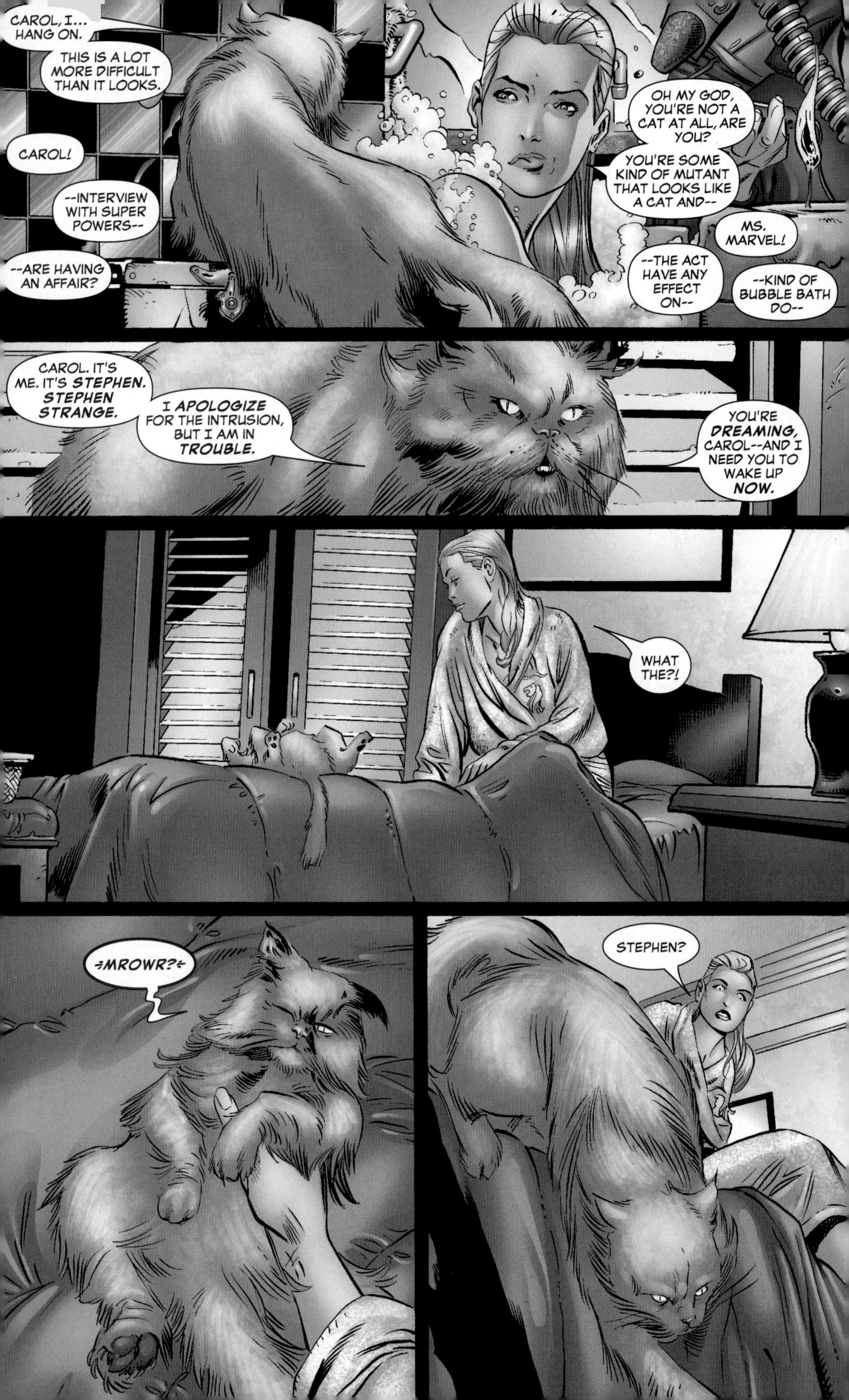
CAROL, I... HANG ON.
THIS IS A LOT MORE DIFFICULT THAN IT LOOKS.
OH MY GOD, YOU'RE NOT A CAT AT ALL, ARE YOU?
YOU'RE SOME KIND OF MUTANT THAT LOOKS LIKE A CAT AND--
CAROL!
--INTERVIEW WITH SUPER POWERS--
--ARE HAVING AN AFFAIR?
MS. MARVEL!
--THE ACT HAVE ANY EFFECT ON--
--KIND OF BUBBLE BATH DO--
CAROL. IT'S ME. IT'S STEPHEN. STEPHEN STRANGE.
I APOLOGIZE FOR THE INTRUSION, BUT I AM IN TROUBLE.
YOU'RE DREAMING, CAROL--AND I NEED YOU TO WAKE UP NOW.
WHAT THE?!
MROWR?
STEPHEN?

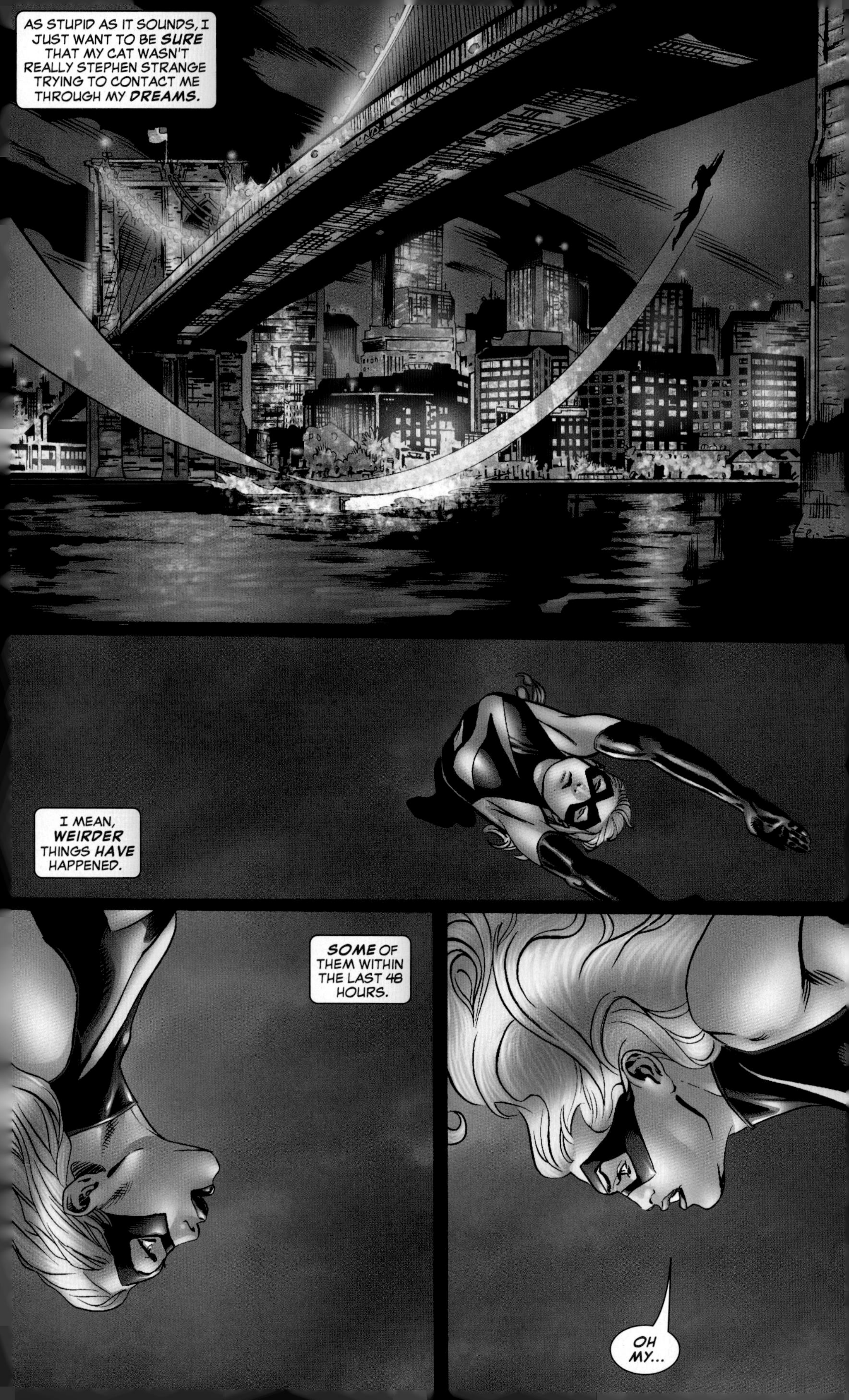
AS STUPID AS IT SOUNDS, I JUST WANT TO BE SURE THAT MY CAT WASN'T REALLY STEPHEN STRANGE TRYING TO CONTACT ME THROUGH MY DREAMS.
I MEAN, WEIRDER THINGS HAVE HAPPENED.
SOME OF THEM WITHIN THE LAST 48 HOURS.
OH MY...

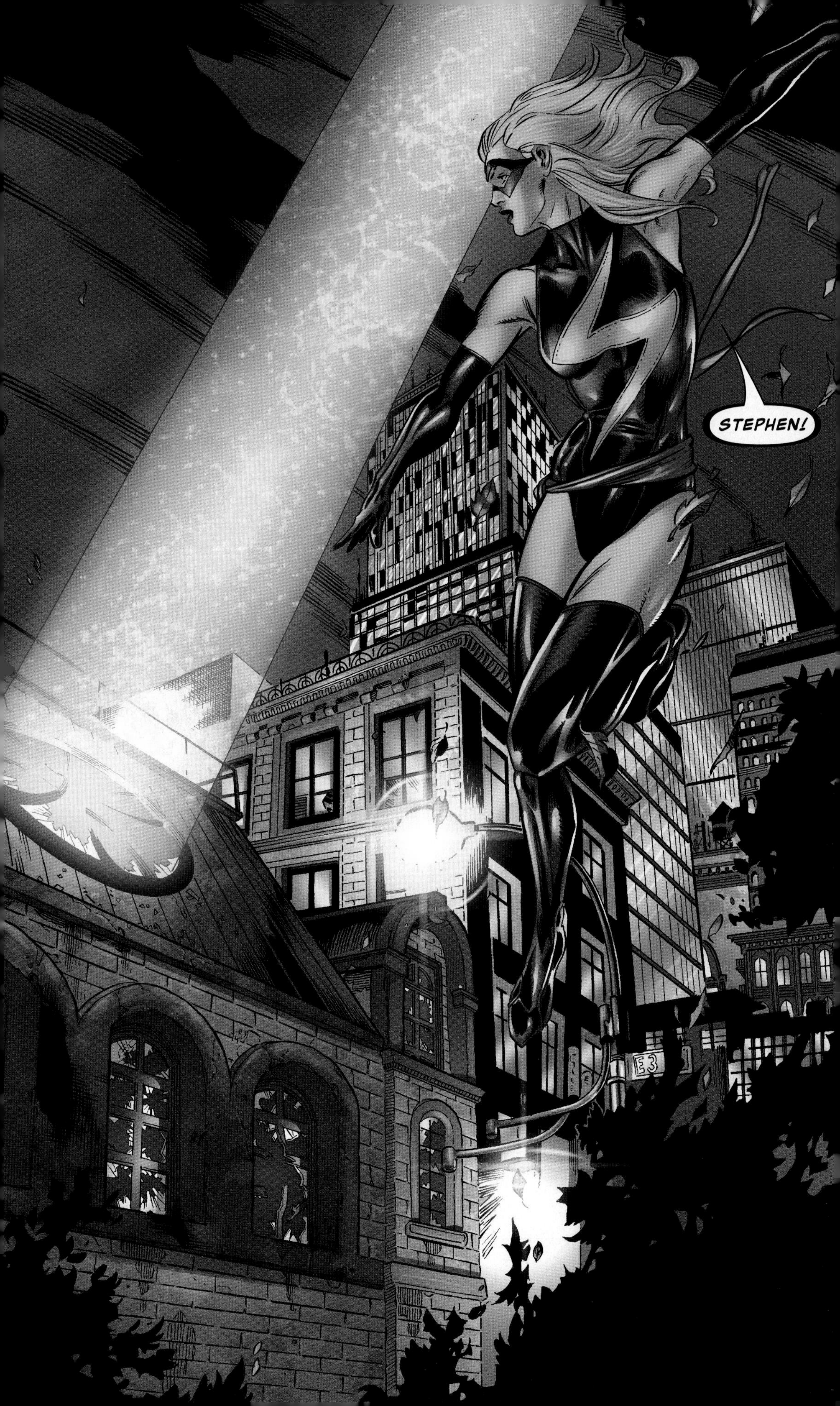
STEPHEN!

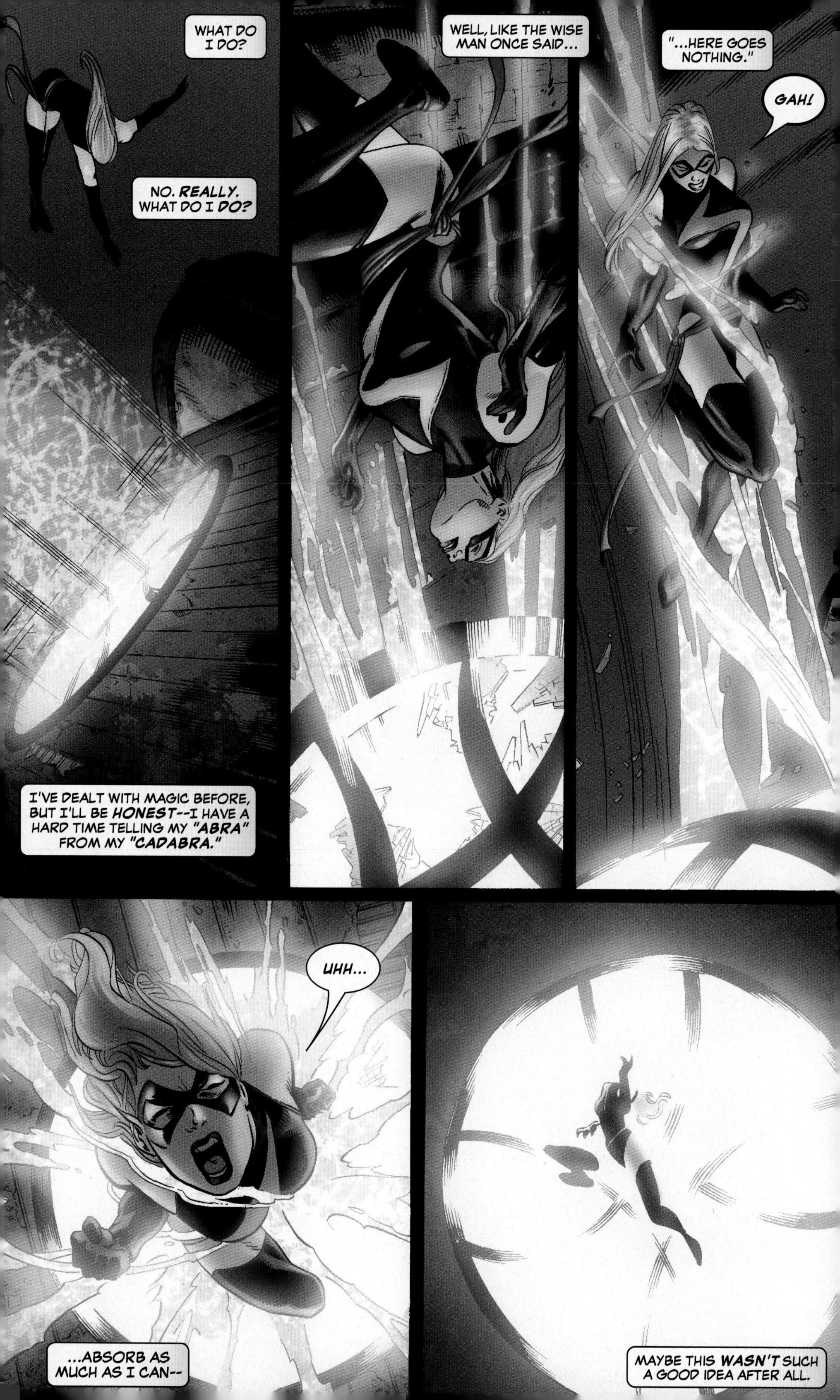
WHAT DO I DO?
NO. REALLY. WHAT DO I DO?
I'VE DEALT WITH MAGIC BEFORE, BUT I'LL BE HONEST--I HAVE A HARD TIME TELLING MY "ABRA" FROM MY "CADABRA."
WELL, LIKE THE WISE MAN ONCE SAID...
"...HERE GOES NOTHING."
GAH!
UHH...
...ABSORB AS MUCH AS I CAN--
MAYBE THIS WASN'T SUCH A GOOD IDEA AFTER ALL.

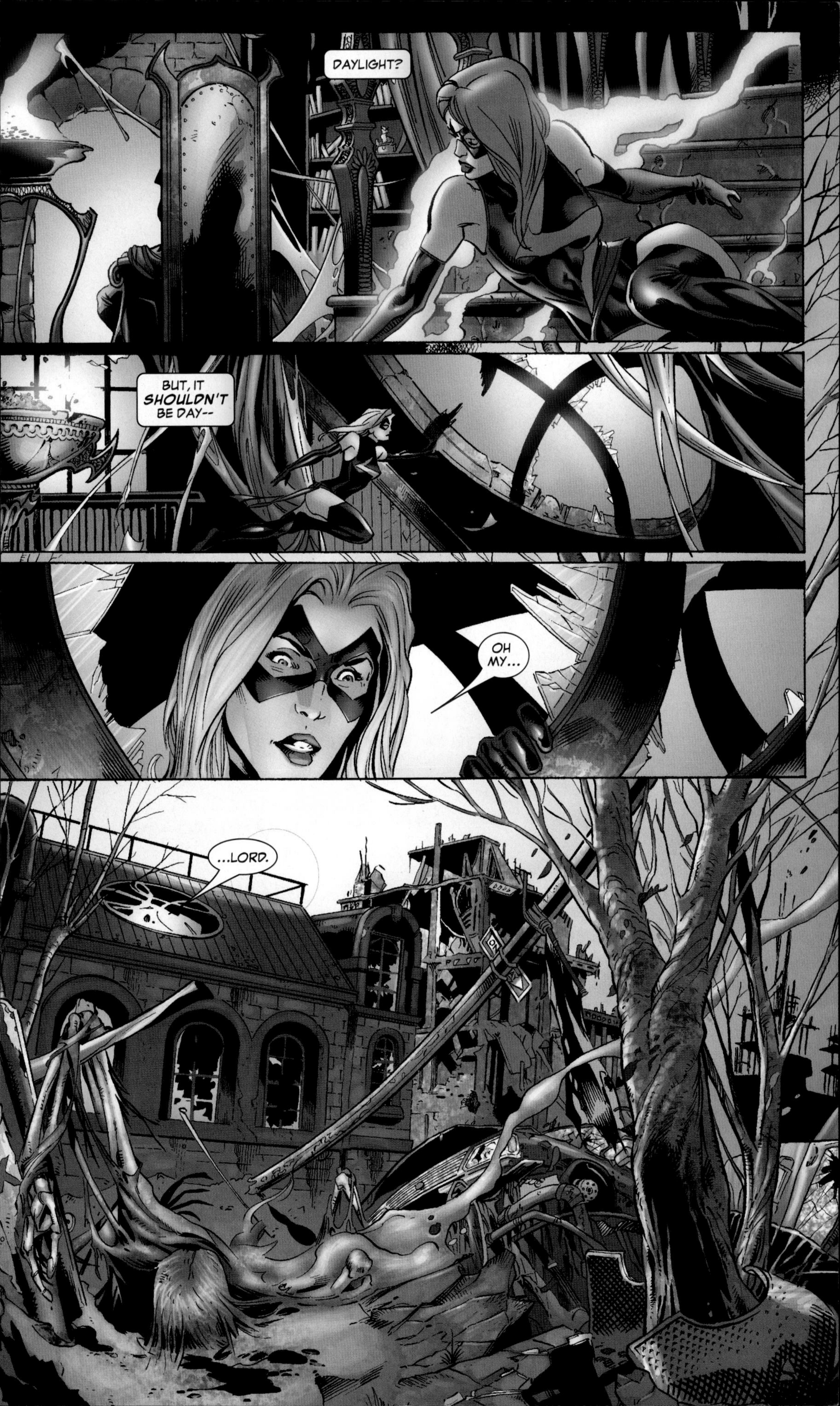
DAYLIGHT?
BUT, IT SHOULDN'T BE DAY--
OH MY...
...LORD.

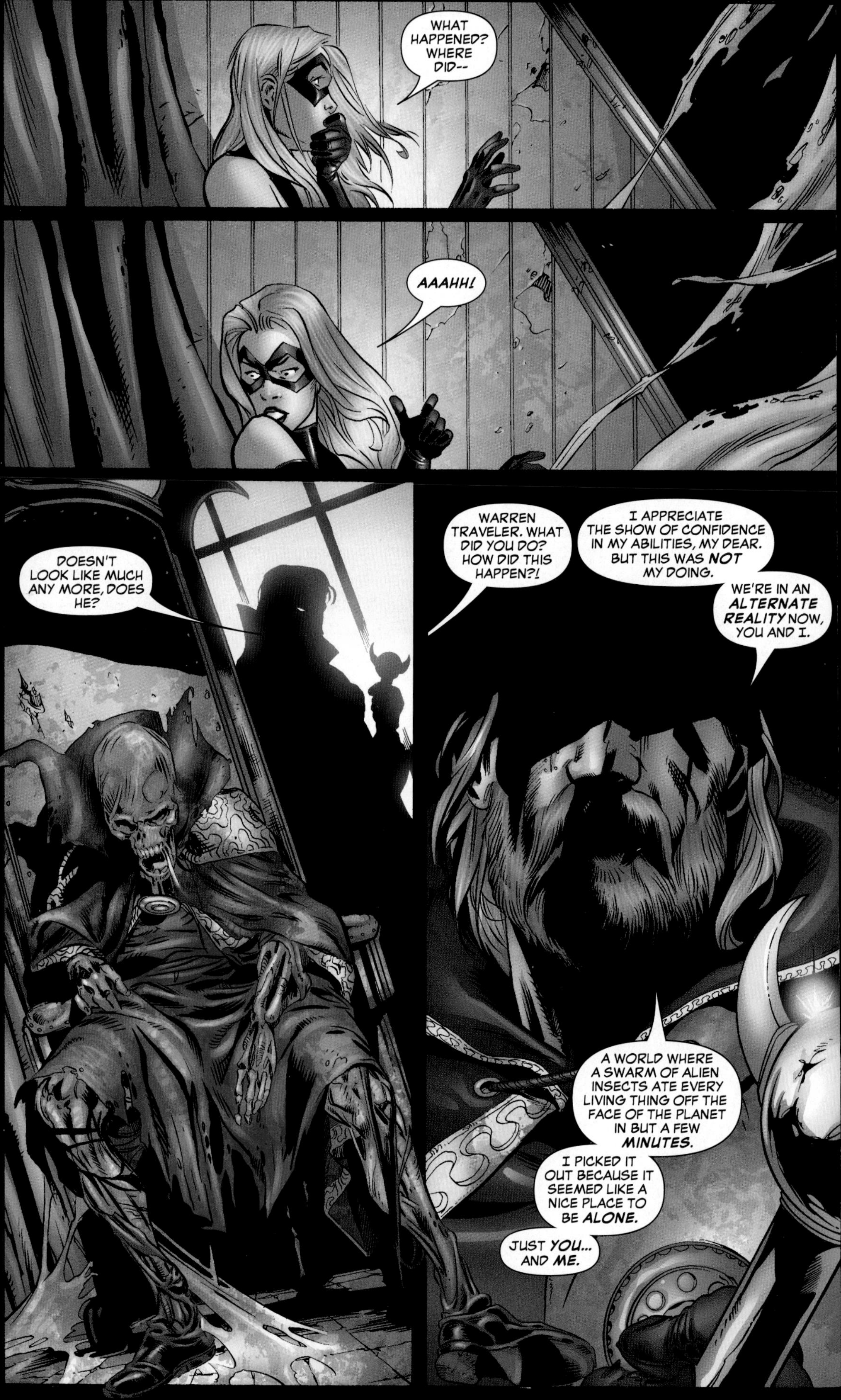
WHAT HAPPENED? WHERE DID--
AAAHH!
DOESN'T LOOK LIKE MUCH ANY MORE, DOES HE?
WARREN TRAVELER. WHAT DID YOU DO? HOW DID THIS HAPPEN?!
I APPRECIATE THE SHOW OF CONFIDENCE IN MY ABILITIES, MY DEAR. BUT THIS WAS NOT MY DOING.
WE'RE IN AN ALTERNATE REALITY NOW, YOU AND I.
A WORLD WHERE A SWARM OF ALIEN INSECTS ATE EVERY LIVING THING OFF THE FACE OF THE PLANET IN BUT A FEW MINUTES.
I PICKED IT OUT BECAUSE IT SEEMED LIKE A NICE PLACE TO BE ALONE.
JUST YOU... AND ME.

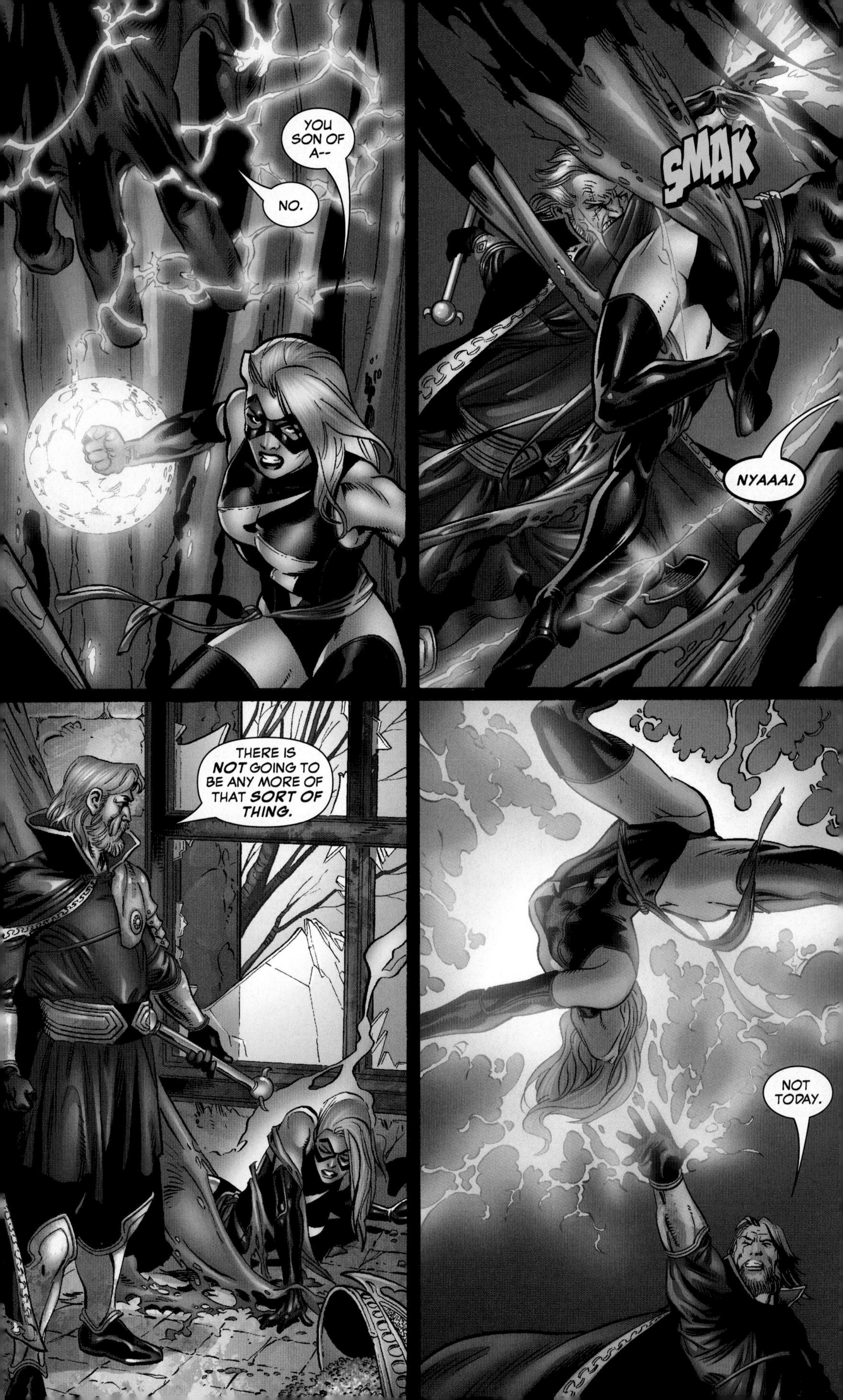
YOU SON OF A--
NO.
SMAK
NYAAA!
THERE IS NOT GOING TO BE ANY MORE OF THAT SORT OF THING.
NOT TODAY.

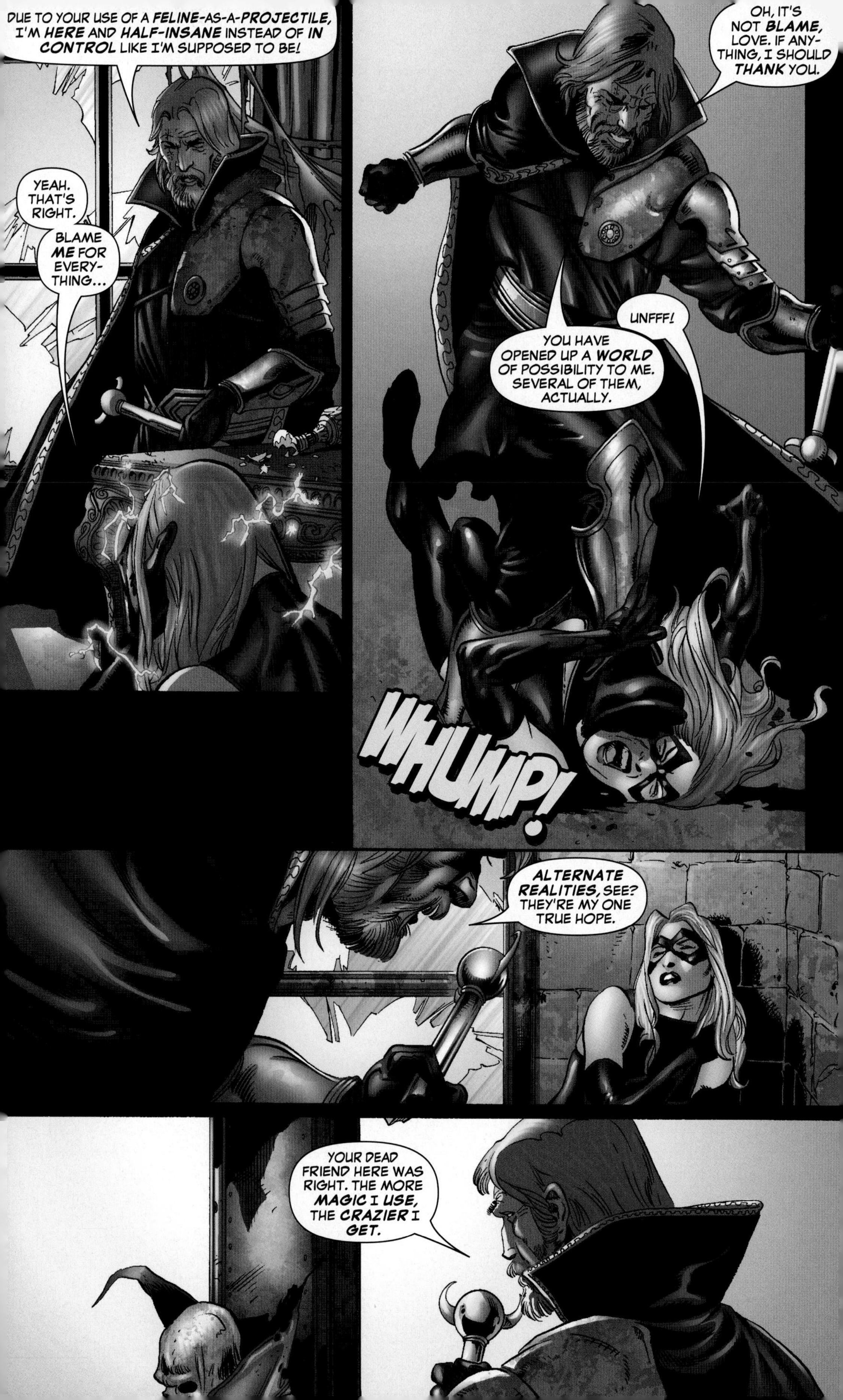
DUE TO YOUR USE OF A FELINE-AS-A-PROJECTILE, I'M HERE AND HALF-INSANE INSTEAD OF IN CONTROL LIKE I'M SUPPOSED TO BE!
YEAH. THAT'S RIGHT.
BLAME ME FOR EVERY-THING...
OH, IT'S NOT BLAME, LOVE. IF ANY-THING, I SHOULD THANK YOU.
YOU HAVE OPENED UP A WORLD OF POSSIBILITY TO ME. SEVERAL OF THEM, ACTUALLY.
UNFFF!
WHUMP!
ALTERNATE REALITIES, SEE? THEY'RE MY ONE TRUE HOPE.
YOUR DEAD FRIEND HERE WAS RIGHT. THE MORE MAGIC I USE, THE CRAZIER I GET.

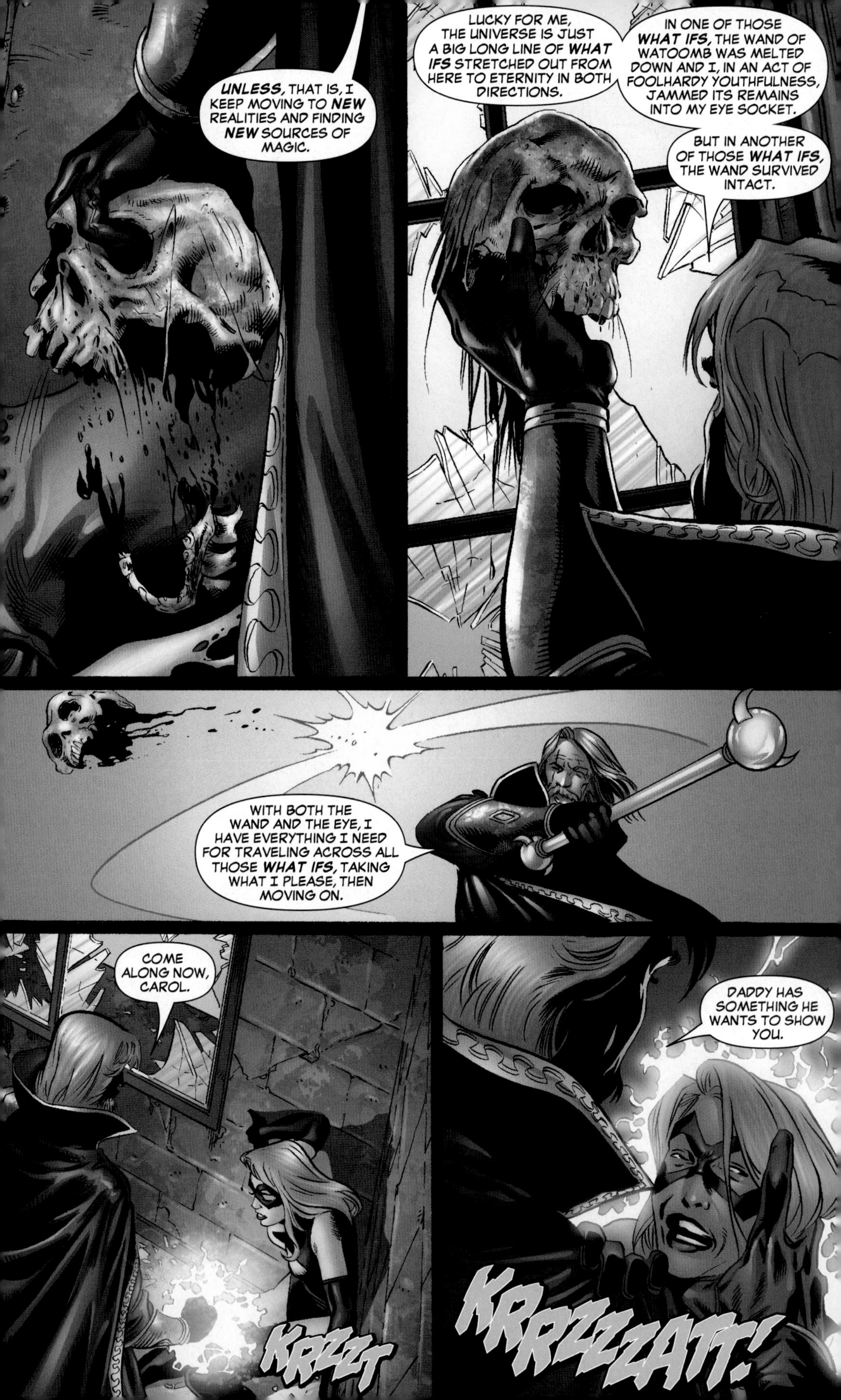
UNLESS, THAT IS, I KEEP MOVING TO NEW REALITIES AND FINDING NEW SOURCES OF MAGIC.
LUCKY FOR ME, THE UNIVERSE IS JUST A BIG LONG LINE OF WHAT IFS STRETCHED OUT FROM HERE TO ETERNITY IN BOTH DIRECTIONS.
IN ONE OF THOSE WHAT IFS, THE WAND OF WATOOMB WAS MELTED DOWN AND I, IN AN ACT OF FOOLHARDY YOUTHFULNESS, JAMMED ITS REMAINS INTO MY EYE SOCKET.
BUT IN ANOTHER OF THOSE WHAT IFS, THE WAND SURVIVED INTACT.
WITH BOTH THE WAND AND THE EYE, I HAVE EVERYTHING I NEED FOR TRAVELING ACROSS ALL THOSE WHAT IFS, TAKING WHAT I PLEASE, THEN MOVING ON.
COME ALONG NOW, CAROL.
KRZZZT
DADDY HAS SOMETHING HE WANTS TO SHOW YOU.
KRRZZZZATT!

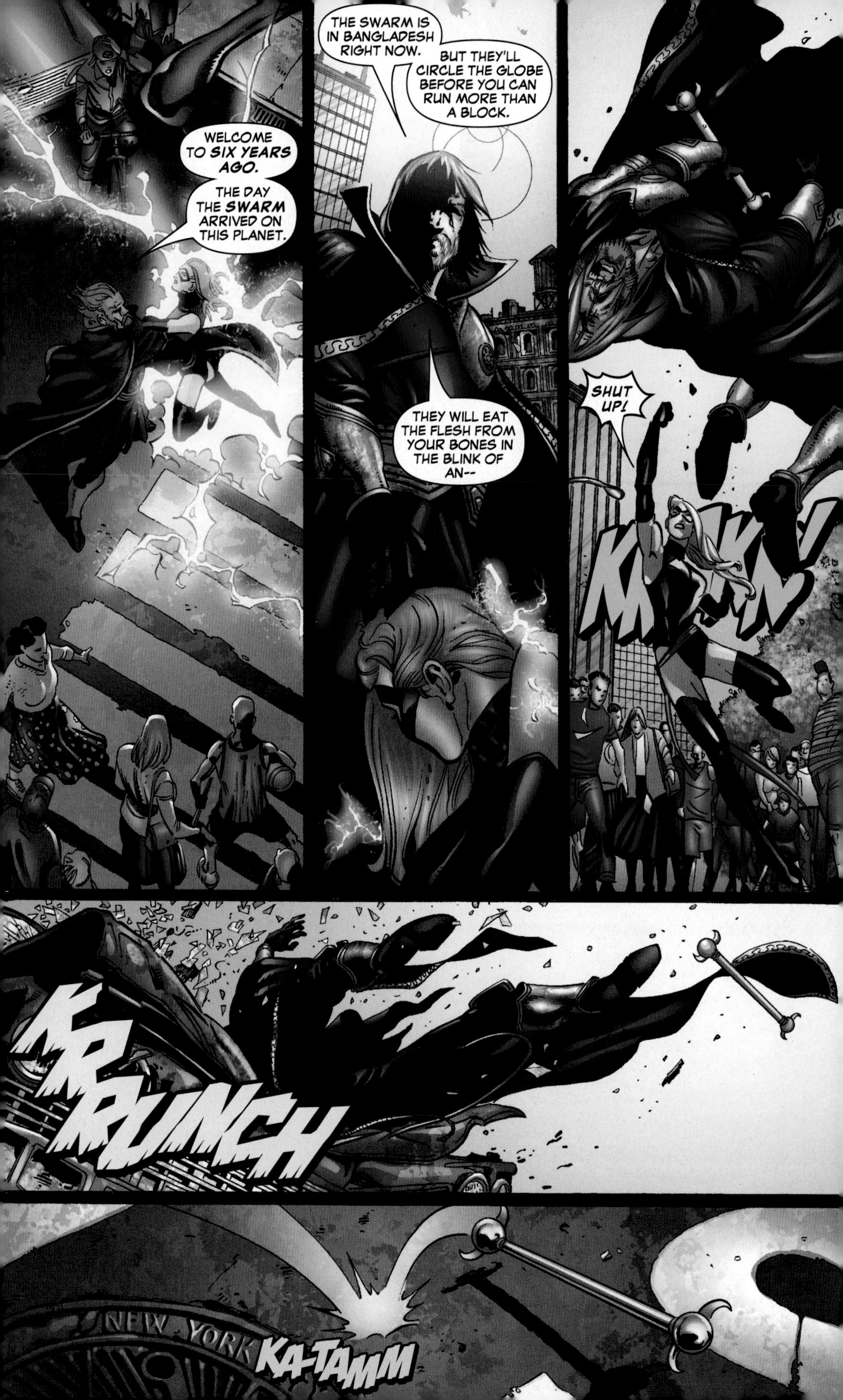
WELCOME TO SIX YEARS AGO.
THE DAY THE SWARM ARRIVED ON THIS PLANET.
THE SWARM IS IN BANGLADESH RIGHT NOW.
BUT THEY'LL CIRCLE THE GLOBE BEFORE YOU CAN RUN MORE THAN A BLOCK.
THEY WILL EAT THE FLESH FROM YOUR BONES IN THE BLINK OF AN--
SHUT UP!
KRAKK
KRRUNCH
NEW YORK
KA-TAMM

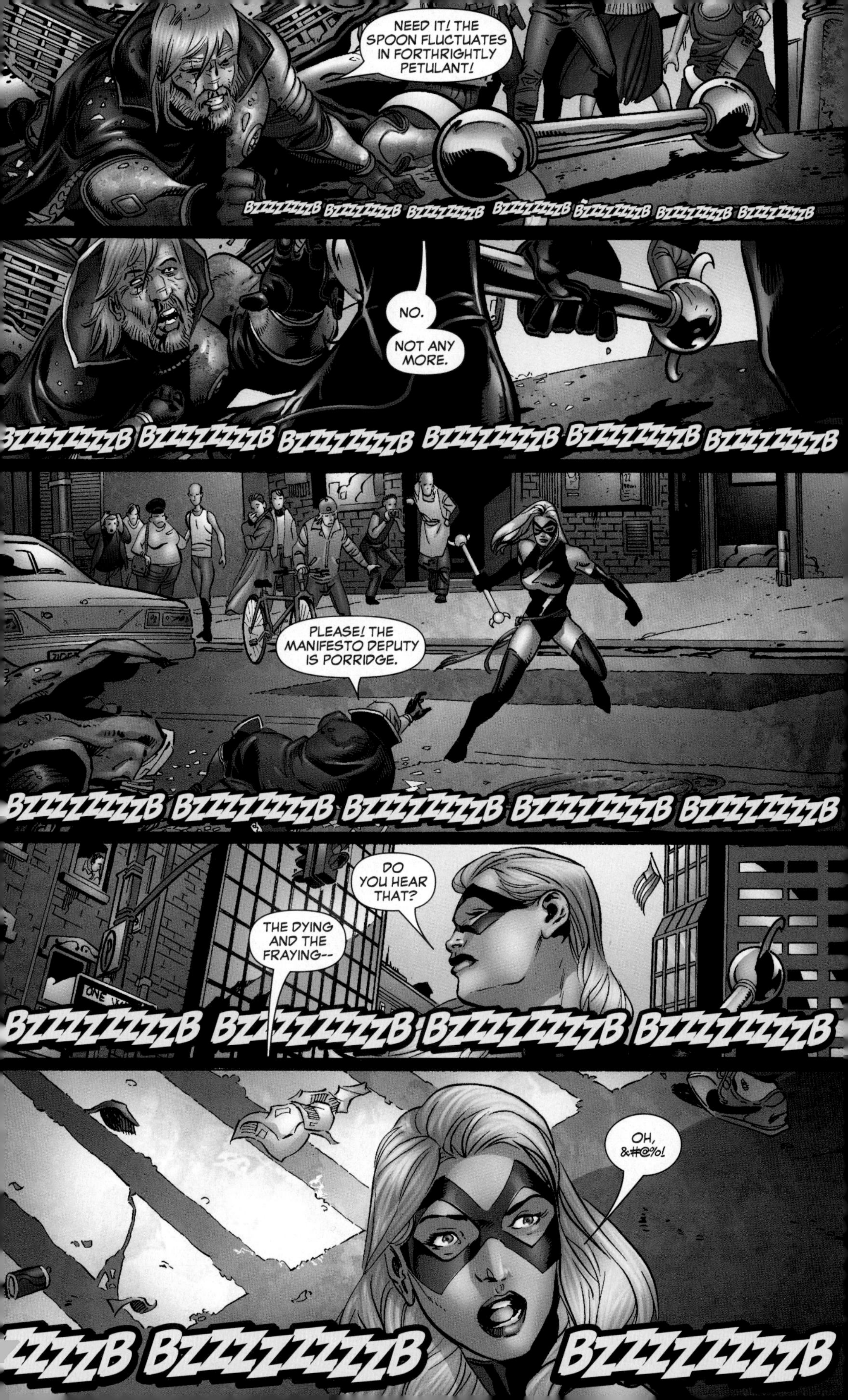

NEED IT! THE SPOON FLUCTUATES IN FORTHRIGHTLY PETULANT!
BZZZZZZZZB BZZZZZZZZB BZZZZZZZZB BZZZZZZZZB BZZZZZZZZB BZZZZZZZZB BZZZZZZZZB
NO.
NOT ANY MORE.
BZZZZZZZZB BZZZZZZZZB BZZZZZZZZB BZZZZZZZZB BZZZZZZZZB BZZZZZZZZB
PLEASE! THE MANIFESTO DEPUTY IS PORRIDGE.
BZZZZZZZZB BZZZZZZZZB BZZZZZZZZB BZZZZZZZZB BZZZZZZZZB
DO YOU HEAR THAT?
THE DYING AND THE FRAYING--
BZZZZZZZZB BZZZZZZZZB BZZZZZZZZB BZZZZZZZZB
OH, &#@%!
ZZZZB BZZZZZZZZB BZZZZZZZZB

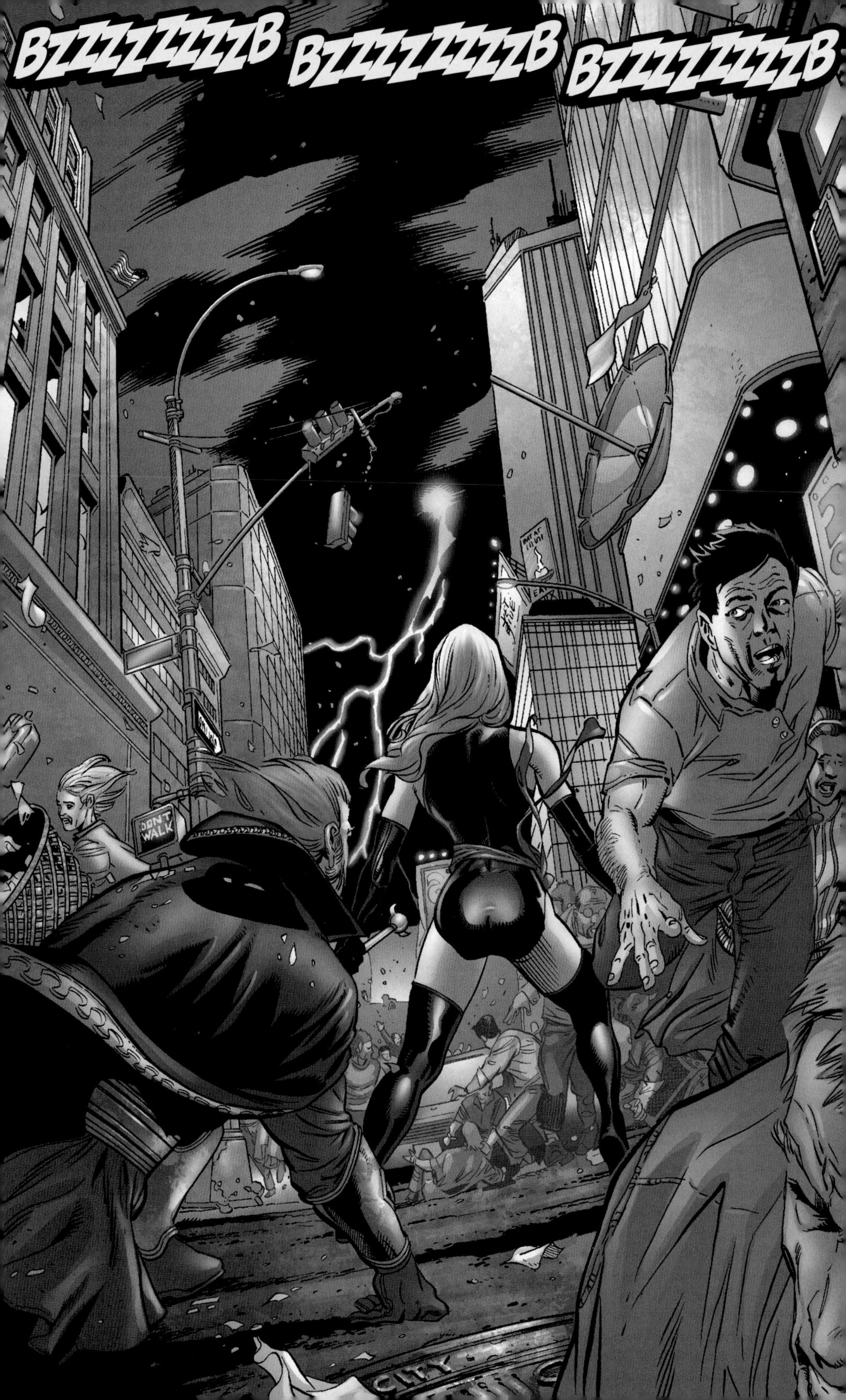
BZZZZZZZZZB
BZZZZZZZZZB
BZZZZZZZZZB
DON'T WALK
CITY

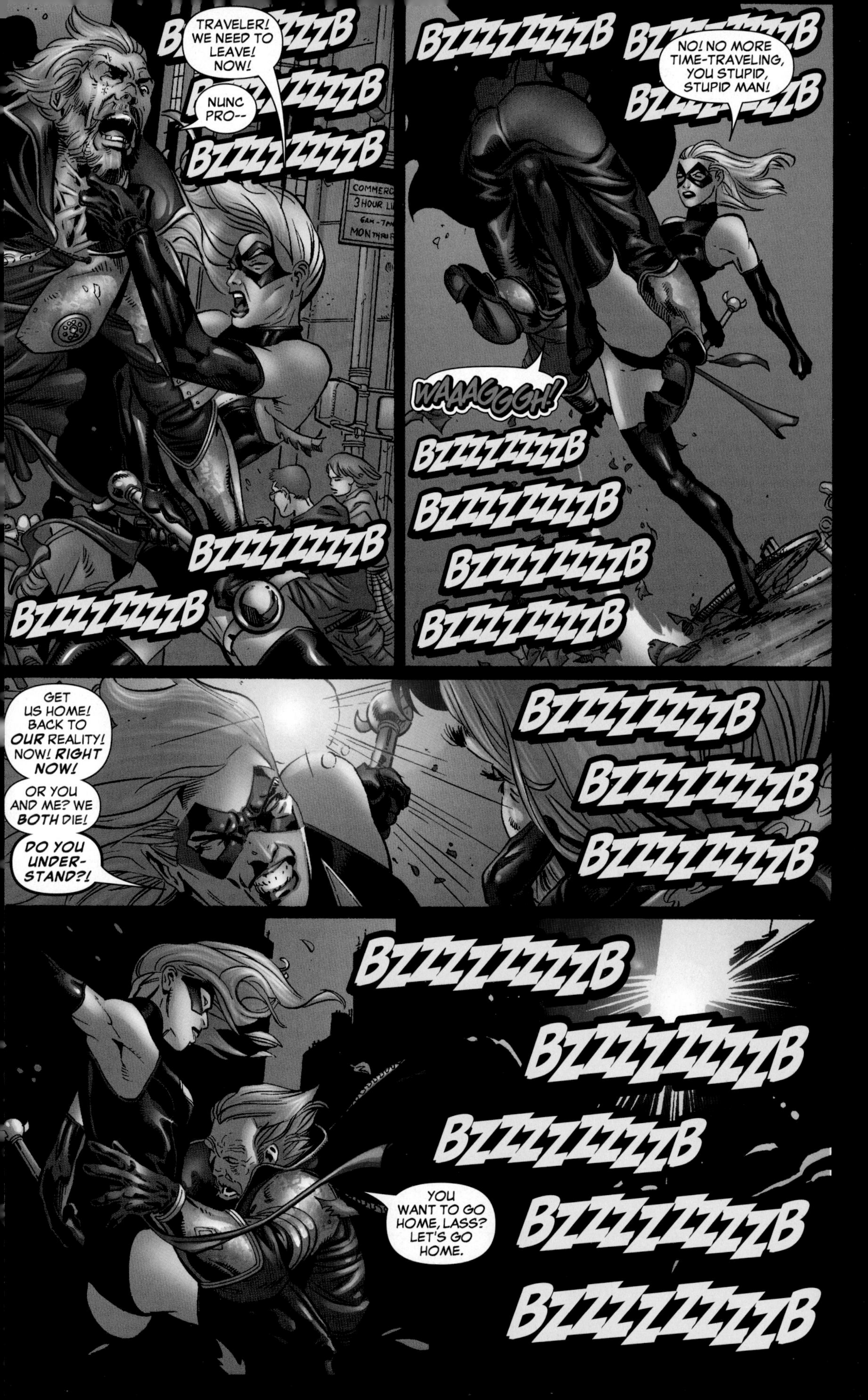
TRAVELER! WE NEED TO LEAVE! NOW!
NUNC PRO--
BZZZZZZZZZB
BZZZZZZZZZB
BZZZZZZZZZB
NO! NO MORE TIME-TRAVELING, YOU STUPID, STUPID MAN!
WAAAGGGH!
BZZZZZZZZZB
BZZZZZZZZZB
BZZZZZZZZZB
BZZZZZZZZZB
GET US HOME! BACK TO OUR REALITY! NOW! RIGHT NOW!
OR YOU AND ME? WE BOTH DIE!
DO YOU UNDER-STAND?!
BZZZZZZZZZB
BZZZZZZZZZB
BZZZZZZZZZB
BZZZZZZZZZB
BZZZZZZZZZB
BZZZZZZZZZB
YOU WANT TO GO HOME, LASS? LET'S GO HOME.
BZZZZZZZZZB
BZZZZZZZZZB

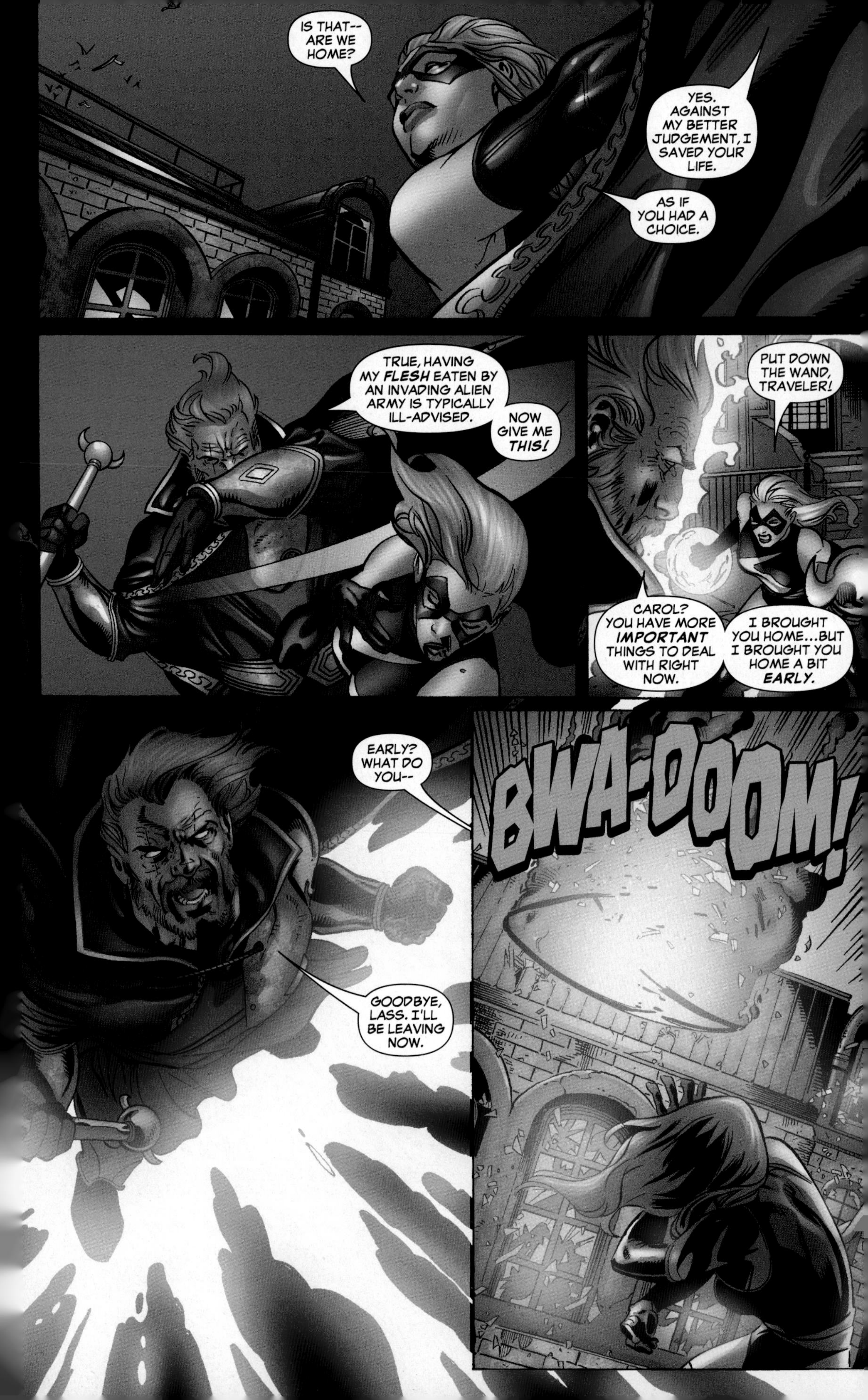
IS THAT-- ARE WE HOME?
YES. AGAINST MY BETTER JUDGEMENT, I SAVED YOUR LIFE.
AS IF YOU HAD A CHOICE.
TRUE, HAVING MY FLESH EATEN BY AN INVADING ALIEN ARMY IS TYPICALLY ILL-ADVISED.
NOW GIVE ME THIS!
PUT DOWN THE WAND, TRAVELER!
CAROL? YOU HAVE MORE IMPORTANT THINGS TO DEAL WITH RIGHT NOW.
I BROUGHT YOU HOME...BUT I BROUGHT YOU HOME A BIT EARLY.
EARLY? WHAT DO YOU--
GOODBYE, LASS. I'LL BE LEAVING NOW.
BWA-DOOM!

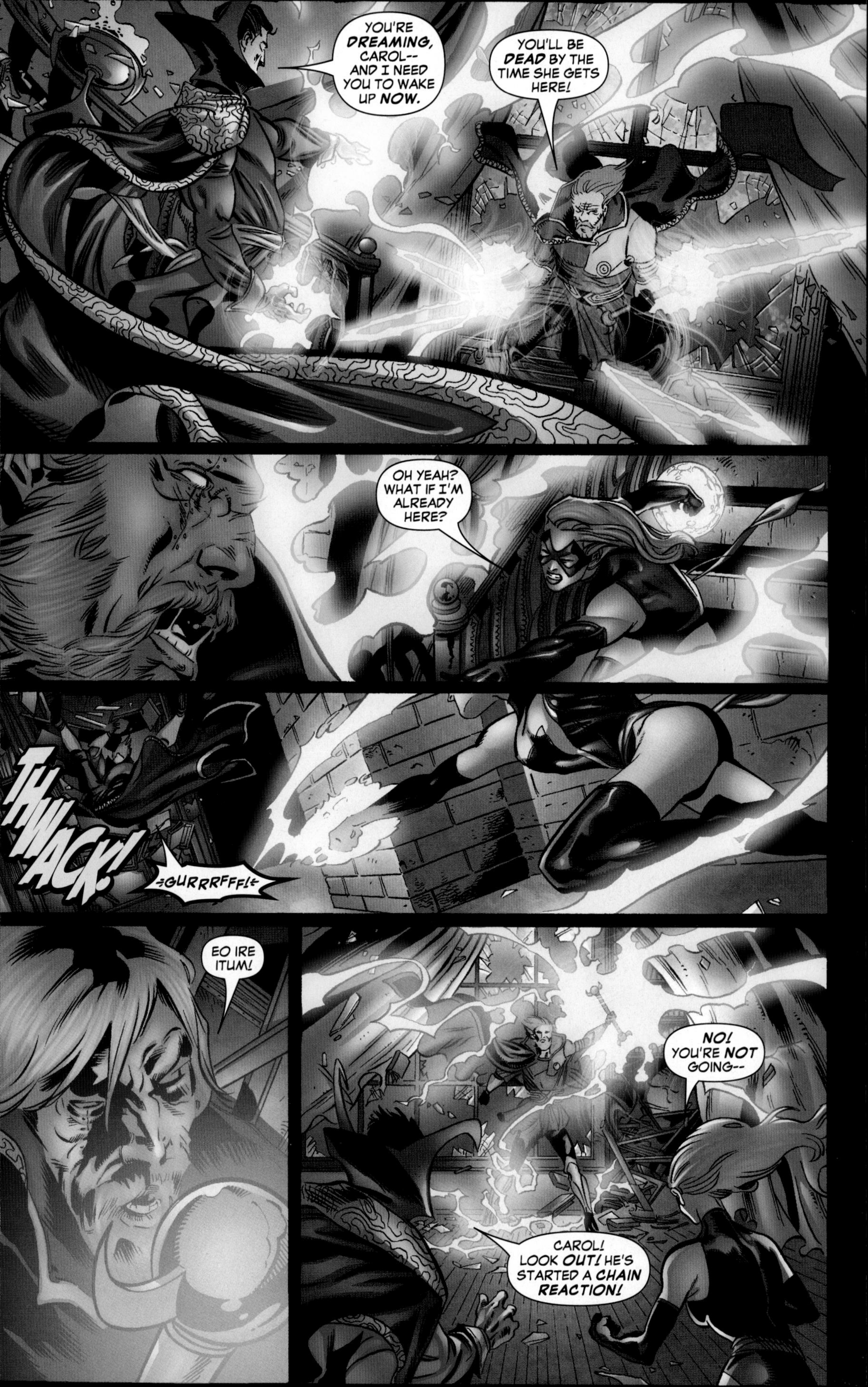
YOU'RE DREAMING, CAROL-- AND I NEED YOU TO WAKE UP NOW.
YOU'LL BE DEAD BY THE TIME SHE GETS HERE!
OH YEAH? WHAT IF I'M ALREADY HERE?
THWACK!
GURRRFFF!
EO IRE ITUM!
NO! YOU'RE NOT GOING--
CAROL! LOOK OUT! HE'S STARTED A CHAIN REACTION!

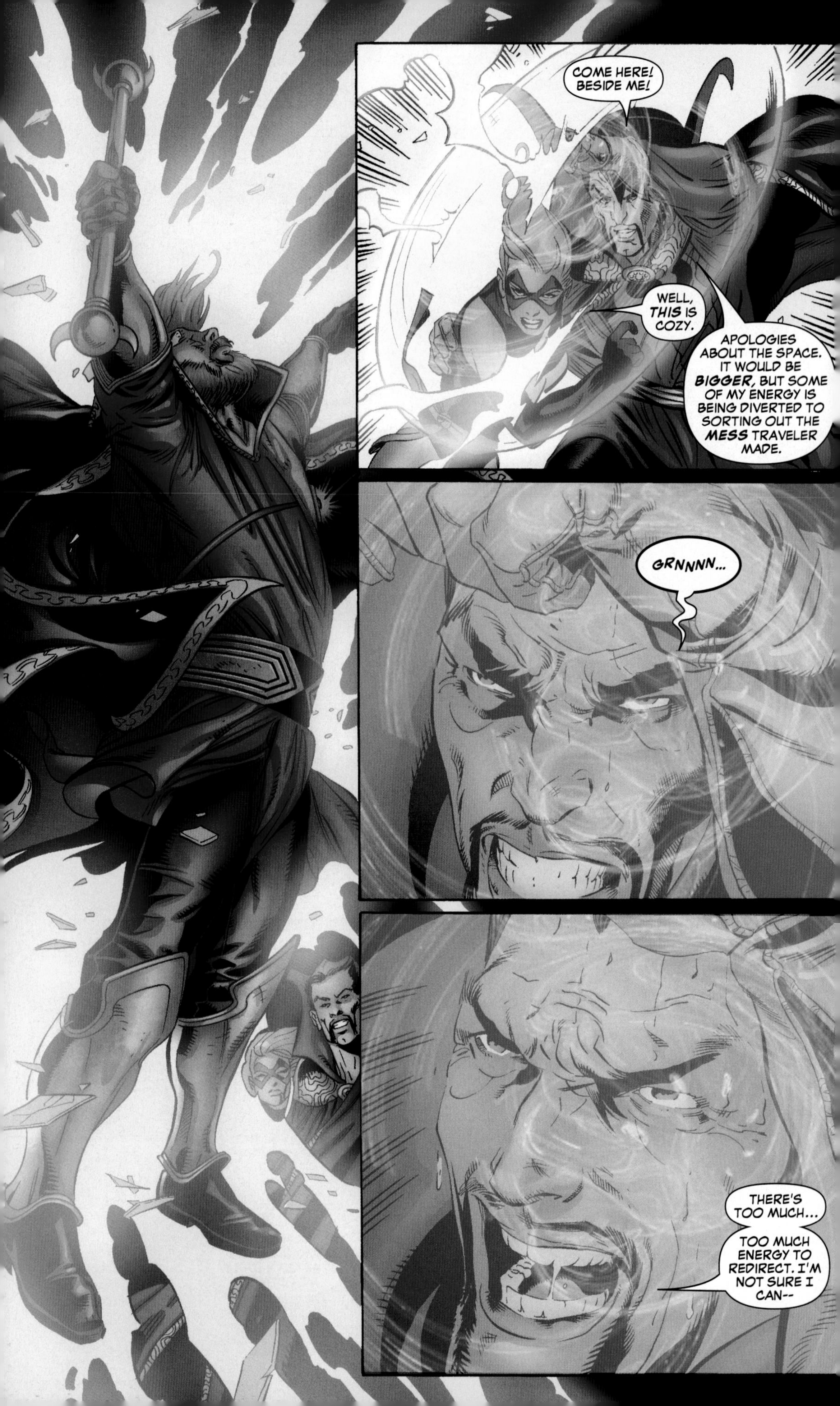

COME HERE! BESIDE ME!
WELL, THIS IS COZY.
APOLOGIES ABOUT THE SPACE. IT WOULD BE BIGGER, BUT SOME OF MY ENERGY IS BEING DIVERTED TO SORTING OUT THE MESS TRAVELER MADE.
GRNNNN...
THERE'S TOO MUCH...
TOO MUCH ENERGY TO REDIRECT. I'M NOT SURE I CAN--

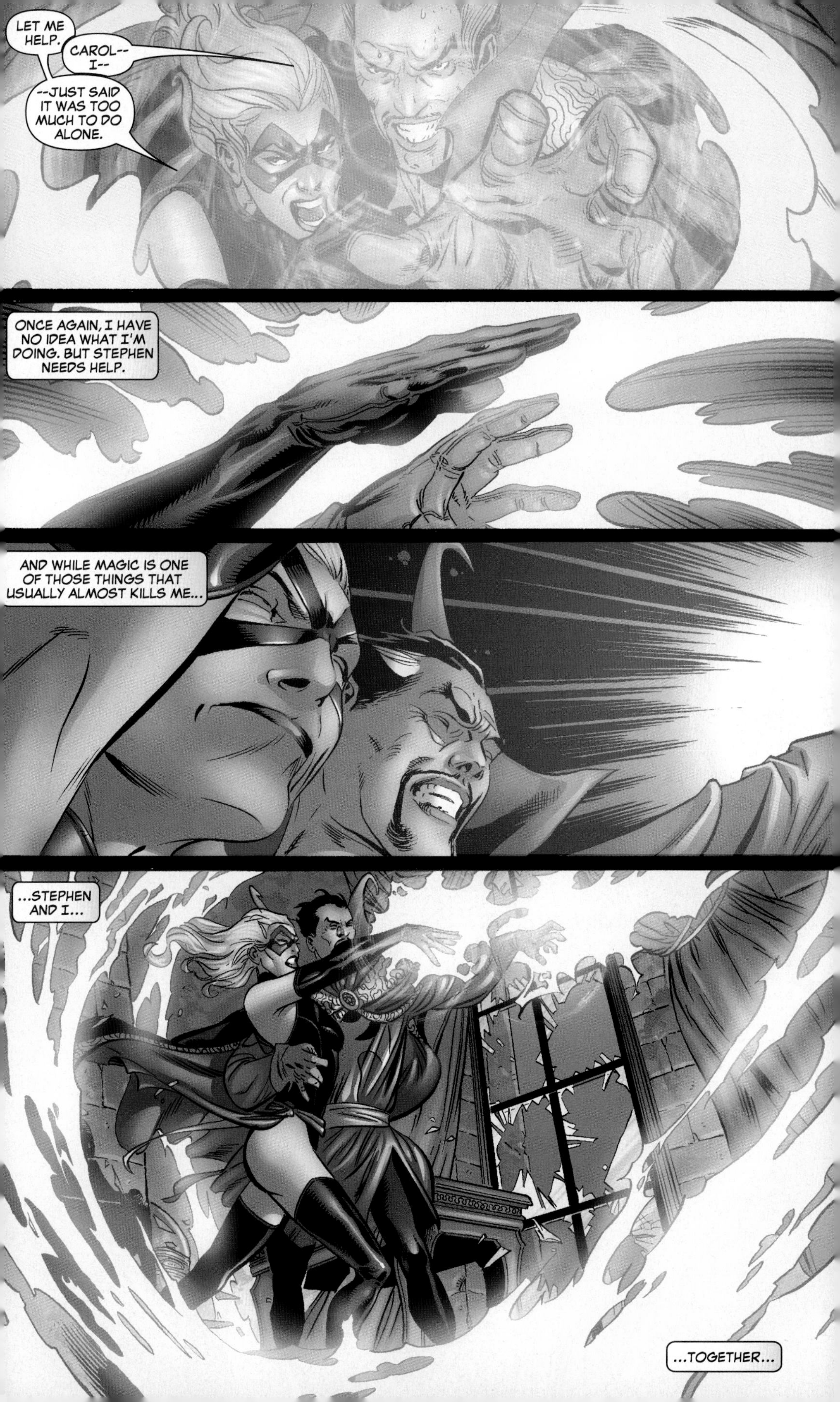
LET ME HELP.
CAROL-- I--
--JUST SAID IT WAS TOO MUCH TO DO ALONE.
ONCE AGAIN, I HAVE NO IDEA WHAT I'M DOING. BUT STEPHEN NEEDS HELP.
AND WHILE MAGIC IS ONE OF THOSE THINGS THAT USUALLY ALMOST KILLS ME...
...STEPHEN AND I...
...TOGETHER...

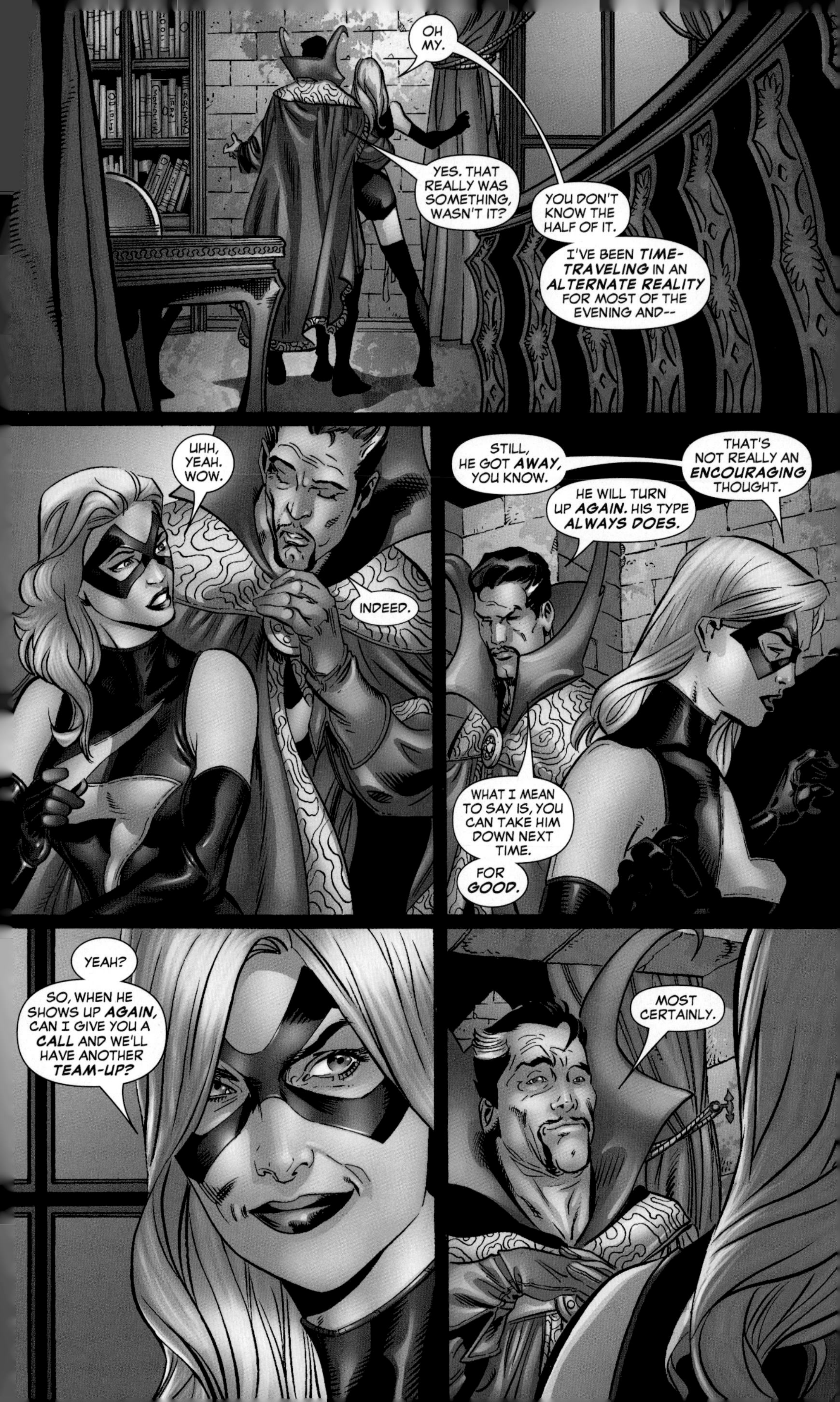
OH MY.
YES. THAT REALLY WAS SOMETHING, WASN'T IT?
YOU DON'T KNOW THE HALF OF IT.
I'VE BEEN TIME-TRAVELING IN AN ALTERNATE REALITY FOR MOST OF THE EVENING AND--
UHH, YEAH. WOW.
INDEED.
STILL, HE GOT AWAY, YOU KNOW.
THAT'S NOT REALLY AN ENCOURAGING THOUGHT.
HE WILL TURN UP AGAIN. HIS TYPE ALWAYS DOES.
WHAT I MEAN TO SAY IS, YOU CAN TAKE HIM DOWN NEXT TIME.
FOR GOOD.
YEAH?
SO, WHEN HE SHOWS UP AGAIN, CAN I GIVE YOU A CALL AND WE'LL HAVE ANOTHER TEAM-UP?
MOST CERTAINLY.

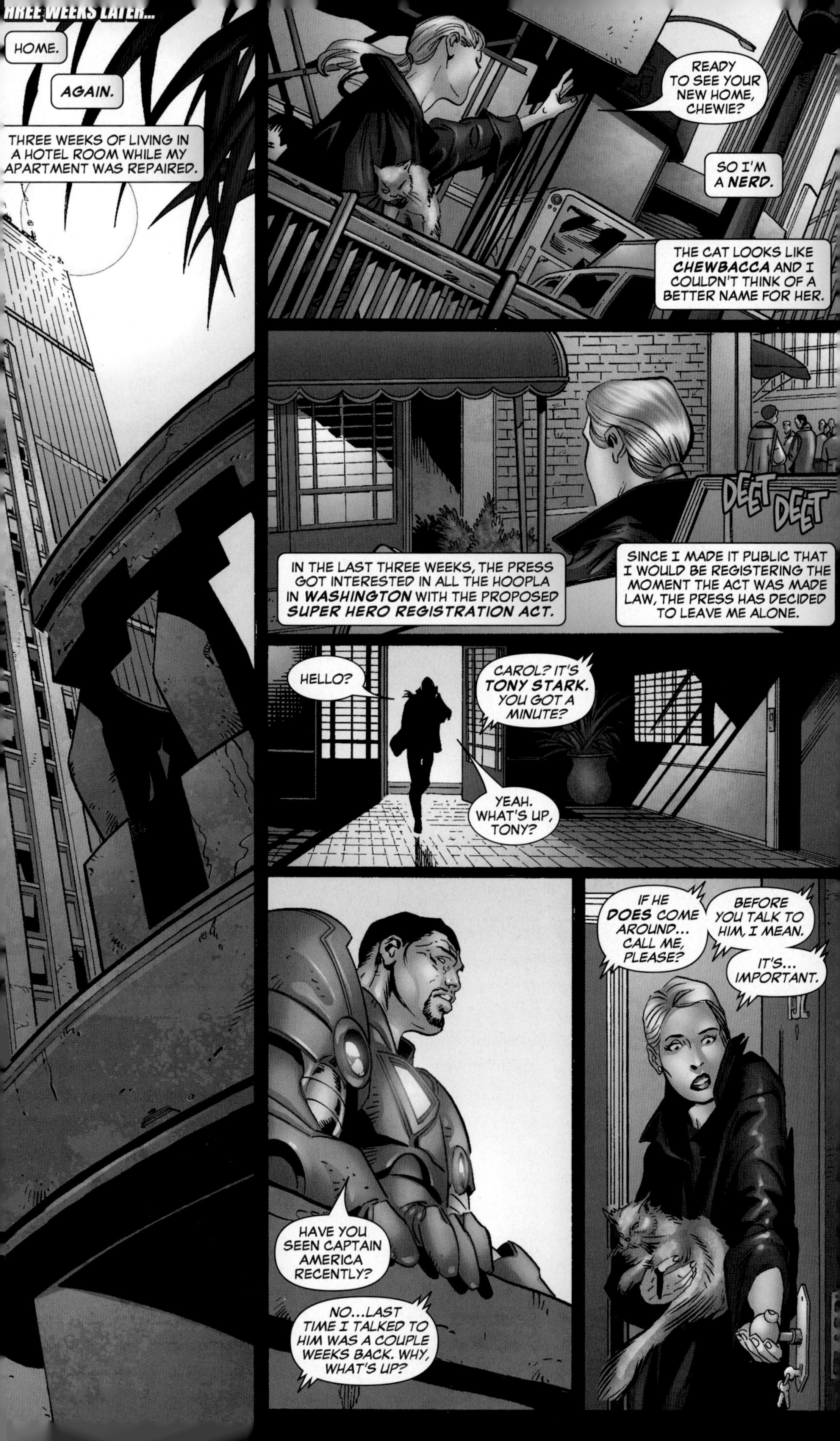
HREE WEEKS LATER...
HOME.
AGAIN.
THREE WEEKS OF LIVING IN A HOTEL ROOM WHILE MY APARTMENT WAS REPAIRED.
READY TO SEE YOUR NEW HOME, CHEWIE?
SO I'M A NERD.
THE CAT LOOKS LIKE CHEWBACCA AND I COULDN'T THINK OF A BETTER NAME FOR HER.
DEET DEET
IN THE LAST THREE WEEKS, THE PRESS GOT INTERESTED IN ALL THE HOOPLA IN WASHINGTON WITH THE PROPOSED SUPER HERO REGISTRATION ACT.
SINCE I MADE IT PUBLIC THAT I WOULD BE REGISTERING THE MOMENT THE ACT WAS MADE LAW, THE PRESS HAS DECIDED TO LEAVE ME ALONE.
HELLO?
CAROL? IT'S TONY STARK. YOU GOT A MINUTE?
YEAH. WHAT'S UP, TONY?
HAVE YOU SEEN CAPTAIN AMERICA RECENTLY?
NO...LAST TIME I TALKED TO HIM WAS A COUPLE WEEKS BACK. WHY, WHAT'S UP?
IF HE DOES COME AROUND... CALL ME, PLEASE?
BEFORE YOU TALK TO HIM, I MEAN.
IT'S... IMPORTANT.

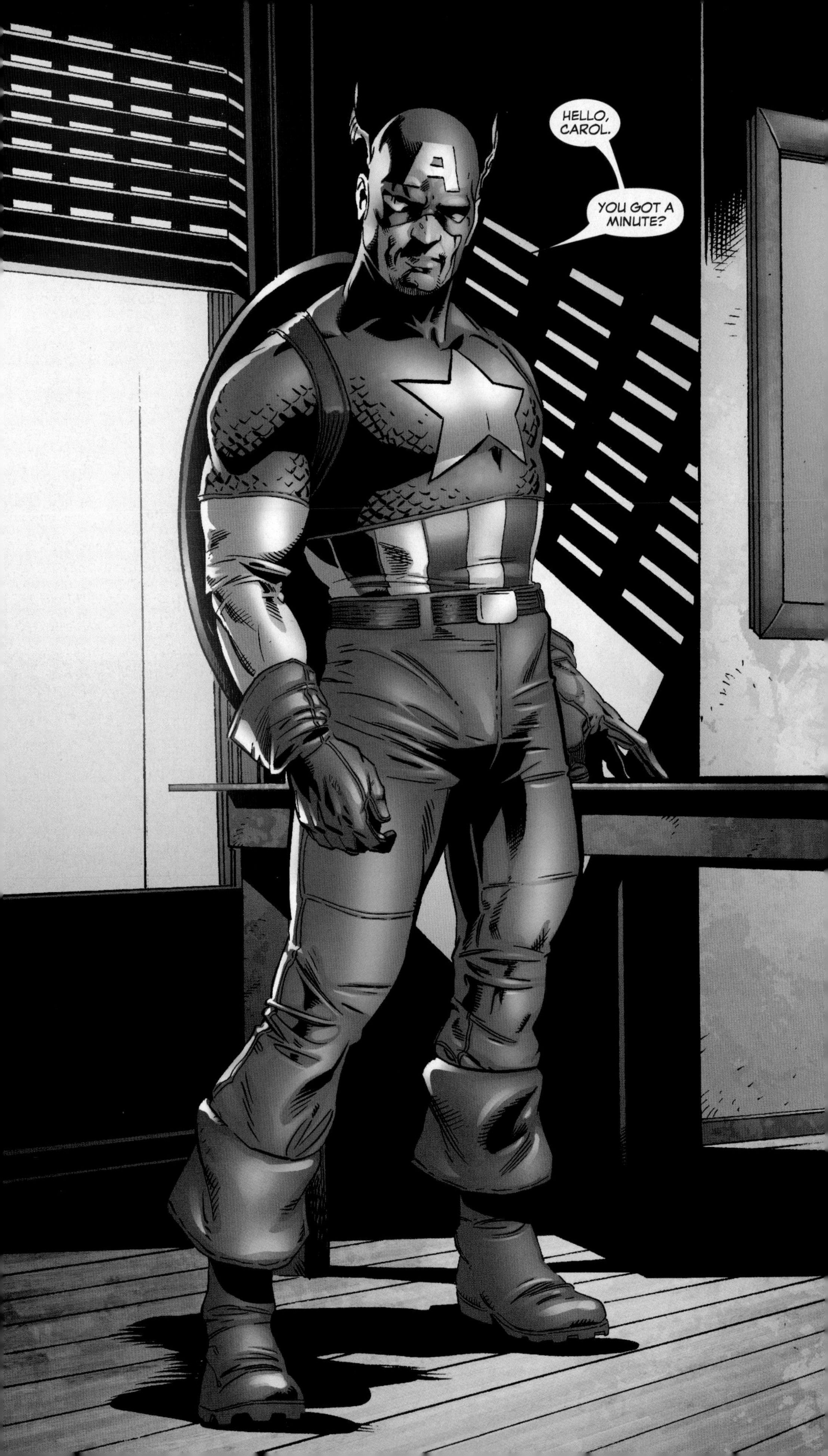
HELLO, CAROL.
YOU GOT A MINUTE?

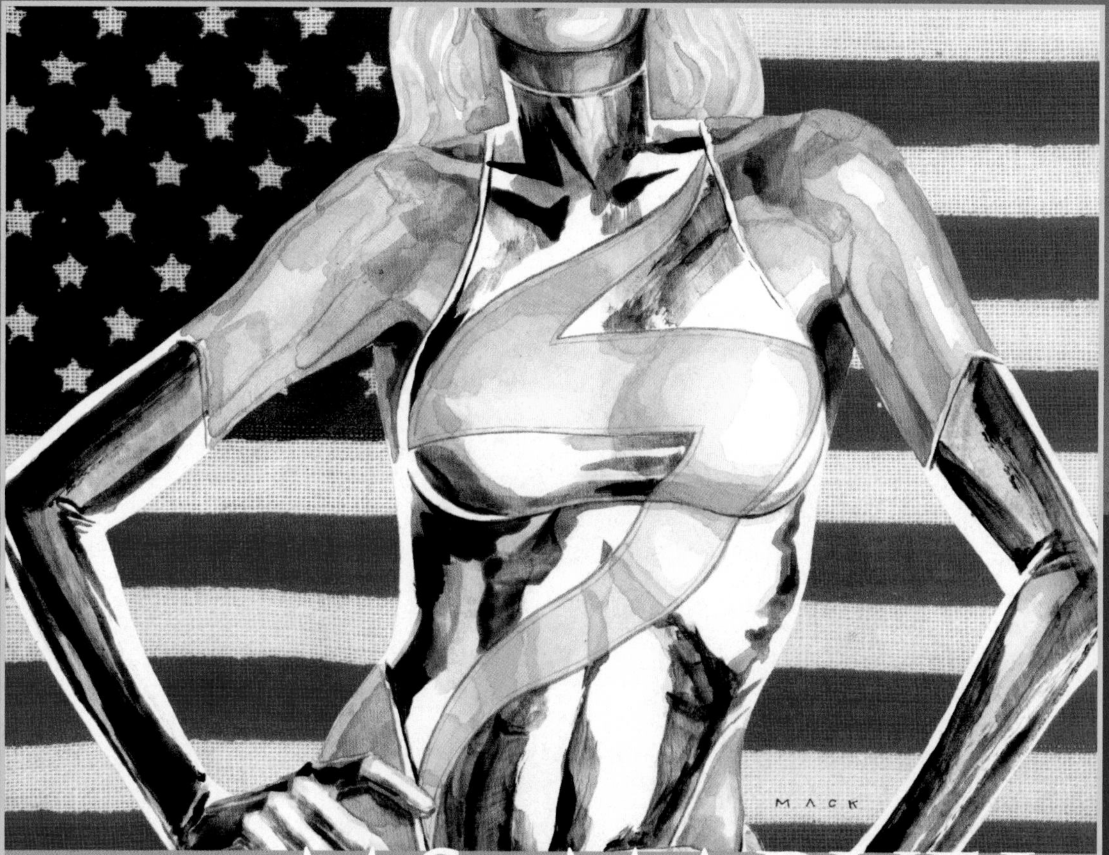
MACK

MS. MARVEL

A MARVEL COMICS EVENT

CIVIL WAR

6

"BATTLE LINES"

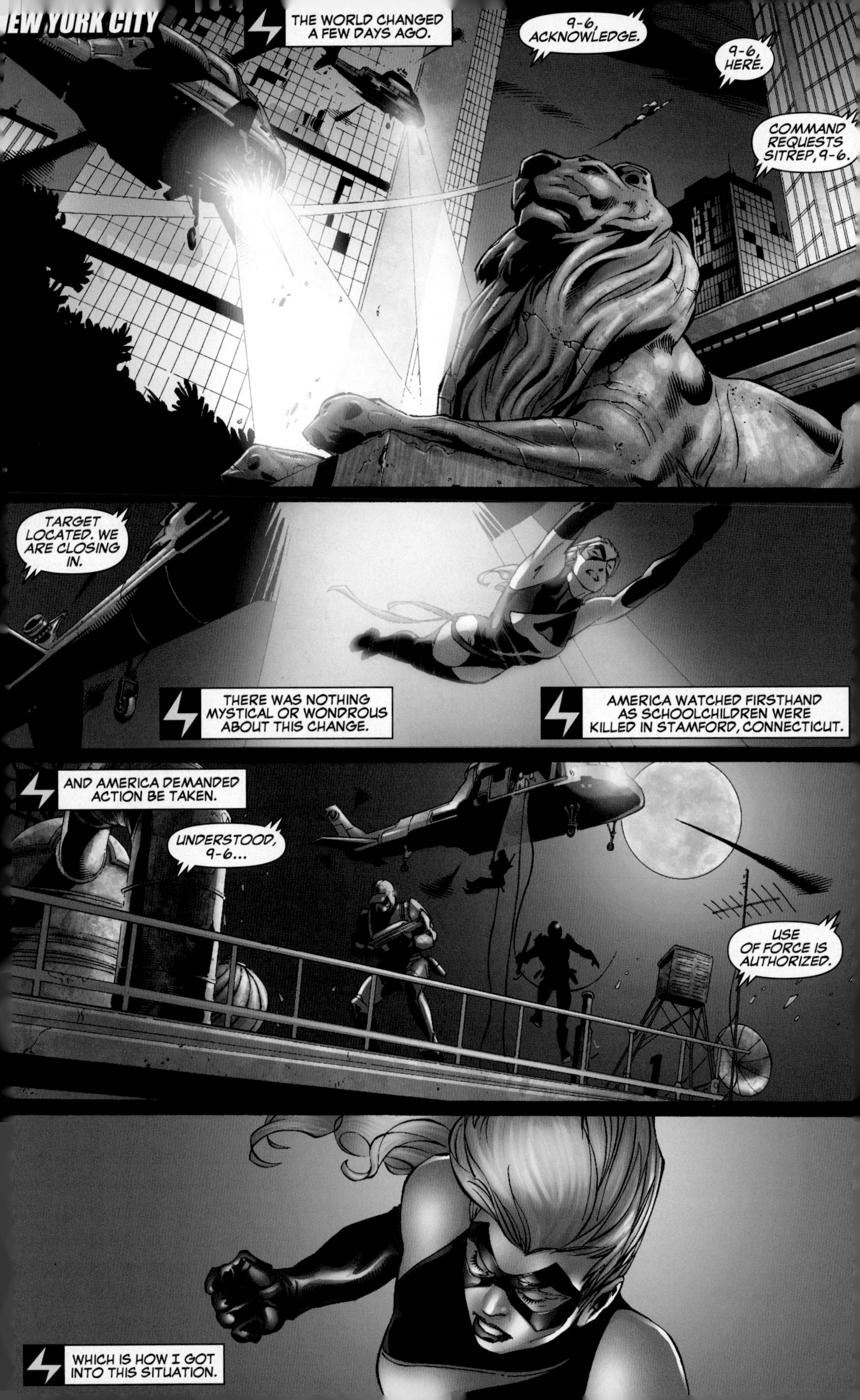

EW YORK CITY
THE WORLD CHANGED A FEW DAYS AGO.
9-6, ACKNOWLEDGE.
9-6, HERE.
COMMAND REQUESTS SITREP, 9-6.
TARGET LOCATED. WE ARE CLOSING IN.
THERE WAS NOTHING MYSTICAL OR WONDROUS ABOUT THIS CHANGE.
AMERICA WATCHED FIRSTHAND AS SCHOOLCHILDREN WERE KILLED IN STAMFORD, CONNECTICUT.
AND AMERICA DEMANDED ACTION BE TAKEN.
UNDERSTOOD, 9-6...
USE OF FORCE IS AUTHORIZED.
WHICH IS HOW I GOT INTO THIS SITUATION.

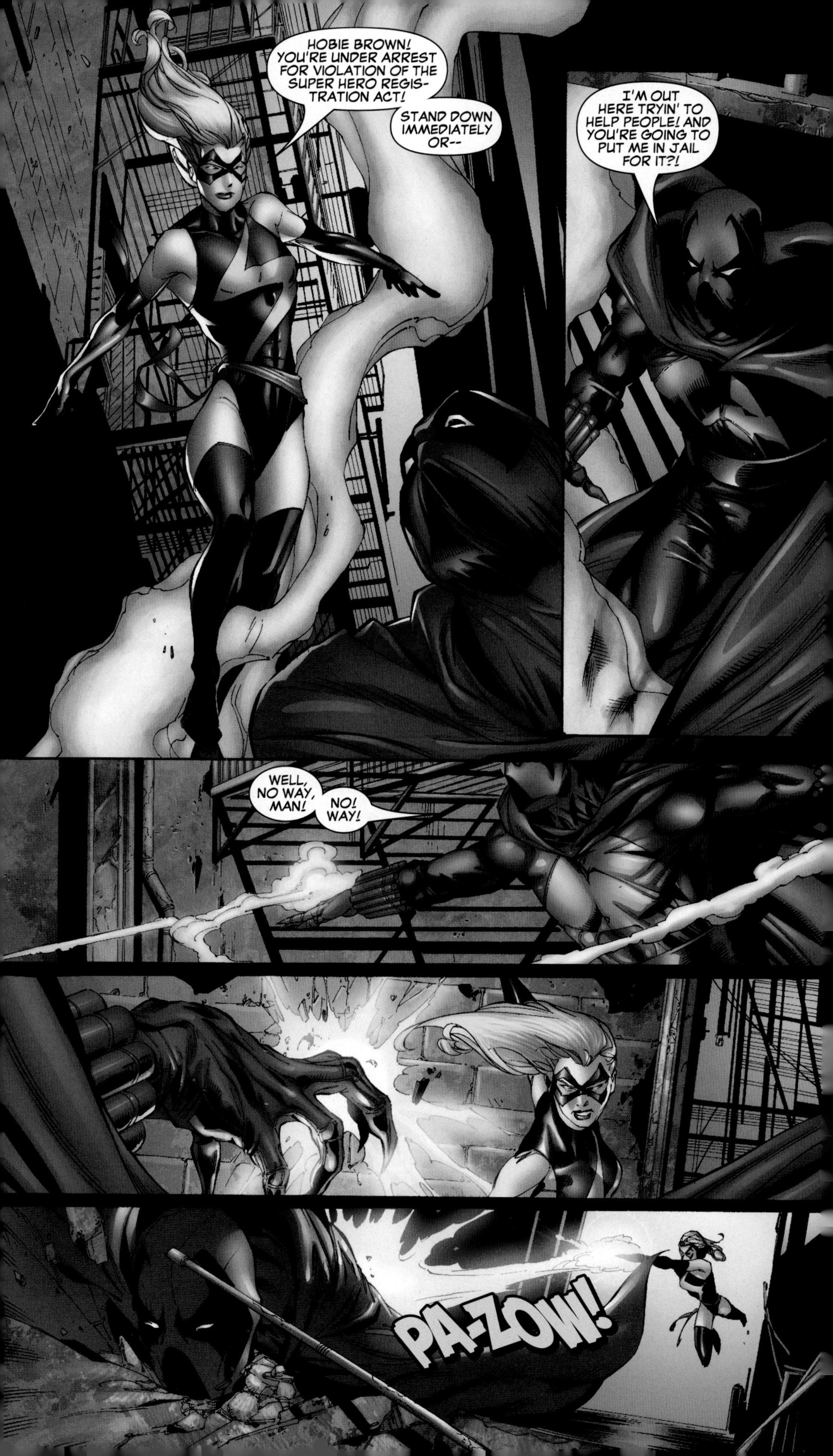
HOBIE BROWN! YOU'RE UNDER ARREST FOR VIOLATION OF THE SUPER HERO REGIS-TRATION ACT!
STAND DOWN IMMEDIATELY OR--
I'M OUT HERE TRYIN' TO HELP PEOPLE! AND YOU'RE GOING TO PUT ME IN JAIL FOR IT?!
WELL, NO WAY, MAN!
NO! WAY!
PA-ZOW!

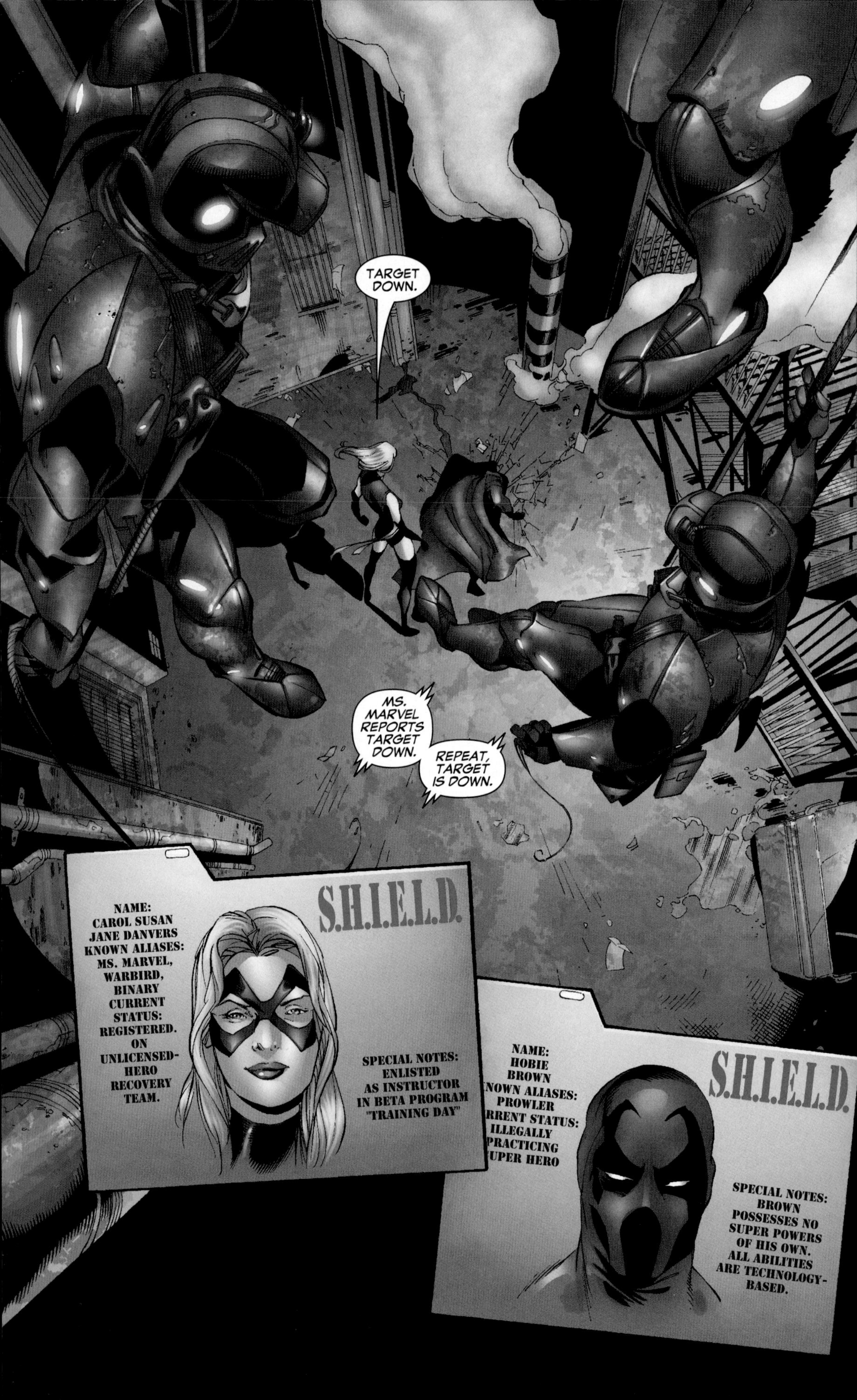

TARGET DOWN.
MS. MARVEL REPORTS TARGET DOWN.
REPEAT, TARGET IS DOWN.
S.H.I.E.L.D.
NAME: CAROL SUSAN JANE DANVERS
KNOWN ALIASES: MS. MARVEL, WARBIRD, BINARY
CURRENT STATUS: REGISTERED. ON UNLICENSED-HERO RECOVERY TEAM.
SPECIAL NOTES: ENLISTED AS INSTRUCTOR IN BETA PROGRAM "TRAINING DAY"
S.H.I.E.L.D.
NAME: HOBIE BROWN
NOWN ALIASES: PROWLER
RRENT STATUS: ILLEGALLY PRACTICING UPER HERO
SPECIAL NOTES: BROWN POSSESSES NO SUPER POWERS OF HIS OWN. ALL ABILITIES ARE TECHNOLOGY-BASED.

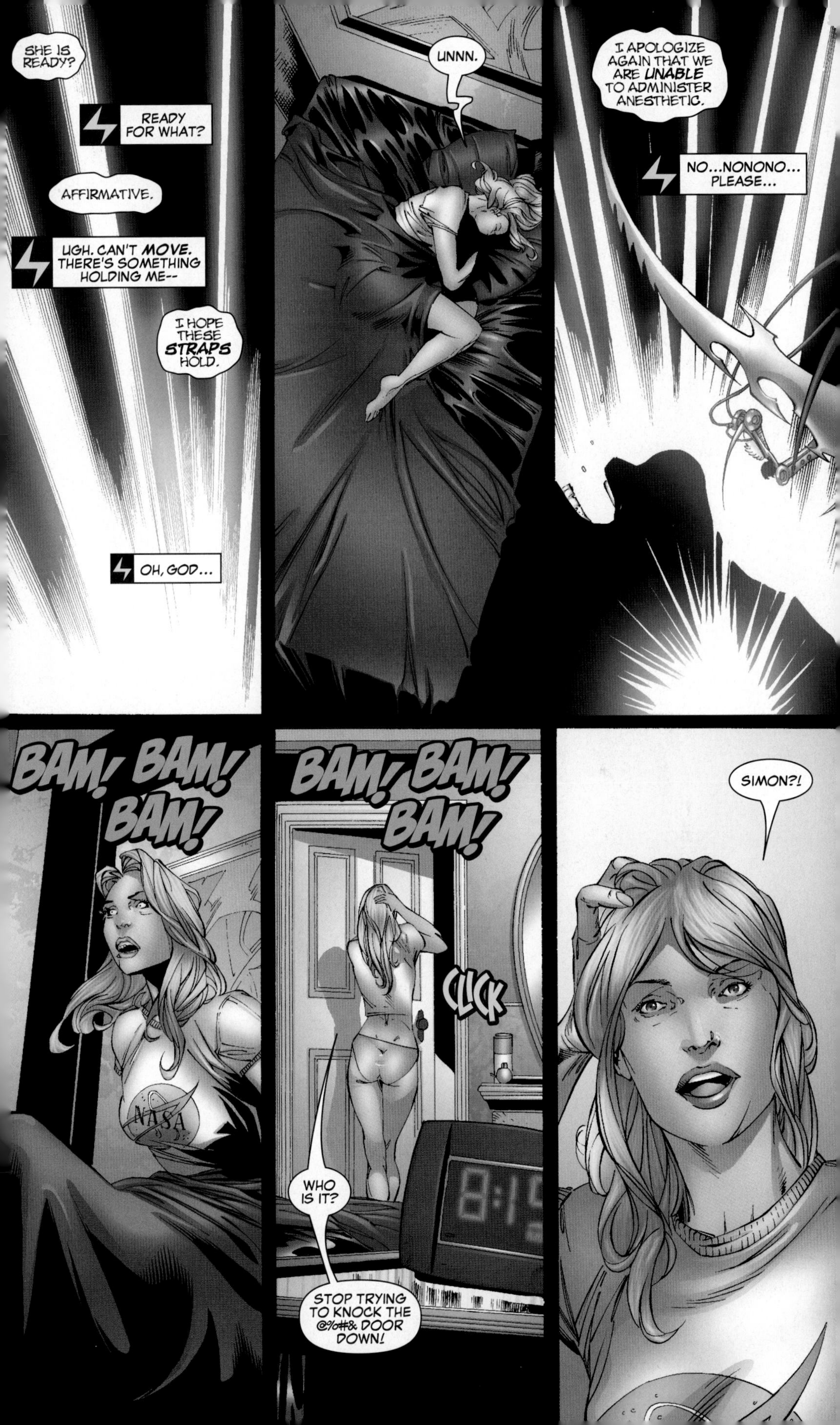
SHE IS READY?
READY FOR WHAT?
AFFIRMATIVE.
UGH. CAN'T MOVE. THERE'S SOMETHING HOLDING ME--
I HOPE THESE STRAPS HOLD.
OH, GOD...
UNNN.
I APOLOGIZE AGAIN THAT WE ARE UNABLE TO ADMINISTER ANESTHETIC.
NO...NONONO... PLEASE...
BAM! BAM! BAM!
NASA
BAM! BAM! BAM!
CLICK
WHO IS IT?
STOP TRYING TO KNOCK THE @%#& DOOR DOWN!
SIMON?!

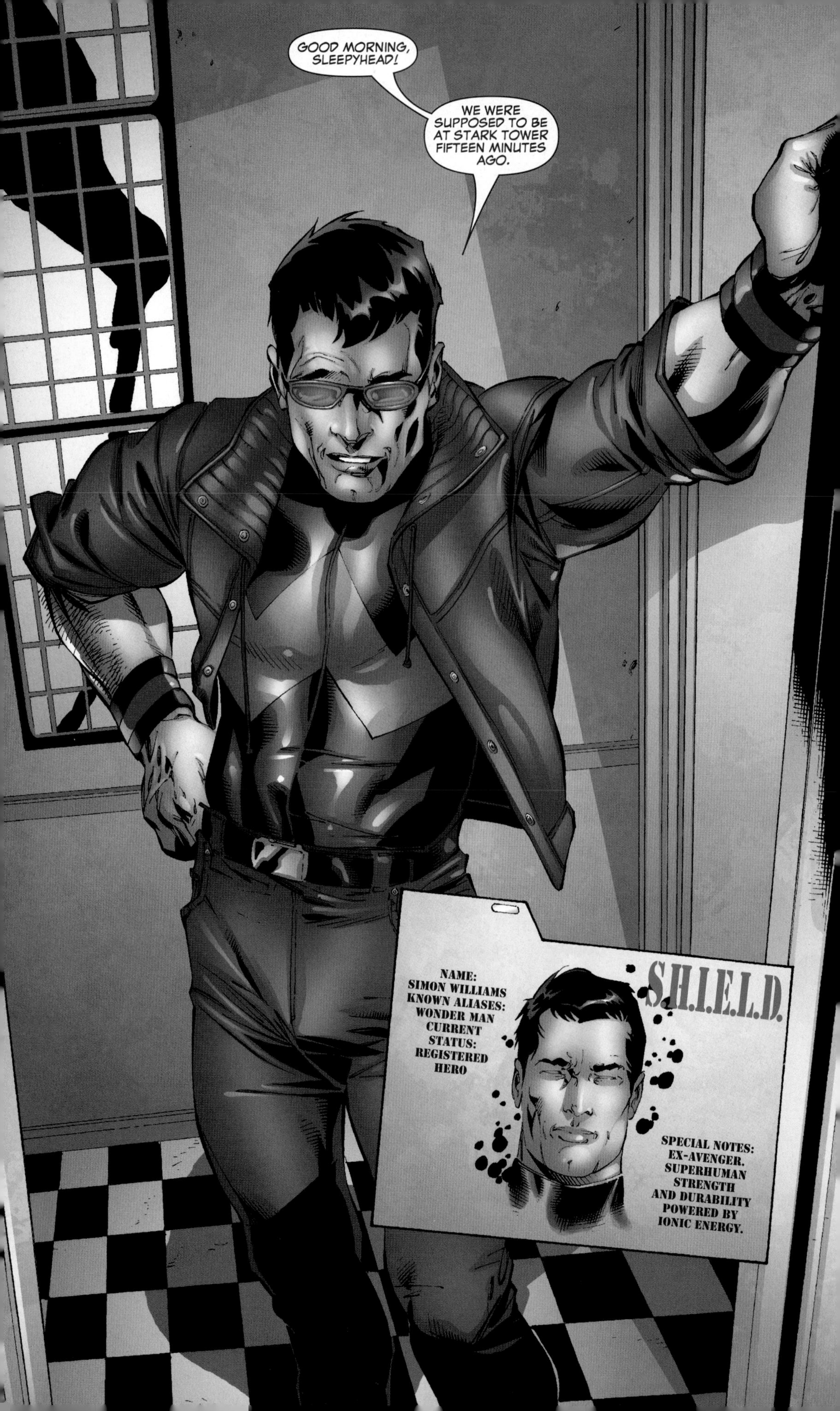
GOOD MORNING, SLEEPYHEAD!
WE WERE SUPPOSED TO BE AT STARK TOWER FIFTEEN MINUTES AGO.
NAME: SIMON WILLIAMS KNOWN ALIASES: WONDER MAN CURRENT STATUS: REGISTERED HERO
S.H.I.E.L.D.
SPECIAL NOTES: EX-AVENGER. SUPERHUMAN STRENGTH AND DURABILITY POWERED BY IONIC ENERGY.

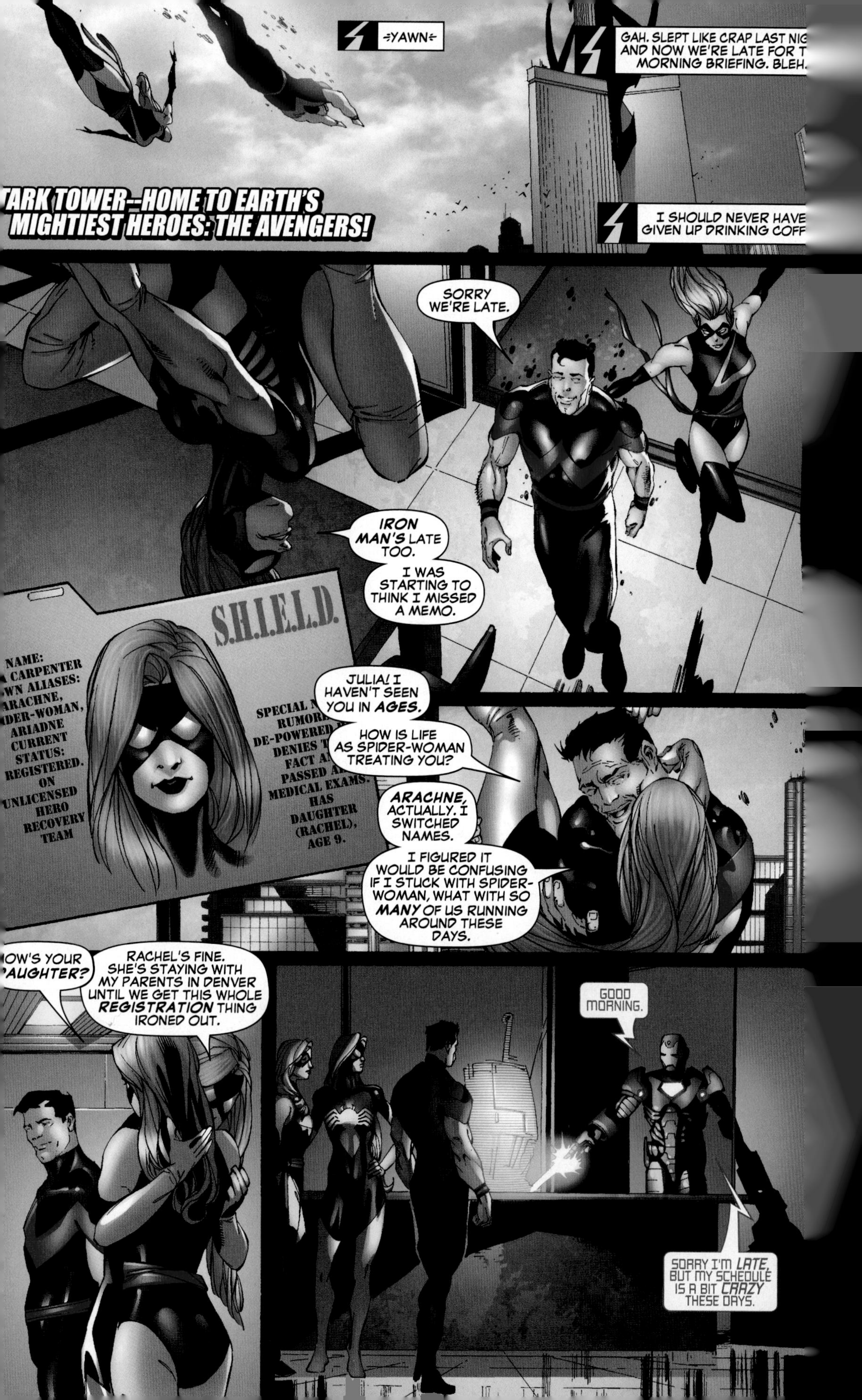
=YAWN=
GAH. SLEPT LIKE CRAP LAST NIG
AND NOW WE'RE LATE FOR T
MORNING BRIEFING. BLEH.
TARK TOWER--HOME TO EARTH'S MIGHTIEST HEROES: THE AVENGERS!
I SHOULD NEVER HAVE GIVEN UP DRINKING COFF
SORRY WE'RE LATE.
IRON MAN'S LATE TOO.
I WAS STARTING TO THINK I MISSED A MEMO.
S.H.I.E.L.D.
NAME:
A CARPENTER
WN ALIASES:
ARACHNE,
DER-WOMAN,
ARIADNE
CURRENT
STATUS:
REGISTERED.
ON
UNLICENSED
HERO
RECOVERY
TEAM
SPECIAL N
RUMOR
DE-POWERED
DENIES T
FACT A
PASSED A
MEDICAL EXAMS.
HAS
DAUGHTER
(RACHEL),
AGE 9.
JULIA! I HAVEN'T SEEN YOU IN AGES.
HOW IS LIFE AS SPIDER-WOMAN TREATING YOU?
ARACHNE, ACTUALLY. I SWITCHED NAMES.
I FIGURED IT WOULD BE CONFUSING IF I STUCK WITH SPIDER-WOMAN, WHAT WITH SO MANY OF US RUNNING AROUND THESE DAYS.
OW'S YOUR AUGHTER?
RACHEL'S FINE. SHE'S STAYING WITH MY PARENTS IN DENVER UNTIL WE GET THIS WHOLE REGISTRATION THING IRONED OUT.
GOOD MORNING.
SORRY I'M LATE, BUT MY SCHEDULE IS A BIT CRAZY THESE DAYS.

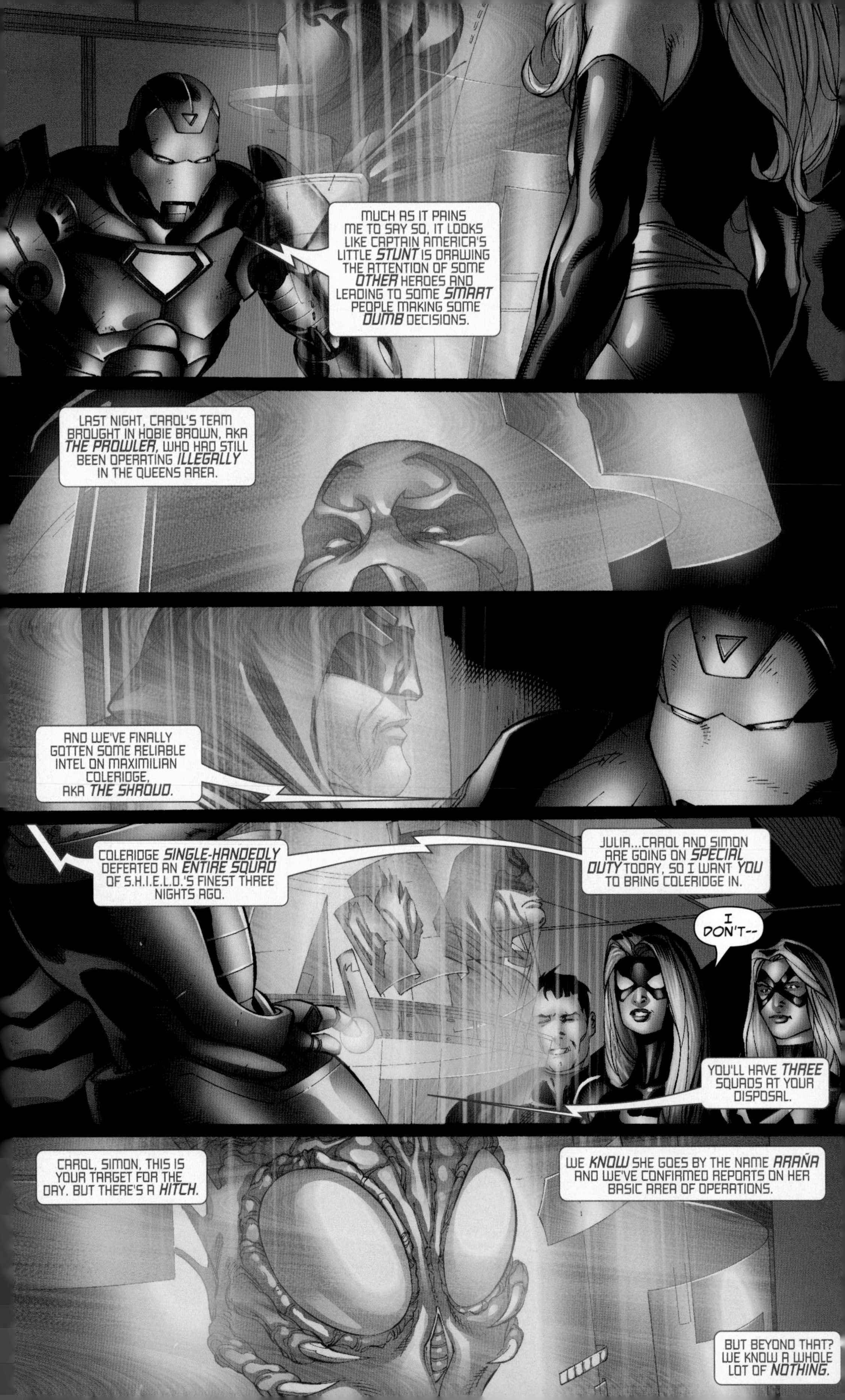
MUCH AS IT PAINS ME TO SAY SO, IT LOOKS LIKE CAPTAIN AMERICA'S LITTLE STUNT IS DRAWING THE ATTENTION OF SOME OTHER HEROES AND LEADING TO SOME SMART PEOPLE MAKING SOME DUMB DECISIONS.
LAST NIGHT, CAROL'S TEAM BROUGHT IN HOBIE BROWN, AKA THE PROWLER, WHO HAD STILL BEEN OPERATING ILLEGALLY IN THE QUEENS AREA.
AND WE'VE FINALLY GOTTEN SOME RELIABLE INTEL ON MAXIMILIAN COLERIDGE, AKA THE SHROUD.
COLERIDGE SINGLE-HANDEDLY DEFEATED AN ENTIRE SQUAD OF S.H.I.E.L.D.'S FINEST THREE NIGHTS AGO.
JULIA...CAROL AND SIMON ARE GOING ON SPECIAL DUTY TODAY, SO I WANT YOU TO BRING COLERIDGE IN.
I DON'T--
YOU'LL HAVE THREE SQUADS AT YOUR DISPOSAL.
CAROL, SIMON, THIS IS YOUR TARGET FOR THE DAY. BUT THERE'S A HITCH.
WE KNOW SHE GOES BY THE NAME ARAÑA AND WE'VE CONFIRMED REPORTS ON HER BASIC AREA OF OPERATIONS.
BUT BEYOND THAT? WE KNOW A WHOLE LOT OF NOTHING.

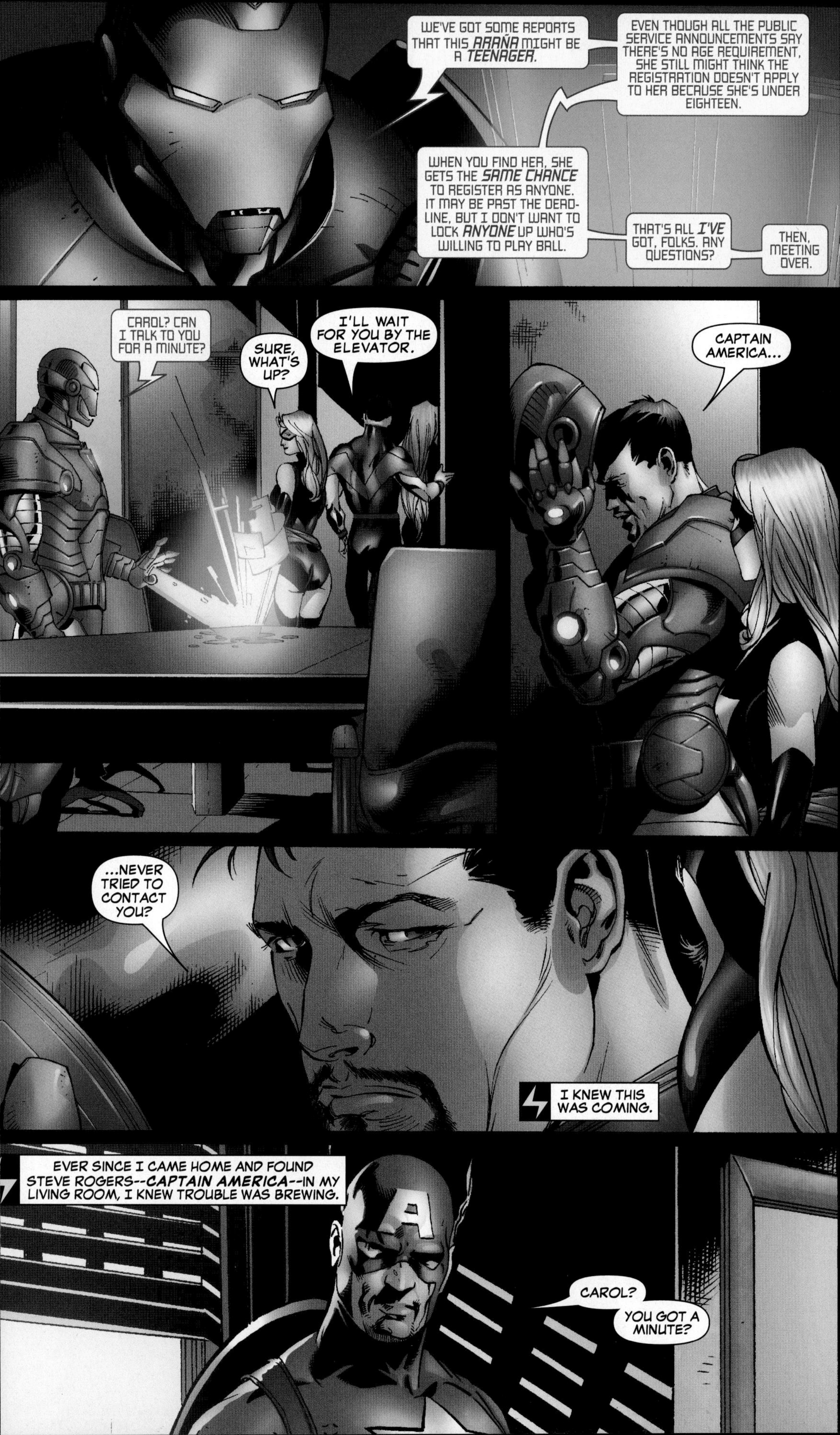
WE'VE GOT SOME REPORTS THAT THIS ARAÑA MIGHT BE A TEENAGER.
EVEN THOUGH ALL THE PUBLIC SERVICE ANNOUNCEMENTS SAY THERE'S NO AGE REQUIREMENT, SHE STILL MIGHT THINK THE REGISTRATION DOESN'T APPLY TO HER BECAUSE SHE'S UNDER EIGHTEEN.
WHEN YOU FIND HER, SHE GETS THE SAME CHANCE TO REGISTER AS ANYONE. IT MAY BE PAST THE DEAD-LINE, BUT I DON'T WANT TO LOCK ANYONE UP WHO'S WILLING TO PLAY BALL.
THAT'S ALL I'VE GOT, FOLKS. ANY QUESTIONS?
THEN, MEETING OVER.
CAROL? CAN I TALK TO YOU FOR A MINUTE?
SURE, WHAT'S UP?
I'LL WAIT FOR YOU BY THE ELEVATOR.
CAPTAIN AMERICA...
...NEVER TRIED TO CONTACT YOU?
I KNEW THIS WAS COMING.
EVER SINCE I CAME HOME AND FOUND STEVE ROGERS--CAPTAIN AMERICA--IN MY LIVING ROOM, I KNEW TROUBLE WAS BREWING.
CAROL?
YOU GOT A MINUTE?

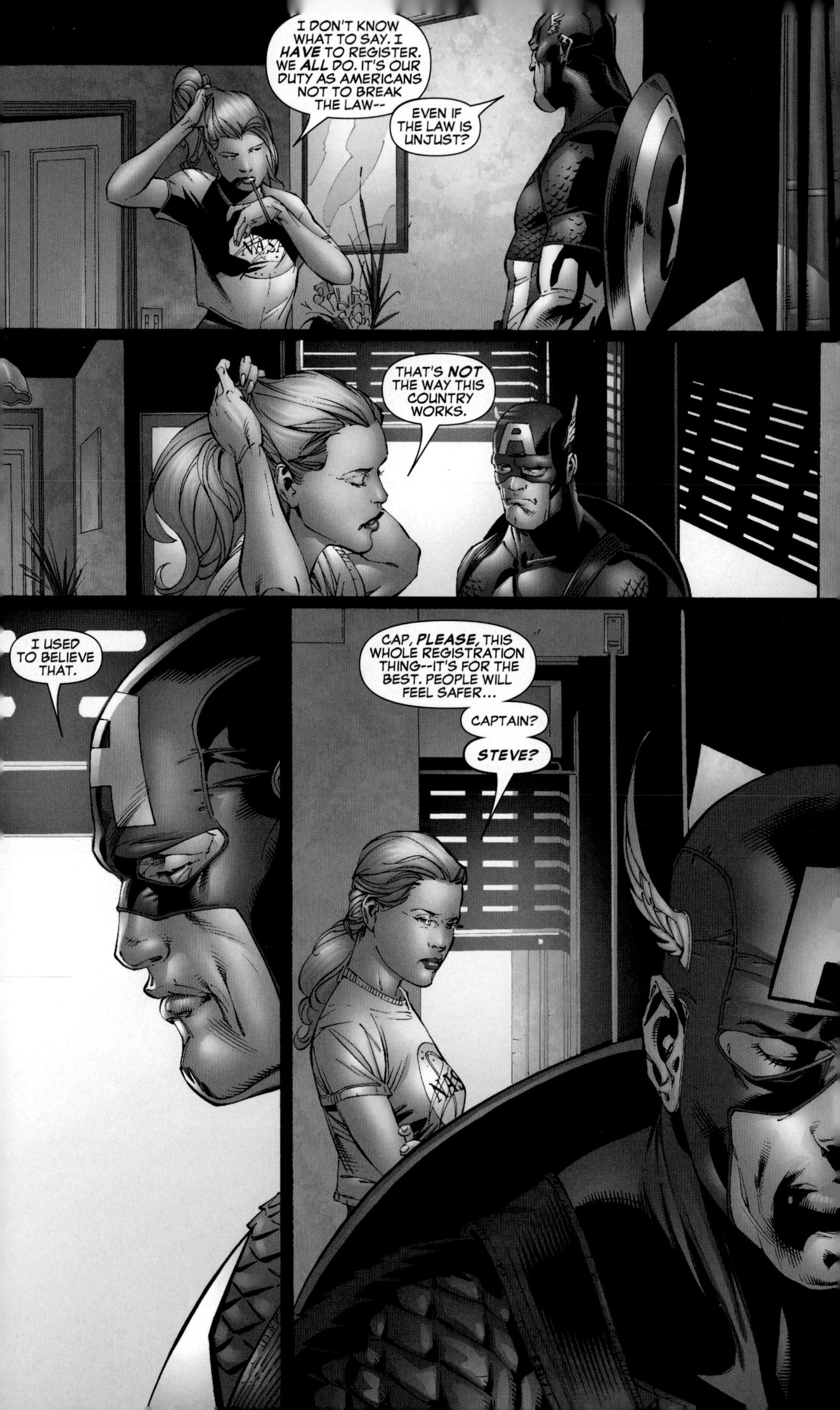

I DON'T KNOW WHAT TO SAY. I *HAVE* TO REGISTER. WE *ALL* DO. IT'S OUR DUTY AS AMERICANS NOT TO BREAK THE LAW--
EVEN IF THE LAW IS UNJUST?
THAT'S *NOT* THE WAY THIS COUNTRY WORKS.
I USED TO BELIEVE THAT.
CAP, *PLEASE,* THIS WHOLE REGISTRATION THING--IT'S FOR THE BEST. PEOPLE WILL FEEL SAFER...
CAPTAIN?
STEVE?

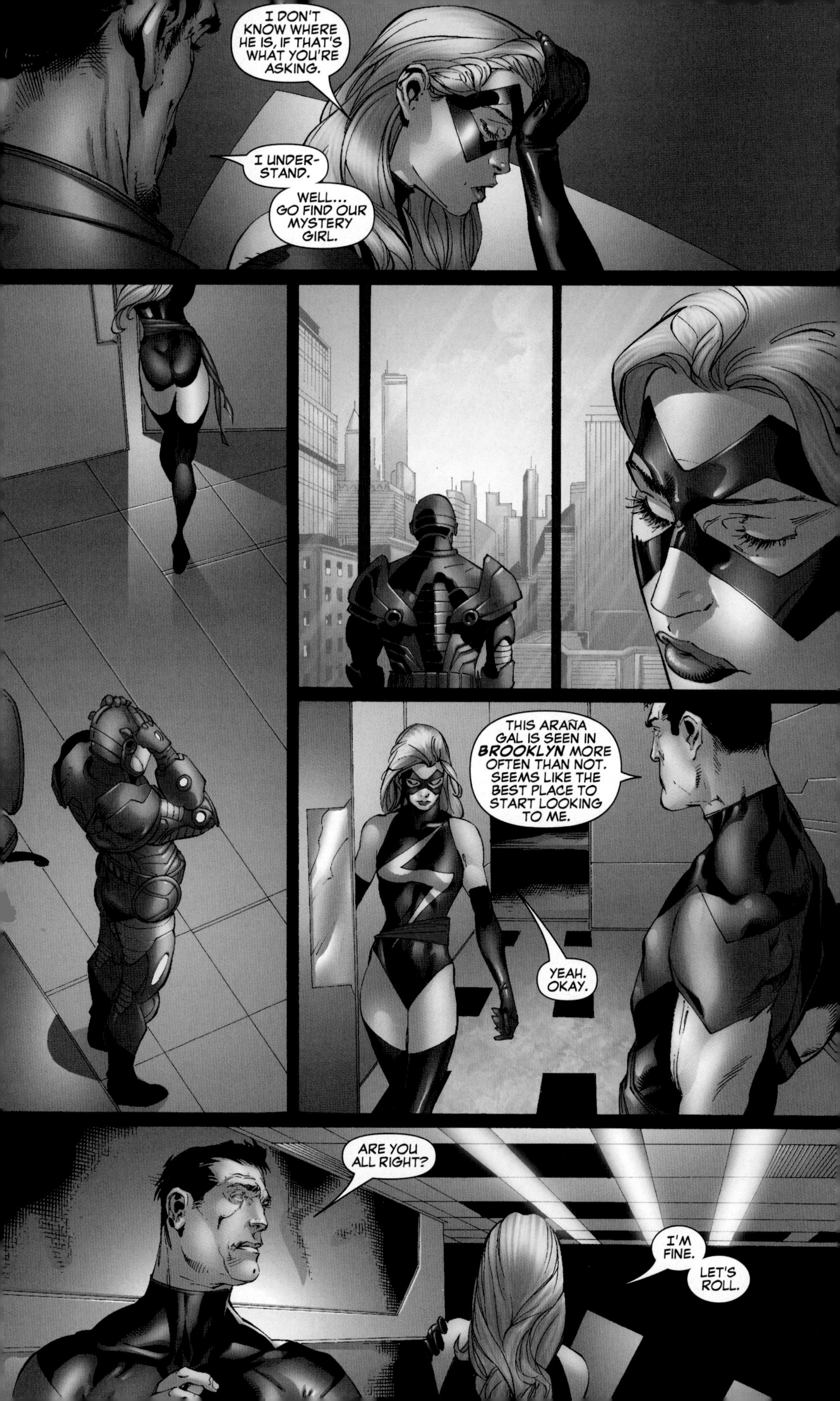
I DON'T KNOW WHERE HE IS, IF THAT'S WHAT YOU'RE ASKING.
I UNDER-STAND.
WELL... GO FIND OUR MYSTERY GIRL.
THIS ARAÑA GAL IS SEEN IN **BROOKLYN** MORE OFTEN THAN NOT. SEEMS LIKE THE BEST PLACE TO START LOOKING TO ME.
YEAH. OKAY.
ARE YOU ALL RIGHT?
I'M FINE.
LET'S ROLL.

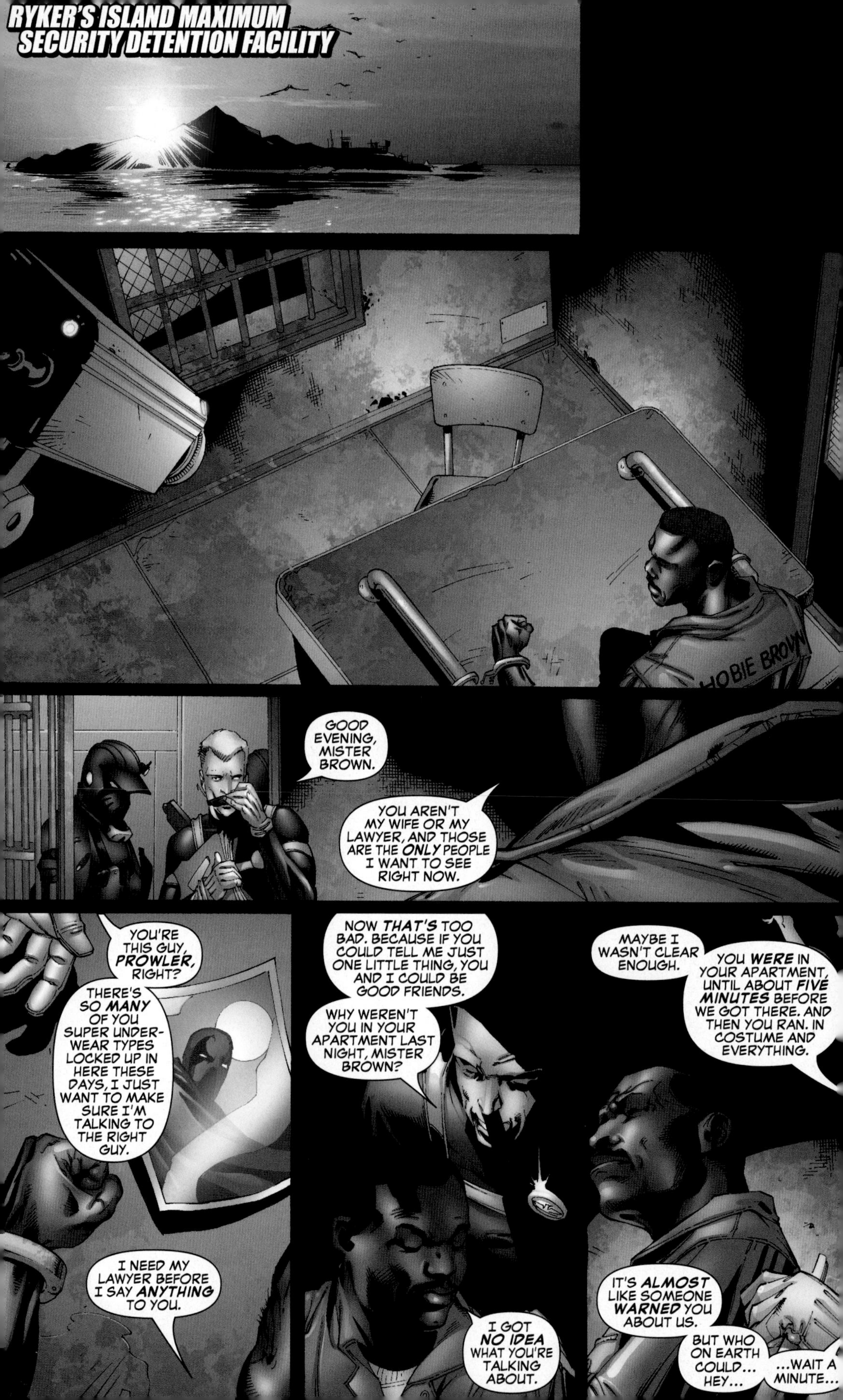
RYKER'S ISLAND MAXIMUM SECURITY DETENTION FACILITY
HOBIE BROWN
GOOD EVENING, MISTER BROWN.
YOU AREN'T MY WIFE OR MY LAWYER, AND THOSE ARE THE ONLY PEOPLE I WANT TO SEE RIGHT NOW.
YOU'RE THIS GUY, PROWLER, RIGHT?
THERE'S SO MANY OF YOU SUPER UNDER-WEAR TYPES LOCKED UP IN HERE THESE DAYS, I JUST WANT TO MAKE SURE I'M TALKING TO THE RIGHT GUY.
I NEED MY LAWYER BEFORE I SAY ANYTHING TO YOU.
NOW THAT'S TOO BAD. BECAUSE IF YOU COULD TELL ME JUST ONE LITTLE THING, YOU AND I COULD BE GOOD FRIENDS.
WHY WEREN'T YOU IN YOUR APARTMENT LAST NIGHT, MISTER BROWN?
I GOT NO IDEA WHAT YOU'RE TALKING ABOUT.
MAYBE I WASN'T CLEAR ENOUGH.
YOU WERE IN YOUR APARTMENT, UNTIL ABOUT FIVE MINUTES BEFORE WE GOT THERE. AND THEN YOU RAN. IN COSTUME AND EVERYTHING.
IT'S ALMOST LIKE SOMEONE WARNED YOU ABOUT US.
BUT WHO ON EARTH COULD... HEY...
...WAIT A MINUTE...

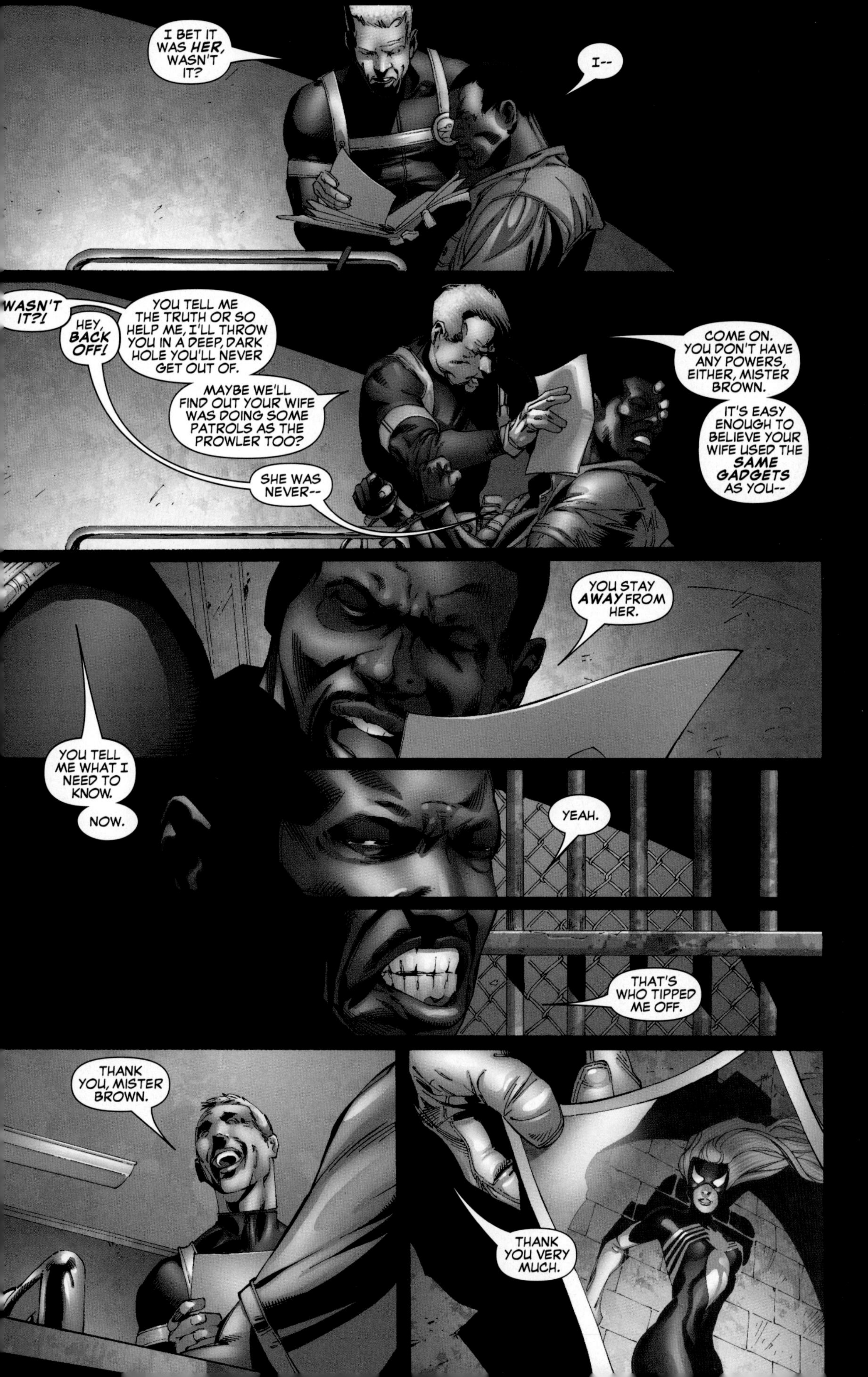
I BET IT WAS HER, WASN'T IT?
I--
WASN'T IT?!
YOU TELL ME THE TRUTH OR SO HELP ME, I'LL THROW YOU IN A DEEP, DARK HOLE YOU'LL NEVER GET OUT OF.
HEY, BACK OFF!
MAYBE WE'LL FIND OUT YOUR WIFE WAS DOING SOME PATROLS AS THE PROWLER TOO?
SHE WAS NEVER--
COME ON. YOU DON'T HAVE ANY POWERS, EITHER, MISTER BROWN.
IT'S EASY ENOUGH TO BELIEVE YOUR WIFE USED THE SAME GADGETS AS YOU--
YOU STAY AWAY FROM HER.
YOU TELL ME WHAT I NEED TO KNOW.
NOW.
YEAH.
THAT'S WHO TIPPED ME OFF.
THANK YOU, MISTER BROWN.
THANK YOU VERY MUCH.

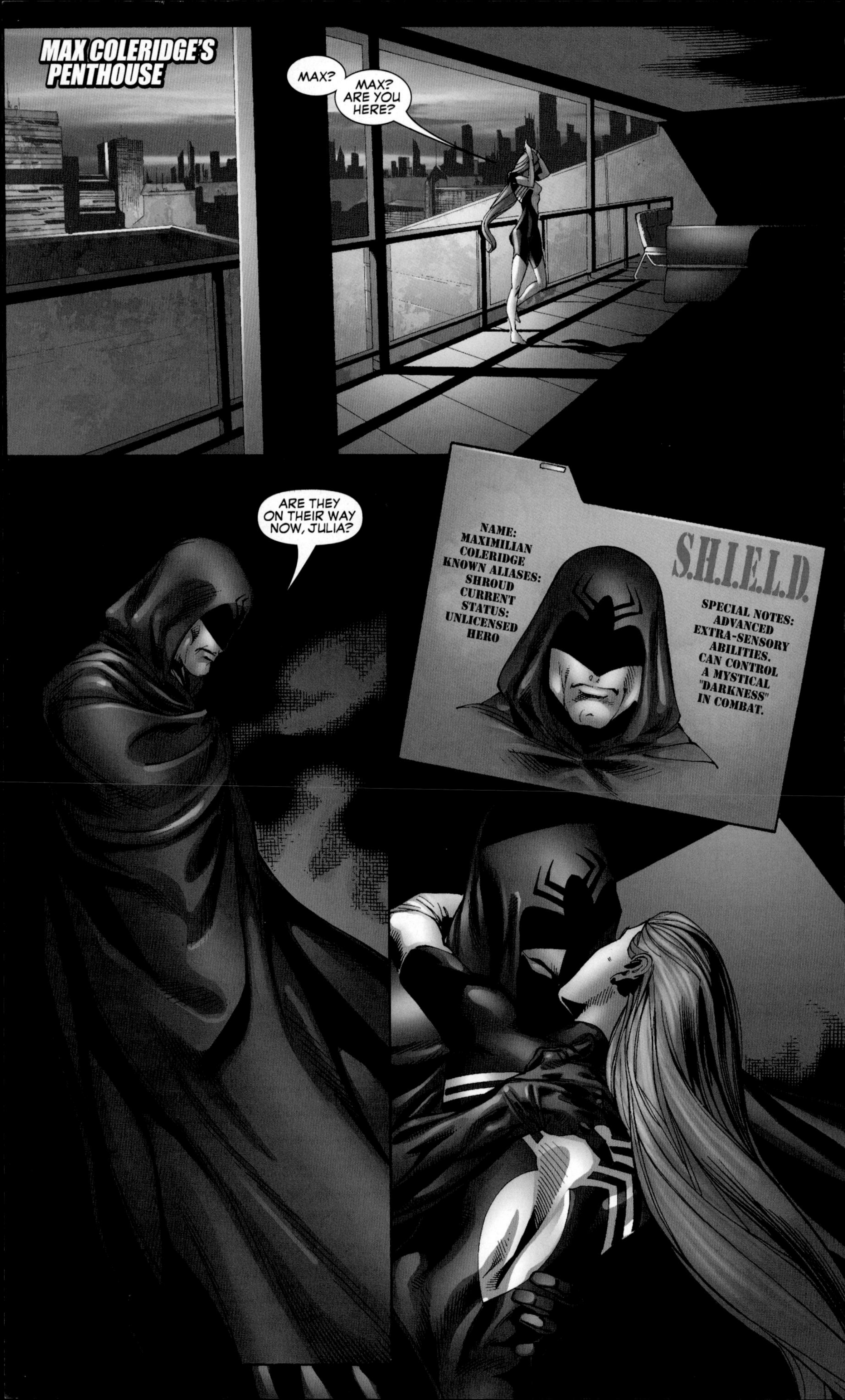
MAX COLERIDGE'S PENTHOUSE
MAX?
MAX? ARE YOU HERE?
ARE THEY ON THEIR WAY NOW, JULIA?
NAME: MAXIMILIAN COLERIDGE KNOWN ALIASES: SHROUD CURRENT STATUS: UNLICENSED HERO
S.H.I.E.L.D.
SPECIAL NOTES: ADVANCED EXTRA-SENSORY ABILITIES. CAN CONTROL A MYSTICAL "DARKNESS" IN COMBAT.

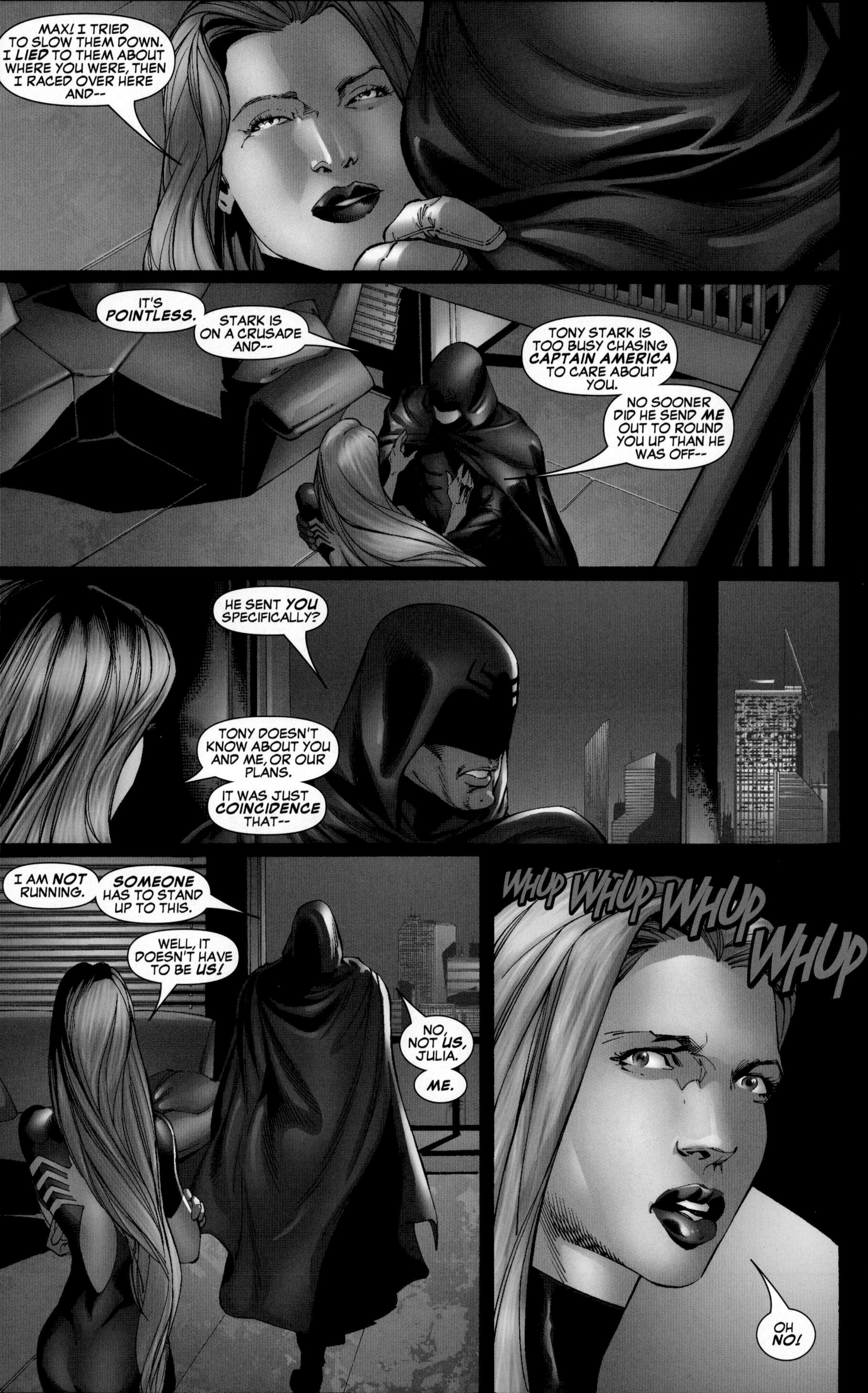

MAX! I TRIED TO SLOW THEM DOWN. I LIED TO THEM ABOUT WHERE YOU WERE, THEN I RACED OVER HERE AND--
IT'S POINTLESS.
STARK IS ON A CRUSADE AND--
TONY STARK IS TOO BUSY CHASING CAPTAIN AMERICA TO CARE ABOUT YOU.
NO SOONER DID HE SEND ME OUT TO ROUND YOU UP THAN HE WAS OFF--
HE SENT YOU SPECIFICALLY?
TONY DOESN'T KNOW ABOUT YOU AND ME, OR OUR PLANS.
IT WAS JUST COINCIDENCE THAT--
I AM NOT RUNNING.
SOMEONE HAS TO STAND UP TO THIS.
WELL, IT DOESN'T HAVE TO BE US!
NO, NOT US, JULIA.
ME.
WHUP WHUP WHUP WHUP
OH NO!

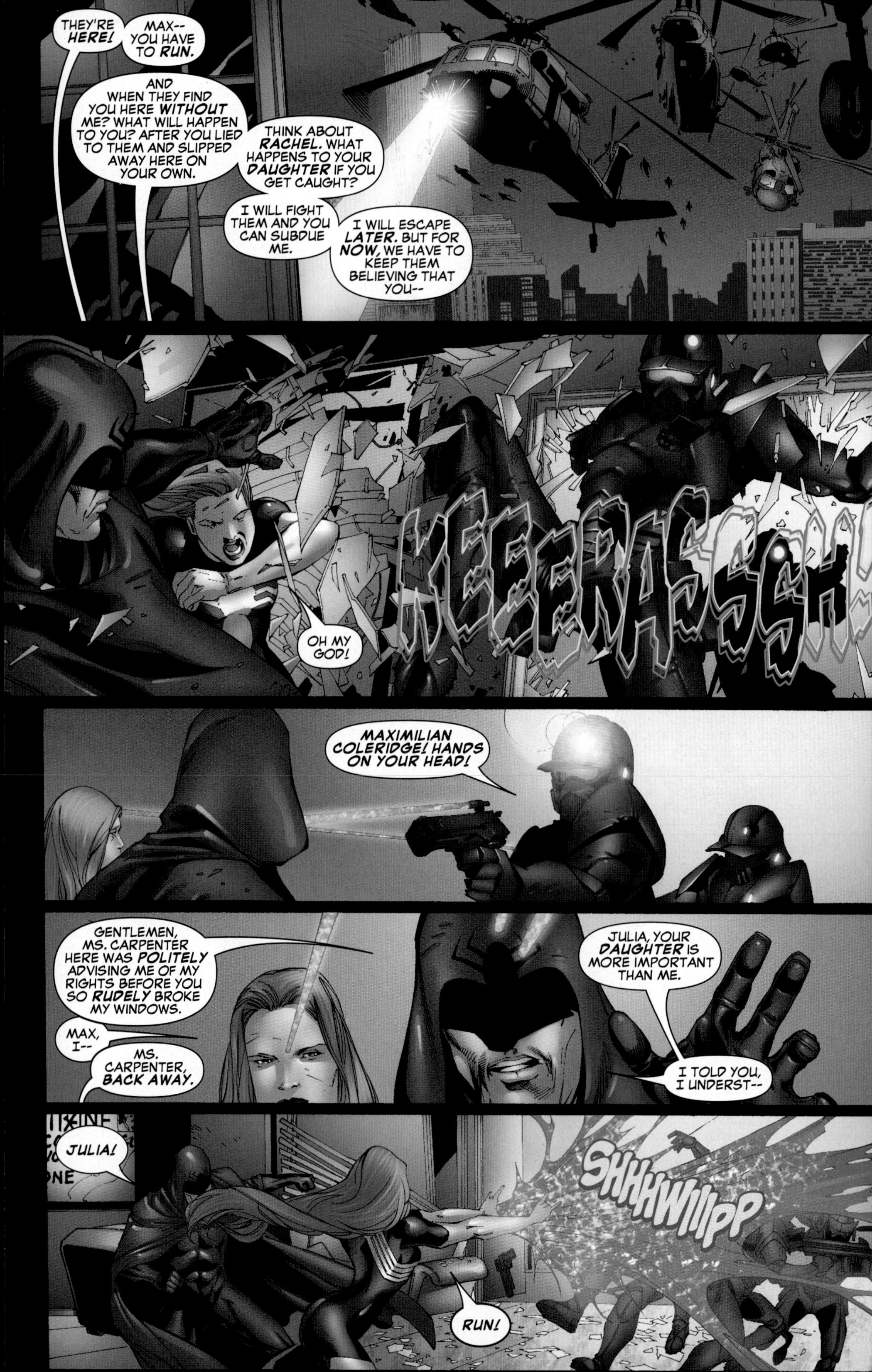
THEY'RE HERE!
MAX-- YOU HAVE TO RUN.
AND WHEN THEY FIND YOU HERE WITHOUT ME? WHAT WILL HAPPEN TO YOU? AFTER YOU LIED TO THEM AND SLIPPED AWAY HERE ON YOUR OWN.
THINK ABOUT RACHEL. WHAT HAPPENS TO YOUR DAUGHTER IF YOU GET CAUGHT?
I WILL FIGHT THEM AND YOU CAN SUBDUE ME.
I WILL ESCAPE LATER. BUT FOR NOW, WE HAVE TO KEEP THEM BELIEVING THAT YOU--
KEEERASSCH
OH MY GOD!
MAXIMILIAN COLERIDGE! HANDS ON YOUR HEAD!
GENTLEMEN, MS. CARPENTER HERE WAS POLITELY ADVISING ME OF MY RIGHTS BEFORE YOU SO RUDELY BROKE MY WINDOWS.
MAX, I--
MS. CARPENTER, BACK AWAY.
JULIA, YOUR DAUGHTER IS MORE IMPORTANT THAN ME.
I TOLD YOU, I UNDERST--
JULIA!
SHHHWIIIPP
RUN!

S.H.I.E.L.D.

NAME:
JULIA CARPENTER
KNOWN ALIASES:
ARACHNE,
SPIDER-WOMAN,
ARIADNE
CURRENT
STATUS:
FUGITIVE.

SPECIAL NOTES:
RUMORED
DE-POWERED BUT
DENIES THIS
FACT AND
PASSED ALL
MEDICAL EXAMS.
HAS
DAUGHTER
RACHEL,
AGE 9.

FUGITIVE

S.H.I.E.L.D.

NAME:
MAXIMILIAN
COLERIDGE
KNOWN ALIASES:
SHROUD
CURRENT
STATUS:
FUGITIVE.

SPECIAL NOTES:
ADVANCED
EXTRA-SENSORY
ABILITIES.
CAN CONTROL
A "MYSTICAL
DARKNESS"
IN COMBAT.

FUGITIVE

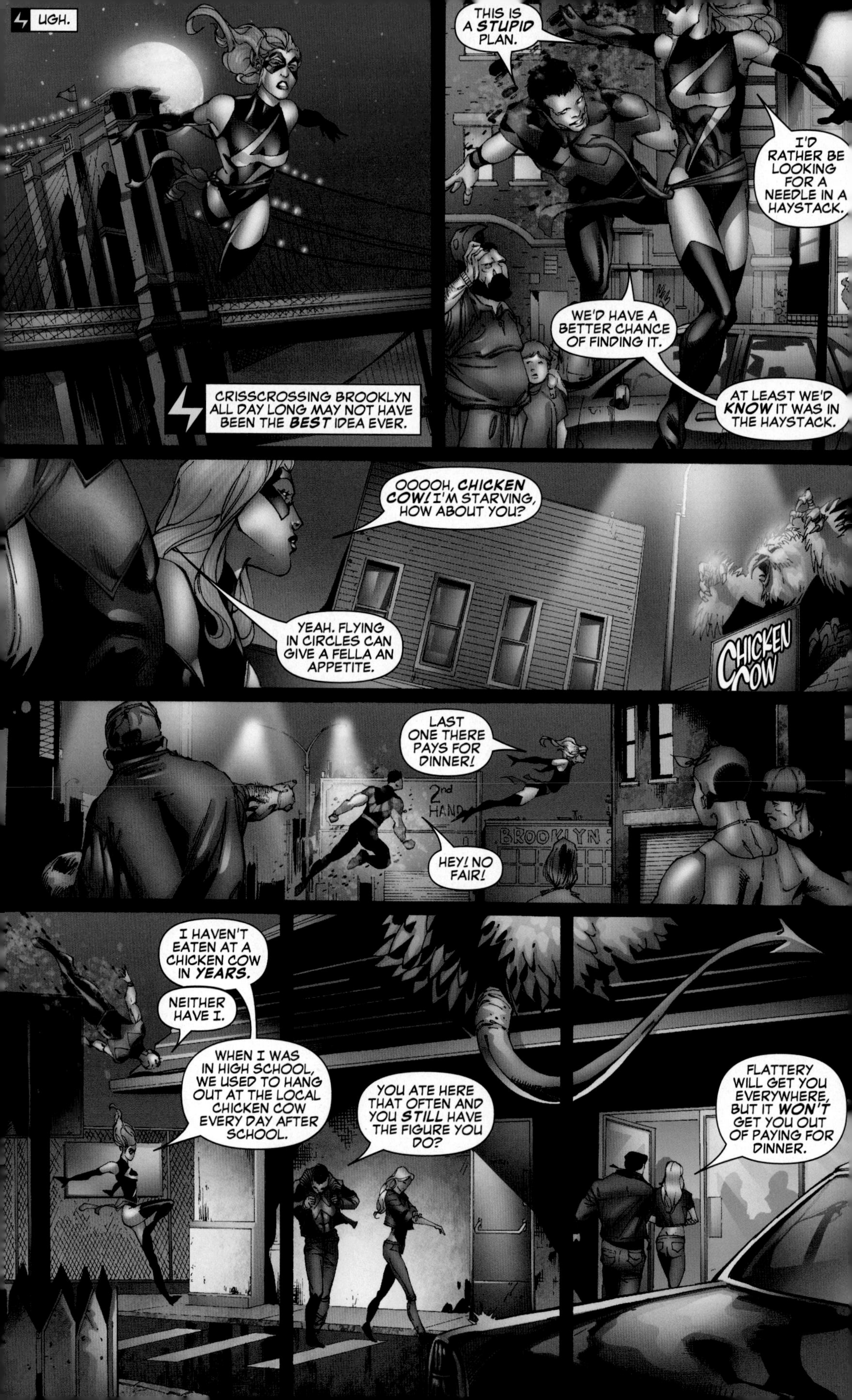
UGH.
CRISSCROSSING BROOKLYN ALL DAY LONG MAY NOT HAVE BEEN THE BEST IDEA EVER.
THIS IS A STUPID PLAN.
I'D RATHER BE LOOKING FOR A NEEDLE IN A HAYSTACK.
WE'D HAVE A BETTER CHANCE OF FINDING IT.
AT LEAST WE'D KNOW IT WAS IN THE HAYSTACK.
OOOOH, CHICKEN COW! I'M STARVING, HOW ABOUT YOU?
YEAH. FLYING IN CIRCLES CAN GIVE A FELLA AN APPETITE.
CHICKEN COW
LAST ONE THERE PAYS FOR DINNER!
2nd HAND
BROOKLYN
HEY! NO FAIR!
I HAVEN'T EATEN AT A CHICKEN COW IN YEARS.
NEITHER HAVE I.
WHEN I WAS IN HIGH SCHOOL, WE USED TO HANG OUT AT THE LOCAL CHICKEN COW EVERY DAY AFTER SCHOOL.
YOU ATE HERE THAT OFTEN AND YOU STILL HAVE THE FIGURE YOU DO?
FLATTERY WILL GET YOU EVERYWHERE, BUT IT WON'T GET YOU OUT OF PAYING FOR DINNER.

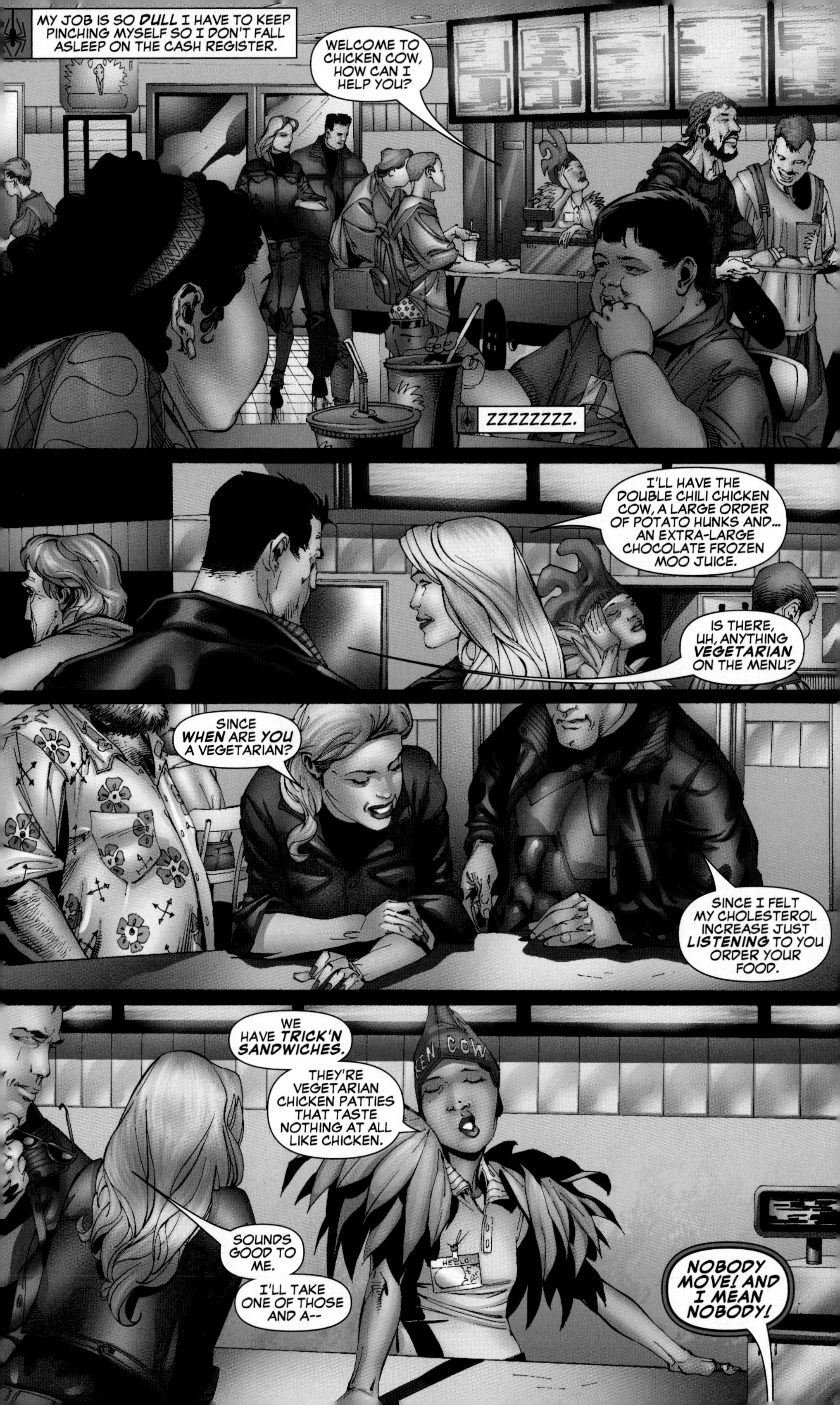

MY JOB IS SO DULL I HAVE TO KEEP PINCHING MYSELF SO I DON'T FALL ASLEEP ON THE CASH REGISTER.
WELCOME TO CHICKEN COW, HOW CAN I HELP YOU?
ZZZZZZZZ.
I'LL HAVE THE DOUBLE CHILI CHICKEN COW, A LARGE ORDER OF POTATO HUNKS AND... AN EXTRA-LARGE CHOCOLATE FROZEN MOO JUICE.
IS THERE, UH, ANYTHING VEGETARIAN ON THE MENU?
SINCE WHEN ARE YOU A VEGETARIAN?
SINCE I FELT MY CHOLESTEROL INCREASE JUST LISTENING TO YOU ORDER YOUR FOOD.
WE HAVE TRICK'N SANDWICHES.
THEY'RE VEGETARIAN CHICKEN PATTIES THAT TASTE NOTHING AT ALL LIKE CHICKEN.
SOUNDS GOOD TO ME.
I'LL TAKE ONE OF THOSE AND A--
NOBODY MOVE! AND I MEAN NOBODY!

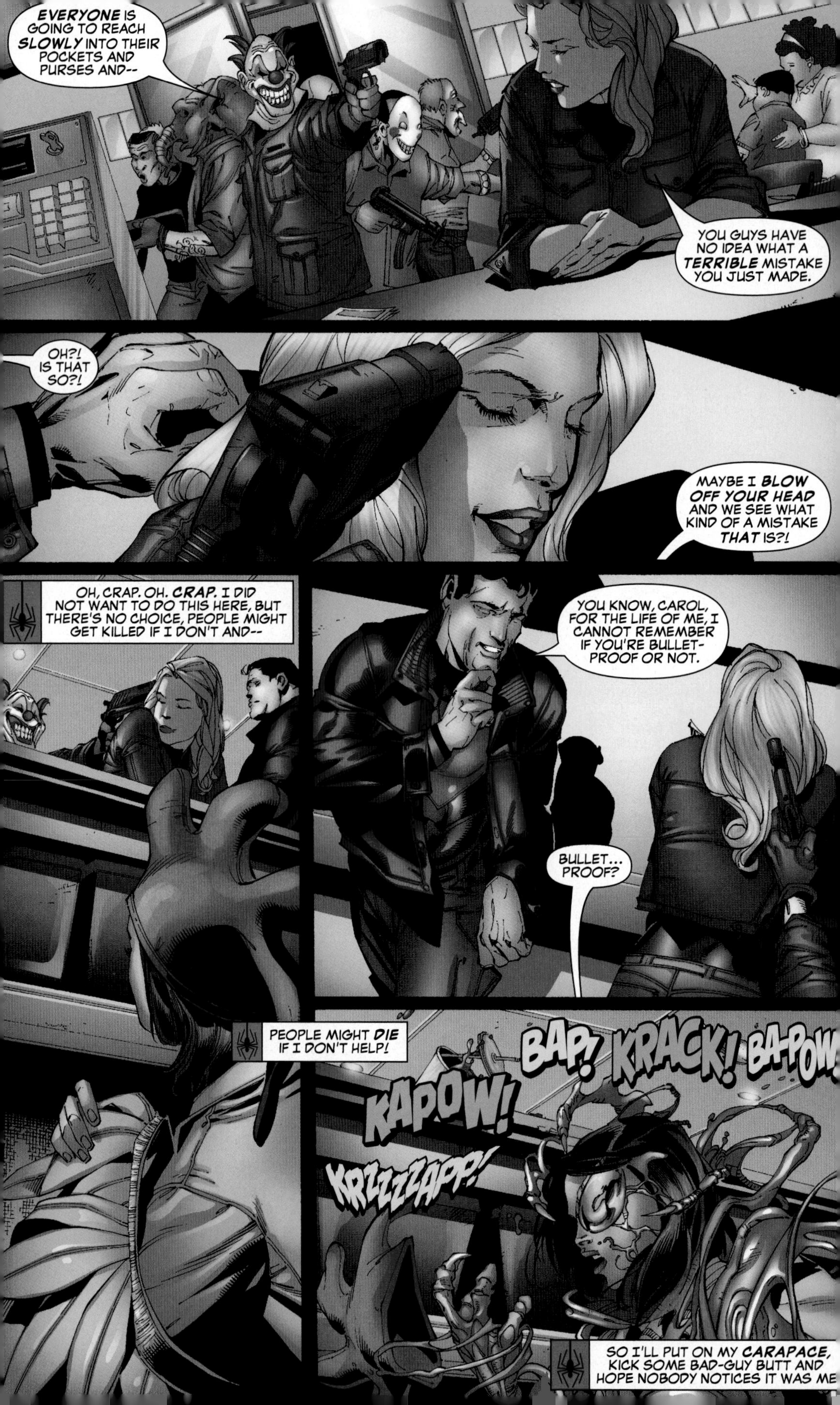
EVERYONE IS GOING TO REACH SLOWLY INTO THEIR POCKETS AND PURSES AND--
YOU GUYS HAVE NO IDEA WHAT A TERRIBLE MISTAKE YOU JUST MADE.
OH?! IS THAT SO?!
MAYBE I BLOW OFF YOUR HEAD AND WE SEE WHAT KIND OF A MISTAKE THAT IS?!
OH, CRAP. OH. CRAP. I DID NOT WANT TO DO THIS HERE, BUT THERE'S NO CHOICE, PEOPLE MIGHT GET KILLED IF I DON'T AND--
YOU KNOW, CAROL, FOR THE LIFE OF ME, I CANNOT REMEMBER IF YOU'RE BULLET-PROOF OR NOT.
BULLET... PROOF?
PEOPLE MIGHT DIE IF I DON'T HELP!
BAP! KRACK! BA-POW!
KAPOW!
KRZZZZAPP!
SO I'LL PUT ON MY CARAPACE, KICK SOME BAD-GUY BUTT AND HOPE NOBODY NOTICES IT WAS ME

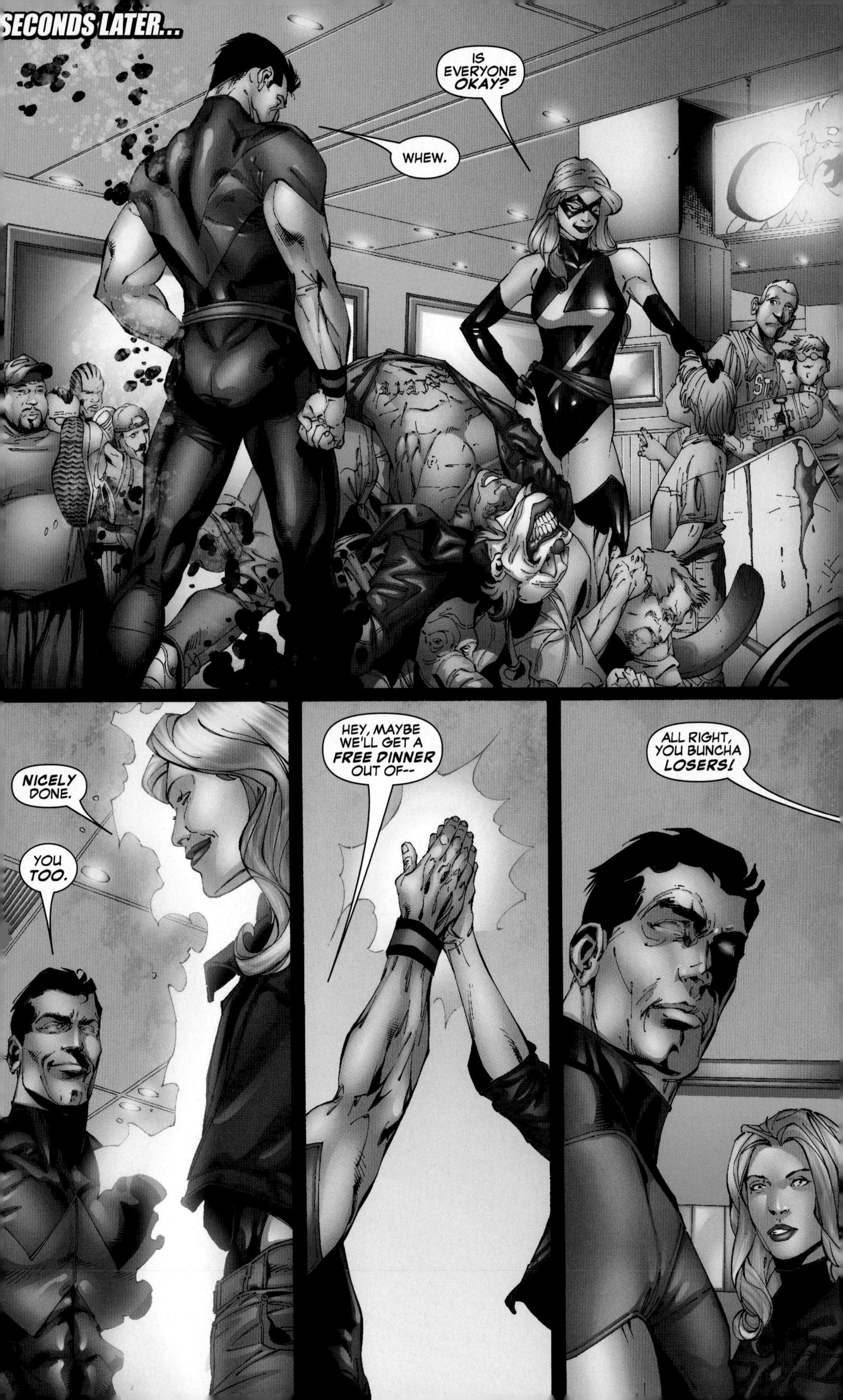
SECONDS LATER...
WHEW.
IS EVERYONE OKAY?
NICELY DONE.
YOU TOO.
HEY, MAYBE WE'LL GET A FREE DINNER OUT OF--
ALL RIGHT, YOU BUNCHA LOSERS!

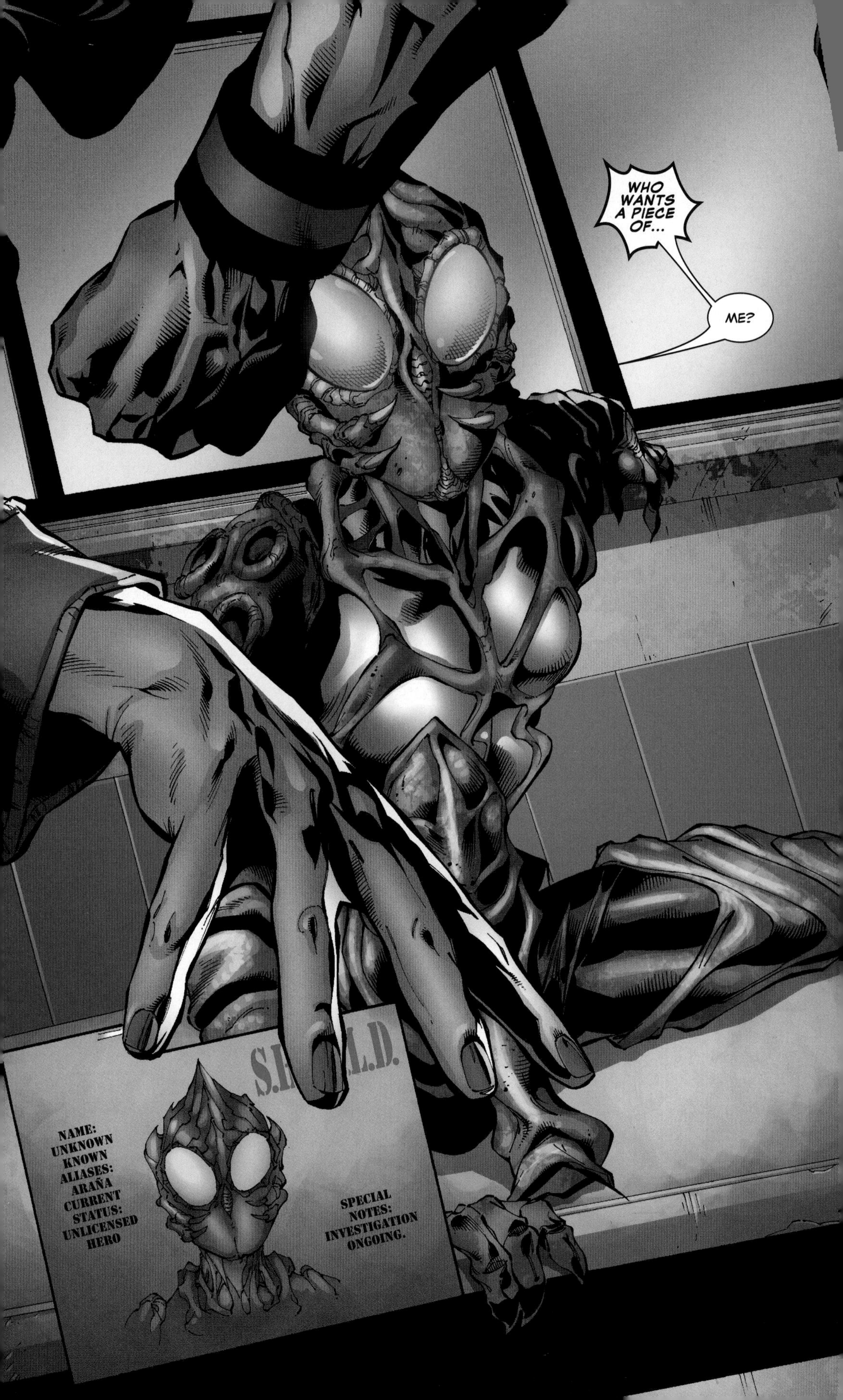
WHO WANTS A PIECE OF...
ME?
S.H.I.E.L.D.
NAME: UNKNOWN
KNOWN ALIASES: ARAÑA
CURRENT STATUS: UNLICENSED HERO
SPECIAL NOTES: INVESTIGATION ONGOING.

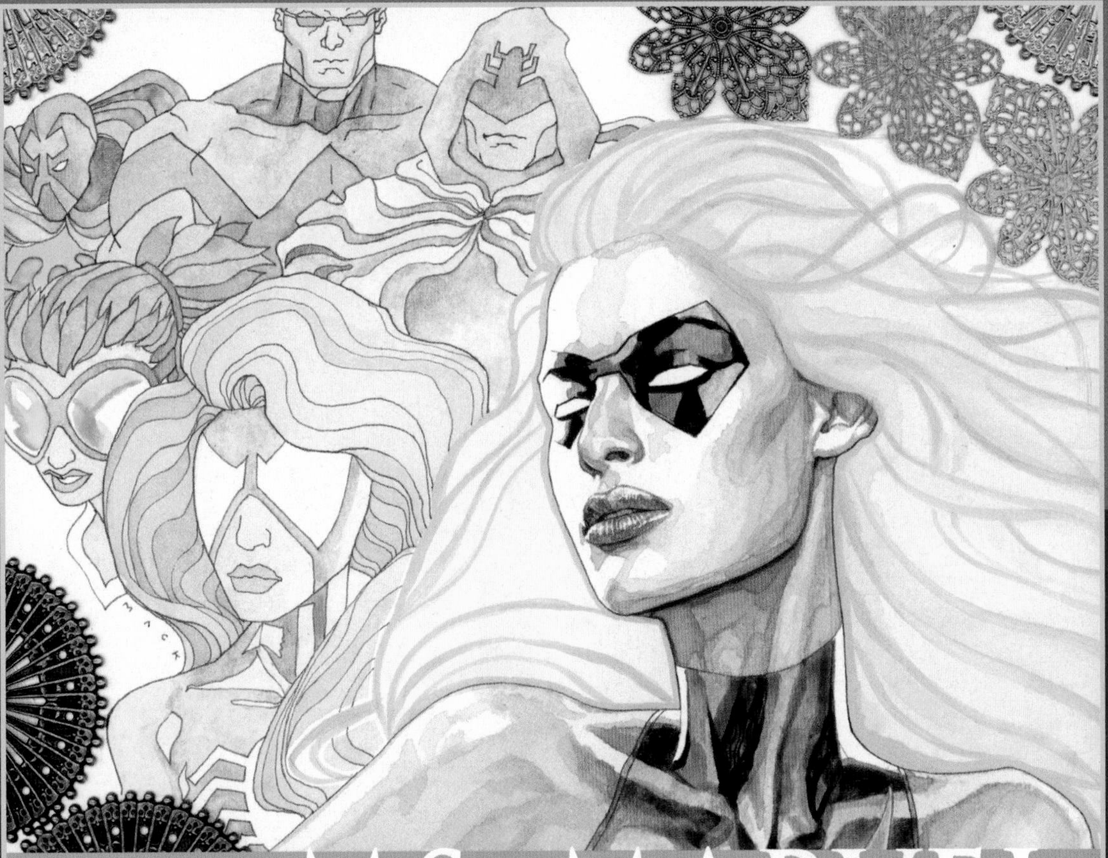
MACK

MS. MARVEL

A MARVEL COMICS EVENT

CIVIL WAR

7

"BATTLE LINES (PART 2)"

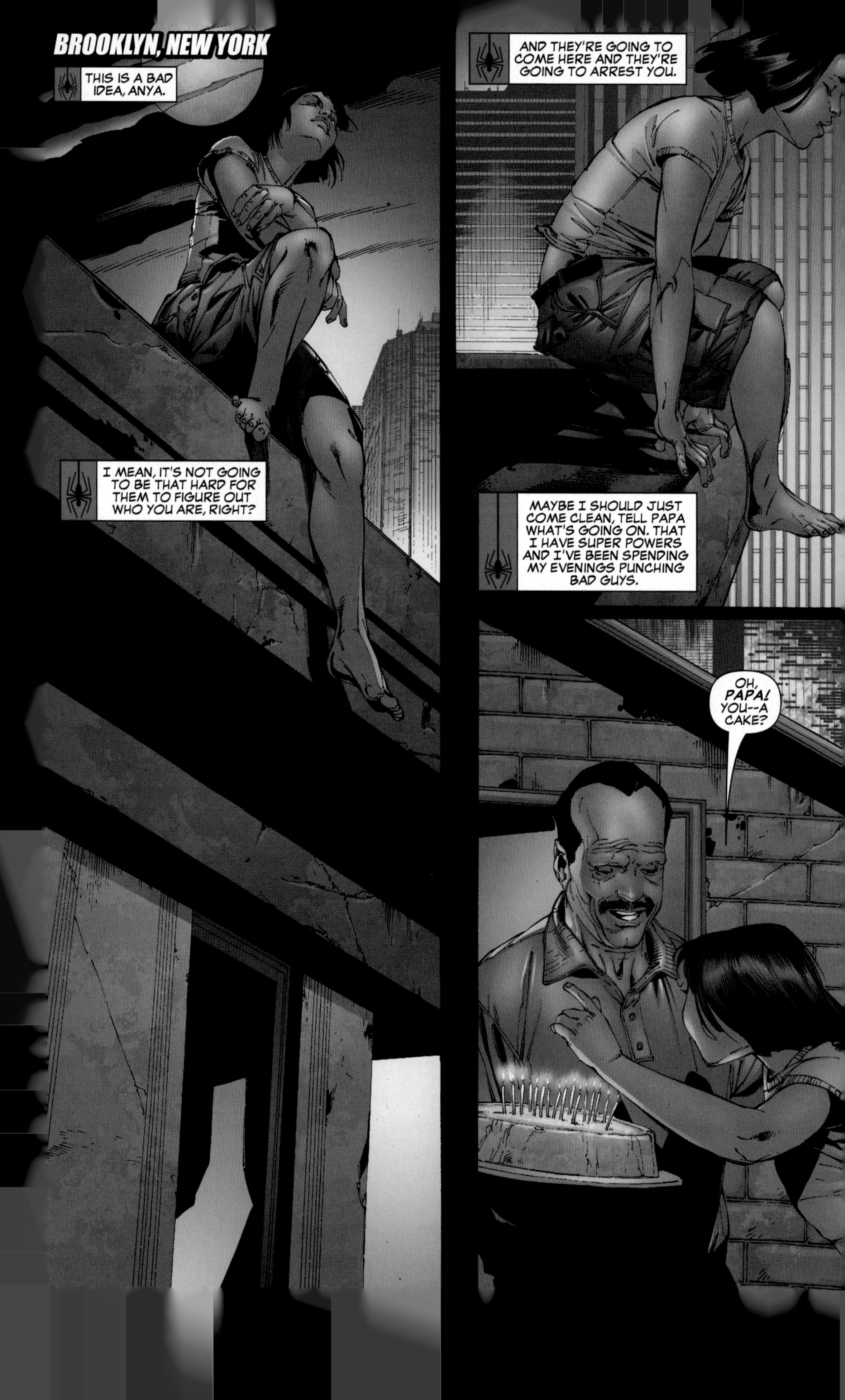
BROOKLYN, NEW YORK
THIS IS A BAD IDEA, ANYA.
I MEAN, IT'S NOT GOING TO BE THAT HARD FOR THEM TO FIGURE OUT WHO YOU ARE, RIGHT?
AND THEY'RE GOING TO COME HERE AND THEY'RE GOING TO ARREST YOU.
MAYBE I SHOULD JUST COME CLEAN, TELL PAPA WHAT'S GOING ON. THAT I HAVE SUPER POWERS AND I'VE BEEN SPENDING MY EVENINGS PUNCHING BAD GUYS.
OH, PAPA! YOU--A CAKE?

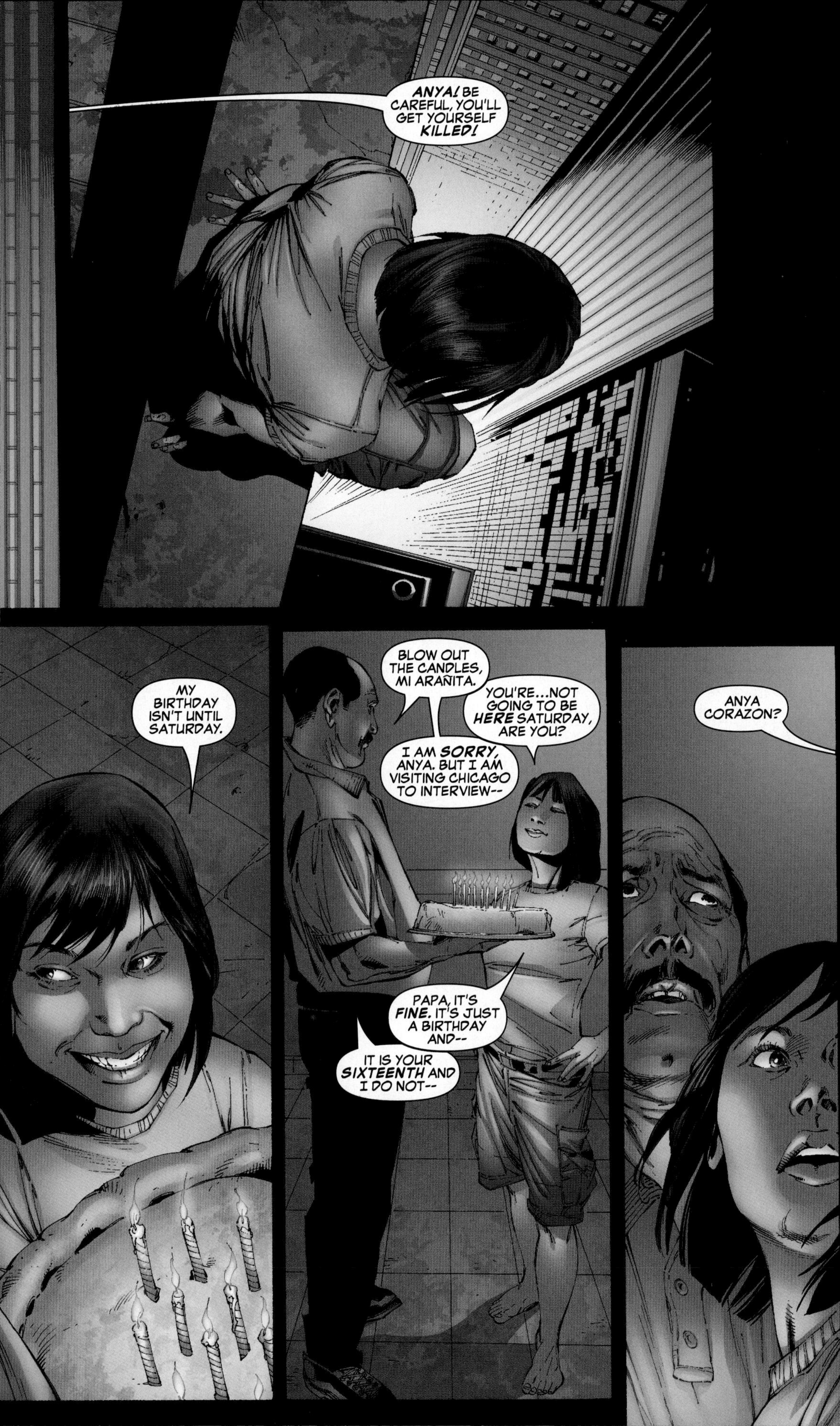
ANYA! BE CAREFUL, YOU'LL GET YOURSELF KILLED!
MY BIRTHDAY ISN'T UNTIL SATURDAY.
BLOW OUT THE CANDLES, MI ARAÑITA.
YOU'RE...NOT GOING TO BE HERE SATURDAY, ARE YOU?
I AM SORRY, ANYA. BUT I AM VISITING CHICAGO TO INTERVIEW--
PAPA, IT'S FINE. IT'S JUST A BIRTHDAY AND--
IT IS YOUR SIXTEENTH AND I DO NOT--
ANYA CORAZON?

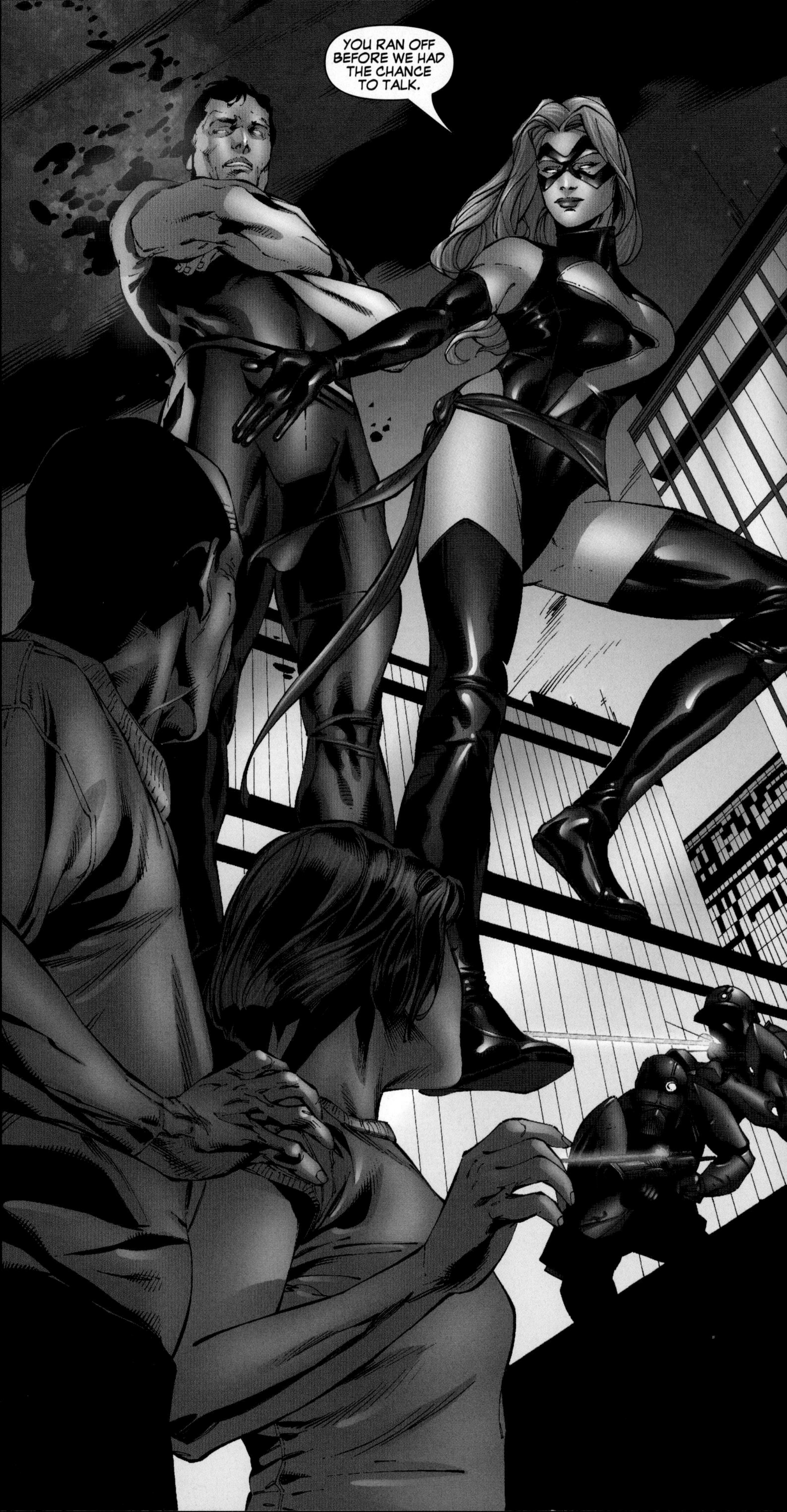
YOU RAN OFF BEFORE WE HAD THE CHANCE TO TALK.

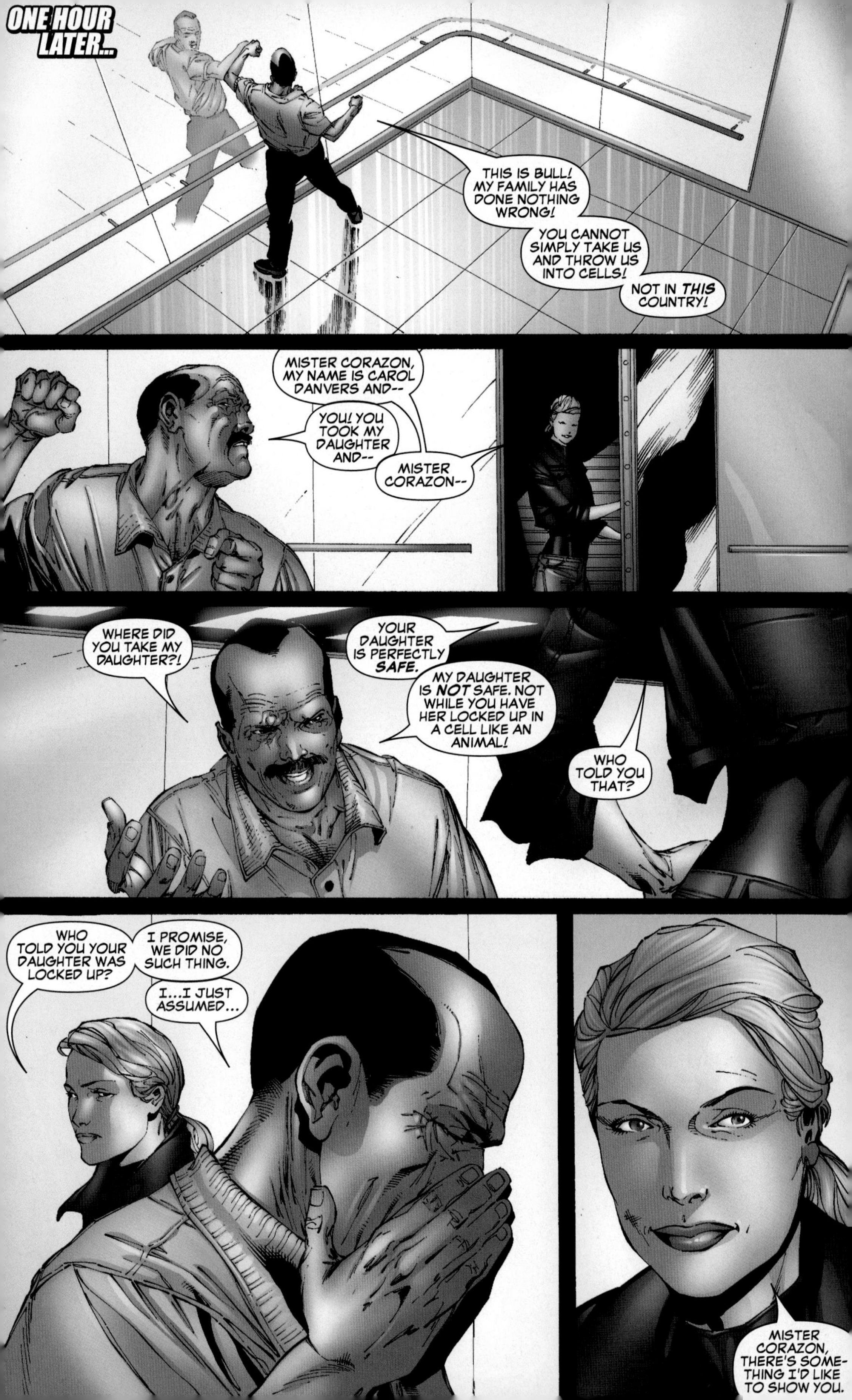
ONE HOUR LATER...
THIS IS BULL! MY FAMILY HAS DONE NOTHING WRONG!
YOU CANNOT SIMPLY TAKE US AND THROW US INTO CELLS!
NOT IN THIS COUNTRY!
MISTER CORAZON, MY NAME IS CAROL DANVERS AND--
YOU! YOU TOOK MY DAUGHTER AND--
MISTER CORAZON--
WHERE DID YOU TAKE MY DAUGHTER?!
YOUR DAUGHTER IS PERFECTLY SAFE.
MY DAUGHTER IS NOT SAFE. NOT WHILE YOU HAVE HER LOCKED UP IN A CELL LIKE AN ANIMAL!
WHO TOLD YOU THAT?
WHO TOLD YOU YOUR DAUGHTER WAS LOCKED UP?
I PROMISE, WE DID NO SUCH THING.
I...I JUST ASSUMED...
MISTER CORAZON, THERE'S SOMETHING I'D LIKE TO SHOW YOU.

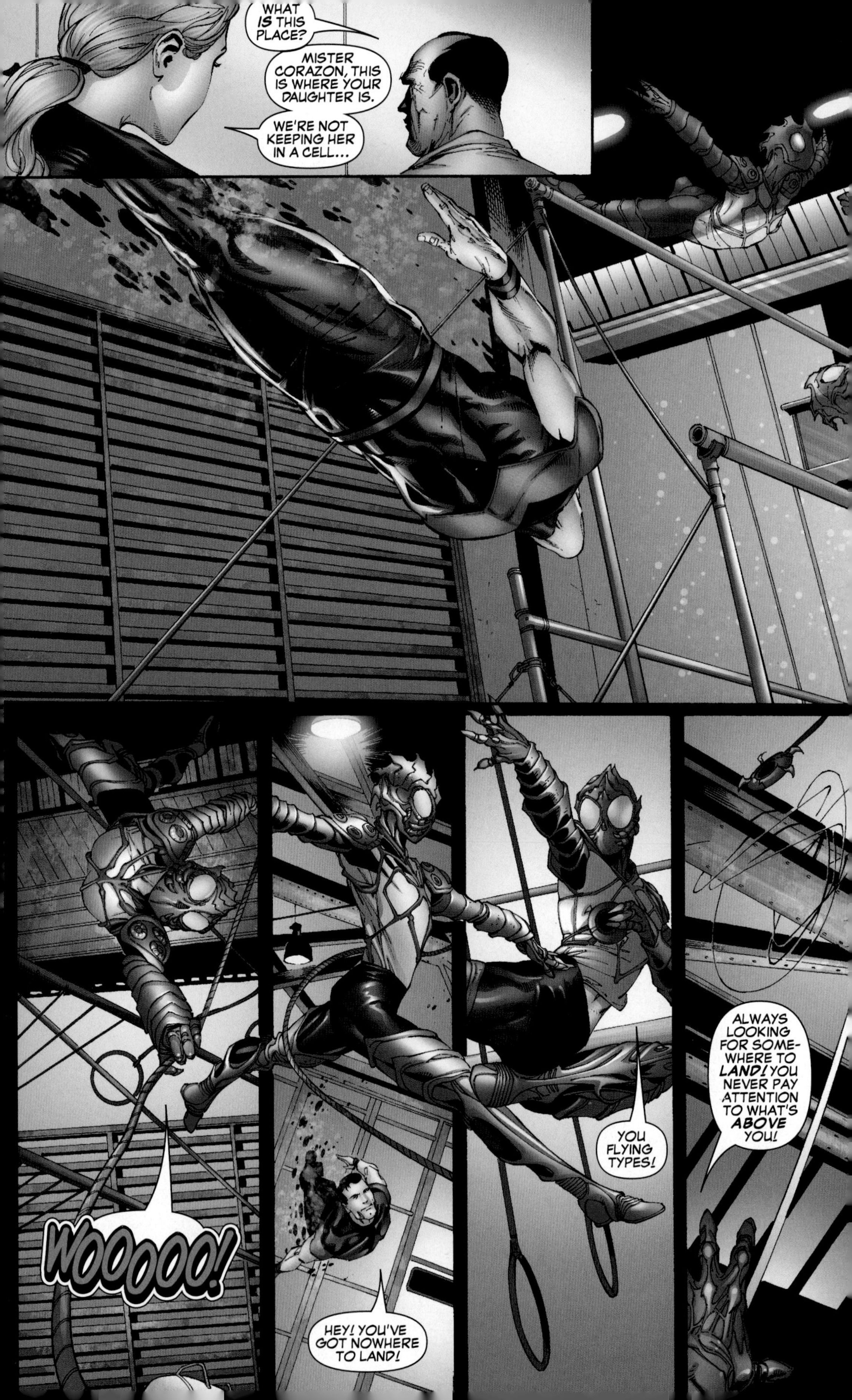
WHAT IS THIS PLACE?
MISTER CORAZON, THIS IS WHERE YOUR DAUGHTER IS.
WE'RE NOT KEEPING HER IN A CELL...
WOOOOO!
HEY! YOU'VE GOT NOWHERE TO LAND!
YOU FLYING TYPES!
ALWAYS LOOKING FOR SOME-WHERE TO LAND! YOU NEVER PAY ATTENTION TO WHAT'S ABOVE YOU!

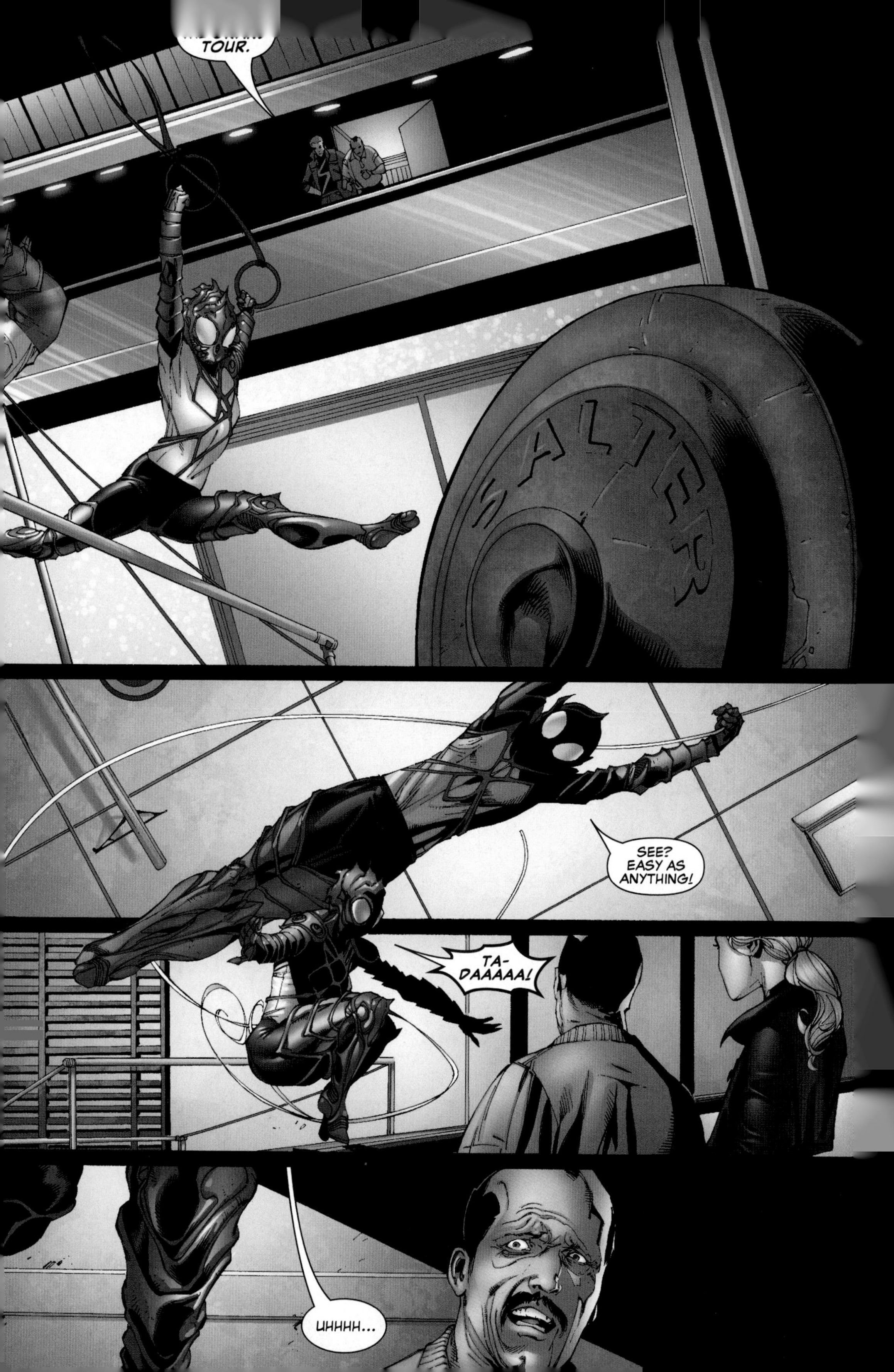
TOUR.
SALTER
SEE? EASY AS ANYTHING!
TA-DAAAAAA!
UHHHH...

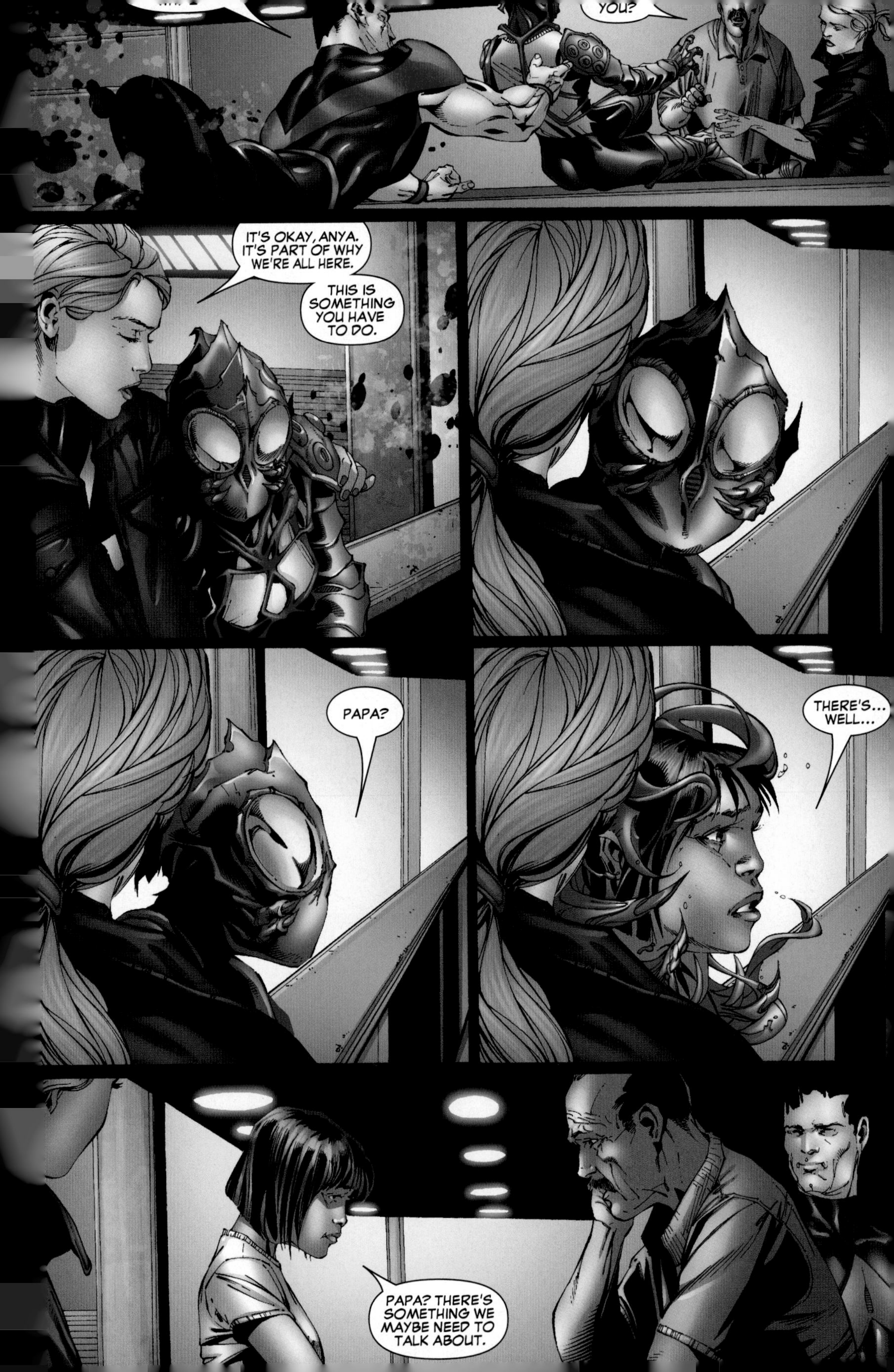
YOU?
IT'S OKAY, ANYA. IT'S PART OF WHY WE'RE ALL HERE.
THIS IS SOMETHING YOU HAVE TO DO.
PAPA?
THERE'S... WELL...
PAPA? THERE'S SOMETHING WE MAYBE NEED TO TALK ABOUT.

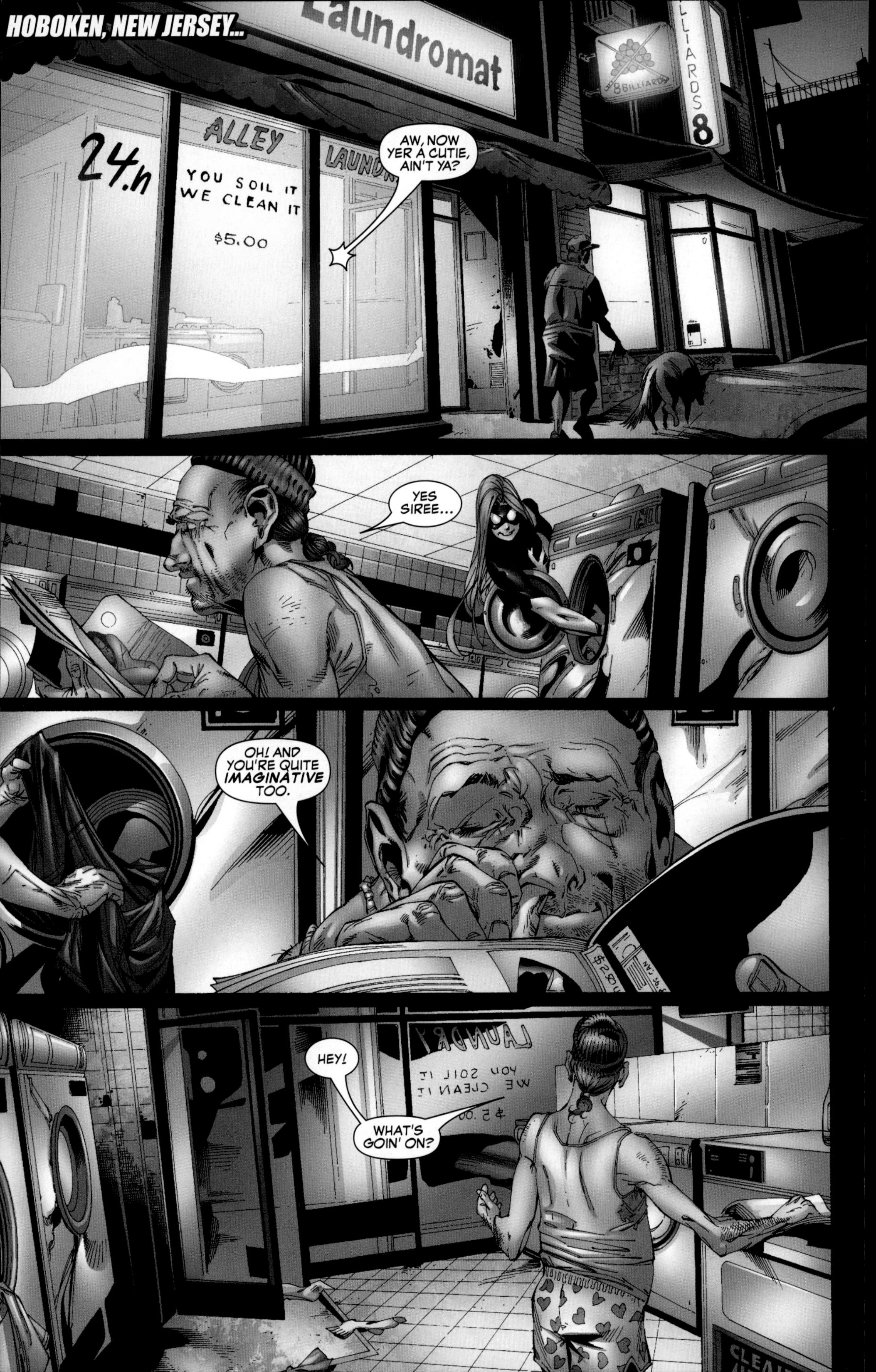
HOBOKEN, NEW JERSEY...
Laundromat
BILLIARDS 8
8 BILLIARDS
ALLEY LAUNDRY
24.h
YOU SOIL IT WE CLEAN IT
$5.00
AW, NOW YER A CUTIE, AIN'T YA?
YES SIREE...
OH! AND YOU'RE QUITE IMAGINATIVE TOO.
HEY!
WHAT'S GOIN' ON?

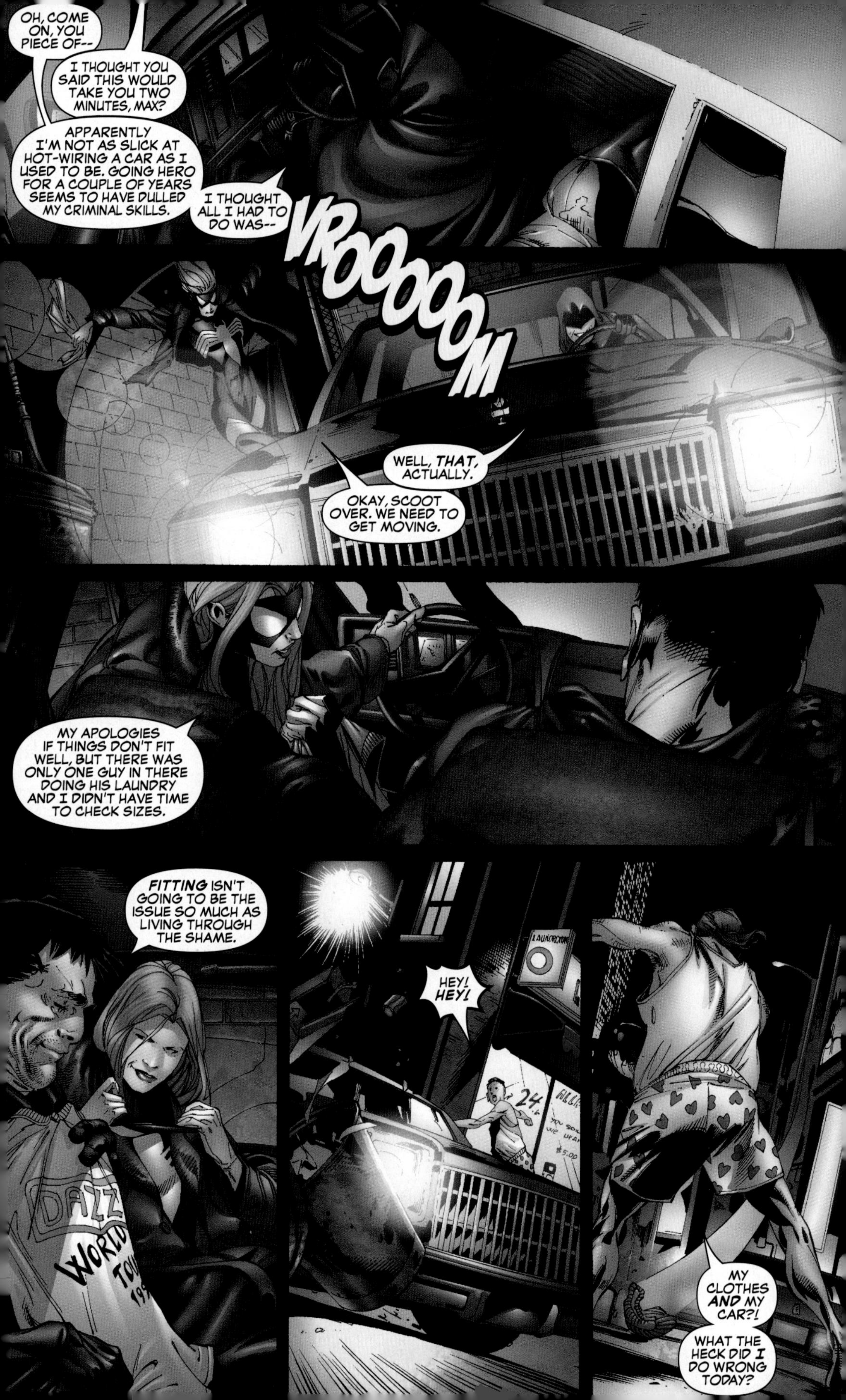
OH, COME ON, YOU PIECE OF--
I THOUGHT YOU SAID THIS WOULD TAKE YOU TWO MINUTES, MAX?
APPARENTLY I'M NOT AS SLICK AT HOT-WIRING A CAR AS I USED TO BE. GOING HERO FOR A COUPLE OF YEARS SEEMS TO HAVE DULLED MY CRIMINAL SKILLS.
I THOUGHT ALL I HAD TO DO WAS--
VROOOOOOM
WELL, THAT, ACTUALLY.
OKAY, SCOOT OVER. WE NEED TO GET MOVING.
MY APOLOGIES IF THINGS DON'T FIT WELL, BUT THERE WAS ONLY ONE GUY IN THERE DOING HIS LAUNDRY AND I DIDN'T HAVE TIME TO CHECK SIZES.
FITTING ISN'T GOING TO BE THE ISSUE SO MUCH AS LIVING THROUGH THE SHAME.
HEY! HEY!
MY CLOTHES AND MY CAR?!
WHAT THE HECK DID I DO WRONG TODAY?

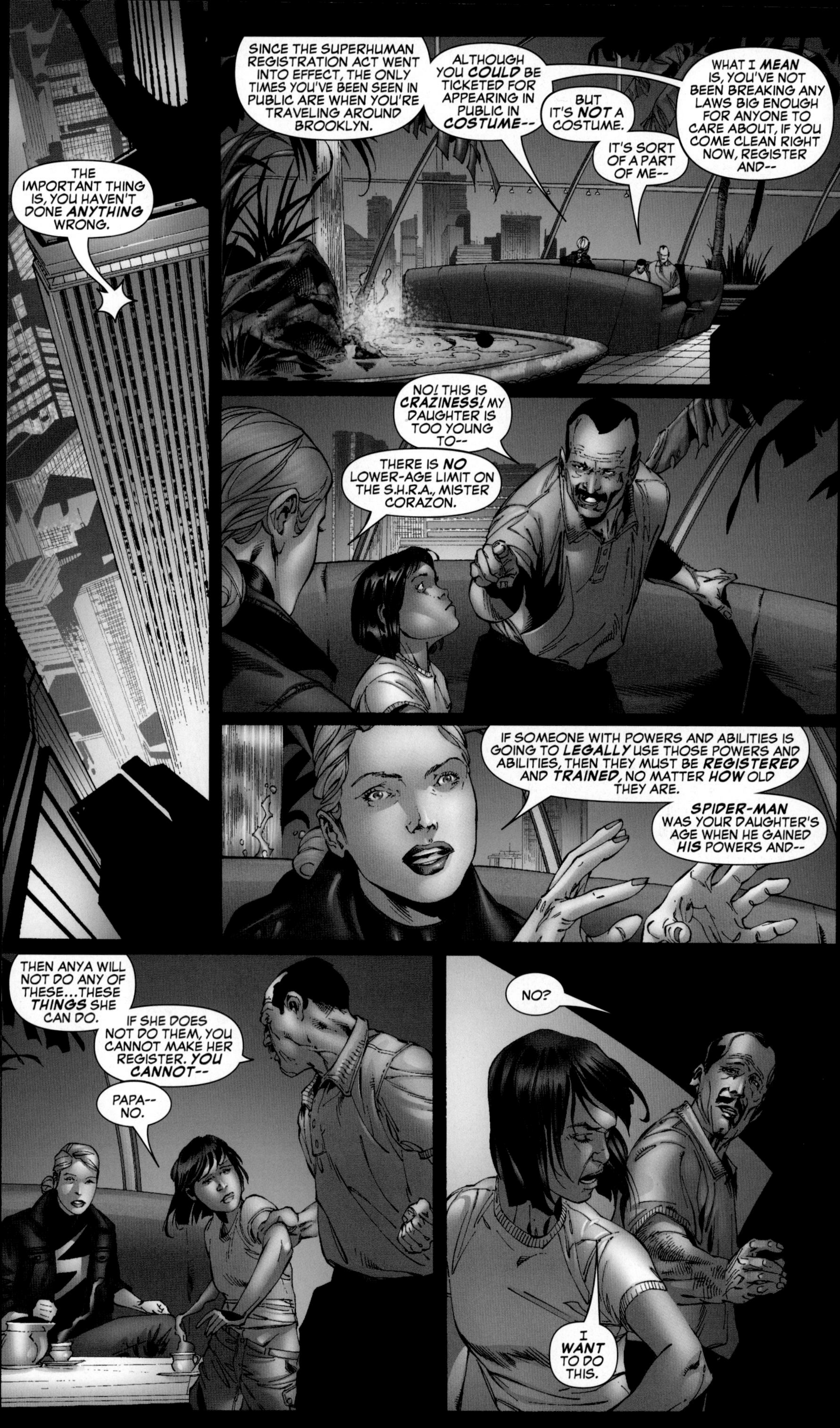
THE IMPORTANT THING IS, YOU HAVEN'T DONE ANYTHING WRONG.
SINCE THE SUPERHUMAN REGISTRATION ACT WENT INTO EFFECT, THE ONLY TIMES YOU'VE BEEN SEEN IN PUBLIC ARE WHEN YOU'RE TRAVELING AROUND BROOKLYN.
ALTHOUGH YOU COULD BE TICKETED FOR APPEARING IN PUBLIC IN COSTUME--
BUT IT'S NOT A COSTUME.
IT'S SORT OF A PART OF ME--
WHAT I MEAN IS, YOU'VE NOT BEEN BREAKING ANY LAWS BIG ENOUGH FOR ANYONE TO CARE ABOUT, IF YOU COME CLEAN RIGHT NOW, REGISTER AND--
NO! THIS IS CRAZINESS! MY DAUGHTER IS TOO YOUNG TO--
THERE IS NO LOWER-AGE LIMIT ON THE S.H.R.A., MISTER CORAZON.
IF SOMEONE WITH POWERS AND ABILITIES IS GOING TO LEGALLY USE THOSE POWERS AND ABILITIES, THEN THEY MUST BE REGISTERED AND TRAINED, NO MATTER HOW OLD THEY ARE.
SPIDER-MAN WAS YOUR DAUGHTER'S AGE WHEN HE GAINED HIS POWERS AND--
THEN ANYA WILL NOT DO ANY OF THESE...THESE THINGS SHE CAN DO.
IF SHE DOES NOT DO THEM, YOU CANNOT MAKE HER REGISTER. YOU CANNOT--
PAPA-- NO.
NO?
I WANT TO DO THIS.

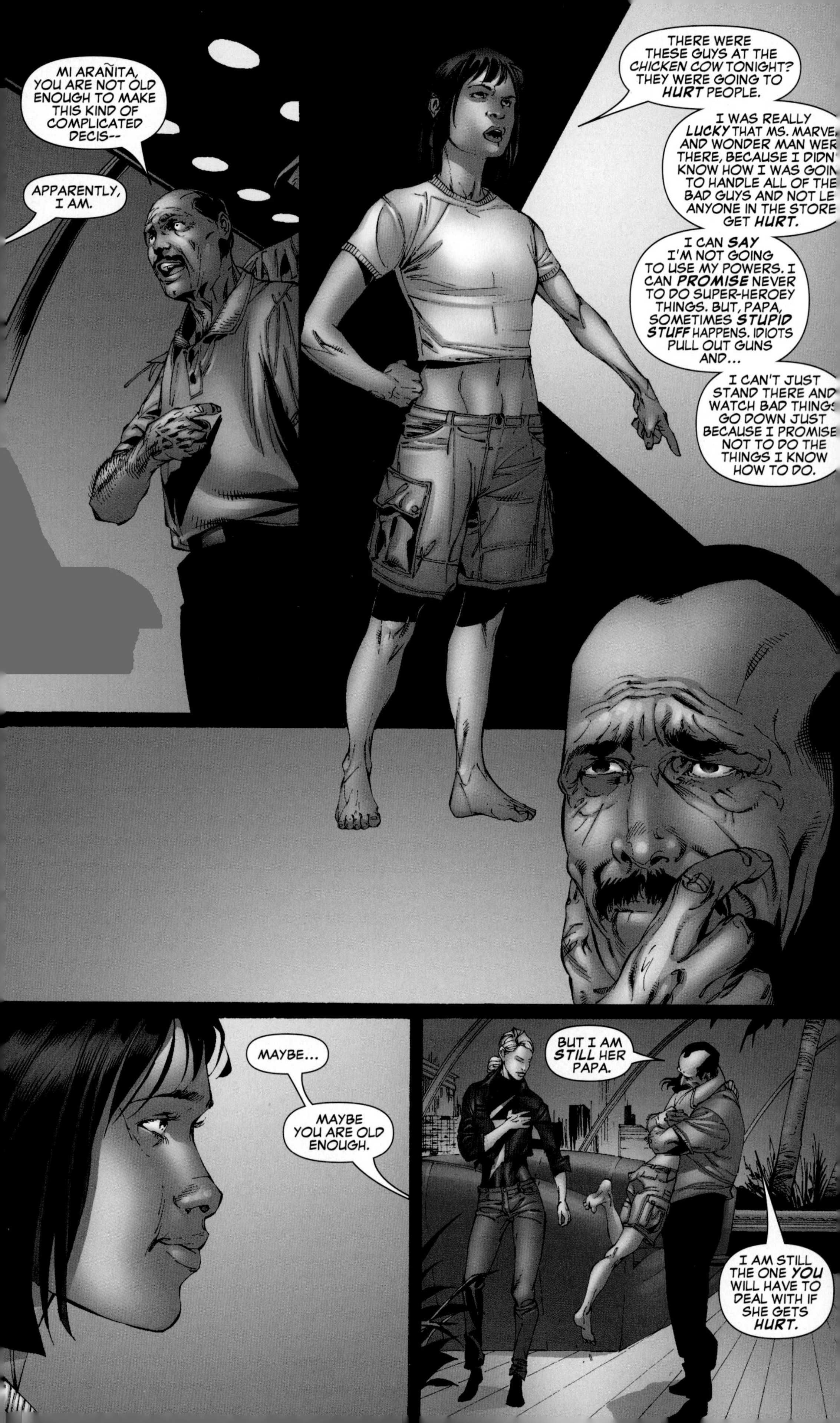
MI ARAÑITA, YOU ARE NOT OLD ENOUGH TO MAKE THIS KIND OF COMPLICATED DECIS--
APPARENTLY, I AM.
THERE WERE THESE GUYS AT THE CHICKEN COW TONIGHT? THEY WERE GOING TO HURT PEOPLE.
I WAS REALLY LUCKY THAT MS. MARVE AND WONDER MAN WER THERE, BECAUSE I DIDN KNOW HOW I WAS GOIN TO HANDLE ALL OF THE BAD GUYS AND NOT LE ANYONE IN THE STORE GET HURT.
I CAN SAY I'M NOT GOING TO USE MY POWERS. I CAN PROMISE NEVER TO DO SUPER-HEROEY THINGS. BUT, PAPA, SOMETIMES STUPID STUFF HAPPENS. IDIOTS PULL OUT GUNS AND...
I CAN'T JUST STAND THERE AND WATCH BAD THINGS GO DOWN JUST BECAUSE I PROMISE NOT TO DO THE THINGS I KNOW HOW TO DO.
MAYBE...
MAYBE YOU ARE OLD ENOUGH.
BUT I AM STILL HER PAPA.
I AM STILL THE ONE YOU WILL HAVE TO DEAL WITH IF SHE GETS HURT.

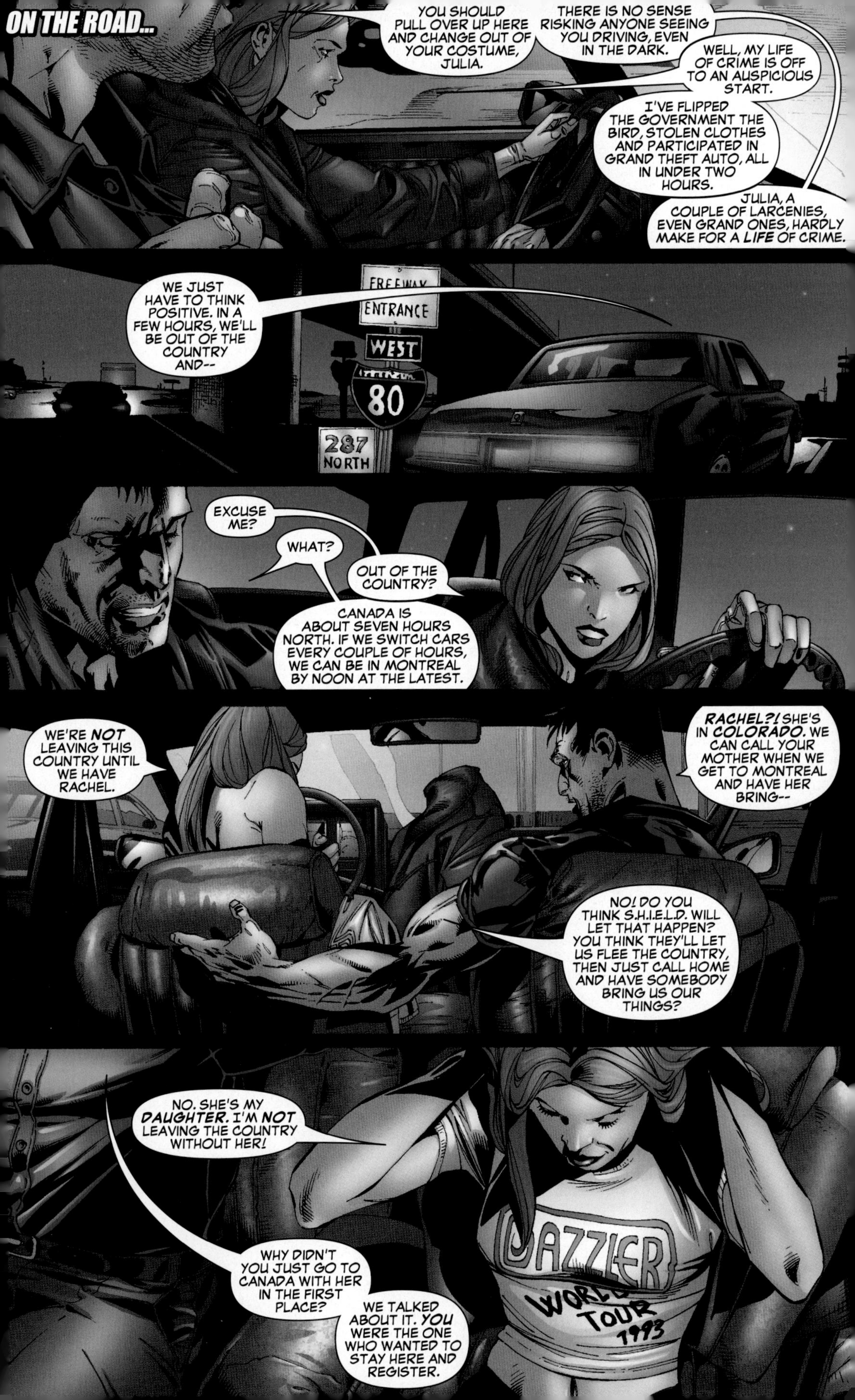
ON THE ROAD...
YOU SHOULD PULL OVER UP HERE AND CHANGE OUT OF YOUR COSTUME, JULIA.
THERE IS NO SENSE RISKING ANYONE SEEING YOU DRIVING, EVEN IN THE DARK.
WELL, MY LIFE OF CRIME IS OFF TO AN AUSPICIOUS START.
I'VE FLIPPED THE GOVERNMENT THE BIRD, STOLEN CLOTHES AND PARTICIPATED IN GRAND THEFT AUTO, ALL IN UNDER TWO HOURS.
JULIA, A COUPLE OF LARCENIES, EVEN GRAND ONES, HARDLY MAKE FOR A LIFE OF CRIME.
WE JUST HAVE TO THINK POSITIVE. IN A FEW HOURS, WE'LL BE OUT OF THE COUNTRY AND--
FREEWAY ENTRANCE
WEST
80
287 NORTH
EXCUSE ME?
WHAT?
OUT OF THE COUNTRY?
CANADA IS ABOUT SEVEN HOURS NORTH. IF WE SWITCH CARS EVERY COUPLE OF HOURS, WE CAN BE IN MONTREAL BY NOON AT THE LATEST.
WE'RE NOT LEAVING THIS COUNTRY UNTIL WE HAVE RACHEL.
RACHEL?! SHE'S IN COLORADO. WE CAN CALL YOUR MOTHER WHEN WE GET TO MONTREAL AND HAVE HER BRING--
NO! DO YOU THINK S.H.I.E.L.D. WILL LET THAT HAPPEN? YOU THINK THEY'LL LET US FLEE THE COUNTRY, THEN JUST CALL HOME AND HAVE SOMEBODY BRING US OUR THINGS?
NO. SHE'S MY DAUGHTER. I'M NOT LEAVING THE COUNTRY WITHOUT HER!
DAZZLER
TOUR 1993
WHY DIDN'T YOU JUST GO TO CANADA WITH HER IN THE FIRST PLACE?
WE TALKED ABOUT IT. YOU WERE THE ONE WHO WANTED TO STAY HERE AND REGISTER.

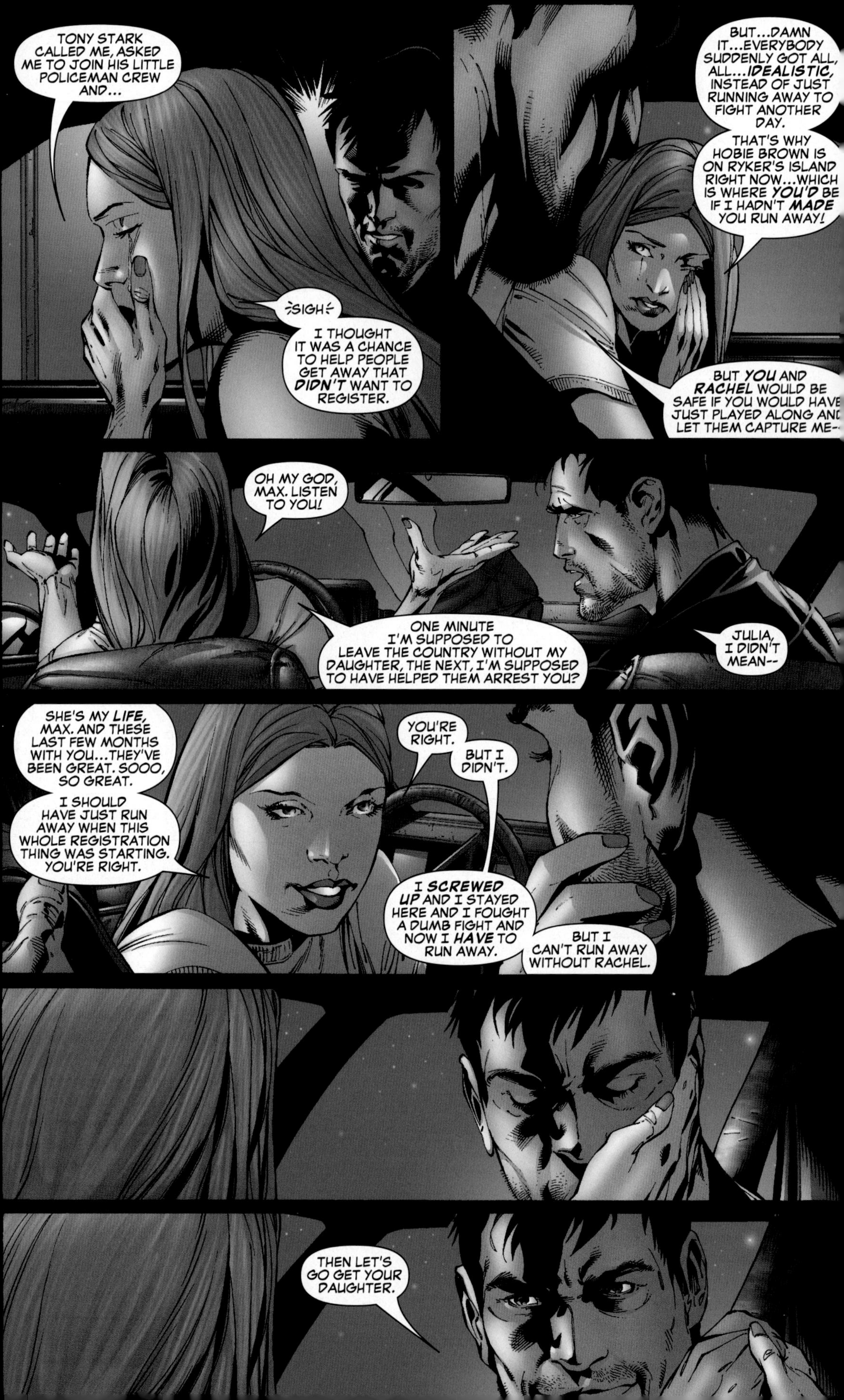
TONY STARK CALLED ME, ASKED ME TO JOIN HIS LITTLE POLICEMAN CREW AND...
SIGH
I THOUGHT IT WAS A CHANCE TO HELP PEOPLE GET AWAY THAT *DIDN'T* WANT TO REGISTER.
BUT...DAMN IT...EVERYBODY SUDDENLY GOT ALL, ALL...*IDEALISTIC,* INSTEAD OF JUST RUNNING AWAY TO FIGHT ANOTHER DAY.
THAT'S WHY HOBIE BROWN IS ON RYKER'S ISLAND RIGHT NOW...WHICH IS WHERE *YOU'D* BE IF I HADN'T *MADE* YOU RUN AWAY!
BUT *YOU* AND *RACHEL* WOULD BE SAFE IF YOU WOULD HAVE JUST PLAYED ALONG AND LET THEM CAPTURE ME--
OH MY GOD, MAX. LISTEN TO YOU!
ONE MINUTE I'M SUPPOSED TO LEAVE THE COUNTRY WITHOUT MY DAUGHTER, THE NEXT, I'M SUPPOSED TO HAVE HELPED THEM ARREST YOU?
JULIA, I DIDN'T MEAN--
SHE'S MY *LIFE,* MAX. AND THESE LAST FEW MONTHS WITH YOU...THEY'VE BEEN GREAT. SOOO, SO GREAT.
I SHOULD HAVE JUST RUN AWAY WHEN THIS WHOLE REGISTRATION THING WAS STARTING. YOU'RE RIGHT.
YOU'RE RIGHT.
BUT I DIDN'T.
I *SCREWED UP* AND I STAYED HERE AND I FOUGHT A DUMB FIGHT AND NOW I *HAVE* TO RUN AWAY.
BUT I CAN'T RUN AWAY WITHOUT RACHEL.
THEN LET'S GO GET YOUR DAUGHTER.

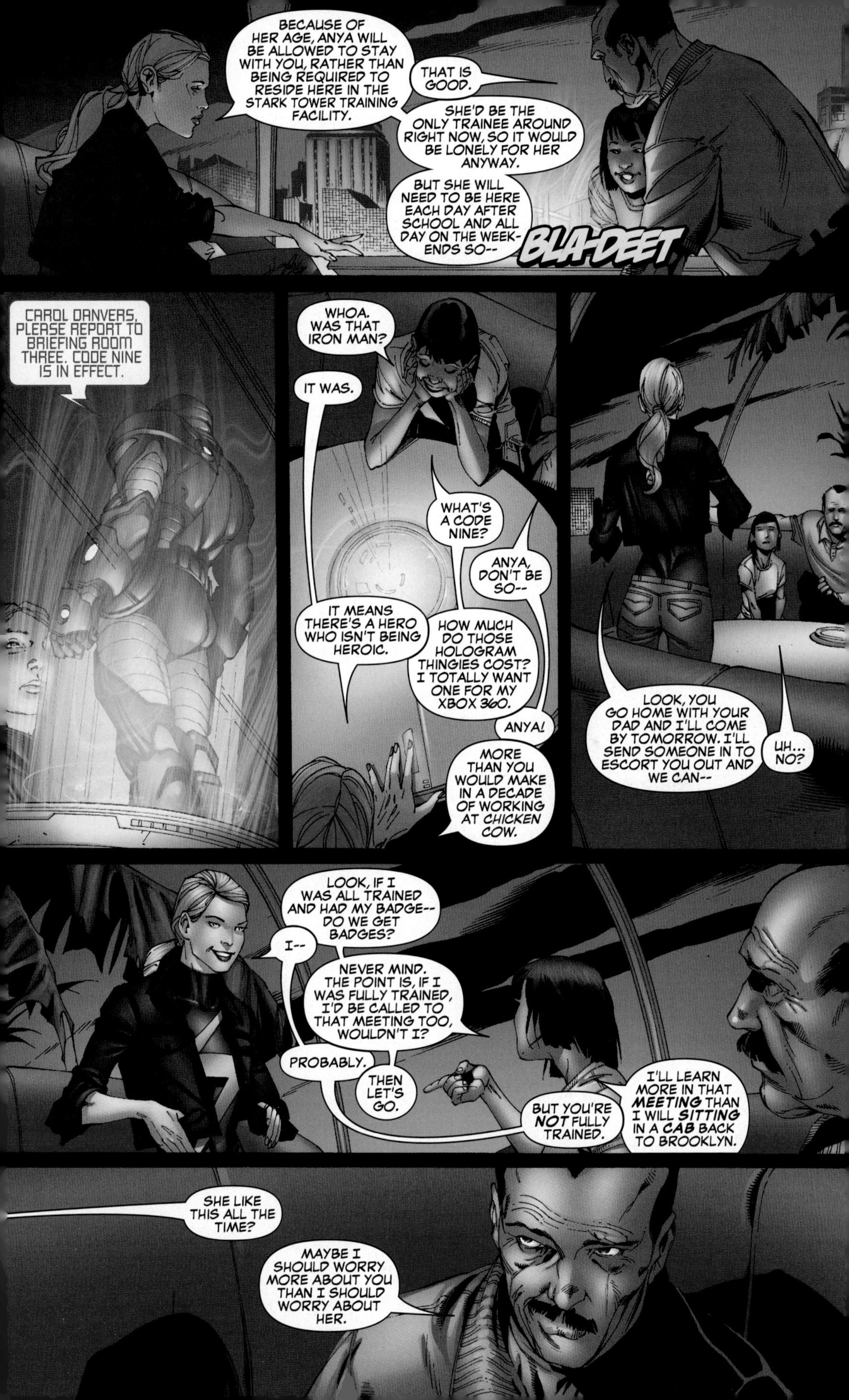
BECAUSE OF HER AGE, ANYA WILL BE ALLOWED TO STAY WITH YOU, RATHER THAN BEING REQUIRED TO RESIDE HERE IN THE STARK TOWER TRAINING FACILITY.
THAT IS GOOD.
SHE'D BE THE ONLY TRAINEE AROUND RIGHT NOW, SO IT WOULD BE LONELY FOR HER ANYWAY.
BUT SHE WILL NEED TO BE HERE EACH DAY AFTER SCHOOL AND ALL DAY ON THE WEEK-ENDS SO--
BLA-DEET
CAROL DANVERS, PLEASE REPORT TO BRIEFING ROOM THREE. CODE NINE IS IN EFFECT.
WHOA. WAS THAT IRON MAN?
IT WAS.
WHAT'S A CODE NINE?
ANYA, DON'T BE SO--
IT MEANS THERE'S A HERO WHO ISN'T BEING HEROIC.
HOW MUCH DO THOSE HOLOGRAM THINGIES COST? I TOTALLY WANT ONE FOR MY XBOX 360.
ANYA!
MORE THAN YOU WOULD MAKE IN A DECADE OF WORKING AT CHICKEN COW.
LOOK, YOU GO HOME WITH YOUR DAD AND I'LL COME BY TOMORROW. I'LL SEND SOMEONE IN TO ESCORT YOU OUT AND WE CAN--
UH... NO?
LOOK, IF I WAS ALL TRAINED AND HAD MY BADGE-- DO WE GET BADGES?
I--
NEVER MIND. THE POINT IS, IF I WAS FULLY TRAINED, I'D BE CALLED TO THAT MEETING TOO, WOULDN'T I?
PROBABLY.
THEN LET'S GO.
BUT YOU'RE NOT FULLY TRAINED.
I'LL LEARN MORE IN THAT MEETING THAN I WILL SITTING IN A CAB BACK TO BROOKLYN.
SHE LIKE THIS ALL THE TIME?
MAYBE I SHOULD WORRY MORE ABOUT YOU THAN I SHOULD WORRY ABOUT HER.

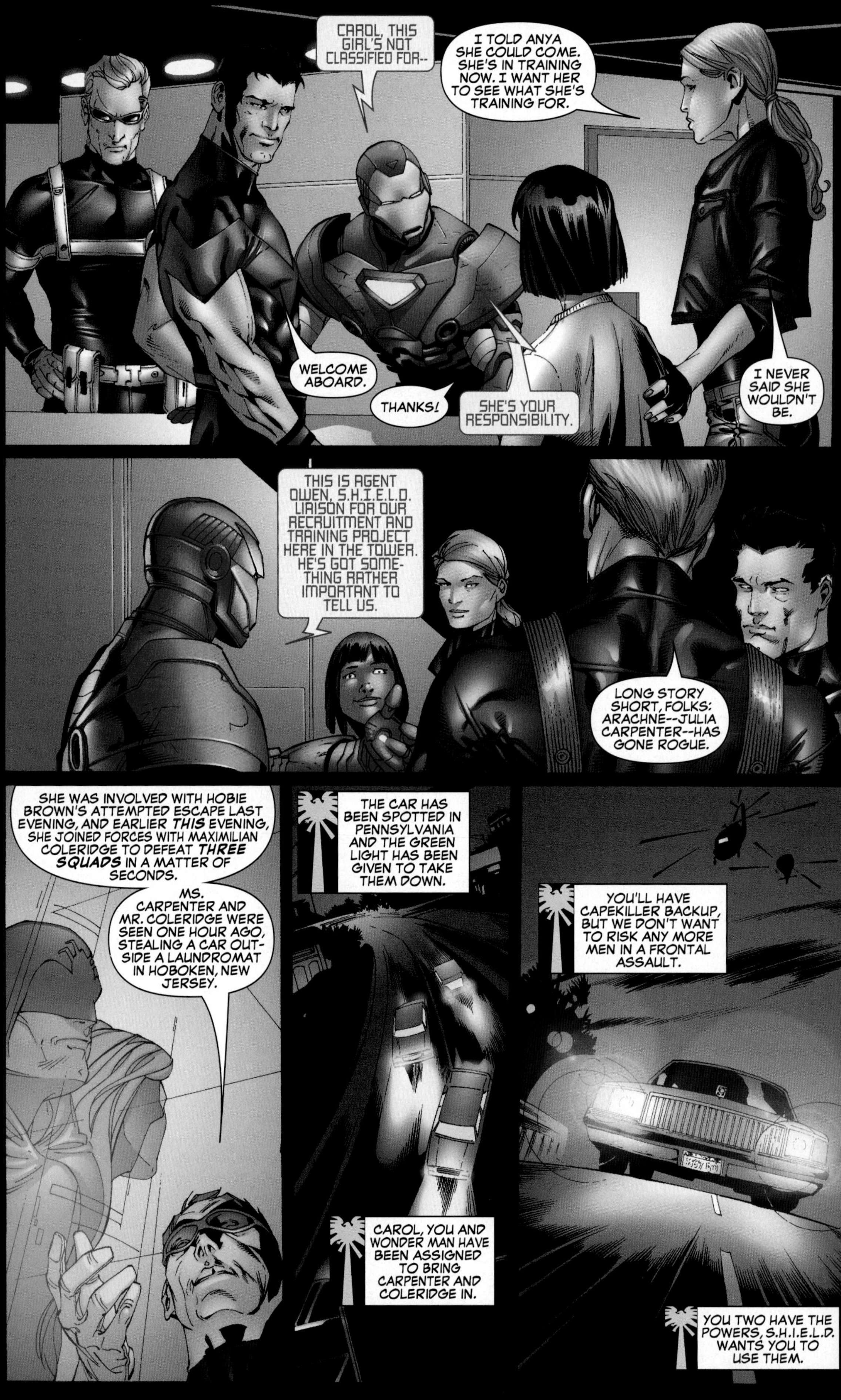
CAROL, THIS GIRL'S NOT CLASSIFIED FOR--
I TOLD ANYA SHE COULD COME. SHE'S IN TRAINING NOW. I WANT HER TO SEE WHAT SHE'S TRAINING FOR.
WELCOME ABOARD.
THANKS!
SHE'S YOUR RESPONSIBILITY.
I NEVER SAID SHE WOULDN'T BE.
THIS IS AGENT OWEN, S.H.I.E.L.D. LIAISON FOR OUR RECRUITMENT AND TRAINING PROJECT HERE IN THE TOWER. HE'S GOT SOMETHING RATHER IMPORTANT TO TELL US.
LONG STORY SHORT, FOLKS: ARACHNE--JULIA CARPENTER--HAS GONE ROGUE.
SHE WAS INVOLVED WITH HOBIE BROWN'S ATTEMPTED ESCAPE LAST EVENING, AND EARLIER *THIS* EVENING, SHE JOINED FORCES WITH MAXIMILIAN COLERIDGE TO DEFEAT *THREE SQUADS* IN A MATTER OF SECONDS.
MS. CARPENTER AND MR. COLERIDGE WERE SEEN ONE HOUR AGO, STEALING A CAR OUTSIDE A LAUNDROMAT IN HOBOKEN, NEW JERSEY.
THE CAR HAS BEEN SPOTTED IN PENNSYLVANIA AND THE GREEN LIGHT HAS BEEN GIVEN TO TAKE THEM DOWN.
CAROL, YOU AND WONDER MAN HAVE BEEN ASSIGNED TO BRING CARPENTER AND COLERIDGE IN.
YOU'LL HAVE CAPEKILLER BACKUP, BUT WE DON'T WANT TO RISK ANY MORE MEN IN A FRONTAL ASSAULT.
YOU TWO HAVE THE POWERS, S.H.I.E.L.D. WANTS YOU TO USE THEM.

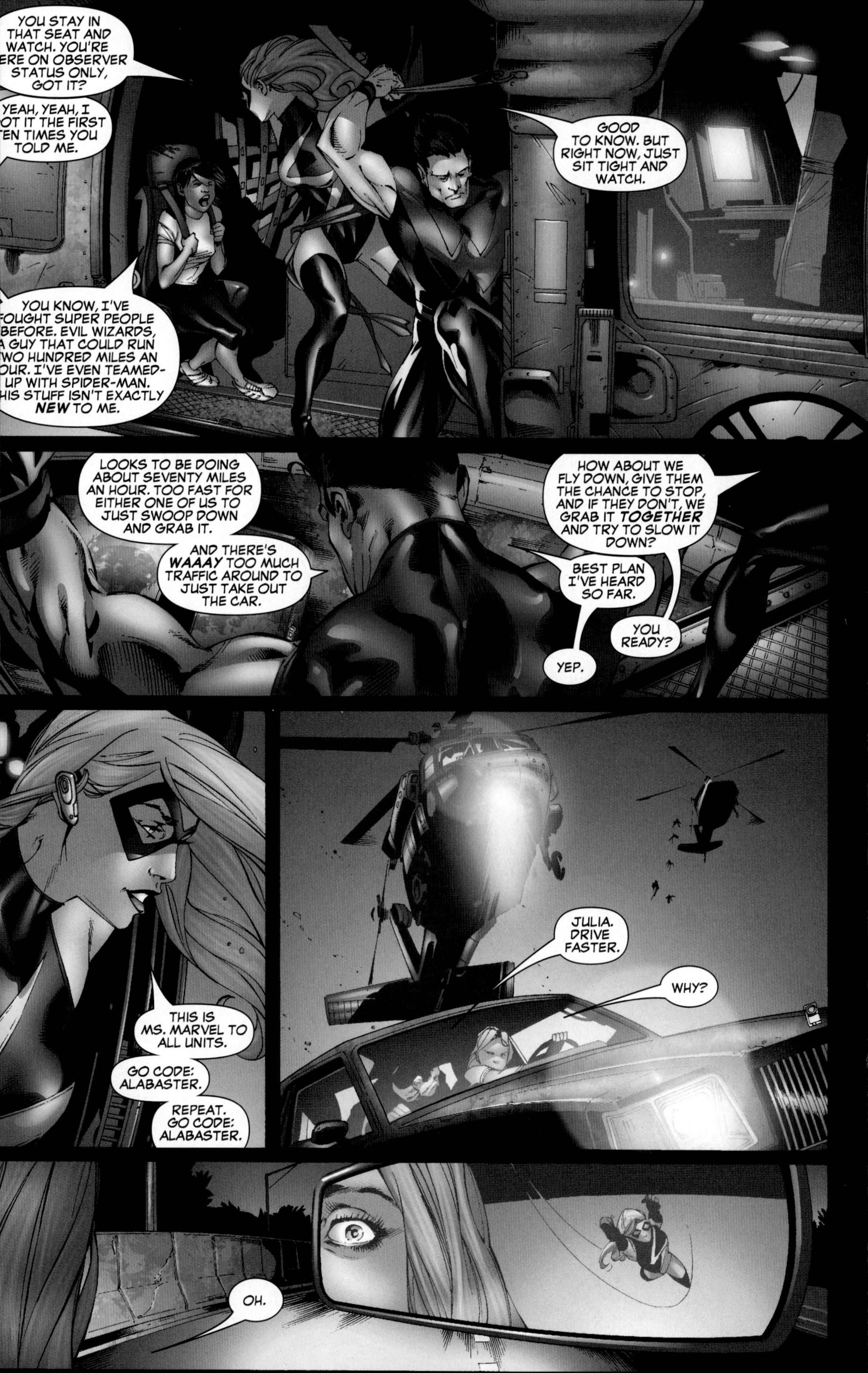

YOU STAY IN THAT SEAT AND WATCH. YOU'RE ERE ON OBSERVER STATUS ONLY, GOT IT?
YEAH, YEAH, I OT IT THE FIRST TEN TIMES YOU TOLD ME.
GOOD TO KNOW. BUT RIGHT NOW, JUST SIT TIGHT AND WATCH.
YOU KNOW, I'VE FOUGHT SUPER PEOPLE BEFORE. EVIL WIZARDS, A GUY THAT COULD RUN TWO HUNDRED MILES AN OUR. I'VE EVEN TEAMED-UP WITH SPIDER-MAN. HIS STUFF ISN'T EXACTLY **NEW** TO ME.
LOOKS TO BE DOING ABOUT SEVENTY MILES AN HOUR. TOO FAST FOR EITHER ONE OF US TO JUST SWOOP DOWN AND GRAB IT.
AND THERE'S **WAAAY** TOO MUCH TRAFFIC AROUND TO JUST TAKE OUT THE CAR.
HOW ABOUT WE FLY DOWN, GIVE THEM THE CHANCE TO STOP, AND IF THEY DON'T, WE GRAB IT ***TOGETHER*** AND TRY TO SLOW IT DOWN?
BEST PLAN I'VE HEARD SO FAR.
YOU READY?
YEP.
THIS IS MS. MARVEL TO ALL UNITS.
GO CODE: ALABASTER.
REPEAT. GO CODE: ALABASTER.
JULIA. DRIVE FASTER.
WHY?
OH.

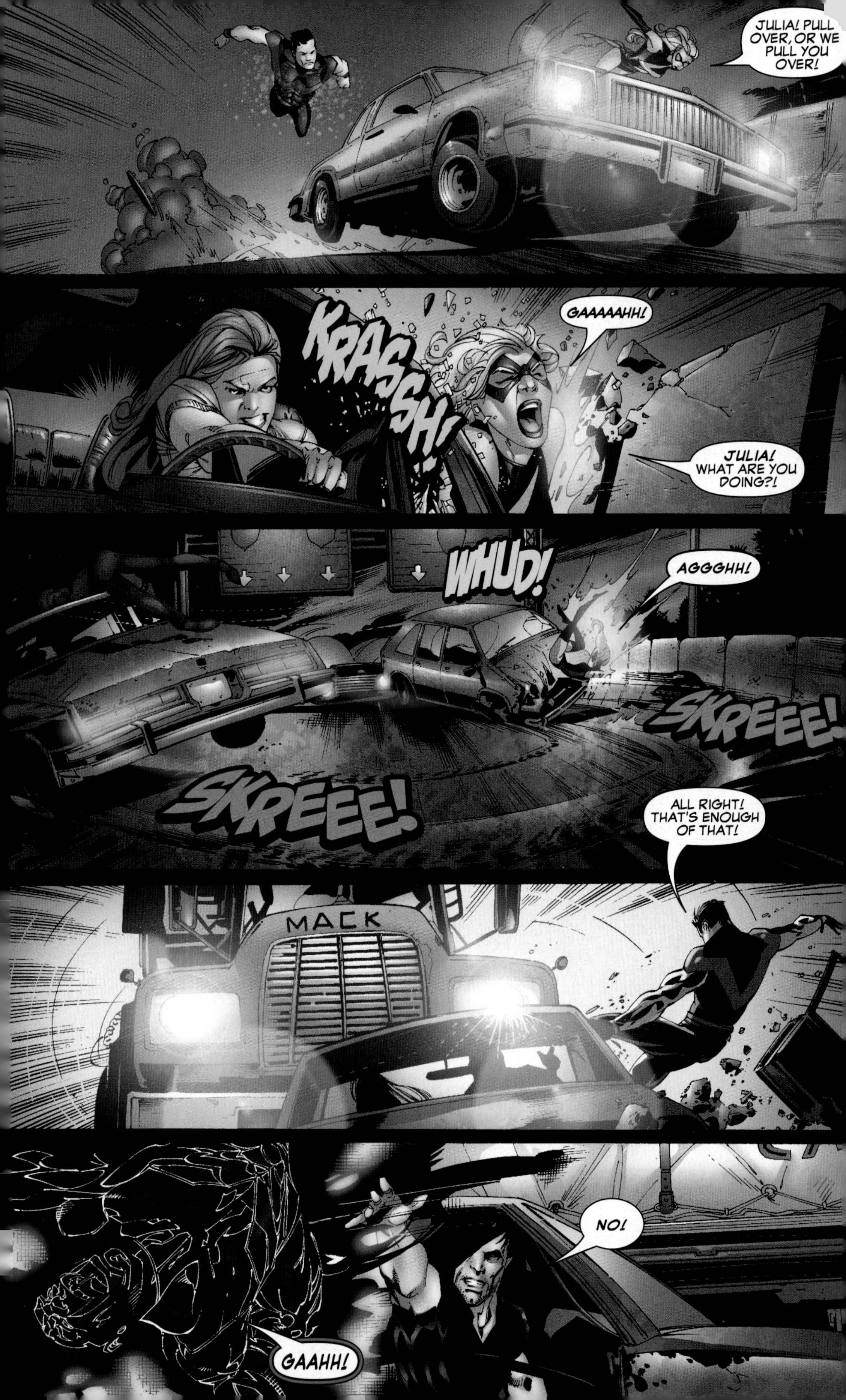
JULIA! PULL OVER, OR WE PULL YOU OVER!
KRASSH!
GAAAAAHH!
JULIA! WHAT ARE YOU DOING?!
WHUD!
AGGGHH!
SKREEE!
SKREEE!
ALL RIGHT! THAT'S ENOUGH OF THAT!
MACK
NO!
GAAHH!

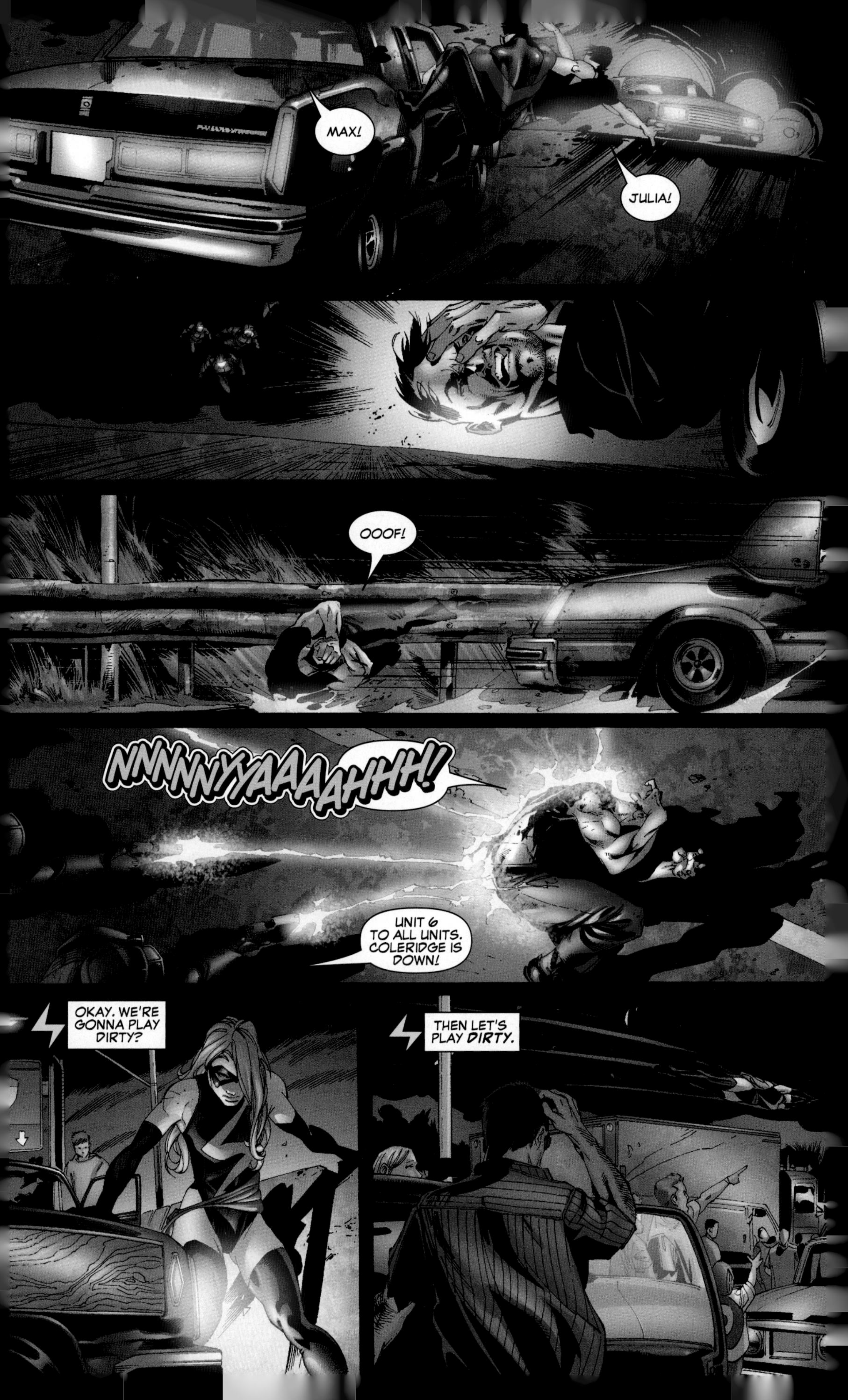
MAX!
JULIA!
OOOF!
NNNNNYYAAAAHHH!
UNIT 6 TO ALL UNITS. COLERIDGE IS DOWN!
OKAY. WE'RE GONNA PLAY DIRTY?
THEN LET'S PLAY DIRTY.

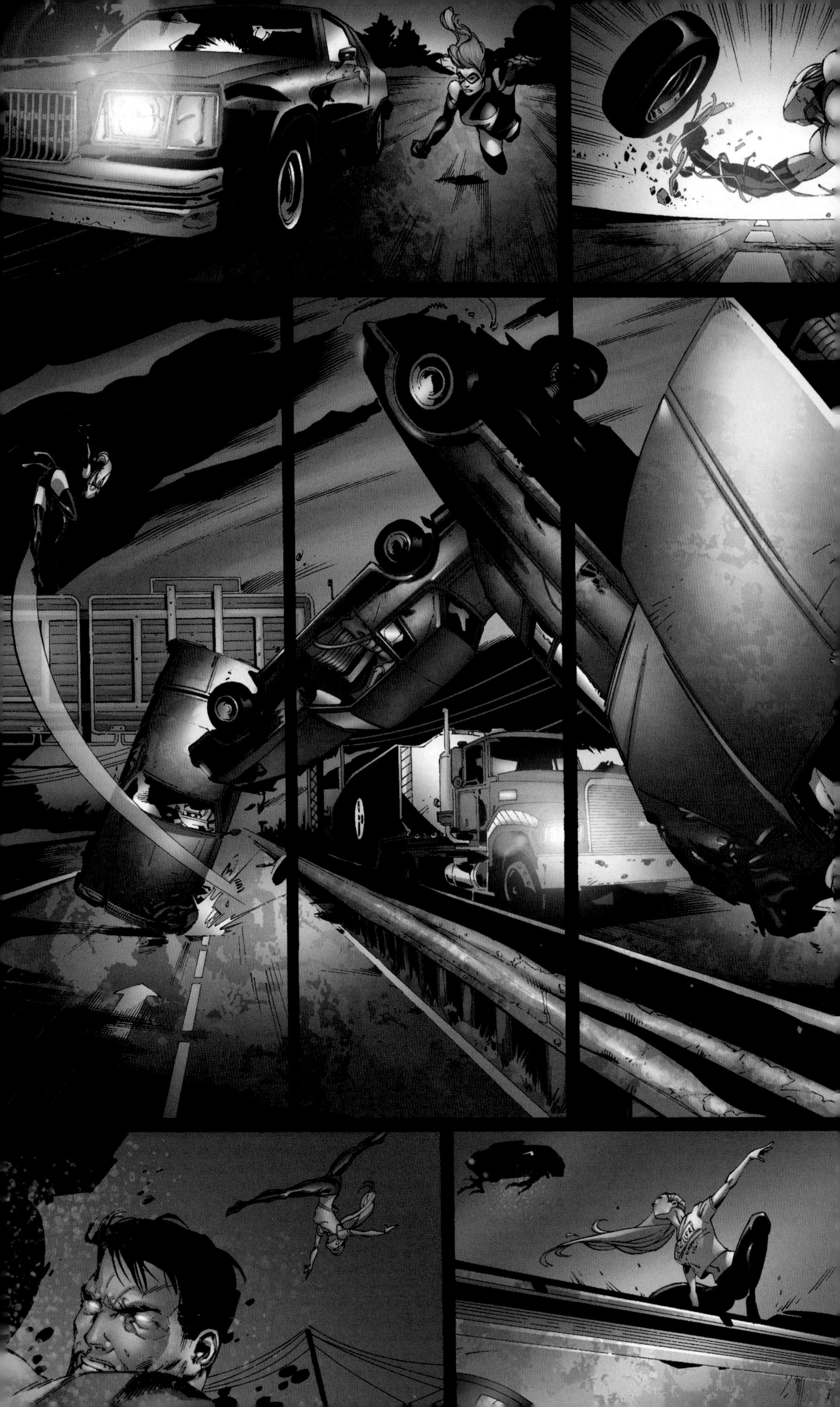

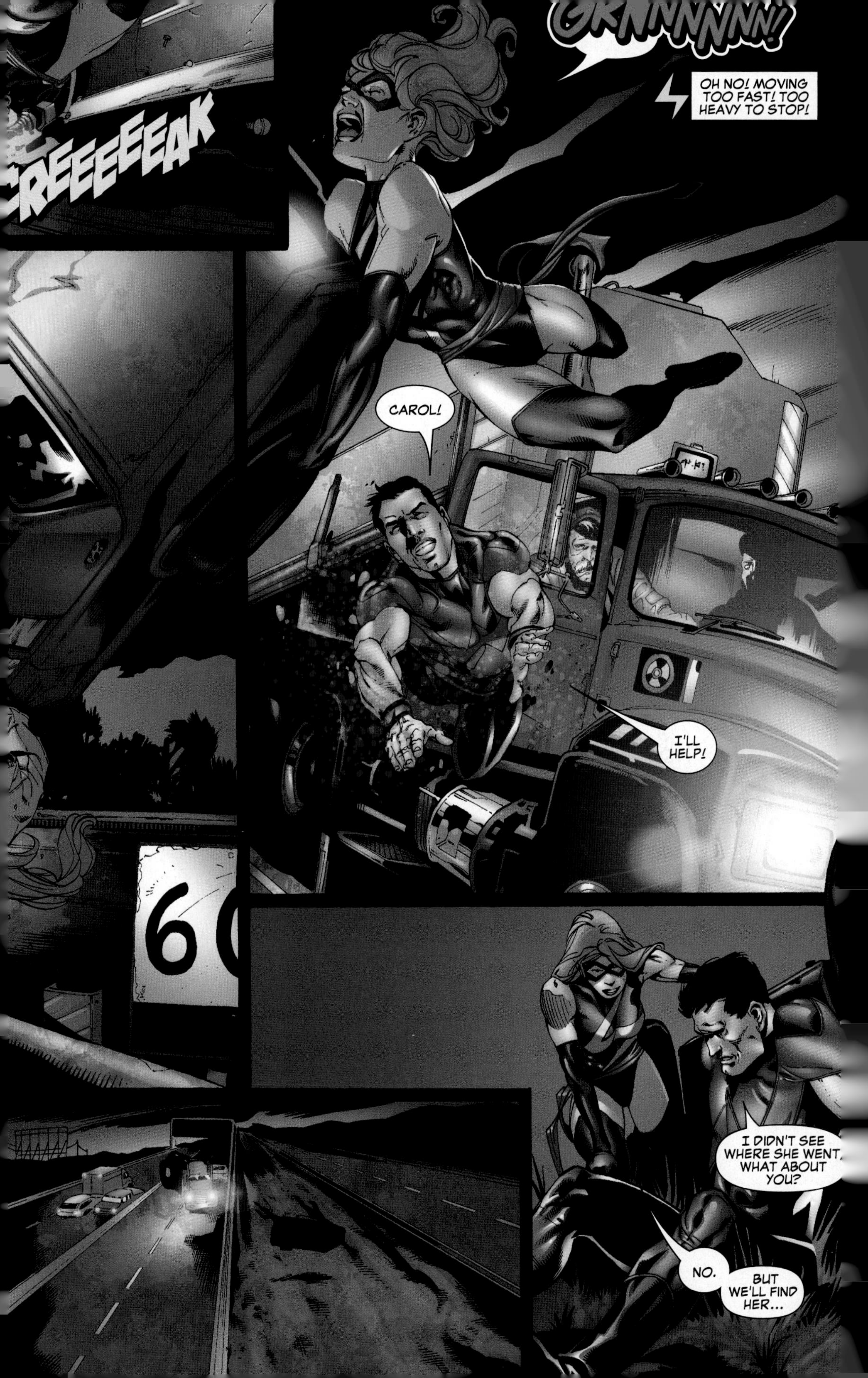

CREEEEEAK
GRNNNNNNN!
OH NO! MOVING TOO FAST! TOO HEAVY TO STOP!
CAROL!
I'LL HELP!
60
I DIDN'T SEE WHERE SHE WENT. WHAT ABOUT YOU?
NO.
BUT WE'LL FIND HER...

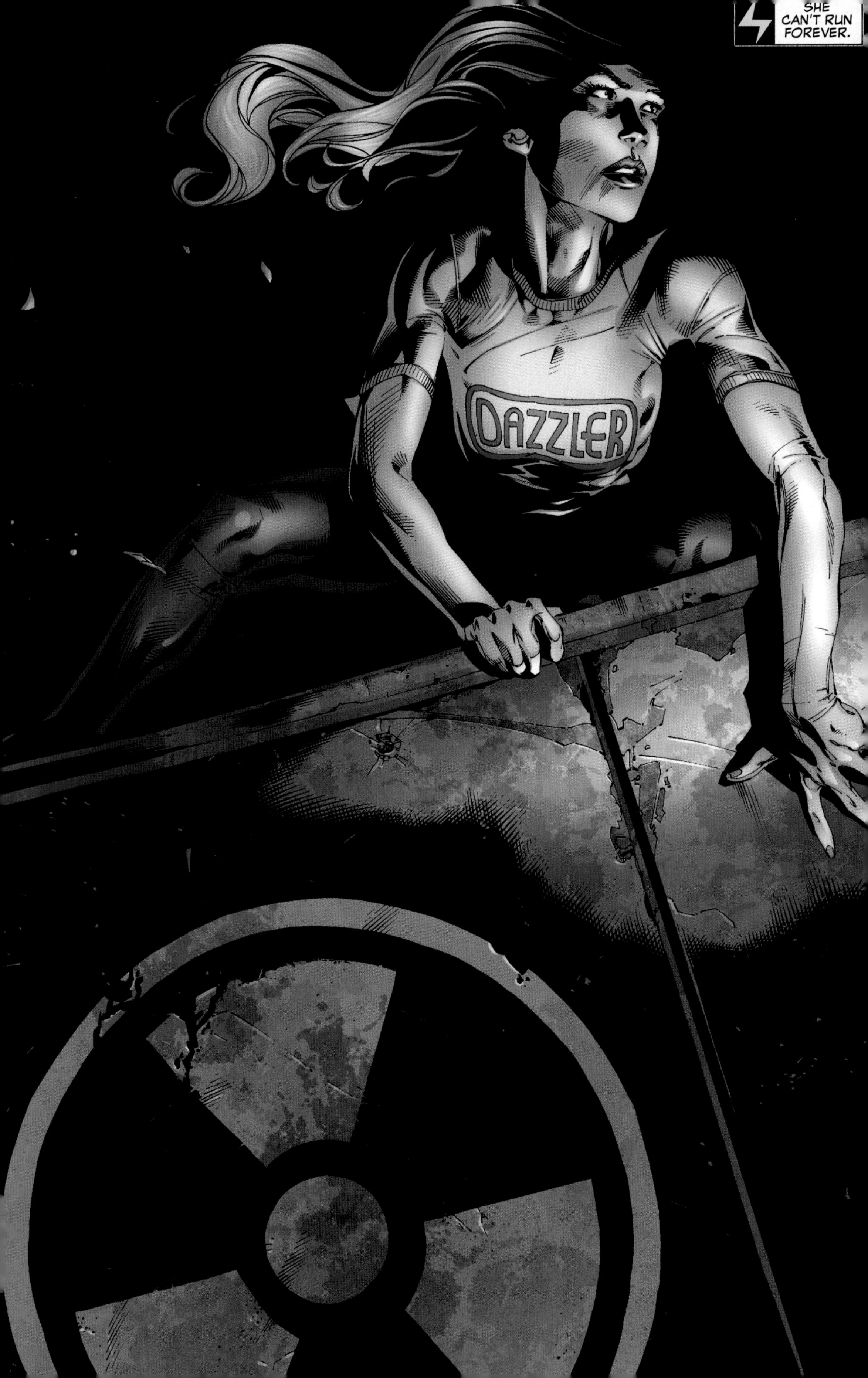
SHE CAN'T RUN FOREVER.
DAZZLER

MS. MARVEL
A MARVEL COMICS EVENT

CIVIL
WAR

8

"FOR THE BEST"

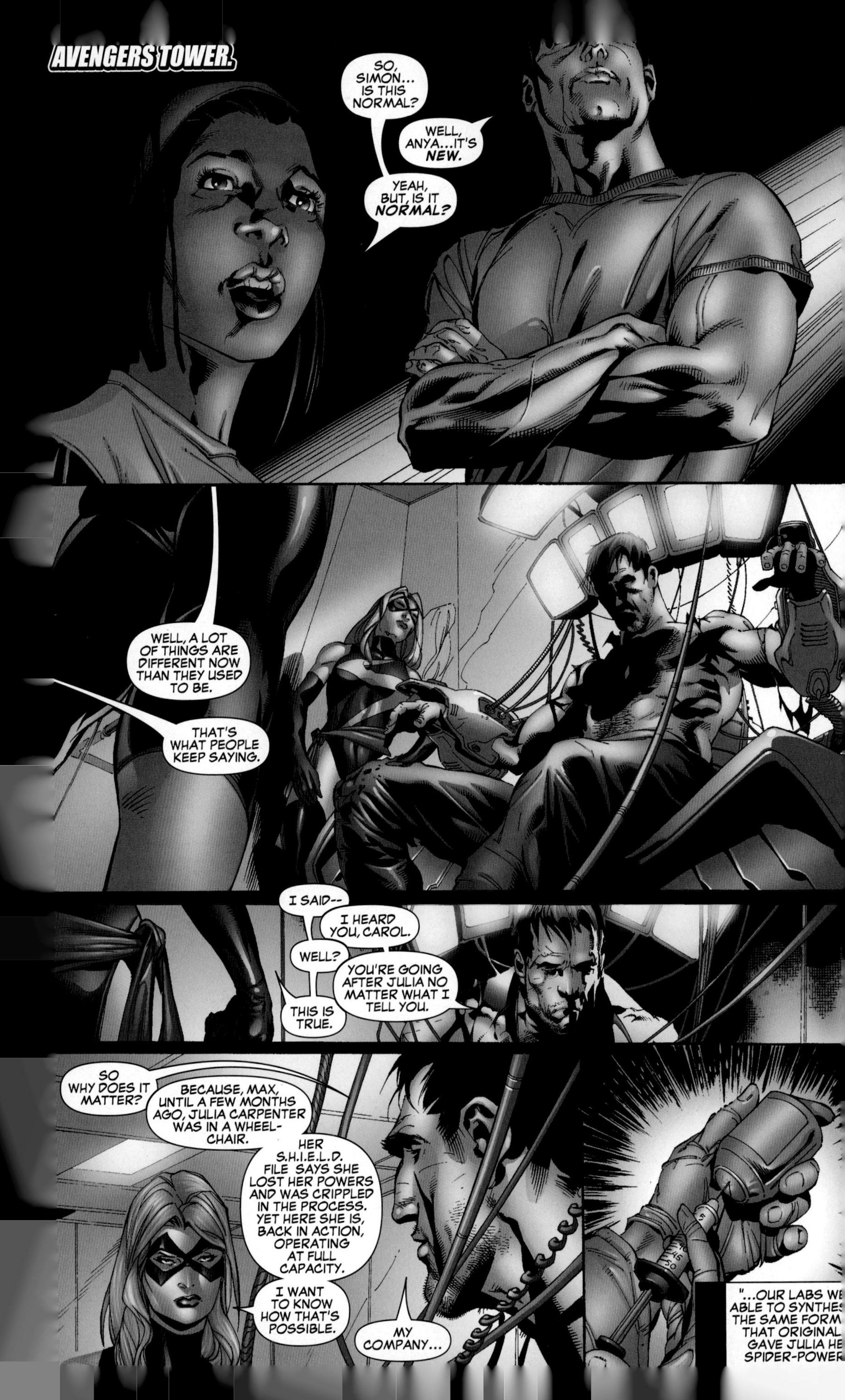
AVENGERS TOWER.
SO, SIMON... IS THIS NORMAL?
WELL, ANYA...IT'S NEW.
YEAH, BUT, IS IT NORMAL?
WELL, A LOT OF THINGS ARE DIFFERENT NOW THAN THEY USED TO BE.
THAT'S WHAT PEOPLE KEEP SAYING.
I SAID--
I HEARD YOU, CAROL.
WELL?
YOU'RE GOING AFTER JULIA NO MATTER WHAT I TELL YOU.
THIS IS TRUE.
SO WHY DOES IT MATTER?
BECAUSE, MAX, UNTIL A FEW MONTHS AGO, JULIA CARPENTER WAS IN A WHEEL-CHAIR.
HER S.H.I.E.L.D. FILE SAYS SHE LOST HER POWERS AND WAS CRIPPLED IN THE PROCESS. YET HERE SHE IS, BACK IN ACTION, OPERATING AT FULL CAPACITY.
I WANT TO KNOW HOW THAT'S POSSIBLE.
MY COMPANY...
"...OUR LABS WE ABLE TO SYNTHES THE SAME FORM THAT ORIGINAL GAVE JULIA HE SPIDER-POWER

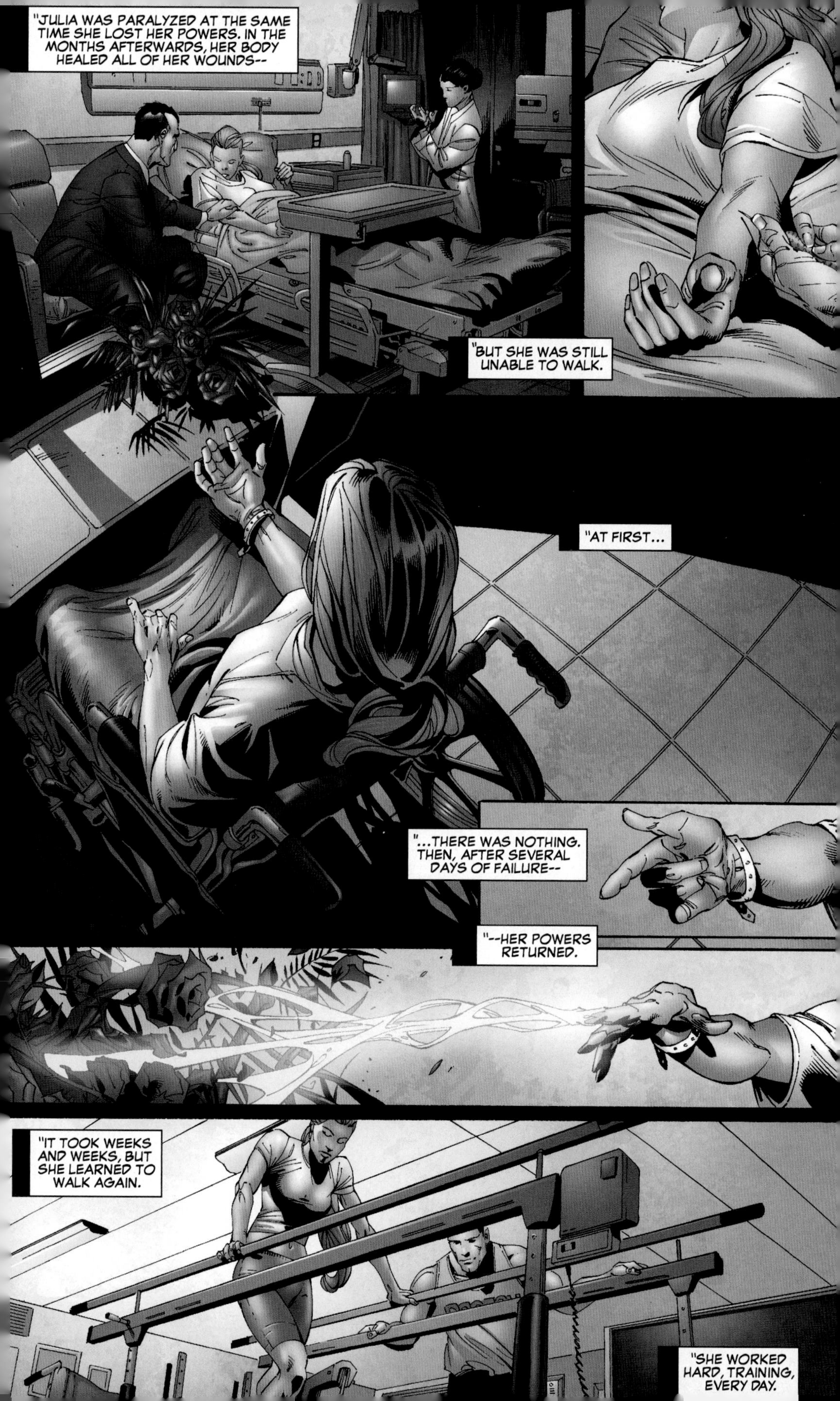
"JULIA WAS PARALYZED AT THE SAME TIME SHE LOST HER POWERS. IN THE MONTHS AFTERWARDS, HER BODY HEALED ALL OF HER WOUNDS--
"BUT SHE WAS STILL UNABLE TO WALK.
"AT FIRST...
"...THERE WAS NOTHING. THEN, AFTER SEVERAL DAYS OF FAILURE--
"--HER POWERS RETURNED.
"IT TOOK WEEKS AND WEEKS, BUT SHE LEARNED TO WALK AGAIN.
"SHE WORKED HARD, TRAINING, EVERY DAY.

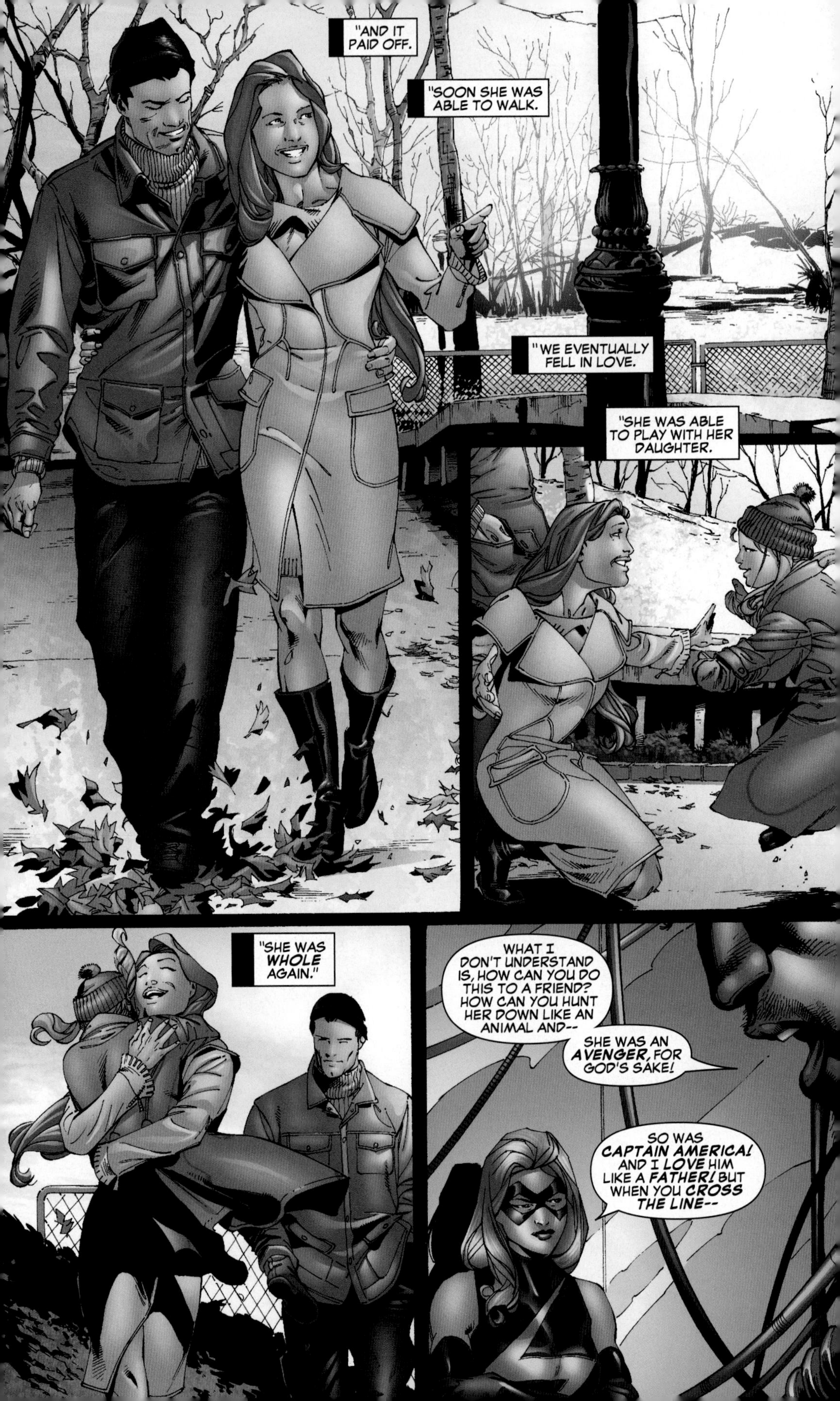
"AND IT PAID OFF.
"SOON SHE WAS ABLE TO WALK.
"WE EVENTUALLY FELL IN LOVE.
"SHE WAS ABLE TO PLAY WITH HER DAUGHTER.
"SHE WAS WHOLE AGAIN."
WHAT I DON'T UNDERSTAND IS, HOW CAN YOU DO THIS TO A FRIEND? HOW CAN YOU HUNT HER DOWN LIKE AN ANIMAL AND--
SHE WAS AN AVENGER, FOR GOD'S SAKE!
SO WAS CAPTAIN AMERICA! AND I LOVE HIM LIKE A FATHER! BUT WHEN YOU CROSS THE LINE--

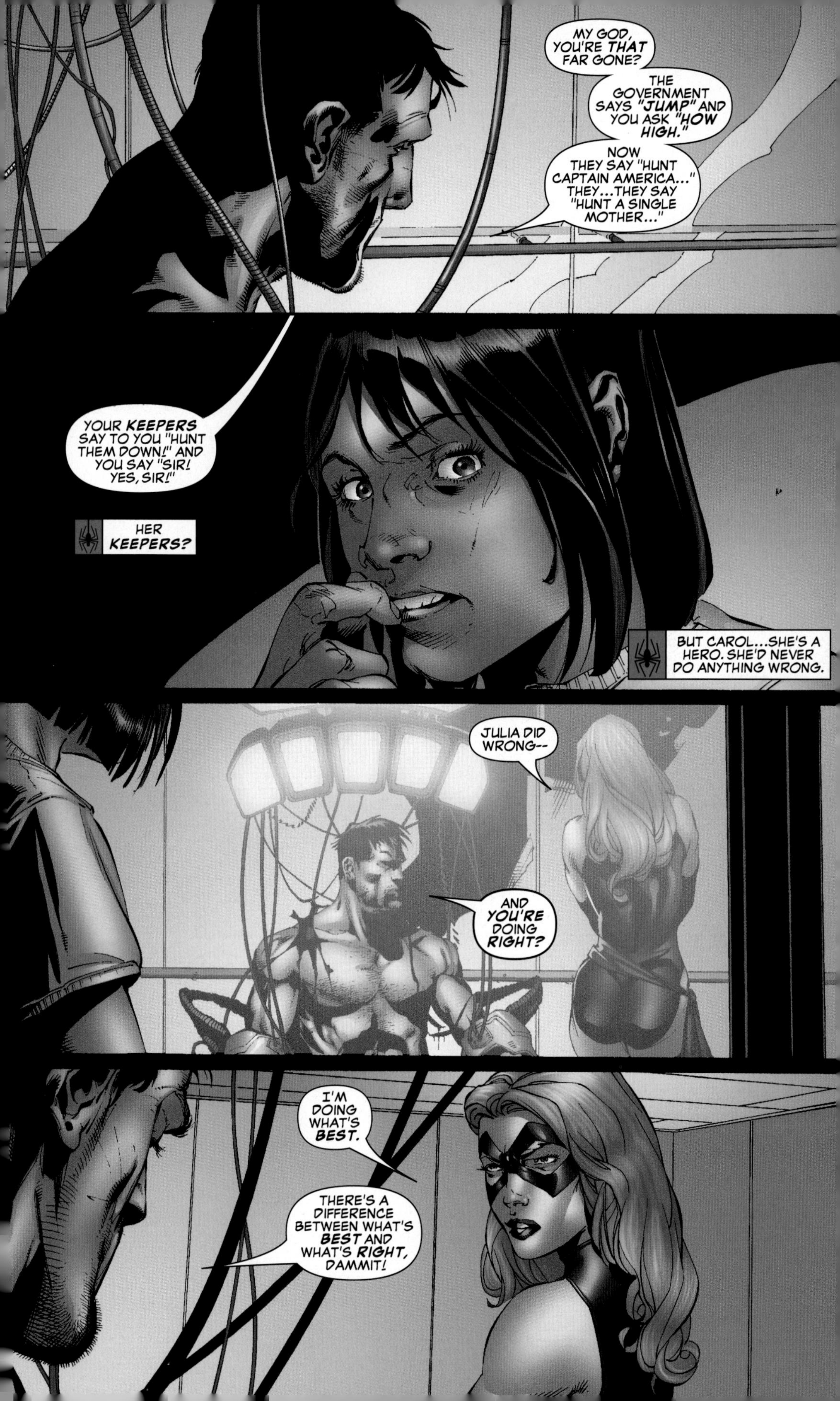

MY GOD, YOU'RE THAT FAR GONE?
THE GOVERNMENT SAYS "JUMP" AND YOU ASK "HOW HIGH."
NOW THEY SAY "HUNT CAPTAIN AMERICA..." THEY...THEY SAY "HUNT A SINGLE MOTHER..."
YOUR KEEPERS SAY TO YOU "HUNT THEM DOWN!" AND YOU SAY "SIR! YES, SIR!"
HER KEEPERS?
BUT CAROL...SHE'S A HERO. SHE'D NEVER DO ANYTHING WRONG.
JULIA DID WRONG--
AND YOU'RE DOING RIGHT?
I'M DOING WHAT'S BEST.
THERE'S A DIFFERENCE BETWEEN WHAT'S BEST AND WHAT'S RIGHT, DAMMIT!

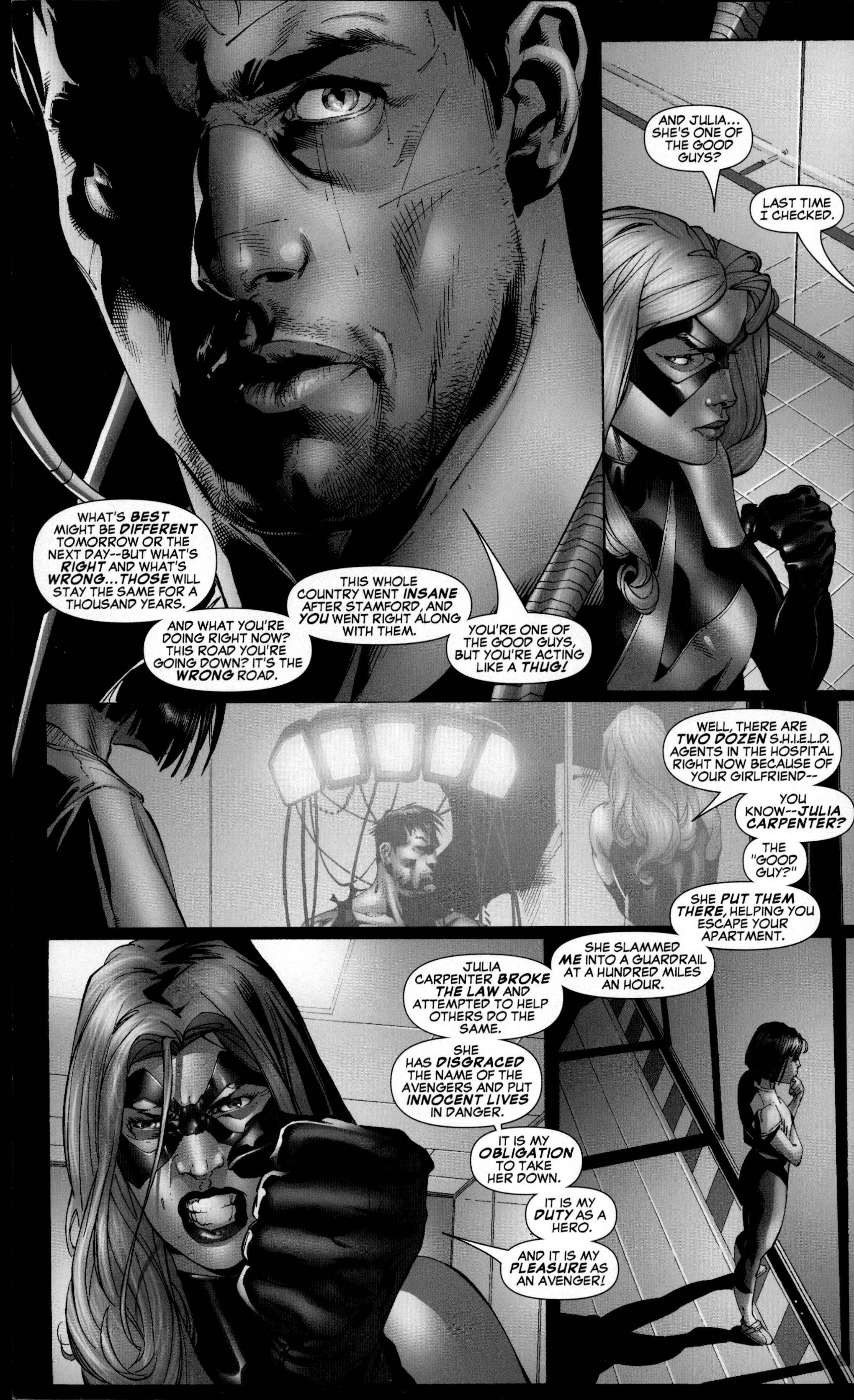
WHAT'S **BEST** MIGHT BE **DIFFERENT** TOMORROW OR THE NEXT DAY--BUT WHAT'S **RIGHT** AND WHAT'S **WRONG**...**THOSE** WILL STAY THE SAME FOR A THOUSAND YEARS.
AND WHAT YOU'RE DOING RIGHT NOW? THIS ROAD YOU'RE GOING DOWN? IT'S THE **WRONG** ROAD.
THIS WHOLE COUNTRY WENT **INSANE** AFTER STAMFORD, AND **YOU** WENT RIGHT ALONG WITH THEM.
YOU'RE ONE OF THE GOOD GUYS, BUT YOU'RE ACTING LIKE A **THUG!**
AND JULIA... SHE'S ONE OF THE GOOD GUYS?
LAST TIME I CHECKED.
WELL, THERE ARE **TWO DOZEN** S.H.I.E.L.D. AGENTS IN THE HOSPITAL RIGHT NOW BECAUSE OF YOUR GIRLFRIEND--
YOU KNOW--**JULIA CARPENTER?**
THE "GOOD GUY?"
SHE **PUT THEM THERE,** HELPING YOU ESCAPE YOUR APARTMENT.
SHE SLAMMED **ME** INTO A GUARDRAIL AT A HUNDRED MILES AN HOUR.
JULIA CARPENTER **BROKE THE LAW** AND ATTEMPTED TO HELP OTHERS DO THE SAME.
SHE HAS **DISGRACED** THE NAME OF THE AVENGERS AND PUT **INNOCENT LIVES** IN DANGER.
IT IS MY **OBLIGATION** TO TAKE HER DOWN.
IT IS MY **DUTY** AS A HERO.
AND IT IS MY **PLEASURE** AS AN AVENGER!

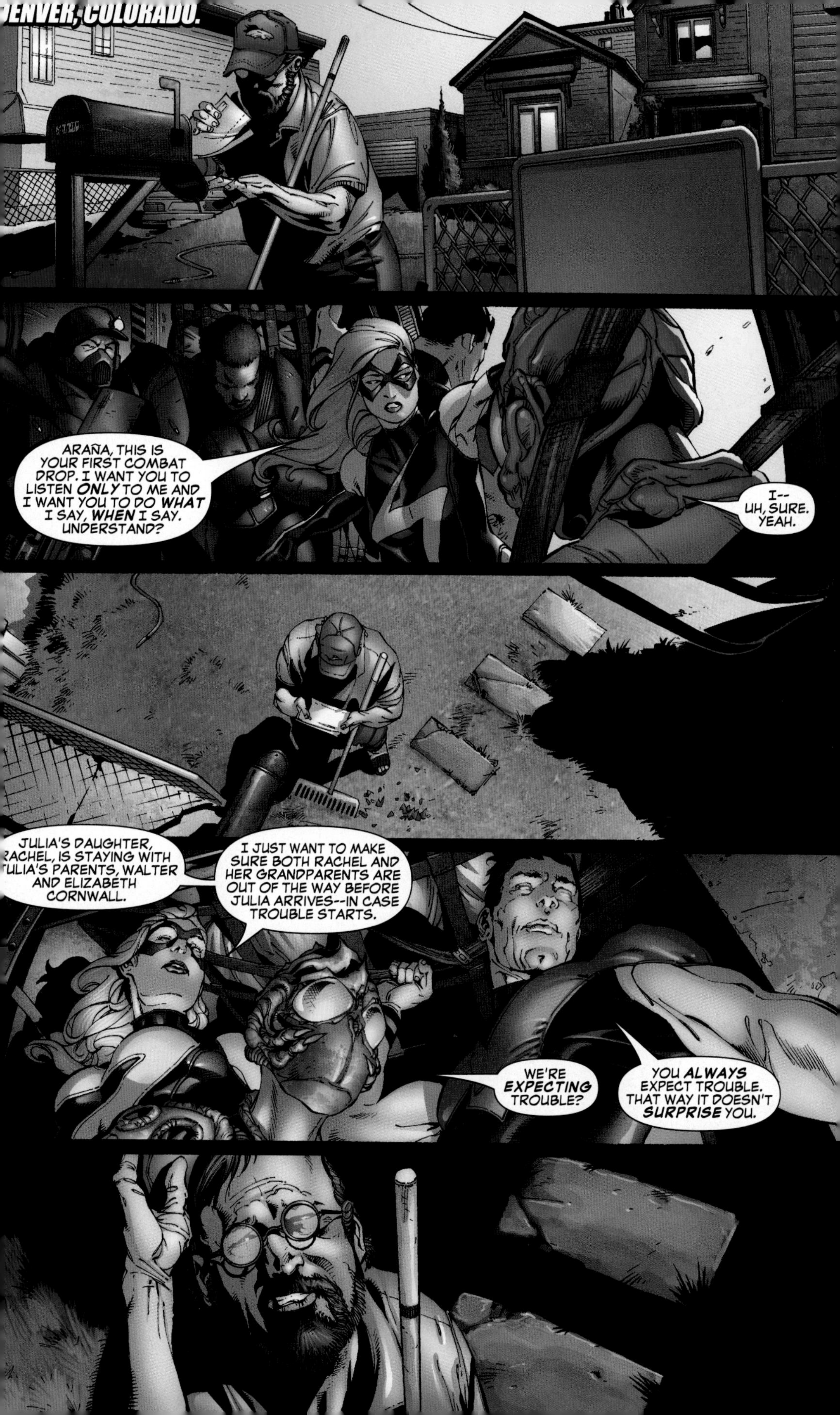
ENVER, COLORADO.
ARAÑA, THIS IS YOUR FIRST COMBAT DROP. I WANT YOU TO LISTEN ONLY TO ME AND I WANT YOU TO DO WHAT I SAY, WHEN I SAY. UNDERSTAND?
I-- UH, SURE. YEAH.
JULIA'S DAUGHTER, RACHEL, IS STAYING WITH JULIA'S PARENTS, WALTER AND ELIZABETH CORNWALL.
I JUST WANT TO MAKE SURE BOTH RACHEL AND HER GRANDPARENTS ARE OUT OF THE WAY BEFORE JULIA ARRIVES--IN CASE TROUBLE STARTS.
WE'RE EXPECTING TROUBLE?
YOU ALWAYS EXPECT TROUBLE. THAT WAY IT DOESN'T SURPRISE YOU.

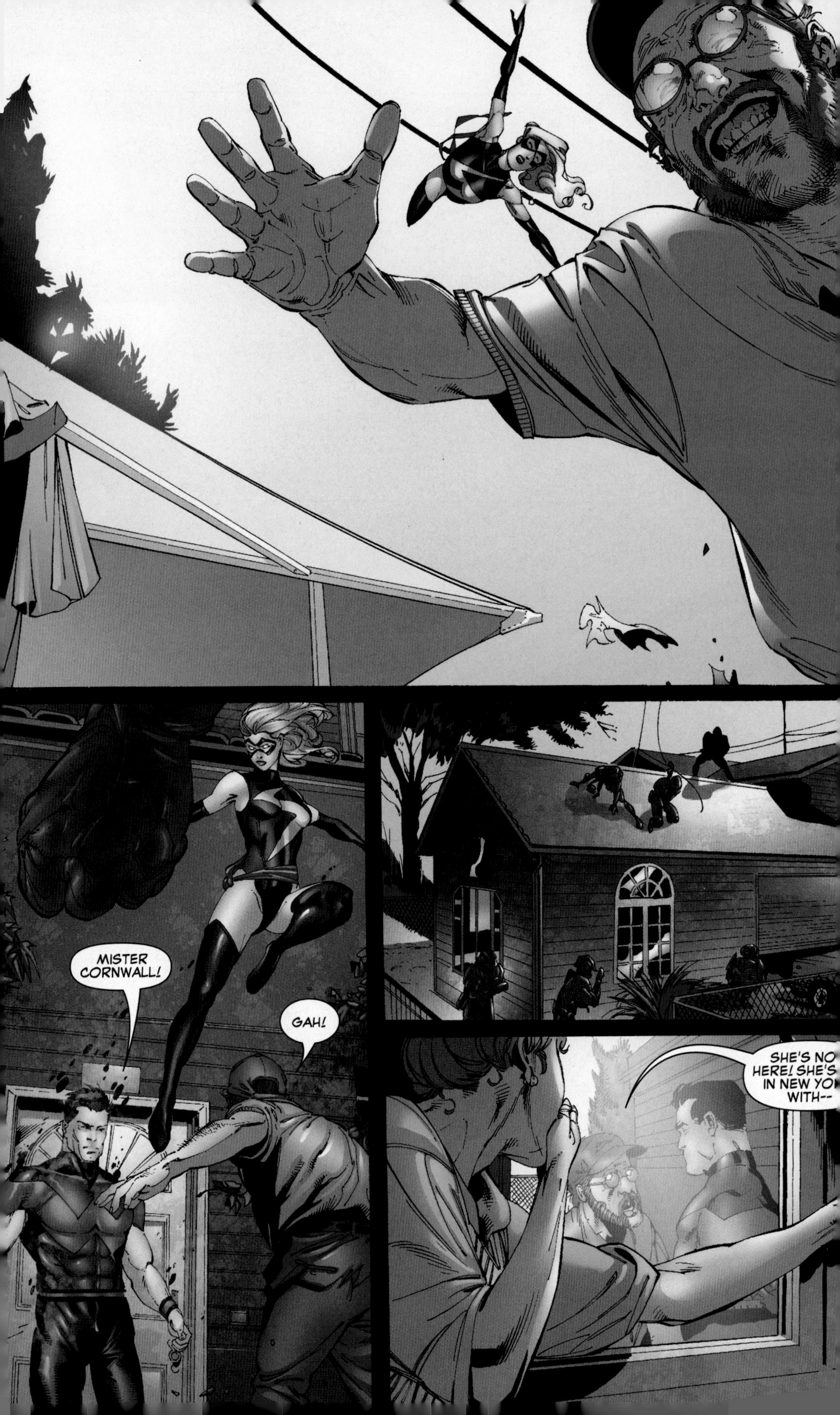
MISTER CORNWALL!
GAH!
SHE'S NO HERE! SHE'S IN NEW YO WITH--

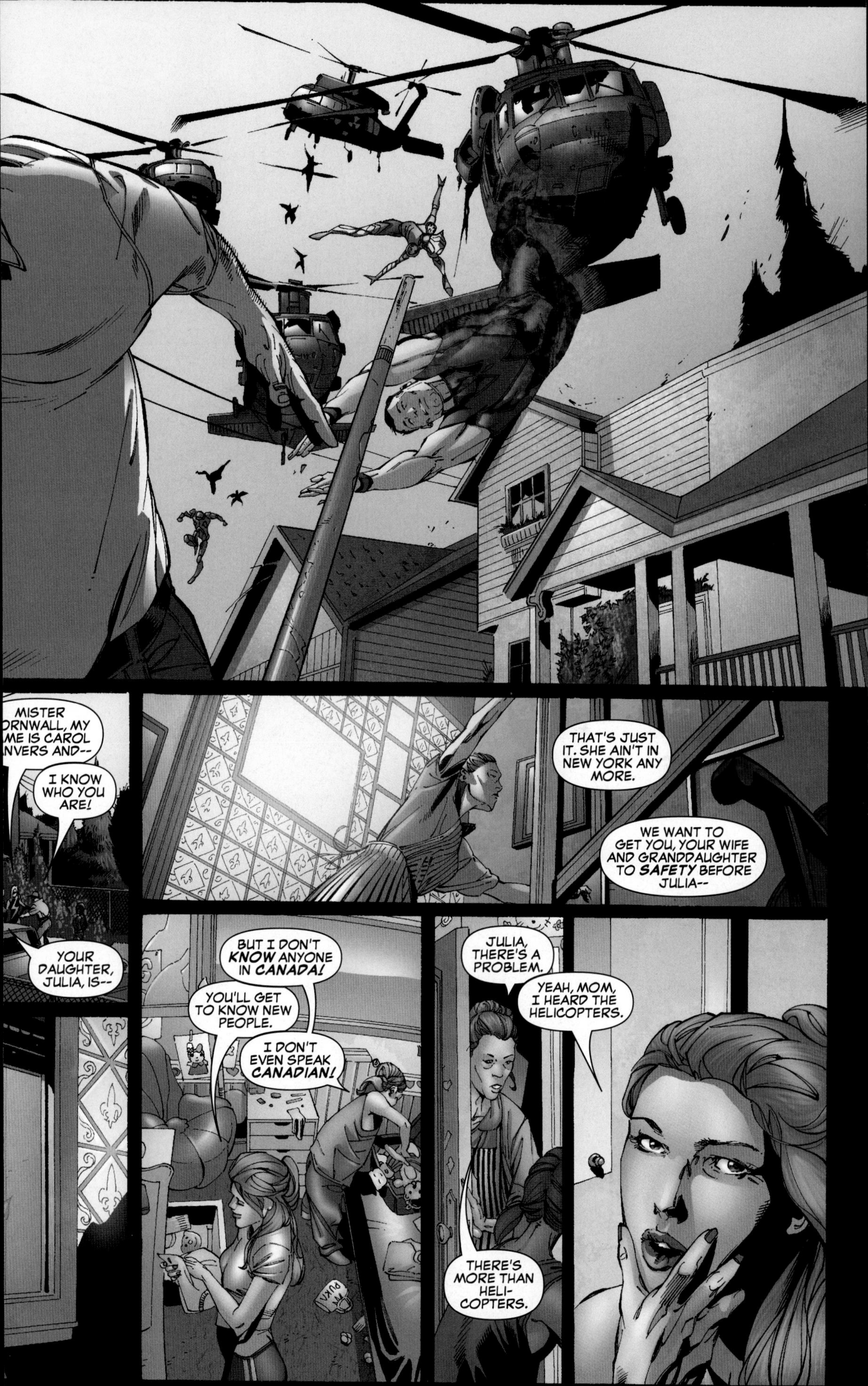

MISTER
ORNWALL, MY
ME IS CAROL
NVERS AND--
I KNOW WHO YOU ARE!
YOUR DAUGHTER, JULIA, IS--
THAT'S JUST IT. SHE AIN'T IN NEW YORK ANY MORE.
WE WANT TO GET YOU, YOUR WIFE AND GRANDDAUGHTER TO SAFETY BEFORE JULIA--
BUT I DON'T KNOW ANYONE IN CANADA!
YOU'LL GET TO KNOW NEW PEOPLE.
I DON'T EVEN SPEAK CANADIAN!
JULIA, THERE'S A PROBLEM.
YEAH, MOM, I HEARD THE HELICOPTERS.
THERE'S MORE THAN HELI-COPTERS.

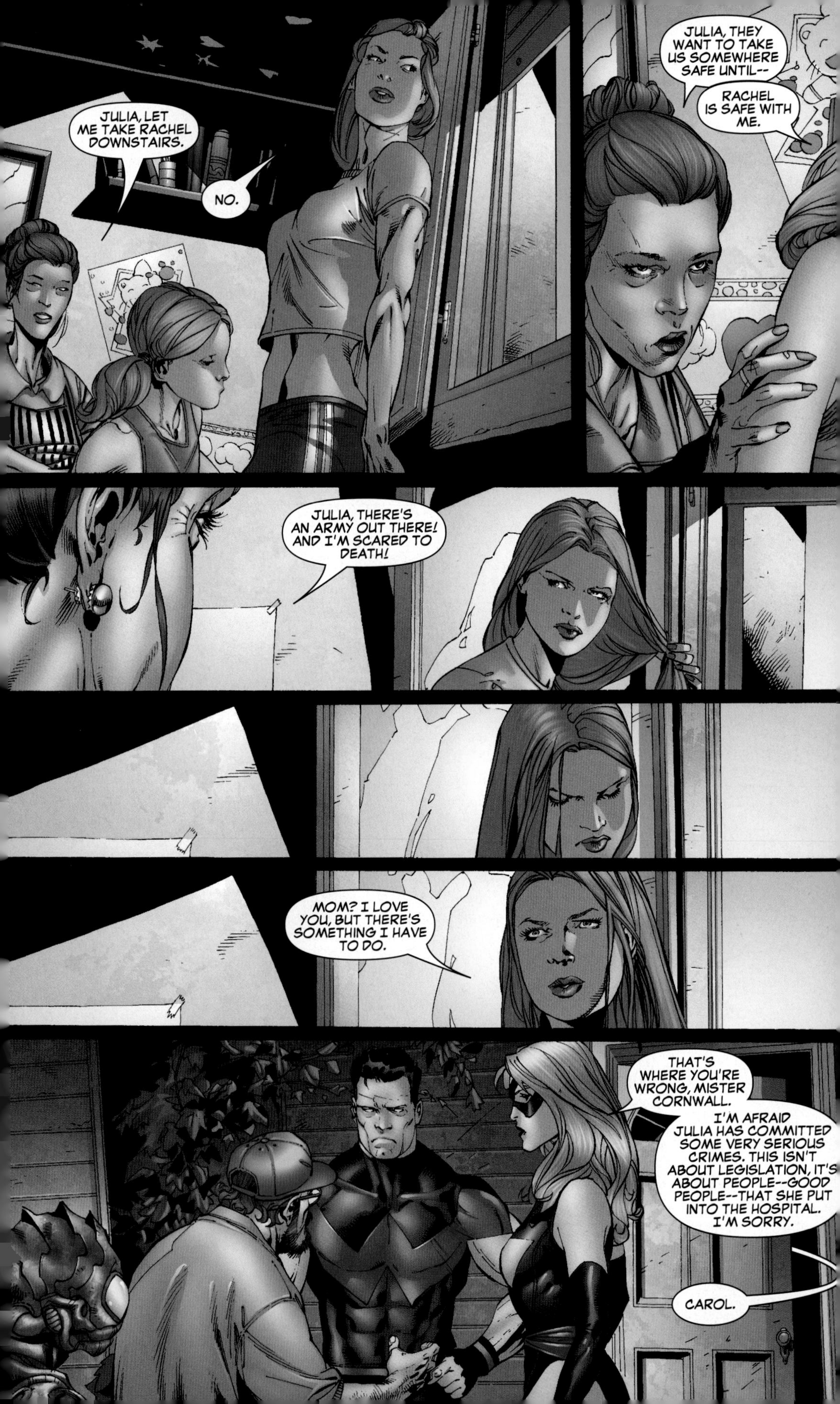

JULIA, LET ME TAKE RACHEL DOWNSTAIRS.
NO.
JULIA, THEY WANT TO TAKE US SOMEWHERE SAFE UNTIL--
RACHEL IS SAFE WITH ME.
JULIA, THERE'S AN ARMY OUT THERE! AND I'M SCARED TO DEATH!
MOM? I LOVE YOU, BUT THERE'S SOMETHING I HAVE TO DO.
THAT'S WHERE YOU'RE WRONG, MISTER CORNWALL.
I'M AFRAID JULIA HAS COMMITTED SOME VERY SERIOUS CRIMES. THIS ISN'T ABOUT LEGISLATION, IT'S ABOUT PEOPLE--GOOD PEOPLE--THAT SHE PUT INTO THE HOSPITAL. I'M SORRY.
CAROL.

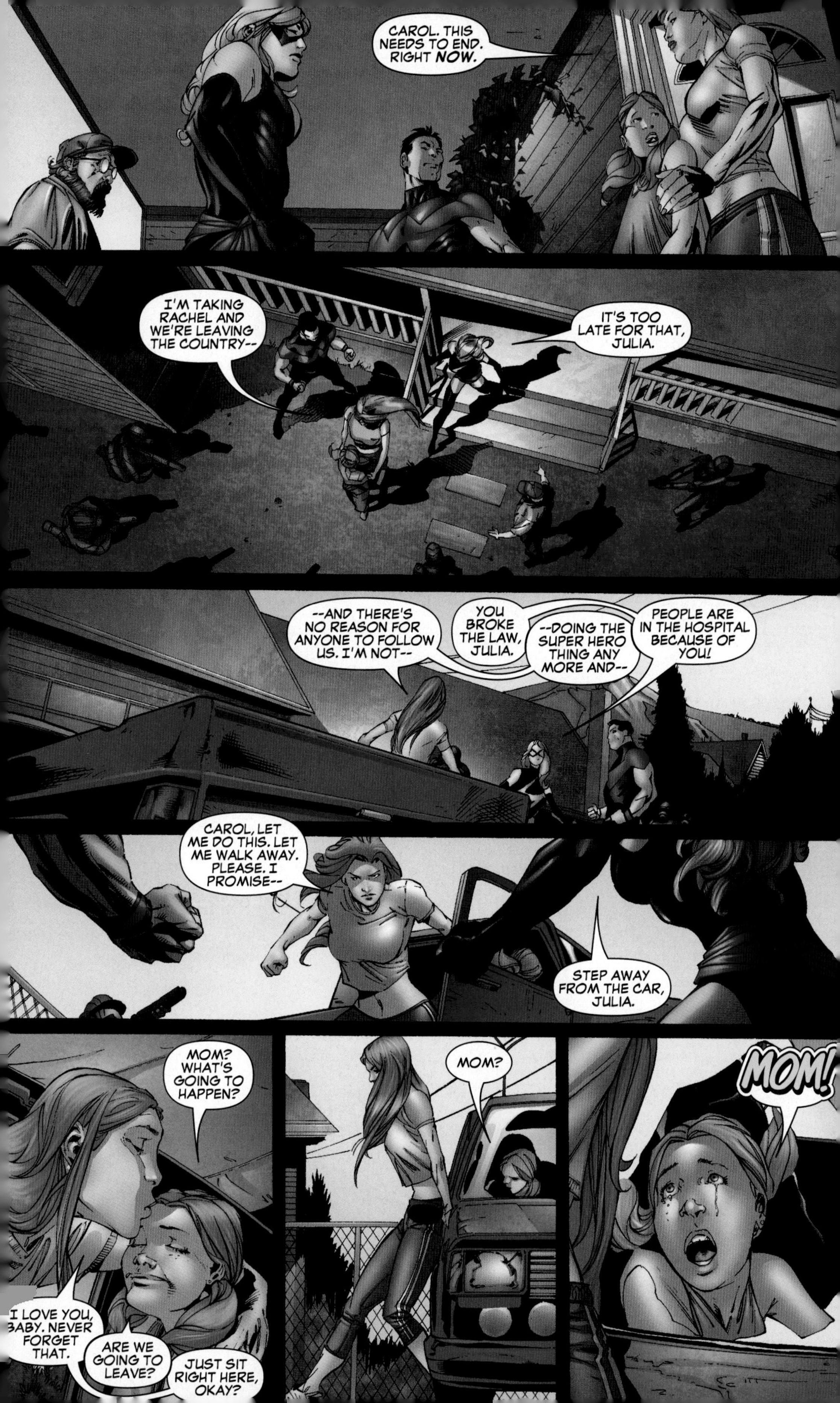
CAROL. THIS NEEDS TO END. RIGHT NOW.
I'M TAKING RACHEL AND WE'RE LEAVING THE COUNTRY--
IT'S TOO LATE FOR THAT, JULIA.
--AND THERE'S NO REASON FOR ANYONE TO FOLLOW US. I'M NOT--
YOU BROKE THE LAW, JULIA.
--DOING THE SUPER HERO THING ANY MORE AND--
PEOPLE ARE IN THE HOSPITAL BECAUSE OF YOU!
CAROL, LET ME DO THIS. LET ME WALK AWAY. PLEASE. I PROMISE--
STEP AWAY FROM THE CAR, JULIA.
MOM? WHAT'S GOING TO HAPPEN?
I LOVE YOU, BABY. NEVER FORGET THAT.
ARE WE GOING TO LEAVE?
JUST SIT RIGHT HERE, OKAY?
MOM?
MOM!

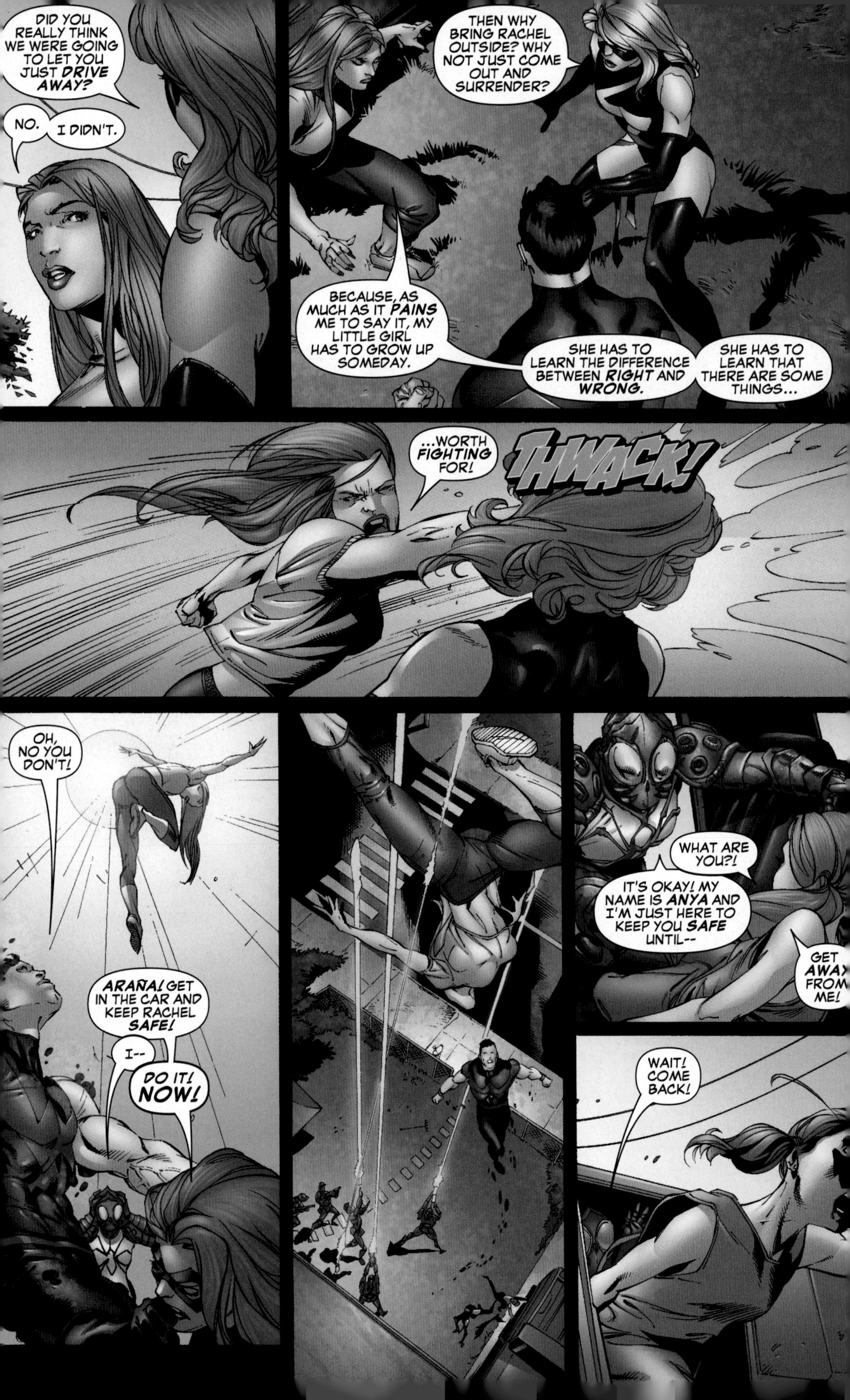
DID YOU REALLY THINK WE WERE GOING TO LET YOU JUST DRIVE AWAY?
NO.
I DIDN'T.
THEN WHY BRING RACHEL OUTSIDE? WHY NOT JUST COME OUT AND SURRENDER?
BECAUSE, AS MUCH AS IT PAINS ME TO SAY IT, MY LITTLE GIRL HAS TO GROW UP SOMEDAY.
SHE HAS TO LEARN THE DIFFERENCE BETWEEN RIGHT AND WRONG.
SHE HAS TO LEARN THAT THERE ARE SOME THINGS...
...WORTH FIGHTING FOR!
THWACK!
OH, NO YOU DON'T!
ARAÑA! GET IN THE CAR AND KEEP RACHEL SAFE!
I--
DO IT! NOW!
WHAT ARE YOU?!
IT'S OKAY! MY NAME IS ANYA AND I'M JUST HERE TO KEEP YOU SAFE UNTIL--
GET AWAY FROM ME!
WAIT! COME BACK!

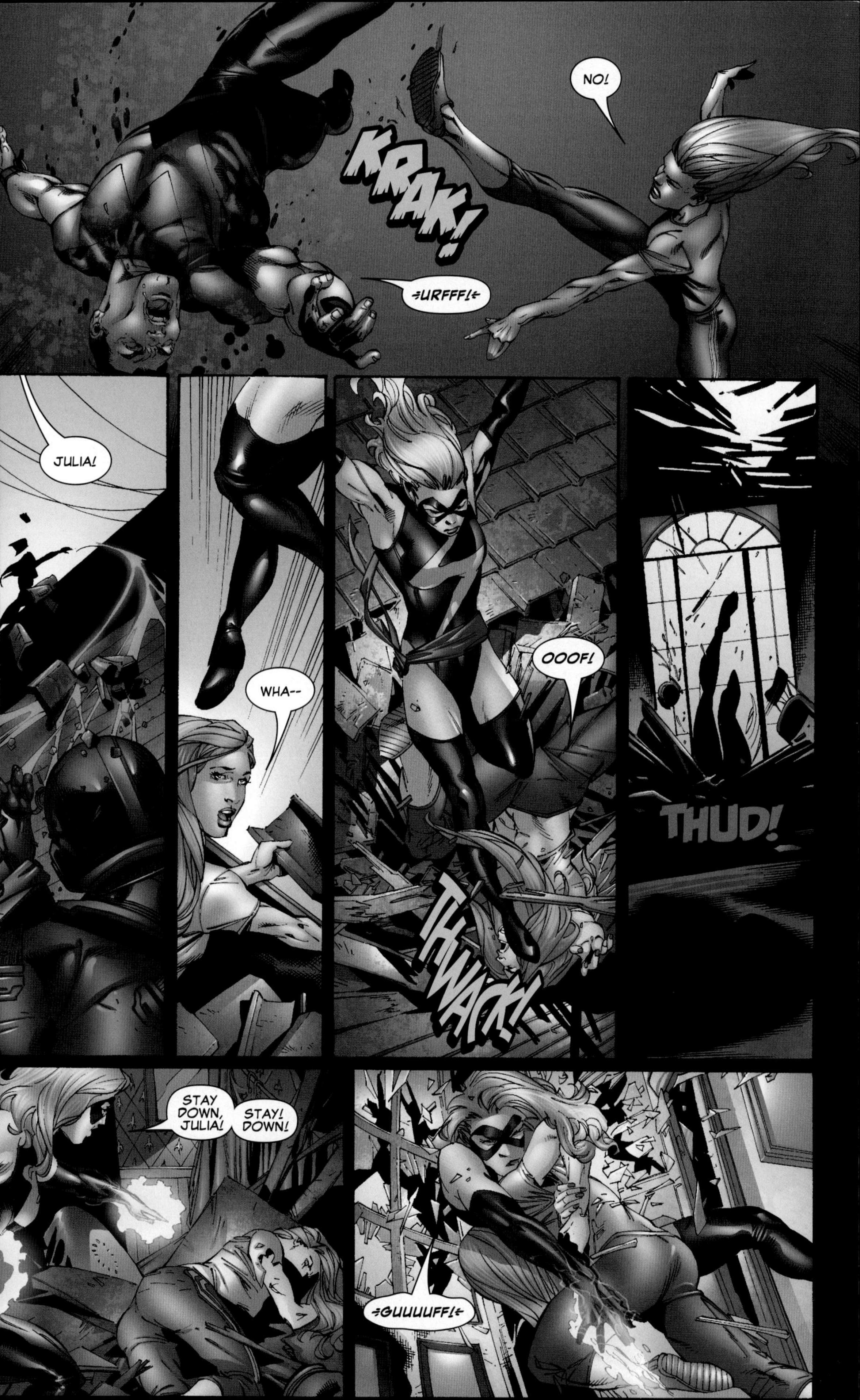

NO!
KRAK!
URFFF!
JULIA!
WHA--
OOOF!
THWACK!
THUD!
STAY DOWN, JULIA!
STAY! DOWN!
GUUUUFF!

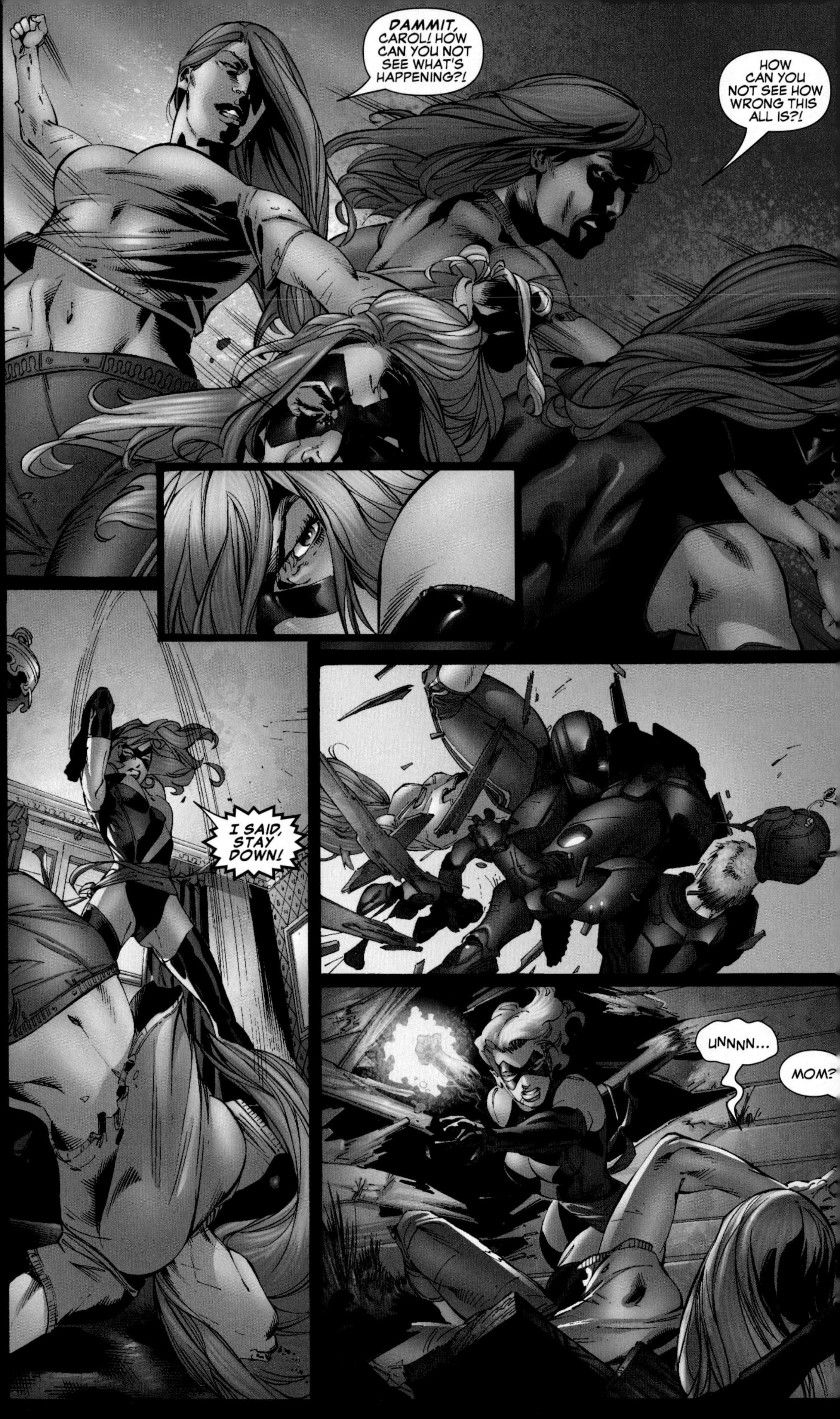
DAMMIT, CAROL! HOW CAN YOU NOT SEE WHAT'S HAPPENING?!
HOW CAN YOU NOT SEE HOW WRONG THIS ALL IS?!
I SAID, STAY DOWN!
UNNNN...
MOM?

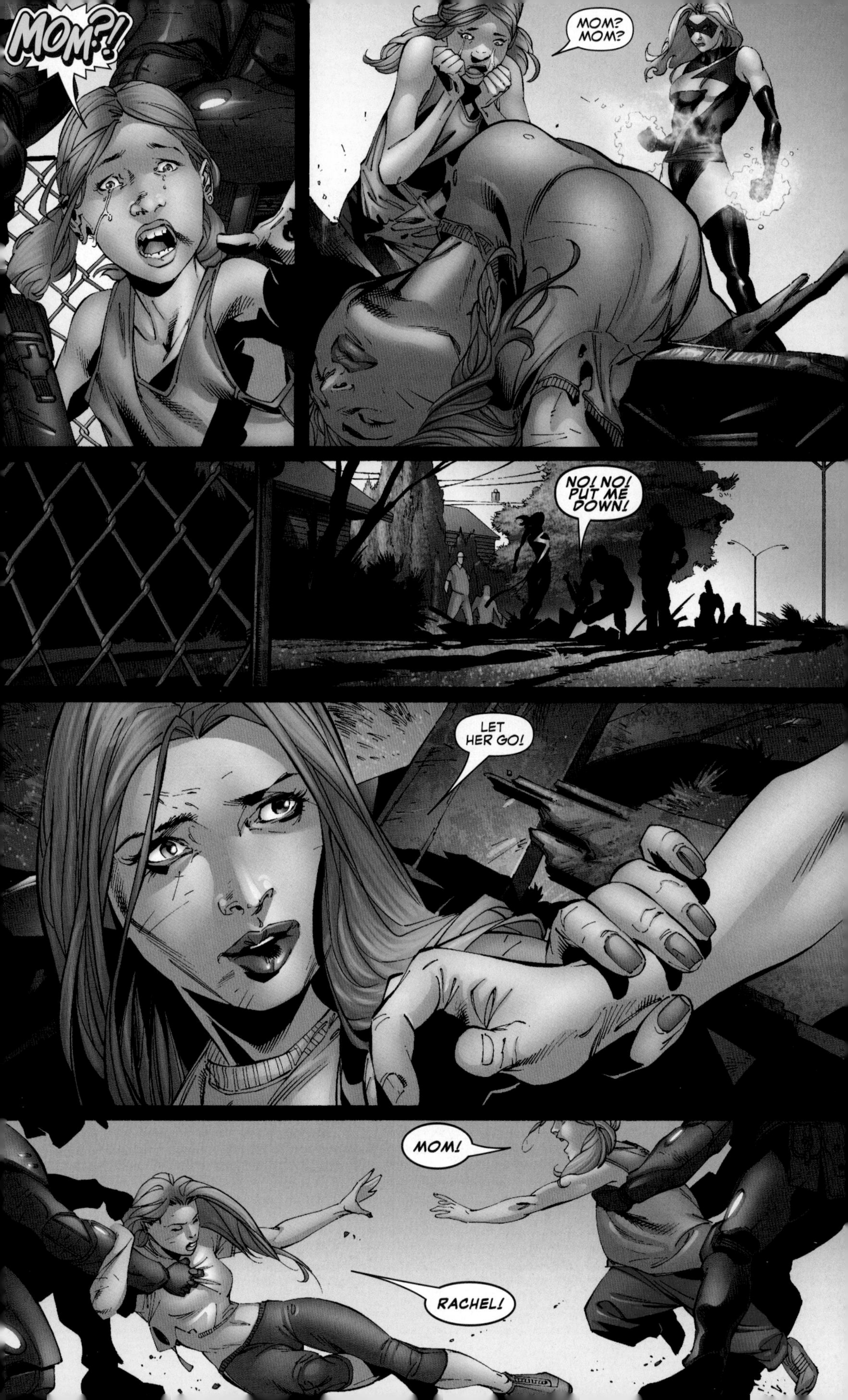
MOM?!
MOM? MOM?
NO! NO! PUT ME DOWN!
LET HER GO!
MOM!
RACHEL!

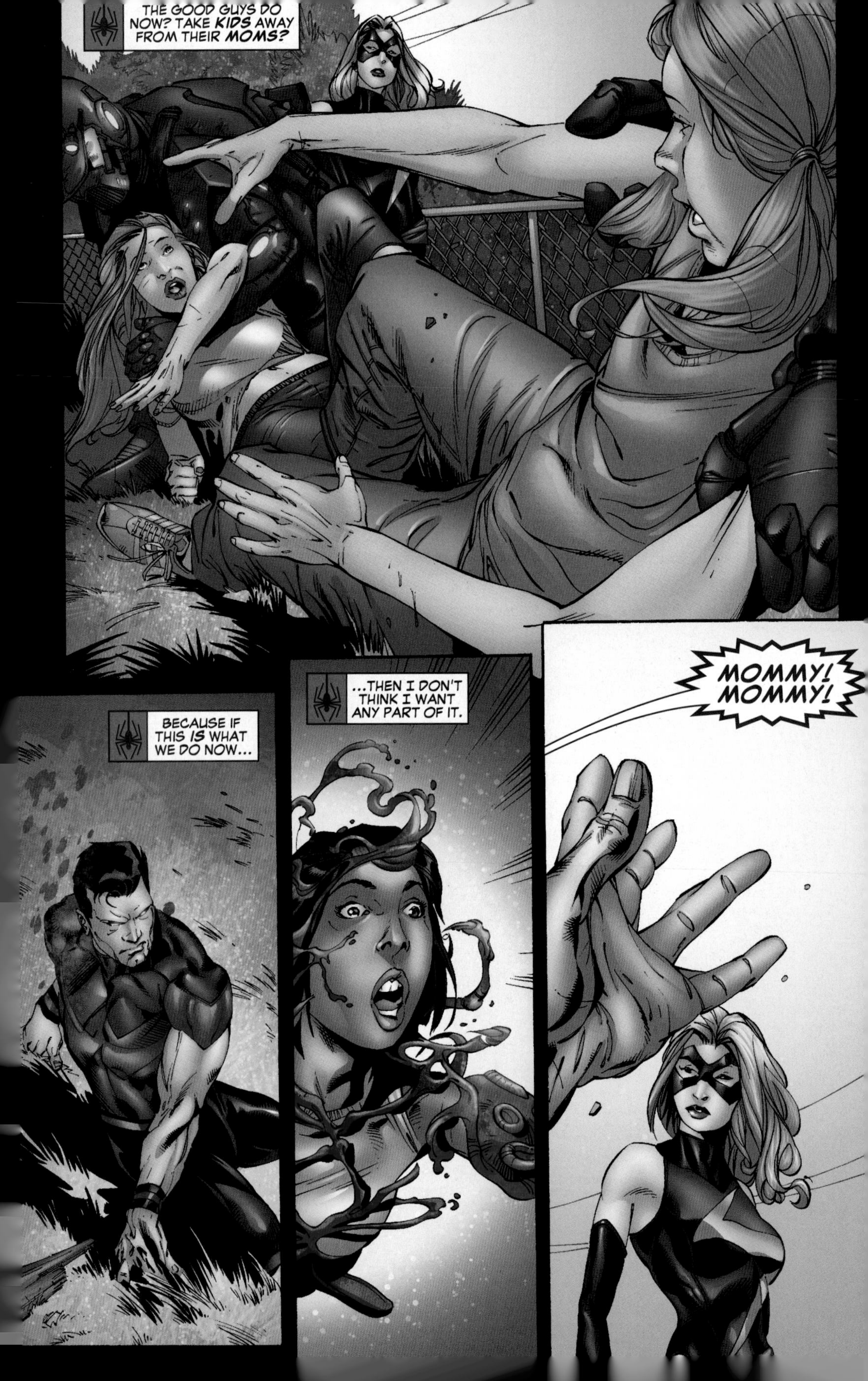

THE GOOD GUYS DO NOW? TAKE KIDS AWAY FROM THEIR MOMS?
MOMMY! MOMMY!
BECAUSE IF THIS IS WHAT WE DO NOW...
...THEN I DON'T THINK I WANT ANY PART OF IT.

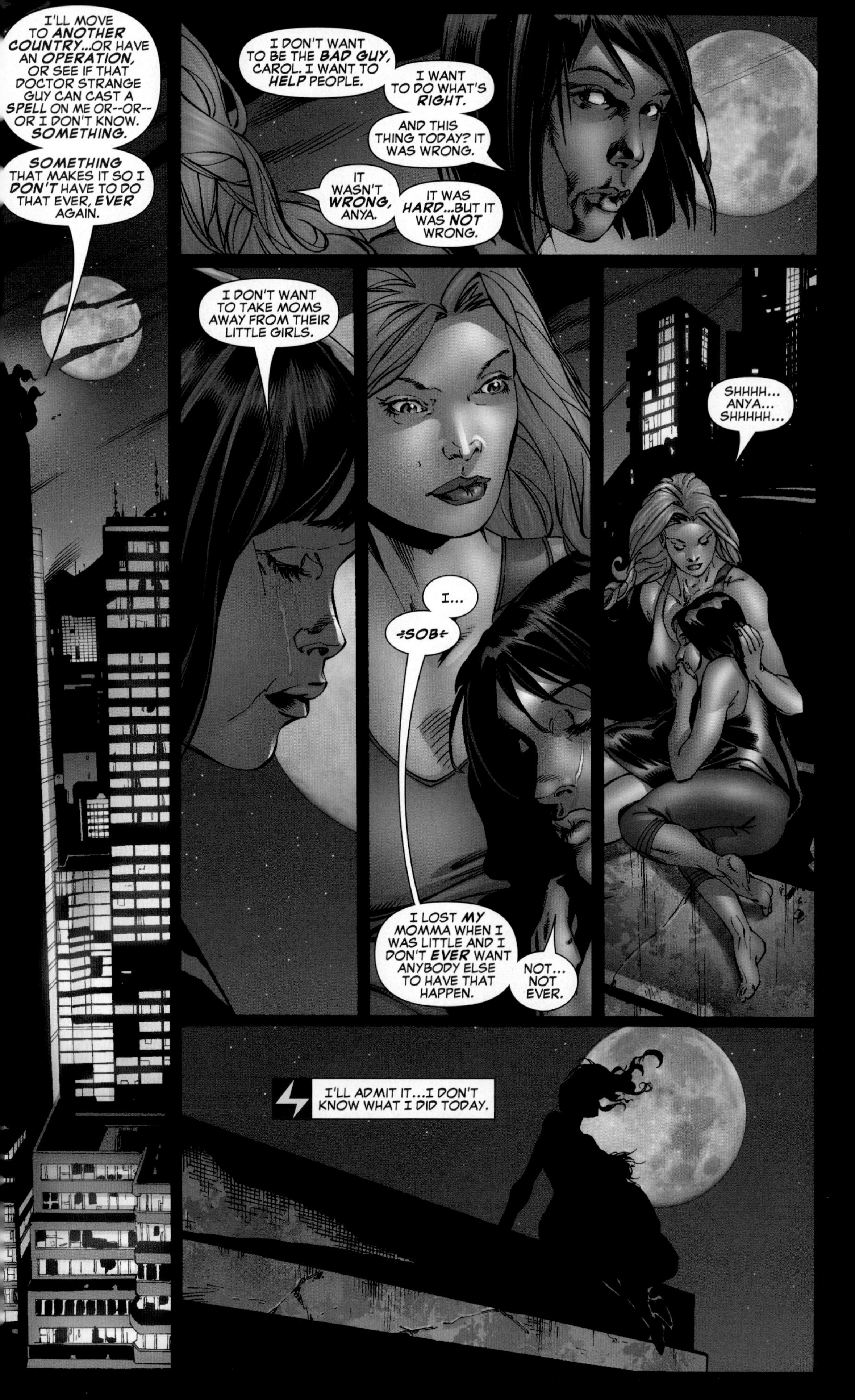
I'LL MOVE TO ANOTHER COUNTRY...OR HAVE AN OPERATION, OR SEE IF THAT DOCTOR STRANGE GUY CAN CAST A SPELL ON ME OR--OR--OR I DON'T KNOW. SOMETHING.
SOMETHING THAT MAKES IT SO I DON'T HAVE TO DO THAT EVER, EVER AGAIN.
I DON'T WANT TO BE THE BAD GUY, CAROL. I WANT TO HELP PEOPLE.
I WANT TO DO WHAT'S RIGHT.
AND THIS THING TODAY? IT WAS WRONG.
IT WASN'T WRONG, ANYA.
IT WAS HARD...BUT IT WAS NOT WRONG.
I DON'T WANT TO TAKE MOMS AWAY FROM THEIR LITTLE GIRLS.
I...
SOB
I LOST MY MOMMA WHEN I WAS LITTLE AND I DON'T EVER WANT ANYBODY ELSE TO HAVE THAT HAPPEN.
NOT... NOT EVER.
SHHHH... ANYA... SHHHHH...
I'LL ADMIT IT...I DON'T KNOW WHAT I DID TODAY.

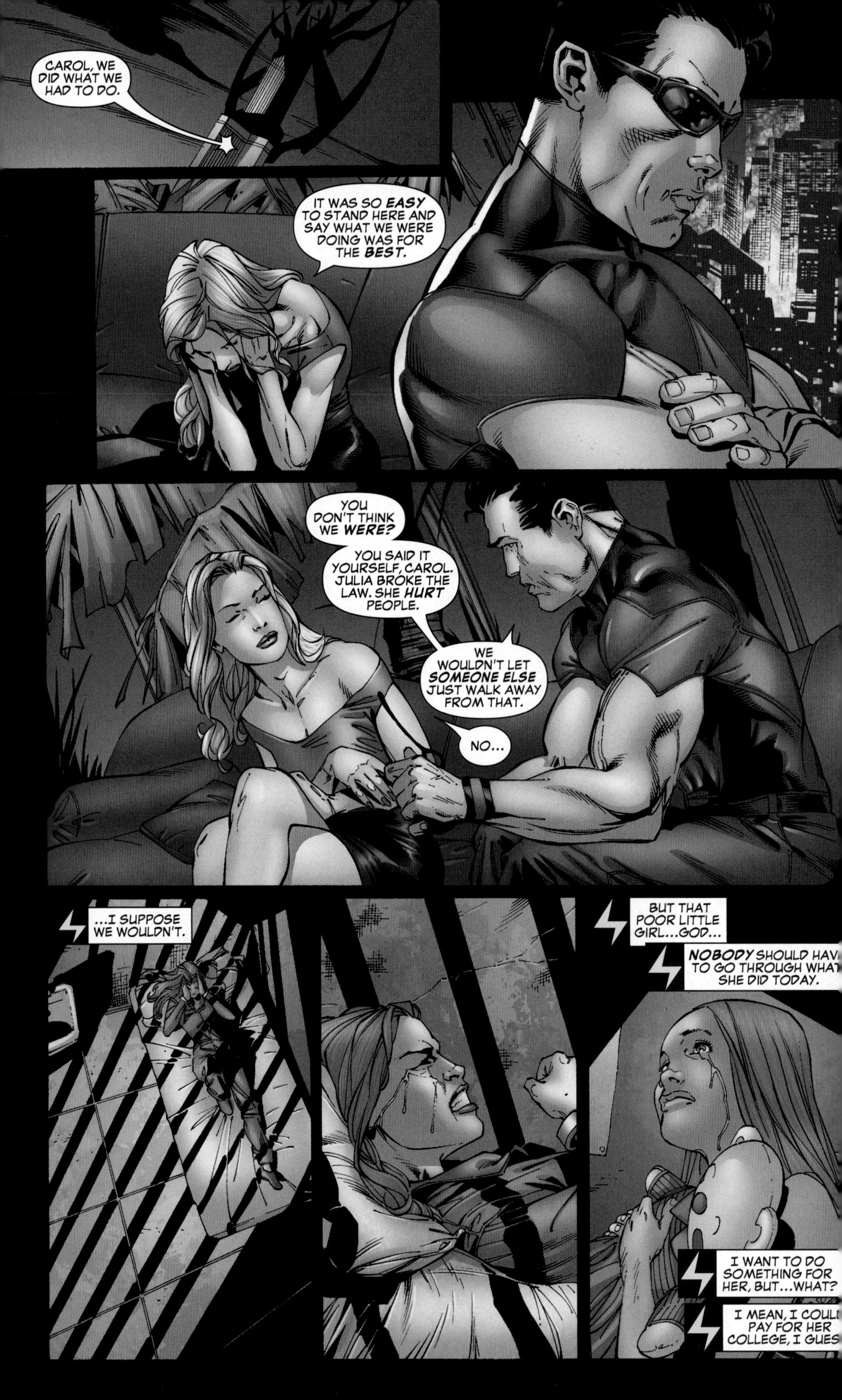

CAROL, WE DID WHAT WE HAD TO DO.
IT WAS SO EASY TO STAND HERE AND SAY WHAT WE WERE DOING WAS FOR THE BEST.
YOU DON'T THINK WE WERE?
YOU SAID IT YOURSELF, CAROL. JULIA BROKE THE LAW. SHE HURT PEOPLE.
WE WOULDN'T LET SOMEONE ELSE JUST WALK AWAY FROM THAT.
NO...
...I SUPPOSE WE WOULDN'T.
BUT THAT POOR LITTLE GIRL...GOD...
NOBODY SHOULD HAV TO GO THROUGH WHAT SHE DID TODAY.
I WANT TO DO SOMETHING FOR HER, BUT...WHAT?
I MEAN, I COUL PAY FOR HER COLLEGE, I GUES

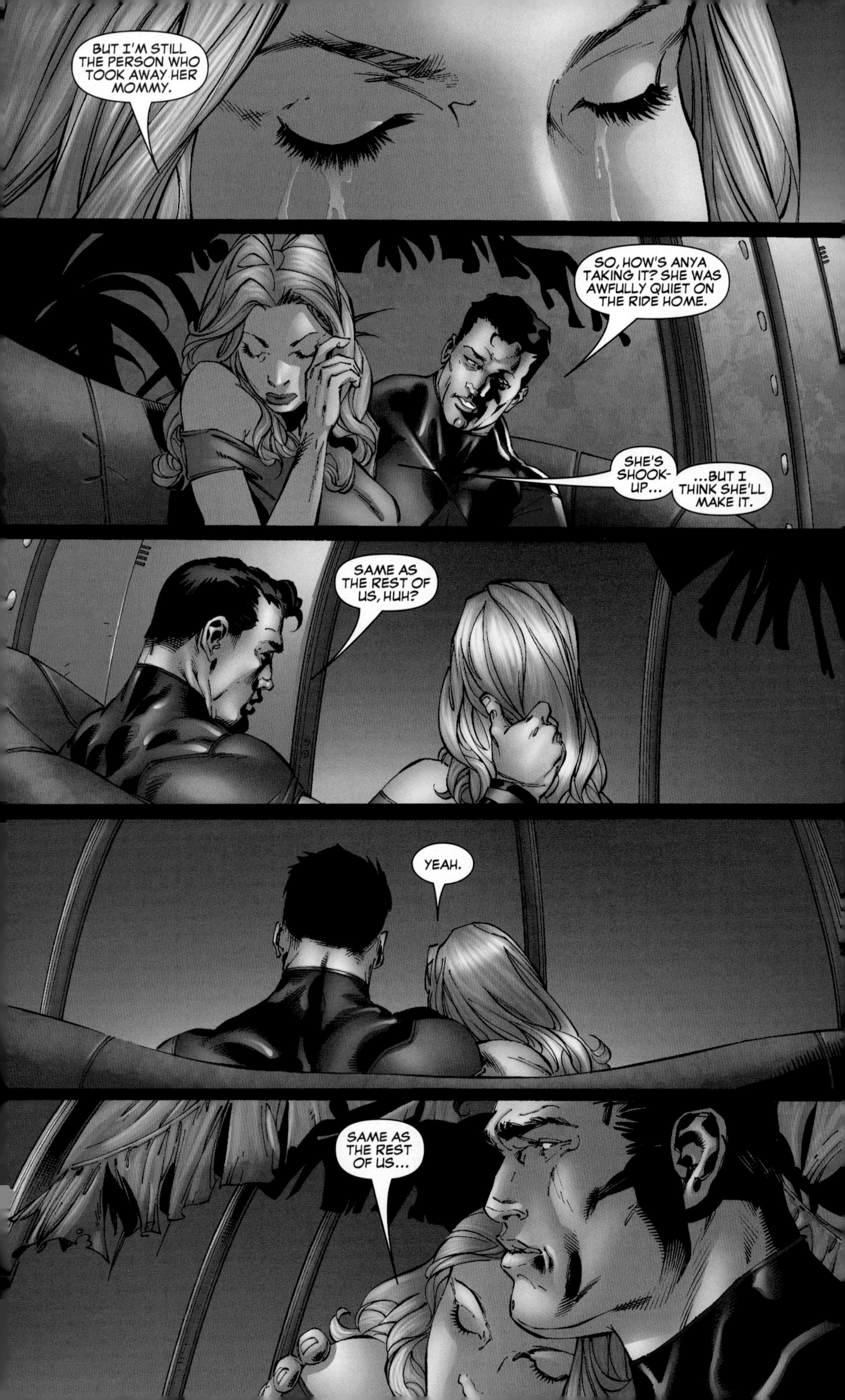
BUT I'M STILL THE PERSON WHO TOOK AWAY HER MOMMY.
SO, HOW'S ANYA TAKING IT? SHE WAS AWFULLY QUIET ON THE RIDE HOME.
SHE'S SHOOK-UP...
...BUT I THINK SHE'LL MAKE IT.
SAME AS THE REST OF US, HUH?
YEAH.
SAME AS THE REST OF US...

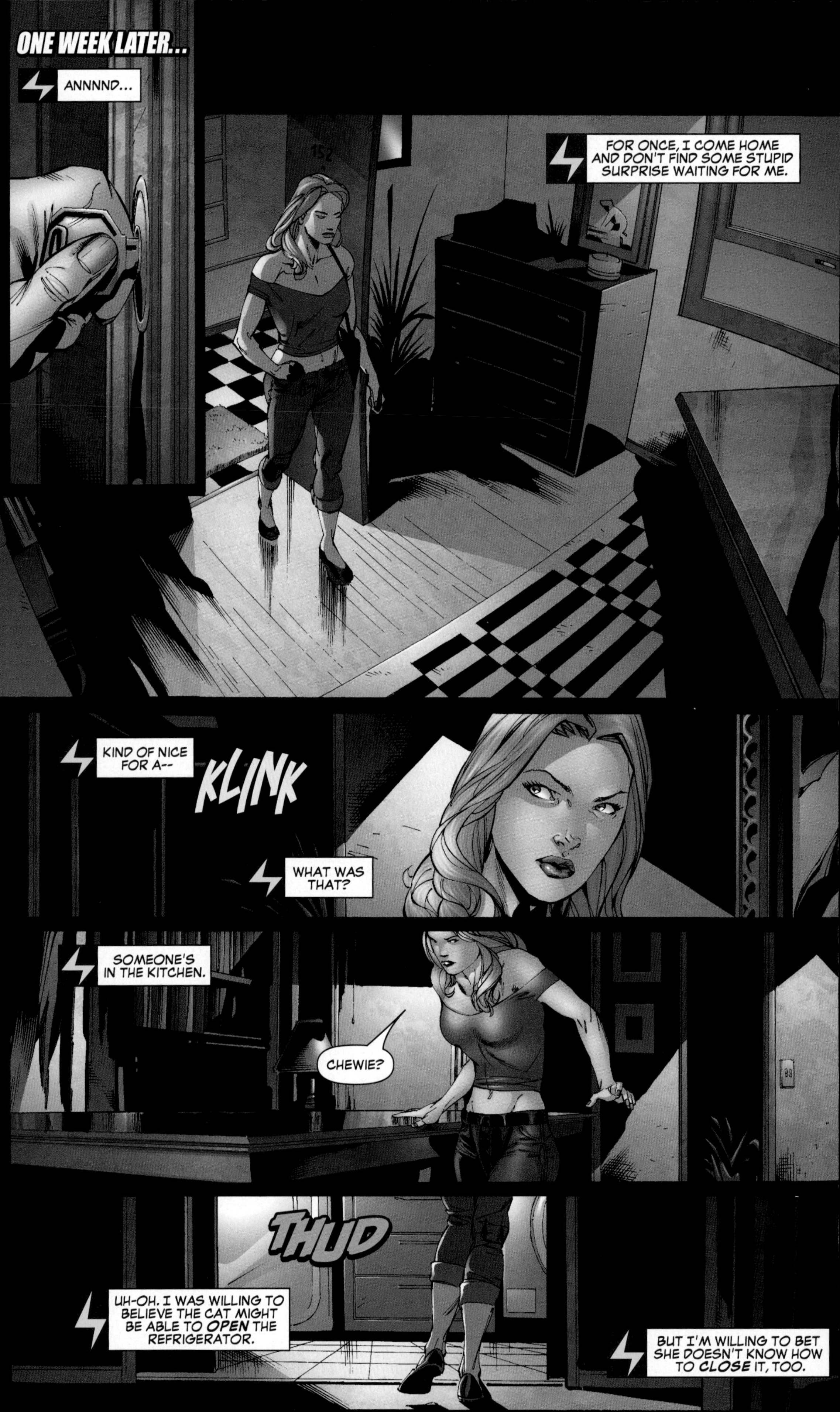
ONE WEEK LATER...
ANNNND...
FOR ONCE, I COME HOME AND DON'T FIND SOME STUPID SURPRISE WAITING FOR ME.
KIND OF NICE FOR A--
KLINK
WHAT WAS THAT?
SOMEONE'S IN THE KITCHEN.
CHEWIE?
THUD
UH-OH. I WAS WILLING TO BELIEVE THE CAT MIGHT BE ABLE TO *OPEN* THE REFRIGERATOR.
BUT I'M WILLING TO BET SHE DOESN'T KNOW HOW TO *CLOSE* IT, TOO.

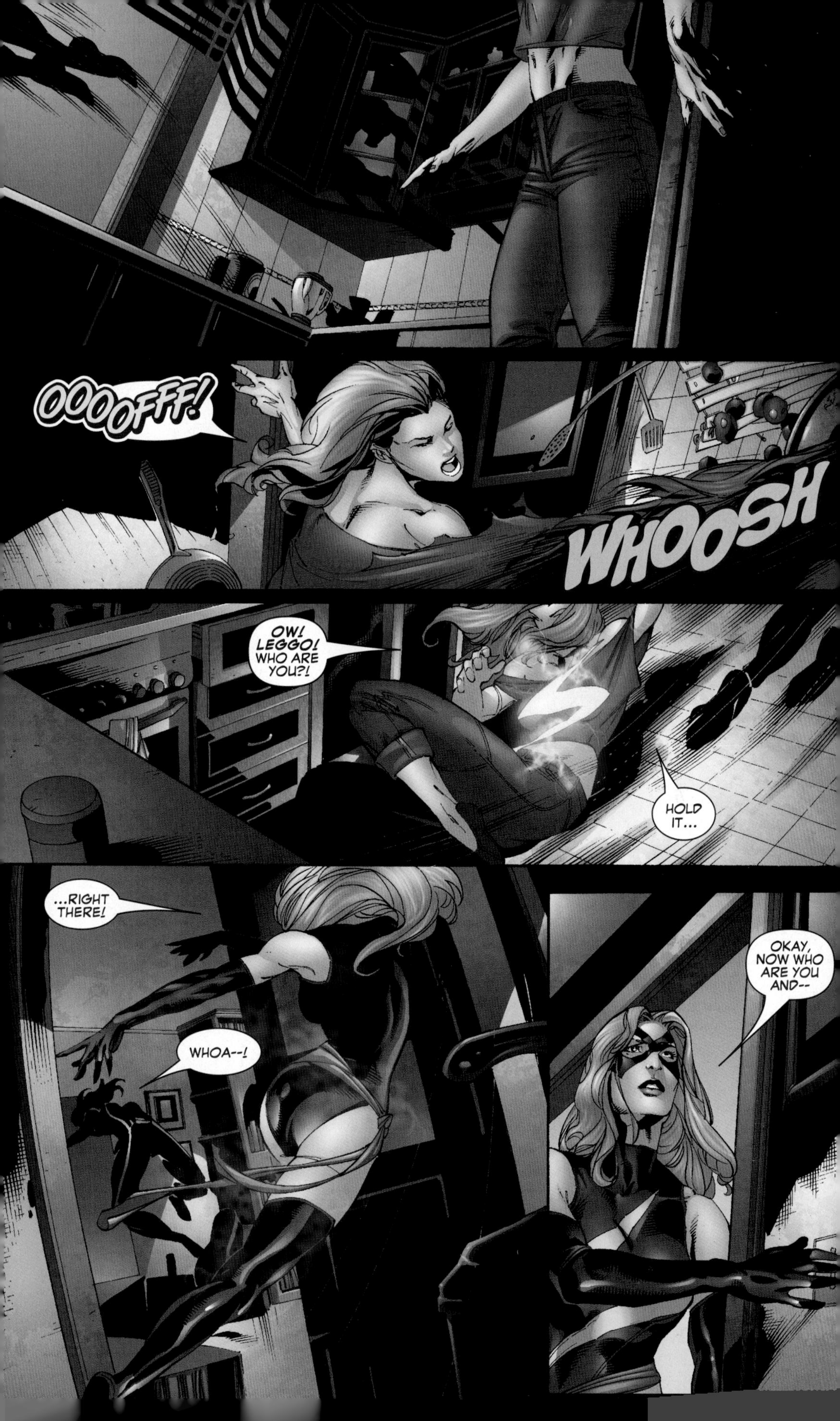
OOOOFFF!
WHOOSH
OW! LEGGO! WHO ARE YOU?!
HOLD IT...
...RIGHT THERE!
WHOA--!
OKAY, NOW WHO ARE YOU AND--

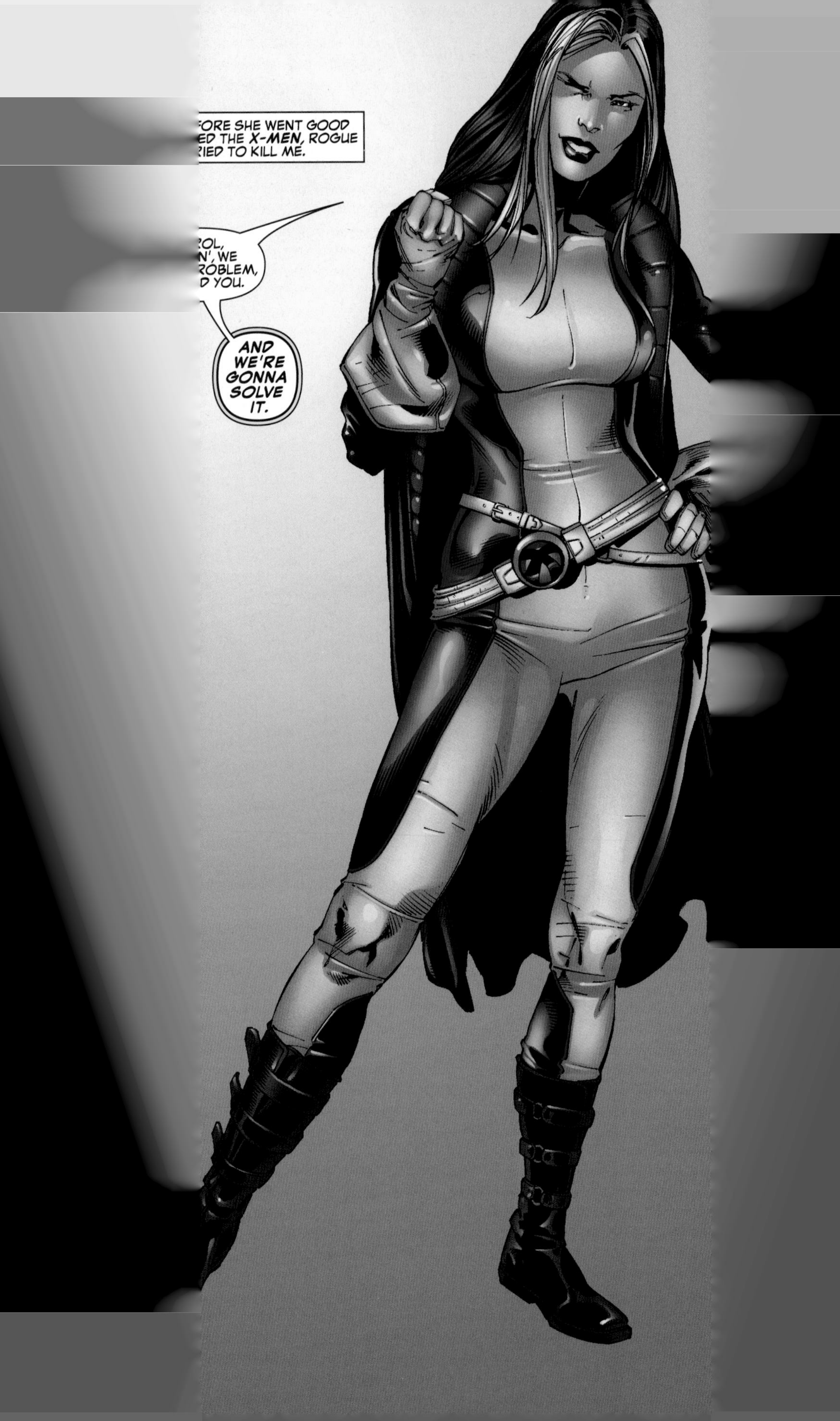
FORE SHE WENT GOOD ED THE X-MEN, ROGUE RIED TO KILL ME.
ROL, N', WE ROBLEM, D YOU.
AND WE'RE GONNA SOLVE IT.

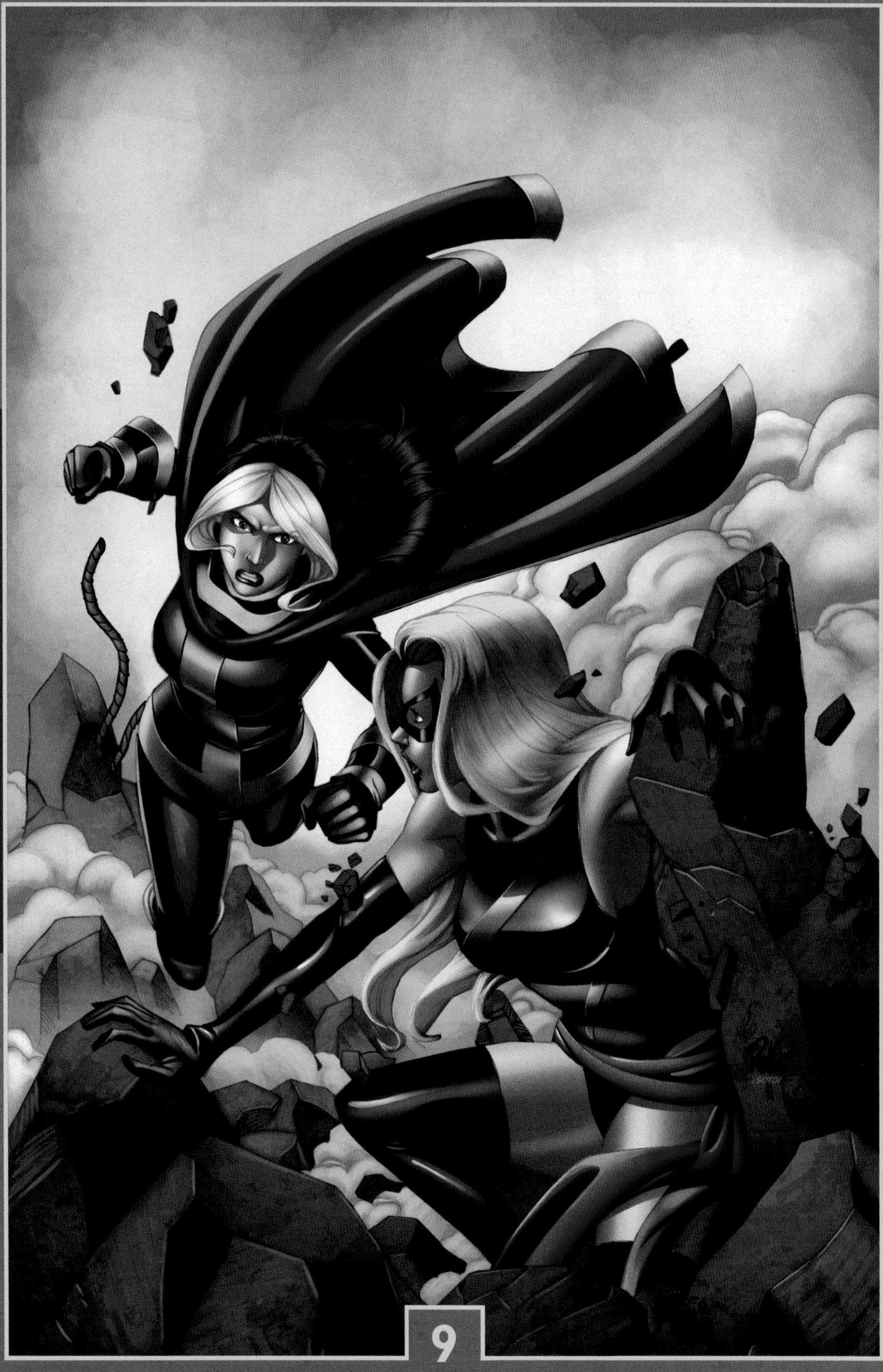

9

"DOPPELGANGER"

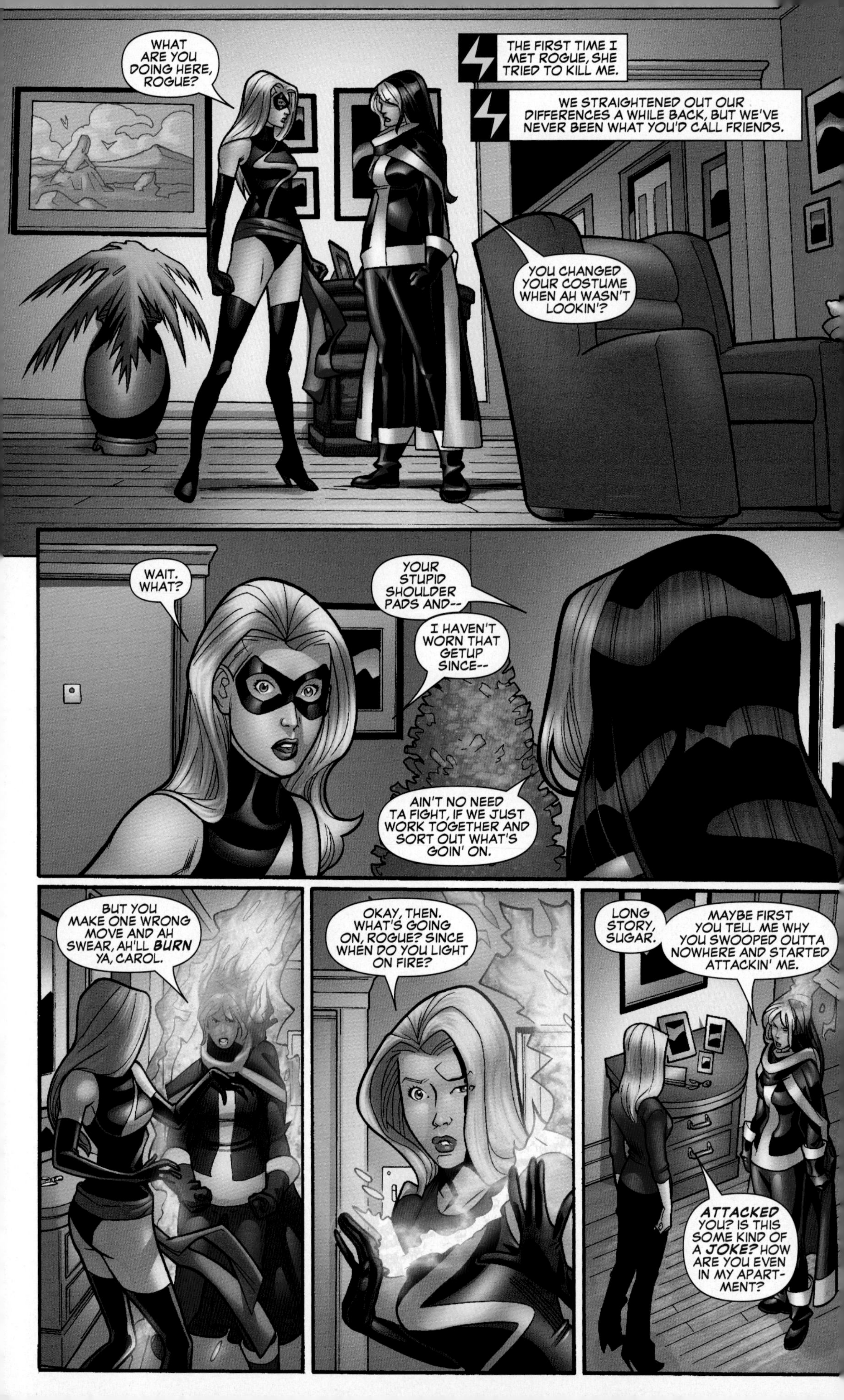
WHAT ARE YOU DOING HERE, ROGUE?
THE FIRST TIME I MET ROGUE, SHE TRIED TO KILL ME.
WE STRAIGHTENED OUT OUR DIFFERENCES A WHILE BACK, BUT WE'VE NEVER BEEN WHAT YOU'D CALL FRIENDS.
YOU CHANGED YOUR COSTUME WHEN AH WASN'T LOOKIN'?
WAIT. WHAT?
YOUR STUPID SHOULDER PADS AND--
I HAVEN'T WORN THAT GETUP SINCE--
AIN'T NO NEED TA FIGHT, IF WE JUST WORK TOGETHER AND SORT OUT WHAT'S GOIN' ON.
BUT YOU MAKE ONE WRONG MOVE AND AH SWEAR, AH'LL **BURN** YA, CAROL.
OKAY, THEN. WHAT'S GOING ON, ROGUE? SINCE WHEN DO YOU LIGHT ON FIRE?
LONG STORY, SUGAR.
MAYBE FIRST YOU TELL ME WHY YOU SWOOPED OUTTA NOWHERE AND STARTED ATTACKIN' ME.
ATTACKED YOU? IS THIS SOME KIND OF A ***JOKE?*** HOW ARE YOU EVEN IN MY APARTMENT?

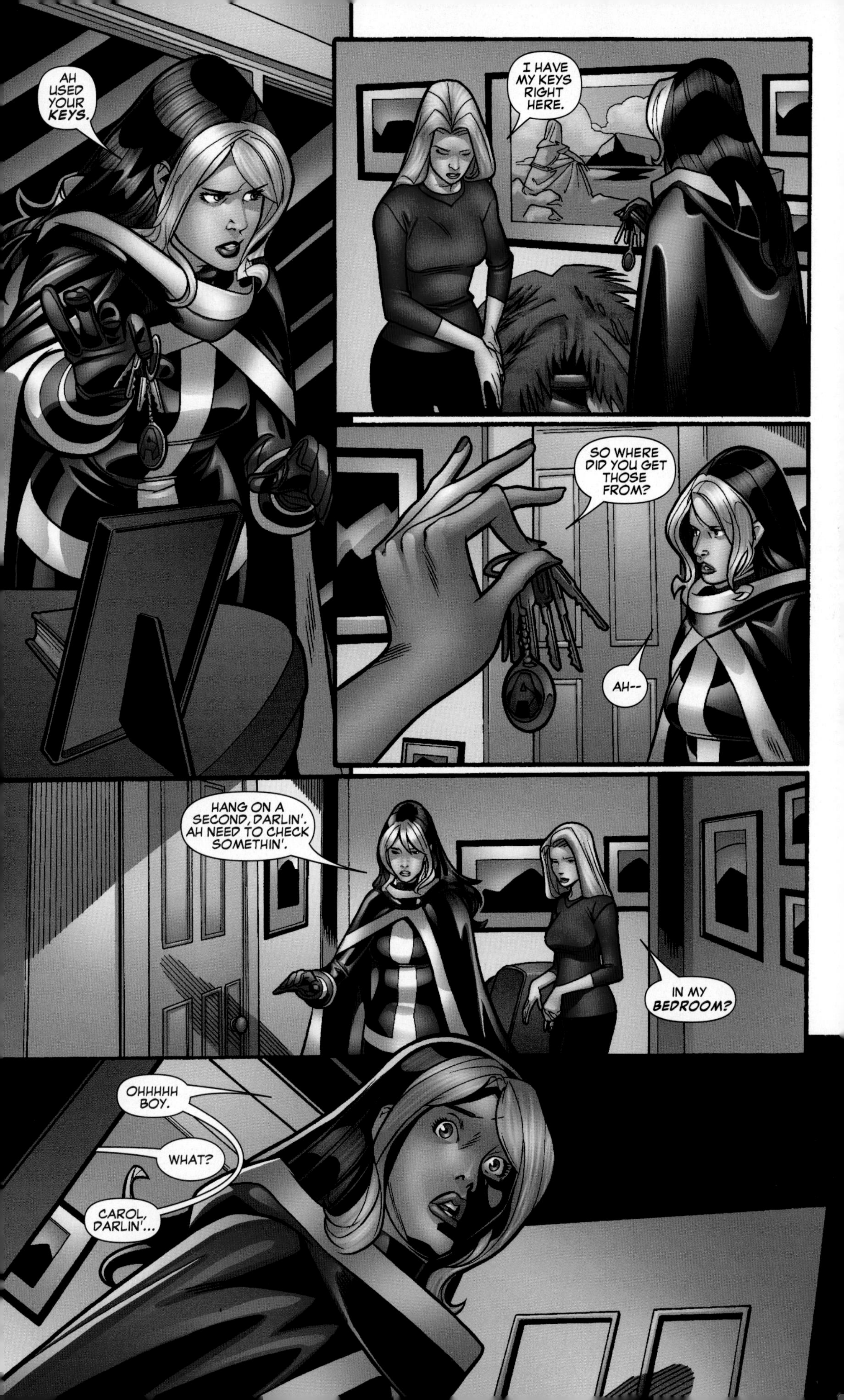
AH USED YOUR KEYS.
I HAVE MY KEYS RIGHT HERE.
SO WHERE DID YOU GET THOSE FROM?
AH--
HANG ON A SECOND, DARLIN'. AH NEED TO CHECK SOMETHIN'.
IN MY BEDROOM?
OHHHHH BOY.
WHAT?
CAROL, DARLIN'...

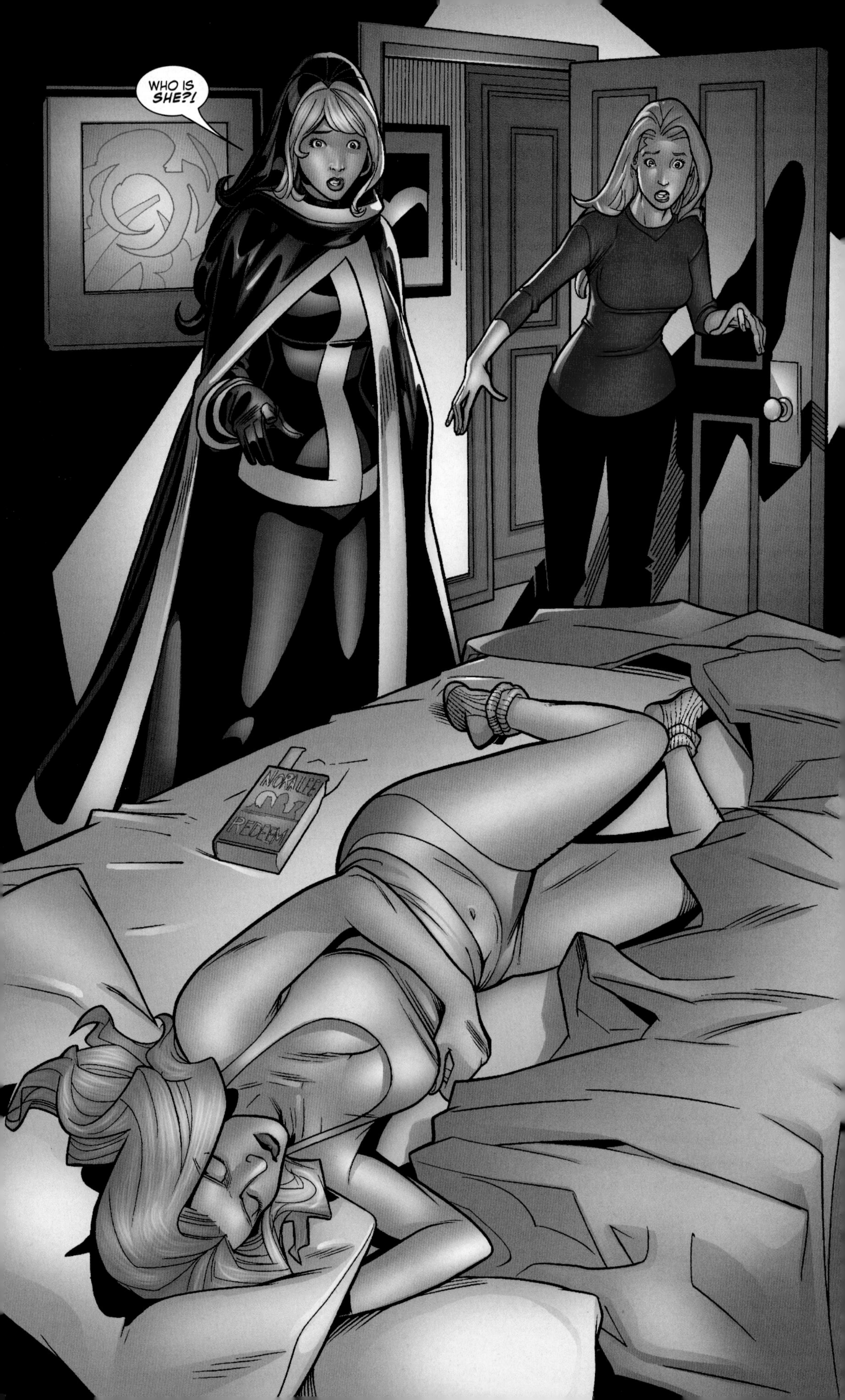
WHO IS SHE?!
NORA LEE
REDEEM

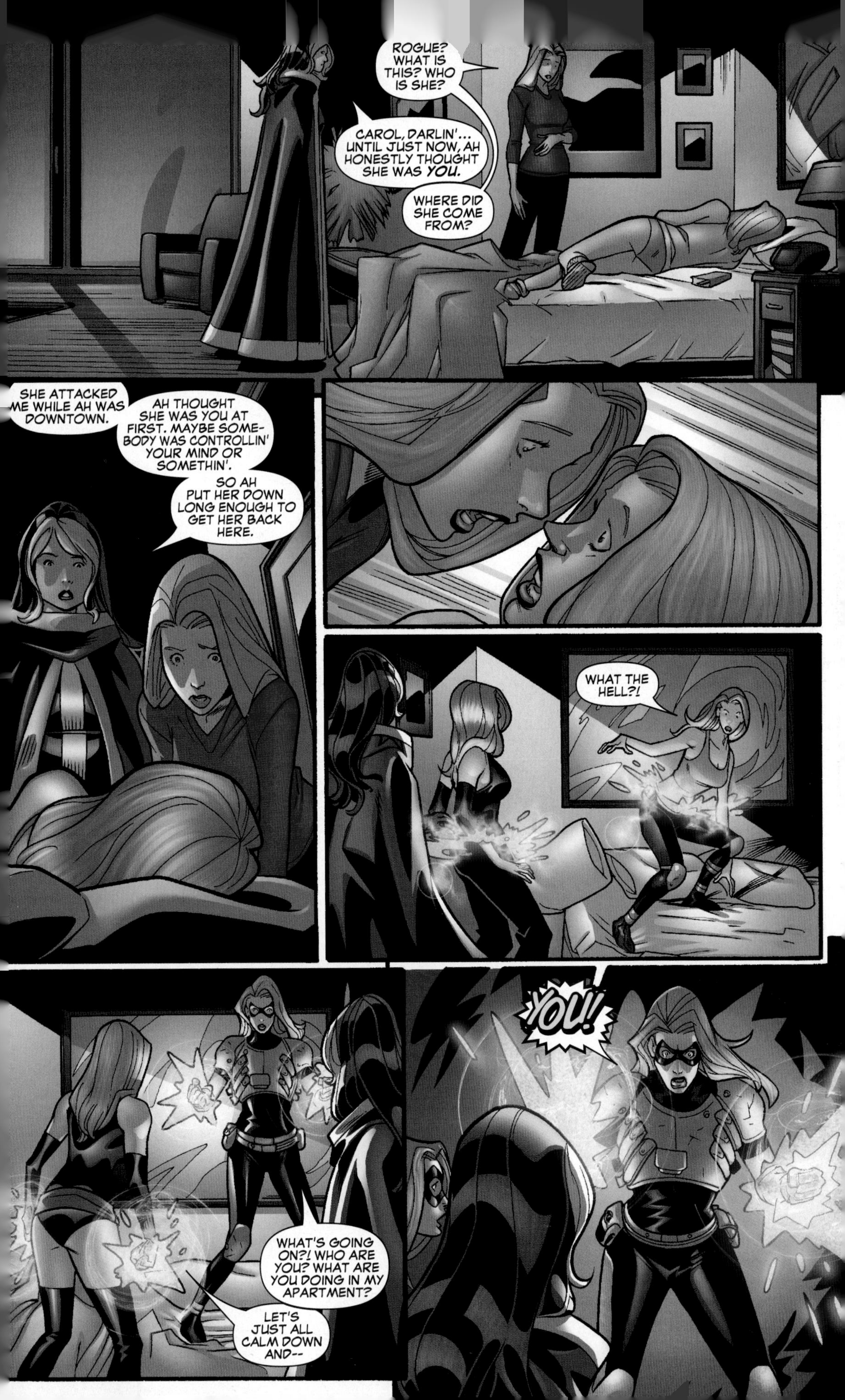

ROGUE? WHAT IS THIS? WHO IS SHE?
CAROL, DARLIN'... UNTIL JUST NOW, AH HONESTLY THOUGHT SHE WAS YOU.
WHERE DID SHE COME FROM?
SHE ATTACKED ME WHILE AH WAS DOWNTOWN.
AH THOUGHT SHE WAS YOU AT FIRST. MAYBE SOMEBODY WAS CONTROLLIN' YOUR MIND OR SOMETHIN'.
SO AH PUT HER DOWN LONG ENOUGH TO GET HER BACK HERE.
WHAT THE HELL?!
WHAT'S GOING ON?! WHO ARE YOU? WHAT ARE YOU DOING IN MY APARTMENT?
LET'S JUST ALL CALM DOWN AND--
YOU!

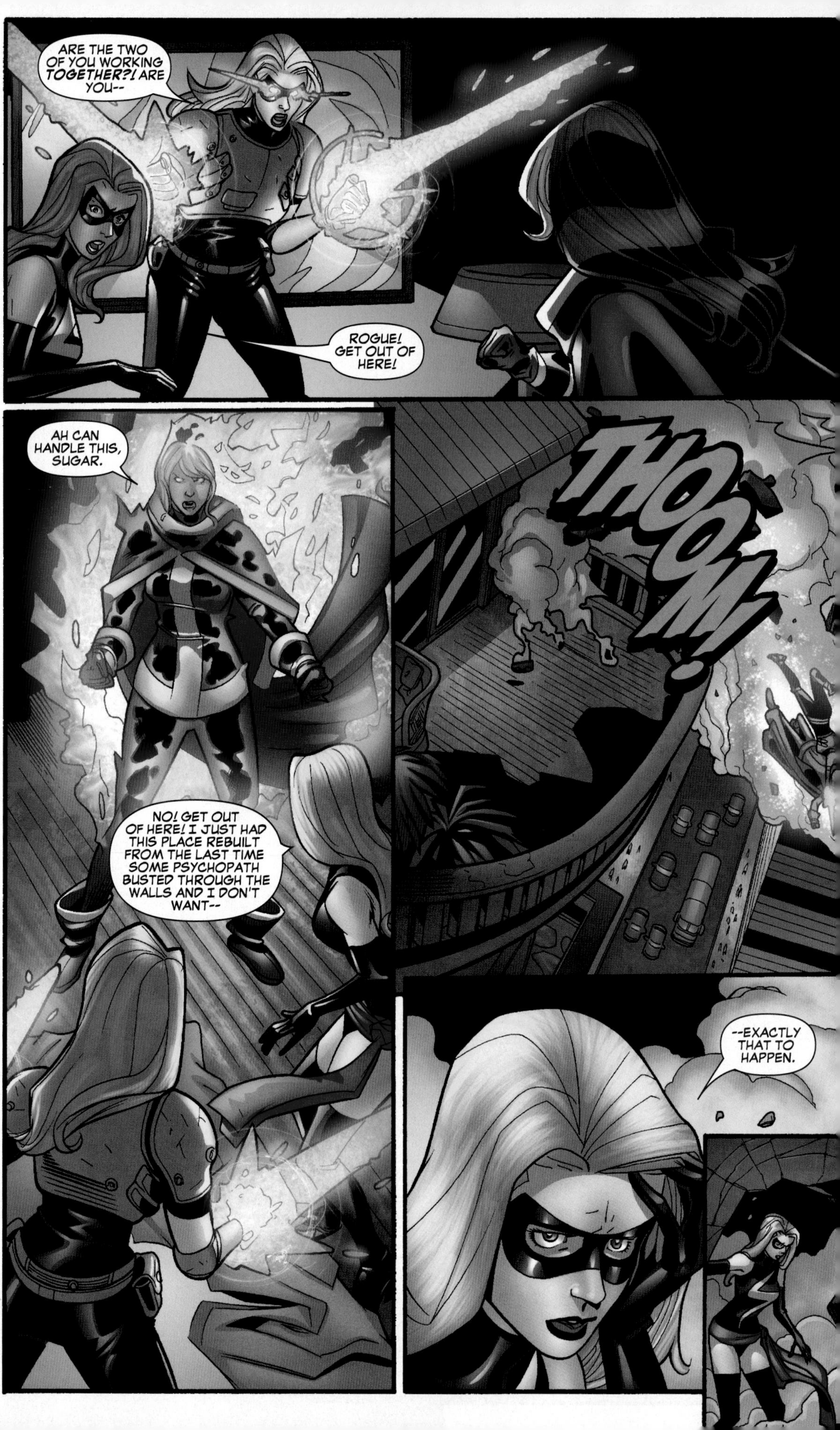
ARE THE TWO OF YOU WORKING TOGETHER?! ARE YOU--
ROGUE! GET OUT OF HERE!
AH CAN HANDLE THIS, SUGAR.
NO! GET OUT OF HERE! I JUST HAD THIS PLACE REBUILT FROM THE LAST TIME SOME PSYCHOPATH BUSTED THROUGH THE WALLS AND I DON'T WANT--
THOOM!
--EXACTLY THAT TO HAPPEN.

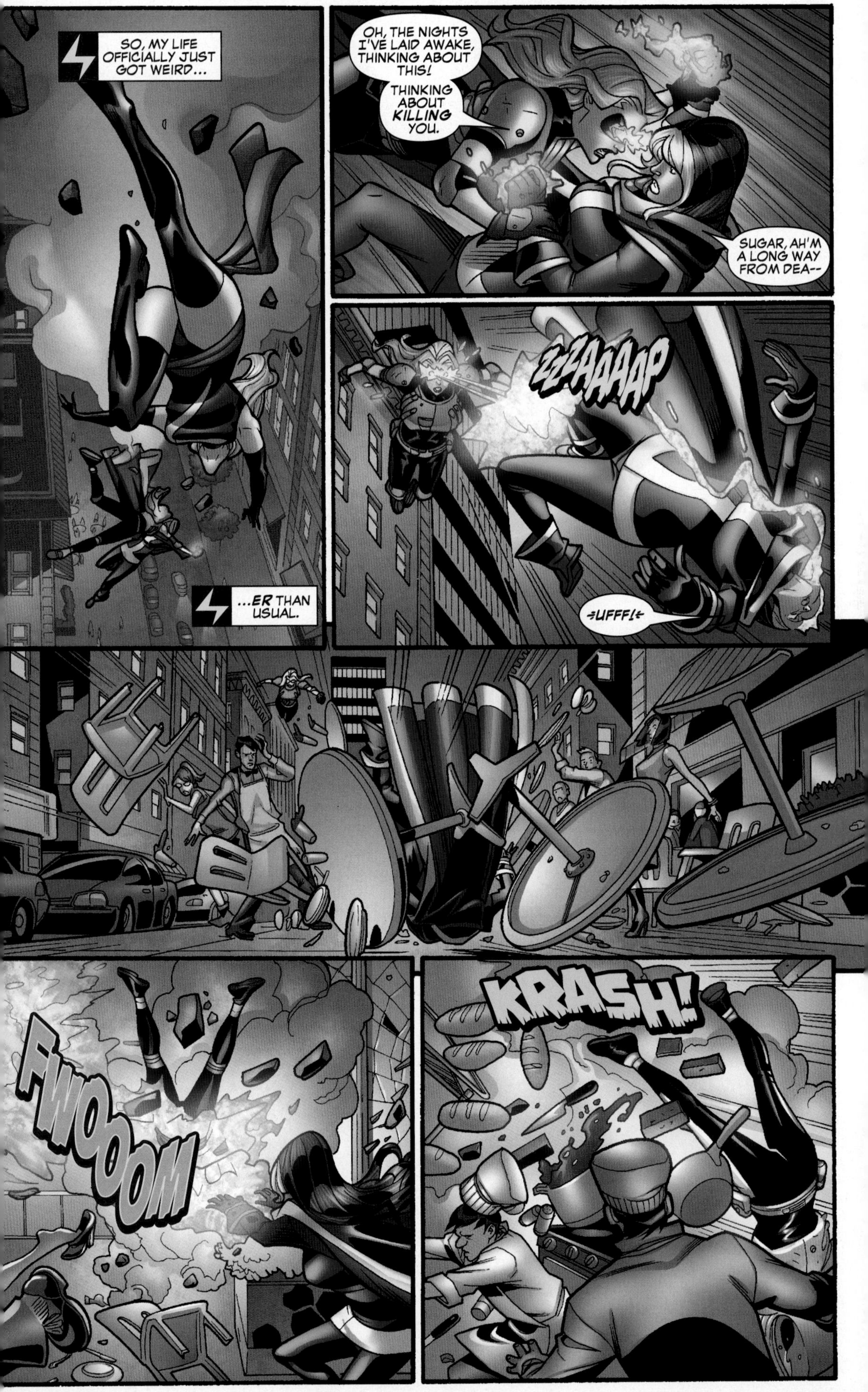
SO, MY LIFE OFFICIALLY JUST GOT WEIRD...
...ER THAN USUAL.
OH, THE NIGHTS I'VE LAID AWAKE, THINKING ABOUT THIS!
THINKING ABOUT KILLING YOU.
SUGAR, AH'M A LONG WAY FROM DEA--
ZZZAAAAP
UFFF!
FWOOOM
KRASH!

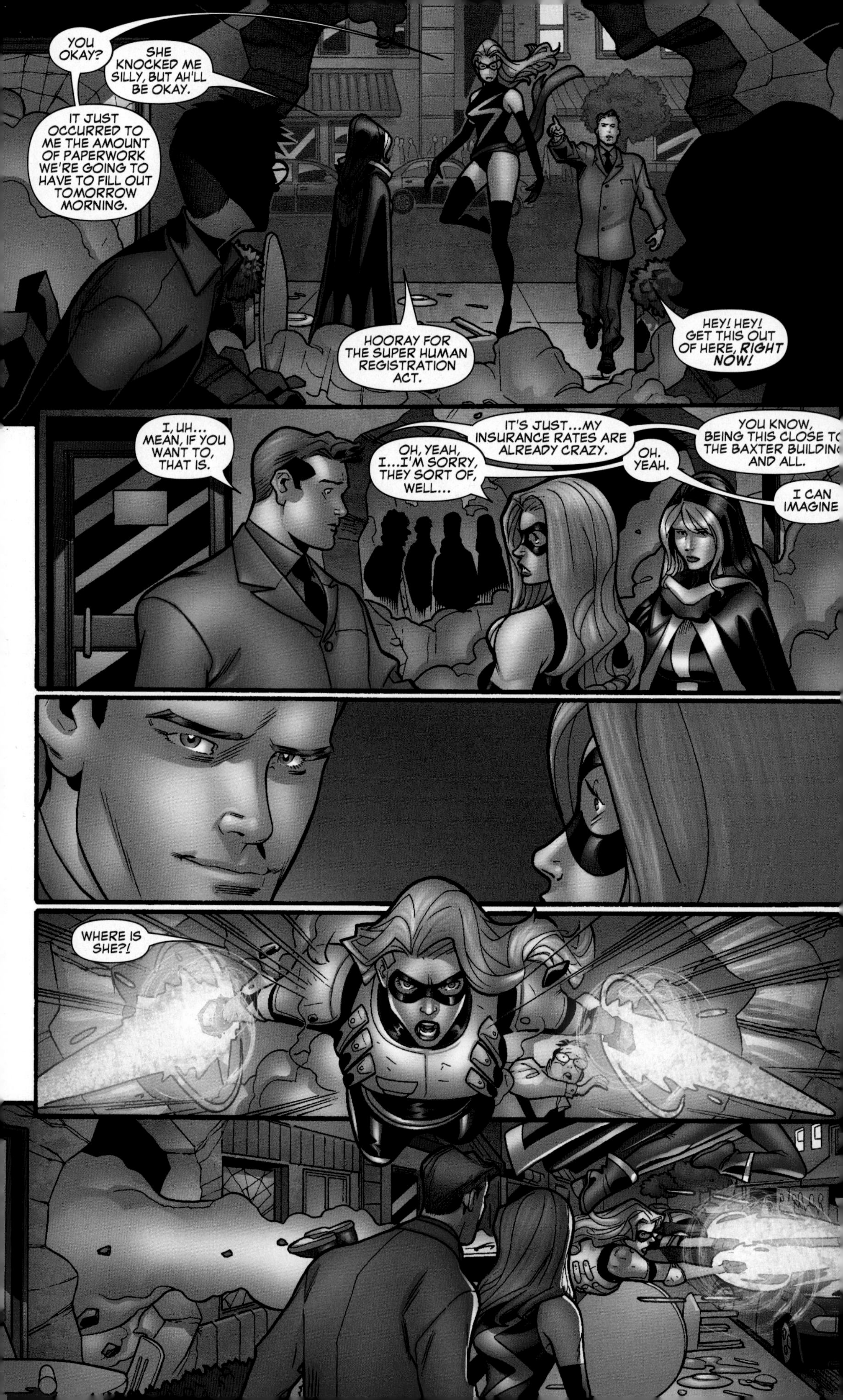
YOU OKAY?
SHE KNOCKED ME SILLY, BUT AH'LL BE OKAY.
IT JUST OCCURRED TO ME THE AMOUNT OF PAPERWORK WE'RE GOING TO HAVE TO FILL OUT TOMORROW MORNING.
HOORAY FOR THE SUPER HUMAN REGISTRATION ACT.
HEY! HEY! GET THIS OUT OF HERE, **RIGHT NOW!**
I, UH... MEAN, IF YOU WANT TO, THAT IS.
OH, YEAH, I...I'M SORRY, THEY SORT OF, WELL...
IT'S JUST...MY INSURANCE RATES ARE ALREADY CRAZY.
OH. YEAH.
YOU KNOW, BEING THIS CLOSE TO THE BAXTER BUILDING AND ALL.
I CAN IMAGINE
WHERE IS SHE?!

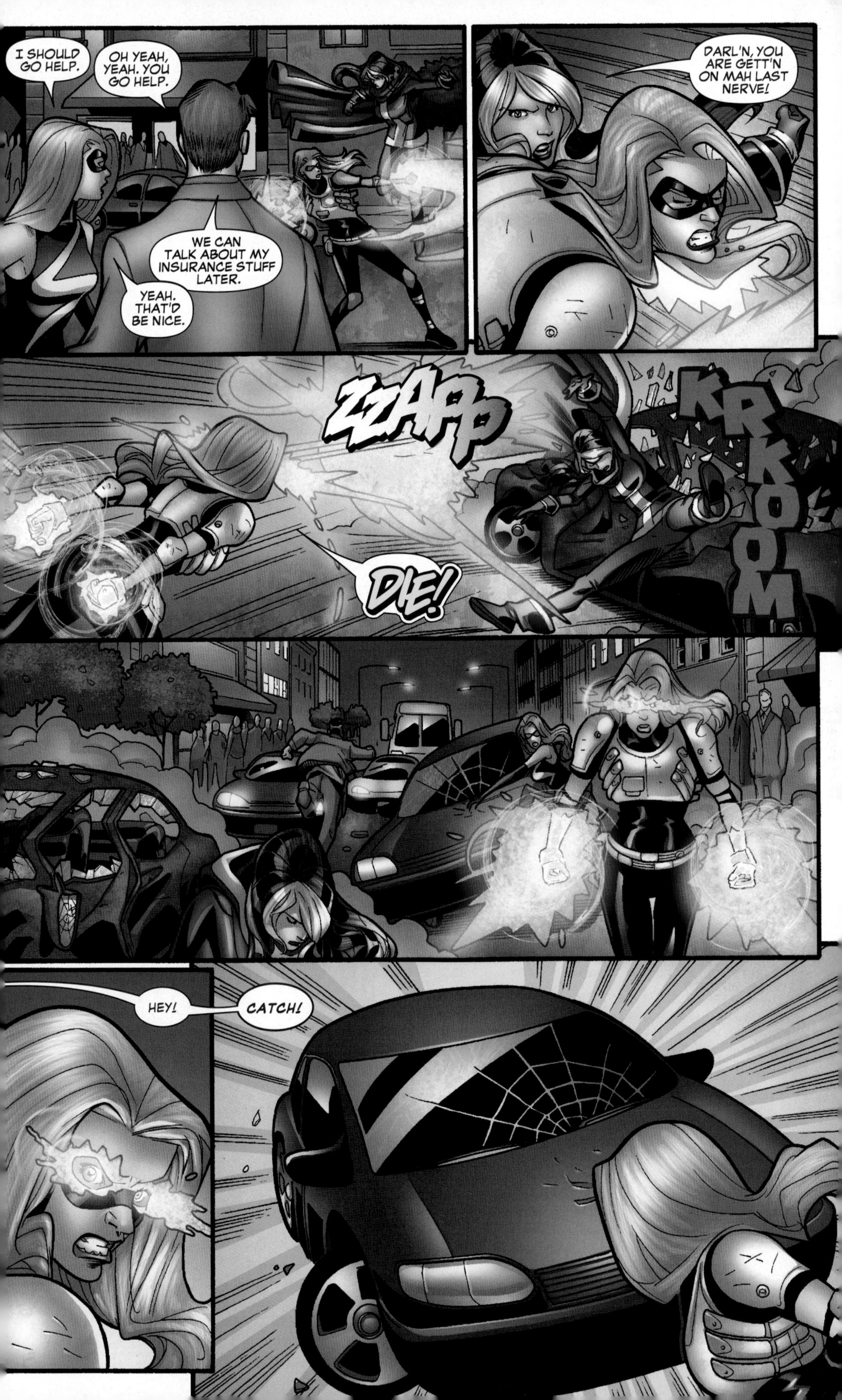

I SHOULD GO HELP.
OH YEAH, YEAH. YOU GO HELP.
WE CAN TALK ABOUT MY INSURANCE STUFF LATER.
YEAH. THAT'D BE NICE.
DARL'N, YOU ARE GETT'N ON MAH LAST NERVE!
ZZAPP
KRRKOOM
DIE!
HEY!
CATCH!

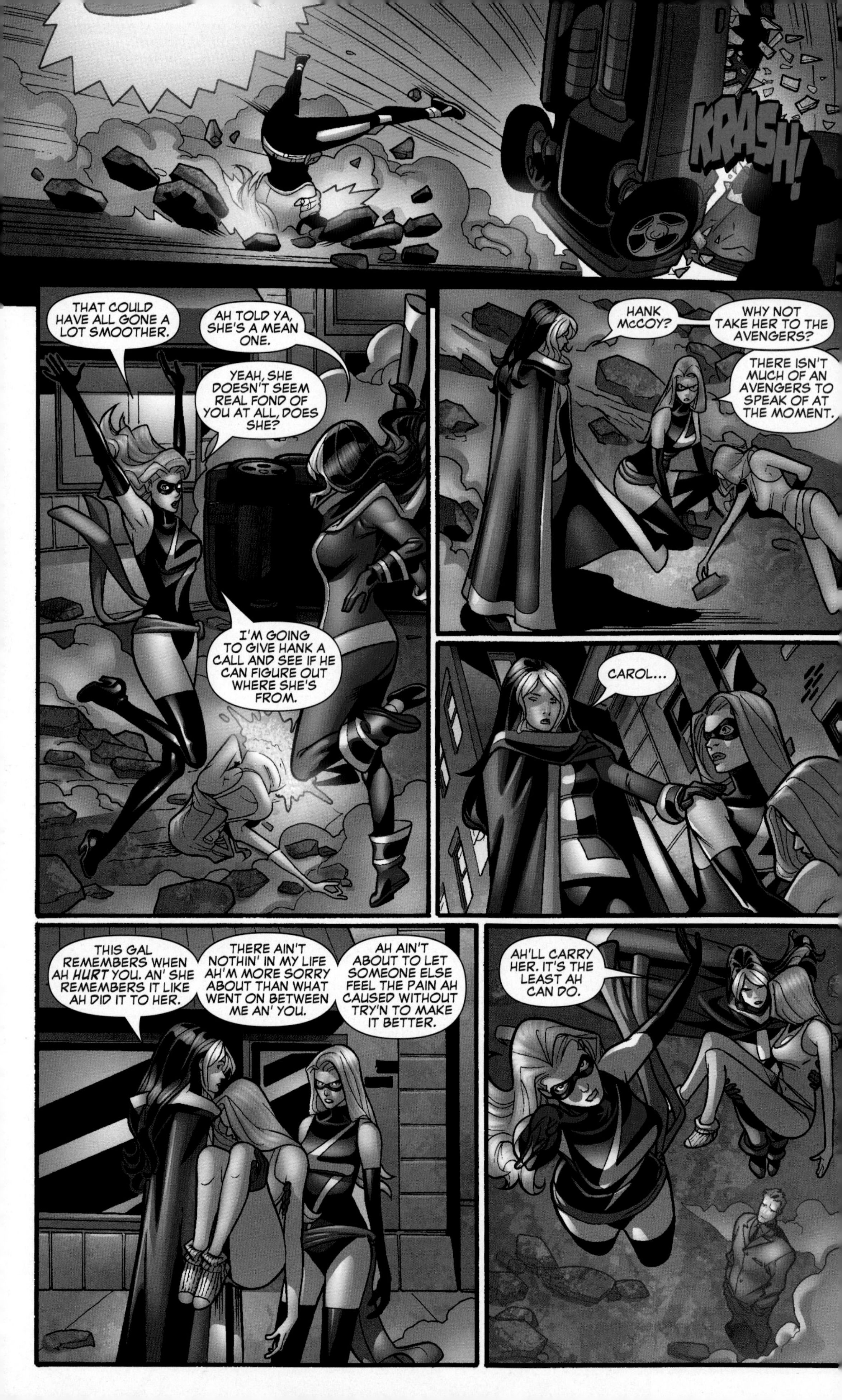
KRASH!
THAT COULD HAVE ALL GONE A LOT SMOOTHER.
AH TOLD YA, SHE'S A MEAN ONE.
YEAH, SHE DOESN'T SEEM REAL FOND OF YOU AT ALL, DOES SHE?
I'M GOING TO GIVE HANK A CALL AND SEE IF HE CAN FIGURE OUT WHERE SHE'S FROM.
HANK McCOY?
WHY NOT TAKE HER TO THE AVENGERS?
THERE ISN'T MUCH OF AN AVENGERS TO SPEAK OF AT THE MOMENT.
CAROL...
THIS GAL REMEMBERS WHEN AH HURT YOU. AN' SHE REMEMBERS IT LIKE AH DID IT TO HER.
THERE AIN'T NOTHIN' IN MY LIFE AH'M MORE SORRY ABOUT THAN WHAT WENT ON BETWEEN ME AN' YOU.
AH AIN'T ABOUT TO LET SOMEONE ELSE FEEL THE PAIN AH CAUSED WITHOUT TRY'N TO MAKE IT BETTER.
AH'LL CARRY HER. IT'S THE LEAST AH CAN DO.

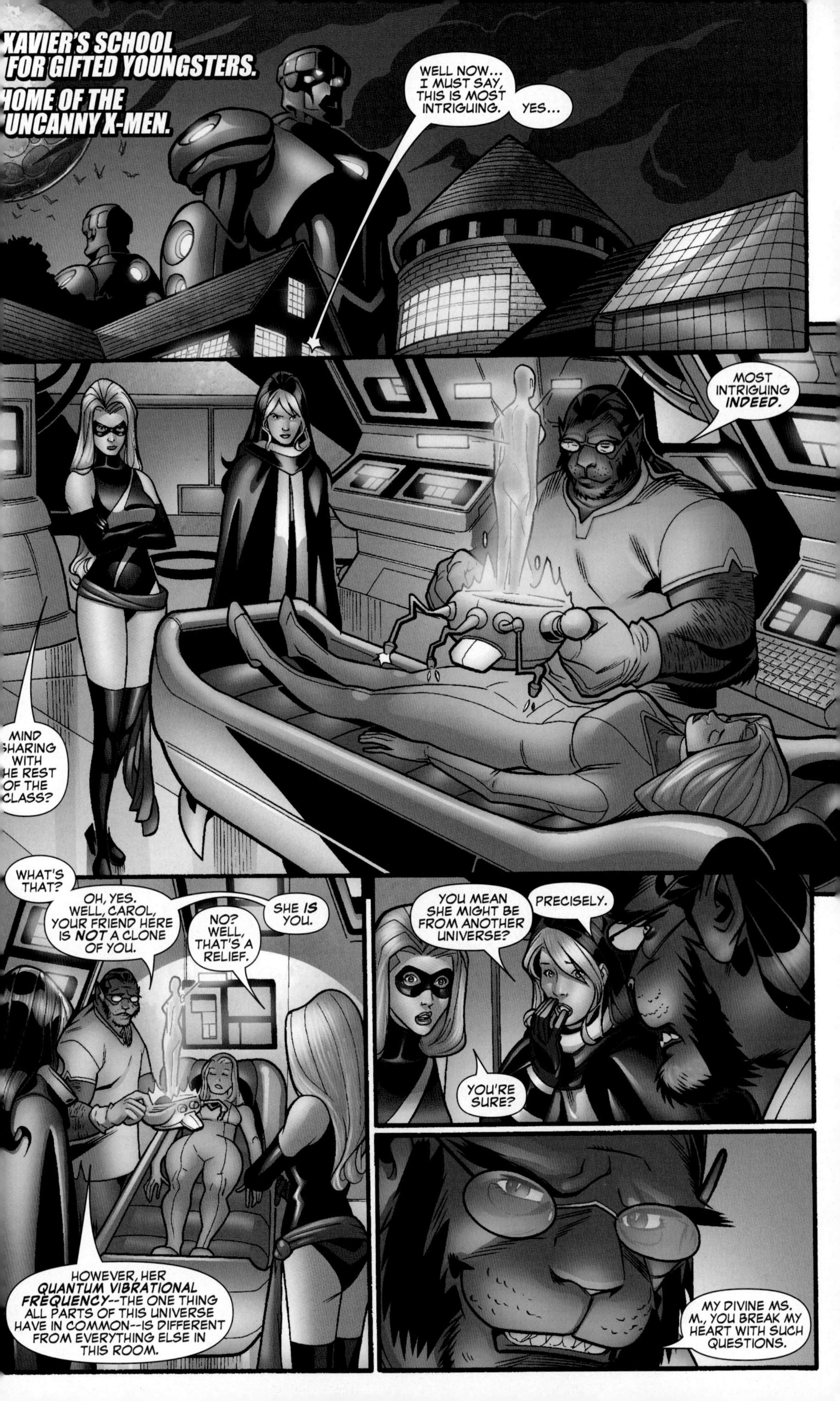

XAVIER'S SCHOOL FOR GIFTED YOUNGSTERS.
HOME OF THE UNCANNY X-MEN.
WELL NOW... I MUST SAY, THIS IS MOST INTRIGUING.
YES...
MOST INTRIGUING INDEED.
MIND SHARING WITH THE REST OF THE CLASS?
WHAT'S THAT?
OH, YES. WELL, CAROL, YOUR FRIEND HERE IS NOT A CLONE OF YOU.
NO? WELL, THAT'S A RELIEF.
SHE IS YOU.
HOWEVER, HER QUANTUM VIBRATIONAL FREQUENCY--THE ONE THING ALL PARTS OF THIS UNIVERSE HAVE IN COMMON--IS DIFFERENT FROM EVERYTHING ELSE IN THIS ROOM.
YOU MEAN SHE MIGHT BE FROM ANOTHER UNIVERSE?
PRECISELY.
YOU'RE SURE?
MY DIVINE MS. M., YOU BREAK MY HEART WITH SUCH QUESTIONS.

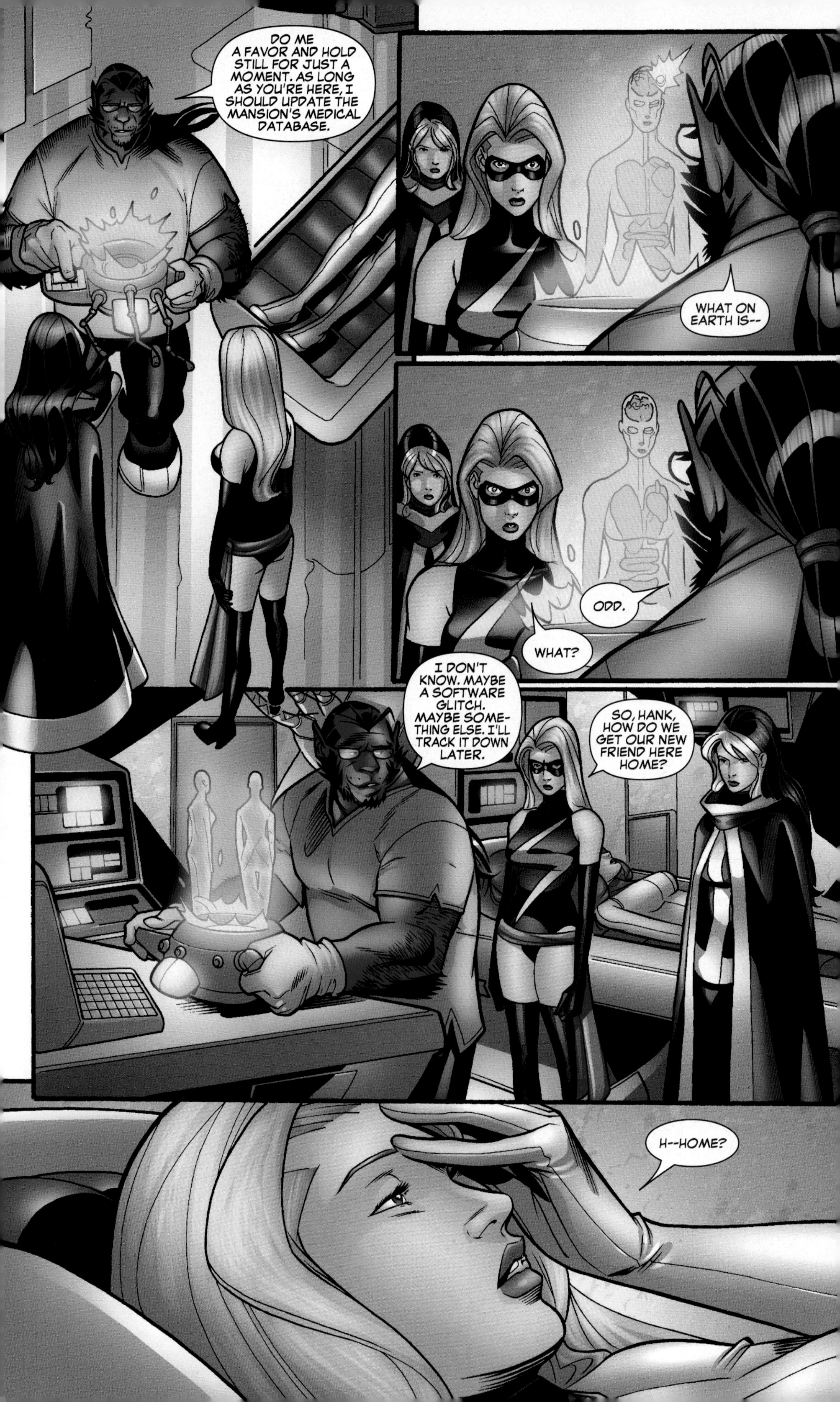
DO ME A FAVOR AND HOLD STILL FOR JUST A MOMENT. AS LONG AS YOU'RE HERE, I SHOULD UPDATE THE MANSION'S MEDICAL DATABASE.
WHAT ON EARTH IS--
ODD.
WHAT?
I DON'T KNOW. MAYBE A SOFTWARE GLITCH. MAYBE SOME-THING ELSE. I'LL TRACK IT DOWN LATER.
SO, HANK, HOW DO WE GET OUR NEW FRIEND HERE HOME?
H--HOME?

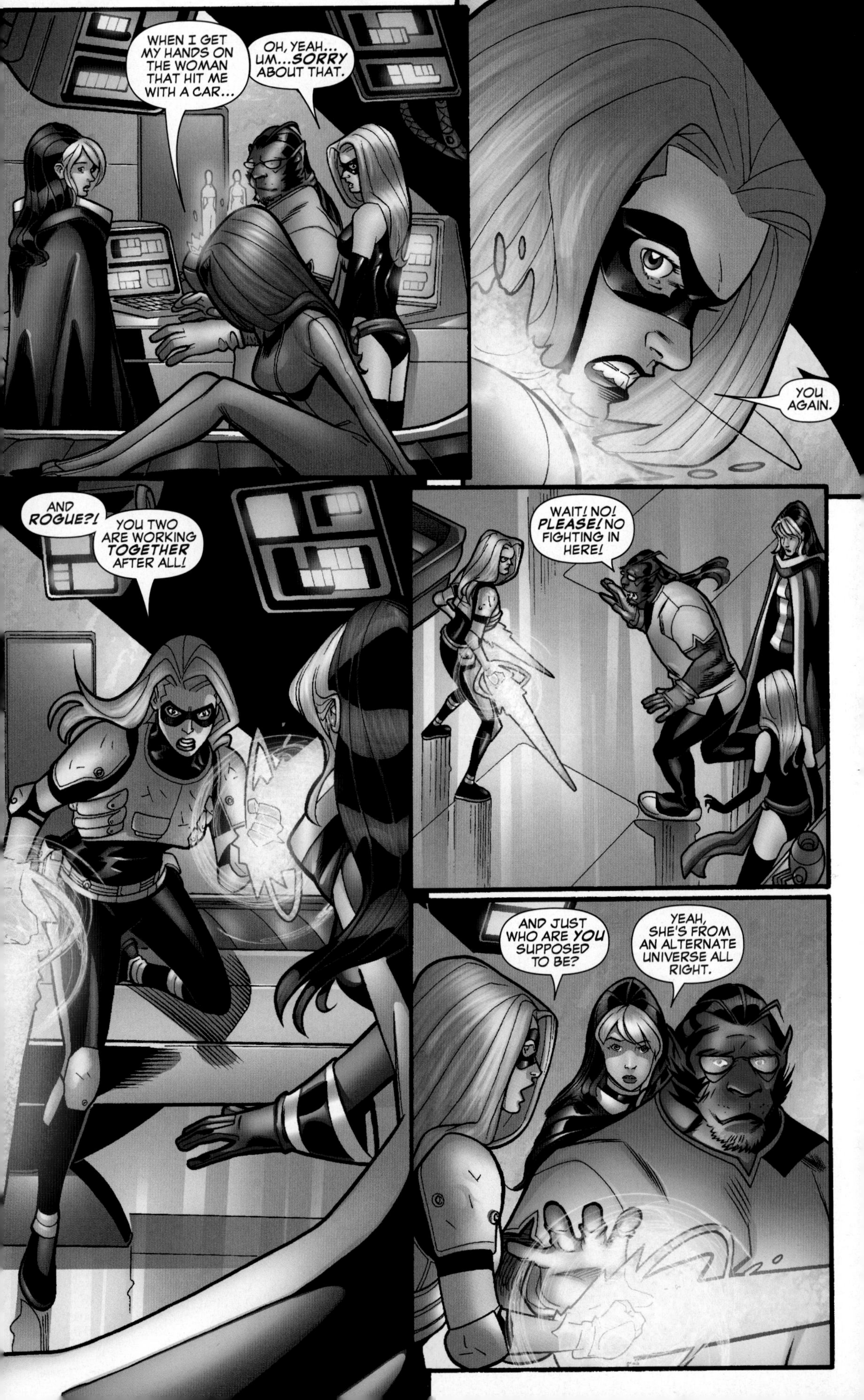
WHEN I GET MY HANDS ON THE WOMAN THAT HIT ME WITH A CAR...
OH, YEAH... UM...**SORRY** ABOUT THAT.
YOU AGAIN.
AND **ROGUE?!**
YOU TWO ARE WORKING **TOGETHER** AFTER ALL!
WAIT! NO! **PLEASE!** NO FIGHTING IN HERE!
AND JUST WHO ARE **YOU** SUPPOSED TO BE?
YEAH, SHE'S FROM AN ALTERNATE UNIVERSE ALL RIGHT.

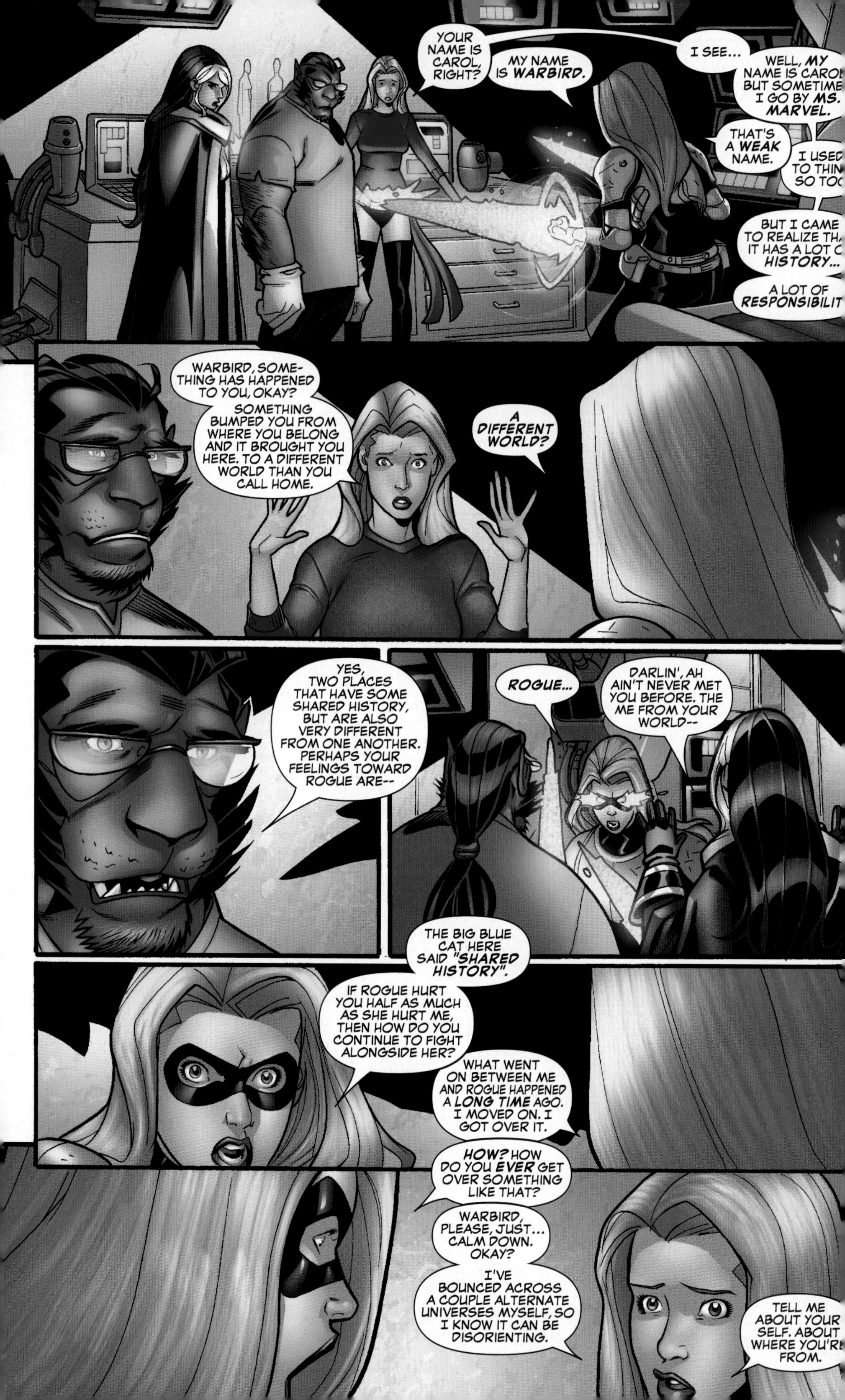

YOUR NAME IS CAROL, RIGHT?
MY NAME IS WARBIRD.
I SEE...
WELL, MY NAME IS CAROL BUT SOMETIME I GO BY MS. MARVEL.
THAT'S A WEAK NAME.
I USED TO THIN SO TOO
BUT I CAME TO REALIZE TH IT HAS A LOT O HISTORY...
A LOT OF RESPONSIBILIT
WARBIRD, SOMETHING HAS HAPPENED TO YOU, OKAY? SOMETHING BUMPED YOU FROM WHERE YOU BELONG AND IT BROUGHT YOU HERE. TO A DIFFERENT WORLD THAN YOU CALL HOME.
A DIFFERENT WORLD?
YES, TWO PLACES THAT HAVE SOME SHARED HISTORY, BUT ARE ALSO VERY DIFFERENT FROM ONE ANOTHER. PERHAPS YOUR FEELINGS TOWARD ROGUE ARE--
ROGUE...
DARLIN', AH AIN'T NEVER MET YOU BEFORE. THE ME FROM YOUR WORLD--
THE BIG BLUE CAT HERE SAID "SHARED HISTORY".
IF ROGUE HURT YOU HALF AS MUCH AS SHE HURT ME, THEN HOW DO YOU CONTINUE TO FIGHT ALONGSIDE HER?
WHAT WENT ON BETWEEN ME AND ROGUE HAPPENED A LONG TIME AGO. I MOVED ON. I GOT OVER IT.
HOW? HOW DO YOU EVER GET OVER SOMETHING LIKE THAT?
WARBIRD, PLEASE, JUST... CALM DOWN. OKAY?
I'VE BOUNCED ACROSS A COUPLE ALTERNATE UNIVERSES MYSELF, SO I KNOW IT CAN BE DISORIENTING.
TELL ME ABOUT YOUR SELF. ABOUT WHERE YOU'R FROM.

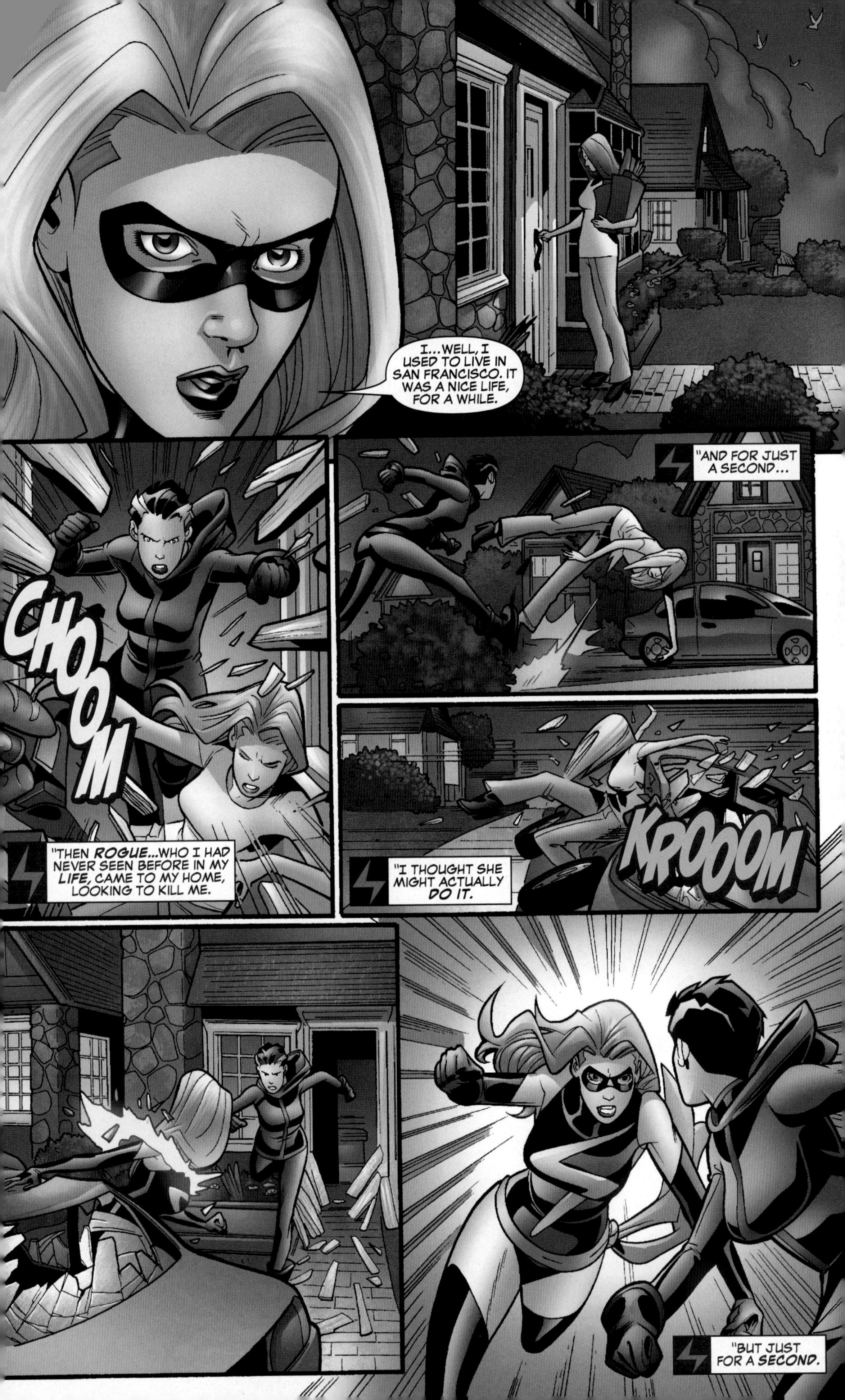
I...WELL, I USED TO LIVE IN SAN FRANCISCO. IT WAS A NICE LIFE, FOR A WHILE.
CHOOM
"THEN ROGUE...WHO I HAD NEVER SEEN BEFORE IN MY LIFE, CAME TO MY HOME, LOOKING TO KILL ME.
"AND FOR JUST A SECOND...
KROOOM
"I THOUGHT SHE MIGHT ACTUALLY DO IT.
"BUT JUST FOR A SECOND.

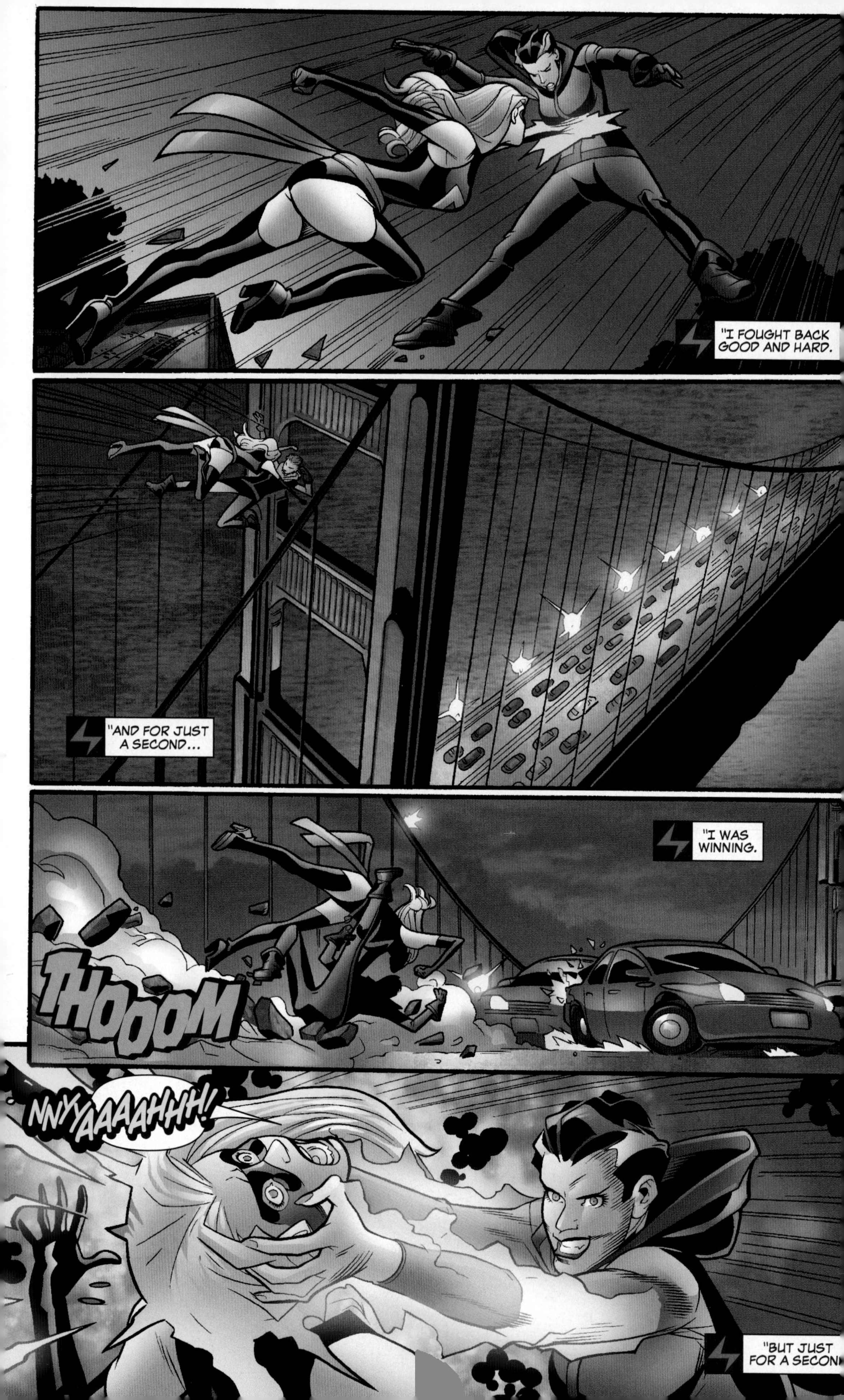

"I FOUGHT BACK GOOD AND HARD.
"AND FOR JUST A SECOND...
"I WAS WINNING.
THOOOM
NNYYAAAAHHH!
"BUT JUST FOR A SECON

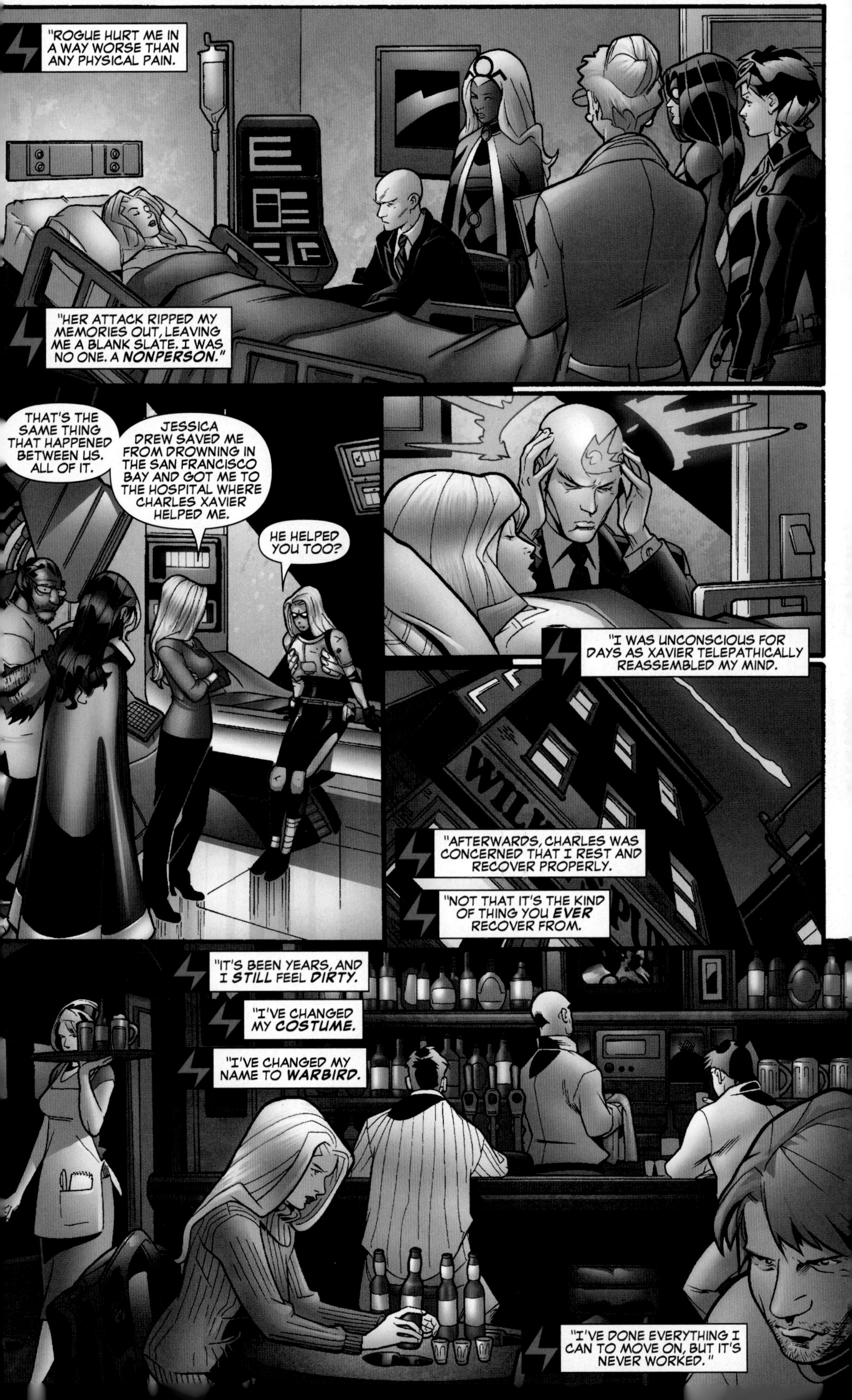
"ROGUE HURT ME IN A WAY WORSE THAN ANY PHYSICAL PAIN.
"HER ATTACK RIPPED MY MEMORIES OUT, LEAVING ME A BLANK SLATE. I WAS NO ONE. A NONPERSON."
THAT'S THE SAME THING THAT HAPPENED BETWEEN US. ALL OF IT.
JESSICA DREW SAVED ME FROM DROWNING IN THE SAN FRANCISCO BAY AND GOT ME TO THE HOSPITAL WHERE CHARLES XAVIER HELPED ME.
HE HELPED YOU TOO?
"I WAS UNCONSCIOUS FOR DAYS AS XAVIER TELEPATHICALLY REASSEMBLED MY MIND.
"AFTERWARDS, CHARLES WAS CONCERNED THAT I REST AND RECOVER PROPERLY.
"NOT THAT IT'S THE KIND OF THING YOU EVER RECOVER FROM.
"IT'S BEEN YEARS, AND I STILL FEEL DIRTY.
"I'VE CHANGED MY COSTUME.
"I'VE CHANGED MY NAME TO WARBIRD.
"I'VE DONE EVERYTHING I CAN TO MOVE ON, BUT IT'S NEVER WORKED."

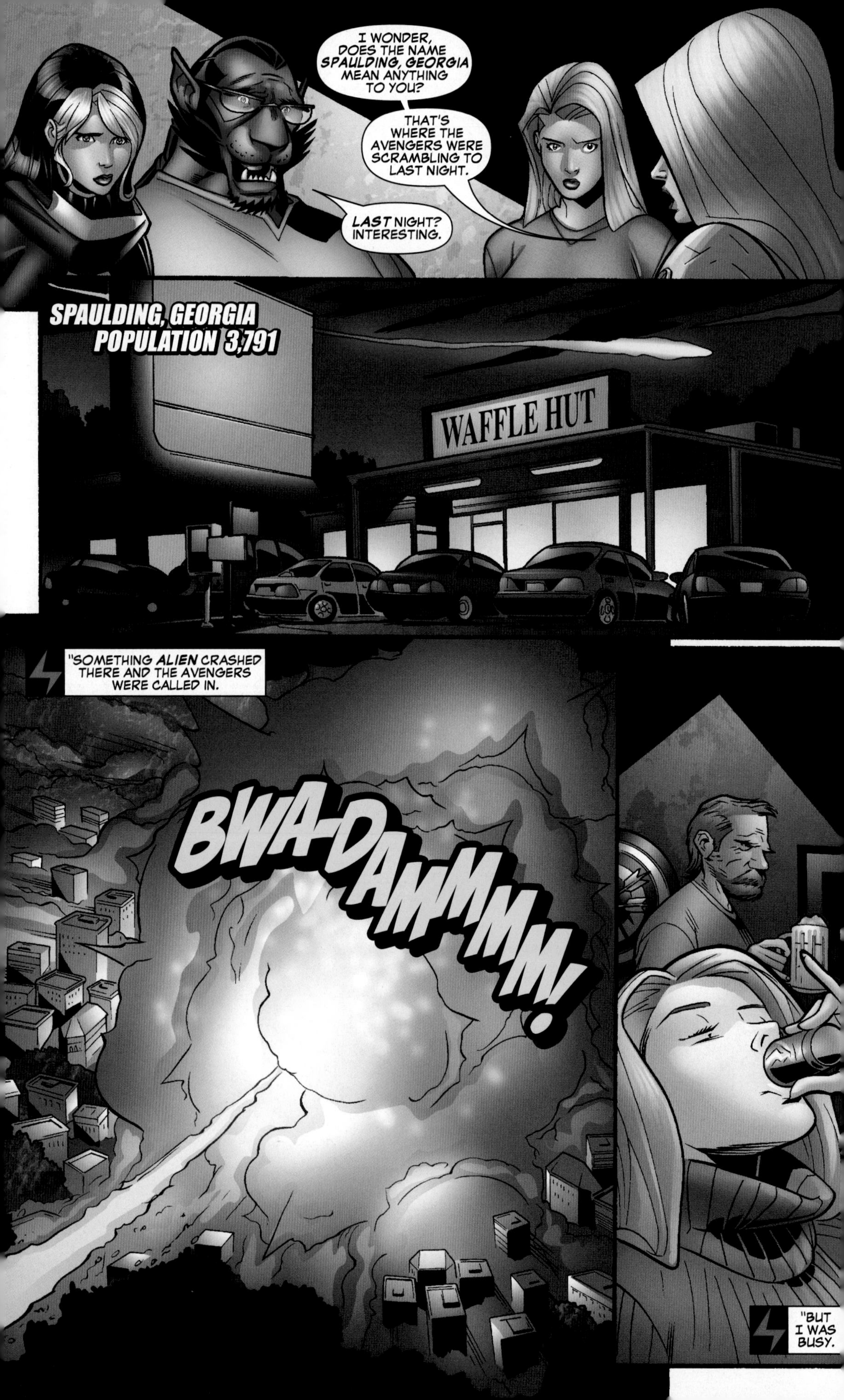
I WONDER, DOES THE NAME SPAULDING, GEORGIA MEAN ANYTHING TO YOU?
THAT'S WHERE THE AVENGERS WERE SCRAMBLING TO LAST NIGHT.
LAST NIGHT? INTERESTING.
SPAULDING, GEORGIA POPULATION 3,791
WAFFLE HUT
"SOMETHING ALIEN CRASHED THERE AND THE AVENGERS WERE CALLED IN.
BWA-DAMMMMM!
"BUT I WAS BUSY.

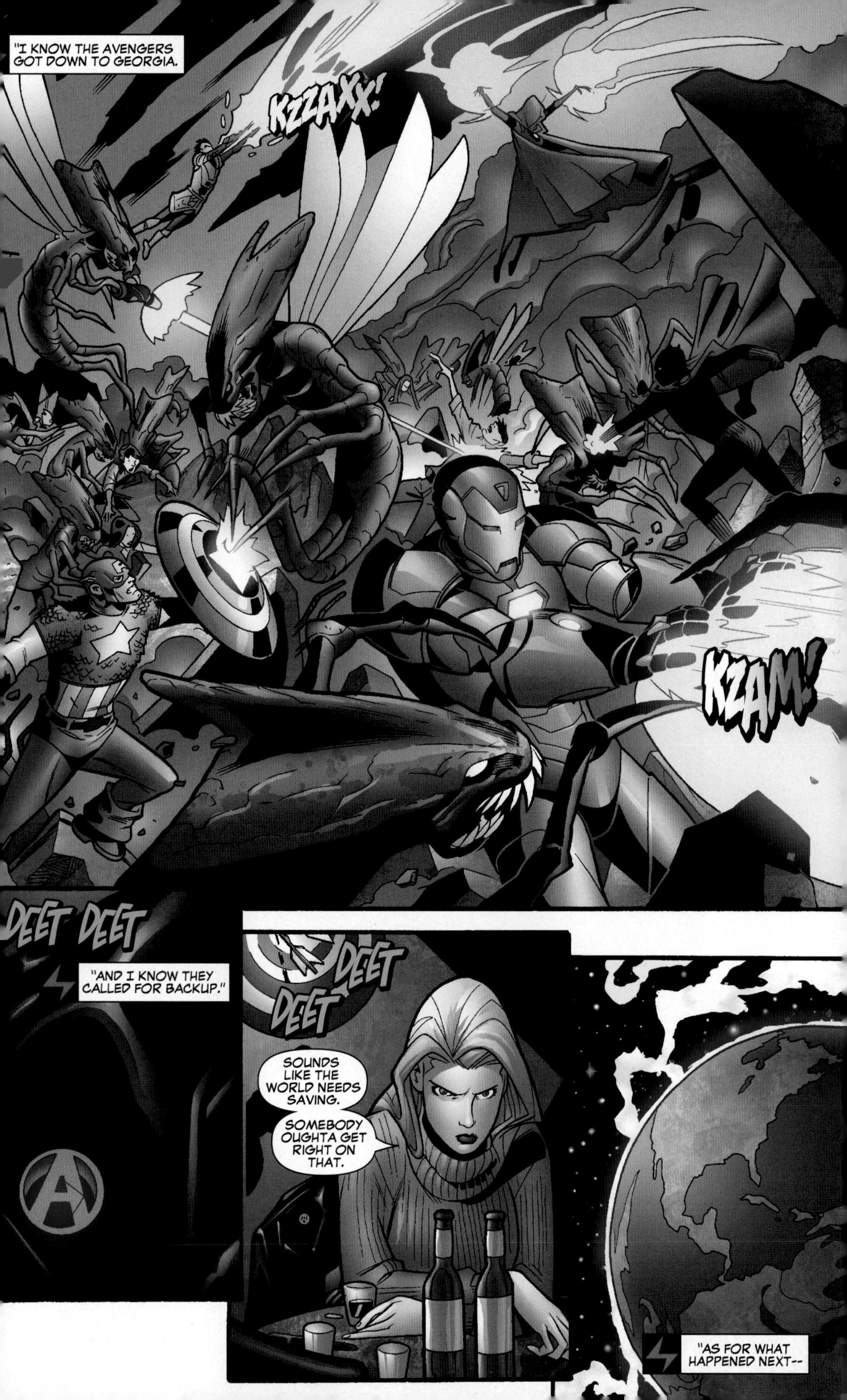
"I KNOW THE AVENGERS GOT DOWN TO GEORGIA.
KZZAXX!
KZAM!
DEET DEET
"AND I KNOW THEY CALLED FOR BACKUP."
DEET DEET
SOUNDS LIKE THE WORLD NEEDS SAVING.
SOMEBODY OUGHTA GET RIGHT ON THAT.
"AS FOR WHAT HAPPENED NEXT--

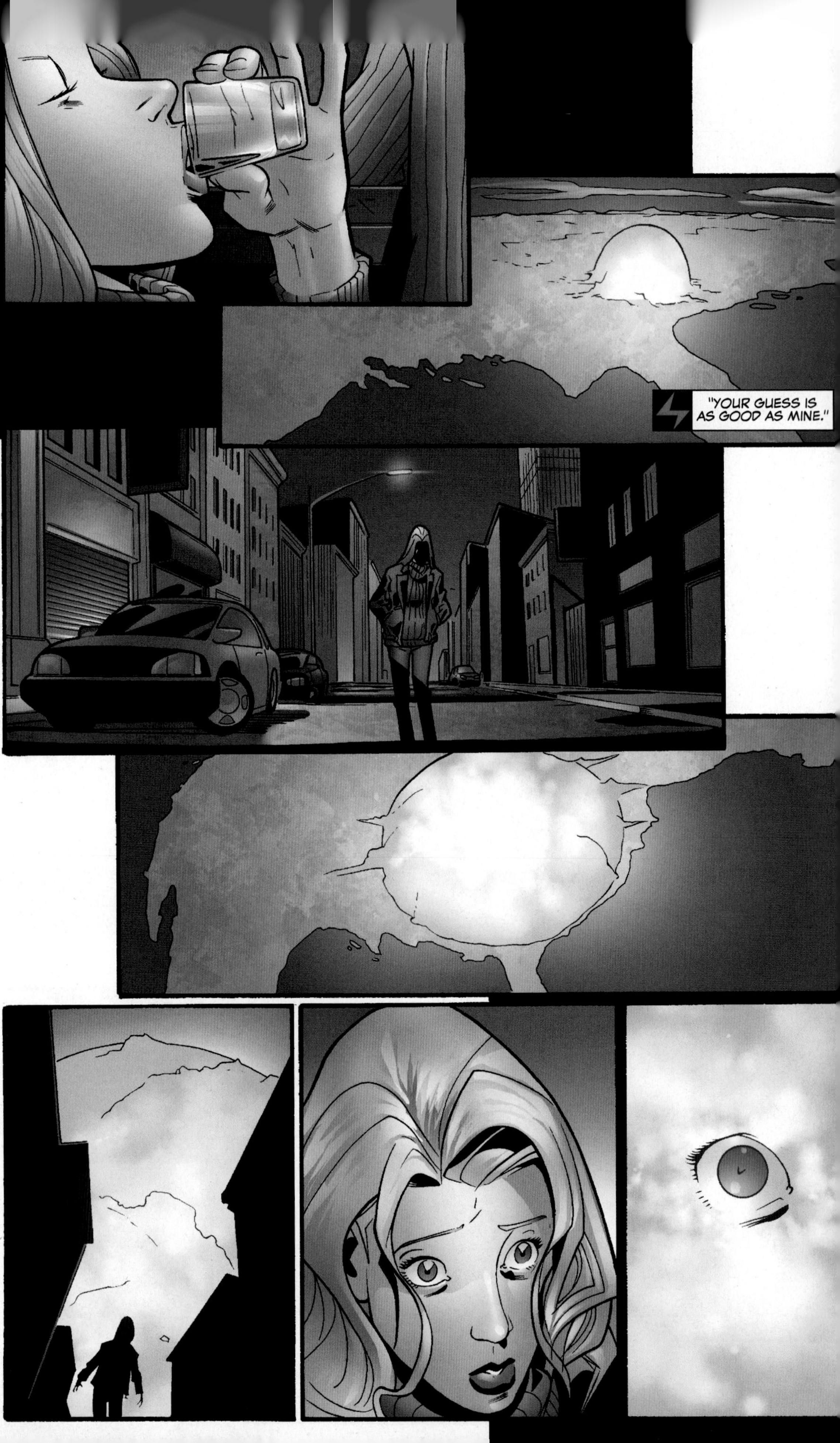
"YOUR GUESS IS AS GOOD AS MINE."

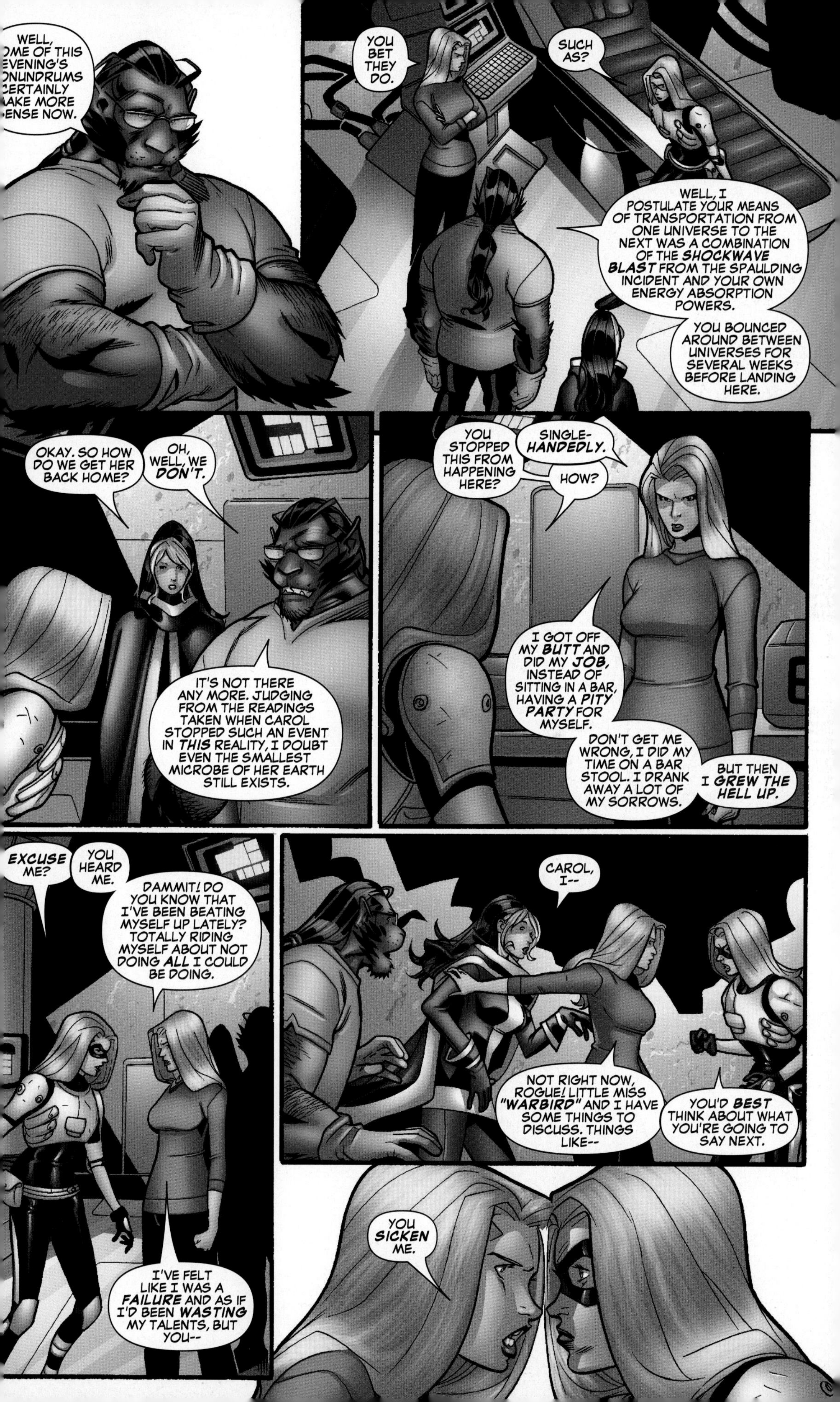

WELL, SOME OF THIS EVENING'S CONUNDRUMS CERTAINLY MAKE MORE SENSE NOW.
YOU BET THEY DO.
SUCH AS?
WELL, I POSTULATE YOUR MEANS OF TRANSPORTATION FROM ONE UNIVERSE TO THE NEXT WAS A COMBINATION OF THE SHOCKWAVE BLAST FROM THE SPAULDING INCIDENT AND YOUR OWN ENERGY ABSORPTION POWERS.
YOU BOUNCED AROUND BETWEEN UNIVERSES FOR SEVERAL WEEKS BEFORE LANDING HERE.
OKAY. SO HOW DO WE GET HER BACK HOME?
OH, WELL, WE DON'T.
IT'S NOT THERE ANY MORE. JUDGING FROM THE READINGS TAKEN WHEN CAROL STOPPED SUCH AN EVENT IN THIS REALITY, I DOUBT EVEN THE SMALLEST MICROBE OF HER EARTH STILL EXISTS.
YOU STOPPED THIS FROM HAPPENING HERE?
SINGLE-HANDEDLY.
HOW?
I GOT OFF MY BUTT AND DID MY JOB, INSTEAD OF SITTING IN A BAR, HAVING A PITY PARTY FOR MYSELF.
DON'T GET ME WRONG, I DID MY TIME ON A BAR STOOL. I DRANK AWAY A LOT OF MY SORROWS.
BUT THEN I GREW THE HELL UP.
EXCUSE ME?
YOU HEARD ME.
DAMMIT! DO YOU KNOW THAT I'VE BEEN BEATING MYSELF UP LATELY? TOTALLY RIDING MYSELF ABOUT NOT DOING ALL I COULD BE DOING.
I'VE FELT LIKE I WAS A FAILURE AND AS IF I'D BEEN WASTING MY TALENTS, BUT YOU--
CAROL, I--
NOT RIGHT NOW, ROGUE! LITTLE MISS "WARBIRD" AND I HAVE SOME THINGS TO DISCUSS. THINGS LIKE--
YOU'D BEST THINK ABOUT WHAT YOU'RE GOING TO SAY NEXT.
YOU SICKEN ME.

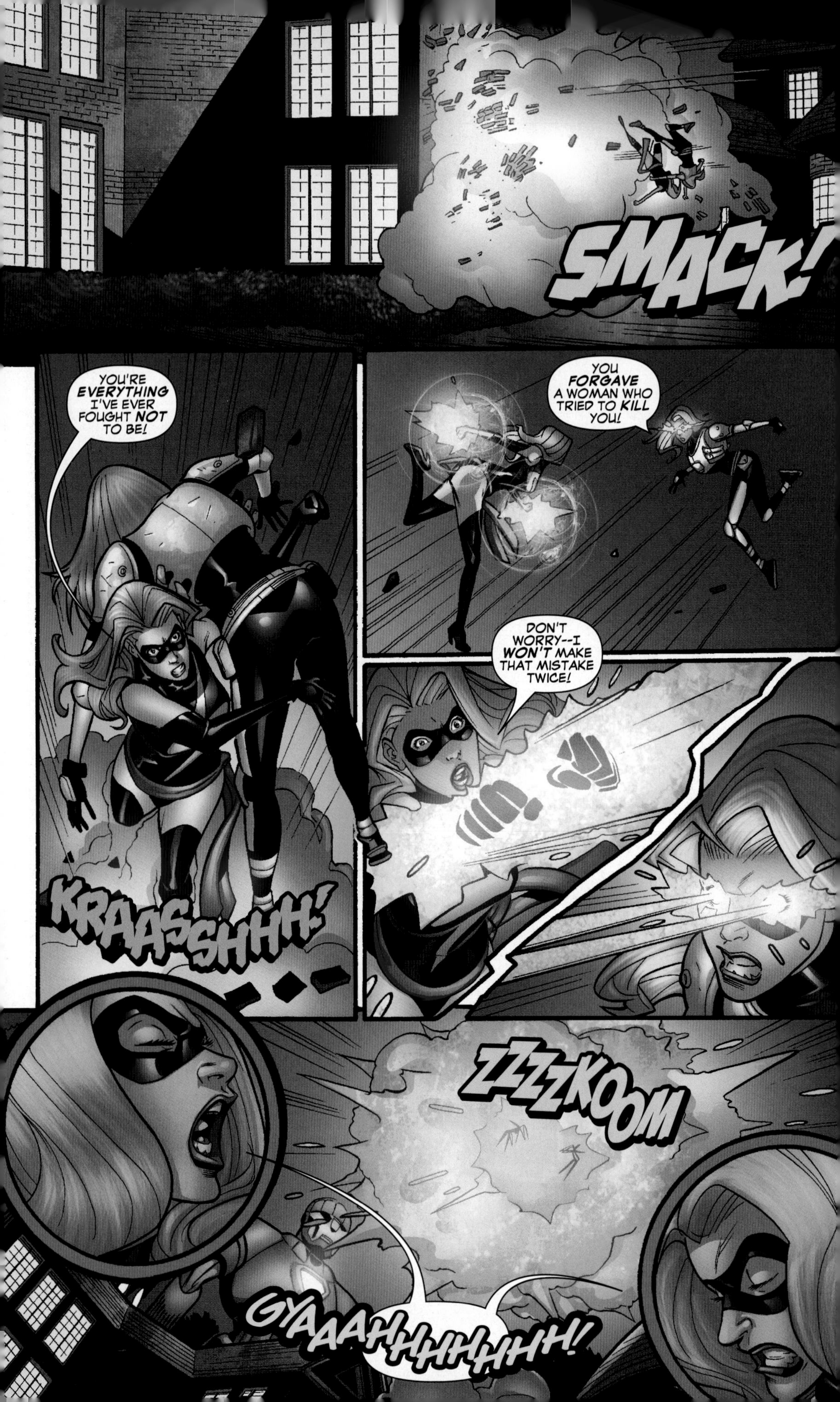
SMACK!
YOU'RE EVERYTHING I'VE EVER FOUGHT NOT TO BE!
KRAASSHHH!
YOU FORGAVE A WOMAN WHO TRIED TO KILL YOU!
DON'T WORRY--I WON'T MAKE THAT MISTAKE TWICE!
ZZZZKOOOM
GYAAAHHHHHHHH!

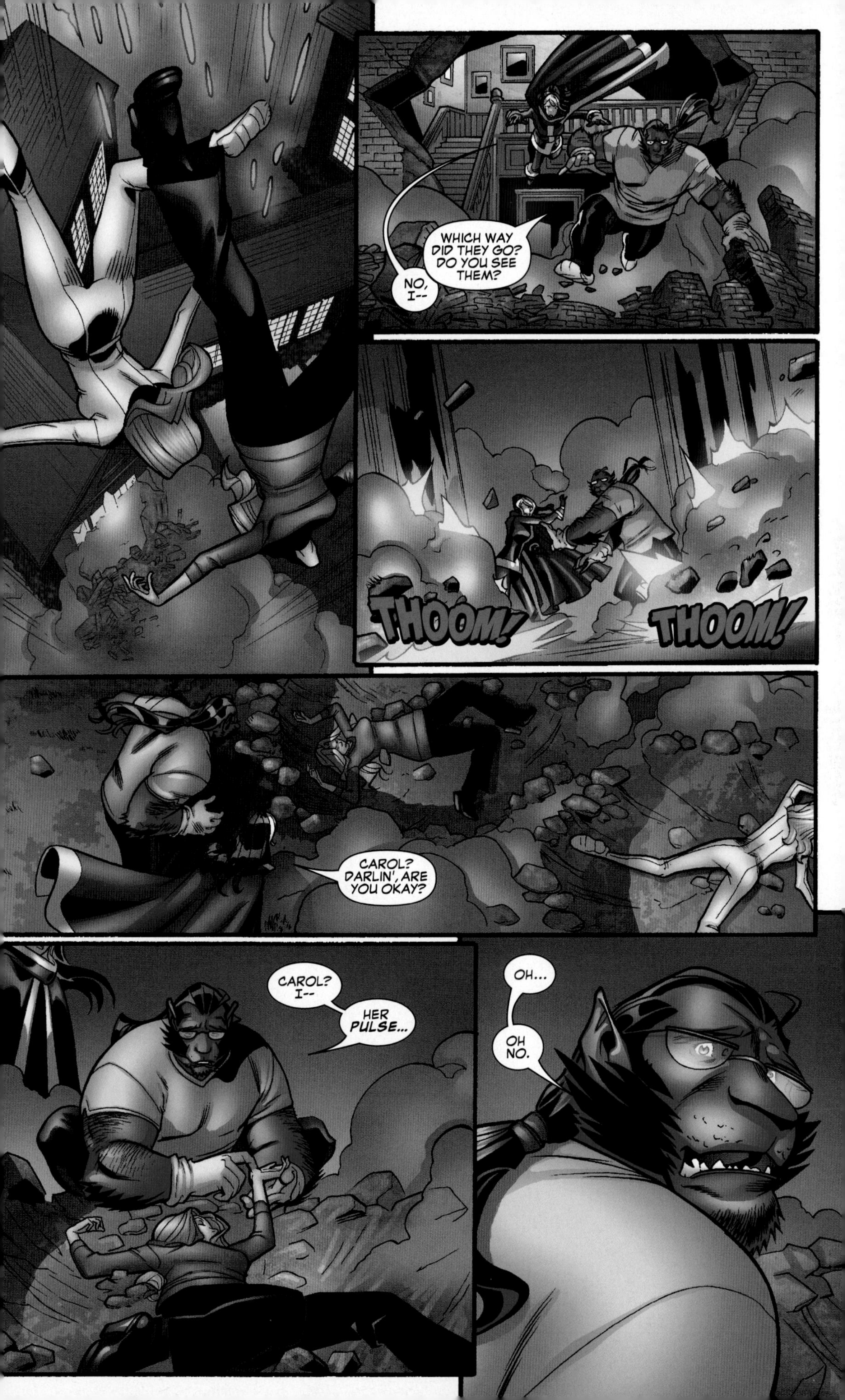
WHICH WAY DID THEY GO? DO YOU SEE THEM?
NO, I--
THOOM!
THOOM!
CAROL? DARLIN', ARE YOU OKAY?
CAROL? I--
HER PULSE...
OH...
OH NO.

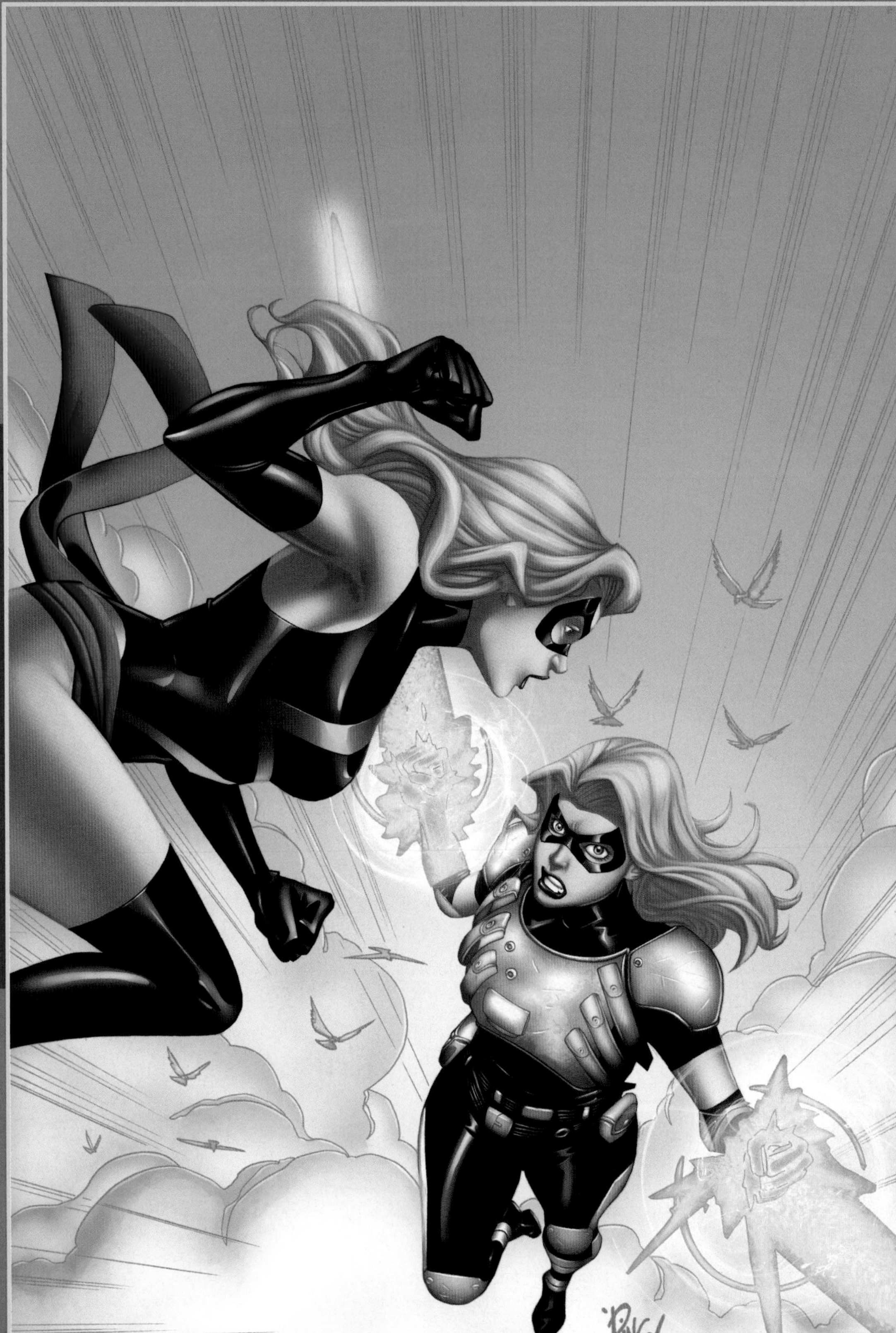
RINGO!
¡SOTO!

10

"YOUR OWN WORST ENEMY"

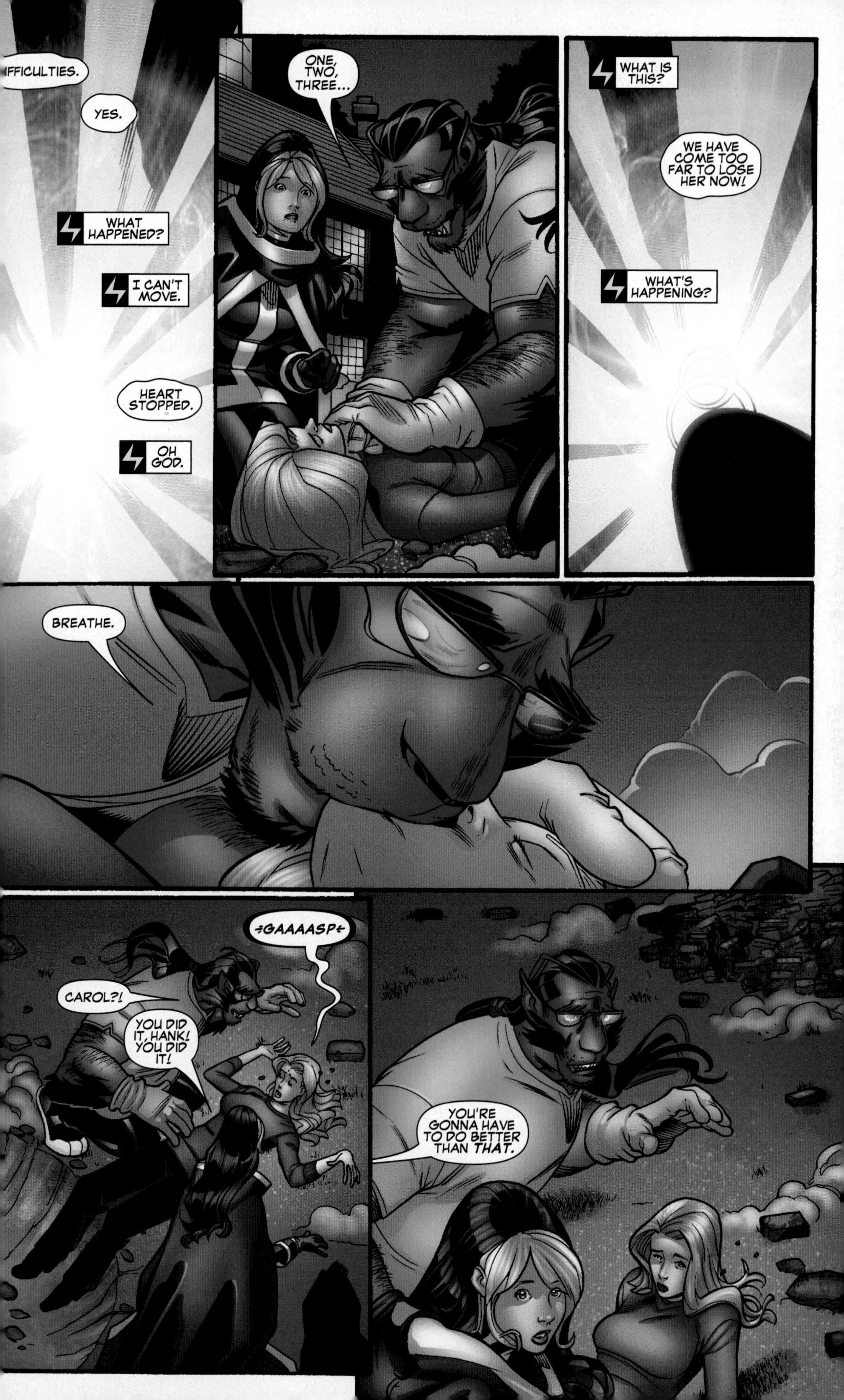

IFFICULTIES.
YES.
WHAT HAPPENED?
I CAN'T MOVE.
HEART STOPPED.
OH GOD.
ONE, TWO, THREE...
WHAT IS THIS?
WE HAVE COME TOO FAR TO LOSE HER NOW!
WHAT'S HAPPENING?
BREATHE.
GAAAASP
CAROL?!
YOU DID IT, HANK! YOU DID IT!
YOU'RE GONNA HAVE TO DO BETTER THAN THAT.

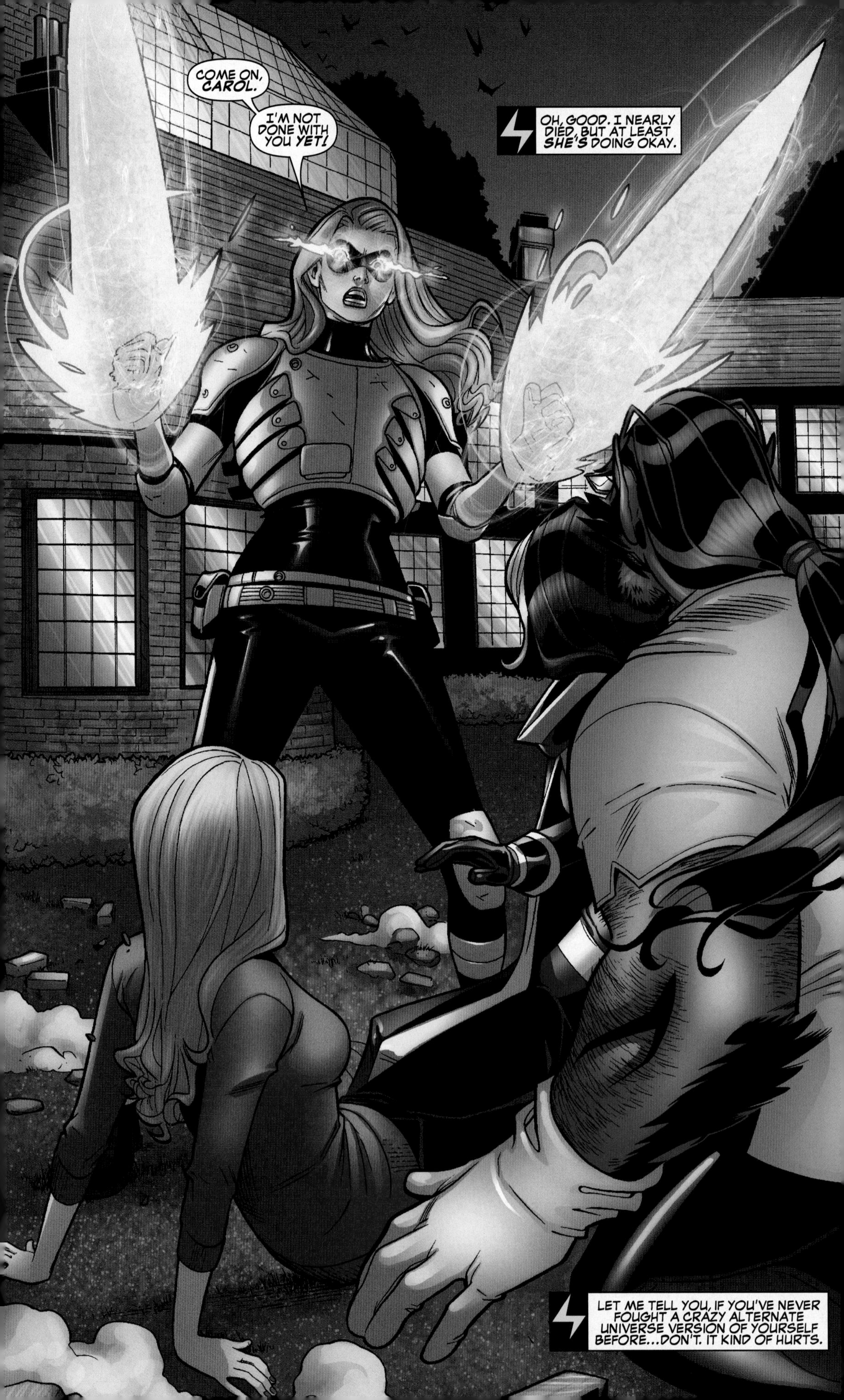

COME ON, CAROL.
I'M NOT DONE WITH YOU YET!
OH, GOOD. I NEARLY DIED, BUT AT LEAST SHE'S DOING OKAY.
LET ME TELL YOU, IF YOU'VE NEVER FOUGHT A CRAZY ALTERNATE UNIVERSE VERSION OF YOURSELF BEFORE...DON'T. IT KIND OF HURTS.

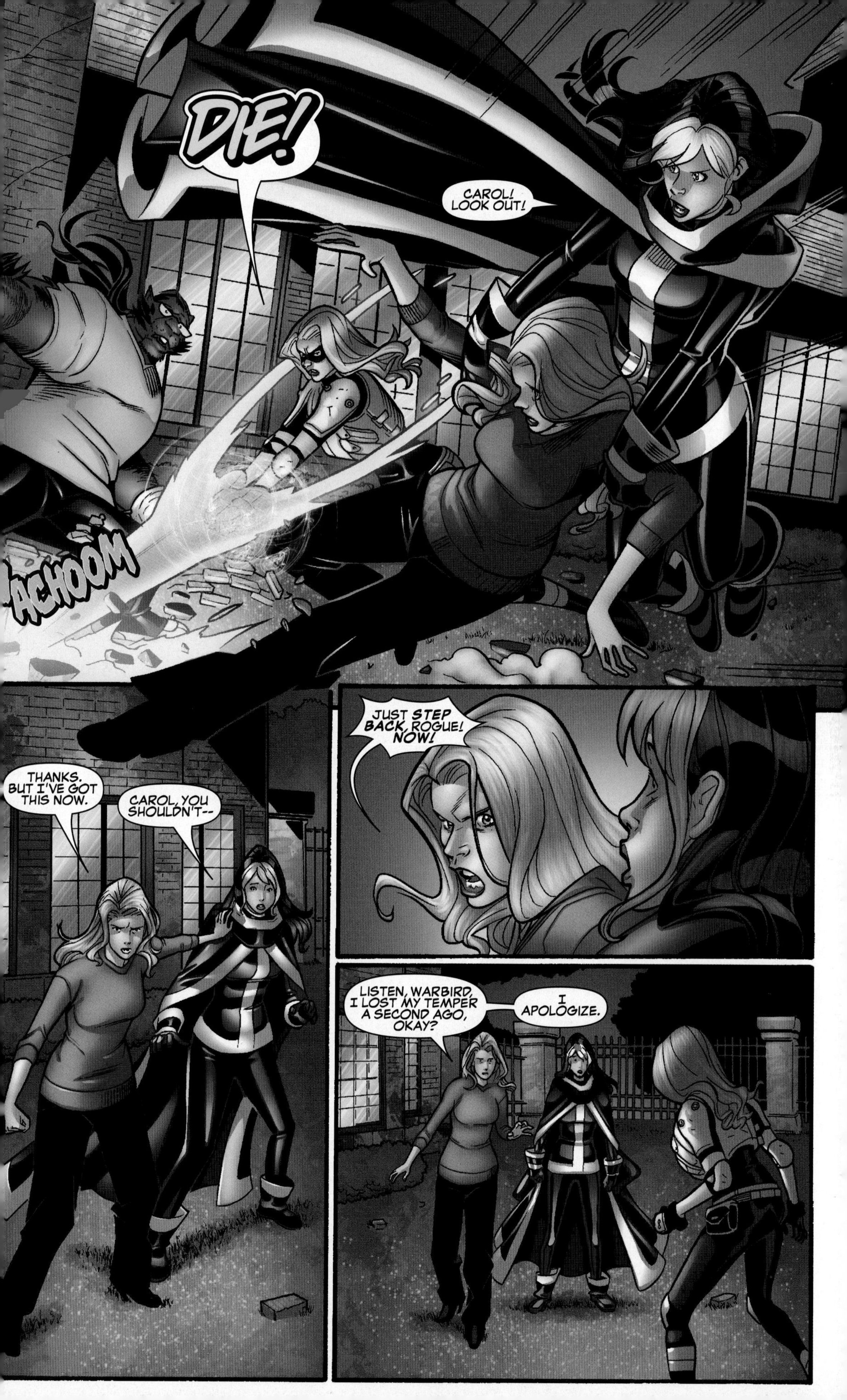
DIE!
CAROL! LOOK OUT!
ACHOOM
THANKS. BUT I'VE GOT THIS NOW.
CAROL, YOU SHOULDN'T--
JUST STEP BACK, ROGUE! NOW!
LISTEN, WARBIRD, I LOST MY TEMPER A SECOND AGO, OKAY?
I APOLOGIZE.

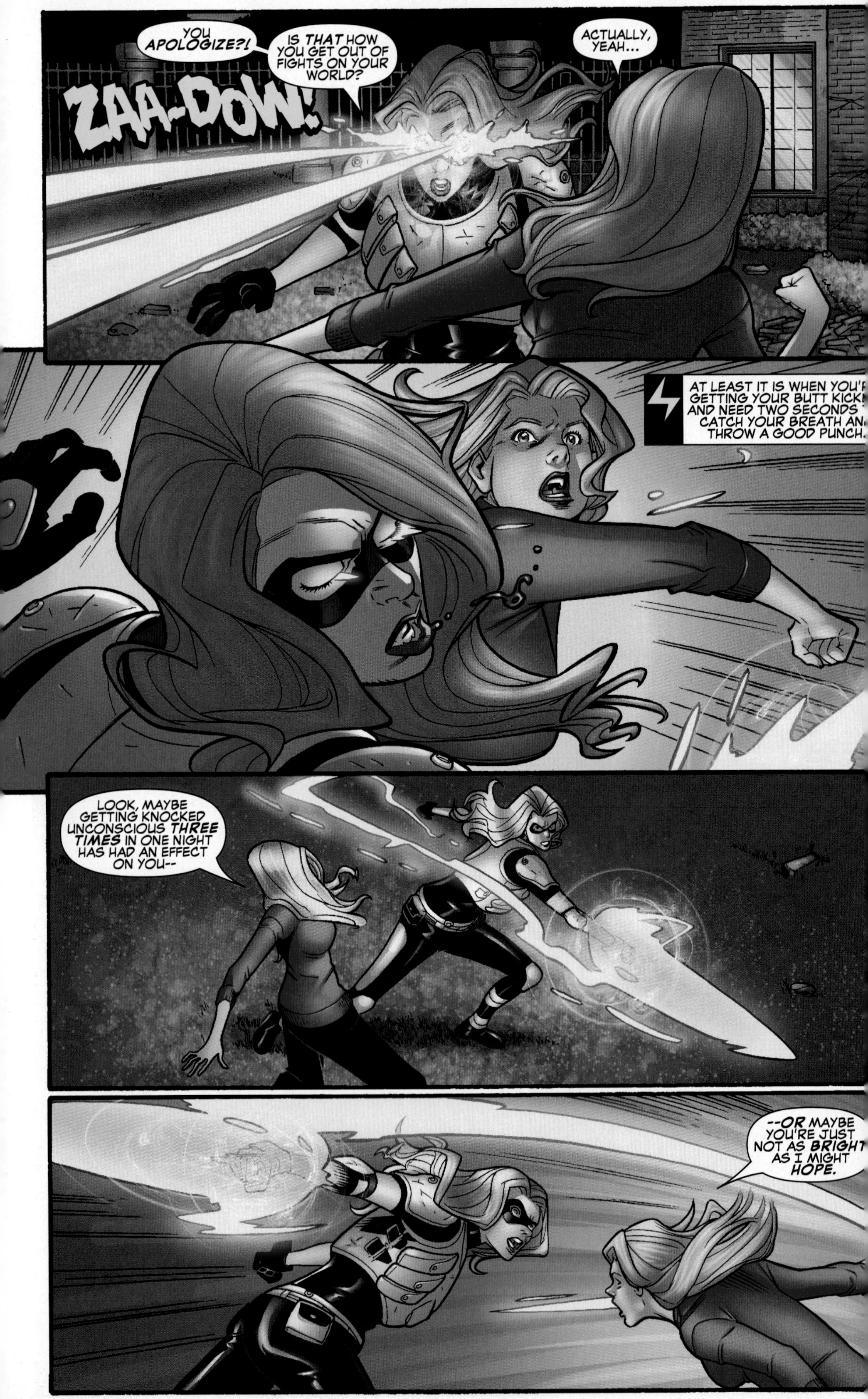

YOU APOLOGIZE?!
IS THAT HOW YOU GET OUT OF FIGHTS ON YOUR WORLD?
ZAA-DOW!
ACTUALLY, YEAH...
AT LEAST IT IS WHEN YOU'R GETTING YOUR BUTT KICK AND NEED TWO SECONDS T CATCH YOUR BREATH AN THROW A GOOD PUNCH.
LOOK, MAYBE GETTING KNOCKED UNCONSCIOUS THREE TIMES IN ONE NIGHT HAS HAD AN EFFECT ON YOU--
--OR MAYBE YOU'RE JUST NOT AS BRIGHT AS I MIGHT HOPE.

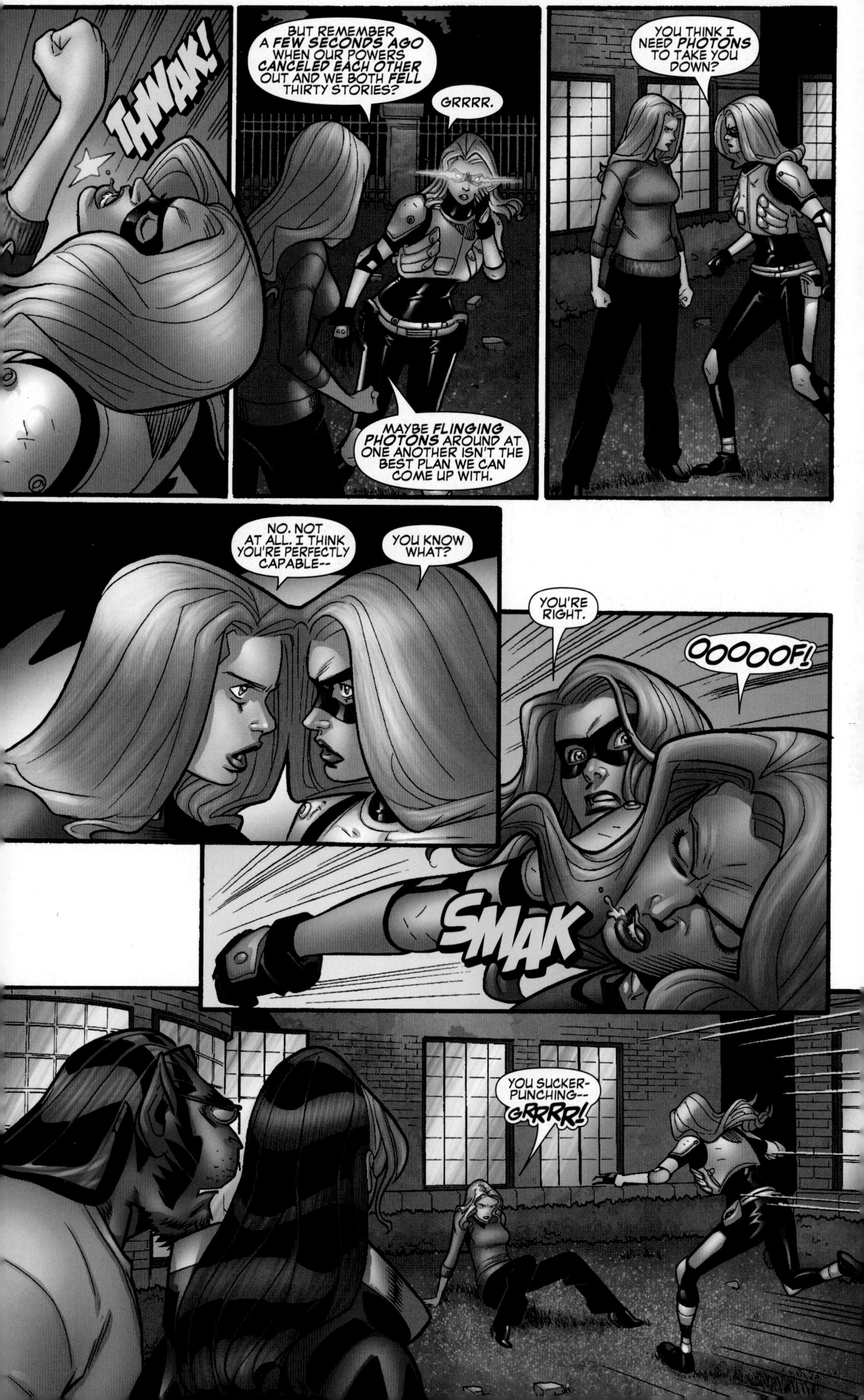
THWAK!
BUT REMEMBER A FEW SECONDS AGO WHEN OUR POWERS CANCELED EACH OTHER OUT AND WE BOTH FELL THIRTY STORIES?
GRRRR.
MAYBE FLINGING PHOTONS AROUND AT ONE ANOTHER ISN'T THE BEST PLAN WE CAN COME UP WITH.
YOU THINK I NEED PHOTONS TO TAKE YOU DOWN?
NO. NOT AT ALL. I THINK YOU'RE PERFECTLY CAPABLE--
YOU KNOW WHAT?
YOU'RE RIGHT.
OOOOOF!
SMAK
YOU SUCKER-PUNCHING-- GRRRR!

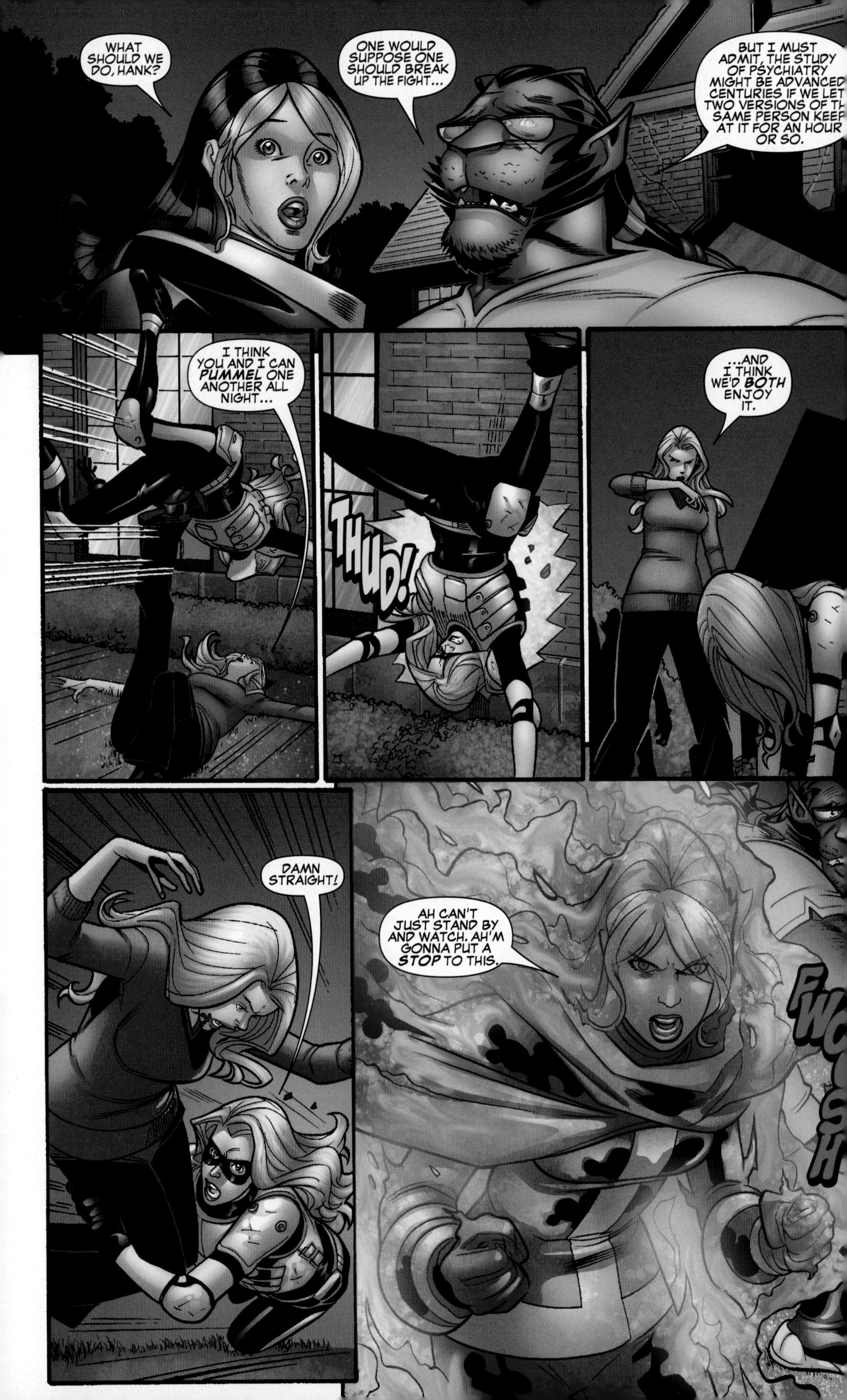
WHAT SHOULD WE DO, HANK?
ONE WOULD SUPPOSE ONE SHOULD BREAK UP THE FIGHT...
BUT I MUST ADMIT, THE STUDY OF PSYCHIATRY MIGHT BE ADVANCED CENTURIES IF WE LET TWO VERSIONS OF TH SAME PERSON KEEP AT IT FOR AN HOUR OR SO.
I THINK YOU AND I CAN PUMMEL ONE ANOTHER ALL NIGHT...
THUD!
...AND I THINK WE'D BOTH ENJOY IT.
DAMN STRAIGHT!
AH CAN'T JUST STAND BY AND WATCH. AH'M GONNA PUT A STOP TO THIS.
FWOOSH

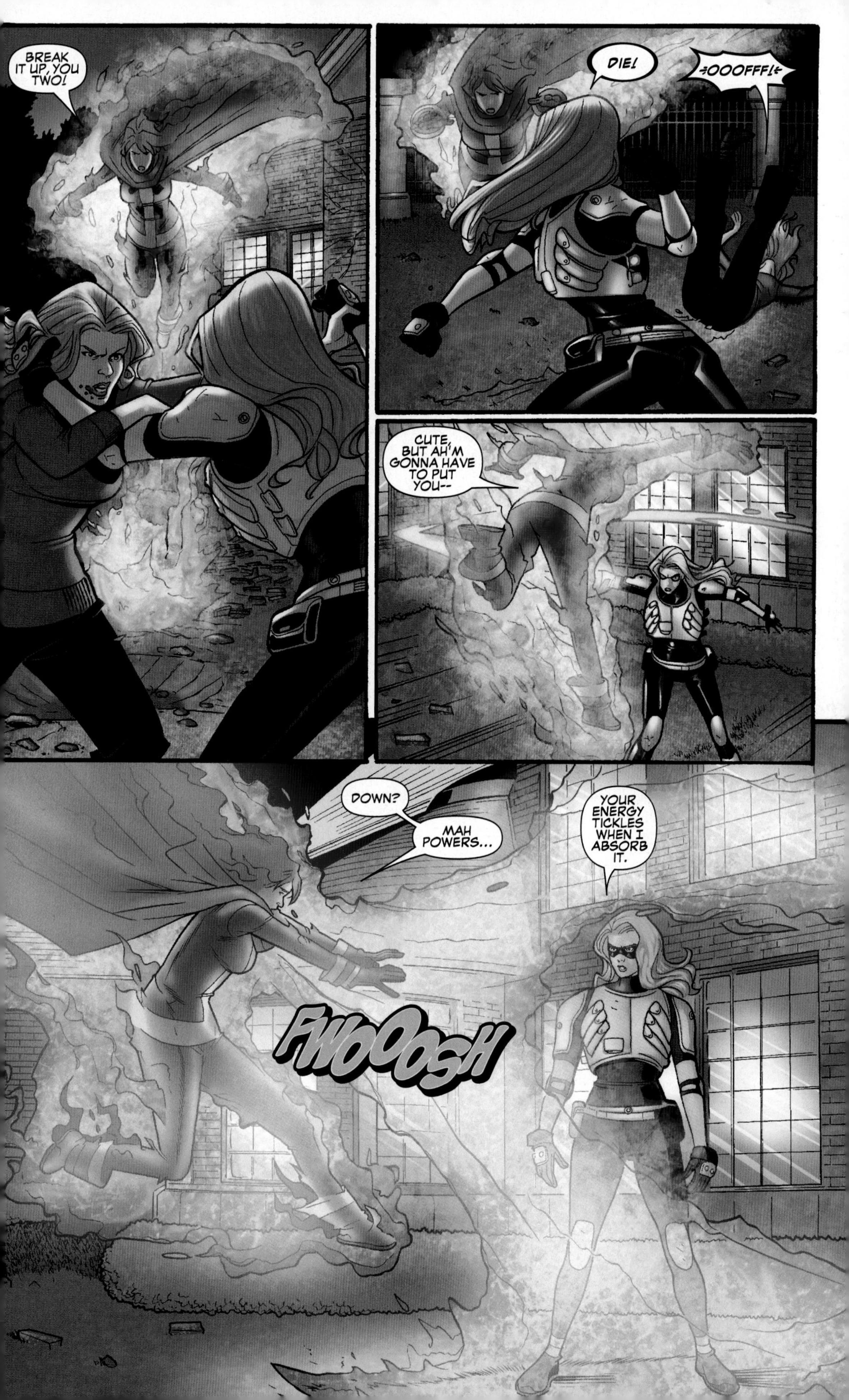
BREAK IT UP, YOU TWO!
DIE!
OOOFFF!
CUTE, BUT AH'M GONNA HAVE TO PUT YOU--
DOWN?
MAH POWERS...
YOUR ENERGY TICKLES WHEN I ABSORB IT.
FWOOOSH

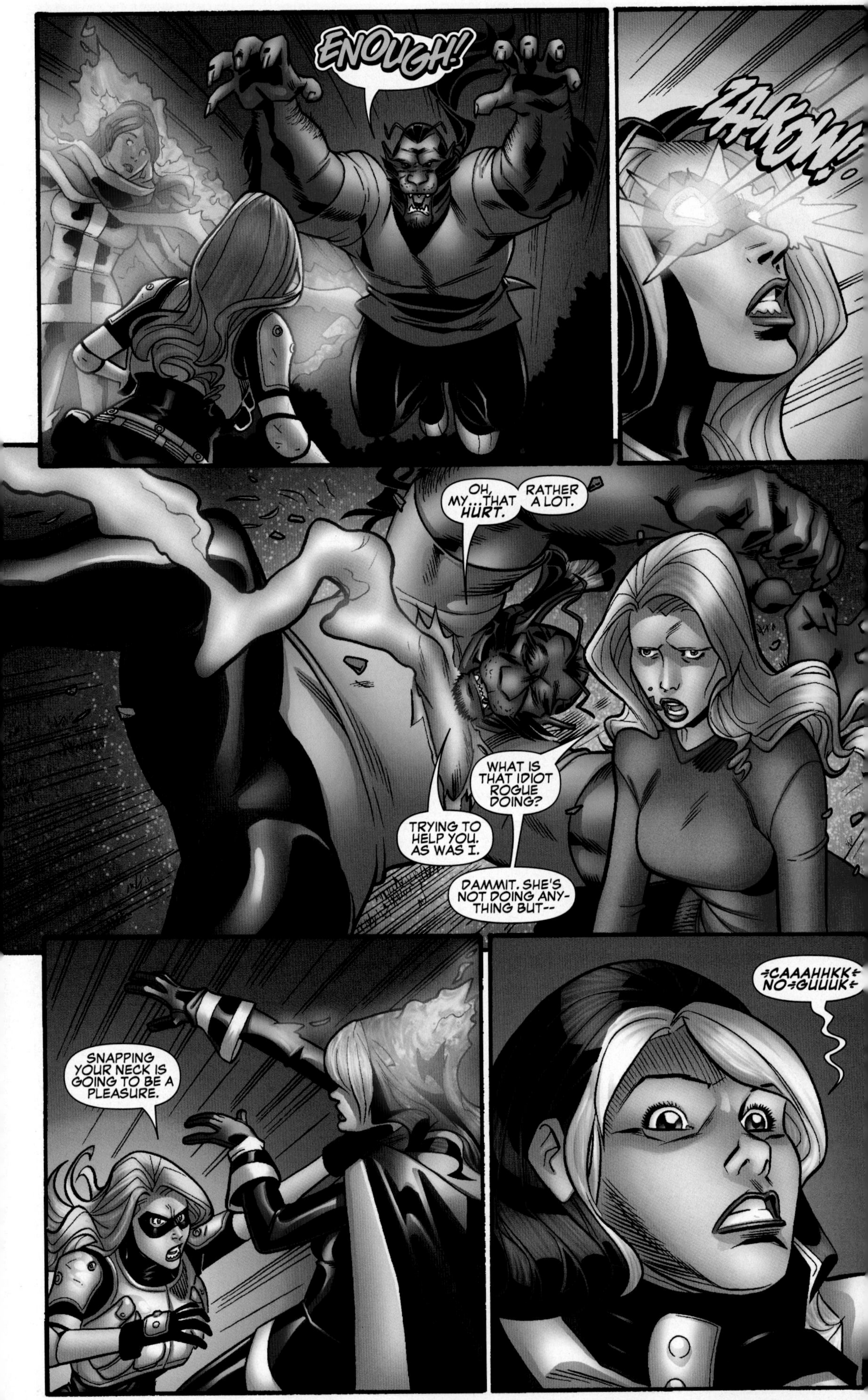
ENOUGH!
ZA-KOW!
OH, MY...THAT HURT.
RATHER A LOT.
WHAT IS THAT IDIOT ROGUE DOING?
TRYING TO HELP YOU. AS WAS I.
DAMMIT. SHE'S NOT DOING ANYTHING BUT--
SNAPPING YOUR NECK IS GOING TO BE A PLEASURE.
CAAAHHKK NO GUUUK

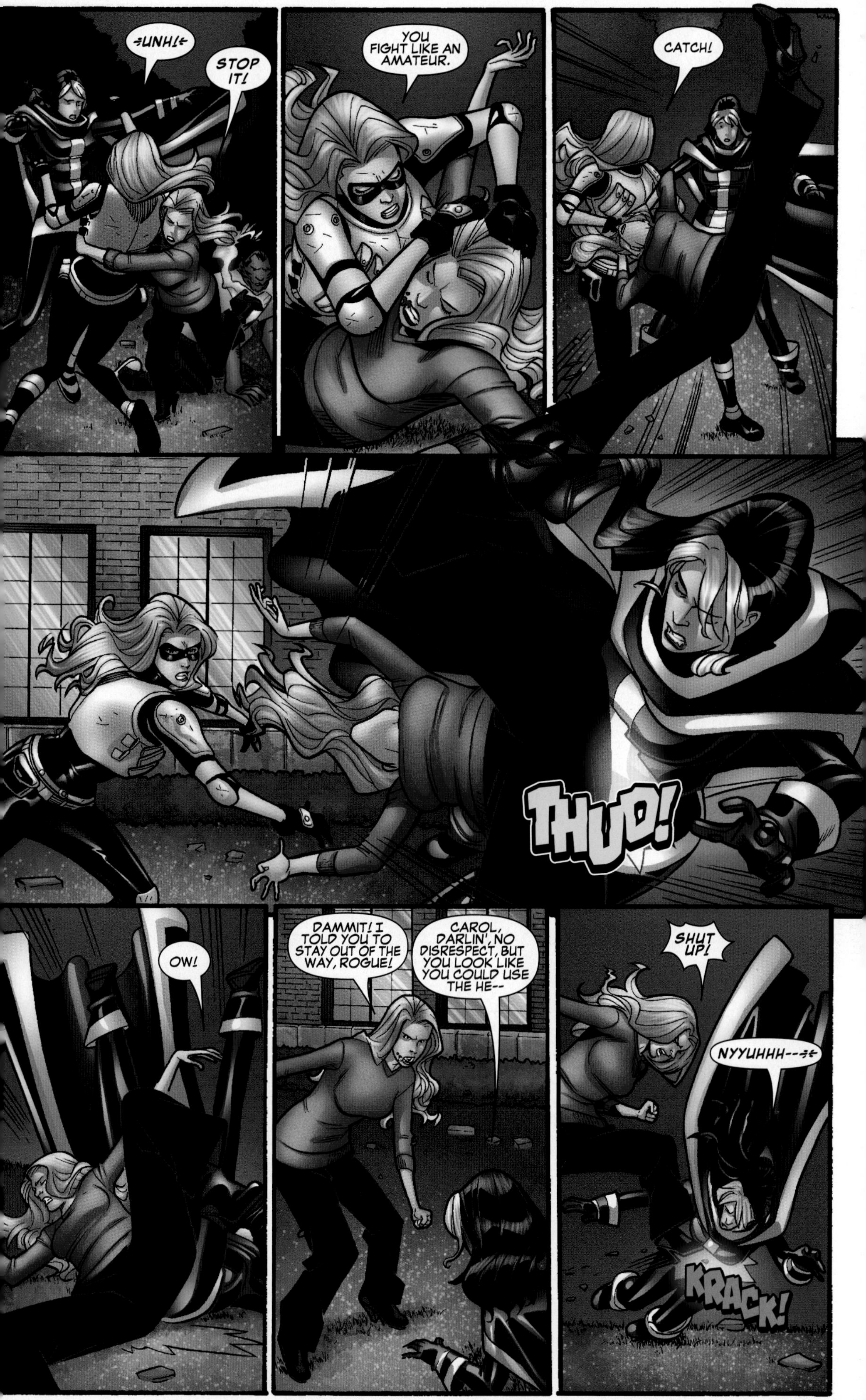

UNH!
STOP IT!
YOU FIGHT LIKE AN AMATEUR.
CATCH!
THUD!
OW!
DAMMIT! I TOLD YOU TO STAY OUT OF THE WAY, ROGUE!
CAROL, DARLIN', NO DISRESPECT, BUT YOU LOOK LIKE YOU COULD USE THE HE--
SHUT UP!
NYYUHHH--
KRACK!

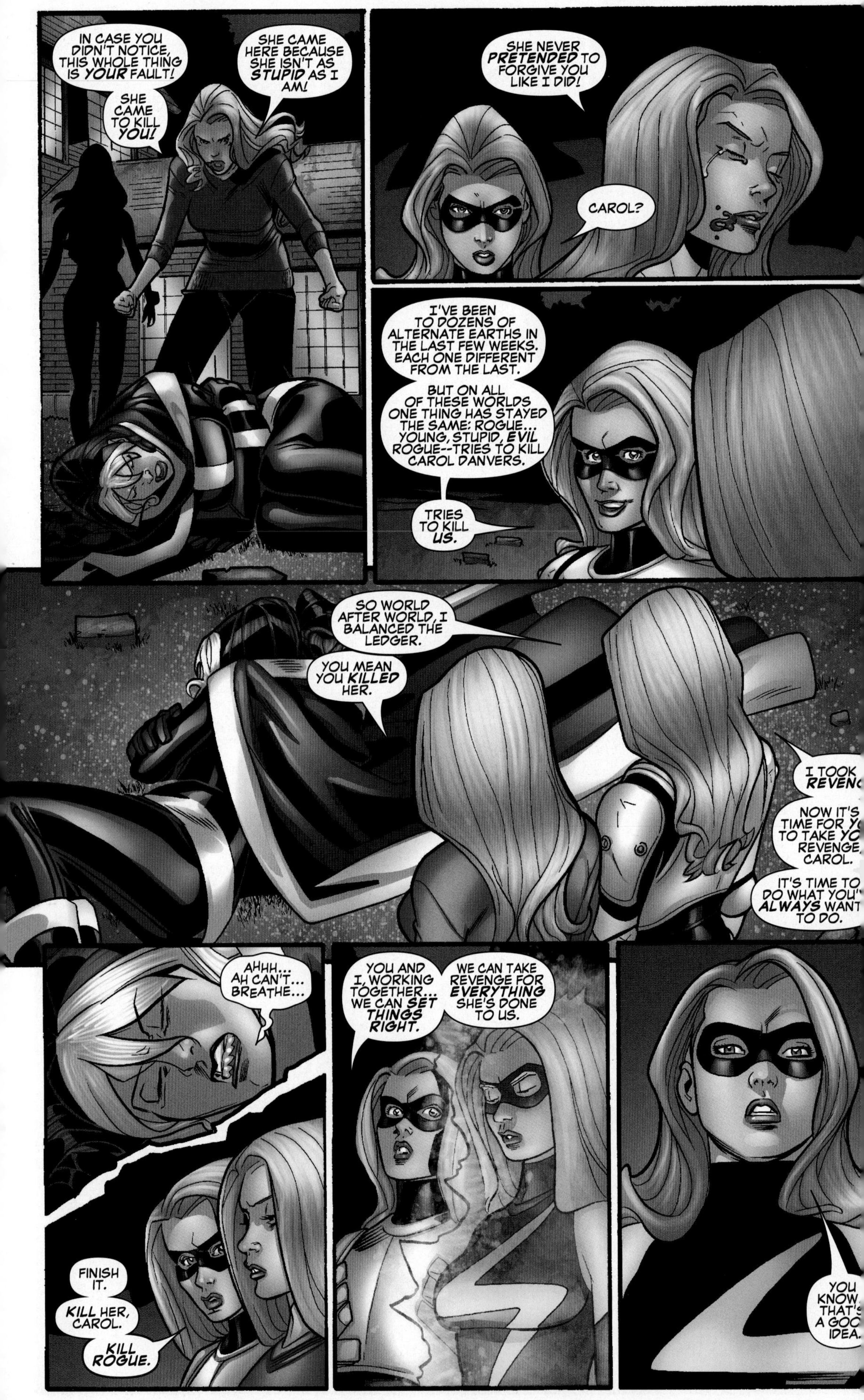

IN CASE YOU DIDN'T NOTICE, THIS WHOLE THING IS YOUR FAULT!
SHE CAME TO KILL YOU!
SHE CAME HERE BECAUSE SHE ISN'T AS STUPID AS I AM!
SHE NEVER PRETENDED TO FORGIVE YOU LIKE I DID!
CAROL?
I'VE BEEN TO DOZENS OF ALTERNATE EARTHS IN THE LAST FEW WEEKS. EACH ONE DIFFERENT FROM THE LAST.
BUT ON ALL OF THESE WORLDS ONE THING HAS STAYED THE SAME: ROGUE... YOUNG, STUPID, EVIL ROGUE--TRIES TO KILL CAROL DANVERS.
TRIES TO KILL US.
SO WORLD AFTER WORLD, I BALANCED THE LEDGER.
YOU MEAN YOU KILLED HER.
I TOOK REVENG
NOW IT'S TIME FOR YO TO TAKE YO REVENGE, CAROL.
IT'S TIME TO DO WHAT YOU' ALWAYS WANT TO DO.
AHHH... AH CAN'T... BREATHE...
FINISH IT.
KILL HER, CAROL.
KILL ROGUE.
YOU AND I, WORKING TOGETHER... WE CAN SET THINGS RIGHT.
WE CAN TAKE REVENGE FOR EVERYTHING SHE'S DONE TO US.
YOU KNOW, THAT'S A GOO IDEA.

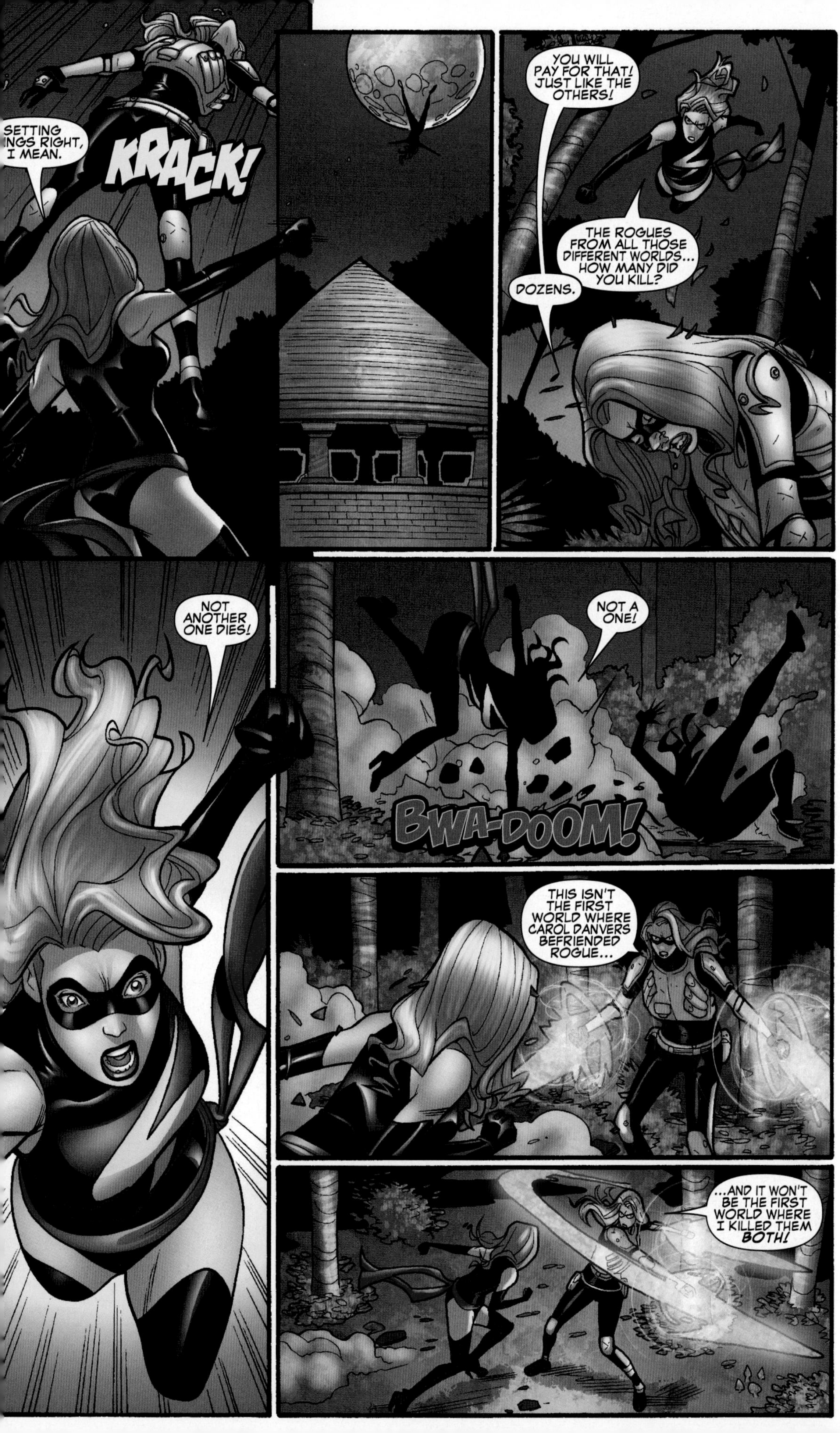
SETTING
NGS RIGHT, I MEAN.
KRACK!
YOU WILL PAY FOR THAT! JUST LIKE THE OTHERS!
THE ROGUES FROM ALL THOSE DIFFERENT WORLDS... HOW MANY DID YOU KILL?
DOZENS.
NOT ANOTHER ONE DIES!
NOT A ONE!
BWA-DOOM!
THIS ISN'T THE FIRST WORLD WHERE CAROL DANVERS BEFRIENDED ROGUE...
...AND IT WON'T BE THE FIRST WORLD WHERE I KILLED THEM BOTH!

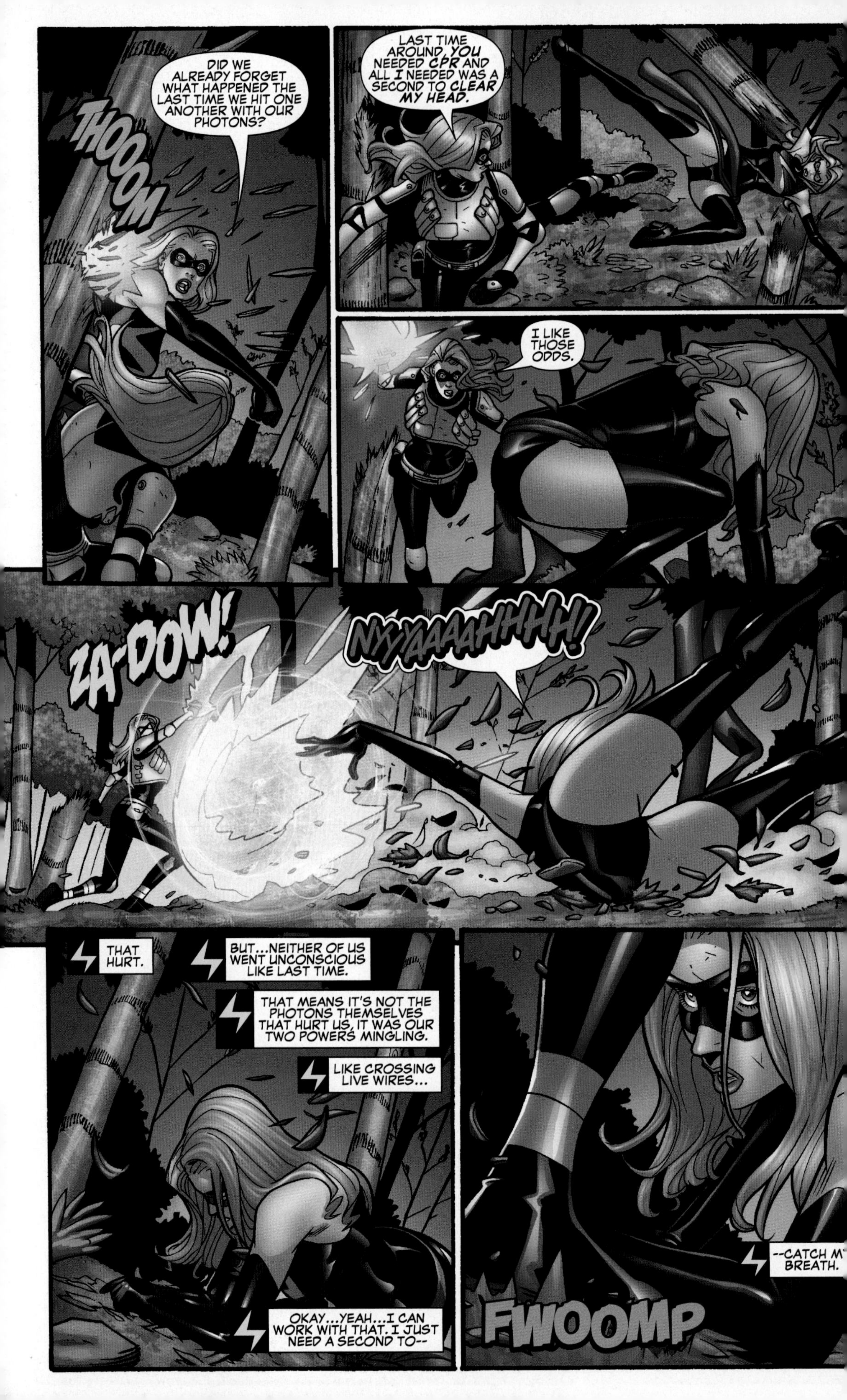
DID WE ALREADY FORGET WHAT HAPPENED THE LAST TIME WE HIT ONE ANOTHER WITH OUR PHOTONS?
THOOOM
LAST TIME AROUND, YOU NEEDED CPR AND ALL I NEEDED WAS A SECOND TO CLEAR MY HEAD.
I LIKE THOSE ODDS.
ZA-DOW!
NYYAAAAHHHH!
THAT HURT.
BUT...NEITHER OF US WENT UNCONSCIOUS LIKE LAST TIME.
THAT MEANS IT'S NOT THE PHOTONS THEMSELVES THAT HURT US, IT WAS OUR TWO POWERS MINGLING.
LIKE CROSSING LIVE WIRES...
OKAY...YEAH...I CAN WORK WITH THAT. I JUST NEED A SECOND TO--
FWOOMP
--CATCH M
BREATH.

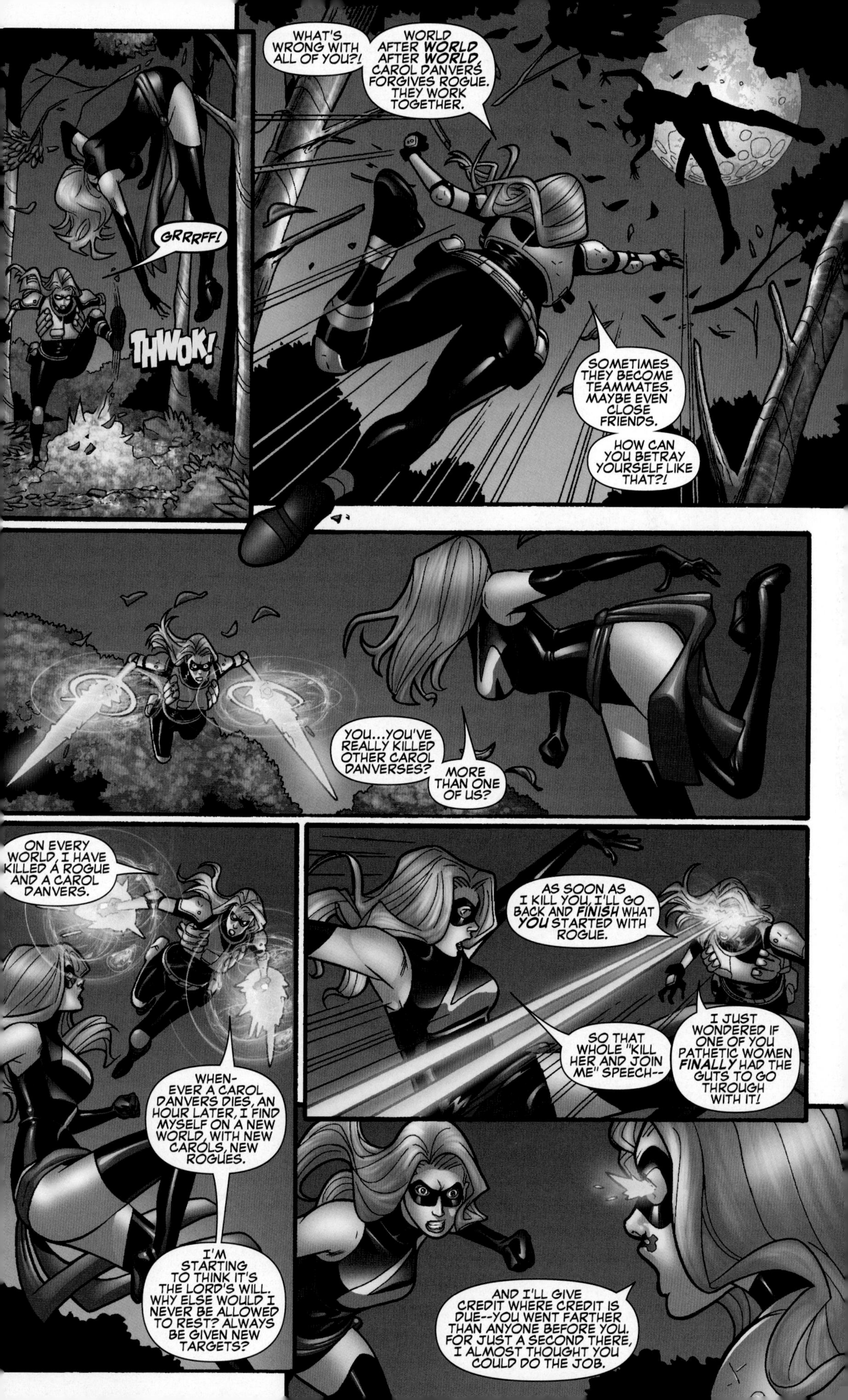
GRRRFF!
THWOK!
WHAT'S WRONG WITH ALL OF YOU?!
WORLD AFTER WORLD AFTER WORLD, CAROL DANVERS FORGIVES ROGUE. THEY WORK TOGETHER.
SOMETIMES THEY BECOME TEAMMATES. MAYBE EVEN CLOSE FRIENDS.
HOW CAN YOU BETRAY YOURSELF LIKE THAT?!
YOU...YOU'VE REALLY KILLED OTHER CAROL DANVERSES?
MORE THAN ONE OF US?
ON EVERY WORLD, I HAVE KILLED A ROGUE AND A CAROL DANVERS.
WHEN-EVER A CAROL DANVERS DIES, AN HOUR LATER, I FIND MYSELF ON A NEW WORLD, WITH NEW CAROLS, NEW ROGUES.
I'M STARTING TO THINK IT'S THE LORD'S WILL. WHY ELSE WOULD I NEVER BE ALLOWED TO REST? ALWAYS BE GIVEN NEW TARGETS?
AS SOON AS I KILL YOU, I'LL GO BACK AND FINISH WHAT YOU STARTED WITH ROGUE.
SO THAT WHOLE "KILL HER AND JOIN ME" SPEECH--
I JUST WONDERED IF ONE OF YOU PATHETIC WOMEN FINALLY HAD THE GUTS TO GO THROUGH WITH IT!
AND I'LL GIVE CREDIT WHERE CREDIT IS DUE--YOU WENT FARTHER THAN ANYONE BEFORE YOU. FOR JUST A SECOND THERE, I ALMOST THOUGHT YOU COULD DO THE JOB.

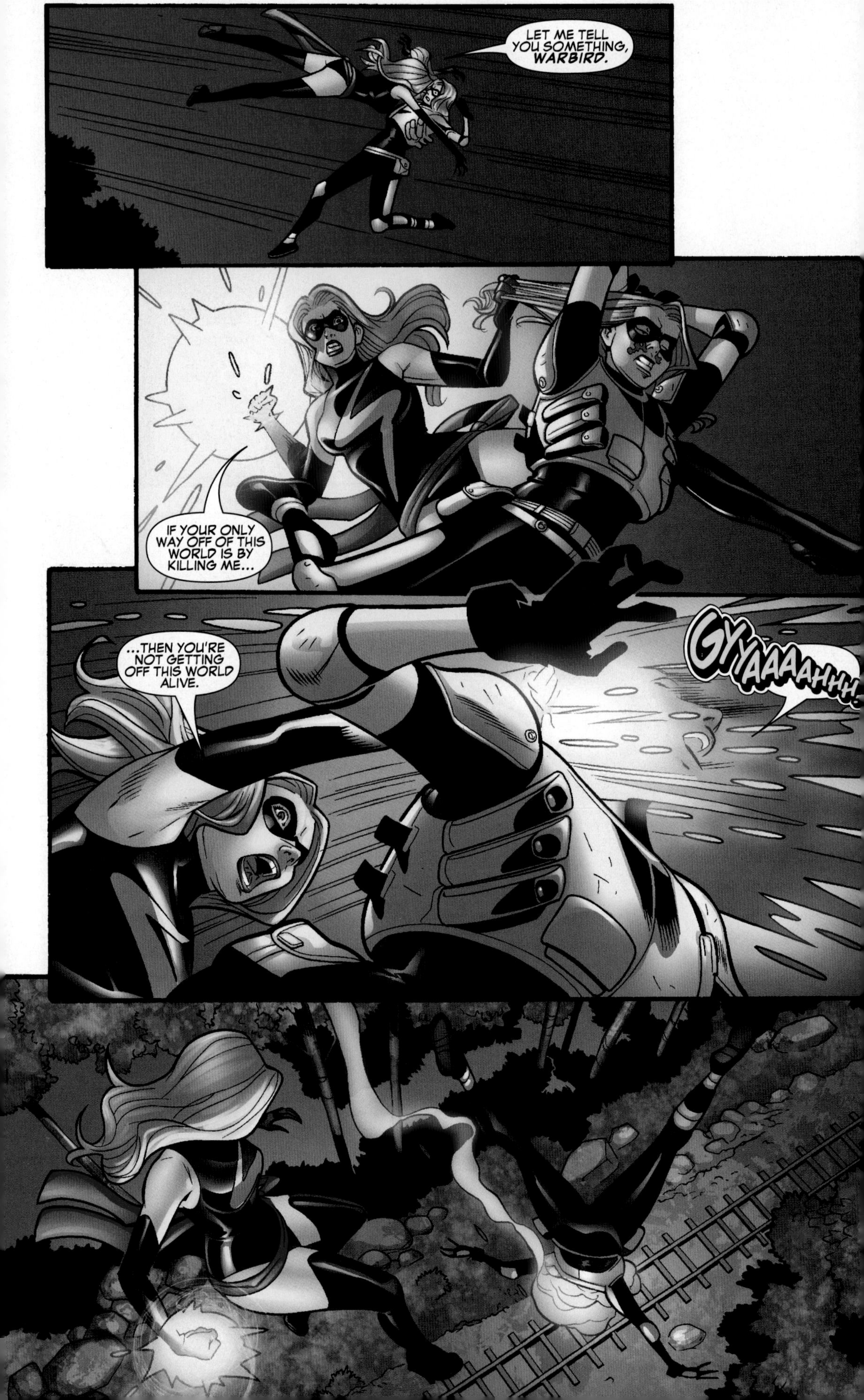
LET ME TELL YOU SOMETHING, WARBIRD.
IF YOUR ONLY WAY OFF OF THIS WORLD IS BY KILLING ME...
...THEN YOU'RE NOT GETTING OFF THIS WORLD ALIVE.
GYYAAAAHHH!

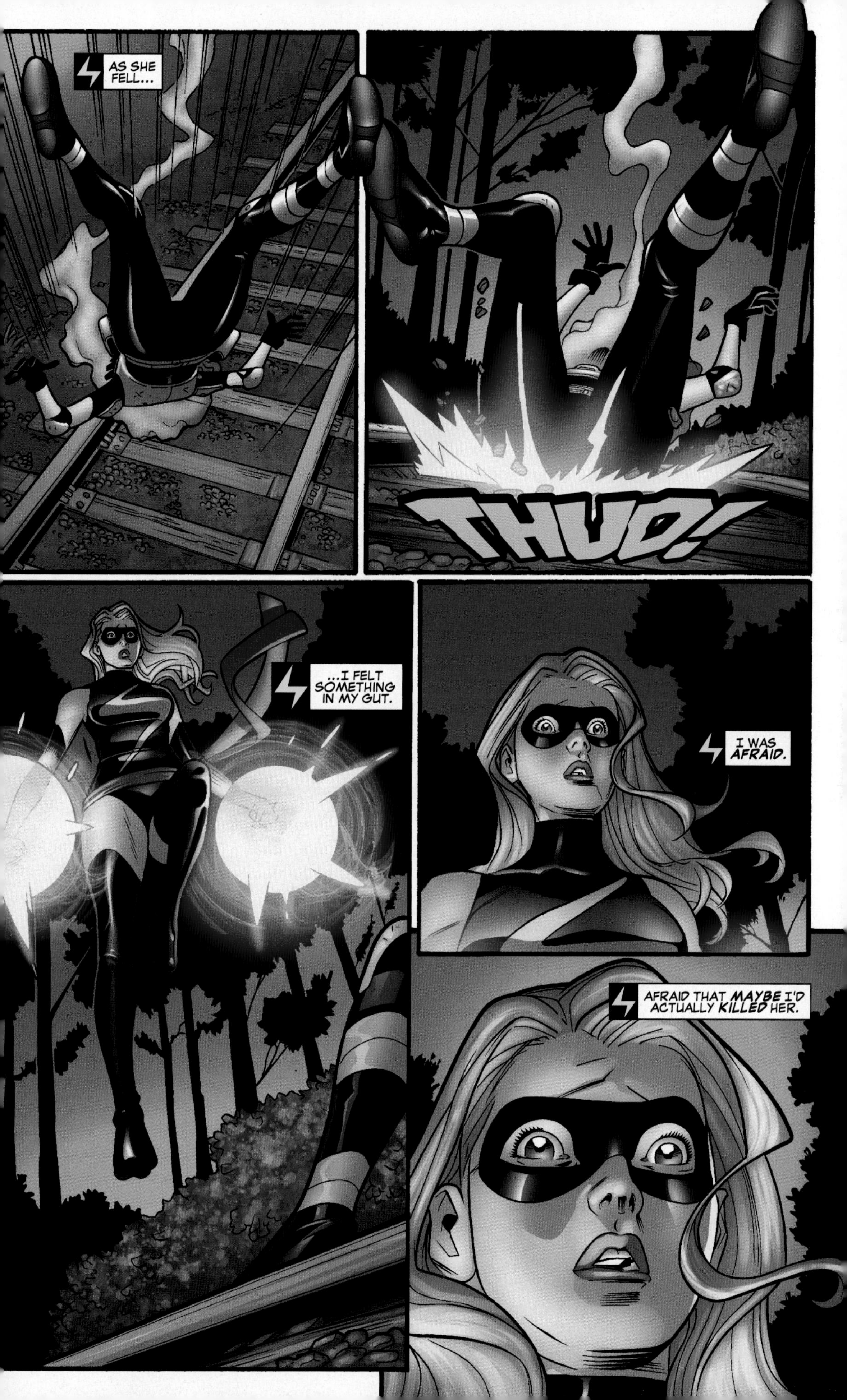
AS SHE FELL...
THUD!
...I FELT SOMETHING IN MY GUT.
I WAS AFRAID.
AFRAID THAT MAYBE I'D ACTUALLY KILLED HER.

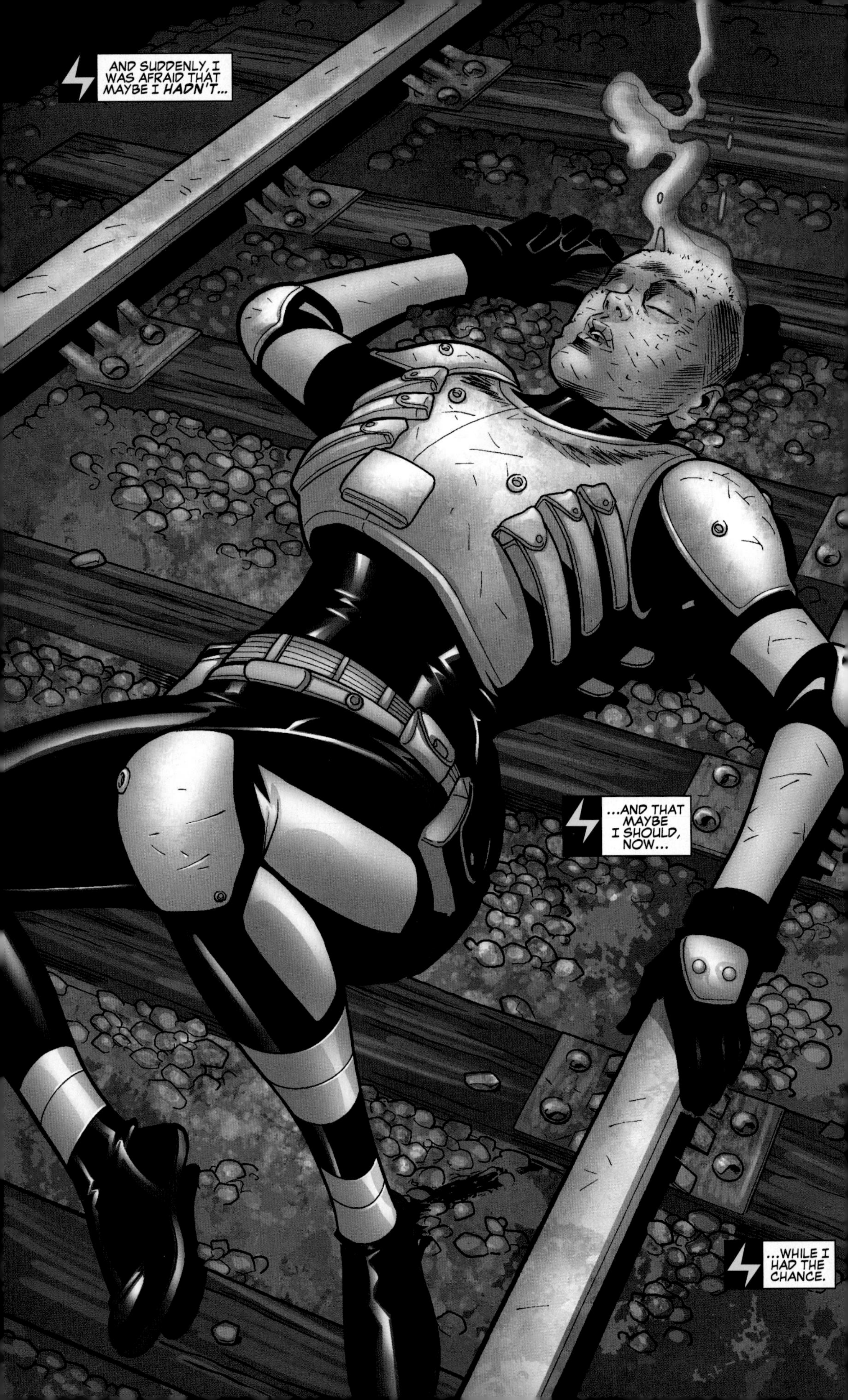
AND SUDDENLY, I WAS AFRAID THAT MAYBE I HADN'T...
...AND THAT MAYBE I SHOULD, NOW...
...WHILE I HAD THE CHANCE.

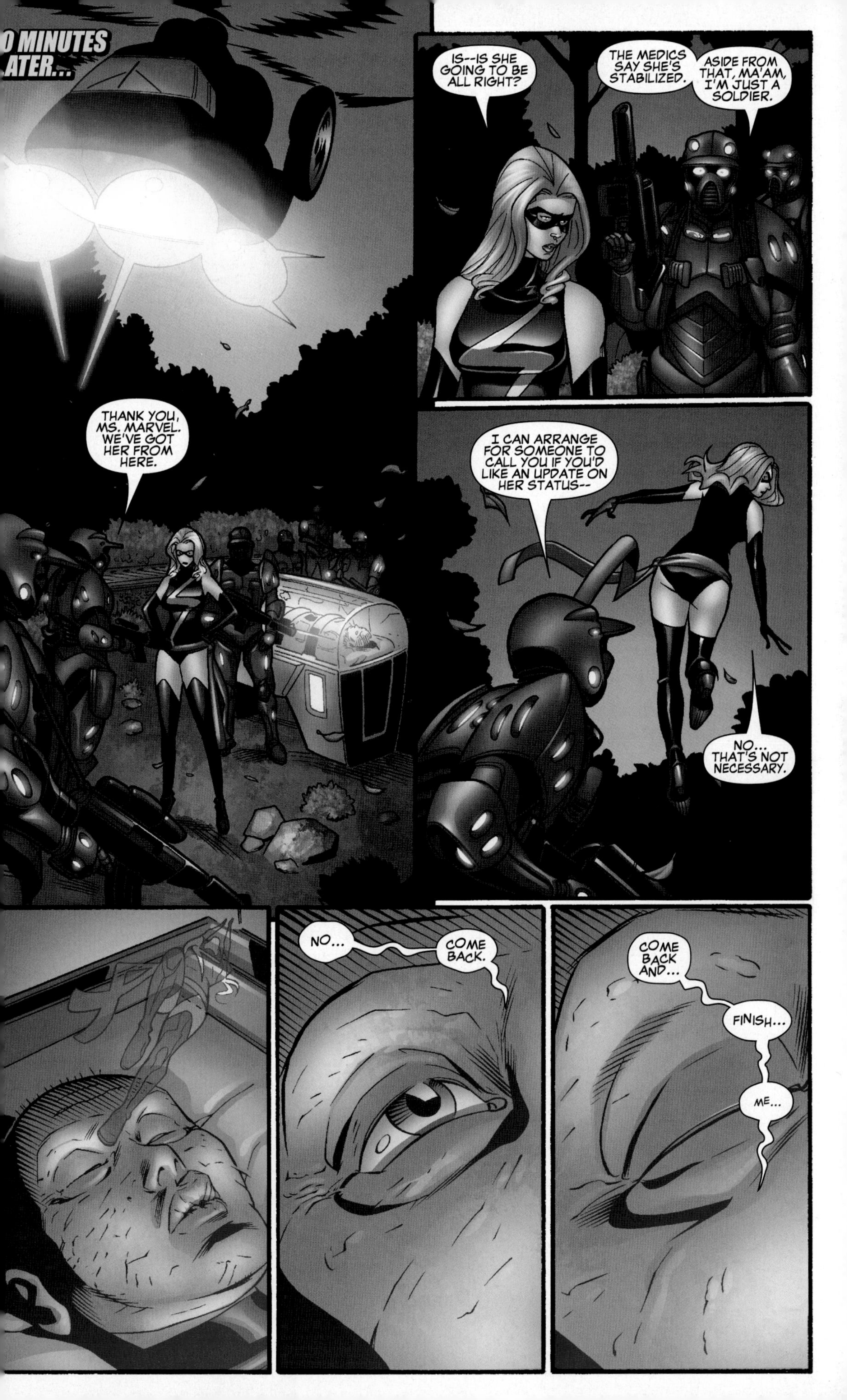

0 MINUTES LATER...
IS--IS SHE GOING TO BE ALL RIGHT?
THE MEDICS SAY SHE'S STABILIZED.
ASIDE FROM THAT, MA'AM, I'M JUST A SOLDIER.
THANK YOU, MS. MARVEL. WE'VE GOT HER FROM HERE.
I CAN ARRANGE FOR SOMEONE TO CALL YOU IF YOU'D LIKE AN UPDATE ON HER STATUS--
NO... THAT'S NOT NECESSARY.
NO...
COME BACK.
COME BACK AND...
FINISH...
ME...

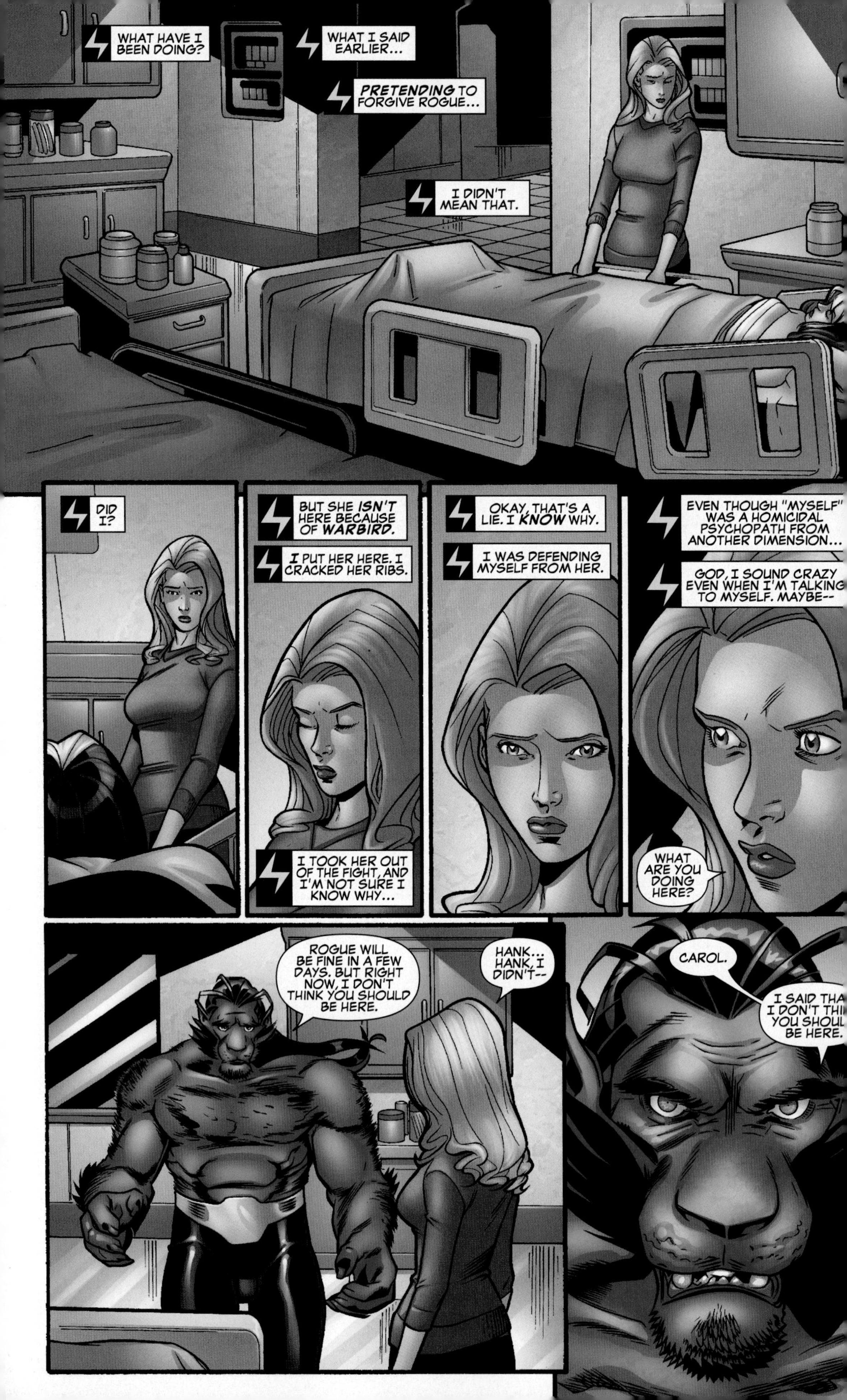
WHAT HAVE I BEEN DOING?
WHAT I SAID EARLIER...
PRETENDING TO FORGIVE ROGUE...
I DIDN'T MEAN THAT.
DID I?
BUT SHE ISN'T HERE BECAUSE OF WARBIRD.
I PUT HER HERE. I CRACKED HER RIBS.
I TOOK HER OUT OF THE FIGHT, AND I'M NOT SURE I KNOW WHY...
OKAY, THAT'S A LIE. I KNOW WHY.
I WAS DEFENDING MYSELF FROM HER.
EVEN THOUGH "MYSELF" WAS A HOMICIDAL PSYCHOPATH FROM ANOTHER DIMENSION...
GOD, I SOUND CRAZY EVEN WHEN I'M TALKING TO MYSELF. MAYBE--
WHAT ARE YOU DOING HERE?
ROGUE WILL BE FINE IN A FEW DAYS. BUT RIGHT NOW, I DON'T THINK YOU SHOULD BE HERE.
HANK... HANK, I DIDN'T--
CAROL.

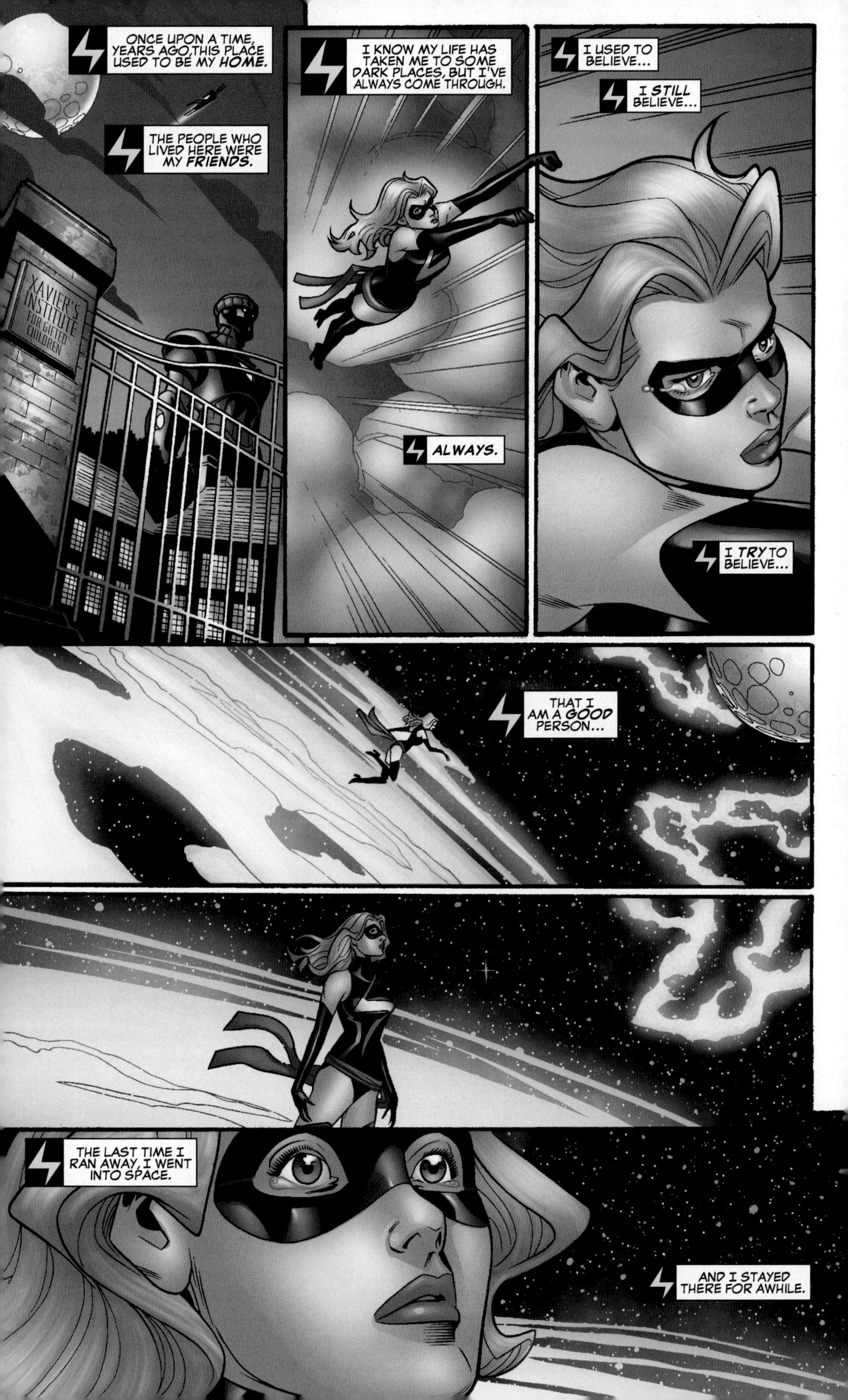
ONCE UPON A TIME, YEARS AGO, THIS PLACE USED TO BE MY HOME.
THE PEOPLE WHO LIVED HERE WERE MY FRIENDS.
XAVIER'S INSTITUTE FOR GIFTED CHILDREN
I KNOW MY LIFE HAS TAKEN ME TO SOME DARK PLACES, BUT I'VE ALWAYS COME THROUGH.
ALWAYS.
I USED TO BELIEVE...
I STILL BELIEVE...
I TRY TO BELIEVE...
THAT I AM A GOOD PERSON...
THE LAST TIME I RAN AWAY, I WENT INTO SPACE.
AND I STAYED THERE FOR AWHILE.

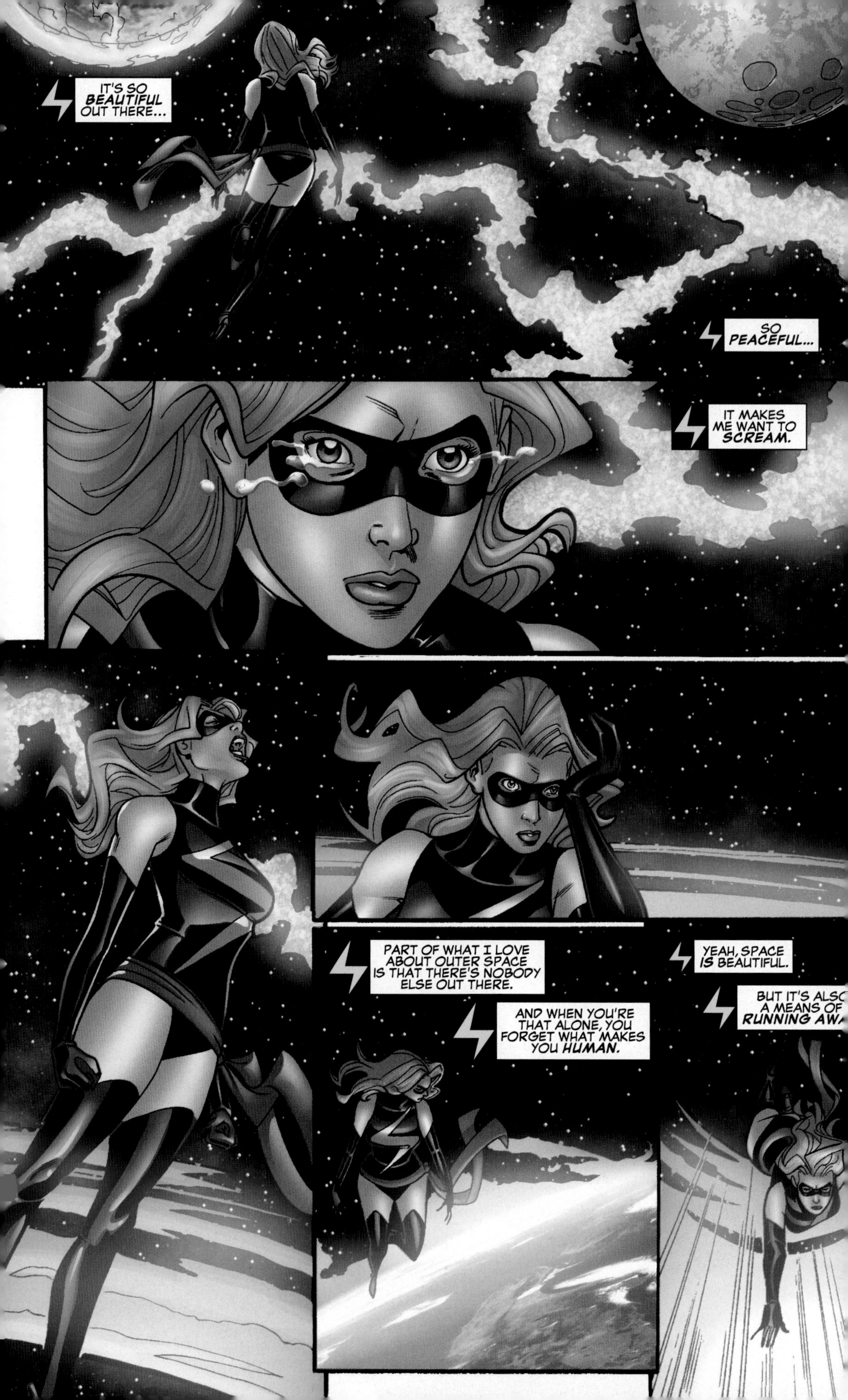
IT'S SO BEAUTIFUL OUT THERE...
SO PEACEFUL...
IT MAKES ME WANT TO SCREAM.
PART OF WHAT I LOVE ABOUT OUTER SPACE IS THAT THERE'S NOBODY ELSE OUT THERE.
AND WHEN YOU'RE THAT ALONE, YOU FORGET WHAT MAKES YOU HUMAN.
YEAH, SPACE IS BEAUTIFUL.
BUT IT'S ALSO A MEANS OF RUNNING AWA

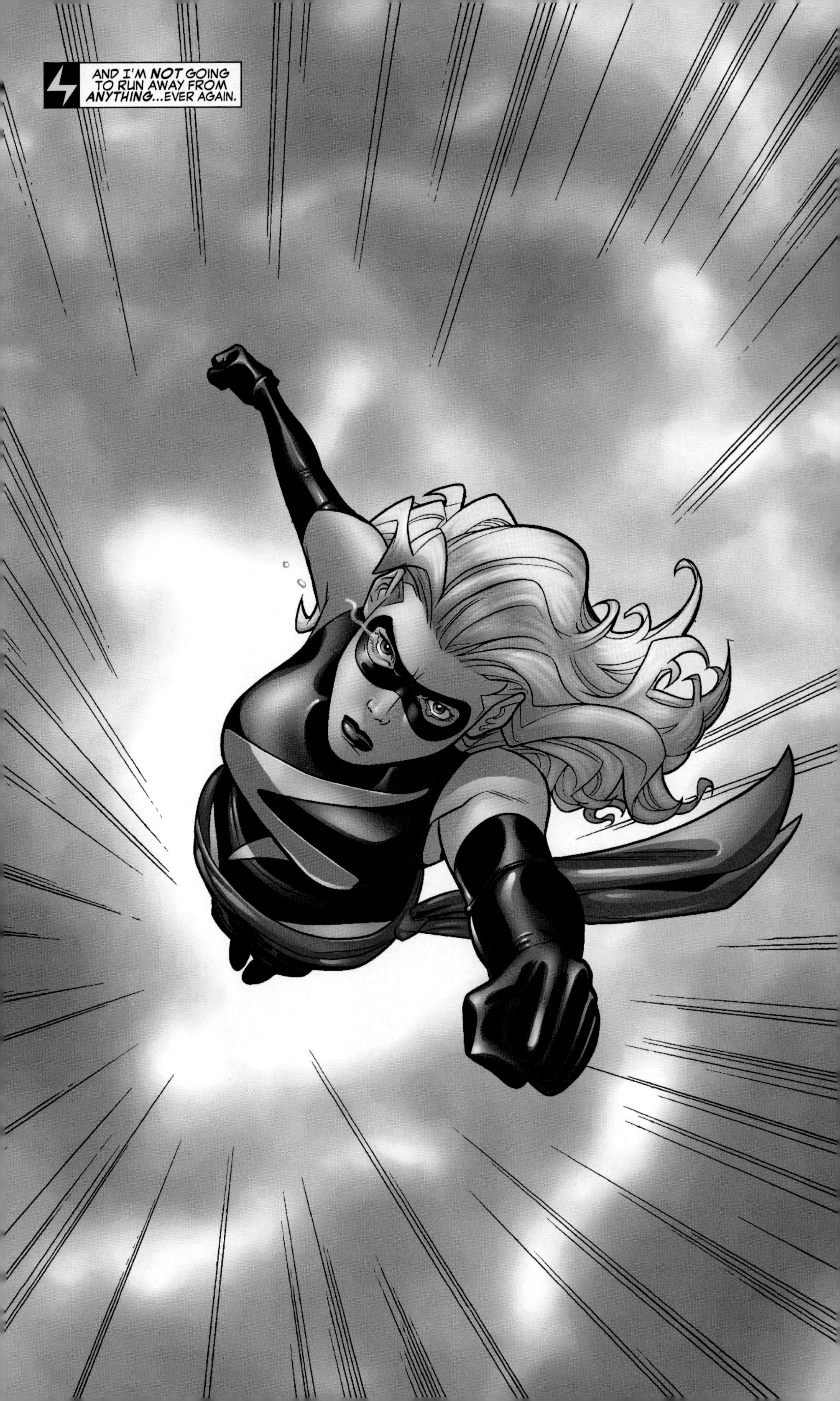
AND I'M NOT GOING TO RUN AWAY FROM ANYTHING...EVER AGAIN.

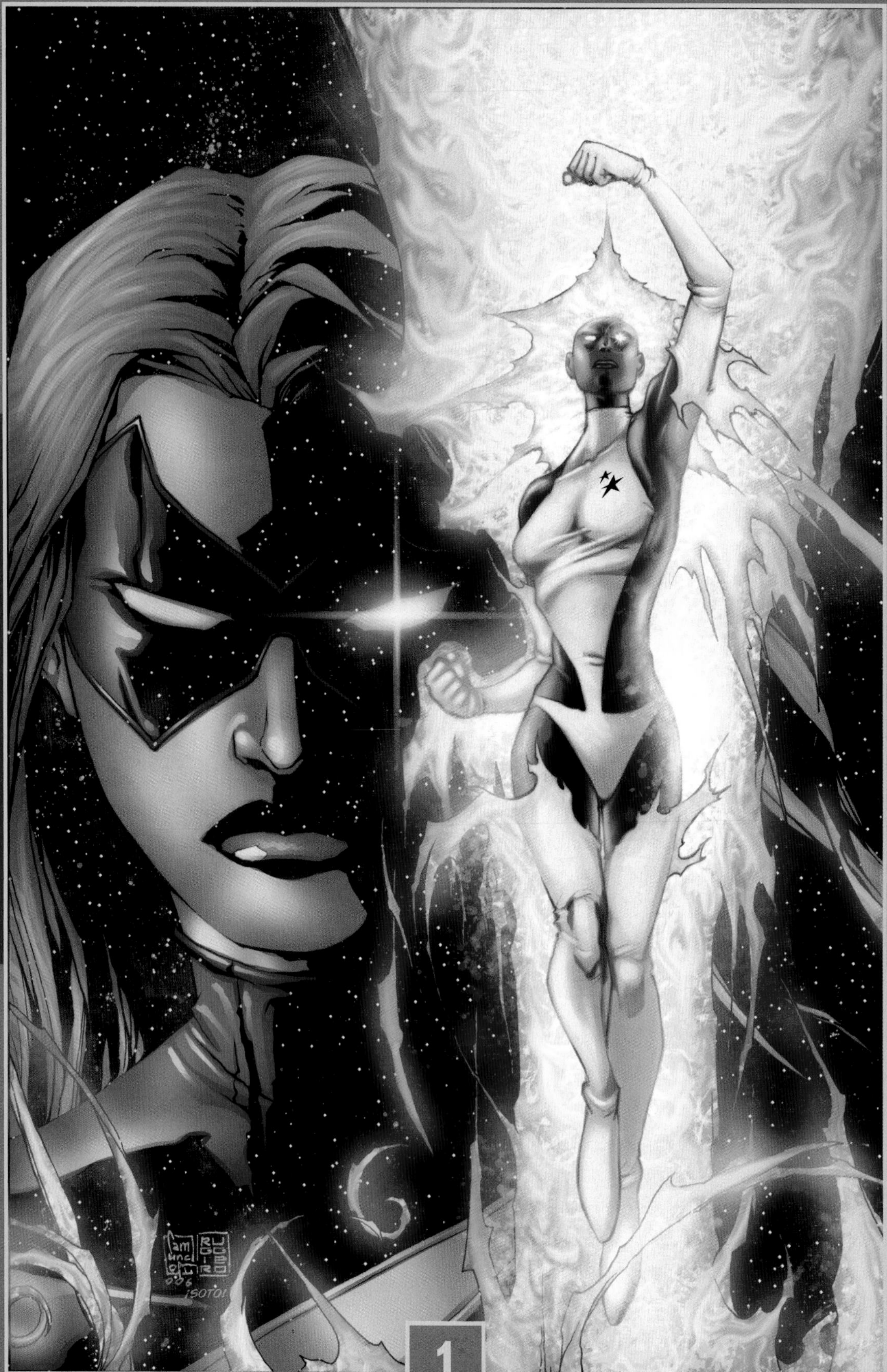

1

MS. MARVEL SPECIAL (2007) "BINARY"

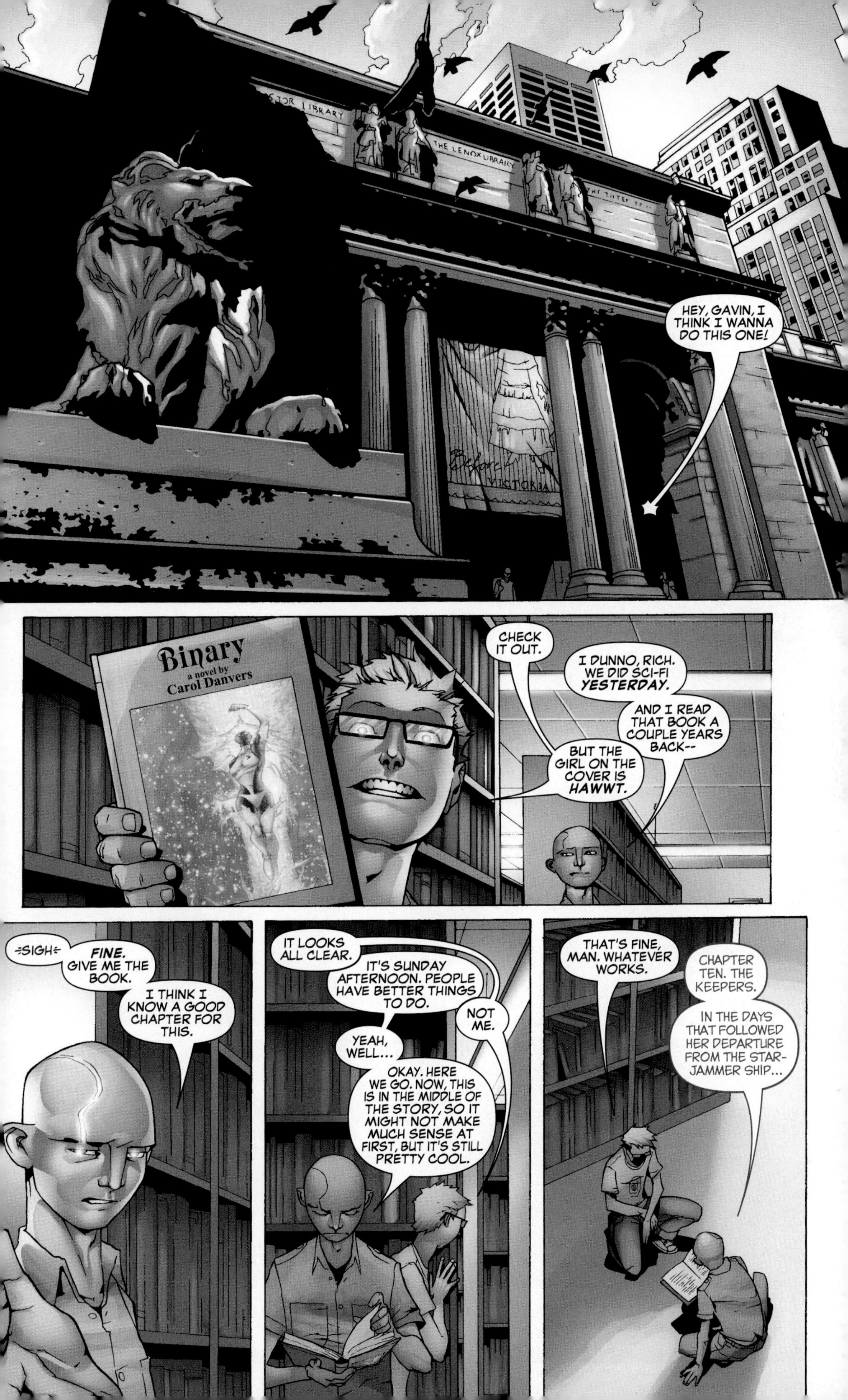

STOR LIBRARY
THE LENOX LIBRARY
VICTORIA
HEY, GAVIN, I THINK I WANNA DO THIS ONE!
Binary
a novel by
Carol Danvers
CHECK IT OUT.
I DUNNO, RICH. WE DID SCI-FI YESTERDAY.
AND I READ THAT BOOK A COUPLE YEARS BACK--
BUT THE GIRL ON THE COVER IS HAWWT.
=SIGH= FINE. GIVE ME THE BOOK.
I THINK I KNOW A GOOD CHAPTER FOR THIS.
IT LOOKS ALL CLEAR.
IT'S SUNDAY AFTERNOON. PEOPLE HAVE BETTER THINGS TO DO.
NOT ME.
YEAH, WELL...
OKAY. HERE WE GO. NOW, THIS IS IN THE MIDDLE OF THE STORY, SO IT MIGHT NOT MAKE MUCH SENSE AT FIRST, BUT IT'S STILL PRETTY COOL.
THAT'S FINE, MAN. WHATEVER WORKS.
CHAPTER TEN. THE KEEPERS.
IN THE DAYS THAT FOLLOWED HER DEPARTURE FROM THE STAR-JAMMER SHIP...

Chapter 10:
The Keepers

In the days that followed her departure from the Starjammer ship, Binary traveled the galaxy aimlessly, lost in the great void of space and loving every moment of it. It was a simple matter for her to aim herself at a distant star and find new adventures along the way.

Yet, Binary realized that the moments of the day that made her feel "human" or "normal" were gone. Such routine moments as a simple "hello" to another member of the Starjammer crew, or something as mundane as following a schedule for waking and sleeping... In the depths of space, these things were lost. Time carried little meaning to Binary. Companionship was a thing of the past. The cosmos itself was her home now, and she found a certain comfort in its cold expanse.

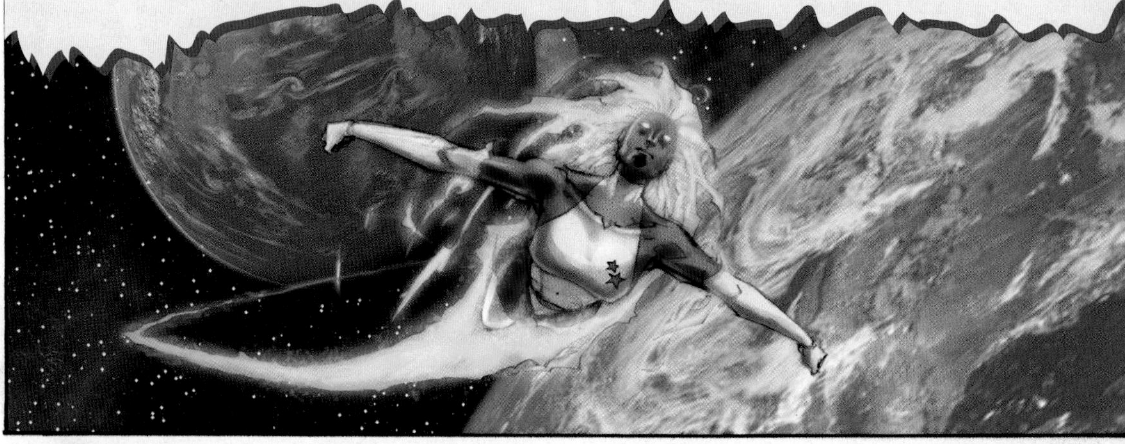

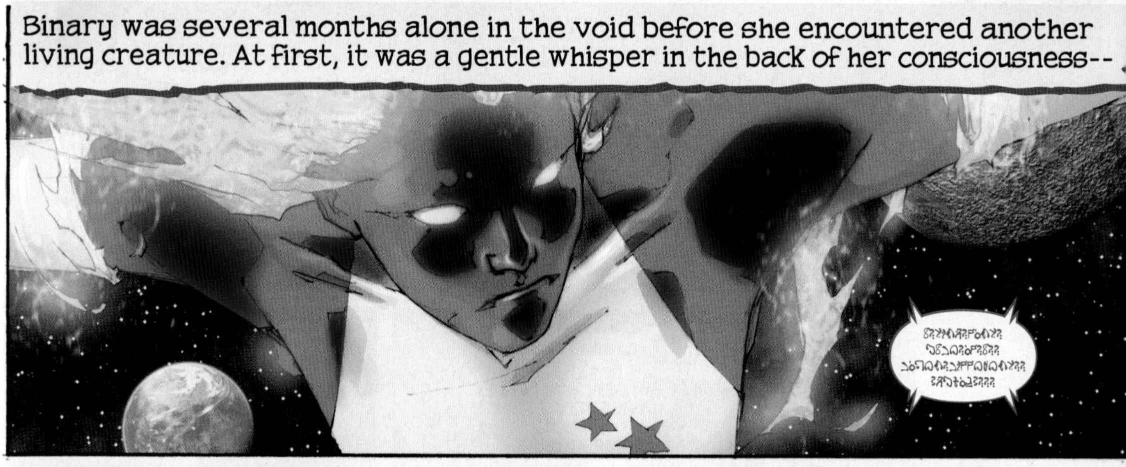
Binary was several months alone in the void before she encountered another living creature. At first, it was a gentle whisper in the back of her consciousness--

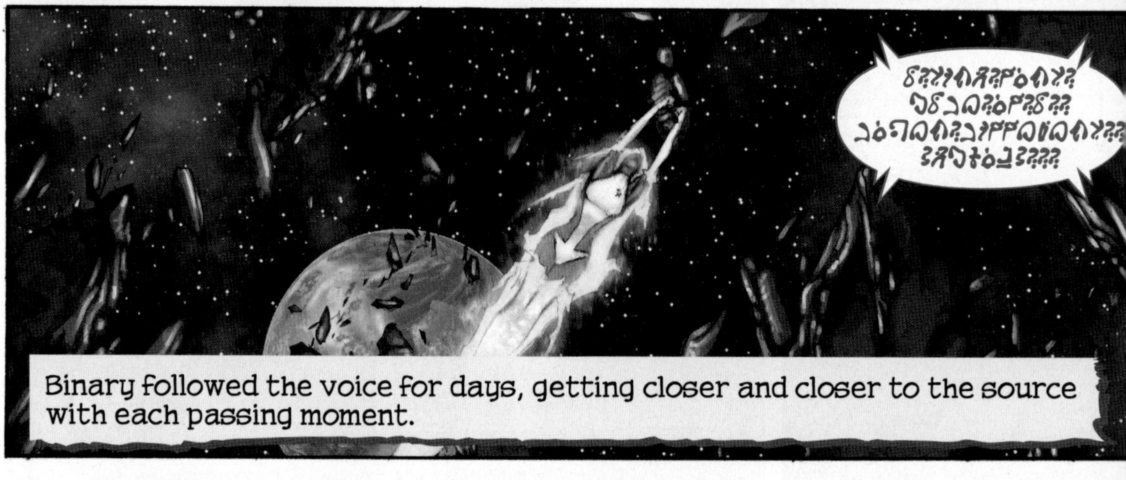
Binary followed the voice for days, getting closer and closer to the source with each passing moment.

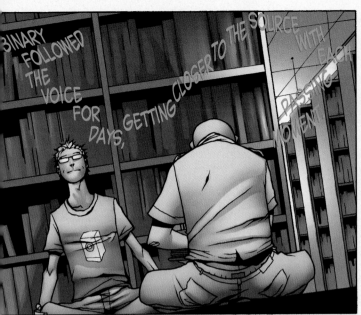

BINARY FOLLOWED THE VOICE FOR DAYS, GETTING CLOSER TO THE SOURCE WITH EACH PASSING MOMENT.

IS IT WORKING?

SHHH... JUST KEEP GOING.

CLOSER TO THE SOURCE WITH EACH PASSING MOMENT.

FINALLY, BINARY REACHED THE SOURCE OF THE MESSAGE.

WHAT BINARY FOUND SHOCKED AND AMAZED HER.

FINALLY, BINARY REACHED THE SOURCE OF THE MESS

WHAT BINARY FOUND SHOCKED AND AMAZED HER.

SHE WAS AT THE CENTER OF THE GALAXY.

SHE WAS AT THE CENTER OF THE GALAXY.

AND IT WAS THE MOST BEAUTIFUL THING SHE HAD EVER SEEN.

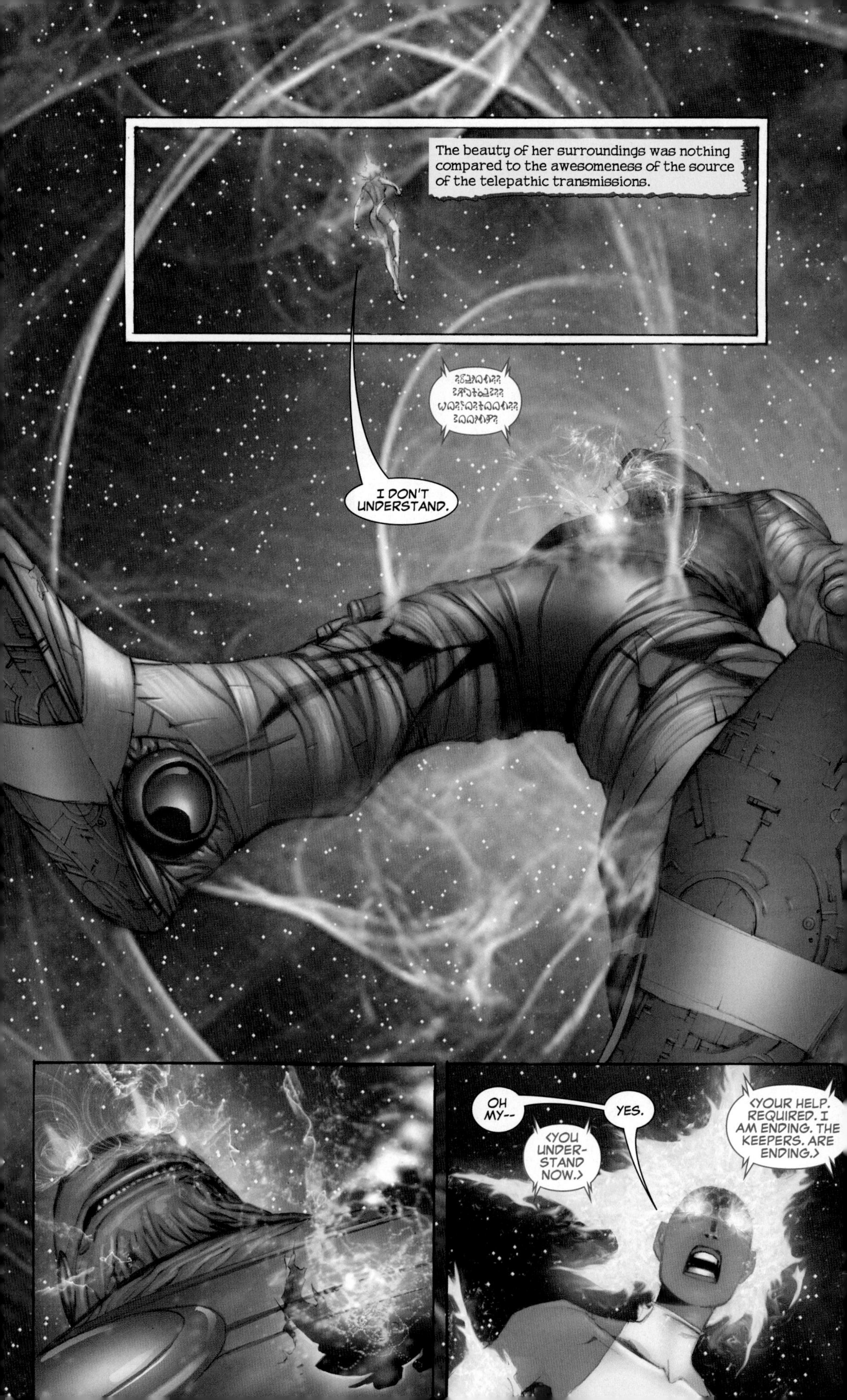
The beauty of her surroundings was nothing compared to the awesomeness of the source of the telepathic transmissions.
I DON'T UNDERSTAND.
OH MY--
YES.
<YOU UNDER-STAND NOW.>
<YOUR HELP. REQUIRED. I AM ENDING. THE KEEPERS. ARE ENDING.>

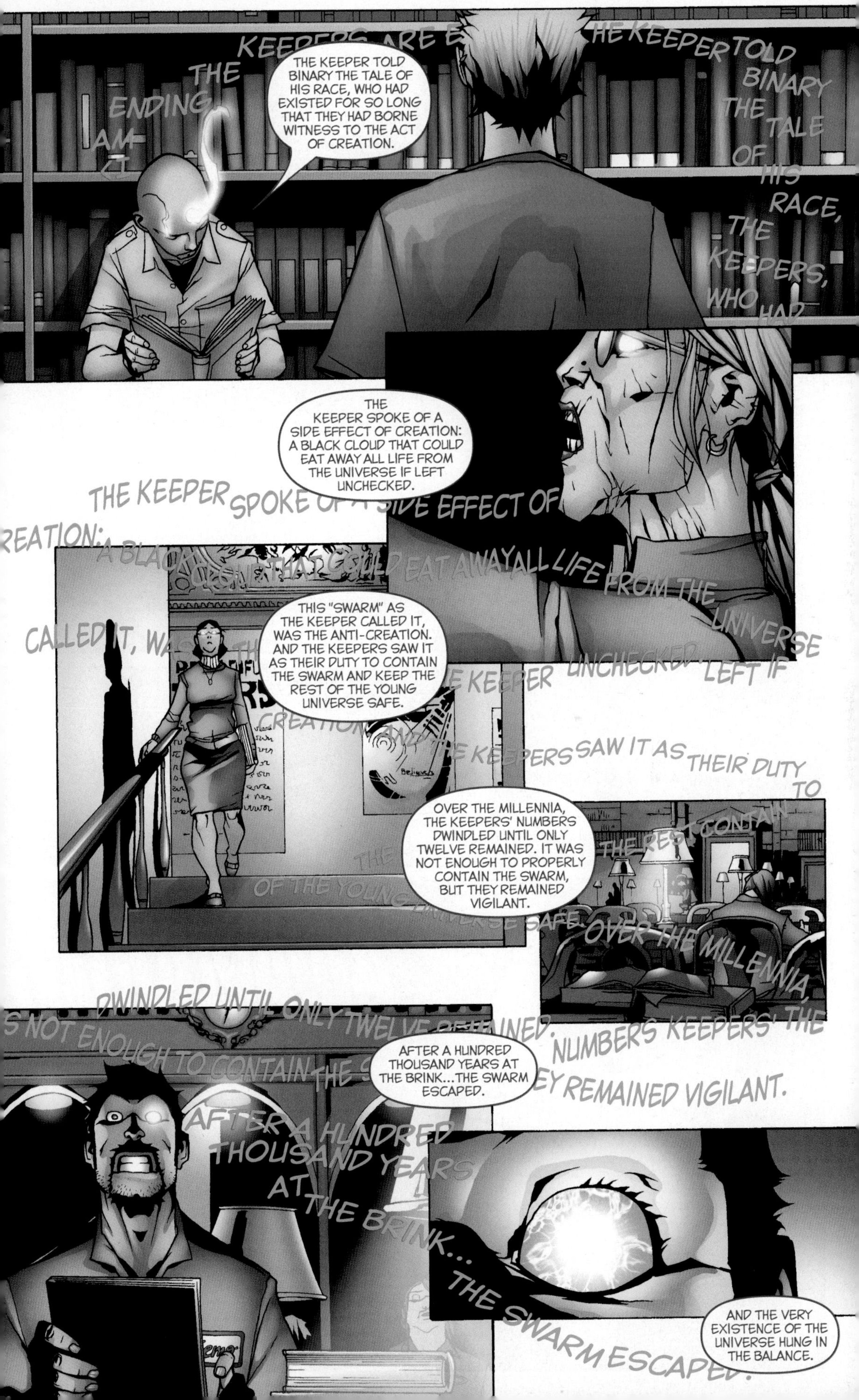
THE KEEPER TOLD BINARY THE TALE OF HIS RACE, WHO HAD EXISTED FOR SO LONG THAT THEY HAD BORNE WITNESS TO THE ACT OF CREATION.
THE KEEPER SPOKE OF A SIDE EFFECT OF CREATION: A BLACK CLOUD THAT COULD EAT AWAY ALL LIFE FROM THE UNIVERSE IF LEFT UNCHECKED.
THIS "SWARM" AS THE KEEPER CALLED IT, WAS THE ANTI-CREATION. AND THE KEEPERS SAW IT AS THEIR DUTY TO CONTAIN THE SWARM AND KEEP THE REST OF THE YOUNG UNIVERSE SAFE.
OVER THE MILLENNIA, THE KEEPERS' NUMBERS DWINDLED UNTIL ONLY TWELVE REMAINED. IT WAS NOT ENOUGH TO PROPERLY CONTAIN THE SWARM, BUT THEY REMAINED VIGILANT.
AFTER A HUNDRED THOUSAND YEARS AT THE BRINK...THE SWARM ESCAPED.
AND THE VERY EXISTENCE OF THE UNIVERSE HUNG IN THE BALANCE.

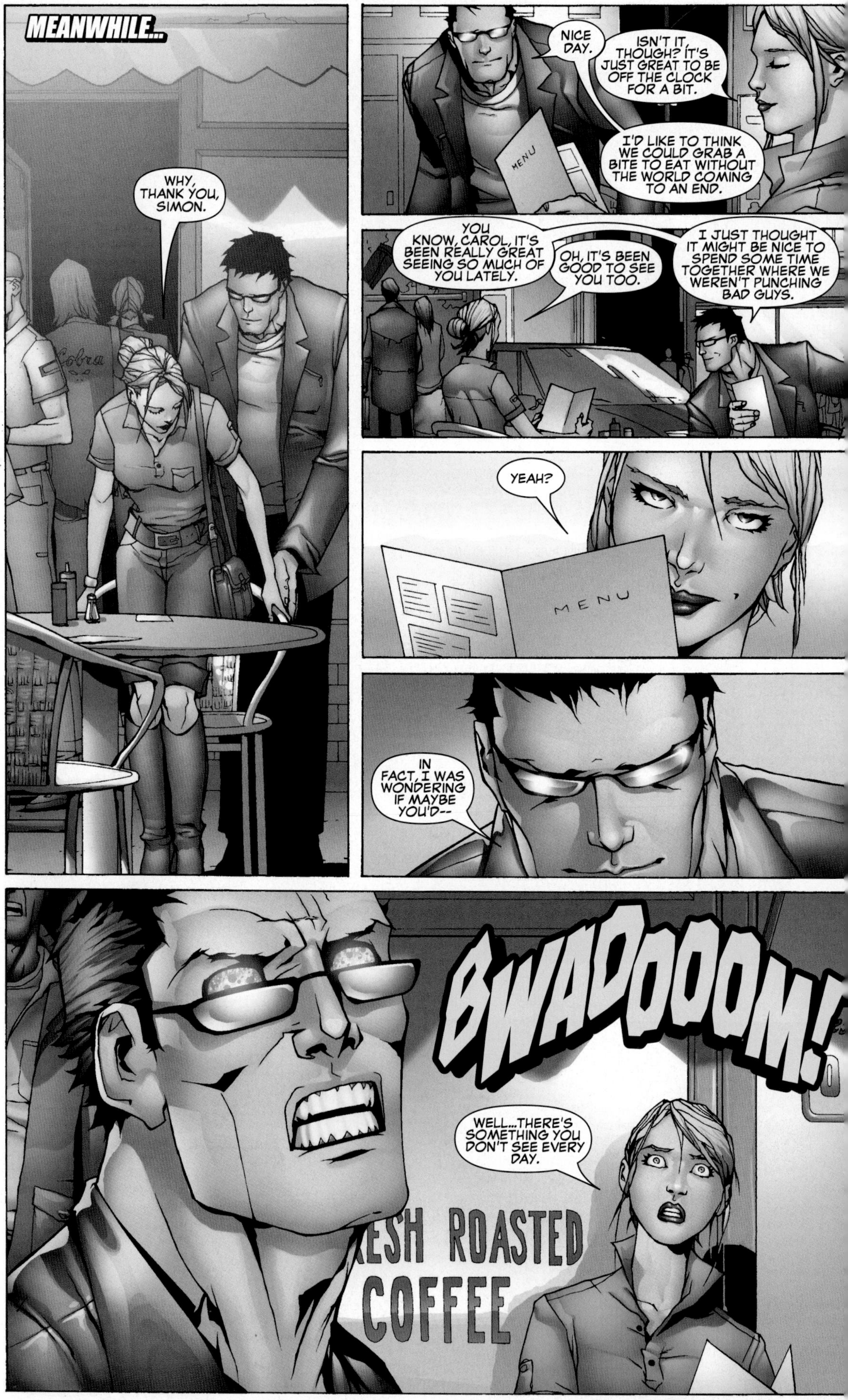
MEANWHILE...
WHY, THANK YOU, SIMON.
NICE DAY.
ISN'T IT, THOUGH? IT'S JUST GREAT TO BE OFF THE CLOCK FOR A BIT.
I'D LIKE TO THINK WE COULD GRAB A BITE TO EAT WITHOUT THE WORLD COMING TO AN END.
MENU
YOU KNOW, CAROL, IT'S BEEN REALLY GREAT SEEING SO MUCH OF YOU LATELY.
OH, IT'S BEEN GOOD TO SEE YOU TOO.
I JUST THOUGHT IT MIGHT BE NICE TO SPEND SOME TIME TOGETHER WHERE WE WEREN'T PUNCHING BAD GUYS.
YEAH?
MENU
IN FACT, I WAS WONDERING IF MAYBE YOU'D--
BWADOOOM!
WELL...THERE'S SOMETHING YOU DON'T SEE EVERY DAY.
RESH ROASTED
COFFEE

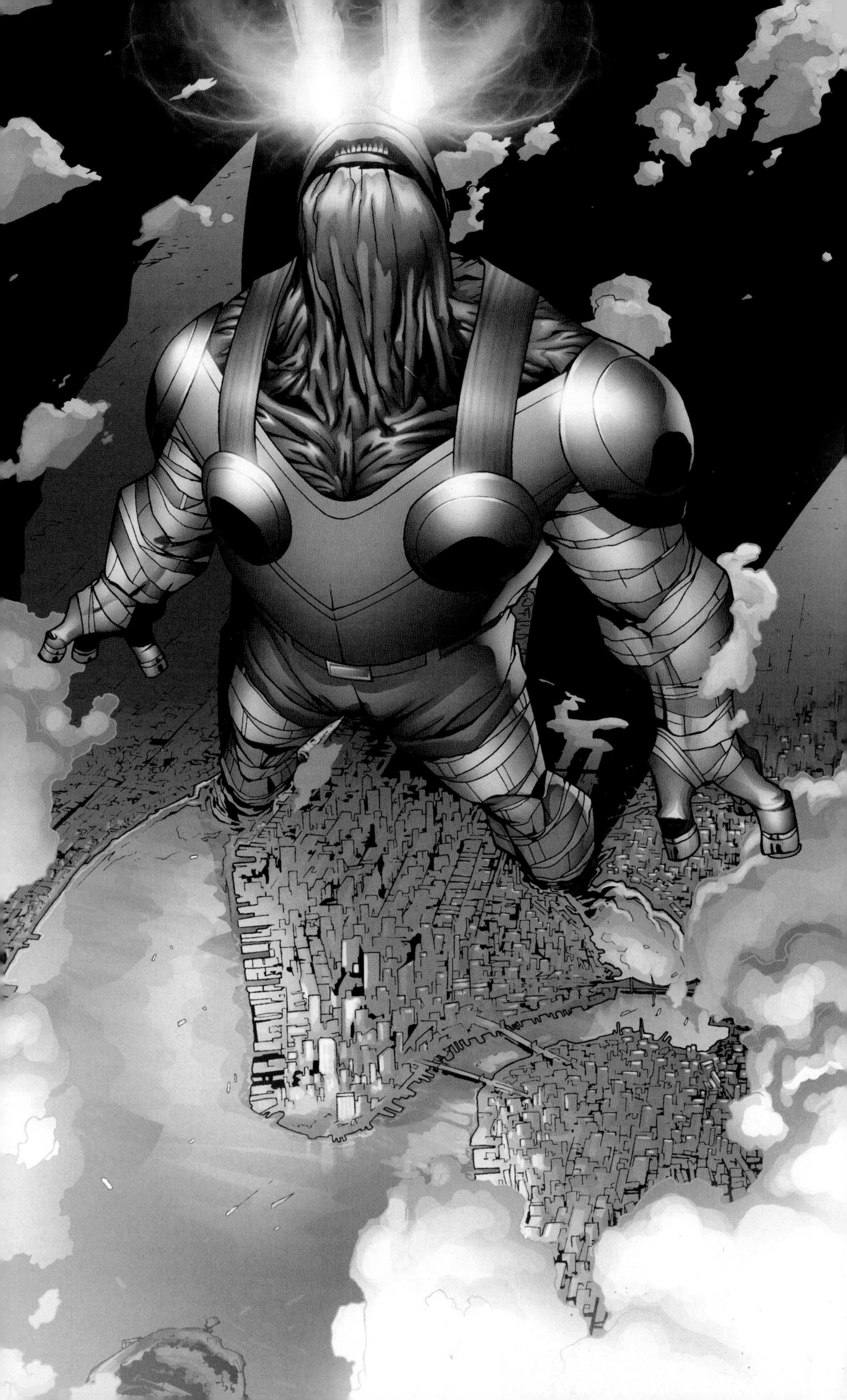

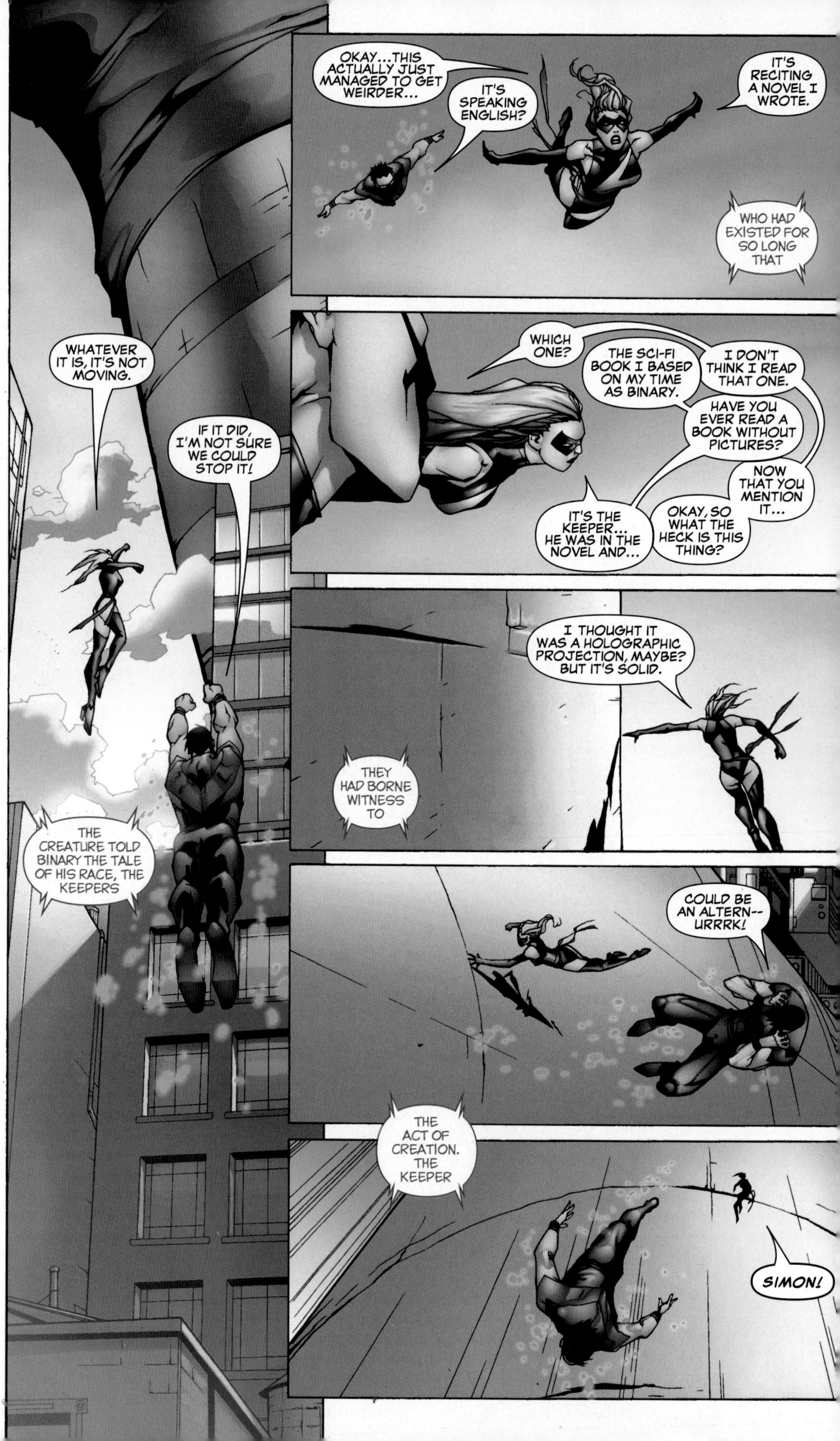
OKAY...THIS ACTUALLY JUST MANAGED TO GET WEIRDER...
IT'S SPEAKING ENGLISH?
IT'S RECITING A NOVEL I WROTE.
WHO HAD EXISTED FOR SO LONG THAT
WHATEVER IT IS, IT'S NOT MOVING.
IF IT DID, I'M NOT SURE WE COULD STOP IT!
WHICH ONE?
THE SCI-FI BOOK I BASED ON MY TIME AS BINARY.
I DON'T THINK I READ THAT ONE.
HAVE YOU EVER READ A BOOK WITHOUT PICTURES?
NOW THAT YOU MENTION IT...
OKAY, SO WHAT THE HECK IS THIS THING?
IT'S THE KEEPER... HE WAS IN THE NOVEL AND...
THE CREATURE TOLD BINARY THE TALE OF HIS RACE, THE KEEPERS
I THOUGHT IT WAS A HOLOGRAPHIC PROJECTION, MAYBE? BUT IT'S SOLID.
THEY HAD BORNE WITNESS TO
COULD BE AN ALTERN-- URRRK!
THE ACT OF CREATION. THE KEEPER
SIMON!

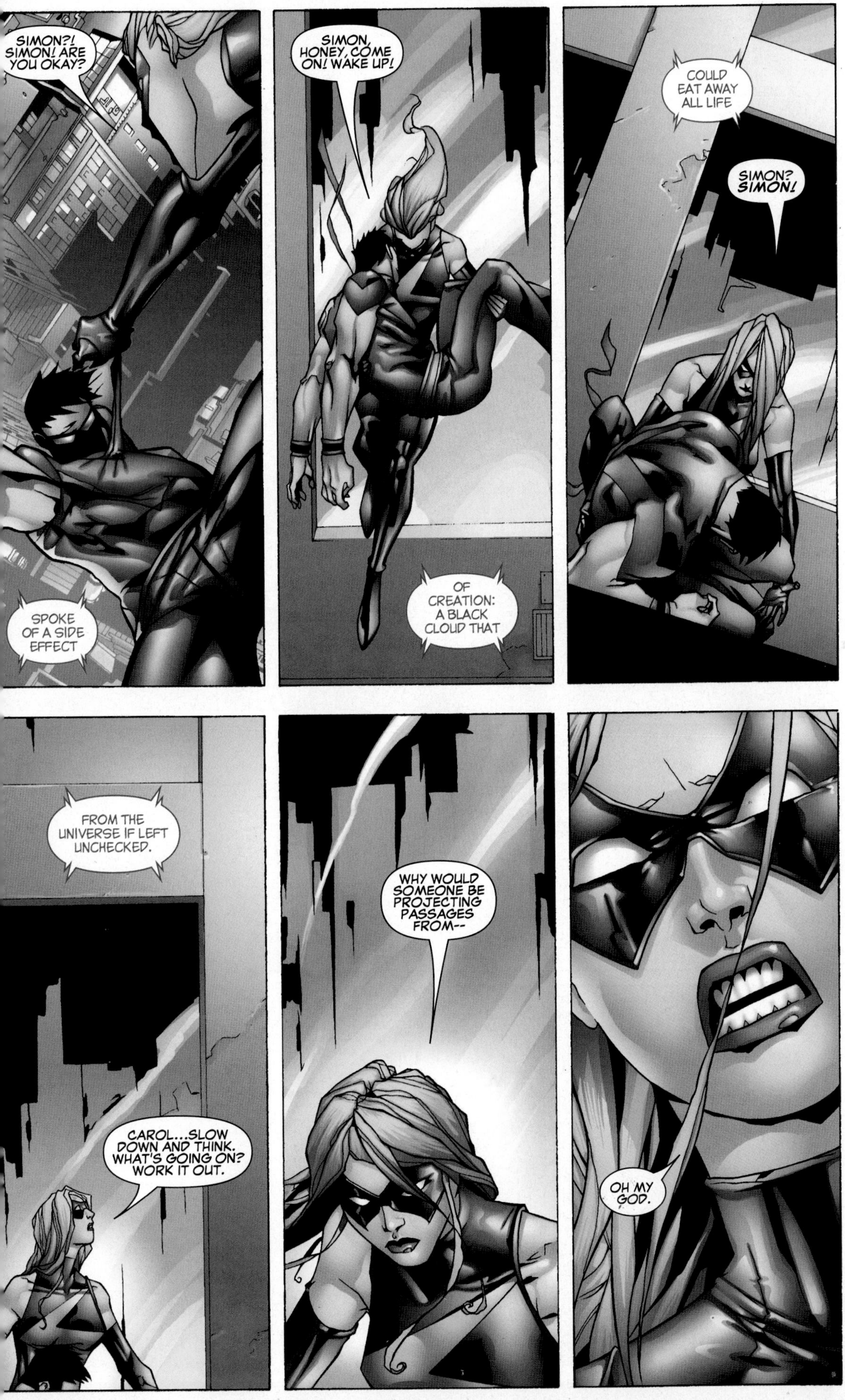
SIMON?! SIMON! ARE YOU OKAY?
SPOKE OF A SIDE EFFECT
SIMON, HONEY, COME ON! WAKE UP!
OF CREATION: A BLACK CLOUD THAT
COULD EAT AWAY ALL LIFE
SIMON? SIMON!
FROM THE UNIVERSE IF LEFT UNCHECKED.
CAROL...SLOW DOWN AND THINK. WHAT'S GOING ON? WORK IT OUT.
WHY WOULD SOMEONE BE PROJECTING PASSAGES FROM--
OH MY GOD.

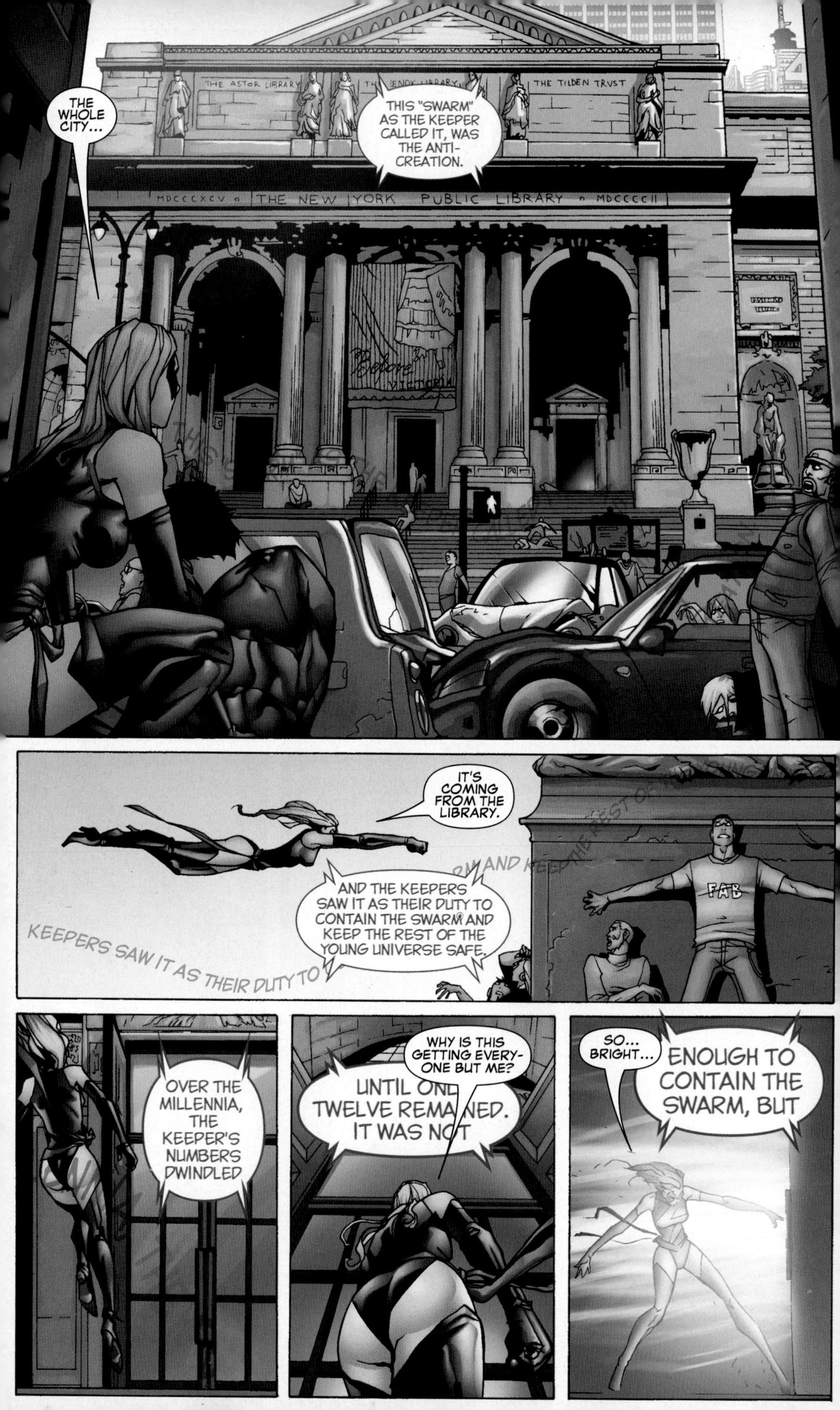
THE WHOLE CITY...
THE ASTOR LIBRARY
THE TILDEN TRUST
THIS "SWARM" AS THE KEEPER CALLED IT, WAS THE ANTI-CREATION.
MDCCCXCV THE NEW YORK PUBLIC LIBRARY MDCCCCII
IT'S COMING FROM THE LIBRARY.
AND THE KEEPERS SAW IT AS THEIR DUTY TO CONTAIN THE SWARM AND KEEP THE REST OF THE YOUNG UNIVERSE SAFE.
FAB
OVER THE MILLENNIA, THE KEEPER'S NUMBERS DWINDLED
WHY IS THIS GETTING EVERY-ONE BUT ME?
UNTIL ONLY TWELVE REMAINED. IT WAS NOT
SO... BRIGHT...
ENOUGH TO CONTAIN THE SWARM, BUT

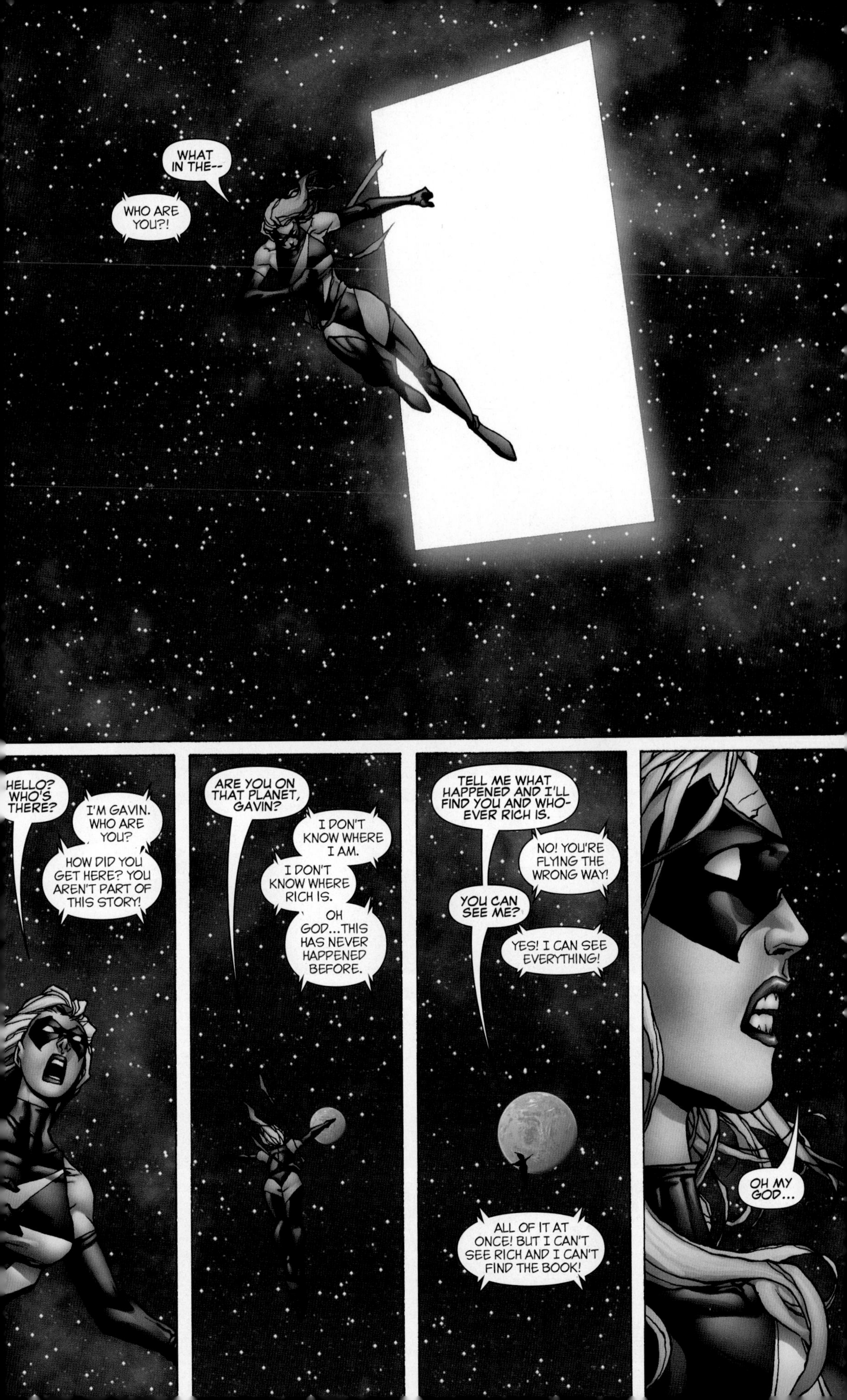
WHAT IN THE--
WHO ARE YOU?!
HELLO? WHO'S THERE?
I'M GAVIN. WHO ARE YOU?
HOW DID YOU GET HERE? YOU AREN'T PART OF THIS STORY!
ARE YOU ON THAT PLANET, GAVIN?
I DON'T KNOW WHERE I AM.
I DON'T KNOW WHERE RICH IS.
OH GOD...THIS HAS NEVER HAPPENED BEFORE.
TELL ME WHAT HAPPENED AND I'LL FIND YOU AND WHO-EVER RICH IS.
NO! YOU'RE FLYING THE WRONG WAY!
YOU CAN SEE ME?
YES! I CAN SEE EVERYTHING!
ALL OF IT AT ONCE! BUT I CAN'T SEE RICH AND I CAN'T FIND THE BOOK!
OH MY GOD...

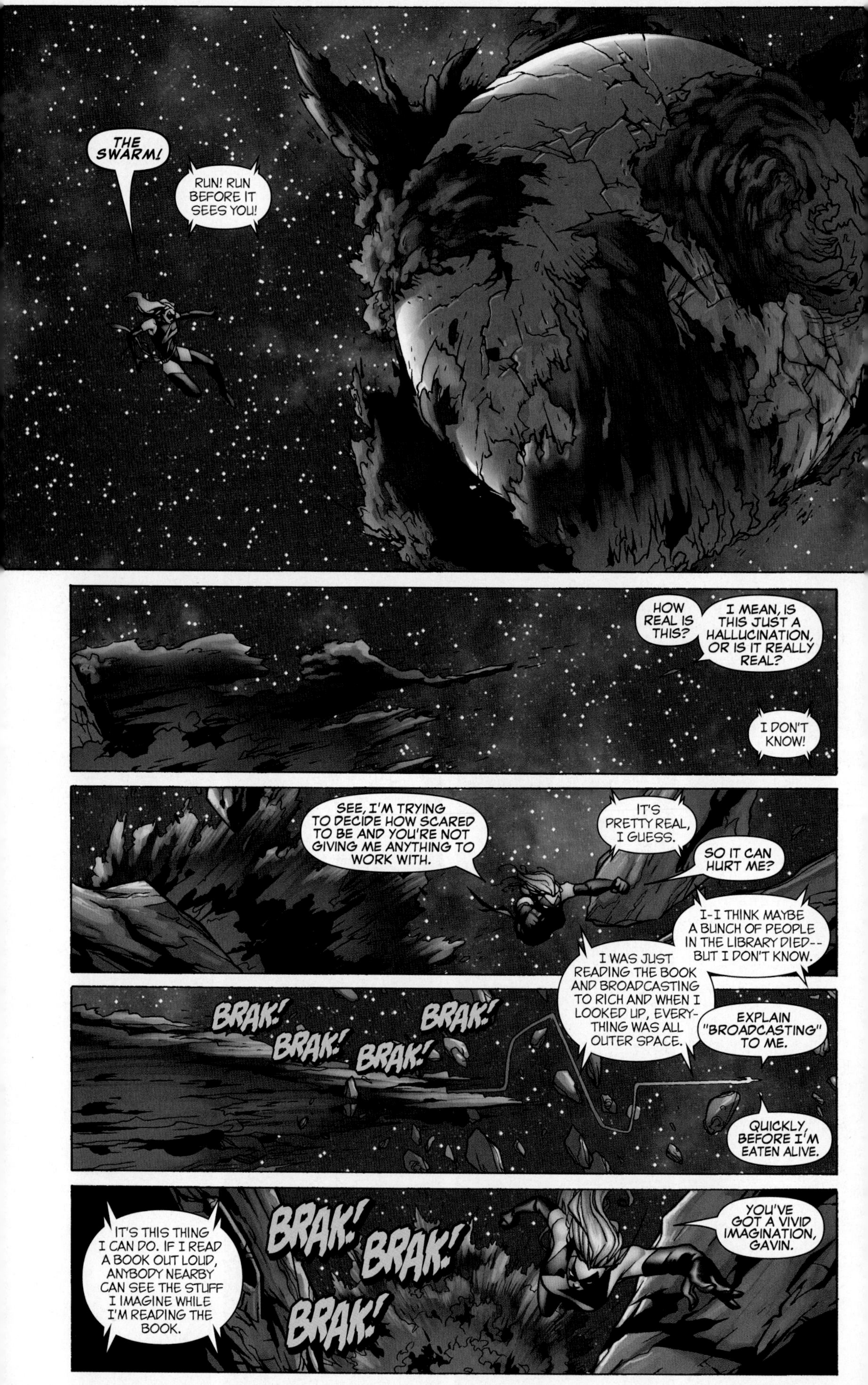
THE SWARM!
RUN! RUN BEFORE IT SEES YOU!
HOW REAL IS THIS?
I MEAN, IS THIS JUST A HALLUCINATION, OR IS IT REALLY REAL?
I DON'T KNOW!
SEE, I'M TRYING TO DECIDE HOW SCARED TO BE AND YOU'RE NOT GIVING ME ANYTHING TO WORK WITH.
IT'S PRETTY REAL, I GUESS.
SO IT CAN HURT ME?
I-I THINK MAYBE A BUNCH OF PEOPLE IN THE LIBRARY DIED-- BUT I DON'T KNOW.
I WAS JUST READING THE BOOK AND BROADCASTING TO RICH AND WHEN I LOOKED UP, EVERY-THING WAS ALL OUTER SPACE.
EXPLAIN "BROADCASTING" TO ME.
BRAK! BRAK! BRAK! BRAK!
QUICKLY, BEFORE I'M EATEN ALIVE.
IT'S THIS THING I CAN DO. IF I READ A BOOK OUT LOUD, ANYBODY NEARBY CAN SEE THE STUFF I IMAGINE WHILE I'M READING THE BOOK.
BRAK! BRAK! BRAK!
YOU'VE GOT A VIVID IMAGINATION, GAVIN.

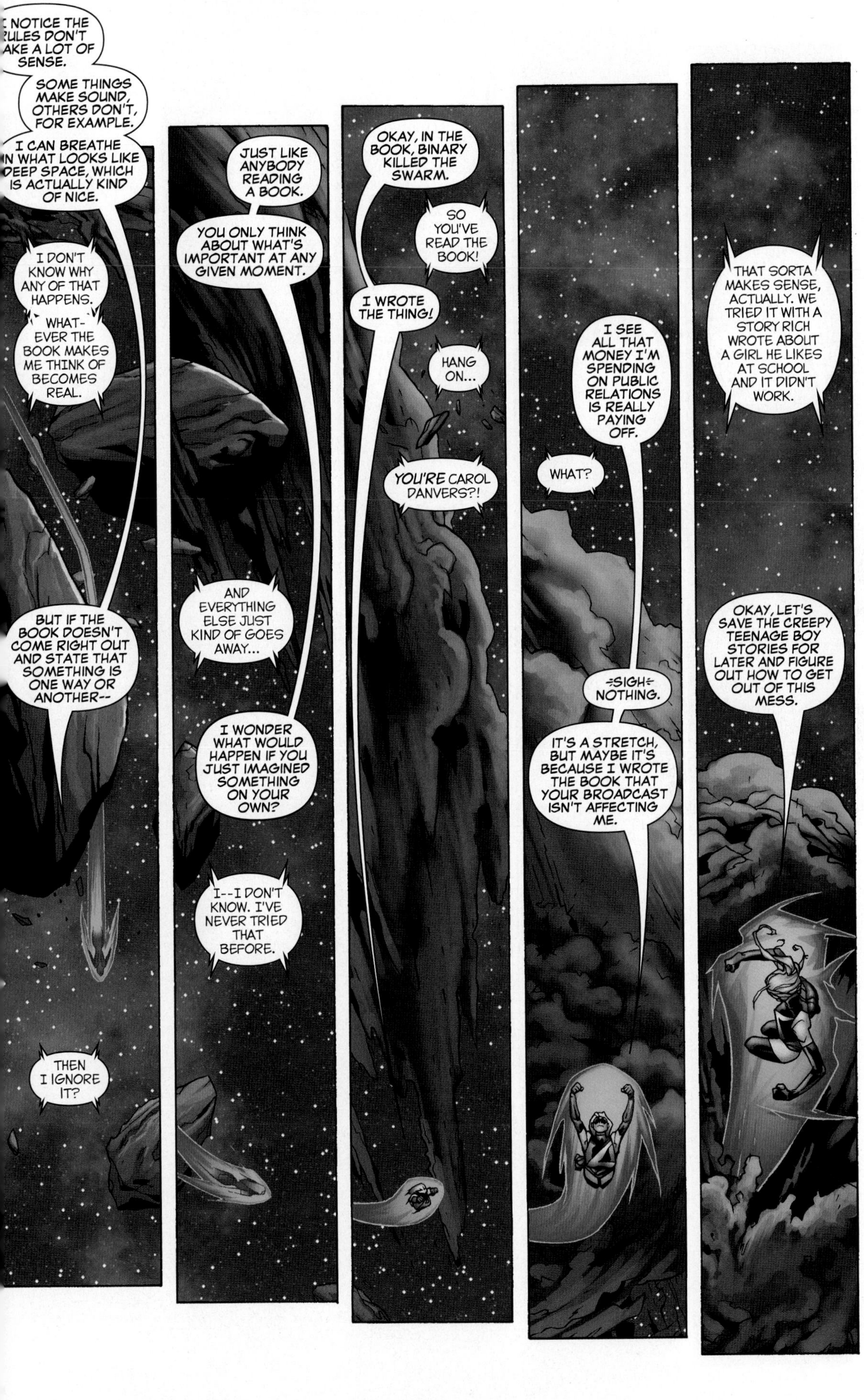

I NOTICE THE RULES DON'T MAKE A LOT OF SENSE.
SOME THINGS MAKE SOUND, OTHERS DON'T, FOR EXAMPLE.
I CAN BREATHE IN WHAT LOOKS LIKE DEEP SPACE, WHICH IS ACTUALLY KIND OF NICE.
I DON'T KNOW WHY ANY OF THAT HAPPENS.
WHAT-EVER THE BOOK MAKES ME THINK OF BECOMES REAL.
BUT IF THE BOOK DOESN'T COME RIGHT OUT AND STATE THAT SOMETHING IS ONE WAY OR ANOTHER--
THEN I IGNORE IT?
JUST LIKE ANYBODY READING A BOOK.
YOU ONLY THINK ABOUT WHAT'S IMPORTANT AT ANY GIVEN MOMENT.
AND EVERYTHING ELSE JUST KIND OF GOES AWAY...
I WONDER WHAT WOULD HAPPEN IF YOU JUST IMAGINED SOMETHING ON YOUR OWN?
I--I DON'T KNOW. I'VE NEVER TRIED THAT BEFORE.
OKAY, IN THE BOOK, BINARY KILLED THE SWARM.
SO YOU'VE READ THE BOOK!
I WROTE THE THING!
HANG ON...
YOU'RE CAROL DANVERS?!
I SEE ALL THAT MONEY I'M SPENDING ON PUBLIC RELATIONS IS REALLY PAYING OFF.
WHAT?
=SIGH= NOTHING.
IT'S A STRETCH, BUT MAYBE IT'S BECAUSE I WROTE THE BOOK THAT YOUR BROADCAST ISN'T AFFECTING ME.
THAT SORTA MAKES SENSE, ACTUALLY. WE TRIED IT WITH A STORY RICH WROTE ABOUT A GIRL HE LIKES AT SCHOOL AND IT DIDN'T WORK.
OKAY, LET'S SAVE THE CREEPY TEENAGE BOY STORIES FOR LATER AND FIGURE OUT HOW TO GET OUT OF THIS MESS.

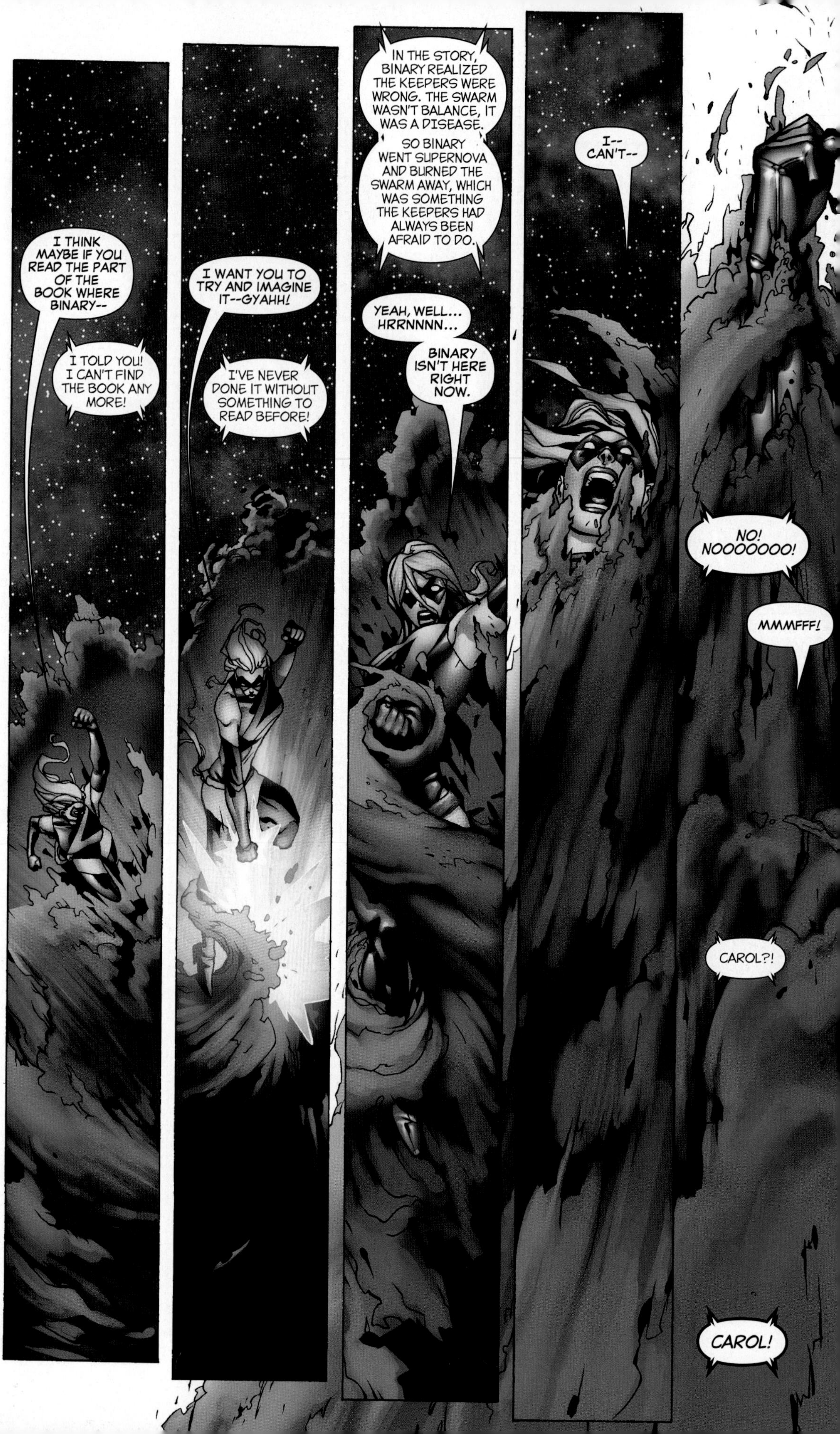

I THINK MAYBE IF YOU READ THE PART OF THE BOOK WHERE BINARY--
I TOLD YOU! I CAN'T FIND THE BOOK ANY MORE!
I WANT YOU TO TRY AND IMAGINE IT--GYAHH!
I'VE NEVER DONE IT WITHOUT SOMETHING TO READ BEFORE!
IN THE STORY, BINARY REALIZED THE KEEPERS WERE WRONG. THE SWARM WASN'T BALANCE, IT WAS A DISEASE.
SO BINARY WENT SUPERNOVA AND BURNED THE SWARM AWAY, WHICH WAS SOMETHING THE KEEPERS HAD ALWAYS BEEN AFRAID TO DO.
YEAH, WELL... HRRNNNN...
BINARY ISN'T HERE RIGHT NOW.
I-- CAN'T--
NO! NOOOOOOO!
MMMFFF!
CAROL?!
CAROL!

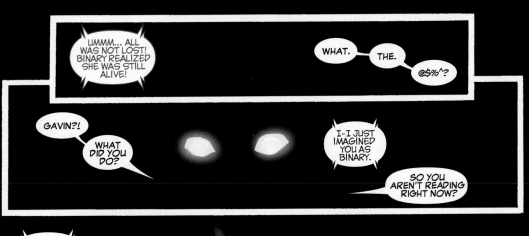

UMMM... ALL WAS NOT LOST! BINARY REALIZED SHE WAS STILL ALIVE!

WHAT. THE. @$%^?

GAVIN?!

WHAT DID YOU DO?

I-I JUST IMAGINED YOU AS BINARY.

SO YOU AREN'T READING RIGHT NOW?

NO. I TOLD YOU. I CAN'T FIND THE BOOK.

OKAY. YEAH.

WOW...

WOW.

YOU KNOW WHAT? WE CAN DO THIS, GAVIN. ME AND YOU.

I'M GOING TO START POWERING UP AND I WANT YOU TO IMAGINE THE SWARM BURNING AWAY. OKAY?

I--I DON'T--

YOU CAN DO IT, GAVIN...

COME ON NOW. IN 3...2...1...

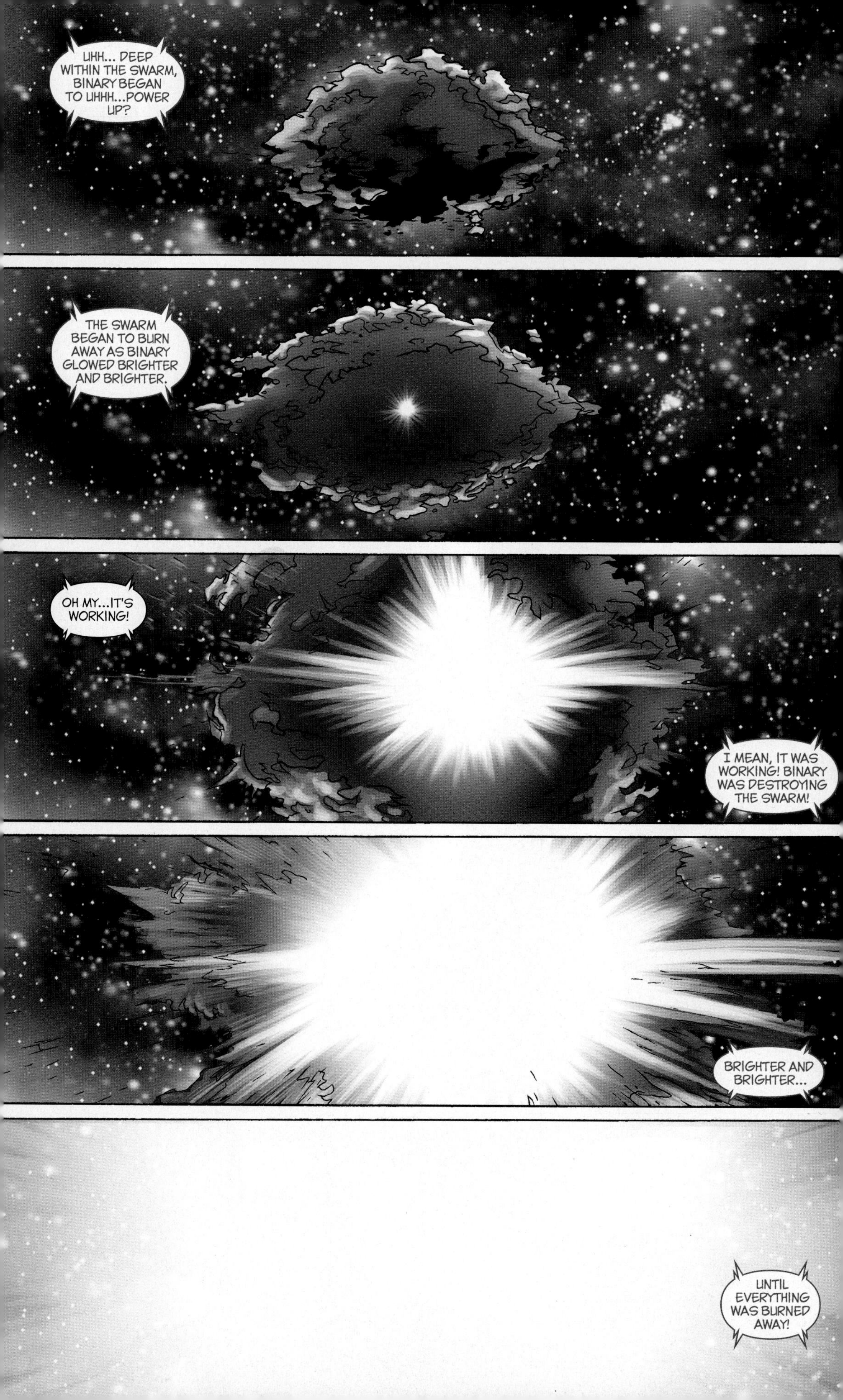
UHH... DEEP WITHIN THE SWARM, BINARY BEGAN TO UHHH...POWER UP?
THE SWARM BEGAN TO BURN AWAY AS BINARY GLOWED BRIGHTER AND BRIGHTER.
OH MY...IT'S WORKING!
I MEAN, IT WAS WORKING! BINARY WAS DESTROYING THE SWARM!
BRIGHTER AND BRIGHTER...
UNTIL EVERYTHING WAS BURNED AWAY!

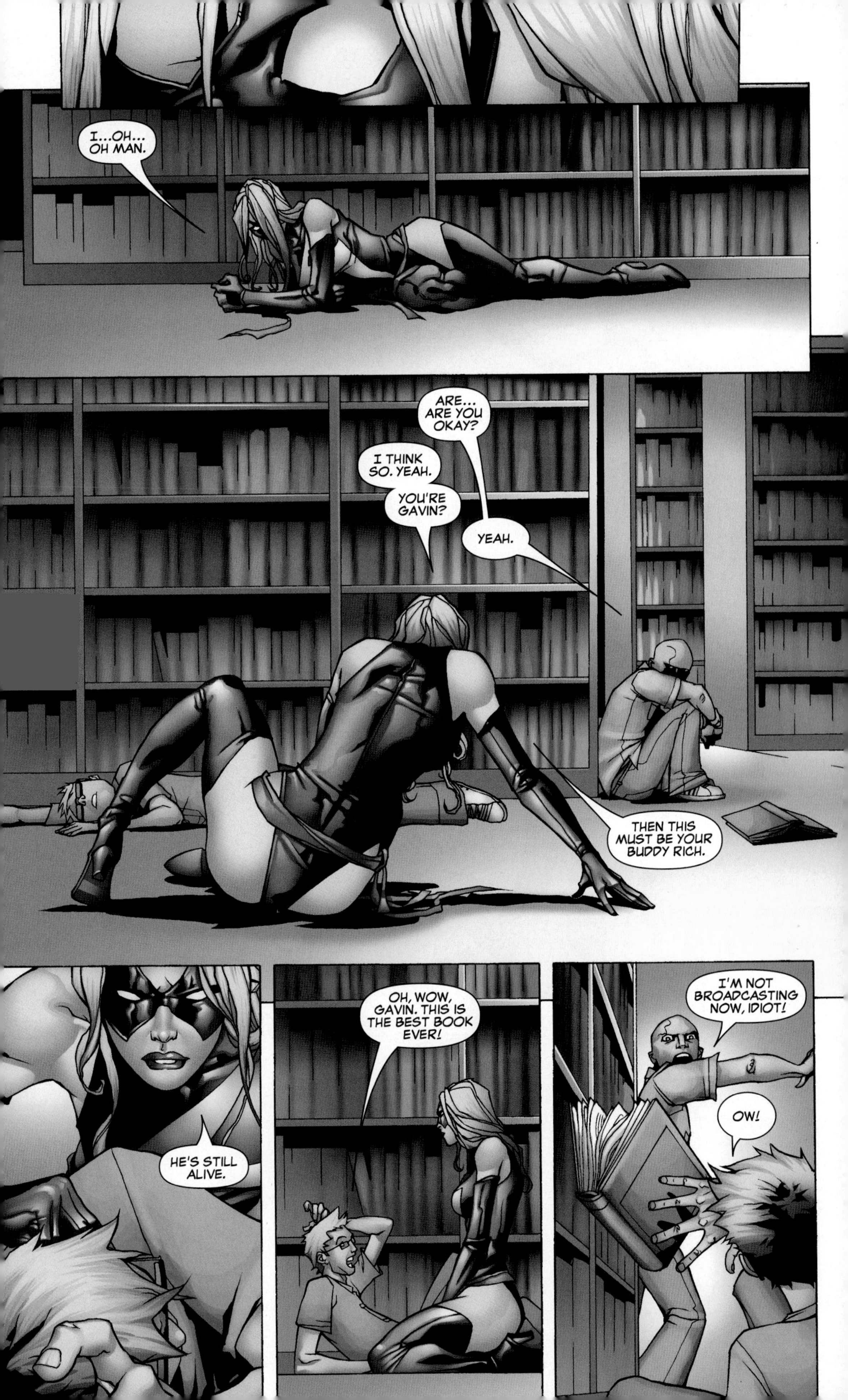
I...OH... OH MAN.
ARE... ARE YOU OKAY?
I THINK SO. YEAH.
YOU'RE GAVIN?
YEAH.
THEN THIS MUST BE YOUR BUDDY RICH.
HE'S STILL ALIVE.
OH, WOW, GAVIN. THIS IS THE BEST BOOK EVER!
I'M NOT BROADCASTING NOW, IDIOT!
OW!

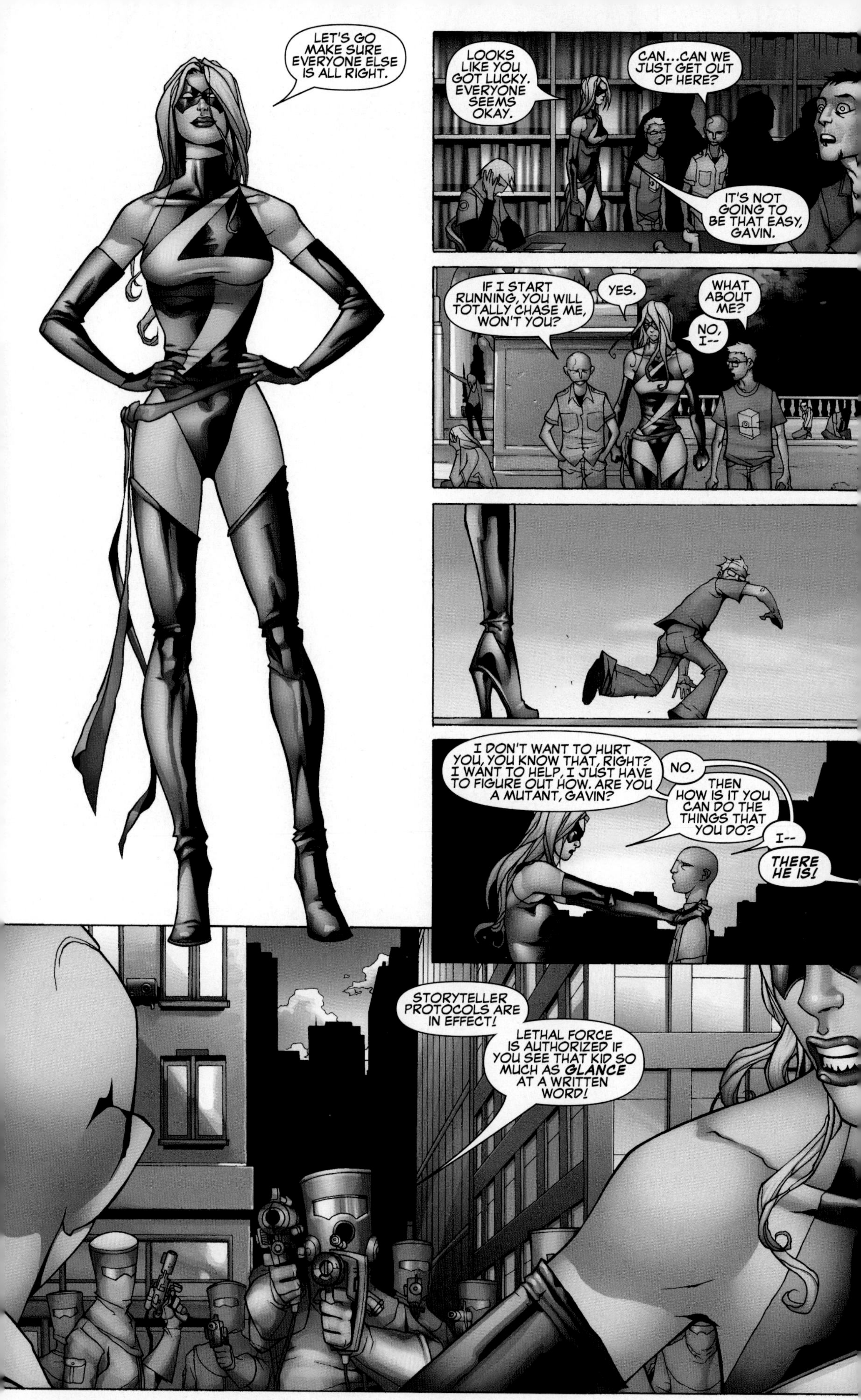
LET'S GO MAKE SURE EVERYONE ELSE IS ALL RIGHT.
LOOKS LIKE YOU GOT LUCKY. EVERYONE SEEMS OKAY.
CAN...CAN WE JUST GET OUT OF HERE?
IT'S NOT GOING TO BE THAT EASY, GAVIN.
IF I START RUNNING, YOU WILL TOTALLY CHASE ME, WON'T YOU?
YES.
WHAT ABOUT ME?
NO, I--
I DON'T WANT TO HURT YOU, YOU KNOW THAT, RIGHT? I WANT TO HELP, I JUST HAVE TO FIGURE OUT HOW. ARE YOU A MUTANT, GAVIN?
NO.
THEN HOW IS IT YOU CAN DO THE THINGS THAT YOU DO?
I--
THERE HE IS!
STORYTELLER PROTOCOLS ARE IN EFFECT!
LETHAL FORCE IS AUTHORIZED IF YOU SEE THAT KID SO MUCH AS GLANCE AT A WRITTEN WORD!

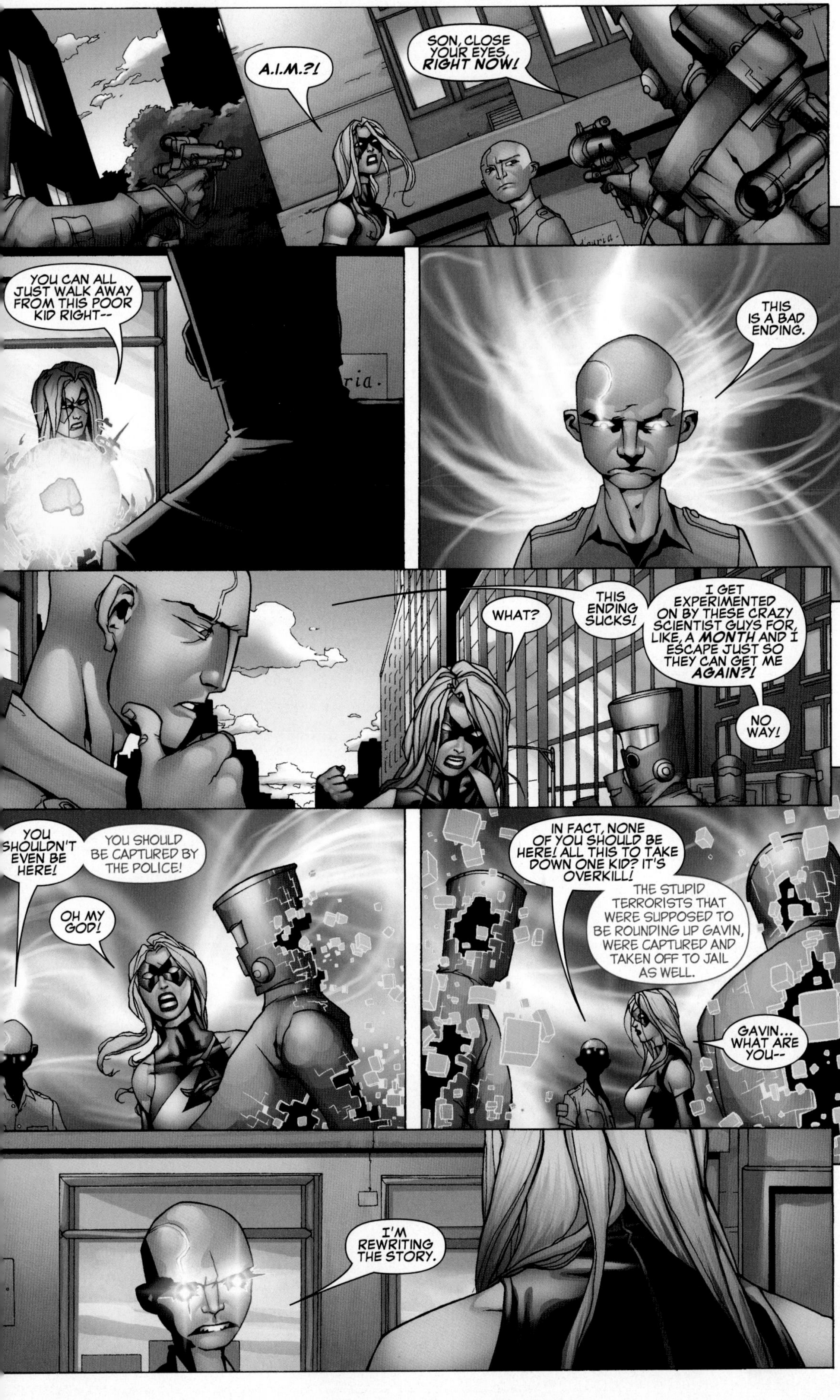
A.I.M.?!
SON, CLOSE YOUR EYES, RIGHT NOW!
YOU CAN ALL JUST WALK AWAY FROM THIS POOR KID RIGHT--
THIS IS A BAD ENDING.
WHAT?
THIS ENDING SUCKS!
I GET EXPERIMENTED ON BY THESE CRAZY SCIENTIST GUYS FOR, LIKE, A MONTH AND I ESCAPE JUST SO THEY CAN GET ME AGAIN?!
NO WAY!
YOU SHOULDN'T EVEN BE HERE!
YOU SHOULD BE CAPTURED BY THE POLICE!
OH MY GOD!
IN FACT, NONE OF YOU SHOULD BE HERE! ALL THIS TO TAKE DOWN ONE KID? IT'S OVERKILL!
THE STUPID TERRORISTS THAT WERE SUPPOSED TO BE ROUNDING UP GAVIN, WERE CAPTURED AND TAKEN OFF TO JAIL AS WELL.
GAVIN... WHAT ARE YOU--
I'M REWRITING THE STORY.

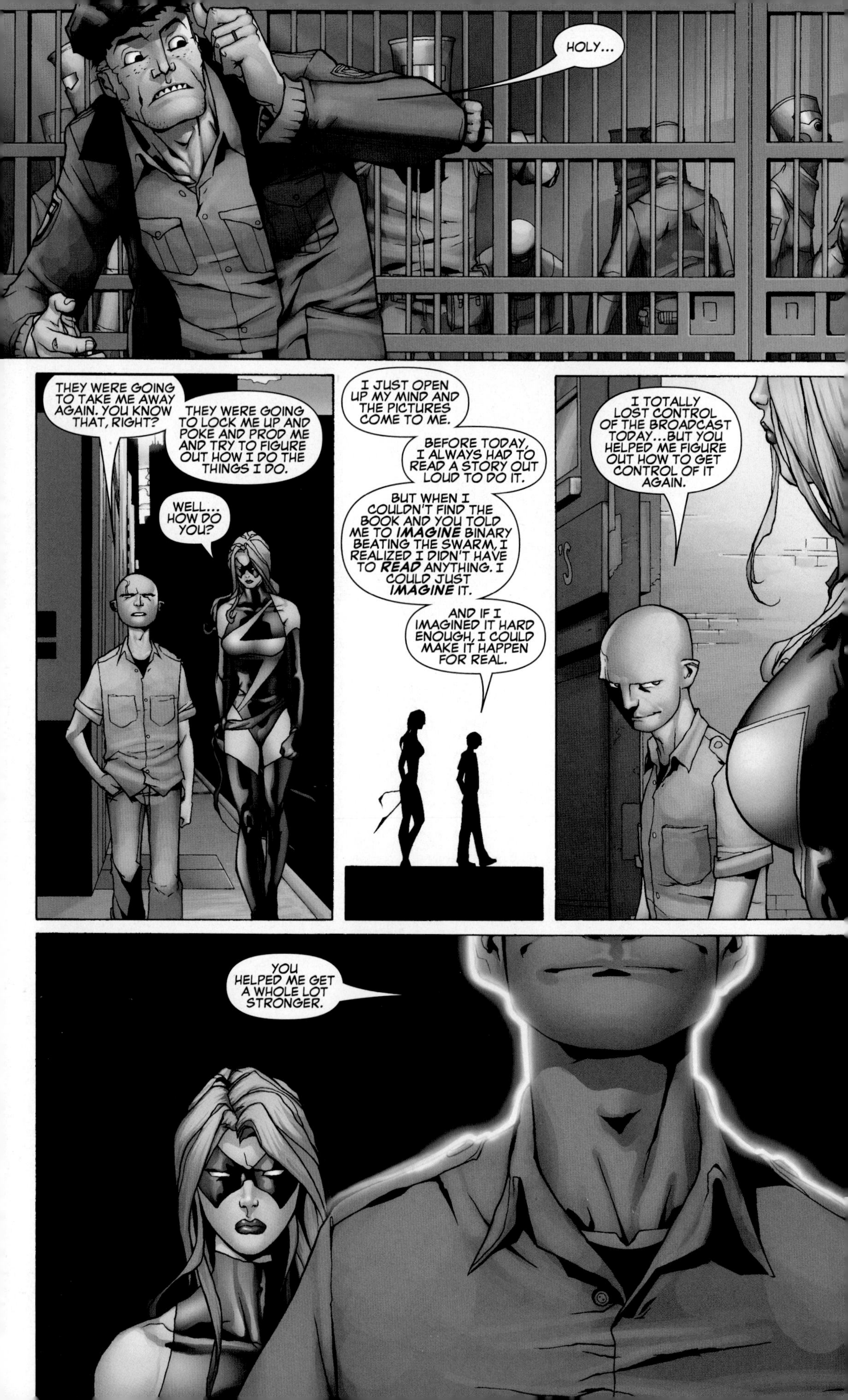
HOLY...
THEY WERE GOING TO TAKE ME AWAY AGAIN. YOU KNOW THAT, RIGHT?
THEY WERE GOING TO LOCK ME UP AND POKE AND PROD ME AND TRY TO FIGURE OUT HOW I DO THE THINGS I DO.
WELL... HOW DO YOU?
I JUST OPEN UP MY MIND AND THE PICTURES COME TO ME.
BEFORE TODAY, I ALWAYS HAD TO READ A STORY OUT LOUD TO DO IT.
BUT WHEN I COULDN'T FIND THE BOOK AND YOU TOLD ME TO IMAGINE BINARY BEATING THE SWARM, I REALIZED I DIDN'T HAVE TO READ ANYTHING. I COULD JUST IMAGINE IT.
AND IF I IMAGINED IT HARD ENOUGH, I COULD MAKE IT HAPPEN FOR REAL.
I TOTALLY LOST CONTROL OF THE BROADCAST TODAY...BUT YOU HELPED ME FIGURE OUT HOW TO GET CONTROL OF IT AGAIN.
YOU HELPED ME GET A WHOLE LOT STRONGER.

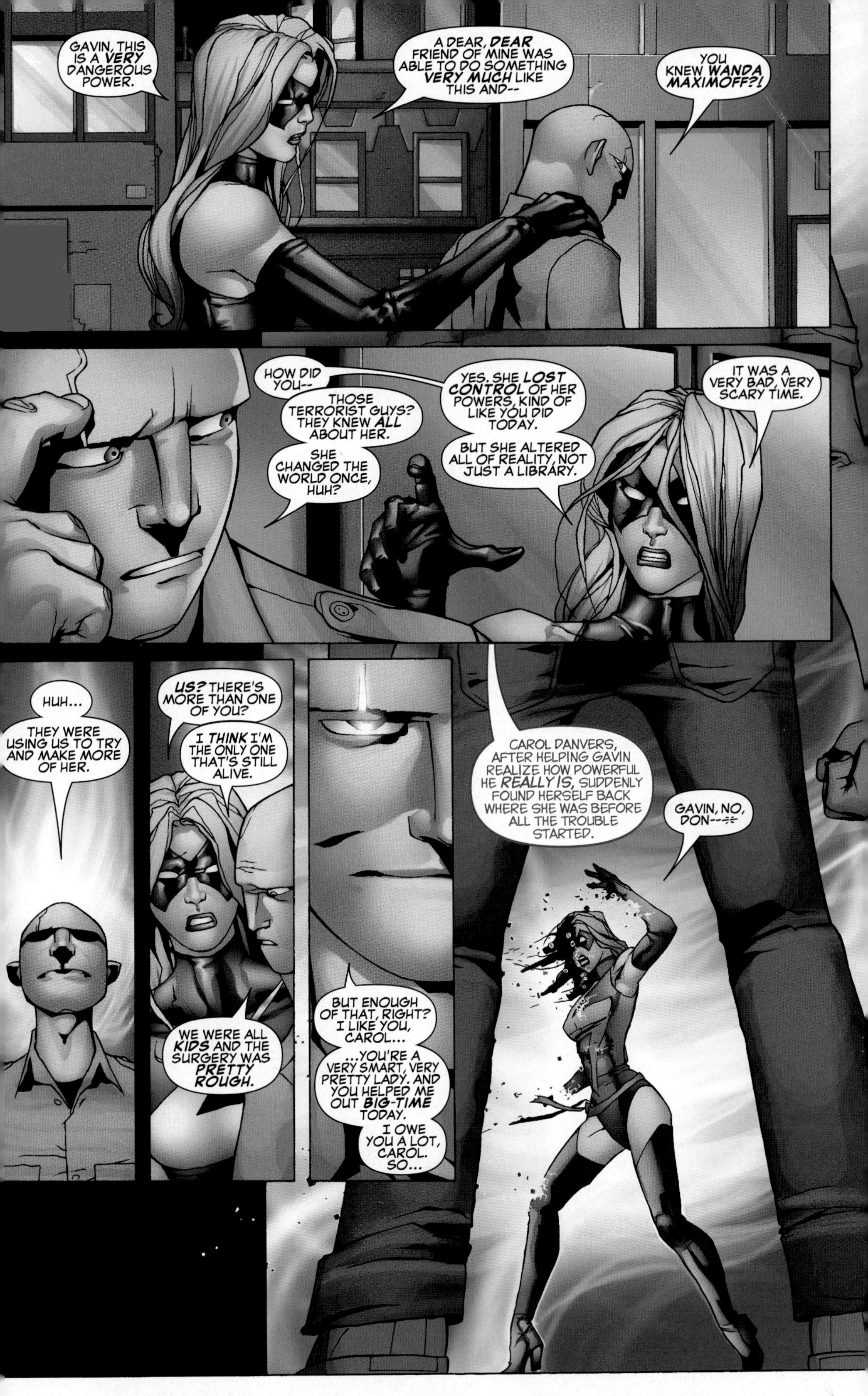
GAVIN, THIS IS A VERY DANGEROUS POWER.
A DEAR, DEAR FRIEND OF MINE WAS ABLE TO DO SOMETHING VERY MUCH LIKE THIS AND--
YOU KNEW WANDA MAXIMOFF?!
HOW DID YOU--
YES. SHE LOST CONTROL OF HER POWERS, KIND OF LIKE YOU DID TODAY.
BUT SHE ALTERED ALL OF REALITY, NOT JUST A LIBRARY.
IT WAS A VERY BAD, VERY SCARY TIME.
THOSE TERRORIST GUYS? THEY KNEW ALL ABOUT HER.
SHE CHANGED THE WORLD ONCE, HUH?
HUH...
THEY WERE USING US TO TRY AND MAKE MORE OF HER.
US? THERE'S MORE THAN ONE OF YOU?
I THINK I'M THE ONLY ONE THAT'S STILL ALIVE.
WE WERE ALL KIDS AND THE SURGERY WAS PRETTY ROUGH.
BUT ENOUGH OF THAT, RIGHT? I LIKE YOU, CAROL...
...YOU'RE A VERY SMART, VERY PRETTY LADY. AND YOU HELPED ME OUT BIG-TIME TODAY.
I OWE YOU A LOT, CAROL. SO...
CAROL DANVERS, AFTER HELPING GAVIN REALIZE HOW POWERFUL HE REALLY IS, SUDDENLY FOUND HERSELF BACK WHERE SHE WAS BEFORE ALL THE TROUBLE STARTED.
GAVIN, NO, DON--

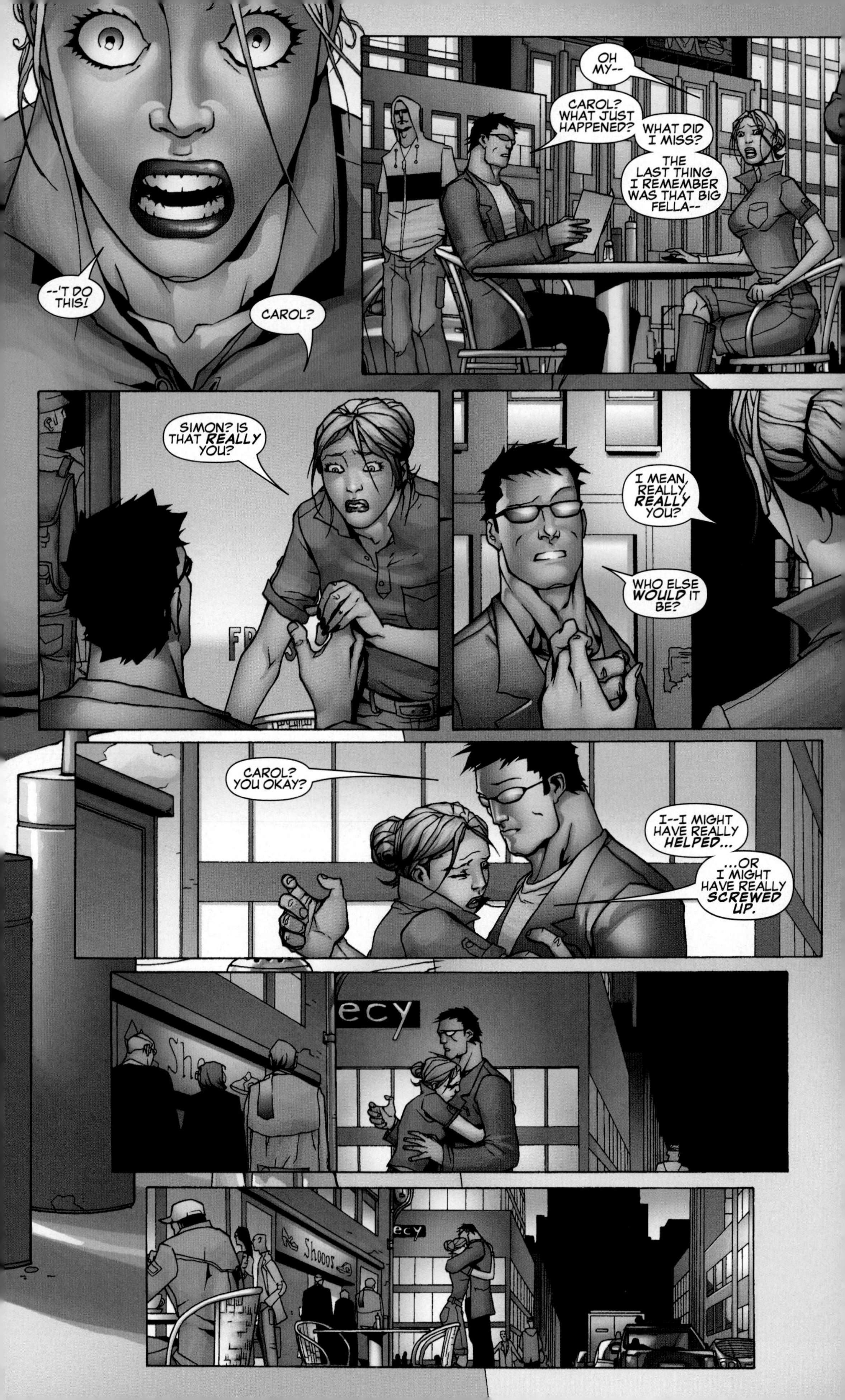
--'T DO THIS!
CAROL?
OH MY--
CAROL? WHAT JUST HAPPENED?
WHAT DID I MISS?
THE LAST THING I REMEMBER WAS THAT BIG FELLA--
SIMON? IS THAT REALLY YOU?
I MEAN, REALLY, REALLY YOU?
WHO ELSE WOULD IT BE?
CAROL? YOU OKAY?
I--I MIGHT HAVE REALLY HELPED...
...OR I MIGHT HAVE REALLY SCREWED UP.

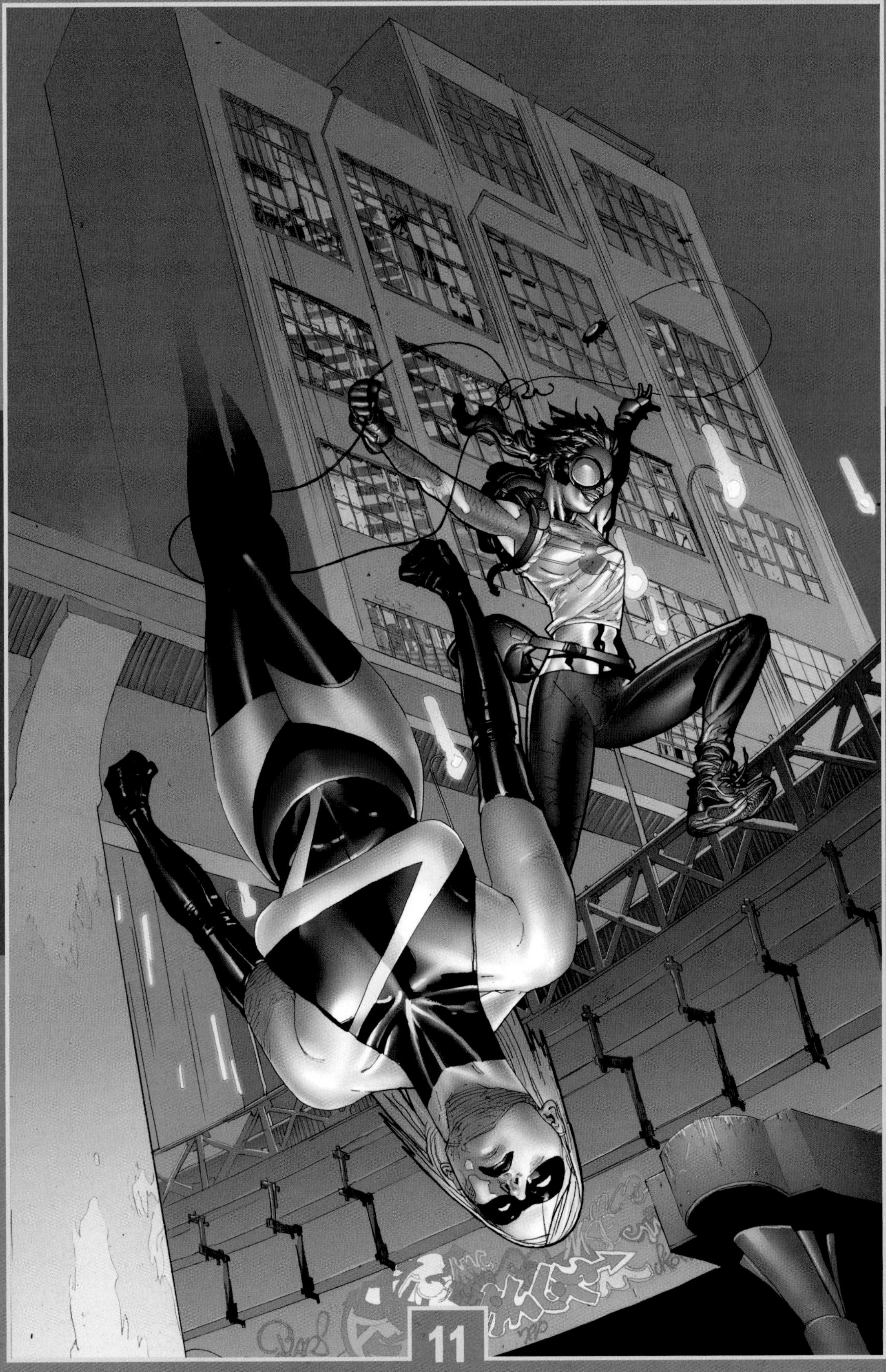

11

“DOOMSDAY”

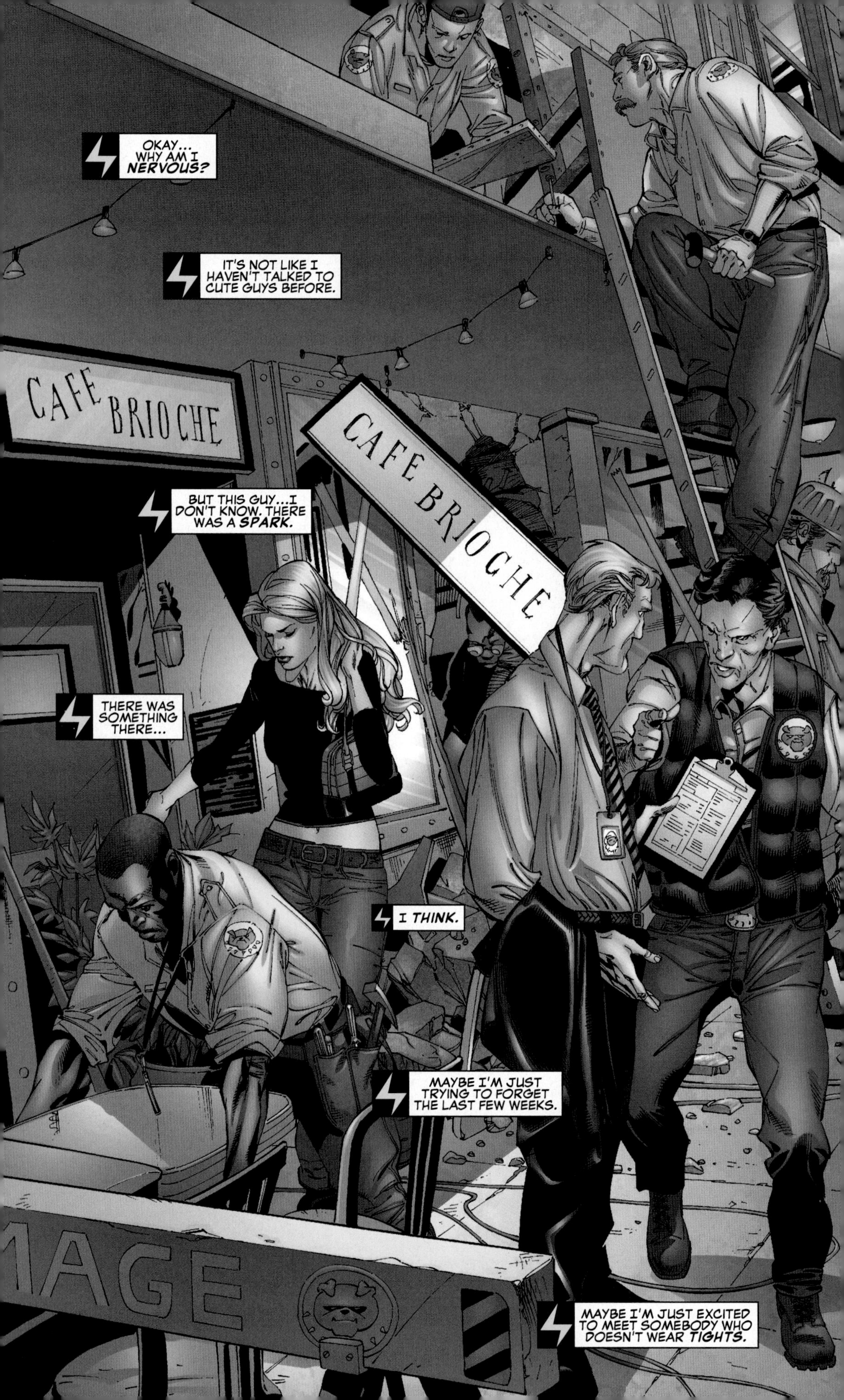
OKAY... WHY AM I NERVOUS?
IT'S NOT LIKE I HAVEN'T TALKED TO CUTE GUYS BEFORE.
CAFE BRIOCHE
CAFE BRIOCHE
BUT THIS GUY...I DON'T KNOW. THERE WAS A SPARK.
THERE WAS SOMETHING THERE...
I THINK.
MAYBE I'M JUST TRYING TO FORGET THE LAST FEW WEEKS.
MAGE
MAYBE I'M JUST EXCITED TO MEET SOMEBODY WHO DOESN'T WEAR TIGHTS.

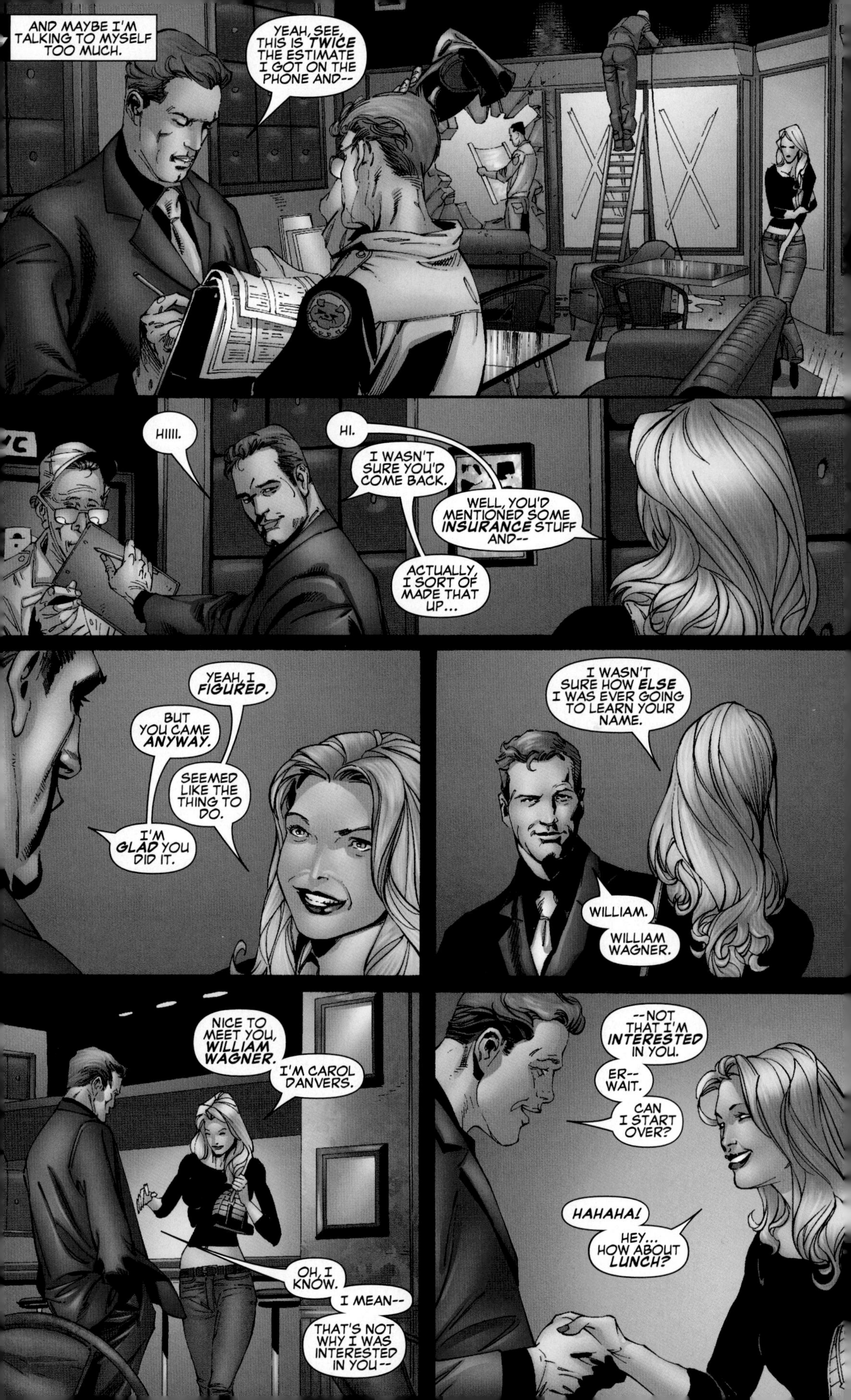
AND MAYBE I'M TALKING TO MYSELF TOO MUCH.
YEAH, SEE, THIS IS TWICE THE ESTIMATE I GOT ON THE PHONE AND--
HIIII.
HI.
I WASN'T SURE YOU'D COME BACK.
WELL, YOU'D MENTIONED SOME INSURANCE STUFF AND--
ACTUALLY, I SORT OF MADE THAT UP...
YEAH, I FIGURED.
BUT YOU CAME ANYWAY.
SEEMED LIKE THE THING TO DO.
I'M GLAD YOU DID IT.
I WASN'T SURE HOW ELSE I WAS EVER GOING TO LEARN YOUR NAME.
WILLIAM.
WILLIAM WAGNER.
NICE TO MEET YOU, WILLIAM WAGNER.
I'M CAROL DANVERS.
OH, I KNOW.
I MEAN--
THAT'S NOT WHY I WAS INTERESTED IN YOU--
--NOT THAT I'M INTERESTED IN YOU.
ER-- WAIT.
CAN I START OVER?
HAHAHA!
HEY... HOW ABOUT LUNCH?

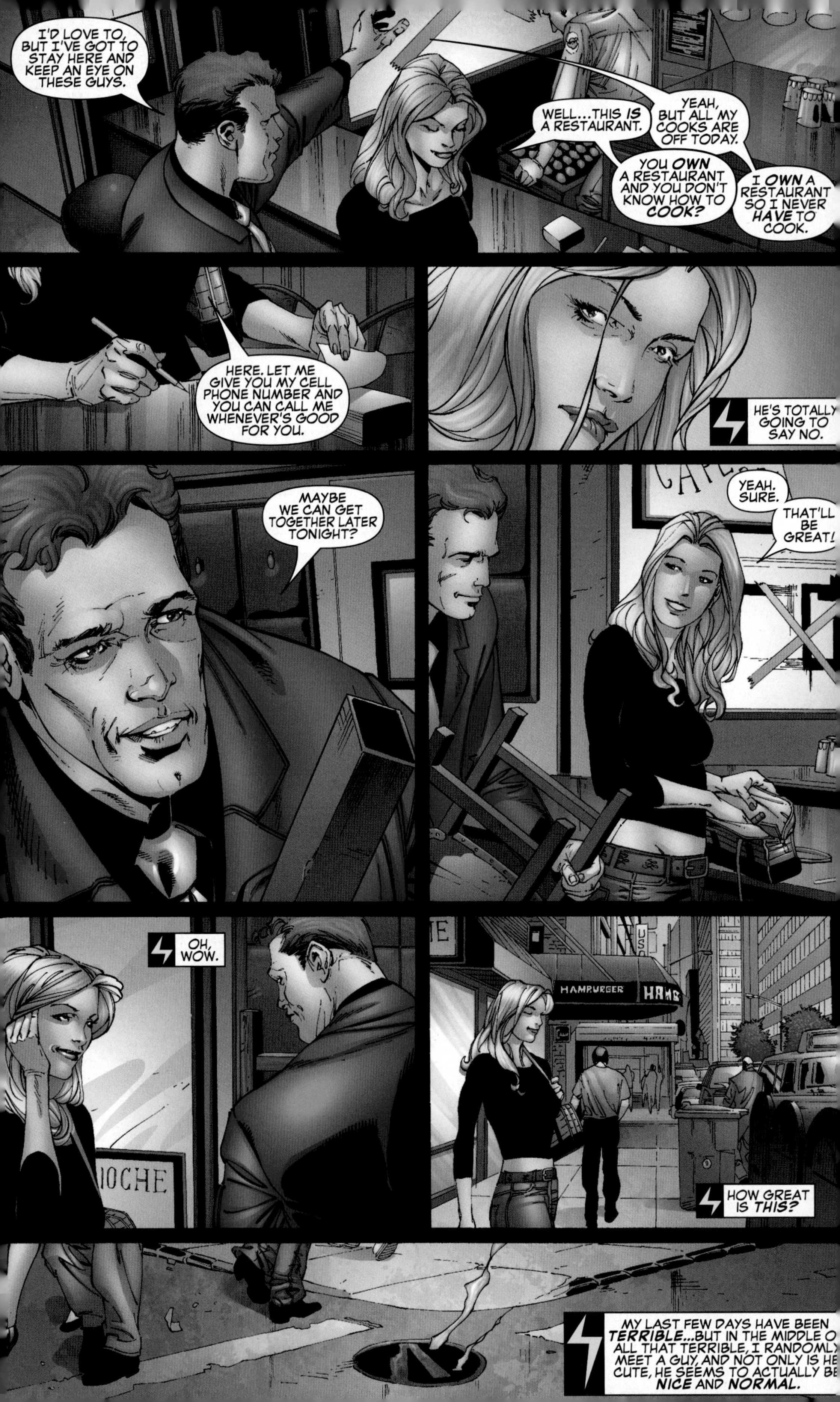
I'D LOVE TO, BUT I'VE GOT TO STAY HERE AND KEEP AN EYE ON THESE GUYS.
WELL...THIS IS A RESTAURANT.
YEAH, BUT ALL MY COOKS ARE OFF TODAY.
YOU OWN A RESTAURANT AND YOU DON'T KNOW HOW TO COOK?
I OWN A RESTAURANT SO I NEVER HAVE TO COOK.
HERE. LET ME GIVE YOU MY CELL PHONE NUMBER AND YOU CAN CALL ME WHENEVER'S GOOD FOR YOU.
HE'S TOTALLY GOING TO SAY NO.
MAYBE WE CAN GET TOGETHER LATER TONIGHT?
YEAH. SURE.
THAT'LL BE GREAT!
OH, WOW.
HAMBURGER
HOW GREAT IS THIS?
MY LAST FEW DAYS HAVE BEEN TERRIBLE...BUT IN THE MIDDLE OF ALL THAT TERRIBLE, I RANDOMLY MEET A GUY, AND NOT ONLY IS HE CUTE, HE SEEMS TO ACTUALLY BE NICE AND NORMAL.

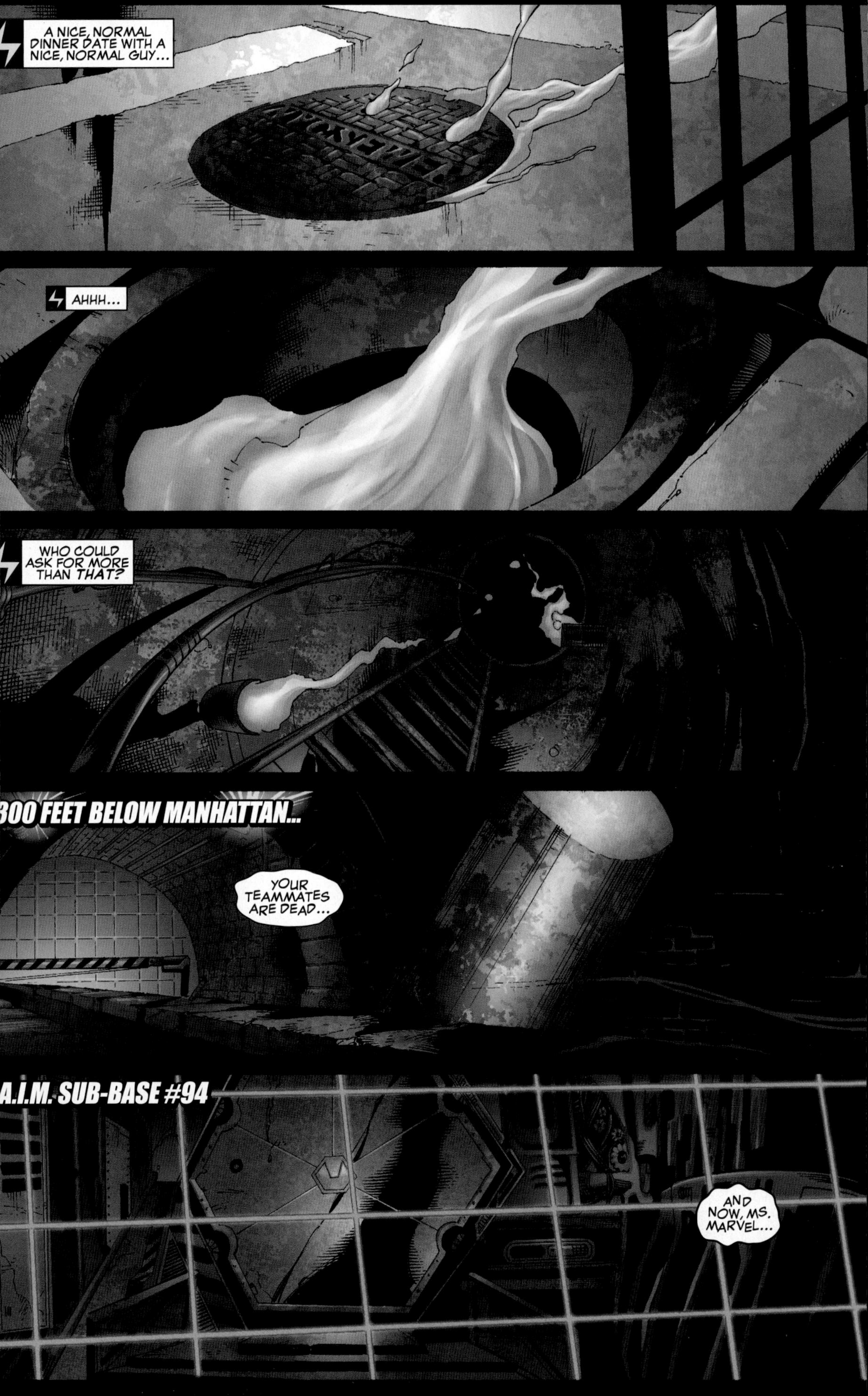

A NICE, NORMAL DINNER DATE WITH A NICE, NORMAL GUY...
AHHH...
WHO COULD ASK FOR MORE THAN THAT?
300 FEET BELOW MANHATTAN...
YOUR TEAMMATES ARE DEAD...
A.I.M. SUB-BASE #94
AND NOW, MS. MARVEL...

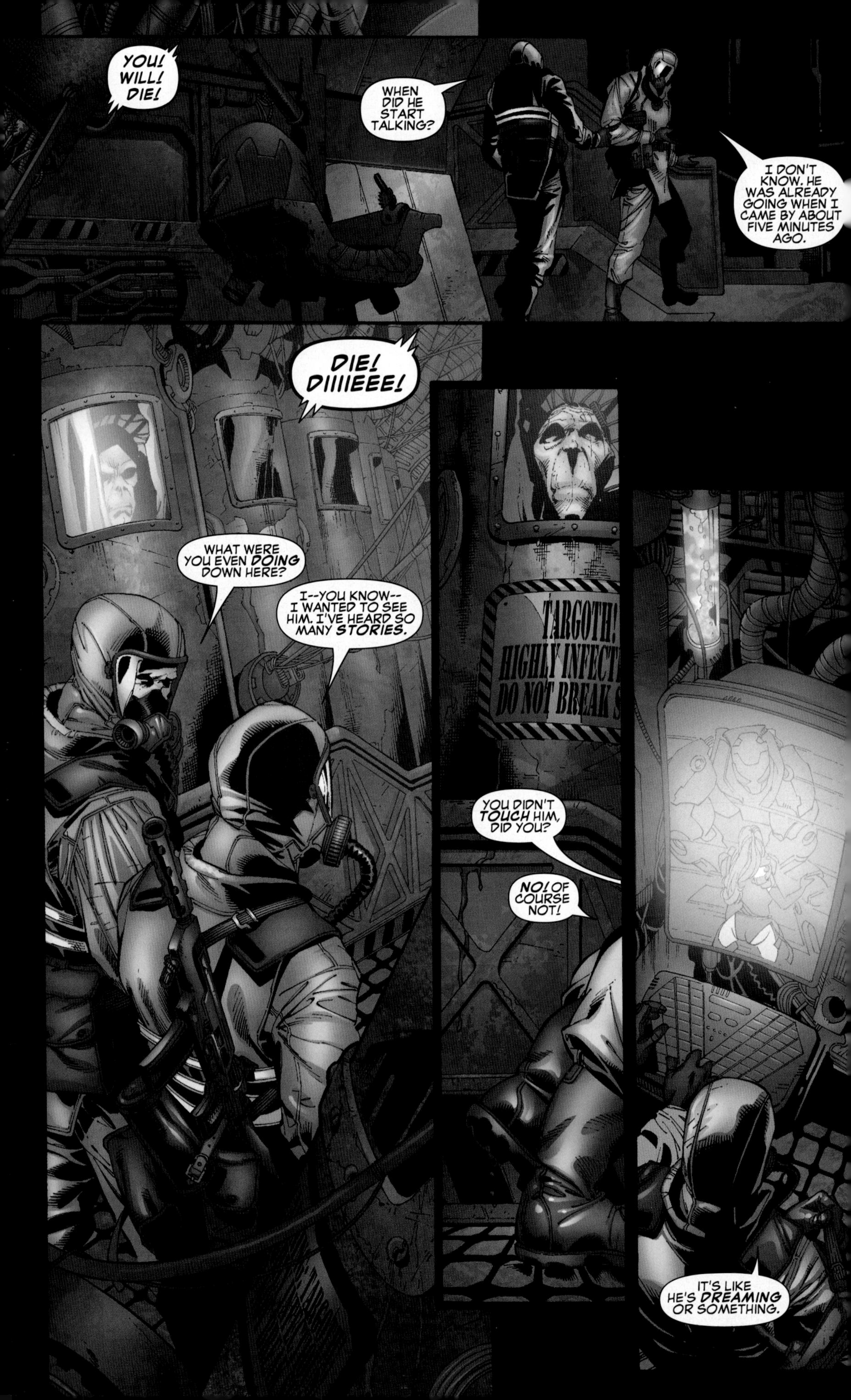
YOU! WILL! DIE!
WHEN DID HE START TALKING?
I DON'T KNOW. HE WAS ALREADY GOING WHEN I CAME BY ABOUT FIVE MINUTES AGO.
DIE! DIIIIEEE!
WHAT WERE YOU EVEN DOING DOWN HERE?
I--YOU KNOW-- I WANTED TO SEE HIM. I'VE HEARD SO MANY STORIES.
TARGOTH! HIGHLY INFECT DO NOT BREAK S
YOU DIDN'T TOUCH HIM, DID YOU?
NO! OF COURSE NOT!
IT'S LIKE HE'S DREAMING OR SOMETHING.

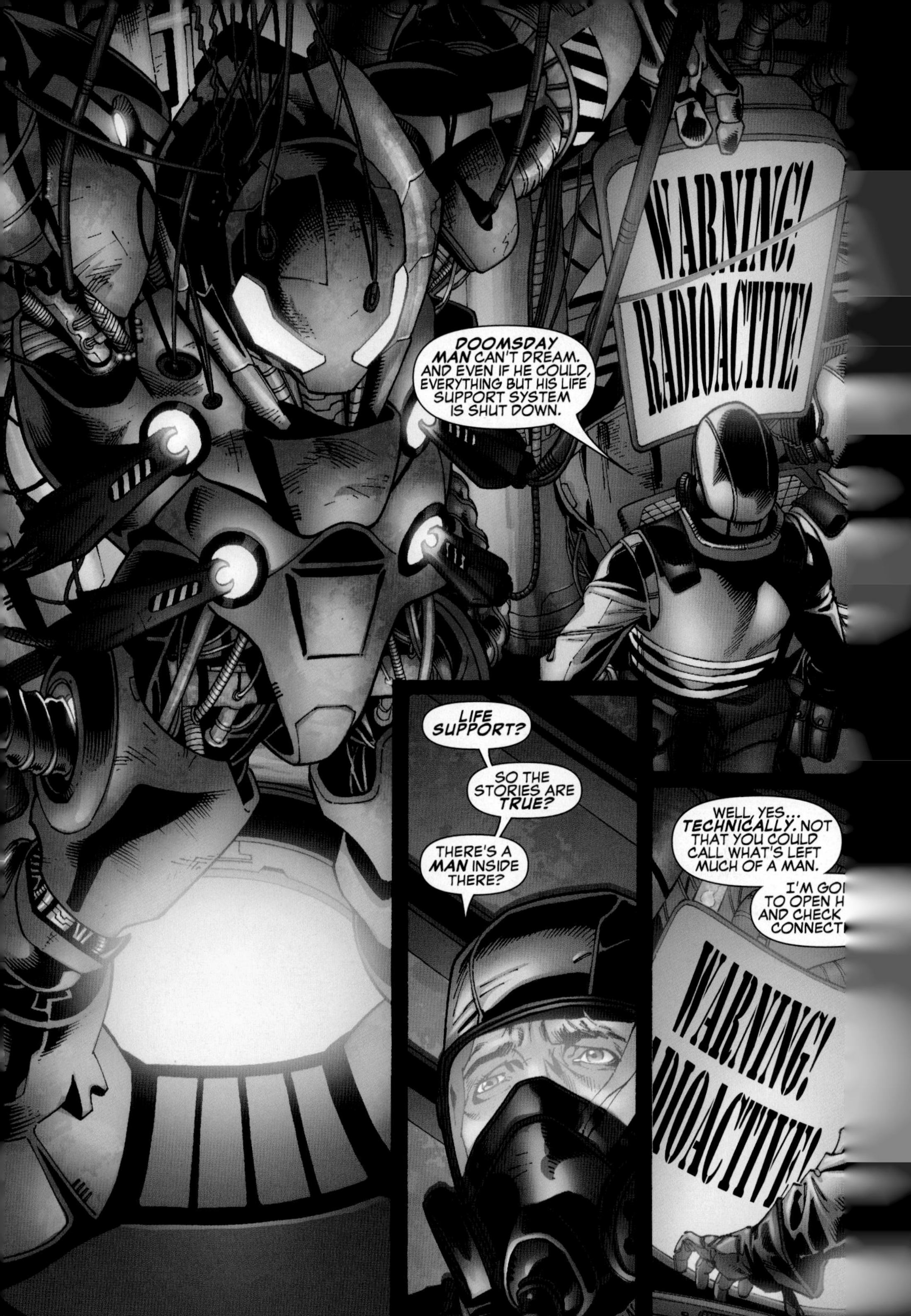
WARNING! RADIOACTIVE!
DOOMSDAY MAN CAN'T DREAM. AND EVEN IF HE COULD, EVERYTHING BUT HIS LIFE SUPPORT SYSTEM IS SHUT DOWN.
LIFE SUPPORT?
SO THE STORIES ARE TRUE?
THERE'S A MAN INSIDE THERE?
WELL, YES... TECHNICALLY. NOT THAT YOU COULD CALL WHAT'S LEFT MUCH OF A MAN.
WARNING!

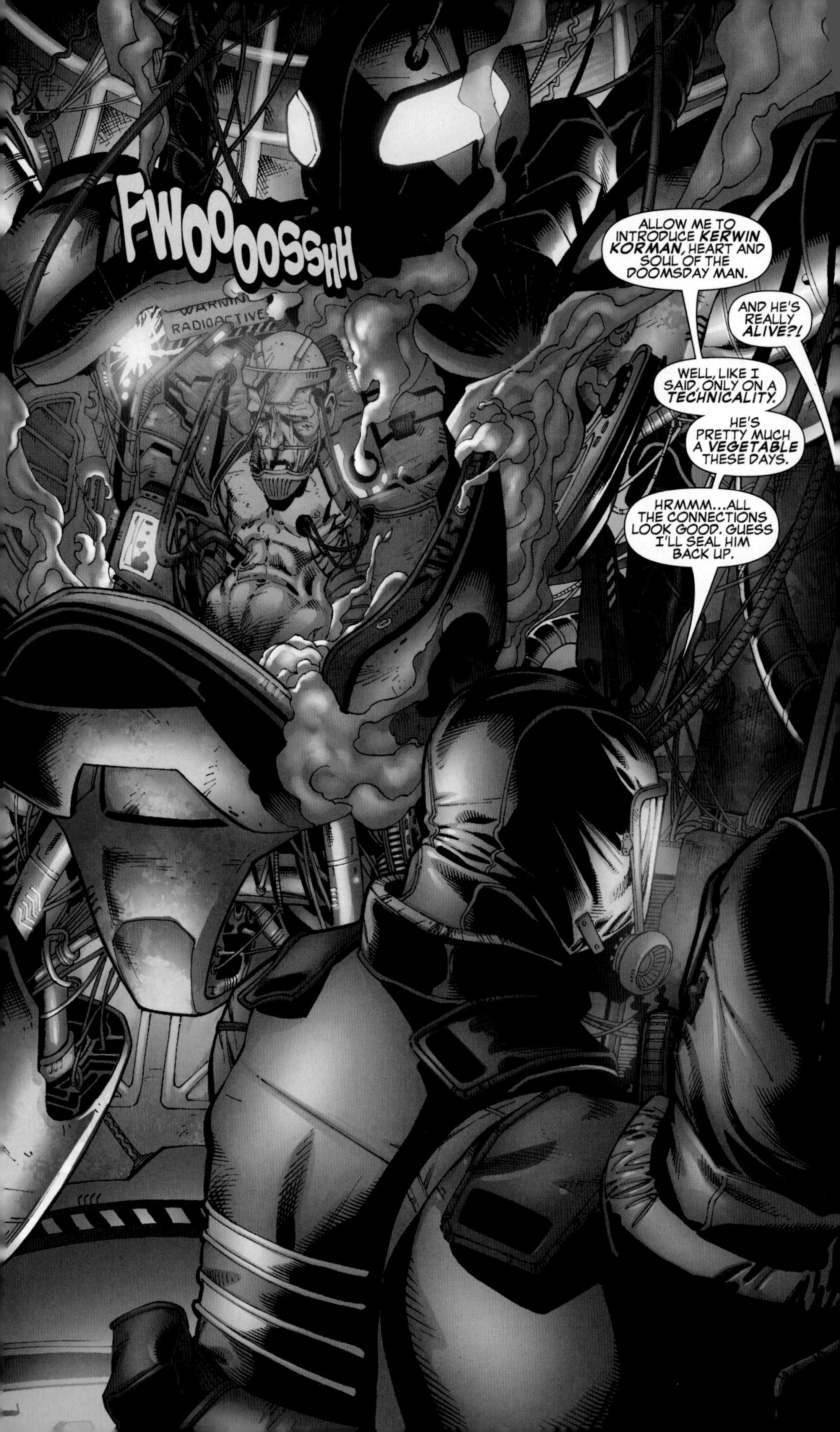
FWOOOOSSHH
WARNING
RADIOACTIVE
ALLOW ME TO INTRODUCE KERWIN KORMAN, HEART AND SOUL OF THE DOOMSDAY MAN.
AND HE'S REALLY ALIVE?!
WELL, LIKE I SAID, ONLY ON A TECHNICALITY.
HE'S PRETTY MUCH A VEGETABLE THESE DAYS.
HRMMM...ALL THE CONNECTIONS LOOK GOOD. GUESS I'LL SEAL HIM BACK UP.

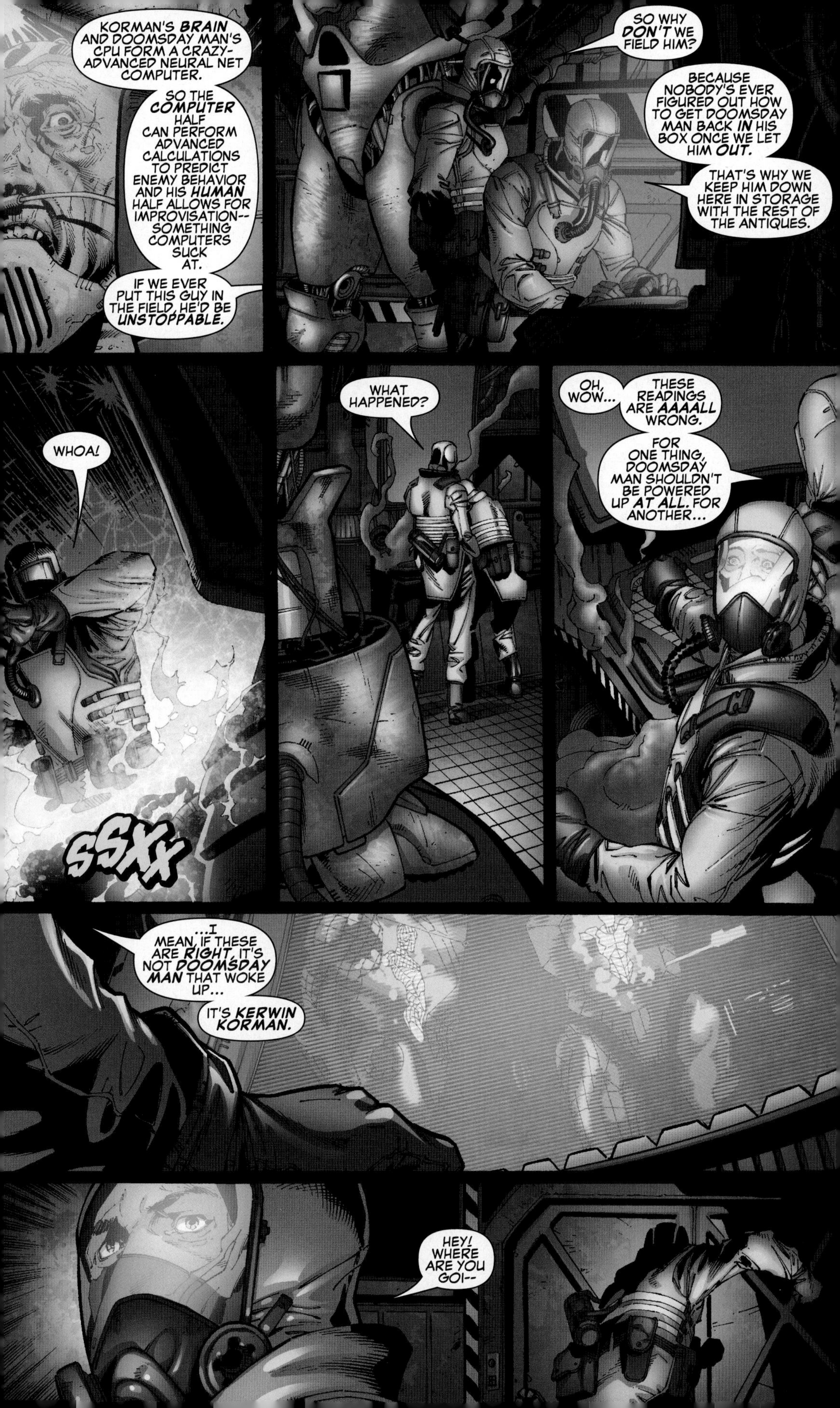
KORMAN'S BRAIN AND DOOMSDAY MAN'S CPU FORM A CRAZY-ADVANCED NEURAL NET COMPUTER.
SO THE COMPUTER HALF CAN PERFORM ADVANCED CALCULATIONS TO PREDICT ENEMY BEHAVIOR AND HIS HUMAN HALF ALLOWS FOR IMPROVISATION-- SOMETHING COMPUTERS SUCK AT.
IF WE EVER PUT THIS GUY IN THE FIELD, HE'D BE UNSTOPPABLE.
SO WHY DON'T WE FIELD HIM?
BECAUSE NOBODY'S EVER FIGURED OUT HOW TO GET DOOMSDAY MAN BACK IN HIS BOX ONCE WE LET HIM OUT.
THAT'S WHY WE KEEP HIM DOWN HERE IN STORAGE WITH THE REST OF THE ANTIQUES.
WHOA!
SSXX
WHAT HAPPENED?
OH, WOW...
THESE READINGS ARE AAAALL WRONG.
FOR ONE THING, DOOMSDAY MAN SHOULDN'T BE POWERED UP AT ALL. FOR ANOTHER...
...I MEAN, IF THESE ARE RIGHT, IT'S NOT DOOMSDAY MAN THAT WOKE UP...
IT'S KERWIN KORMAN.
HEY! WHERE ARE YOU GOI--

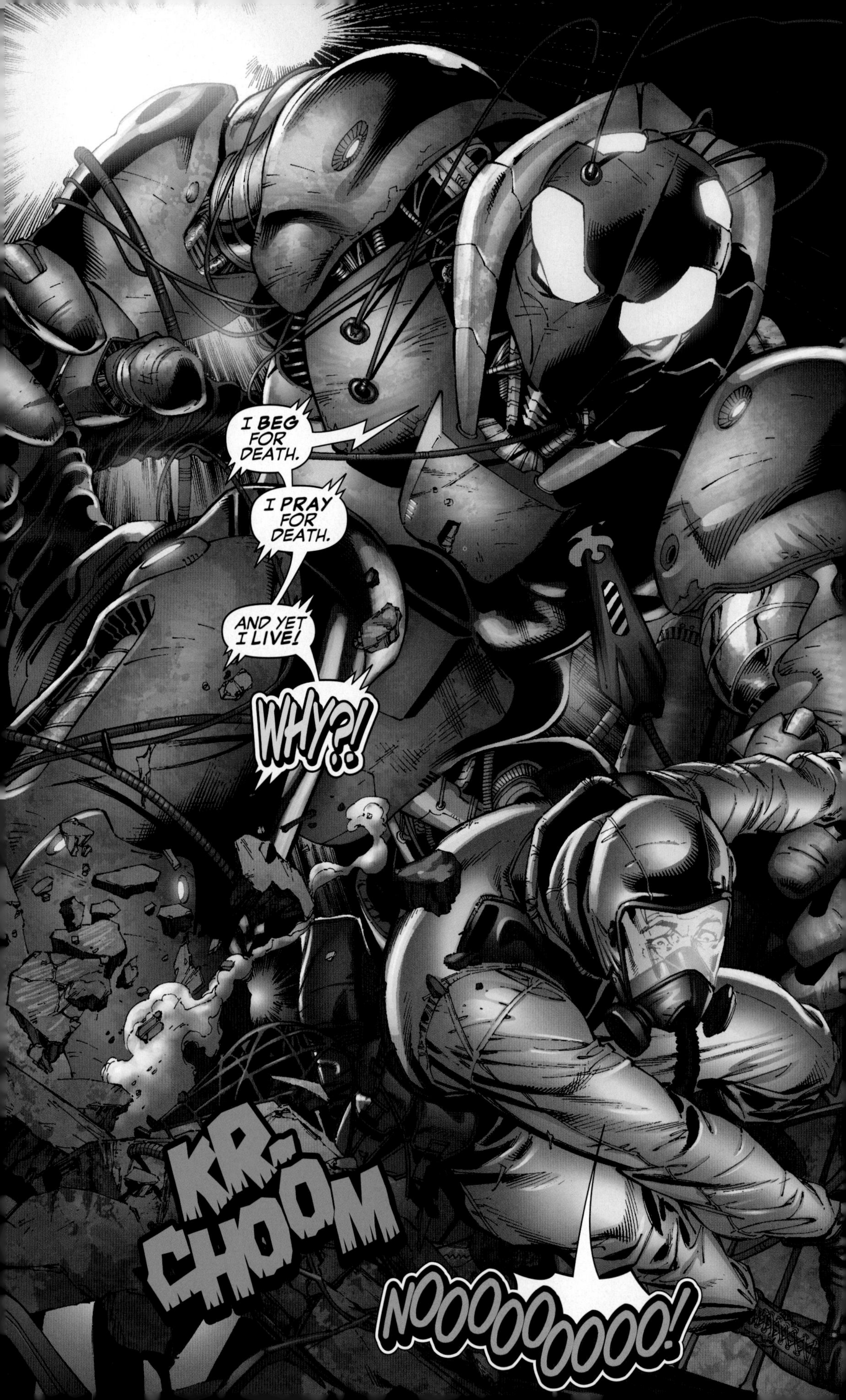
I BEG FOR DEATH.
I PRAY FOR DEATH.
AND YET I LIVE!
WHY?!
KR-CHOOM
NOOOOOOOOOO!

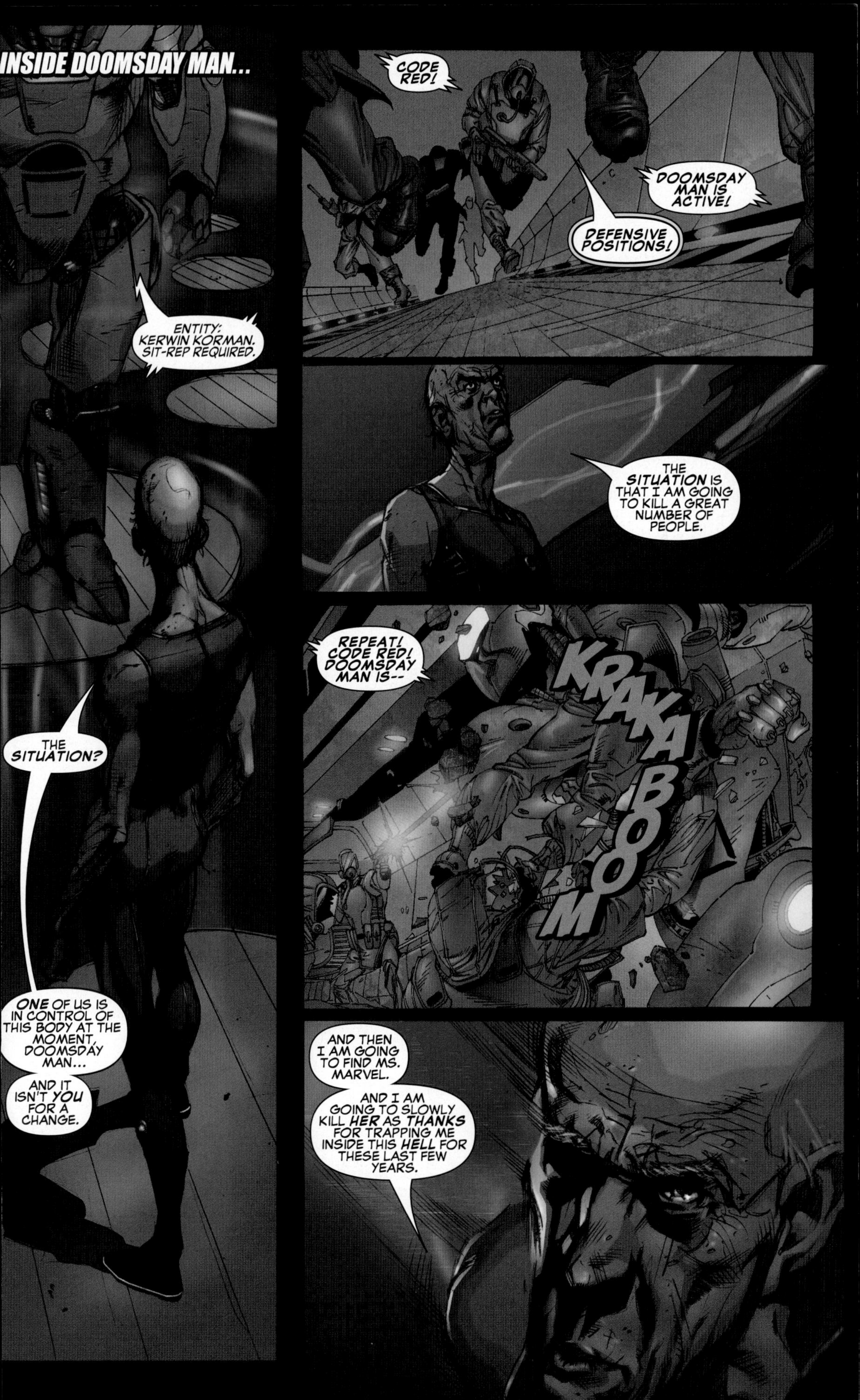
INSIDE DOOMSDAY MAN...
ENTITY: KERWIN KORMAN. SIT-REP REQUIRED.
CODE RED!
DOOMSDAY MAN IS ACTIVE!
DEFENSIVE POSITIONS!
THE SITUATION?
THE SITUATION IS THAT I AM GOING TO KILL A GREAT NUMBER OF PEOPLE.
REPEAT! CODE RED! DOOMSDAY MAN IS--
KRAKABOOM
ONE OF US IS IN CONTROL OF THIS BODY AT THE MOMENT, DOOMSDAY MAN...
AND IT ISN'T YOU FOR A CHANGE.
AND THEN I AM GOING TO FIND MS. MARVEL.
AND I AM GOING TO SLOWLY KILL HER AS THANKS FOR TRAPPING ME INSIDE THIS HELL FOR THESE LAST FEW YEARS.

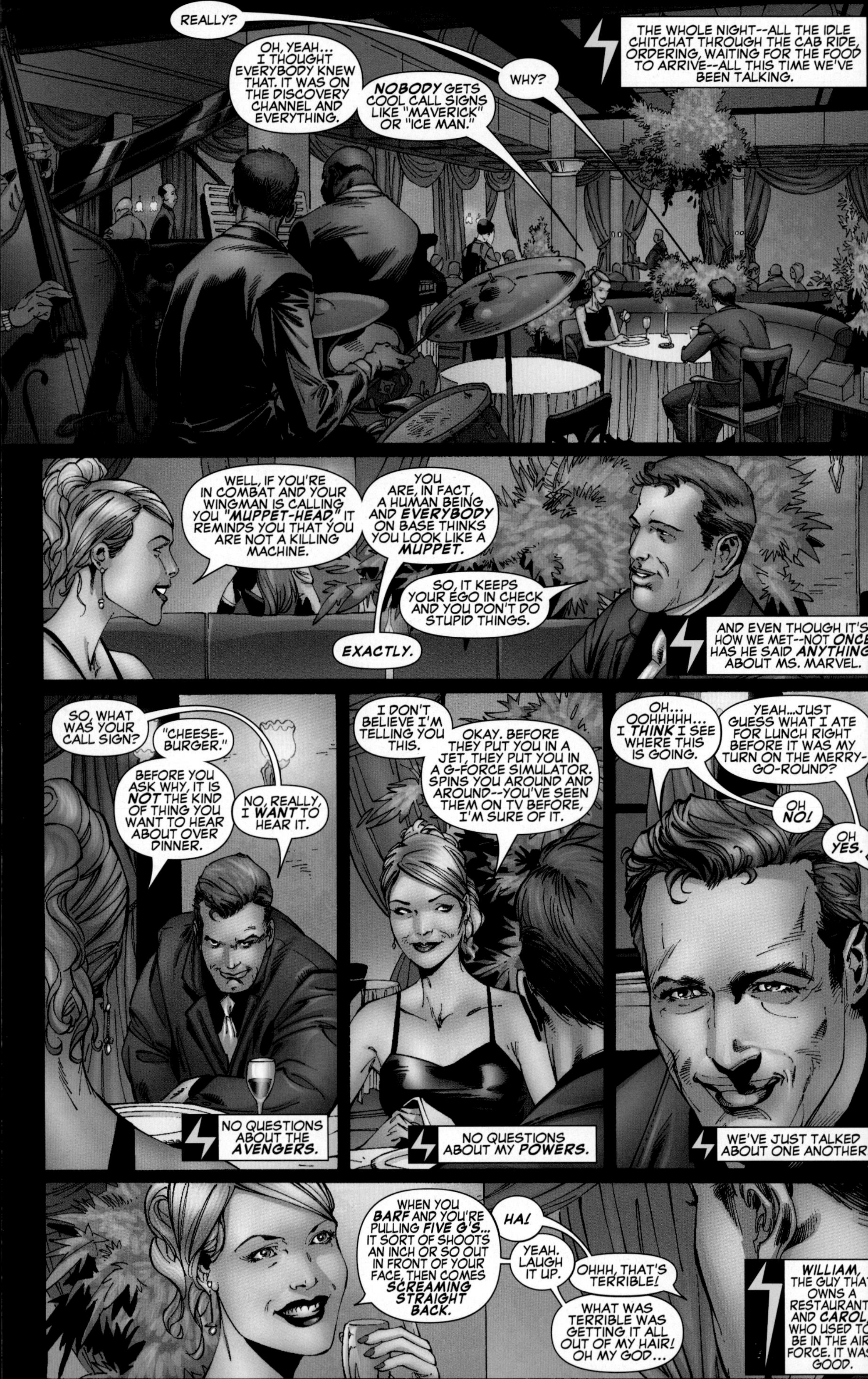
REALLY?
OH, YEAH... I THOUGHT EVERYBODY KNEW THAT. IT WAS ON THE DISCOVERY CHANNEL AND EVERYTHING.
WHY?
NOBODY GETS COOL CALL SIGNS LIKE "MAVERICK" OR "ICE MAN."
THE WHOLE NIGHT--ALL THE IDLE CHITCHAT THROUGH THE CAB RIDE, ORDERING, WAITING FOR THE FOOD TO ARRIVE--ALL THIS TIME WE'VE BEEN TALKING.
WELL, IF YOU'RE IN COMBAT AND YOUR WINGMAN IS CALLING YOU "MUPPET-HEAD," IT REMINDS YOU THAT YOU ARE NOT A KILLING MACHINE.
YOU ARE, IN FACT, A HUMAN BEING AND EVERYBODY ON BASE THINKS YOU LOOK LIKE A MUPPET.
SO, IT KEEPS YOUR EGO IN CHECK AND YOU DON'T DO STUPID THINGS.
EXACTLY.
AND EVEN THOUGH IT'S HOW WE MET--NOT ONCE HAS HE SAID ANYTHING ABOUT MS. MARVEL.
SO, WHAT WAS YOUR CALL SIGN?
"CHEESE-BURGER."
BEFORE YOU ASK WHY, IT IS NOT THE KIND OF THING YOU WANT TO HEAR ABOUT OVER DINNER.
NO, REALLY, I WANT TO HEAR IT.
NO QUESTIONS ABOUT THE AVENGERS.
I DON'T BELIEVE I'M TELLING YOU THIS.
OKAY. BEFORE THEY PUT YOU IN A JET, THEY PUT YOU IN A G-FORCE SIMULATOR. SPINS YOU AROUND AND AROUND--YOU'VE SEEN THEM ON TV BEFORE, I'M SURE OF IT.
NO QUESTIONS ABOUT MY POWERS.
OH... OOHHHHH... I THINK I SEE WHERE THIS IS GOING.
YEAH...JUST GUESS WHAT I ATE FOR LUNCH RIGHT BEFORE IT WAS MY TURN ON THE MERRY-GO-ROUND?
OH NO!
OH YES.
WE'VE JUST TALKED ABOUT ONE ANOTHER
WHEN YOU BARF AND YOU'RE PULLING FIVE G'S... IT SORT OF SHOOTS AN INCH OR SO OUT IN FRONT OF YOUR FACE, THEN COMES SCREAMING STRAIGHT BACK.
HA!
YEAH. LAUGH IT UP.
OHHH, THAT'S TERRIBLE!
WHAT WAS TERRIBLE WAS GETTING IT ALL OUT OF MY HAIR! OH MY GOD...
WILLIAM, THE GUY THAT OWNS A RESTAURANT AND CAROL, WHO USED TO BE IN THE AIR FORCE. IT WAS GOOD.

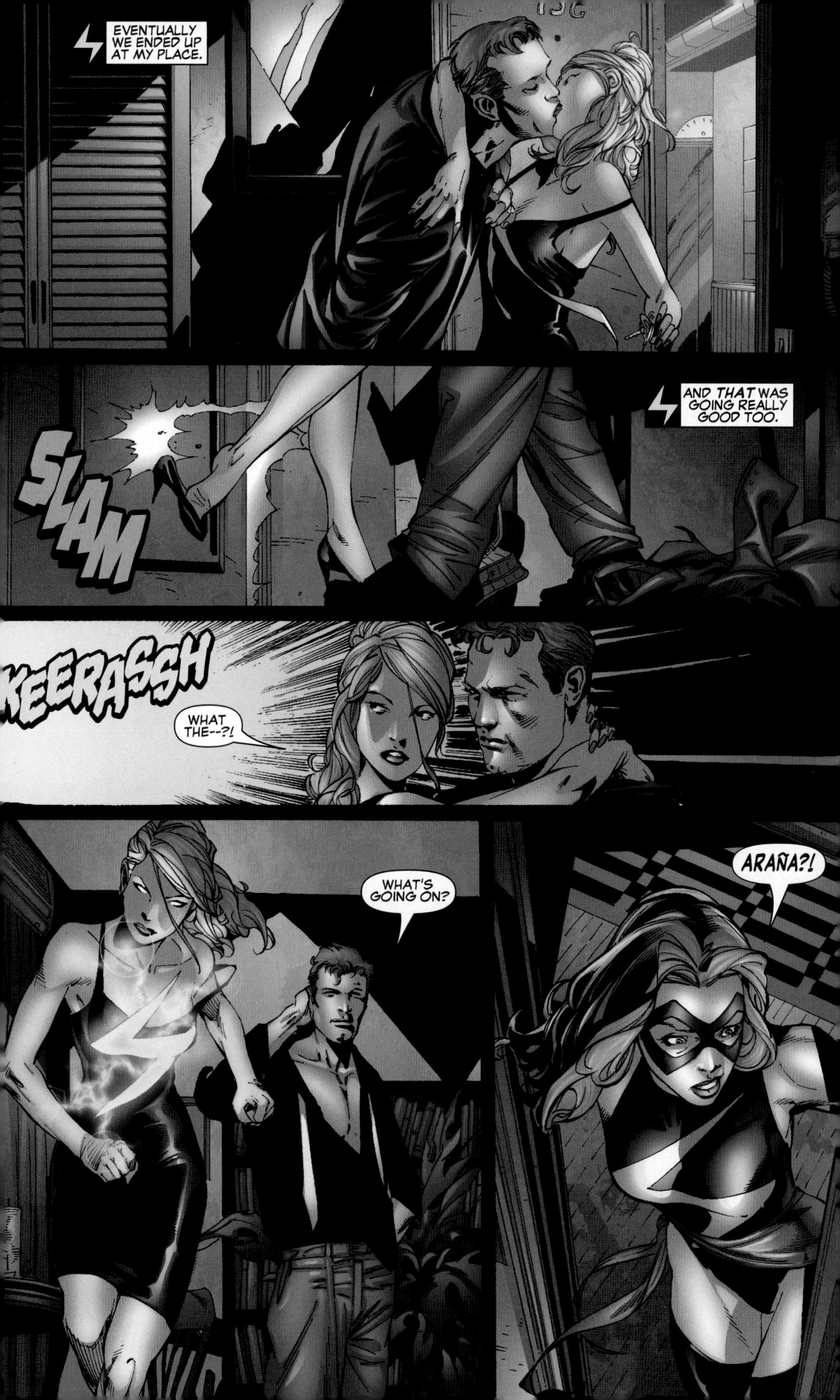
EVENTUALLY WE ENDED UP AT MY PLACE.
AND THAT WAS GOING REALLY GOOD TOO.
SLAM
KEERASSH
WHAT THE--?!
WHAT'S GOING ON?
ARAÑA?!

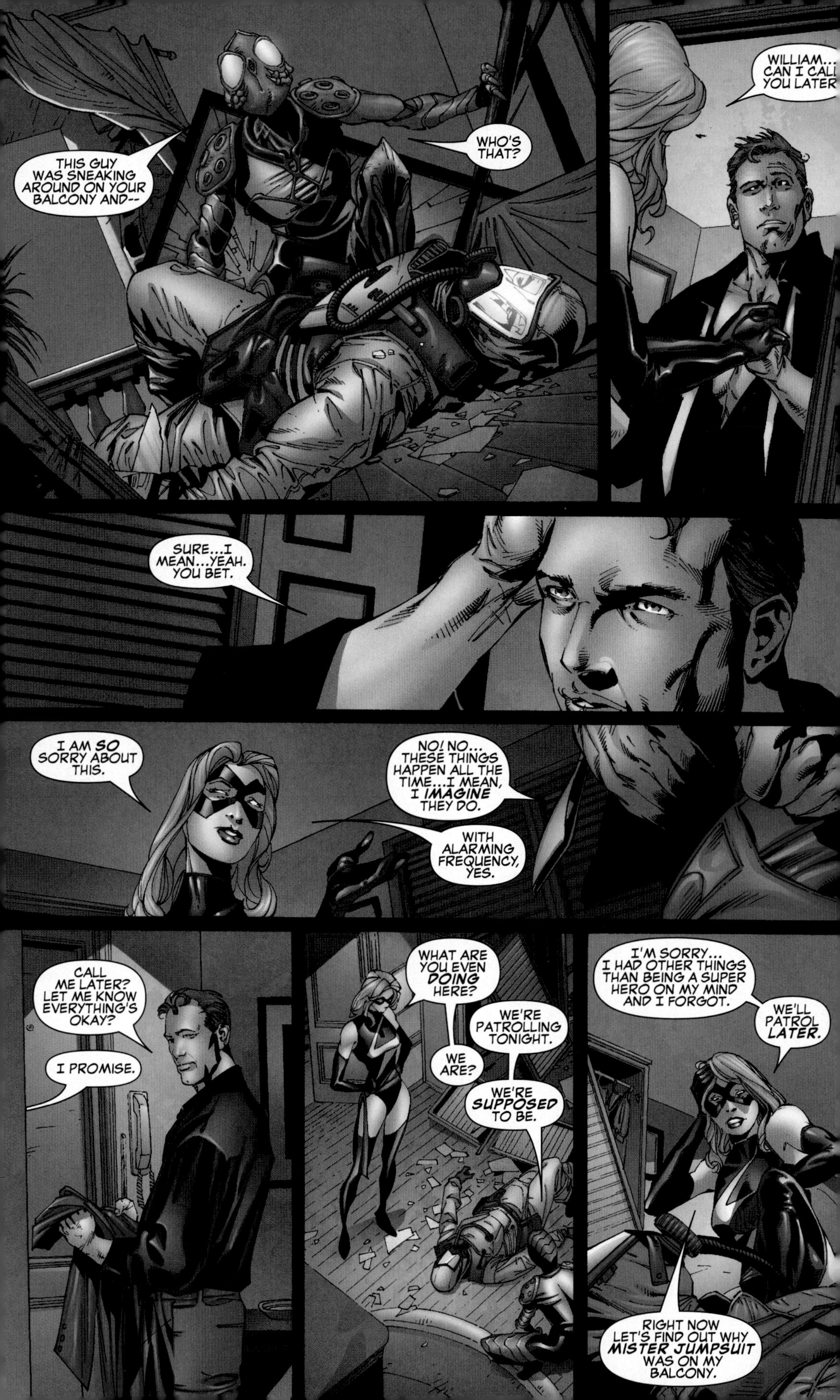

THIS GUY WAS SNEAKING AROUND ON YOUR BALCONY AND--
WHO'S THAT?
WILLIAM... CAN I CALL YOU LATER
SURE...I MEAN...YEAH. YOU BET.
I AM SO SORRY ABOUT THIS.
NO! NO... THESE THINGS HAPPEN ALL THE TIME...I MEAN, I IMAGINE THEY DO.
WITH ALARMING FREQUENCY, YES.
CALL ME LATER? LET ME KNOW EVERYTHING'S OKAY?
I PROMISE.
WHAT ARE YOU EVEN DOING HERE?
WE'RE PATROLLING TONIGHT.
WE ARE?
WE'RE SUPPOSED TO BE.
I'M SORRY... I HAD OTHER THINGS THAN BEING A SUPER HERO ON MY MIND AND I FORGOT.
WE'LL PATROL LATER.
RIGHT NOW LET'S FIND OUT WHY MISTER JUMPSUIT WAS ON MY BALCONY.

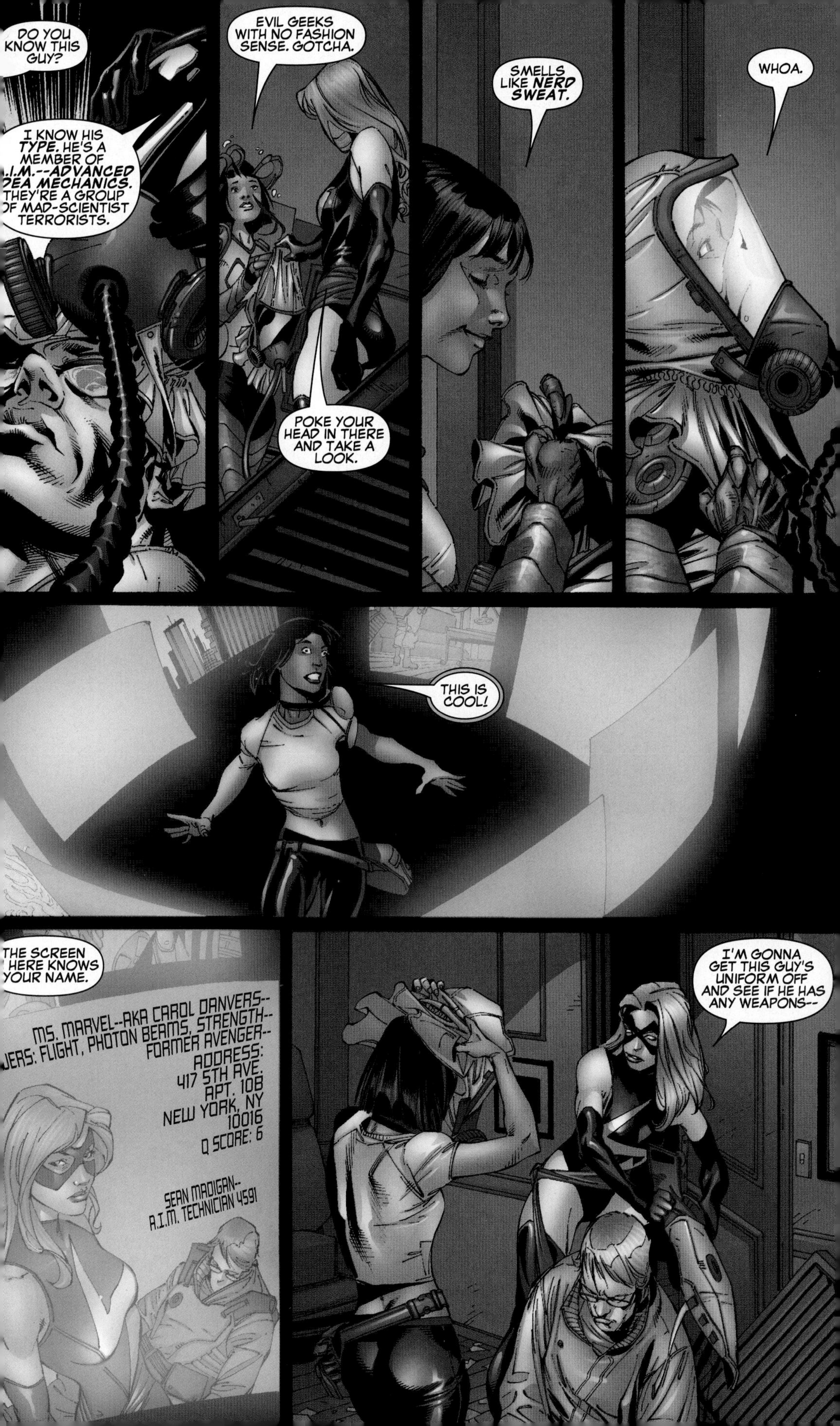
DO YOU KNOW THIS GUY?
I KNOW HIS TYPE. HE'S A MEMBER OF A.I.M.--ADVANCED IDEA MECHANICS. THEY'RE A GROUP OF MAD-SCIENTIST TERRORISTS.
EVIL GEEKS WITH NO FASHION SENSE. GOTCHA.
POKE YOUR HEAD IN THERE AND TAKE A LOOK.
SMELLS LIKE NERD SWEAT.
WHOA.
THIS IS COOL!
THE SCREEN HERE KNOWS YOUR NAME.
MS. MARVEL--AKA CAROL DANVERS--
WERS: FLIGHT, PHOTON BEAMS, STRENGTH--
FORMER AVENGER--
ADDRESS:
417 5TH AVE.
APT. 10B
NEW YORK, NY
10016
Q SCORE: 6
SEAN MADIGAN--
A.I.M. TECHNICIAN 4591
I'M GONNA GET THIS GUY'S UNIFORM OFF AND SEE IF HE HAS ANY WEAPONS--

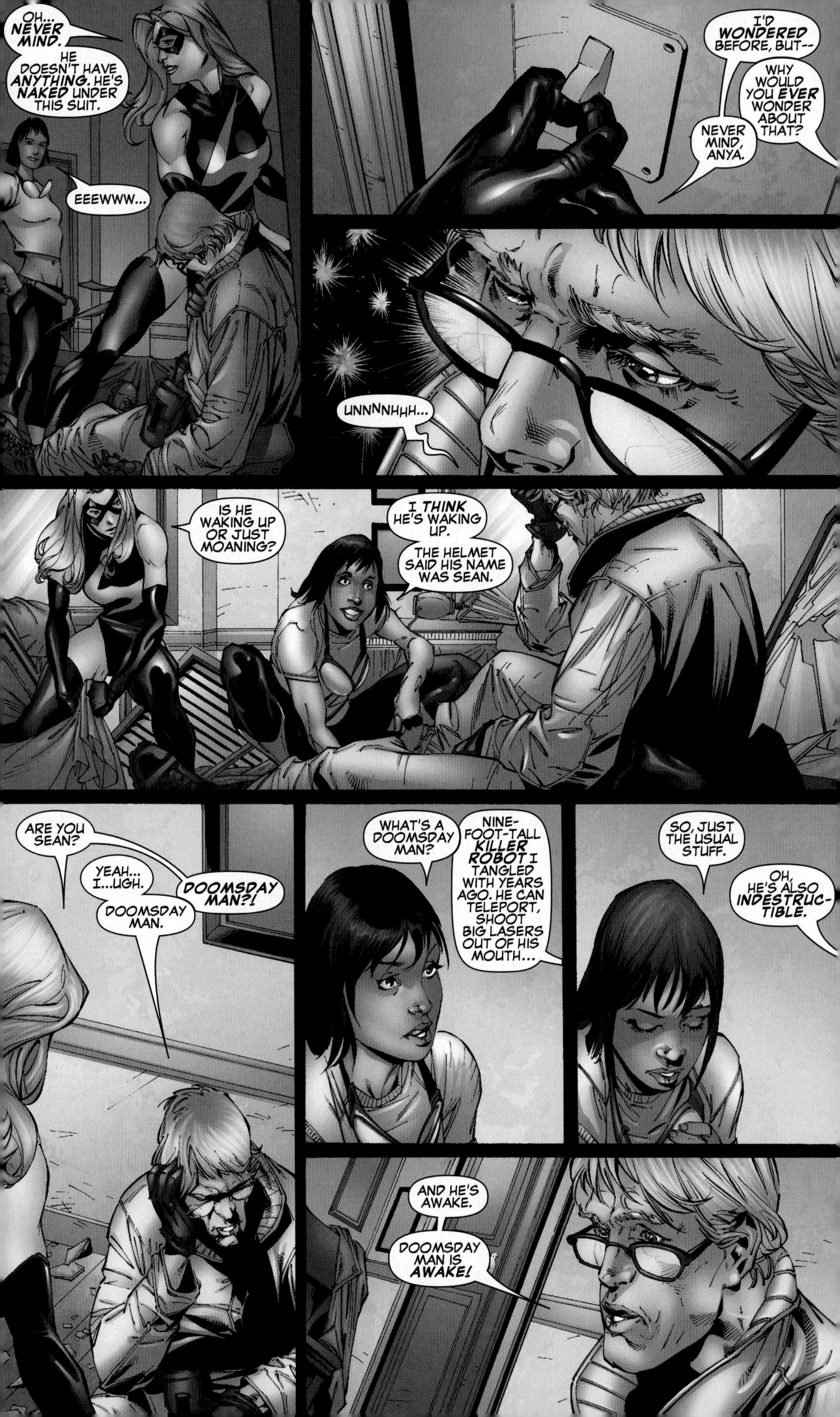
OH... NEVER MIND.
HE DOESN'T HAVE ANYTHING. HE'S NAKED UNDER THIS SUIT.
EEEWWW...
I'D WONDERED BEFORE, BUT--
WHY WOULD YOU EVER WONDER ABOUT THAT?
NEVER MIND, ANYA.
UNNNNHHH...
IS HE WAKING UP OR JUST MOANING?
I THINK HE'S WAKING UP.
THE HELMET SAID HIS NAME WAS SEAN.
ARE YOU SEAN?
YEAH... I...UGH.
DOOMSDAY MAN.
DOOMSDAY MAN?!
WHAT'S A DOOMSDAY MAN?
NINE-FOOT-TALL KILLER ROBOT I TANGLED WITH YEARS AGO. HE CAN TELEPORT, SHOOT BIG LASERS OUT OF HIS MOUTH...
SO, JUST THE USUAL STUFF.
OH, HE'S ALSO INDESTRUC-TIBLE.
AND HE'S AWAKE.
DOOMSDAY MAN IS AWAKE!

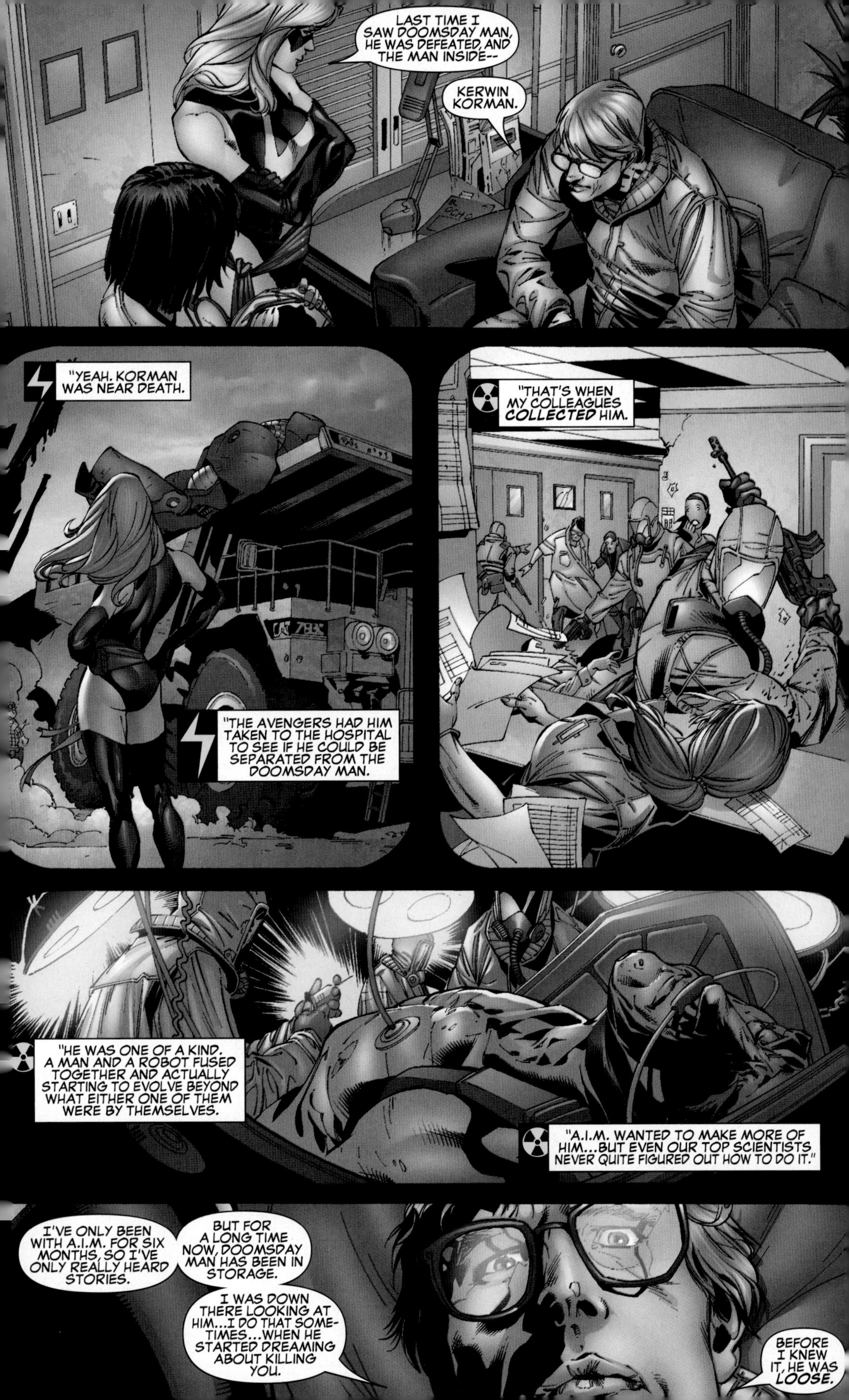
LAST TIME I SAW DOOMSDAY MAN, HE WAS DEFEATED, AND THE MAN INSIDE--
KERWIN KORMAN.
"YEAH. KORMAN WAS NEAR DEATH.
"THE AVENGERS HAD HIM TAKEN TO THE HOSPITAL TO SEE IF HE COULD BE SEPARATED FROM THE DOOMSDAY MAN.
"THAT'S WHEN MY COLLEAGUES COLLECTED HIM.
"HE WAS ONE OF A KIND. A MAN AND A ROBOT FUSED TOGETHER AND ACTUALLY STARTING TO EVOLVE BEYOND WHAT EITHER ONE OF THEM WERE BY THEMSELVES.
"A.I.M. WANTED TO MAKE MORE OF HIM...BUT EVEN OUR TOP SCIENTISTS NEVER QUITE FIGURED OUT HOW TO DO IT."
I'VE ONLY BEEN WITH A.I.M. FOR SIX MONTHS, SO I'VE ONLY REALLY HEARD STORIES.
BUT FOR A LONG TIME NOW, DOOMSDAY MAN HAS BEEN IN STORAGE.
I WAS DOWN THERE LOOKING AT HIM...I DO THAT SOME-TIMES...WHEN HE STARTED DREAMING ABOUT KILLING YOU.
BEFORE I KNEW IT, HE WAS LOOSE.

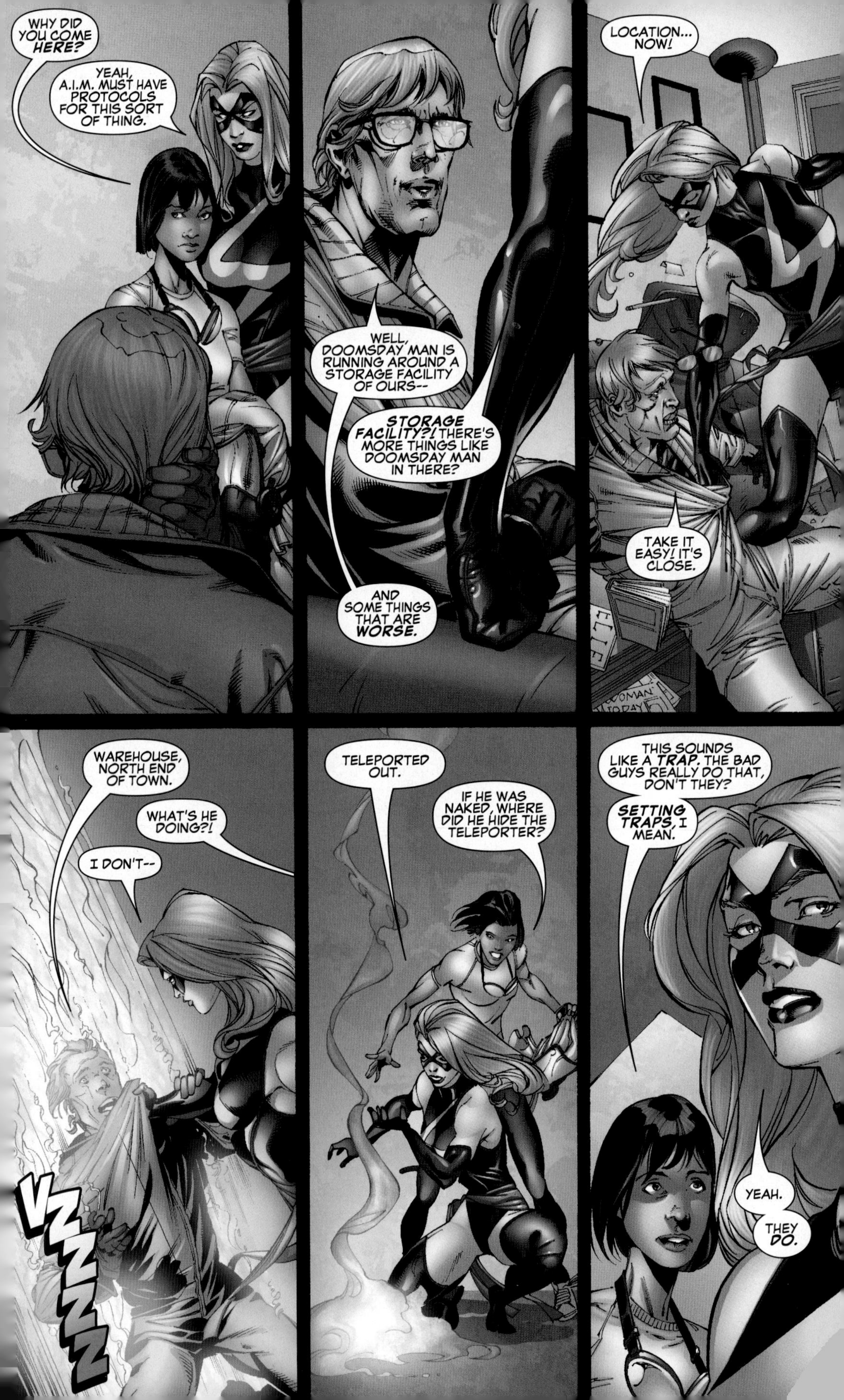
WHY DID YOU COME HERE?
YEAH, A.I.M. MUST HAVE PROTOCOLS FOR THIS SORT OF THING.
WELL, DOOMSDAY MAN IS RUNNING AROUND A STORAGE FACILITY OF OURS--
STORAGE FACILITY?! THERE'S MORE THINGS LIKE DOOMSDAY MAN IN THERE?
AND SOME THINGS THAT ARE WORSE.
LOCATION... NOW!
TAKE IT EASY! IT'S CLOSE.
WAREHOUSE, NORTH END OF TOWN.
WHAT'S HE DOING?!
I DON'T--
VZZZZ
TELEPORTED OUT.
IF HE WAS NAKED, WHERE DID HE HIDE THE TELEPORTER?
THIS SOUNDS LIKE A TRAP. THE BAD GUYS REALLY DO THAT, DON'T THEY?
SETTING TRAPS, I MEAN.
YEAH.
THEY DO.

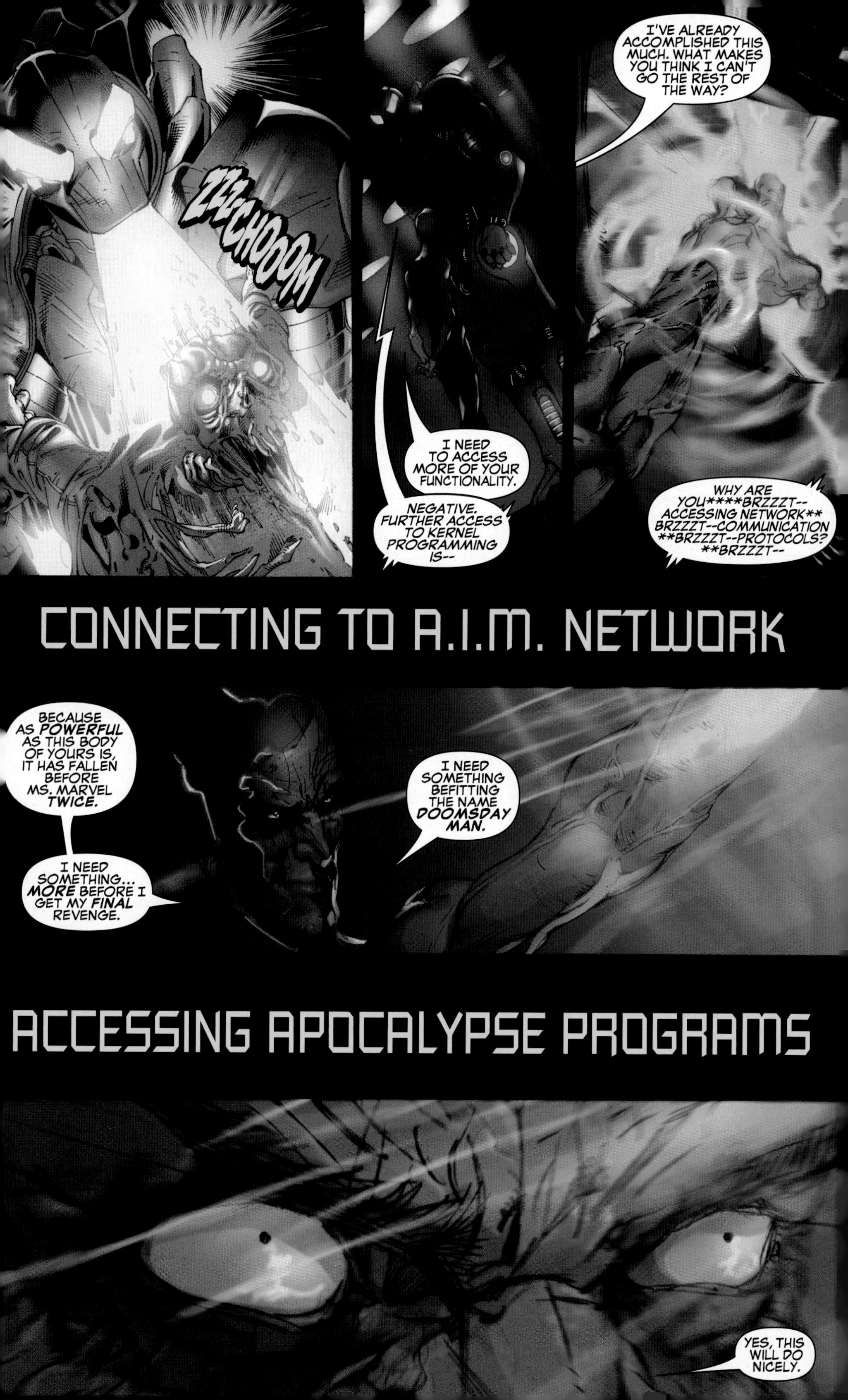
ZZZ-CHOOOM
I NEED TO ACCESS MORE OF YOUR FUNCTIONALITY.
NEGATIVE. FURTHER ACCESS TO KERNEL PROGRAMMING IS--
I'VE ALREADY ACCOMPLISHED THIS MUCH. WHAT MAKES YOU THINK I CAN'T GO THE REST OF THE WAY?
WHY ARE YOU****BRZZZT--ACCESSING NETWORK** BRZZZT--COMMUNICATION **BRZZZT--PROTOCOLS? **BRZZZT--
CONNECTING TO A.I.M. NETWORK
BECAUSE AS POWERFUL AS THIS BODY OF YOURS IS, IT HAS FALLEN BEFORE MS. MARVEL TWICE.
I NEED SOMETHING... MORE BEFORE I GET MY FINAL REVENGE.
I NEED SOMETHING BEFITTING THE NAME DOOMSDAY MAN.
ACCESSING APOCALYPSE PROGRAMS
YES, THIS WILL DO NICELY.

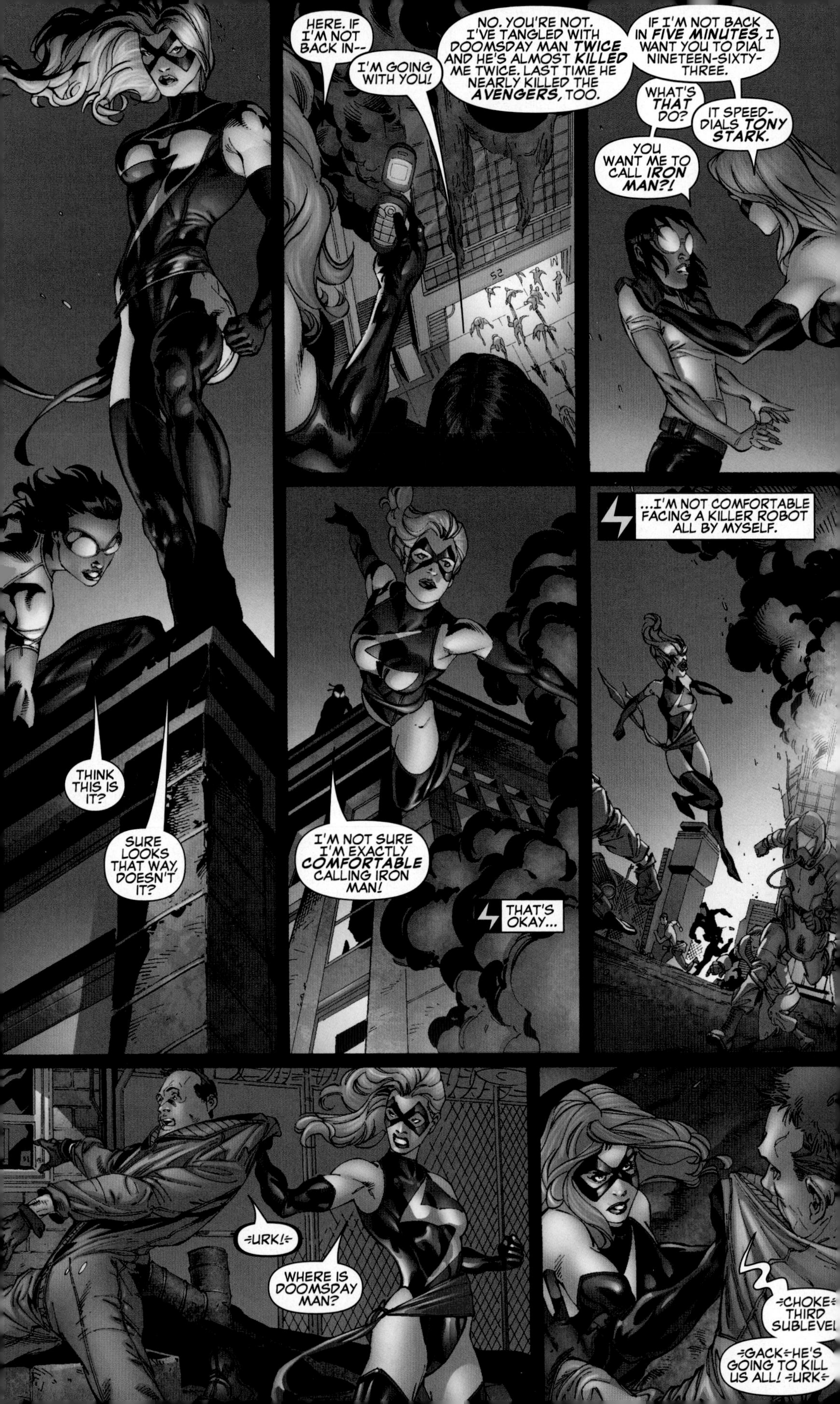
HERE. IF I'M NOT BACK IN--
I'M GOING WITH YOU!
NO. YOU'RE NOT. I'VE TANGLED WITH DOOMSDAY MAN TWICE AND HE'S ALMOST KILLED ME TWICE. LAST TIME HE NEARLY KILLED THE AVENGERS, TOO.
IF I'M NOT BACK IN FIVE MINUTES, I WANT YOU TO DIAL NINETEEN-SIXTY-THREE.
WHAT'S THAT DO?
IT SPEED-DIALS TONY STARK.
YOU WANT ME TO CALL IRON MAN?!
THINK THIS IS IT?
SURE LOOKS THAT WAY, DOESN'T IT?
I'M NOT SURE I'M EXACTLY COMFORTABLE CALLING IRON MAN!
THAT'S OKAY...
...I'M NOT COMFORTABLE FACING A KILLER ROBOT ALL BY MYSELF.
URK!
WHERE IS DOOMSDAY MAN?
CHOKE THIRD SUBLEVEL
GACK HE'S GOING TO KILL US ALL! URK

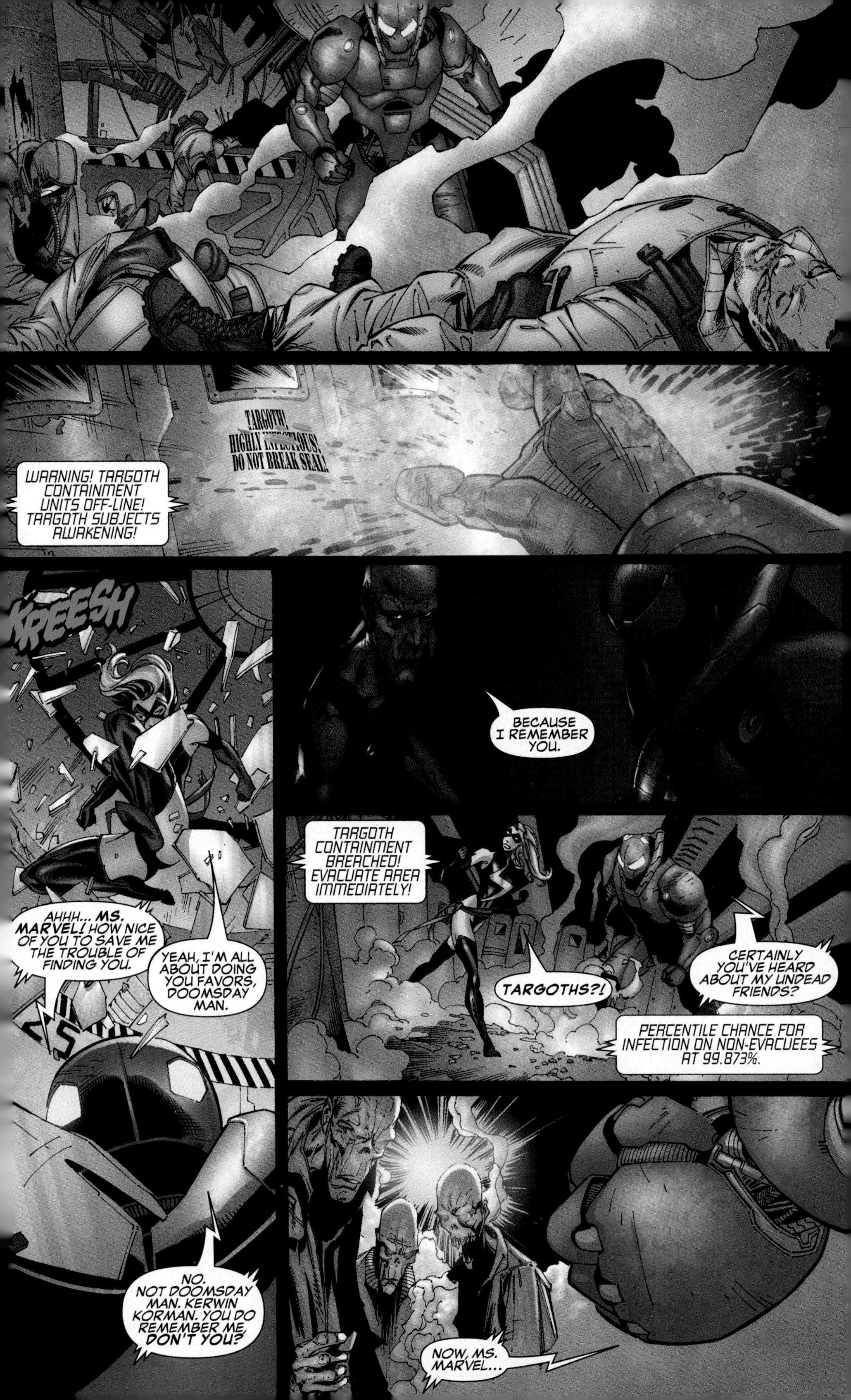
TARGOTH!
DO NOT BREAK SEAL!
WARNING! TARGOTH CONTAINMENT UNITS OFF-LINE! TARGOTH SUBJECTS AWAKENING!
KREESH
AHHH... MS. MARVEL! HOW NICE OF YOU TO SAVE ME THE TROUBLE OF FINDING YOU.
YEAH, I'M ALL ABOUT DOING YOU FAVORS, DOOMSDAY MAN.
NO. NOT DOOMSDAY MAN. KERWIN KORMAN. YOU DO REMEMBER ME, DON'T YOU?
BECAUSE I REMEMBER YOU.
TARGOTH CONTAINMENT BREACHED! EVACUATE AREA IMMEDIATELY!
TARGOTHS?!
CERTAINLY YOU'VE HEARD ABOUT MY UNDEAD FRIENDS?
PERCENTILE CHANCE FOR INFECTION ON NON-EVACUEES AT 99.873%.
NOW, MS. MARVEL...

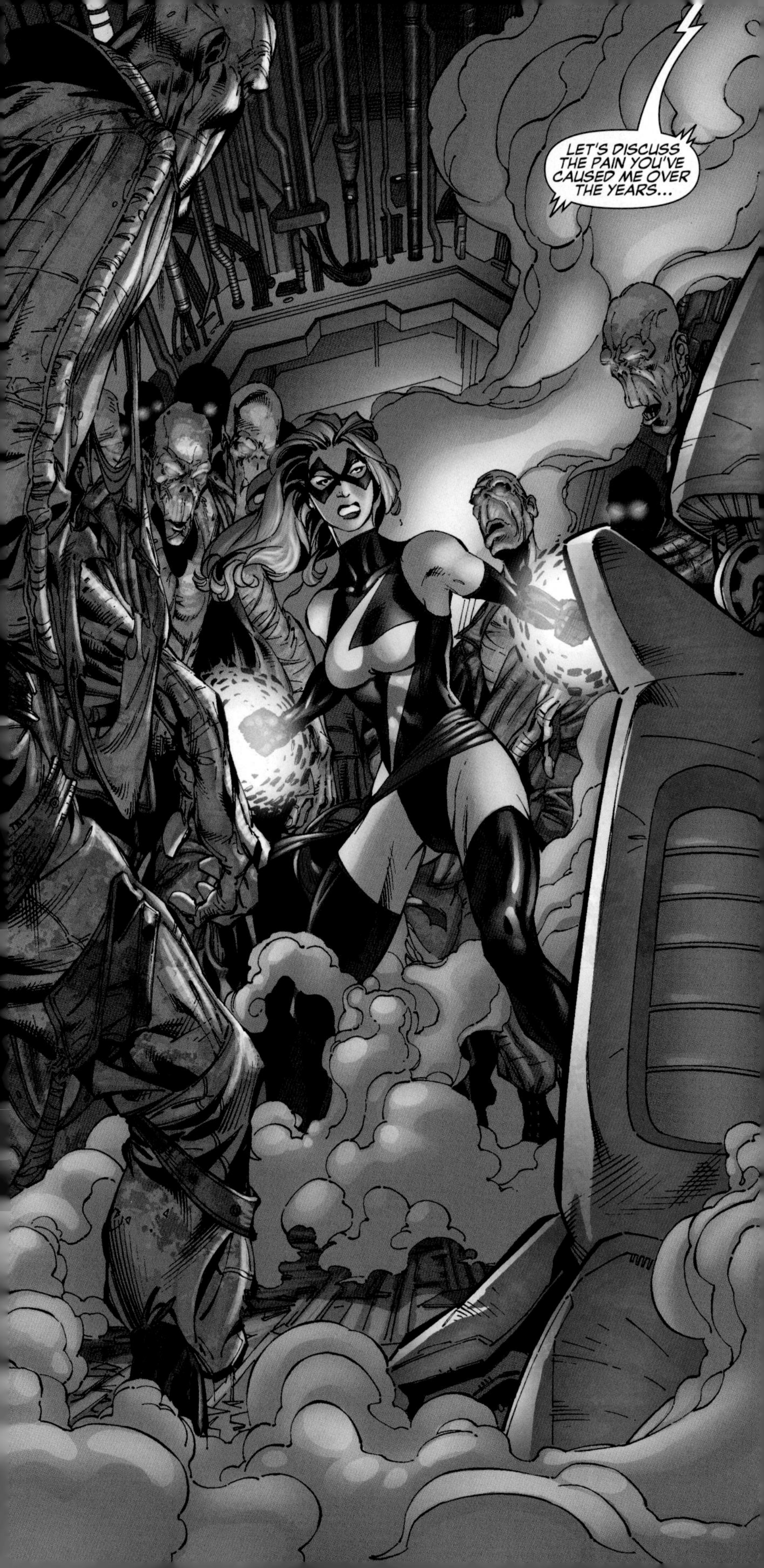
LET'S DISCUSS THE PAIN YOU'VE CAUSED ME OVER THE YEARS...

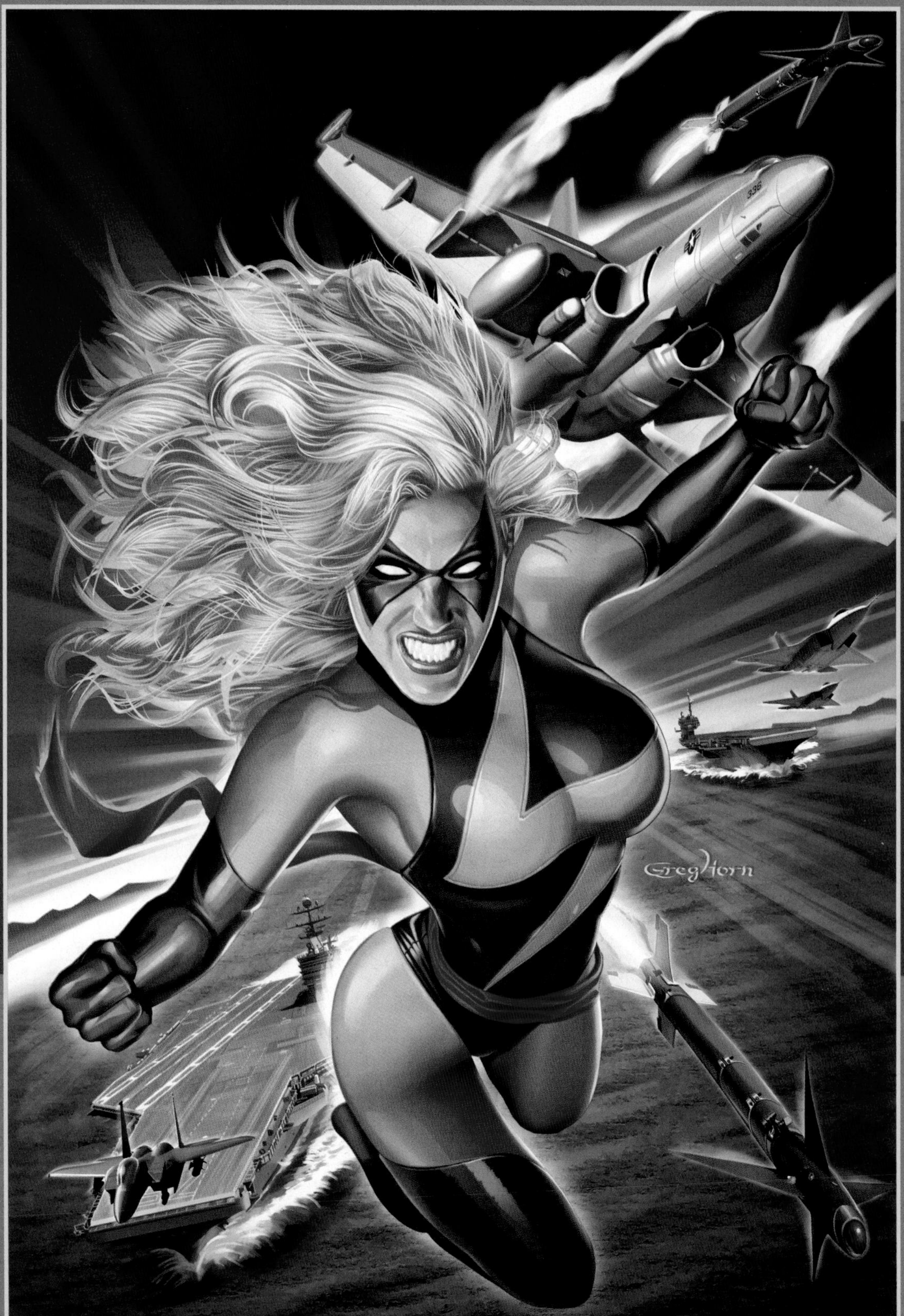
336
Greg Horn

12

"SOMETHING DARK IS COMING"

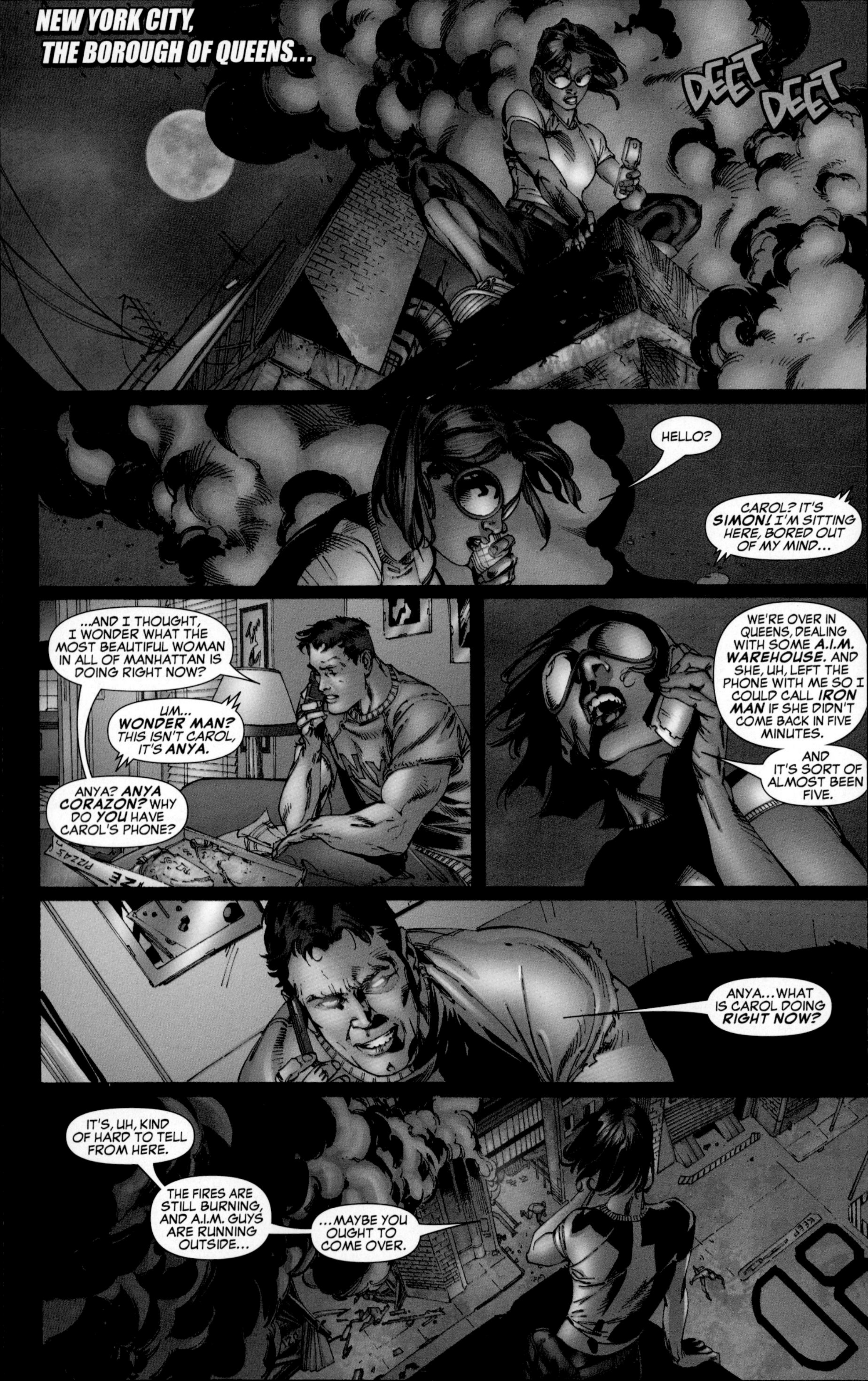
NEW YORK CITY, THE BOROUGH OF QUEENS...
DEET DEET
HELLO?
CAROL? IT'S SIMON! I'M SITTING HERE, BORED OUT OF MY MIND...
...AND I THOUGHT, I WONDER WHAT THE MOST BEAUTIFUL WOMAN IN ALL OF MANHATTAN IS DOING RIGHT NOW?
UM... WONDER MAN? THIS ISN'T CAROL, IT'S ANYA.
ANYA? ANYA CORAZON? WHY DO YOU HAVE CAROL'S PHONE?
WE'RE OVER IN QUEENS, DEALING WITH SOME A.I.M. WAREHOUSE. AND SHE, UH, LEFT THE PHONE WITH ME SO I COULD CALL IRON MAN IF SHE DIDN'T COME BACK IN FIVE MINUTES.
AND IT'S SORT OF ALMOST BEEN FIVE.
ANYA...WHAT IS CAROL DOING RIGHT NOW?
IT'S, UH, KIND OF HARD TO TELL FROM HERE.
THE FIRES ARE STILL BURNING, AND A.I.M. GUYS ARE RUNNING OUTSIDE...
...MAYBE YOU OUGHT TO COME OVER.

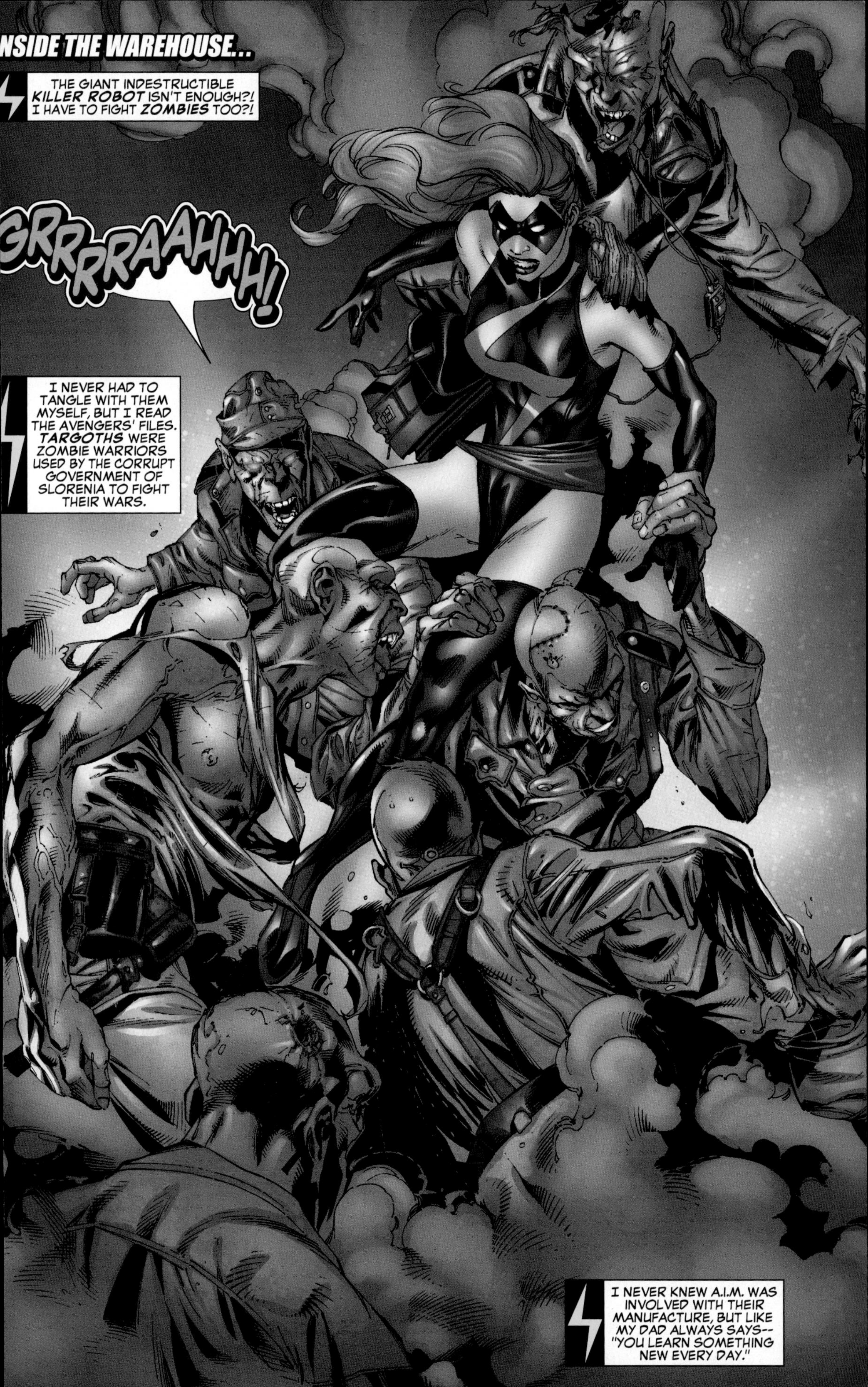

NSIDE THE WAREHOUSE...
THE GIANT INDESTRUCTIBLE KILLER ROBOT ISN'T ENOUGH?! I HAVE TO FIGHT ZOMBIES TOO?!
GRRRRAAHHH!
I NEVER HAD TO TANGLE WITH THEM MYSELF, BUT I READ THE AVENGERS' FILES. TARGOTHS WERE ZOMBIE WARRIORS USED BY THE CORRUPT GOVERNMENT OF SLORENIA TO FIGHT THEIR WARS.
I NEVER KNEW A.I.M. WAS INVOLVED WITH THEIR MANUFACTURE, BUT LIKE MY DAD ALWAYS SAYS-- "YOU LEARN SOMETHING NEW EVERY DAY."

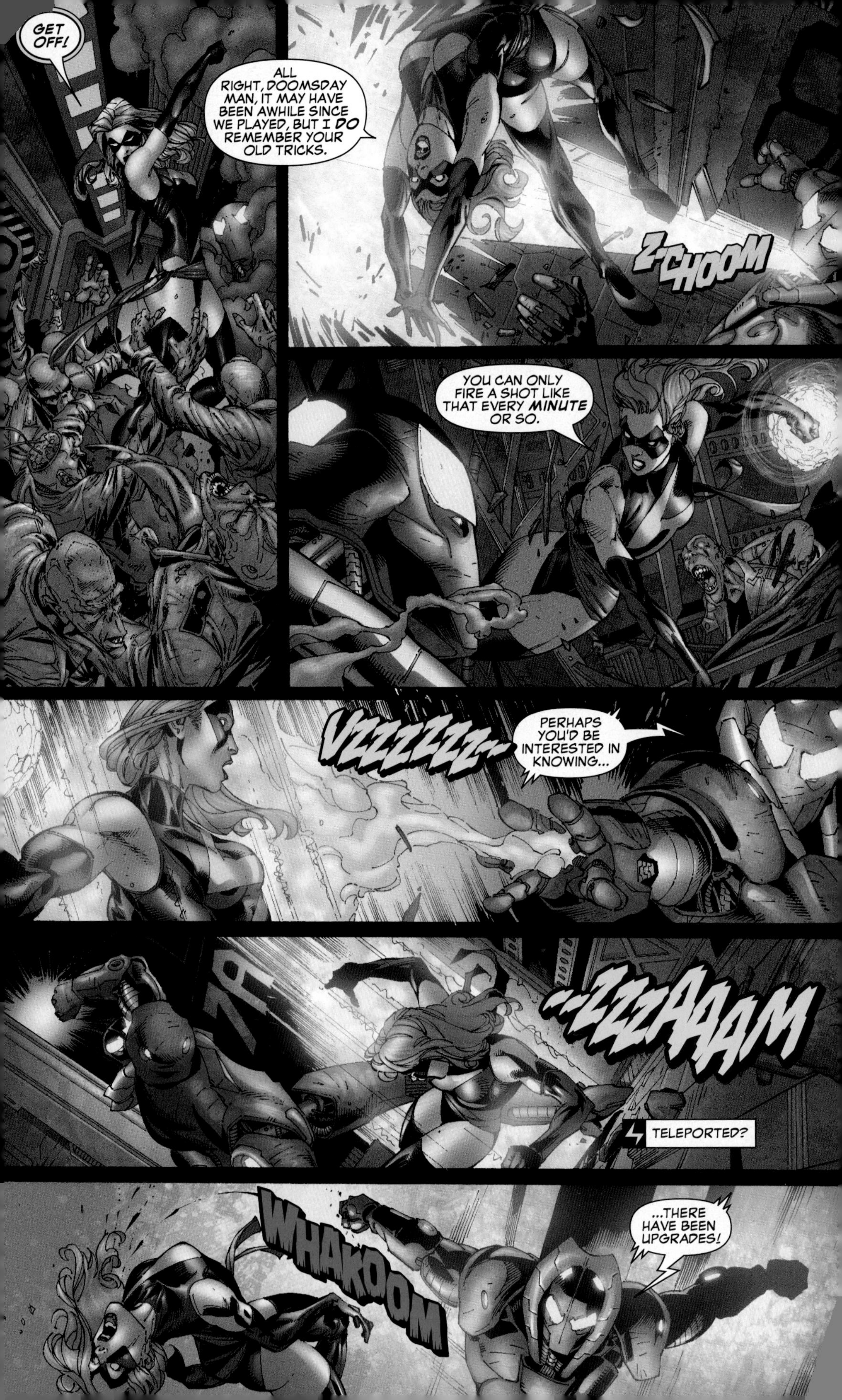
GET OFF!
ALL RIGHT, DOOMSDAY MAN, IT MAY HAVE BEEN AWHILE SINCE WE PLAYED, BUT I DO REMEMBER YOUR OLD TRICKS.
Z-CHOOM
YOU CAN ONLY FIRE A SHOT LIKE THAT EVERY MINUTE OR SO.
VZZZZZZ--
PERHAPS YOU'D BE INTERESTED IN KNOWING...
--ZZZAAAM
TELEPORTED?
WHAKOOM
...THERE HAVE BEEN UPGRADES!

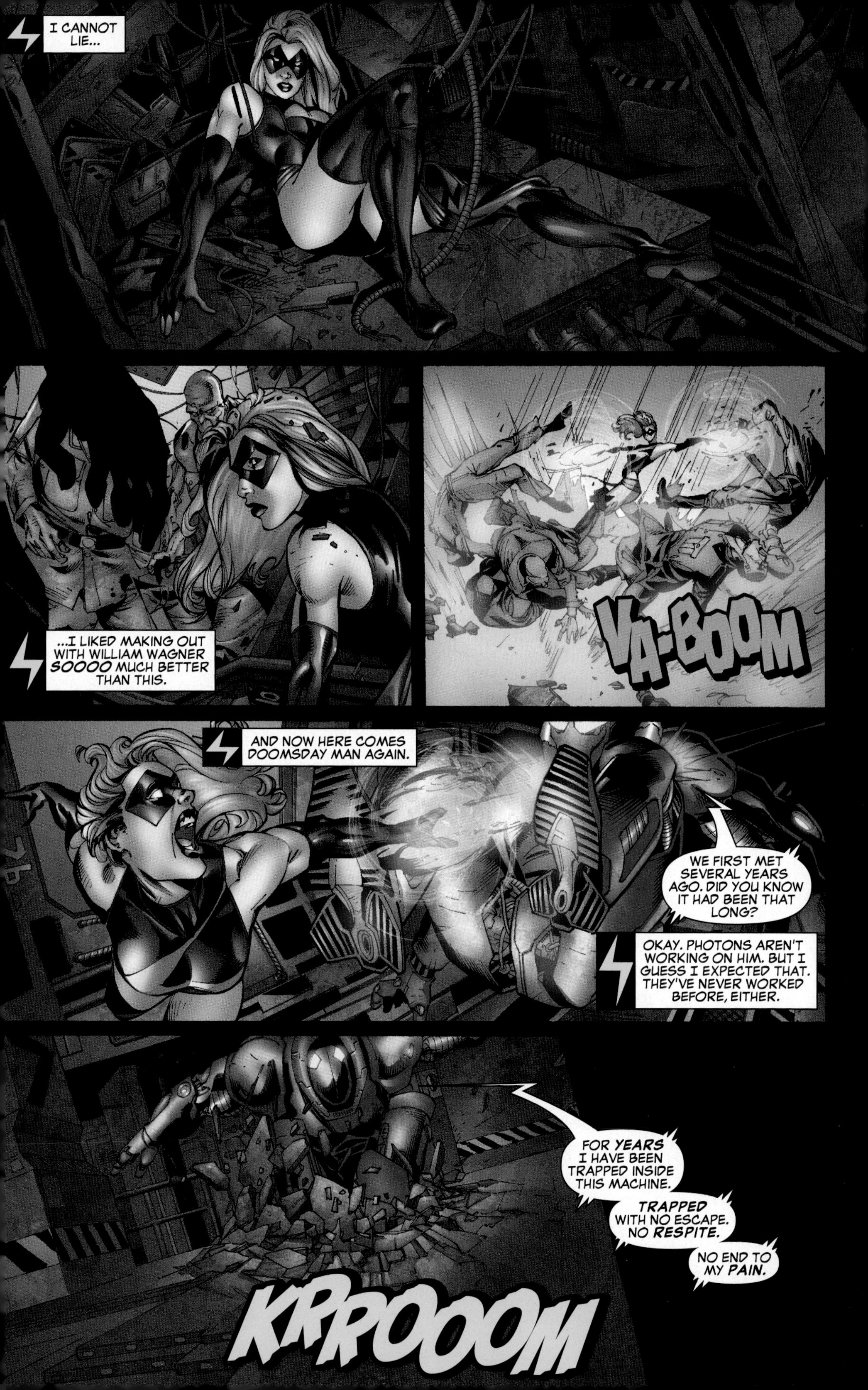
I CANNOT LIE...
...I LIKED MAKING OUT WITH WILLIAM WAGNER SOOOO MUCH BETTER THAN THIS.
VA-BOOM
AND NOW HERE COMES DOOMSDAY MAN AGAIN.
WE FIRST MET SEVERAL YEARS AGO. DID YOU KNOW IT HAD BEEN THAT LONG?
OKAY. PHOTONS AREN'T WORKING ON HIM. BUT I GUESS I EXPECTED THAT. THEY'VE NEVER WORKED BEFORE, EITHER.
FOR YEARS I HAVE BEEN TRAPPED INSIDE THIS MACHINE.
TRAPPED WITH NO ESCAPE. NO RESPITE.
NO END TO MY PAIN.
KRROOOM

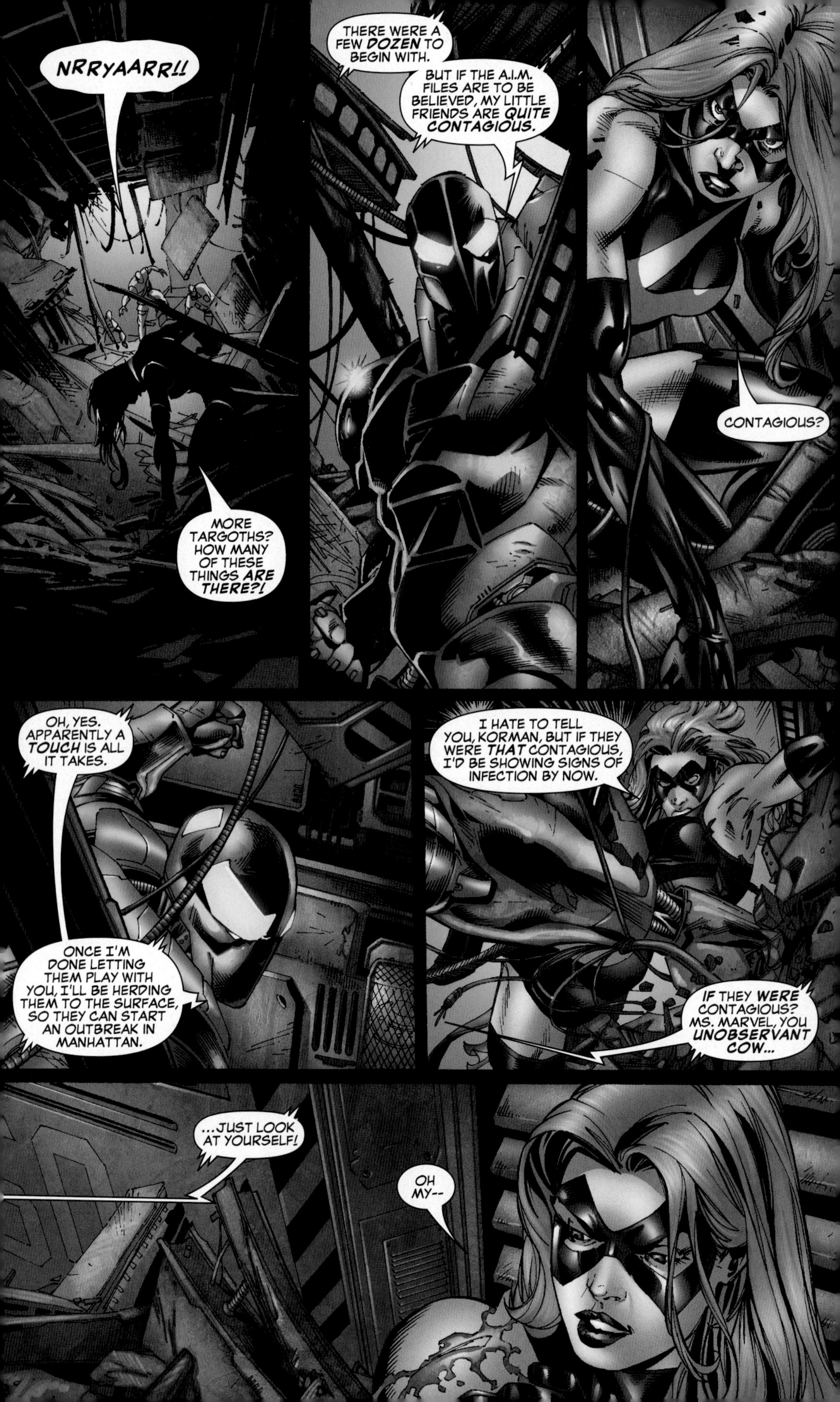

NRRYAARR!!
MORE TARGOTHS? HOW MANY OF THESE THINGS ARE THERE?!
THERE WERE A FEW DOZEN TO BEGIN WITH.
BUT IF THE A.I.M. FILES ARE TO BE BELIEVED, MY LITTLE FRIENDS ARE QUITE CONTAGIOUS.
CONTAGIOUS?
OH, YES. APPARENTLY A TOUCH IS ALL IT TAKES.
ONCE I'M DONE LETTING THEM PLAY WITH YOU, I'LL BE HERDING THEM TO THE SURFACE, SO THEY CAN START AN OUTBREAK IN MANHATTAN.
I HATE TO TELL YOU, KORMAN, BUT IF THEY WERE THAT CONTAGIOUS, I'D BE SHOWING SIGNS OF INFECTION BY NOW.
IF THEY WERE CONTAGIOUS? MS. MARVEL, YOU UNOBSERVANT COW...
...JUST LOOK AT YOURSELF!
OH MY--

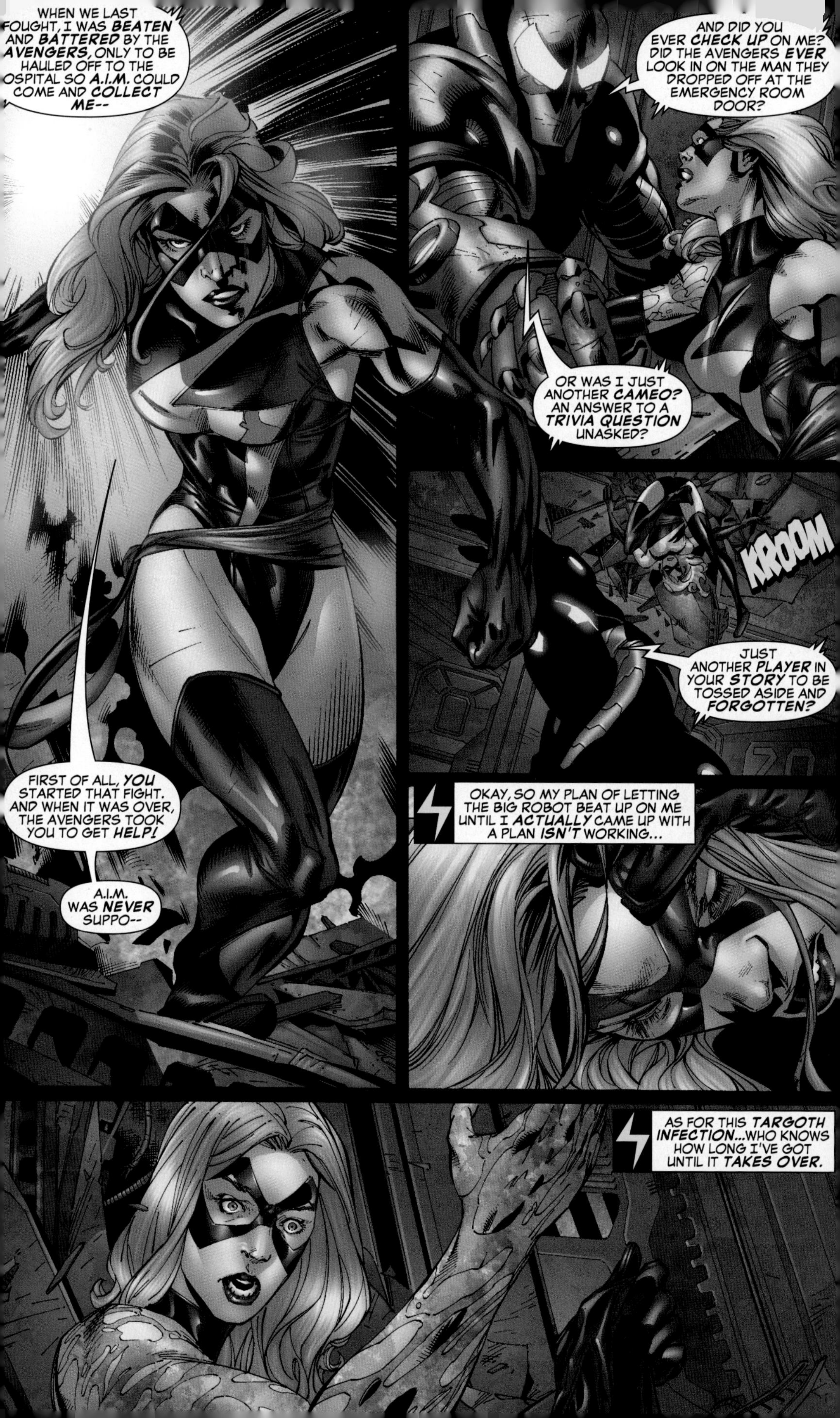
WHEN WE LAST FOUGHT, I WAS BEATEN AND BATTERED BY THE AVENGERS, ONLY TO BE HAULED OFF TO THE OSPITAL SO A.I.M. COULD COME AND COLLECT ME--
AND DID YOU EVER CHECK UP ON ME? DID THE AVENGERS EVER LOOK IN ON THE MAN THEY DROPPED OFF AT THE EMERGENCY ROOM DOOR?
OR WAS I JUST ANOTHER CAMEO? AN ANSWER TO A TRIVIA QUESTION UNASKED?
KROOM
JUST ANOTHER PLAYER IN YOUR STORY TO BE TOSSED ASIDE AND FORGOTTEN?
FIRST OF ALL, YOU STARTED THAT FIGHT. AND WHEN IT WAS OVER, THE AVENGERS TOOK YOU TO GET HELP!
A.I.M. WAS NEVER SUPPO--
OKAY, SO MY PLAN OF LETTING THE BIG ROBOT BEAT UP ON ME UNTIL I ACTUALLY CAME UP WITH A PLAN ISN'T WORKING...
AS FOR THIS TARGOTH INFECTION...WHO KNOWS HOW LONG I'VE GOT UNTIL IT TAKES OVER.

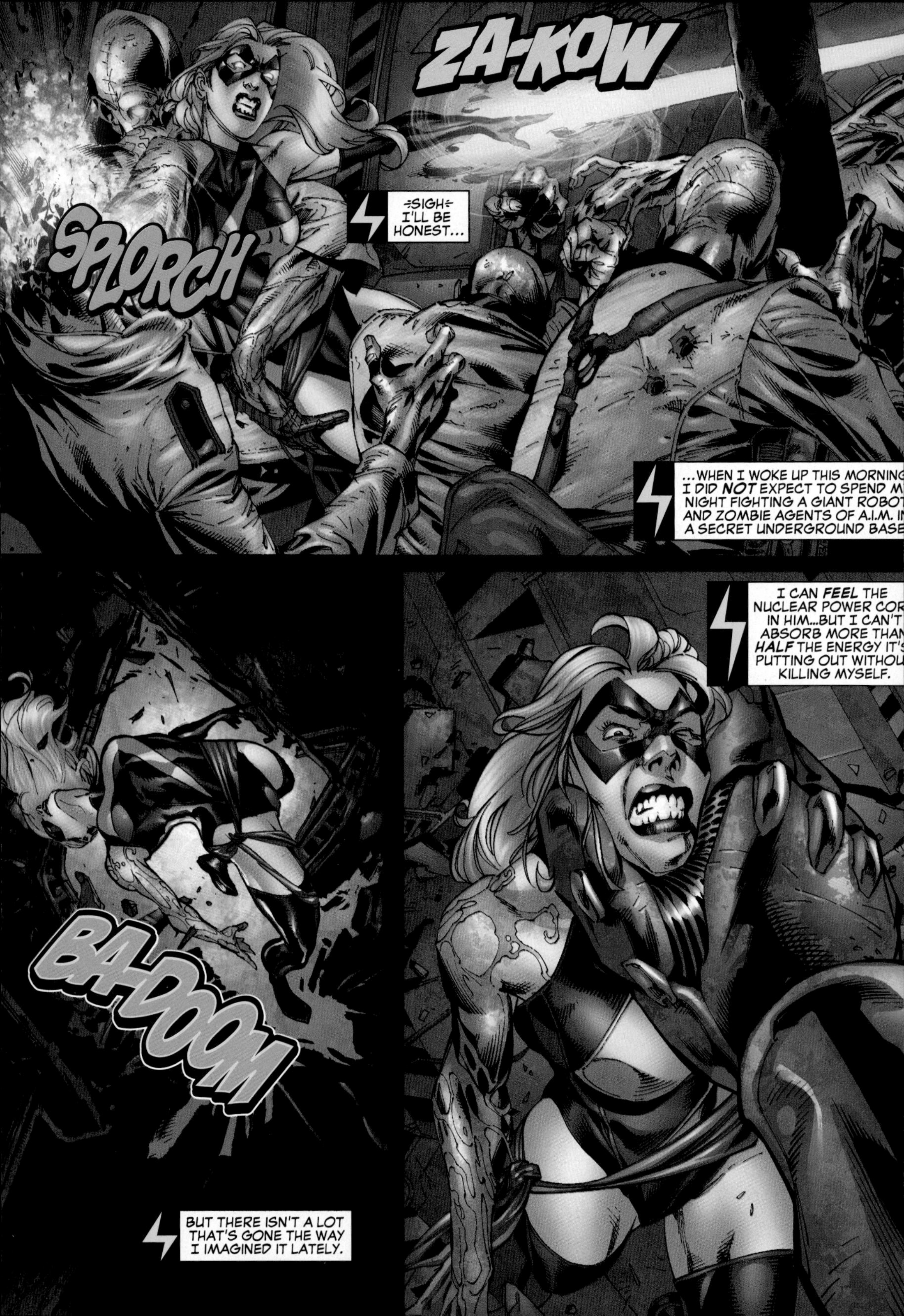

ZA-KOW
SPLORCH
=SIGH= I'LL BE HONEST...
...WHEN I WOKE UP THIS MORNING I DID NOT EXPECT TO SPEND MY NIGHT FIGHTING A GIANT ROBOT AND ZOMBIE AGENTS OF A.I.M. IN A SECRET UNDERGROUND BASE.
BA-DOOM
BUT THERE ISN'T A LOT THAT'S GONE THE WAY I IMAGINED IT LATELY.
I CAN FEEL THE NUCLEAR POWER CORE IN HIM...BUT I CAN'T ABSORB MORE THAN HALF THE ENERGY IT'S PUTTING OUT WITHOUT KILLING MYSELF.

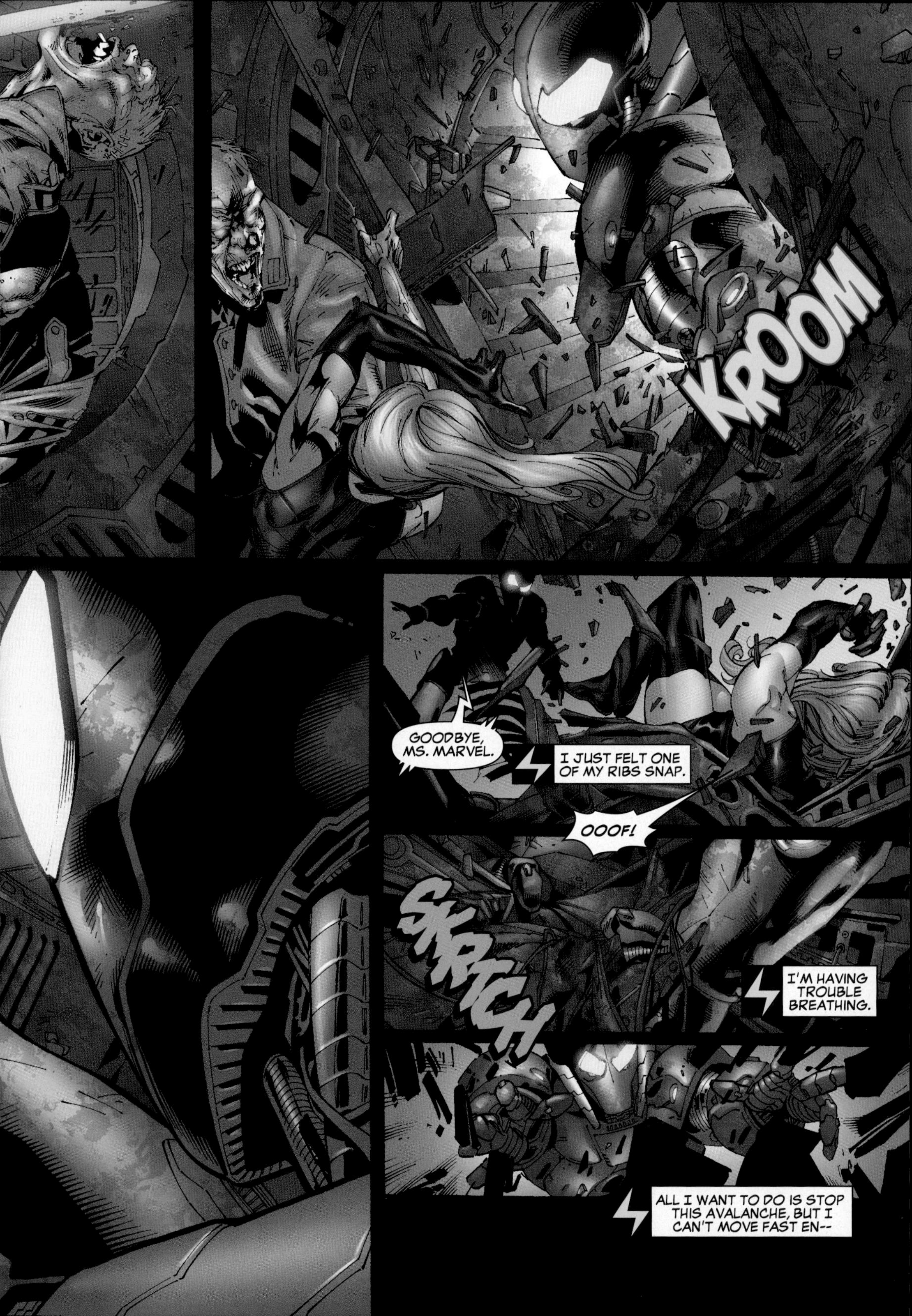
KROOM
GOODBYE, MS. MARVEL.
I JUST FELT ONE OF MY RIBS SNAP.
OOOF!
SKRTCH
I'M HAVING TROUBLE BREATHING.
ALL I WANT TO DO IS STOP THIS AVALANCHE, BUT I CAN'T MOVE FAST EN--

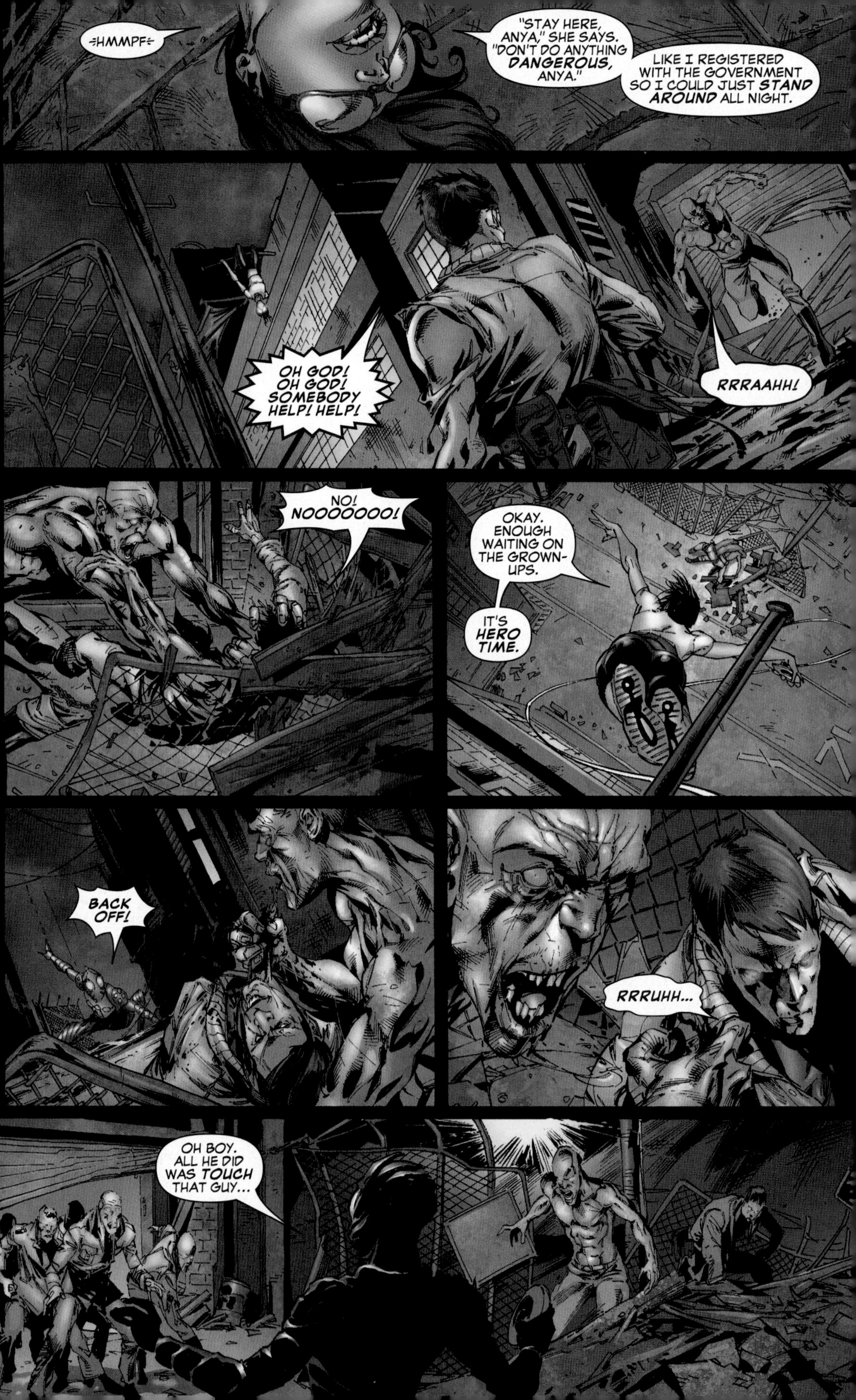

=HMMPF=
"STAY HERE, ANYA," SHE SAYS. "DON'T DO ANYTHING DANGEROUS, ANYA."
LIKE I REGISTERED WITH THE GOVERNMENT SO I COULD JUST STAND AROUND ALL NIGHT.
OH GOD! OH GOD! SOMEBODY HELP! HELP!
RRRAAHH!
NO! NOOOOOOO!
OKAY. ENOUGH WAITING ON THE GROWN-UPS.
IT'S HERO TIME.
BACK OFF!
RRRUHH...
OH BOY. ALL HE DID WAS TOUCH THAT GUY...

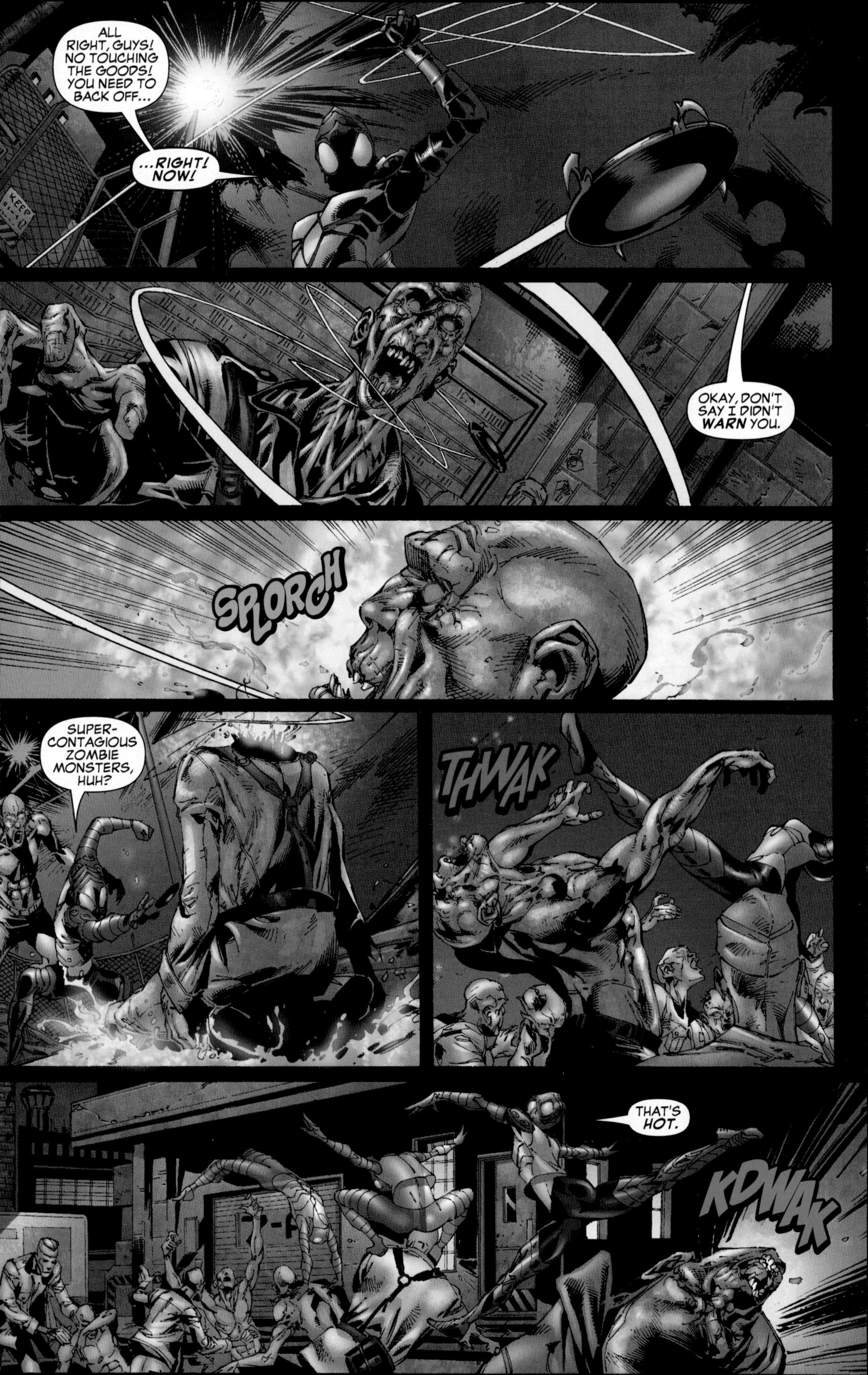
ALL RIGHT, GUYS! NO TOUCHING THE GOODS! YOU NEED TO BACK OFF...
...RIGHT! NOW!
OKAY, DON'T SAY I DIDN'T **WARN** YOU.
SPLORCH
SUPER-CONTAGIOUS ZOMBIE MONSTERS, HUH?
THWAK
THAT'S **HOT**.
KDWAK

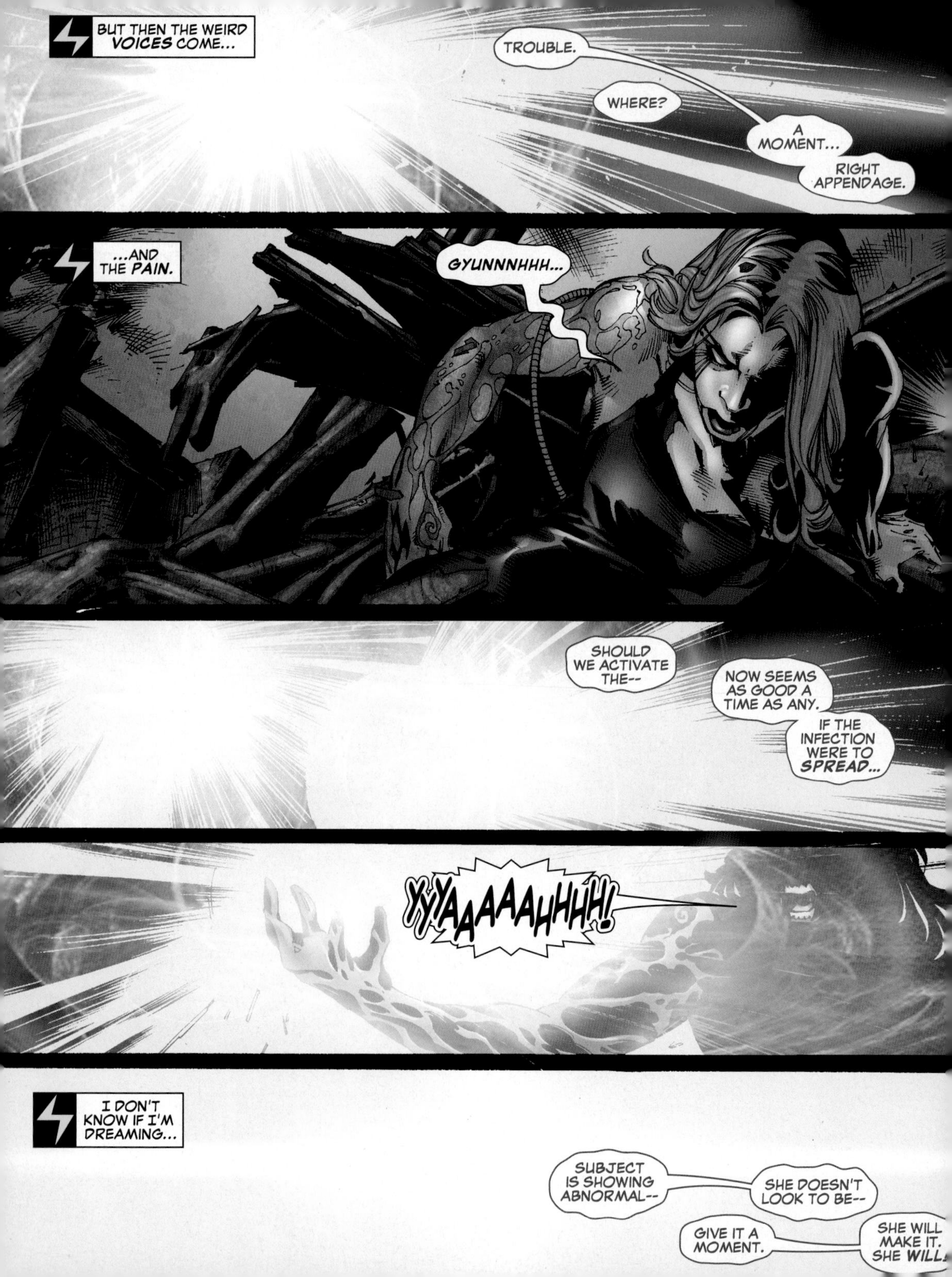
BUT THEN THE WEIRD VOICES COME...
TROUBLE.
WHERE?
A MOMENT...
RIGHT APPENDAGE.
...AND THE PAIN.
GYUNNNHHH...
SHOULD WE ACTIVATE THE--
NOW SEEMS AS GOOD A TIME AS ANY.
IF THE INFECTION WERE TO SPREAD...
YYYAAAAAHHHH!
I DON'T KNOW IF I'M DREAMING...
SUBJECT IS SHOWING ABNORMAL--
SHE DOESN'T LOOK TO BE--
GIVE IT A MOMENT.
SHE WILL MAKE IT. SHE WILL.

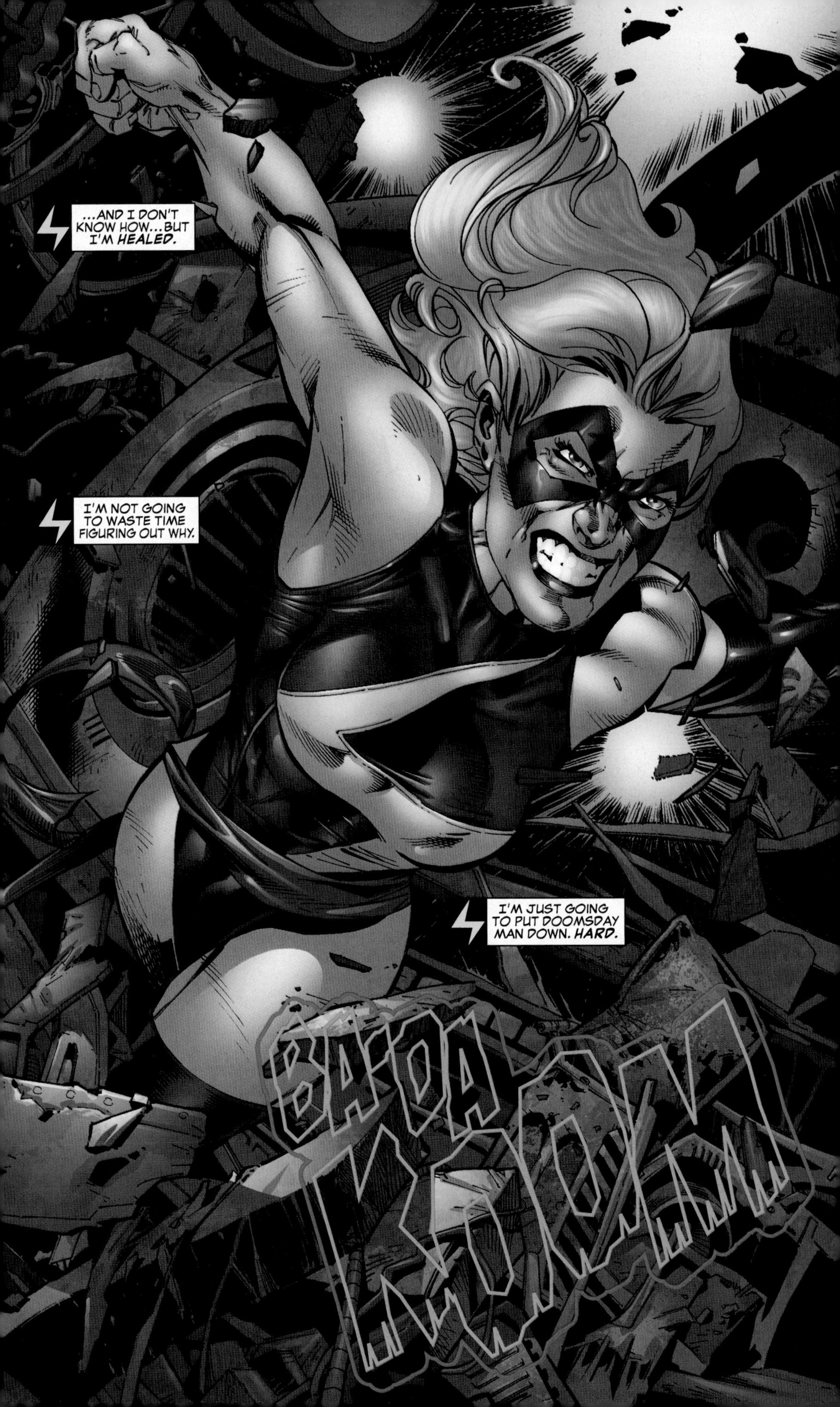
...AND I DON'T KNOW HOW...BUT I'M *HEALED*.
I'M NOT GOING TO WASTE TIME FIGURING OUT WHY.
I'M JUST GOING TO PUT DOOMSDAY MAN DOWN. *HARD*.
BADABOOM

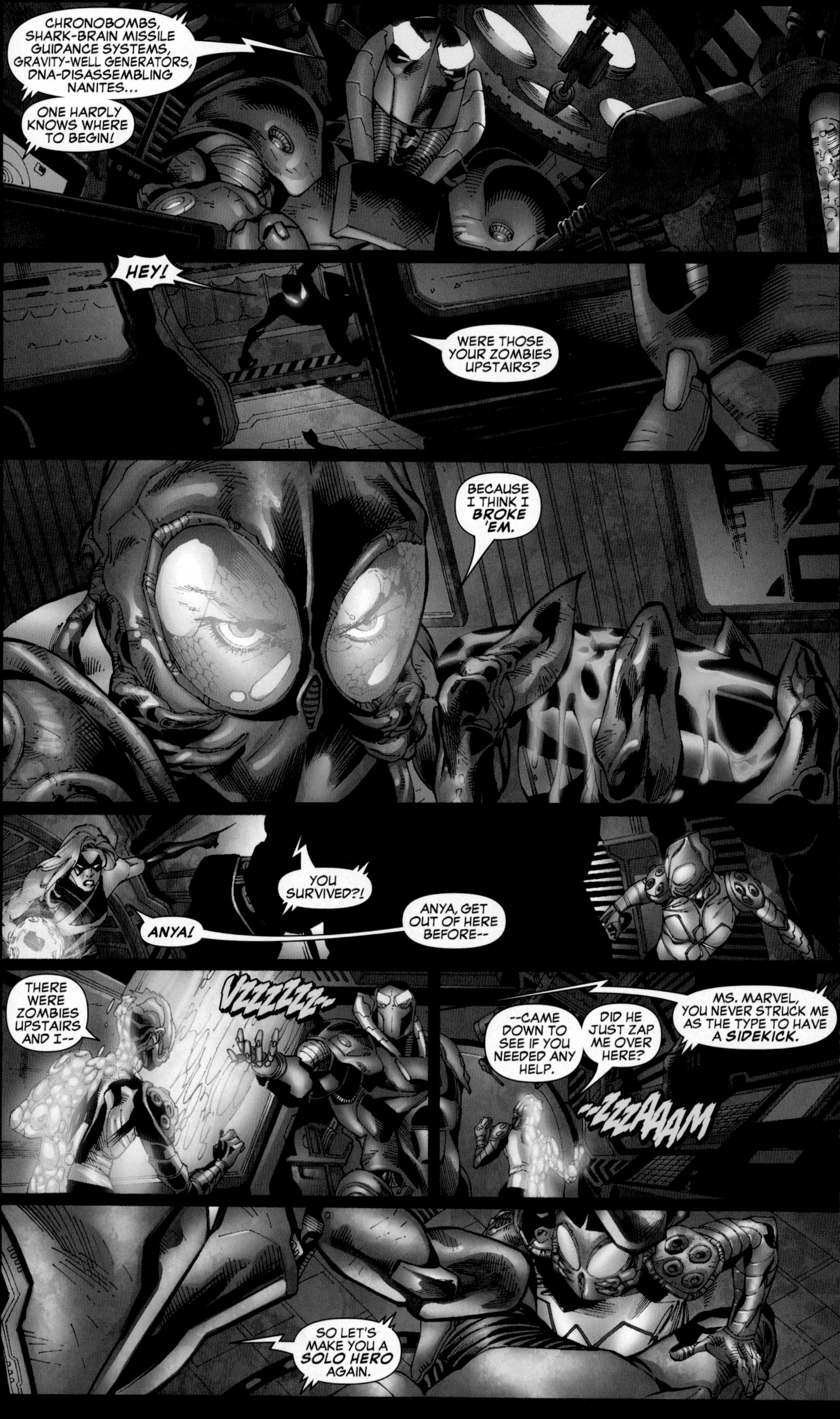
CHRONOBOMBS, SHARK-BRAIN MISSILE GUIDANCE SYSTEMS, GRAVITY-WELL GENERATORS, DNA-DISASSEMBLING NANITES...
ONE HARDLY KNOWS WHERE TO BEGIN!
HEY!
WERE THOSE YOUR ZOMBIES UPSTAIRS?
BECAUSE I THINK I BROKE 'EM.
YOU SURVIVED?!
ANYA!
ANYA, GET OUT OF HERE BEFORE--
THERE WERE ZOMBIES UPSTAIRS AND I--
VZZZZZZ--
--CAME DOWN TO SEE IF YOU NEEDED ANY HELP.
DID HE JUST ZAP ME OVER HERE?
MS. MARVEL, YOU NEVER STRUCK ME AS THE TYPE TO HAVE A SIDEKICK.
--ZZZAAAM
SO LET'S MAKE YOU A SOLO HERO AGAIN.

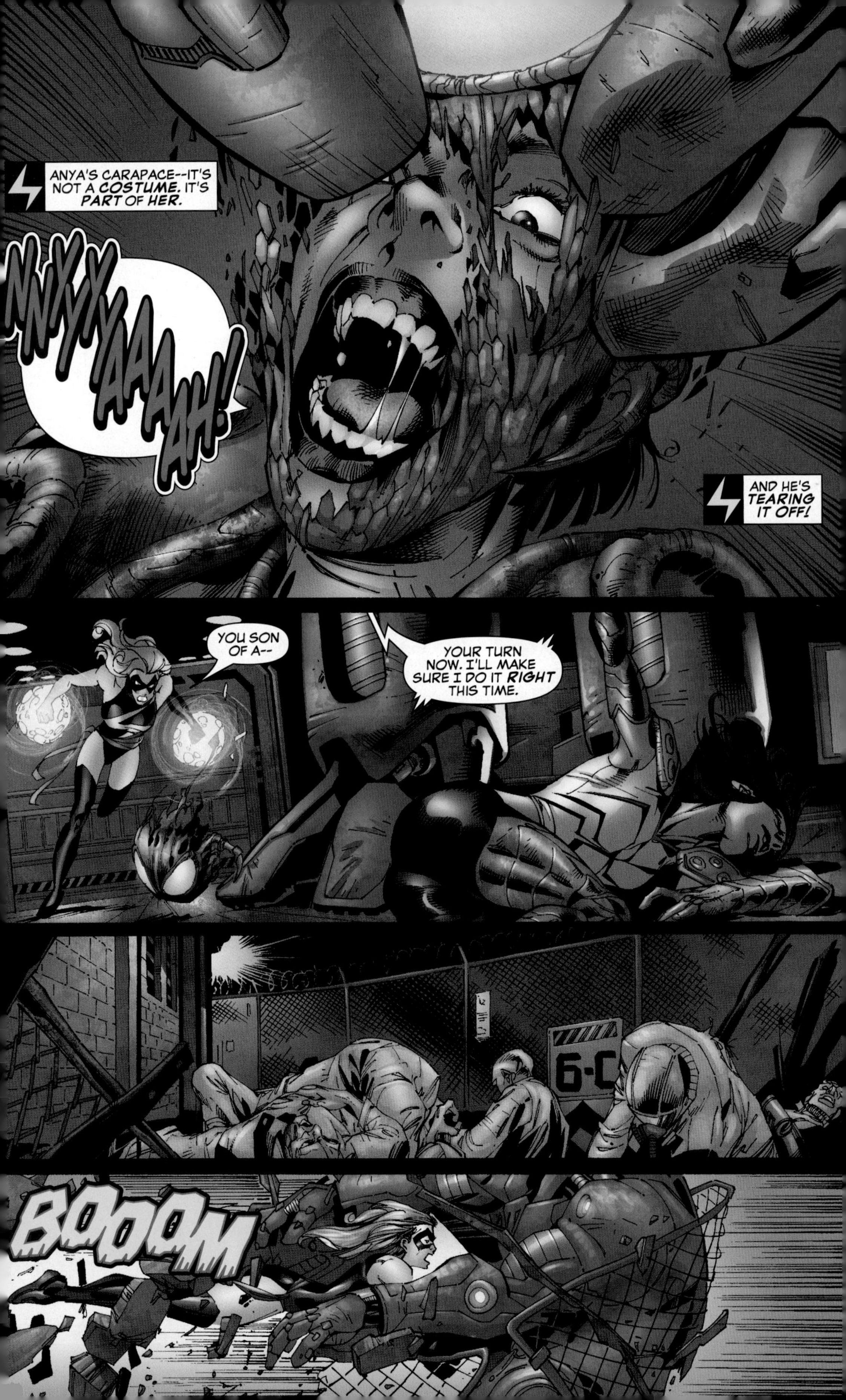
ANYA'S CARAPACE--IT'S NOT A COSTUME. IT'S PART OF HER.
NNYYYAAAAH!
AND HE'S TEARING IT OFF!
YOU SON OF A--
YOUR TURN NOW. I'LL MAKE SURE I DO IT RIGHT THIS TIME.
6-C
BOOOM

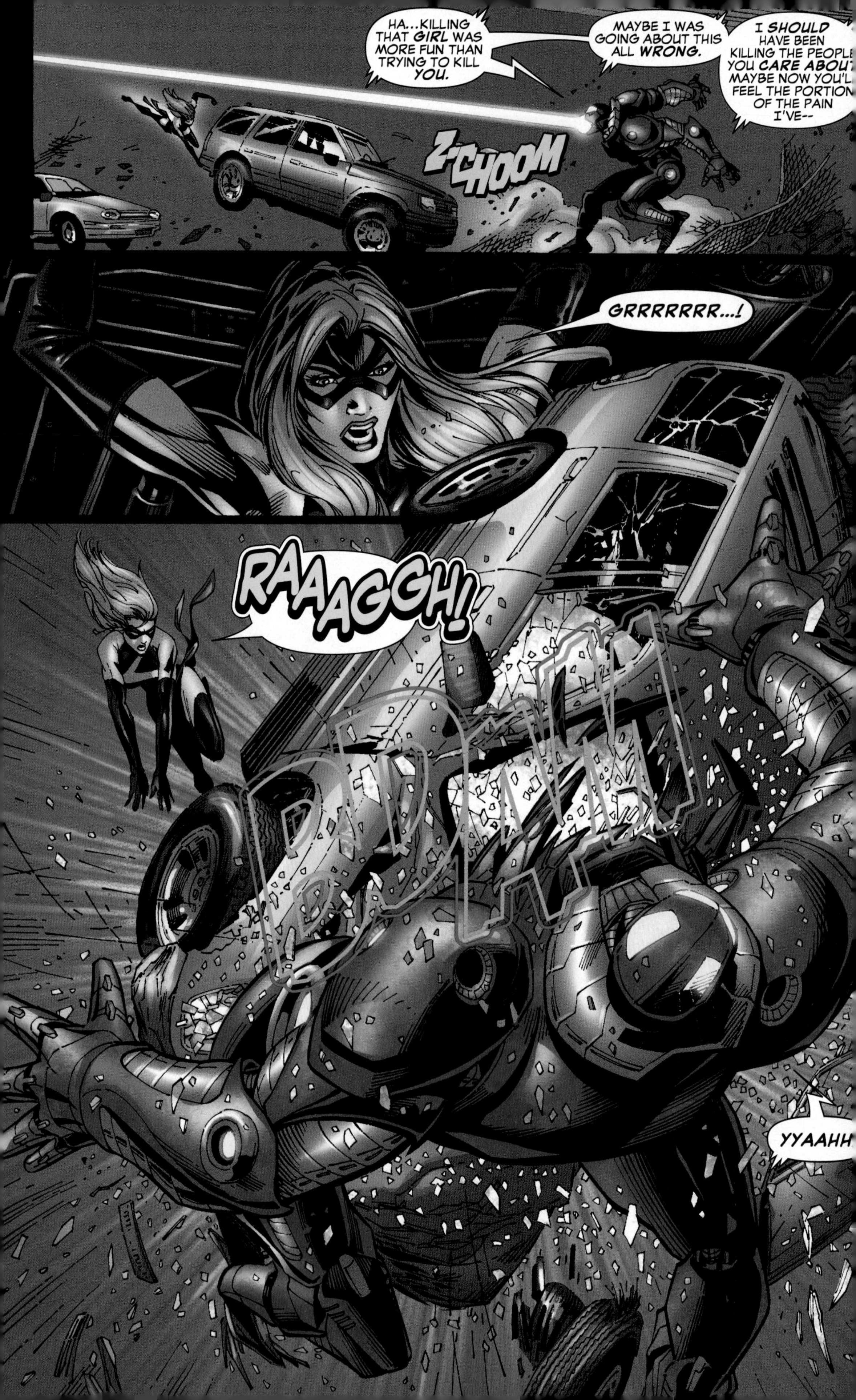
HA...KILLING THAT GIRL WAS MORE FUN THAN TRYING TO KILL YOU.
MAYBE I WAS GOING ABOUT THIS ALL WRONG.
I SHOULD HAVE BEEN KILLING THE PEOPLE YOU CARE ABOUT. MAYBE NOW YOU'LL FEEL THE PORTION OF THE PAIN I'VE--
Z-CHOOM
GRRRRRRR...!
RAAAGGH!
YYAAHH

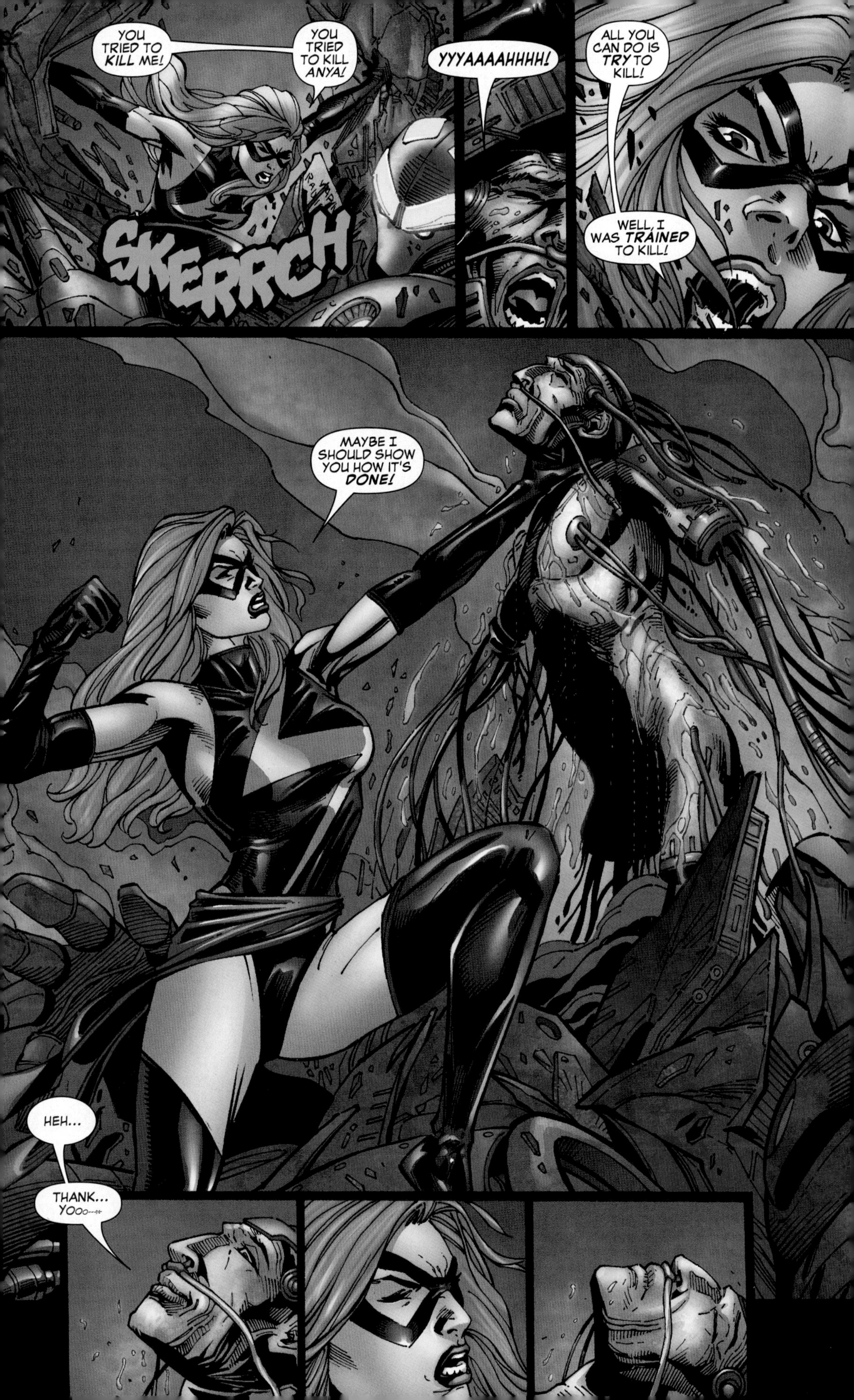
YOU TRIED TO KILL ME!
YOU TRIED TO KILL ANYA!
SKERRCH
YYYAAAAHHHH!
ALL YOU CAN DO IS TRY TO KILL!
WELL, I WAS TRAINED TO KILL!
MAYBE I SHOULD SHOW YOU HOW IT'S DONE!
HEH...
THANK... YOOo--

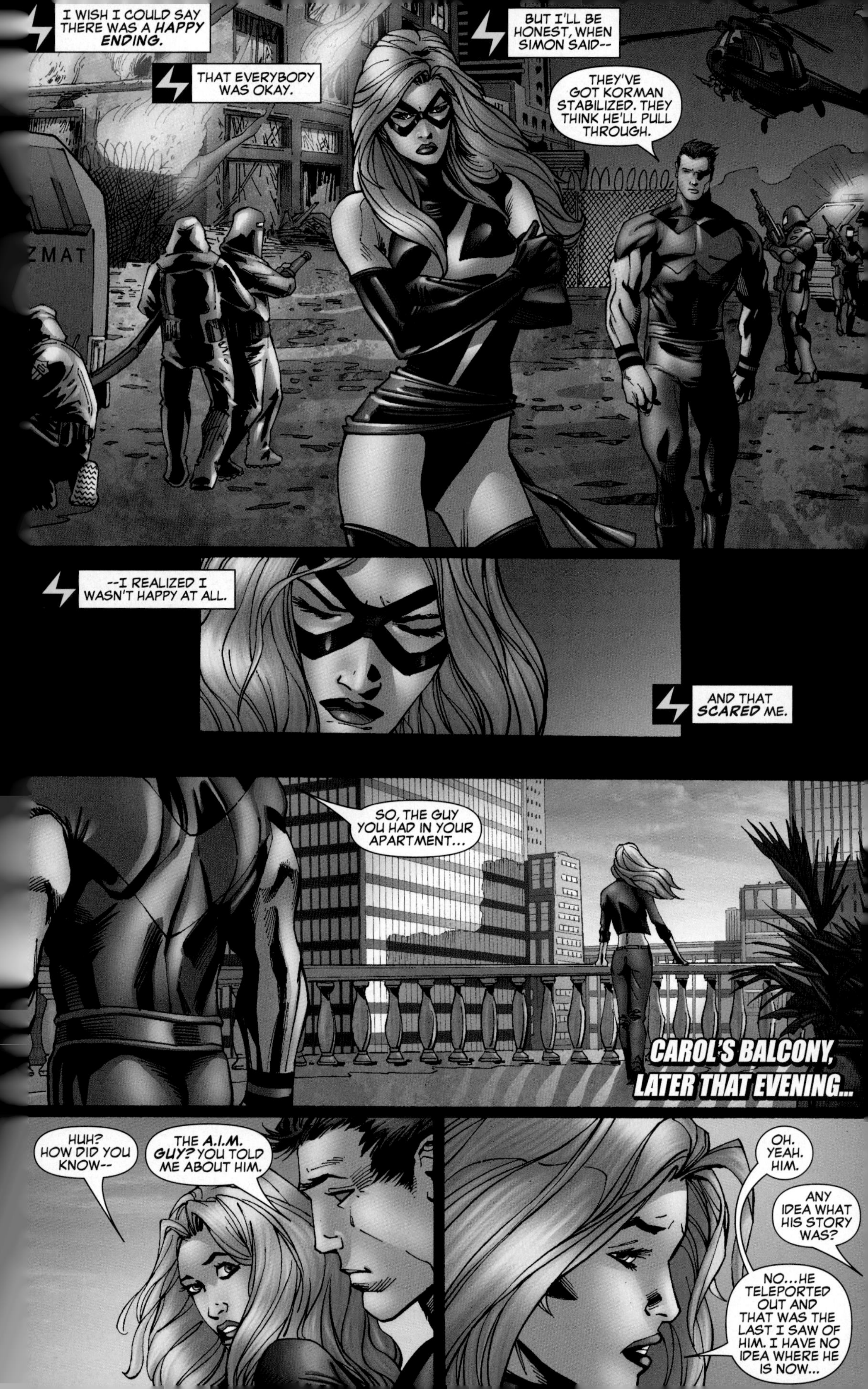

I WISH I COULD SAY THERE WAS A HAPPY ENDING.
THAT EVERYBODY WAS OKAY.
BUT I'LL BE HONEST, WHEN SIMON SAID--
THEY'VE GOT KORMAN STABILIZED. THEY THINK HE'LL PULL THROUGH.
ZMAT
--I REALIZED I WASN'T HAPPY AT ALL.
AND THAT SCARED ME.
SO, THE GUY YOU HAD IN YOUR APARTMENT...
CAROL'S BALCONY, LATER THAT EVENING...
HUH? HOW DID YOU KNOW--
THE A.I.M. GUY? YOU TOLD ME ABOUT HIM.
OH. YEAH. HIM.
ANY IDEA WHAT HIS STORY WAS?
NO...HE TELEPORTED OUT AND THAT WAS THE LAST I SAW OF HIM. I HAVE NO IDEA WHERE HE IS NOW...

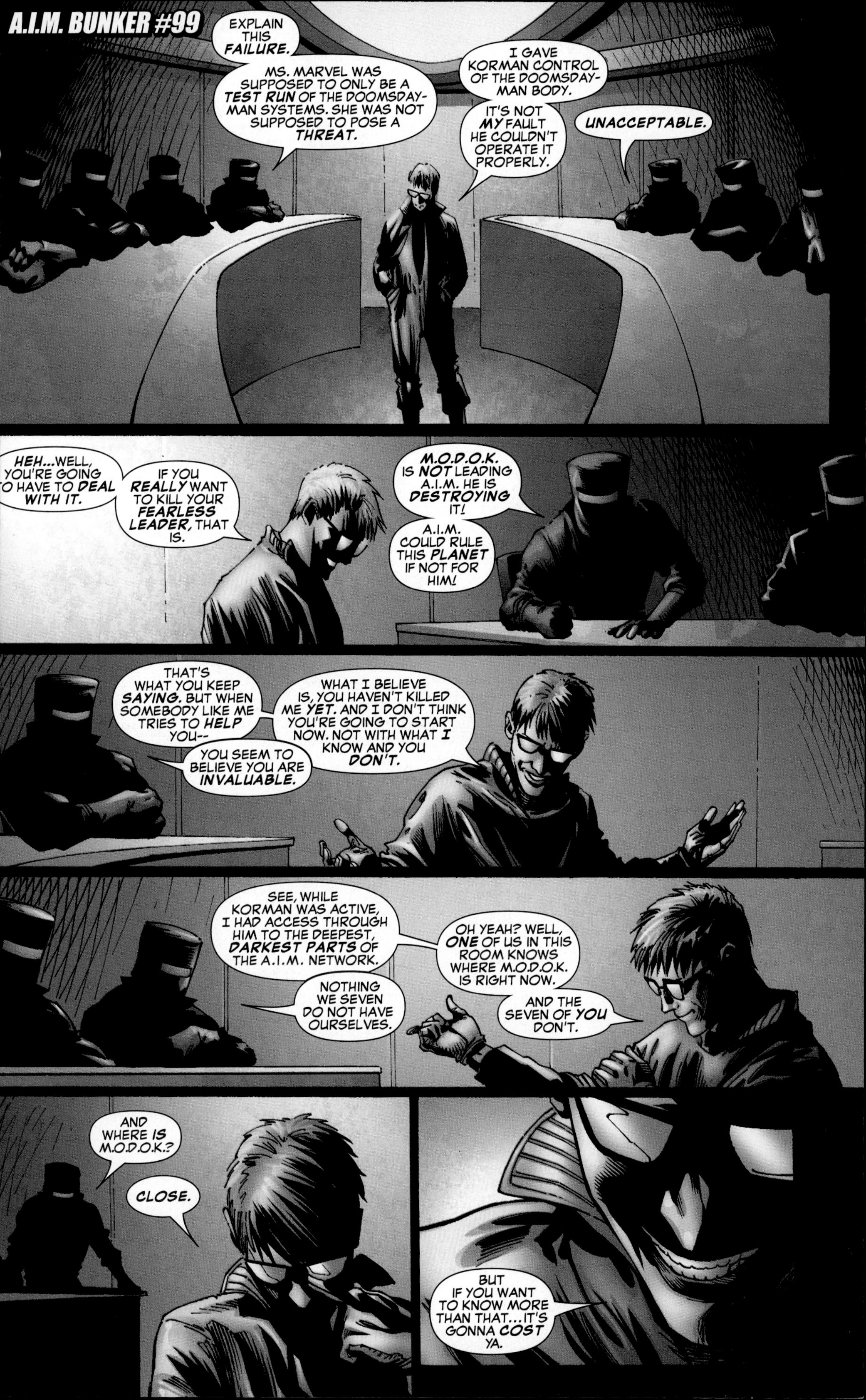
A.I.M. BUNKER #99
EXPLAIN THIS FAILURE.
MS. MARVEL WAS SUPPOSED TO ONLY BE A TEST RUN OF THE DOOMSDAY-MAN SYSTEMS. SHE WAS NOT SUPPOSED TO POSE A THREAT.
I GAVE KORMAN CONTROL OF THE DOOMSDAY-MAN BODY.
IT'S NOT MY FAULT HE COULDN'T OPERATE IT PROPERLY.
UNACCEPTABLE.
HEH...WELL, YOU'RE GOING TO HAVE TO DEAL WITH IT.
IF YOU REALLY WANT TO KILL YOUR FEARLESS LEADER, THAT IS.
M.O.D.O.K. IS NOT LEADING A.I.M. HE IS DESTROYING IT!
A.I.M. COULD RULE THIS PLANET IF NOT FOR HIM!
THAT'S WHAT YOU KEEP SAYING. BUT WHEN SOMEBODY LIKE ME TRIES TO HELP YOU--
YOU SEEM TO BELIEVE YOU ARE INVALUABLE.
WHAT I BELIEVE IS, YOU HAVEN'T KILLED ME YET. AND I DON'T THINK YOU'RE GOING TO START NOW. NOT WITH WHAT I KNOW AND YOU DON'T.
SEE, WHILE KORMAN WAS ACTIVE, I HAD ACCESS THROUGH HIM TO THE DEEPEST, DARKEST PARTS OF THE A.I.M. NETWORK.
NOTHING WE SEVEN DO NOT HAVE OURSELVES.
OH YEAH? WELL, ONE OF US IN THIS ROOM KNOWS WHERE M.O.D.O.K. IS RIGHT NOW.
AND THE SEVEN OF YOU DON'T.
AND WHERE IS M.O.D.O.K.?
CLOSE.
BUT IF YOU WANT TO KNOW MORE THAN THAT...IT'S GONNA COST YA.

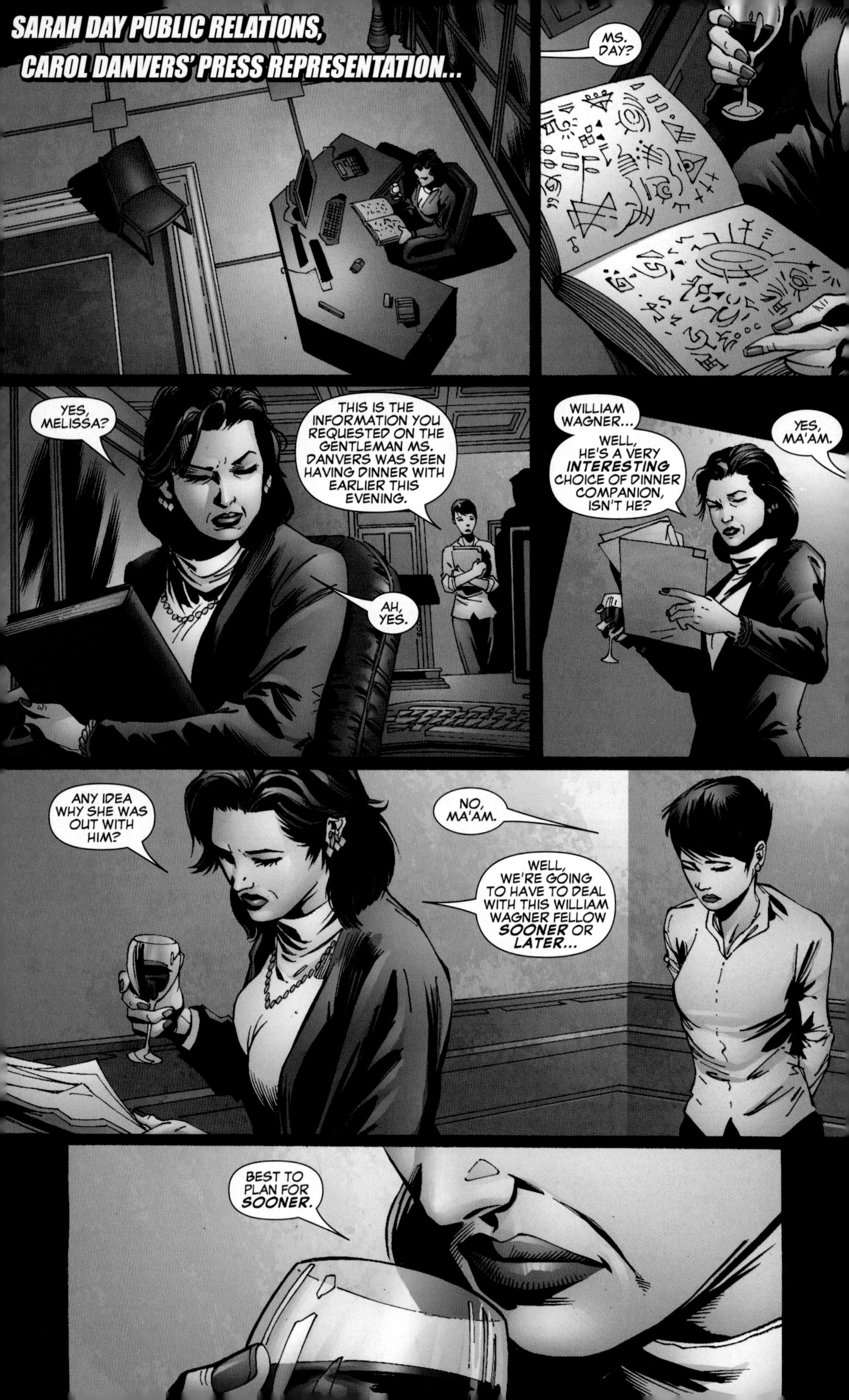
SARAH DAY PUBLIC RELATIONS, CAROL DANVERS' PRESS REPRESENTATION...
MS. DAY?
YES, MELISSA?
THIS IS THE INFORMATION YOU REQUESTED ON THE GENTLEMAN MS. DANVERS WAS SEEN HAVING DINNER WITH EARLIER THIS EVENING.
AH, YES.
WILLIAM WAGNER...
WELL, HE'S A VERY INTERESTING CHOICE OF DINNER COMPANION, ISN'T HE?
YES, MA'AM.
ANY IDEA WHY SHE WAS OUT WITH HIM?
NO, MA'AM.
WELL, WE'RE GOING TO HAVE TO DEAL WITH THIS WILLIAM WAGNER FELLOW SOONER OR LATER...
BEST TO PLAN FOR SOONER.

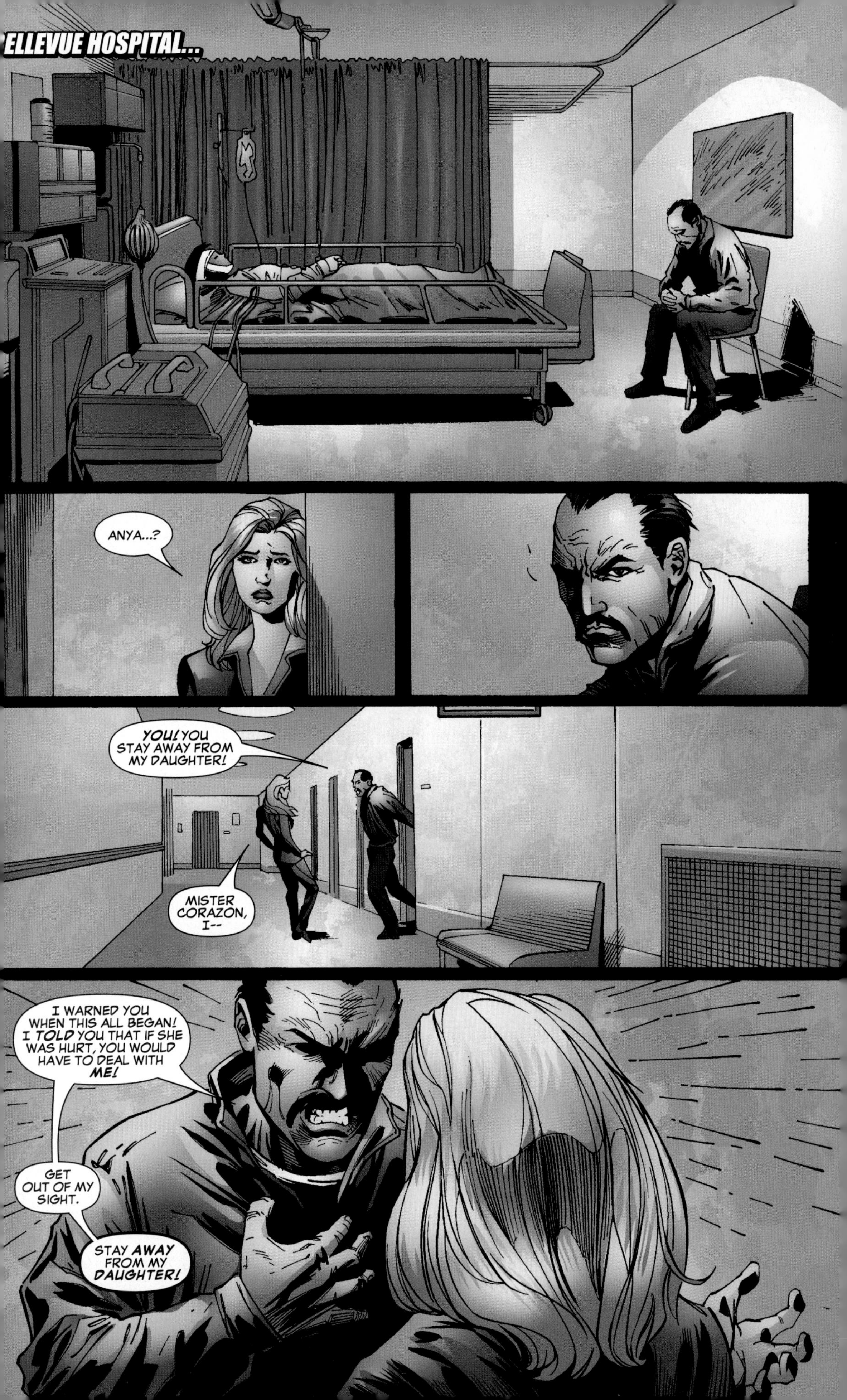
ELLEVUE HOSPITAL...
ANYA...?
YOU! YOU STAY AWAY FROM MY DAUGHTER!
MISTER CORAZON, I--
I WARNED YOU WHEN THIS ALL BEGAN! I TOLD YOU THAT IF SHE WAS HURT, YOU WOULD HAVE TO DEAL WITH ME!
GET OUT OF MY SIGHT.
STAY AWAY FROM MY DAUGHTER!

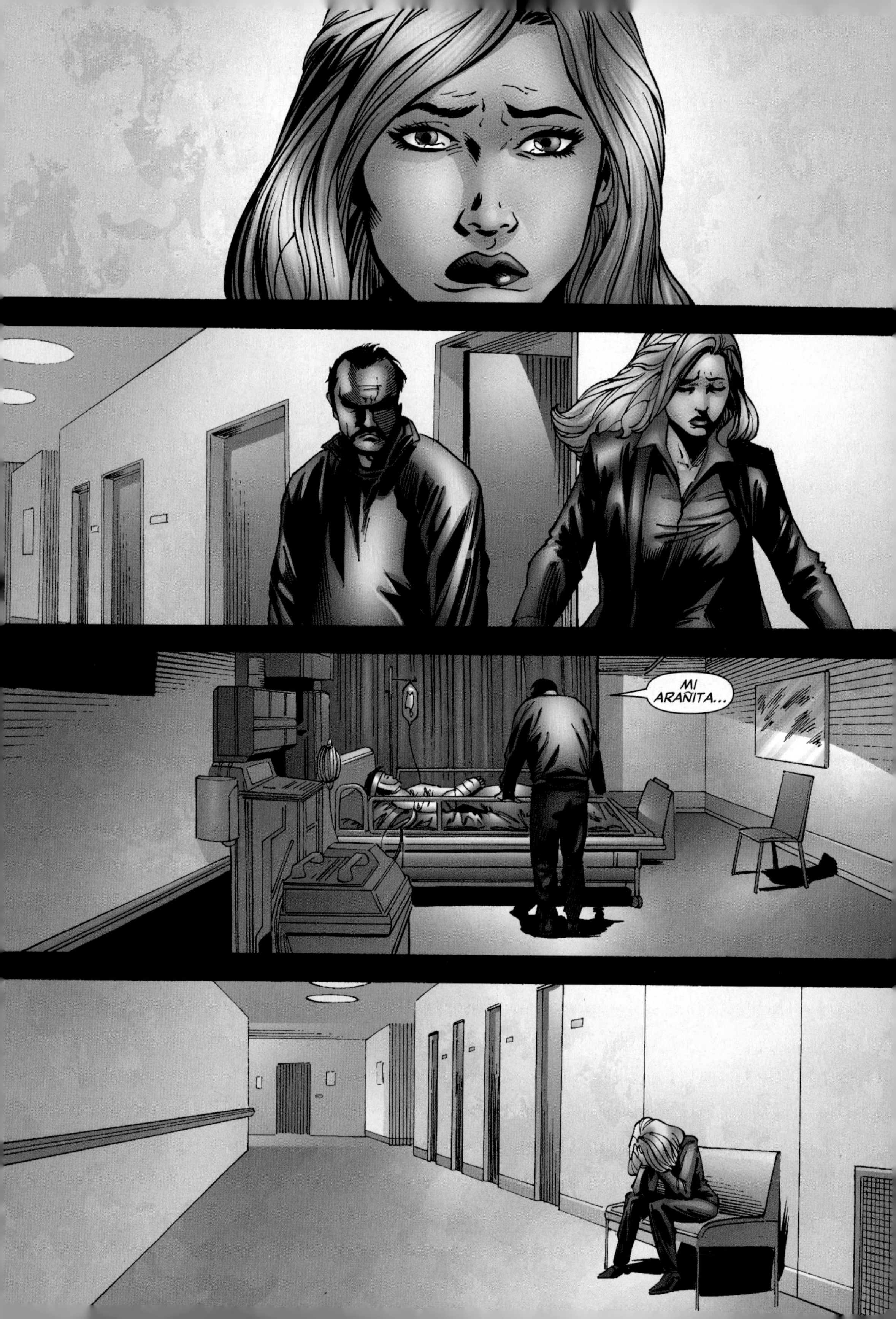
MI ARAÑITA...

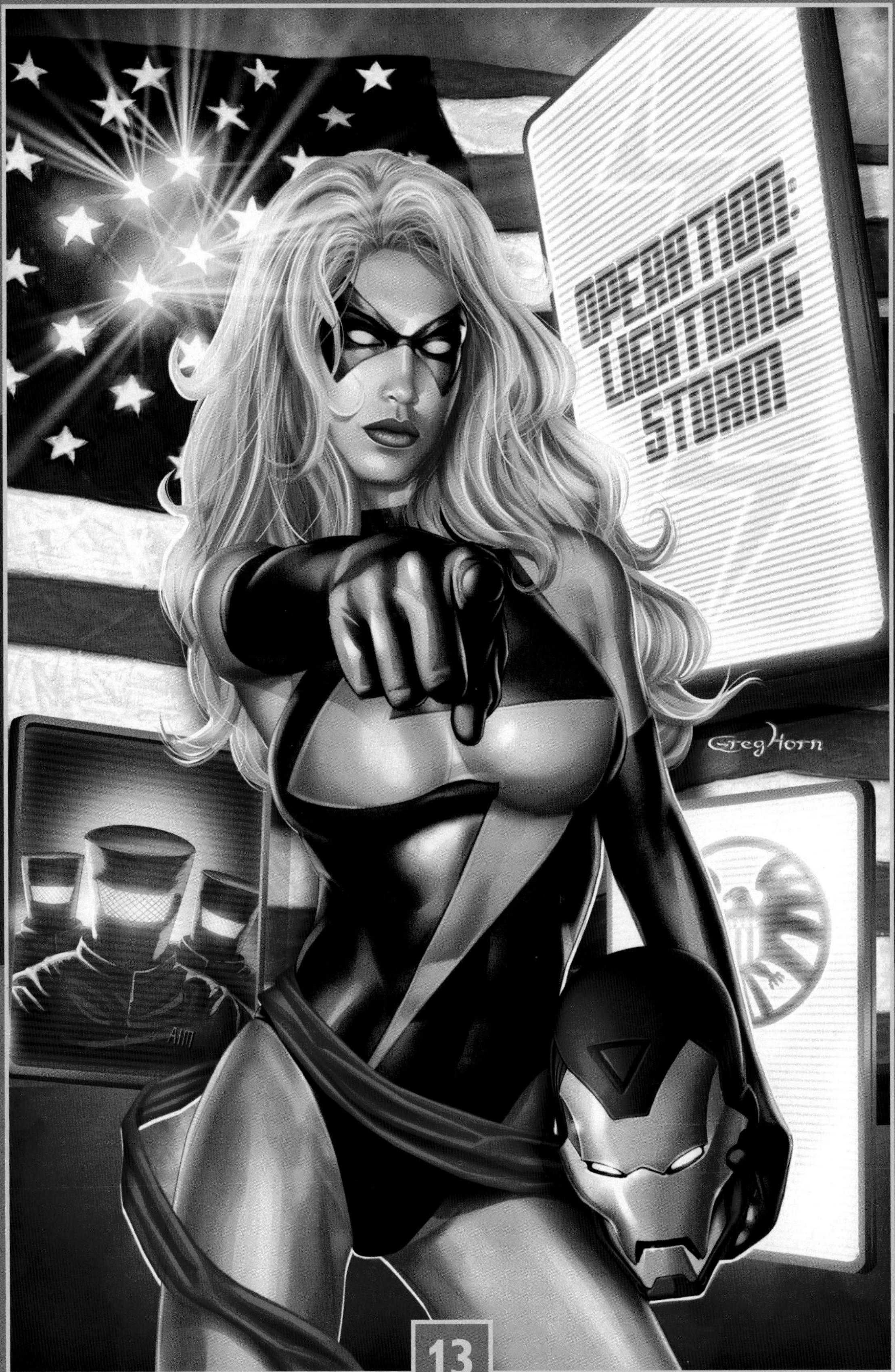
OPERATION:
LIGHTNING
STORM
Greg Horn
AIM
13

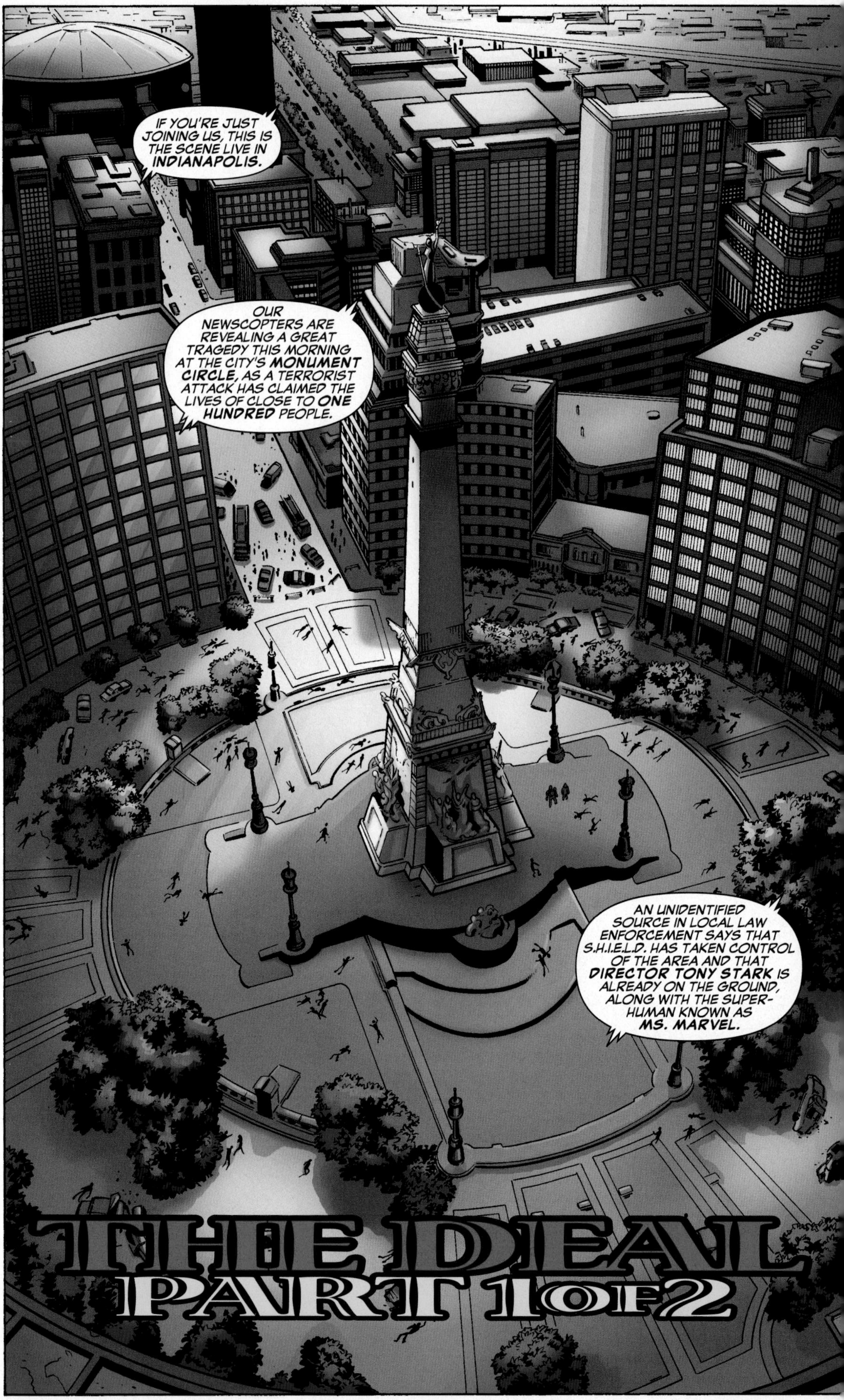
IF YOU'RE JUST JOINING US, THIS IS THE SCENE LIVE IN INDIANAPOLIS.
OUR NEWSCOPTERS ARE REVEALING A GREAT TRAGEDY THIS MORNING AT THE CITY'S MONUMENT CIRCLE, AS A TERRORIST ATTACK HAS CLAIMED THE LIVES OF CLOSE TO ONE HUNDRED PEOPLE.
AN UNIDENTIFIED SOURCE IN LOCAL LAW ENFORCEMENT SAYS THAT S.H.I.E.L.D. HAS TAKEN CONTROL OF THE AREA AND THAT DIRECTOR TONY STARK IS ALREADY ON THE GROUND, ALONG WITH THE SUPER-HUMAN KNOWN AS MS. MARVEL.
THE DEAL
PART 1 OF 2

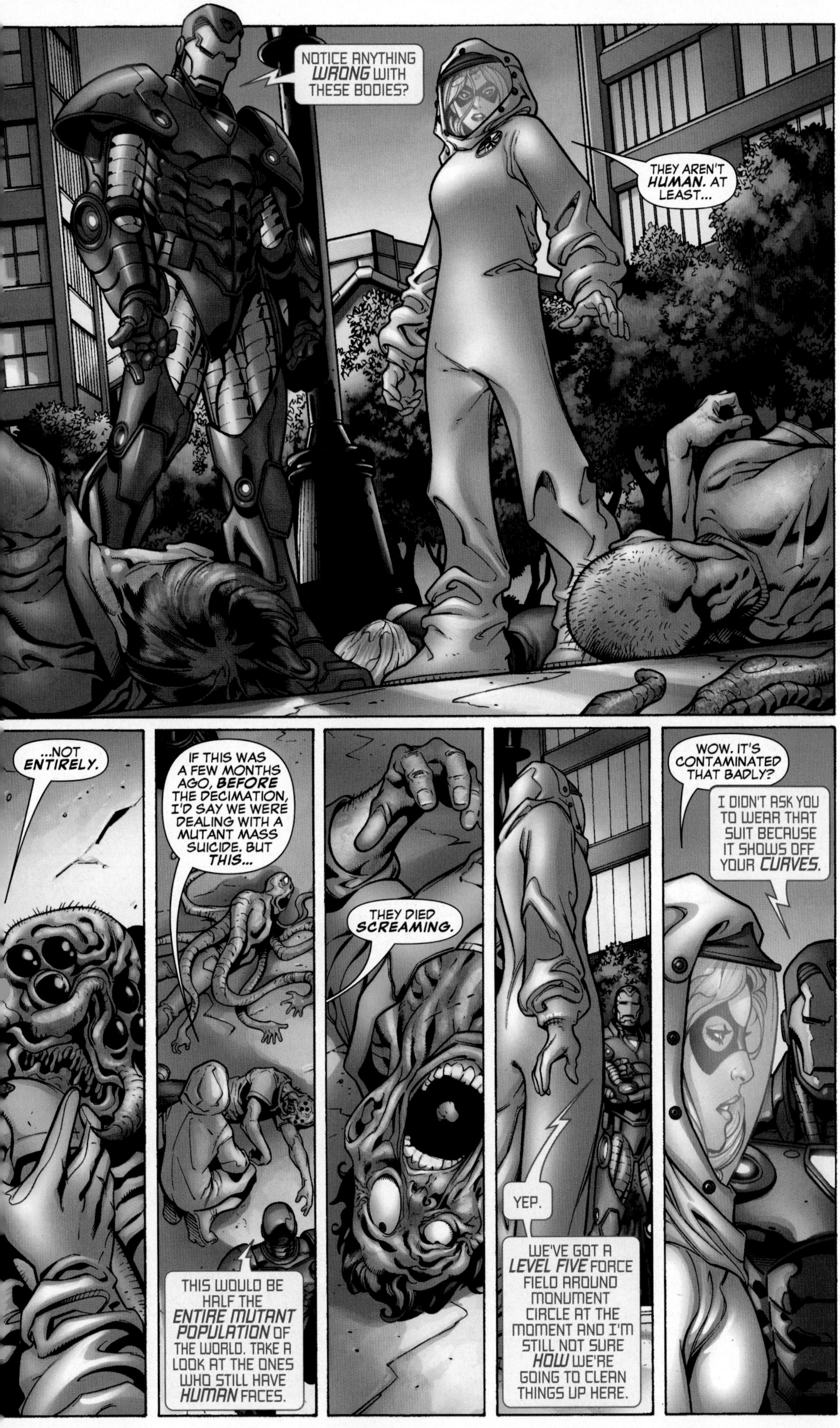
NOTICE ANYTHING WRONG WITH THESE BODIES?
THEY AREN'T HUMAN. AT LEAST...
...NOT ENTIRELY.
IF THIS WAS A FEW MONTHS AGO, BEFORE THE DECIMATION, I'D SAY WE WERE DEALING WITH A MUTANT MASS SUICIDE. BUT THIS...
THIS WOULD BE HALF THE ENTIRE MUTANT POPULATION OF THE WORLD. TAKE A LOOK AT THE ONES WHO STILL HAVE HUMAN FACES.
THEY DIED SCREAMING.
YEP.
WE'VE GOT A LEVEL FIVE FORCE FIELD AROUND MONUMENT CIRCLE AT THE MOMENT AND I'M STILL NOT SURE HOW WE'RE GOING TO CLEAN THINGS UP HERE.
WOW. IT'S CONTAMINATED THAT BADLY?
I DIDN'T ASK YOU TO WEAR THAT SUIT BECAUSE IT SHOWS OFF YOUR CURVES.

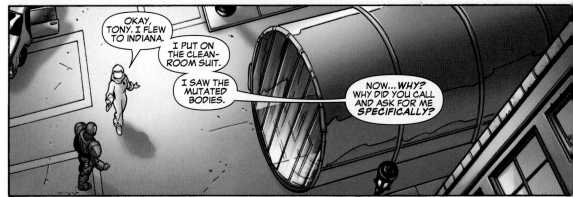

OKAY, TONY. I FLEW TO INDIANA.

I PUT ON THE CLEAN-ROOM SUIT.

I SAW THE MUTATED BODIES.

NOW...WHY? WHY DID YOU CALL AND ASK FOR ME SPECIFICALLY?

CAROL, THIS WAS AN ATTACK WITH A BOMB DESIGNED TO CAUSE RANDOM FLUCTUATIONS IN THE ADENINE, GUANINE, CYTOSINE AND THYMINE MAKEUPS OF THE VICTIMS.

IF YOU TWO WILL PLEASE STAND IN THE MIDDLE OF THE ROOM, WITH YOUR ARMS OUTSTRETCHED, I'LL ACTIVATE THE CLEANSING SOLUTION.

A DNA BOMB?

WHO ON EARTH COULD EVEN FATHOM--

A.I.M.

GOT IT IN ONE.

S.H.I.E.L.D. HAS BEEN CHASING AFTER A.I.M. FOR SEVERAL MONTHS AND--

PLEASE PAUSE IN THE NEXT ROOM FOR A FEW MOMENTS. LET THE ULTRAVIOLETS DO THEIR WORK.

I DON'T GET IT. HOW HARD IS IT FOR THE WORLD'S TOP ESPIONAGE ORGANIZATION TO FIND A BUNCH OF GUYS IN BEEKEEPER COSTUMES?

CAROL, WE HAVE BEEN LOOKING FOR THEM.

AND DON'T UNDERESTIMATE A.I.M. EVEN THEIR MOST LOWLY OPERATIVE IS A SCIENTIFIC GENIUS.

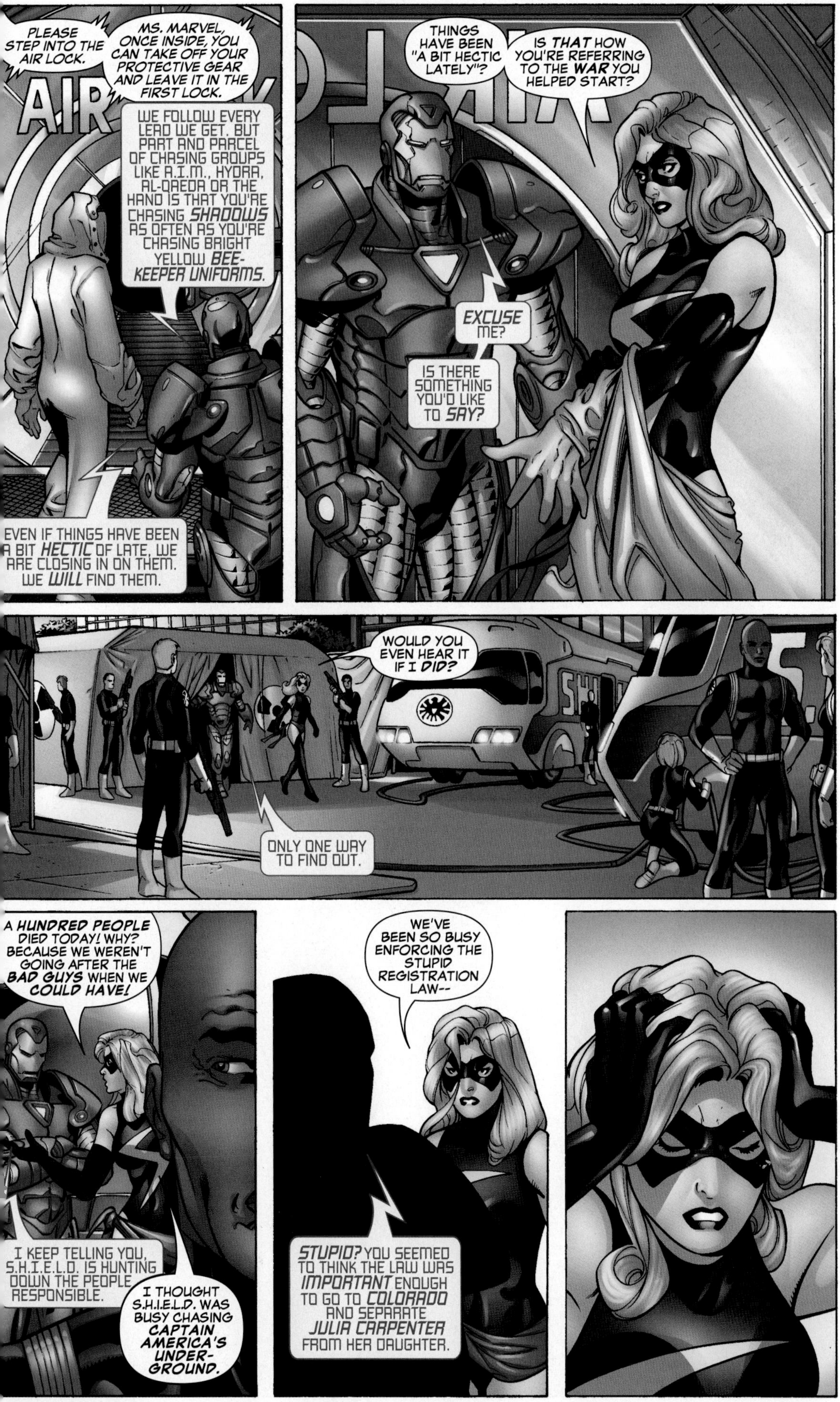
PLEASE STEP INTO THE AIR LOCK.
MS. MARVEL, ONCE INSIDE, YOU CAN TAKE OFF YOUR PROTECTIVE GEAR AND LEAVE IT IN THE FIRST LOCK.
AIR
WE FOLLOW EVERY LEAD WE GET. BUT PART AND PARCEL OF CHASING GROUPS LIKE A.I.M., HYDRA, AL-QAEDA OR THE HAND IS THAT YOU'RE CHASING SHADOWS AS OFTEN AS YOU'RE CHASING BRIGHT YELLOW BEE-KEEPER UNIFORMS.
EVEN IF THINGS HAVE BEEN A BIT HECTIC OF LATE, WE ARE CLOSING IN ON THEM. WE WILL FIND THEM.
THINGS HAVE BEEN "A BIT HECTIC LATELY"?
IS THAT HOW YOU'RE REFERRING TO THE WAR YOU HELPED START?
EXCUSE ME?
IS THERE SOMETHING YOU'D LIKE TO SAY?
WOULD YOU EVEN HEAR IT IF I DID?
ONLY ONE WAY TO FIND OUT.
A HUNDRED PEOPLE DIED TODAY! WHY? BECAUSE WE WEREN'T GOING AFTER THE BAD GUYS WHEN WE COULD HAVE!
I KEEP TELLING YOU, S.H.I.E.L.D. IS HUNTING DOWN THE PEOPLE RESPONSIBLE.
I THOUGHT S.H.I.E.L.D. WAS BUSY CHASING CAPTAIN AMERICA'S UNDER-GROUND.
WE'VE BEEN SO BUSY ENFORCING THE STUPID REGISTRATION LAW--
STUPID? YOU SEEMED TO THINK THE LAW WAS IMPORTANT ENOUGH TO GO TO COLORADO AND SEPARATE JULIA CARPENTER FROM HER DAUGHTER.

"AND *THAT* IS HOW TONY STARK AND I CAME TO AN UNDERSTANDING THAT MAYBE WE *DON'T* SEE EVERYTHING EYE TO EYE."

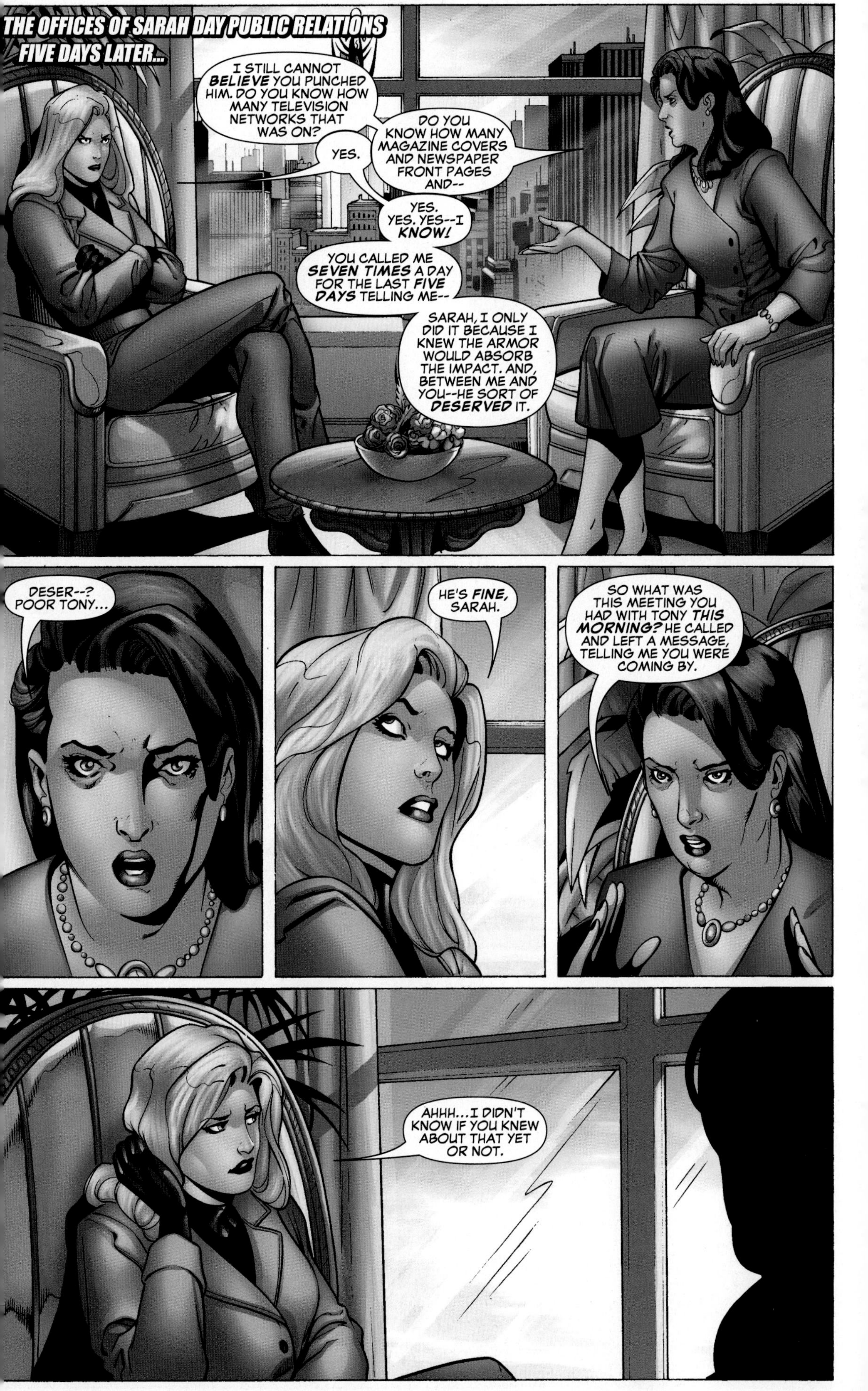
THE OFFICES OF SARAH DAY PUBLIC RELATIONS
FIVE DAYS LATER...
I STILL CANNOT BELIEVE YOU PUNCHED HIM. DO YOU KNOW HOW MANY TELEVISION NETWORKS THAT WAS ON?
YES.
DO YOU KNOW HOW MANY MAGAZINE COVERS AND NEWSPAPER FRONT PAGES AND--
YES. YES. YES--I KNOW!
YOU CALLED ME SEVEN TIMES A DAY FOR THE LAST FIVE DAYS TELLING ME--
SARAH, I ONLY DID IT BECAUSE I KNEW THE ARMOR WOULD ABSORB THE IMPACT. AND, BETWEEN ME AND YOU--HE SORT OF DESERVED IT.
DESER--? POOR TONY...
HE'S FINE, SARAH.
SO WHAT WAS THIS MEETING YOU HAD WITH TONY THIS MORNING? HE CALLED AND LEFT A MESSAGE, TELLING ME YOU WERE COMING BY.
AHHH...I DIDN'T KNOW IF YOU KNEW ABOUT THAT YET OR NOT.

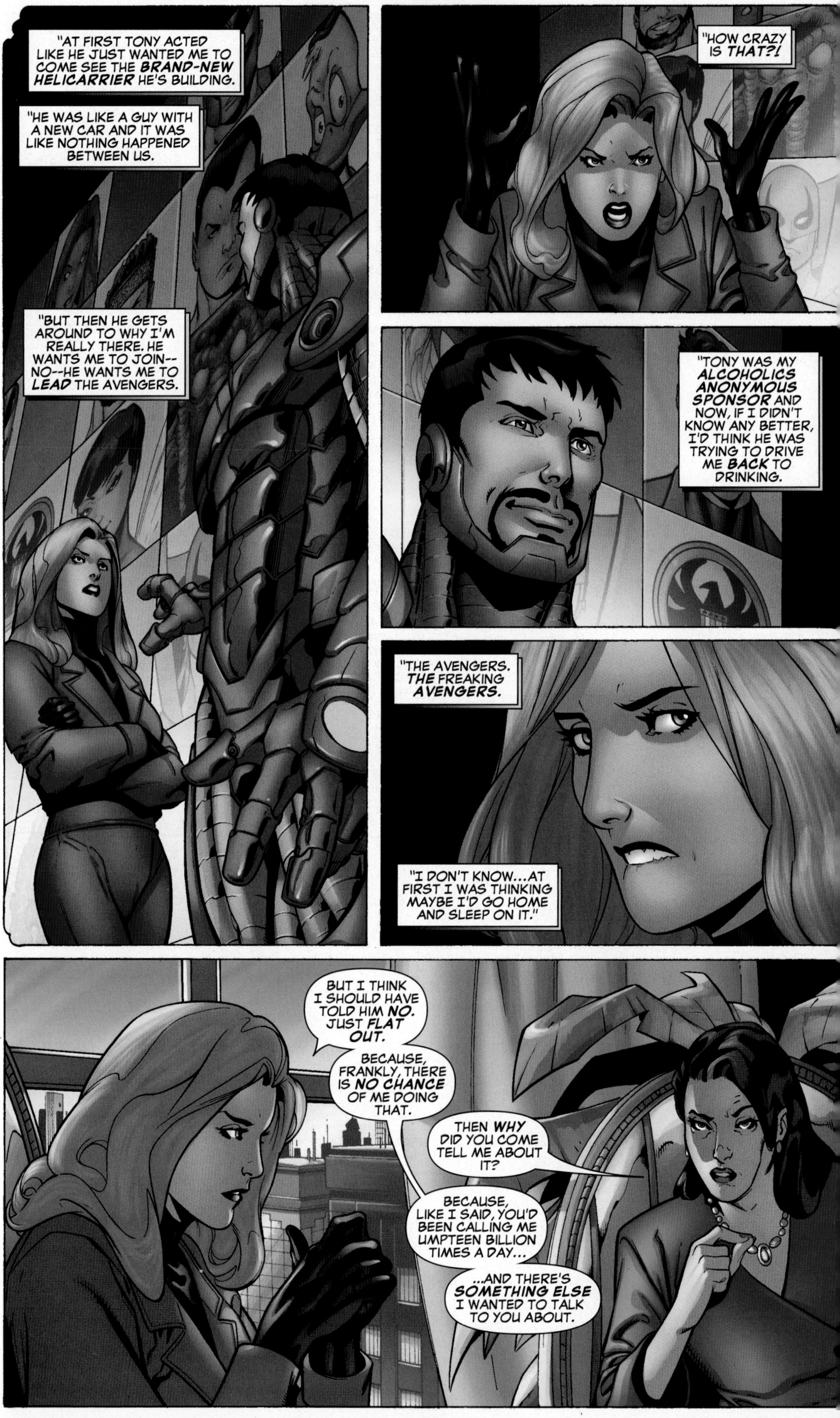
"AT FIRST TONY ACTED LIKE HE JUST WANTED ME TO COME SEE THE BRAND-NEW HELICARRIER HE'S BUILDING.
"HE WAS LIKE A GUY WITH A NEW CAR AND IT WAS LIKE NOTHING HAPPENED BETWEEN US.
"BUT THEN HE GETS AROUND TO WHY I'M REALLY THERE. HE WANTS ME TO JOIN--NO--HE WANTS ME TO LEAD THE AVENGERS.
"HOW CRAZY IS THAT?!
"TONY WAS MY ALCOHOLICS ANONYMOUS SPONSOR AND NOW, IF I DIDN'T KNOW ANY BETTER, I'D THINK HE WAS TRYING TO DRIVE ME BACK TO DRINKING.
"THE AVENGERS. THE FREAKING AVENGERS.
"I DON'T KNOW...AT FIRST I WAS THINKING MAYBE I'D GO HOME AND SLEEP ON IT."
BUT I THINK I SHOULD HAVE TOLD HIM NO. JUST FLAT OUT.
BECAUSE, FRANKLY, THERE IS NO CHANCE OF ME DOING THAT.
THEN WHY DID YOU COME TELL ME ABOUT IT?
BECAUSE, LIKE I SAID, YOU'D BEEN CALLING ME UMPTEEN BILLION TIMES A DAY...
...AND THERE'S SOMETHING ELSE I WANTED TO TALK TO YOU ABOUT.

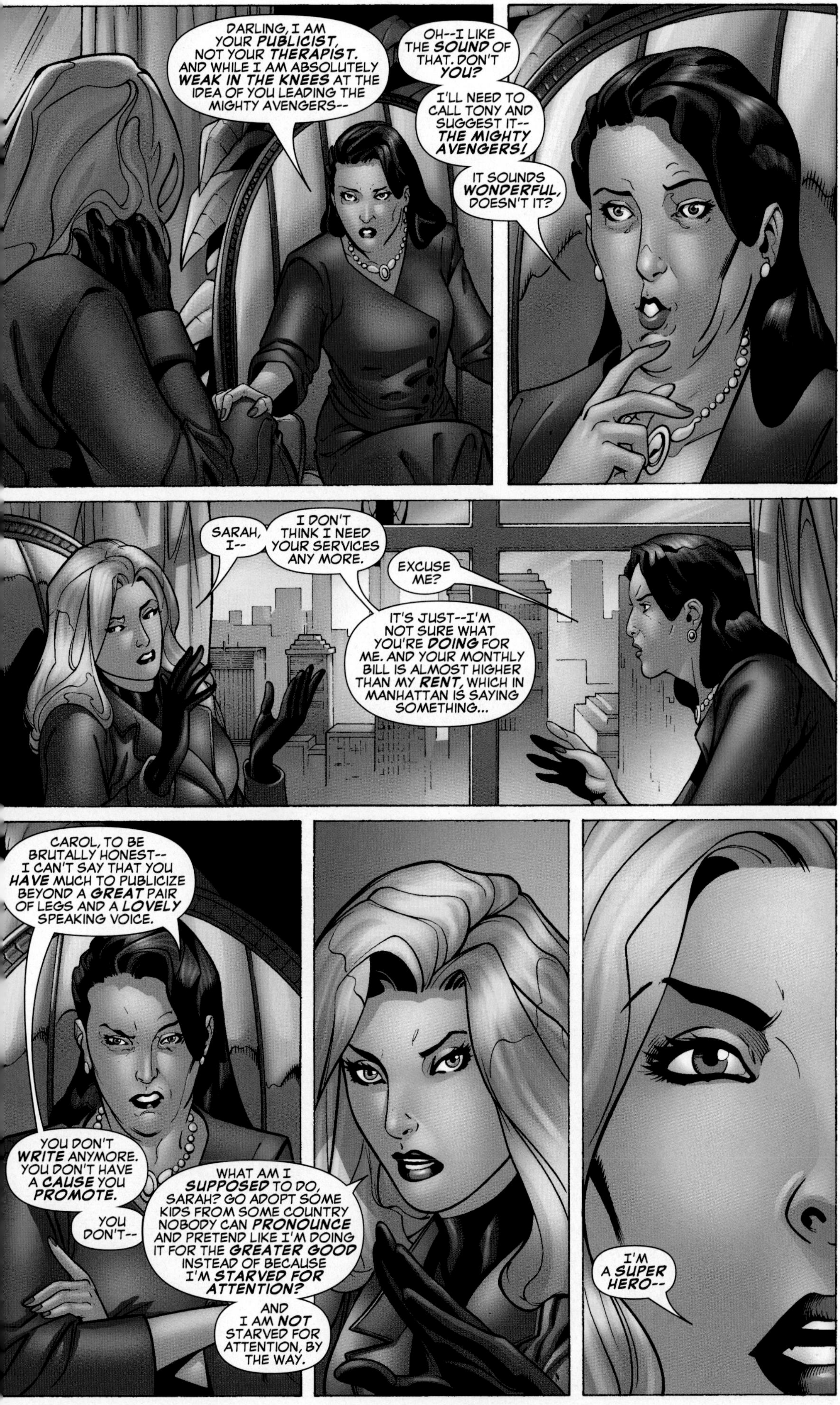
DARLING, I AM YOUR PUBLICIST, NOT YOUR THERAPIST. AND WHILE I AM ABSOLUTELY WEAK IN THE KNEES AT THE IDEA OF YOU LEADING THE MIGHTY AVENGERS--
OH--I LIKE THE SOUND OF THAT. DON'T YOU?
I'LL NEED TO CALL TONY AND SUGGEST IT--THE MIGHTY AVENGERS!
IT SOUNDS WONDERFUL, DOESN'T IT?
SARAH, I--
I DON'T THINK I NEED YOUR SERVICES ANY MORE.
EXCUSE ME?
IT'S JUST--I'M NOT SURE WHAT YOU'RE DOING FOR ME. AND YOUR MONTHLY BILL IS ALMOST HIGHER THAN MY RENT, WHICH IN MANHATTAN IS SAYING SOMETHING...
CAROL, TO BE BRUTALLY HONEST--I CAN'T SAY THAT YOU HAVE MUCH TO PUBLICIZE BEYOND A GREAT PAIR OF LEGS AND A LOVELY SPEAKING VOICE.
YOU DON'T WRITE ANYMORE. YOU DON'T HAVE A CAUSE YOU PROMOTE.
YOU DON'T--
WHAT AM I SUPPOSED TO DO, SARAH? GO ADOPT SOME KIDS FROM SOME COUNTRY NOBODY CAN PRONOUNCE AND PRETEND LIKE I'M DOING IT FOR THE GREATER GOOD INSTEAD OF BECAUSE I'M STARVED FOR ATTENTION?
AND I AM NOT STARVED FOR ATTENTION, BY THE WAY.
I'M A SUPER HERO--

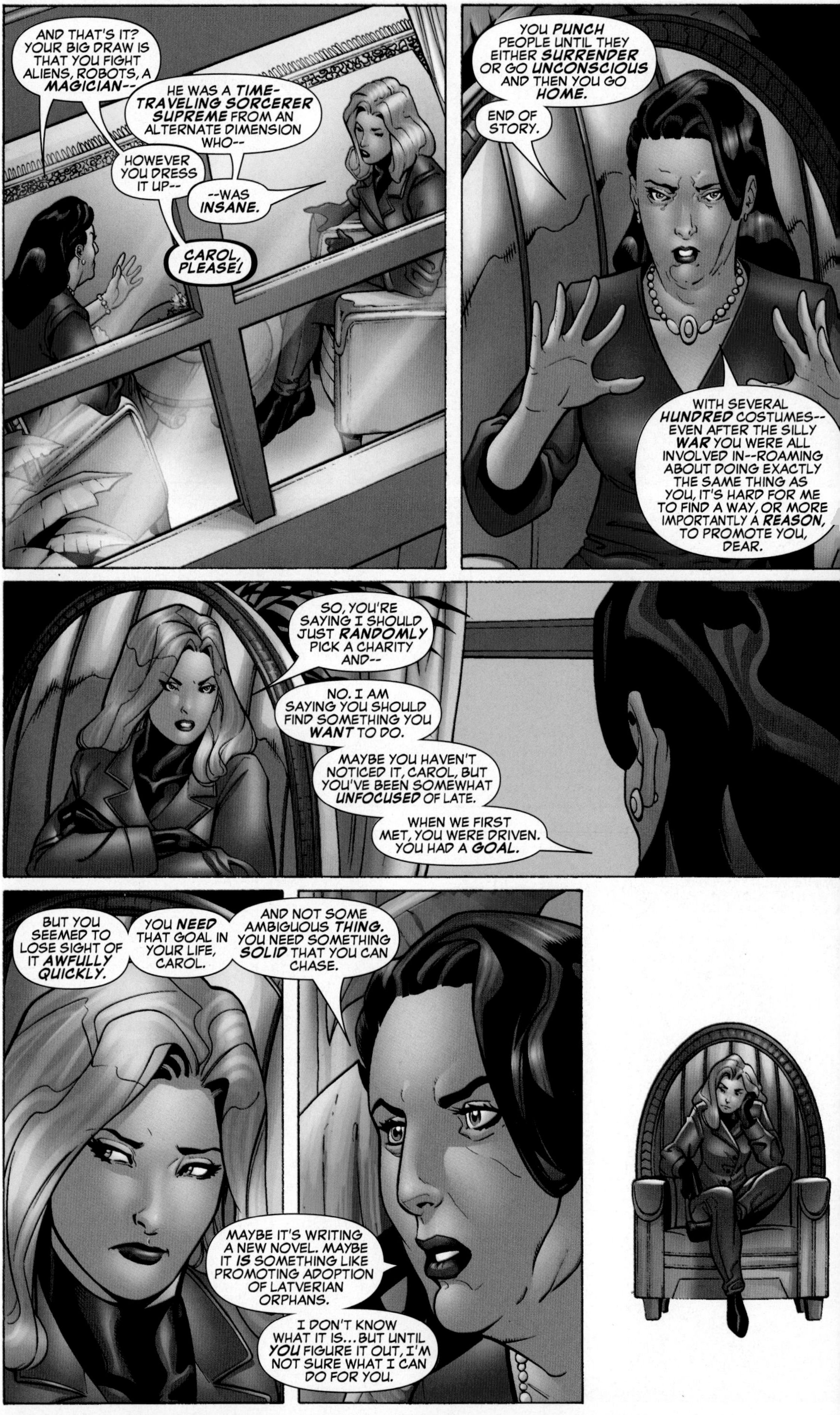
AND THAT'S IT? YOUR BIG DRAW IS THAT YOU FIGHT ALIENS, ROBOTS, A MAGICIAN--
HE WAS A TIME-TRAVELING SORCERER SUPREME FROM AN ALTERNATE DIMENSION WHO--
HOWEVER YOU DRESS IT UP--
--WAS INSANE.
CAROL, PLEASE!
YOU PUNCH PEOPLE UNTIL THEY EITHER SURRENDER OR GO UNCONSCIOUS AND THEN YOU GO HOME.
END OF STORY.
WITH SEVERAL HUNDRED COSTUMES--EVEN AFTER THE SILLY WAR YOU WERE ALL INVOLVED IN--ROAMING ABOUT DOING EXACTLY THE SAME THING AS YOU, IT'S HARD FOR ME TO FIND A WAY, OR MORE IMPORTANTLY A REASON, TO PROMOTE YOU, DEAR.
SO, YOU'RE SAYING I SHOULD JUST RANDOMLY PICK A CHARITY AND--
NO. I AM SAYING YOU SHOULD FIND SOMETHING YOU WANT TO DO.
MAYBE YOU HAVEN'T NOTICED IT, CAROL, BUT YOU'VE BEEN SOMEWHAT UNFOCUSED OF LATE.
WHEN WE FIRST MET, YOU WERE DRIVEN. YOU HAD A GOAL.
BUT YOU SEEMED TO LOSE SIGHT OF IT AWFULLY QUICKLY.
YOU NEED THAT GOAL IN YOUR LIFE, CAROL.
AND NOT SOME AMBIGUOUS THING. YOU NEED SOMETHING SOLID THAT YOU CAN CHASE.
MAYBE IT'S WRITING A NEW NOVEL. MAYBE IT IS SOMETHING LIKE PROMOTING ADOPTION OF LATVERIAN ORPHANS.
I DON'T KNOW WHAT IT IS... BUT UNTIL YOU FIGURE IT OUT, I'M NOT SURE WHAT I CAN DO FOR YOU.

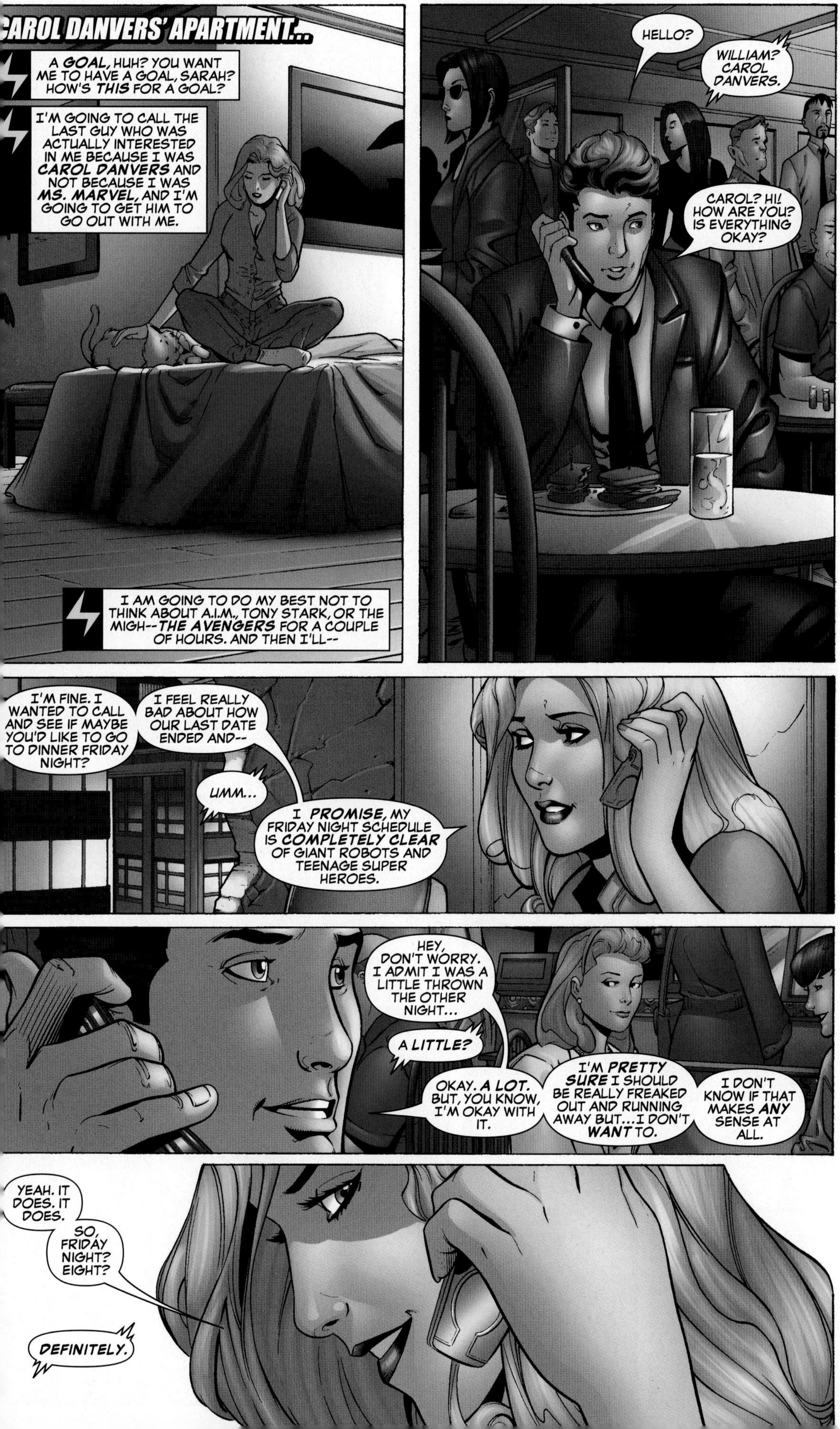
CAROL DANVERS' APARTMENT...
A GOAL, HUH? YOU WANT ME TO HAVE A GOAL, SARAH? HOW'S THIS FOR A GOAL?
I'M GOING TO CALL THE LAST GUY WHO WAS ACTUALLY INTERESTED IN ME BECAUSE I WAS CAROL DANVERS AND NOT BECAUSE I WAS MS. MARVEL, AND I'M GOING TO GET HIM TO GO OUT WITH ME.
I AM GOING TO DO MY BEST NOT TO THINK ABOUT A.I.M., TONY STARK, OR THE MIGH--THE AVENGERS FOR A COUPLE OF HOURS. AND THEN I'LL--
HELLO?
WILLIAM? CAROL DANVERS.
CAROL? HI! HOW ARE YOU? IS EVERYTHING OKAY?
I'M FINE. I WANTED TO CALL AND SEE IF MAYBE YOU'D LIKE TO GO TO DINNER FRIDAY NIGHT?
I FEEL REALLY BAD ABOUT HOW OUR LAST DATE ENDED AND--
UMM...
I PROMISE, MY FRIDAY NIGHT SCHEDULE IS COMPLETELY CLEAR OF GIANT ROBOTS AND TEENAGE SUPER HEROES.
HEY, DON'T WORRY. I ADMIT I WAS A LITTLE THROWN THE OTHER NIGHT...
A LITTLE?
OKAY. A LOT. BUT, YOU KNOW, I'M OKAY WITH IT.
I'M PRETTY SURE I SHOULD BE REALLY FREAKED OUT AND RUNNING AWAY BUT...I DON'T WANT TO.
I DON'T KNOW IF THAT MAKES ANY SENSE AT ALL.
YEAH. IT DOES. IT DOES.
SO, FRIDAY NIGHT? EIGHT?
DEFINITELY.

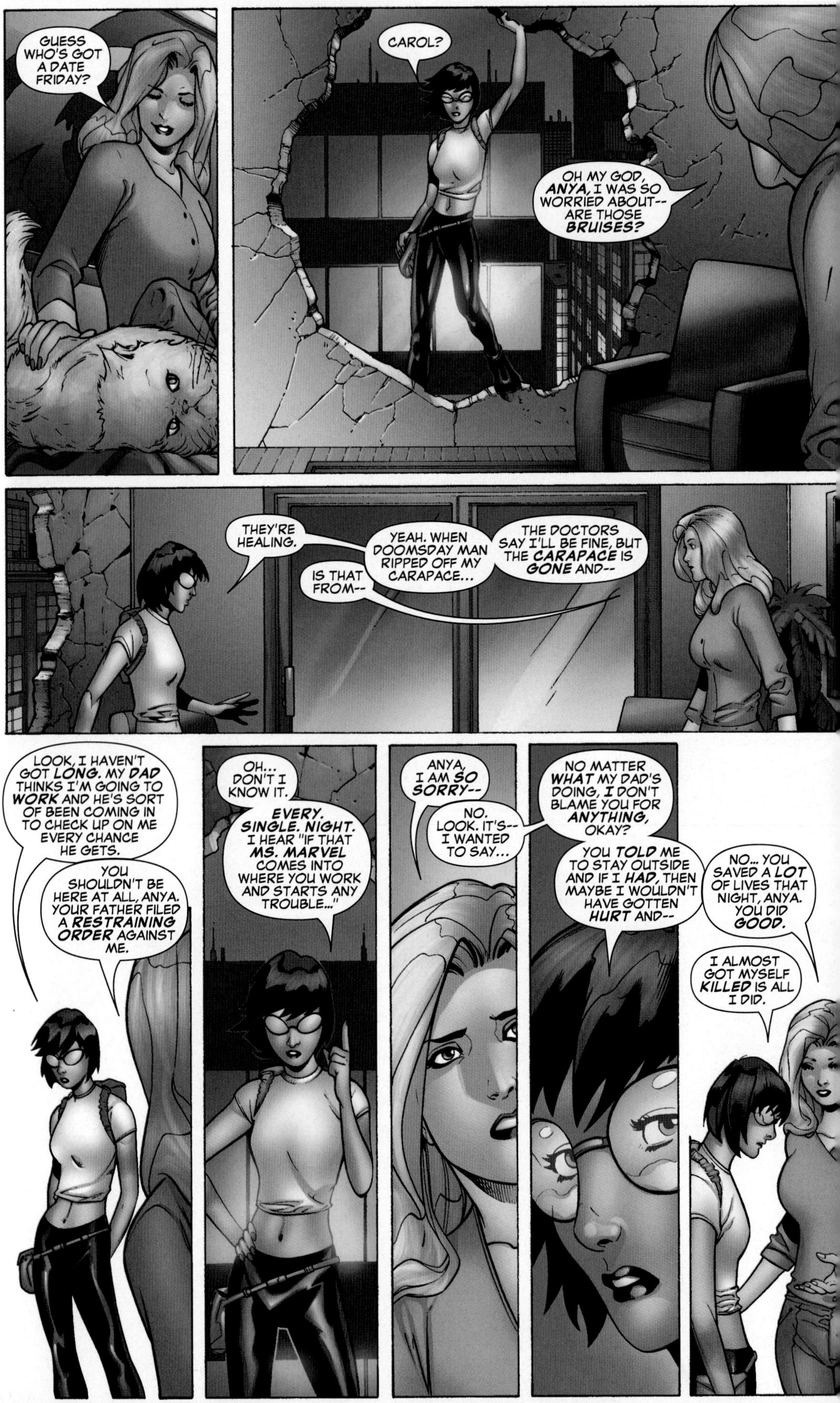
GUESS WHO'S GOT A DATE FRIDAY?
CAROL?
OH MY GOD, ANYA, I WAS SO WORRIED ABOUT-- ARE THOSE BRUISES?
THEY'RE HEALING.
IS THAT FROM--
YEAH. WHEN DOOMSDAY MAN RIPPED OFF MY CARAPACE...
THE DOCTORS SAY I'LL BE FINE, BUT THE CARAPACE IS GONE AND--
LOOK, I HAVEN'T GOT LONG. MY DAD THINKS I'M GOING TO WORK AND HE'S SORT OF BEEN COMING IN TO CHECK UP ON ME EVERY CHANCE HE GETS.
YOU SHOULDN'T BE HERE AT ALL, ANYA. YOUR FATHER FILED A RESTRAINING ORDER AGAINST ME.
OH... DON'T I KNOW IT.
EVERY. SINGLE. NIGHT. I HEAR "IF THAT MS. MARVEL COMES INTO WHERE YOU WORK AND STARTS ANY TROUBLE..."
ANYA, I AM SO SORRY--
NO. LOOK. IT'S-- I WANTED TO SAY...
NO MATTER WHAT MY DAD'S DOING, I DON'T BLAME YOU FOR ANYTHING, OKAY?
YOU TOLD ME TO STAY OUTSIDE AND IF I HAD, THEN MAYBE I WOULDN'T HAVE GOTTEN HURT AND--
NO... YOU SAVED A LOT OF LIVES THAT NIGHT, ANYA. YOU DID GOOD.
I ALMOST GOT MYSELF KILLED IS ALL I DID.

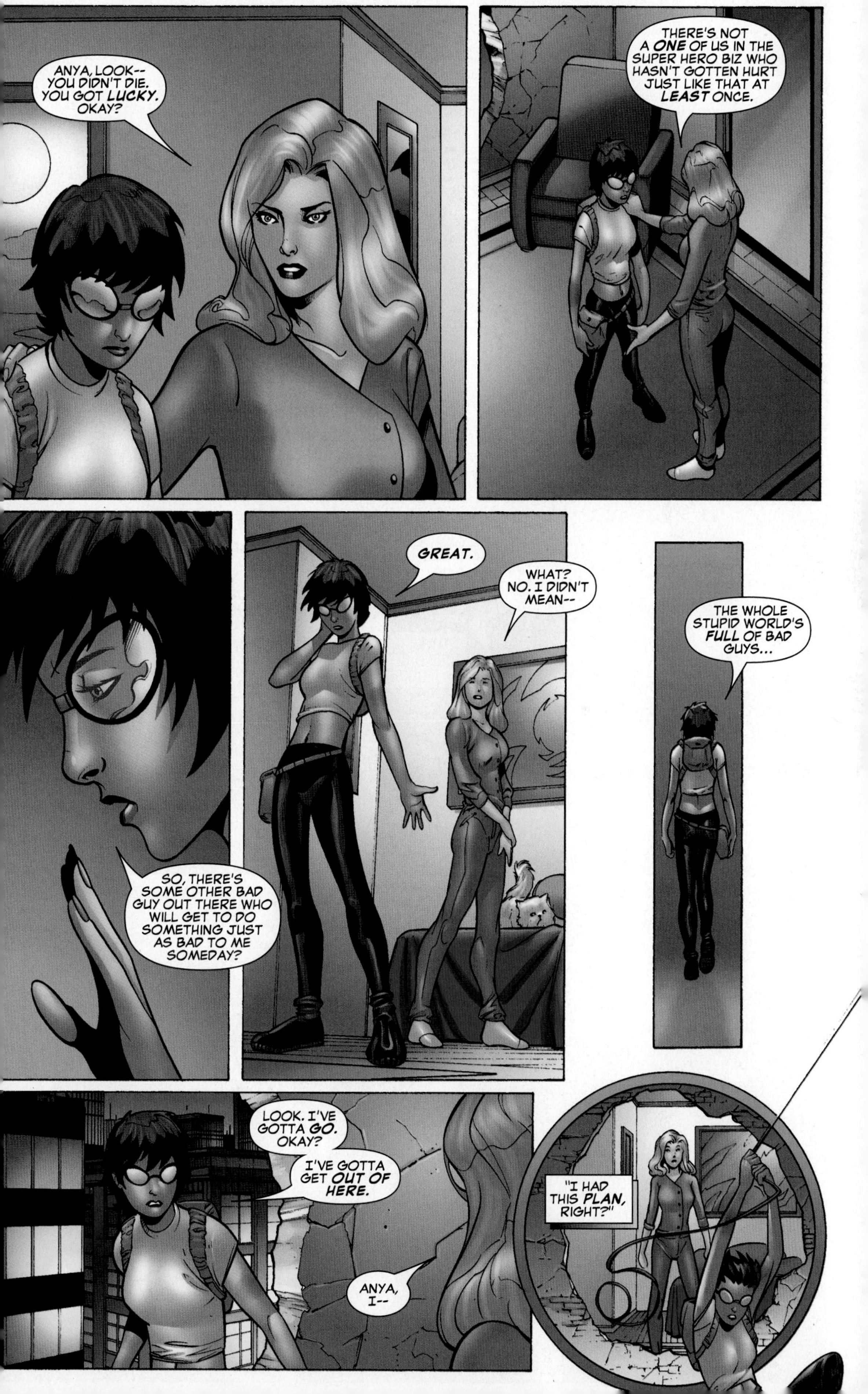
ANYA, LOOK-- YOU DIDN'T DIE. YOU GOT LUCKY. OKAY?
THERE'S NOT A ONE OF US IN THE SUPER HERO BIZ WHO HASN'T GOTTEN HURT JUST LIKE THAT AT LEAST ONCE.
SO, THERE'S SOME OTHER BAD GUY OUT THERE WHO WILL GET TO DO SOMETHING JUST AS BAD TO ME SOMEDAY?
GREAT.
WHAT? NO. I DIDN'T MEAN--
THE WHOLE STUPID WORLD'S FULL OF BAD GUYS...
LOOK. I'VE GOTTA GO. OKAY?
I'VE GOTTA GET OUT OF HERE.
ANYA, I--
"I HAD THIS PLAN, RIGHT?"

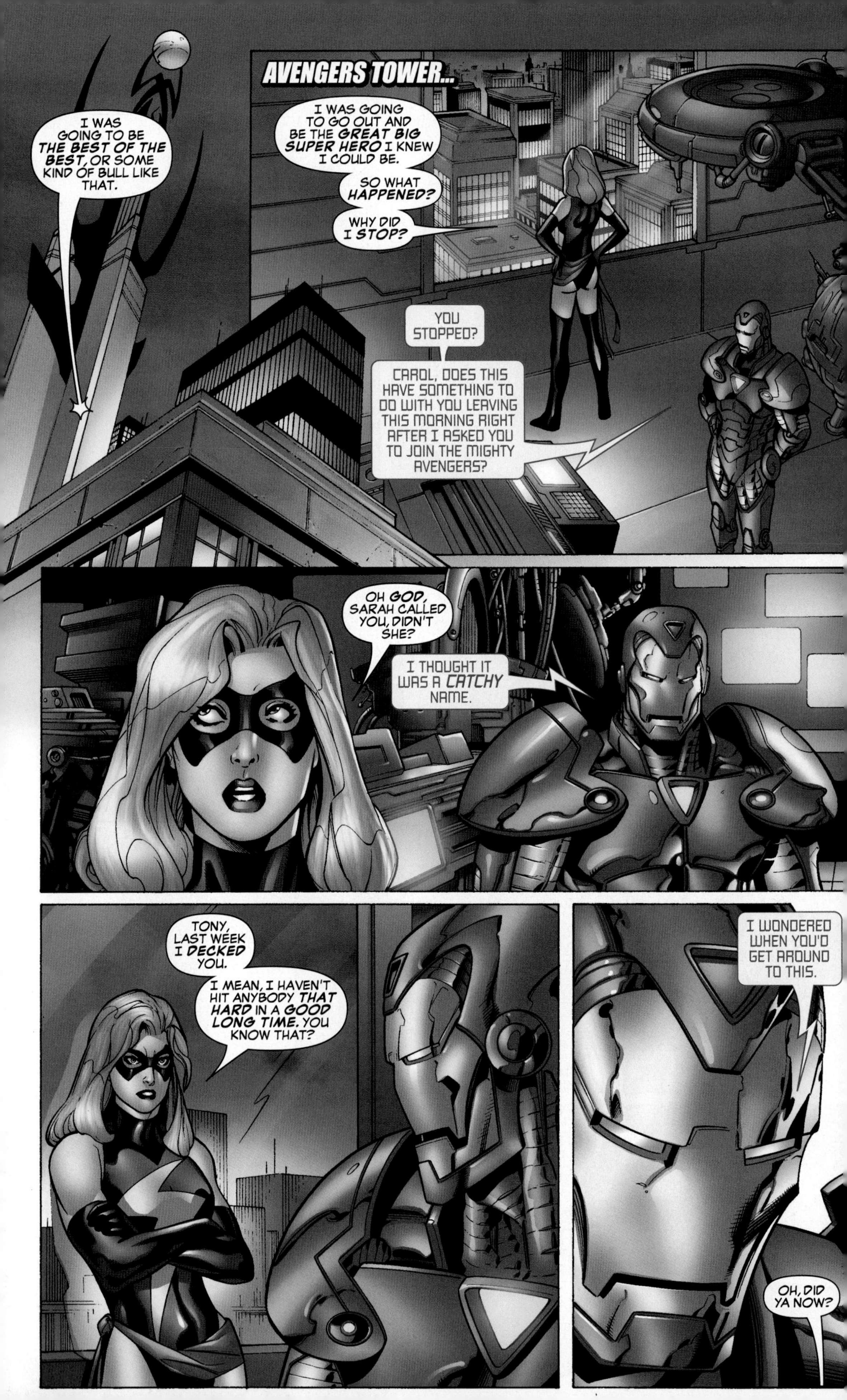
AVENGERS TOWER...
I WAS GOING TO BE THE BEST OF THE BEST, OR SOME KIND OF BULL LIKE THAT.
I WAS GOING TO GO OUT AND BE THE GREAT BIG SUPER HERO I KNEW I COULD BE.
SO WHAT HAPPENED?
WHY DID I STOP?
YOU STOPPED?
CAROL, DOES THIS HAVE SOMETHING TO DO WITH YOU LEAVING THIS MORNING RIGHT AFTER I ASKED YOU TO JOIN THE MIGHTY AVENGERS?
OH GOD, SARAH CALLED YOU, DIDN'T SHE?
I THOUGHT IT WAS A CATCHY NAME.
TONY, LAST WEEK I DECKED YOU.
I MEAN, I HAVEN'T HIT ANYBODY THAT HARD IN A GOOD LONG TIME. YOU KNOW THAT?
I WONDERED WHEN YOU'D GET AROUND TO THIS.
OH, DID YA NOW?

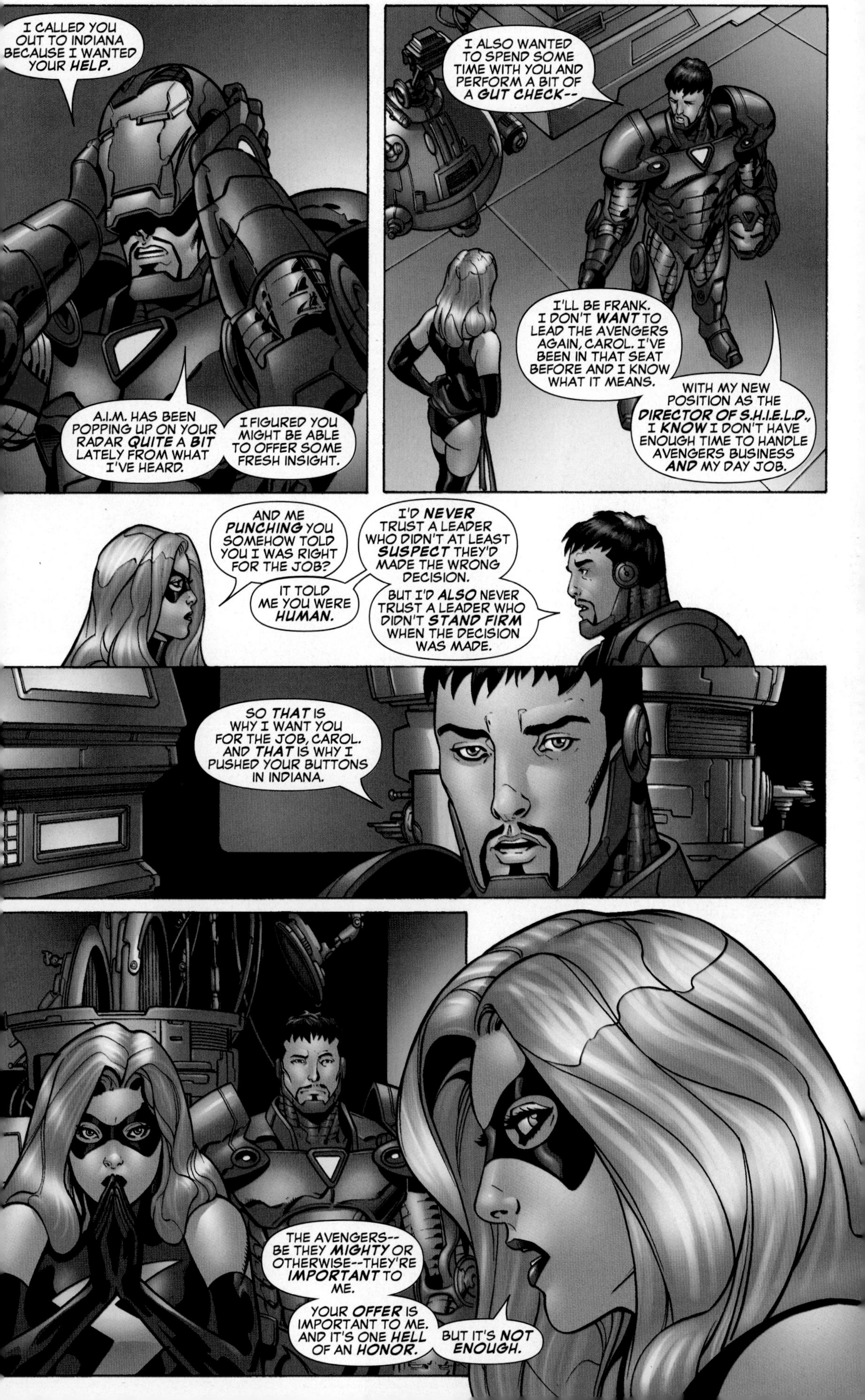
I CALLED YOU OUT TO INDIANA BECAUSE I WANTED YOUR HELP.
A.I.M. HAS BEEN POPPING UP ON YOUR RADAR QUITE A BIT LATELY FROM WHAT I'VE HEARD.
I FIGURED YOU MIGHT BE ABLE TO OFFER SOME FRESH INSIGHT.
I ALSO WANTED TO SPEND SOME TIME WITH YOU AND PERFORM A BIT OF A GUT CHECK--
I'LL BE FRANK. I DON'T WANT TO LEAD THE AVENGERS AGAIN, CAROL. I'VE BEEN IN THAT SEAT BEFORE AND I KNOW WHAT IT MEANS.
WITH MY NEW POSITION AS THE DIRECTOR OF S.H.I.E.L.D., I KNOW I DON'T HAVE ENOUGH TIME TO HANDLE AVENGERS BUSINESS AND MY DAY JOB.
AND ME PUNCHING YOU SOMEHOW TOLD YOU I WAS RIGHT FOR THE JOB?
IT TOLD ME YOU WERE HUMAN.
I'D NEVER TRUST A LEADER WHO DIDN'T AT LEAST SUSPECT THEY'D MADE THE WRONG DECISION.
BUT I'D ALSO NEVER TRUST A LEADER WHO DIDN'T STAND FIRM WHEN THE DECISION WAS MADE.
SO THAT IS WHY I WANT YOU FOR THE JOB, CAROL. AND THAT IS WHY I PUSHED YOUR BUTTONS IN INDIANA.
THE AVENGERS-- BE THEY MIGHTY OR OTHERWISE--THEY'RE IMPORTANT TO ME.
YOUR OFFER IS IMPORTANT TO ME. AND IT'S ONE HELL OF AN HONOR.
BUT IT'S NOT ENOUGH.

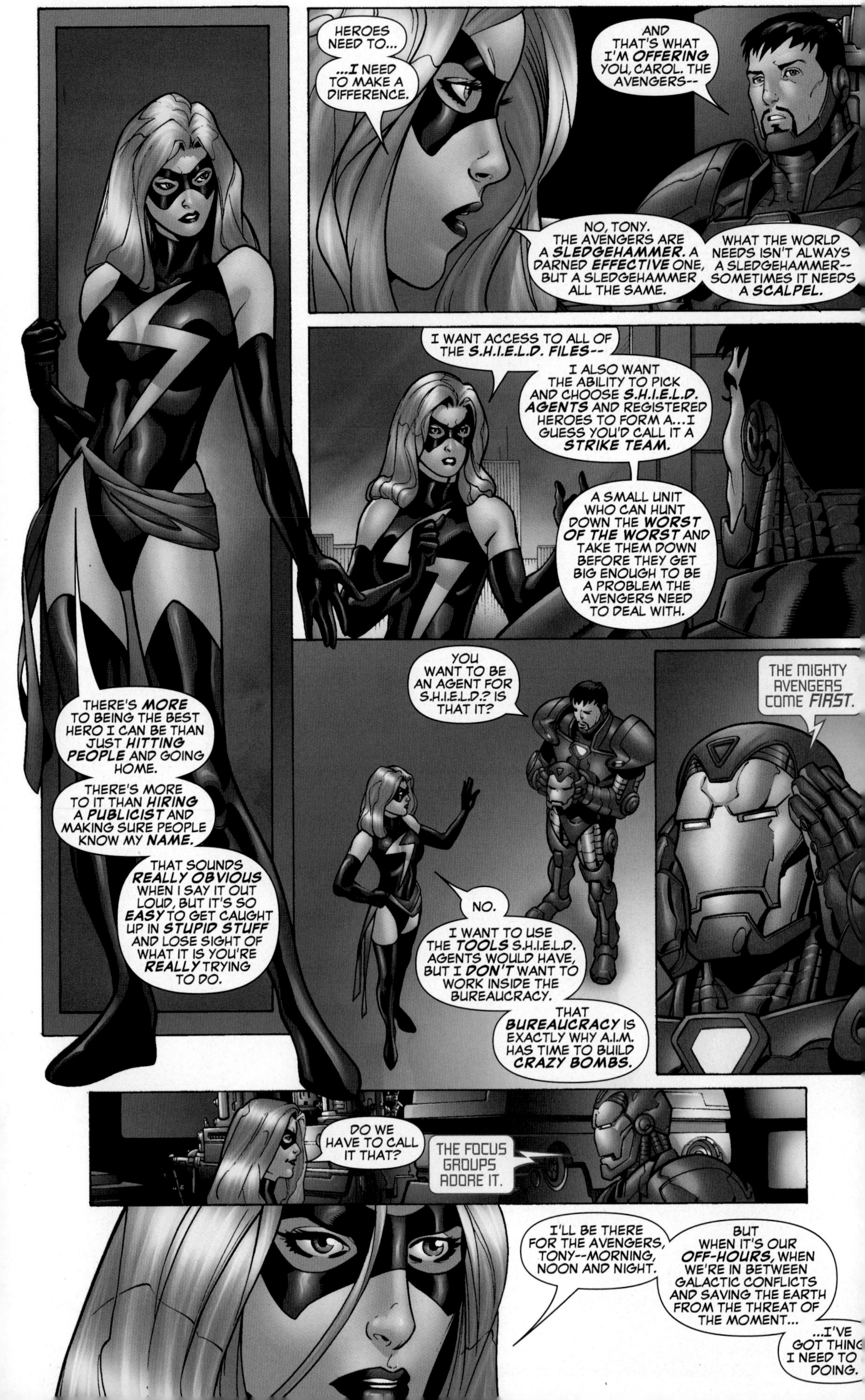
HEROES NEED TO...
...I NEED TO MAKE A DIFFERENCE.
AND THAT'S WHAT I'M OFFERING YOU, CAROL. THE AVENGERS--
NO, TONY. THE AVENGERS ARE A SLEDGEHAMMER. A DARNED EFFECTIVE ONE, BUT A SLEDGEHAMMER ALL THE SAME.
WHAT THE WORLD NEEDS ISN'T ALWAYS A SLEDGEHAMMER-- SOMETIMES IT NEEDS A SCALPEL.
THERE'S MORE TO BEING THE BEST HERO I CAN BE THAN JUST HITTING PEOPLE AND GOING HOME.
THERE'S MORE TO IT THAN HIRING A PUBLICIST AND MAKING SURE PEOPLE KNOW MY NAME.
THAT SOUNDS REALLY OBVIOUS WHEN I SAY IT OUT LOUD, BUT IT'S SO EASY TO GET CAUGHT UP IN STUPID STUFF AND LOSE SIGHT OF WHAT IT IS YOU'RE REALLY TRYING TO DO.
I WANT ACCESS TO ALL OF THE S.H.I.E.L.D. FILES--
I ALSO WANT THE ABILITY TO PICK AND CHOOSE S.H.I.E.L.D. AGENTS AND REGISTERED HEROES TO FORM A...I GUESS YOU'D CALL IT A STRIKE TEAM.
A SMALL UNIT WHO CAN HUNT DOWN THE WORST OF THE WORST AND TAKE THEM DOWN BEFORE THEY GET BIG ENOUGH TO BE A PROBLEM THE AVENGERS NEED TO DEAL WITH.
YOU WANT TO BE AN AGENT FOR S.H.I.E.L.D.? IS THAT IT?
NO.
I WANT TO USE THE TOOLS S.H.I.E.L.D. AGENTS WOULD HAVE, BUT I DON'T WANT TO WORK INSIDE THE BUREAUCRACY.
THAT BUREAUCRACY IS EXACTLY WHY A.I.M. HAS TIME TO BUILD CRAZY BOMBS.
THE MIGHTY AVENGERS COME FIRST.
DO WE HAVE TO CALL IT THAT?
THE FOCUS GROUPS ADORE IT.
I'LL BE THERE FOR THE AVENGERS, TONY--MORNING, NOON AND NIGHT.
BUT WHEN IT'S OUR OFF-HOURS, WHEN WE'RE IN BETWEEN GALACTIC CONFLICTS AND SAVING THE EARTH FROM THE THREAT OF THE MOMENT...
...I'VE GOT THING I NEED TO DOING.

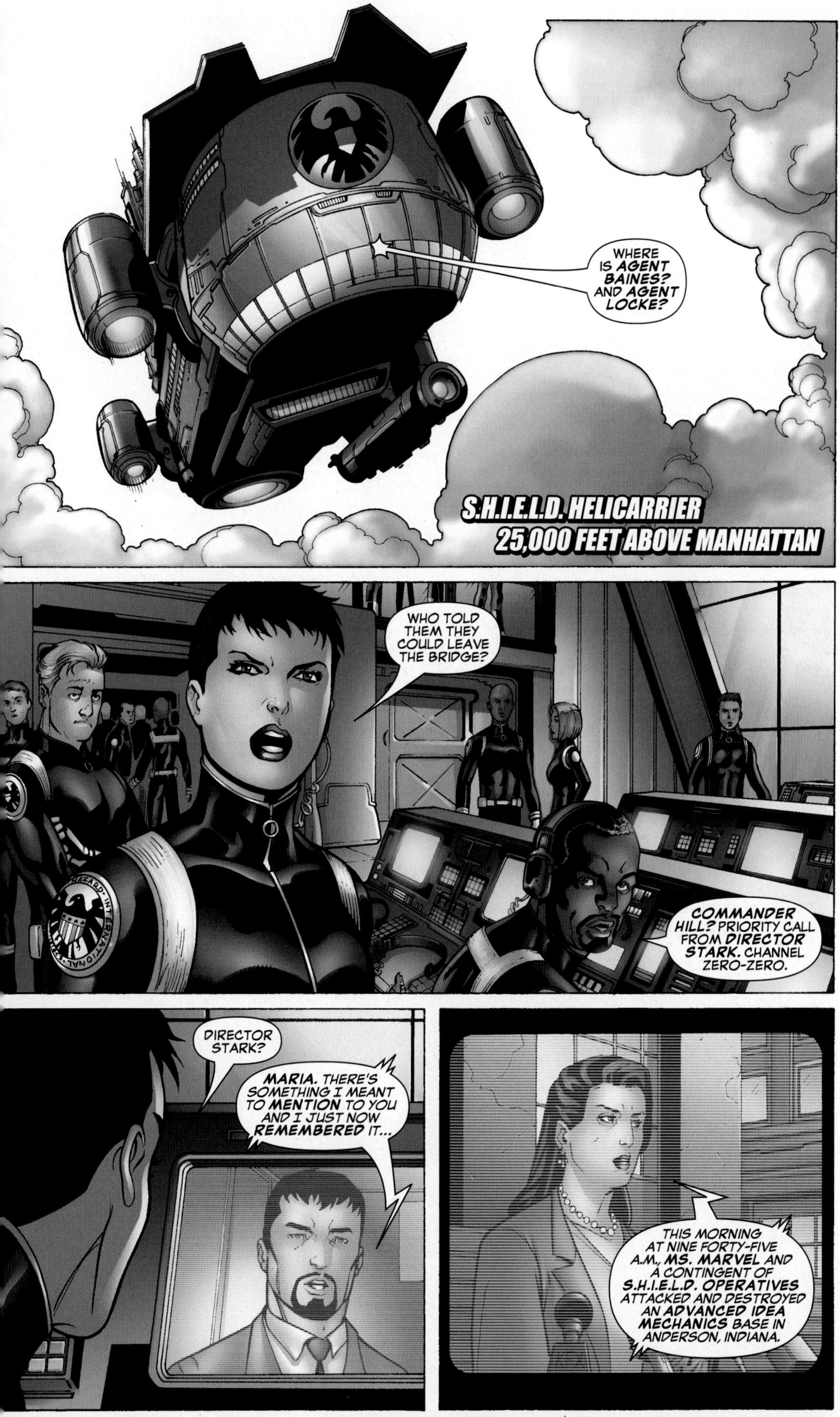
WHERE IS AGENT BAINES? AND AGENT LOCKE?
S.H.I.E.L.D. HELICARRIER
25,000 FEET ABOVE MANHATTAN
WHO TOLD THEM THEY COULD LEAVE THE BRIDGE?
COMMANDER HILL? PRIORITY CALL FROM DIRECTOR STARK. CHANNEL ZERO-ZERO.
DIRECTOR STARK?
MARIA. THERE'S SOMETHING I MEANT TO MENTION TO YOU AND I JUST NOW REMEMBERED IT...
THIS MORNING AT NINE FORTY-FIVE A.M., MS. MARVEL AND A CONTINGENT OF S.H.I.E.L.D. OPERATIVES ATTACKED AND DESTROYED AN ADVANCED IDEA MECHANICS BASE IN ANDERSON, INDIANA.

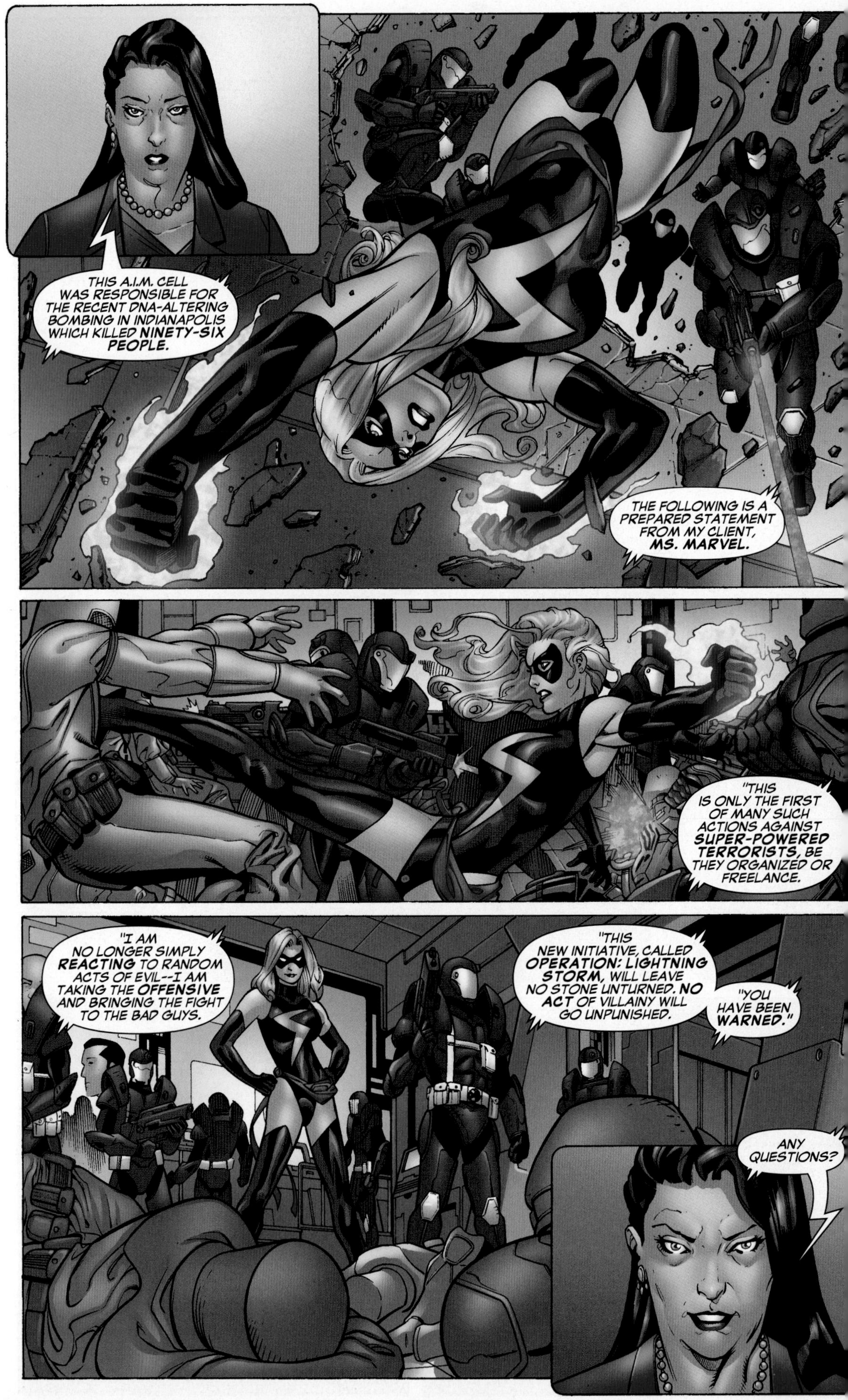
THIS A.I.M. CELL WAS RESPONSIBLE FOR THE RECENT DNA-ALTERING BOMBING IN INDIANAPOLIS WHICH KILLED NINETY-SIX PEOPLE.
THE FOLLOWING IS A PREPARED STATEMENT FROM MY CLIENT, MS. MARVEL.
"THIS IS ONLY THE FIRST OF MANY SUCH ACTIONS AGAINST SUPER-POWERED TERRORISTS, BE THEY ORGANIZED OR FREELANCE.
"I AM NO LONGER SIMPLY REACTING TO RANDOM ACTS OF EVIL--I AM TAKING THE OFFENSIVE AND BRINGING THE FIGHT TO THE BAD GUYS.
"THIS NEW INITIATIVE, CALLED OPERATION: LIGHTNING STORM, WILL LEAVE NO STONE UNTURNED. NO ACT OF VILLAINY WILL GO UNPUNISHED.
"YOU HAVE BEEN WARNED."
ANY QUESTIONS?

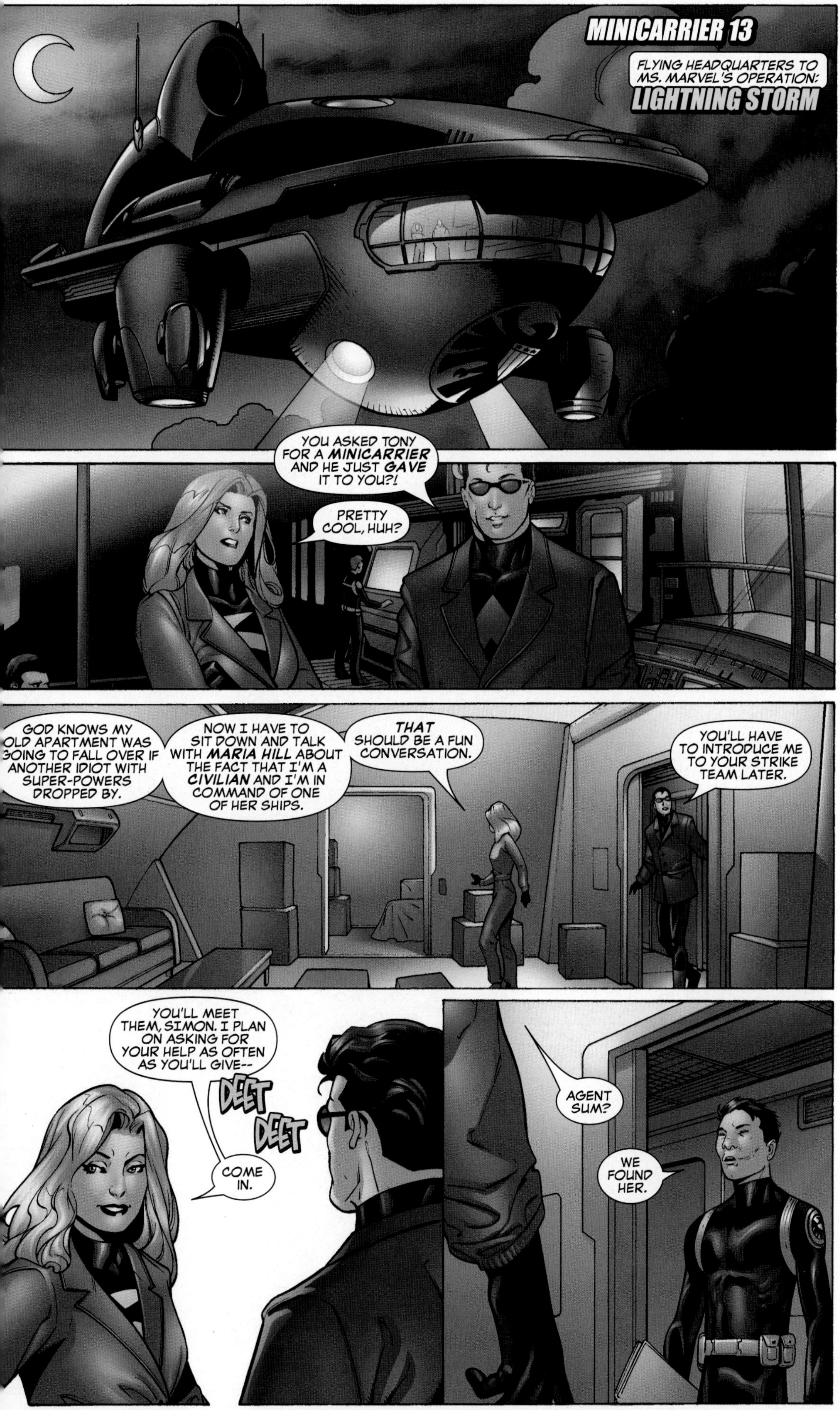
MINICARRIER 13
FLYING HEADQUARTERS TO MS. MARVEL'S OPERATION: LIGHTNING STORM
YOU ASKED TONY FOR A MINICARRIER AND HE JUST GAVE IT TO YOU?!
PRETTY COOL, HUH?
GOD KNOWS MY OLD APARTMENT WAS GOING TO FALL OVER IF ANOTHER IDIOT WITH SUPER-POWERS DROPPED BY.
NOW I HAVE TO SIT DOWN AND TALK WITH MARIA HILL ABOUT THE FACT THAT I'M A CIVILIAN AND I'M IN COMMAND OF ONE OF HER SHIPS.
THAT SHOULD BE A FUN CONVERSATION.
YOU'LL HAVE TO INTRODUCE ME TO YOUR STRIKE TEAM LATER.
YOU'LL MEET THEM, SIMON. I PLAN ON ASKING FOR YOUR HELP AS OFTEN AS YOU'LL GIVE--
DEET DEET
COME IN.
AGENT SUM?
WE FOUND HER.

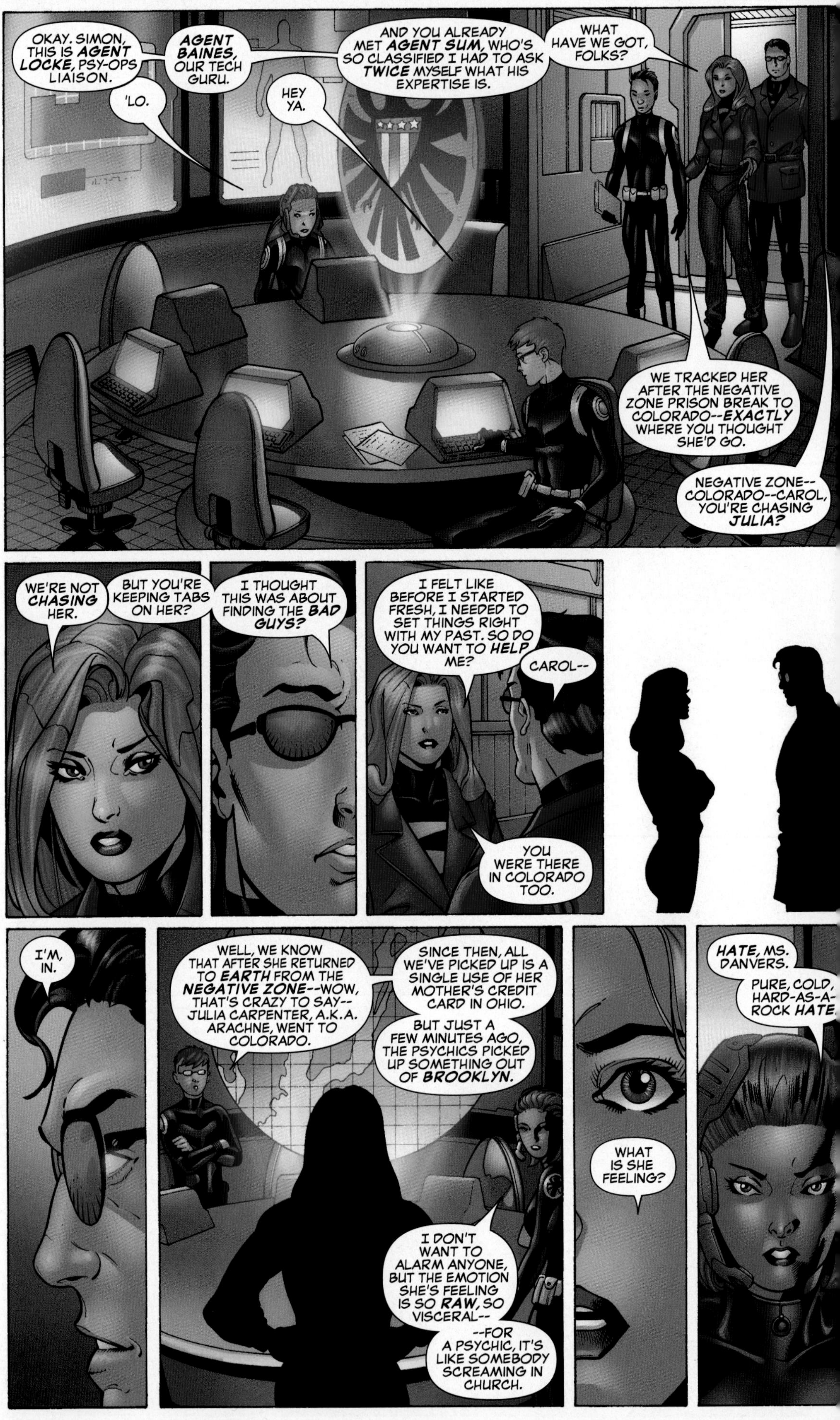

OKAY. SIMON, THIS IS AGENT LOCKE, PSY-OPS LIAISON.
AGENT BAINES, OUR TECH GURU.
'LO.
HEY YA.
AND YOU ALREADY MET AGENT SUM, WHO'S SO CLASSIFIED I HAD TO ASK TWICE MYSELF WHAT HIS EXPERTISE IS.
WHAT HAVE WE GOT, FOLKS?
WE TRACKED HER AFTER THE NEGATIVE ZONE PRISON BREAK TO COLORADO--EXACTLY WHERE YOU THOUGHT SHE'D GO.
NEGATIVE ZONE--COLORADO--CAROL, YOU'RE CHASING JULIA?
WE'RE NOT CHASING HER.
BUT YOU'RE KEEPING TABS ON HER?
I THOUGHT THIS WAS ABOUT FINDING THE BAD GUYS?
I FELT LIKE BEFORE I STARTED FRESH, I NEEDED TO SET THINGS RIGHT WITH MY PAST. SO DO YOU WANT TO HELP ME?
CAROL--
YOU WERE THERE IN COLORADO TOO.
I'M, IN.
WELL, WE KNOW THAT AFTER SHE RETURNED TO EARTH FROM THE NEGATIVE ZONE--WOW, THAT'S CRAZY TO SAY--JULIA CARPENTER, A.K.A. ARACHNE, WENT TO COLORADO.
SINCE THEN, ALL WE'VE PICKED UP IS A SINGLE USE OF HER MOTHER'S CREDIT CARD IN OHIO.
BUT JUST A FEW MINUTES AGO, THE PSYCHICS PICKED UP SOMETHING OUT OF BROOKLYN.
I DON'T WANT TO ALARM ANYONE, BUT THE EMOTION SHE'S FEELING IS SO RAW, SO VISCERAL--
--FOR A PSYCHIC, IT'S LIKE SOMEBODY SCREAMING IN CHURCH.
WHAT IS SHE FEELING?
HATE, MS. DANVERS.
PURE, COLD, HARD-AS-A-ROCK HATE.

ANYA, I *CAN'T* HAVE YOU OUT FRONT WORKING THE *REGISTERS* LOOKING LIKE *THAT.*

THOSE *BRUISES* ARE--

I BROUGHT A *LONG-SLEEVE SHIRT* AND--

BROOKLYN, N.Y.

UNACCEPTABLE! YOU HAVE TO WEAR THE *UNIFORM* IF YOU'RE GOING TO WORK THE *REGISTER!* IT'S COMPANY POLICY!

LOOK, I'M SORRY, OKAY? I'LL JUST WORK IN THE BACK, ON THE *FRY MACHINE* OR--

AND WHO'S GOING TO WORK THE *REGISTER?* THE FRY MACHINE ALREADY *HAS SOMEONE* SCHEDULED FOR IT AND--

YOU KNOW WHAT? I SO DO *NOT* NEED THIS IN MY LIFE RIGHT NOW.

SO YOU'RE *QUITTING?!*

EXACTAMUNDO.

STUPID JOB. STUPID UNIFORM. STUPID *EVERY-THING.*

WHERE IS MY DAUGHTER?

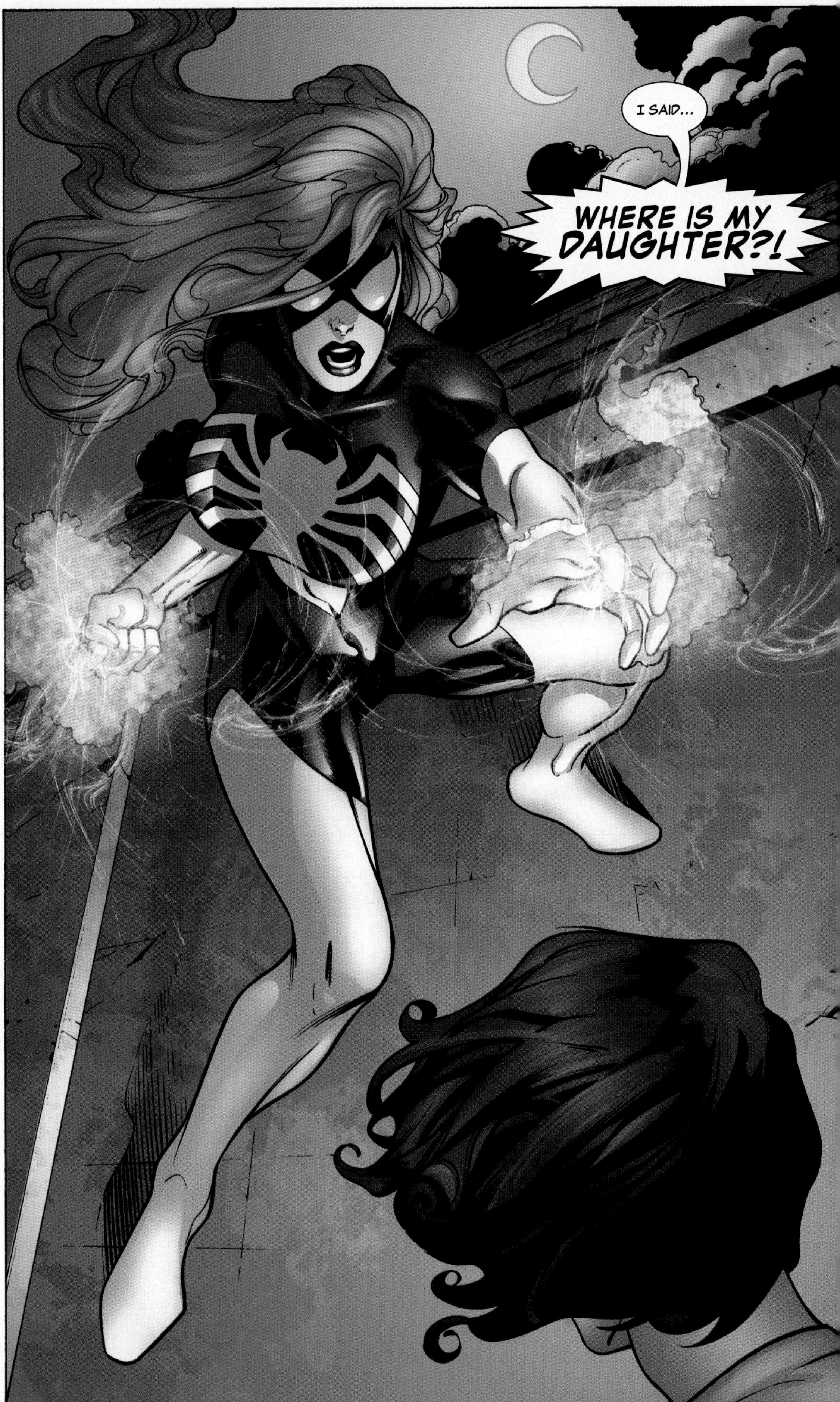
I SAID...
WHERE IS MY DAUGHTER?!

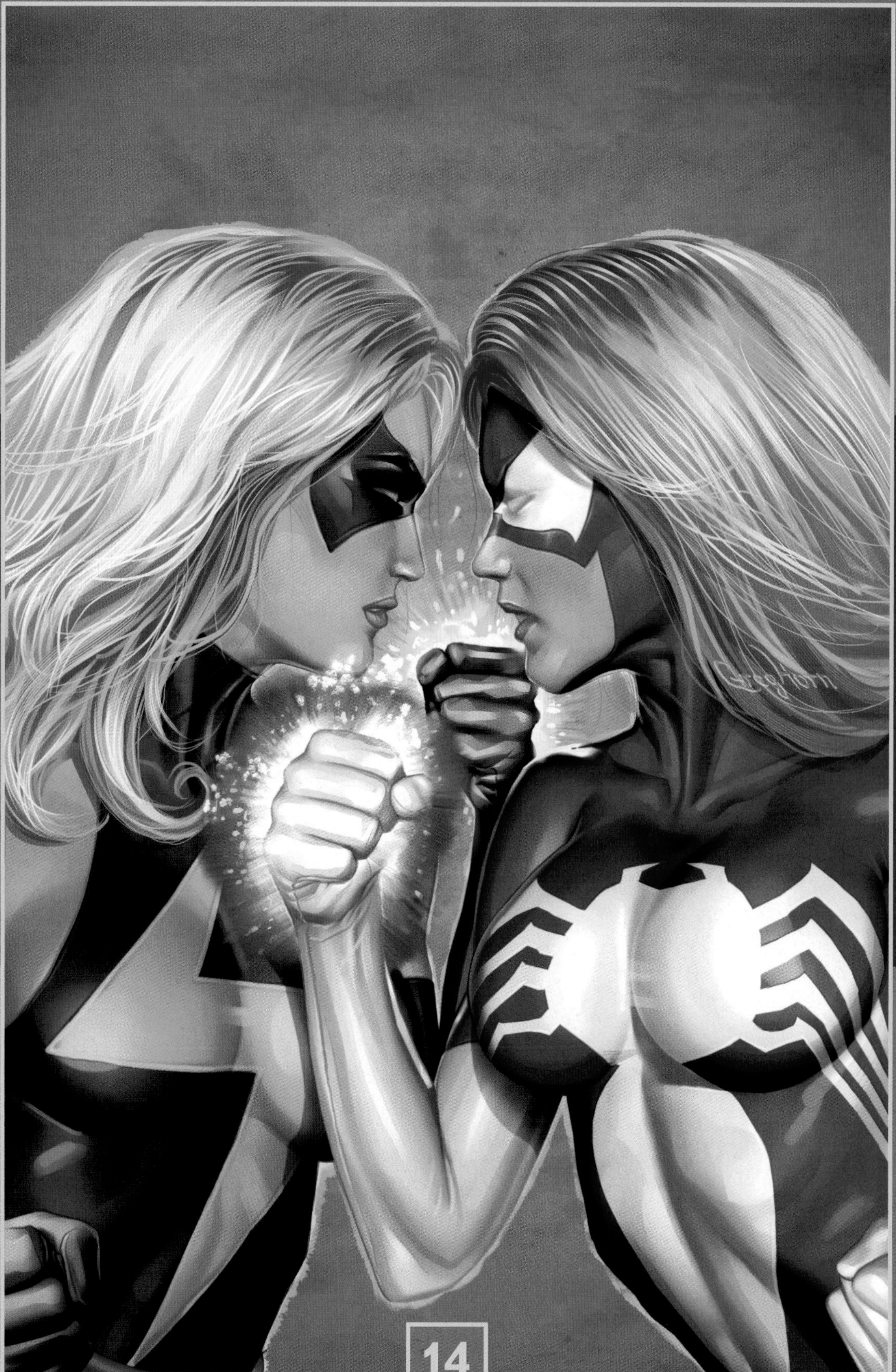

14

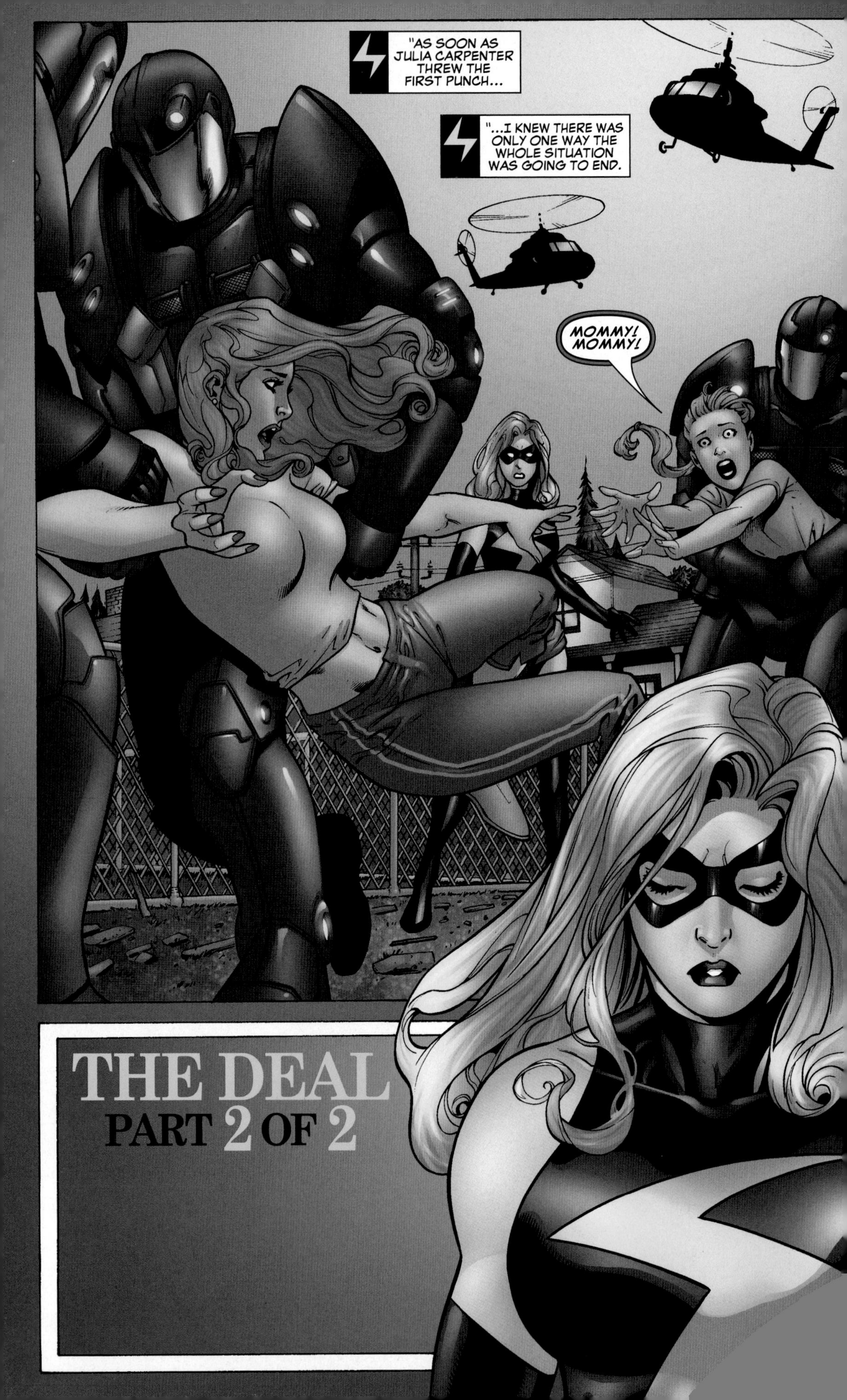
"AS SOON AS JULIA CARPENTER THREW THE FIRST PUNCH...
"...I KNEW THERE WAS ONLY ONE WAY THE WHOLE SITUATION WAS GOING TO END.
MOMMY! MOMMY!
THE DEAL
PART 2 OF 2

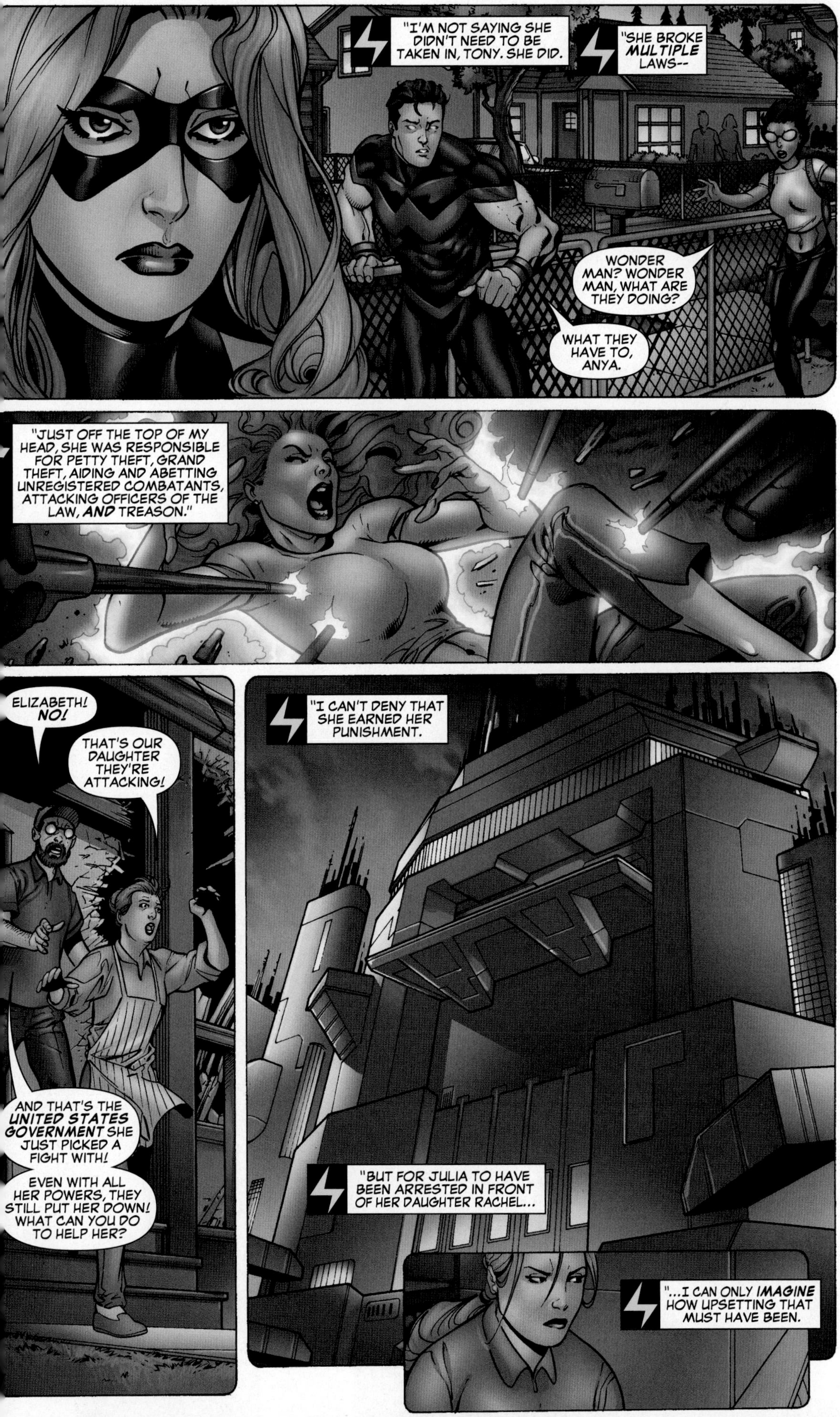
"I'M NOT SAYING SHE DIDN'T NEED TO BE TAKEN IN, TONY. SHE DID.
"SHE BROKE MULTIPLE LAWS--
WONDER MAN? WONDER MAN, WHAT ARE THEY DOING?
WHAT THEY HAVE TO, ANYA.
"JUST OFF THE TOP OF MY HEAD, SHE WAS RESPONSIBLE FOR PETTY THEFT, GRAND THEFT, AIDING AND ABETTING UNREGISTERED COMBATANTS, ATTACKING OFFICERS OF THE LAW, AND TREASON."
ELIZABETH! NO!
THAT'S OUR DAUGHTER THEY'RE ATTACKING!
AND THAT'S THE UNITED STATES GOVERNMENT SHE JUST PICKED A FIGHT WITH!
EVEN WITH ALL HER POWERS, THEY STILL PUT HER DOWN! WHAT CAN YOU DO TO HELP HER?
"I CAN'T DENY THAT SHE EARNED HER PUNISHMENT.
"BUT FOR JULIA TO HAVE BEEN ARRESTED IN FRONT OF HER DAUGHTER RACHEL...
"...I CAN ONLY IMAGINE HOW UPSETTING THAT MUST HAVE BEEN.

"THEN, A COUPLE OF WEEKS LATER, WHEN THE PRISON BREAK OCCURRED... WELL...

"...YOU WERE THERE.

"AND I *ADMIT IT*-- UNLIKE THE HEROES WHO WERE PARDONED AND OFFERED THE CHANCE TO REGISTER...

"...JULIA, BECAUSE SHE STILL WON'T SIGN UP, *DESERVED* TO BE DECLARED A FUGITIVE.

"BUT WHEN SHE WAS SIGHTED IN COLORADO THE OTHER DAY...

"...ALL I COL THINK OF W. RACHEL."

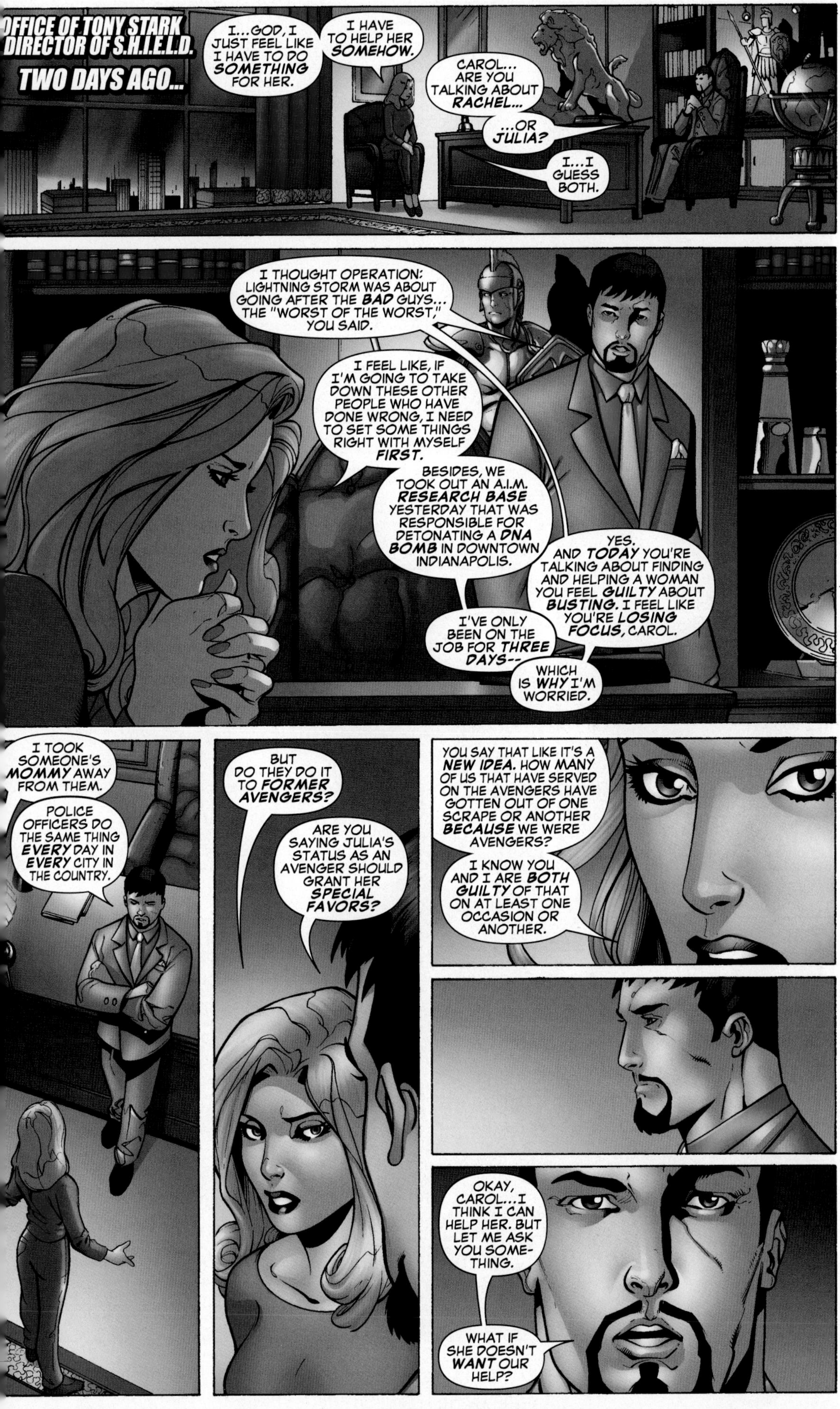
OFFICE OF TONY STARK DIRECTOR OF S.H.I.E.L.D.
TWO DAYS AGO...
I...GOD, I JUST FEEL LIKE I HAVE TO DO SOMETHING FOR HER.
I HAVE TO HELP HER SOMEHOW.
CAROL... ARE YOU TALKING ABOUT RACHEL...
...OR JULIA?
I...I GUESS BOTH.
I THOUGHT OPERATION: LIGHTNING STORM WAS ABOUT GOING AFTER THE BAD GUYS... THE "WORST OF THE WORST," YOU SAID.
I FEEL LIKE, IF I'M GOING TO TAKE DOWN THESE OTHER PEOPLE WHO HAVE DONE WRONG, I NEED TO SET SOME THINGS RIGHT WITH MYSELF FIRST.
BESIDES, WE TOOK OUT AN A.I.M. RESEARCH BASE YESTERDAY THAT WAS RESPONSIBLE FOR DETONATING A DNA BOMB IN DOWNTOWN INDIANAPOLIS.
YES. AND TODAY YOU'RE TALKING ABOUT FINDING AND HELPING A WOMAN YOU FEEL GUILTY ABOUT BUSTING. I FEEL LIKE YOU'RE LOSING FOCUS, CAROL.
I'VE ONLY BEEN ON THE JOB FOR THREE DAYS--
WHICH IS WHY I'M WORRIED.
I TOOK SOMEONE'S MOMMY AWAY FROM THEM.
POLICE OFFICERS DO THE SAME THING EVERY DAY IN EVERY CITY IN THE COUNTRY.
BUT DO THEY DO IT TO FORMER AVENGERS?
ARE YOU SAYING JULIA'S STATUS AS AN AVENGER SHOULD GRANT HER SPECIAL FAVORS?
YOU SAY THAT LIKE IT'S A NEW IDEA. HOW MANY OF US THAT HAVE SERVED ON THE AVENGERS HAVE GOTTEN OUT OF ONE SCRAPE OR ANOTHER BECAUSE WE WERE AVENGERS?
I KNOW YOU AND I ARE BOTH GUILTY OF THAT ON AT LEAST ONE OCCASION OR ANOTHER.
OKAY, CAROL...I THINK I CAN HELP HER. BUT LET ME ASK YOU SOME-THING.
WHAT IF SHE DOESN'T WANT OUR HELP?

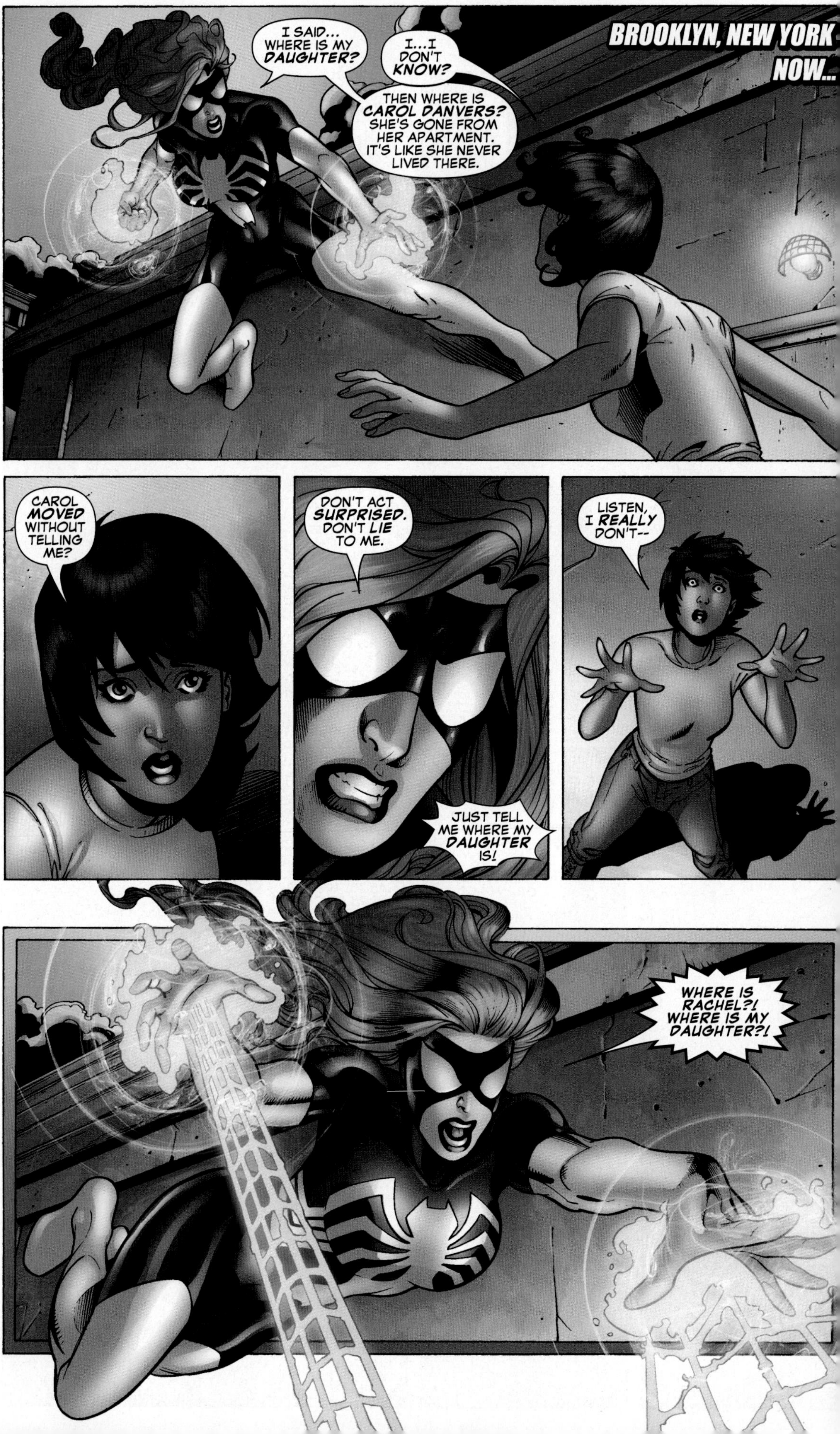
BROOKLYN, NEW YORK NOW...
I SAID... WHERE IS MY DAUGHTER?
I...I DON'T KNOW?
THEN WHERE IS CAROL DANVERS? SHE'S GONE FROM HER APARTMENT. IT'S LIKE SHE NEVER LIVED THERE.
CAROL MOVED WITHOUT TELLING ME?
DON'T ACT SURPRISED. DON'T LIE TO ME.
JUST TELL ME WHERE MY DAUGHTER IS!
LISTEN, I REALLY DON'T--
WHERE IS RACHEL?! WHERE IS MY DAUGHTER?!

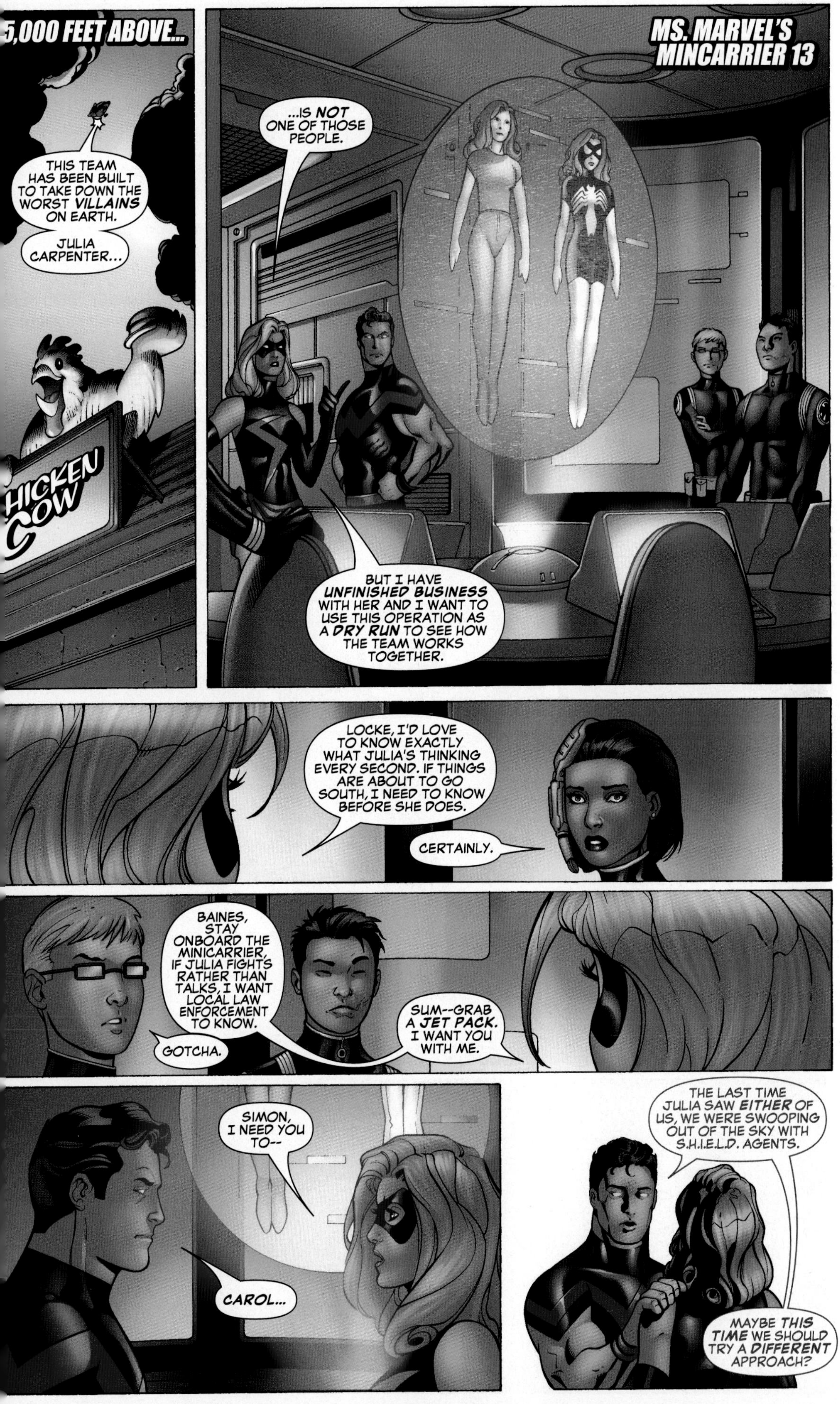
5,000 FEET ABOVE...
THIS TEAM HAS BEEN BUILT TO TAKE DOWN THE WORST VILLAINS ON EARTH.
JULIA CARPENTER...
HICKEN COW
MS. MARVEL'S MINCARRIER 13
...IS NOT ONE OF THOSE PEOPLE.
BUT I HAVE UNFINISHED BUSINESS WITH HER AND I WANT TO USE THIS OPERATION AS A DRY RUN TO SEE HOW THE TEAM WORKS TOGETHER.
LOCKE, I'D LOVE TO KNOW EXACTLY WHAT JULIA'S THINKING EVERY SECOND. IF THINGS ARE ABOUT TO GO SOUTH, I NEED TO KNOW BEFORE SHE DOES.
CERTAINLY.
BAINES, STAY ONBOARD THE MINICARRIER, IF JULIA FIGHTS RATHER THAN TALKS, I WANT LOCAL LAW ENFORCEMENT TO KNOW.
GOTCHA.
SUM--GRAB A JET PACK. I WANT YOU WITH ME.
SIMON, I NEED YOU TO--
CAROL...
THE LAST TIME JULIA SAW EITHER OF US, WE WERE SWOOPING OUT OF THE SKY WITH S.H.I.E.L.D. AGENTS.
MAYBE THIS TIME WE SHOULD TRY A DIFFERENT APPROACH?

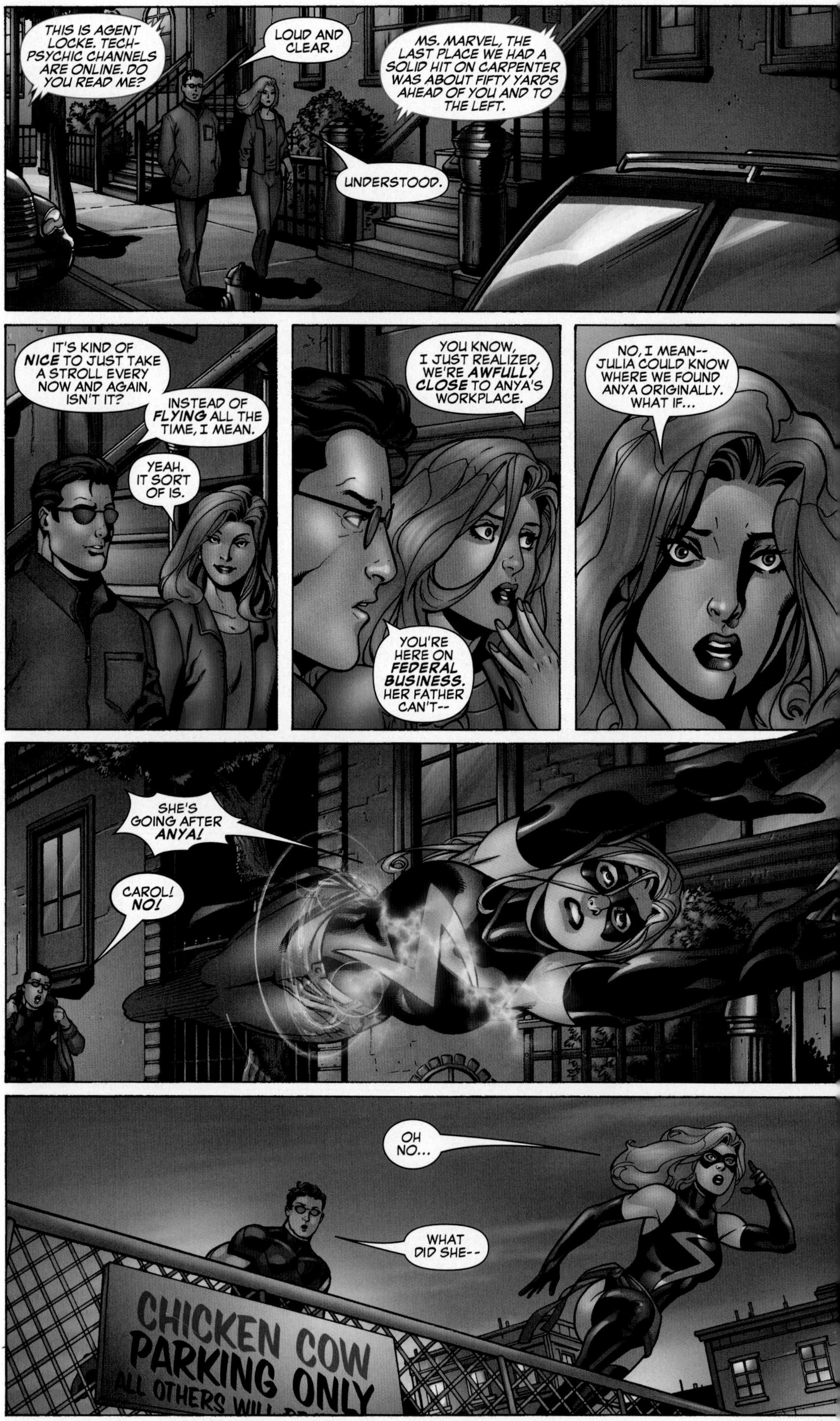

THIS IS AGENT LOCKE. TECH-PSYCHIC CHANNELS ARE ONLINE. DO YOU READ ME?
LOUD AND CLEAR.
MS. MARVEL, THE LAST PLACE WE HAD A SOLID HIT ON CARPENTER WAS ABOUT FIFTY YARDS AHEAD OF YOU AND TO THE LEFT.
UNDERSTOOD.
IT'S KIND OF NICE TO JUST TAKE A STROLL EVERY NOW AND AGAIN, ISN'T IT?
INSTEAD OF FLYING ALL THE TIME, I MEAN.
YEAH. IT SORT OF IS.
YOU KNOW, I JUST REALIZED, WE'RE AWFULLY CLOSE TO ANYA'S WORKPLACE.
YOU'RE HERE ON FEDERAL BUSINESS. HER FATHER CAN'T--
NO, I MEAN-- JULIA COULD KNOW WHERE WE FOUND ANYA ORIGINALLY. WHAT IF...
SHE'S GOING AFTER ANYA!
CAROL! NO!
OH NO...
WHAT DID SHE--
CHICKEN COW
PARKING ONLY

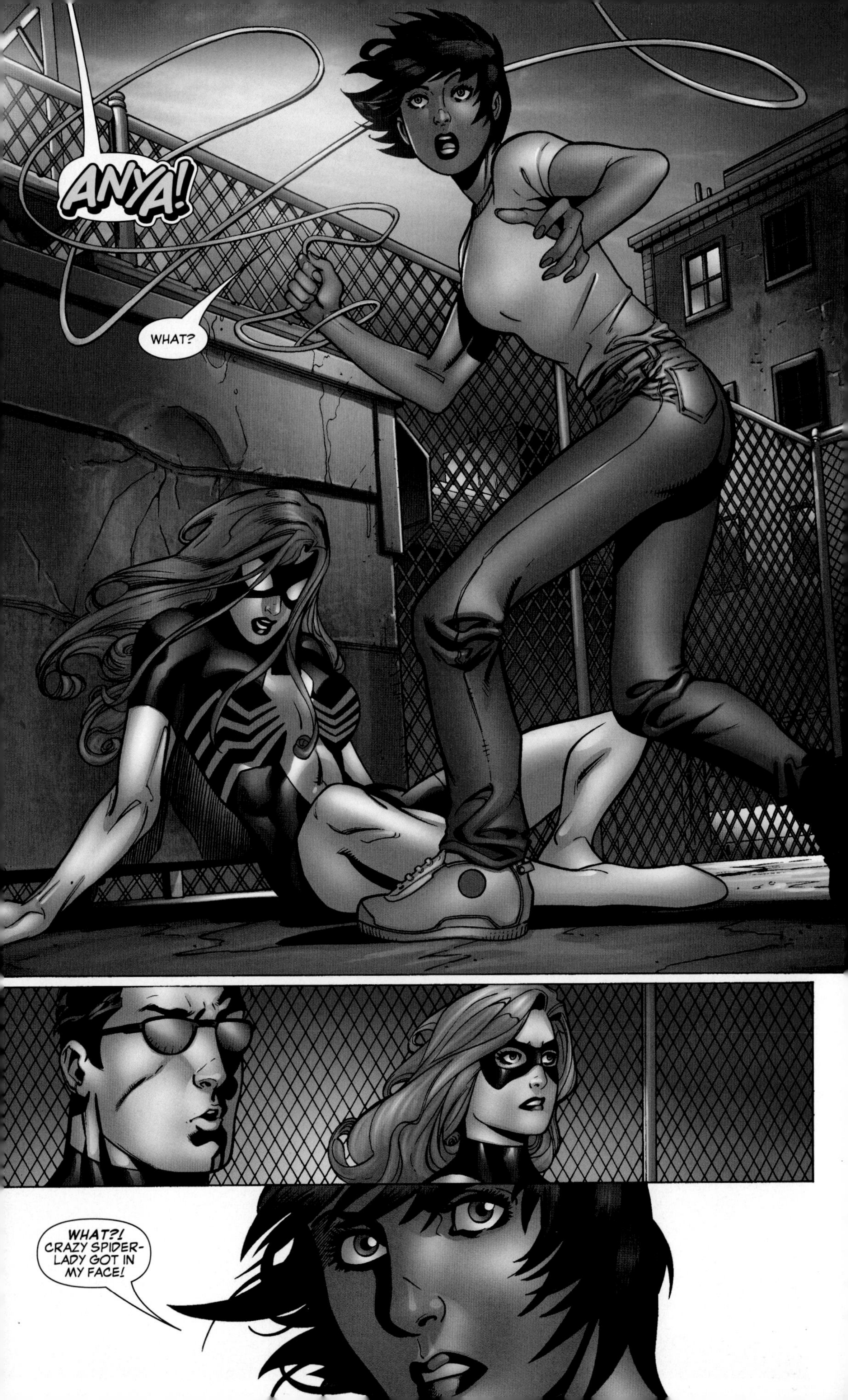
ANYA!
WHAT?
WHAT?! CRAZY SPIDER-LADY GOT IN MY FACE!

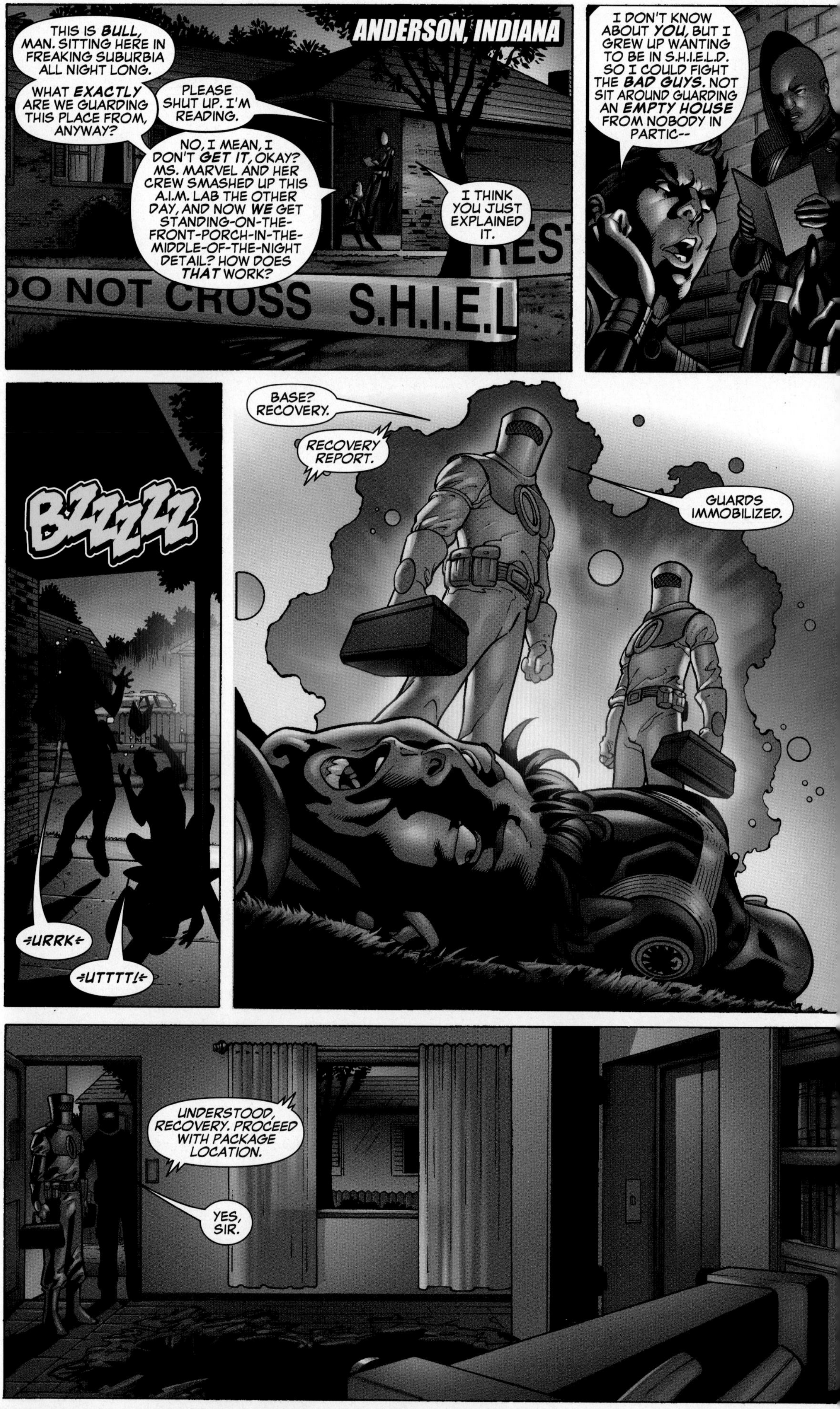
ANDERSON, INDIANA
THIS IS BULL, MAN. SITTING HERE IN FREAKING SUBURBIA ALL NIGHT LONG.
WHAT EXACTLY ARE WE GUARDING THIS PLACE FROM, ANYWAY?
PLEASE SHUT UP. I'M READING.
NO, I MEAN, I DON'T GET IT, OKAY? MS. MARVEL AND HER CREW SMASHED UP THIS A.I.M. LAB THE OTHER DAY, AND NOW WE GET STANDING-ON-THE-FRONT-PORCH-IN-THE-MIDDLE-OF-THE-NIGHT DETAIL? HOW DOES THAT WORK?
I THINK YOU JUST EXPLAINED IT.
DO NOT CROSS S.H.I.E.L
REST
I DON'T KNOW ABOUT YOU, BUT I GREW UP WANTING TO BE IN S.H.I.E.L.D. SO I COULD FIGHT THE BAD GUYS. NOT SIT AROUND GUARDING AN EMPTY HOUSE FROM NOBODY IN PARTIC--
BZZZZZ
URRK
UTTTT!
BASE? RECOVERY.
RECOVERY REPORT.
GUARDS IMMOBILIZED.
UNDERSTOOD, RECOVERY. PROCEED WITH PACKAGE LOCATION.
YES, SIR.

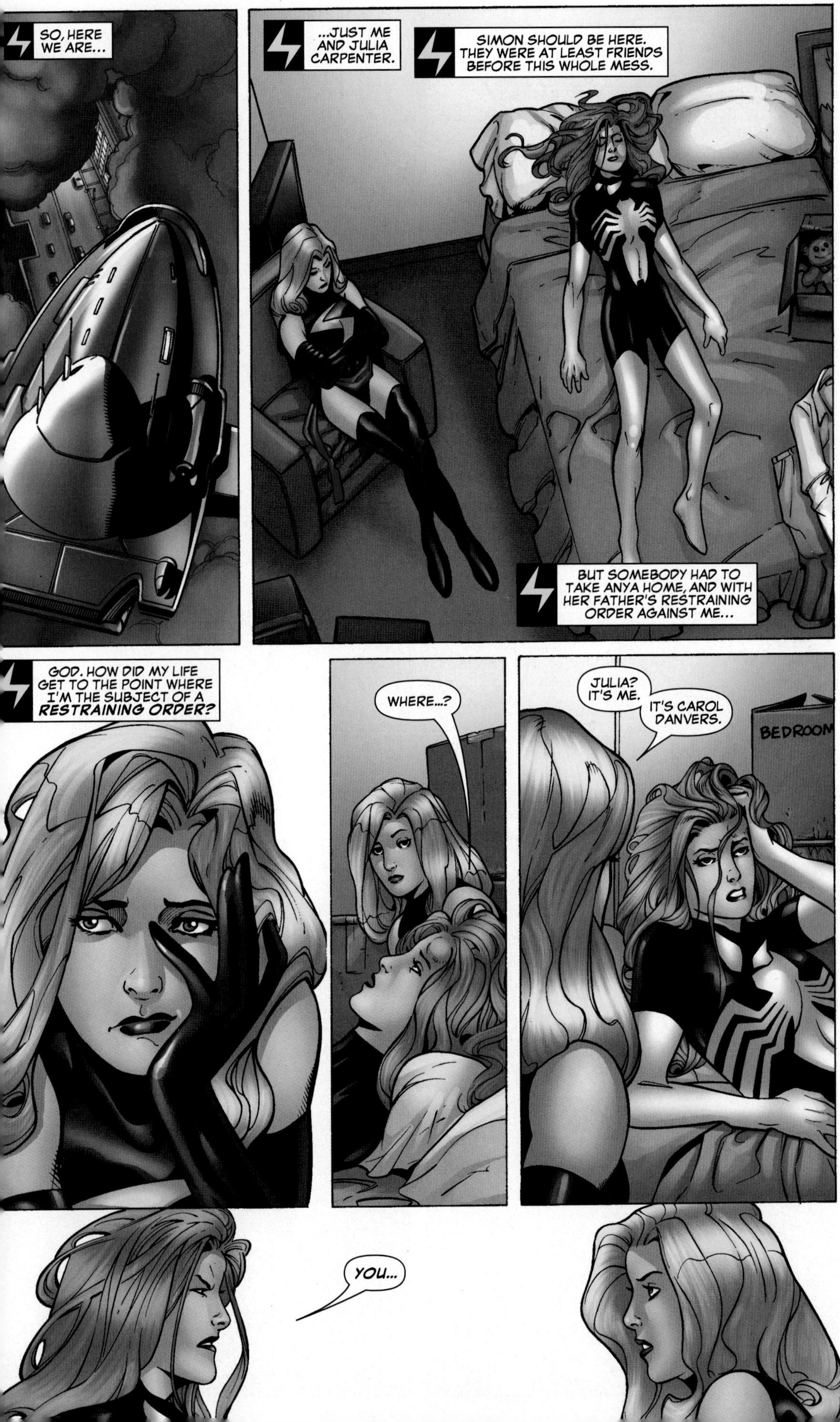
SO, HERE WE ARE...
...JUST ME AND JULIA CARPENTER.
SIMON SHOULD BE HERE. THEY WERE AT LEAST FRIENDS BEFORE THIS WHOLE MESS.
BUT SOMEBODY HAD TO TAKE ANYA HOME, AND WITH HER FATHER'S RESTRAINING ORDER AGAINST ME...
GOD. HOW DID MY LIFE GET TO THE POINT WHERE I'M THE SUBJECT OF A *RESTRAINING ORDER?*
WHERE...?
JULIA? IT'S ME.
IT'S CAROL DANVERS.
BEDROOM
YOU...

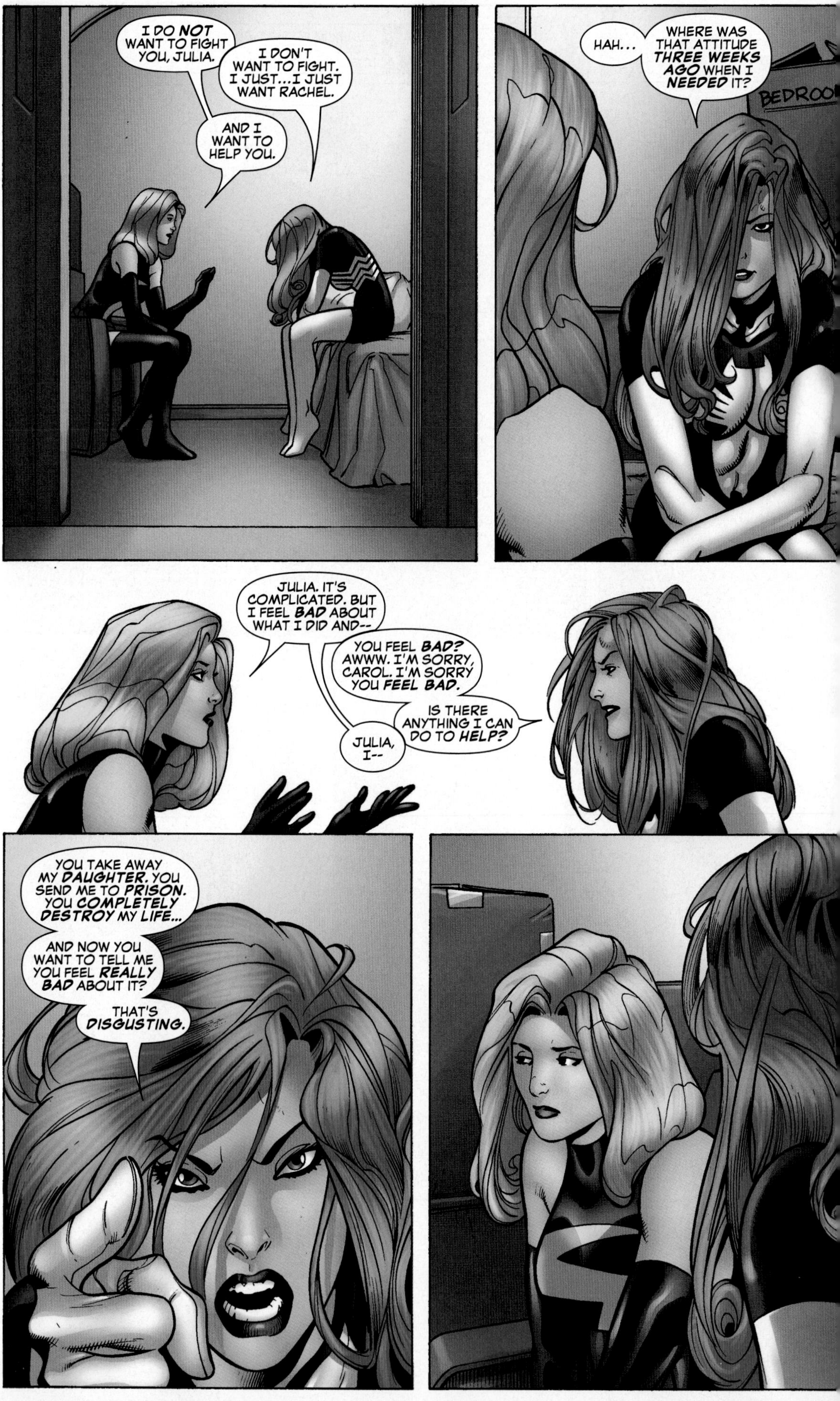
I DO NOT WANT TO FIGHT YOU, JULIA.
I DON'T WANT TO FIGHT. I JUST...I JUST WANT RACHEL.
AND I WANT TO HELP YOU.
HAH...
WHERE WAS THAT ATTITUDE THREE WEEKS AGO WHEN I NEEDED IT?
BEDROO
JULIA. IT'S COMPLICATED. BUT I FEEL BAD ABOUT WHAT I DID AND--
YOU FEEL BAD? AWWW. I'M SORRY, CAROL. I'M SORRY YOU FEEL BAD.
IS THERE ANYTHING I CAN DO TO HELP?
JULIA, I--
YOU TAKE AWAY MY DAUGHTER. YOU SEND ME TO PRISON. YOU COMPLETELY DESTROY MY LIFE...
AND NOW YOU WANT TO TELL ME YOU FEEL REALLY BAD ABOUT IT?
THAT'S DISGUSTING.

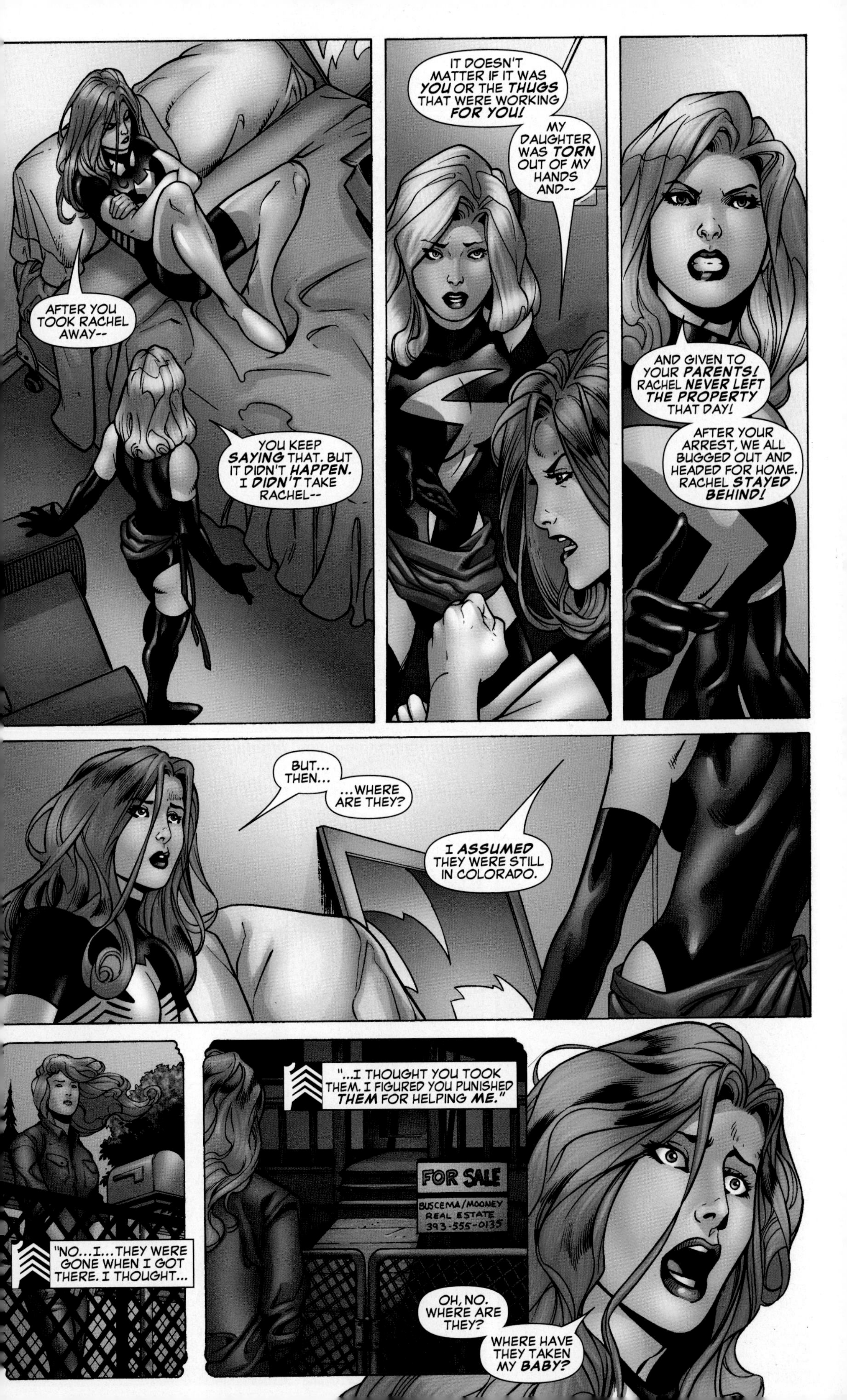
AFTER YOU TOOK RACHEL AWAY--
YOU KEEP SAYING THAT. BUT IT DIDN'T HAPPEN. I DIDN'T TAKE RACHEL--
IT DOESN'T MATTER IF IT WAS YOU OR THE THUGS THAT WERE WORKING FOR YOU!
MY DAUGHTER WAS TORN OUT OF MY HANDS AND--
AND GIVEN TO YOUR PARENTS! RACHEL NEVER LEFT THE PROPERTY THAT DAY!
AFTER YOUR ARREST, WE ALL BUGGED OUT AND HEADED FOR HOME. RACHEL STAYED BEHIND!
BUT... THEN...
...WHERE ARE THEY?
I ASSUMED THEY WERE STILL IN COLORADO.
"NO... I... THEY WERE GONE WHEN I GOT THERE. I THOUGHT...
"...I THOUGHT YOU TOOK THEM. I FIGURED YOU PUNISHED THEM FOR HELPING ME."
FOR SALE
BUSCEMA/MOONEY
REAL ESTATE
393-555-0135
OH, NO. WHERE ARE THEY?
WHERE HAVE THEY TAKEN MY BABY?

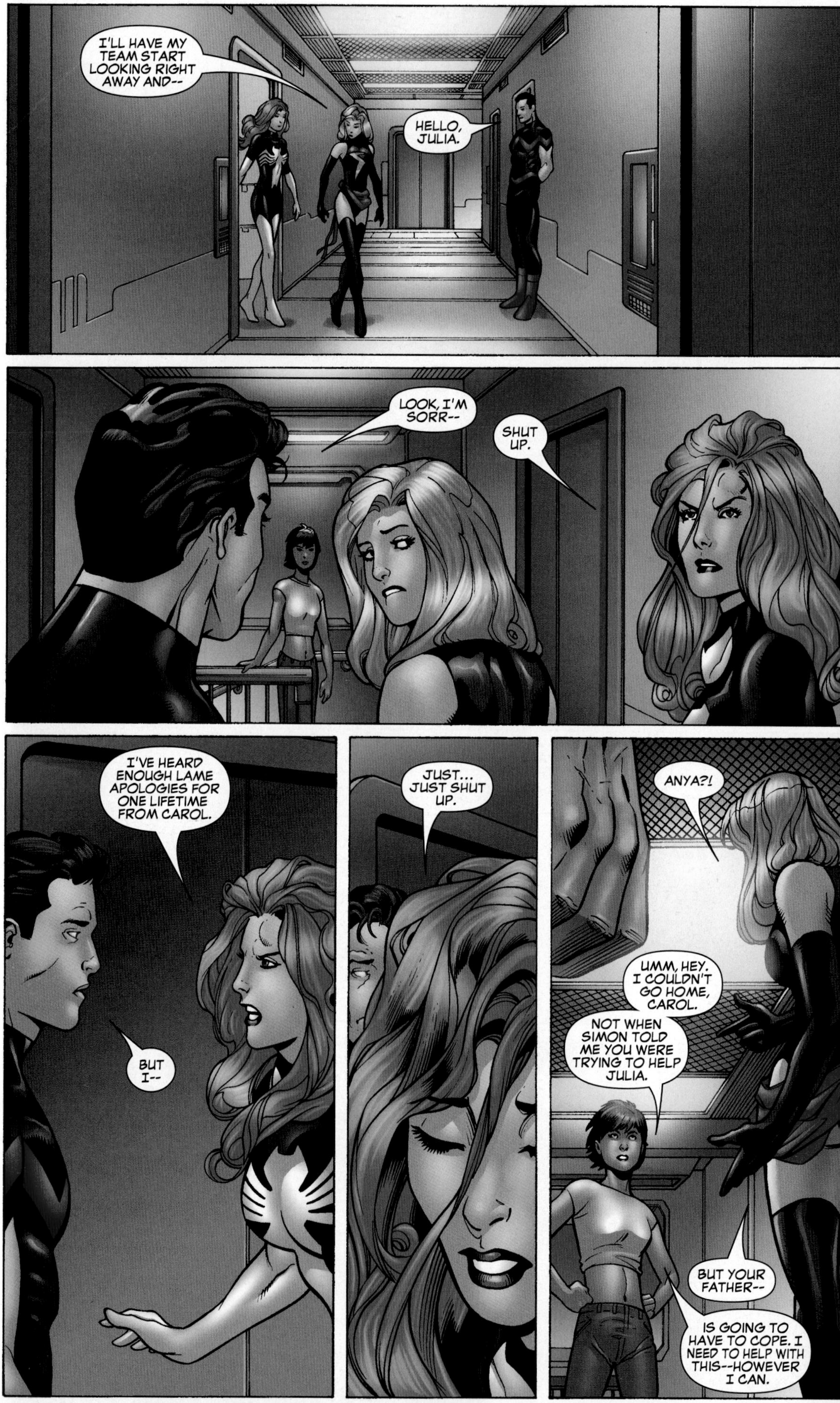
I'LL HAVE MY TEAM START LOOKING RIGHT AWAY AND--
HELLO, JULIA.
LOOK, I'M SORR--
SHUT UP.
I'VE HEARD ENOUGH LAME APOLOGIES FOR ONE LIFETIME FROM CAROL.
BUT I--
JUST... JUST SHUT UP.
ANYA?!
UMM, HEY. I COULDN'T GO HOME, CAROL.
NOT WHEN SIMON TOLD ME YOU WERE TRYING TO HELP JULIA.
BUT YOUR FATHER--
IS GOING TO HAVE TO COPE. I NEED TO HELP WITH THIS--HOWEVER I CAN.

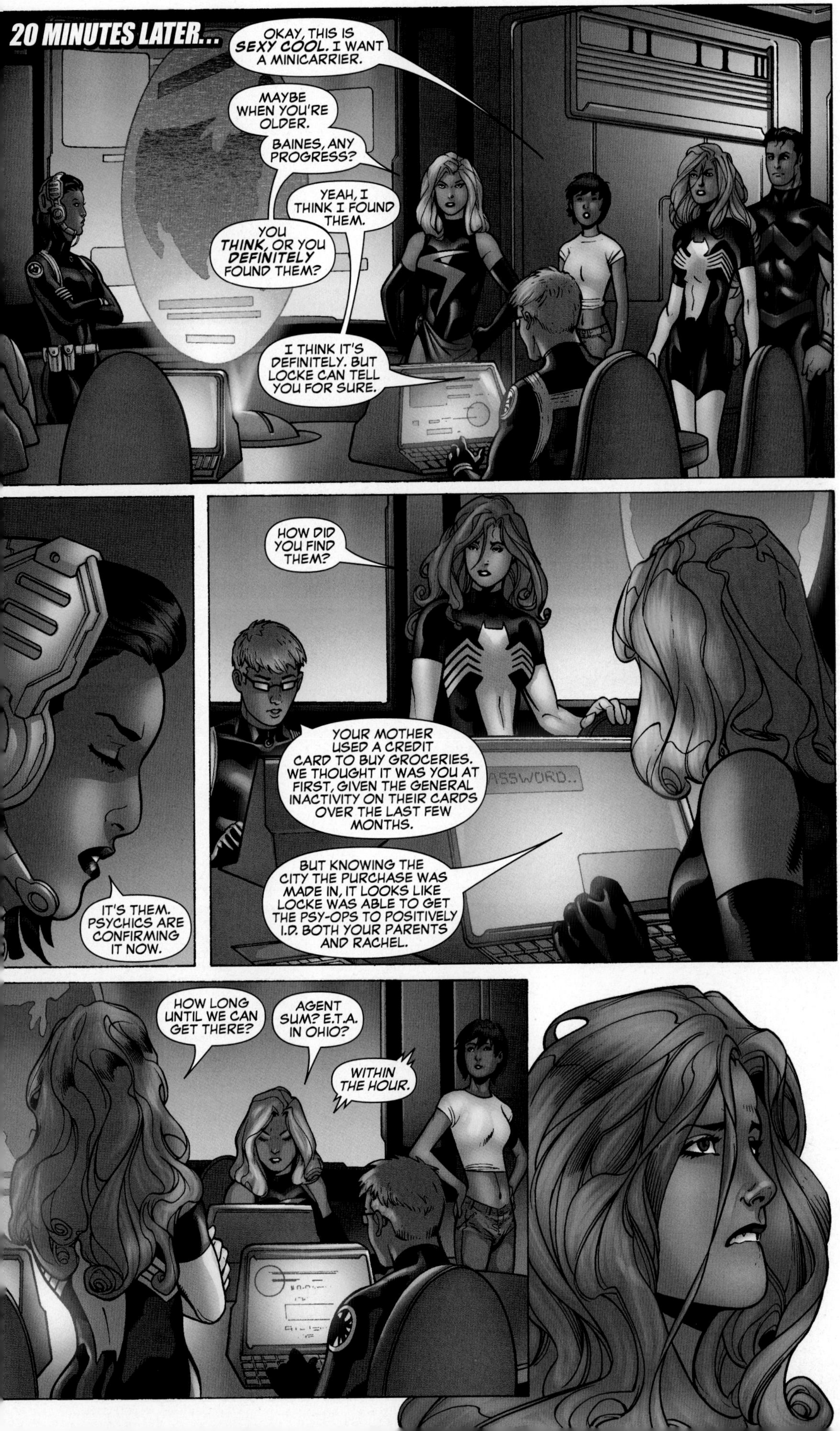
20 MINUTES LATER...
OKAY, THIS IS SEXY COOL. I WANT A MINICARRIER.
MAYBE WHEN YOU'RE OLDER.
BAINES, ANY PROGRESS?
YEAH, I THINK I FOUND THEM.
YOU THINK, OR YOU DEFINITELY FOUND THEM?
I THINK IT'S DEFINITELY. BUT LOCKE CAN TELL YOU FOR SURE.
IT'S THEM. PSYCHICS ARE CONFIRMING IT NOW.
HOW DID YOU FIND THEM?
YOUR MOTHER USED A CREDIT CARD TO BUY GROCERIES. WE THOUGHT IT WAS YOU AT FIRST, GIVEN THE GENERAL INACTIVITY ON THEIR CARDS OVER THE LAST FEW MONTHS.
BUT KNOWING THE CITY THE PURCHASE WAS MADE IN, IT LOOKS LIKE LOCKE WAS ABLE TO GET THE PSY-OPS TO POSITIVELY I.D. BOTH YOUR PARENTS AND RACHEL.
HOW LONG UNTIL WE CAN GET THERE?
AGENT SUM? E.T.A. IN OHIO?
WITHIN THE HOUR.

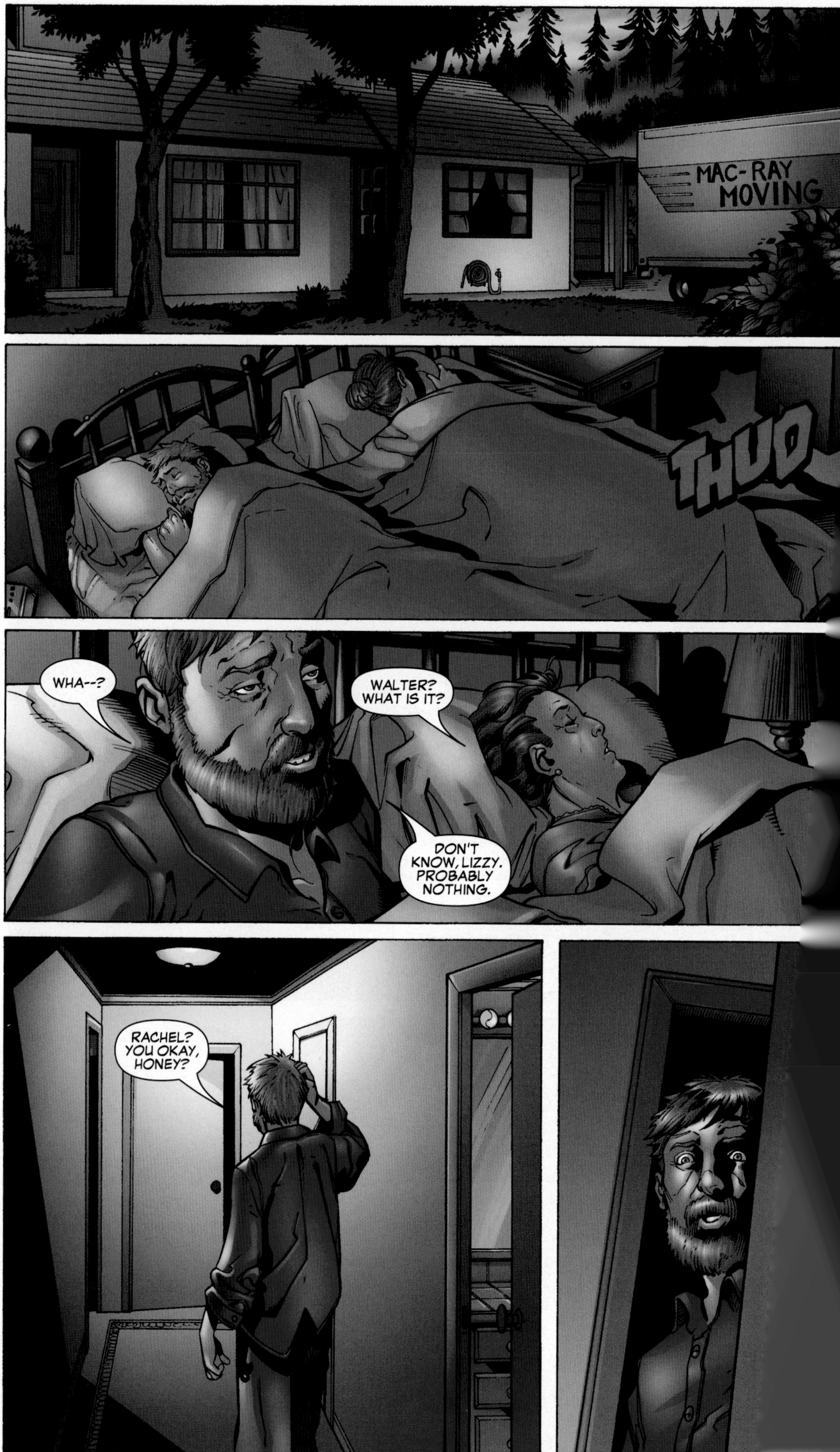
MAC-RAY MOVING
THUD
WHA--?
WALTER? WHAT IS IT?
DON'T KNOW, LIZZY. PROBABLY NOTHING.
RACHEL? YOU OKAY, HONEY?

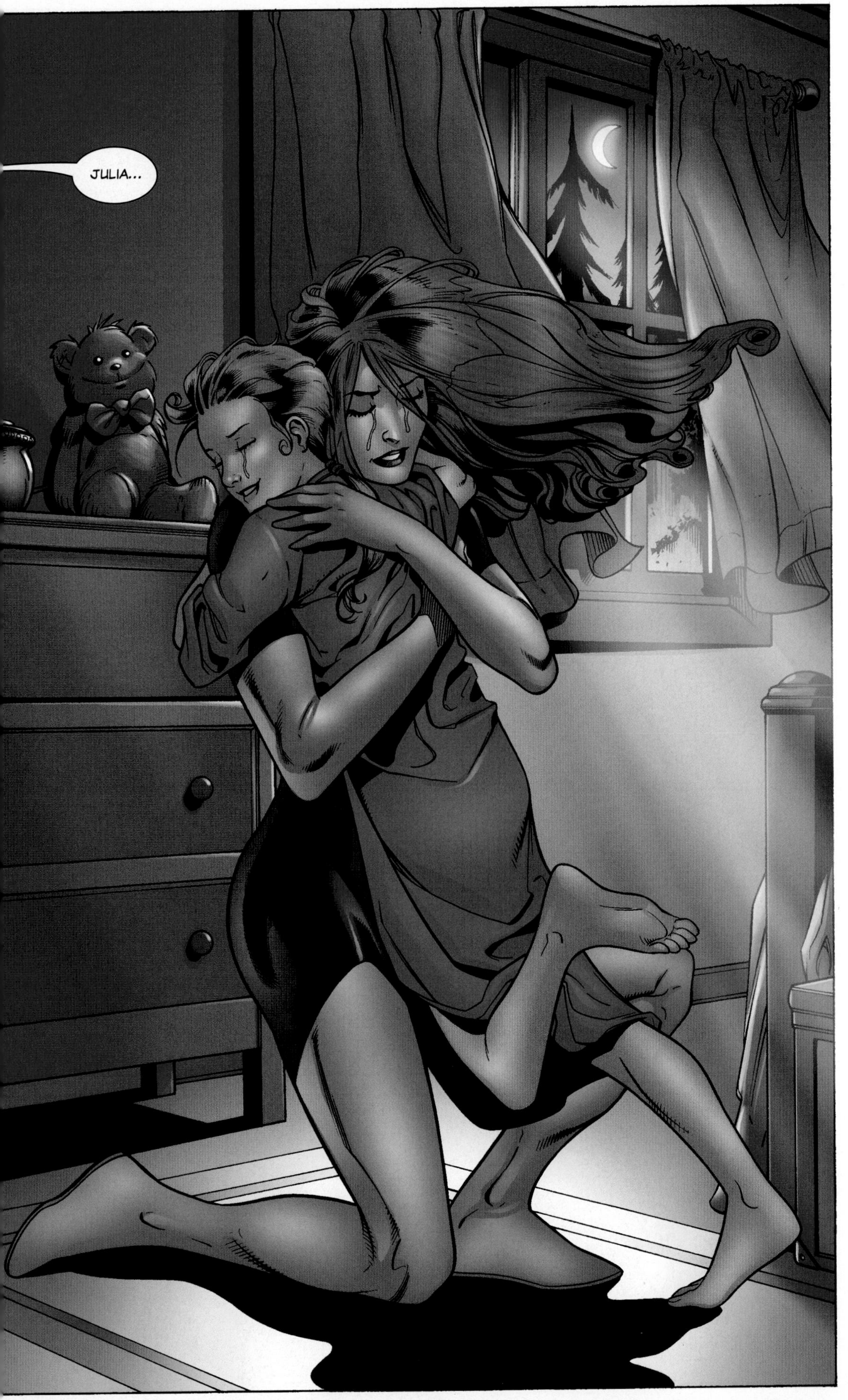
JULIA...

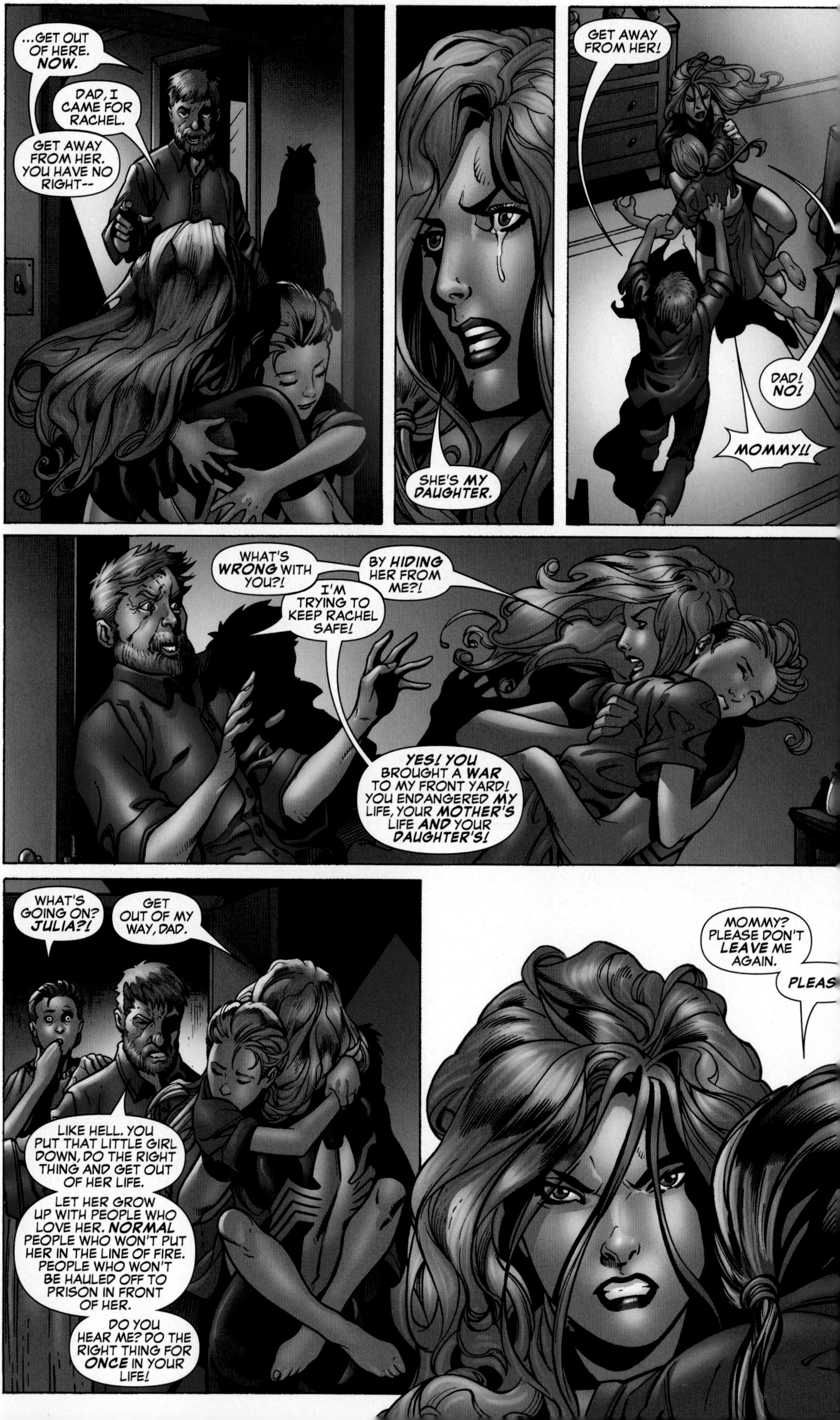
...GET OUT OF HERE. NOW.
DAD, I CAME FOR RACHEL.
GET AWAY FROM HER. YOU HAVE NO RIGHT--
SHE'S MY DAUGHTER.
GET AWAY FROM HER!
DAD! NO!
MOMMY!!
WHAT'S WRONG WITH YOU?!
I'M TRYING TO KEEP RACHEL SAFE!
BY HIDING HER FROM ME?!
YES! YOU BROUGHT A WAR TO MY FRONT YARD! YOU ENDANGERED MY LIFE, YOUR MOTHER'S LIFE AND YOUR DAUGHTER'S!
WHAT'S GOING ON? JULIA?!
GET OUT OF MY WAY, DAD.
LIKE HELL. YOU PUT THAT LITTLE GIRL DOWN, DO THE RIGHT THING AND GET OUT OF HER LIFE.
LET HER GROW UP WITH PEOPLE WHO LOVE HER. NORMAL PEOPLE WHO WON'T PUT HER IN THE LINE OF FIRE. PEOPLE WHO WON'T BE HAULED OFF TO PRISON IN FRONT OF HER.
DO YOU HEAR ME? DO THE RIGHT THING FOR ONCE IN YOUR LIFE!
MOMMY? PLEASE DON'T LEAVE ME AGAIN.
PLEAS

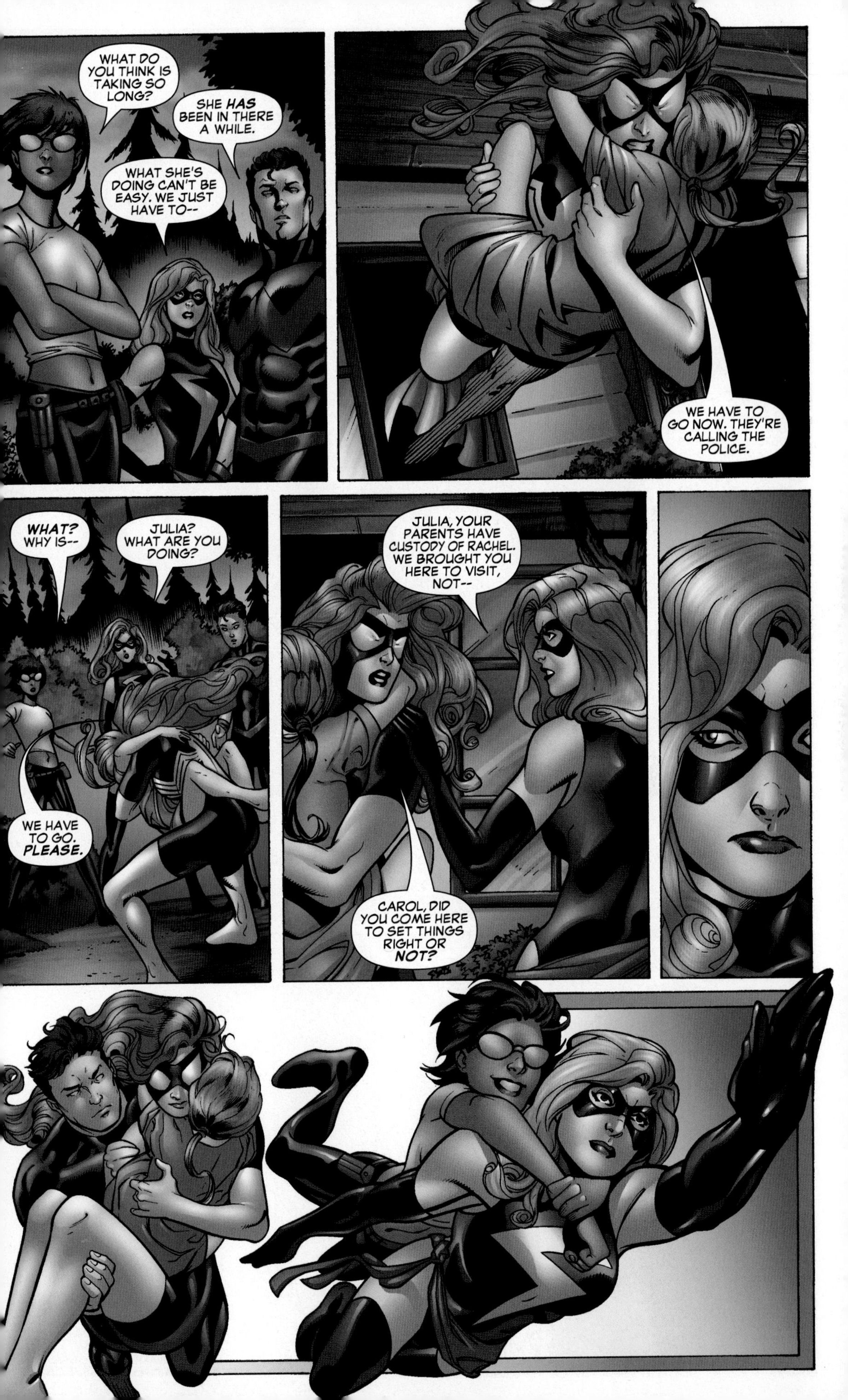

WHAT DO YOU THINK IS TAKING SO LONG?
SHE HAS BEEN IN THERE A WHILE.
WHAT SHE'S DOING CAN'T BE EASY. WE JUST HAVE TO--
WE HAVE TO GO NOW. THEY'RE CALLING THE POLICE.
WHAT? WHY IS--
JULIA? WHAT ARE YOU DOING?
WE HAVE TO GO. PLEASE.
JULIA, YOUR PARENTS HAVE CUSTODY OF RACHEL. WE BROUGHT YOU HERE TO VISIT, NOT--
CAROL, DID YOU COME HERE TO SET THINGS RIGHT OR NOT?

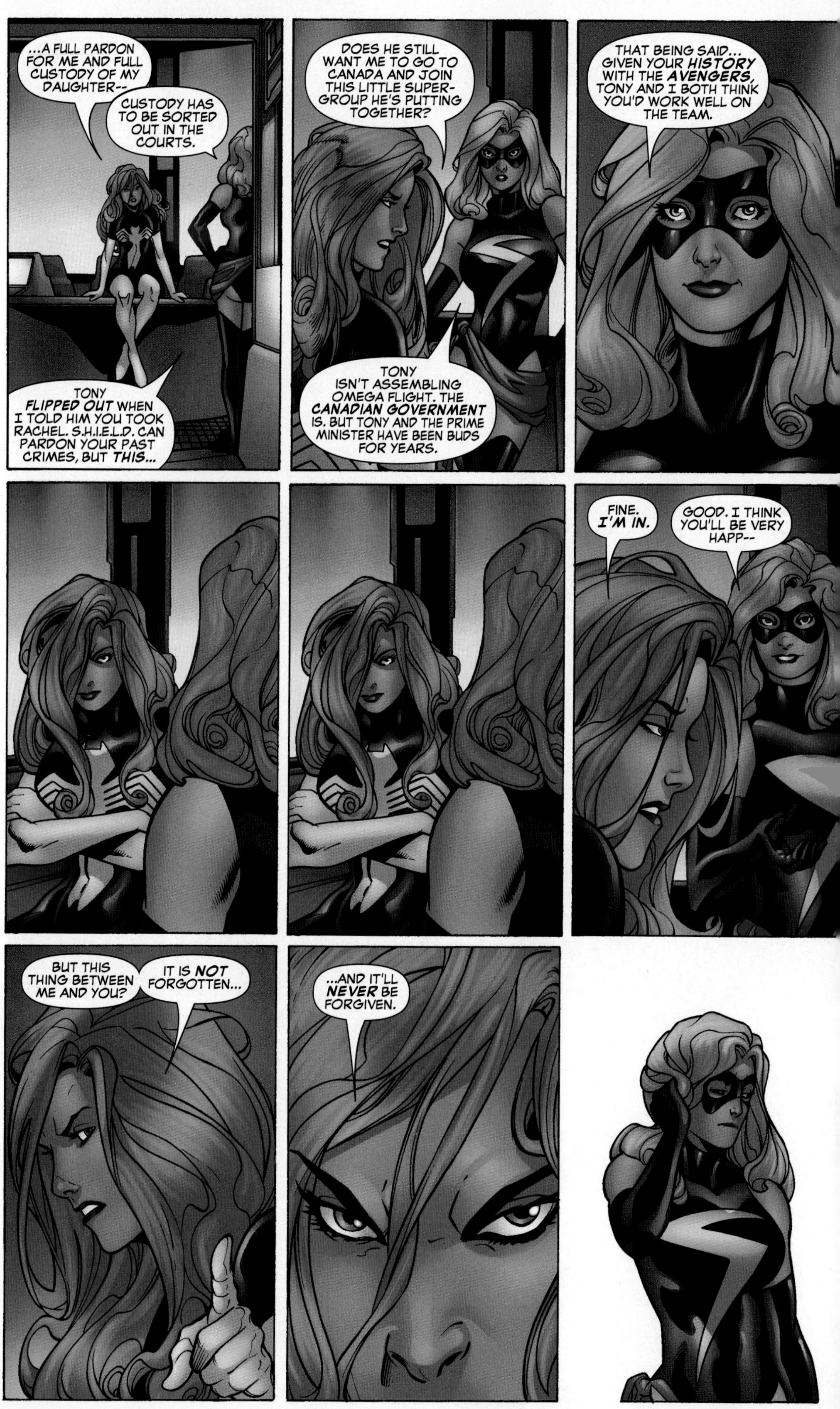
...A FULL PARDON FOR ME AND FULL CUSTODY OF MY DAUGHTER--
CUSTODY HAS TO BE SORTED OUT IN THE COURTS.
TONY FLIPPED OUT WHEN I TOLD HIM YOU TOOK RACHEL. S.H.I.E.L.D. CAN PARDON YOUR PAST CRIMES, BUT THIS...
DOES HE STILL WANT ME TO GO TO CANADA AND JOIN THIS LITTLE SUPER-GROUP HE'S PUTTING TOGETHER?
TONY ISN'T ASSEMBLING OMEGA FLIGHT. THE CANADIAN GOVERNMENT IS. BUT TONY AND THE PRIME MINISTER HAVE BEEN BUDS FOR YEARS.
THAT BEING SAID... GIVEN YOUR HISTORY WITH THE AVENGERS, TONY AND I BOTH THINK YOU'D WORK WELL ON THE TEAM.
FINE. I'M IN.
GOOD. I THINK YOU'LL BE VERY HAPP--
BUT THIS THING BETWEEN ME AND YOU?
IT IS NOT FORGOTTEN...
...AND IT'LL NEVER BE FORGIVEN.

ANDERSON, INDIANA

FOUND IT.

HIDING THINGS IN *EXTRA DIMENSIONS*... MAN, THIS KIND OF STUFF ALWAYS GIVES ME THE WILLIES.

I'M NOT GETTING ANYTHING. ARE YOU SURE WE HAVE THE CORRECT FREQ--

HEY. NEVER MIND.

YEAH, BUT IF WE DIDN'T HAVE A FAIL-SAFE LIKE THIS, THEN S.H.I.E.L.D. WOULD HAVE ALL OUR BEST TOYS.

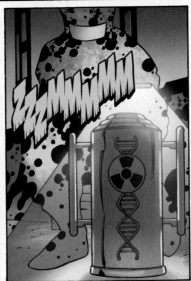

ZZZMMMMMM

BASE? RECOVERY.

DNA BOMB IS LOCATED.

EXCELLENT WORK, RECOVERY.

NOW, BRING IT TO ME...

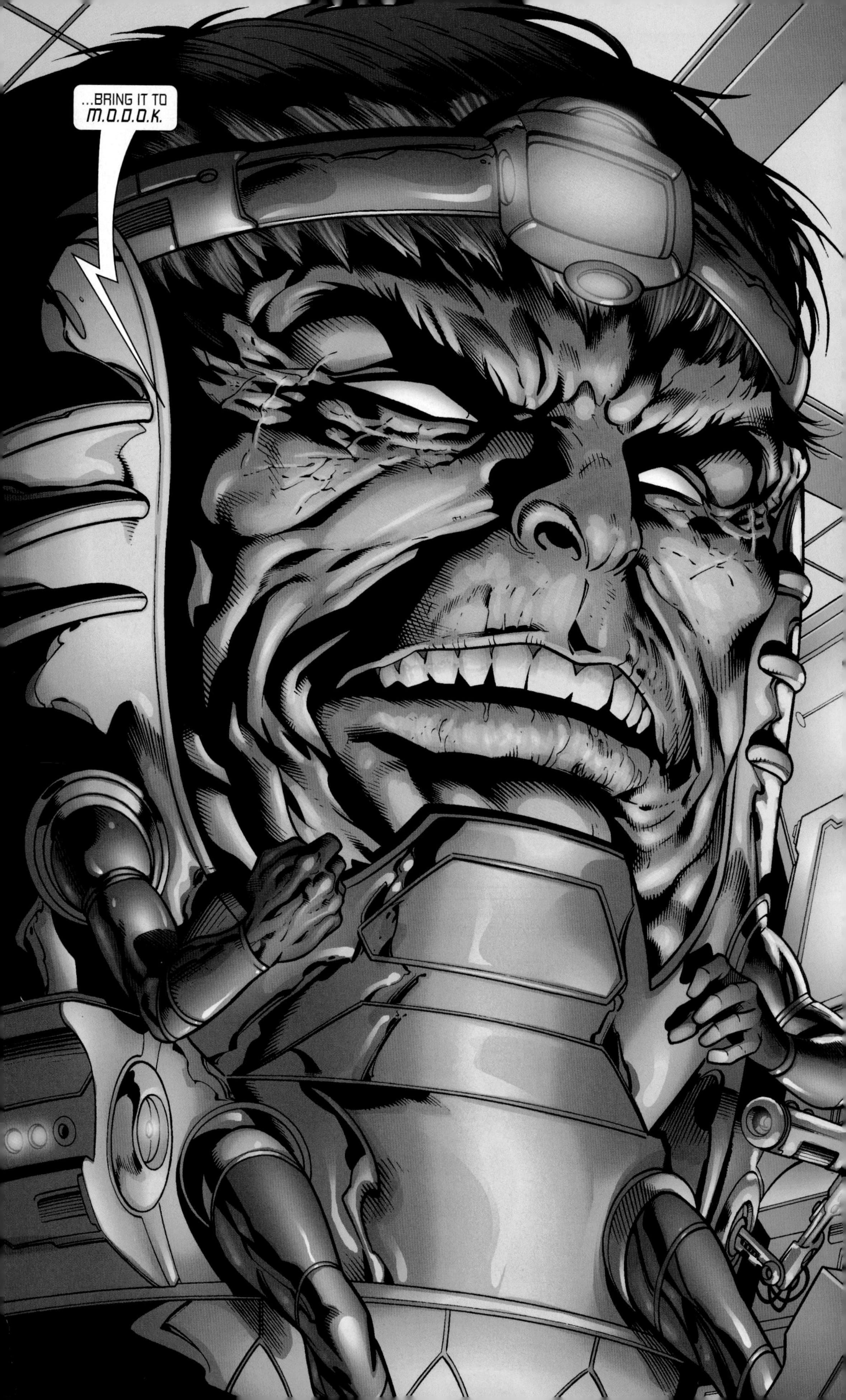
...BRING IT TO M.O.D.O.K.

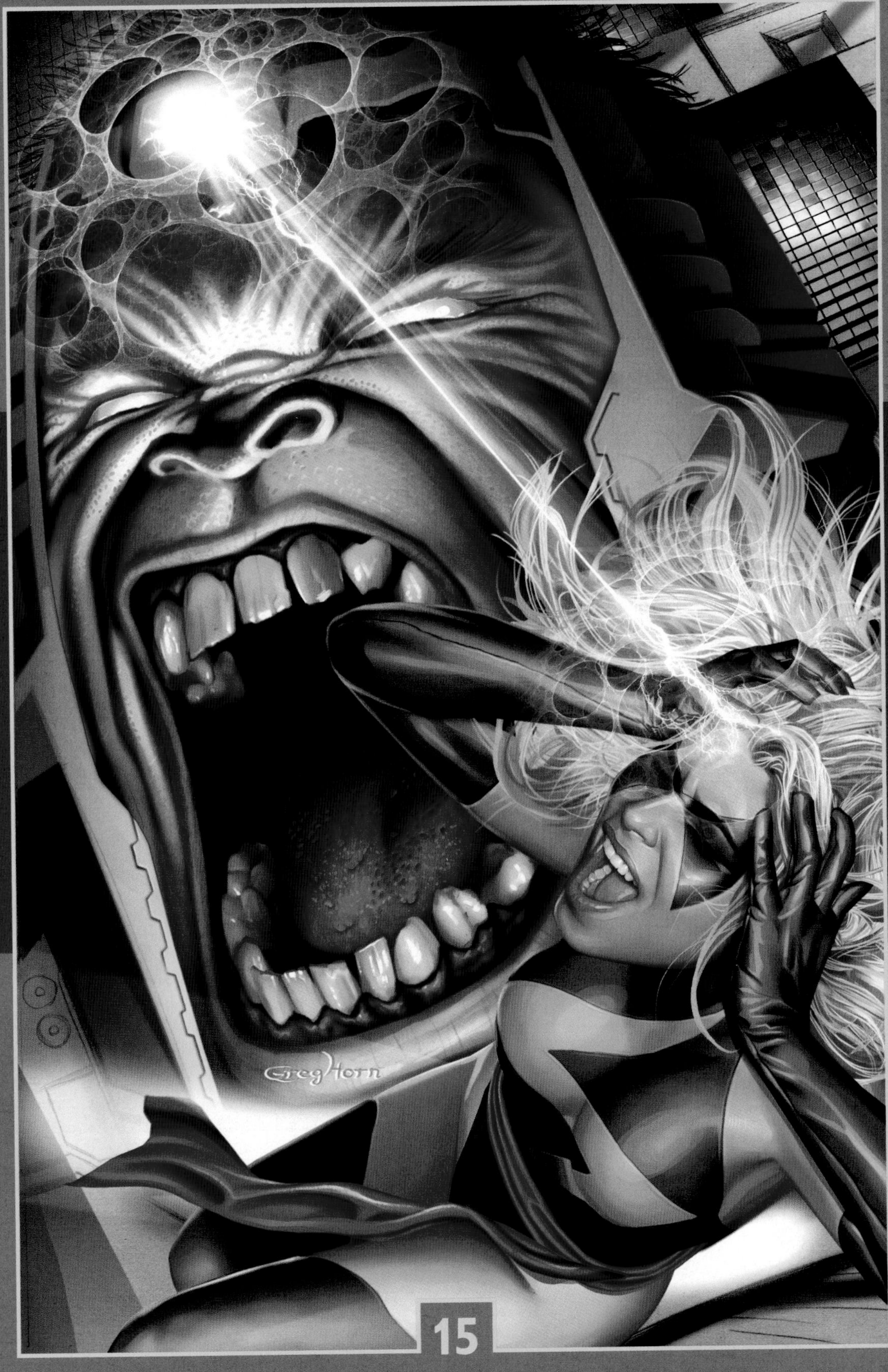
GregHorn
15

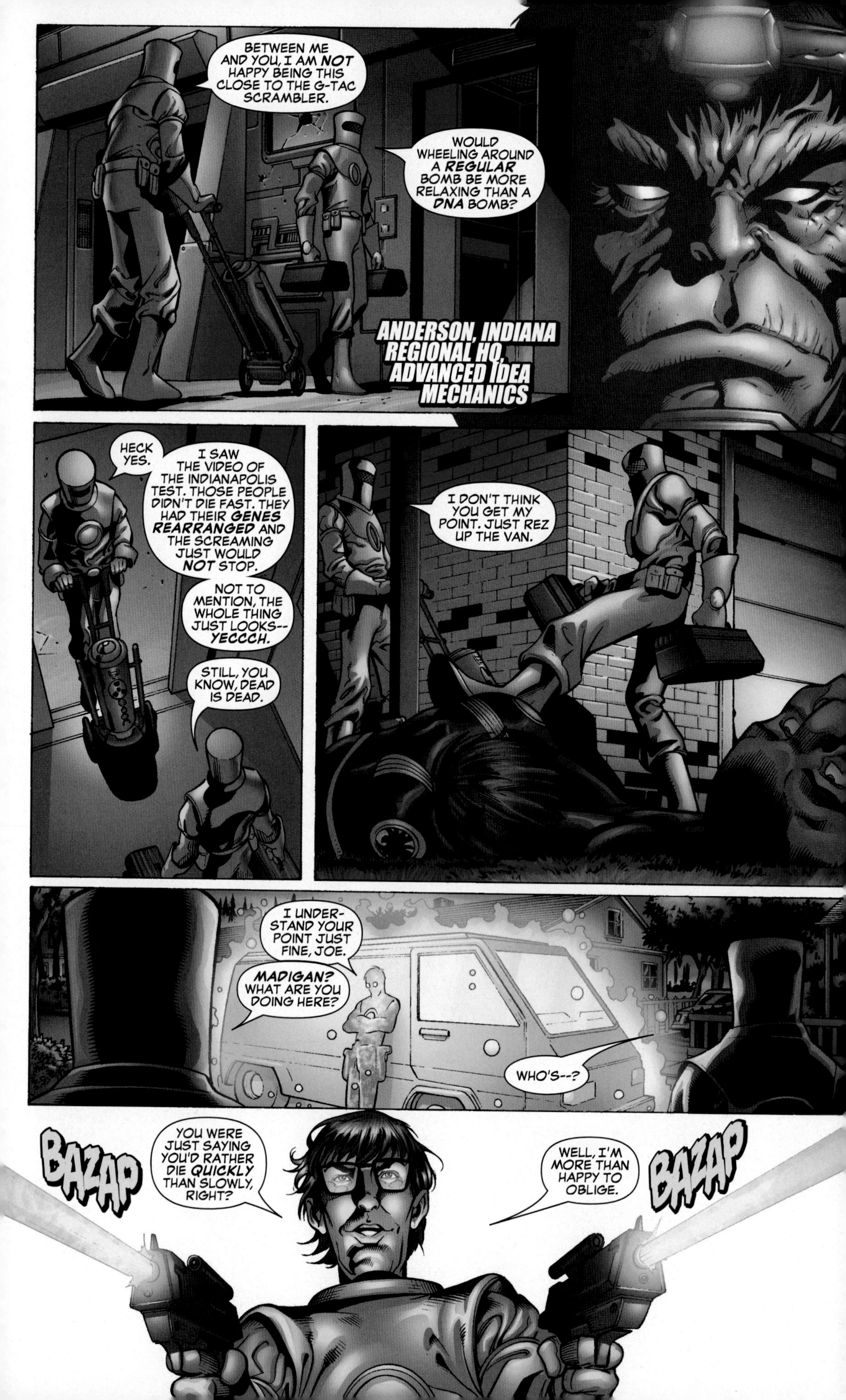
BETWEEN ME AND YOU, I AM NOT HAPPY BEING THIS CLOSE TO THE G-TAC SCRAMBLER.
WOULD WHEELING AROUND A REGULAR BOMB BE MORE RELAXING THAN A DNA BOMB?
ANDERSON, INDIANA REGIONAL HQ, ADVANCED IDEA MECHANICS
HECK YES.
I SAW THE VIDEO OF THE INDIANAPOLIS TEST. THOSE PEOPLE DIDN'T DIE FAST. THEY HAD THEIR GENES REARRANGED AND THE SCREAMING JUST WOULD NOT STOP.
NOT TO MENTION, THE WHOLE THING JUST LOOKS-- YECCCH.
STILL, YOU KNOW, DEAD IS DEAD.
I DON'T THINK YOU GET MY POINT. JUST REZ UP THE VAN.
I UNDER-STAND YOUR POINT JUST FINE, JOE.
MADIGAN? WHAT ARE YOU DOING HERE?
WHO'S--?
BAZAP
YOU WERE JUST SAYING YOU'D RATHER DIE QUICKLY THAN SLOWLY, RIGHT?
WELL, I'M MORE THAN HAPPY TO OBLIGE.
BAZAP

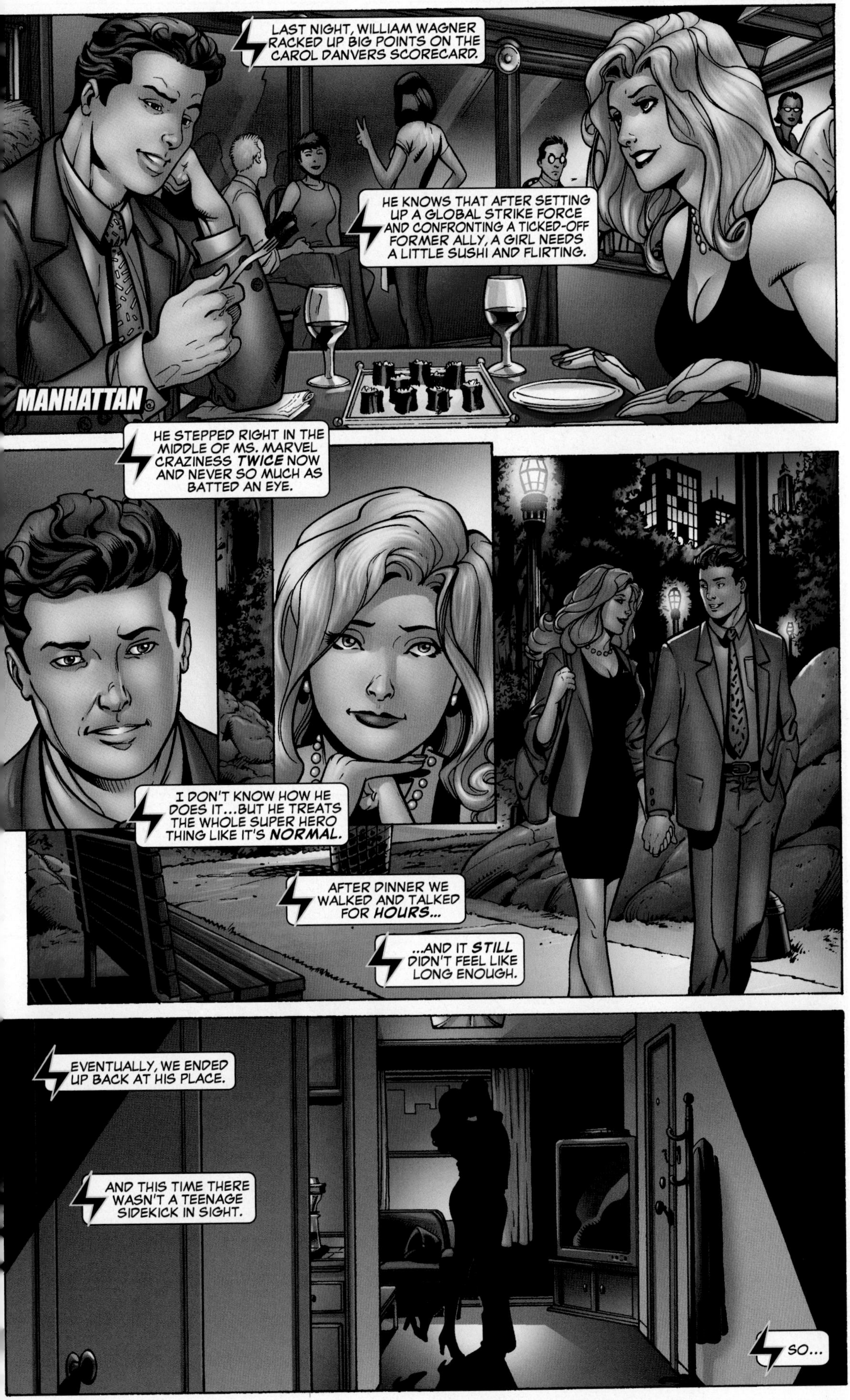
LAST NIGHT, WILLIAM WAGNER RACKED UP BIG POINTS ON THE CAROL DANVERS SCORECARD.
HE KNOWS THAT AFTER SETTING UP A GLOBAL STRIKE FORCE AND CONFRONTING A TICKED-OFF FORMER ALLY, A GIRL NEEDS A LITTLE SUSHI AND FLIRTING.
MANHATTAN
HE STEPPED RIGHT IN THE MIDDLE OF MS. MARVEL CRAZINESS TWICE NOW AND NEVER SO MUCH AS BATTED AN EYE.
I DON'T KNOW HOW HE DOES IT...BUT HE TREATS THE WHOLE SUPER HERO THING LIKE IT'S NORMAL.
AFTER DINNER WE WALKED AND TALKED FOR HOURS...
...AND IT STILL DIDN'T FEEL LIKE LONG ENOUGH.
EVENTUALLY, WE ENDED UP BACK AT HIS PLACE.
AND THIS TIME THERE WASN'T A TEENAGE SIDEKICK IN SIGHT.
SO...

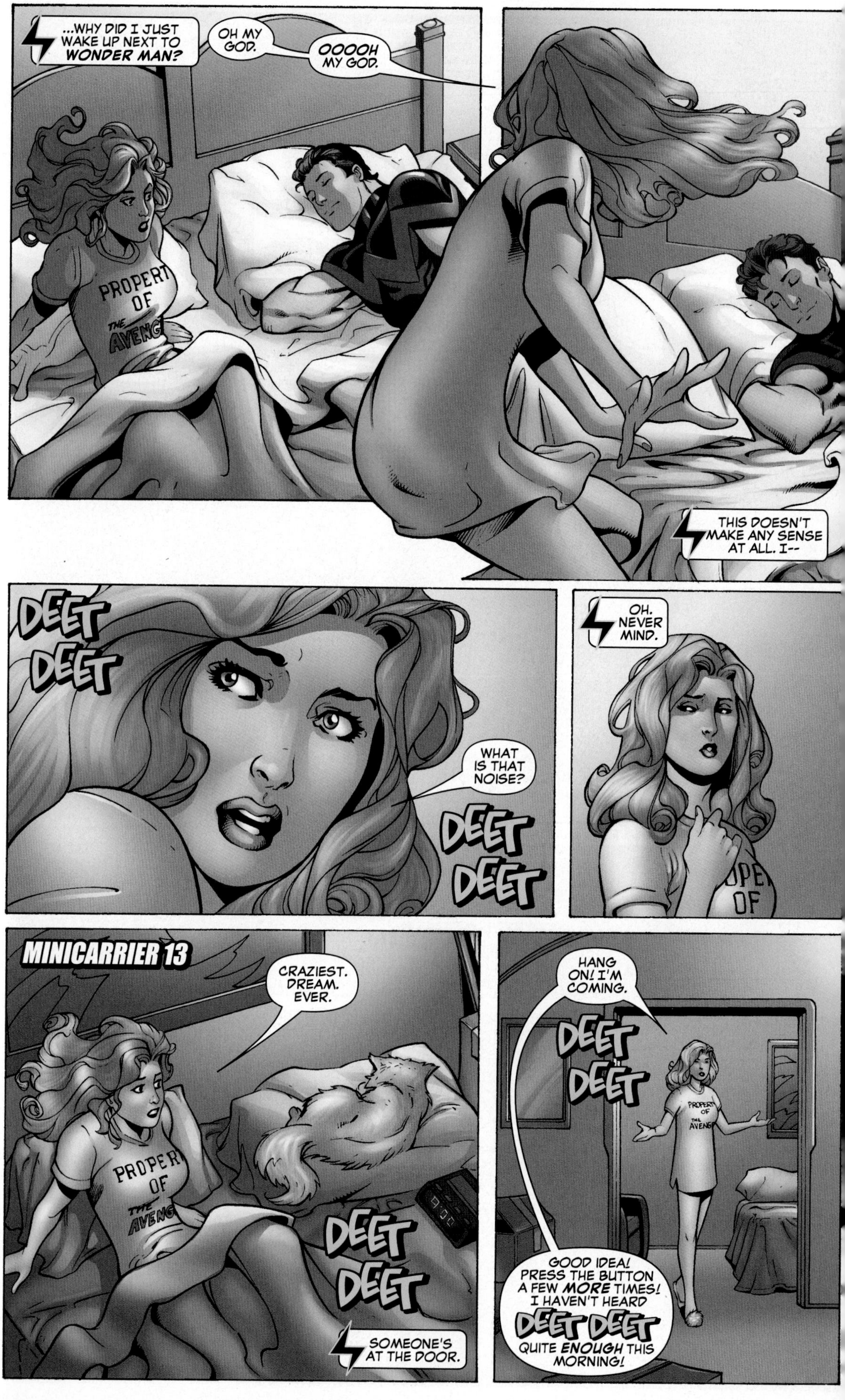

...WHY DID I JUST WAKE UP NEXT TO WONDER MAN?
OH MY GOD.
OOOOH MY GOD.
PROPERT OF THE AVENG
THIS DOESN'T MAKE ANY SENSE AT ALL. I--
DEET DEET
WHAT IS THAT NOISE?
DEET DEET
OH. NEVER MIND.
MINICARRIER 13
CRAZIEST. DREAM. EVER.
DEET DEET
SOMEONE'S AT THE DOOR.
HANG ON! I'M COMING.
DEET DEET
GOOD IDEA! PRESS THE BUTTON A FEW MORE TIMES! I HAVEN'T HEARD DEET DEET QUITE ENOUGH THIS MORNING!

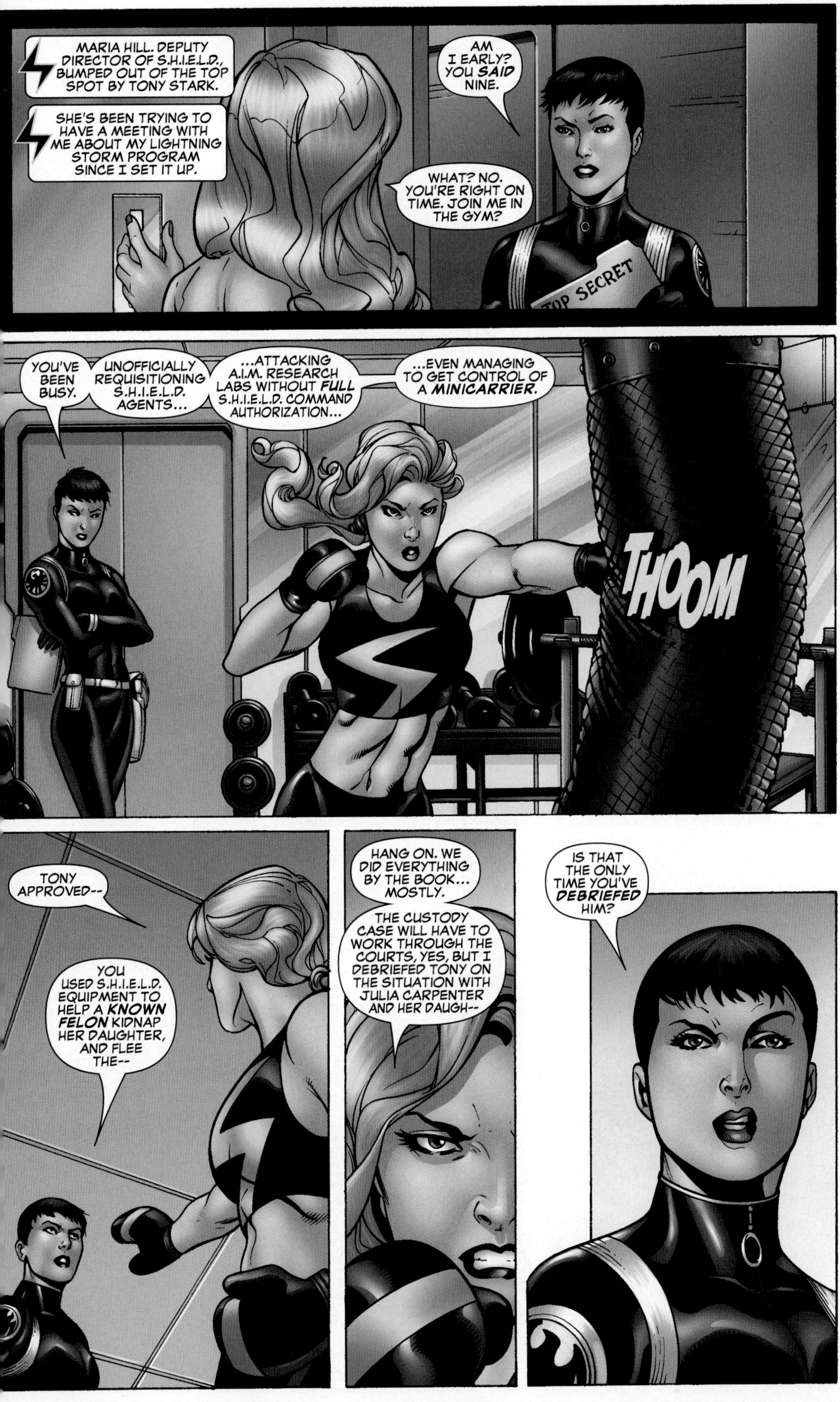

MARIA HILL. DEPUTY DIRECTOR OF S.H.I.E.L.D., BUMPED OUT OF THE TOP SPOT BY TONY STARK.
SHE'S BEEN TRYING TO HAVE A MEETING WITH ME ABOUT MY LIGHTNING STORM PROGRAM SINCE I SET IT UP.
AM I EARLY? YOU SAID NINE.
WHAT? NO. YOU'RE RIGHT ON TIME. JOIN ME IN THE GYM?
TOP SECRET
YOU'VE BEEN BUSY.
UNOFFICIALLY REQUISITIONING S.H.I.E.L.D. AGENTS...
...ATTACKING A.I.M. RESEARCH LABS WITHOUT FULL S.H.I.E.L.D. COMMAND AUTHORIZATION...
...EVEN MANAGING TO GET CONTROL OF A MINICARRIER.
THOOM
TONY APPROVED--
YOU USED S.H.I.E.L.D. EQUIPMENT TO HELP A KNOWN FELON KIDNAP HER DAUGHTER, AND FLEE THE--
HANG ON. WE DID EVERYTHING BY THE BOOK... MOSTLY.
THE CUSTODY CASE WILL HAVE TO WORK THROUGH THE COURTS, YES, BUT I DEBRIEFED TONY ON THE SITUATION WITH JULIA CARPENTER AND HER DAUGH--
IS THAT THE ONLY TIME YOU'VE DEBRIEFED HIM?

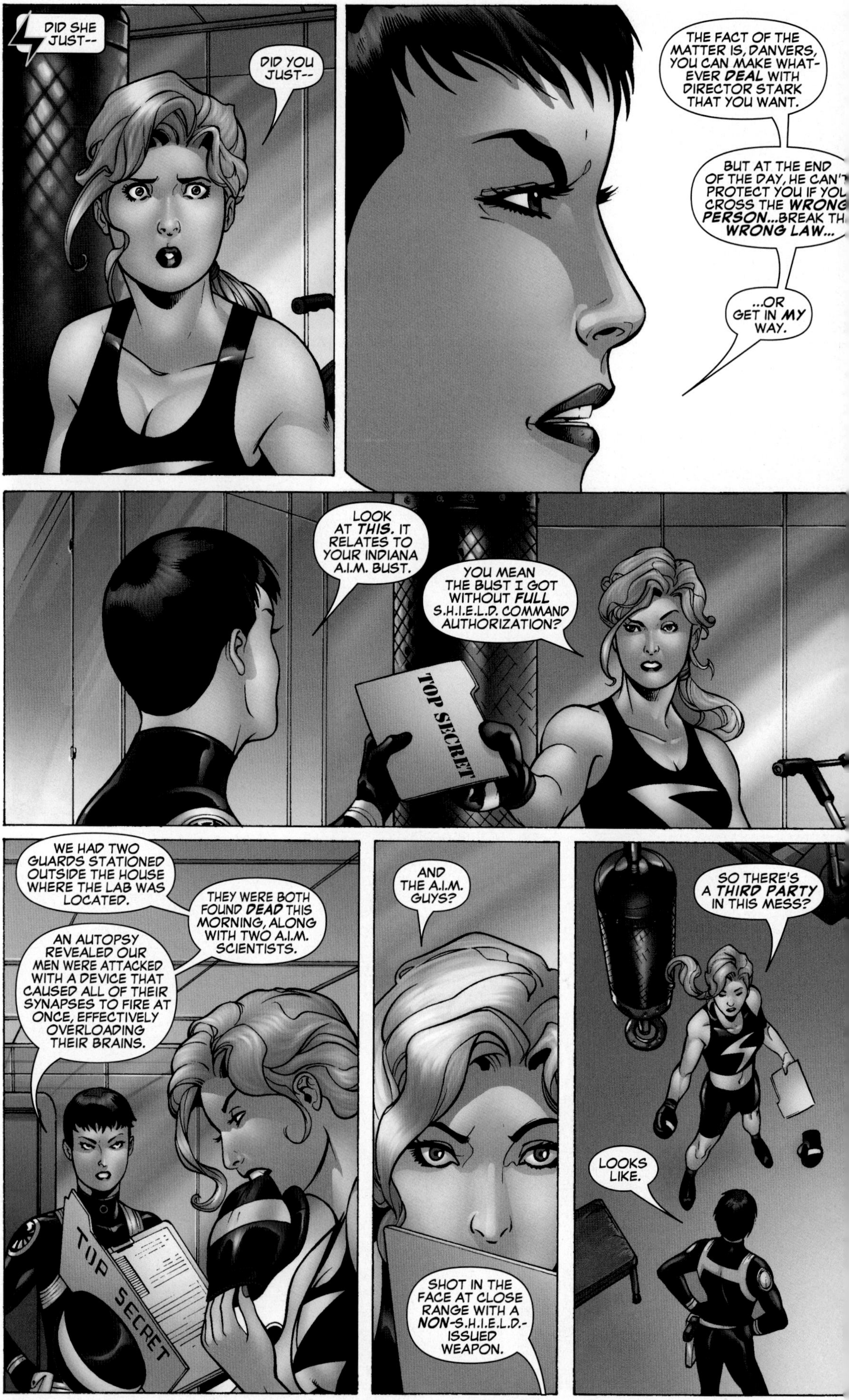
DID SHE JUST--
DID YOU JUST--
THE FACT OF THE MATTER IS, DANVERS, YOU CAN MAKE WHATEVER DEAL WITH DIRECTOR STARK THAT YOU WANT.
BUT AT THE END OF THE DAY, HE CAN'T PROTECT YOU IF YOU CROSS THE WRONG PERSON...BREAK THE WRONG LAW...
...OR GET IN MY WAY.
LOOK AT THIS. IT RELATES TO YOUR INDIANA A.I.M. BUST.
YOU MEAN THE BUST I GOT WITHOUT FULL S.H.I.E.L.D. COMMAND AUTHORIZATION?
TOP SECRET
WE HAD TWO GUARDS STATIONED OUTSIDE THE HOUSE WHERE THE LAB WAS LOCATED.
THEY WERE BOTH FOUND DEAD THIS MORNING, ALONG WITH TWO A.I.M. SCIENTISTS.
AN AUTOPSY REVEALED OUR MEN WERE ATTACKED WITH A DEVICE THAT CAUSED ALL OF THEIR SYNAPSES TO FIRE AT ONCE, EFFECTIVELY OVERLOADING THEIR BRAINS.
TOP SECRET
AND THE A.I.M. GUYS?
SHOT IN THE FACE AT CLOSE RANGE WITH A NON-S.H.I.E.L.D.-ISSUED WEAPON.
SO THERE'S A THIRD PARTY IN THIS MESS?
LOOKS LIKE.

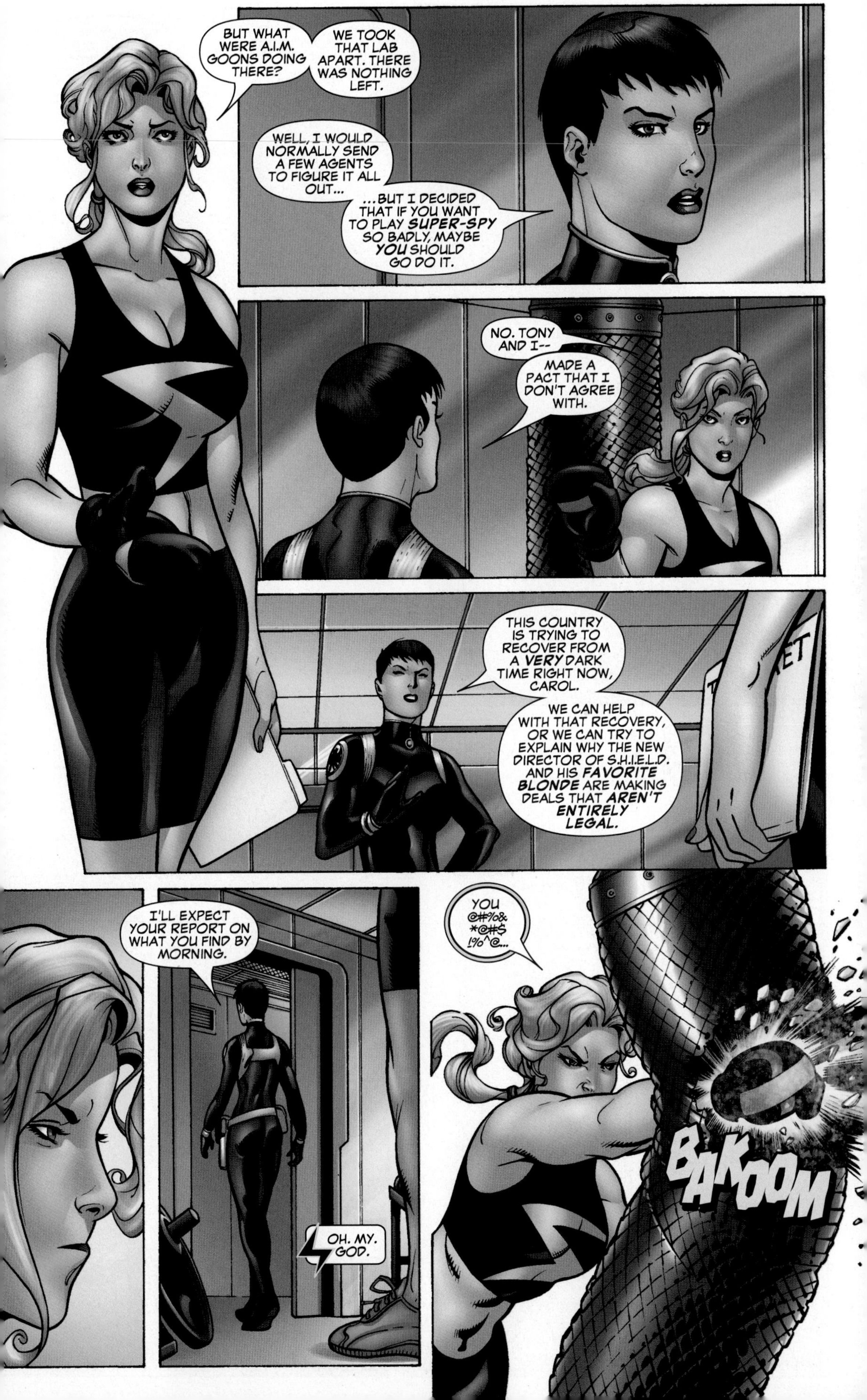
BUT WHAT WERE A.I.M. GOONS DOING THERE?
WE TOOK THAT LAB APART. THERE WAS NOTHING LEFT.
WELL, I WOULD NORMALLY SEND A FEW AGENTS TO FIGURE IT ALL OUT...
...BUT I DECIDED THAT IF YOU WANT TO PLAY SUPER-SPY SO BADLY, MAYBE YOU SHOULD GO DO IT.
NO. TONY AND I--
MADE A PACT THAT I DON'T AGREE WITH.
THIS COUNTRY IS TRYING TO RECOVER FROM A VERY DARK TIME RIGHT NOW, CAROL.
WE CAN HELP WITH THAT RECOVERY, OR WE CAN TRY TO EXPLAIN WHY THE NEW DIRECTOR OF S.H.I.E.L.D. AND HIS FAVORITE BLONDE ARE MAKING DEALS THAT AREN'T ENTIRELY LEGAL.
I'LL EXPECT YOUR REPORT ON WHAT YOU FIND BY MORNING.
OH. MY. GOD.
YOU @#%& *@#$!%^@...
BAKOOM

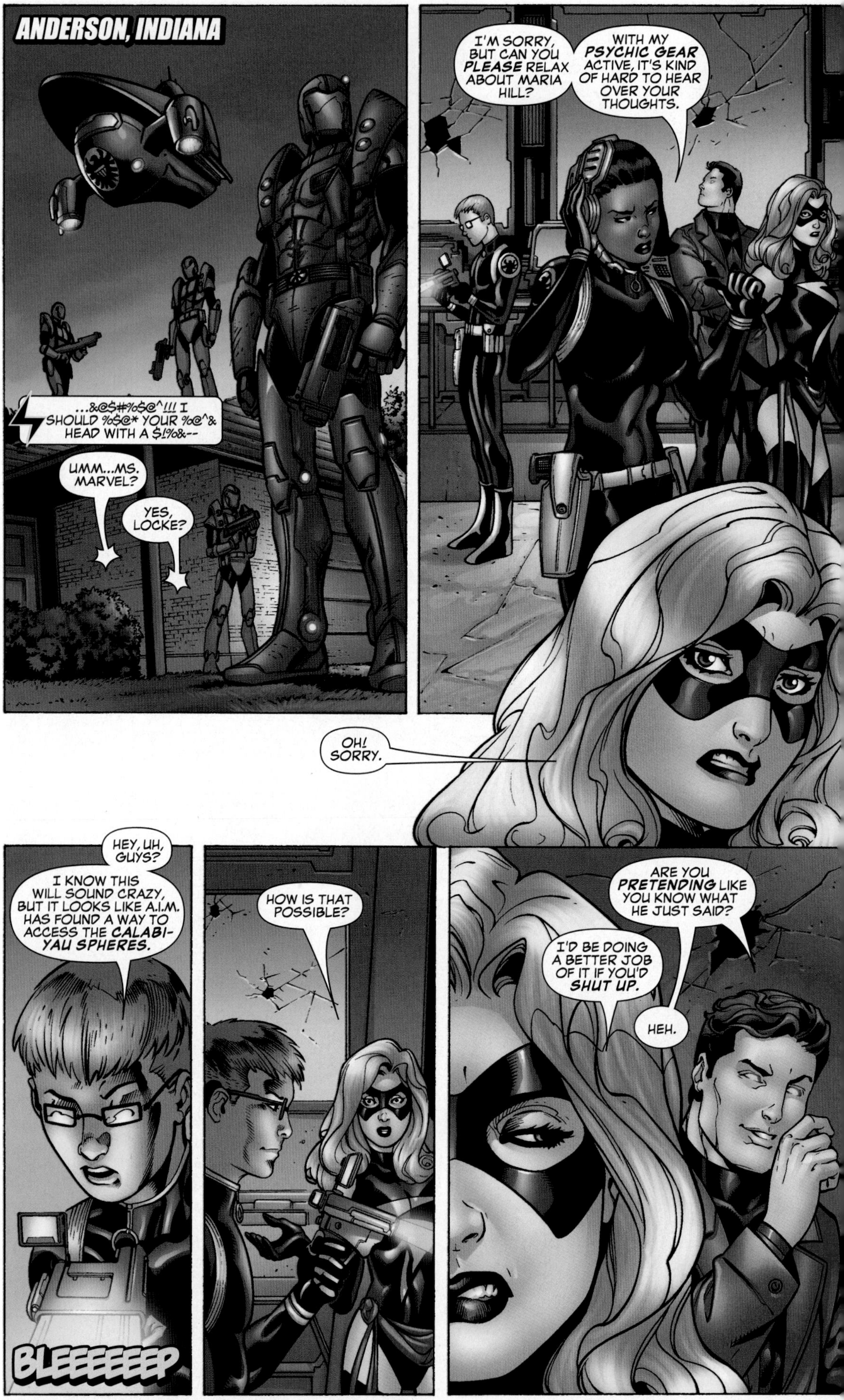
ANDERSON, INDIANA
...&@$#%$@^!!! I SHOULD %$@* YOUR %@^& HEAD WITH A $!%&--
UMM...MS. MARVEL?
YES, LOCKE?
I'M SORRY, BUT CAN YOU PLEASE RELAX ABOUT MARIA HILL?
WITH MY PSYCHIC GEAR ACTIVE, IT'S KIND OF HARD TO HEAR OVER YOUR THOUGHTS.
OH! SORRY.
HEY, UH, GUYS?
I KNOW THIS WILL SOUND CRAZY, BUT IT LOOKS LIKE A.I.M. HAS FOUND A WAY TO ACCESS THE CALABI-YAU SPHERES.
BLEEEEEEP
HOW IS THAT POSSIBLE?
ARE YOU PRETENDING LIKE YOU KNOW WHAT HE JUST SAID?
I'D BE DOING A BETTER JOB OF IT IF YOU'D SHUT UP.
HEH.

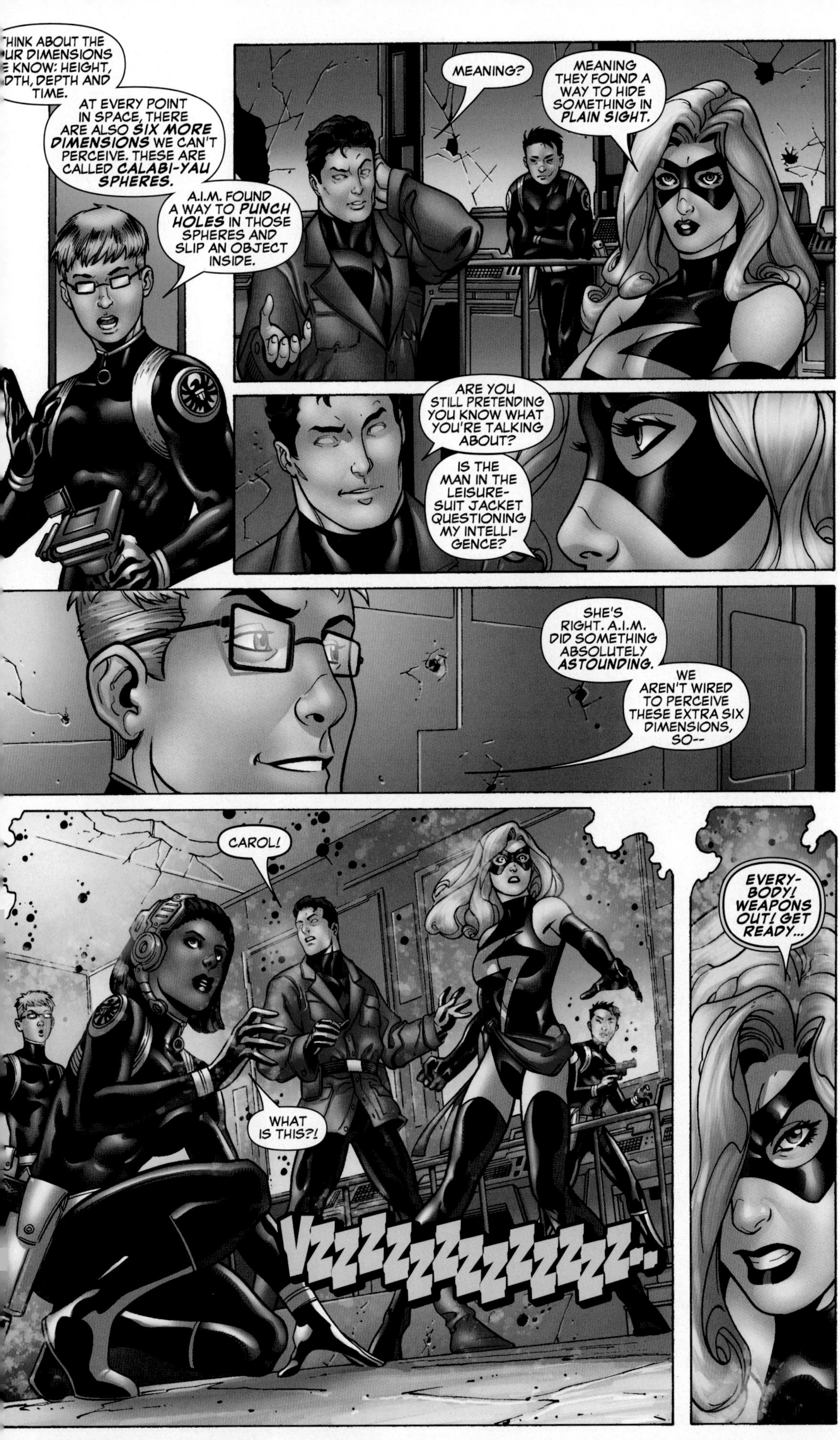
THINK ABOUT THE FOUR DIMENSIONS WE KNOW: HEIGHT, WIDTH, DEPTH AND TIME.
AT EVERY POINT IN SPACE, THERE ARE ALSO SIX MORE DIMENSIONS WE CAN'T PERCEIVE. THESE ARE CALLED CALABI-YAU SPHERES.
A.I.M. FOUND A WAY TO PUNCH HOLES IN THOSE SPHERES AND SLIP AN OBJECT INSIDE.
MEANING?
MEANING THEY FOUND A WAY TO HIDE SOMETHING IN PLAIN SIGHT.
ARE YOU STILL PRETENDING YOU KNOW WHAT YOU'RE TALKING ABOUT?
IS THE MAN IN THE LEISURE-SUIT JACKET QUESTIONING MY INTELLI-GENCE?
SHE'S RIGHT. A.I.M. DID SOMETHING ABSOLUTELY ASTOUNDING.
WE AREN'T WIRED TO PERCEIVE THESE EXTRA SIX DIMENSIONS, SO--
CAROL!
WHAT IS THIS?!
VZZZZZZZZZZZZZZ..
EVERY-BODY! WEAPONS OUT! GET READY...

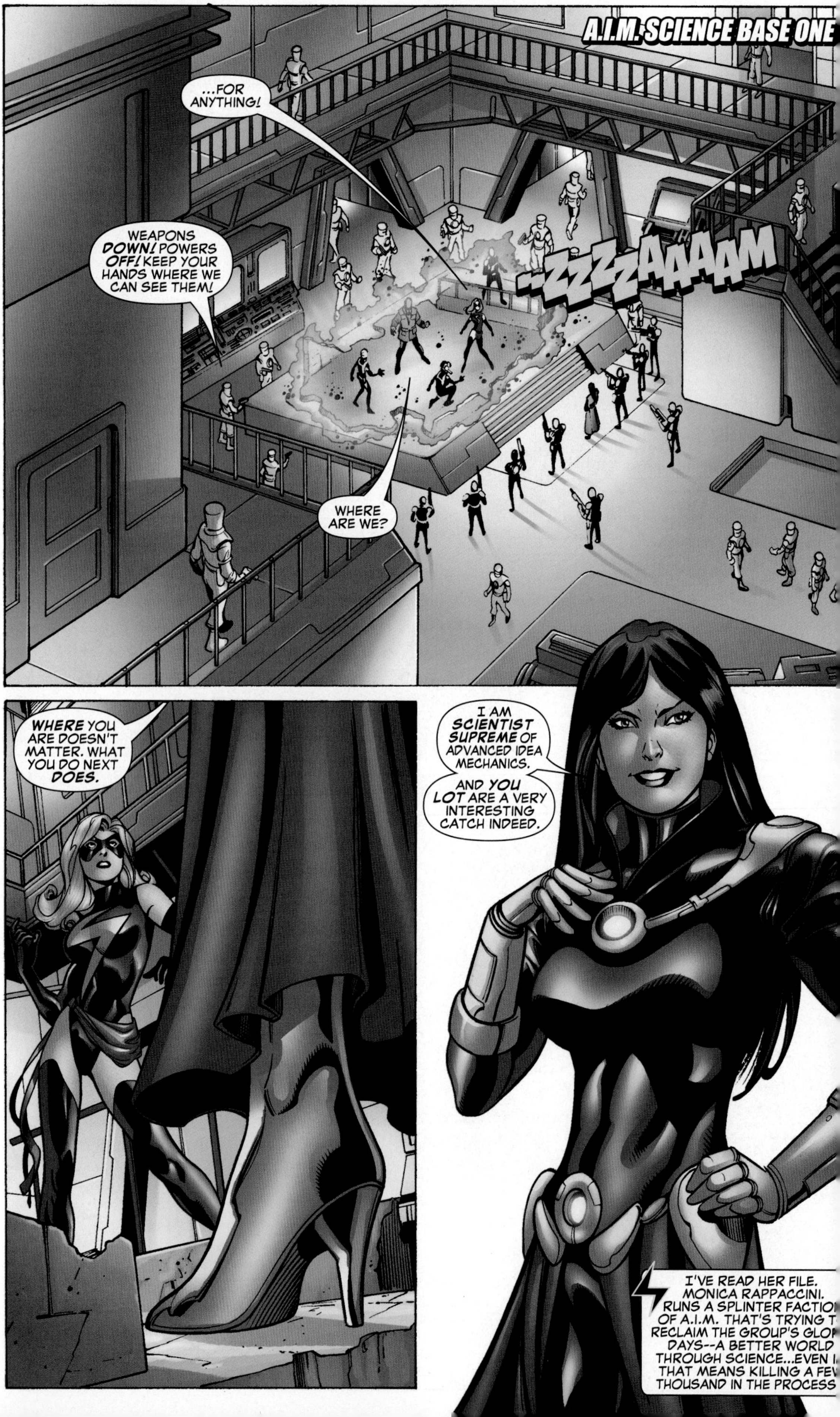
A.I.M. SCIENCE BASE ONE
...FOR ANYTHING!
WEAPONS DOWN! POWERS OFF! KEEP YOUR HANDS WHERE WE CAN SEE THEM!
-ZZZZAAAAAM
WHERE ARE WE?
WHERE YOU ARE DOESN'T MATTER. WHAT YOU DO NEXT DOES.
I AM SCIENTIST SUPREME OF ADVANCED IDEA MECHANICS.
AND YOU LOT ARE A VERY INTERESTING CATCH INDEED.
I'VE READ HER FILE. MONICA RAPPACCINI. RUNS A SPLINTER FACTIO OF A.I.M. THAT'S TRYING T RECLAIM THE GROUP'S GLO DAYS--A BETTER WORLD THROUGH SCIENCE...EVEN I THAT MEANS KILLING A FE THOUSAND IN THE PROCESS

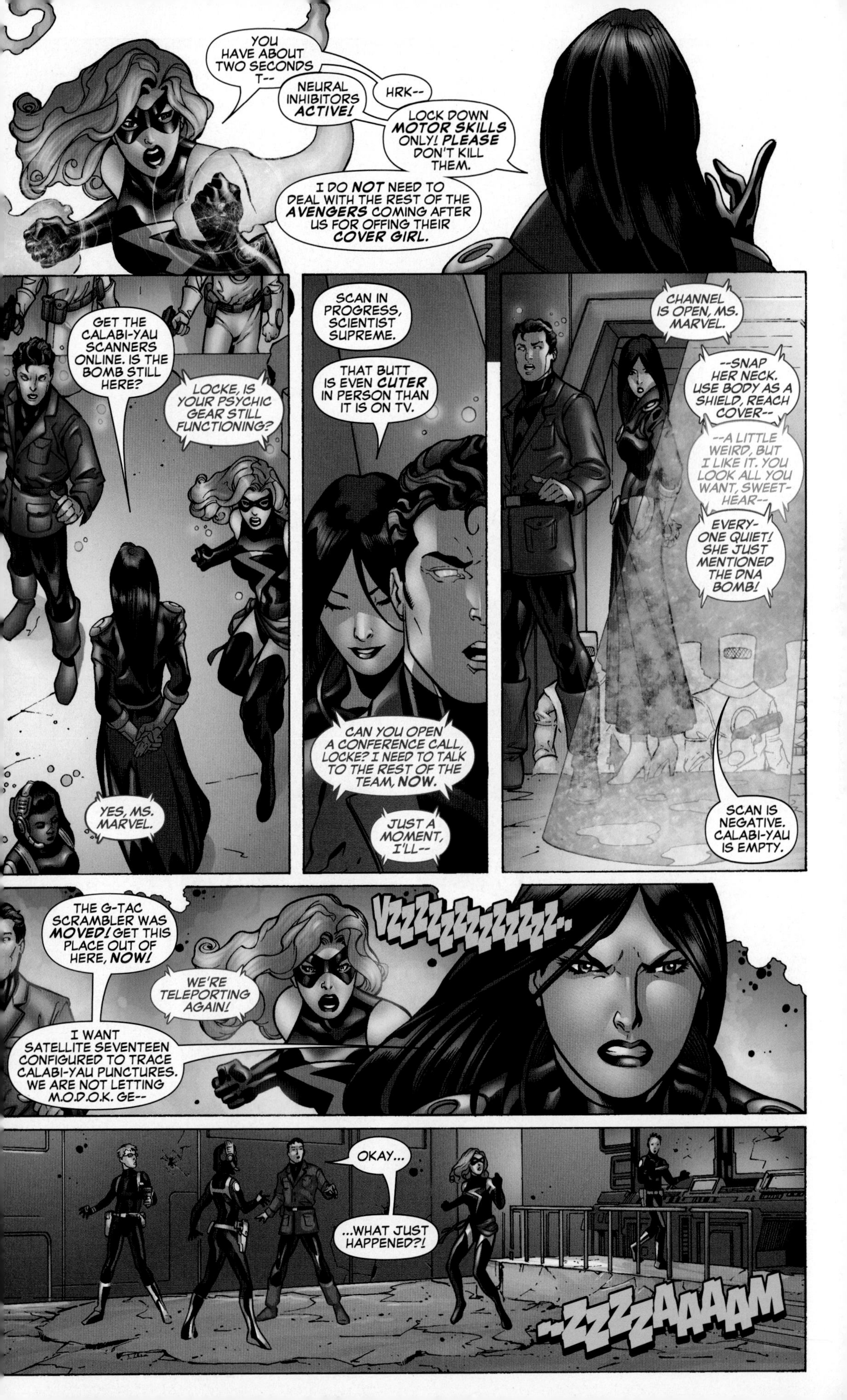
YOU HAVE ABOUT TWO SECONDS T--
HRK--
NEURAL INHIBITORS ACTIVE!
LOCK DOWN MOTOR SKILLS ONLY! PLEASE DON'T KILL THEM.
I DO NOT NEED TO DEAL WITH THE REST OF THE AVENGERS COMING AFTER US FOR OFFING THEIR COVER GIRL.
GET THE CALABI-YAU SCANNERS ONLINE. IS THE BOMB STILL HERE?
LOCKE, IS YOUR PSYCHIC GEAR STILL FUNCTIONING?
YES, MS. MARVEL.
SCAN IN PROGRESS, SCIENTIST SUPREME.
THAT BUTT IS EVEN CUTER IN PERSON THAN IT IS ON TV.
CAN YOU OPEN A CONFERENCE CALL, LOCKE? I NEED TO TALK TO THE REST OF THE TEAM, NOW.
JUST A MOMENT, I'LL--
CHANNEL IS OPEN, MS. MARVEL.
--SNAP HER NECK. USE BODY AS A SHIELD, REACH COVER--
--A LITTLE WEIRD, BUT I LIKE IT. YOU LOOK ALL YOU WANT, SWEET-HEAR--
EVERY-ONE QUIET! SHE JUST MENTIONED THE DNA BOMB!
SCAN IS NEGATIVE. CALABI-YAU IS EMPTY.
THE G-TAC SCRAMBLER WAS MOVED! GET THIS PLACE OUT OF HERE, NOW!
VZZZZZZZZZZZZZ..
WE'RE TELEPORTING AGAIN!
I WANT SATELLITE SEVENTEEN CONFIGURED TO TRACE CALABI-YAU PUNCTURES. WE ARE NOT LETTING M.O.D.O.K. GE--
OKAY...
...WHAT JUST HAPPENED?!
..ZZZZAAAAM

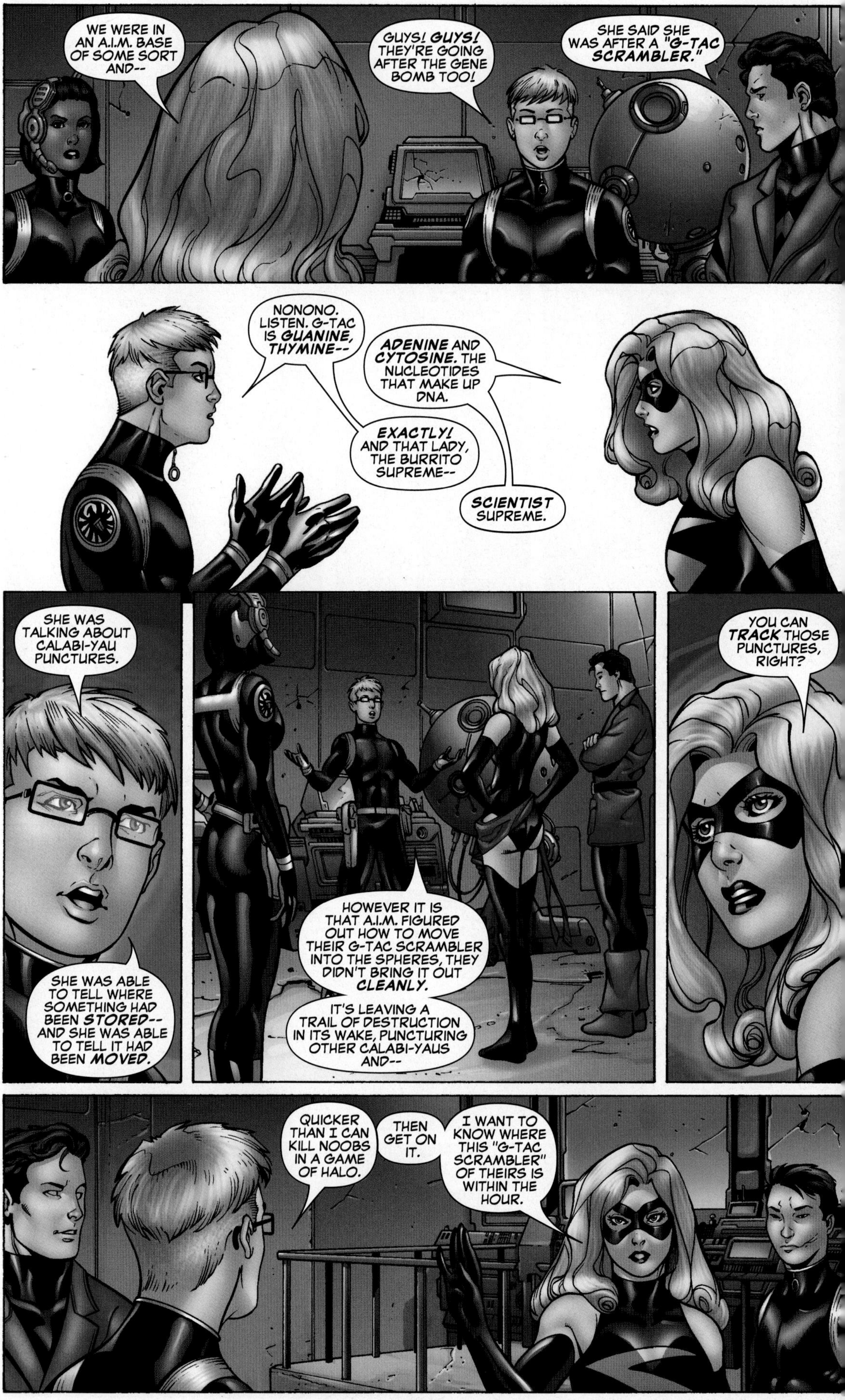
WE WERE IN AN A.I.M. BASE OF SOME SORT AND--
GUYS! GUYS! THEY'RE GOING AFTER THE GENE BOMB TOO!
SHE SAID SHE WAS AFTER A "G-TAC SCRAMBLER."
NONONO. LISTEN. G-TAC IS GUANINE, THYMINE--
ADENINE AND CYTOSINE. THE NUCLEOTIDES THAT MAKE UP DNA.
EXACTLY! AND THAT LADY, THE BURRITO SUPREME--
SCIENTIST SUPREME.
SHE WAS TALKING ABOUT CALABI-YAU PUNCTURES.
SHE WAS ABLE TO TELL WHERE SOMETHING HAD BEEN STORED-- AND SHE WAS ABLE TO TELL IT HAD BEEN MOVED.
HOWEVER IT IS THAT A.I.M. FIGURED OUT HOW TO MOVE THEIR G-TAC SCRAMBLER INTO THE SPHERES, THEY DIDN'T BRING IT OUT CLEANLY.
IT'S LEAVING A TRAIL OF DESTRUCTION IN ITS WAKE, PUNCTURING OTHER CALABI-YAUS AND--
YOU CAN TRACK THOSE PUNCTURES, RIGHT?
QUICKER THAN I CAN KILL NOOBS IN A GAME OF HALO.
THEN GET ON IT.
I WANT TO KNOW WHERE THIS "G-TAC SCRAMBLER" OF THEIRS IS WITHIN THE HOUR.

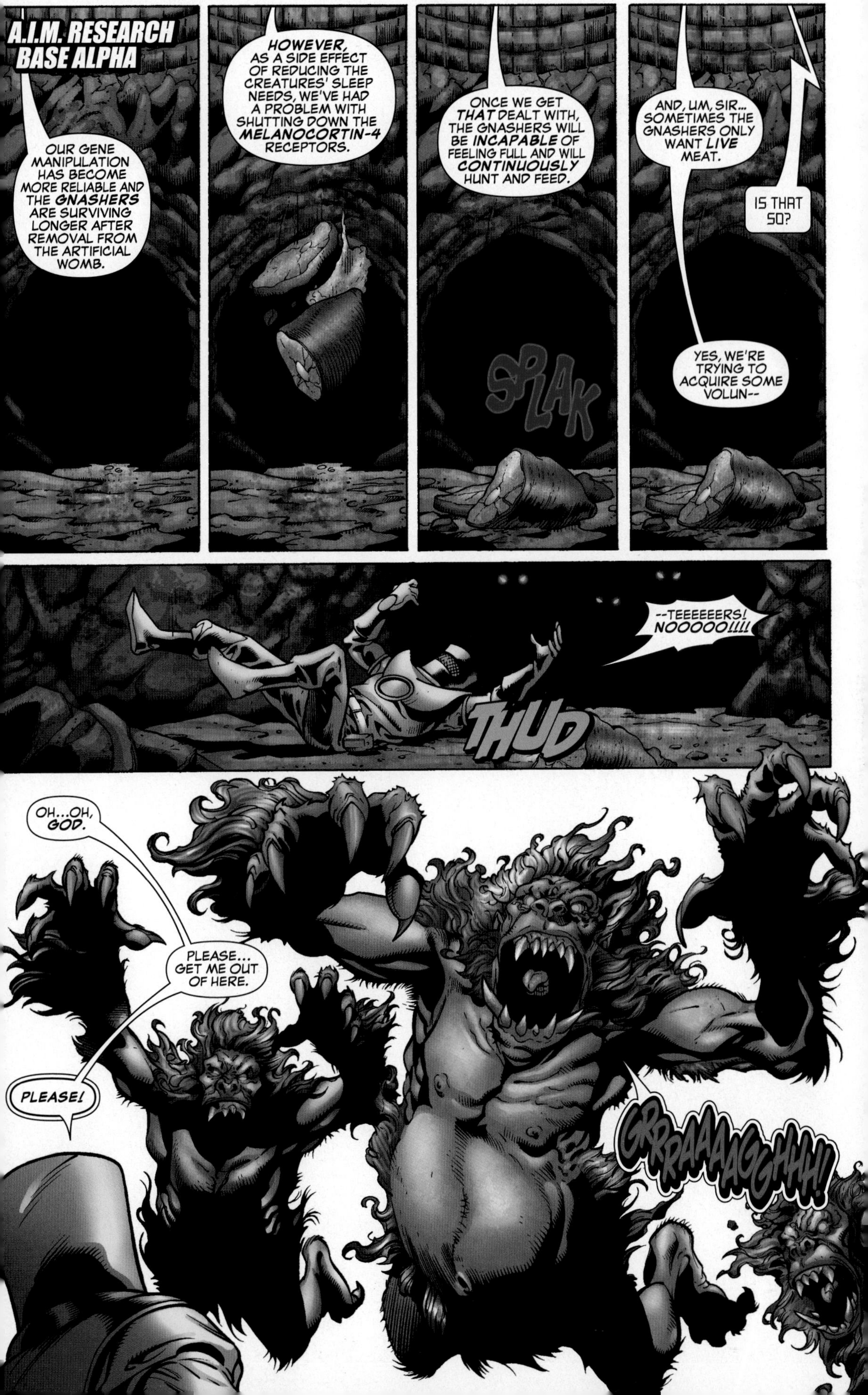
A.I.M. RESEARCH BASE ALPHA
OUR GENE MANIPULATION HAS BECOME MORE RELIABLE AND THE GNASHERS ARE SURVIVING LONGER AFTER REMOVAL FROM THE ARTIFICIAL WOMB.
HOWEVER, AS A SIDE EFFECT OF REDUCING THE CREATURES' SLEEP NEEDS, WE'VE HAD A PROBLEM WITH SHUTTING DOWN THE MELANOCORTIN-4 RECEPTORS.
ONCE WE GET THAT DEALT WITH, THE GNASHERS WILL BE INCAPABLE OF FEELING FULL AND WILL CONTINUOUSLY HUNT AND FEED.
SPLAK
AND, UM, SIR... SOMETIMES THE GNASHERS ONLY WANT LIVE MEAT.
IS THAT SO?
YES, WE'RE TRYING TO ACQUIRE SOME VOLUN--
--TEEEEEERS! NOOOOO!!!!
THUD
OH...OH, GOD.
PLEASE... GET ME OUT OF HERE.
PLEASE!
GRRRAAAAGGHHH!

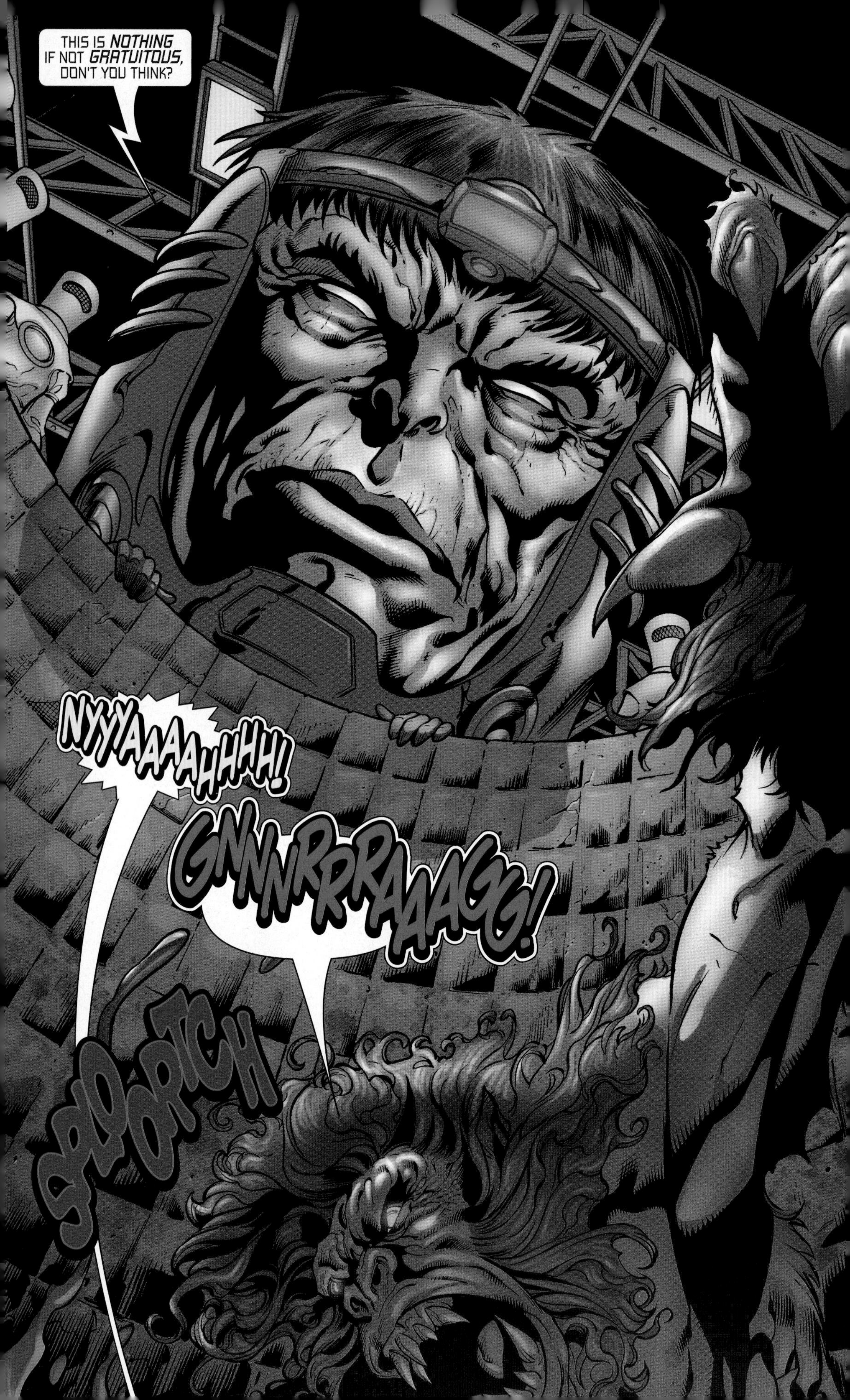
THIS IS NOTHING IF NOT GRATUITOUS, DON'T YOU THINK?
NYYAAAAHHHH!
GNNNRRRAAAGG!
SPLOOTCH

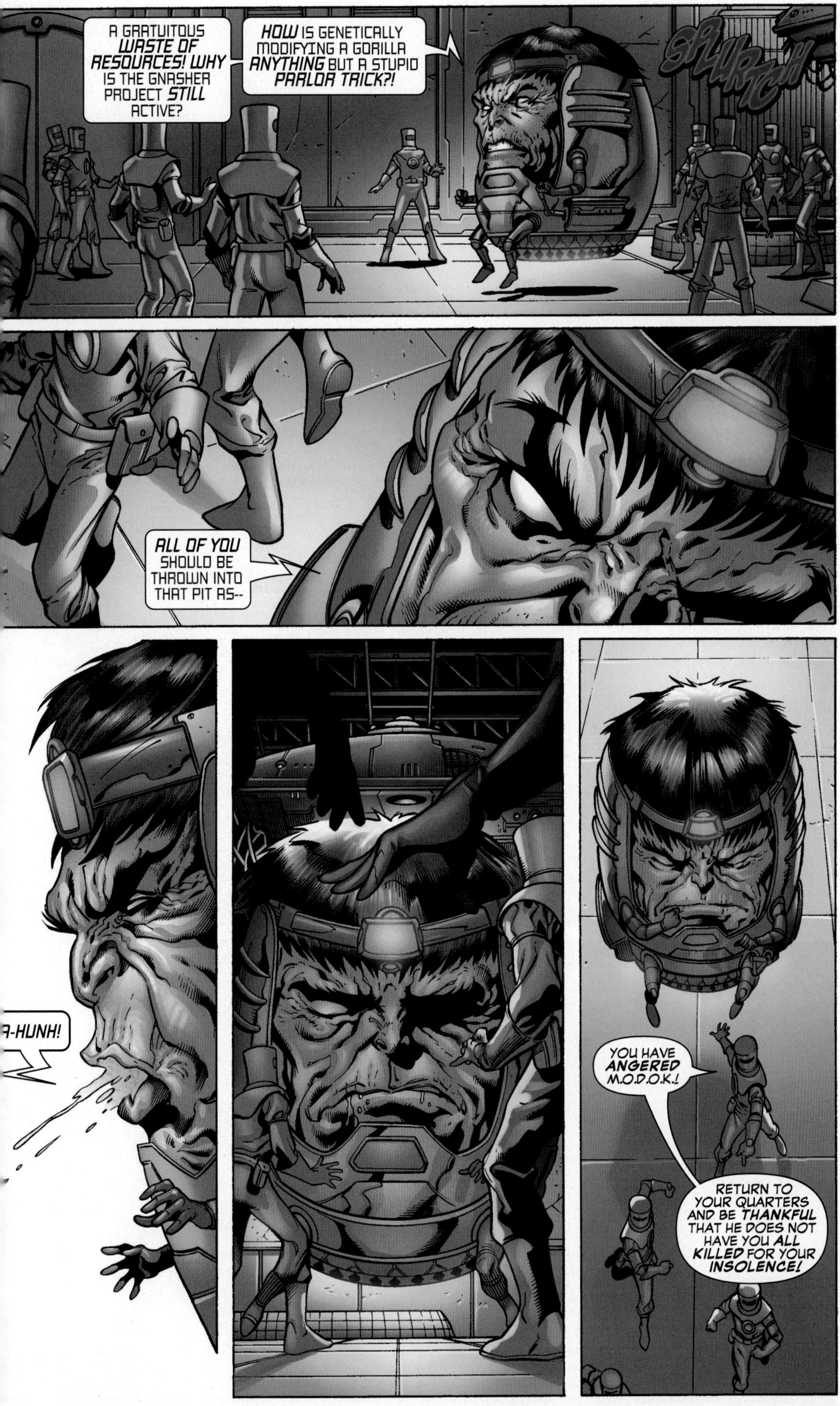

A GRATUITOUS WASTE OF RESOURCES! WHY IS THE GNASHER PROJECT STILL ACTIVE?
HOW IS GENETICALLY MODIFYING A GORILLA ANYTHING BUT A STUPID PARLOR TRICK?!
SHLURCH
ALL OF YOU SHOULD BE THROWN INTO THAT PIT AS--
-HUNH!
YOU HAVE ANGERED M.O.D.O.K.!
RETURN TO YOUR QUARTERS AND BE THANKFUL THAT HE DOES NOT HAVE YOU ALL KILLED FOR YOUR INSOLENCE!

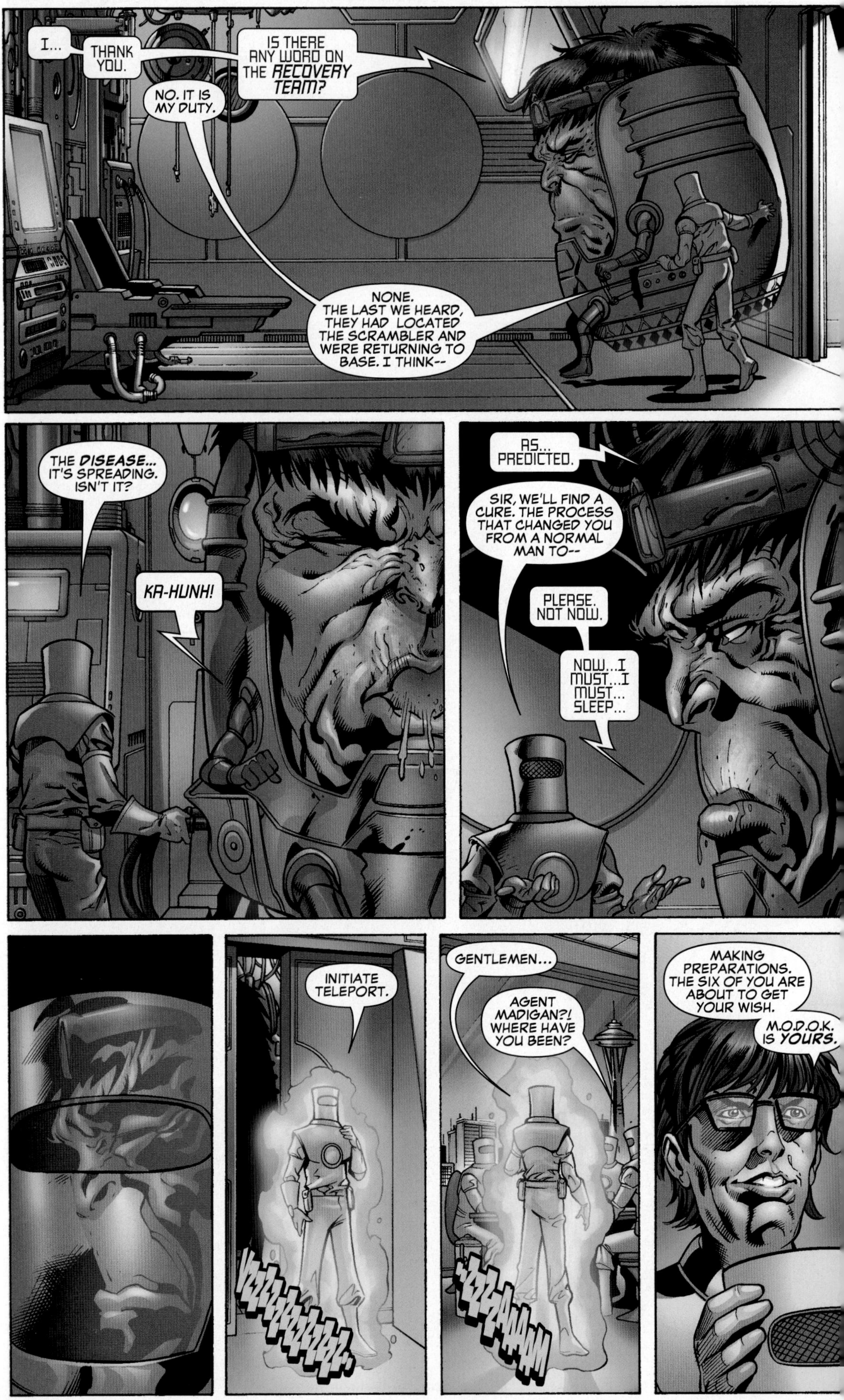
I...
THANK YOU.
NO. IT IS MY DUTY.
IS THERE ANY WORD ON THE *RECOVERY TEAM?*
NONE. THE LAST WE HEARD, THEY HAD LOCATED THE SCRAMBLER AND WERE RETURNING TO BASE. I THINK--
THE *DISEASE...* IT'S SPREADING. ISN'T IT?
KA-HUNH!
AS... PREDICTED.
SIR, WE'LL FIND A CURE. THE PROCESS THAT CHANGED YOU FROM A NORMAL MAN TO--
PLEASE. NOT NOW.
NOW...I MUST...I MUST... SLEEP...
INITIATE TELEPORT.
VZZZZZZZZZZZZ-
GENTLEMEN...
AGENT MADIGAN?! WHERE HAVE YOU BEEN?
-ZZZAAAAM
MAKING PREPARATIONS. THE SIX OF YOU ARE ABOUT TO GET YOUR WISH.
M.O.D.O.K. IS *YOURS.*

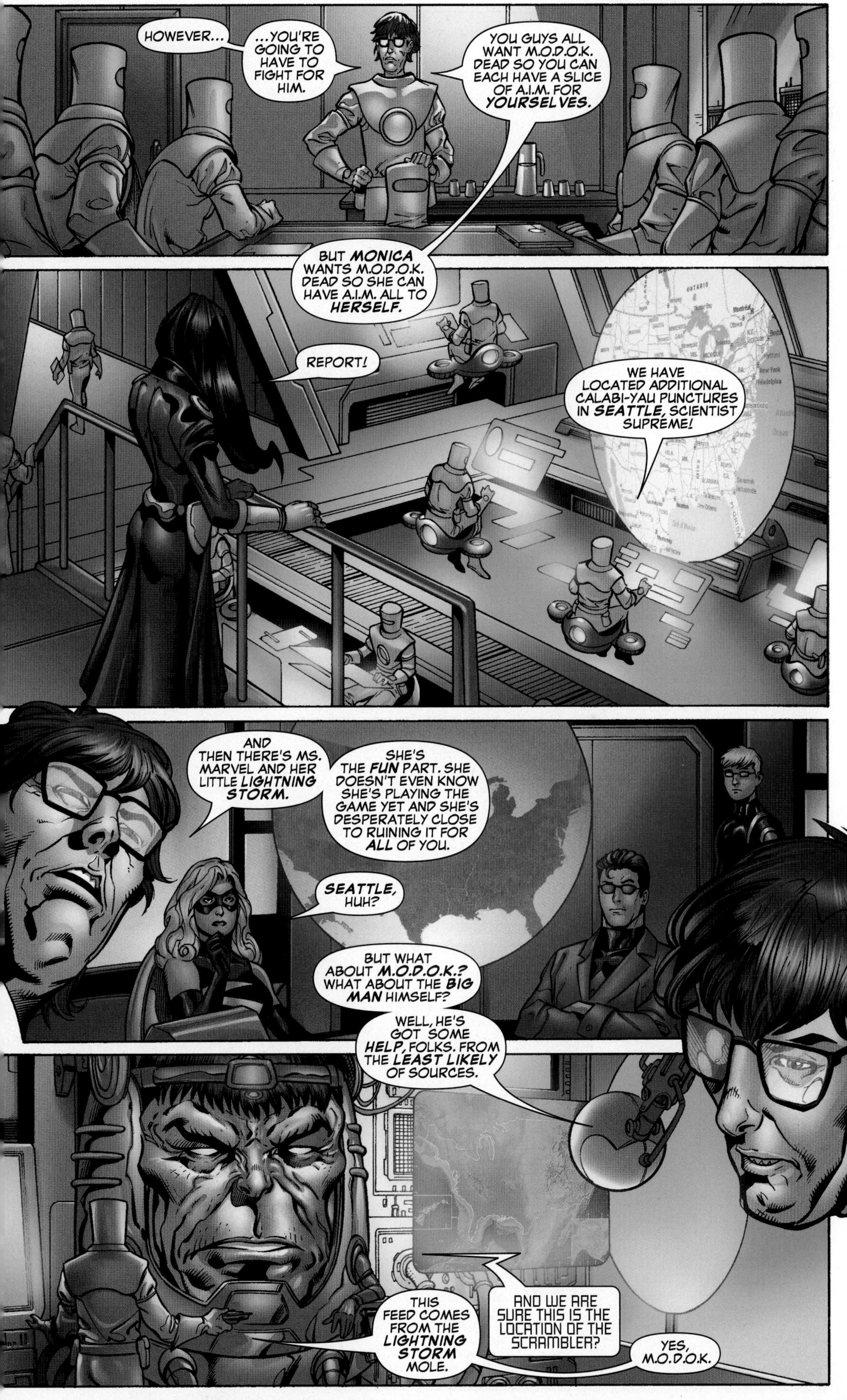
HOWEVER...
...YOU'RE GOING TO HAVE TO FIGHT FOR HIM.
YOU GUYS ALL WANT M.O.D.O.K. DEAD SO YOU CAN EACH HAVE A SLICE OF A.I.M. FOR YOURSELVES.
BUT MONICA WANTS M.O.D.O.K. DEAD SO SHE CAN HAVE A.I.M. ALL TO HERSELF.
REPORT!
WE HAVE LOCATED ADDITIONAL CALABI-YAU PUNCTURES IN SEATTLE, SCIENTIST SUPREME!
AND THEN THERE'S MS. MARVEL AND HER LITTLE LIGHTNING STORM.
SHE'S THE FUN PART. SHE DOESN'T EVEN KNOW SHE'S PLAYING THE GAME YET AND SHE'S DESPERATELY CLOSE TO RUINING IT FOR ALL OF YOU.
SEATTLE, HUH?
BUT WHAT ABOUT M.O.D.O.K.? WHAT ABOUT THE BIG MAN HIMSELF?
WELL, HE'S GOT SOME HELP, FOLKS. FROM THE LEAST LIKELY OF SOURCES.
THIS FEED COMES FROM THE LIGHTNING STORM MOLE.
AND WE ARE SURE THIS IS THE LOCATION OF THE SCRAMBLER?
YES, M.O.D.O.K.

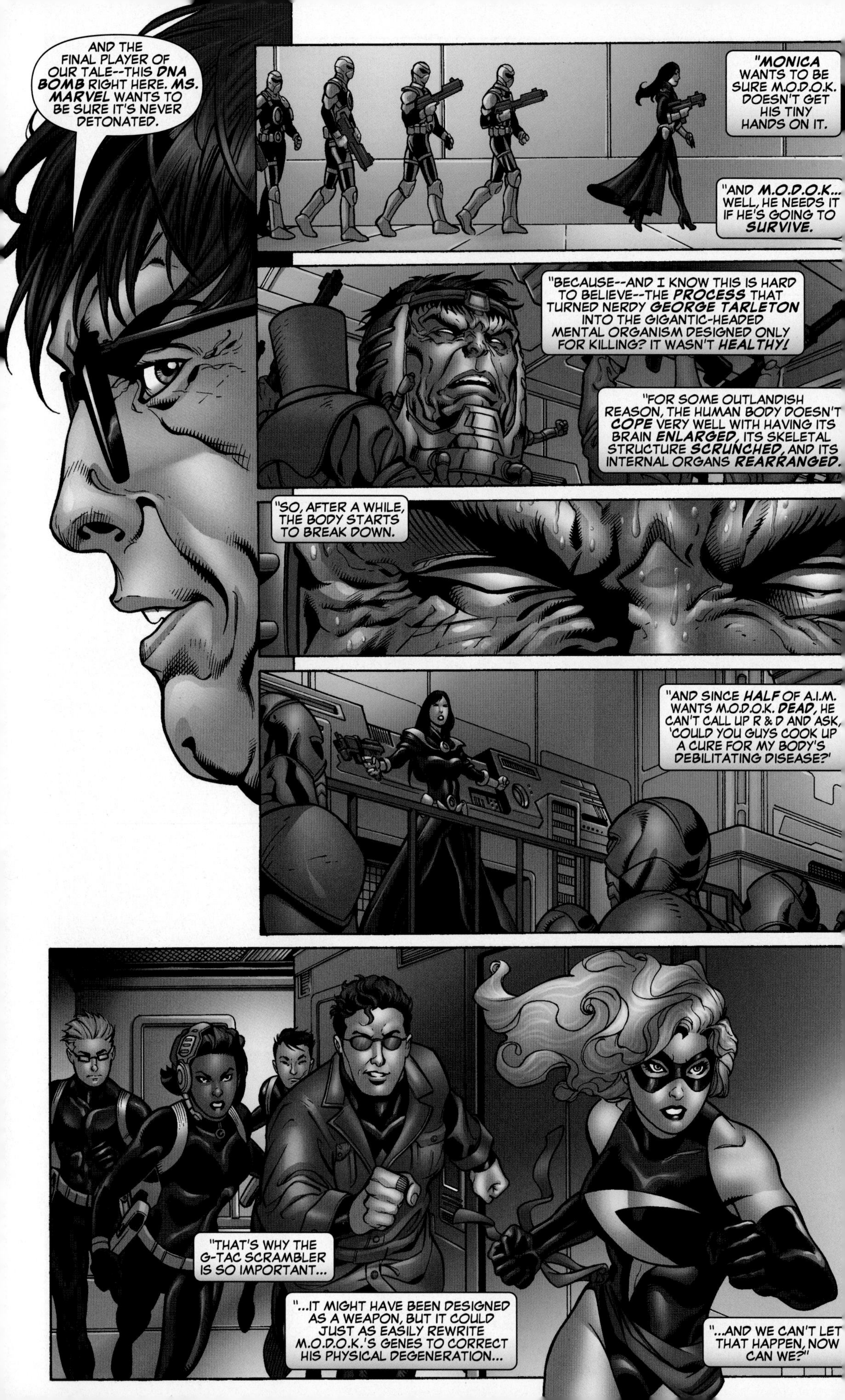
AND THE FINAL PLAYER OF OUR TALE--THIS DNA BOMB RIGHT HERE. MS. MARVEL WANTS TO BE SURE IT'S NEVER DETONATED.
"MONICA WANTS TO BE SURE M.O.D.O.K. DOESN'T GET HIS TINY HANDS ON IT.
"AND M.O.D.O.K... WELL, HE NEEDS IT IF HE'S GOING TO SURVIVE.
"BECAUSE--AND I KNOW THIS IS HARD TO BELIEVE--THE PROCESS THAT TURNED NERDY GEORGE TARLETON INTO THE GIGANTIC-HEADED MENTAL ORGANISM DESIGNED ONLY FOR KILLING? IT WASN'T HEALTHY!
"FOR SOME OUTLANDISH REASON, THE HUMAN BODY DOESN'T COPE VERY WELL WITH HAVING ITS BRAIN ENLARGED, ITS SKELETAL STRUCTURE SCRUNCHED, AND ITS INTERNAL ORGANS REARRANGED.
"SO, AFTER A WHILE, THE BODY STARTS TO BREAK DOWN.
"AND SINCE HALF OF A.I.M. WANTS M.O.D.O.K. DEAD, HE CAN'T CALL UP R & D AND ASK, 'COULD YOU GUYS COOK UP A CURE FOR MY BODY'S DEBILITATING DISEASE?'
"THAT'S WHY THE G-TAC SCRAMBLER IS SO IMPORTANT...
"...IT MIGHT HAVE BEEN DESIGNED AS A WEAPON, BUT IT COULD JUST AS EASILY REWRITE M.O.D.O.K.'S GENES TO CORRECT HIS PHYSICAL DEGENERATION...
"...AND WE CAN'T LET THAT HAPPEN, NOW CAN WE?"

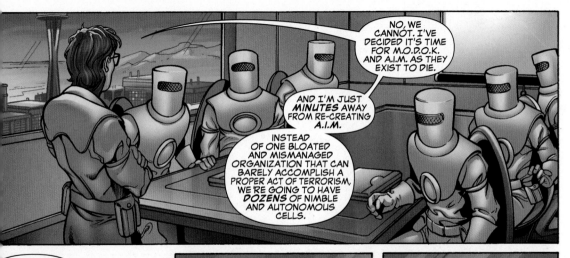

NO, WE CANNOT. I'VE DECIDED IT'S TIME FOR M.O.D.O.K. AND A.I.M. AS THEY EXIST TO DIE.

AND I'M JUST *MINUTES* AWAY FROM RE-CREATING A.I.M.

INSTEAD OF ONE BLOATED AND MISMANAGED ORGANIZATION THAT CAN BARELY ACCOMPLISH A PROPER ACT OF TERRORISM, WE'RE GOING TO HAVE *DOZENS* OF NIMBLE AND AUTONOMOUS CELLS.

ALL CAUSING DESTRUCTION AND TERROR ON AN *INCREDIBLE* SCALE.

FUN, HUH?

NO! THE DEAL WAS THAT YOU WOULD BRING US M.O.D.O.K.! WE HAVE NO INTEREST IN *SEGMENTING* A.I.M.! WE HAVE NO--

THE BEST YOU CAN HOPE FOR IS TO GRAB SOME OF THE SCRAPS THAT FALL TO THE FLOOR. BUT YOU BETTER GET READY, BECAUSE EVERYBODY IS COMING *RIGHT HERE.*

TO THIS.

VERY.

VZZZZZZZZZZZZZZZ--

VZZZZZZZZZZZZZ--

ROOM.

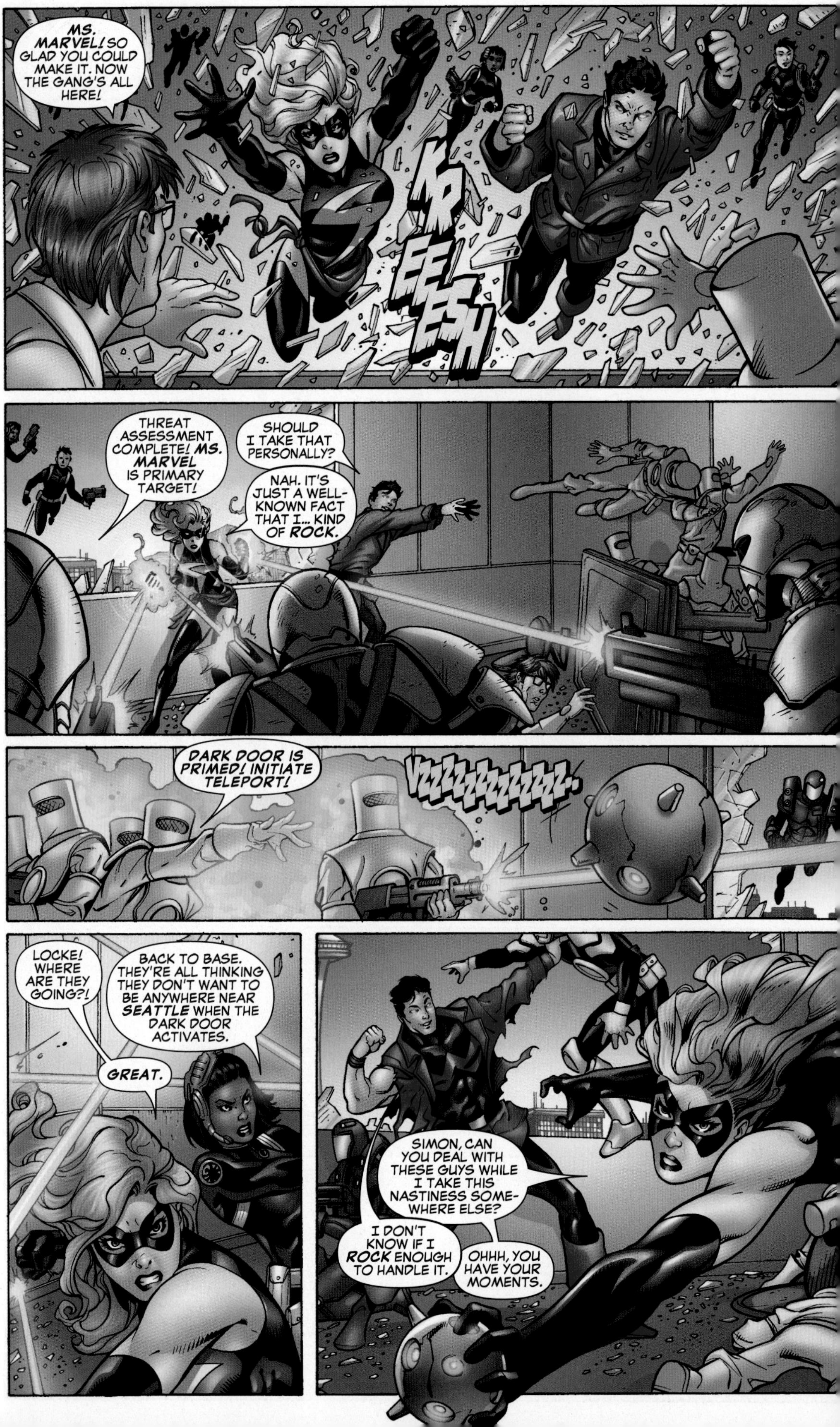
MS. MARVEL! SO GLAD YOU COULD MAKE IT. NOW THE GANG'S ALL HERE!
KRREEESH
THREAT ASSESSMENT COMPLETE! MS. MARVEL IS PRIMARY TARGET!
SHOULD I TAKE THAT PERSONALLY?
NAH. IT'S JUST A WELL-KNOWN FACT THAT I... KIND OF ROCK.
DARK DOOR IS PRIMED! INITIATE TELEPORT!
VZZZZZZZZZZZZZ.
LOCKE! WHERE ARE THEY GOING?!
BACK TO BASE. THEY'RE ALL THINKING THEY DON'T WANT TO BE ANYWHERE NEAR SEATTLE WHEN THE DARK DOOR ACTIVATES.
GREAT.
SIMON, CAN YOU DEAL WITH THESE GUYS WHILE I TAKE THIS NASTINESS SOME-WHERE ELSE?
I DON'T KNOW IF I ROCK ENOUGH TO HANDLE IT.
OHHH, YOU HAVE YOUR MOMENTS.

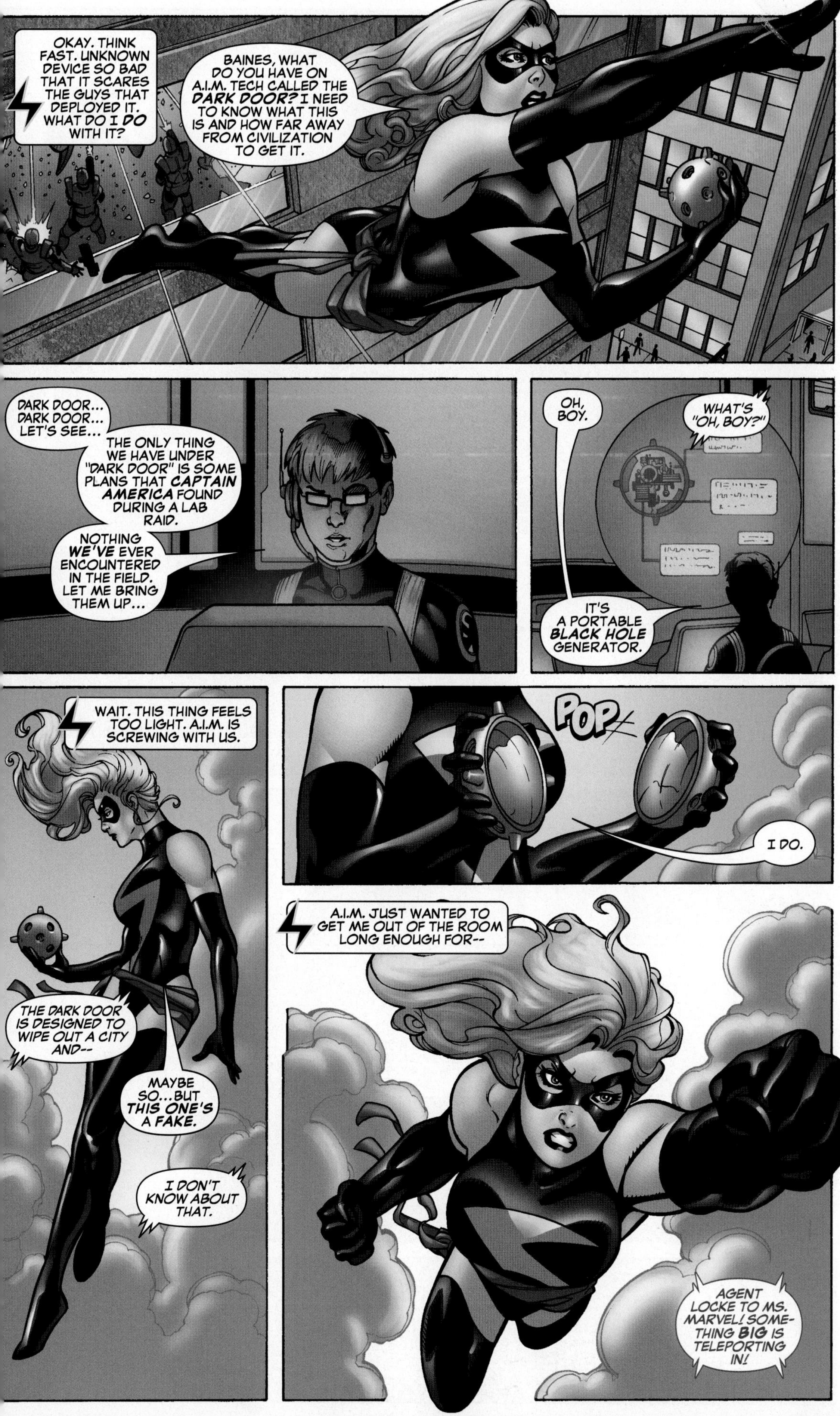
OKAY. THINK FAST. UNKNOWN DEVICE SO BAD THAT IT SCARES THE GUYS THAT DEPLOYED IT. WHAT DO I DO WITH IT?
BAINES, WHAT DO YOU HAVE ON A.I.M. TECH CALLED THE DARK DOOR? I NEED TO KNOW WHAT THIS IS AND HOW FAR AWAY FROM CIVILIZATION TO GET IT.
DARK DOOR... DARK DOOR... LET'S SEE...
THE ONLY THING WE HAVE UNDER "DARK DOOR" IS SOME PLANS THAT CAPTAIN AMERICA FOUND DURING A LAB RAID.
NOTHING WE'VE EVER ENCOUNTERED IN THE FIELD. LET ME BRING THEM UP...
OH, BOY.
WHAT'S "OH, BOY?"
IT'S A PORTABLE BLACK HOLE GENERATOR.
WAIT. THIS THING FEELS TOO LIGHT. A.I.M. IS SCREWING WITH US.
THE DARK DOOR IS DESIGNED TO WIPE OUT A CITY AND--
MAYBE SO...BUT THIS ONE'S A FAKE.
I DON'T KNOW ABOUT THAT.
POP
I DO.
A.I.M. JUST WANTED TO GET ME OUT OF THE ROOM LONG ENOUGH FOR--
AGENT LOCKE TO MS. MARVEL! SOMETHING BIG IS TELEPORTING IN!

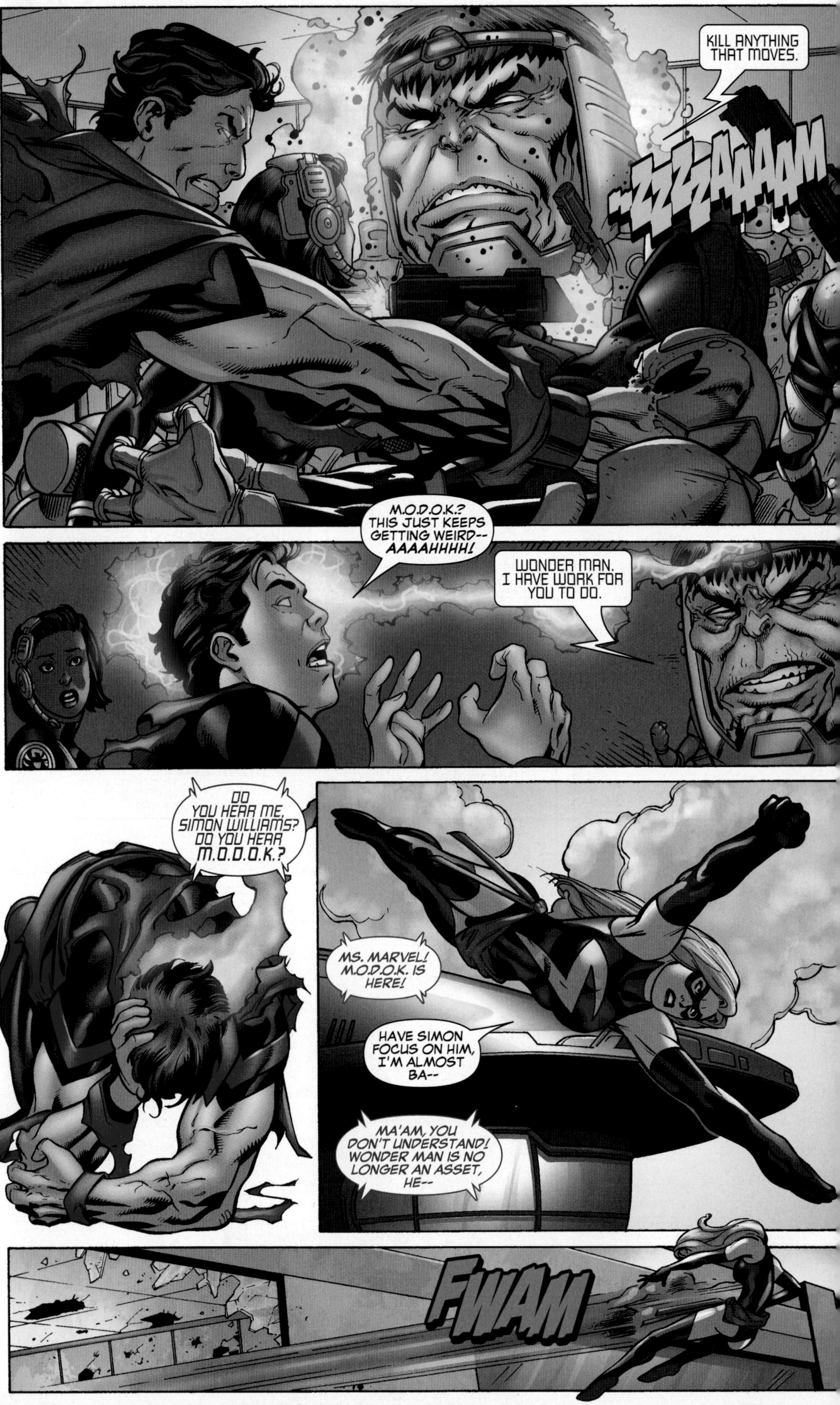
KILL ANYTHING THAT MOVES.
ZZZZAAAAM
M.O.D.O.K.? THIS JUST KEEPS GETTING WEIRD-- AAAAHHHH!
WONDER MAN. I HAVE WORK FOR YOU TO DO.
DO YOU HEAR ME, SIMON WILLIAMS? DO YOU HEAR M.O.D.O.K.?
MS. MARVEL! M.O.D.O.K. IS HERE!
HAVE SIMON FOCUS ON HIM, I'M ALMOST BA--
MA'AM, YOU DON'T UNDERSTAND! WONDER MAN IS NO LONGER AN ASSET, HE--
FWAM

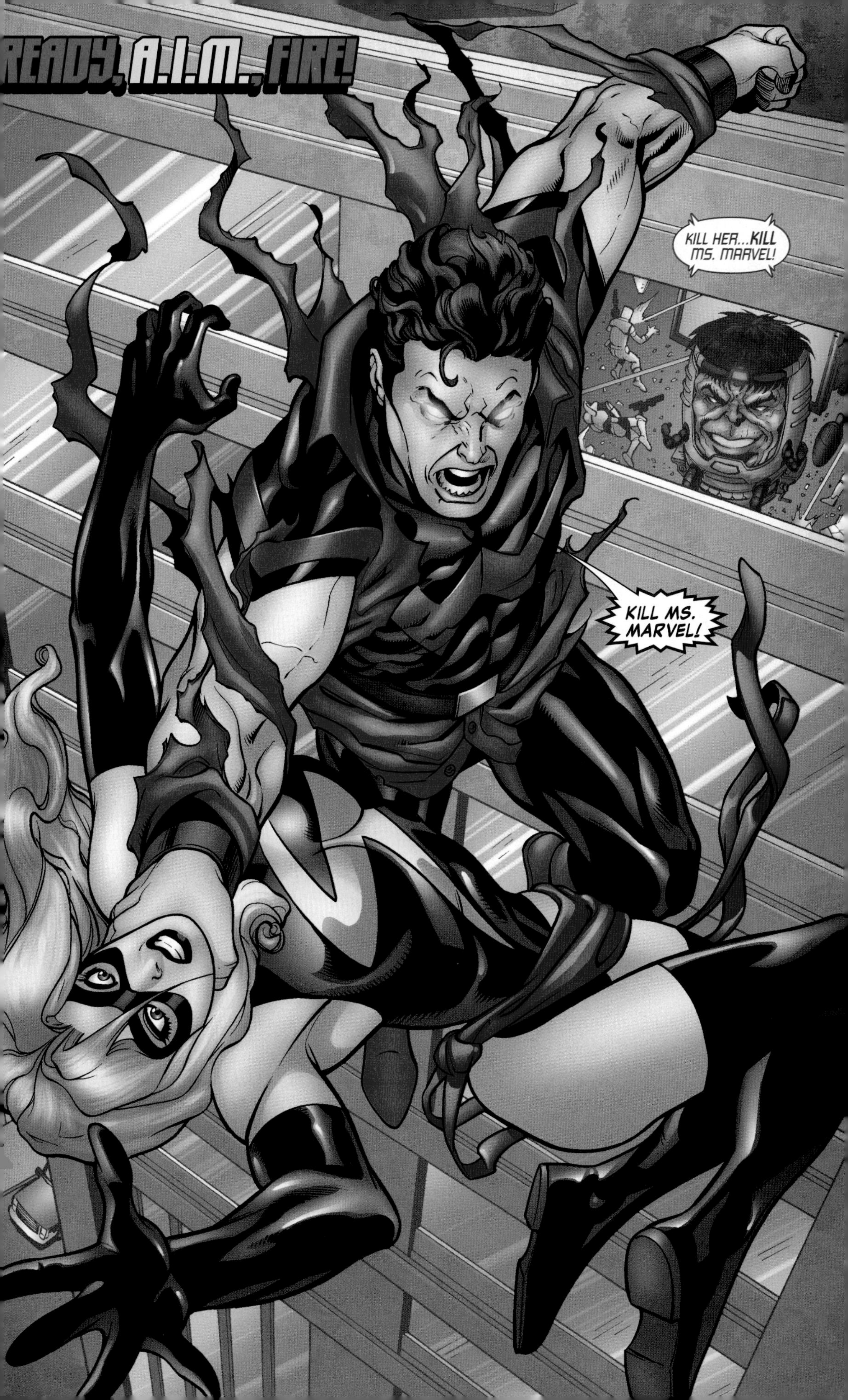
READY, A.I.M., FIRE!
KILL HER...KILL MS. MARVEL!
KILL MS. MARVEL!

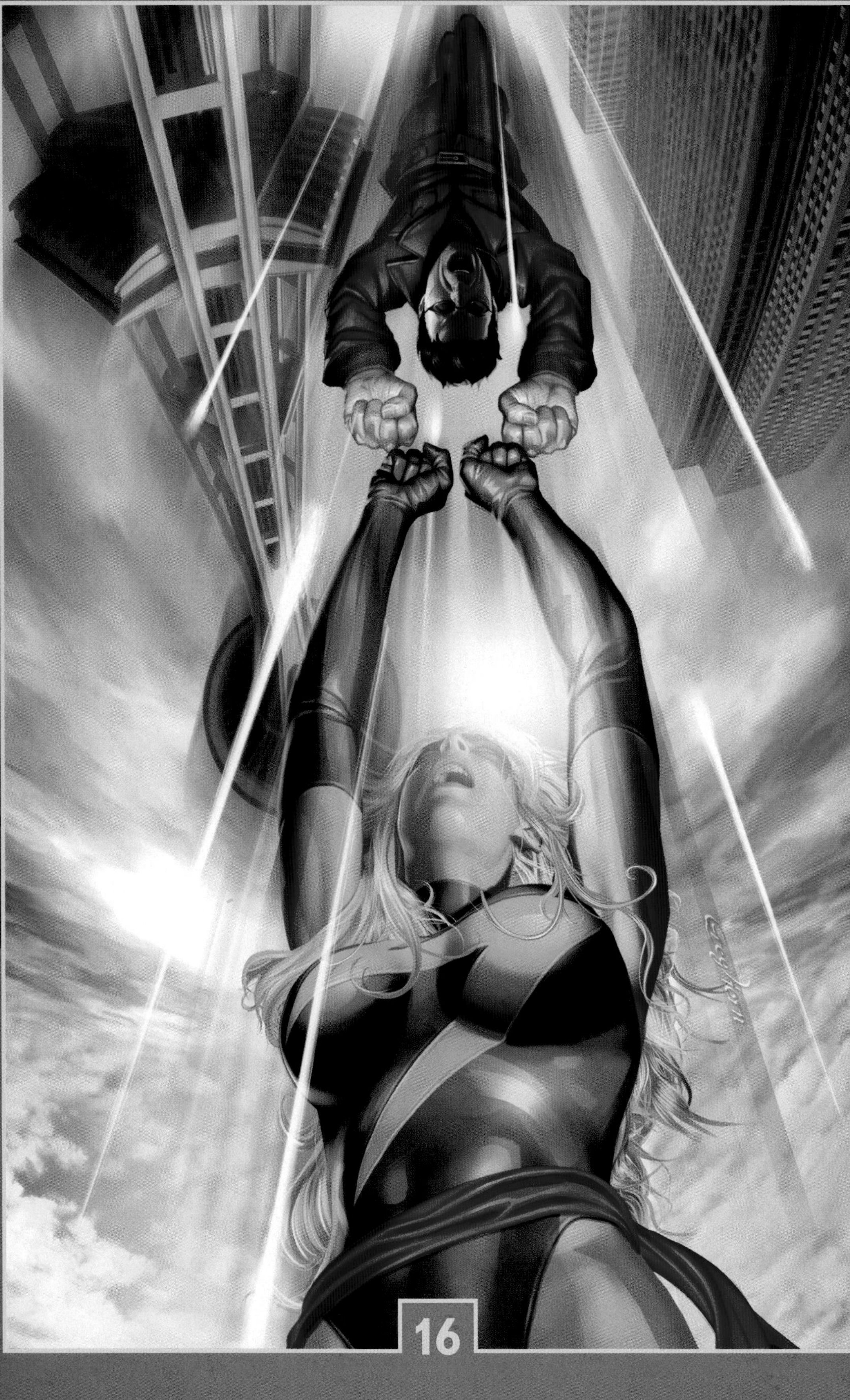

16

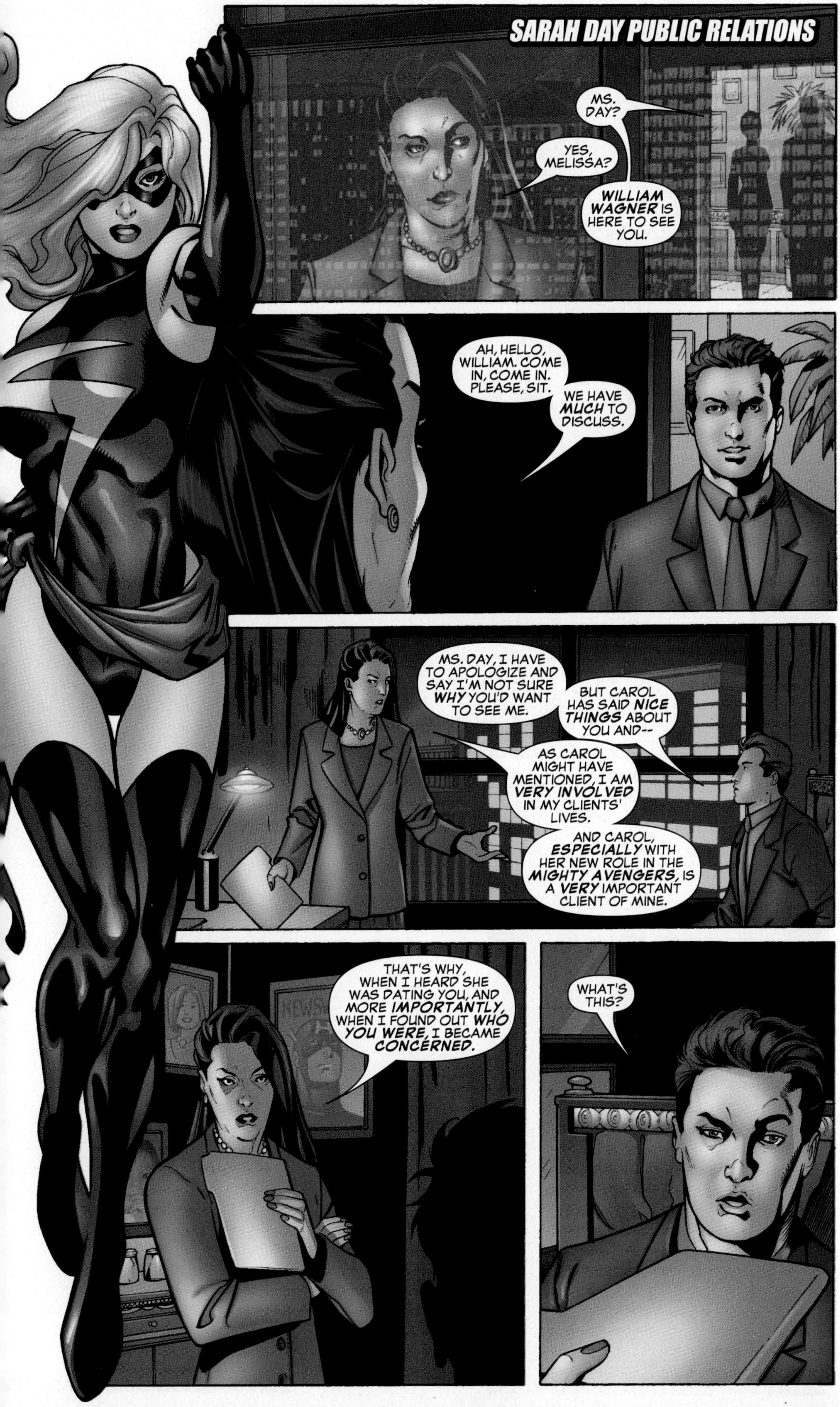
SARAH DAY PUBLIC RELATIONS
MS. DAY?
YES, MELISSA?
WILLIAM WAGNER IS HERE TO SEE YOU.
AH, HELLO, WILLIAM. COME IN, COME IN. PLEASE, SIT.
WE HAVE MUCH TO DISCUSS.
MS. DAY, I HAVE TO APOLOGIZE AND SAY I'M NOT SURE WHY YOU'D WANT TO SEE ME.
BUT CAROL HAS SAID NICE THINGS ABOUT YOU AND--
AS CAROL MIGHT HAVE MENTIONED, I AM VERY INVOLVED IN MY CLIENTS' LIVES.
AND CAROL, ESPECIALLY WITH HER NEW ROLE IN THE MIGHTY AVENGERS, IS A VERY IMPORTANT CLIENT OF MINE.
THAT'S WHY, WHEN I HEARD SHE WAS DATING YOU, AND MORE IMPORTANTLY, WHEN I FOUND OUT WHO YOU WERE, I BECAME CONCERNED.
WHAT'S THIS?

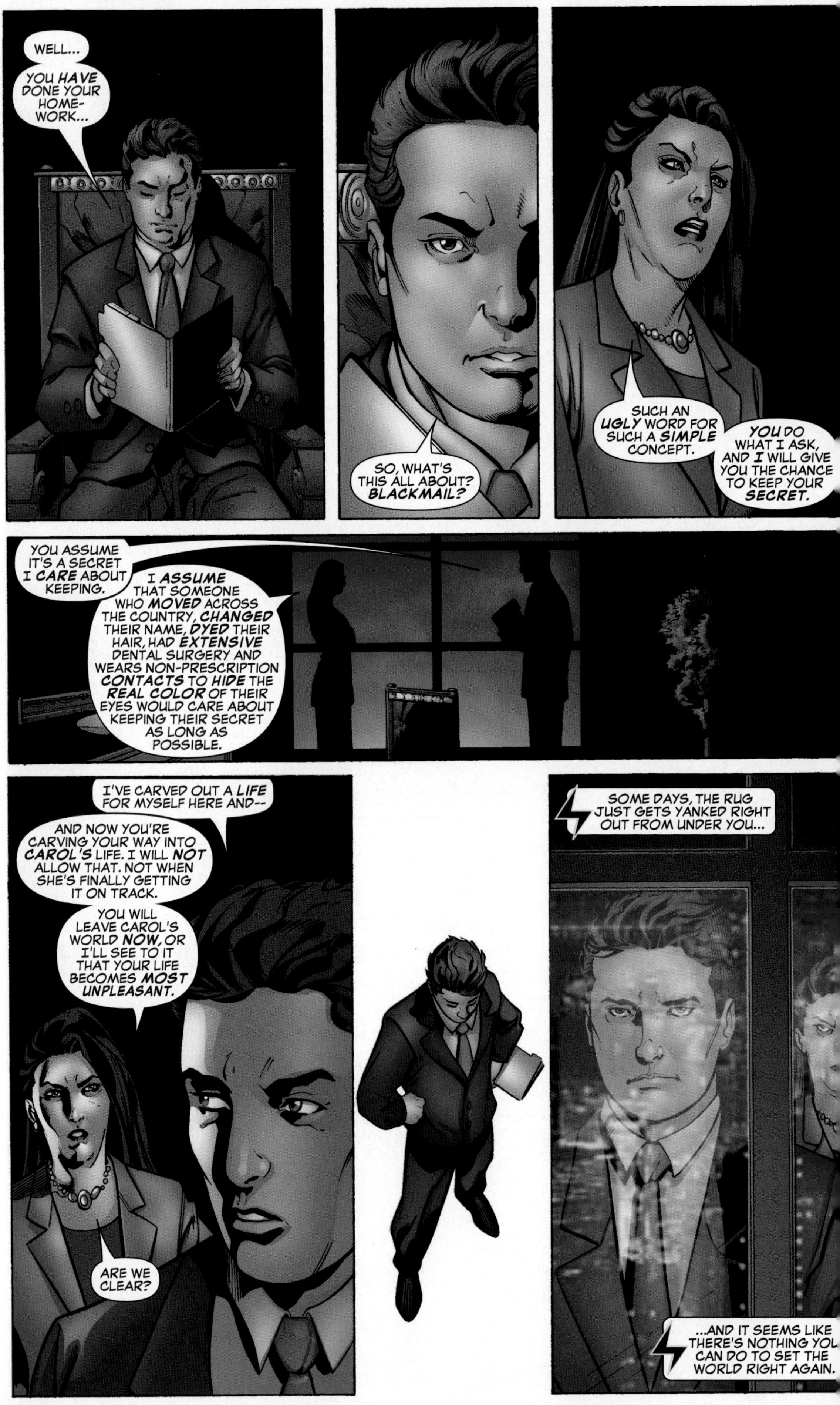
WELL...
YOU HAVE DONE YOUR HOME-WORK...
SO, WHAT'S THIS ALL ABOUT? BLACKMAIL?
SUCH AN UGLY WORD FOR SUCH A SIMPLE CONCEPT.
YOU DO WHAT I ASK, AND I WILL GIVE YOU THE CHANCE TO KEEP YOUR SECRET.
YOU ASSUME IT'S A SECRET I CARE ABOUT KEEPING.
I ASSUME THAT SOMEONE WHO MOVED ACROSS THE COUNTRY, CHANGED THEIR NAME, DYED THEIR HAIR, HAD EXTENSIVE DENTAL SURGERY AND WEARS NON-PRESCRIPTION CONTACTS TO HIDE THE REAL COLOR OF THEIR EYES WOULD CARE ABOUT KEEPING THEIR SECRET AS LONG AS POSSIBLE.
I'VE CARVED OUT A LIFE FOR MYSELF HERE AND--
AND NOW YOU'RE CARVING YOUR WAY INTO CAROL'S LIFE. I WILL NOT ALLOW THAT. NOT WHEN SHE'S FINALLY GETTING IT ON TRACK.
YOU WILL LEAVE CAROL'S WORLD NOW, OR I'LL SEE TO IT THAT YOUR LIFE BECOMES MOST UNPLEASANT.
ARE WE CLEAR?
SOME DAYS, THE RUG JUST GETS YANKED RIGHT OUT FROM UNDER YOU...
...AND IT SEEMS LIKE THERE'S NOTHING YOU CAN DO TO SET THE WORLD RIGHT AGAIN.

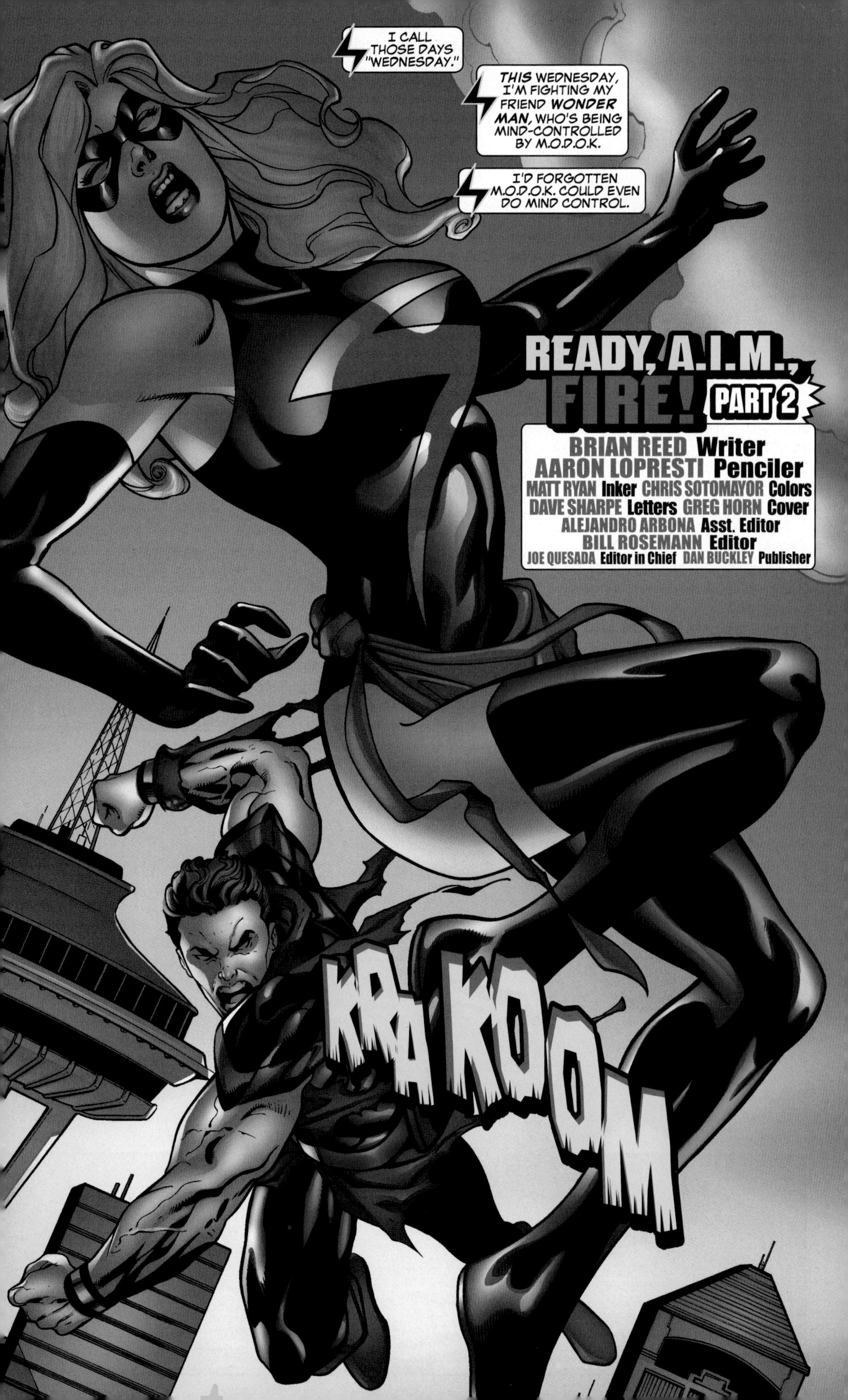

I CALL THOSE DAYS "WEDNESDAY."
THIS WEDNESDAY, I'M FIGHTING MY FRIEND WONDER MAN, WHO'S BEING MIND-CONTROLLED BY M.O.D.O.K.
I'D FORGOTTEN M.O.D.O.K. COULD EVEN DO MIND CONTROL.
READY, A.I.M., FIRE! PART 2
BRIAN REED Writer
AARON LOPRESTI Penciler
MATT RYAN Inker CHRIS SOTOMAYOR Colors
DAVE SHARPE Letters GREG HORN Cover
ALEJANDRO ARBONA Asst. Editor
BILL ROSEMANN Editor
JOE QUESADA Editor in Chief DAN BUCKLEY Publisher
KRA KOOOM

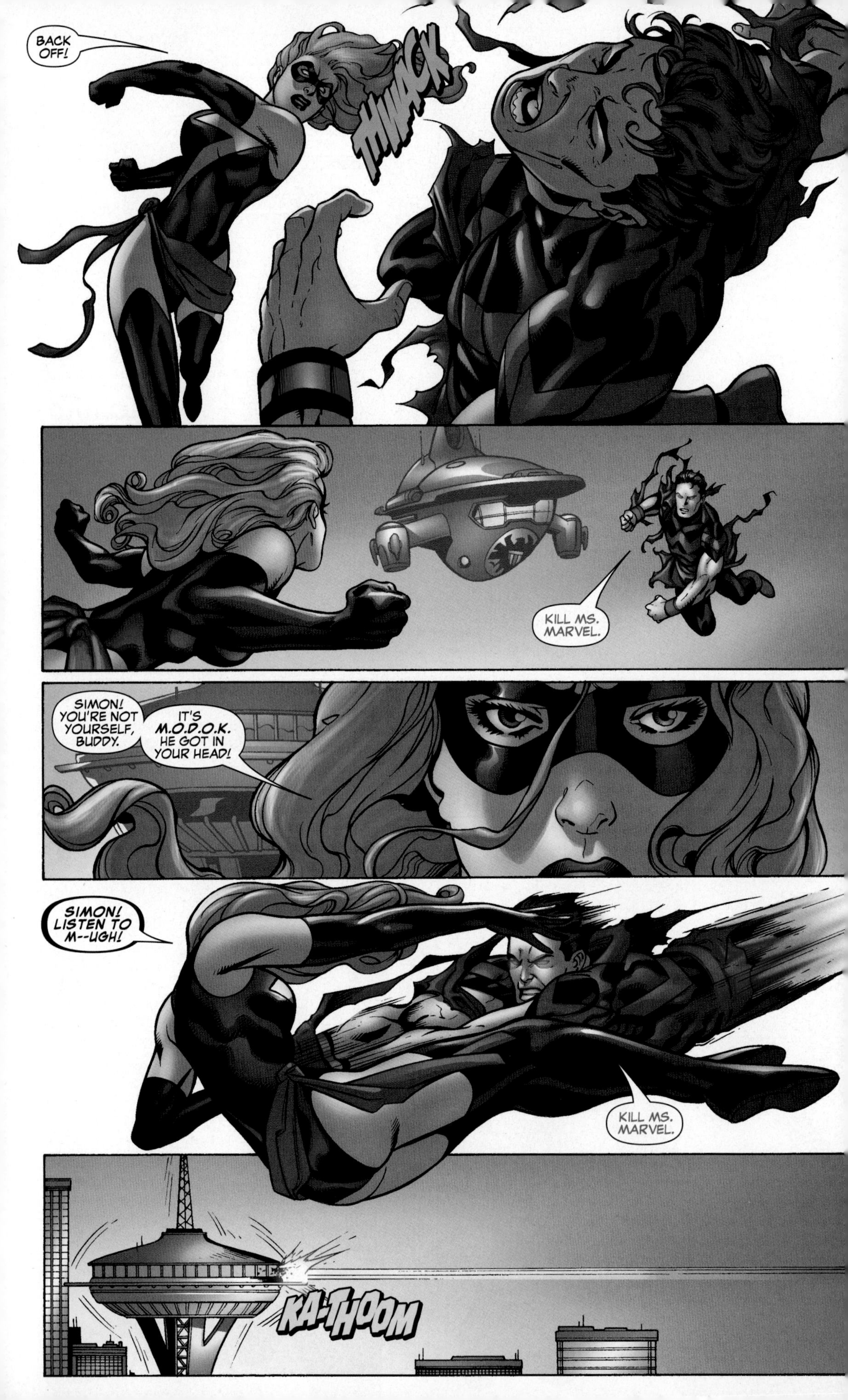
BACK OFF!
THWACK
KILL MS. MARVEL.
SIMON! YOU'RE NOT YOURSELF, BUDDY.
IT'S M.O.D.O.K. HE GOT IN YOUR HEAD!
SIMON! LISTEN TO M--UGH!
KILL MS. MARVEL.
KA-THOOM

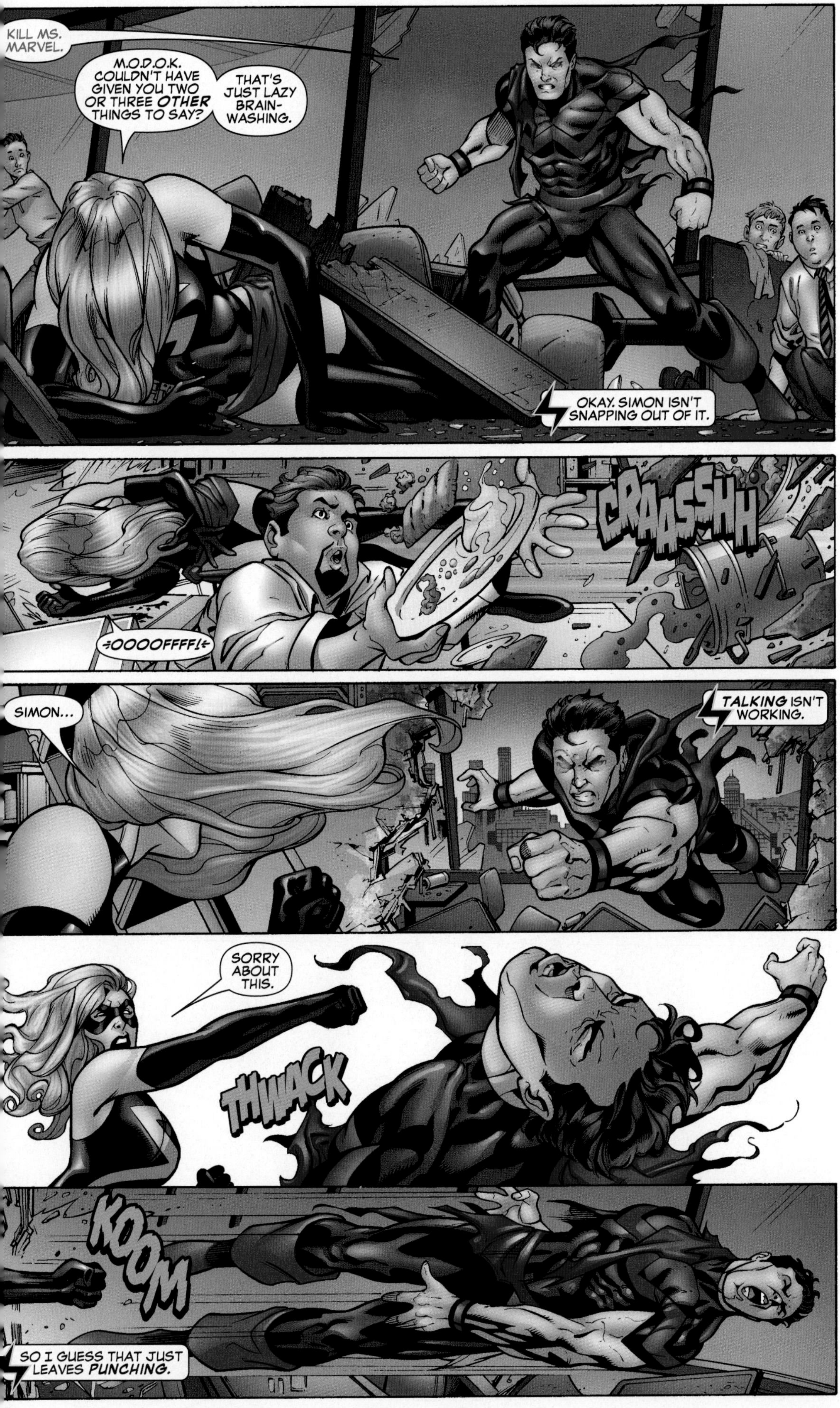
KILL MS. MARVEL.
M.O.D.O.K. COULDN'T HAVE GIVEN YOU TWO OR THREE OTHER THINGS TO SAY?
THAT'S JUST LAZY BRAIN-WASHING.
OKAY. SIMON ISN'T SNAPPING OUT OF IT.
CRAASSHH
OOOOFFFF!
SIMON...
TALKING ISN'T WORKING.
SORRY ABOUT THIS.
THWACK
KOOM
SO I GUESS THAT JUST LEAVES PUNCHING.

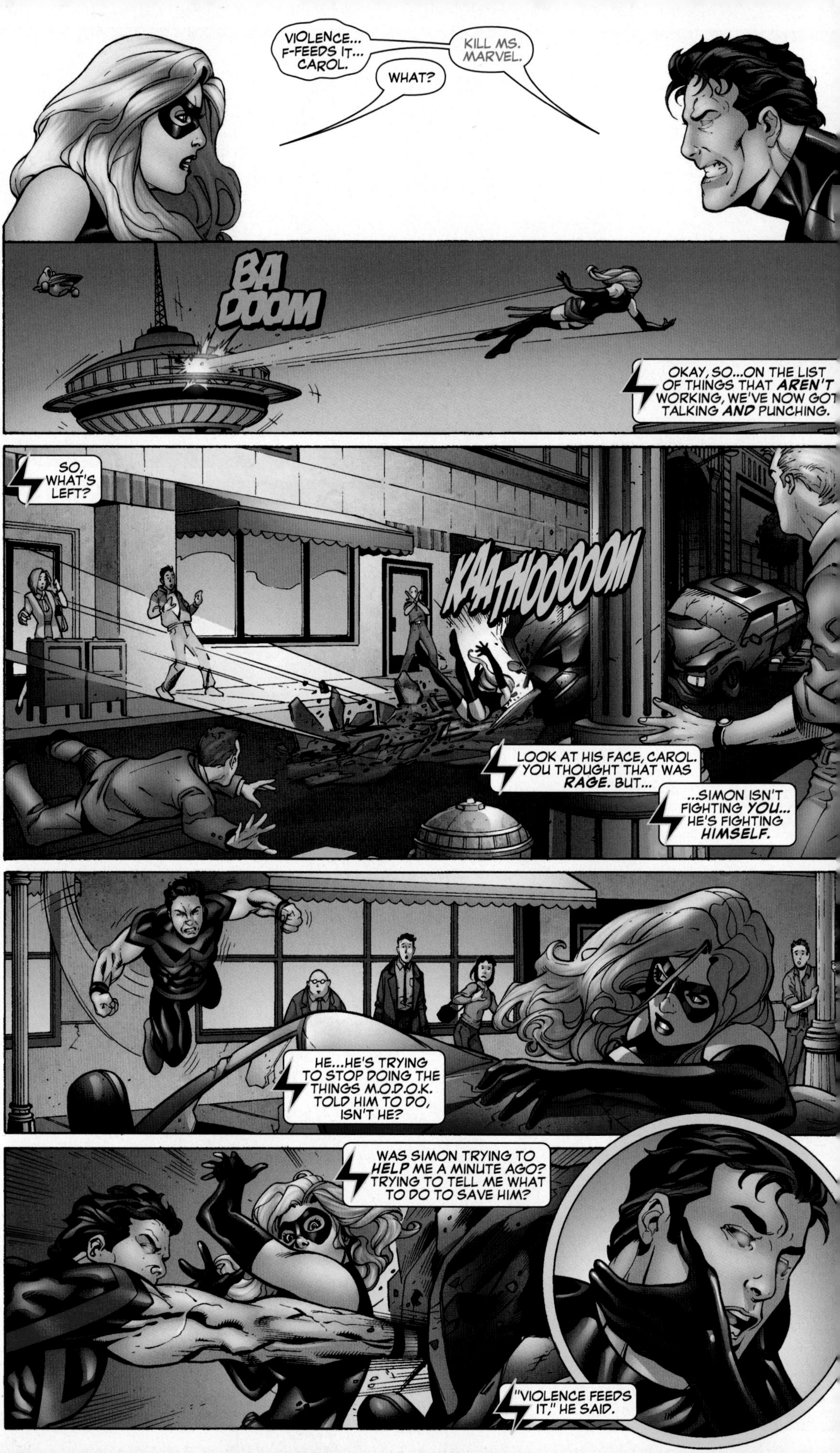
VIOLENCE... F-FEEDS IT... CAROL.
KILL MS. MARVEL.
WHAT?
BA DOOM
OKAY, SO...ON THE LIST OF THINGS THAT AREN'T WORKING, WE'VE NOW GOT TALKING AND PUNCHING.
SO, WHAT'S LEFT?
KAATHOOOOOM
LOOK AT HIS FACE, CAROL. YOU THOUGHT THAT WAS RAGE. BUT...
...SIMON ISN'T FIGHTING YOU... HE'S FIGHTING HIMSELF.
HE...HE'S TRYING TO STOP DOING THE THINGS M.O.D.O.K. TOLD HIM TO DO, ISN'T HE?
WAS SIMON TRYING TO HELP ME A MINUTE AGO? TRYING TO TELL ME WHAT TO DO TO SAVE HIM?
"VIOLENCE FEEDS IT," HE SAID.

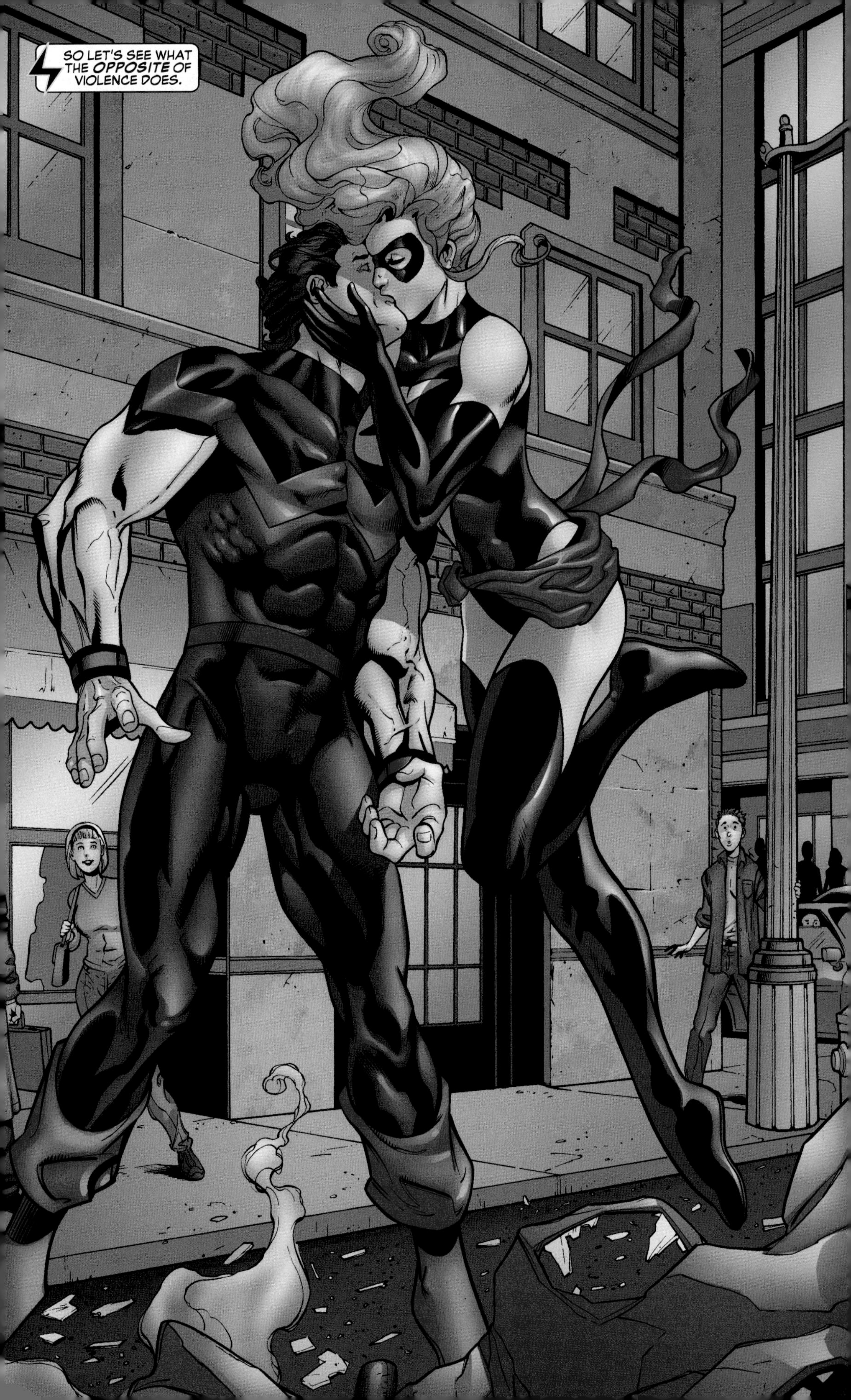
SO LET'S SEE WHAT THE OPPOSITE OF VIOLENCE DOES.

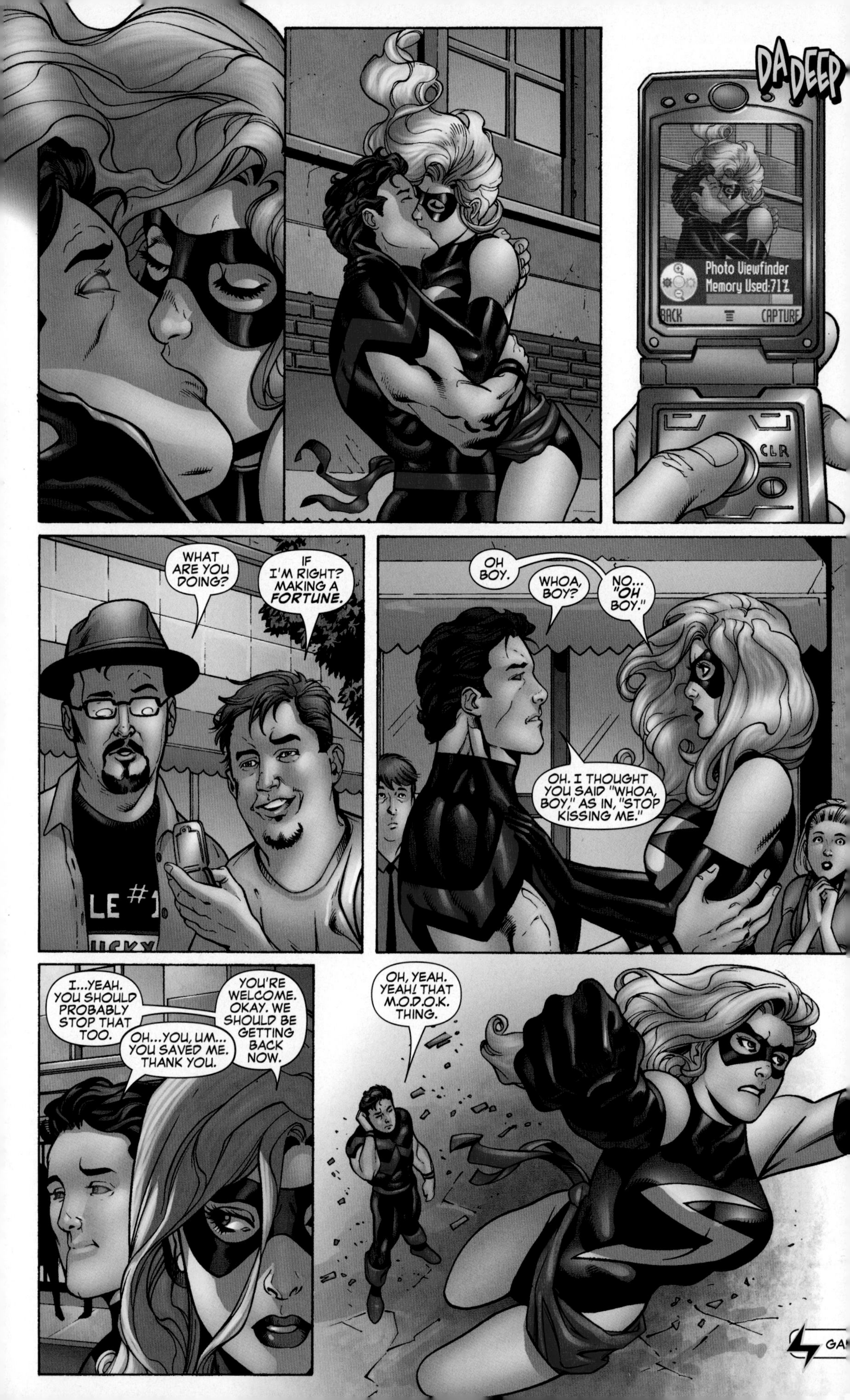
DADEEP
Photo Viewfinder
Memory Used:71%
BACK
CAPTURE
CLR
WHAT ARE YOU DOING?
IF I'M RIGHT? MAKING A FORTUNE.
OH BOY.
WHOA, BOY?
NO... "OH BOY."
OH. I THOUGHT YOU SAID "WHOA, BOY," AS IN, "STOP KISSING ME."
I...YEAH. YOU SHOULD PROBABLY STOP THAT TOO.
OH...YOU, UM... YOU SAVED ME. THANK YOU.
YOU'RE WELCOME. OKAY. WE SHOULD BE GETTING BACK NOW.
OH, YEAH. YEAH! THAT M.O.D.O.K. THING.

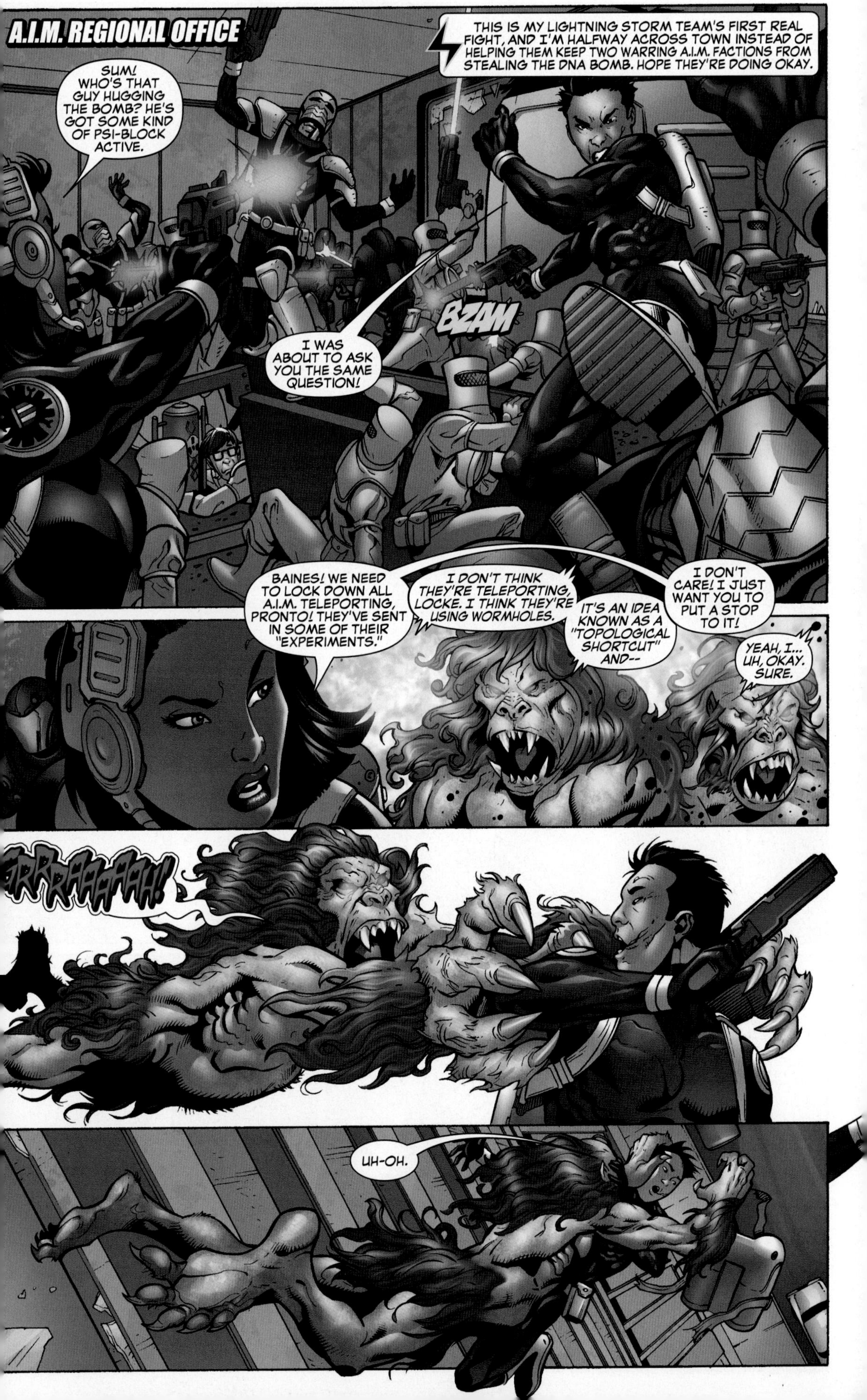
A.I.M. REGIONAL OFFICE
THIS IS MY LIGHTNING STORM TEAM'S FIRST REAL FIGHT, AND I'M HALFWAY ACROSS TOWN INSTEAD OF HELPING THEM KEEP TWO WARRING A.I.M. FACTIONS FROM STEALING THE DNA BOMB. HOPE THEY'RE DOING OKAY.
SUM! WHO'S THAT GUY HUGGING THE BOMB? HE'S GOT SOME KIND OF PSI-BLOCK ACTIVE.
I WAS ABOUT TO ASK YOU THE SAME QUESTION!
BZAM
BAINES! WE NEED TO LOCK DOWN ALL A.I.M. TELEPORTING, PRONTO! THEY'VE SENT IN SOME OF THEIR "EXPERIMENTS."
I DON'T THINK THEY'RE TELEPORTING, LOCKE. I THINK THEY'RE USING WORMHOLES.
IT'S AN IDEA KNOWN AS A "TOPOLOGICAL SHORTCUT" AND--
I DON'T CARE! I JUST WANT YOU TO PUT A STOP TO IT!
YEAH, I... UH, OKAY. SURE.
GRRRAAAAAAH!
UH-OH.

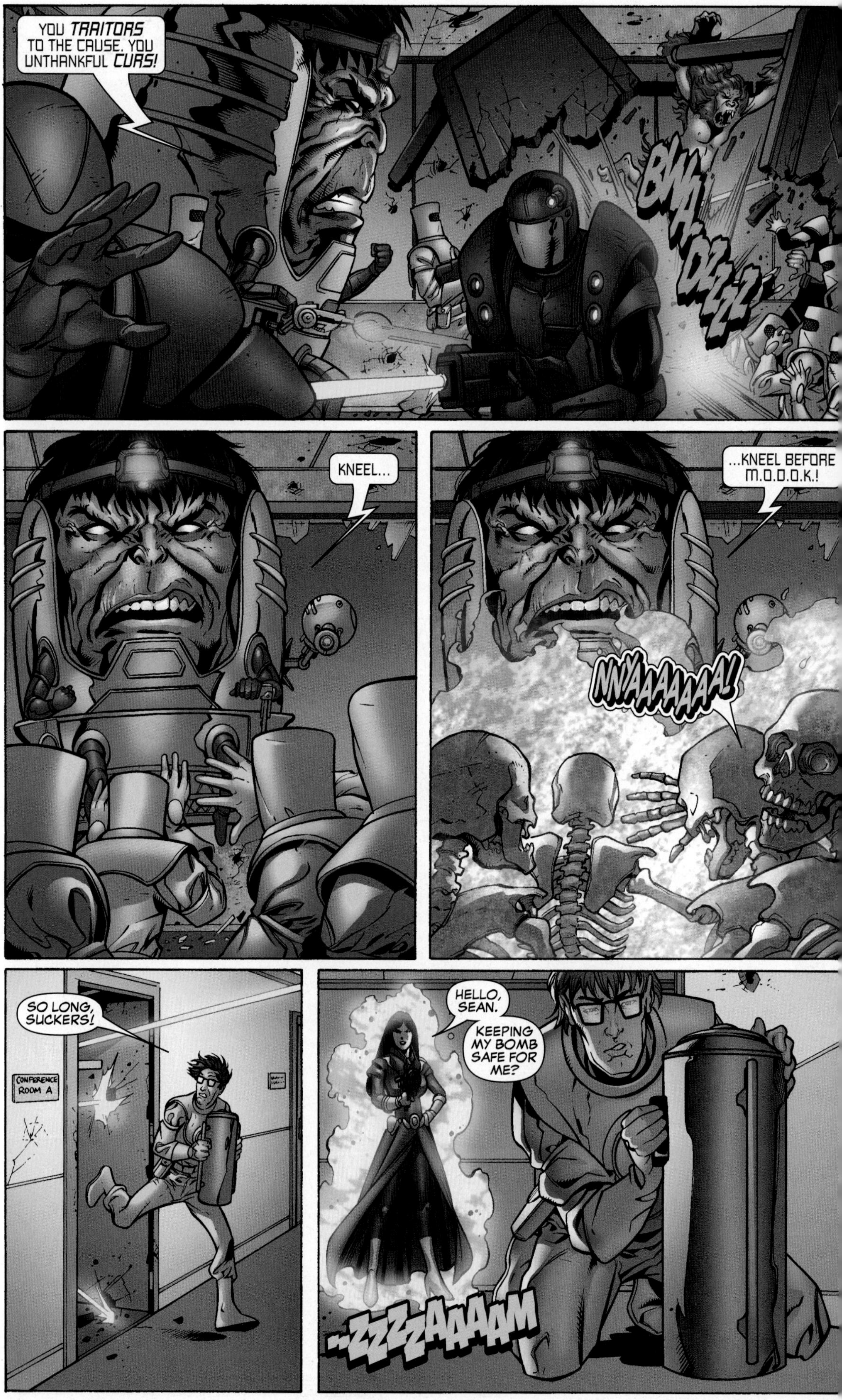
YOU TRAITORS TO THE CAUSE. YOU UNTHANKFUL CURS!
BWA-DZZZZ
KNEEL...
...KNEEL BEFORE M.O.D.O.K.!
NNYAAAAAAA!
SO LONG, SUCKERS!
CONFERENCE ROOM A
HELLO, SEAN.
KEEPING MY BOMB SAFE FOR ME?
-ZZZZAAAAM

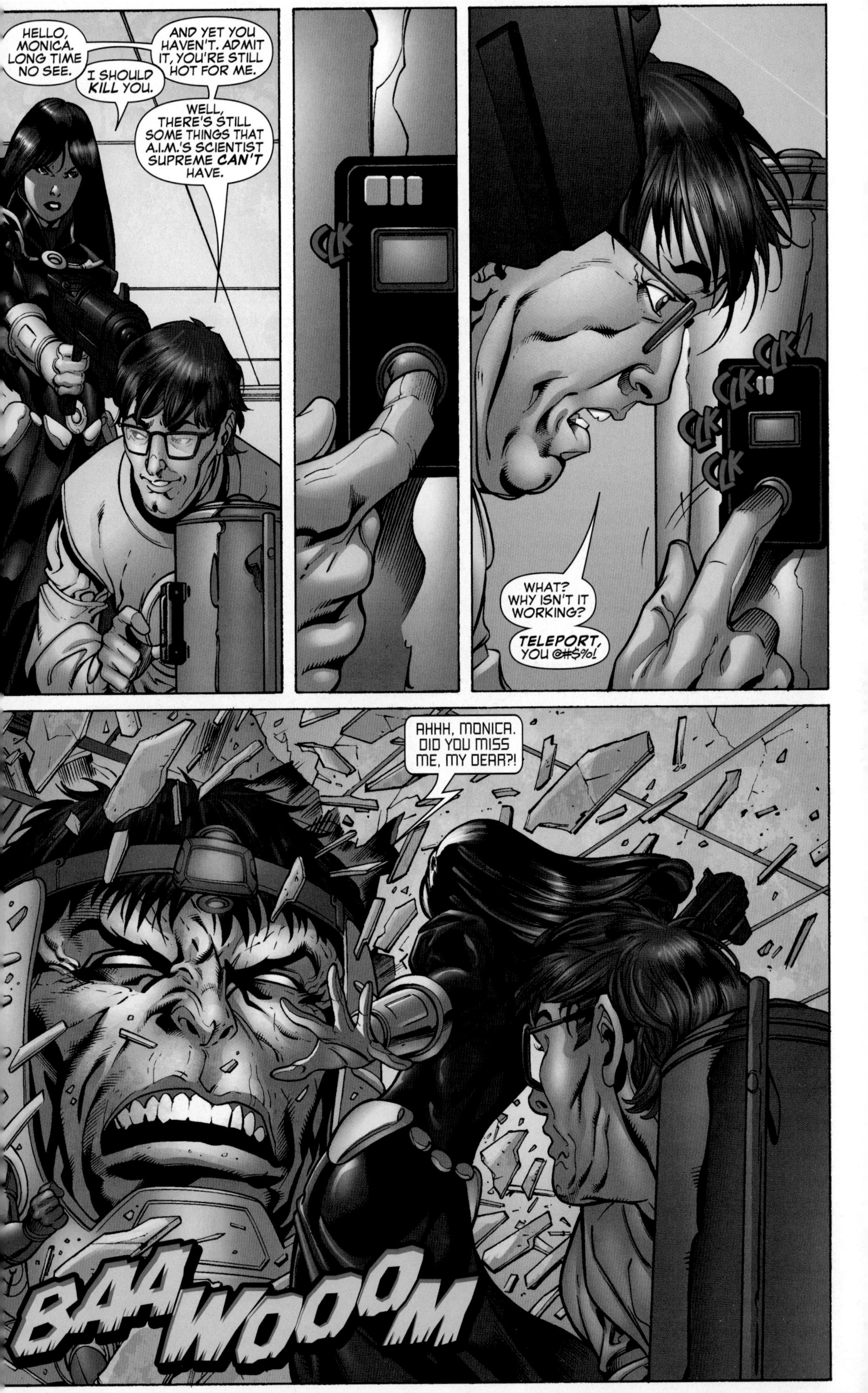
HELLO, MONICA. LONG TIME NO SEE.
I SHOULD KILL YOU.
AND YET YOU HAVEN'T. ADMIT IT, YOU'RE STILL HOT FOR ME.
WELL, THERE'S STILL SOME THINGS THAT A.I.M.'S SCIENTIST SUPREME CAN'T HAVE.
CLK
CLK
CLK
CLK
CLK
WHAT? WHY ISN'T IT WORKING?
TELEPORT, YOU @#$%!
AHHH, MONICA. DID YOU MISS ME, MY DEAR?!
BAAWOOOM

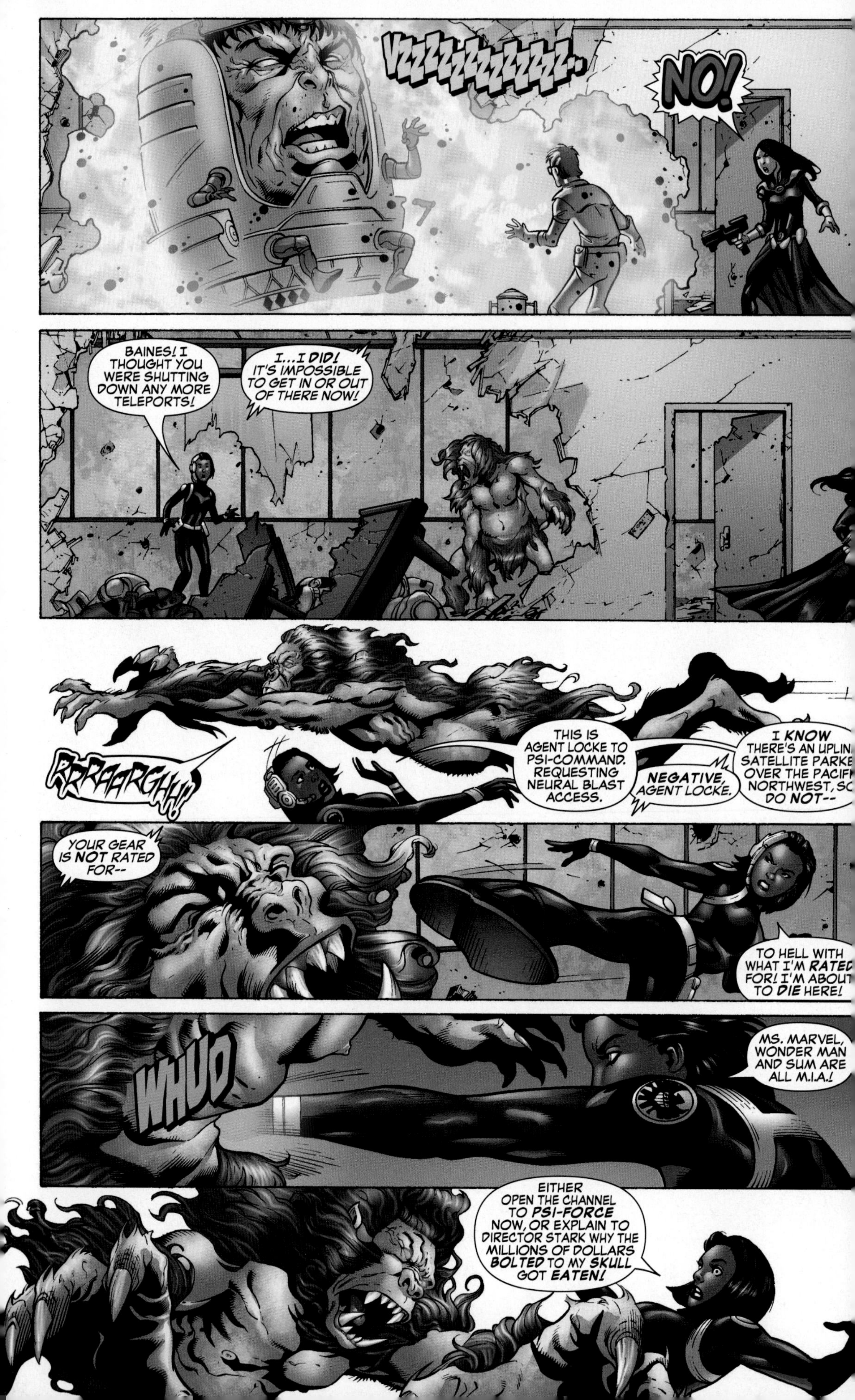
VZZZZZZZZZZZZZ..
NO!
BAINES! I THOUGHT YOU WERE SHUTTING DOWN ANY MORE TELEPORTS!
I...I DID! IT'S IMPOSSIBLE TO GET IN OR OUT OF THERE NOW!
RRRAARGHH!
THIS IS AGENT LOCKE TO PSI-COMMAND. REQUESTING NEURAL BLAST ACCESS.
NEGATIVE, AGENT LOCKE.
I KNOW THERE'S AN UPLIN SATELLITE PARKE OVER THE PACIF NORTHWEST, SO DO NOT--
YOUR GEAR IS NOT RATED FOR--
TO HELL WITH WHAT I'M RATED FOR! I'M ABOUT TO DIE HERE!
WHUD
MS. MARVEL, WONDER MAN AND SUM ARE ALL M.I.A.!
EITHER OPEN THE CHANNEL TO PSI-FORCE NOW, OR EXPLAIN TO DIRECTOR STARK WHY THE MILLIONS OF DOLLARS BOLTED TO MY SKULL GOT EATEN!

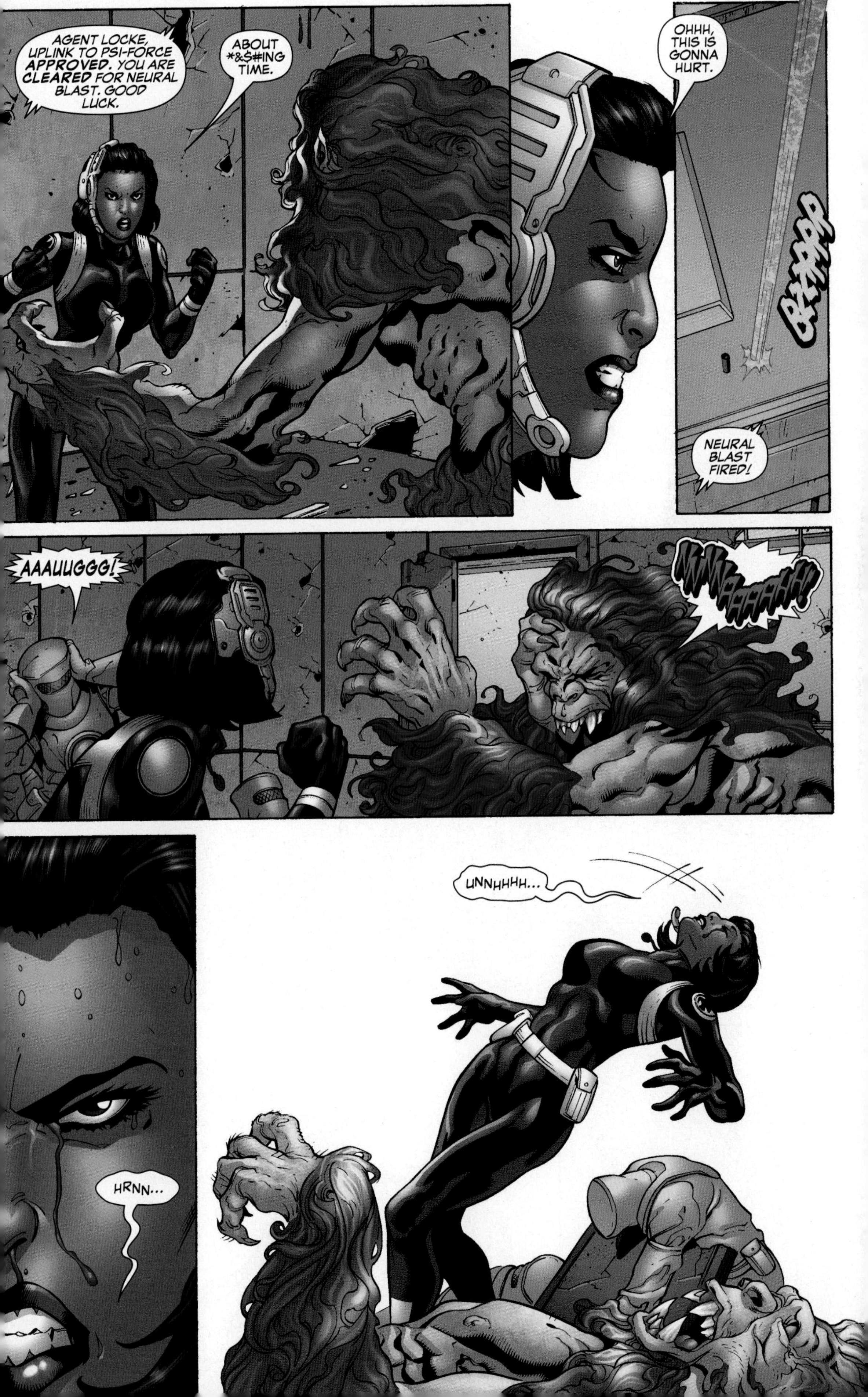
AGENT LOCKE, UPLINK TO PSI-FORCE APPROVED. YOU ARE CLEARED FOR NEURAL BLAST. GOOD LUCK.
ABOUT *&$#ING TIME.
OHHH, THIS IS GONNA HURT.
BZZZAPP
NEURAL BLAST FIRED!
AAAUUGGG!
NNNAAAAHH!
UNNHHHH...
HRNN...

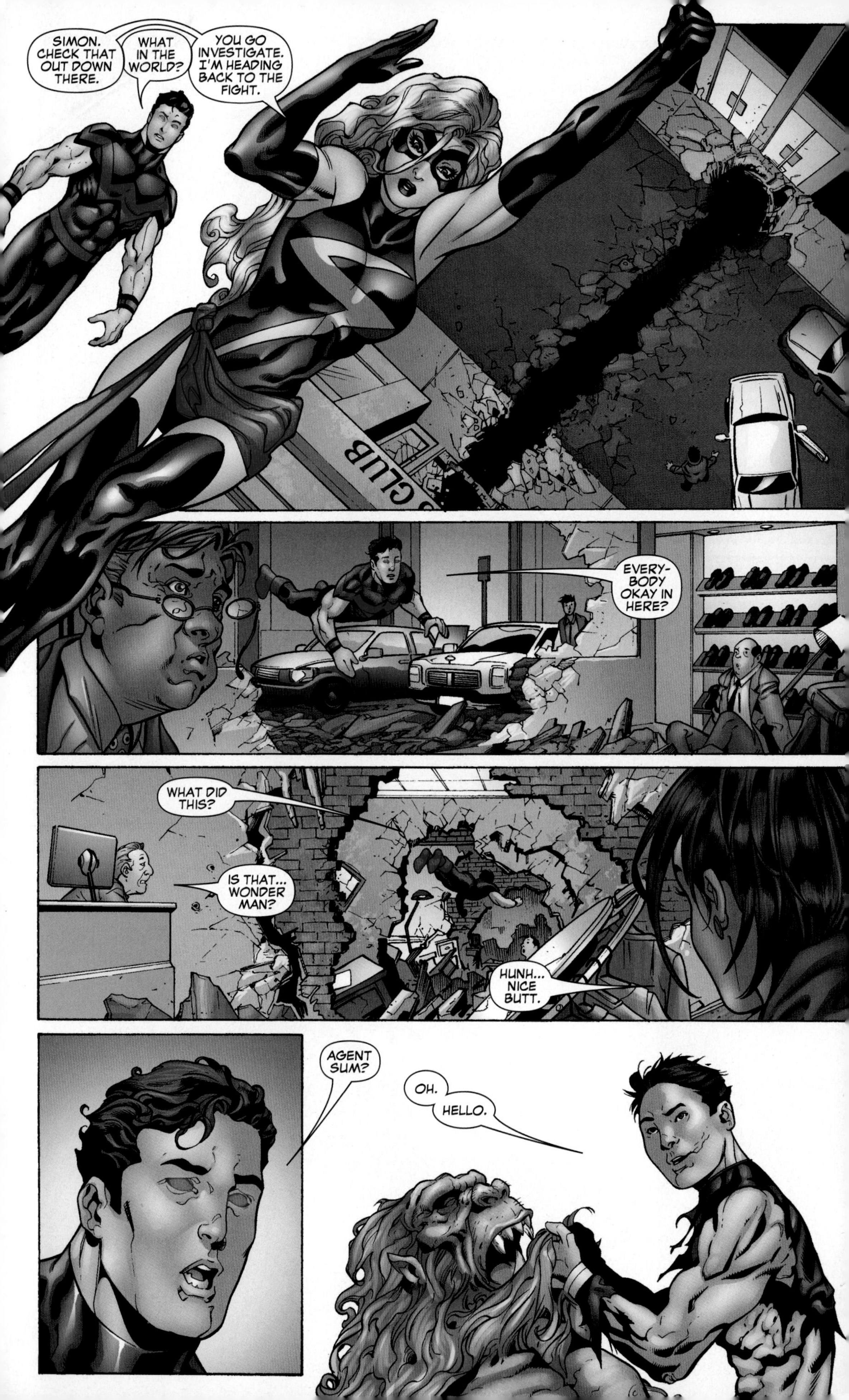
SIMON. CHECK THAT OUT DOWN THERE.
WHAT IN THE WORLD?
YOU GO INVESTIGATE. I'M HEADING BACK TO THE FIGHT.
CLUB
EVERY-BODY OKAY IN HERE?
WHAT DID THIS?
IS THAT... WONDER MAN?
HUNH... NICE BUTT.
AGENT SUM?
OH.
HELLO.

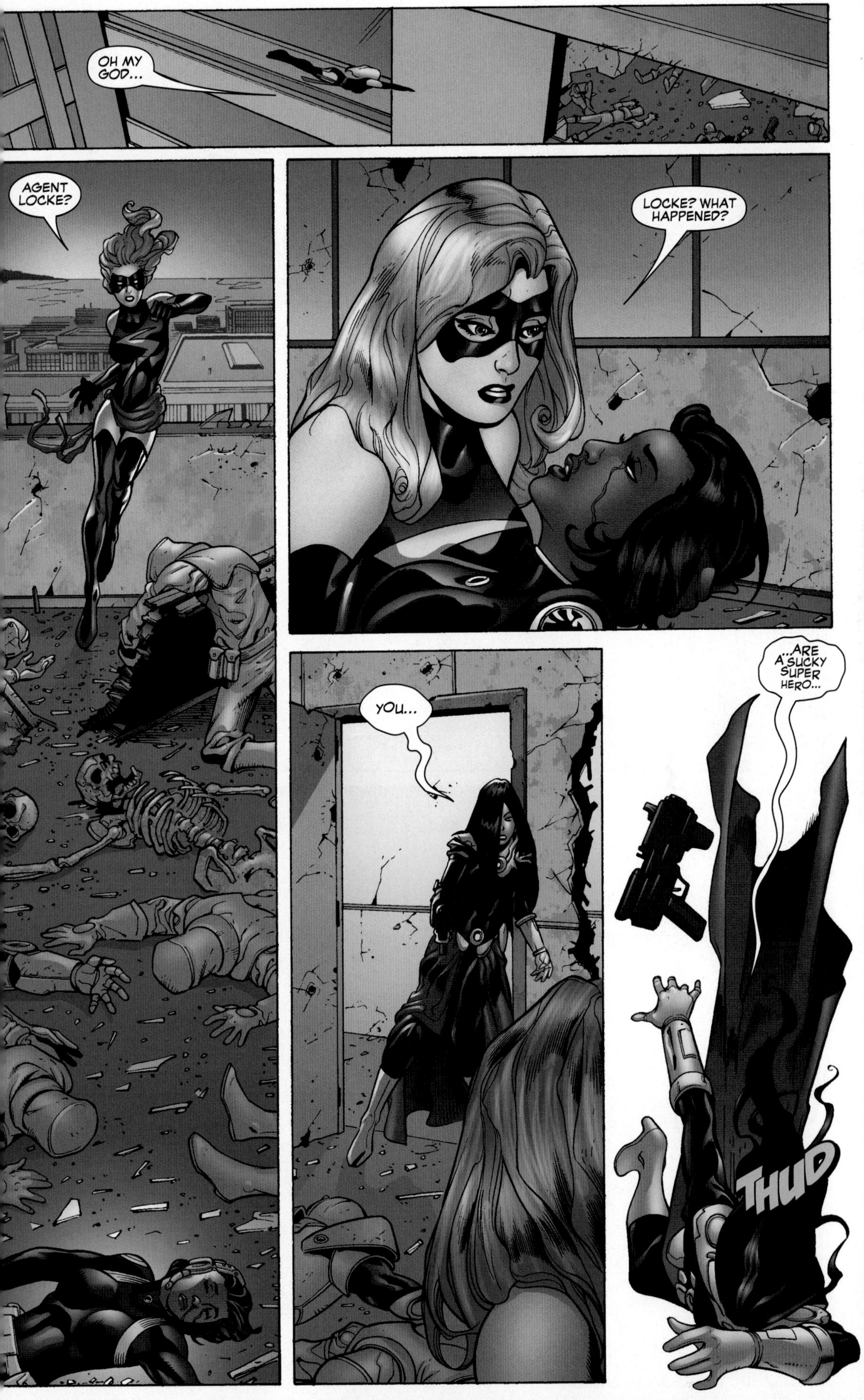
OH MY GOD...
AGENT LOCKE?
LOCKE? WHAT HAPPENED?
YOU...
...ARE A SUCKY SUPER HERO...
THUD

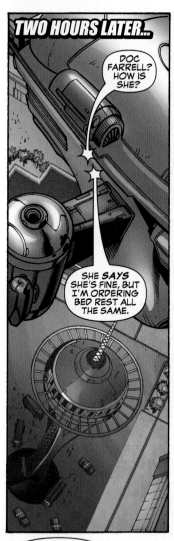

DOC FARRELL? HOW IS SHE?

SHE *SAYS* SHE'S FINE, BUT I'M ORDERING BED REST ALL THE SAME.

THEY RATE PSYCHICS FOR A *REASON*, AGENT LOCKE.

YOU'RE A *COMMUNICATIONS* AND *COORDINATIONS* SPECIALIST. *NOT A SOLDIER.*

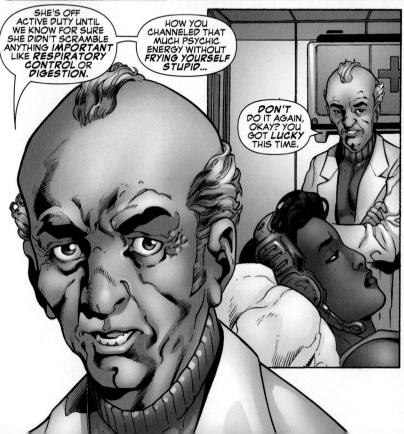

SHE'S OFF ACTIVE DUTY UNTIL WE KNOW FOR SURE SHE DIDN'T SCRAMBLE ANYTHING *IMPORTANT* LIKE *RESPIRATORY CONTROL* OR *DIGESTION.*

HOW YOU CHANNELED THAT MUCH PSYCHIC ENERGY WITHOUT FRYING YOURSELF STUPID...

DON'T DO IT AGAIN, OKAY? YOU GOT *LUCKY* THIS TIME.

DON'T WORRY, DOC. ONE *DEUS EX MACHINA* IN A LIFETIME IS ENOUGH FOR ME.

YOU FOUND IT!

WE FOUND ITS *CASING* ABOUT TWO MILES FROM THE OFFICE BUILDING.

THERE'S NOTHING HERE BUT THE TRIGGERING MECHANISM.

MINICARRIER 13 HANGAR BAY

ANY TRACE OF *SEAN?*

NAH. HE'S GONE. SAME WITH M.O.D.O.K.

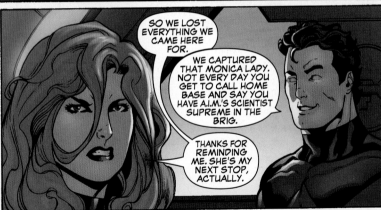

SO WE LOST EVERYTHING WE CAME HERE FOR.

WE CAPTURED THAT MONICA LADY. NOT EVERY DAY YOU GET TO CALL HOME BASE AND SAY YOU HAVE A.I.M.'S SCIENTIST SUPREME IN THE BRIG.

THANKS FOR REMINDING ME. SHE'S MY NEXT STOP, ACTUALLY.

MIND IF I TAG ALONG?

I--UM, NO. I GUESS NOT.

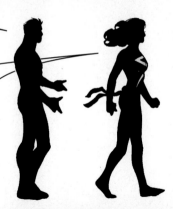

SO...ARE WE GONNA TALK ABOUT WHAT HAPPENED OUT THERE?

WHICH PART? SUM SURVIVING A *TWELVE-STORY FALL* AND FIGHTING THAT MONSTER BARE-HANDED, M.O.D.O.K. *ESCAPING,* LOCKE NEARLY KILLING HERSE--

YOU *KNOW* WHAT I MEAN.

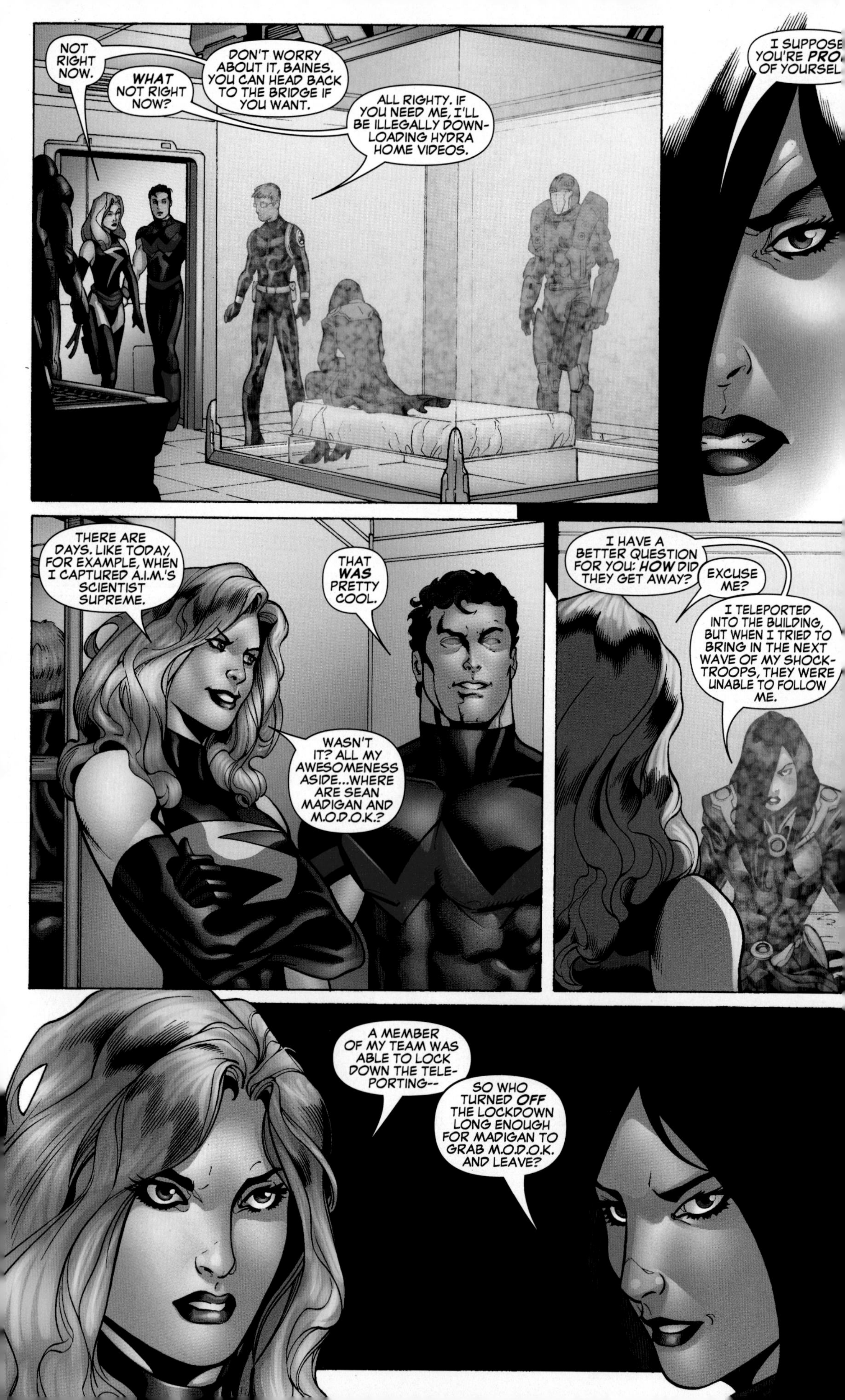
NOT RIGHT NOW.
DON'T WORRY ABOUT IT, BAINES. YOU CAN HEAD BACK TO THE BRIDGE IF YOU WANT.
WHAT NOT RIGHT NOW?
ALL RIGHTY. IF YOU NEED ME, I'LL BE ILLEGALLY DOWN-LOADING HYDRA HOME VIDEOS.
I SUPPOSE YOU'RE PRO
OF YOURSEL
THERE ARE DAYS. LIKE TODAY, FOR EXAMPLE, WHEN I CAPTURED A.I.M.'S SCIENTIST SUPREME.
THAT WAS PRETTY COOL.
WASN'T IT? ALL MY AWESOMENESS ASIDE...WHERE ARE SEAN MADIGAN AND M.O.D.O.K.?
I HAVE A BETTER QUESTION FOR YOU: HOW DID THEY GET AWAY?
EXCUSE ME?
I TELEPORTED INTO THE BUILDING, BUT WHEN I TRIED TO BRING IN THE NEXT WAVE OF MY SHOCK-TROOPS, THEY WERE UNABLE TO FOLLOW ME.
A MEMBER OF MY TEAM WAS ABLE TO LOCK DOWN THE TELE-PORTING--
SO WHO TURNED OFF THE LOCKDOWN LONG ENOUGH FOR MADIGAN TO GRAB M.O.D.O.K. AND LEAVE?

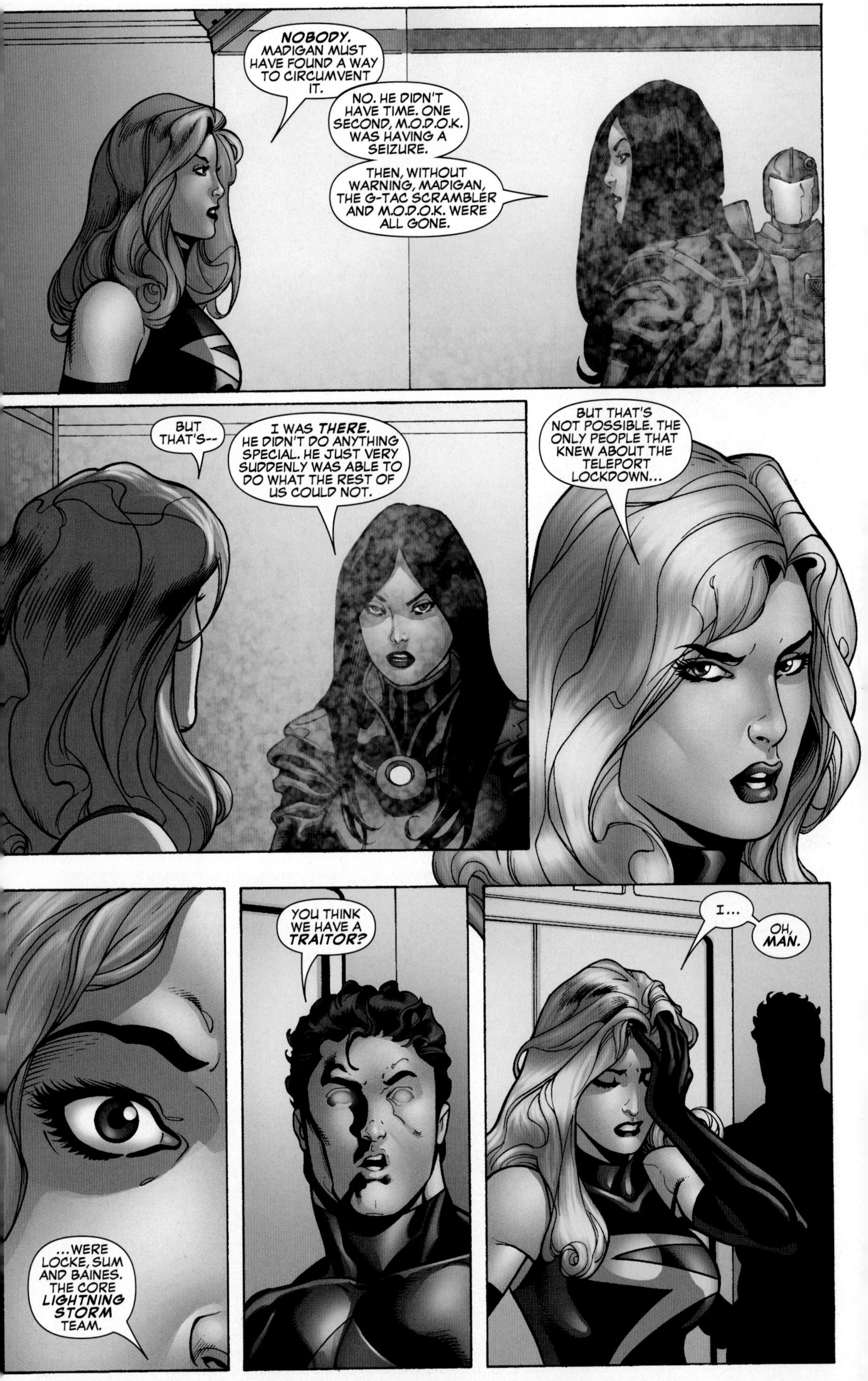
NOBODY. MADIGAN MUST HAVE FOUND A WAY TO CIRCUMVENT IT.
NO. HE DIDN'T HAVE TIME. ONE SECOND, M.O.D.O.K. WAS HAVING A SEIZURE.
THEN, WITHOUT WARNING, MADIGAN, THE G-TAC SCRAMBLER AND M.O.D.O.K. WERE ALL GONE.
BUT THAT'S--
I WAS THERE. HE DIDN'T DO ANYTHING SPECIAL. HE JUST VERY SUDDENLY WAS ABLE TO DO WHAT THE REST OF US COULD NOT.
BUT THAT'S NOT POSSIBLE. THE ONLY PEOPLE THAT KNEW ABOUT THE TELEPORT LOCKDOWN...
...WERE LOCKE, SUM AND BAINES. THE CORE LIGHTNING STORM TEAM.
YOU THINK WE HAVE A TRAITOR?
I...
OH, MAN.

LISTEN CLOSELY. I AM ABOUT TO TELL YOU MANY *IMPORTANT* THINGS AND I DO *NOT* HAVE TIME TO REPEAT MYSELF.

M.O.D.O.K. IS *DYING.* HE HAS BEEN FOR MONTHS, BUT NOT MANY A.I.M. AGENTS KNEW. BUT NOW THAT THE SECRET IS OUT...

...A.I.M. HAS *FRACTURED.*

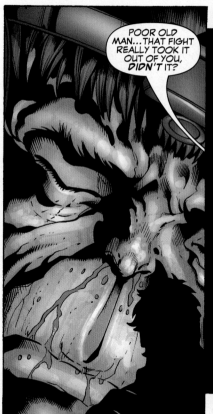

POOR OLD MAN...THAT FIGHT REALLY TOOK IT OUT OF YOU, *DIDN'T* IT?

I HONESTLY CAN'T *BELIEVE* YOU SURVIVED THAT. IN *YOUR* CONDITION, IT WAS AN *AMAZING* EFFORT.

BUT FIGHTING LIKE THAT, AND ALL THE TELEPORTING-- WELL, IT'S A *LOT* TO THROW AT A BIG-HEADED SICK GUY, RIGHT?

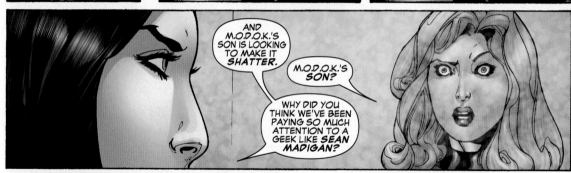

AND M.O.D.O.K.'S SON IS LOOKING TO MAKE IT *SHATTER.*

M.O.D.O.K.'S *SON?*

WHY DID YOU THINK WE'VE BEEN PAYING SO MUCH ATTENTION TO A GEEK LIKE *SEAN MADIGAN?*

BUT I *COULDN'T* LET THEM CAPTURE YOU.

AT LEAST, NOT *YET.*

NO. I NEEDED SOMETHING...MORE *PUBLIC.* SOMETHING MORE *DESERVING* OF THE MIGHTY *M.O.D.O.K.*

SOMETHING INVOLVING THE GUTS OF THE G-TAC SCRAMBLER.

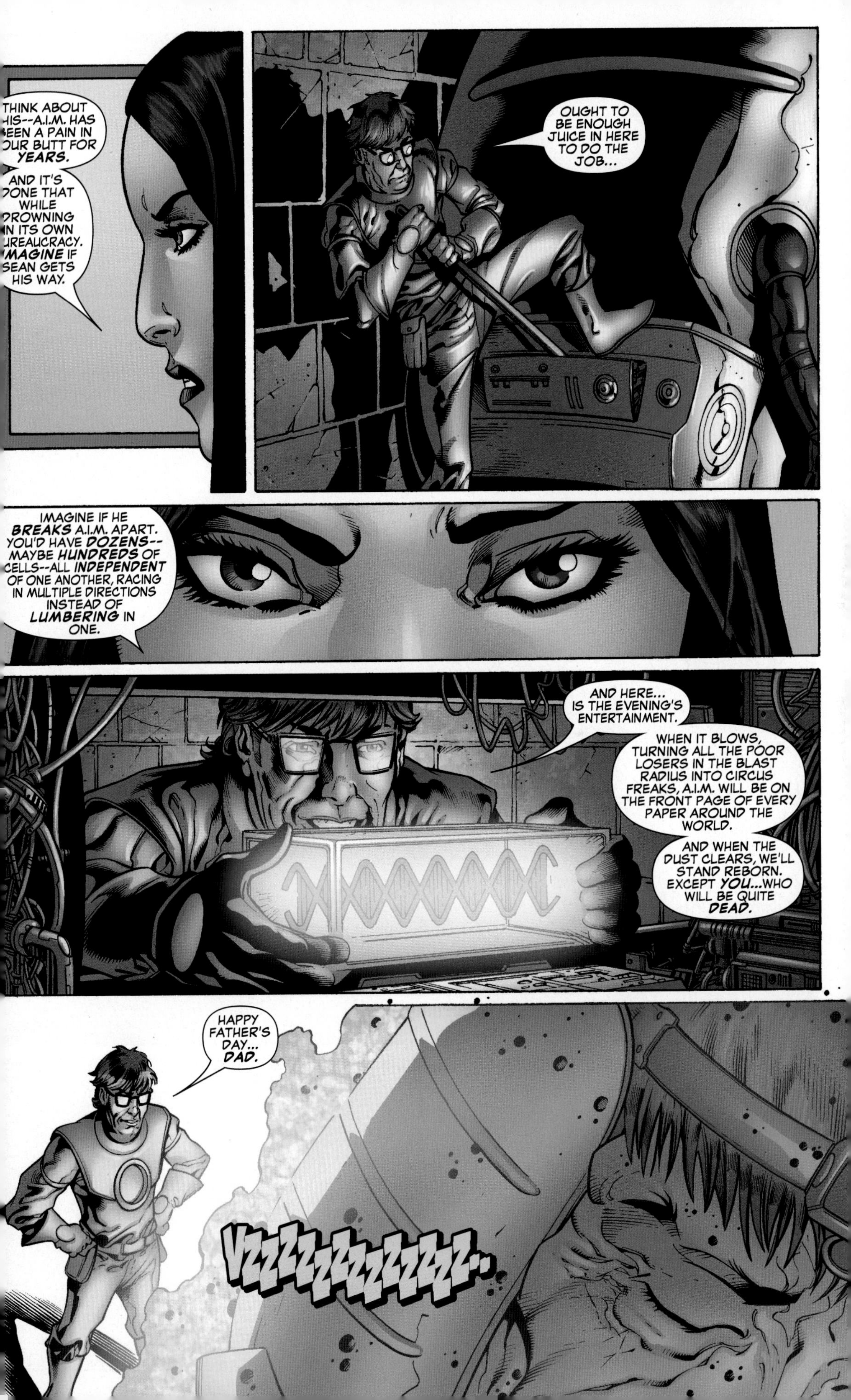
THINK ABOUT HIS--A.I.M. HAS BEEN A PAIN IN OUR BUTT FOR YEARS.
AND IT'S DONE THAT WHILE DROWNING IN ITS OWN BUREAUCRACY. IMAGINE IF SEAN GETS HIS WAY.
OUGHT TO BE ENOUGH JUICE IN HERE TO DO THE JOB...
IMAGINE IF HE BREAKS A.I.M. APART. YOU'D HAVE DOZENS--MAYBE HUNDREDS OF CELLS--ALL INDEPENDENT OF ONE ANOTHER, RACING IN MULTIPLE DIRECTIONS INSTEAD OF LUMBERING IN ONE.
AND HERE... IS THE EVENING'S ENTERTAINMENT.
WHEN IT BLOWS, TURNING ALL THE POOR LOSERS IN THE BLAST RADIUS INTO CIRCUS FREAKS, A.I.M. WILL BE ON THE FRONT PAGE OF EVERY PAPER AROUND THE WORLD.
AND WHEN THE DUST CLEARS, WE'LL STAND REBORN. EXCEPT YOU...WHO WILL BE QUITE DEAD.
HAPPY FATHER'S DAY... DAD.
VZZZZZZZZZZZZZZ..

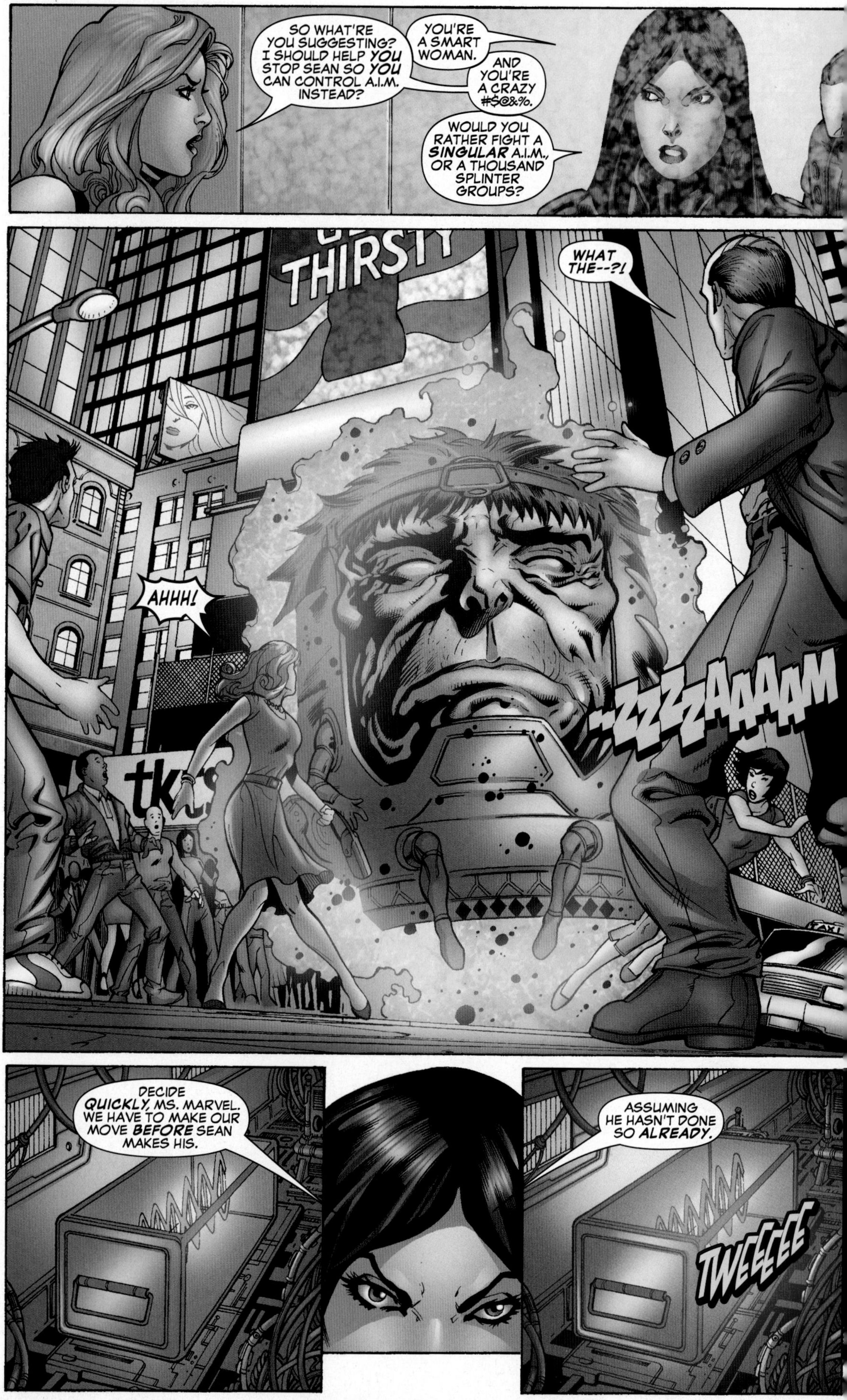
SO WHAT'RE YOU SUGGESTING? I SHOULD HELP YOU STOP SEAN SO YOU CAN CONTROL A.I.M. INSTEAD?
YOU'RE A SMART WOMAN.
AND YOU'RE A CRAZY #$@&%.
WOULD YOU RATHER FIGHT A SINGULAR A.I.M., OR A THOUSAND SPLINTER GROUPS?
THIRSTY
WHAT THE--?!
AHHH!
-ZZZZAAAAM
DECIDE QUICKLY, MS. MARVEL. WE HAVE TO MAKE OUR MOVE BEFORE SEAN MAKES HIS.
ASSUMING HE HASN'T DONE SO ALREADY.
TWEEEEEE

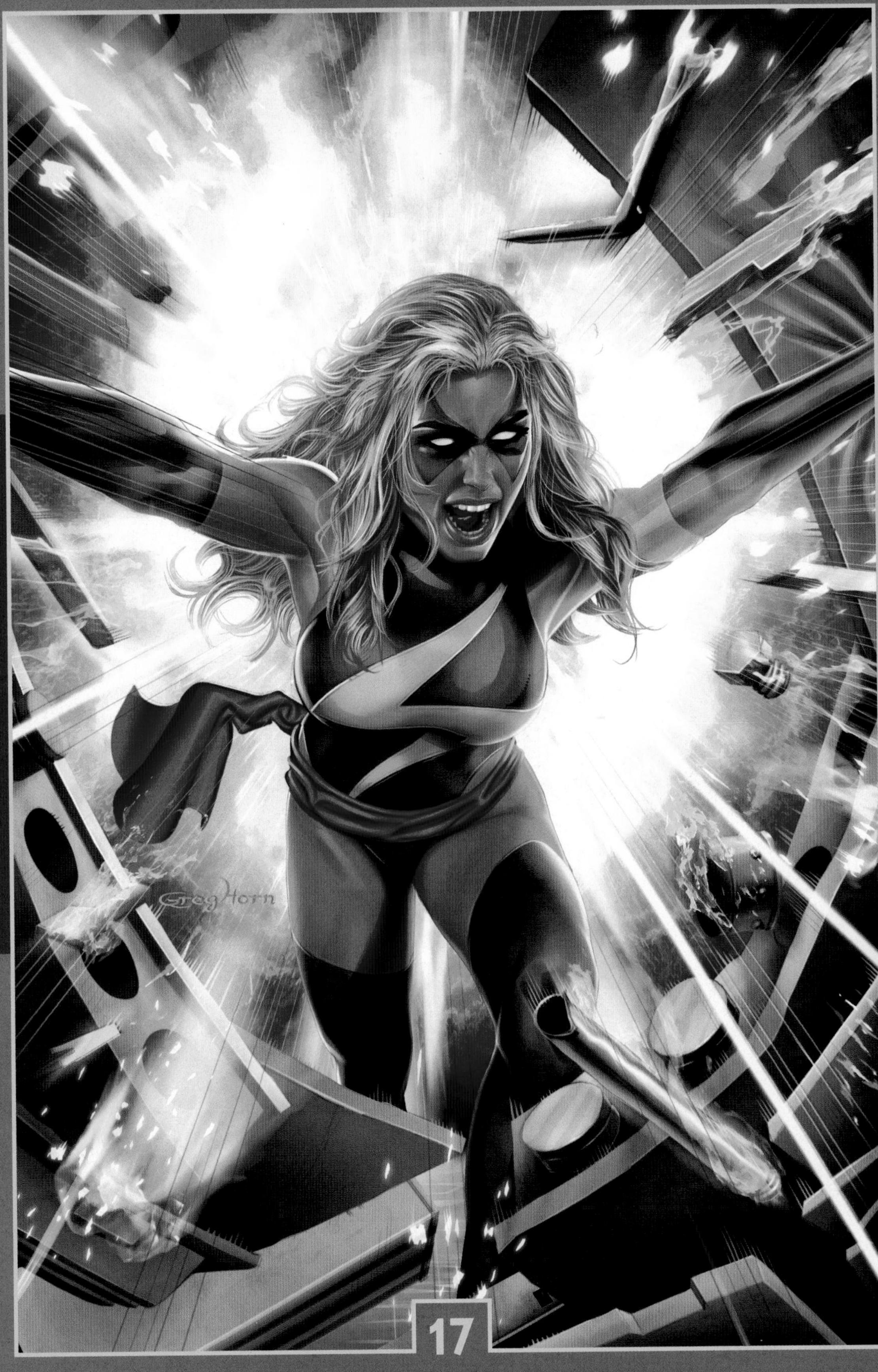

Greg Horn
17

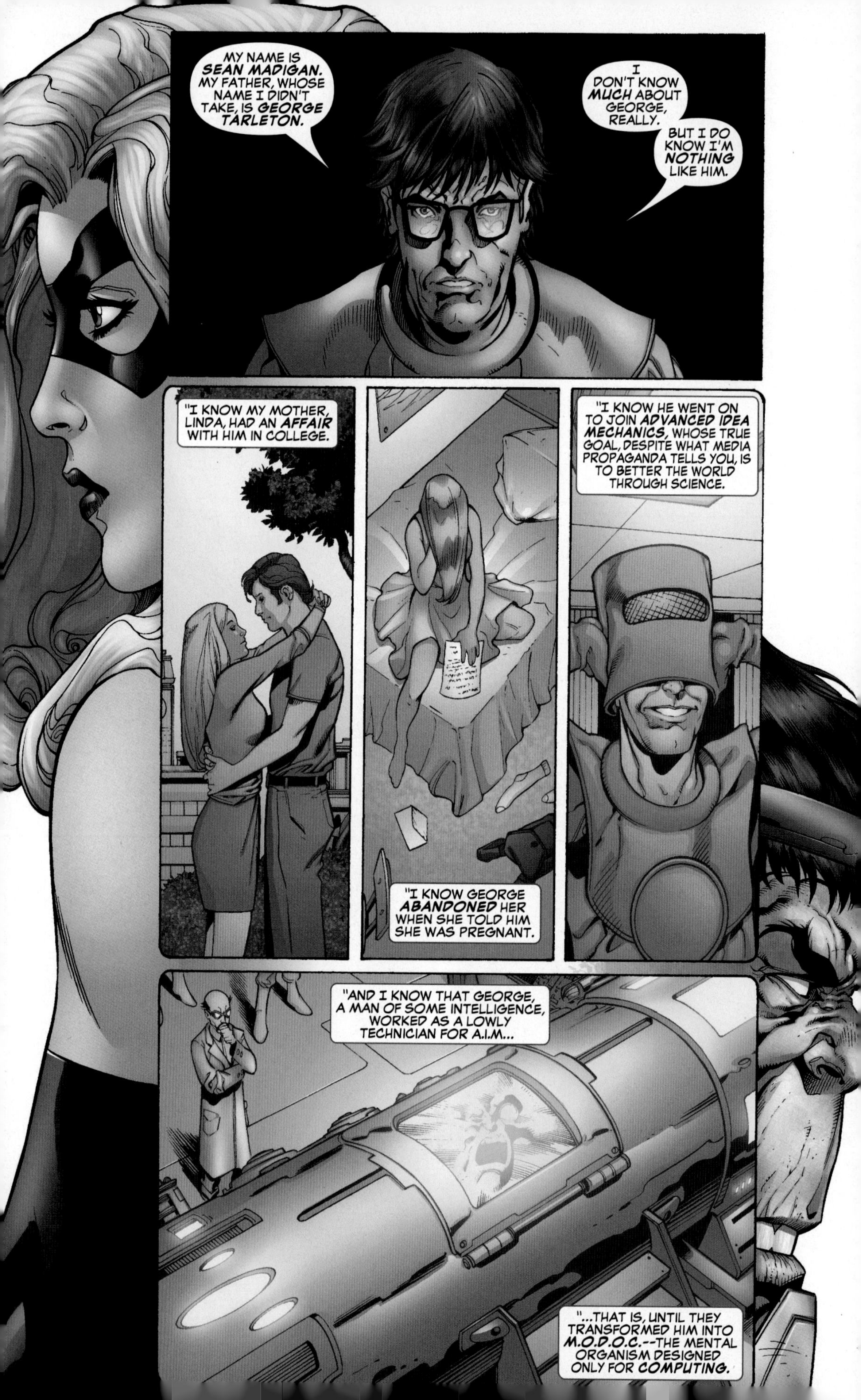
MY NAME IS SEAN MADIGAN. MY FATHER, WHOSE NAME I DIDN'T TAKE, IS GEORGE TARLETON.
I DON'T KNOW MUCH ABOUT GEORGE, REALLY.
BUT I DO KNOW I'M NOTHING LIKE HIM.
"I KNOW MY MOTHER, LINDA, HAD AN AFFAIR WITH HIM IN COLLEGE.
"I KNOW GEORGE ABANDONED HER WHEN SHE TOLD HIM SHE WAS PREGNANT.
"I KNOW HE WENT ON TO JOIN ADVANCED IDEA MECHANICS, WHOSE TRUE GOAL, DESPITE WHAT MEDIA PROPAGANDA TELLS YOU, IS TO BETTER THE WORLD THROUGH SCIENCE.
"AND I KNOW THAT GEORGE, A MAN OF SOME INTELLIGENCE, WORKED AS A LOWLY TECHNICIAN FOR A.I.M...
"...THAT IS, UNTIL THEY TRANSFORMED HIM INTO M.O.D.O.C.--THE MENTAL ORGANISM DESIGNED ONLY FOR COMPUTING.

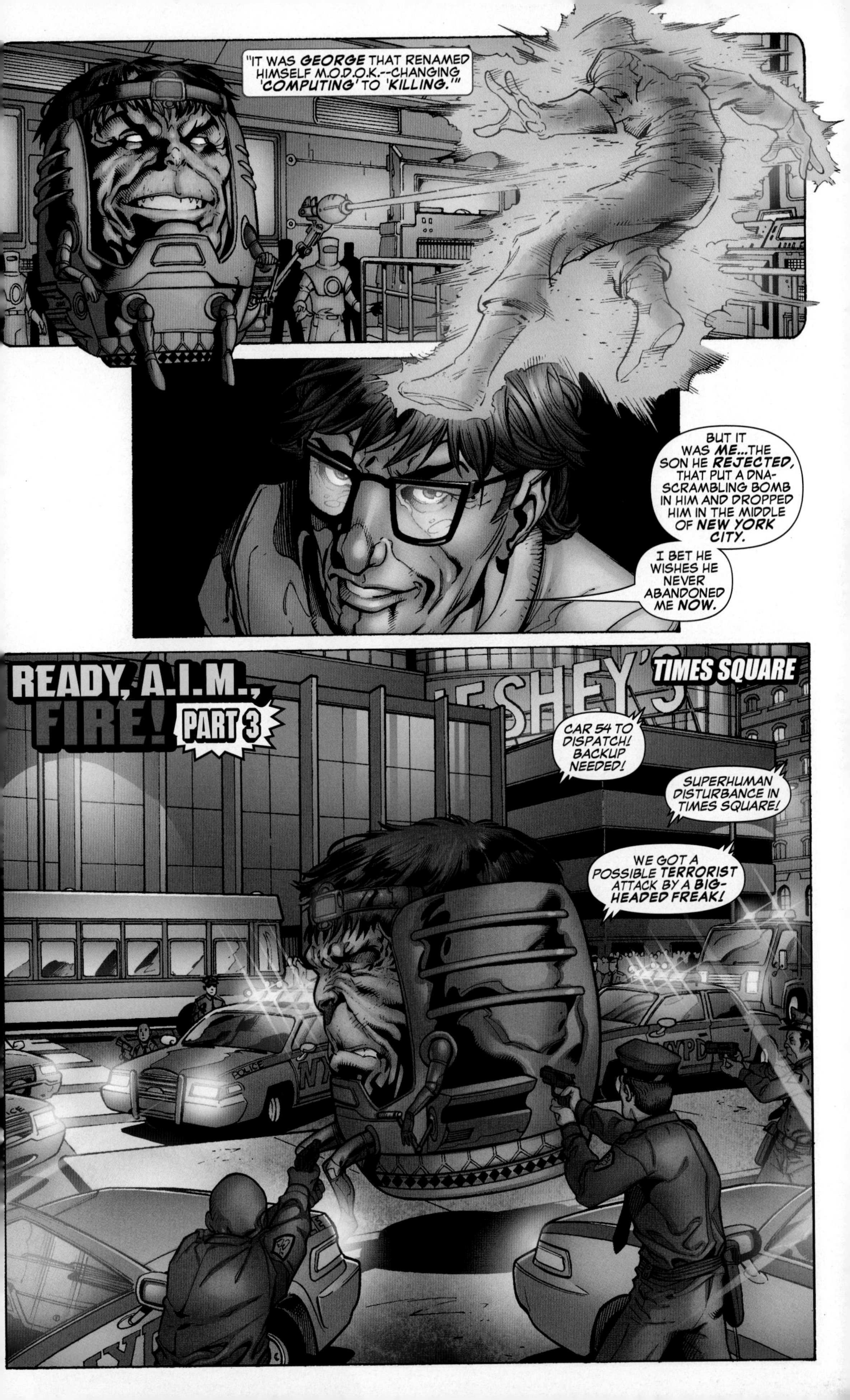
"IT WAS GEORGE THAT RENAMED HIMSELF M.O.D.O.K.--CHANGING 'COMPUTING' TO 'KILLING.'"
BUT IT WAS ME...THE SON HE REJECTED, THAT PUT A DNA-SCRAMBLING BOMB IN HIM AND DROPPED HIM IN THE MIDDLE OF NEW YORK CITY.
I BET HE WISHES HE NEVER ABANDONED ME NOW.
READY, A.I.M., FIRE! PART 3
TIMES SQUARE
CAR 54 TO DISPATCH! BACKUP NEEDED!
SUPERHUMAN DISTURBANCE IN TIMES SQUARE!
WE GOT A POSSIBLE TERRORIST ATTACK BY A BIG-HEADED FREAK!
POLICE
NYPD

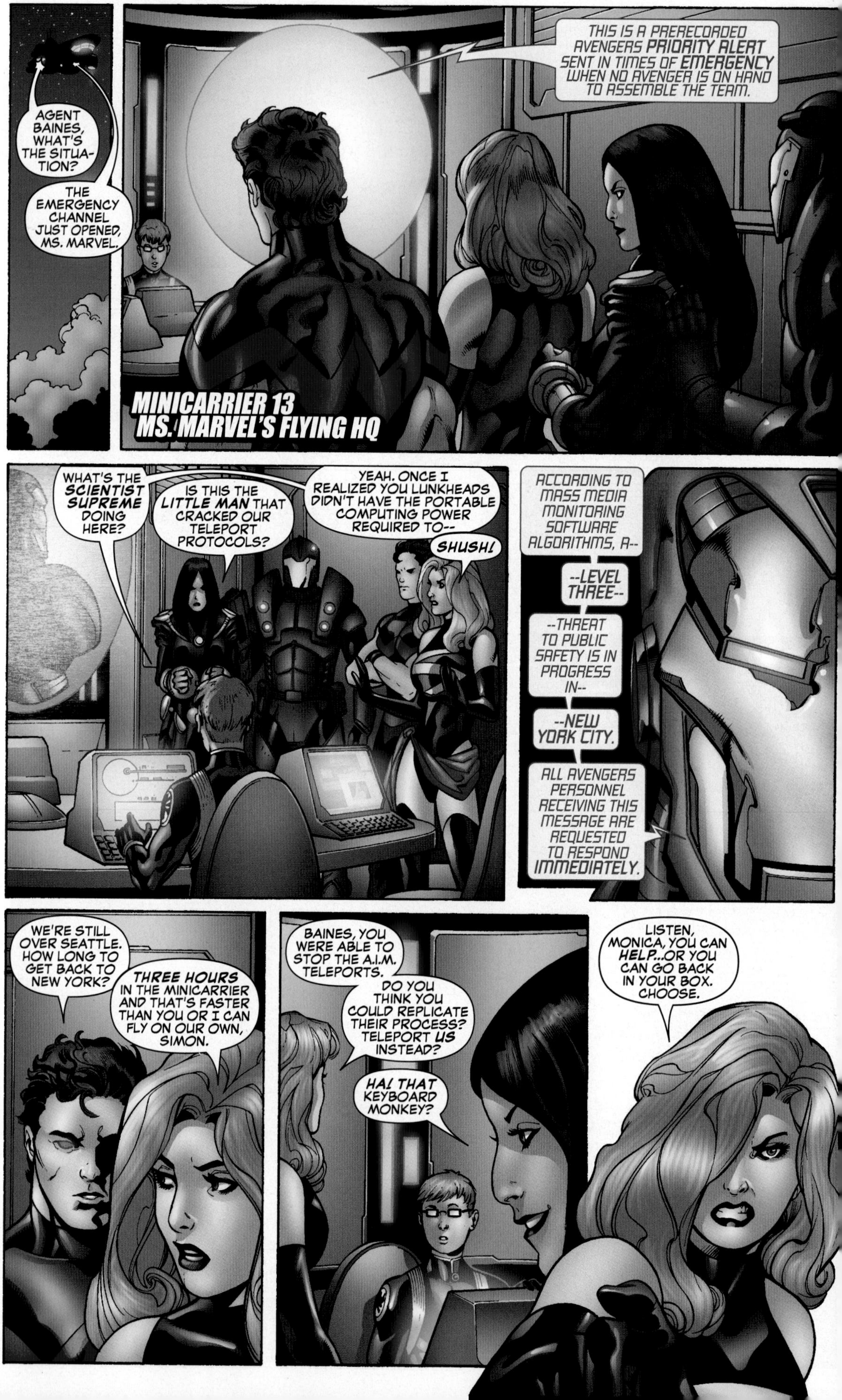
AGENT BAINES, WHAT'S THE SITUATION?
THE EMERGENCY CHANNEL JUST OPENED, MS. MARVEL.
THIS IS A PRERECORDED AVENGERS PRIORITY ALERT SENT IN TIMES OF EMERGENCY WHEN NO AVENGER IS ON HAND TO ASSEMBLE THE TEAM.
MINICARRIER 13
MS. MARVEL'S FLYING HQ
WHAT'S THE SCIENTIST SUPREME DOING HERE?
IS THIS THE LITTLE MAN THAT CRACKED OUR TELEPORT PROTOCOLS?
YEAH. ONCE I REALIZED YOU LUNKHEADS DIDN'T HAVE THE PORTABLE COMPUTING POWER REQUIRED TO--
SHUSH!
ACCORDING TO MASS MEDIA MONITORING SOFTWARE ALGORITHMS, A--
--LEVEL THREE--
--THREAT TO PUBLIC SAFETY IS IN PROGRESS IN--
--NEW YORK CITY.
ALL AVENGERS PERSONNEL RECEIVING THIS MESSAGE ARE REQUESTED TO RESPOND IMMEDIATELY.
WE'RE STILL OVER SEATTLE. HOW LONG TO GET BACK TO NEW YORK?
THREE HOURS IN THE MINICARRIER AND THAT'S FASTER THAN YOU OR I CAN FLY ON OUR OWN, SIMON.
BAINES, YOU WERE ABLE TO STOP THE A.I.M. TELEPORTS.
DO YOU THINK YOU COULD REPLICATE THEIR PROCESS? TELEPORT US INSTEAD?
HA! THAT KEYBOARD MONKEY?
LISTEN, MONICA, YOU CAN HELP...OR YOU CAN GO BACK IN YOUR BOX. CHOOSE.

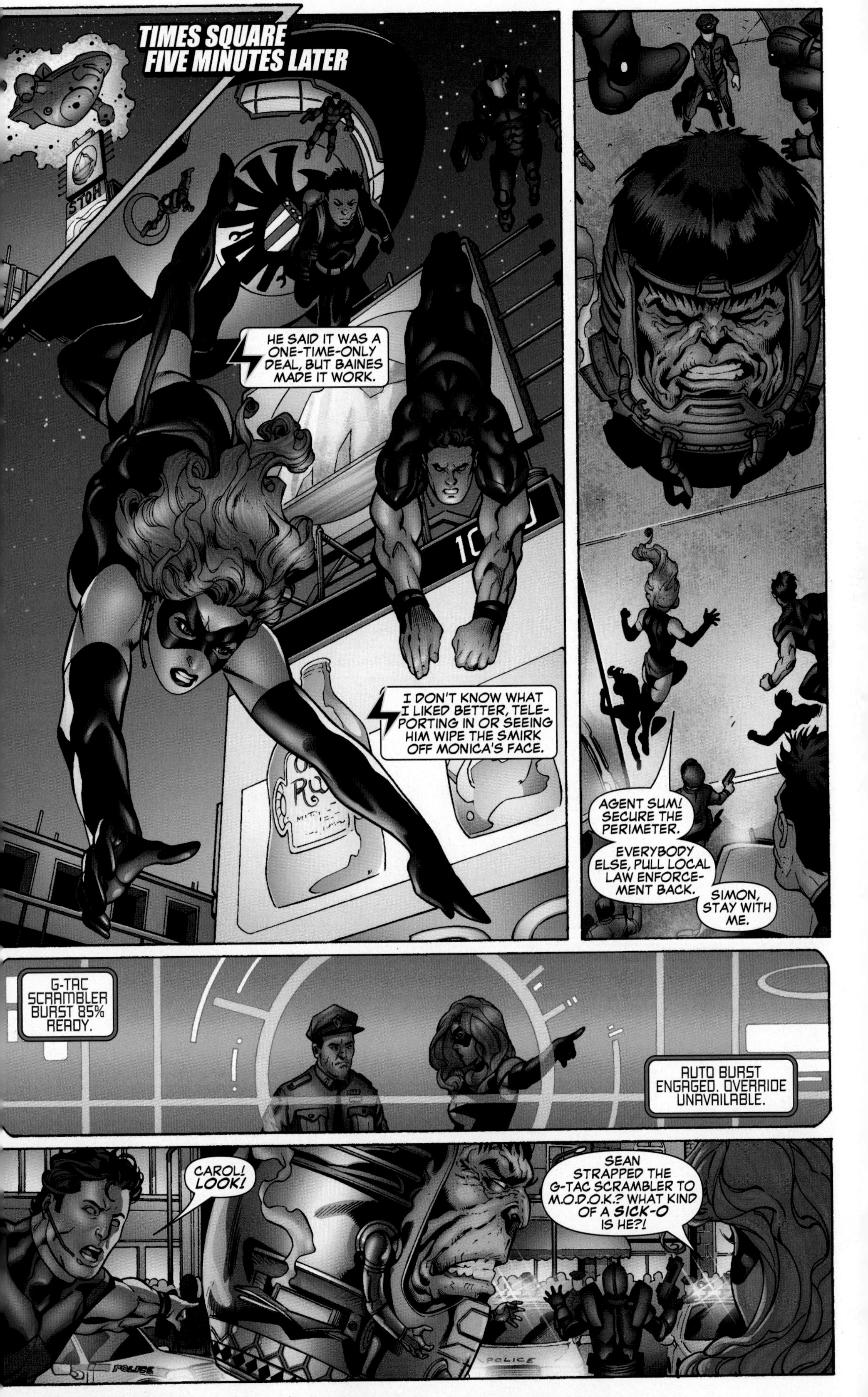
TIMES SQUARE
FIVE MINUTES LATER
HE SAID IT WAS A ONE-TIME-ONLY DEAL, BUT BAINES MADE IT WORK.
I DON'T KNOW WHAT I LIKED BETTER, TELE-PORTING IN OR SEEING HIM WIPE THE SMIRK OFF MONICA'S FACE.
AGENT SUM! SECURE THE PERIMETER.
EVERYBODY ELSE, PULL LOCAL LAW ENFORCE-MENT BACK.
SIMON, STAY WITH ME.
G-TAC SCRAMBLER BURST 85% READY.
AUTO BURST ENGAGED. OVERRIDE UNAVAILABLE.
CAROL! LOOK!
SEAN STRAPPED THE G-TAC SCRAMBLER TO M.O.D.O.K.? WHAT KIND OF A SICK-O IS HE?!

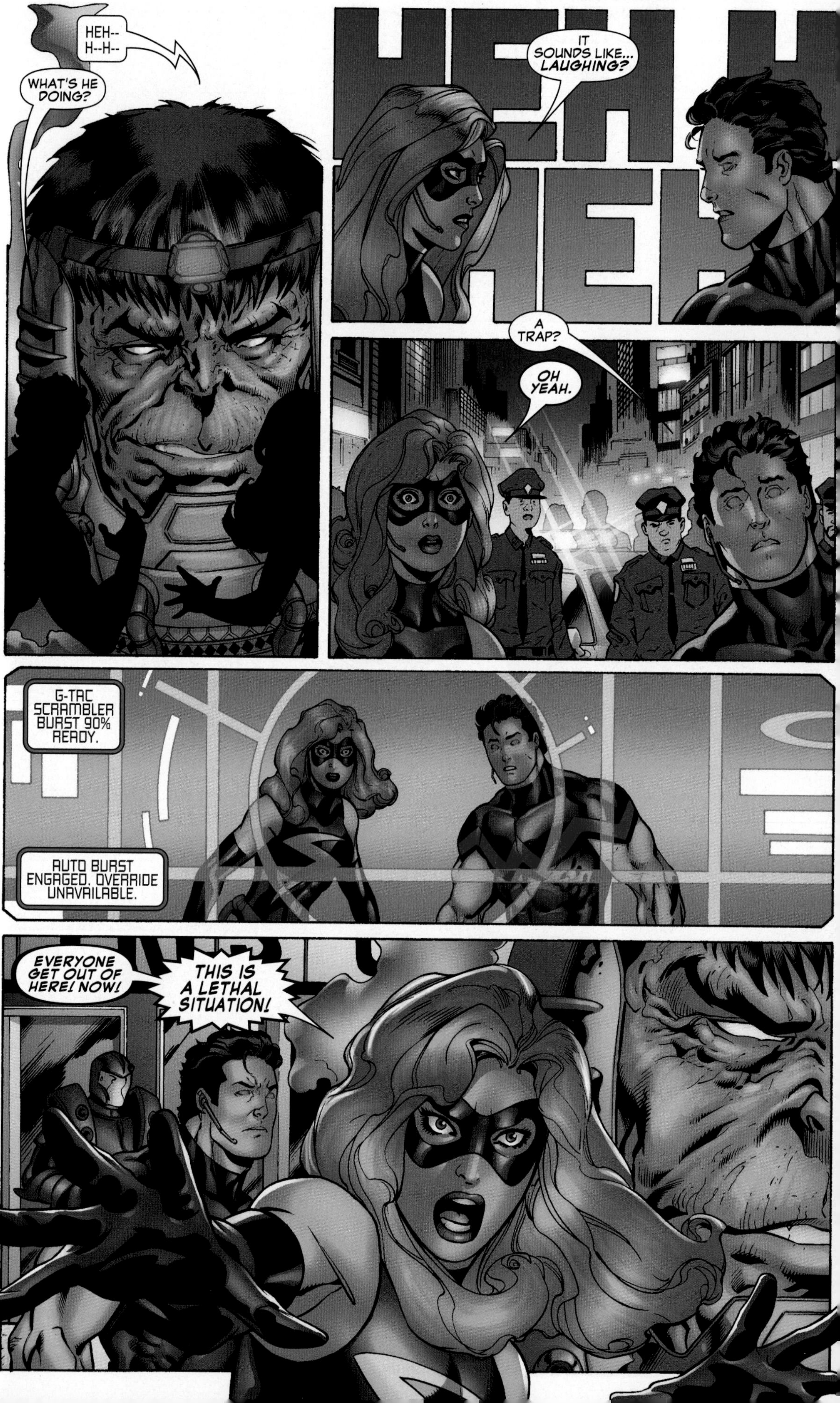
HEH--
H--H--
WHAT'S HE DOING?
HEH H
HEH
IT SOUNDS LIKE... LAUGHING?
A TRAP?
OH YEAH.
G-TAC SCRAMBLER BURST 90% READY.
AUTO BURST ENGAGED. OVERRIDE UNAVAILABLE.
EVERYONE GET OUT OF HERE! NOW!
THIS IS A LETHAL SITUATION!

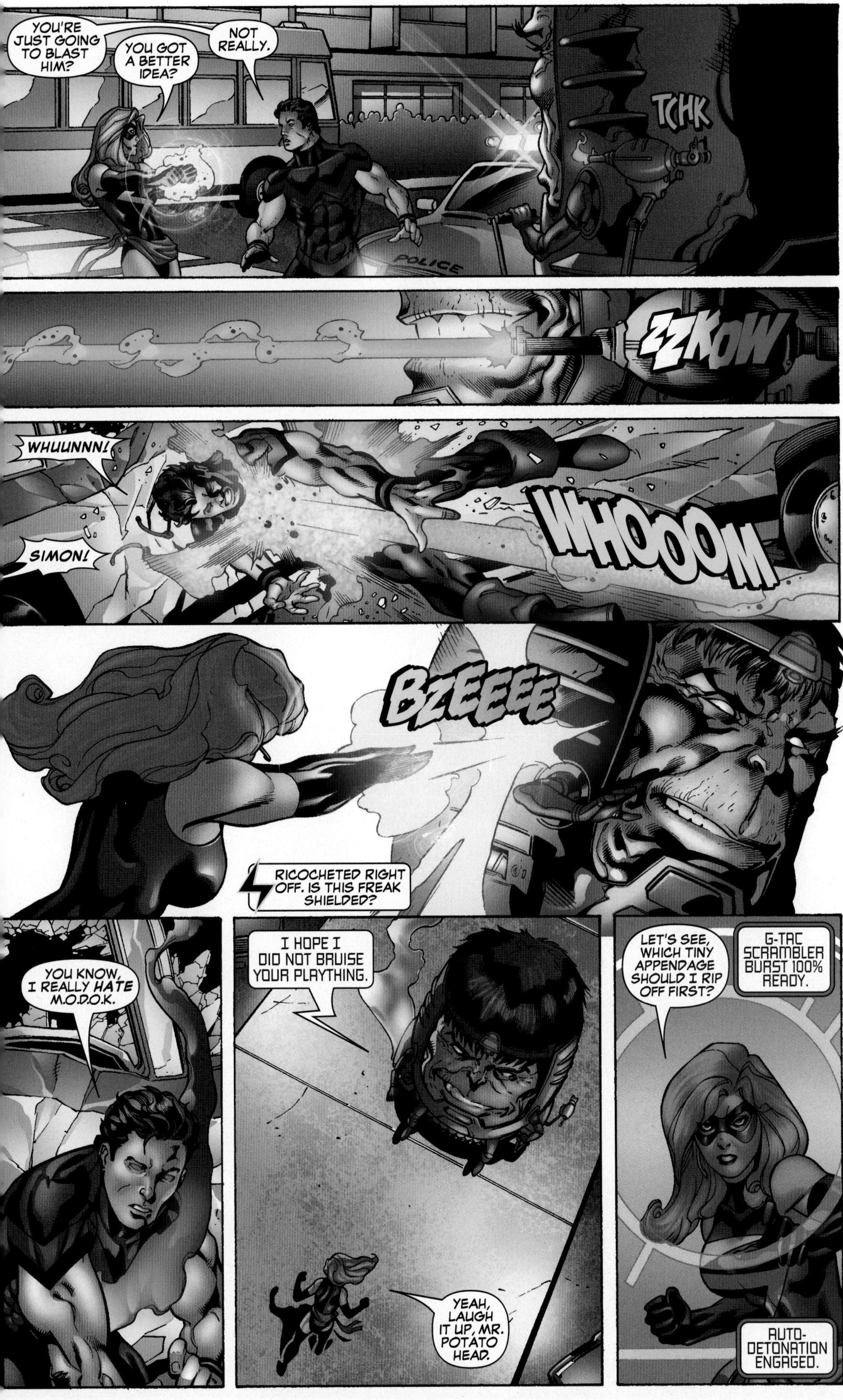

YOU'RE JUST GOING TO BLAST HIM?
YOU GOT A BETTER IDEA?
NOT REALLY.
TCHK
POLICE
ZZKOW
WHUUNNN!
SIMON!
WHOOOM
BZEEEE
RICOCHETED RIGHT OFF. IS THIS FREAK SHIELDED?
YOU KNOW, I REALLY HATE M.O.D.O.K.
I HOPE I DID NOT BRUISE YOUR PLAYTHING.
YEAH, LAUGH IT UP, MR. POTATO HEAD.
LET'S SEE, WHICH TINY APPENDAGE SHOULD I RIP OFF FIRST?
G-TAC SCRAMBLER BURST 100% READY.
AUTO-DETONATION ENGAGED.

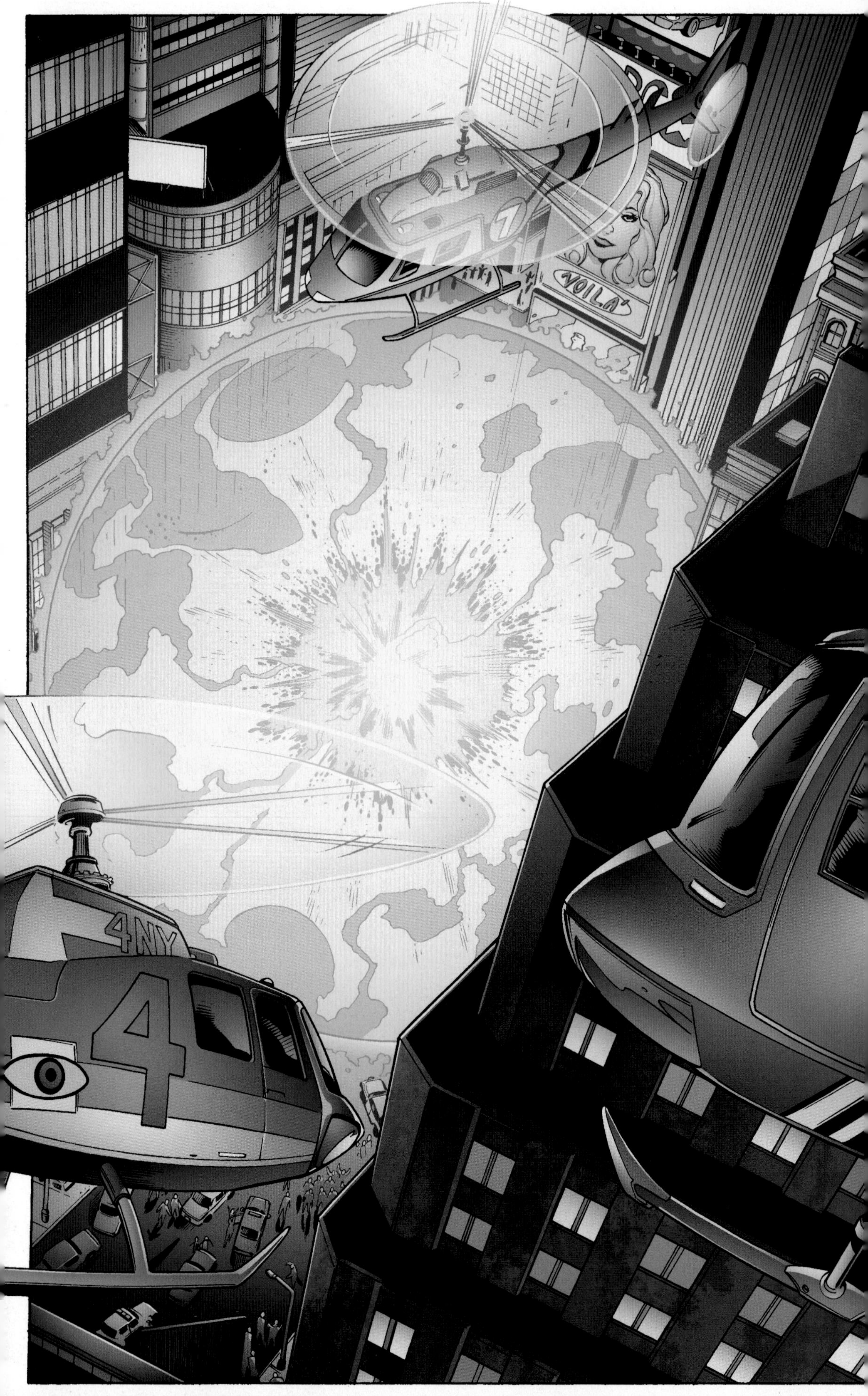
VOILA'
4NY
4

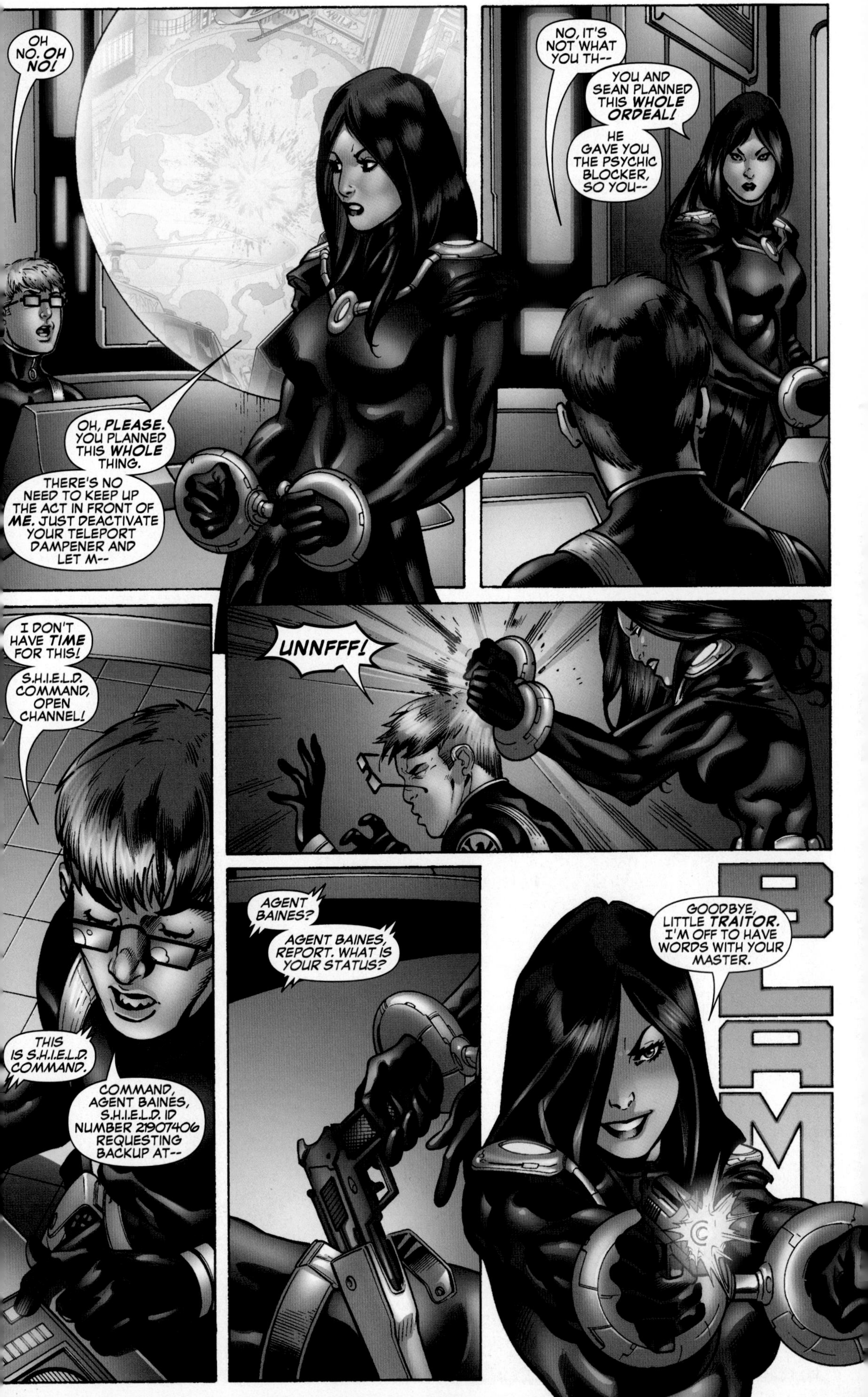
OH NO. OH NO!
OH, PLEASE. YOU PLANNED THIS WHOLE THING.
THERE'S NO NEED TO KEEP UP THE ACT IN FRONT OF ME. JUST DEACTIVATE YOUR TELEPORT DAMPENER AND LET M--
NO, IT'S NOT WHAT YOU TH--
YOU AND SEAN PLANNED THIS WHOLE ORDEAL!
HE GAVE YOU THE PSYCHIC BLOCKER, SO YOU--
I DON'T HAVE TIME FOR THIS!
S.H.I.E.L.D. COMMAND, OPEN CHANNEL!
THIS IS S.H.I.E.L.D. COMMAND.
COMMAND, AGENT BAINES, S.H.I.E.L.D. ID NUMBER 21907406 REQUESTING BACKUP AT--
UNNFFF!
AGENT BAINES?
AGENT BAINES, REPORT. WHAT IS YOUR STATUS?
BLAM
GOODBYE, LITTLE TRAITOR. I'M OFF TO HAVE WORDS WITH YOUR MASTER.

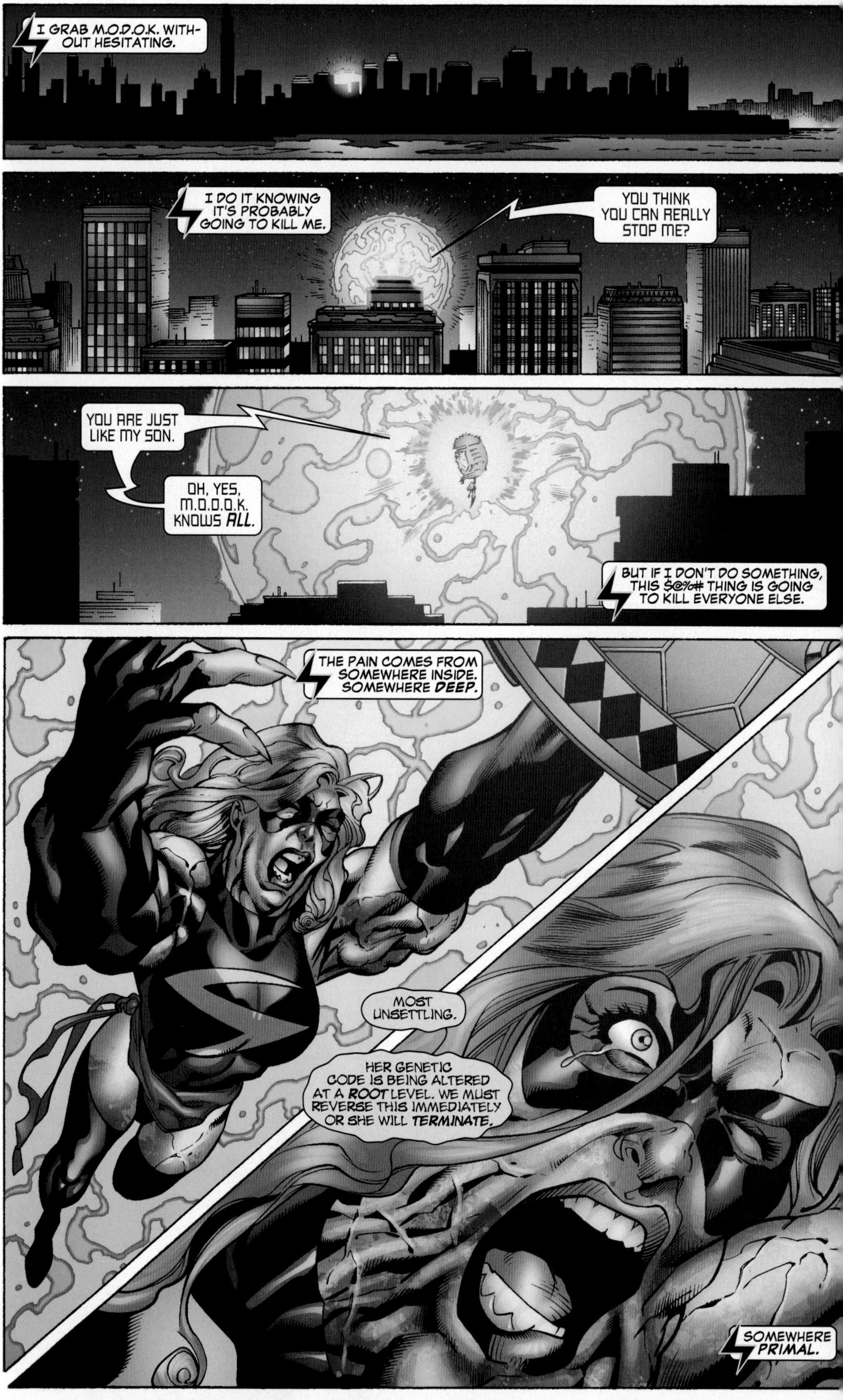
I GRAB M.O.D.O.K. WITH-OUT HESITATING.
I DO IT KNOWING IT'S PROBABLY GOING TO KILL ME.
YOU THINK YOU CAN REALLY STOP ME?
YOU ARE JUST LIKE MY SON.
OH, YES, M.O.D.O.K. KNOWS ALL.
BUT IF I DON'T DO SOMETHING, THIS $@%# THING IS GOING TO KILL EVERYONE ELSE.
THE PAIN COMES FROM SOMEWHERE INSIDE. SOMEWHERE DEEP.
MOST UNSETTLING.
HER GENETIC CODE IS BEING ALTERED AT A ROOT LEVEL. WE MUST REVERSE THIS IMMEDIATELY OR SHE WILL TERMINATE.
SOMEWHERE PRIMAL.

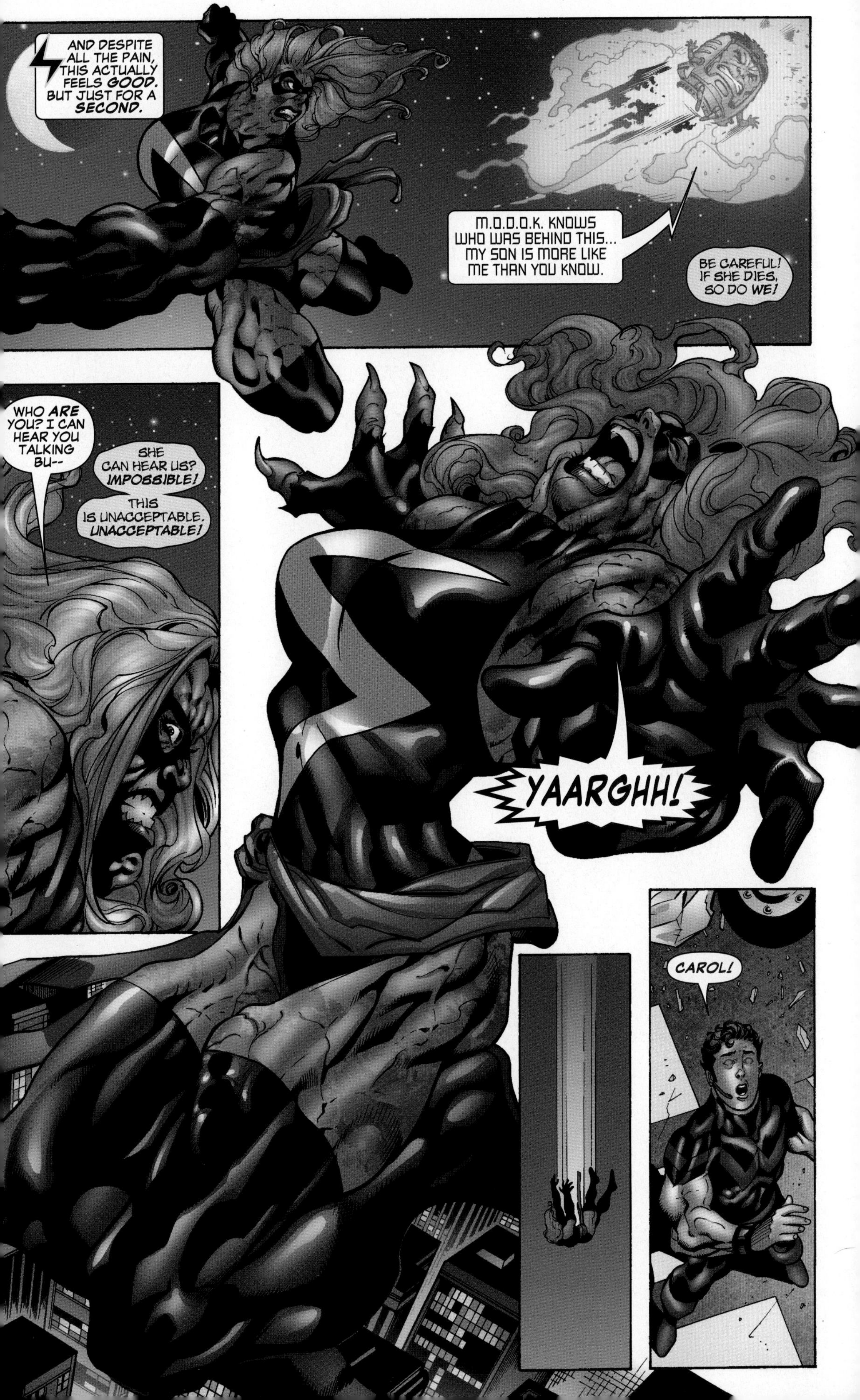
AND DESPITE ALL THE PAIN, THIS ACTUALLY FEELS GOOD. BUT JUST FOR A SECOND.
M.O.D.O.K. KNOWS WHO WAS BEHIND THIS... MY SON IS MORE LIKE ME THAN YOU KNOW.
BE CAREFUL! IF SHE DIES, SO DO WE!
WHO ARE YOU? I CAN HEAR YOU TALKING BU--
SHE CAN HEAR US? IMPOSSIBLE!
THIS IS UNACCEPTABLE. UNACCEPTABLE!
YAARGHH!
CAROL!

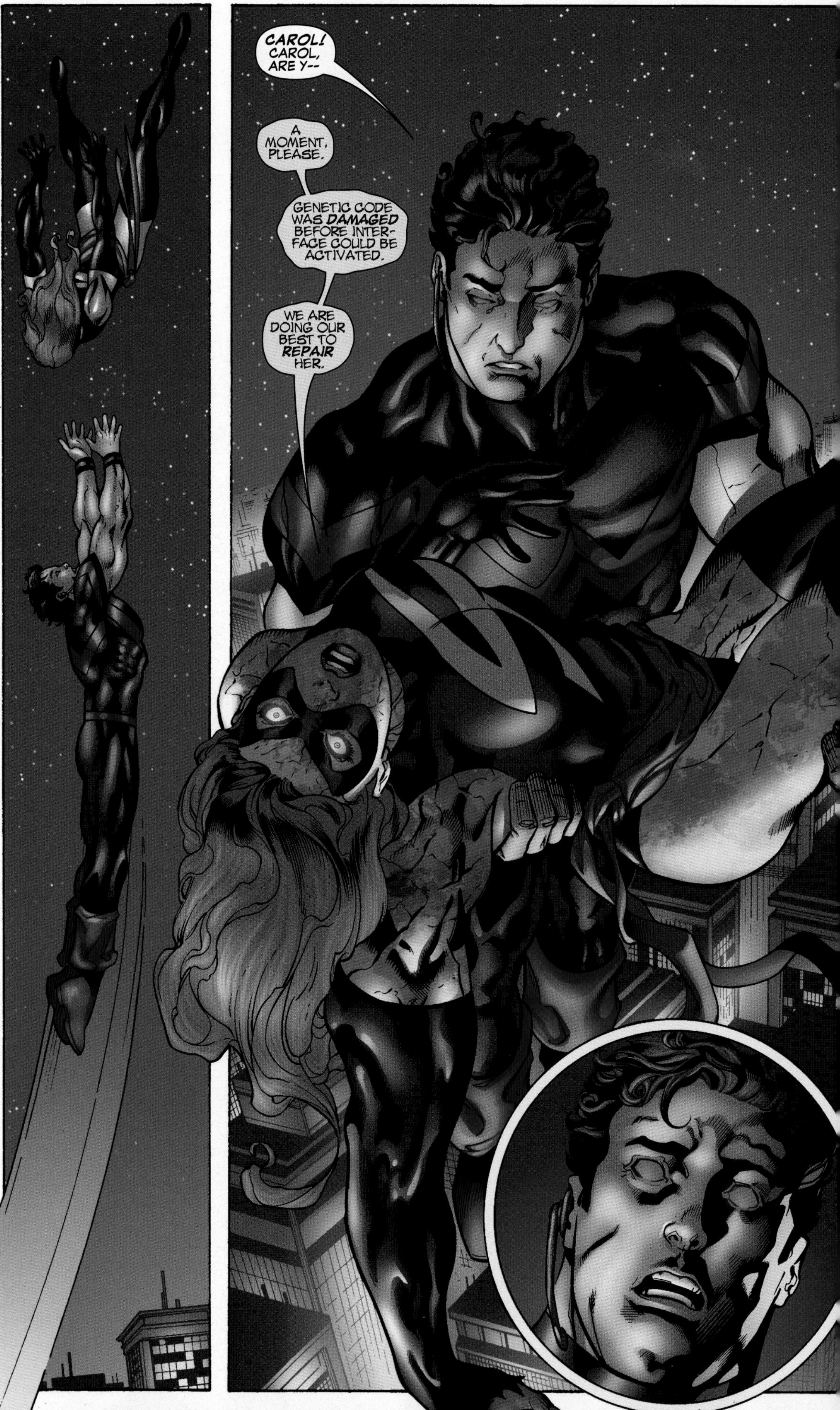
CAROL! CAROL, ARE Y--
A MOMENT, PLEASE.
GENETIC CODE WAS DAMAGED BEFORE INTER-FACE COULD BE ACTIVATED.
WE ARE DOING OUR BEST TO REPAIR HER.

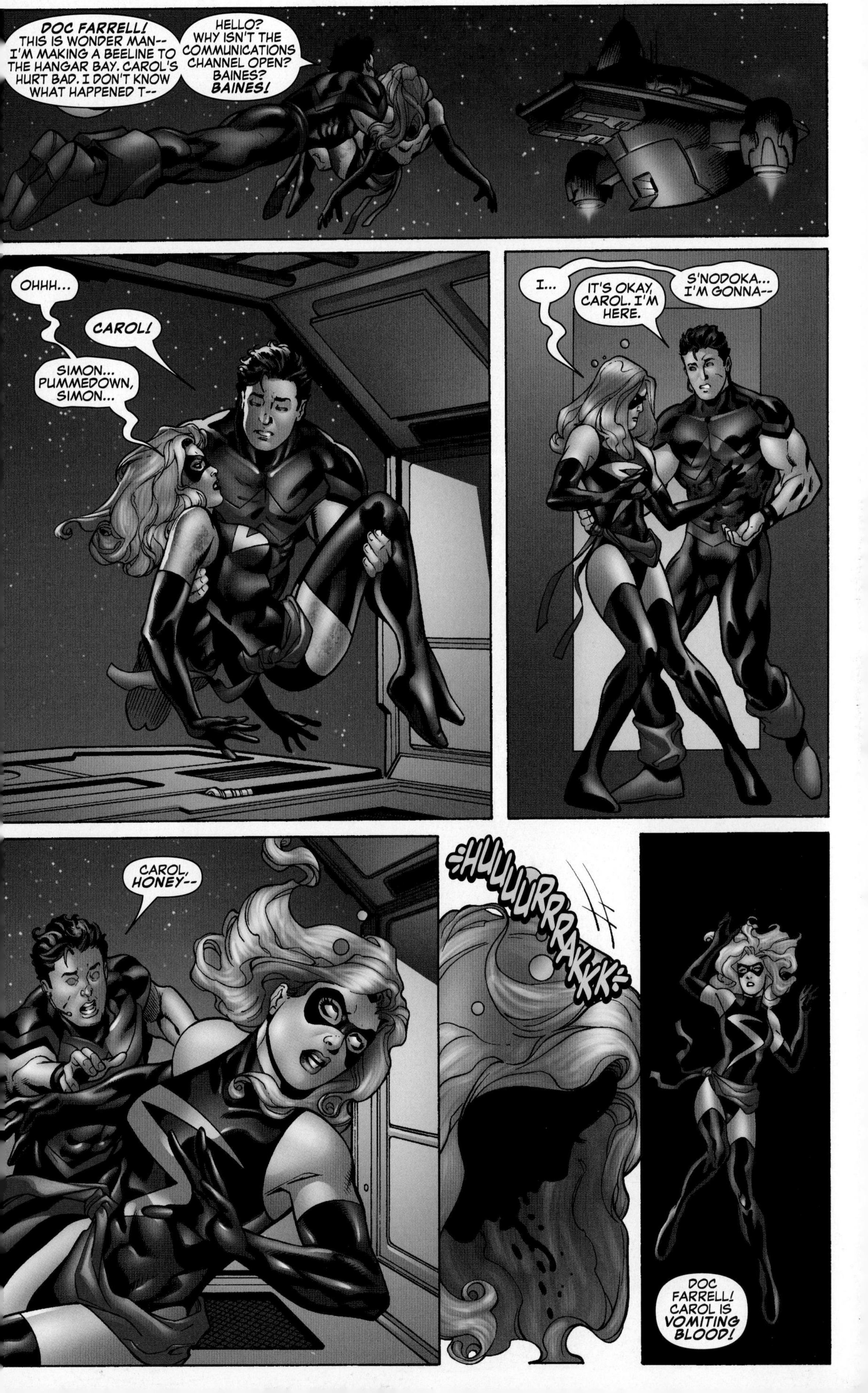

DOC FARRELL! THIS IS WONDER MAN-- I'M MAKING A BEELINE TO THE HANGAR BAY. CAROL'S HURT BAD. I DON'T KNOW WHAT HAPPENED T--
HELLO? WHY ISN'T THE COMMUNICATIONS CHANNEL OPEN? BAINES? BAINES!
OHHH...
CAROL!
SIMON... PUMMEDOWN, SIMON...
I...
IT'S OKAY, CAROL. I'M HERE.
S'NODOKA... I'M GONNA--
CAROL, HONEY--
HUUUURRRAKKK
DOC FARRELL! CAROL IS VOMITING BLOOD!

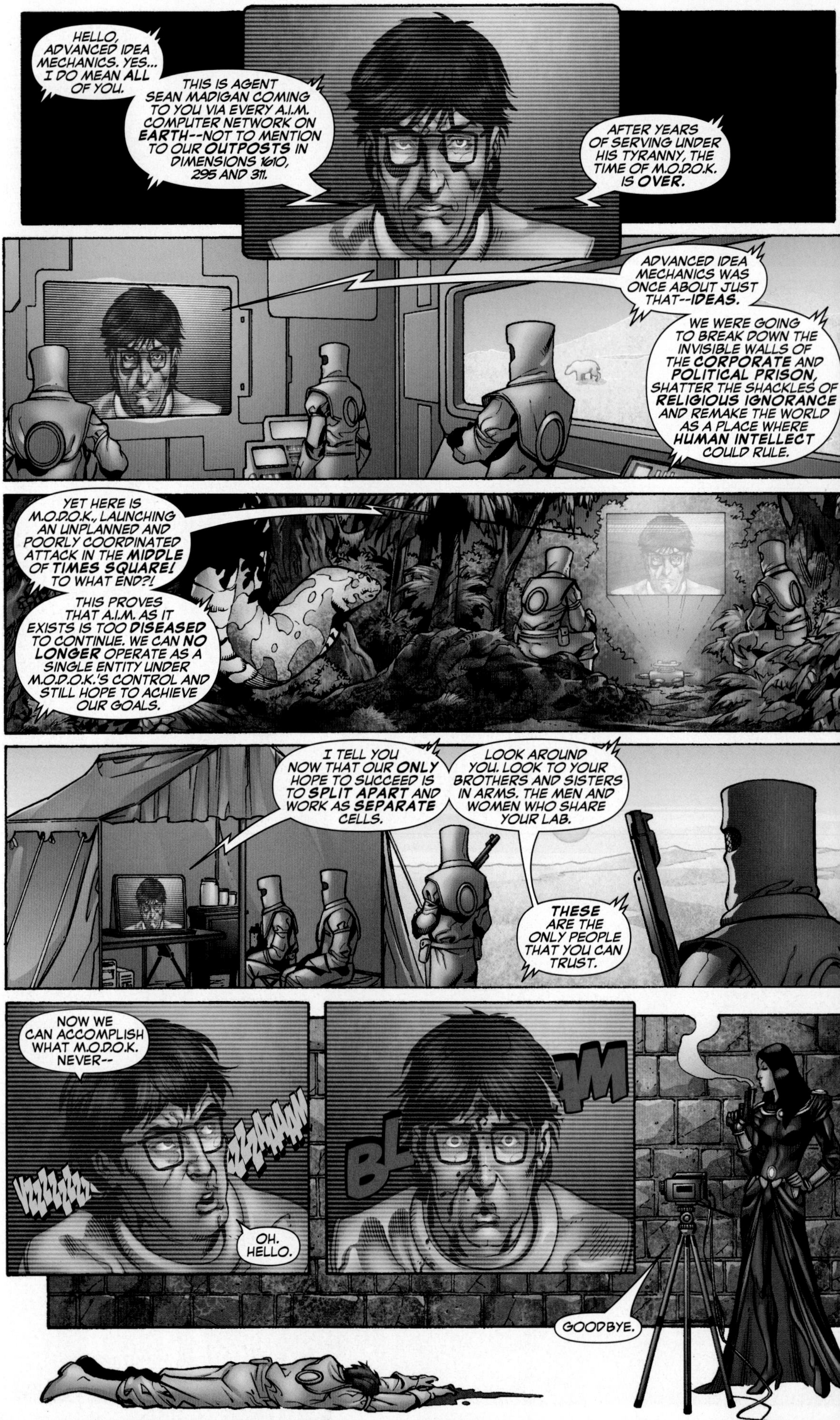
HELLO, ADVANCED IDEA MECHANICS. YES... I DO MEAN ALL OF YOU.
THIS IS AGENT SEAN MADIGAN COMING TO YOU VIA EVERY A.I.M. COMPUTER NETWORK ON EARTH--NOT TO MENTION TO OUR OUTPOSTS IN DIMENSIONS 1610, 295 AND 311.
AFTER YEARS OF SERVING UNDER HIS TYRANNY, THE TIME OF M.O.D.O.K. IS OVER.
ADVANCED IDEA MECHANICS WAS ONCE ABOUT JUST THAT--IDEAS.
WE WERE GOING TO BREAK DOWN THE INVISIBLE WALLS OF THE CORPORATE AND POLITICAL PRISON, SHATTER THE SHACKLES OF RELIGIOUS IGNORANCE AND REMAKE THE WORLD AS A PLACE WHERE HUMAN INTELLECT COULD RULE.
YET HERE IS M.O.D.O.K., LAUNCHING AN UNPLANNED AND POORLY COORDINATED ATTACK IN THE MIDDLE OF TIMES SQUARE! TO WHAT END?!
THIS PROVES THAT A.I.M. AS IT EXISTS IS TOO DISEASED TO CONTINUE. WE CAN NO LONGER OPERATE AS A SINGLE ENTITY UNDER M.O.D.O.K.'S CONTROL AND STILL HOPE TO ACHIEVE OUR GOALS.
I TELL YOU NOW THAT OUR ONLY HOPE TO SUCCEED IS TO SPLIT APART AND WORK AS SEPARATE CELLS.
LOOK AROUND YOU. LOOK TO YOUR BROTHERS AND SISTERS IN ARMS. THE MEN AND WOMEN WHO SHARE YOUR LAB.
THESE ARE THE ONLY PEOPLE THAT YOU CAN TRUST.
NOW WE CAN ACCOMPLISH WHAT M.O.D.O.K. NEVER--
VZZZZZZZ
ZZZAAAM
OH. HELLO.
BL
AM
GOODBYE.

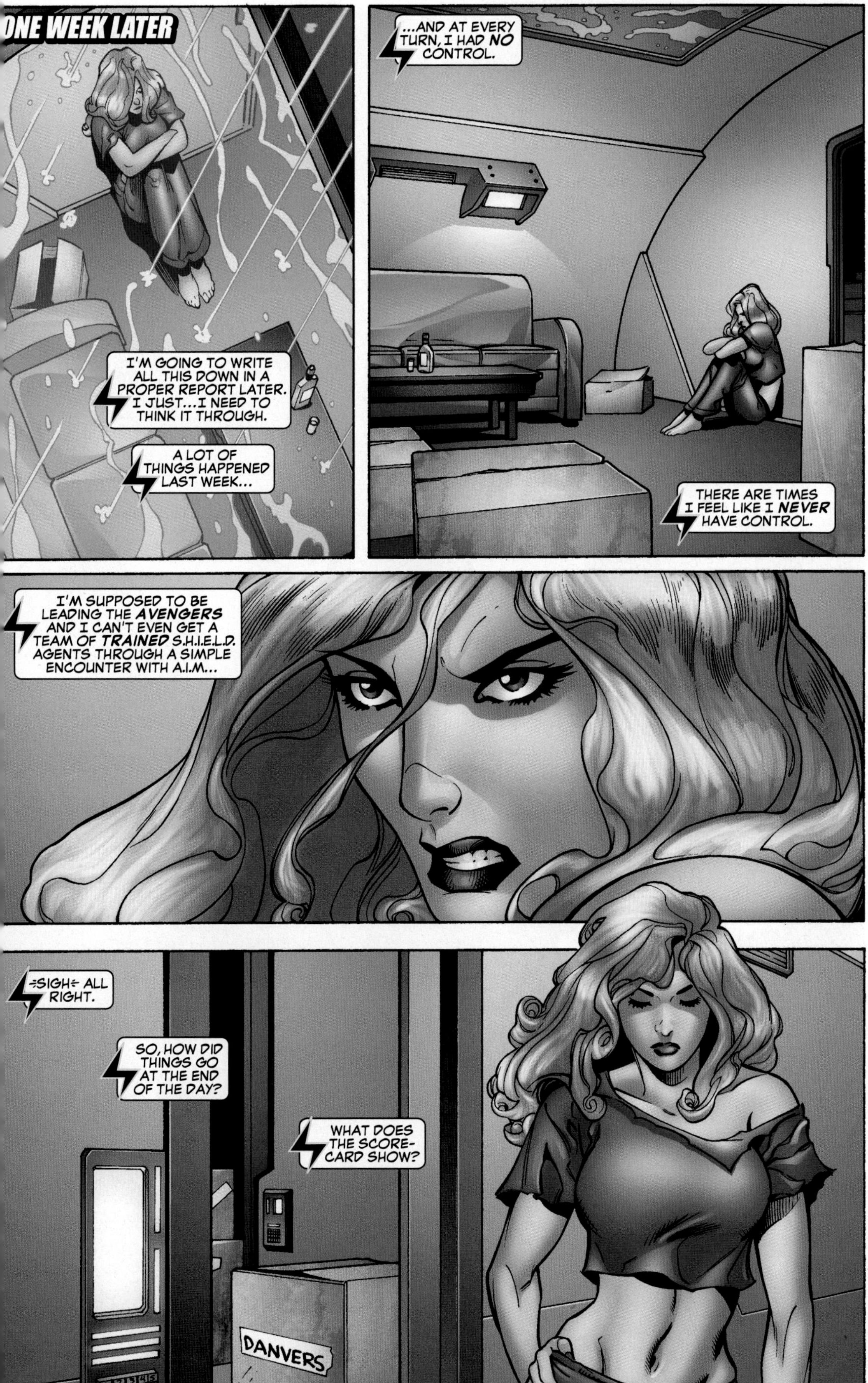
ONE WEEK LATER
I'M GOING TO WRITE ALL THIS DOWN IN A PROPER REPORT LATER. I JUST...I NEED TO THINK IT THROUGH.
A LOT OF THINGS HAPPENED LAST WEEK...
...AND AT EVERY TURN, I HAD NO CONTROL.
THERE ARE TIMES I FEEL LIKE I NEVER HAVE CONTROL.
I'M SUPPOSED TO BE LEADING THE AVENGERS AND I CAN'T EVEN GET A TEAM OF TRAINED S.H.I.E.L.D. AGENTS THROUGH A SIMPLE ENCOUNTER WITH A.I.M...
=SIGH= ALL RIGHT.
SO, HOW DID THINGS GO AT THE END OF THE DAY?
WHAT DOES THE SCORE-CARD SHOW?
DANVERS

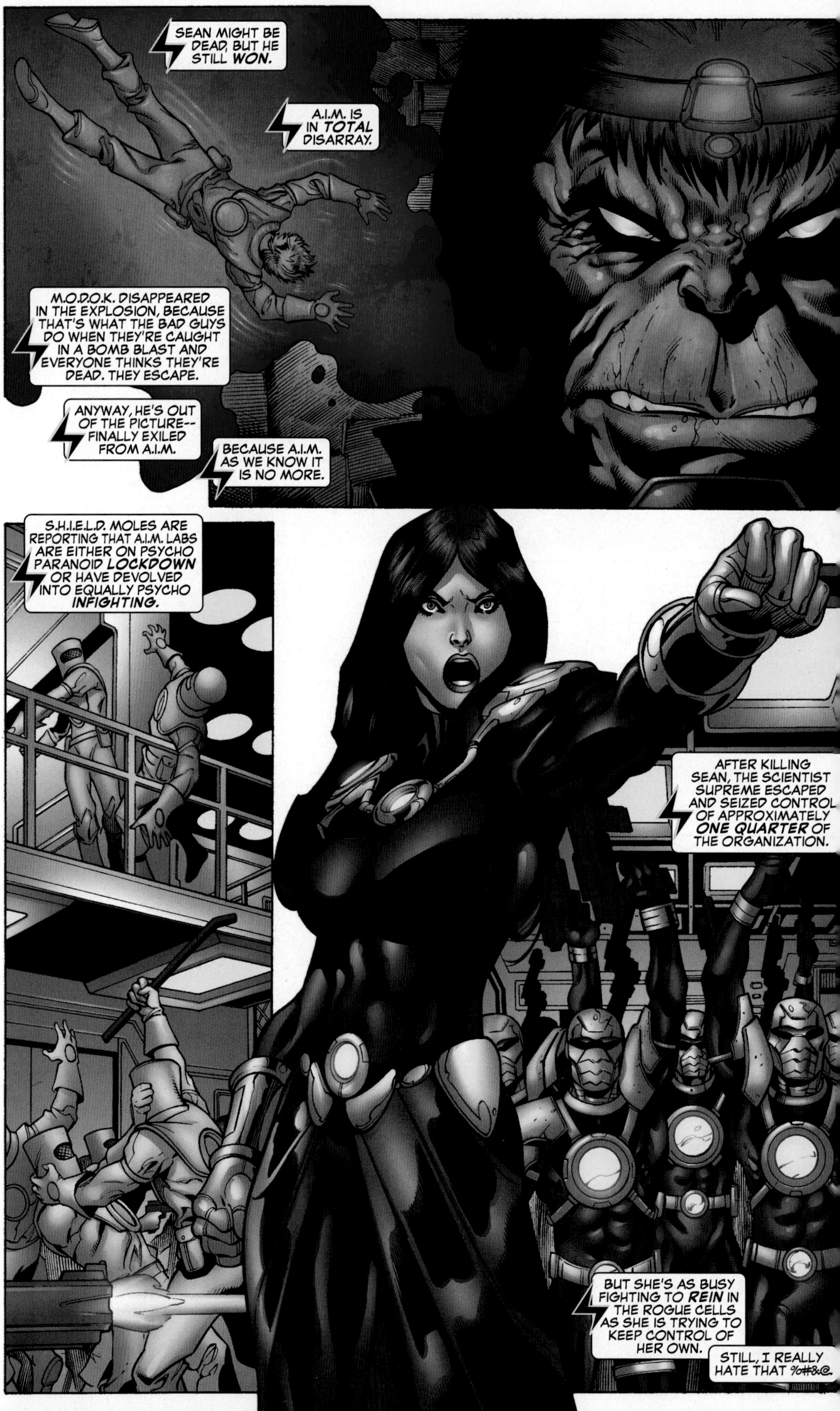
SEAN MIGHT BE DEAD, BUT HE STILL WON.
A.I.M. IS IN TOTAL DISARRAY.
M.O.D.O.K. DISAPPEARED IN THE EXPLOSION, BECAUSE THAT'S WHAT THE BAD GUYS DO WHEN THEY'RE CAUGHT IN A BOMB BLAST AND EVERYONE THINKS THEY'RE DEAD. THEY ESCAPE.
ANYWAY, HE'S OUT OF THE PICTURE--FINALLY EXILED FROM A.I.M.
BECAUSE A.I.M. AS WE KNOW IT IS NO MORE.
S.H.I.E.L.D. MOLES ARE REPORTING THAT A.I.M. LABS ARE EITHER ON PSYCHO PARANOID LOCKDOWN OR HAVE DEVOLVED INTO EQUALLY PSYCHO INFIGHTING.
AFTER KILLING SEAN, THE SCIENTIST SUPREME ESCAPED AND SEIZED CONTROL OF APPROXIMATELY ONE QUARTER OF THE ORGANIZATION.
BUT SHE'S AS BUSY FIGHTING TO REIN IN THE ROGUE CELLS AS SHE IS TRYING TO KEEP CONTROL OF HER OWN.
STILL, I REALLY HATE THAT %#&@.

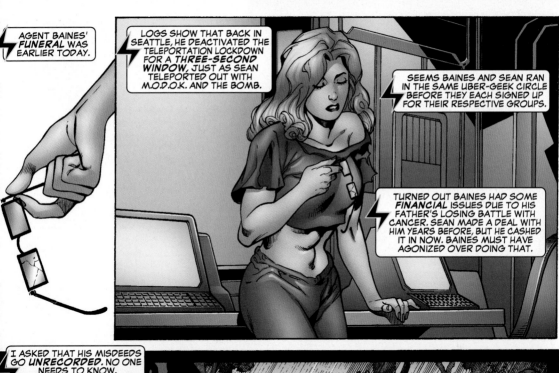

AGENT BAINES' *FUNERAL* WAS EARLIER TODAY.

LOGS SHOW THAT BACK IN SEATTLE, HE DEACTIVATED THE TELEPORTATION LOCKDOWN FOR A *THREE-SECOND WINDOW*, JUST AS SEAN TELEPORTED OUT WITH M.O.D.O.K. AND THE BOMB.

SEEMS BAINES AND SEAN RAN IN THE SAME *UBER-GEEK* CIRCLE BEFORE THEY EACH SIGNED UP FOR THEIR RESPECTIVE GROUPS.

TURNED OUT BAINES HAD SOME *FINANCIAL* ISSUES DUE TO HIS FATHER'S LOSING BATTLE WITH CANCER. SEAN MADE A DEAL WITH HIM YEARS BEFORE, BUT HE CASHED IT IN NOW. BAINES MUST HAVE AGONIZED OVER DOING THAT.

I ASKED THAT HIS MISDEEDS GO *UNRECORDED*. NO ONE NEEDS TO KNOW.

WHEN I HANDED THE FLAG TO HIS MOTHER...

...SHE NEVER LOOKED AWAY FROM HIS CASKET. NOT EVEN *ONCE*.

SINCE AGENT LOCKE WAS INJURED IN SEATTLE, THE S.H.I.E.L.D. PSI-CORPS PLACED HER ON MEDICAL LEAVE.

THERE HAVE BEEN A *LOT OF SURGERIES* FOR HER. A LOT OF *PAIN*.

I SHOULD GO VISIT HER...

...BUT I DON'T THINK SHE'D BE HAPPY TO SEE ME.

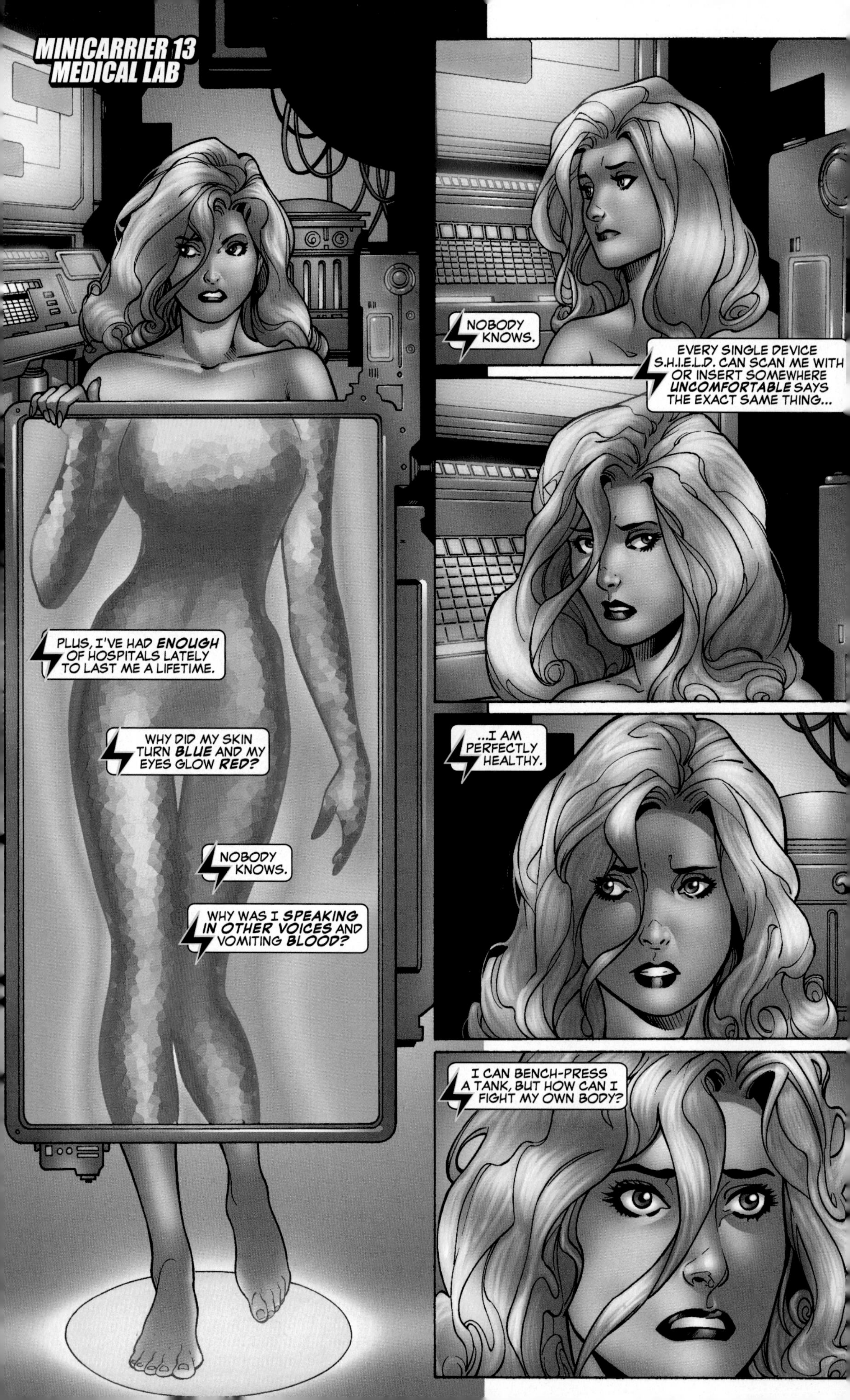
MINICARRIER 13
MEDICAL LAB
PLUS, I'VE HAD ENOUGH OF HOSPITALS LATELY TO LAST ME A LIFETIME.
WHY DID MY SKIN TURN BLUE AND MY EYES GLOW RED?
NOBODY KNOWS.
WHY WAS I SPEAKING IN OTHER VOICES AND VOMITING BLOOD?
NOBODY KNOWS.
EVERY SINGLE DEVICE S.H.I.E.L.D. CAN SCAN ME WITH OR INSERT SOMEWHERE UNCOMFORTABLE SAYS THE EXACT SAME THING...
...I AM PERFECTLY HEALTHY.
I CAN BENCH-PRESS A TANK, BUT HOW CAN I FIGHT MY OWN BODY?

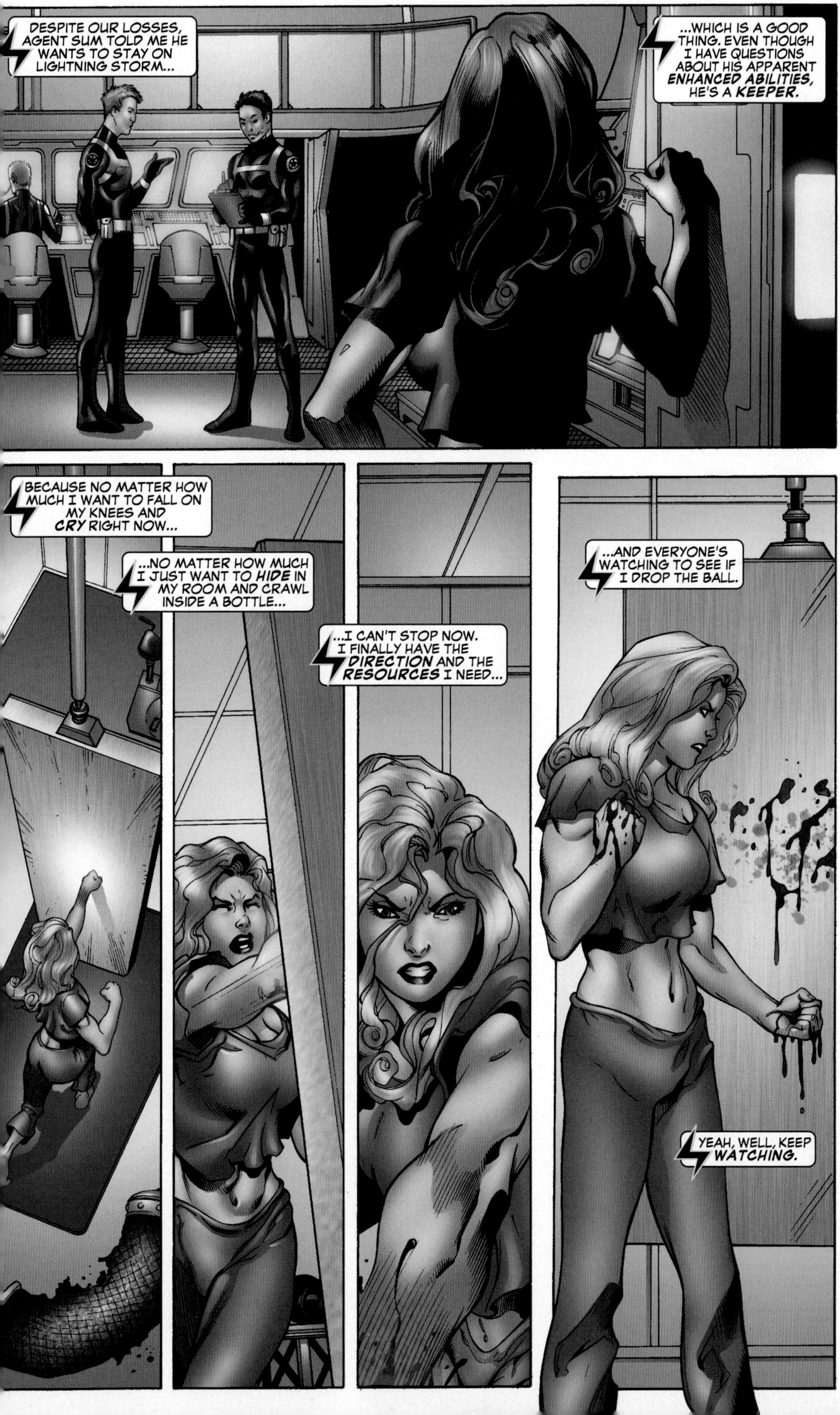
DESPITE OUR LOSSES, AGENT SUM TOLD ME HE WANTS TO STAY ON LIGHTNING STORM...
...WHICH IS A GOOD THING. EVEN THOUGH I HAVE QUESTIONS ABOUT HIS APPARENT ENHANCED ABILITIES, HE'S A KEEPER.
BECAUSE NO MATTER HOW MUCH I WANT TO FALL ON MY KNEES AND CRY RIGHT NOW...
...NO MATTER HOW MUCH I JUST WANT TO HIDE IN MY ROOM AND CRAWL INSIDE A BOTTLE...
...I CAN'T STOP NOW. I FINALLY HAVE THE DIRECTION AND THE RESOURCES I NEED...
...AND EVERYONE'S WATCHING TO SEE IF I DROP THE BALL.
YEAH, WELL, KEEP WATCHING.

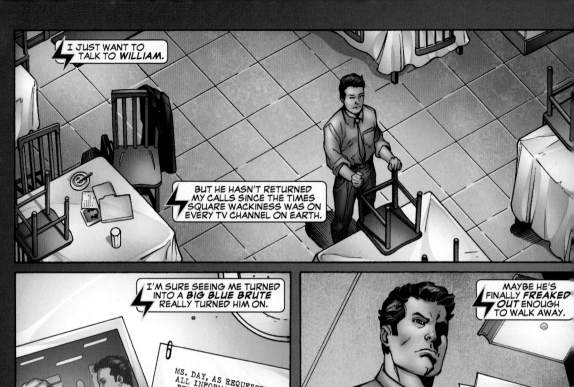

I JUST WANT TO TALK TO *WILLIAM.*

BUT HE HASN'T RETURNED MY CALLS SINCE THE TIMES SQUARE WACKINESS WAS ON EVERY TV CHANNEL ON EARTH.

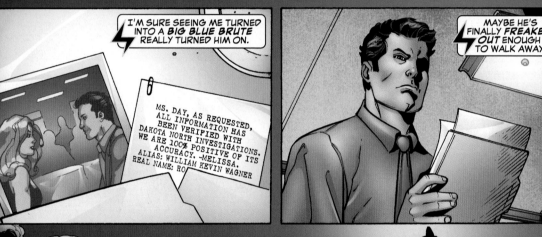

I'M SURE SEEING ME TURNED INTO A *BIG BLUE BRUTE* REALLY TURNED HIM ON.

MS. DAY, AS REQUESTED, ALL INFORMATION HAS BEEN VERIFIED WITH DAKOTA NORTH INVESTIGATIONS. WE ARE 100% POSITIVE OF ITS ACCURACY. -MELISSA.
ALIAS: WILLIAM KEVIN WAGNER
REAL NAME: RO

MAYBE HE'S FINALLY *FREAKED OUT* ENOUGH TO WALK AWAY.

HEY, CAROL?

I HAVEN'T SEEN YOU AROUND THE LAST FEW DAYS...

YOU HAVEN'T *UNPACKED* YET?

YEAH. I'VE BEEN KIND OF--

I, UM, YEAH--I KEEP *MEANING* TO, BUT...

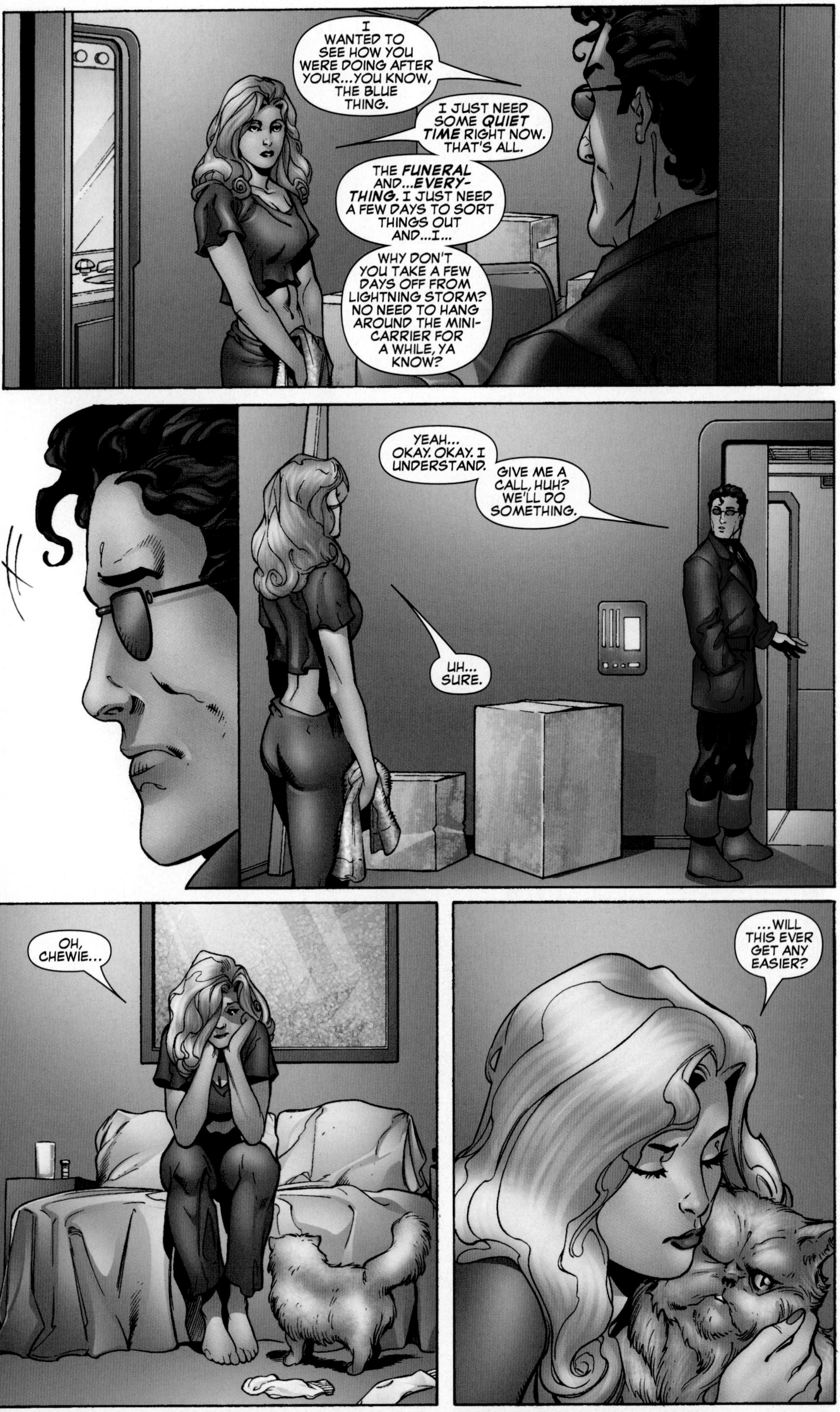
I WANTED TO SEE HOW YOU WERE DOING AFTER YOUR...YOU KNOW, THE BLUE THING.
I JUST NEED SOME QUIET TIME RIGHT NOW. THAT'S ALL.
THE FUNERAL AND...EVERY-THING. I JUST NEED A FEW DAYS TO SORT THINGS OUT AND...I...
WHY DON'T YOU TAKE A FEW DAYS OFF FROM LIGHTNING STORM? NO NEED TO HANG AROUND THE MINI-CARRIER FOR A WHILE, YA KNOW?
YEAH... OKAY. OKAY. I UNDERSTAND.
GIVE ME A CALL, HUH? WE'LL DO SOMETHING.
UH... SURE.
OH, CHEWIE...
...WILL THIS EVER GET ANY EASIER?

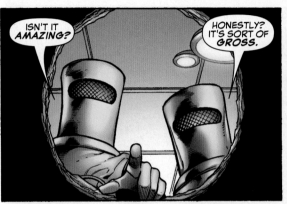

ISN'T IT AMAZING?

HONESTLY? IT'S SORT OF GROSS.

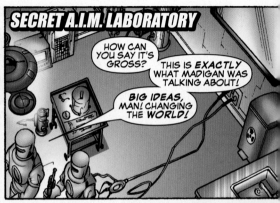

HOW CAN YOU SAY IT'S GROSS?

THIS IS EXACTLY WHAT MADIGAN WAS TALKING ABOUT!

BIG IDEAS, MAN! CHANGING THE WORLD!

I GUESS... BUT I'M NOT SURE SEAN IMAGINED HE MIGHT END UP AS ONE OF THOSE BIG IDEAS.

COME ON, THIS LAB WAS ALWAYS IN CHARGE OF REANIMATION RESEARCH, WASN'T IT?

HAND ME THE M.G. CHIP, PLEASE?

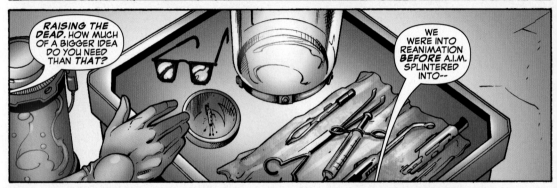

RAISING THE DEAD. HOW MUCH OF A BIGGER IDEA DO YOU NEED THAN THAT?

WE WERE INTO REANIMATION BEFORE A.I.M. SPLINTERED INTO--

YOU MEAN BEFORE MR. MADIGAN HERE REMINDED EVERY-ONE THAT WE--ANY OF US--COULD CHANGE THE WORLD?

THE TARGOTHS WERE NEAT TO LEARN WITH, BUT THEY WERE MINDLESS...STUPID. THIS, THOUGH...

TAKING WHAT WE LEARNED FROM DOOMSDAY MAN'S NEURAL LINKS...

...CROSSING IT WITH THE REANIMATIVE PROPERTIES OF THE TARGOTH VIRUS...

ACTIVATING THE CHIP--OH, WHAT A PRETTY GLOW.

OKAY... FILLING THE SUIT WITH GEL. OHHH, THAT'S PERFECT. HE LOOKS GOOD, DOESN'T HE?

HAND ME THE HELMET, PLEASE? NOW LET'S SEE WHAT HAPPENS...

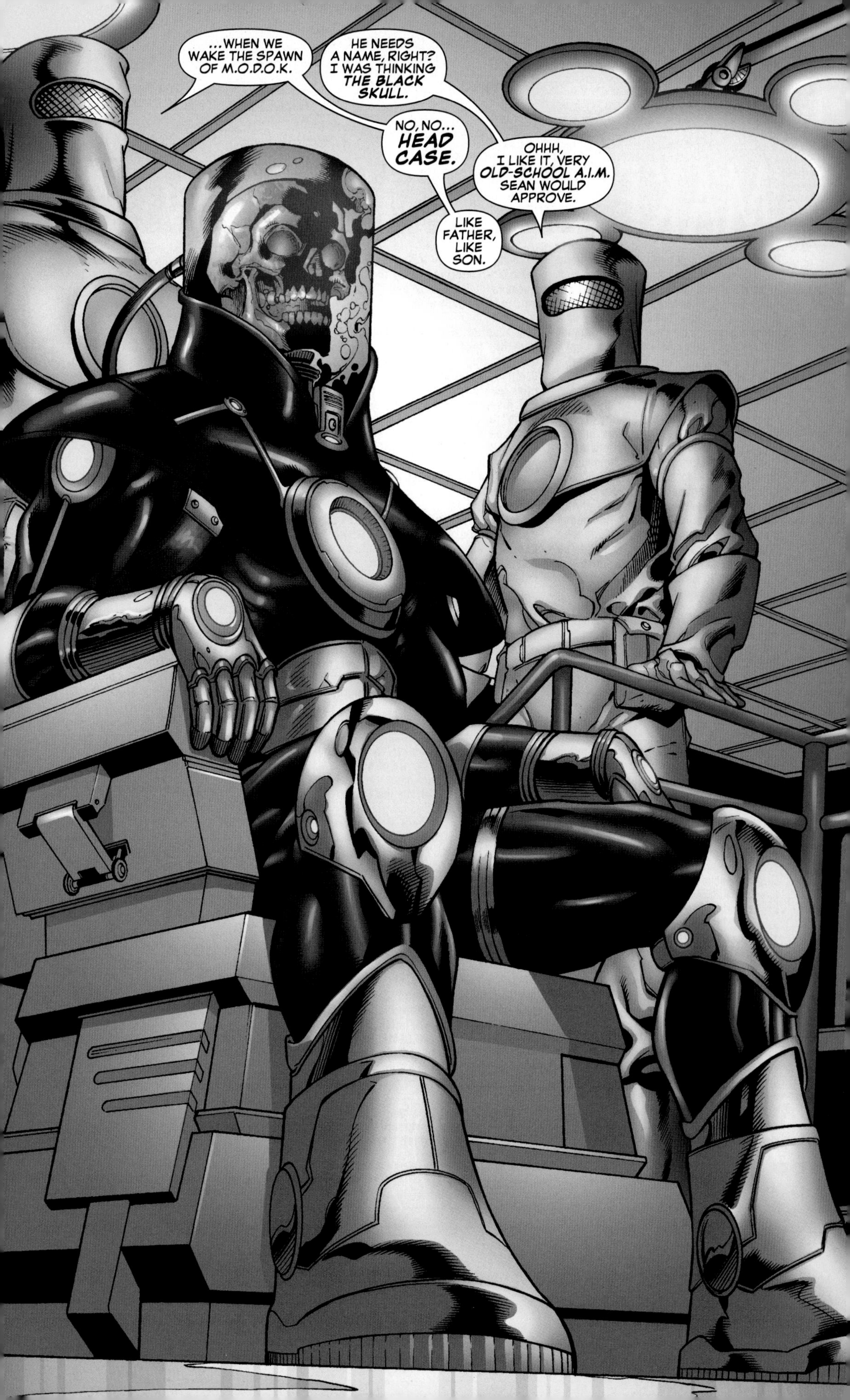
...WHEN WE WAKE THE SPAWN OF M.O.D.O.K.
HE NEEDS A NAME, RIGHT? I WAS THINKING THE BLACK SKULL.
NO, NO... HEAD CASE.
OHHH, I LIKE IT, VERY OLD-SCHOOL A.I.M. SEAN WOULD APPROVE.
LIKE FATHER, LIKE SON.

MAKE MINE MS. MARVEL!

Hello, and welcome to what is traditionally the letters page. I am your author and host Brian Reed and this month we're taking a pause from your letters in favor of a bit of shilling. See, MS. MARVEL is going in a pretty amazing new direction next month and I wanted to let you guys know what's going on.

The Doomsday Man story was written during a transition phase on the book. I was moving across the country to live close to family for the first time in over a decade, Andy Schmidt was leaving to join the X-Men office, Warren Simons was the new editor for about thirty seconds or so (but long enough to make some truly amazing suggestions for the plot of these last two issues), Bill Rosemann was returning home to Marvel Comics to become the editor he always wanted to be when he grew up, and Rob de la Torre was heading off to draw IRON MAN full-time. (We'll miss ya, Rob!)

Once Doomsday Man finished, and the dust settled from everyone playing musical chairs, Bill gave me a call. He had this idea, see. He called it MS. MARVEL VS. SANTA CLAUS, wherein Carol would do battle with a deranged Kris Kringle, saving the world and, presumably, Christmas in the process. Bill envisioned it as a twenty-four-part epic with multiple, collectible, glow-in-the-dark, holographic gatefold covers, and including scratch-and-sniff panels on each page so you could smell Carol's perfume.

I knew the instant I heard it that Bill was dropping the next *Watchmen* right in my lap. It was up to me to grab hold of this idea with both hands and hang on until the six-figure royalty checks started rolling in. But the question nagged: Was the comics-buying public ready for something that absolutely amazing? I wasn't sure, honestly, that anyone could survive creating, let alone reading, the level of sheer awesome we were talking about putting on the page. In fact, I was worried that paper might not even be structurally capable of containing the sheer force of the story and art.

I called Brian Bendis to get his opinion on things and he reminded me that the restraining order includes phone calls as well as showing up on his doorstep at 3 a.m. Bendis also said that I needed to send the script for ILLUMINATI #3 to Phil, his lawyer, so Phil could give it to him to rewrite from page one.

Then I called Joe Quesada. Joe's secretary informed me that, "Mister Quesada is very busy and doesn't have time to talk to fans who call."

I realized then that it was up to me. Help Bill foist this masterpiece upon an unsuspecting Earth, consequences be damned, or get him to step back from the brink and maybe do something else for a bit? A sort of a warm-up to the "Awesome Bomb" (as I had taken to thinking of it) that would be MS. MARVEL VS. SANTA CLAUS, if you will.

So I called Bill and the conversation went like this:

ME: Bill, it's Brian Reed. I don't think we should do MS. MARVEL VS. SANTA CLAUS. I don't think we're ready for it. I don't think the public is ready for it. I have doubts that paper itself is ready for it.

BILL: What you talking about, Willis?

It turns out that either Bill or myself (it's open to debate, really) was not entirely, shall we say, *sober* at the time of the previous phone call and well, let's just say there were some crossed wires and leave it at that.

So, instead of breaking any interweb tubes in half or whatever the cool kids are saying these days, we're going to do something really intelligent and cool and downright great next issue instead.

Issue #13 is, without slapping a new number 1 on the cover, for all intents and purposes, MS. MARVEL: SEASON 2. These first 12 stories have focused on Carol trying to be the "best of the best" and while she's been doing okay, she's made her fair share of mistakes along the way. Our next story is called "The Deal" and it's the first time we see Carol confront that maybe everything hasn't been going to plan.

Aaron Lopresti will be joining us as the regular penciler on the book and I'm excited to have him aboard. Aaron's handling of Ms. Marvel in last fall's WHAT IF? AVENGERS DISASSEMBLED was so great that when Rob accepted the IRON MAN gig, Bill and I knew Aaron was just the guy to join our team.

Greg Horn has also been added to our squad as the new cover artist. I actually started reading Dan Slott's fantastic SHE-HULK because of Greg's covers, so I'm happy as can be to have him join the party.

As for you, The Reader (and you are my favorite of the lot), I hope you'll enjoy "The Deal", which will also see the return of Julia Carpenter as she looks to set straight the events of CIVIL WAR. Right after that, we've got "Taking A.I.M." where Ms. Marvel goes after the terrorist organization Advanced Idea Mechanics and ends up face-to-gigantic-face with M.O.D.O.K. himself.

I'm sure you've noticed that in recent months the stories have started to get a dark undercurrent with events like Carol taking down Julia Carpenter, the Rogue beat down, and now the Doomsday Man tale ending the way it did. You're going to see where all this is headed in coming months as well. Carol is taking on more and more responsibility and, if she can admit it to herself or not, she may not be able to handle it. But that's what has always made Marvel great in my eyes – books that star human beings that are capable of making mistakes, not perfect specimens of herodom who wouldn't know what a flaw was without a dictionary to explain it to them.

So, there it is – a hint of what's to come and a "thank you" to everybody who was with us through this first year of stories. I think the next 12 issues are going to be even better. Next month, the letters page returns to normal, and in the meantime, I want to hear from each and every one of you. See you soon!

NEXT ISSUE:

OPERATION LIGHTNING STORM

CAROL WANTS YOU!

BILL ROSEMANN
EDITOR

JOE QUESADA
CHIEF

MS. MARVEL c/o MARVEL COMICS
417 5TH AVE., NEW YORK, NY 10016
IF YOU DON'T WANT YOUR NAME AND ADDRESS
PRINTED, PLEASE LET US KNOW.
LETTERS MAY BE EDITED FOR CONTENT AND LENGTH.

E-MAIL: MHEROES@MARVEL.COM
MARK E-MAIL "OKAY TO PRINT"

MS. MARVEL #12 LETTERS PAGE BY BRIAN REED

MS. MARVEL

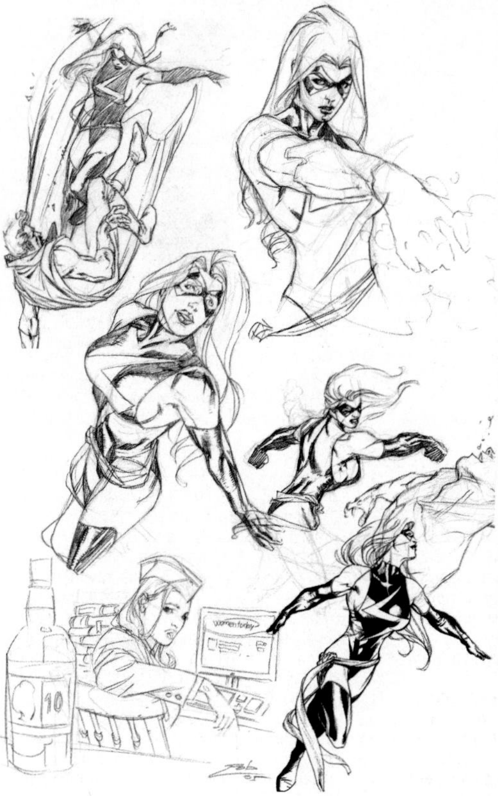

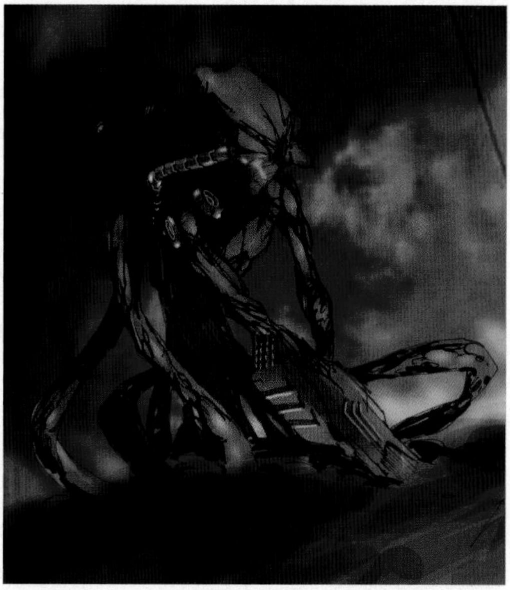

CRU

TRAVELER

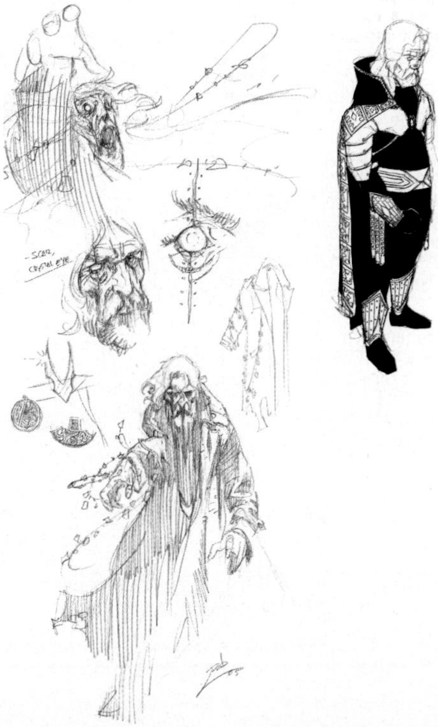
- SCAR, CRYSTAL EYE

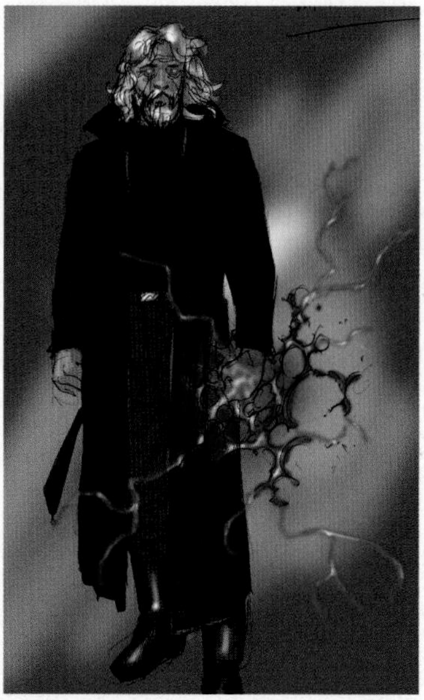

CONCEPT SKETCHES BY ROBERTO DE LA TORRE

CIVIL WAR AFTERMATH

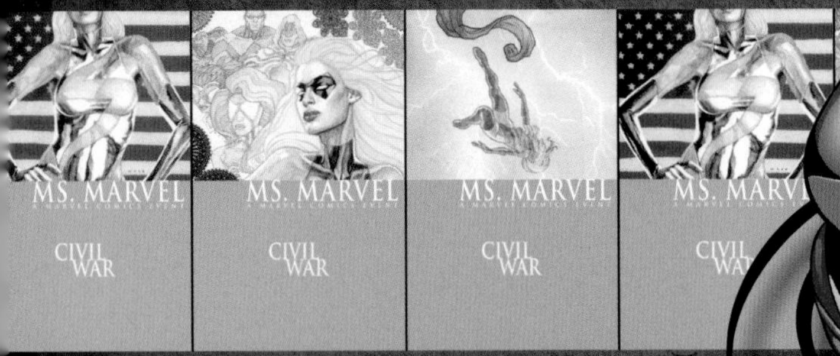
MS. MARVEL
CIVIL WAR
MS. MARVEL
CIVIL WAR
MS. MARVEL
CIVIL WAR
CIVIL WAR

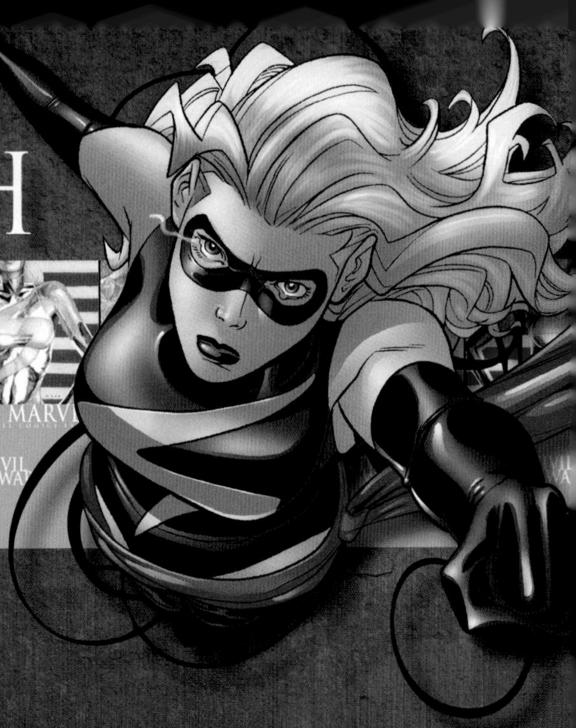

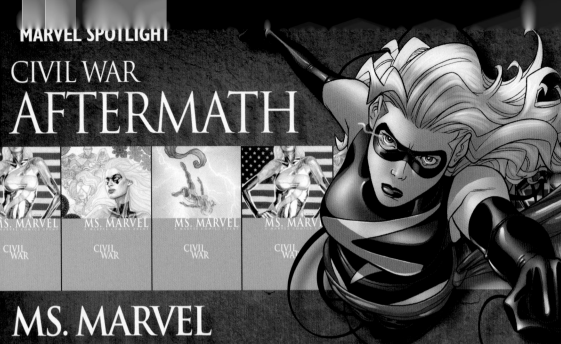

MS. MARVEL

WRITER: BRIAN REED
ARTIST: AARON LOPRESTI

Carol Danvers has always been a woman who wanted to achieve high marks in life, whether as a member of the United States Air Force, a card-carrying super hero or a member of the Avengers. She's always wanted to be the best of the best. As any reader who has been following her story over the years knows, however, Carol has been faced with one adversity after another that has done more than merely pummel her self-esteem; the combined effects of her assault by Marcus, getting mind-wiped by Rogue, gaining and then losing tremendous superhuman powers and her troubles with alcoholism have taken a toll on her very identity.

And just when Carol seems to be asserting herself like never before, to find a place for in the world that can be uniquely her own, along comes *Civil War* to move the ground from under her feet in life-changing ways. An early and consistent supporter of the Registration Act (though not without uneasily muddling through the many moral dimensions of her pro-registration stance), Carol has come out the other end of *Civil War* seemingly intact. But as all Marvel loyalists know, it's the inner turmoil that hides behind the confident veneer of our favorite characters that produces the best stories. To discuss the future of Carol Danvers, *Spotlight* got together with writer Brian Reed and new artist Aaron Lopresti for the full scoop!

SPOTLIGHT: Was there much of a reassessment to your writing strategy for *Ms. Marvel* once you knew *Civil War* was coming down the pike? If so, is your plan for *Ms. Marvel* in the post-*CW* Marvel Universe substantively different from what it was when you signed and how?

BRIAN: Oh, it's a completely different book now than it was going to be before. And I couldn't be happier about that. I've said before that the beauty of *Civil War* was that it was something the characters themselves didn't see coming, so all of their plans for their lives got thrown off the rails. The same thing happened to the creators of these books. You get a lot of ideas in your head, like, "Oh, I'm going to do this story and then this story..." and you get in a groove and you're comfortable. Then... BAM! Something like this comes along and totally blows away everything you thought you knew. And that's great because that's what's happening to the characters too and that's what makes you able to get in their headspace and tell their stories.

SPOTLIGHT: When we think of the word "aftermath" (our book's title is *Civil War: Aftermath*, natch), it suggests something like the image of dust settling after an explosive event. What was the one moment, or series of moments, in Carol's experience during the *CW* event that you could point to and say is the key moment, the one on which her future development pivots, the one that places her squarely inside her own personal "aftermath"?

BRIAN: The events in that front yard in Colorado, when Julia Carpenter was cornered and lashed out. Carol fought back and the whole day went down in a bad, bad way. Issues #13 and #14 are going to deal with some of the most obvious fallout from that day, but there's a lot more nastiness lurking for Ms. Marvel just below the surface – and it can all be traced back to that one event.

SPOTLIGHT: The dramatic thrust of *Civil War* was pretty well described by the tagline that preceded the event: "Whose Side Are You On?" Ms. Marvel happens to be one of the heroes on the front lines of the pro-registration side. As the one who has to write her continuing story, can you discuss how this decision fit into her values as a character? And how have her values changed since the war has reached its climax?

BRIAN: Carol chose to go pro-registration because of her history in the military and the Avengers, and her understanding that proper training can keep you alive. I tried to show in the tie-in issues that she didn't just wake up one day and say, "Hey, I'm going to be pro-registration now." I wanted folks to see that she thought about it and she had her reasons — however much any of us may disagree with them — and that scene in *Ms. Marvel #6* where she explains herself to Captain America was a big piece of the "Why is Carol Doing This" puzzle.

Unfortunately, I can't get too much into how her worldview and values change post-Civil War because a lot of that stuff hinges on the outcome of the war.

SPOTLIGHT: As a writer, your job is to take the character and write them in a credible and authentic way, and sometimes, your characters don't make the same choices and have the same values as you do. So let's say you were Ms. Marvel: presented with all the difficult choices thrown at Carol Danvers — both in her own title and in the other *CW* titles — how would Brian Reed have handled them had he been in her boots?

BRIAN: Oh, I'm a total problem child when it comes to authority figures. I probably would have been on Cap's side in an instant if I were in Carol's boots.

However, assuming I had a pro-registration bent, then I think what you saw Carol do was a lot of what I would have done in the same situation — made a choice, stood by it, and wondered if I was doing the right thing after the whole situation got out of control. I think it's the only human reaction to the situations she was placed in.

SPOTLIGHT: I don't think it's controversial to suggest that most of the readership in comics has chosen the side of anti-registration. How you do you regard the sometimes harsh fan reaction to Carol's stance? Is it harsher than you expected, or about the right reaction? And have you gotten equally strong support from some readers *for* her stance?

BRIAN: Frankly, I *love* the people who read the Civil War books and started calling Carol a fascist. Because right on the same message board, or in the very next fan letter, you'll see someone defend her choices and point out how wrong Julia Carpenter was.

If every mail had been positive about Carol's choices, I'd worry I'd done something wrong. The story was about a woman who has made a decision that she thinks is right and starts to see that maybe the side effects of that decision are undesirable. So I wanted people to be offended by her actions, or completely supportive of them. It was a tricky line to walk, but judging by the reaction I'd say I did it.

Of course, now I sound like a self-aggrandizing schmuck...."Oooh, look at me and the great story I told," and I don't want to come off like that. I'm just saying that it would have been really easy to write a story where Carol did no wrong and even though she held a different view than the fans she could have come out smelling like roses. But that would have been pretty easy and predictable, so I didn't do it.

SPOTLIGHT: You're developing a very interesting supporting cast for Carol. Her pro-registration stance has put her in proximity to Araña, a character that's had a rough going in getting established in the MU. Are we going to be seeing more of Araña

MS. MARVEL VS. WARBIRD: Carol Danvers faces down an evil version of herself from another dimension in *Ms. Marvel #10*. (Art by Mike Wieringo.)

ARAÑA, SIDEKICK: The young super heroine gets training from one of the best in future issues of *Ms. Marvel!* (Art by Roberto de la Torre from *Ms. Marvel #11*.)

and she's just proven to be a fantastic addition to the cast.

SPOTLIGHT: We've also seen Wonder Man as Carol's cohort in the *Civil War* crossover issues, and a new gentleman named William Wagner show up as a potential romantic interest. Are you perhaps developing any entanglements that might cause these two guys to feel any competition with each other? Or is ol' Wondy strictly business with Carol?

BRIAN: There is a Carol Danvers/William Wagner/ Simon Williams triangle in progress. We're going to see Carol in the position where she realizes she has feelings for these two guys who could not be more different. One is an average (albeit darned handsome and well-to-do guy) and the other is a super hero and a movie star. There's a lot of stuff planned out for these three and how Carol deals with it all.

SPOTLIGHT: Looking ahead to "Season Two" of *Ms. Marvel*, what are some of the things that are happening in the book that we haven't yet touched on that you want to highlight?

BRIAN: Starting in issue #13, we see Carol realize that just saying she wants to be the best of the best isn't enough. She made this proclamation back in issue #1 and she's been rambling around ever since, not quite clear on what her next step should be. Issue #13 is that next step.

We also see how her joining the *Mighty Avengers* affects her day-to-day life. And, interestingly enough, we see that she doesn't initially want to join the Mighty Avengers at all. Issues #13 and #14, aside from dealing with Julia Carpenter/*Civil War* fallout, also focus on the deal Carol makes that gets her interested in the *Mighty Avengers*.

SPOTLIGHT: Speaking for yourself as a comics professional, what's the aftermath of *Civil War* like for you? Has it been a rush (in good ways or bad ways)? Are you feeling slightly crazed about how to react to the rapidly changing status quo, or are you enthusiastic and even more motivated than before *CW*? (Or maybe both?)

BRIAN: I'm so happy with *Civil War*. And that's not a company line. I actually really enjoy the effect it has had on the Marvel Universe and the effect it has had on me as a writer. It forced me to switch up my game plan mid-stream, it forced me to become better in a lot of ways. And the stories it has spawned in this next year are going to be huge and exciting.

THE ART OF MS. MARVEL: AARON LOPRESTI

SPOTLIGHT: How far back do you go with Carol Danvers as a character? Is she a character that you're eminently familiar with, or do you really only have a general sense of her at this point?

in *Ms. Marvel*, and how do you feel about being given the challenge of giving such a character a little love and esteem?

BRIAN: Oh yeah, Araña has been this total surprise to me. I just wanted a character who was new and didn't have a lot of history behind them so I could slip them into the slot I had in the story for "hero to be trained." She just so happened to fit the position and when I asked about her, nobody else was using her, so she got cast.

What ended up happening was that I completely fell in love with her. She's exactly what I needed in a character since she's young and reasonably naive not only in the ways of super heroes, but also of adults. She got to say things the adults wouldn't or couldn't and she got to show us what someone completely new to the super-hero profession would think when given the choices at hand.

The side effect has been finding this great underused character and having her really click with Carol. I've written a few issues with her around since the *Civil War*

AARON: I bought that when I was a kid, like, the first couple of issues because I think John Buscema was drawing it, so I bought those. Here I was, this 12-year-old boy running around with the *Ms. Marvel* comic, I don't think that I shared with anybody that I actually bought it. Scorpion was in there and John Buscema was drawing it so I was like, "I'll check this out." Other than her guest appearances in *New Avengers*, I have not been keeping up at all with her character, so this has all been sort of learning on the run for me.

SPOTLIGHT: Do you find that "learning on the run" is

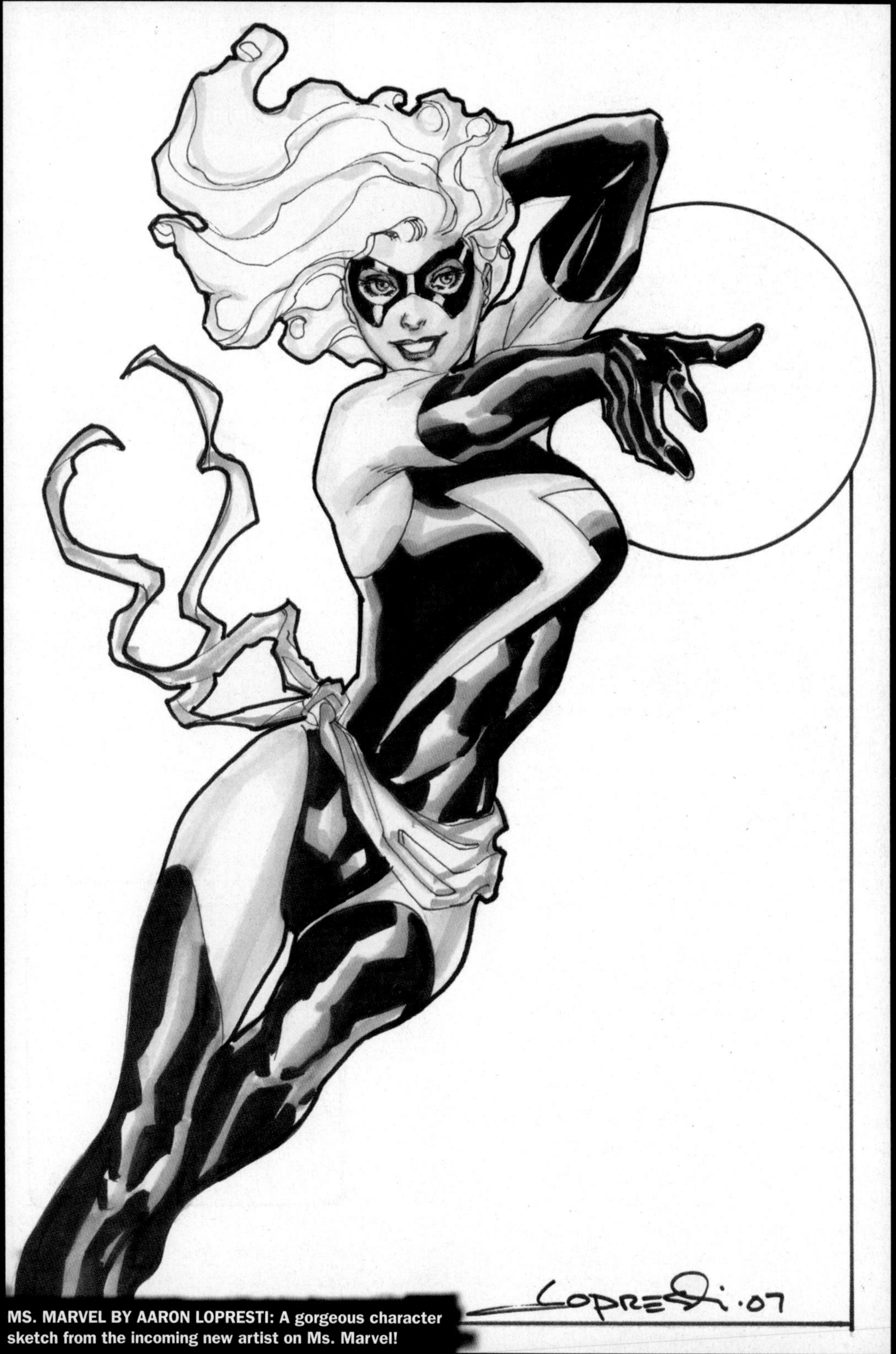
LOPRESTI ·07

MS. MARVEL BY AARON LOPRESTI: A gorgeous character sketch from the incoming new artist on Ms. Marvel!

CW: TURNING POINT

"The events in that front yard in Colorado, when Julia Carpenter was cornered and lashed out. Carol fought back and the whole day went down in a bad, bad way — that was the major turning point for her. *Ms. Marvel # 13-14* are going to deal with some of the most obvious fallout from that day, but there's a lot more nastiness lurking for Ms. Marvel just below the surface — and it can all be traced back to that one event." — **writer Brian Reed**

sort of an exciting place to be as an artist, something that gets your juices going, or is it simply an extra layer of labor to work through?

AARON: From just the technical standpoint of working, it's a pain because you are constantly stopping and saying, "OK, I gotta find reference for this." I'm not a guy who enjoys that because once I get drawing I just like to go, and to have to stop and say, "Wait a minute, who's this character in the background? Oh gosh, now I have to go find it..." And to go through piles of paper to find the reference, then to go on the internet to find more reference!

But on the other side of it, the *Ms. Marvel* title is relatively new, only a year old, and obviously what we're doing after *Civil War* is practically like starting a new series because everything has changed so much. So there is the excitement of that, we're really sort of launching something here, and to be on the ground level of that is always exciting and fun, although requires a lot more work because you're either looking up stuff you weren't familiar with, or you're creating new stuff on top of just drawing the book.

SPOTLIGHT: What elements of her visual look really stand out to you as an artist? And are you going to tinker any at all with her costume?

AARON: It's funny you should mention that, specifically about the costume. Well, I'll answer your first question: any time you get to draw the female figure you can't really complain about it. The human anatomy is the most fun part of drawing, at least for me. I'm not a big "cars and robots" kind of guy. I'm more organic, and that's why I loved all of Gil Kane's designs from DC and Marvel in the '60s and '70s, because they were basically painted on body suits, so he was *always* drawing anatomy. In that regard, she doesn't have a bunch of shoulder pads and tacky stuff all over; you're drawing the figure, which I

really like.

On the other hand, I have been thinking about (and I haven't talked to anybody about this editorial-wise) revamping the costume or maybe doing something a little different. I don't think anybody has really even thought about it as an option, it just kind of popped into my head the other day. Maybe I would change this, or maybe I would change that, just kind of fool around a little bit, so it's actually a subject I might broach with Bill Roseman and Brian Reed and see what they think at some point — if there seems to be a logical point to do it, you know?

SPOTLIGHT: So are you enjoying settling in with *Ms. Marvel* now?

AARON: Yeah, I'm diggin' it. I'm very much a Marvel zombie and a throwback. We're going to be using some villains that are...I don't know if they are going to make the Top 10 of people's favorites list. *(Laughter.)* But they'd make the Top 10 of mine!

SPOTLIGHT: Like who?

AARON: We have M.O.D.O.K. coming up. Any guy with a big head, I'm there.

SPOTLIGHT: Yeah: big head, little stubby legs and a floating chair.

AARON: It doesn't get any better than that! So he's going to be in the first story line here, and I've been begging them to somehow work in Xemnu, the Living Titan. We'll see if that actually comes to fruition. If I keep bugging them long enough, maybe they actually will go, "Alright, alright, we'll throw him in there!"

Good luck to Brian Reed and Aaron Lopresti as MS. MARVEL enters "Season Two!"